POSTCODE ATLAS

Great Britain and Northern Ireland

CONTENTS

Key to map symbols	i
Structure of postcodes	ii
Map of postcode areas	iii
Index of postcode areas	iv
Britain postcode maps	2-109
(4.1 miles to 1 inch)	
Northern Ireland map	110-111
(8.3 miles to 1 inch)	
Conurbation maps	112-120
(1.6 miles to 1 inch)	
West Midlands	112-113
Manchester	114-115
Leeds and Bradford	116-117
Liverpool	118
Newcastle upon Tyne	119
Glasgow	120

London key to map pages and symbols	121
London mapping	122-129
(3.2 inches to 1 mile)	
Administrative areas	130-145
Counties mapping	146-151
(19.7 miles to inch)	
London boroughs map	152-153
(2.6 miles to 1 inch)	
Index to London street names	154-166
Index to Great Britain place names	167-223
Index to Northern Ireland place names	224

Published by Collins
An imprint of HarperCollinsPublishers
77-85 Fulham Palace Road, Hammersmith, London W6 8JB

www.collins.co.uk

Copyright © HarperCollinsPublishers Ltd 2004

Collins® is a registered trademark of HarperCollinsPublishers Limited

Postcode boundaries and codes copyright © Royal Mail Group plc

The postcode boundary information published in this atlas is compiled from the Postcode Address File (PAF) and reproduced with the permission of Royal Mail Group plc. The copyright and database rights in PAF are owned by Royal Mail Group plc. Details included in this atlas are subject to change without notice.

Mapping generated from Collins Bartholomew digital databases

The grid on this mapping is the National Grid taken from the Ordnance Survey map with the permission of the controller of Her Majesty's Stationery Office.

Printed in Hong Kong   ISBN 0 00 719197 9   RV11837   BDB   Imp 001

e-mail: roadcheck@harpercollins.co.uk

HarperCollinsPublishers

Key to map symbols

Postcode information

PL   Area code

   Area boundary

35   District code

   District boundary

Britain postcode map symbols (pages 2-109)

M4   Motorway

M6 Toll   Toll Motorway

30   29 Maidstone   Motorway junction with full / limited access

Birch   Sarn   Motorway service areas (off road, full, limited access)

A48   Primary route dual / single carriageway

   Primary route with passing places

A5   'A' road dual / single carriageway

   'A' road with passing places

B1403   'B' road dual / single carriageway

   'B' road with passing places

   Minor road

   Restricted access due to road condition or private ownership

   Roads projected or under construction

32b   Multi-level junction (occasionally with junction number)

   Roundabout

   Road tunnel

   Steep hill (arrows point downhill)

   Level crossing

Toll   Toll

Caen.....6(7½)   Car ferry route with journey times; daytime and (night-time)

   Railway line and station

   Railway tunnel

✈   Airport with scheduled services

Ⓗ   Heliport

   Built up area

□ □ □   Towns, villages and other settlements

   National boundary

   County / Unitary Authority boundary

   Woodland

468   ▲ 941   Spot / Summit height in metres

   Lake, dam and river

   Canal / Dry canal / Canal tunnel

   Beach

ℹ   ℹ   Tourist information office (all year / seasonal)

```
0        2        4        6        8       10 miles
0    2    4    6    8    10   12   14   16 km
    1:260,000 (approx)   4.1 miles to 1 inch   2.6 km to 1 cm
```

Northern Ireland map symbols (pages 110-111)

M1   Motorway

2   3   Motorway junction with full access / limited access

A1   N16   Primary / National route

A21   N56   'A' / Secondary road

B180   R170   'B' / Regional road

   Dual carriageway

   Motorway / Road under construction

   Steep hill (arrows point downhill)

   Car ferry

   Railway line

   Canal

   Lake / Lough

   River

313 ▲   Summit height in metres

✈ ✈   Airport

   International boundary

   District boundary

   Beach

   Built up areas

ℹ   ℹ   Tourist information office (all year / seasonal)

Conurbation map symbols (pages 112-120)

M73   Motorway

M6 Toll   Toll motorway

5   4 FRANKLEY SERVICES   Motorway junctions with full / limited access

   Motorway service area

A725   Primary route dual / single carriageway

A4054   'A' road dual / single carriageway

B7078   'B' road dual / single carriageway

   Minor road dual / single carriageway

○ ○ ○ ○   Roundabout

   Car ferry

   Railway line and station

Ⓢ ▣ •   Subway / Metro / Light rail station

   Railway tunnel

   Airport with scheduled services

Ⓟ   Park and ride

   Built up areas

   Public building

   County / Unitary Authority boundary

   Woodland / Park

▲ 266   Spot height in metres

Postcodes operate at five levels.

Level 1. Areas are denoted by the first one or two letters of the code, eg GL. These areas are then divided into districts.

Level 2. Districts are denoted by the number or numbers in the first part of the postcode, eg GL52. Districts are further subdivided into sectors.

Level 3. Subdistricts are a further special division of districts and only occur in London, eg EC1A.

Level 4. Sectors are denoted by the number in the second part of the postcode, eg GL52 5.

Level 5. The final two letters of the code denote a group of houses or an individual building, eg GL52 5HH.

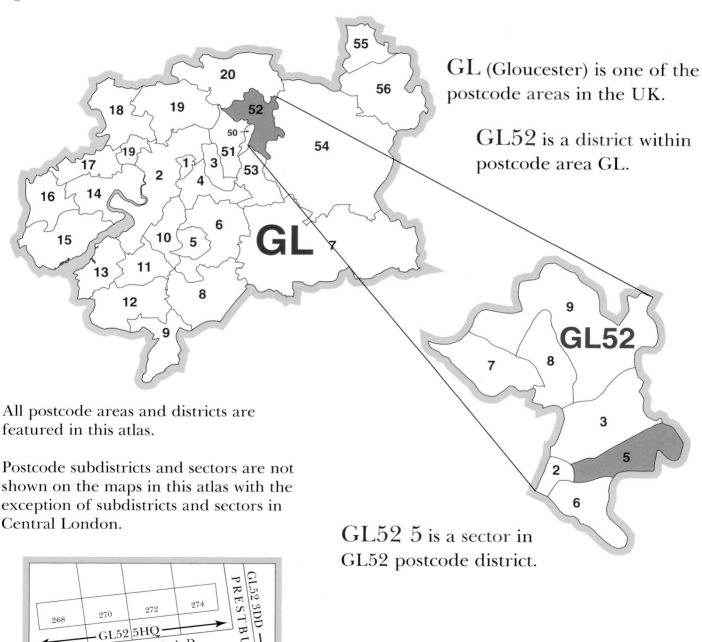

GL (Gloucester) is one of the postcode areas in the UK.

GL52 is a district within postcode area GL.

All postcode areas and districts are featured in this atlas.

Postcode subdistricts and sectors are not shown on the maps in this atlas with the exception of subdistricts and sectors in Central London.

GL52 5 is a sector in GL52 postcode district.

GL52 5HH is the postcode. It pinpoints a group of houses and in some cases individual business premises.

Map of postcode areas

Atlantic
Ocean

North
Sea

ZE

KW

Thurso
KW

HS

Ullapool

IV

HS

IV

Inverness

AB

Aberdeen

HS

PH

Fort
William

PH

DD

PA

PA

Perth
KY

Dundee

FK

G

EDINBURGH

PA

Glasgow

EH

PA

KA

ML

TD

KA

NE

Newcastle
upon Tyne

Londonderry

DG

Stranraer

SR

BT

Carlisle
CA

DH

Middlesbrough

BELFAST

DL

TS

Isle of
Man

IM

LA

HG

YO

Lancaster

REPUBLIC
OF
IRELAND

Irish
Sea

LL

BD

FY PR BB

HX LS WF

HU

Leeds

BL OL HD

DN

Liverpool

L WN M

WA

SK

S

CH

CW

NG

Lincoln
LN

LL

ST

DE

Nottingham

SY

TF WS

LE

PE

Norwich
NR

Aberystwyth

WV

Birmingham

NN

Cambridge

IP

DY B CV

Ipswich

LD

HR

WR

MK

SG

CB

CO

SA

NP

GL

Oxford

LU

CM

HP AL

SS

Swansea

CF

BS

SN

SL

LONDON

CARDIFF

Bristol

RG

KT

ME

TA

BA

GU

CT

EX

DT BH

SP

SO

PO

RH

TN

Folkestone

Exeter

Southampton

BN

PL

TQ

PO

Brighton

Plymouth

Isles of
Scilly

TR

TR

English Channel

Channel
Islands GY

iii

JE

FRANCE

London inset

HP WD AL SG EN CM

HA N E IG

SL UB W WC EC RM SS

TW SW SE BR DA ME

KT S M CR

GU RH TN

Postcode	Area	Postcode	Area	Postcode	Area
AB	Aberdeen	HG	Harrogate	PL	Plymouth
AL	St Albans	HP	Hemel	PO	Portsmouth
B	Birmingham		Hempstead	PR	Preston
BA	Bath	HR	Hereford	RG	Reading
BB	Blackburn	HS	Hebrides	RH	Redhill
BD	Bradford	HU	Kingston upon	RM	Romford
BH	Bournemouth		Hull	S	Sheffield
BL	Bolton	HX	Halifax	SA	Swansea
BN	Brighton	IG	Ilford	SE	London SE
BR	Bromley	IM	Isle of Man	SG	Stevenage
BS	Bristol	IP	Ipswich	SK	Stockport
BT	Northern Ireland	IV	Inverness	SL	Slough
CA	Carlisle	JE	Jersey	SM	Sutton
CB	Cambridge	KA	Kilmarnock	SN	Swindon
CF	Cardiff	KT	Kingston-upon-	SO	Southampton
CH	Chester		Thames	SP	Salisbury
CM	Chelmsford	KW	Kirkwall	SR	Sunderland
CO	Colchester	KY	Kirkcaldy	SS	Southend-on-
CR	Croydon	L	Liverpool		Sea
CT	Canterbury	LA	Lancaster	ST	Stoke-on-Trent
CV	Coventry	LD	Llandrindod	SW	London SW
CW	Crewe		Wells	SY	Shrewsbury
DA	Dartford	LE	Leicester	TA	Taunton
DD	Dundee	LL	Llandudno	TD	Galashiels
DE	Derby	LN	Lincoln	TF	Telford
DG	Dumfries	LS	Leeds	TN	Royal Tunbridge
DH	Durham	LU	Luton		Wells
DL	Darlington	M	Manchester	TQ	Torquay
DN	Doncaster	ME	Medway	TR	Truro
DT	Dorchester	MK	Milton Keynes	TS	Teesside
DY	Dudley	ML	Motherwell	TW	Twickenham
E	London E	N	London N	UB	Southall
EC	London EC	NE	Newcastle upon	W	London W
EH	Edinburgh		Tyne	WA	Warrington
EN	Enfield	NG	Nottingham	WC	London WC
EX	Exeter	NN	Northampton	WD	Watford
FK	Falkirk	NP	Newport	WF	Wakefield
FY	Blackpool	NR	Norwich	WN	Wigan
G	Glasgow	NW	London NW	WR	Worcester
GL	Gloucester	OL	Oldham	WS	Walsall
GU	Guildford	OX	Oxford	WV	Wolverhampton
GY	Guernsey	PA	Paisley	YO	York
HA	Harrow	PE	Peterborough	ZE	Lerwick
HD	Huddersfield	PH	Perth		

iv

ISLES OF SCILLY

TR

LIZARD POINT

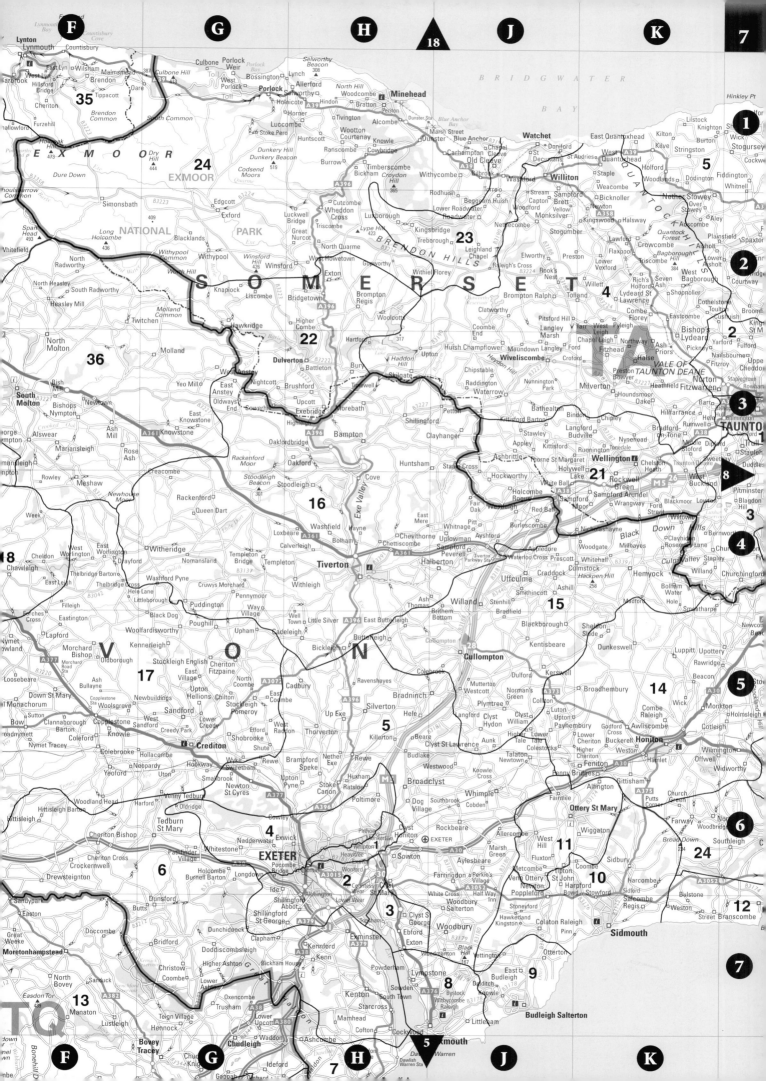

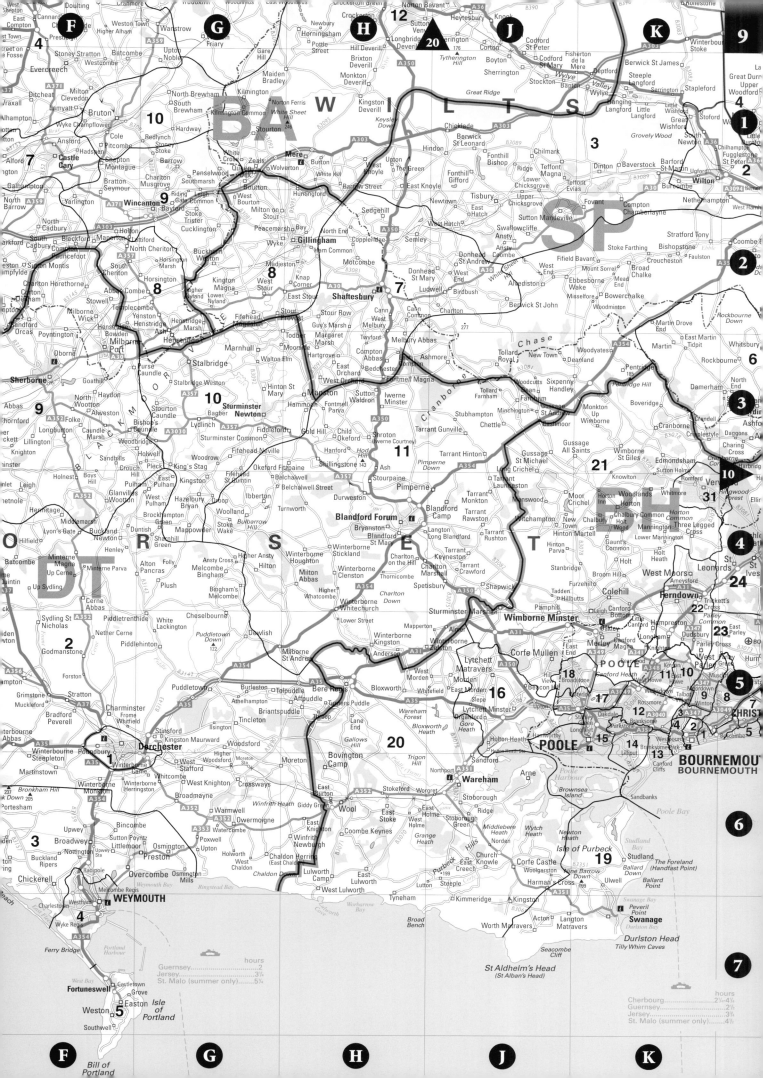

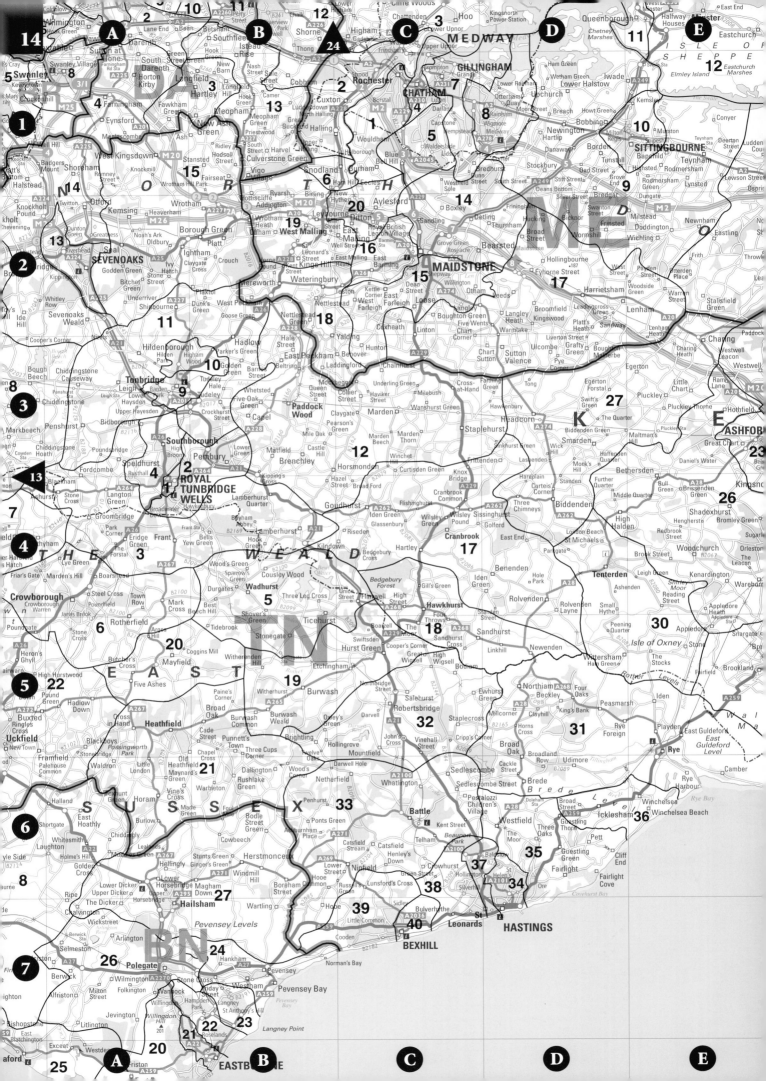

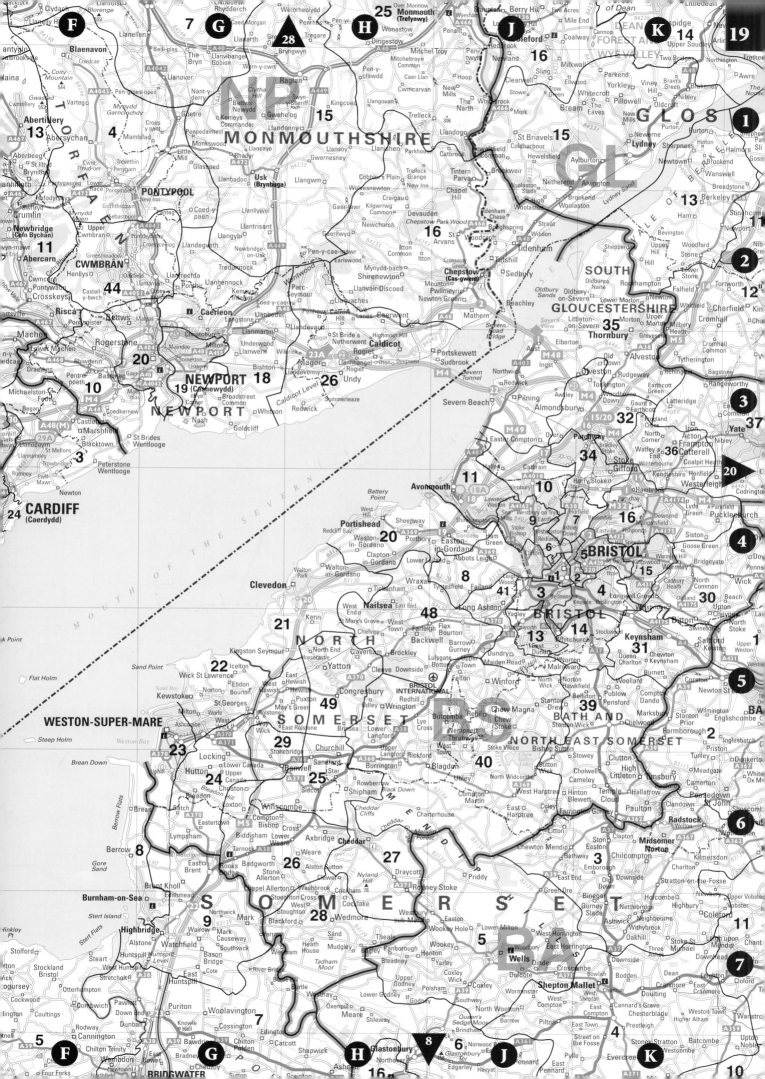

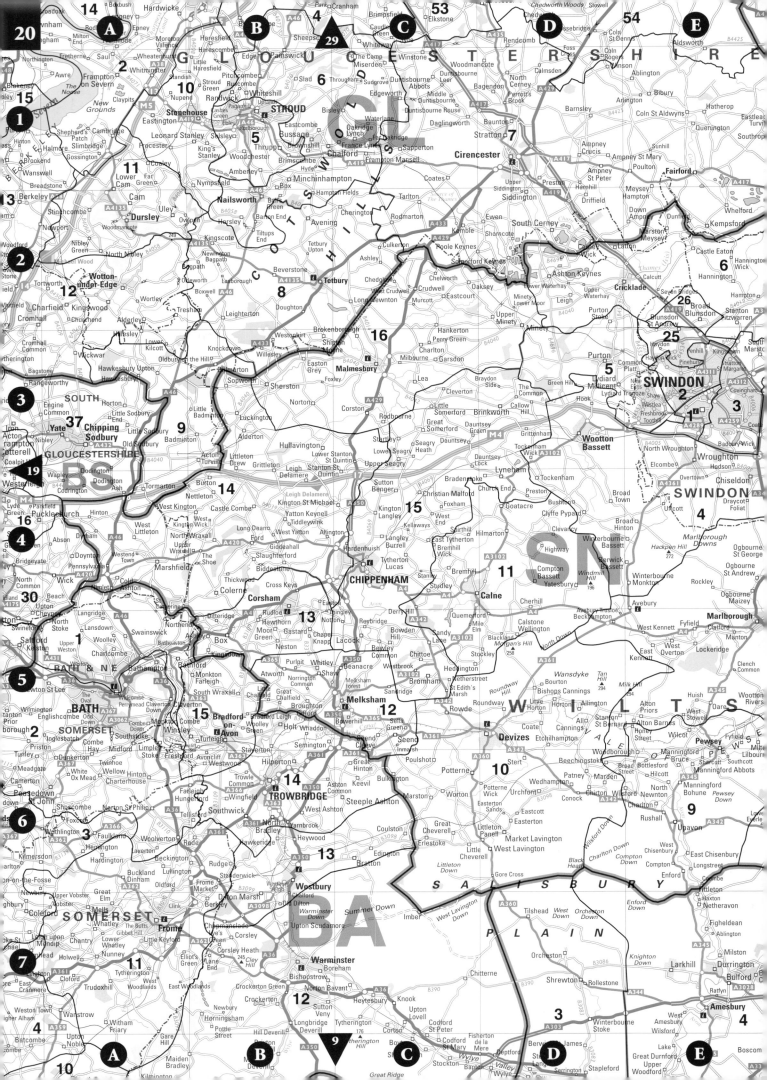

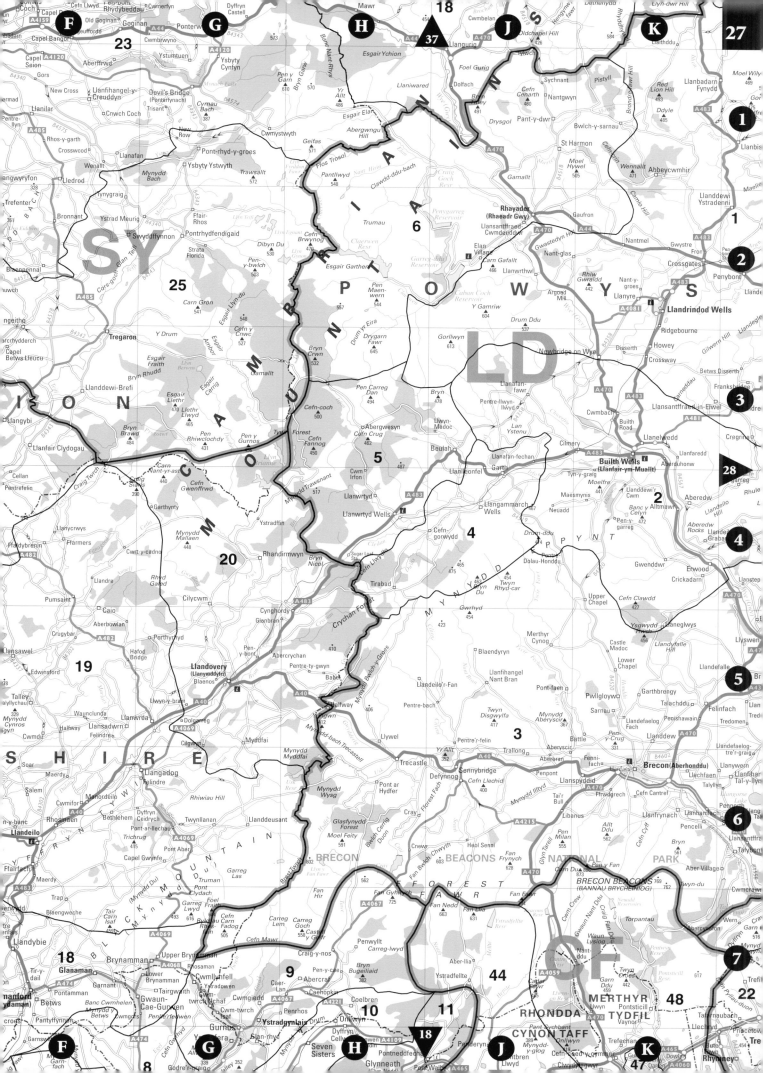

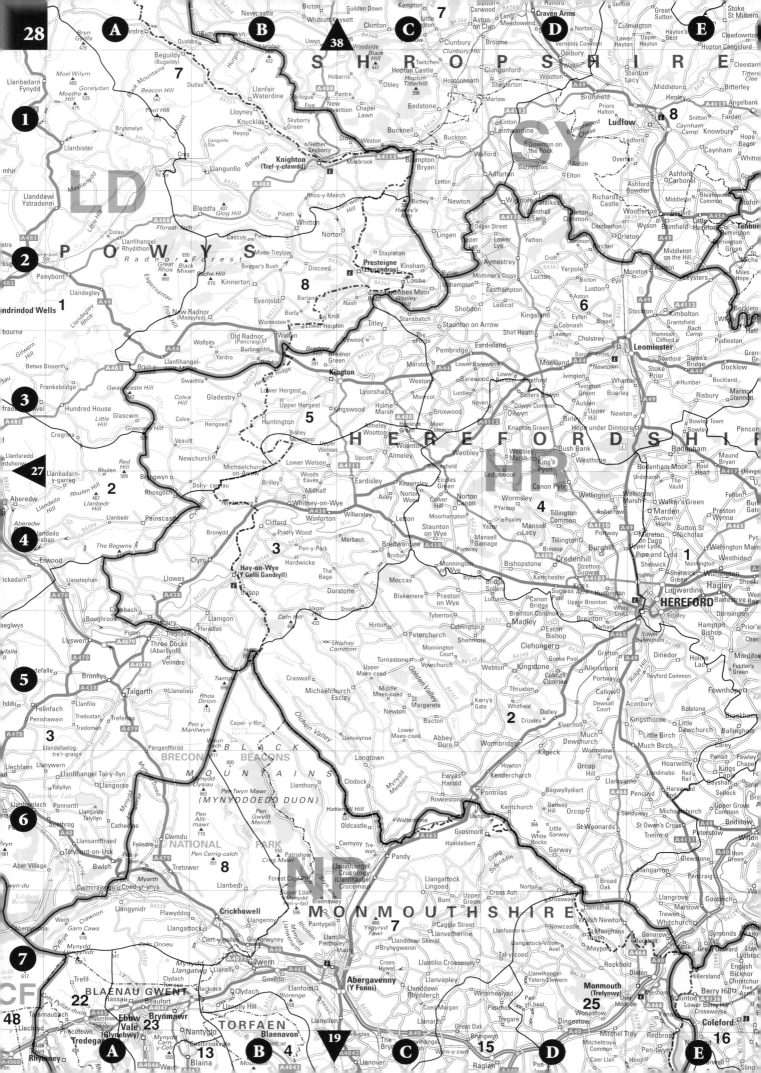

See pages 112 - 113 for postcode detail

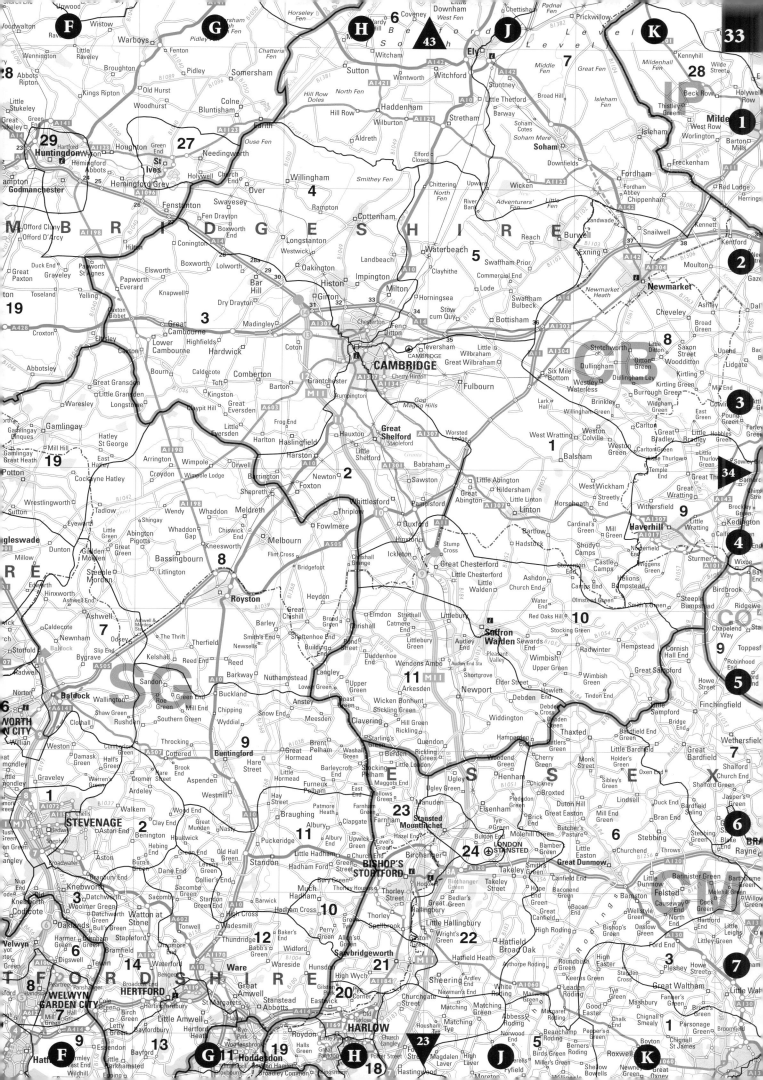

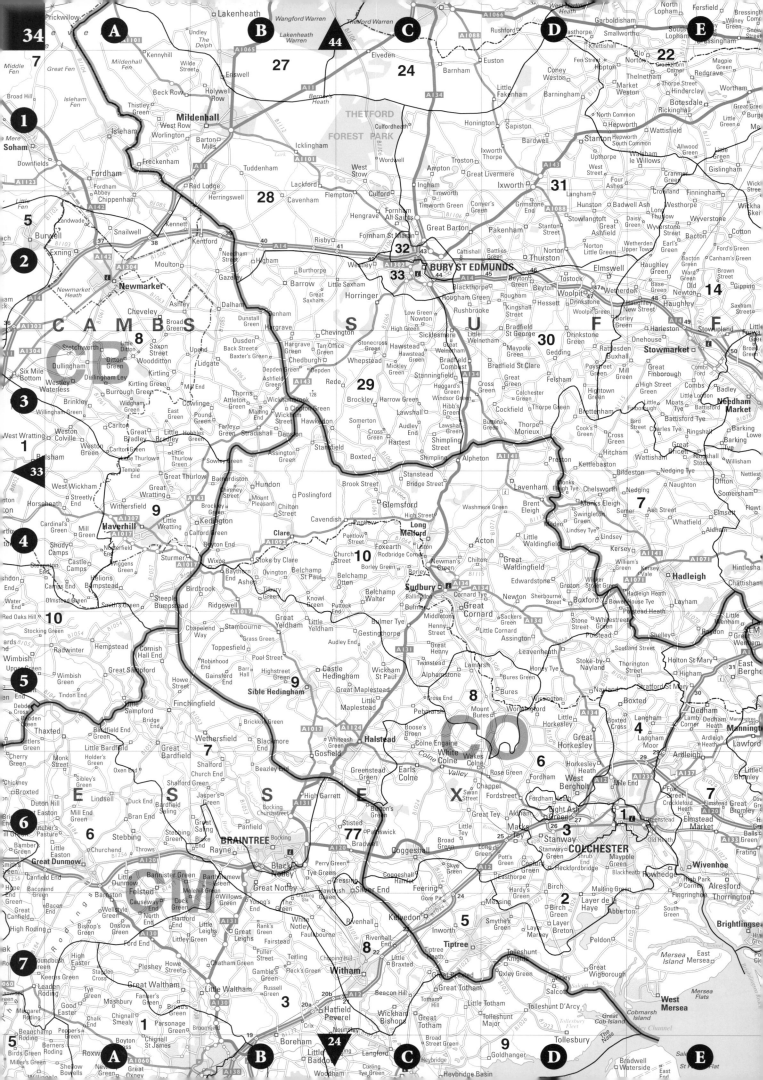

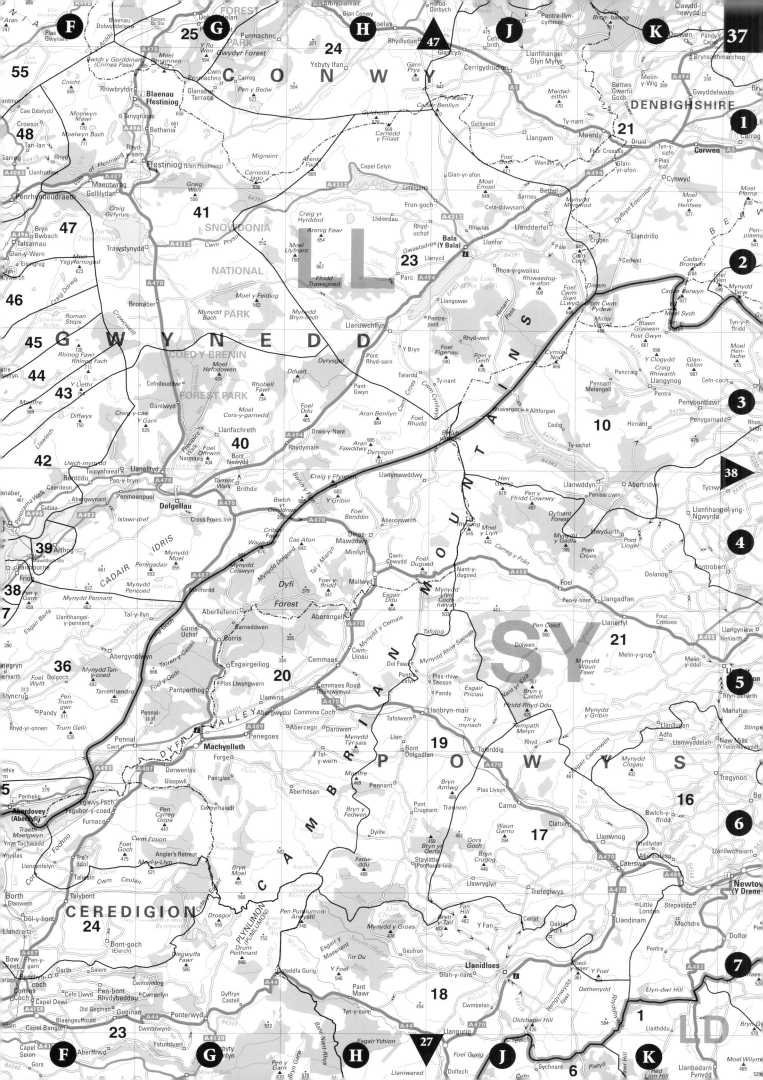

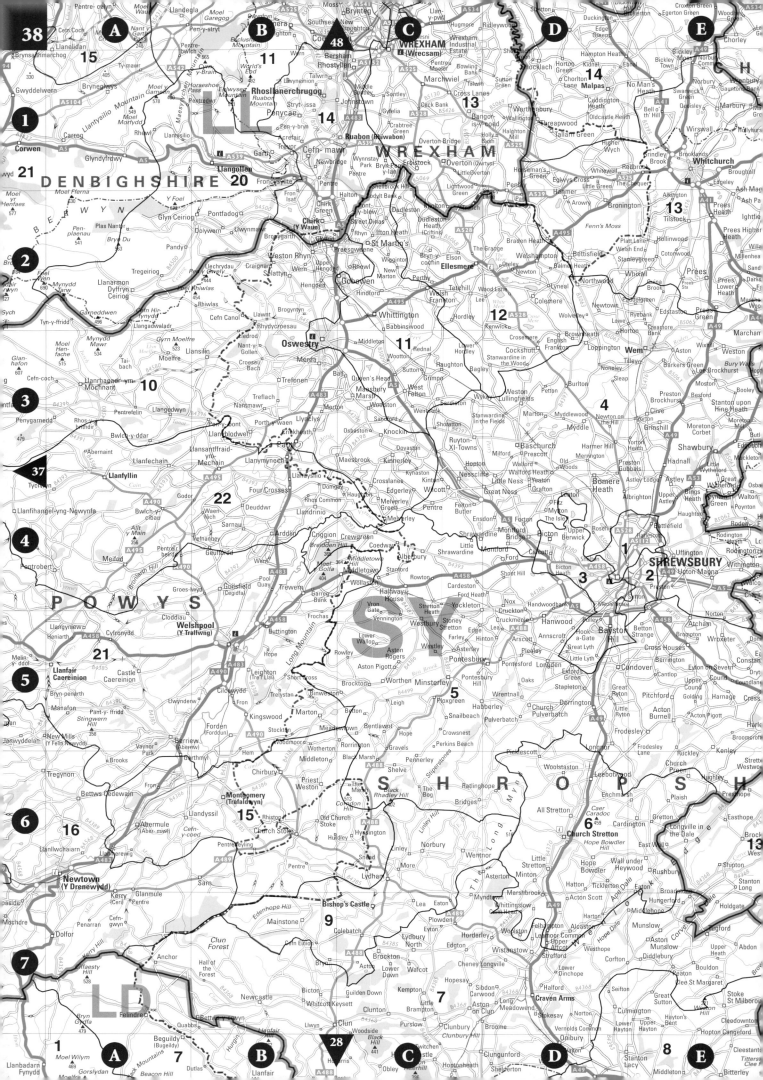

See pages 112 - 113 for postcode detail

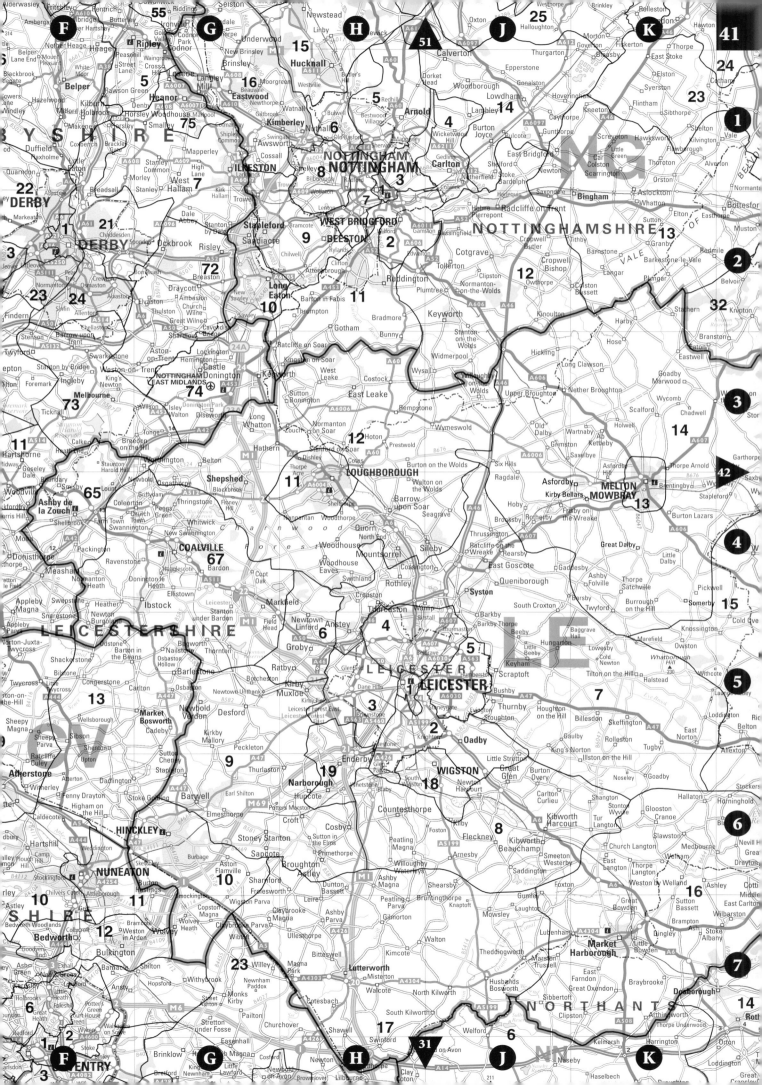

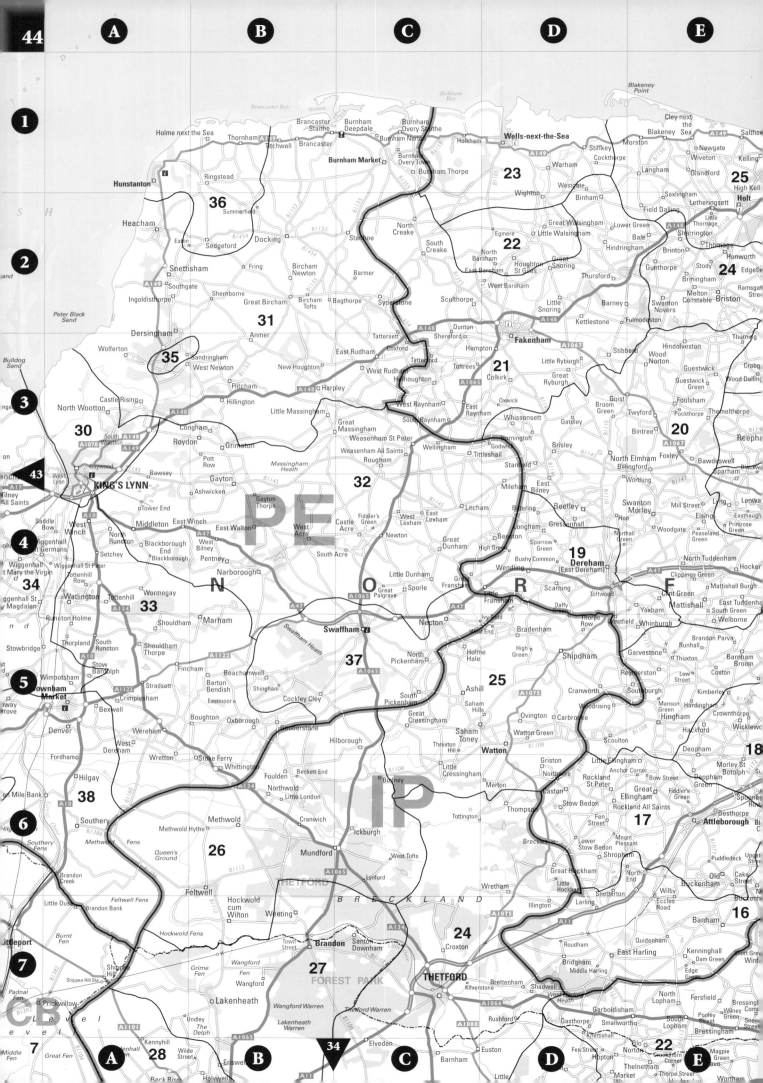

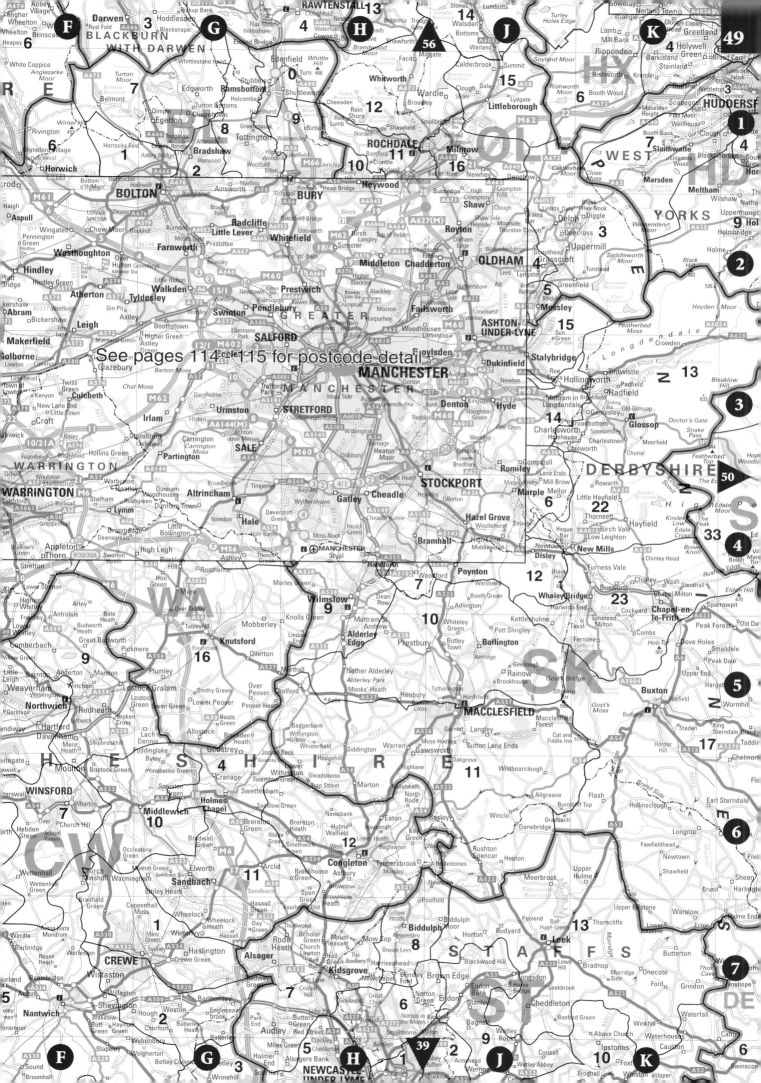

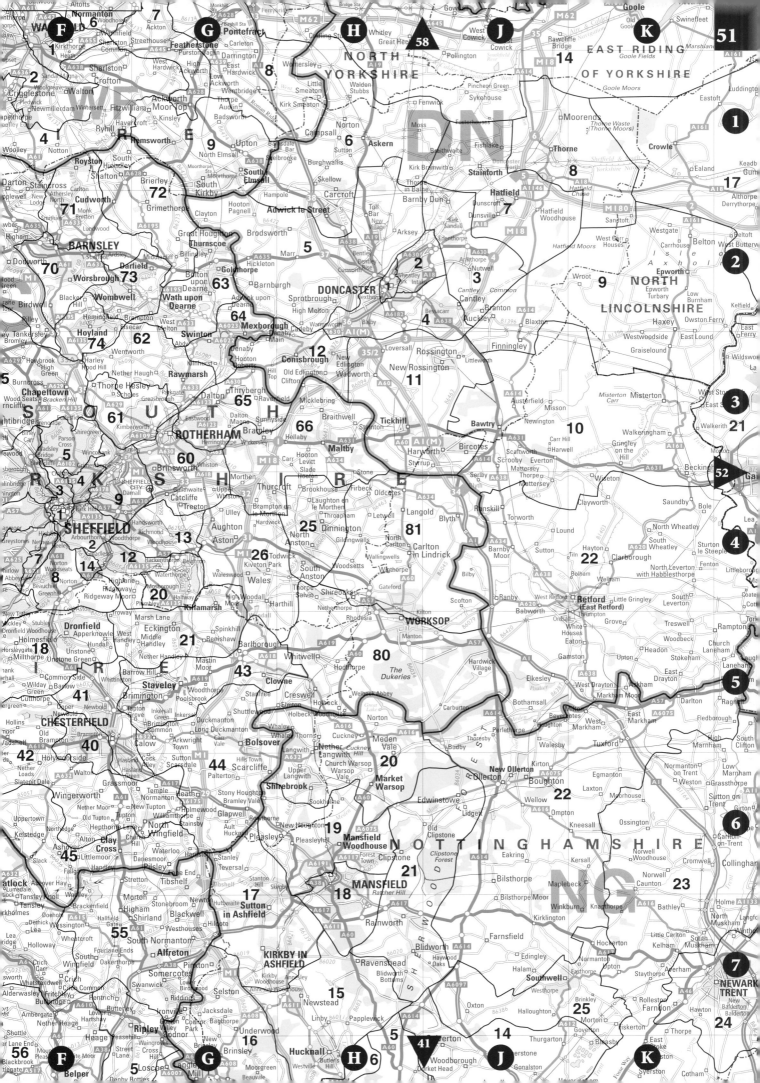

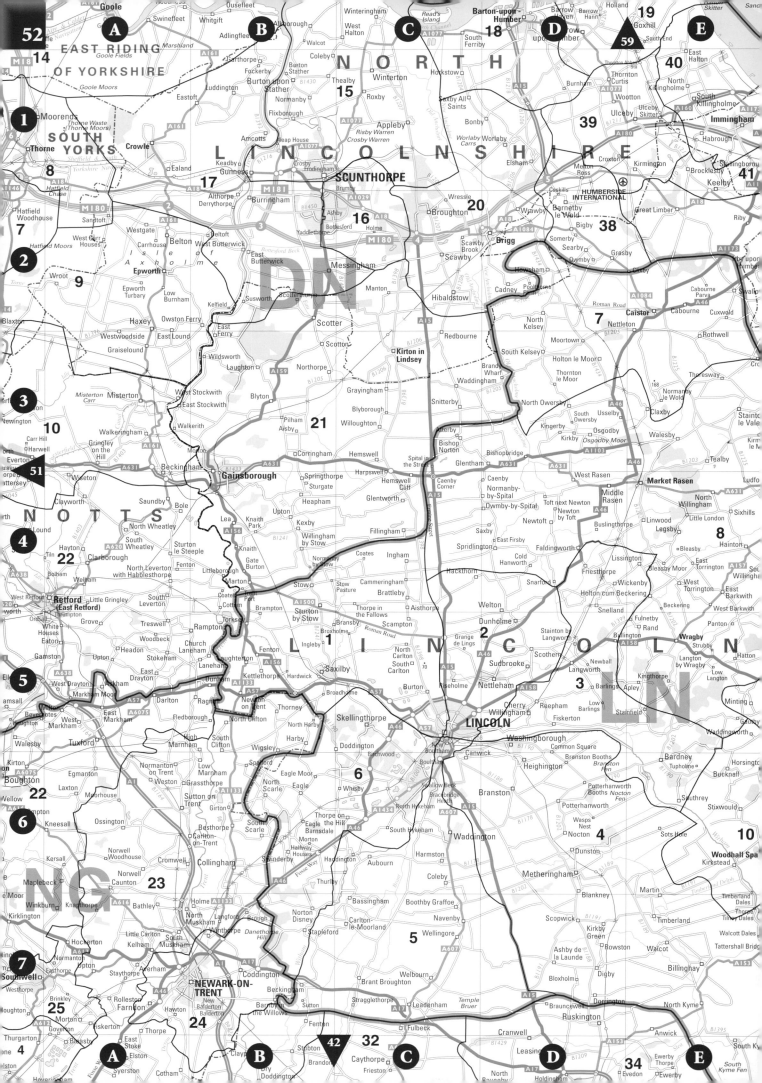

A B C D E

19
18

1

2

3

same scale as main map

Point of
Ayre

Rue
Point

The Ayres

A16

The
Lhen   Glentruan   Cranstal

Sartfield   A10   Dhowin   A17   Bride

A19   A9
Jurby Head   Jurby
Jurby West   Sandygate   East   B7   Regaby   Shellag Point

ISLE
OF
MAN

IM

Ballasalla
Crawyn   St Judes   A13   Dhoor   Ramsey Bay
The Cronk   A10 A13   A13
The Curraghs   Kella   Sulby   8   Ramsey
Orrisdale   A3   A3   Churchtown   Port e
Orrisdale Head   A10   Ballaugh   A14   7   Glen Auldyn   Vullen

Ravensdale   Slieau Managh   A18   Dreemskerry   A15   Maughold Head
Kirk Michael   Slieau   A14   383   North Barrule   Ballajora   Maughold
Curn   Slieau   565
351   Dhoo   Corrany
Ballacarnane Beg   424   Clagh   Glen
6   Slieau   551   Ouyr   Mona
Barregarrow   Freoaghane   621   469
Gob y Deigan   Sartfell   488   Snaefell   Slieau   Dhoon
Knocksharry   454   B10   546   Lhean   Port Cornaa
Cronk-   Little   B10   Beinn-   Bulgham Bay
y-Voddy   London   Injebreck   y-Phott
St Patrick's Isle   Peel   Colden   B22   Laxey
Ballaugh   Lambfell Moar   487
Contrary Head   A1   Laxey Head
A20   Injebreck   Ballacannell
Ballig   Reservoir   A18   Laxey
Knockaloe Moar   Slieau   Bay
Patrick   Ruy   Baldwin   Baldrine
A27   A30   St   Greeba   478
5   John's   Mountain   B20   Garwick Bay
Glenmaye   422   4   Sulby   Clay Head
333   Lower   Hilberry
Dalby   Foxdale   Crosby   A23   A2   A11
Point   A1   Glen Vine   A22
Dalby Mountain   Garth   Strang   Onchan   3
Dalby   280   Eairy   2   Onchan Head
Niarbyl   Foxdale   A24   Union Mills   A16   1
Island   A36   A26   Cooil   DOUGLAS
483   Stugga   Braaid   Douglas
Niarbyl   South   Close   B35   Bay
Bay   Barrule   Clark   Newtown   Quine's
Stroin   341   B30   Hill
Vuigh   A27   Ballamodha   St Mark's   Ballaveare   A37   Douglas
A36   Ronague   A3   A5   A25   Little Ness   Head
Lingague   9   Grenaby
Ballakilpheric   B41   hours
Bradda Head   Bradda   Colby   Ballabeg   Ballasalla   Belfast (Summer Only)..............2¾
Port Erin   Ballafesson   Santon Head   Dublin (Summer Only)..........2¾-4¾
Croit e Caley   Balladoole   Port   Heysham...............................3½
Cregneash   Derbyhaven   Grenaugh   Liverpool.............................2¾-4
Calf   The   Port   ISLE OF MAN
of Man   A31   Howe   St Mary   Castletown
Spanish   Perwick   Castletown   St Michael's Island
Head   Bay   Bay   Langness
Chicken   Dreswick
Rock   Point

4

5

6

7

A B C D E

See pages 116 - 117 for postcode detail

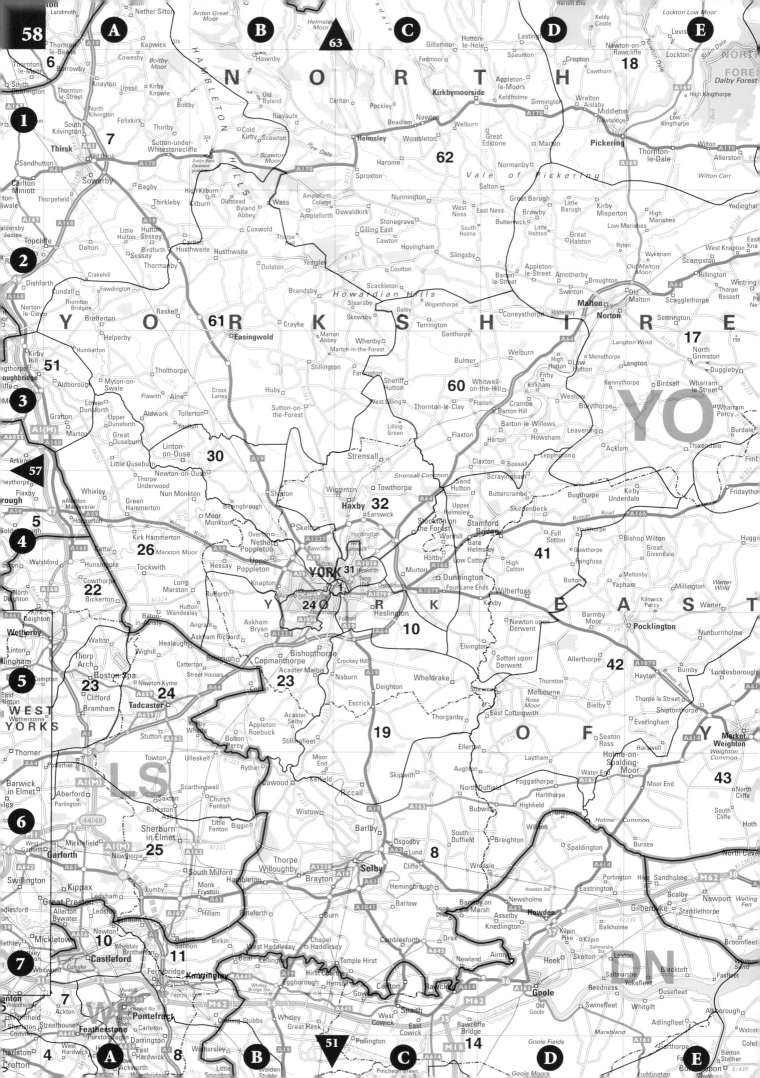

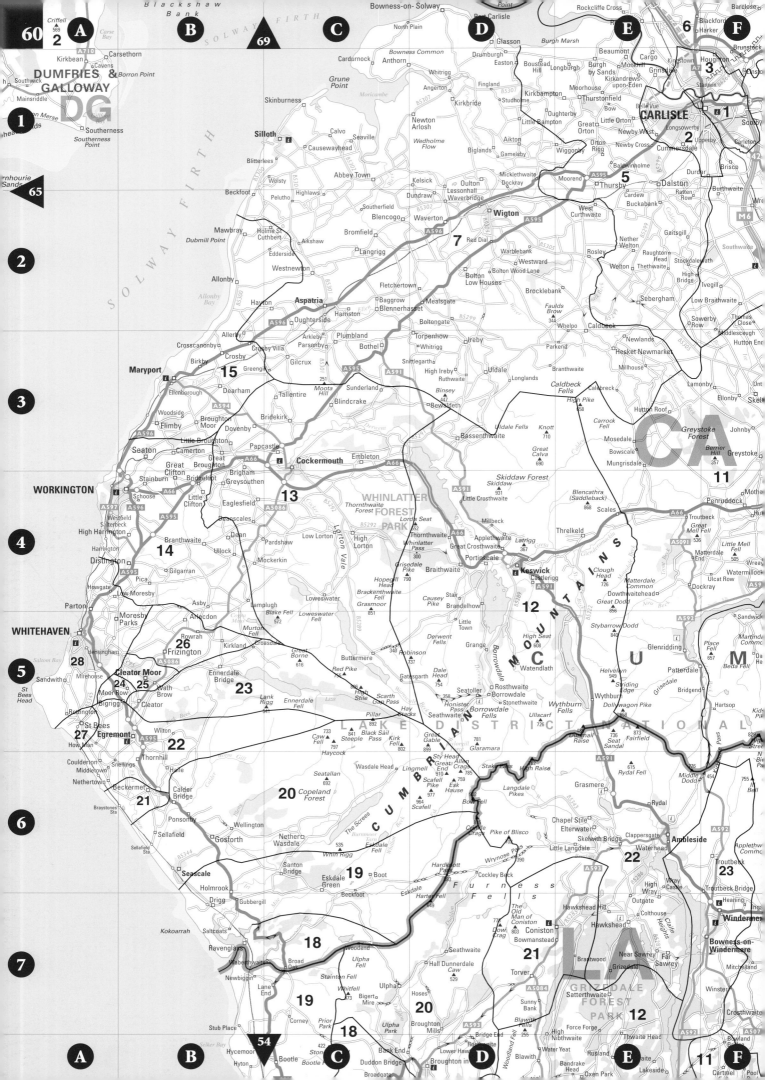

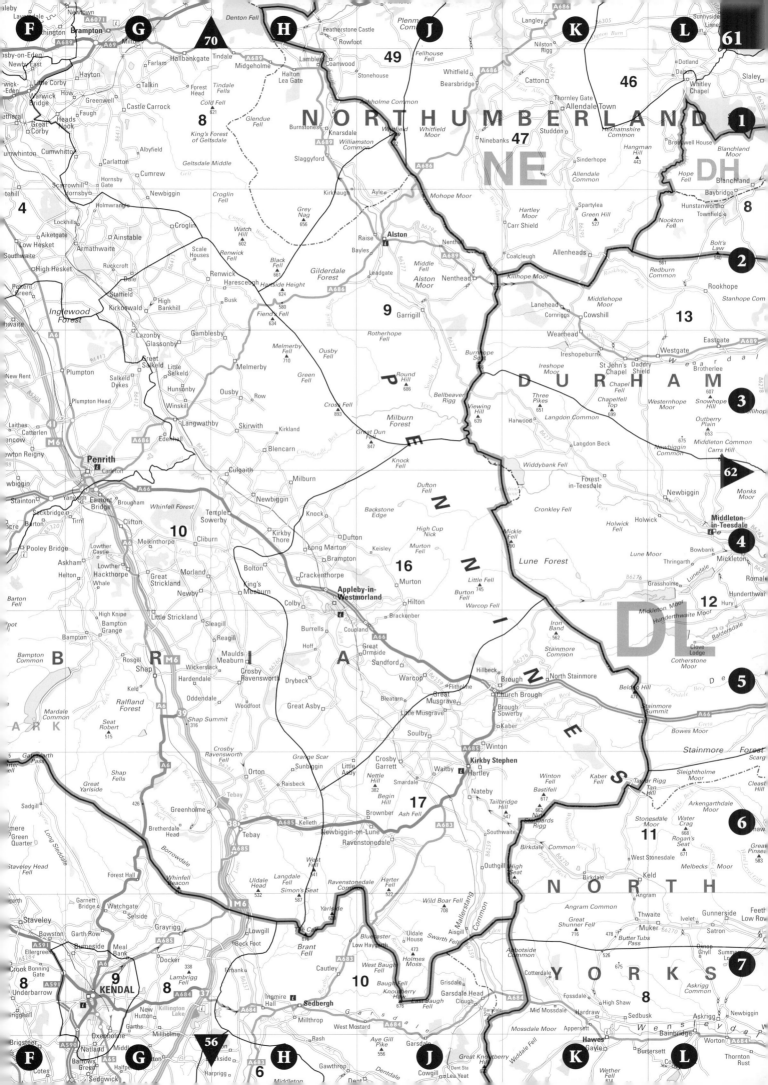

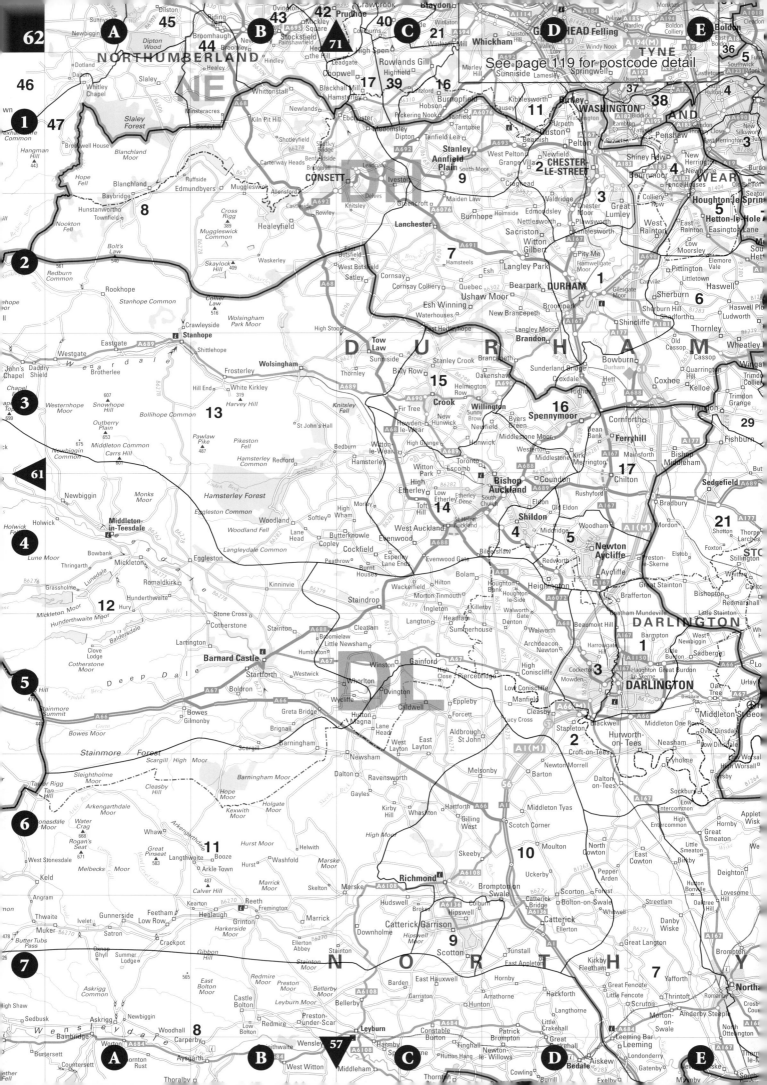

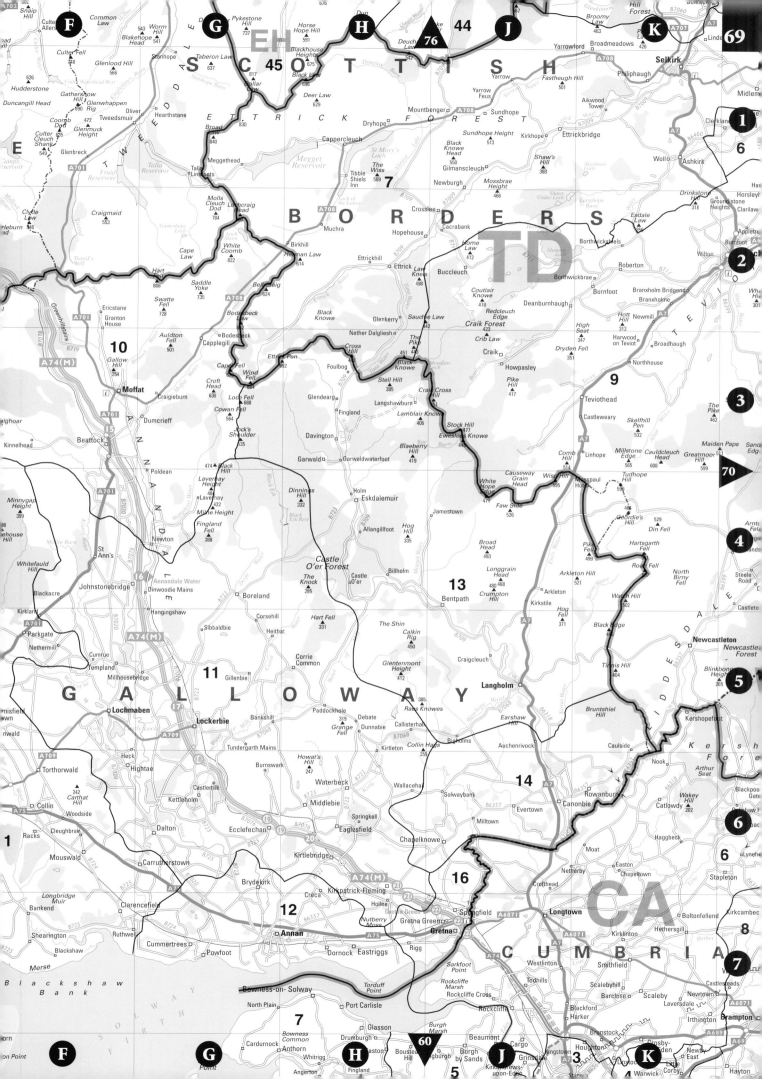

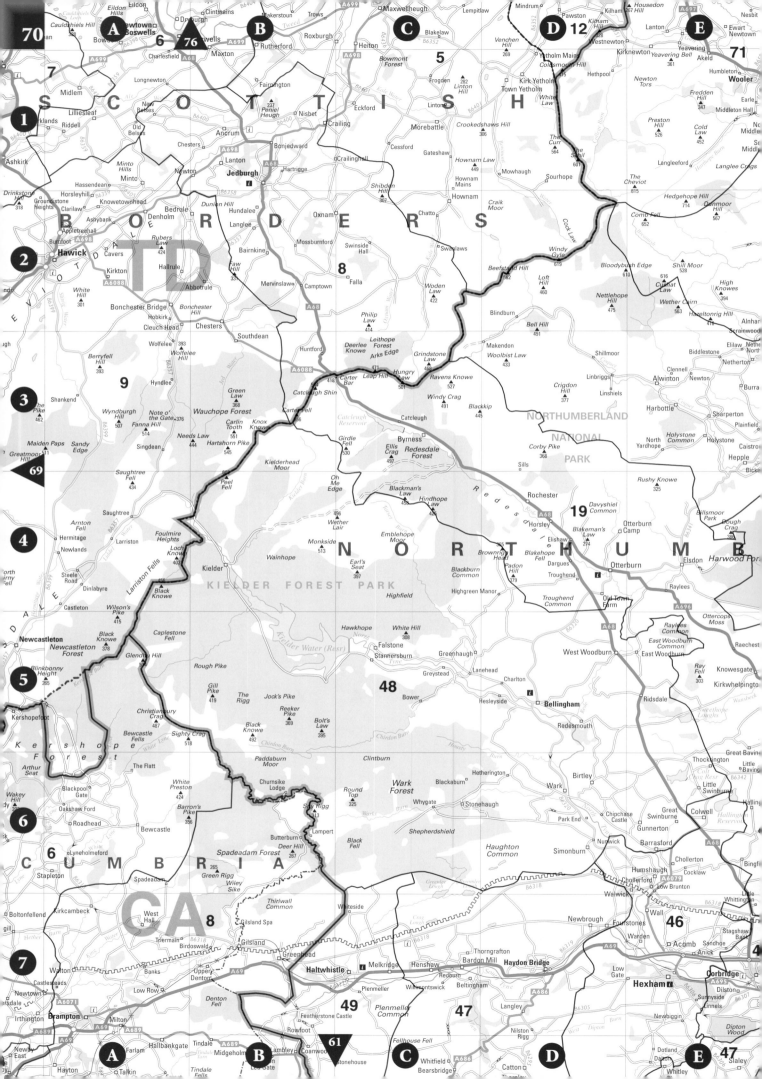

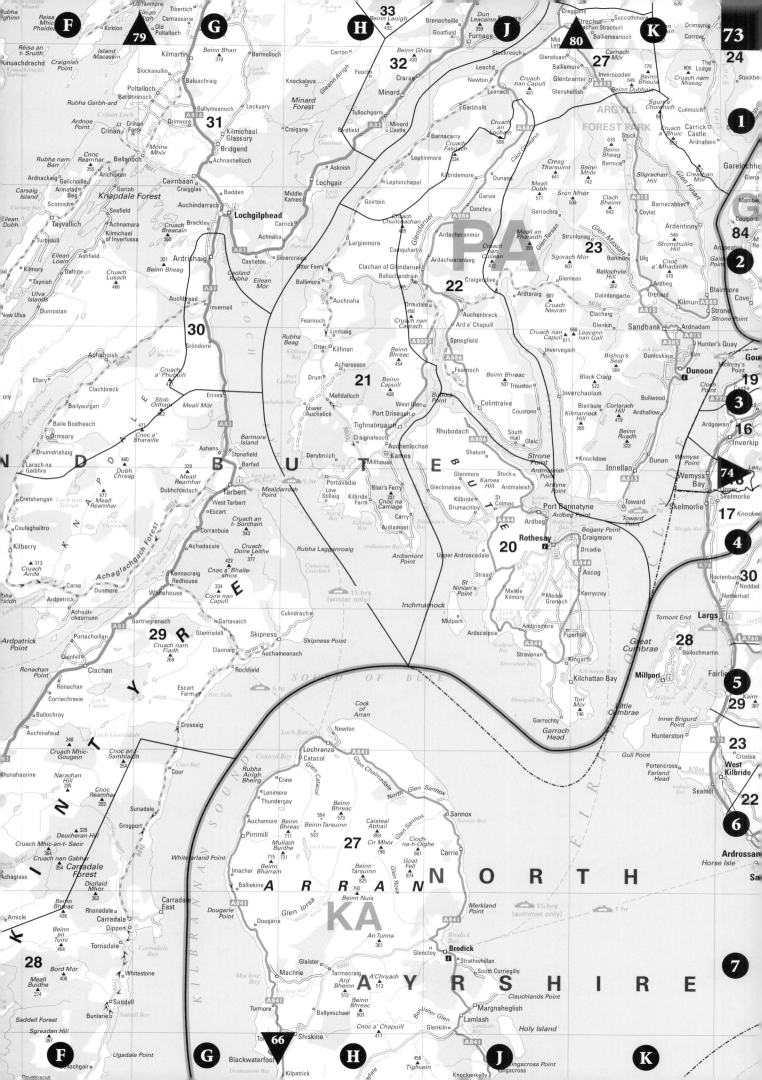

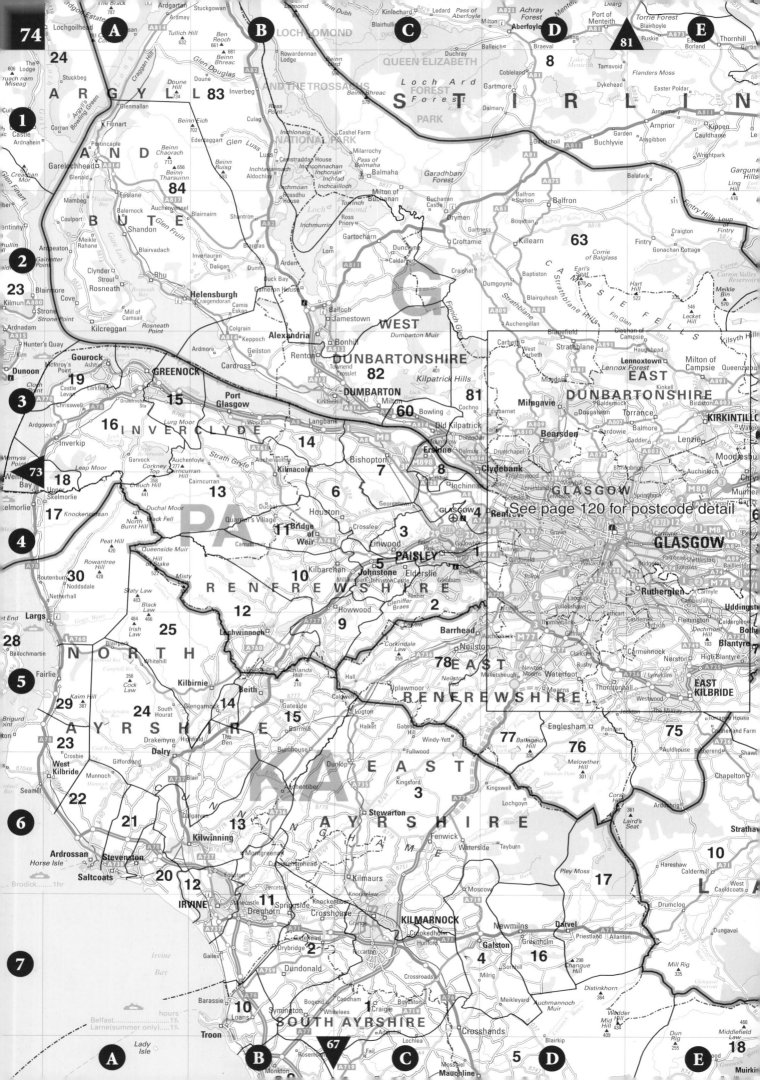

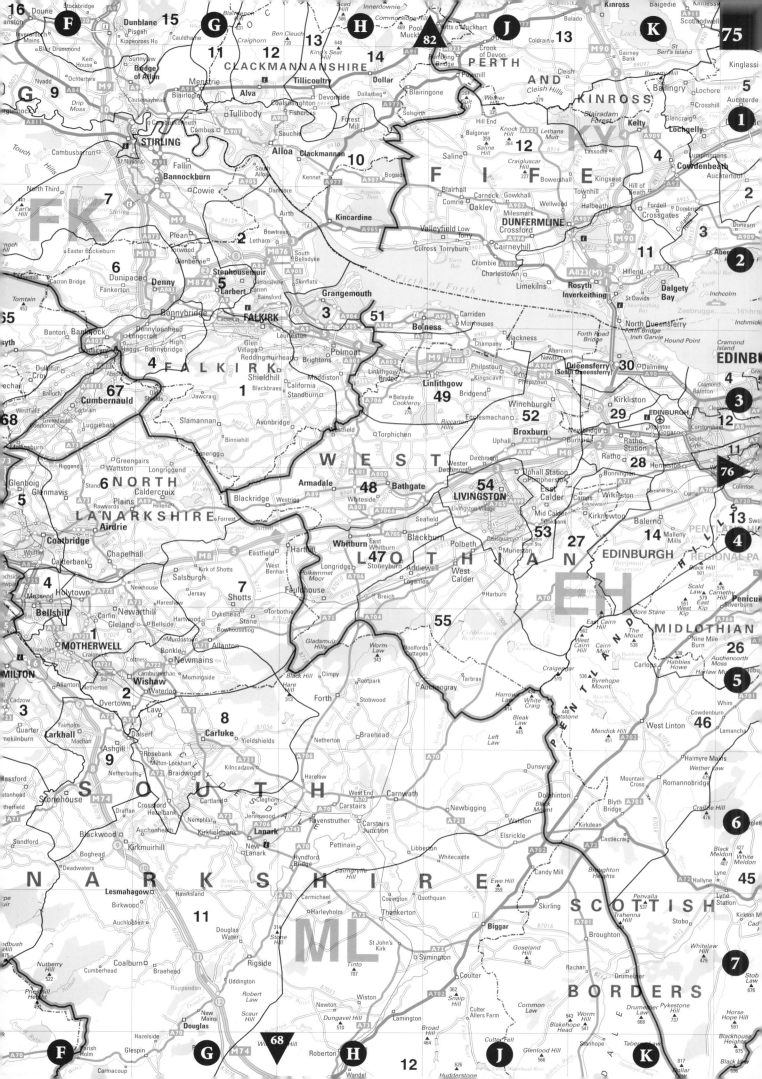

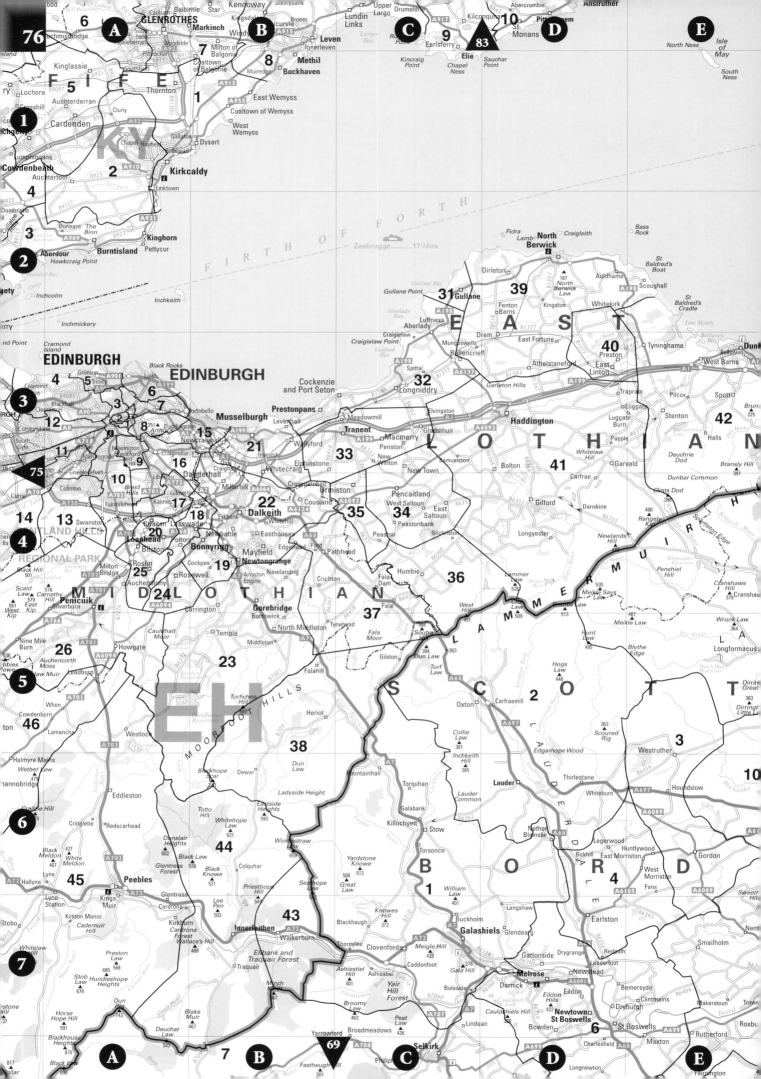

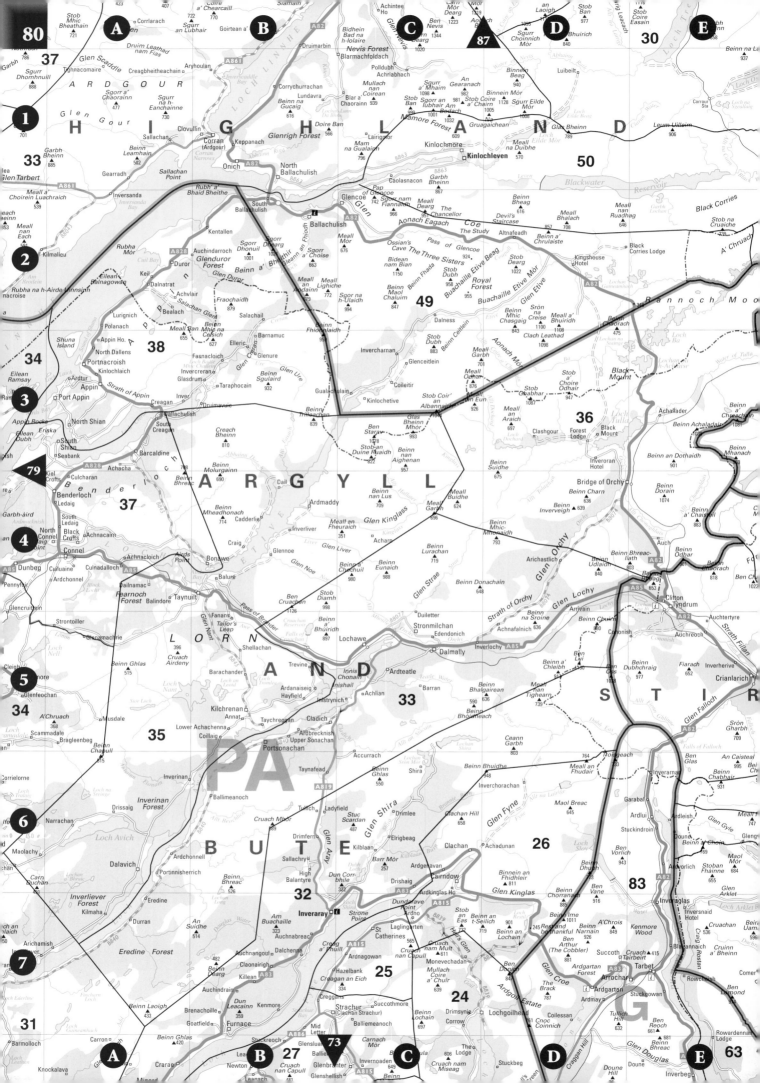

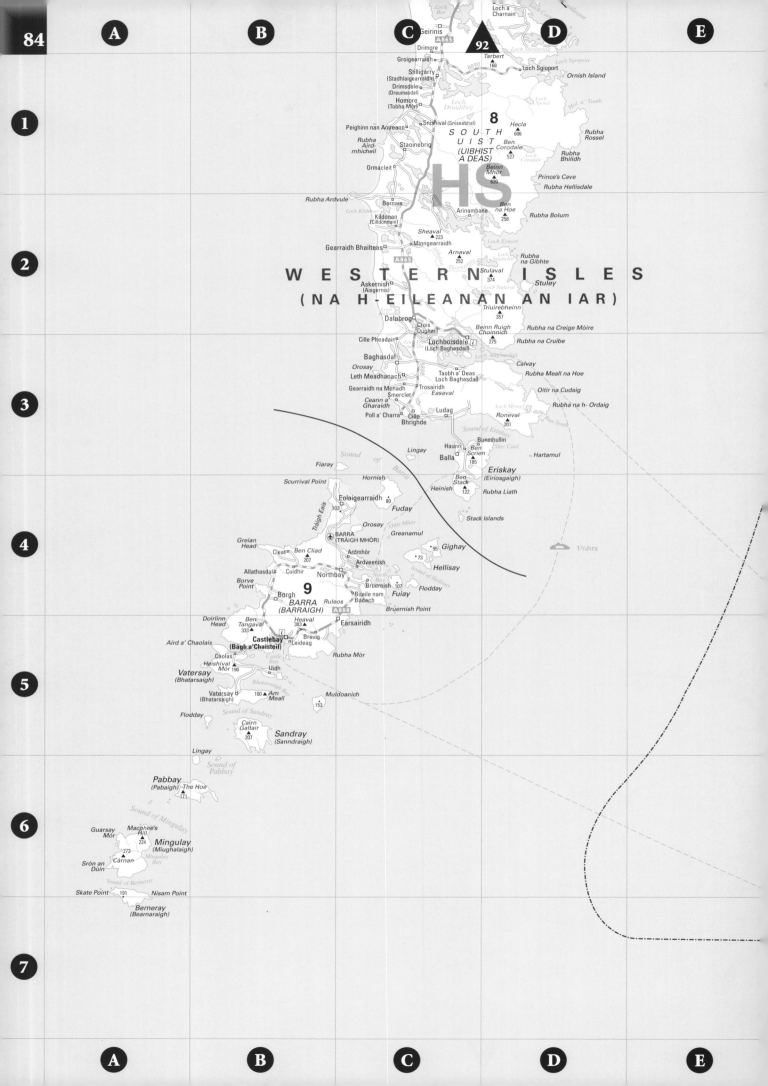

A   B   C   A865   92   D   E

Loch a
Charnain

Geirinis
Drimore
Groigearraidh
Tarbert
168
Loch Sgioport
Loch Shirlaveag

Stilligarry
(Stadhlaigearraidh)
Ornish Island

Drimsdale
(Dreumasdal)
Loch
Druidibeg
Mol a' Tuath

Homore
(Tobha Mòr)

8
SOUTH
UIST
(UIBHIST
A DEAS)
Hecla
606
Rubha
Rossel

Peighinn nan Aoireann
Snishival (Sniseabhal)

Ben
Corodale
527
Rubha
Bhilidh

Rubha
Aird-
mhicheil
Staoinebrig
HS

Ormacleit
Beinn
Mhòr
620
Prince's Cave

Rubha Hellisdale

Rubha Ardvule
Bornais
Ben
na Hoe
258
Rubha Bolum

Kildonan
(Cilldonnain)
Loch Kildonan
Arinambane

Sheaval
223

WESTERN ISLES
Minngearraidh

(NA H-EILEANAN AN IAR)

Gearraidh Bhailteas
Arnaval
252
Rubha
na Gibhte

A865
Stulaval
374
Stuley

Triuirebheinn
357
Rubha na Creige Mòire

Dalabrog
Crois
Dughaill
Beinn Ruigh
Choinnich
275
Rubha na Cruibe

Cille Pheadair
Lochboisdale
(Loch Baghasdail)
Calvay

Baghasdal
Rubha Meall na Hoe

Orosay
Taobh a' Deas
Loch Baghasdail
Oitir na Cudaig

Leth Meadhanach
Trosairidh
Easaval
Rubha na h- Ordaig

Gearraidh na Monadh
Smerclet

Ceann a'
Gharaidh
Ludag
Roneval
201

Poll a' Charra
Cille
Bhrighde
Sound of Eriskay

Bunmhullin

Lingay
Haunn
Ben
Scrien
185
Hartamul

Sound   of   Barra
Balla
Eriskay
(Eiriosgaigh)

Fiaray
Ben
Stack
122
Rubha Liath

Scurrival Point
Hornish
Heinish

Eolaigearraidh
80
Fuday
Stack Islands

Tràigh Eais
Orosay
Oitir Mhòr
Greanamul
Gighay
95

BARRA
(TRAIGH MHÒR)
73
Hellisay
1¾hrs

Greian
Head
Cleat
Ben Cliad
207
Ardmhòr
Ardveenish
Sound of Hellisay

Allathasdale
Cuidhir
Northbay
Bruernish
107
Flodday
Fuiay

Borve
Point
Bòrgh
9
BARRA
(BARRAIGH)
Ruleos
Buaile nam
Bodach

Doirlinn
Head
Ben
Tangaval
333
Heaval
383
Eàrsairidh
Bruernish Point

Aird a' Chaolais
Castlebay
(Bàgh a'Chaisteil)
Brevig
Leideag

Rubha Mòr

Caolas
Heishival
Mòr 190
Uidh
Castle
Bay

Vatersay
(Bhatarsaigh)
Bhatarsaigh Bay

Vatersay
(Bhatarsaigh)
100
Am
Meall
Muldoanich

Flodday
153

Sound of Sandray

Lingay
Sandray
(Sanndraigh)

Cairn
Galtair
207

Sound of
Pabbay

Pabbay
(Pabaigh)
The Hoe
171

Sound   of   Mingulay

Guarsay
Mòr
Macphee's
Hill
224
Mingulay
(Miughalaigh)

273
Càrnan
Mingulay
Bay

Sròn an
Dùin

Sound of Berneray

Skate Point
191
Nisam Point

Berneray
(Bearnaraigh)

A   B   C   D   E

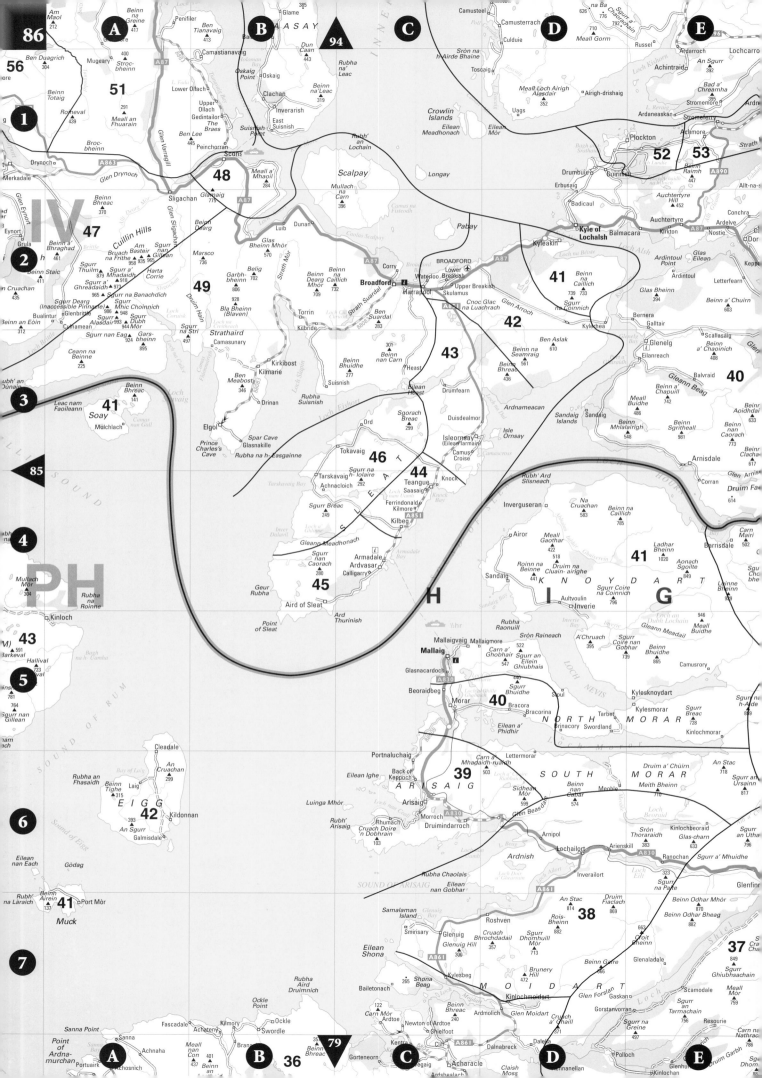

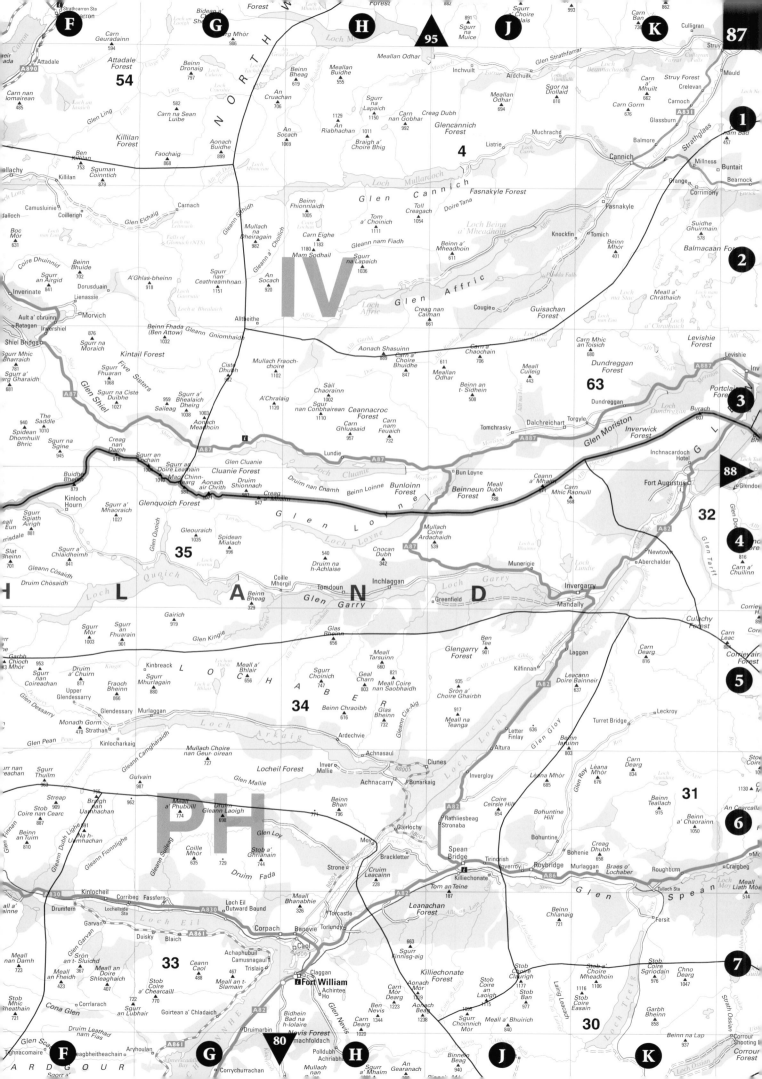

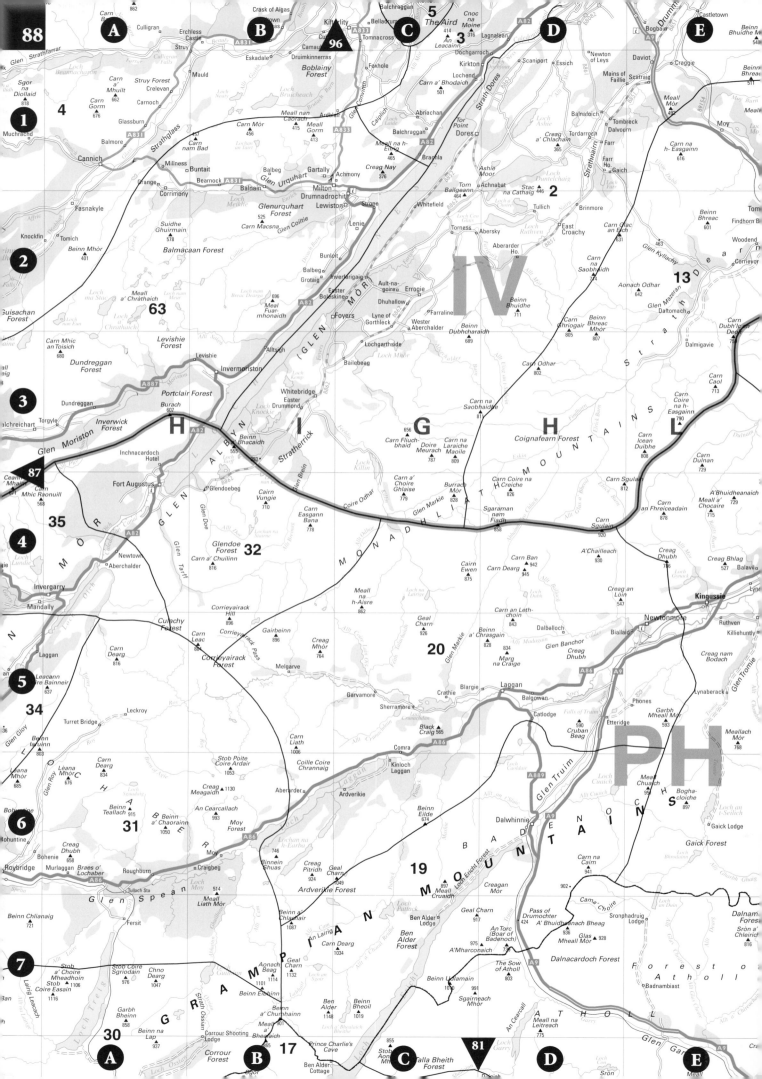

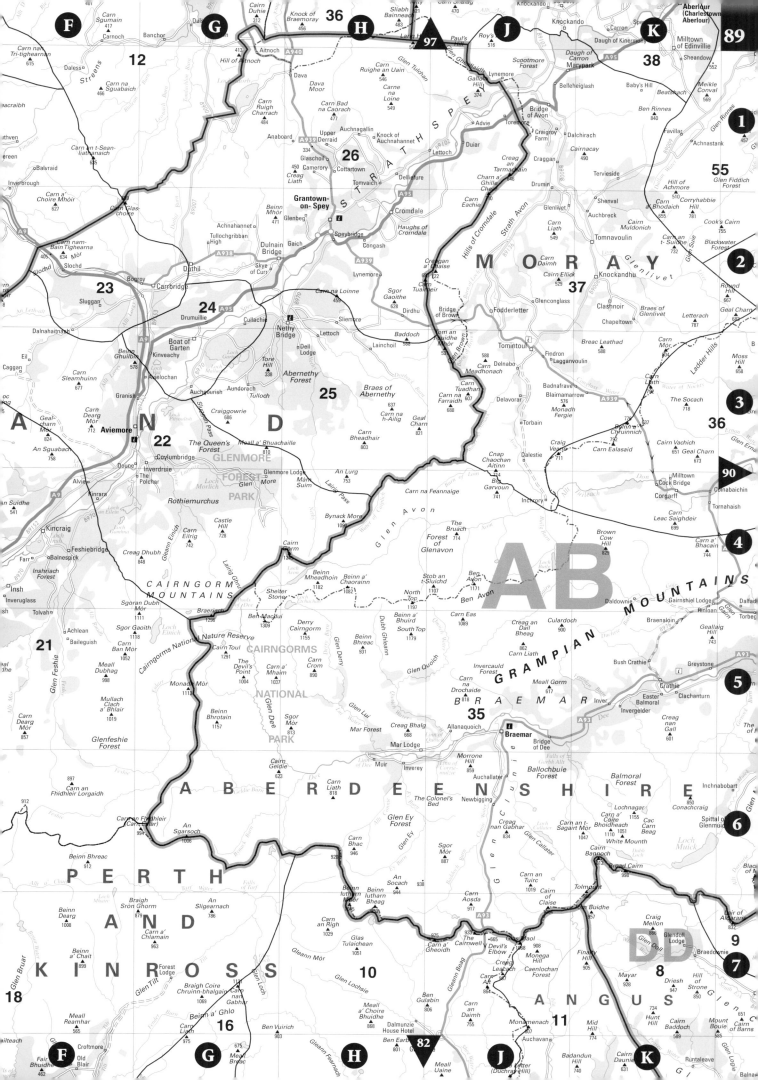

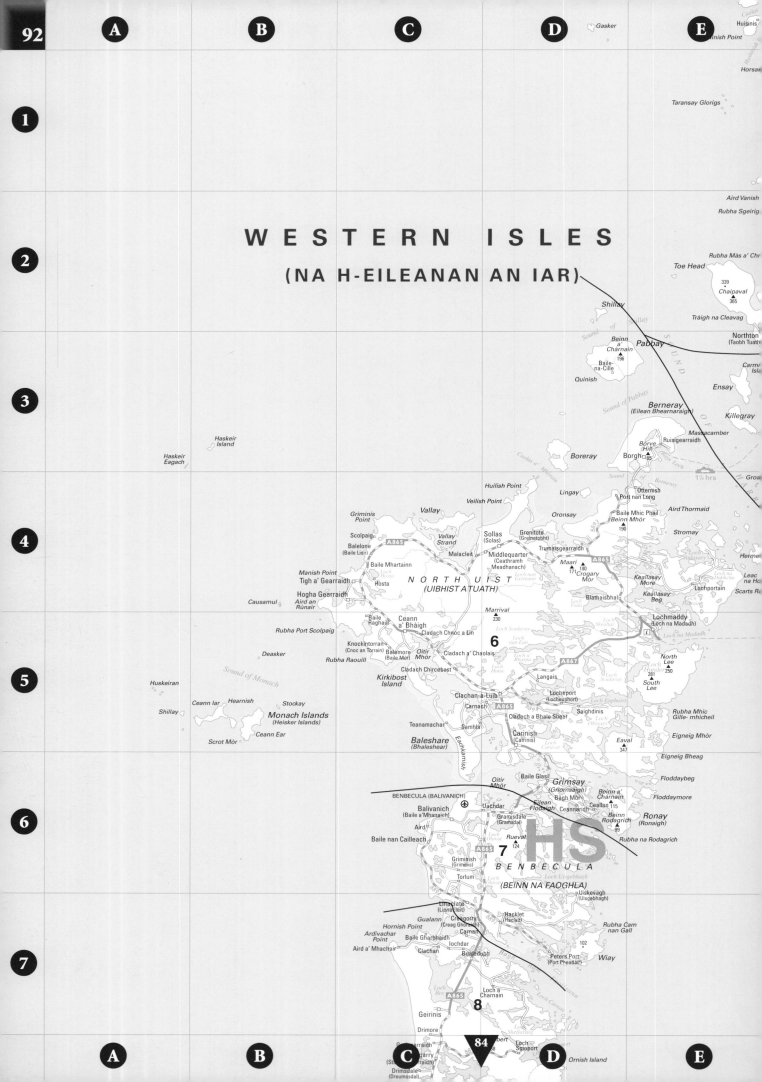

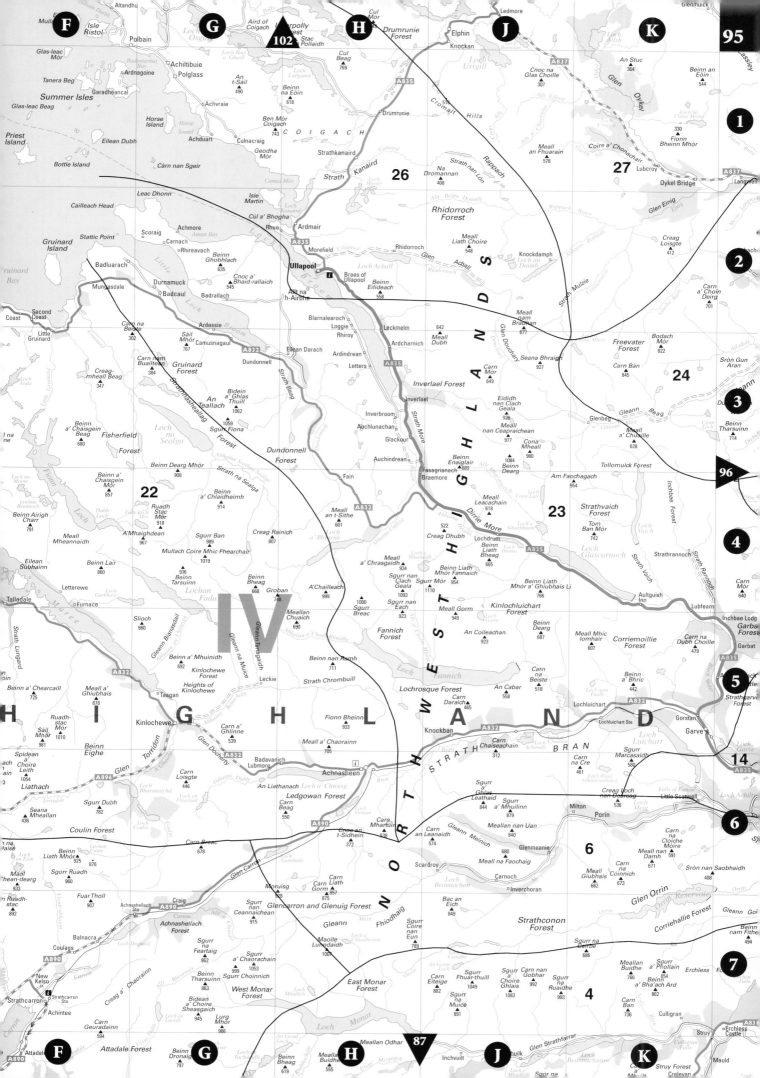

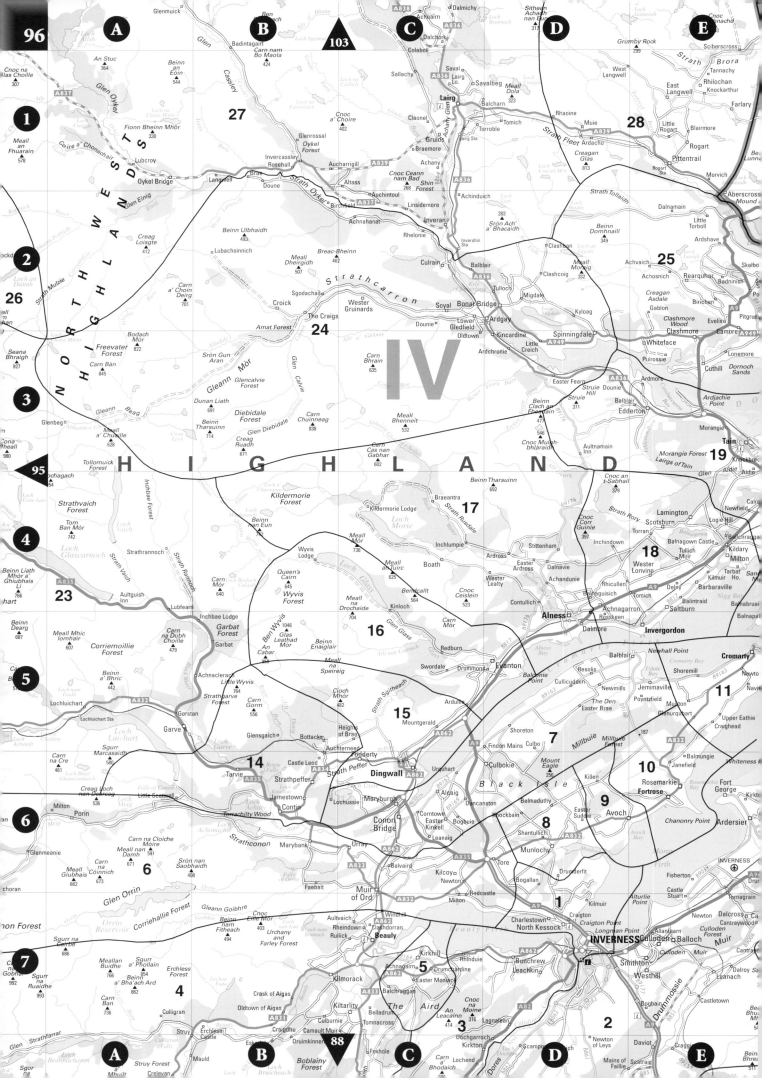

A B C D E

1

2

WESTERN ISLES
(NA H-EILEANAN AN IAR)

Rinn Druir Tallig
Aird Mhòr Bragair
Labost
Rubh' an Dùnain
Fibhig
Brag
Shawbost (Siabost)
Siabost Bho Dheas
Siabost Bho Thuath
Bàgh Dail Beag
Pairc
Aird Mhòr
Dail Beag
Dail Mòr
Gearrannan
Beinn Bragar Choinn
Beinn 261 210
Craigeam
Mullach Charlabhaigh
Borghastan
Beinn Rahacleit
Carloway (Carlabhagh)
248
Loch Carlabhagh
Creag Mhòr
Cirbhig
3
Little Bernera
Loch   East Loch Roag
Gallan Head
Camas Sandig
Pabaidh Mòr
Bostadh
Tobson
Crothair
Tolastadh a' Chaolais
Great Breacleit
West Loch Roag
Aird Uig
Bhaltos
Geodha Nasavig
Forsnaval 205
Nisa Mhòr
Vacsay
Vuia Mòr
Bernera
Kirkibost (Cìrebost)
Breascleit
Loch nam Breac
Miavaig (Miabhaig)
Reef (Riof)
Hacklete (Tacleit)
Barraglom
Fiùrvig Bàgh
Cradhlastadh
Timsgearraidh
Uigen
Vuia Beg
Iarsiadar
Crùlabhig
Eilean Kearstay
Callanish (Calanais)
Aird Mhòr Mangurstadh
Camas Uig
Cairisiadar
Floday
Geisiadar
Ben Drovinish 185
Lundale
A858
4
Mangurstadh
Eadar dha Fhadhail
Suainaval 429
Linsiadar
Garrynahine (Gearraidh na h-Aibhne)
Loch a' Bharbhais
Loch Ceann Thùlabhig
Griomarstaidh
Aird Fenish
Ungisiadar
Teahaval 256
Loch Langavat
Loch Clett Sheonais
Loch Suainaval
Aird Breanais
Mealisval 574
Einacleit
Loch Crosteam
Loch nam Falco
Islibhig
Tahaval 515
Abhainn Grioda
Scealascro
B8011
HS
5
Breanais
Mealasta
Cracaval 514
Loch Grunavat
Giosla
Skeun 265
Beinn Mheadhonach
Calltraiseal Bheag 226
Beinn Mohal 207
Loch Airigh na h-Airde
Loch Fuaran
2
Tamanaisval 467
Kinlochroag (Ceann Lochroag)
Coduinn 241
228
Roineval 281
Balalla (Baile Ailei)
Mealasta Island
Griomaval
Maghannan
Loch na Craobhaig
Loch Morsgail
Calltraiseal Mhòr
Loch Coirrigend
Scalaval 260
Loch Smandail
Sìldinis
6
Liongam
Aird Bheag
Loch Boshnval
Loch Benisval
Morsgail Forest
Beinn a' Bhoth 308
Sleiteachal Mhòr 248
Airidh a' Bhruaich
Kearstay
Gob na h-Airde Mòire
Aird Mhòr
Kintarvie
Aird an Troim
Ceann Loch Shipho
Sgeir Moil Duinn
Sròn Romul 308
Loch Crossbost
Màs a Chnoic-chuairtich 386
Mullach na Reidheachd 295
Rapaire 450
Loch Langavat
Kearnaval
Beinn a' Mhuil
A859
Sidheen an Airgid 381
Mòr Mhonadh 401
Feirihis
Scarp
Sgianait 425
Liuthaid 492
Ath Linne
Beinn na h-Uamha 389
Beann Mc 247
Gasker
Huisinis
Husival Mòr 489
Tirga Mòr 679
Loch Westmaul
Stulaval 579
Mullach a' Ruisg
Muaithabhal
Hushinish Point
Loch a' Ghlinne
Ullaval 659
N O R T H   H A R R I S
Aird a' Mhulaidh
Seaforth Island
Beinn Mhòr 572
Pa
Arda Beaga
Leosaval 412
Oreval 662
(CEANN A TUATH NA HEARADH)
Kendale
Horsanish
Gobhaig
Forest of Harris
Cleiseval 511
Uisgnaval Mòr 729
Mulla-fo-dheas 743
Clisham 799
Clett Ard 328
Maraig (Maaruig)
Kenmore
Rubha Bhuic
Abhainnsuidhe
3
Taransay Glorigs
Soay Beg
Soay Mòr
Miabhag
Tolmachan
Bun Abhainn Eadarra
Sgaoth Aird 559
A859
Straiaval 389
Toddun 528
Caiteshal 449
Tathas Crìon
7
Taransay (Tarasaigh)
WEST LOCH TARBERT
Aird Asaig
Rhenigidale (Reinigeadal)
Beinn a' Chaolais
Bhala
Ben Raah 267
Beinn Dhubh 506
Taobh Siar
Tarbert (Tairbeart)
Sgeir h-Eighe
Aird Vanish
Paible
Beinn Reamhar 467
Losgaintir
So   Harris Forest
93
Beesdale
Urgha
Carragrich
Uiseval 334
Eilean Mòr a' Bhàigh
Rubha Sgeirigin
Sound of T
Sgeotasaigh
Kyles Scalpay (Caolas Scalpai)

A B C D E

A   **B**   **C**   **D**   **E**

1

2

3

◀ 101

4

5

6

7

Duslic

Cape Wrath

Stack Kearv

Kearva

Geodha Ruadh na Fola

Cnoc a' Ghiubhais
297

Bay of Keisgaig

Loch Keisgaig

Am Balg

Beinn Dearg
423

Am Buachaille

Sandwood Bay

Creag Riabhach
485

Rubh' an Fhir Leithe

An Grianan
467

Meall Moine
464

Strath Shinary

Sheigra

Blairmore

Beinn a' Chraisg
257

Balchrick

Oldshore Beg

Oldshoremore

An Socach
358

Eilean an Ròin Mòr

Kinlochbervie

Rubha na Leacaig

Badcall

Achriesgill

Bàgh Loch an Ròin

Achlyness

Rhiconich

Ardmore Point

Ceathramh Garbh

Rubha Ruadh

Fanagmore

Tarbet

Foindle

A838

Handa Island

Laxford Bridge

Badnabay

A894

A838

Loch Stack

Scourie Bay

Scourie More

Scourie

Ben Stack
721

Rubh' Aird an t- Sionnaich

Badcall

Ben Auskaird
386

Strath Achfary

Stack Achfary

Reay Forest

Eilean a' Bhreitheimh

Rubh' a' Mhucard

Ben Strome
426

Loch an Leathaid Bhuain

Meall Mòr

Calbha Beag

A894

Meall Beag

Calbha Mòr

Ben Aird da Bh

Point of Stoer

Sgeir nan Gall

Oldany Island

Eddrachillis Bay

Kylestrome

Cirean Geardail
161

Rubha nan Còsan

Eilean Chrona

Ardvar

Glendhu Forest

Culkein

Raffin

Clashnessie Bay

Drumbeg

Loch Nedd

Unapool

Ben Aird da Bh
530

Cluas Deas

Achnacarnin

Nedd

Gleann Leireag

Newton

A894

Clashmore

Clashnessie

Sàil Gorm
776

Balchladich

Rubh' a' Mhill Dheirg

Stoer

Quinag
808

Loch na Gainimh

Clachtoll

Spidean Coinich
764

A894

Bay of Stoer

Inver

Glas Bheinn
776

Rubha Leumair

Little Assynt

A837

Achmelvich Bay

Rhicarn

Beinn Uidhe
740

Achmelvich

Ardroe

Loch Assynt

Beinn Gharbh
540

Inchnadam

Rubha Rodha

Baddidarach

Lochinver

Inchnadamph

Soyea Island

Strathan

Gleann Dub

Kirkaig Point

A'Chleit

Badnaban

Inverkirkaig

Glencanisp Forest

Stronechrubie

A837

Rubha Coigeach

Rubha na Brèige

Eilean Mòr

Rhegreanoch

Canisp
846

Feochag Bay

Suilven
731

Breabe
814

Camus Coille

Enard Bay

Rubh' a' Choin

Mea Bhragl

Camas Eilean Ghlais

Polly Bay

Cul Mòr

Ledbeg

Rubha Mòr

Reiff

Brae of Achnahaird

26

Loch Sionascaig

Ledmore

Altandhu

Aird of Coigach

Inverpolly Forest

Drumrunie Forest

Elphin

Eilean Mullagrach

Isle Ristol

Polbain

95

Stac Pollaidh
613

Cul Beag

Knockan

A835

Glas-leac

Achiltibu

Polgla

An t-Sàil

A8

Tanera Beg

Ardvegoine

Beinn

Cnoc na Glas Choille
307

Loch Urigill

Loch Borralan

T H E   M I N C H

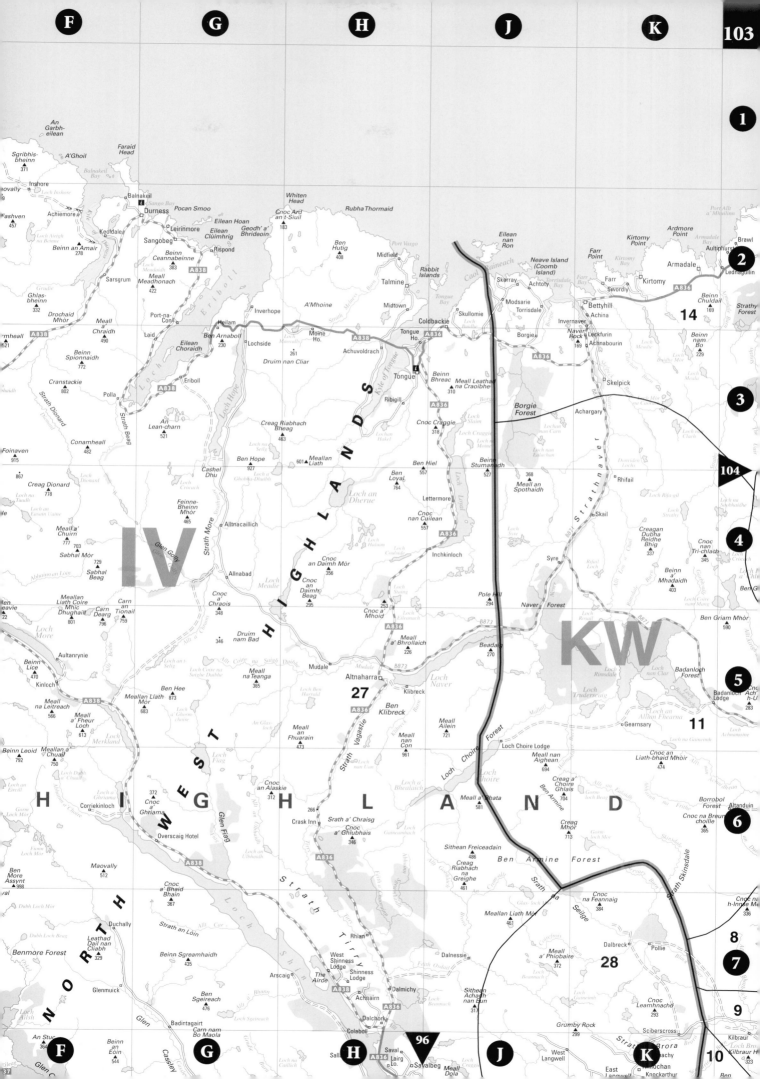

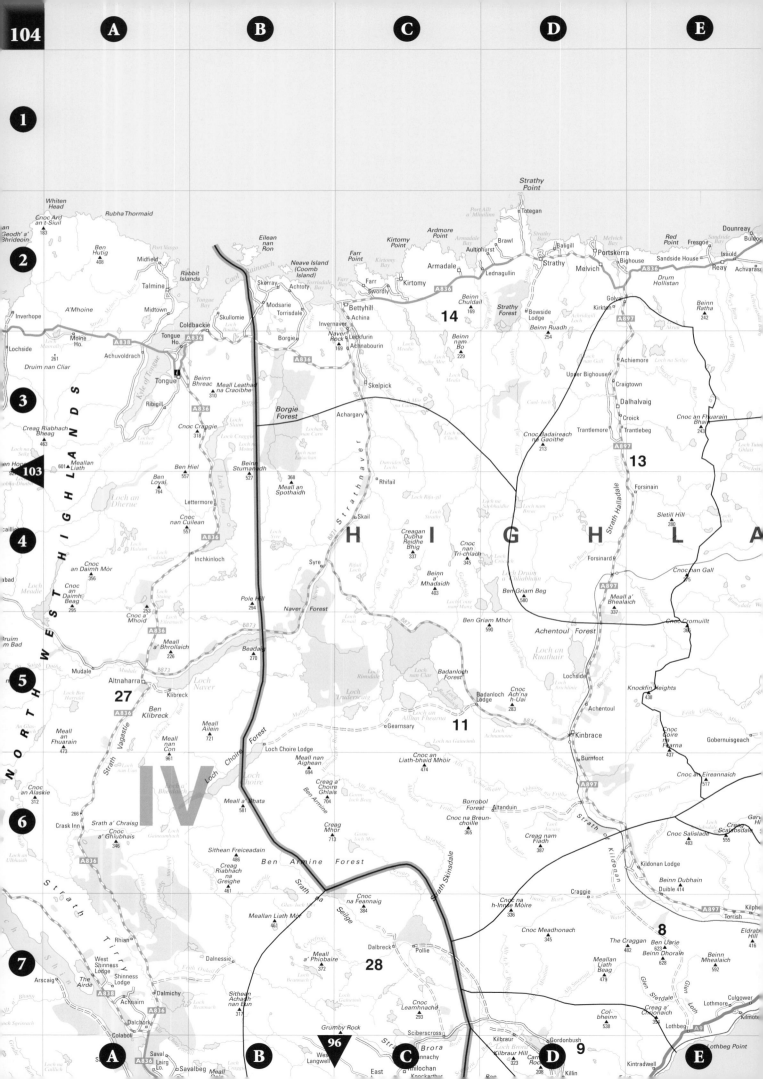

same scale as main map

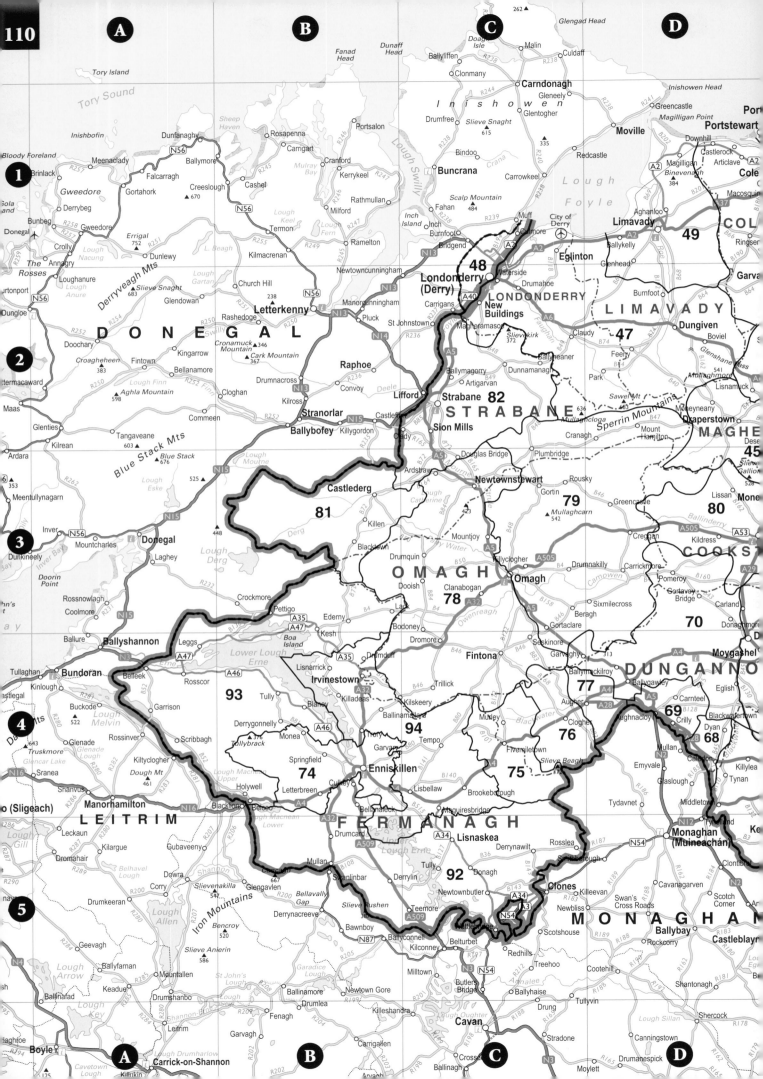

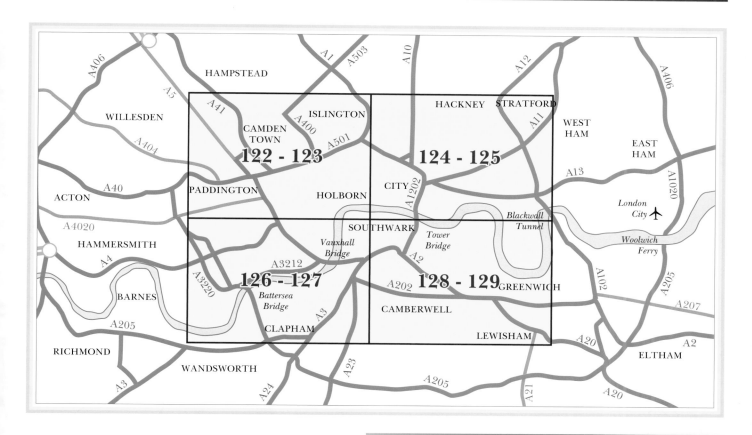

London key to symbols

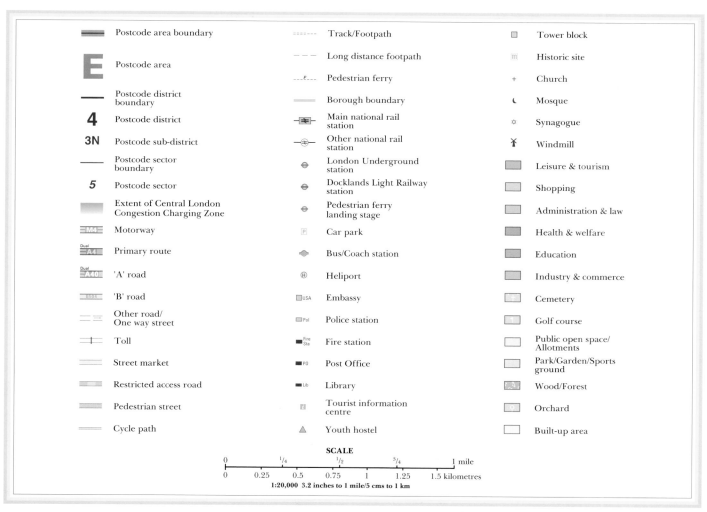

	Postcode area boundary		Track/Footpath		Tower block
E	Postcode area		Long distance footpath		Historic site
	Postcode district boundary		Pedestrian ferry	+	Church
4	Postcode district		Borough boundary		Mosque
3N	Postcode sub-district		Main national rail station		Synagogue
	Postcode sector boundary		Other national rail station		Windmill
5	Postcode sector		London Underground station		Leisure & tourism
	Extent of Central London Congestion Charging Zone		Docklands Light Railway station		Shopping
M4	Motorway		Pedestrian ferry landing stage		Administration & law
Dual A4	Primary route	P	Car park		Health & welfare
Dual A40	'A' road		Bus/Coach station		Education
B504	'B' road	H	Heliport		Industry & commerce
	Other road/ One way street	USA	Embassy		Cemetery
	Toll	Pol	Police station		Golf course
	Street market	Fire Sta	Fire station		Public open space/ Allotments
	Restricted access road	PO	Post Office		Park/Garden/Sports ground
	Pedestrian street	Lib	Library		Wood/Forest
	Cycle path		Tourist information centre		Orchard
			Youth hostel		Built-up area

SCALE

0	1/4	1/2	3/4	1 mile
0 0.25 0.5 0.75	1	1.25	1.5 kilometres	

1:20,000 3.2 inches to 1 mile/5 cms to 1 km

Notes: Listed below are the administrative areas for Great Britain, Northern Ireland and Isle of Man used in this Postcode Atlas. Where an area is dual language, the English form is given first, followed by the alternative in parenthesis. Each entry includes its standard abbreviation in *italics* which will appear in the index. Population figures are derived from 2001 Census information. A brief description of the area then follows, which includes: adjoining administrative areas; main centres (based on descending order of population); historical, physical and economic characteristics. For English counties or former Metropolitan counties, each district, city or borough authority is listed under the heading, **Districts.**

Aberdeen *Aberdeen* Population: 212,125.
Unitary authority surrounding Aberdeen, Scotland's third largest city, on the NE coast and neighbouring Aberdeenshire. Aberdeen is the major commercial and administrative centre for N Scotland. It is the second largest fishing port in Scotland, with docks at the mouth of the River Dee, and is the oil and gas capital of Europe.

Aberdeenshire *Aber.* Population: 226,871.
Unitary authority on the NE coast of Scotland neighbouring Aberdeen, Angus, Highland, Moray and Perth & Kinross. Main centres are Peterhead, Fraserburgh, Inverurie, Stonehaven, Ellon, Banchory, Portlethan and Huntly. Aberdeenshire is split geographically into two main areas. The W is dominated by the Grampian Mountains and is largely unpopulated. The undulating lowlands of the E are mainly rural and are populated by farming and fishing communities. The major rivers are the Dee, which flows through Royal Deeside, and the Don.

Angus *Angus* Population: 108,400.
Unitary authority on the E coast of Scotland neighbouring Aberdeenshire, Dundee and Perth & Kinross. The chief centres are Arbroath, Forfar, Montrose, Carnoustie, the ancient cathedral city of Brechin, Kirriemuir and Monifieth. Angus occupies an area of 2200 square km and is an important agricultural area. It combines ancient relics and castles with highland terrain and market towns. Rivers include the North Esk, Isla and Prosen Water.

Antrim *Antrim* Population: 48,366
Covering around 4% of the total area of Northern Ireland, Antrim borders the eastern and northern shores of Lough Neagh, the largest freshwater lake in the United Kingdom. Major towns include Antrim, Crumlin, Templepatrick, Toombridge, internationally famous for its eel industry and Randalstown. Chief industries are heavy engineering, construction, transport and distribution, plus agriculture and tourism.

Ards *Ards* Population: 73,244
Designated as an Area of Outstanding Natural Beauty (AONB). Over half the area is a peninsula created by Strangford Lough. Newtownards is the largest town, with smaller ones being Donaghdee, Portaferry, where the ferry can be caught to the other side of the lough, Kircubbin, Ballygowan, Comber, Millisle and Portavogie. The Copeland Islands lie about a mile offshore and there are several small islands in Strangford Lough itself. Main industries are agriculture and tourism.

Argyll & Bute *Arg. & B.* Population: 91,306.
Unitary authority on the W coast of Scotland combining mainland and island life and neighbouring Highland, Inverclyde, North Ayrshire, Perth & Kinross, Stirling and West Dunbartonshire. The main towns are Helensburgh, Dunoon, Oban, Campbeltown, Rothesay and Lochgilphead. It includes the former districts of Argyll and Bute as well as the islands of Islay, Jura, Colonsay and Mull. The main industries are fishing, agriculture, whisky production and tourism.

Armagh *Armagh* Population: 54,263.
The southern border of Armagh abuts the Republic of Ireland and the city of Armagh is home to the Archbishops of both the Church of Ireland and the Roman Catholic Church. Other towns include Keady, Tandragee, Richill, Loughgall and Markethill. Chief industries are agriculture (particularly orchard fruits), food processing, small scale manufacturing and tourism, with IT as an emerging sector.

Bath & North East Somerset *B. & N.E.Som.* Population: 169,040.
Unitary authority in SW England neighbouring Bristol, North Somerset, Somerset, South Gloucestershire and Wiltshire. It surrounds the city of Bath, and includes the towns of Keynsham, Radstock and Midsomer Norton. The Georgian spa of Bath is considered to be one of the most beautiful cities in Britain, and is an important commercial and ecclesiastical centre popular with tourists. The River Avon flows through the area.

Ballymena *Ballymena* Population: 58,610.
The river Bann, which forms the western border, affords some of the best coarse fishing in Europe. To the east are the Antrim Hills. The main town is Ballymena, where around half the population live. Other towns include Broughshane, Cullybackey and Ahoghill. Main industries are agriculture, textiles, manufacturing and tourism.

Ballymoney *Ballymoney* Population: 26,894.
This predominantly rural district contains much of the Antrim Coast & Glens AONB, in the north-east corner of Northern Ireland. Ballymoney is the principle town, lying on the main A26 road. Many small villages dot the area, with agriculture being the main industry. There are a high proportion of self-employed and small businesses, along with textiles and pharmaceuticals.

Banbridge *Banbr.* Population: 41,392.
Crossed by the river Bann and dotted with glacial drumlins, Banbridge is a peaceful, unspoilt district, with the rugged Slieve Croob mountain in the east. Banbridge is the main town, while the historic cathedral town of Dromore on the river Lagan is the other major settlement. Other villages include Scarva, Loughbrickland and Gilford. Main industries are textiles (linen), construction, light engineering and agriculture.

Bedfordshire *Beds.* Population: 381,572.
S midland county of England bounded by Buckinghamshire, Cambridgeshire, Hertfordshire, Luton, Milton Keynes and Northamptonshire. Main centres are the county town of Bedford, Dunstable, Leighton Buzzard, Kempston and Biggleswade. The N end of the Chiltern Hills runs through the S and SE of the county, which is otherwise mostly flat. Most of Bedfordshire is rural, and includes many stately homes. Industries include light engineering, brick manufacture, mineral extraction and vegetable growing. Chief river is the Great Ouse.
Districts: Bedford; Mid Bedfordshire; South Bedfordshire.

Belfast *Belfast.* Population: 277,391.
Belfast has the highest population and population density of all the Northern Ireland Districts. The city of Belfast sits on the river Lagan at the mouth of Belfast Lough and is a lively, vibrant city. There are no other settlements of significance within the area. A busy port, shipbuilding is still a major industry, the Titanic was built here, along with aircraft manufacturing, textiles, construction, oil refining, brewing, retail and tourism. Belfast city airport handles tourist and business flights.

Blackburn with Darwen *B'burn.* Population: 137,470.
Unitary authority in NW England surrounding Blackburn and Darwen and neighbouring Greater Manchester and Lancashire. Blackburn is a market and retail centre with a wide spread of industry including textiles, brewing and electronic engineering.

Blackpool *B'pool* Population: 142,283.
Unitary authority on the NW coast of England surrounding Blackpool and neighbouring Lancashire. Blackpool receives around 7.2 million visitors each year, making it the most popular seaside resort in Europe. Attractions including the Tower, Pleasure Beach, Winter Gardens and Illuminations.

Blaenau Gwent *B.Gwent* Population: 70,064.
Unitary authority in S Wales bounded by Caerphilly, Monmouthshire, Powys and Torfaen. The chief towns are Ebbw Vale, Tredegar, Bryn-mawr and Abertillery. The area was previously dependent upon coal, iron and steel industries but has since developed a broader industrial base. Part of the Brecon Beacons are in the N of the area.

Bournemouth *Bourne.* Population: 163,444.
Unitary authority on the S coast of England surrounding Bournemouth and neighbouring Dorset and Poole. Bournemouth is a major resort, conference and commercial centre.

Bracknell Forest *Brack.F.* Population: 109,617.
Unitary authority to the W of Greater London and bounded by Hampshire, Surrey, Windsor & Maidenhead and Wokingham. Bracknell is the chief town, while to the N of the area there are the villages of Winkfield and Binfield. To the S lies forest and heathland, and the towns of Crowthorne and Sandhurst. Bracknell has many hi-tech industries, and is a shopping and leisure centre.

Bridgend (Pen-y-Bont ar Ogwr). *Bridgend* Population: 128,645.
Unitary authority in S Wales bounded by Neath Port Talbot, Rhondda Cynon Taff, Vale of Glamorgan and the sea. Main centres are Bridgend, Maesteg and Porthcawl. The area is mountainous to the N, having ribbon development along river valleys; there is greater urbanisation in the S.

Brighton & Hove *B. & H.* Population: 247,817.
Unitary authority on the S coast of England neighbouring East Sussex and West Sussex. It encompasses the seaside resort of Brighton, which is a major commercial and conference centre, and the surrounding area which includes Hove, Portslade-by-Sea, Portslade, Rottingdean, Saltdean and part of the South Downs.

Bristol *Bristol* Population: 380,615.
Unitary authority in SW England neighbouring Bath & North East Somerset, North Somerset, South Gloucestershire and the Bristol Channel. The area includes the city of Bristol and surrounding urban area, including Avonmouth. Bristol is an important industrial and commercial centre of W England. A former major port, its character varies from docks and a busy city centre, to parks and gardens and Georgian terracing. The city hosts the Balloon Fiesta and Harbour Regatta. River Avon forms part of the W border of the area.

Buckinghamshire *Bucks.* Population: 479,026.
S midland county of England bounded by Bedfordshire, Greater London, Hertfordshire, Northamptonshire, Oxfordshire, Surrey, Windsor & Maidenhead and Wokingham. Chief towns are High Wycombe, the county town of Aylesbury, Amersham, Chesham, Marlow and Beaconsfield, around which, and other smaller towns, is a variety of light industry, as well as extensive residential areas. The chalk downs of the Chiltern Hills traverse the S part of the county, which is otherwise mostly flat. The River Thames flows along its S border.
Districts: Aylesbury Vale; Chiltern; South Bucks; Wycombe.

Caerphilly (Caerffili). *Caerp.* Population: 169,519.
Unitary authority in S Wales bordered by Blaenau Gwent, Cardiff, Merthyr Tydfil, Rhondda Cynon Taff and Torfaen. The chief centres are Caerphilly, Gelligaer, Risca, Bargoed, Blackwood and Bedwas. The geography of the area varies from open moorland to busy market towns. The former mining industry has been replaced by electronics and automotive companies, with tourism also being important to the local economy. Rivers include the Rhymney and Sirhowy.

Cambridgeshire *Cambs.* Population: 552,658.
County of E England bounded by Bedfordshire, Essex, Hertfordshire, Lincolnshire, Norfolk, Northamptonshire, Peterborough and Suffolk. Cambridgeshire is mostly flat, with fenland to N and E, although there are low chalk hills in the S and SE. Chief centres are the city and county town of Cambridge, Wisbech, St. Ives, March, Huntingdon, St. Neots and the cathedral city of Ely. Agriculture is a major industry with sugar beet, potatoes and corn all important crops; soft fruit and vegetable cultivation and canning are also significant rural industries. There has been recent growth of medical, pharmaceutical and hi-tech industries around Cambridge. Rivers include the Cam, Nene, and Great Ouse.
Districts: Cambridge; East Cambridgeshire; Fenland; Huntingdonshire; South Cambridgeshire.

Cardiff (Caerdydd). *Cardiff* Population: 305,353.
Unitary authority in S Wales surrounding the city of Cardiff and bordered by Caerphilly, Newport, Rhondda Cynon Taff, Vale of Glamorgan and the Bristol Channel. Cardiff, the capital of Wales, is a major administrative, commercial, cultural and tourism centre. It contains the Welsh Office, Welsh National Stadium, remains of medieval castle, cathedral at Llandarff and university. Cardiff docks, which were formerly used to export Welsh coal, are part of an ongoing major redevelopment. The city has excellent shopping facilities, notably at the St. David's Centre. The birthplace of Roald Dahl.

Carmarthenshire (Sir Gaerfyrddin). *Carmar.* Population: 172,842.
Unitary authority in S Wales bounded by Ceredigion, Neath Port Talbot, Pembrokeshire, Powys, Swansea and the sea. The chief towns are Llanelli, Carmarthen and Ammanford. The geography varies from the Brecon Beacons in the E, to the river valleys in the N, and the fishing villages, beaches and coastal towns in the S. The 50m coastline runs along the S of the area. Rivers include the Tywi, Cothi, Gwendaeth Fach and Gwendaeth Fawr.

Carrickfergus *Carrick.* Population: 37,659.
A small district, with Belfast Lough at its eastern boundary. The main town of Carrickfergus is an ancient harbour with the impressive Carrickfergus Norman Castle built on a volcanic dyke. Smaller towns include Greenisland and Whitehead. Main industries are construction, manufacturing, retailing and tourism.

Castlereagh *Castle.* Population: 66,488.
To the south-east of Belfast, the main town of the district is Castlereagh, with other towns being Carryduff and Dundonald, which still has a Norman motte. Agriculture is the main industry but many people work in the shipbuilding and aircraft industries in Belfast.

Ceredigion *Cere.* Population: 74,941.
Unitary authority in W Wales bounded by Carmarthenshire, Gwynedd, Pembrokeshire, Powys and the sea at Cardigan Bay. The main towns are Aberystwyth, Cardigan, Aberaeron,

Lampeter, Tregaron and Llandysul. Part of the Cambrian Mountains lie in the E of the area and the 50m coast has many sandy beaches. Tourism and agriculture are the most important industries. The main river is the Teifi.

Cheshire *Ches.* Population: 673,788.
County of NW England bounded by Derbyshire, Greater Manchester, Halton, Merseyside, Staffordshire, Shropshire, Warrington and the Welsh authorities of Flintshire and Wrexham. Chief centres are the cathedral city of Chester and the towns of Ellesmere Port, Crewe, Macclesfield, Northwich, Wilmslow, Winsford and Congleton. The country is mainly flat, except in the NE, where the foothills of The Pennines enter the county. The rural areas, which are mostly in the S and W, are noted for dairy products. Much of the county is industrialised; there are large salt mines with an associated chemicals industry in the N, silk and cotton mills, and engineering. Chief rivers are the Dane, Dee, and Weaver. In the NW the county reaches the estuaries of the River Dee and River Mersey.
Districts: Chester; Congleton; Crewe & Nantwich; Ellesmere Port & Neston; Macclesfield; Vale Royal.

Clackmannanshire *Clack.* Population: 48,077.
Unitary authority in central Scotland neighbouring Fife, Perth & Kinross and Stirling. The N includes the Ochil Hills, while the lowland surrounding the Forth estuary contains the chief towns which are Alloa, Tullibody, Tillicoultry and Alva. Clackmannanshire has over 50 sites of nature conservation and five historic castles and towers. The main rivers are the Devon and the Forth.

Coleraine *Coleraine* Population: 56,315.
This beautiful district borders the coast on its northern edge, with the ports of Portrush, Portstewart and Portballintrae. The resorts of Downhill and Castlerock are popular with tourists, the latter at the outlet of the River Bann. Coleraine is the main town, an ancient but busy shopping centre. Smaller towns include Garvagh and Kilrea. Industries centre on agriculture and tourism.

Conwy *Conwy* Population: 109,596.
Unitary authority in N Wales bordered by Denbighshire, Gwynedd and the sea. The chief towns are Colwyn Bay, Llandudno, Abergele, Rhôs-on-Sea and Conwy. Around 40 per cent of Conwy is within Snowdonia National Park and there are 29m of coastline. The coastal resorts attract tourism which is a key industry, but agriculture and light manufacturing are also important to the local economy. The main river is the Conwy.

Cookstown *Cookstown* Population: 32,581.
With Lough Neagh at its eastern border and the foothills of the Sperrin Mountains to the west, Cookstown has been designated an AONB. The main town of Cookstown has the longest main street in Northern Ireland, with one mile of shops. Another town of significance is Moneymore, with other settlements being scattered, smaller villages. Industries are based around small businesses, agriculture and tourism.

Cornwall *Cornw.* Population: 499,114.
South-westernmost county of England bounded by Devon and the sea. Chief centres are St. Austell, Falmouth, Penzance, the cathedral city and administrative centre of Truro, Redruth, Camborne and Newquay. The coastline is wild and rocky; headlands and cliffs are interspersed with large sandy beaches in the N, and deeply indented with river estuaries in the S. The interior is dominated by areas of moorland, notably the granite mass of Bodmin Moor in the NE. There are also farmlands providing rich cattle-grazing, and deep river valleys. The climate is mild, and flower cultivation is carried on extensively. The many derelict tin mines are witness to the former importance of this industry; there has recently been a partial revival. The chief industry is tourism. China clay is produced in large quantities in the St. Austell area, and there is some fishing. Rivers include the Tamar, forming the boundary with Devon; Fowey, East and West Looe, Fal, Camel, and Lynher.
Districts: Caradon; Carrick; Kerrier; North Cornwall; Penwith; Restormel.

Craigavon *Craigavon* Population: 80,671.
Craigavon's northern boundary is the southern shore of Lough Neagh. The M1 motorway crosses east-west, providing a link to Lisburn, Belfast and Antrim. Its principle towns are Craigavon itself, Lurgan, home to the Carnegie library and Portadown. Main industries include manufacturing, retail, public service and construction.

Cumbria *Cumb.* Population: 487,607.
County of NW England bounded by Durham, Lancashire, Northumberland and North Yorkshire; the Scottish authorities of Dumfries & Galloway and Scottish Borders; and the Solway Firth and Irish Sea. Chief centres are the city of Carlisle and the towns of Barrow-in-Furness, Whitehaven, Workington, Kendal, Penrith and Ulverston. A narrow strip of flat country along the coast widens to a plain in the N and around Carlisle. Otherwise the county is composed of mountains, moorland and lakes, and includes the scenically famous Lake District. Cumbria is mostly rural and uncultivated, with industry centred on Carlisle and the urban centres. Whitehaven, Workington, and Maryport all once relied on coal, while Barrow-in-Furness developed due to shipbuilding and heavy industry. There are links with nuclear technology: Calder Hall, N of Seascale, was Britain's first atomic power station, Sellafield is the site of a nuclear reprocessing plant and Trident submarines were built at Barrow-in-Furness. Tourism in the Lake District and sheep farming are also important industries. The area is noted for its radial drainage, with Windermere and Ullswater being the largest of the lakes and the River Eden being the chief of many rivers.
Districts: Allerdale; Barrow-in-Furness; Carlisle; Copeland; Eden; South Lakeland.

Darlington *Darl.* Population: 97,838.
Unitary authority in NE England surrounding Darlington and neighbouring Durham, North Yorkshire and Stockton-on-Tees. Darlington has a variety of industries, including iron, steel and textiles. The River Tees forms the S border.

Denbighshire (Sir Ddinbych). *Denb.* Population: 93,065.
Unitary authority in N Wales neighbouring Conwy, Flintshire, Gwynedd, Powys, Wrexham and the sea. The chief towns are Rhyl, Prestatyn, Denbigh, Ruthin, the ancient city of St. Asaph, and Llangollen. Main industries are tourism, centred on the coastal resorts of Rhyl and Prestatyn, and agriculture. Rivers include the Morwynion.

Derby *Derby* Population: 221,708.
Unitary authority in central England surrounding the city of Derby and bordered by Derbyshire. Derby has a history dating back to Roman times and is now important in the rail industry; other key industries are manufacturing and aerospace engineering. The River Derwent passes through the area.

Derbyshire *Derbys.* Population: 734,585.
Midland county of England bounded by Cheshire, Derby, Greater Manchester, Leicestershire, Nottinghamshire, South Yorkshire, Staffordshire and West Yorkshire. Chief towns are Chesterfield, Long Eaton, Swadlincote, Ilkeston, Staveley, Dronfield, Alfreton, Heanor and Buxton. The high steep hills in the N, which include the dramatic scenery of The Peak, are the S extremity of The Pennines, and provide grazing for sheep and cattle. There is some textile industry in the towns of the N and W, while the S of the county is dominated by heavy industry,

mining, and quarrying. Tourism is based on the scenic Peak District National Park, most of which falls in the county. Principal rivers are the Dove, forming much of the boundary with Staffordshire and noted for its scenery and fishing, and the Derwent; the Trent flows through the S corner of the county.

Districts: Amber Valley; Bolsover; Chesterfield; Derbyshire Dales; Erewash; High Peak; North East Derbyshire; South Derbyshire.

Devon *Devon* Population: 704,493.

Large county in SW peninsula of England bounded by Cornwall, Dorset, Plymouth, Somerset, Torbay and the Bristol and English Channels. The chief centres are the city of Exeter, Exmouth, Barnstaple, Newton Abbot, Tiverton, Bideford and Teignmouth. The county includes the W end of Exmoor and the whole of the granite mass of Dartmoor, whose summit, High Willhays, is the highest point in S England. Moorland areas apart, the county is largely given over to agriculture, and on the coast, to fishing and tourism. On Dartmoor there are quarries and a military training area; there are china clay workings in the S. Daffodils are grown commercially in River Tamar valley. Chief rivers are Exe, Teign, Dart, Avon, Erme, Tamar and Tavy in the S; and Taw and Torridge in the N. The granite island of Lundy is included in the county for administrative purposes.

Districts: East Devon; Exeter; Mid Devon; North Devon; South Hams; Teignbridge; Torridge; West Devon.

Dorset *Dorset* Population: 390,980.

County in SW England bounded by Bournemouth, Devon, Hampshire, Poole, Somerset, Wiltshire and the English Channel. The chief towns are Weymouth, Christchurch, Wimborne Minster, the county town of Dorchester, Bridport, Swanage and Blandford Forum. The county is hilly, with chalk downs and impressive geological formations along the coastline. Sand, gravel, stone and oil extraction takes place around the Isle of Portland and the Isle of Purbeck. Dorset is also noted for its agricultural and dairy produce. Tourism is an important industry due to the beautiful scenery, the proliferation of prehistoric and Roman remains, and the connection with Thomas Hardy's Wessex. Among numerous minor rivers are the Stour, Frome, and Piddle or Trent.

Districts: Christchurch; East Dorset; North Dorset; Purbeck; West Dorset; Weymouth & Portland.

Down *Down* Population: 63,828.

The southern tip of Down includes part of the beautiful Mourne Mountains, and the eastern edge consists of a long coastline, with the long sandy beach of Dundrum Bay and the shores of Strangford Lough. The main town is Downpatrick, others being Ballynahinch, Crossgar and Saintfield along with the coastal towns of Killyleagh, Newcastle and Ardglass. Industries include engineering and agriculture.

Dumfries & Galloway *D. & G.* Population: 147,765.

Unitary authority in SW Scotland neighbouring East Ayrshire, Scottish Borders, South Ayrshire, South Lanarkshire, the English county of Cumbria and the sea. It comprises the former counties of Dumfries, Kirkcudbright and Wigtown. Chief towns are Dumfries, Stranraer, Annan, Dalbeattie, Lockerbie, Castle Douglas, Newton Stewart and Kirkcudbright. The hilly area to the N is largely given over to sheep-grazing and afforestation, while farther S there is some good-quality arable farmland. At the extreme W of the area is the peninsula known as the Rinns of Galloway, and the port of Stranraer, which provides passenger and car ferry services to Larne in Northern Ireland. Main rivers are the Esk, Annan, Nith, Dee and Cree which descend S to the Solway Firth from the Tweedsmuir Hills, Lowther Hills and the Rhinns of Kells in the N.

Dundee *Dundee* Population: 145,663.

Unitary authority on the E coast of Scotland surrounding the city of Dundee and neighbouring Angus and Perth & Kinross. Dundee is Scotland's fourth largest city and is a centre of excellence in a variety of areas from telecommunications to medical research. The Firth of Tay borders Dundee to the S.

Dungannon *Dungannon* Population: 47,735.

Dungannon includes the scenic Clogher valley, and the Republic of Ireland forms its southern boundary. The north-east corner meets Lough Neagh and the main A4 road bisects it east-west. Dungannon town has almost a quarter of the whole population, with the rest of the area being basically rural. Coalisland still has a linen industry and Tyrone Crystal is famous worldwide. Industries include agriculture, construction, retail and manufacturing.

Durham *Dur.* Population: 493,470.

County in NE England bounded by Cumbria, Darlington, Hartlepool, Northumberland, North Yorkshire, Stockton-on-Tees, Tyne & Wear and the North Sea. Chief centres are the cathedral city and county town of Durham; and the towns of Chester-le-Street, Peterlee, Newton Aycliffe, Bishop Auckland, Seaham and Consett. The W part of the county includes The Peninnes and consists mostly of open moorlands which provide rough sheep-grazing and water for the urban areas from a number of large reservoirs. Economic activity is concentrated on the lowland in the E which is more heavily populated, and was formerly a centre for coal-mining and heavy industry. Diversification has since provided a broad industrial base. The principal rivers are the Tees and the Wear.

Districts: Chester-le-Street; Derwentside; Durham; Easington; Sedgefield; Teesdale; Wear Valley.

East Ayrshire *E.Ayr.* Population: 120,235.

Unitary authority in SW Scotland bounded by Dumfries & Galloway, East Renfrewshire, North Ayrshire, South Ayrshire and South Lanarkshire. The principal towns are Kilmarnock, Cumnock, Stewarton, Galston and Auchinleck. Traditional industries centred on textiles and lace in the Irvine valley, coal mining and engineering. Dairy farming is also an important industry, particularly beef and sheep production. The area is a popular tourist destination, with several castles, battle sites and associations with Robert Burns and Keir Hardie. Rivers include the Irvine, Annick and Cessnock.

East Dunbartonshire *E.Dun.* Population: 108,243.

Unitary authority in central Scotland bounded by Glasgow, North Lanarkshire, Stirling and West Dunbartonshire. The chief centres are Bearsden, Bishopbriggs, Kirkintilloch and Milngavie. Much of the urban and industrial development occurs on the N periphery of Greater Glasgow. The Campsie Fells lie in the N of the area.

East Lothian *E.Loth.* Population: 90,088.

Unitary authority in central Scotland neighbouring Edinburgh, Midlothian, Scottish Borders and the North Sea. The main towns are Musselburgh, Haddington, Tranent, Prestonpans, Dunbar, North Berwick and Cockenzie and Port Seton. There are 43m of varied coastline and the topography includes the Lammermuir Hills in the S, and the ancient volcanoes at North Berwick and Traprain. Much of the urban and industrial development is in the NW and N of the area. Rivers include Whitehead Water, the Tyne, Peffer Burn and Gifford Water.

East Renfrewshire *E.Renf.* Population: 89,311.

Unitary authority in SW Scotland bounded by East Ayrshire, Glasgow, Inverclyde, North Ayrshire, Renfrewshire and South Lanarkshire. The principal centres are Newton Mearns, Clarkston, Barrhead and Giffnock, which lie on the S periphery of Greater Glasgow. Over two-thirds of East Renfrewshire is farmland; the rest being mostly residential, with some light industry.

East Riding of Yorkshire *E.Riding* Population: 314,113.
Unitary authority on the E coast of England neighbouring Kingston upon Hull, North Lincolnshire, North Yorkshire, South Yorkshire and York. The chief centres are Bridlington, Beverley, Goole, Great Driffield, Hornsea, Brough, Hedon and Withernsea. The area is mostly low-lying, except for the central ridge which forms part of The Wolds. The coastline is subject to much erosion, with material being moved from Flamborough Head to the large spit of Spurn Head, at the mouth of the River Humber. Key industries in the area include agriculture, aerospace, gas and oil industries.

East Sussex *E.Suss.* Population: 492,324.
County of SE England bounded by Brighton & Hove, Kent, Surrey, West Sussex and the English Channel. Main towns are Eastbourne, Hastings, Bexhill, Seaford, Crowborough, Hailsham, Peacehaven and the county town of Lewes; Rye is a small historic town in the E of the county. In the W, the coast is backed by the chalk ridge of the South Downs, ending with the white cliffs of the Seven Sisters and Beachy Head, just W of Eastbourne. E of this point, there are extensive areas of reclaimed marshland, which provide good sheep-grazing. Inland is the heavily wooded Weald, a former centre of the iron industry, interspersed with hill ridges, the largest being the open heathland of Ashdown Forest. Rivers, none large, include the Cuckmere, Ouse, Rother, and upper reaches of the Medway.
Districts: Eastbourne; Hastings; Lewes; Rother; Wealden.

Edinburgh *Edin.* Population: 448,624.
Unitary authority on the E coast of central Scotland surrounding the city of Edinburgh and neighbouring East Lothian, Midlothian, West Lothian and the sea at the Firth of Forth. Edinburgh as the capital of Scotland, is a major administrative, cultural, commercial and tourist centre. It contains most of Scotland's national and cultural institutions. Its historic core is centred around Edinburgh Castle and the Royal Mile, attracting much tourism. The city is also a centre for education and scientific research; other important industries are electronics and food and drink production. The river Water of Leith runs through the city to the docks at Leith.

Essex *Essex* Population: 1,310,835.
County of SE England bounded by Cambridgeshire, Greater London, Hertfordshire, Southend, Suffolk, Thurrock and the sea at the Thames estuary and North Sea. Chief towns are Basildon, the county town of Chelmsford, Colchester, Harlow, Brentwood, Clacton-on-Sea, Loughton, Canvey Island, Billericay and Braintree. The landscape is mostly flat or gently undulating, and the low-lying coast is deeply indented with river estuaries. Along the county's S and W sides, there is a concentration of urban development, with a mixture of light engineering and service industries. In the N and central parts are farmlands, orchards, market and nursery gardens. The NE coast has the busy passenger and container port of Harwich, and the popular seaside resort of Clacton-on-Sea. Rivers include the Stour, forming part of the boundary with Suffolk, the Lea, forming part of the boundary with Hertfordshire, and the Blackwater.
Districts: Basildon; Braintree; Brentwood; Castle Point; Chelmsford; Colchester; Epping Forest; Harlow; Maldon; Rochford; Tendring; Uttlesford.

Falkirk *Falk.* Population: 145,191.
Unitary authority in central Scotland surrounding Falkirk and neighbouring Clackmannanshire, Fife, North Lanarkshire, Stirling and West Lothian. Main towns are Falkirk, Grangemouth, Polmont, Stenhousemuir and Bo'ness. Petrochemical and chemical industries are important to the local economy, as well as bus manufacturing, toffees and paper-making. The Firth of Forth borders Falkirk to the N. Other rivers include the Carron and Pow Burn.

Fermanagh *Ferm.* Population: 57,527.
One third of this district is water, mainly taken up by Upper and Lower Lough Erne. Cosequently, there are around 150 inland islands, and the population density is one of the lowest in Northern Ireland. Large areas have been planted with conifers for timber. The north-west and south-west boundaries border the Republic of Ireland. The main town of Enniskillen lies on the River Erne at the junction of the two major loughs and other towns include Irvinestown, Rosslea and Lisnaskea. Main industries are agriculture and tourism, engineering and timber milling.

Fife *Fife* Population: 349,429.
Unitary authority in E Scotland neighbouring Clackmannanshire and Perth & Kinross, and lying between the Firth of Tay and Firth of Forth. Main towns are Dunfermline, Kirkcaldy, Glenrothes, Buckhaven, Cowdenbeath and St. Andrews. Fife comprises the former county of the same name, known since ancient times as the Kingdom of Fife, and is noted for its fine coastline with many distinctive small towns and fishing ports. The historic town of St. Andrews, on the coast between the two firths, is a university town, and the home of the world's premier golf club. Inland, the area is outstandingly fertile, with agriculture being an important industry. The SW of the area is a former coal-mining area.

Flintshire (Sir y Fflint). *Flints.* Population: 148,594.
Unitary authority in N Wales neighbouring Conwy, Denbighshire, Wrexham, the English county of Cheshire and the mouth of the River Dee. Main towns are Buckley, Connah's Quay, Flint, Hawarden, Shotton, Queensferry, Mold and Holywell. Known as the Gateway to N Wales, the landscape varies from the mountains which form the Clwydian Range, to small villages and woodlands.

Glasgow *Glas.* Population: 577,869.
Unitary authority in SW Scotland surrounding Glasgow and bounded by East Dunbartonshire, East Renfrewshire, North Lanarkshire, Renfrewshire, South Lanarkshire and West Dunbartonshire. Glasgow is Scotland's largest city and its principal industrial and shopping centre. The city developed significantly due to heavy industry, notably shipbuilding, being centred on the Clyde. While such industry has declined, Glasgow has emerged as a major cultural centre of Europe, due to its impressive arts and cultural scene. The River Clyde runs through the city.

Gloucestershire *Glos.* Population: 564,559.
County of W England bounded by Herefordshire, Oxfordshire, South Gloucestershire, Swindon, Warwickshire, Wiltshire, Worcestershire and the Welsh authority of Monmouthshire. Main centres are the cathedral city and county town of Gloucester and the towns of Cheltenham, Stroud, Cirencester and Dursley. The limestone mass of the Cotswold Hills dominates the centre of the county, and provides the characteristic pale golden stone of many of its buildings. The River Severn forms a wide valley to the W, ending in a long tidal estuary, beyond which are the hills of the Forest of Dean. Industry is centred on the fertile Severn Vale, with aerospace, light engineering, food production, and service industries in and around the towns; in rural areas market gardening and orchards dominate. The River Thames rises in the county, and forms part of its S boundary in the vicinity of Lechlade. Apart from the Severn and the Thames, there is the River Wye, which forms part of the boundary with Monmouthshire, and many smaller rivers, among them the Chelt, Coln, Evenlode, Leach, Leadon, and Windrush.
Districts: Cheltenham; Cotswold; Forest of Dean; Gloucester; Stroud; Tewkesbury.

Greater London *Gt.Lon.* Population: 7,172,091.
Former metropolitan county of 32 boroughs and the City of
London which together form the conurbation of London, the
capital of the UK. Greater London is the largest financial,
commercial, cultural, distribution and communications centre in
the country, including all but primary industrial sectors. London
developed from the City of London, a walled Roman settlement
on the Thames, and Westminster, which was a Saxon religious
settlement and later a Norman seat of government. The Great
Fire of 1666 destroyed most of the medieval city, and was
followed by a period of rebuilding and rapid, unplanned
expansion. Industrialisation and improved public transport over
the last two centuries have caused major suburban growth, and
the absorption of most of the surrounding settlements and
countryside. Tourism is a major industry, with most attractions
situated in and around the historic core, and along the Thames
bankside. Other notable tourist areas include Greenwich,
Hampstead, Kew and Richmond. Industrial activity is
widespread, with major concentrations in the E along the
Thames. Leisure facilities include national and major sports
stadiums, and many big parks and gardens. Airports at
Heathrow and docklands. The main river is the Thames.
Districts: Barking & Dagenham; Barnet; Bexley; Brent; Bromley;
Camden; City of London; City of Westminster; Croydon; Ealing; Enfield;
Greenwich; Hackney; Hammersmith & Fulham; Haringey; Harrow;
Havering; Hillingdon; Hounslow; Islington; Kensington & Chelsea;
Kingston upon Thames; Lambeth; Lewisham; Merton; Newham;
Redbridge; Richmond upon Thames; Southwark; Sutton; Tower Hamlets;
Waltham Forest; Wandsworth.

Greater Manchester *Gt.Man.* Population: 2,482,328.
Former metropolitan county of NW England neighbouring
Blackburn with Darwen, Cheshire, Derbyshire, Lancashire,
Merseyside, Warrington and West Yorkshire. It comprises the
near-continuous urban complex which includes the adjoining
cities of Manchester and Salford; and towns including Bolton,
Stockport, Oldham, Rochdale, Wigan, Bury and Sale. The
conurbation is framed by the wild moorland of The Pennines to
the N and the Peak District and Cheshire Plain to the S.
Development occurred during the 18c and 19c, creating a series
of cotton producing textile towns, while Manchester established
itself as the commercial and trading hub, later becoming an
inland port linked to Liverpool via the canal network. As textile
production declined, the industrial base of the area broadened to
include brewing, food production, electronics, plastics, printing,
light engineering, financial, leisure and service sectors. Retail is
based on town shopping centres and malls such as the Arndale
and Trafford Centres. There are many major sporting venues in
the area, and cultural facilities include the G-MEX centre,
numerous universities, museums and galleries and a diverse
nightlife. The area is served by Manchester Airport. Main rivers
are Irwell and Mersey.
Districts: Bolton; Bury; Manchester; Oldham; Rochdale; Salford;
Stockport; Tameside; Trafford; Wigan.

Gwynedd *Gwyn.* Population: 116,843.
Unitary authority in NW Wales bounded by Ceredigion, Conwy,
Denbighshire, Isle of Anglesey, Powys and the sea. Main centres
are the cathedral city of Bangor, Caernarfon, Ffestiniog, Blaenau
Ffestiniog, Llanddeiniolen, Pwllheli, Llanllynfi, Bethesda and
Porthmadog. The whole mainland area, except the Lleyn
Peninsula in the NW, is extremely mountainous and contains the
scenically famous Snowdonia National Park. There is
slate-quarrying in the Ffestiniog valley, otherwise sheep-farming
and tourism are the principal occupations; the coastline has been
much developed for the holiday trade. The area contains many
lakes and reservoirs, among them are Llyn Trawsfynedd, Llyn
Celyn and Llyn Tegid. Of the many rivers, the Wnion and the
Dyfi, which flows through part of the area, are most significant.

Halton *Halton* Population: 118,208.
Unitary authority in NW England neighbouring Cheshire,
Merseyside and Warrington. The principal towns are Runcorn
and Widnes, separated by the River Mersey. The area is
industrialised, being dominated by petro-chemicals and chemicals
industries due to the nearby salt mines and port facilities.

Hampshire *Hants.* Population: 1,240,103.
County of S England bounded by Bracknell Forest, Dorset,
Portsmouth, Southampton, Surrey, West Berkshire, West Sussex,
Wiltshire, Wokingham and the English Channel. Main towns are
Basingstoke, Gosport, Waterlooville, Farnborough, Aldershot,
Eastleigh, Havant, the ancient city and county town of
Winchester, Andover and Fleet. The centre of the county
consists largely of chalk downs interspersed with fertile valleys.
In the SW is the New Forest, while in the NE is the military area
centred on Aldershot. The much indented coastline borders The
Solent and looks across to the Isle of Wight. Main industries are
in the service sector, with chemicals and pharmaceuticals also
important. The chief rivers are the Itchen and Test, both chalk
streams flowing into Southampton Water, and the Meon flowing
into The Solent.
Districts: Basingstoke & Deane; East Hampshire; Eastleigh; Fareham;
Gosport; Hart; Havant; New Forest; Rushmoor; Test Valley; Winchester.

Hartlepool *Hart.* Population: 88,611.
Unitary authority on the NE coast of England surrounding
Hartlepool and bordering Darlington, Durham, Stockton-on-Tees
and the North Sea. Fishing is a major industry and a marina has
been created from part of the old docks. The mouth of the River
Tees forms part of the E border.

Herefordshire *Here.* Population: 174,871.
Unitary authority in W England bounded by Gloucestershire,
Shropshire, Worcestershire and the Welsh authorities of
Monmouthshire and Powys. Main centres are the cathedral city
of Hereford and the towns of Ross-on-Wye, Leominster and
Ledbury. Herefordshire lies between the Malvern Hills to the E
and the Black Mountains to the W. It is mainly rural, with dairy
farming, orchards and market gardening in evidence. The main
river is the Wye, which provides excellent fishing.

Hertfordshire *Herts.* Population: 1,033,977.
S midland county of England bounded by Bedfordshire,
Buckinghamshire, Cambridgeshire, Essex, Greater London and
Luton. Chief centres are Watford, the cathedral city of St.
Albans, Hemel Hempstead, Stevenage, Cheshunt, Welwyn
Garden City, Hoddesdon, Hitchin, Letchworth and Hatfield; the
county town is Hertford. The Chilterns rise along the W border,
and there are chalk hills in the N around Royston; otherwise the
landscape is mostly flat or gently undulating. There is a mixture
of rural and urban life, with agricultural and hi-tech industries
represented. While the urban centres in the S lie on the N
periphery of the Greater London conurbation, there are many
villages with the traditional large green or common. The more
urban S part of the county includes a dense network of major
roads bypassing, and leading N from London. Rivers include the
Colne, Ivel, and Lee.
Districts: Broxbourne; Dacorum; East Herts; Hertsmere; North
Hertfordshire; St. Albans; Stevenage; Three Rivers; Watford; Welwyn
Hatfield.

Highland *High.* Population: 208,914.
Unitary authority covering a large part of N Scotland and
neighbouring Aberdeenshire, Argyll & Bute, Moray and Perth &
Kinross. It contains a mixture of mainland and island life,
comprising the former districts of Badenoch and Strathspey,
Caithness, Inverness, Lochaber, Nairn, Ross and Cromarty, Skye
and Lochalsh and Sutherland. Main towns are Inverness, Fort
William, Thurso, Nairn, Wick, Alness and Dingwall. Overall,

Highland is very sparsely inhabited, being wild and remote in character. It is scenically outstanding, containing as it does part of the Cairngorm Mountains, Ben Nevis, and the North West Highlands. Many of the finest sea and inland lochs in Scotland are also here, such as Loch Ness, Loch Linnhe, Loch Torridon and Loch Broom. The discovery of North Sea oil has made an impact on the towns and villages around the Moray Firth. Elsewhere, tourism, crofting, fishing and skiing are important locally.

Inverclyde *Inclyde* Population: 84,203.
Unitary authority on the W coast of central Scotland, on the S bank of the River Clyde. It is bordered by North Ayrshire, Renfrewshire and the Firth of Clyde. The chief towns are Greenock, Port Glasgow, Gourock and Kilmacolm.

Isle of Anglesey (Sir Ynys Môn). *I.o.A.* Population: 66,829.
Unitary authority island of NW Wales divided from Gwynedd and the mainland by the Menai Strait, and with Holy Island lying to the W. Main towns are Holyhead, Llangefni, Amlwch and Menai Bridge. Anglesey has 125m of coastline and 16 beaches. Agriculture is an important industry to the island, with other industries including aluminium smelting and food processing. Holyhead is an important port terminus for the Republic of Ireland. Rivers include the Braint and Cefni.

Isle of Man *I.o.M.* Population: 76,315.
Self-governing island in the Irish Sea, situated in the centre of the British Isles. The chief towns are Douglas, Ramsey, Peel, Castletown, Port St. Mary, Port Erin and Laxey. Apart from the N tip, the topography is generally mountainous, rising to a peak at Snaefell. The main industries are agriculture, fishing and tourism as well as financial services and manufacturing. The island is synonymous with motorsport, being the home of the internationally renowned Tourist Trophy Circuit. Rivers include the Glen Auldyn and Neb.

Isle of Wight *I.o.W.* Population: 132,731.
County and island with an area of 147 square miles or 381 square km, separated from the S coast of England by The Solent. Chief towns are the capital, Newport, Ryde, Cowes, Shanklin, Sandown, Ventnor and Yarmouth. The island is geologically diverse, composed of sedimentary rocks and contains many important fossil remains. Tourism flourishes owing to the mild climate and the natural beauty of the island. There are Royal associations as Queen Victoria lived and died at Osborne House in the N of the island. There is a strong naval tradition, with the island historically acting as a defence for Portsmouth. Cowes is internationally famous for yachting. There are ferry and hovercraft connections at Cowes, Ryde, and Yarmouth (ferry to Lymington). Chief river is the Medina.

Isles of Scilly *I.o.S.* Population: 2153.
Group of some 140 islands 48m/45km SW of Land's End, Cornwall, of which five are inhabited: Bryher, St. Agnes, St. Martin's, St. Mary's and Tresco. Chief industries are fishing, and the growing of early flowers and vegetables due to the exceptionally mild climate.

Kent *Kent* Population: 1,329,718.
South-easternmost county of England bounded by East Sussex, Greater London, Medway, Surrey and the sea at the Thames estuary and the Strait of Dover. Chief centres are the county town of Maidstone, Royal Tunbridge Wells, Dartford, Margate, Ashford, Gravesend, Folkestone, Sittingbourne, Ramsgate, the cathedral city of Canterbury, Tonbridge and Dover. The chalk ridge of the North Downs runs along the N side, then SE to Folkestone and Dover. The River Medway cuts through the chalk in the vicinity of Maidstone, and there are low lying areas to the E of Canterbury and of Tonbridge, on Romney Marsh in

the S, and bordering the Thames estuary in the N. Chief industrial areas are around Maidstone, Ashford and Tonbridge; Dover and Folkestone are major ports, with the Channel Tunnel terminus to the N of Folkestone; Sheerness is a port of growing importance. Industrial activity includes mineral extraction, cement manufacture and papermaking. On the highly productive agricultural land, Kent's reputation as the Garden of England is earned, with market gardening, fruit and hop production. Romney Marsh is used for extensive sheep-grazing. Rivers include the Medway, Stour, and Beult.
Districts: Ashford; Canterbury; Dartford; Dover; Gravesham; Maidstone; Sevenoaks; Shepway; Swale; Thanet; Tonbridge & Malling; Tunbridge Wells.

Kingston upon Hull *Hull* Population: 243,589.
Unitary authority on the E coast of England surrounding the city of Kingston upon Hull and bounded by East Riding of Yorkshire and the mouth of the River Humber. Kingston upon Hull is a major sea port and a great industrial city, with key industries including chemicals, food processing, pharmaceuticals and engineering. The River Hull passes through the area, and the River Humber forms the S border.

Lancashire *Lancs.* Population: 1,134,974.
County of NW England bounded by Blackburn with Darwen, Cumbria, Greater Manchester, Merseyside, North Yorkshire, West Yorkshire and the Irish Sea. Chief towns are the administrative centre of Preston, Burnley, Morecambe, the historic county town of Lancaster, Skelmersdale, Lytham St. Anne's, Leyland, Accrington and Chorley; Fleetwood and Heysham are ports. The inland side of the county is hilly and includes the wild and impressive Forest of Bowland. The W side contains the coastal plain, where vegetables are extensively cultivated. The S is largely urban; industries include cotton spinning and weaving, chemicals, glass, rubber, electrical goods, and motor vehicles. The principal rivers are the Lune and the Ribble.
Districts: Burnley; Chorley; Fylde; Hyndburn; Lancaster; Pendle; Preston; Ribble Valley; Rossendale; South Ribble; West Lancashire; Wyre.

Larne *Larne* Population: 30,832.
On the east coast of Northern Ireland, Larne port is one of the main points of entry to Northern Ireland and is also an important centre for freight. The northern part of the district contains the southern tip of the Antrim Hills and the coastline has an amazing range of geological features, from the most ancient rocks, to remains from the last glaciation. Other towns include Carnlough, Ballygalley and Portmuck on the coast, and Kilwaughter, Ballynure and Ballycarry inland. Industries are based around freight, agriculture and tourism.

Leicester *Leic.* Population: 279,921.
Unitary authority in central England surrounding Leicester and bounded by Leicestershire. It is one of the leading shopping regions in the Midlands. Traditional industries such as hosiery and footwear, as well as hi-tech industries, are important to the local economy. Leicester is aiming to be one of the most environmentally-friendly cities in Europe. It is involved in pioneering electronic toll road schemes in order to encourage the use of public transport. The Rivers Sence and Soar run through the area.

Leicestershire *Leics.* Population: 609,578.
Midland county of England bounded by Derbyshire, Leicester, Lincolnshire, Northamptonshire, Nottinghamshire, Rutland, Staffordshire and Warwickshire. Chief towns are Loughborough, Hinckley, Wigston, Coalville, Melton Mowbray, Oadby, Market Harborough, Shepshed and Ashby de la Zouch. The landscape is mostly of low, rolling hills. E and W of Leicester are areas of higher ground, notably Charnwood Forest. The W is largely

industrial; industries include light engineering, hosiery, and footwear. The E is rural, with large fields and scattered woods, and is noted for field sports and food production. Part of the legacy left by the Roman occupation of Leicestershire are the Great North Road, Watling Street and Fosse Way which dissect the county. River Soar traverses the county from S to N, while River Welland forms part of the boundary with Northamptonshire to the S.

Districts: Blaby; Charnwood; Harborough; Hinckley & Bosworth; Melton; North West Leicestershire; Oadby & Wigston.

Limavady *Limavady* Population: 32,422.
There are two AONBs in this district, which contains the Sperrin mountains to the south and the wide, fertile valley of the river Roe in the centre. To the north is Lough Foyle and the long, sandy beach of Magilligan Strand. Main towns are Limavady, Dungiven and Ballykelly and a car ferry runs across Lough Foyle from Magilligan Point to the Inishowen Peninsula in the Republic of Ireland. Industries include agriculture, services, small-scale manufacturing, construction and tourism.

Lincolnshire *Lincs.* Population: 646,645.
County of E England bounded by Cambridgeshire, Leicestershire, Norfolk, Northamptonshire, North East Lincolnshire, North Lincolnshire, Nottinghamshire, Peterborough, Rutland and the North Sea. Main towns are the cathedral city and county town of Lincoln and the towns of Boston, Grantham, Gainsborough, Spalding, Stamford, Skegness and Louth. Much of the county is flat and includes a large area of The Fens in the S. This reclaimed marshland is richly fertile, producing large crops of peas (for canning), sugar beet, potatoes, corn, and around Spalding, flower bulbs. Two ranges of hills traverse the county N and S: the narrow limestone ridge, a continuation of the Cotswold Hills, running from Grantham to Scunthorpe, and the chalk Wolds, about 12m/20km wide, running N from Spilsby and Horncastle. Apart from agriculture, industries include manufacture of agricultural machinery and tourism, which is centred on historic Lincoln, and the coastal resorts of Skegness and Mablethorpe. The rivers, of which the chief are the Witham and Welland, are largely incorporated into the extensive land-drainage system, and scarcely distinguishable from man-made channels.

Districts: Boston; East Lindsey; Lincoln; North Kesteven; South Holland; South Kesteven; West Lindsey.

Lisburn *Lisburn* Population: 108,694.
This district borders Belfast in the east and touches Lough Neagh in the west. Lisburn city itself sits in the valley of the River Lagan, with other towns being Dunmurry, Hillsborough, Magheraberry and Derriaghy. The Giants' Ring is a massive 656 feet (200m) diameter earthwork near the village of Drumbo. Industries include textiles (linen) and light engineering.

Londonderry/Derry *London.* Population: 105,066.
The city of Londonderry (Derry) is an important seaport and the second city of Northern Ireland, sitting astride the wide estuary of the river Foyle. The city walls, erected in 1619, are complete and some of the finest in Europe. Other towns include New Buildings and Eglinton, with several small villages scattered in the rural areas. In the south, are the forested glens of the Sperrin Mountains. Agriculture is the main industry, along with textiles (linen), distilling and chemicals.

Luton *Luton* Population: 184,371.
Unitary authority in SE England surrounding Luton and bounded by Bedfordshire and Hertfordshire. Luton is one of the major centres of employment and manufacturing in SE England, with automotive, electrical and retail industries among the most important. The production and export of high fashion

and straw hats remains a feature of the local economy. London Luton Airport is situated in the SE of the area, and the River Lea rises nearby.

Magherafelt *Magh.* Population: 39,780.
The Sperrin Mountains form the western boundary and the River Bann, the eastern. The main town of Magherafelt is the administrative and marketing centre of the district and is also well known for its arts festival. Other small towns include Maghera and Draperstown. Agriculture is the main industry, along with some manufacturing and construction.

Medway *Med.* Population: 249,488.
Unitary authority on SE coast of England S of the River Thames estuary and neighbouring Kent. The chief centres are Gillingham, the naval base of Chatham, Strood and the cathedral city of Rochester. The S part of the area, surrounding the River Medway, is largely urban and industrialised. The marshland to the N includes Kingsnorth Power Station and the Isle of Grain, but is mostly rural, and contains Northward Hill Nature Reserve which is a haven for birds.

Merseyside *Mersey.* Population: 1,362,026.
Former metropolitan county of NW England. It neighbours Cheshire, Greater Manchester, Halton, Lancashire, Warrington and the sea. It comprises the near-continuous urban complex which includes the city of Liverpool and the towns of St. Helens, Birkenhead, Southport, Bootle, Wallasey, Bebington, Huyton and Crosby. The county straddles the long, wide estuary of the River Mersey, which accounts for the development of the area. During the 18c, growing Imperial trade of goods and slaves, led to the explosion of urban development surrounding the docks at Liverpool, Birkenhead and Bootle. Liverpool went on to become Britain's premier transatlantic port and a significant terminus during the migration flows of the 19c, leading to an ethnically diverse city culture. Over the last century the docks have declined, leaving behind an impressive waterfront and cityscape as testament to a mercantile and maritime heritage. Inland, the urban spread has reached the industrial town of St. Helens which is famed for glass production. To the N are the residential areas of Crosby, Formby and the coastal resort of Southport. The area includes race courses at Aintree and Haydock, and an airport at Speke.

Districts: Knowsley; Liverpool; St. Helens; Sefton; Wirral.

Merthyr Tydfil *M.Tyd.* Population: 55,981.
Unitary authority in S Wales bounded by Caerphilly, Powys and Rhondda Cynon Taff. Main centres are the town of Merthyr Tydfil and the villages of Treharris, Abercanaid and Troedyrhiw. The area stretches from the Brecon Beacons, along the Taff Valley, to the centre of the former Welsh coal mining district. The local economy has diversified from primary industry, with Merthyr Tydfil being an important centre for public administration, shopping and employment for the region. The River Taff flows through the area.

Middlesbrough *Middbro.* Population: 134,855.
Unitary authority in NE England surrounding Middlesbrough and bounded by North Yorkshire, Redcar & Cleveland and Stockton-on-Tees. Middlesbrough is an industrial town, with chemical and petro-chemical industries in evidence. It is also an important sub-regional shopping and entertainment centre between Leeds and Newcastle upon Tyne.

Midlothian *Midloth.* Population: 80,941.
Unitary authority in central Scotland neighbouring East Lothian, Edinburgh and Scottish Borders. Main towns are Penicuik, Bonnyrigg, Dalkeith, Gorebridge and Loanhead. The area is mostly rural, including the rolling moorland of the Pentland Hills and Moorfoot Hills in the S. To the N, the urban area is

comprised of satellite towns to the SE of Edinburgh. Rivers include Tyne Water and South Esk.

Milton Keynes *M.K.* Population: 207,057.
S midland unitary authority of England bounded by Bedfordshire, Buckinghamshire and Northamptonshire. The area includes the city of Milton Keynes, Bletchley, Newport Pagnell, Great Linford, Stony Stratford and Wolverton. Over the past 30 years, the area has undergone the fastest rate of growth in the country, attracting numerous industries. The Great Ouse and Ouzel rivers pass through the area.

Monmouthshire (Sir Fynwy). *Mon.* Population: 84,885.
Unitary authority in SE Wales bounded by Blaenau Gwent, Newport, Powys, Torfaen, the English areas of Gloucestershire, Herefordshire and the Bristol Channel. The main towns are Abergavenny, Caldicot, Chepstow and Monmouth. Part of the Brecon Beacons are found in NW Monmouthshire, whereas the SW area is mainly flat. Agriculture, mineral extraction and the service sector are important to the local economy. Rivers include the Wye, which forms part of E border, and the Usk, Trothy and Monnow.

Moray *Moray* Population: 86,940.
Unitary authority in N Scotland neighboured by Aberdeenshire, Highland and the sea. Main towns are Elgin, Forres, Buckie, Lossiemouth and Keith. The area is mainly mountainous, including part of the Cairngorm Mountains in the S. It is dissected by many deep river valleys, most notably that of the River Spey. Along with the local grain and peat, the abundant waters provide the raw materials for half of Scotland's malt whisky distilleries, leading to the Whisky Trail and much tourism through Speyside.

Moyle *Moyle* Population: 15,933.
This is Northern Ireland's smallest district by population but it is famous for the amazing basalt columns of the Giant's Causeway on the north coast, a UNESCO World Heritage Site. The entire Causeway Coast has been designated as an AONB. Ballycastle is the largest town, others being Cushendun, Cushendall and Bushmills, which has the worlds oldest licensed distillery. Off the north coast is Rathlin Island where Northern Ireland's largest seabird colony breeds under the management of the RSPB. The main industry is agriculture, with some light industry and tourism.

Neath Port Talbot (Castell-nedd Port Talbot). *N.P.T.*
Population: 134,468.
Unitary authority in S Wales neighbouring Bridgend, Powys, Rhondda Cynon Taff, Swansea and the sea. The chief centres are Neath, Port Talbot, Pontardawe, Baglan, Glyncorrwg and Briton Ferry. The area is mostly mountainous, divided up by the river valleys of the Tawe, Neath, Afan and Dulais, which all flow out to sea at Swansea Bay. The lower valley of the River Neath is heavily industrialised.

Newport (Casnewydd). *Newport* Population: 137,011.
Unitary authority on the S coast of Wales, N of the mouth of the River Severn, and bounded by Caerphilly, Cardiff, Monmouthshire and Torfaen. Main centres are Newport, Liswerry, Malpas and Caerleon. Steel manufacturing and hi-tech industries are important to the local economy. The rivers Ebbw and Usk run through the area.

Newry & Mourne *N. & M.* Population: 87,058.
Bordering the Republic of Ireland on its southern edge, the district contains the beautiful Mourne mountains in the east and has two areas designated as AONBs. Newry is the main town and has been an important centre for cross-border trade development. Warrenpoint is a modern port. Other towns

include Killkeel, with its important fishing industry, Rostrevor, Bessbrook and Annalong. Besides fishing, industries are mainly agriculture and tourism.

Newtownabbey *Newtown.* Population: 79,995.
Bordering the north-western shore of Belfast Lough, this small district is a mix of the urban and rural. It has a high population density compared to the rest of Northern Ireland. The main town is Newtownabbey, others being Ballyclare, which hosts one of the oldest horse fairs in Ireland, Mossley and Mallusk which is a busy commercial centre. There are many small businesses in the area as well as agriculture.

Norfolk *Norf.* Population: 796,728.
County of E England bounded by Cambridgeshire, Lincolnshire, Suffolk and the North Sea. Chief centres are the cathedral city and county town of Norwich, Great Yarmouth on the E coast, the expanding port of King's Lynn near the mouth of the Great Ouse and The Wash, Thetford, which is known as the Breckland 'capital', East Dereham and Wymondham. Norfolk is mainly flat or gently undulating, with fenland in the W characterised by large drainage channels emptying into The Wash. In the SW is Breckland, an expanse of heath and conifer forest used for military training; other afforested areas are near King's Lynn and North Walsham. NE of Norwich are The Broads, an area of meres and rivers popular for boating; reeds for thatching are grown here. The N Norfolk coastline is an Area of Outstanding Natural Beauty and Heritage Coast, and includes the popular resorts of Cromer and Sheringham. Otherwise the county is almost entirely agricultural, with farming an important activity; service and manufacturing industries are also significant. Rivers include the Great Ouse, Bure, Nar, Wensum, Wissey, and Yare; the Little Ouse and Waveney both enter the county briefly, but mainly form the boundary with Suffolk.
Districts: Breckland; Broadland; Great Yarmouth; King's Lynn & West Norfolk; North Norfolk; Norwich; South Norfolk.

North Ayrshire *N.Ayr.* Population: 135,817.
Unitary authority in central Scotland including the islands of Arran, Great Cumbrae and Little Cumbrae. It is bounded by East Ayrshire, East Renfrewshire, Inverclyde, Renfrewshire, South Ayrshire and the sea. The principal towns are Irvine, Kilwinning, Saltcoats, Largs, Ardrossan, Stevenston and Kirbirnie. The area includes mountains and part of Clyde Muirshiel Regional Park in the N, and the lower lands of Cunninghame in the S. There is a maritime heritage to the area; ferry routes operate from Largs and Ardrossan. Rivers include the Garnock, Dusk Water and Noddsdale Water.

North Down *N.Down* Population: 76,323.
On the southern shore of Belfast Lough, this is another high population density district. The main town of Bangor is an important maritime resort with a large, modern marina and shopping centre. Other towns are Helen's Bay and Holywood. Main industries include light engineering, food processing, retail and tourism.

North East Lincolnshire *N.E.Lincs.* Population: 157,979.
Unitary authority in NE England, S of the mouth of the River Humber and bounded by Lincolnshire, North Lincolnshire and the North Sea. Chief towns are Grimsby, Cleethorpes and Immingham. Grimsby and Cleethorpes together are the shopping and commercial centres of the area. Fishing, food, tourism, chemical and port industries are all important to the local economy. The main rivers are the Humber and Freshney.

North Lanarkshire *N.Lan.* Population: 321,067.
Unitary authority in central Scotland neighbouring East Dunbartonshire, Falkirk, Glasgow, South Lanarkshire, Stirling and West Lothian. The chief centres are Cumbernauld,

Coatbridge, Airdrie, Motherwell, Wishaw and Bellshill. North Lanarkshshire contains a mixture of urban and rural areas, and formerly depended heavily upon the coal, engineering and steel industries. Regeneration and diversification have occurred in recent years.

North Lincolnshire *N.Lincs.* Population: 152,849.

Unitary authority in NE England neighbouring East Riding of Yorkshire, Leicestershire, Norfolk, North East Lincolnshire, Nottinghamshire, Peterborough, Rutland, South Yorkshire and the River Humber. The main centres are Scunthorpe, Bottesford, Barton-upon-Humber and Brigg. The area is mainly rural, but does include oil refineries, steel and manufacturing industries; the River Humber provides pool and wharf facilities. Rivers include the Humber, Trent and the Old Ancholme.

North Somerset *N.Som.* Population: 188,564.

Unitary authority in W England, S of the mouth of the River Severn, and neighbouring Bath & North East Somerset, Bristol, Somerset and the Bristol Channel. Chief towns are Weston-super-Mare, Clevedon, Nailsea and Portishead. The area is largely rural with tourism, centred on the coastal resort of Weston-super-Mare, being a major industry. Bristol International Airport is located in the E of the area.

North Yorkshire *N.Yorks.* Population: 569,660.

Large county of N England bounded by Cumbria, Darlington, Durham, East Riding of Yorkshire, Lancashire, Middlesbrough, Redcar & Cleveland, South Yorkshire, Stockton-on-Tees, West Yorkshire, York and the North Sea. Main centres are Harrogate, Scarborough, Hetton, Selby, the cathedral city of Ripon, the county town of Northallerton, Whitby, Skipton and Knaresborough. Apart from the wide plain around York, through which flow River Ouse and its tributaries, and the smaller Vale of Pickering, watered by the Derwent and its tributary the Rye, the county is dominated by two ranges of hills; The Pennines in the W and the Cleveland Hills in the NE. The plains are pastoral and agricultural, while the hills provide rough sheep-grazing. The county includes the popular resorts of Scarborough and Whitby, and the majority of the North York Moors and Yorkshire Dales National Parks which promote tourism. Other economic activities include light engineering, service and hi-tech industries. Principal rivers are the Ouse, fed by the Derwent, Swale, Ure, Nidd and Wharfe, and draining into the Humber; the Esk, flowing into the North Sea at Whitby; and in the W, the Ribble, passing out into Lancashire and the Irish Sea.

Districts: Craven; Hambleton; Harrogate; Richmondshire; Ryedale; Scarborough; Selby.

Northamptonshire *Northants.* Population: 629,676.

Midland county of England bounded by Bedfordshire, Buckinghamshire, Cambridgeshire, Leicestershire, Lincolnshire, Milton Keynes, Oxfordshire, Peterborough, Rutland and Warwickshire. Chief towns are Northampton, Corby, Kettering, Wellingborough, Rushden and Daventry. The county consists largely of undulating agricultural country rising locally to low hills, especially along the W border. Large fields and scattered woods provide terrain for field sports. Northamptonshire still retains its rural and agricultural charm, despite undergoing rapid population growth recently. There are many villages of architectural, scenic and historic interest. Industrial development is modest, concentrating on the traditional footwear manufacture. Corby is undergoing regeneration following the decline of its steel industry. Tourism is set to increase due to the county's natural Middle England ambience, and the seasonal opening of the Althorp Estate, the family home and resting place of Diana, Princess of Wales. The principal rivers are the Nene and Welland.

Districts: Corby; Daventry; East Northamptonshire; Kettering; Northampton; South Northamptonshire; Wellingborough.

Northumberland *Northumb.* Population: 307,190.

Northernmost county of England bounded by Cumbria, Durham and Tyne & Wear, the Scottish authority of Scottish Borders and the North Sea. The principal towns are Blyth, Ashington, Cramlington, Bedlington, Morpeth, Berwick-upon-Tweed, Prudhoe and Hexham. There is some industry in the SE coastal area, otherwise the county is almost entirely rural, the greater part being high moorland, culminating in the Cheviot Hills along the Scottish border. The most spectacular stretches of Hadrian's Wall traverse the county to the N of Haltwhistle and Hexham. There is extensive afforestation, including Kielder Forest Park and part of the Northumberland National Park in the NW; parts of these forests are used for military training. The large reservoir, Kielder Water, also occurs in the NW of the area. Rivers include the Aln, Blyth, Breamish, Coquet, East and West Allen, North and South Tyne, Till, and Wansbeck. The Tweed forms part of the Scottish border and flows out to sea at Berwick-upon-Tweed.

Districts: Alnwick; Berwick-upon-Tweed; Blyth Valley; Castle Morpeth; Tynedale; Wansbeck.

Nottingham *Nott.* Population: 266,988.

Unitary authority in central England surrounding the city of Nottingham and bounded by Nottinghamshire. The city of Nottingham has a long history, having been granted many Royal Charters; Nottingham Castle and Wollaton Hall are among its many historical buildings. It is also an industrial and engineering centre, and a university city. Its main industries include the manufacture of chemicals, tobacco, cycles, lace and hosiery. The River Trent flows through the city.

Nottinghamshire *Notts.* Population: 748,510.

Midland county of England bounded by Derbyshire, Leicestershire, Lincolnshire, North Lincolnshire, Nottingham and South Yorkshire. Principal towns are Mansfield, Carlton, Sutton in Ashfield, Arnold, Worksop, Newark-on-Trent, West Bridgford, Beeston, Stapleford, Hucknall and Kirkby in Ashfield. Much of the county is rural, with extensive woodlands in the central area of The Dukeries, part of the larger Sherwood Forest. Cattle-grazing is the chief farming activity. Around the large towns there is much industry, including iron and steel, engineering, knitwear, pharmaceuticals, and coal-mining. The county has associations with Robin Hood, at Sherwood Forest, and D.H. Lawrence, at Eastwood. The most important river is the Trent.

Districts: Ashfield; Bassetlaw; Broxtowe; Gedling; Mansfield; Newark & Sherwood; Rushcliffe.

Omagh *Omagh.* Population: 47,952.

One of the largest districts by area of Northern Ireland, the borders are mainly hills, with the town of Omagh in a central valley, at the confluence of several rivers where almost one third of the total population live. The area is primarily rural, with small towns and villages scattered throughout the landscape. These include Fintona, Dromore and Carrickmore. Agriculture is the main industry.

Orkney *Ork.* Population: 19,245.

Group of some fifteen main islands and numerous smaller islands, islets and rocks. Designated an Islands Area for administrative purposes, and lying N of the NE end of the Scottish mainland across the Pentland Firth. Kirkwall is the capital, situated on the island Mainland, 24m/38km N of Duncansby Head. Stromness is the only other town. About twenty of the islands are inhabited. In general the islands are low-lying but have steep, high cliffs on W side. The climate is generally mild for the latitude but storms are frequent. Fishing and farming (mainly cattle-rearing) are the chief industries. The oil industry is also represented, with an oil terminal on the island of Flotta, and oil service bases at Car Ness and Stromness,

Mainland and at Lyness, Hoy. Lesser industries include whisky distilling, knitwear and tourism. The islands are noted for their unique prehistoric and archaeological remains. The main airport is at Grimsetter, near Kirkwall, with most of the populated islands being served by airstrips. Ferries also operate from the Scottish mainland, and between islands in the group.

Oxfordshire *Oxon.* Population: 605,488.
S midland county of England bounded by Buckinghamshire, Gloucestershire, Northamptonshire, Reading, Swindon, Warwickshire, West Berkshire, Wiltshire and Wokingham. Chief centres are the county town, cathedral and university city of Oxford and towns of Banbury, Abingdon, Bicester, Witney, Didcot, Thame and Henley-on-Thames. Burford and Chipping Norton are small Cotswold towns in the W and NW respectively. The landscape is predominantly flat or gently undulating, forming part of the Thames Valley. High ground occurs where the Chiltern Hills enter the county in the SE and the Cotswold Hills in the NW. The county is largely agricultural, with industries centred on the towns. Scientific, medical and research establishments are attracted by the proximity of Oxford's universities. Printing and publishing industries have their greatest concentration outside London. The motor industry is well represented with car manufacture at Cowley, Oxford, and the county has the world's largest concentration of performance car development and manufacturing. Tourism, attracted to stately homes, notably Blenheim Palace, and Oxford city centre, is also important. Chief rivers are the Thames (or Isis), Cherwell, Ock, Thame, and Windrush.
Districts: Cherwell; Oxford; South Oxfordshire; Vale of White Horse; West Oxfordshire.

Pembrokeshire (Sir Benfro). *Pembs.* Population: 114,131.
Unitary authority in the SW corner of Wales neighbouring Carmarthenshire, Ceredigion and the sea. The chief centres are Haverfordwest, Pembroke Dock, Pembroke, Tenby, Saundersfoot, Neyland, Fishguard and the ancient cathedral city of St. David's. Key industries are tourism, agriculture and oil refining. The deep estuarial waters of Milford Haven provide a berth for oil tankers. A large part of Pembrokeshire's coastline forms Britain's only coastal National Park. Ferries sail from Fishguard and Pembroke Dock to Rosslare in the Republic of Ireland.

Perth & Kinross *P. & K.* Population: 134,949.
Unitary authority in Scotland bounded by Aberdeenshire, Angus, Argyll & Bute, Clackmannanshire, Fife, Highland and Stirling. Chief centres are the city of Perth, Blairgowrie, Crieff, Kinross, Auchterarder and Pitlochry. The area is mountainous, containing large areas of remote open moorland, especially in the N and W; the vast upland expanses of Breadalbane, Rannoch and Atholl, form the S edge of the Grampian Mountains. The lower land of the S and E is more heavily populated and is dominated by the ancient city of Perth. The area is rich in history as it links the Highlands to the N with the central belt and lowlands to the S via important mountain passes, most notably the Pass of Dromochter. The area has many castles, and Scottish Kings were traditionally enthroned at Scone Abbey, to the N of Perth. There are many lochs, including Loch Rannoch and Loch Tay. Main industries are tourism and whisky production. The world famous Gleneagles golf course is in the S of the area. Rivers include the Tay, Almond and Earn.

Peterborough *Peter.* Population: 156,061.
Unitary authority in E England neighbouring Cambridgeshire, Lincolnshire, Northamptonshire and Rutland. The area includes the city of Peterborough, which lies at the heart of an important agricultural area. Developing as a railway hub, it has become a major industrial, distribution and shopping centre. The River Nene passes through Peterborough.

Plymouth *Plym.* Population: 240,720.
Unitary authority on the SW coast of England surrounding the city of Plymouth and neighbouring Cornwall and Devon. Plymouth stands at the mouth of the River Tamar and is the largest city on the S coast of England. It has strong mercantile and naval traditions; it is closely linked with Sir Francis Drake, and has maintained a Royal Naval Dockyard for 300 years. Plymouth is a regional shopping centre and a popular resort.

Poole *Poole* Population: 138,288.
Unitary authority on S coast of England surrounding Poole and bordered by Bournemouth and Dorset. Poole Harbour is the second largest natural harbour in the world, which enabled Poole to prosper through trading, especially with Newfoundland. Poole has now attracted a variety of industries including boat-building, fishing, pottery, engineering and electronics. Ferries run to the Channel Islands and France.

Portsmouth *Ports.* Population: 186,701.
Unitary authority on the S coast of England surrounding the city of Portsmouth and bordered by Hampshire. Portsmouth developed as a strategic port around Portsmouth Harbour, and it is still the home of the Royal Navy. It has become a culturally diverse centre, attracting a wide range of industries which include leisure, tourism, financial services, distribution, manufacturing and hi-tech industries.

Powys *Powys* Population: 126,354.
Large unitary authority in central Wales bordering Blaenau Gwent, Caerphilly, Carmarthenshire, Ceredigion, Denbighshire, Gwynedd, Merthyr Tydfil, Monmouthshire, Neath Port Talbot, Rhondda Cynon Taff, Wrexham and the English areas of Herefordshire and Shropshire. Main centres are Newtown, Gurnos, Brecon, Welshpool, Ystradgynlais, Llanllwchaiarn, Llandrindod Wells, Knighton, Llanidloes, Builth Wells and Machynlleth. Powys is almost entirely rural, with mountainous terrain; most of the Brecon Beacons National Park falls within the S part of the area, while the Cambrian Mountains are in the W. There is considerable afforestation, and a number of large reservoirs, including Lake Vyrnwy. To the N of Brecon, on Mynydd Eppynt, is an extensive military training area. Main economic activities are agriculture, which is predominantly based around hill farming. Tourism is significant, owing to the natural beauty of the area, and innovative attractions such as the Centre for Alternative Technology. Industrial development is gradually increasing. Among the many rivers, the largest are the Severn, Usk, and Wye.

Reading *Read.* Population: 143,096.
Unitary authority in S England to W of Greater London, surrounding Reading and bordered by Oxfordshire, West Berkshire, Windsor & Maidenhead and Wokingham. Reading developed as a crossing point of the River Thames and River Kennet. Traditional industries include brewing and food production, notably biscuits. These are accompanied by an increasing sector of hi-tech and computer-based companies, attracted by Reading's location in the M4 corridor. Reading has also established itself as a major entertainments centre.

Redcar & Cleveland *R. & C.* Population: 139,132.
Unitary authority on the NE coast of England neighbouring Hartlepool, Middlesbrough and North Yorkshire. The main centres are Redcar, South Bank, Eston, Guisborough, Marske-by-the-Sea, Saltburn-by-the-Sea, Loftus and Skelton. The area is one of great contrasts. It combines rural villages, market towns and coastal resorts, along with heavily populated urban areas and industrialised port facilities. Industries include steel-making, due to the local ironstone, and chemicals, based around the River Tees to the NW of the area. The coastal towns attract some tourism. The River Tees forms part of the border to the W.

Renfrewshire *Renf.* Population: 172,867.

Unitary authority in central Scotland bordering East Renfrewshire, Glasgow, Inverclyde, North Ayrshire, West Dunbartonshire and the Firth of Clyde. Main centres are Paisley, Renfrew, Johnstone, Erskine and Linwood. The area emerges W from the Greater Glasgow periphery into a contrasting countryside of highlands, lochs and glens. Industry is centred on the urban area and includes electronics, engineering, food and drink production and service sectors; in rural areas to the W, agriculture is still important. The W part of the area includes some of Clyde Muirshiels Regional Park; Glasgow Airport is in the E.

Rhondda Cynon Taff (Rhondda Cynon Taf). *R.C.T.* Population: 231,946.

Unitary authority in S Wales bounded by Bridgend, Caerphilly, Cardiff, Merthyr Tydfil, Neath Port Talbot, Powys and Vale of Glamorgan. The principal towns are Treorchy, Aberdare, Pontypridd, Ferndale and Mountain Ash. Rhondda Cynon Taff is a mountainous area, dissected by deep narrow valleys, with urbanisation typified by ribbon development. The area was the former heart of the Welsh coal mining industry, and has experienced a sharp economic decline as pits closed. Diversification into light engineering and service sectors are gradually improving the industrial base. Main rivers are the Rhondda and Cynon.

Rutland *Rut.* Population: 34,563.

Unitary authority in E England neighbouring Leicestershire, Lincolnshire, Northamptonshire and Peterborough. The main town is Oakham. Agriculture is the main industry; other important industries are engineering, cement-making, plastics, clothing and tourism. The area includes the large reservoir, Rutland Water, which is an important feature for leisure, tourism and wildlife.

Scottish Borders *Sc.Bord.* Population: 106,764.

Administrative region of SE Scotland bordering Dumfries & Galloway, East Lothian, Midlothian, South Lanarkshire, West Lothian, the English counties of Cumbria and Northumberland and the North Sea. It comprises the former counties of Berwick, Peebles, Roxburgh and Selkirk. Main towns are Hawick, Galashiels, Peebles, Kelso, Selkirk and Jedburgh. It extends from the Tweedsmuir Hills in the W to the North Sea on either side of St. Abb's Head in the E, and from the Pentland, Moorfoot and Lammermuir Hills in the N to the Cheviot Hills and the English border in the S. The fertile area of rich farmland between the hills to N and S is known as The Merse. The area around Peebles and Galashiels is noted for woollen manufacture. Elsewhere, the electronics industry is of growing importance. The River Tweed rises in the extreme W and flows between Kelso and Coldstream, finally passing into England, 4m/6km W of Berwick-upon-Tweed.

Shetland *Shet.* Population: 21,988.

Group of over 100 islands, lying beyond Orkney to the NE of the Scottish mainland; Sumburgh Head being about 100m/160km from Duncansby Head. Designated an Islands Area for administrative purposes, the chief islands are Mainland, on which the capital and chief port of Lerwick is situated, Unst and Yell. Some twenty of the islands are inhabited. The islands are mainly low-lying, the highest point being Ronas Hill, on Mainland. The oil industry has made an impact on Shetland, with oil service bases at Lerwick and Sandwick, and a large terminal at Sullom Voe. Other industries include cattle and sheep-rearing, knitwear and fishing. The climate is mild, considering the latitude, but severe storms are frequent. The islands are famous for the small Shetland breed of pony, which is renowned for its strength and hardiness. There is an airport at Sumburgh, on S part of Mainland.

Shropshire *Shrop.* Population: 283,173.

W midland county of England bounded by Cheshire, Herefordshire, Staffordshire, Telford & Wrekin, Worcestershire and the Welsh authorities of Powys and Wrexham. Main towns are the county town of Shrewsbury, Oswestry, Bridgnorth, Market Drayton, Ludlow and Whitchurch. The S and W borders are hilly, with large areas of open moorland, including The Long Mynd and Wenlock Edge, which provide good sheep-grazing. Elsewhere the county undulates towards the Severn Valley, which provides fertile agricultural land served by prosperous market towns. Agricultural output includes dairy, poultry and pig farming, along with corn crops. As the former heart of the Marches of Wales, Shropshire contains the remains of numerous border defences. There are also the remains of several monasteries, for instance, at Much Wenlock and Buildwas. The most important river is the Severn, which flows across the county from W to SE; others include the Clun, Corve, Perry, Rea Brook, and Teme.

Districts: Bridgnorth; North Shropshire; Oswestry; Shrewsbury & Atcham; South Shropshire.

Slough *Slo.* Population: 119,067.

Unitary authority in SE England to the W of London, surrounding Slough and bordering Buckinghamshire, Greater London, Surrey and Windsor & Maidenhead. Slough has grown significantly over the past 30 years, and is a major regional shopping centre. Industry is centred on the large Slough Trading Estate, which was planned after World War I. Numerous sectors are represented in Slough, among them is confectionery.

Somerset *Som.* Population: 498,093.

County in SW England bounded by Bath & North East Somerset, Devon, Dorset, North Somerset, Wiltshire and the Bristol Channel. The chief centres are the county town of Taunton, Yeovil, Bridgwater, Frome, Chard, Street, Burnham-on-Sea, Highbridge, the small cathedral city of Wells, Wellington and Minehead. Somerset consists of several hill ranges, including the Mendip, Polden, Quantock, Brendon Hills, along with most of Exmoor. These uplands are separated by valleys, or, on either side of the River Parrett, by the extensive marshy flats of Sedgemoor. Economic activity is mainly based on agriculture in the fertile vales, with manufacturing, distribution and service industries centred on the urban areas. Tourism is important with attractions including Exmoor National Park, a holiday complex at Minehead and the county's natural rural charm. Somerset also holds one of Europe's largest music festivals at Glastonbury. The chief rivers are Axe, Brue, Parrett, and Tone, draining into the Bristol Channel; and Barle and Exe, rising on Exmoor and flowing into Devon and the English Channel.

Districts: Mendip; Sedgemoor; South Somerset; Taunton Deane; West Somerset.

South Ayrshire *S.Ayr.* Population: 112,097.

Unitary authority in SW Scotland bounded by Dumfries & Galloway, East Ayrshire, North Ayrshire and the sea. The chief towns are Ayr, Troon, Prestwick, Girvan and Maybole. The area consists of a long coastline, with lowlands surrounding Ayr Bay and higher ground to the S. Agriculture is a major economic activity on the uplands. To the N, aerospace and hi-tech industries are located near Prestwick International Airport and Ayr, the main retail centre. Notable sporting venues include a race course at Ayr and open championship golf courses at Troon and Turnberry. Tourism is a major feature of the local economy. The area was the birthplace of Robert the Bruce and Robert Burns; it contains Scotland's first country park at Culzean Castle; and it has a holiday camp on the coast near Ayr. Rivers include the Ayr, Water of Girvan and Stinchar.

South Gloucestershire *S.Glos.* Population: 245,641.
Unitary authority in SW England neighbouring Bath & North East Somerset, Bristol, Gloucestershire and Wiltshire. The chief centres are Kingswood, Chipping Sodbury, Mangotsfield, Frampton Cotterell, Yate, Thornbury, Patchway and Filton. The S part of the area lies on the N and E fringes of Bristol. The Cotswold hills are in the E, and the Severn Vale in the W. Main industries are in the S, and include aerospace engineering; the N is mainly agricultural. South Gloucestershire includes the English side of both Severn road bridges. Badminton Park in the E of the area, is the location for the Badminton Horse Trials. The River Severn borders the area to the NW.

South Lanarkshire *S.Lan.* Population: 302,216.
Unitary authority in central Scotland bordering Dumfries & Galloway, East Ayrshire, East Renfrewshire, Glasgow, North Lanarkshire, Scottish Borders and West Lothian. The main towns are East Kilbride, Hamilton, Blantyre, Larkhall, Carluke, Lanark and Bothwell. Urban development is mainly in the N, merging with the SE periphery of Greater Glasgow. The S part is mostly farmland and not highly populated. Tourism is mainly centred on the picturesque valley of the upper Clyde; there is a race course at Hamilton. The area has associations with the industrial philanthropist, Robert Owen, who built a model village at New Lanark. Rivers include the Clyde, Avon and Dippool Water.

South Yorkshire *S.Yorks.* Population: 1,266,338.
Former metropolitan county of N England bordered by Derbyshire, East Riding of Yorkshire, North Lincolnshire, North Yorkshire, Nottinghamshire and West Yorkshire. It comprises the industrial and urban area around the city of Sheffield and the towns of Rotherham, Barnsley and Doncaster. Located at the heart of a major coalfield, South Yorkshire prospered through the development of heavy industry. Barnsley and Rotherham were coal mining towns, with steel and fine cutlery centred on Sheffield. The decline of these industries has led to the area redefining itself. Sheffield has become a centre of learning, tourism and conferences, aided by its environmental improvements. Barnsley, Rotherham and Doncaster have increased their industrial base, especially via light industries. Leisure and recreation are an important feature of the area, with venues including Barnsley's Metrodome, Doncaster's race course and Dome, and Sheffield's Arena and Don Valley Stadium. Retail has increased with city and town centre redevelopment, and the Meadowhall complex. The surrounding countryside includes country parks at Rother Valley and Thrybergh, with part of the Peak District National Park W and NW of Sheffield. The chief river is the Don.
Districts: Barnsley; Doncaster; Rotherham; Sheffield.

Southampton *S'ham.* Population: 217,445.
Unitary authority on the S coast of England surrounding the city of Southampton, and bordered by Hampshire. Southampton owes much to the deep waters of Southampton Water, which have enabled the development of Europe's busiest cruise port. Water and the waterfront remain very important to the local economy, with marine technology, oceanography, boat shows and yacht races all prominent. The city is also a leading media, recreational, entertainment and retail centre. The chief river is the Itchen.

Southend *S'end* Population: 160,257.
Unitary authority in SE England, N of the mouth of the River Thames, surrounding Southend-on-Sea and bordering Essex. Southend is a commerical, residential, shopping and holiday centre, with tourism among its main industries. It includes a 7m shoreline from Leigh-on-Sea to Shoeburyness, a famous pier and a sea life centre.

Staffordshire *Staffs.* Population: 806,744.
Midland county of England bounded by Cheshire, Derbyshire, Leicestershire, Shropshire, Stoke-on-Trent, Telford & Wrekin, Warwickshire, West Midlands and Worcestershire. Chief centres are Newcastle-under-Lyme, Tamworth, the county town of Stafford, Burton upon Trent, Cannock, Burntwood, the cathedral city of Lichfield, Kidsgrove, Rugeley and Leek. The urban development occurs around the West Midlands conurbation in the S, where main industries include engineering, iron and steel, rubber goods and leather production, while to the N, there is an urban concentration around Stoke-on-Trent. Burton upon Trent is noted for brewing. The ancient hunting forest and former mining district of Cannock Chase is in the centre of the county and contains preserved tracts of moorland. In the NE lies part of the Peak District National Park. The rest of the county is predominantly agricultural, with milk, wheat and sugar beet produced. To the E of Leek, moorland broken up by limestone walls extends across the Manifold valley to the Derbyshire border. In additon to the Trent, which dominates much of the county, rivers include the Blithe, Manifold, Sow and Tame. River Dove forms the boundary with Derbyshire.
Districts: Cannock Chase; East Staffordshire; Lichfield; Newcastle-under-Lyme; South Staffordshire; Stafford; Staffordshire Moorlands; Tamworth.

Stirling *Stir.* Population: 86,212.
Unitary authority in central Scotland neighbouring Argyll & Bute, Clackmannanshire, East Dunbartonshire, Falkirk, North Lanarkshire, Perth & Kinross and West Dunbartonshire. The chief centres are Stirling, the ancient cathedral city of Dunblane, Bannockburn, Bridge of Allan and Callander. The fertile agricultural lands of the Forth valley are in the centre of the area, bounded by mountains: The Trossachs and the mountain peaks of Ben Lomond, Ben More and Ben Lui in the N, while in the S are the Campsie Fells. Tourism is an important industry with Stirling including many sites of historical significance to Scotland, particularly during the struggle to retain independence. There are associations with Rob Roy, and the battle site of Bannockburn. Other features include The Trossachs, part of the Loch Lomond Regional Park and the Queen Elizabeth Forest Park. There are several lochs, including Loch Lomond, which forms part of the W border, and Loch Katrine. Scotland's only lake named as such, Lake of Menteith, is also in Stirling. The main river is the Forth.

Stockton-on-Tees *Stock.* Population: 178,408.
Unitary authority in NE England neighbouring Darlington, Durham, Hartlepool, Middlesbrough, North Yorkshire and Redcar & Cleveland. The main centres are Stockton-on-Tees, Billingham, Thornaby-on-Tees, Eaglescliffe, Egglescliffe and Yarm. The area has a diverse mix of picturesque villages, large-scale urbanisation and heavy industry. The area has recently undergone major renewal and regeneration, with industries now including electronics, food technology and chemical production. Stockton is the main shopping centre for the area, and includes the Teesside Retail Park. The main river is the Tees, which is controlled by the Tees Barrage. This has created Britain's largest purpose-built whitewater canoeing course.

Stoke-on-Trent *Stoke* Population: 240,636.
Unitary authority in England surrounding the city of Stoke-on-Trent and neighbouring Staffordshire. The city has six town centres: Burslem, Fenton, Hanley, Longton, Stoke-upon-Trent and Tunstall. Hanley is where most current city centre activities are located. The area forms The Potteries, and is the largest claywear producer in the world, although now it is largely a finishing centre for imported pottery. There are a wide variety of other industries, including steel, engineering, paper, glass and furniture. Stoke-on-Trent is a centre of employment, leisure and shopping for the surrounding areas. It

is noted for its environmental approach, particularly with land reclamation which accounts for around 10 per cent of the city area; sites include Festival Park, Central Forest Park and Westport Lake. The River Trent flows through the area.

Strabane *Strabane* Population: 38,248.
To the east lie the Sperrin Mountains (an AONB) with the Republic of Ireland border and the River Mourne to the west. The main town of the district is Strabane, an historic market town. Other towns include Castlederg in the Derg valley, Newtonstewart, with Baronscourt forest nearby, Sion Mills, with its model linen village, Plumbridge and Mount Hamilton. Main industries are agriculture, manufacturing and tourism.

Suffolk *Suff.* Population: 668,553.
Easternmost county of England bounded by Cambridgeshire, Essex, Norfolk and the North Sea. Main towns are the county town of Ipswich, Lowestoft, Bury St. Edmunds, Felixstowe, Sudbury, Haverhill, Newmarket, Stowmarket and Woodbridge. The county is low-lying and gently undulating. It is almost entirely agricultural, with cereal crops and oil seed rape in abundance. The low coastline, behind which are areas of heath and marsh, afforested in places, is subject to much erosion; it is deeply indented with long river estuaries which provide good sailing. The NW corner of the county forms part of Breckland. The central region includes many notable historic Wool Towns, for instance, Lavenham. Apart from agriculture, industries include electronics, telecommunications, printing and port facilities. Lowestoft is a prominent fishing port and Felixstowe is a container port of growing importance. River Stour forms the S boundary with Essex, and the Little Ouse and Waveney form most of the N boundary with Norfolk. The many other small rivers include the Alde with its estuary the Ore, Deben, and Gipping with its estuary the Orwell, in the E and Lark in the W.
Districts: Babergh; Forest Heath; Ipswich; Mid Suffolk; St. Edmundsbury; Suffolk Coastal; Waveney.

Surrey *Surr.* Population: 1,059,015.
County of SE England bounded by Bracknell Forest, East Sussex, Greater London, Hampshire, Kent, Slough, West Sussex and Windsor & Maidenhead. The prinicpal towns are Woking, the cathedral and university town of Guildford, Staines, Leatherhead, Farnham, Epsom, Ewell, Sunbury, Walton-on-Thames, Weybridge, Egham, Redhill, Reigate, Esher, Camberley, Frimley and Godalming. The chalk ridge of the North Downs, gently sloping on the N side but forming a steep escarpment on the S, traverses the county from E to W. Extensive sandy heaths in the W are much used for military training. The county is heavily wooded, and contains many traces of the former iron industry in the predominantly rural S. Much of the urbanised E and N areas include commuter or dormitory towns which form the residential outskirts of the Greater London conurbation. Industries include the agricultural activites of dairy farming and horticulture. Tourism and recreation are also important, with Surrey including numerous stately homes, Wentworth golf course, four race courses, and a theme park at Thorpe Park. The chief river is the Thames, into which flow the Wey and the Mole.
Districts: Elmbridge; Epsom & Ewell; Guildford; Mole Valley; Reigate & Banstead; Runnymede; Spelthorne; Surrey Heath; Tandridge; Waverley; Woking.

Swansea (Abertawe). *Swan.* Population: 223,301.
Unitary authority in S Wales bordering Carmarthenshire, Neath Port Talbot and the sea. Main centres are the city of Swansea, Gorseinon, The Mumbles, Sketty, Cockett and Clydach. The area includes mountains in the N, the urban centre surrounding Swansea, and the Gower peninsula in the S. Swansea originally developed as a port serving the W coalfield of S Wales. The area gained an international reputation for tin-plating and copper and nickel production. Swansea is now a regional shopping and commercial centre, including a university and marina development. The Gower peninsula attracts many tourists with its fine beaches and cliff scenery; hang-gliding is popular at Rhossili Down, and there are associations with Dylan Thomas. The Mumbles is a popular resort, formerly connected to Swansea via a tramway. The chief river is the Tawe.

Swindon *Swin.* Population: 180,051.
Unitary authority in SW England neighbouring Gloucestershire, Oxfordshire and Wiltshire. Main centres are Swindon, Stratton St. Margaret, Highworth and Wroughton. The area is located between the Cotswold Hills and Wiltshire Downs, on the fringes of the Thames Valley. Originally a railway town, Swindon has experienced rapid recent growth and is now a centre for car manufacture and central commercial operations. The town is a regional shopping centre with a redeveloped town centre and the Designer Outlet Village. The River Thames borders the area to the N and the River Cole to the E.

Telford & Wrekin *Tel. & W.* Population: 158,325.
Unitary authority in W England bordered by Shropshire and Staffordshire. Main centres are Telford, Wellington, Madeley, Donnington, Oakengates, Hadley and Newport. The area was the cradle of the Industrial Revolution, with notable firsts including Darby's discovery of the iron smelting process at Coalbrookdale, the casting and construction of the first cold blast iron bridge at Ironbridge, and the construction of the first iron ship. The new town of Telford, named after the famous engineer, surveyor and road builder, Thomas Telford, is the major commercial centre. The River Severn runs S through the area.

Thurrock *Thur.* Population: 143,128.
Unitary authority in SE England, N of the mouth of the River Thames. It is bounded by Essex and Greater London. The main centres are Grays, South Ockendon, Stanford-le-Hope, Corringham and Tilbury. The area is a mix of old and modern, rural and urban. In the N there are historic villages set in agricultural land, while in the S, there are the modern urban developments, and industrial activities surrounding oil refining and the container port of Tilbury. Grays is the commercial centre of Thurrock, with the major retail centre being Thurrock Lakeside. The area includes the N stretch of the Dartford Tunnel and Queen Elizabeth II Bridge, both of which cross the River Thames.

Torbay *Torbay* Population: 129,706.
Unitary authority located on the SW coast of England neighbouring Devon. The major towns are Torquay, Paignton and Brixham. The area, situated on Tor Bay, is among Britain's main holiday resorts, and is widely regarded as the English Riviera. Tourism is the main industry, with Torbay receiving over 1.5 million visitors per year. Excellent leisure, recreation and conference facilities are added attractions.

Torfaen (Tor-faen). *Torfaen* Population: 90,949.
Unitary authority in S Wales bounded by Blaenau Gwent, Caerphilly, Monmouthshire and Newport. The principal towns are Cwmbran, Pontypool and Blaenavon. Torfaen contains rugged mountains with a 12-mile-long valley running N to S from Blaenavon to Cwmbran. The area is a manufacturing centre which includes electronics, engineering and automotive companies. The industrial past of the area has led to the growth of tourist attractions, with notable sites including The Valley Inheritance at Pontypool, and Big Pit National Mining Museum of Wales and 19c ironworks at Blaenavon. The river Afon Llwyd runs through the area.

Tyne & Wear *T. & W.* Population: 1,075,938.
Maritime county of NE England bordered by Durham and

Northumberland. It comprises the urban complex around the cities of Newcastle upon Tyne and Sunderland, South Shields, Gateshead, Washington and Wallsend. Named after its two important rivers, the area developed largely through the coal mining and ship-building industries. As these industries declined, the area has undergone urban and industrial regeneration. Newcastle upon Tyne is now a commercial, university and cultural centre, with a historic heart including a cathedral, 12c castle and the Tyne Bridge; the historic Quayside has recently been developed. Sunderland gained city status in 1992, and is now a centre for car manufacture, with recreational facilities including the Crowtree Leisure Complex and the National Glass Centre. Elsewhere, Wallsend has hi-tech and off-shore industries; South Tyneside has electronics industries, and tourism, via its Catherine Cookson links. Gateshead has an international athletics stadium, Europe's largest undercover shopping centre, the Metrocentre, and the modern symbol of renewal, the Angel of the North. The area is served by the Port of Tyne and Newcastle International Airport.
Districts: Gateshead; Newcastle upon Tyne; North Tyneside; South Tyneside; Sunderland.

Vale of Glamorgan (Bro Morgannwg). *V. of Glam.* Population: 119,292.
Unitary authority on the S coast of Wales neighbouring Bridgend, Cardiff and Rhondda Cynon Taff. The chief towns are Barry, Penarth and Llantwit Major. Vale of Glamorgan is a lowland area between Cardiff and Bridgend, with some agricultural activities, and tourism at the resorts of Barry and Penarth. Cardiff International Airport is situated in the SE near Rhoose. Main river is the Ely, which passes through the area.

Warrington *Warr.* Population: 191,080.
Unitary authority in NW England surrounding Warrington and bounded by Cheshire, Greater Manchester, Halton and Merseyside. The area developed as a main crossing point of the River Mersey and latterly the Manchester Ship Canal. During industrialisation it became an important strategic trading centre for the NW region. In 1968, Warrington was granted New Town status, leading to traditional industries such as chemicals, brewing and food processing being joined by hi-tech industries and research and development facilities. Warrington retains its importance as a regional shopping, leisure and commercial centre. The River Mersey flows through the area.

Warwickshire *Warks.* Population: 505,860.
Midland county of England bounded by Gloucestershire, Leicestershire, Northamptonshire, Oxfordshire, Staffordshire, West Midlands and Worcestershire. Chief towns are Nuneaton, Rugby, Royal Leamington Spa, Bedworth, the county town of Warwick, Stratford-upon-Avon and Kenilworth. Warwickshire consists of mostly flat or undulating farmland, although the foothills of the Cotswold Hills spill over the SW border. Main manufacturing activites occur in an industrial belt extending NW from Rugby to the boundary with Staffordshire. They include motor and component industries, service sectors, electrical and general engineering. Tourism is centred on the historic town of Warwick with its medieval castle, and Stratford-upon-Avon with its Shakespeare associations. The principal river is the Avon.
Districts: North Warwickshire; Nuneaton & Bedworth; Rugby; Stratford-on-Avon; Warwick.

West Berkshire *W.Berks.* Population: 144,483.
Unitary authority in S England bordered by Hampshire, Oxfordshire, Reading, Wiltshire and Wokingham. The chief centres are Newbury, Thatcham and Hungerford. West Berkshire is a mixture of old market towns, historic buildings and waterways, and includes the famous Newbury racecourse. Rivers include the Kennet and the Pang.

West Dunbartonshire *W.Dun.* Population: 93,378.
Unitary authority in central Scotland bordered by Argyll & Bute, East Dunbartonshire, Glasgow, Inverclyde, Renfrewshire and Stirling. The chief towns are Clydebank, Dumbarton, Alexandria and Bonhill. The area is mountainous, containing the Kilpatrick Hills, and is bounded by Loch Lomond in the N and the Firth of Clyde in the S. The urban SE area of West Dunbartonshire forms part of the NW periphery of Greater Glasgow. There is a broad base of light manufacturing and service sector industries. Tourism and leisure are a feature, with the SE tip of Loch Lomond Regional Park and the whole of Balloch Castle Country Park falling within the area. West Dunbartonshire includes the Erskine Bridge which spans the River Clyde, other rivers include the Leven.

West Lothian *W.Loth.* Population: 158,714.
Unitary authority in central Scotland neighbouring Edinburgh, Falkirk, Midlothian, North Lanarkshire, Scottish Borders and South Lanarkshire. The chief towns are Livingston, Bathgate, Linlithgow, Broxburn, Whitburn and Armadale. The area undulates to the S of the Firth of Forth, and rises to moorland at the foot of the Pentland Hills in the S. The main urban areas are situated along commuter corridors between Glasgow, Edinburgh and Falkirk; elsewhere the area is mostly rural. Hi-tech and computing industries are in evidence.

West Midlands *W.Mid.* Population: 2,555,592.
Former metropolitan county of central England bordered by Staffordshire, Warwickshire and Worcestershire. It comprises the urban complex around the cities of Birmingham and Coventry, and the towns of Wolverhampton, Dudley, Walsall, West Bromwich, Sutton Coldfield and Solihull. The West Midlands developed as a manufacturing and engineering centre which specialised in the metalworking and motor trades. The area around Dudley, Walsall and Wolverhampton became known as the Black Country, with heavy industry centred on the local deposits of coal, iron ore and limestone. Other local trades included glassware, saddlery and lock-making. Birmingham became Britain's second city by specialising in 1001 trades from confectionery to cars, and has developed into the major business, industrial, commercial and cultural centre for the area. As the traditional industries have declined, there has been a shift towards service, leisure and recreation sectors of the economy; several significant corporate service centres and venues, such as the National Exhibition Centre and the Indoor Arena, are in the West Midlands. The area is served by Birmingham International Airport. Rivers include the Tame and the Cole.
Districts: Birmingham; Coventry; Dudley; Sandwell; Solihull; Walsall; Wolverhampton.

West Sussex *W.Suss.* Population: 753,614.
County of S England bounded by Brighton & Hove, East Sussex, Hampshire, Surrey and the English Channel. Main towns are Worthing, Crawley, Bognor Regis, Littlehampton, Horsham, Haywards Heath, East Grinstead, the cathedral city and county town of Chichester, Burgess Hill and Shoreham-by-Sea. N of a level coastal strip run the South Downs, a steep-sided chalk ridge which is thickly wooded in parts. The remaining inland area, The Weald, is largely well-wooded farmland, although there is industrial development around Crawley, Gatwick (London) Airport, Horsham, and Haywards Heath, as well as among the predominantly residential towns on the coast. Tourism is a major activity throughout the county. There are many castles and stately homes, such as Arundel Castle and Goodwood House, the popular seaside resorts of Bognor Regis and Worthing, race courses at Goodwood and Fontwell, Chichester Harbour, which is a centre for yachtsmen and wildfowl, historic Chichester itself, and numerous picturesque villages. The N of the county includes Gatwick (London) Airport. The rivers, none large, include the Adur and Arun, with its tributary the Rother; the

Medway rises in the E of the county.

Districts: Adur; Arun; Chichester; Crawley; Horsham; Mid Sussex; Worthing.

West Yorkshire *W.Yorks.* Population: 2,079,211.

Former metropolitan county of N England bordering Derbyshire, Greater Manchester, Lancashire, North Yorkshire and South Yorkshire. It comprises the area around the cities of Leeds, Bradford and Wakefield, and the towns of Huddersfield, Halifax, Dewsbury, Keighley, Batley, Morley, Castleford, Brighouse, Pudsey, Pontefract and Shipley. West Yorkshire developed as a centre for wool and textiles, manufacturing and engineering, creating an industrial urban landscape set against rural moorland. As the traditional industries have declined, the area has undergone regeneration and diversification, moving towards tertiary economic sectors. Leeds is the industrial, administrative, commercial and cultural centre of the area, containing regional government offices and many corporate service centres and head offices. Emerging economic activities across West Yorkshire have included printing, distribution, chemicals, food and drink production, hi-tech industries and financial services. Haworth with its Brontë associations, Holmfirth and the moorlands are the centres of tourism. The area includes Leeds Bradford International Airport. The chief rivers are the Aire and the Calder, while the Wharfe forms its N boundary below Addingham.

Districts: Bradford; Calderdale; Kirklees; Leeds; Wakefield.

Western Isles (Na h-Eileanan an Iar. Also known as Outer Hebrides.) *W.Isles* Population: 26,502.

String of islands off the W coast of Scotland and separated from Skye and the mainland by The Minch. They extend for some 130m/209km from Butt of Lewis in the N, to Barra Head in the S. Stornoway, situated on the Isle of Lewis, is the main town; elsewhere, there are mainly scattered coastal villages and settlements. The chief islands are Isle of Lewis, North Uist, Benbecula, South Uist and Barra. North Harris and South Harris form significant areas in the S part of the Isle of Lewis. The topography of the islands consists of undulating moorland, mountains and lochs. The main industries are fishing, grazing and, on the Isle of Lewis, tweed manufacture. There are airfields with scheduled passenger flights on the Isle of Lewis, Benbecula and Barra.

Wiltshire *Wilts.* Population: 432,973.

County of S England bounded by Bath & North East Somerset, Dorset, Gloucestershire, Hampshire, Oxfordshire, Somerset, South Gloucestershire, Swindon and West Berkshire. Main centres are the cathedral city of Salisbury, the county town of Trowbridge, Chippenham, Warminster, Devizes and Melksham. Wiltshire consists of extensive chalk uplands scattered with prehistoric remains, notably at Avebury and Stonehenge, and interspersed with wide, well-watered valleys. The N of the county is dominated by the Marlborough Downs which are much used for racehorse training, while in the S, the chalk plateau of Salisbury Plain is an important military training area. Between these two upland areas lies the fertile Vale of Pewsey where dairy production and bacon-curing are important agricultural activities. Other industries include electronics, computing, pharmaceuticals, plastics, telecommunications and service sector activities. Wiltshire attracts tourism with its prehistoric remains, stately houses and picturesque market towns and villages. Rivers include the so-called Bristol and Wiltshire Avons, Ebble, Kennet, Nadder, Wylye, and the upper reaches of the Thames.

Districts: Kennet; North Wiltshire; Salisbury; West Wiltshire.

Windsor & Maidenhead *W. & M.* Population: 133,626.

Unitary authority in SE England to the W of Greater London, and bounded by Bracknell Forest, Buckinghamshire, Slough, Surrey and Wokingham. The towns of Maidenhead and Windsor are the main centres for industry, leisure and recreation. The area is particularly noted for its strong Royal connections as it includes Windsor Castle and the former Royal hunting estate of Windsor Great Park. Other popular tourist attractions include Ascot race course, Windsor Legoland and Eton College. The River Thames forms the N boundary.

Wokingham *W'ham* Population: 150,229.

Unitary authority in SE England, to the W of Greater London. The area encompasses Wokingham and is bordered by Bracknell Forest, Buckinghamshire, Hampshire, Oxfordshire, Reading, West Berkshire and Windsor & Maidenhead. The area includes riverside villages in the N, with undulating ridges covered by woodlands and commons in the S. Wokingham is a growing centre for hi-tech and computer industries. The River Thames forms the N border, and the River Blackwater forms the border to the S.

Worcestershire *Worcs.* Population: 542,107.

S midland county of England neighbouring Gloucestershire, Herefordshire, Shropshire, Warwickshire and West Midlands. Main centres are the cathedral city and the county town of Worcester, and the towns of Redditch, Kidderminster, Great Malvern, Bromsgrove, Droitwich Spa, Stourport-on-Severn and Evesham. The urban areas in the N of the county form part of the periphery and commuter belt of the West Midlands conurbation, and attract much of the industrial development. The central and S sections of the county are largely rural, containing the fertile Severn Valley and Vale of Evesham, with market gardening and orchard-growing being the main agricultural activities. Tourism is an important industry, much of it being centred on historic Worcester, with its cathedral, the triennial Three Choirs Festival, Worcester Sauce and china factories. Other popular attractions include boating on the River Severn and visiting the Vale of Evesham whilst the flowers are in full bloom. The main river is the Severn.

Districts: Bromsgrove; Malvern Hills; Redditch; Worcester; Wychavon; Wyre Forest.

Wrexham (Wrecsam). *Wrex.* Population: 128,476.

Unitary authority in NE Wales bordering Denbighshire, Flintshire, Powys and the English counties of Cheshire and Shropshire. Main centres are Wrexham, Rhosllanerchrugog, Gwersyllt, Cefn-mawr and Coedpoeth. The area is mountainous in the SW, containing part of the Berwyn range; the Dee valley lies in the NE. The area was formerly dominated by the iron, coal and limestone industries. Food manufacture, brewing, plastics and hi-tech industries are now important to the local economy. Wrexham is the largest commercial and shopping centre in N Wales. The River Dee flows through the area.

York *York* Population: 181,094.

Unitary authority in N England surrounding the historic cathedral city of York and bordered by East Riding of Yorkshire and North Yorkshire. York is a major archaeological, episcopal, industrial, commercial and cultural centre, situated at the confluence of the River Foss and the River Ouse. The city has a unique history dating from the original Roman military camp, which has led to it becoming one of the main museum and tourist centres in the country. The historic core, situated around the centrepiece of the medieval Minster, is well preserved. Other major attractions include the Jorvik Viking Centre, the medieval city walls and the National Railway Museum. Economic sectors include the confectionery industry, company head offices, Government departmental offices, and research and development establishments. The main river is the Ouse.

WALES Counties

BLAENAU GWENT
BRIDGEND
CAERPHILLY
CARDIFF
CARMARTHENSHIRE
CEREDIGION
CONWY
DENBIGHSHIRE
FLINTSHIRE
GWYNEDD
ISLE OF ANGLESEY
MERTHYR TYDFIL
MONMOUTHSHIRE
NEATH PORT TALBOT
NEWPORT
PEMBROKESHIRE
POWYS
RHONDDA CYNON TAFF
SWANSEA
TORFAEN
VALE OF GLAMORGAN
WREXHAM

ENGLAND
Counties & Districts

BATH AND NORTH
EAST SOMERSET
BEDFORDSHIRE
1 North Bedfordshire
2 Mid Bedfordshire
3 South Bedfordshire
BOURNEMOUTH
BRACKNELL FOREST
BRIGHTON & HOVE
BRISTOL
BUCKINGHAMSHIRE
1 Aylesbury Vale
2 Wycombe
3 Chiltern
4 South Buckinghamshire
CAMBRIDGESHIRE
1 Fenland
2 Huntingdonshire
3 East Cambridgeshire

4 South Cambridgeshire
5 Cambridge
CHESHIRE
1 Ellesmere Port & Neston
2 Vale Royal
3 Macclesfield
4 Chester
5 Crewe & Nantwich
6 Congleton
CORNWALL
1 North Cornwall
2 Caradon
3 Restormel
4 Carrick
5 Kerrier
6 Penwith
DERBY
DERBYSHIRE
1 High Peak
2 Derbyshire Dales
3 North East Derbyshire

4 Chesterfield
5 Bolsover
6 Amber Valley
7 Erewash
8 South Derbyshire
DEVON
1 North Devon
2 Torridge
3 Mid Devon
4 East Devon
5 Exeter
6 Teignbridge
7 West Devon
8 South Hams
DORSET
1 North Dorset
2 East Dorset
3 Christchurch
4 Purbeck
5 West Dorset
6 Weymouth &
  Portland

Scale:
0   10   20   30   40 kilometres
0   10   20   30 miles
1:1,250,000   20 miles to 1 inch/12.5 km to 1 cm

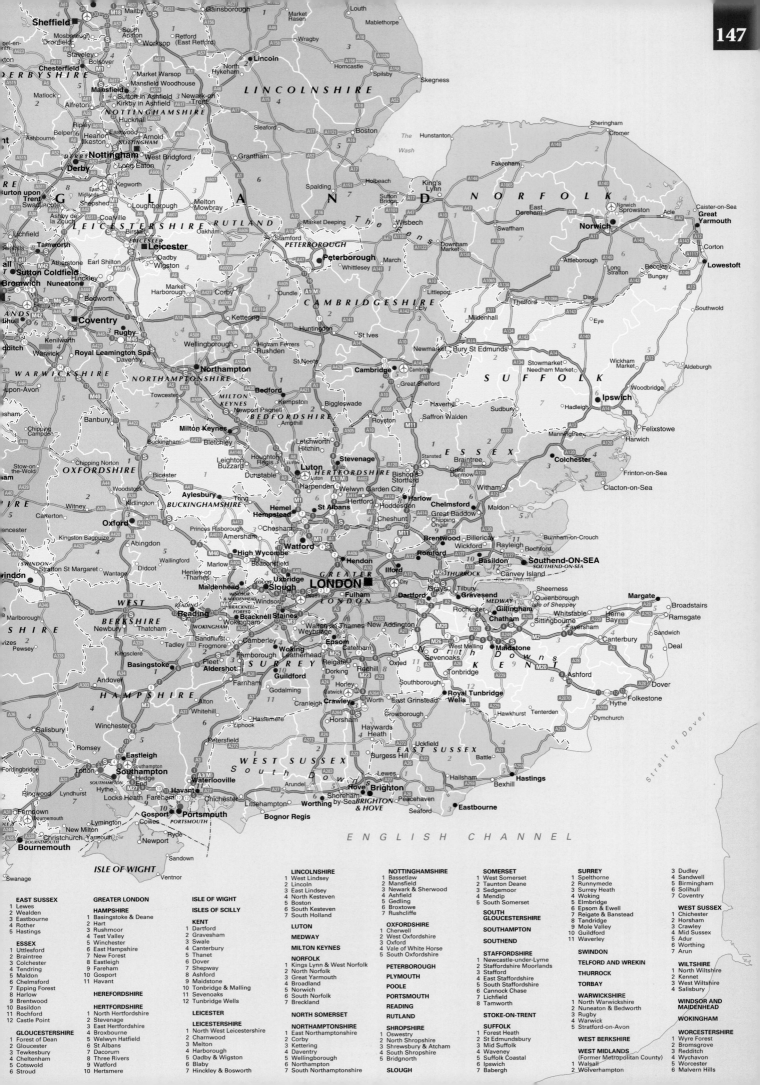

ENGLISH CHANNEL

ISLE OF WIGHT

EAST SUSSEX	**LINCOLNSHIRE**
1 Lewes	1 West Lindsey
2 Wealden	2 Lincoln
3 Eastbourne	3 East Lindsey
4 Rother	4 North Kesteven
5 Hastings	5 Boston
	6 South Kesteven
ESSEX	7 South Holland
1 Uttlesford	
2 Braintree	**NOTTINGHAMSHIRE**
3 Colchester	1 Bassetlaw
4 Tendring	2 Mansfield
5 Maldon	3 Newark & Sherwood
6 Chelmsford	4 Ashfield
7 Epping Forest	5 Gedling
8 Harlow	6 Broxtowe
9 Brentwood	7 Rushcliffe
10 Basildon	
11 Rochford	**OXFORDSHIRE**
12 Castle Point	1 Cherwell
	2 West Oxfordshire
GLOUCESTERSHIRE	3 Oxford
1 Forest of Dean	4 Vale of White Horse
2 Gloucester	5 South Oxfordshire
3 Tewkesbury	
4 Cheltenham	**PETERBOROUGH**
5 Cotswold	
6 Stroud	**PLYMOUTH**
GREATER LONDON	**POOLE**
HAMPSHIRE	**PORTSMOUTH**
1 Basingstoke & Deane	
2 Hart	**READING**
3 Rushmoor	
4 Test Valley	**RUTLAND**
5 Winchester	
6 East Hampshire	**SHROPSHIRE**
7 New Forest	1 Oswestry
8 Eastleigh	2 North Shropshire
9 Fareham	3 Shrewsbury & Atcham
10 Gosport	4 South Shropshire
11 Havant	5 Bridgnorth
HEREFORDSHIRE	**SLOUGH**
HERTFORDSHIRE	
1 North Hertfordshire	
2 Stevenage	
3 East Hertfordshire	
4 Broxbourne	**SOMERSET**
5 Welwyn Hatfield	1 West Somerset
6 St Albans	2 Taunton Deane
7 Dacorum	3 Sedgemoor
8 Three Rivers	4 Mendip
9 Watford	5 South Somerset
10 Hertsmere	
	SOUTH
ISLE OF WIGHT	**GLOUCESTERSHIRE**
ISLES OF SCILLY	**SOUTHAMPTON**
KENT	**SOUTHEND**
1 Dartford	
2 Gravesham	**STAFFORDSHIRE**
3 Swale	1 Newcastle-under-Lyme
4 Canterbury	2 Staffordshire Moorlands
5 Thanet	3 Stafford
6 Dover	4 East Staffordshire
7 Shepway	5 South Staffordshire
8 Ashford	6 Cannock Chase
9 Maidstone	7 Lichfield
10 Tonbridge & Malling	8 Tamworth
11 Sevenoaks	
12 Tunbridge Wells	**STOKE-ON-TRENT**
LEICESTER	**SUFFOLK**
	1 Forest Heath
LEICESTERSHIRE	2 St Edmundsbury
1 North West Leicestershire	3 Mid Suffolk
2 Charnwood	4 Waveney
3 Melton	5 Suffolk Coastal
4 Harborough	6 Ipswich
5 Oadby & Wigston	7 Babergh
6 Blaby	
7 Hinckley & Bosworth	

SURREY	3 Dudley
1 Spelthorne	4 Sandwell
2 Runnymede	5 Birmingham
3 Surrey Heath	6 Solihull
4 Woking	7 Coventry
5 Elmbridge	
6 Epsom & Ewell	**WEST SUSSEX**
7 Reigate & Banstead	1 Chichester
8 Tandridge	2 Horsham
9 Mole Valley	3 Crawley
10 Guildford	4 Mid Sussex
11 Waverley	5 Adur
	6 Worthing
SWINDON	7 Arun
TELFORD AND WREKIN	**WILTSHIRE**
	1 North Wiltshire
THURROCK	2 Kennet
	3 West Wiltshire
TORBAY	4 Salisbury
WARWICKSHIRE	**WINDSOR AND**
1 North Warwickshire	**MAIDENHEAD**
2 Nuneaton & Bedworth	
3 Rugby	**WOKINGHAM**
4 Warwick	
5 Stratford-on-Avon	
	WORCESTERSHIRE
WEST BERKSHIRE	1 Wyre Forest
	2 Bromsgrove
WEST MIDLANDS	3 Redditch
(Former Metropolitan County)	4 Wychavon
1 Walsall	5 Worcester
2 Wolverhampton	6 Malvern Hills

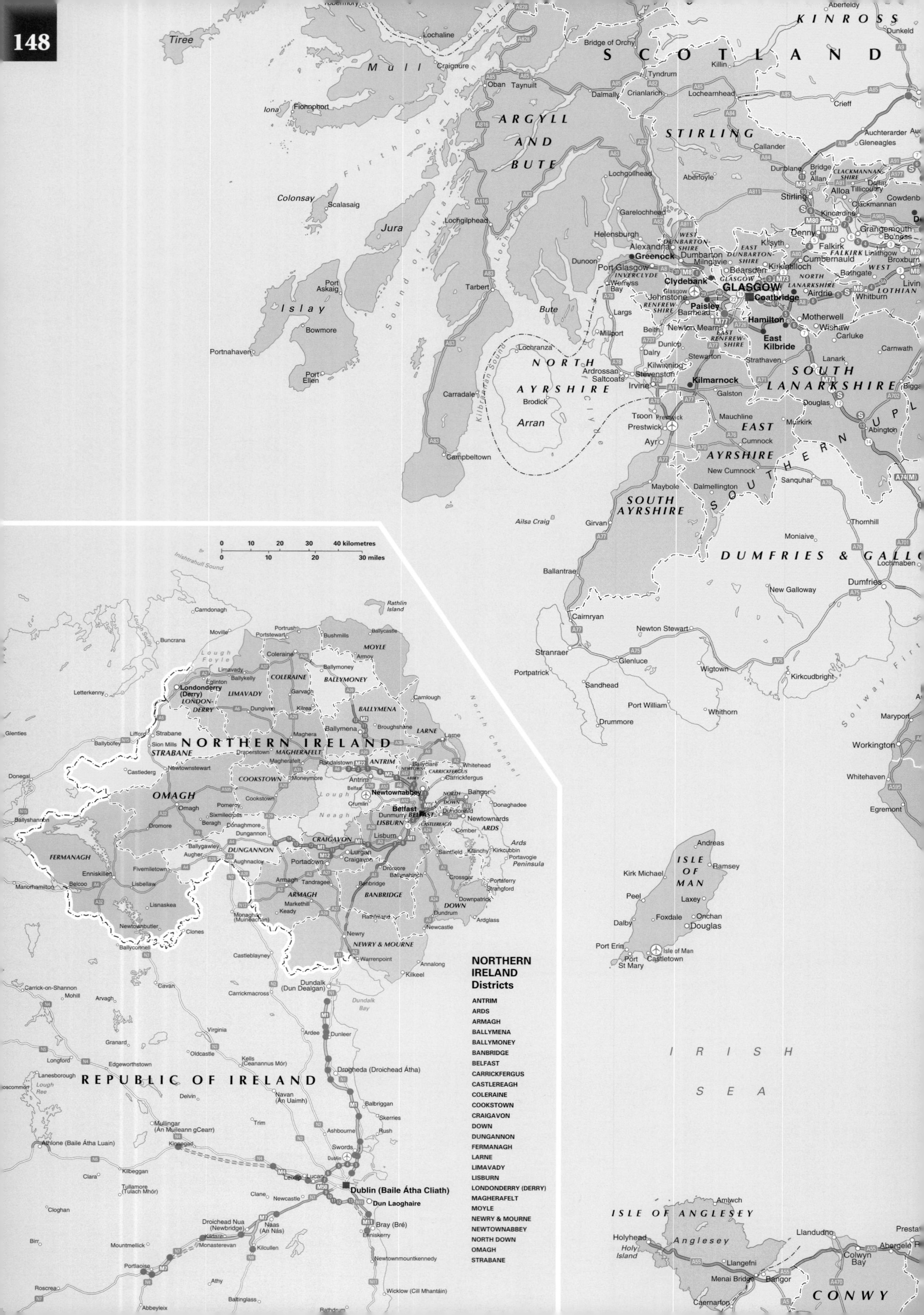
SCOTLAND
KINROSS
ARGYLL AND BUTE
STIRLING
WEST DUNBARTON-SHIRE
EAST DUNBARTON-SHIRE
CLACKMANNAN-SHIRE
FALKIRK
NORTH LANARKSHIRE
WEST LOTHIAN
INVERCLYDE
RENFREW-SHIRE
EAST RENFREW-SHIRE
GLASGOW
NORTH AYRSHIRE
EAST AYRSHIRE
SOUTH AYRSHIRE
SOUTH LANARKSHIRE
SOUTHERN UPLANDS
DUMFRIES & GALLOWAY
Firth of Lorn
Sound of Jura
Loch Fyne
Kilbrannan Sound
Firth of Clyde
Solway Firth
North Channel
IRISH SEA
ISLE OF MAN
ISLE OF ANGLESEY
CONWY
Tiree
Mull
Iona
Colonsay
Jura
Islay
Bute
Arran
Ailsa Craig
Anglesey
Holy Island
Rathlin Island
Tobermory
Lochaline
Craignure
Oban
Taynuilt
Fionnphort
Scalasaig
Port Askaig
Bowmore
Portnahaven
Port Ellen
Lochgilphead
Tarbert
Carradale
Campbeltown
Lochranza
Brodick
Bridge of Orchy
Tyndrum
Killin
Dalmally
Crianlarich
Lochearnhead
Crieff
Callander
Aberfoyle
Lochgoilhead
Garelochhead
Helensburgh
Alexandria
Greenock
Dunoon
Port Glasgow
Dumbarton
Milngavie
Bearsden
Kirkintilloch
Cumbernauld
Clydebank
Wemyss Bay
Largs
Johnstone
Paisley
Barrhead
Coatbridge
Airdrie
Bathgate
Whitburn
Hamilton
Motherwell
Wishaw
Carluke
East Kilbride
Newton Mearns
Millport
Beith
Dunlop
Dalry
Kilwinning
Stewarton
Ardrossan
Saltcoats
Stevenston
Irvine
Kilmarnock
Galston
Troon
Prestwick
Ayr
Mauchline
Cumnock
New Cumnock
Maybole
Dalmellington
Girvan
Ballantrae
Cairnryan
Stranraer
Portpatrick
Glenluce
Sandhead
Port William
Drummore
Newton Stewart
Wigtown
Whithorn
Kirkcudbright
New Galloway
Moniaive
Thornhill
Sanquhar
Dumfries
Lochmaben
Strathaven
Lanark
Carnwath
Douglas
Abington
Muirkirk
Stirling
Dunblane
Bridge of Allan
Alloa
Tillicoultry
Dollar
Clackmannan
Kincardine
Grangemouth
Bo'ness
Denny
Kilsyth
Falkirk
Linlithgow
Broxburn
Auchterarder
Gleneagles
Aberfeldy
Dunkeld
Maryport
Workington
Whitehaven
Egremont
Andreas
Ramsey
Kirk Michael
Peel
Laxey
Foxdale
Onchan
Douglas
Dalby
Port Erin
Port St Mary
Castletown
Isle of Man
Amlwch
Holyhead
Llangefni
Menai Bridge
Bangor
Caernarfon
Llandudno
Colwyn Bay
Abergele
NORTHERN IRELAND
REPUBLIC OF IRELAND
0 10 20 30 40 kilometres
0 10 20 30 miles
Inishtrahull Sound
Lough Swilly
Lough Foyle
Lough Neagh
Dundalk Bay
Lough Ree
Carndonagh
Buncrana
Moville
Portrush
Portstewart
Bushmills
Ballycastle
Coleraine
Limavady
Ballykelly
Eglinton
Londonderry (Derry)
Letterkenny
Ballymoney
Garvagh
Kilrea
Dungiven
Carnlough
Ballymena
Broughshane
Larne
Maghera
Strabane
Lifford
Sion Mills
Ballybofey
Glenties
Donegal
Castlederg
Newtownstewart
Draperstown
Magherafelt
Randalstown
Antrim
Ballyclare
Whitehead
Carrickfergus
Newtownabbey
Bangor
Donaghadee
Belfast
Dundonald
Newtownards
Comber
Crumlin
Dunmurry
Lisburn
Moneymore
Cookstown
Omagh
Pomeroy
Sixmilecross
Beragh
Donaghmore
Dungannon
Dromore
Ballyshannon
Ballygawley
Augher
Aughnacloy
Portadown
Lurgan
Craigavon
Tandragee
Armagh
Markethill
Keady
Banbridge
Rathfriland
Newry
Warrenpoint
Kilkeel
Annalong
Newcastle
Dundrum
Downpatrick
Ardglass
Strangford
Portaferry
Crossgar
Saintfield
Killinchy
Kirkcubbin
Portavogie
Ards Peninsula
Enniskillen
Fivemiletown
Lisbellaw
Belcoo
Manorhamilton
Lisnaskea
Newtownbutler
Clones
Ballyconnell
Monaghan (Muineachán)
Castleblayney
Carrickmacross
Dundalk (Dun Dealgan)
Dunleer
Ardee
Cavan
Carrick-on-Shannon
Mohill
Arvagh
Virginia
Granard
Oldcastle
Kells (Ceanannus Mór)
Longford
Edgeworthstown
Lanesborough
Delvin
Navan (An Uaimh)
Drogheda (Droichead Átha)
Balbriggan
Skerries
Rush
Trim
Mullingar (An Muileann gCearr)
Athlone (Baile Átha Luain)
Kinnegad
Ashbourne
Swords
Dublin
Lucan
Leixlip
Kilbeggan
Clara
Tullamore (Tulach Mhór)
Clane
Newcastle
Dublin (Baile Átha Cliath)
Dun Laoghaire
Cloghan
Droichead Nua (Newbridge)
Naas (An Nás)
Kildare
Monasterevan
Bray (Bré)
Enniskerry
Kilcullen
Birr
Mountmellick
Portlaoise
Newtownmountkennedy
Athy
Roscrea
Baltinglass
Wicklow (Cill Mhantáin)
Abbeyleix
Rathdrum
NORTHERN IRELAND Districts
ANTRIM
ARDS
ARMAGH
BALLYMENA
BALLYMONEY
BANBRIDGE
BELFAST
CARRICKFERGUS
CASTLEREAGH
COLERAINE
COOKSTOWN
CRAIGAVON
DOWN
DUNGANNON
FERMANAGH
LARNE
LIMAVADY
LISBURN
LONDONDERRY (DERRY)
MAGHERAFELT
MOYLE
NEWRY & MOURNE
NEWTOWNABBEY
NORTH DOWN
OMAGH
STRABANE

ENGLAND Counties & Districts

BLACKBURN WITH DARWEN

BLACKPOOL

CHESHIRE
1 Ellesmere Port & Neston
2 Vale Royal
3 Macclesfield
4 Chester
6 Congleton

CUMBRIA
1 Carlisle
2 Allerdale
3 Eden
4 Copeland
5 South Lakeland
6 Barrow-in-Furness

DARLINGTON

DERBYSHIRE
1 High Peak
2 Derbyshire Dales
3 North East Derbyshire
4 Chesterfield
5 Bolsover

DURHAM
1 Chester-le-Street
2 Derwentside
3 Durham
4 Easington
5 Sedgefield
6 Wear Valley
7 Teesdale

EAST RIDING OF YORKSHIRE

GREATER MANCHESTER
(Former Metropolitan County)
1 Wigan
2 Bolton
3 Bury
4 Rochdale
5 Oldham
6 Tameside
7 Stockport
8 Manchester
9 Salford
10 Trafford

HALTON

HARTLEPOOL

ISLE OF MAN

KINGSTON UPON HULL

LANCASHIRE
1 Lancaster
2 Wyre
3 Fylde
4 Preston
5 Ribble Valley
6 Pendle
7 Burnley
8 Rossendale
9 Hyndburn
10 Chorley
11 South Ribble
12 West Lancashire

LINCOLNSHIRE
1 West Lindsey
2 Lincoln
3 East Lindsey
4 North Kesteven

MERSEYSIDE
(Former Metropolitan County)
1 Wirral
2 Sefton
3 Liverpool
4 Knowsley
5 St Helens

MIDDLESBROUGH

NORTH EAST LINCOLNSHIRE

NORTH LINCOLNSHIRE

NORTH YORKSHIRE
1 Scarborough
2 Ryedale
3 Hambleton
4 Richmondshire
5 Craven
6 Harrogate
7 Selby

NORTHUMBERLAND
1 Berwick-upon-Tweed
2 Alnwick
3 Castle Morpeth
4 Wansbeck
5 Blyth Valley
6 Tynedale

NOTTINGHAM

NOTTINGHAMSHIRE
1 Bassetlaw
2 Mansfield
3 Newark & Sherwood
4 Ashfield

REDCAR AND CLEVELAND

SOUTH YORKSHIRE
(Former Metropolitan County)
1 Barnsley
2 Doncaster
3 Rotherham
4 Sheffield

STOCKTON-ON-TEES

TYNE AND WEAR
(Former Metropolitan County)
1 Newcastle upon Tyne
2 North Tyneside
3 South Tyneside
4 Gateshead
5 Sunderland

WARRINGTON

WEST YORKSHIRE
(Former Metropolitan County)
1 Calderdale
2 Bradford
3 Leeds
4 Wakefield
5 Kirklees

YORK

Pentl

Scrabster
Thur
Hal

Durness
Bettyhill
Tongue
Rhiconich
Scourie
Laxford
Bridge

Port Nis

Cai

Sutherland
Kinbrace

Steòrnabhagh
(Stornoway)
Port nan
Giuran

Lochinver
Helm

Gearraidh na h-Aibhne

Eilean Leodhais
(Lewis)

Ledmore
Brora
Golspie

A9

An Tairbeart

Summer
Isles

Ullapool
Bonar
Bridge

Dornoch Firth
Portmahomack

WESTERN ISLES
(NA H-EILEANAN AN IAR)

South
Harris

Aultbea

Easter
Ross

A835

Roghadal

Poolewe

HIGHLAND

Invergordon
Cromarty

Moray Firth
Burgh

Uibhist a' Tuath
(North Uist)

Loch na Madadh
(Lochmaddy)

Gairloch

Wester
Ross

Kinlochewe

Garve

A835

Strathpeffer

Dingwall

Cromarty Firth

A9
Nairn

M

Beinn na Faoghla
(Benbecula)

Uig

Shieldaig

Achnasheen

Muir of Ord
Beauly

A98
Inverness

Inverness

Little Minch

Dunvegan

Skye

Portree

Raasay

Lochcarron

Stromeferry

A832

A9

Uibhist a' Deas
(South Uist)

Sligachan

Kyle of Lochalsh

A87

Kyleakin

Drumnadrochit

A92

Grantown
-on-Spey

Cambridge

A95

Loch Baghasdail (Lochboisdale)

Broadford

Invermoriston

Aviemore

A9

Eilean Barraigh
(Barra)

Elgol

A887

Fort Augustus

Kingussie
Newtonmore

Bagh a' Chaisteil
(Castlebay)

Canna

Ardvasar

Sound of Sleat

Invergarry

A86

Bhatarsaigh
(Vatersay)

Rum
(Rhum)

Mallaig

A82

A889
Dalwhinnie

A9

Eigg

Arisaig

A830

Glenfinnan

A830

Spean
Bridge

A86

Coll

Salen

Fort William

A82

Blair Atholl

Tiree

Tobermory

Lochaline

Craignure

Loch Linnhe

Kinlochleven

Ballachulish

A82

Rannoch
Sta

Kinloch
Rannoch

PERTH A

Aberfeldy

Pitlochry

KINROS

Mull

Iona

Fionnphort

Oban

Taynuilt

A85

Bridge of Orchy

A82

Tyndrum

Killin

SCOTLAND

A9

Dalmally

Crianlarich

A85

Lochearnhead

Crieff

Colonsay

Scalasaig

Jura

Lochgilphead

A816

A83

ARGYLL
AND
BUTE

Firth of Lorn

Sound of Jura

Dalmally

Lochgoilhead

Aberfoyle

STIRLING

Callander

Auchter
Gleneag

A9

Dunblane

Bridge
of Allan

CLACKMANNAN-
SHIRE

Islay

Port
Askaig

Garelochhead

A82

A811

Alloa
Tillicoultry

Dallas
Clackmann

A811

Stirling

Kincardine

A98

Helensburgh

Alexandria

WEST
DUNBARTON-
SHIRE

Denny

M80

M876

Grange

Portnahaven

Bowmore

Loch Tyne

Dunoon

Port Glasgow

Greenock

Dumbarton

DUNBARTON-
SHIRE

Milngavie

Bearsden

Kirkintilloch

Cumbernauld

NORTH
LANARKSHIRE

Klsyth

Falkirk

M9

Linlithgow

FALKIRK

Bathgate

WES

M80

Tarbert

Bute

Largs

INVERCLYDE
Wemyss
Bay

Clydebank

Glasgow

GLASGOW

Paisley

RENFREW-
SHIRE

Johnstone

Barrhead

Coatbridge

Airdrie

Whitburn

M8

LO

Port
Ellen

Millport

Beith

Newton Mearns

EAST
RENFREW-
SHIRE

Hamilton

Motherwell

Wishaw

Carluke

Lochranza

NORTH
AYRSHIRE

Ardrossan
Saltcoats

Dunlop

Dalry

Stewarton

Kilmarnock

East
Kilbride

Lanark

SOUTH
LANARKSHIR

Carradale

Arran

Brodick

Kilwinning

Irvine

Stevenson

Kilbrannan Sound

Troon
Prestwick

Prestwick

Ayr

Galston

Mauchline

Cumnock

EAST

AYRSHIRE

SOUTHERN U

Abin

Douglas

S

Inishtrahull Sound

Campbeltown

Maybole
Dalmellington

New Cumnock

Sanquhar

Rathlin
Island

SOUTH
AYRSHIRE

DUMFRIES &

Carndonagh

SCOTLAND Councils

ABERDEEN
ABERDEENSHIRE
ANGUS
ARGYLL AND BUTE
CLACKMANNANSHIRE
DUMFRIES AND GALLOWAY
DUNDEE
EAST AYRSHIRE
EAST DUNBARTONSHIRE
EAST LOTHIAN
EAST RENFREWSHIRE
EDINBURGH
FALKIRK
FIFE
GLASGOW
HIGHLAND
INVERCLYDE
MIDLOTHIAN
MORAY
NORTH AYRSHIRE
NORTH LANARKSHIRE
ORKNEY
PERTH AND KINROSS
RENFREWSHIRE
SCOTTISH BORDERS
SHETLAND
SOUTH AYRSHIRE
SOUTH LANARKSHIRE
STIRLING
WEST DUNBARTONSHIRE
WEST LOTHIAN
WESTERN ISLES (NA H-EILEANAN AN IAR)

DACORUM

ST. ALBANS

WELWYN
HATFIELD BR

THREE

RIVERS

WATFORD

HERTSMERE

○ Borehamwood

○ Barnet

EN

○ Watford

CHILTERN

○ Rickmansworth

BARNET

○ Finchley

HARIN

SOUTH
BUCKS

HARROW

○ Harrow

HILLINGDON

BRENT

Hampstead ○

ISLINGTON

○ Uxbridge

○ Wembley

CAMDEN

Islingto

EALING

KENSINGTON &
CHELSEA

WESTMINSTER

SLOUGH

○ Ealing

HAMMERSMITH &
FULHAM

WINDSOR &
MAIDENHEAD

River Thames

Heathrow
✈ Airport

HOUNSLOW

Richmond
upon
Thames

Wandsworth ○

LAMBETH

○ Brixton

○ Hounslow

WANDSWORTH

SPELTHORNE

RICHMOND

UPON THAMES

Wimbledon ○

RUNNYMEDE

Kingston
upon Thames

MERTON

○ Esher

ELMBRIDGE

KINGSTON
UPON THAMES

SUTTON

○ Sutton

EPSOM
& EWELL

○ Epsom

○ Woking

○ Banstead

WOKING

REIGATE &

○ Leatherhead

BANSTEAD

GUILDFORD

MOLE VALLEY

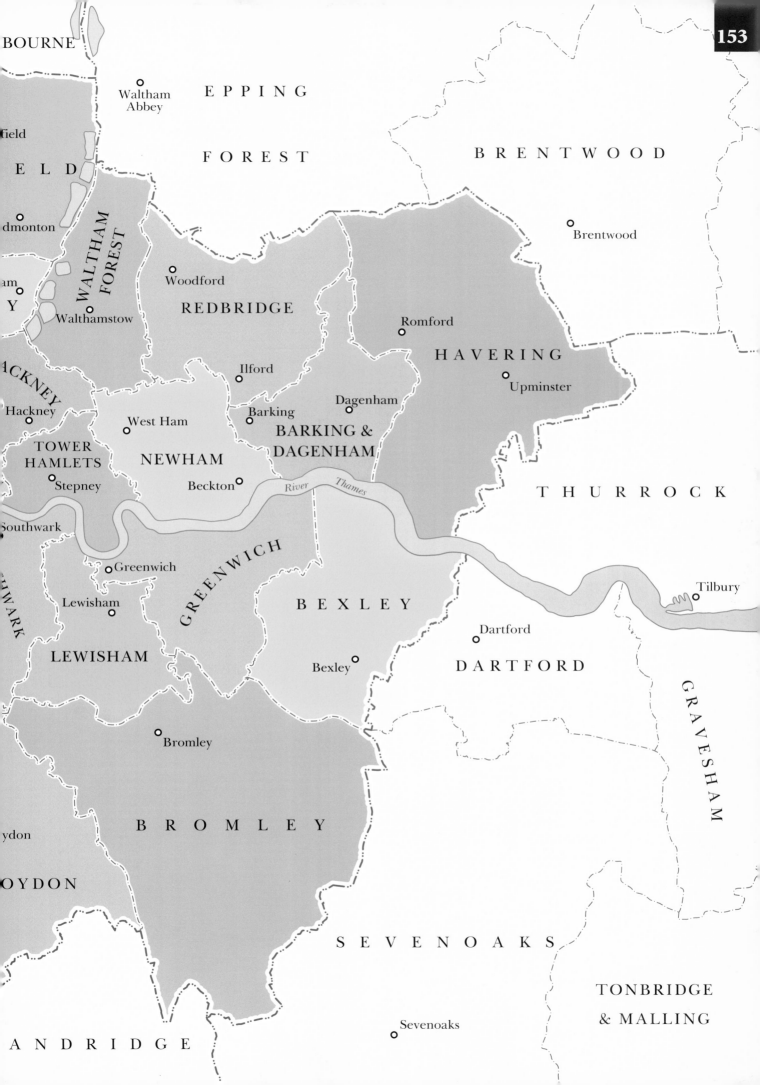

INDEX TO CENTRAL LONDON

General Abbreviations

All	Alley	Cor	Corner	Gdn	Garden	Ms	Mews	Shop	Shopping
Allot	Allotments	Coron	Coroners	Gdns	Gardens	Mt	Mount	Sq	Square
Amb	Ambulance	Cors	Corners	Govt	Government	Mus	Museum	St.	Saint
App	Approach	Cotts	Cottages	Gra	Grange	N	North	St	Street
Arc	Arcade	Cov	Covered	Grd	Ground	NT	National Trust	Sta	Station
Av/Ave	Avenue	Crem	Crematorium	Grds	Grounds	Nat	National	Sts	Streets
Bdy	Broadway	Cres	Crescent	Grn	Green	PH	Public House	Sub	Subway
Bk	Bank	Ct	Court	Grns	Greens	PO	Post Office	Swim	Swimming
Bldgs	Buildings	Cts	Courts	Gro	Grove	Par	Parade	TA	Territorial Army
Boul	Boulevard	Ctyd	Courtyard	Gros	Groves	Pas	Passage	TH	Town Hall
Bowl	Bowling	Dep	Depot	Gt	Great	Pav	Pavilion	Tenn	Tennis
Br/Bri	Bridge	Dev	Development	Ho	House	Pk	Park	Ter	Terrace
Bus	Business	Dr	Drive	Hos	Houses	Pl	Place	Thea	Theatre
C of E	Church of England	Dws	Dwellings	Hosp	Hospital	Pol	Police	Trd	Trading
Cath	Cathedral	E	East	Hts	Heights	Prec	Precinct	Twr	Tower
Cem	Cemetery	Ed	Education	Ind	Industrial	Prim	Primary	Twrs	Towers
Cen	Central, Centre	Elec	Electricity	Int	International	Prom	Promenade	Uni	University
Cft	Croft	Embk	Embankment	Junct	Junction	Pt	Point	Vil	Villa, Villas
Cfts	Crofts	Est	Estate	La	Lane	Quad	Quadrant	Vw	View
Ch	Church	Ex	Exchange	Las	Lanes	RC	Roman Catholic	W	West
Chyd	Churchyard	Exhib	Exhibition	Lib	Library	Rd	Road	Wd	Wood
Cin	Cinema	FB	Footbridge	Lo	Lodge	Rds	Roads	Wds	Woods
Circ	Circus	FC	Football Club	Lwr	Lower	Rec	Recreation	Wf	Wharf
Cl/Clo	Close	Fld	Field	Mag	Magistrates	Res	Reservoir	Wk	Walk
Co	County	Flds	Fields	Mans	Mansions	Ri	Rise	Wks	Works
Coll	College	Fm	Farm	Mem	Memorial	S	South	Yd	Yard
Comm	Community	Gall	Gallery	Mkt	Market	Sch	School		
Conv	Convent	Gar	Garage	Mkts	Markets	Sec	Secondary		

1 Canada Sq **E14** 125 M10

A

Abbey Cl **SW8** 127 K7
Abbey Gdns **NW8** 122 C4
Abbey La **E15** 125 N4
Abbey Orchard St **SW1** 127 K2
Abbey Rd **NW6** 122 B2
Abbey Rd **NW8** 122 C4
Abbey Rd Est **NW8** 122 B3
Abbey St **SE1** 128 C2
Abbeyfield Rd **SE16** 128 G3
Abbot St **E8** 124 D1
Abbots Manor Est **SW1** 127 H3
Abbot's Pl **NW6** 122 B3
Abbotsbury Cl **E15** 125 N4
Abbotsbury Ms **SE15** 128 G9
Abbotshade Rd **SE16** 125 H10
Abbotswood Rd **SE22** 128 C10
Abbott Rd **E14** 125 N7
Abchurch La **EC4** 124 B9
Aberavon Rd **E3** 125 J5
Abercorn Cl **NW8** 122 C5
Abercorn Pl **NW8** 122 C5
Abercorn Way **SE1** 128 E4
Abercrombie St **SW11** 126 E8
Aberdare Gdns **NW6** 122 B2
Aberdeen Pl **NW8** 122 D6
Aberdeen Ter **SE3** 129 P8
Aberdour St **SE1** 128 C3
Aberfeldy St **E14** 125 N8
Abingdon Rd **W8** 126 A2
Abingdon St **SW1** 127 L2
Abingdon Vil **W8** 126 A2
Abinger Gro **SE8** 129 K5
Ablett St **SE16** 128 G4
Acacia Cl **SE8** 129 J3
Acacia Pl **NW8** 122 D4
Acacia Rd **NW8** 122 D4
Acanthus Dr **SE1** 128 E4
Acanthus Rd **SW11** 126 G9
Acfold Rd **SW6** 126 B7
Achilles Cl **SE1** 128 E4
Achilles St **SE14** 129 J6
Ackmar Rd **SW6** 126 A7
Ackroyd Dr **E3** 125 K7
Acland Cres **SE5** 128 B10
Acol Rd **NW6** 122 A2
Acorn Wk **SE16** 125 J10
Acre Dr **SE22** 128 E10
Acre La **SW2** 127 L10
Acton Ms **E8** 124 D3
Acton St **WC1** 123 M5
Ada Gdns **E14** 125 P8
Ada Pl **E2** 124 E3
Ada Rd **SE5** 128 C6
Ada St **E8** 124 F3
Adam & Eve Ms **W8** 126 A2
Adam St **WC2** 123 L9
Adams Row **W1** 122 G9
Adamson Rd **NW3** 122 D2
Adderley St **E14** 125 N8
Addington Rd **E3** 125 L5
Addington Sq **SE5** 128 A6
Adelaide Av **SE4** 129 K10
Adelaide Rd **NW3** 122 D2
Adelina Gro **E1** 124 G7
Adeline Pl **WC1** 123 K7
Adler St **E1** 124 E8
Admiral Pl **SE16** 125 J10
Admiral Sq **SW10** 126 D7
Admiral St **SE8** 129 L8
Admiral Wk **W9** 122 A7
Admirals Gate **SE10** 129 M7
Admirals Way **E14** 129 L1
Adolphus St **SE8** 129 K6
Adpar St **W2** 122 D6
Adrian Ms **SW10** 126 B5
Adys Rd **SE15** 128 D9
Afghan Rd **SW11** 126 E8
Africa Ho **SE16** 128 F2
Agar Gro **NW1** 123 J2
Agar Gro Est **NW1** 123 K2
Agar Pl **NW1** 123 J2
Agar St **WC2** 123 L9
Agdon St **EC1** 123 P6
Agnes St **E14** 125 K8
Ailsa St **E14** 125 N7
Ainger Rd **NW3** 122 F2
Ainsdale Dr **SE1** 128 E4
Ainsley St **E2** 124 F5
Ainsty Est **SE16** 129 H1
Ainsworth Rd **E9** 124 G2
Ainsworth Way **NW8** 122 C3
Air St **W1** 123 J9
Airdrie Cl **N1** 123 M2
Airlie Gdns **W8** 126 A1
Akerman Rd **SW9** 127 P8
Albany Mans **SW11** 126 E6
Albany Rd **SE5** 128 B5
Albany St **NW1** 123 H4
Albatross Way **SE16** 129 H1
Albemarle St **W1** 123 H9
Albert Av **SW8** 127 M6
Albert Br **SW3** 126 E5
Albert Br **SW11** 126 E5
Albert Br Rd **SW11** 126 E6
Albert Embk **SE1** 127 L4
Albert Gdns **E1** 125 H8
Albert Gate **SW1** 126 F1
Albert Pl **W8** 126 B1
Albert Sq **SW8** 127 M6
Albert St **NW1** 123 H3
Albert Ter **NW1** 122 G3
Albert Way **SE15** 128 F6
Alberta Est **SE17** 127 P4
Alberta St **SE17** 127 P4
Albion Av **SW8** 127 K8
Albion Dr **E8** 124 D2
Albion Est **SE16** 129 H1
Albion Ms **N1** 123 N3
Albion Ms **W2** 122 E8
Albion Pl **EC1** 123 P7
Albion Sq **E8** 124 D2
Albion St **SE16** 128 G1
Albion St **W2** 122 E8
Albion Ter **E8** 124 D2
Albion Way **SE13** 129 N10
Albrighton Rd **SE22** 128 C9
Albury St **SE8** 129 L5
Albyn Rd **SE8** 129 L7
Aldbridge St **SE17** 128 C4
Aldebert Ter **SW8** 127 L6
Aldenham St **NW1** 123 K4
Alder Cl **SE15** 128 D5
Aldermanbury **EC2** 124 A8
Alderney Ms **SE1** 128 B2
Alderney Rd **E1** 125 H6
Alderney St **SW1** 127 H3
Aldersgate St **EC1** 124 A7
Alderton Rd **SE24** 128 A9
Alford St **W1** 122 G10
Aldgate **EC3** 124 C8
Aldgate High St **EC3** 124 D8
Aldsworth Cl **W9** 122 B6
Aldwych **WC2** 123 M9
Alexander Pl **SW7** 126 E3
Alexander Sq **SW3** 126 E3
Alexander St **W2** 122 A8
Alexandra Av **SW11** 126 G7
Alexandra Cl **SE8** 129 K5
Alexandra Cotts **SE14** 129 K7
Alexandra Pl **NW8** 122 C3
Alexandra Rd **NW8** 122 C2
Alexandra St **SE14** 129 J6
Alexis St **SE16** 128 E3
Alfred Ms **W1** 123 K7
Alfred Pl **WC1** 123 K7
Alfred Rd **W2** 122 A7
Alfred St **E3** 125 K5
Alfreda St **SW11** 127 H7
Algernon Rd **NW6** 122 A3
Algernon Rd **SE13** 129 M10
Algiers Rd **SE13** 129 L10
Alice La **E3** 125 K3
Alice St **SE1** 128 C2
Alie St **E1** 124 D8
Aliwal Rd **SW11** 126 E10
All Saints St **N1** 123 M4
Allardyce St **SW4** 127 M10
Allen Edwards Dr **SW8** 127 L7
Allen Rd **E3** 125 K4
Allen St **W8** 126 A2
Allensbury Pl **NW1** 123 K2
Allingham St **N1** 124 A4
Allington St **SW1** 127 H2
Allitsen Rd **NW8** 122 E4
Alloa Rd **SE8** 129 H4
Alloway Rd **E3** 125 J5
Allsop Pl **NW1** 122 F6
Alma Gro **SE1** 128 D3
Alma Sq **NW8** 122 C5
Alma St **E15** 125 P1
Alma St **NW5** 123 H1
Almeida St **N1** 123 P2
Almeric Rd **SW11** 126 F10
Almond Cl **SE15** 128 E8
Almond Rd **SE16** 128 F3
Almorah Rd **N1** 124 B2
Alpha Gro **E14** 129 L1
Alpha Pl **NW6** 122 A4
Alpha Pl **SW3** 126 E5
Alpha Rd **SE14** 129 K7
Alpha St **SE15** 128 E8
Alpine Gro **E9** 124 G2
Alpine Rd **SE16** 128 G3
Alsace Rd **SE17** 128 C4
Alscot Rd **SE1** 128 D3
Alscot Way **SE1** 128 D3
Altenburg Gdns **SW11** 126 F10
Althea St **SW6** 126 B9
Alton St **E14** 125 M7
Alverton St **SE8** 129 K4
Alvey Est **SE17** 128 C3
Alvey St **SE17** 128 C4
Alwyne Pl **N1** 124 A1
Alwyne Rd **N1** 124 A2
Alwyne Sq **N1** 124 A1
Alwyne Vil **N1** 123 P2
Alzette Ho **E2** 125 H5
Ambergate St **SE17** 127 P4
Amberley Rd **W9** 122 A7
Ambrosden Av **SW1** 127 J2
Ambrose Ms **SW11** 126 E8
Ambrose St **SE16** 128 F3
Amelia St **SE17** 127 P4
Amersham Gro **SE14** 129 K6
Amersham Rd **SE14** 129 K6
Amersham Vale **SE14** 129 K6
Amiel St **E1** 124 G6
Amies St **SW11** 126 F9
Amott Rd **SE15** 128 E9
Amoy Pl **E14** 125 L8
Ampton St **WC1** 123 M5
Amsterdam Rd **E14** 129 N2
Amwell St **EC1** 123 N5
Anchor Retail Pk **E1** 124 G6
Anchor St **SE16** 128 F3
Andalus Rd **SW9** 127 L9
Anderson Rd **E9** 125 H1
Anderson St **SW3** 126 F4
Anderton Cl **SE5** 128 B9
Andover Pl **NW6** 122 B4
Andrew St **E14** 125 N8
Andrew's Rd **E8** 124 F3
Anerley St **SW11** 126 F8
Angel Ct **EC2** 124 B8
Angel La **E15** 125 P1
Angel Ms **N1** 123 N4
Angel St **EC1** 124 A8
Angell Pk Gdns **SW9** 127 N9
Angell Rd **SW9** 127 N9
Angell Town Est **SW9** 127 N8
Angler's La **NW5** 123 H1
Anglia Ho **E14** 125 J8
Anglo Rd **E3** 125 K4
Angrave Ct **E8** 124 D3
Angus St **SE14** 129 J6
Anhalt Rd **SW11** 126 E6
Ann La **SW10** 126 D6
Ann Moss Way **SE16** 128 G2
Anna Cl **E8** 124 D3
Annabel Cl **E14** 125 M8
Annie Besant Cl **E3** 125 K3
Annis Rd **E9** 125 J1
Ansdell Rd **SE15** 128 G8
Ansdell St **W8** 126 B2
Anselm Rd **SW6** 126 A5
Anstey Rd **SE15** 128 E9
Antill Rd **E3** 125 J5
Antill Ter **E1** 125 H8
Antrim Gro **NW3** 122 F1
Antrim Mans **NW3** 122 E1
Antrim Rd **NW3** 122 F1
Apollo Pl **SW10** 126 D6
Appleby Rd **E8** 124 E2
Appleby St **E2** 124 D4
Appold St **EC2** 124 C7
Approach Rd **E2** 124 G4
Aquila St **NW8** 122 D4
Arabin Rd **SE4** 129 J10
Aragon Twr **SE8** 129 K3
Arbery Rd **E3** 125 J5
Arbour Sq **E1** 125 H8
Arbuthnot Rd **SE14** 129 H8
Arbutus St **E8** 124 C3
Arcadia St **E14** 125 L8
Arch St **SE1** 128 A2
Archangel St **SE16** 129 H1
Archery Cl **W2** 122 E8
Archibald Ms **W1** 122 G9
Archibald St **E3** 125 L5
Arden Cres **E14** 129 L3
Arden Est **N1** 124 C4
Ardleigh Rd **N1** 124 B1
Argon Ms **SW6** 126 A6
Argyle Rd **E1** 125 H6
Argyle Sq **WC1** 123 L5
Argyle St **WC1** 123 L5
Argyle Way **SE16** 128 E4
Argyll Rd **W8** 126 A1
Argyll St **W1** 123 J8
Arica Rd **SE4** 129 J10
Ariel Rd **NW6** 122 A1
Aristotle Rd **SW4** 127 K9
Arklow Rd **SE14** 129 K5
Arlesford Rd **SW9** 127 L9
Arlington Av **N1** 124 A4
Arlington Lo **SW2** 127 M10
Arlington Rd **NW1** 123 H3
Arlington Sq **N1** 124 A3
Arlington St **SW1** 123 J10
Arlington Way **EC1** 123 N5
Armadale Rd **SW6** 126 A6
Armagh Rd **E3** 125 K3
Armoury Rd **SE8** 129 M8
Armstrong Rd **SW7** 126 D2
Arne St **WC2** 123 L8
Arnhem Pl **E14** 129 L2
Arnold Circ **E2** 124 D5
Arnold Est **SE1** 128 D1
Arnold Rd **E3** 125 L5
Arnould Av **SE5** 128 B10
Arnside St **SE17** 128 A5
Arran Wk **N1** 124 A2
Arrow Rd **E3** 125 M5
Artesian Rd **W2** 122 A8
Artillery La **E1** 124 C7
Artillery Row **SW1** 127 K2
Arundel Pl **N1** 123 N1
Arundel Sq **N7** 123 N1
Arundel St **WC2** 123 M9
Ascalon St **SW8** 127 J6
Ash Gro **E8** 124 F3
Ashbridge St **NW8** 122 E6
Ashburn Gdns **SW7** 126 C3
Ashburn Pl **SW7** 126 C3
Ashburnham Gro **SE10** 129 M6
Ashburnham Pl **SE10** 129 M6
Ashburnham Retreat **SE10** 129 M6
Ashburnham Rd **SW10** 126 C6
Ashbury Rd **SW11** 126 F9
Ashby Gro **N1** 124 A2
Ashby Ms **SE4** 129 K8
Ashby Rd **SE4** 129 K8
Ashcombe St **SW6** 126 B8
Ashcroft Rd **E3** 125 J5
Ashdene **SE15** 128 F7
Ashdown Wk **E14** 129 L3
Asher Way **E1** 124 E10
Ashfield St **E1** 124 F7
Ashland Pl **W1** 122 G7
Ashley Cres **SW11** 126 G9
Ashley Gdns **SW1** 127 J2
Ashley Pl **SW1** 127 J2
Ashmead Rd **SE8** 129 L8
Ashmere Gro **SW2** 127 L10
Ashmill St **NW1** 122 E7
Ashmole Pl **SW8** 127 M5
Ashmole St **SW8** 127 M5
Ashton St **E14** 125 N9
Ashwin St **E8** 124 D1
Ashworth Rd **W9** 122 B5
Aspen Way **E14** 125 L9
Aspinall Rd **SE4** 129 H9
Aspinden Rd **SE16** 128 F3
Assembly Pas **E1** 124 G7
Astbury Rd **SE15** 128 G7
Aste St **E14** 129 N1
Astell St **SW3** 126 E4
Astle St **SW11** 126 G8
Aston St **E14** 125 J8
Astoria Wk **SW9** 127 N9
Astwood Ms **SW7** 126 B3
Asylum Rd **SE15** 128 F6
Athelstane Gro **E3** 125 K4
Atherfold Rd **SW9** 127 L9
Atherstone Ms **SW7** 126 C3
Atherton St **SW11** 126 E8
Athlone St **NW5** 122 G1
Athol Sq **E14** 125 N8
Atlantic Rd **SW9** 127 N10
Atlas Ms **N7** 123 M1
Atley Rd **E3** 125 L3
Atterbury St **SW1** 127 K3
Auburn Cl **SE14** 129 J6
Auckland Rd **SW11** 126 E10
Auden Pl **NW1** 122 G3
Audley Cl **SW11** 126 G9
Audrey St **E2** 124 E4
Augusta St **E14** 125 M8
Augustus St **NW1** 123 H4
Aulton Pl **SE11** 127 N4
Austen Ho **NW6** 122 A5
Austin Friars **EC2** 124 B8
Austin Rd **SW11** 126 G7
Austin St **E2** 124 D5
Austral St **SE11** 127 P3
Autumn St **E3** 125 L3
Avalon Rd **SW6** 126 B7
Ave Maria La **EC4** 123 P8
Aveline St **SE11** 127 N4
Avenue, The **SE10** 129 P6
Avenue Cl **NW8** 122 E3
Avenue Rd **NW3** 122 D2
Avenue Rd **NW8** 122 D2
Avery Row **W1** 123 H9
Avignon Rd **SE4** 129 H9
Avis Sq **E1** 125 H8
Avon Rd **SE4** 129 L9
Avondale Ri **SE15** 128 D9
Avondale Sq **SE1** 128 E4
Avonley Rd **SE14** 128 G6
Avonmouth St **SE1** 128 A2
Aybrook St **W1** 122 G7
Aylesbury Rd **SE17** 128 B4
Aylesbury St **EC1** 123 P6
Aylesford St **SW1** 127 K4
Aylesham Cen, The **SE15** 128 E7
Aylward St **E1** 124 G8
Aylwyn Est **SE1** 128 C2
Ayres St **SE1** 128 A1
Aytoun Pl **SW9** 127 M8
Aytoun Rd **SW9** 127 M8
Azenby Rd **SE15** 128 D8

B

Baches St **N1** 124 B5
Back Ch La **E1** 124 E9
Back Hill **EC1** 123 N6
Bacon Gro **SE1** 128 D2
Bacon St **E1** 124 D6
Bacon St **E2** 124 D6
Baddow Wk **N1** 124 A3
Badsworth Rd **SE5** 128 A6
Bagley's La **SW6** 126 B7
Bagshot St **SE17** 128 C4
Baildon St **SE8** 129 K6
Bainbridge St **WC1** 123 K8
Baker St **NW1** 122 F6
Baker St **W1** 122 F7
Baker's Row **EC1** 123 N6

Name	Page	Ref
Bakery Cl SW9	127	M7
Balaclava Rd SE1	128	D3
Balcombe St NW1	122	F6
Balcorne St E9	124	G2
Balderton St W1	122	G8
Baldock St E3	125	M4
Baldwin Cres SE5	128	A7
Baldwin Ter N1	124	A4
Baldwin's Gdns EC1	123	N7
Bale Rd E1	125	J7
Balfe St N1	123	L4
Balfern St SW11	126	E7
Balfour St SE17	128	B3
Ballance Rd E9	125	H1
Ballantine St SW18	126	C10
Ballast Quay SE10	129	P4
Ballater Rd SW2	127	L10
Balls Pond Rd N1	124	B1
Balmer Rd E3	125	K4
Balmes Rd N1	124	B3
Balmoral Gro N7	123	M1
Balmore Cl E14	125	N8
Balniel Gate SW1	127	K4
Baltic St E EC1	124	A6
Baltic St W EC1	124	A6
Balvaird Pl SW1	127	K4
Banbury Rd E9	125	H2
Banbury St SW11	126	E8
Bancroft Rd E1	124	G5
Banfield Rd SE15	128	F10
Bank End SE1	124	A10
Bank St E14	125	L10
Bankton Rd SW2	127	N10
Banner St EC1	124	A6
Bannerman Ho SW8	127	M5
Banstead St SE15	128	G9
Bantry St SE5	128	B6
Barbers Rd E15	125	M4
Barbican, The EC2	124	A7
Barchester St E14	125	M7
Barclay Cl SW6	126	A6
Barclay Rd SW6	126	A6
Bardsley La SE10	129	N5
Barford St N1	123	N3
Barforth Rd SE15	128	F9
Baring St N1	124	B3
Bark Pl W2	122	B9
Barker Dr NW1	123	J2
Barker Ms SW4	127	H10
Barker St SW10	126	C5
Barkston Gdns SW5	126	B3
Barlborough St SE14	128	G6
Barleycorn Way E14	125	K9
Barnaby Pl SW7	126	D3
Barnard Ms SW11	126	E10
Barnard Rd SW11	126	E10
Barnby St NW1	123	J4
Barnes St E14	125	J8
Barnes Ter SE8	129	K4
Barnet Gro E2	124	E5
Barnfield Pl E14	129	L3
Barnham St SE1	128	C1
Barnsbury Gro N7	123	M2
Barnsbury Pk N1	123	N2
Barnsbury Rd N1	123	N4
Barnsbury Sq N1	123	N2
Barnsbury St N1	123	N2
Barnsbury Ter N1	123	M2
Barnsdale Av E14	129	L3
Barnsley St E1	124	F6
Barnwood Cl W9	122	B6
Baron St N1	123	N4
Barons Pl SE1	127	N1
Barrett St W1	122	G8
Barriedale SE14	129	J7
Barrington Rd SW9	127	P9
Barrow Hill Rd NW8	122	E4
Barset Rd SE15	128	G9
Barter St WC1	123	L7
Bartholomew Cl EC1	124	A7
Bartholomew Cl SW18	126	C10
Bartholomew Rd NW5	123	J1
Bartholomew Sq EC1	124	A6
Bartholomew St SE1	128	B2
Bartholomew Vil NW5	123	J1
Bartlett Cl E14	125	L8
Basevi Way SE8	129	M5
Basil St SW3	126	F2
Basing Ct SE15	128	D7
Basingdon Way SE5	128	B10
Basinghall Av EC2	124	B7
Basinghall St EC2	124	A7
Basire St N1	124	A3
Basnett Rd SW11	126	G9
Bassett St NW5	122	G1
Bastwick St EC1	123	P6
Basuto Rd SW6	126	A7
Batavia Rd SE14	129	J6
Batchelor St N1	123	N4
Bateman's Row EC2	124	C6
Bath St EC1	124	B5
Bath Ter SE1	128	A2
Bathurst St W2	122	D9
Batten St SW11	126	E9
Battersea Br SW3	126	D6
Battersea Br Rd SW11	126	D6
Battersea Ch Rd SW11	126	D7
Battersea High St SW11	126	D7
Battersea Pk SW11	126	F6
Battersea Pk Rd SW8	127	H7
Battersea Pk Rd SW11	126	E8
Battle Br La SE1	124	C10
Battle Br Rd NW1	123	L4
Batty St E1	124	E7
Bavent Rd SE5	128	A8
Bawtree Rd SE14	129	J6
Baxendale St E2	124	E5
Baxter Rd N1	124	B1
Bayford St E8	124	F2
Bayham Pl NW1	123	J3
Bayham St NW1	123	J3
Bayley St WC1	123	K7
Baylis Rd SE1	127	N1
Baynes St NW1	123	J2
Bayswater Rd W2	122	D9
Baythorne St E3	125	K7
Bazely St E14	125	N9
Beachy Rd E3	125	L2
Beacon Gate SE14	129	H9
Beaconsfield Rd SE17	128	B4
Beak St W1	123	J9
Beale Pl E3	125	K4
Beale Rd E3	125	K3
Beanacre Cl E9	125	K1
Bear Gdns SE1	124	A10
Bear La SE1	123	P10
Beaton Cl SE15	128	C8
Beatrice Pl W8	126	B2
Beatrice Rd SE1	128	E3
Beatson Wk SE16	125	H10
Beatty St NW1	123	J4
Beauchamp Pl SW3	126	E2
Beauchamp Rd SW11	126	E10
Beaufort Gdns SW3	126	E2
Beaufort St SW3	126	D5
Beaufoy Wk SE11	127	M3
Beaulieu Cl SE5	128	B9
Beaumont Gro E1	125	H6
Beaumont Pl W1	123	J6
Beaumont Sq E1	125	H6
Beaumont St W1	122	G7
Beaumont Wk NW3	122	F2
Beccles St E14	125	K9
Beck Cl SE13	129	M7
Beck Rd E8	124	F3
Beckway St SE17	128	B3
Bedale St SE1	124	B10
Bedford Av WC1	123	K7
Bedford Gdns W8	122	A10
Bedford Ho SW4	127	L10
Bedford Pl WC1	123	L7
Bedford Rd SW4	127	L9
Bedford Row WC1	123	M7
Bedford Sq WC1	123	K7
Bedford St WC2	123	L9
Bedford Way WC1	123	K6
Beech St EC2	124	A7
Beechcroft Rd SW11	126	F7
Beechwood Rd E8	124	D1
Beehive Cl E8	124	D2
Beehive Pl SW9	127	N9
Beeston Pl SW1	127	H2
Belfort Rd SE15	128	G8
Belgrave Gdns NW8	122	B3
Belgrave Ms N SW1	126	G2
Belgrave Ms S SW1	127	G2
Belgrave Ms W SW1	126	G2
Belgrave Pl SW1	126	G2
Belgrave Rd SW1	127	H3
Belgrave Sq SW1	126	G2
Belgrave St E1	125	H8
Belgrave St WC1	123	L5
Belinda Rd SW9	127	P9
Belitha Vil N1	123	M2
Bell La E1	124	D7
Bell St NW1	122	E7
Bell Wf La EC4	124	A9
Bell Yd WC2	123	N8
Bellefields Rd SW9	127	M9
Bellenden Rd SE15	128	D8
Bellevue Pl E1	124	G6
Bells All SW6	126	A8
Bellwood Rd SE15	129	H10
Belmont Cl SW4	127	J9
Belmont Gro SE13	129	P9
Belmont Hill SE13	129	P9
Belmont Pk SE13	129	P10
Belmont Rd SW4	127	J9
Belmont St NW1	122	G2
Belmont St SW8	127	K7
Belsham St E9	124	G1
Belsize Av NW3	122	D1
Belsize Gro NW3	122	E1
Belsize La NW3	122	D1
Belsize Pk NW3	122	D1
Belsize Pk Gdns NW3	122	E1
Belsize Pk Ms NW3	122	D1
Belsize Rd NW6	122	B3
Belsize Sq NW3	122	D1
Belsize Ter NW3	122	D1
Belton Way E3	125	L7
Beltran Rd SW6	126	B8
Belvedere Ms SE15	128	F9
Belvedere Rd SE1	127	P1
Belvedere Rd SE1	123	M10
Belvedere Twr, The SW10	126	C7
Bemerton Est N1	123	M2
Bemerton St N1	123	M3
Ben Jonson Rd E1	125	J7
Benbow St SE8	129	L5
Benedict Rd SW9	127	M9
Bengeworth Rd SE5	128	A9
Benham Cl SW11	126	D9
Benhill Rd SE5	128	B6
Benjamin Cl E8	124	E3
Benjamin St EC1	123	P7
Benledi St E14	125	P8
Benn St E9	125	J1
Bennett Gro SE13	129	M7
Bentham Rd E9	125	H1
Bentinck St W1	122	G8
Benworth St E3	125	K5
Berger Rd E9	125	H1
Berkeley Ho E3	125	L6
Berkeley Sq W1	123	H9
Berkeley St W1	123	H9
Berkley Rd NW1	122	F2
Berkshire Rd E9	125	K1
Bermondsey St SE1	128	C1
Bermondsey Wall E SE16	128	E1
Bermondsey Wall W SE16	128	E1
Bernard St WC1	123	L6
Bernays Gro SW9	127	M10
Berners Ms W1	123	J7
Berners Pl W1	123	J8
Berners Rd N1	123	N4
Berners St W1	123	J7
Bernhardt Cres NW8	122	E6
Berry St EC1	123	P6
Berryfield Rd SE17	127	P4
Berthon St SE8	129	L6
Bertrand St SE13	129	M9
Berwick St W1	123	J8
Bessborough Gdns SW1	127	K4
Bessborough Pl SW1	127	K4
Bessborough St SW1	127	K4
Bessemer Rd SE5	128	A8
Besson St SE14	128	G7
Bestwood St SE8	129	H3
Bethnal Grn Est E2	124	G5
Bethnal Grn Rd E1	124	D6
Bethnal Grn Rd E2	124	D6
Bethwin Rd SE5	127	P6
Betterton St WC2	123	L8
Bevan St N1	124	A3
Bevenden St N1	124	B5
Beverley Ct SE4	129	K9
Bevington Rd SE16	128	E1
Bevis Marks EC3	124	C8
Bewdley St N1	123	N2
Bewick Ms SE15	128	F6
Bewick St SW8	127	H8
Bianca Rd SE15	128	D5
Bibury Cl SE15	128	C5
Bickenhall St W1	122	F7
Bicknell Rd SE5	128	A9
Biddulph Rd W9	122	B5
Bidwell St SE15	128	F7
Biggerstaff Rd E15	125	N3
Bigland St E1	124	F8
Billing Pl SW10	126	B6
Billing Rd SW10	126	B6
Billing St SW10	126	B6
Billingford Cl SE4	129	H10
Billington Rd SE14	129	H6
Billiter St EC3	124	C8
Billson St E14	129	N3
Bina Gdns SW5	126	C3
Binfield Rd SW4	127	L7
Bingfield St N1	123	L3
Bingham St N1	124	B1
Binney St W1	122	G8
Birchfield St E14	125	L9
Birchin La EC3	124	B8
Birchington Rd NW6	122	A3
Bird in Bush Rd SE15	128	E6
Birdcage Wk SW1	127	J1
Birdhurst Rd SW18	126	C10
Birdsfield La E3	125	K3
Birkbeck St E2	124	F5
Birkenhead St WC1	123	L5
Birley St SW11	126	G8
Biscoe Way SE13	129	P9
Bishop St N1	124	A3
Bishops Br W2	122	C8
Bishops Br Rd W2	122	B8
Bishop's Rd SW11	126	E6
Bishops Ter SE11	127	N3
Bishops Way E2	124	F4
Bishopsgate EC2	124	C8
Bisson Rd E15	125	N4
Black Friars La EC4	123	P9
Black Prince Rd SE1	127	M3
Black Prince Rd SE11	127	M3
Blackburn Rd NW6	122	B1
Blackburne's Ms W1	122	G9
Blackfriars Br EC4	123	P9
Blackfriars Br SE1	123	P9
Blackfriars Rd SE1	123	P10
Blackheath Av SE10	129	P6
Blackheath Hill SE10	129	N7
Blackheath Ri SE13	129	N8
Blackheath Rd SE10	129	M7
Blackhorse Rd SE8	129	J4
Blacklands Ter SW3	126	F3
Blackpool Rd SE15	128	F8
Blackstone Est E8	124	F2
Blackthorn St E3	125	L6
Blacktree Ms SW9	127	N9
Blackwall Trd Est E14	125	P7
Blackwall Tunnel E14	125	P10
Blackwall Tunnel Northern App E3	125	L4
Blackwall Tunnel Northern App E14	125	L4
Blackwall Way E14	125	N9
Blackwood St SE17	128	B4
Blair Cl N1	124	A1
Blair St E14	125	N8
Blake Gdns SW6	126	B7
Blaker Rd E15	125	N3
Blakes Rd SE15	128	C6
Blanchard Way E8	124	E1
Blanchedowne SE5	128	B10
Blandford Sq NW1	122	E6
Blandford St W1	122	G7
Blantyre St SW10	126	D6
Blashford NW3	122	F2
Blasker Wk E14	129	L4
Blenheim Gro SE15	128	E8
Blenheim Rd NW8	122	C4
Blenheim Ter NW8	122	C4
Blessington Cl SE13	129	P9
Blessington Rd SE13	129	P9
Bletchley Ct N1	124	B4
Bletchley St N1	124	A4
Bliss Cres SE13	129	M8
Blissett St SE10	129	N7
Blithfield St W8	126	B2
Blomfield Rd W9	122	C7
Blomfield St EC2	124	B7
Blomfield Vil W2	122	B7
Blondel St SW11	126	G8
Blondin St E3	125	L4
Bloomfield Pl W1	123	H9
Bloomfield Ter SW1	126	G4
Bloomsbury Pl WC1	123	L7
Bloomsbury Sq WC1	123	L7
Bloomsbury St WC1	123	K7
Bloomsbury Way WC1	123	L8
Blossom St E1	124	C7
Blount St E14	125	J8
Blucher Rd SE5	128	A6
Blue Anchor La SE16	128	E3
Blue Anchor Yd E1	124	E9
Blundell St N7	123	L2
Blythe St E2	124	F5
Boathouse Wk SE15	128	D6
Bobbin Cl SW4	127	J9
Bocking St E8	124	F3
Bohemia Pl E8	124	F1
Bohn Rd E1	125	J7
Bolden St SE8	129	M8
Bolina Rd SE16	128	G4
Bolingbroke Gro SW11	126	E10
Bolingbroke Wk SW11	126	D6
Bolney St SW8	127	M6
Bolsover St W1	123	H6
Bolton Cres SE5	127	P5
Bolton Gdns SW5	126	B4
Bolton Gdns Ms SW10	126	B4
Bolton Rd NW8	122	B3
Bolton St W1	123	H10
Boltons, The SW10	126	C4
Boltons Pl SW5	126	C4
Bombay St SE16	128	F3
Bonar Rd SE15	128	E6
Bond Ct EC4	124	B8
Bondway SW8	127	L5
Bonfield Rd SE13	129	N10
Bonhill St EC2	124	B6
Bonita Ms SE4	129	H9
Bonner Rd E2	124	G4
Bonner St E2	124	G4
Bonnington Sq SW8	127	M5
Bonny St NW1	123	J2
Bonsor St SE5	128	C6
Boot St N1	124	C5
Borland Rd SE15	128	G10
Borough High St SE1	128	A1
Borough Rd SE1	127	P2
Borthwick St SE8	129	L4
Boscobel Pl SW1	126	G3
Boscobel St NW8	122	D6
Boston Pl NW1	122	F6
Boswell St WC1	123	L7
Boulcott St E1	125	H8
Boulevard, The SW6	126	C7
Boundary La SE17	128	A5
Boundary Rd NW8	122	B3
Boundary St E2	124	D6
Bourdon St W1	123	H9
Bourne Est EC1	123	N7
Bourne St SW1	126	G3
Bourne Ter W2	122	B7
Bournemouth Cl SE15	128	E8
Bournemouth Rd SE15	128	E8
Bousfield Rd SE14	129	H8
Boutflower Rd SW11	126	E10
Bouverie Pl W2	122	D8
Bouverie Rd EC4	123	N8
Bovingdon Rd SW6	126	B7
Bow Back Rivers Wk E15	125	M2
Bow Br Est E3	125	M5
Bow Common La E3	125	K6
Bow Ind Pk E15	125	L2
Bow La EC4	124	A8
Bow Rd E3	125	K5
Bow St WC2	123	L8
Bowden St SE11	127	N4
Bowditch SE8	129	K4
Bowen St E14	125	M8
Bower St E1	125	H8
Bowerdean St SW6	126	B7
Bowerman Av SE14	129	J5
Bowhill Cl SW9	127	N6
Bowl Ct EC2	124	C6
Bowland Rd SW4	127	K10
Bowling Grn La EC1	123	N6
Bowling Grn Pl SE1	128	B1
Bowling Grn St SE11	127	N5
Bowood Rd SW11	126	G10
Bowsprit Pt E14	129	L2
Bowyer Pl SE5	128	B6
Bowyer St SE5	128	A6
Boyd St E1	124	E8
Boyfield St SE1	127	P1
Boyne Rd SE13	129	N9
Boyson Rd SE17	128	B5
Brabazon St E14	125	M8
Brabourn Gro SE15	128	G8
Bracklyn St N1	124	B4
Bradbourne St SW6	126	A8
Bradenham Cl SE17	128	B5
Bradmead SW8	127	H6
Bradstock Rd E9	125	H1
Bradwell St E1	125	H5
Brady St E1	124	F6
Braes St N1	123	P2
Braganza St SE17	127	P4
Braham St E1	124	D8
Braintree St E2	124	G5
Braithwaite Twr W2	122	D7
Bramah Grn SW9	127	N7
Bramcote Gro SE16	128	G4
Bramerton St SW3	126	E5
Bramford Rd SW18	126	C10
Bramham Gdns SW5	126	B4
Bramlands Cl SW11	126	E9
Bramshaw Rd E9	125	H1
Bramwell Ms N1	123	M3
Branch Rd E14	125	J9
Branch St SE15	128	C6
Brand St SE10	129	N6
Brandon Rd N7	123	L2
Brandon St SE17	128	A3
Branscombe St SE13	129	M9
Brassey Sq SW11	126	G9
Braxfield Rd SE4	129	J10
Bray Pl SW3	126	E3
Bray Rd W2	122	E2
Brayards Rd SE15	128	F8
Brayburne Av SW4	127	J7
Bread St EC4	124	A9
Breakspears Rd SE4	129	K9
Bream St E3	125	L2
Bream's Bldgs EC4	123	N8
Breer St SW6	126	B9
Bremner Rd SW7	126	C1
Brendon St W1	122	E8
Brenthouse Rd E9	124	F2
Brenton St E14	125	J8
Bressenden Pl SW1	127	H2
Brewer St W1	123	J9
Brewery Rd N7	123	L2
Brewhouse La E1	124	F10
Brewhouse Wk SE16	125	J10
Brewster Ho E14	125	K9
Briant St SE14	129	H7
Brick La E1	124	D7
Brick La E2	124	D5
Brick St W1	126	B4
Bricklayer's Arms Distribution Cen SE1	128	C3
Bride St N7	123	M1
Bridewain St SE1	128	D2
Bridge App NW1	122	G2
Bridge La SW11	126	E7
Bridge Meadows SE14	129	H5
Bridge Pl SW1	127	H3
Bridge Rd E15	125	P2
Bridge St SW1	127	L1
Bridgefoot SE1	127	L4
Bridgeman Rd N1	123	M2
Bridgeman St NW8	122	E4
Bridgend Rd SW18	126	C10
Bridges Ct SW11	126	D9
Bridgeway St NW1	123	J4
Bridgewater Rd E15	125	N3
Bridport Pl N1	124	B4
Brief St SE5	127	P7
Bright St E14	125	M8
Brightlingsea Pl E14	125	K9
Brighton Rd SW9	127	M10
Brill Pl NW1	123	K4
Brindley St SE14	129	K7
Brinklow Ho W2	122	B7
Brinkworth Way E9	125	K1
Brion Pl E14	125	N7
Brisbane St SE5	128	B6
Bristol Gdns W9	122	B6
Britannia Rd E14	129	L3
Britannia Rd SW6	126	B6
Britannia Row N1	123	P3
Britannia St WC1	123	M5
Britannia Wk N1	124	B5
British St E3	125	K5
Britten St SW3	126	E4
Britton St EC1	123	P6
Brixton Oval SW2	127	N10
Brixton Rd SW9	127	N8
Brixton Sta Rd SW9	127	N10
Broad La EC2	124	C7
Broad Sanctuary SW1	127	K1
Broad Wk NW1	123	H5
Broad Wk W8	122	G10
Broad Wk, The W8	122	B10
Broadfield La NW1	123	L2
Broadhinton Rd SW4	127	H9
Broadgate Gdns NW6	122	B1
Broadley St NW8	122	E7
Broadley Ter NW1	122	E6
Broadwalk Ct W8	125	A10
Broadwalk Pl E14	125	N10
Broadwall SE1	123	N10
Broadway E15	125	P2
Broadway SW1	127	K2
Broadway Mkt E8	124	F3
Broadwick St W1	123	J8
Brock Pl E3	125	M6
Brockham St SE1	128	A2
Brockill Cres SE4	129	J10
Brocklehurst St SE14	129	H6
Brockley Footpath SE15	128	G10
Brockley Gdns SE4	129	K8
Brockley Rd SE4	129	K9
Brodlove La E1	125	H9
Broke Wk E8	124	E3
Brokesley St E3	125	K6
Bromar Rd SE5	128	C9
Bromehead St E1	125	H8
Bromell's Rd SW4	127	J10
Bromfelde Rd SW4	127	K8
Bromfelde Wk SW4	127	K8
Bromfield St N1	123	N4
Bromley Hall Rd E14	125	N7
Bromley High St E3	125	M5
Bromley St E1	125	H7
Brompton Pk Cres SW6	126	B5
Brompton Pl SW3	126	E2
Brompton Rd SW1	126	E2
Brompton Rd SW3	126	E2
Brompton Rd SW7	126	E2
Brompton Sq SW3	126	E2
Bromyard St SE15	128	F6
Bronte Ho NW6	122	A5
Bronti Cl SE17	128	A4
Bronze St SE8	129	L6
Brook Dr SE11	127	N3
Brook Gate W1	122	F9
Brook St W1	123	H8
Brook St W2	122	D9
Brookbank Rd SE13	129	L9
Brookfield Rd E9	125	J1
Brookmill Rd SE8	129	L7
Brook's Ms W1	123	H9
Brooksbank St E9	124	G1
Brooksby St N1	123	N2
Broome Way SE5	128	A6
Broomfield St E14	125	M7
Broomgrove Rd SW9	127	M8
Broomhouse La SW6	126	A8
Broomhouse Rd SW6	126	A8
Brougham Rd E8	124	E3
Brougham St SW11	126	F8
Broughton Dr SW9	127	N10
Broughton Rd SW6	126	B8

Broughton St SW8 122 G8
Brown Hart Gdns W1 122 G9
Brown St W1 122 F8
Brownfield St E14 125 M8
Browning St SE17 128 A4
Brownlow Ms WC1 123 M6
Brownlow Rd E8 124 D3
Brown's Bldgs EC3 124 C8
Broxwood Way NW8 122 E3
Bruce Rd E3 125 M5
Brune St E1 124 D7
Brunel Est W2 122 A7
Brunel Rd SE16 128 G1
Brunswick Ct SE1 128 C1
Brunswick Gdns W8 122 B7
Brunswick PI N1 124 B5
Brunswick PI NW1 122 G6
Brunswick Quay SE16 129 H2
Brunswick Sq WC1 123 L6
Brunswick Vil SE5 128 C7
Brunton PI E14 125 J8
Brushfield St E1 124 C7
Brussels Rd SW11 126 D10
Bruton La W1 123 H9
Bruton PI W1 123 H9
Bruton St W1 123 H9
Bryan Rd SE16 129 K1
Bryanston PI W1 122 F7
Bryanston Sq W1 122 F7
Bryanston St W1 122 F8
Bryant Ct E2 124 D4
Bryant St E15 125 P2
Brymay CI E3 125 L4
Brynmaer Rd SW11 126 F7
Buchan Rd SE15 128 G9
Buck St NW1 123 H2
Buckfast St E2 124 E5
Buckhurst St E1 124 F6
Buckingham Gate SW1 127 J2
Buckingham Palace Rd
  SW1 127 H3
Buckingham Rd N1 124 C1
Buckland Cres NW3 122 D2
Buckland St N1 124 B4
Bucklersbury EC4 124 B8
Buckmaster Rd SW11 126 E10
Bucknall St WC2 123 K8
Bucknell CI SW2 127 M10
Buckner Rd SW2 127 M10
Buckters Rents SE16 125 J10
Budge's Wk W2 122 C9
Bulinga St SW1 127 K3
Bullace Row SE5 128 B6
Bullards PI E2 125 H5
Bullen St SW11 126 E8
Buller CI SE15 128 E6
Bullivant St E14 125 N9
Bulmer PI W11 122 A10
Bulstrode St W1 122 G8
Bunhill Row EC1 124 B6
Bunhouse PI SW1 126 G4
Bunning Way N7 123 L2
Burbage CI SE1 128 B2
Burcham St E14 125 M8
Burchell Rd SE15 128 F7
Burder CI N1 124 C1
Burdett Est E3 125 K6
Burdett Rd E14 125 K6
Burford Rd E15 125 P2
Burge St SE1 128 B2
Burgess St E14 125 L7
Burgh St N1 123 P4
Burgos Gro SE10 129 M7
Burgoyne Rd SW9 127 M9
Burlington Arc W1 123 J9
Burlington Gdns W1 123 J9
Burnaby St SW10 126 C6
Burne St NW1 122 E7
Burney St SE10 129 N6
Burnham NW3 122 E2
Burnham St E2 124 G5
Burnley Rd SW9 127 M8
Burns Rd SW11 126 F8
Burnsall St SW3 126 E4
Burnside CI SE16 125 H10
Burnthwaite Rd SW6 126 A6
Burr CI E1 124 E10
Burrell St SE1 123 P10
Burrells Wf Sq E14 129 M4
Burrow Rd SE22 128 C10
Burslem St E1 124 E8
Burton Gro SE17 128 B2
Burton Rd SW9 127 N8
Burton St WC1 123 K5
Burwell Wk E3 125 L6
Burwood PI W2 122 E8
Bury CI SE16 125 H10
Bury PI WC1 123 L7
Bury St EC3 124 C8
Bury St SW1 123 J10
Bury Wk SW3 126 E4
Busby PI NW5 123 K1
Bush Rd E8 124 F3
Bush Rd SE8 129 H3
Bushberry Rd E9 125 J1
Bushey Hill Rd SE5 128 C7
Bushwood Dr SE1 128 D3
Butcher Row E1 125 H9
Butcher Row E14 125 H9
Bute St SW7 126 D3
Butlers Wf SE1 124 D10
Buttermere Wk E8 124 D1
Buttesland St N1 124 B5
Buxhall Cres E9 125 K1
Buxted Rd E8 124 D2
Buxted Rd SE22 128 C10
Buxton St E1 124 D6
Byam St SW6 126 C8
Bygrove St E14 125 M8
Byng PI WC1 123 K6
Byng St E14 125 L1
Byron CI E8 124 E3
Bythorn St SW9 127 M9
Byward St EC3 124 C9

Bywater PI SE16 125 J10
Bywater St SW3 126 F4

C
Cabbell St NW1 122 E7
Cable St E1 124 E9
Cabot PI E14 125 L10
Cabot Sq E14 125 L10
Cabul Rd SW11 126 E8
Cade Rd SE10 129 P7
Cadet Dr SE1 128 E3
Cadiz St SE17 128 A4
Cadogan Gdns SW3 126 F3
Cadogan Gate SW1 126 F3
Cadogan La SW1 126 G2
Cadogan PI SW1 126 F2
Cadogan Sq SW1 126 F2
Cadogan Sq SW3 126 F3
Cadogan Ter E9 125 K1
Cahir St E14 129 M3
Calabria Rd N5 123 P1
Calais St SE5 127 P7
Caldecot Rd SE5 128 A8
Caldwell St SW9 127 M6
Cale St SW3 126 E4
Caledonia St N1 123 L4
Caledonian Rd N1 123 M4
Caledonian Wf E14 129 P3
Callendar Rd SW7 126 D2
Callow St SW3 126 D5
Calshot St N1 123 M4
Calthorpe St WC1 123 M6
Calvert Av E2 124 C5
Calverton SE5 128 C5
Calvin St E1 124 D6
Calypso Way SE16 129 K2
Cam Rd E15 125 P3
Camberwell Ch St SE5 128 B7
Camberwell Glebe SE5 128 B7
Camberwell Grn SE5 128 B7
Camberwell Gro SE5 128 B7
Camberwell New Rd SE5 127 N6
Camberwell Rd SE5 128 A5
Camberwell Sta Rd SE5 128 A7
Cambria Rd SE5 128 A9
Cambria St SW6 126 B6
Cambridge Av NW6 122 A4
Cambridge Circ WC2 123 K8
Cambridge Cres E2 124 F4
Cambridge Gdns NW6 122 A4
Cambridge Heath Rd E1 124 F4
Cambridge Heath Rd E2 124 F4
Cambridge PI W8 126 B1
Cambridge Rd NW6 122 A5
Cambridge Rd SW11 126 F7
Cambridge Sq W2 122 E8
Cambridge St SW1 127 H4
Camden High St NW1 123 H3
Camden Ms NW1 123 K1
Camden Pk Rd NW1 123 K1
Camden Pas N1 123 P3
Camden Rd NW1 123 J3
Camden Sq NW1 123 K1
Camden St NW1 123 H2
Camden Wk N1 123 P3
Camdenhurst St E14 125 J8
Camellia St SW8 127 L6
Camera PI SW10 126 D5
Camilla Rd SE16 128 F3
Camlet St E2 124 D6
Camley St N1 123 K2
Camomile St EC3 124 C8
Campana Rd SW6 126 A7
Campbell Rd E3 125 L5
Campden Gro W8 126 A1
Campden Hill Gdns W8 122 A10
Campden Hill Rd W8 122 A10
Campden St W8 122 A10
Camplin St SE14 129 H6
Canada Est SE16 128 G2
Canada Sq E14 125 M10
Canada St SE16 129 H1
Canal App SE8 129 J5
Canal CI E1 125 J6
Canal Gro SE15 128 E6
Canal Path E2 124 D3
Canal St SE5 128 B5
Canal Wk N1 124 B3
Cancell Rd SW9 127 N7
Candahar Rd SW11 126 E8
Candle Gro SE15 128 F9
Candy St E3 125 K3
Canfield Gdns NW6 122 C2
Canning Cross SE5 128 C8
Canning Pas W8 126 C2
Canning PI W8 126 C2
Cannon Dr E14 125 L9
Cannon St EC4 124 A8
Cannon St Rd E1 124 F8
Cannon Wf Business Cen
  SE8 129 J3
Canon Beck Rd SE16 128 G1
Canon Row SW1 127 L1
Canon St N1 124 A3
Canonbury Cres N1 124 A2
Canonbury Gro N1 124 A2
Canonbury La N1 123 P2
Canonbury Pk N N1 124 A1
Canonbury Pk S N1 124 A1
Canonbury PI N1 123 P1
Canonbury Rd N1 123 P1
Canonbury Sq N1 123 P1
Canonbury St N1 124 A2
Canonbury Vil N1 123 P2
Canrobert St E2 124 F5
Cantelowes Rd NW1 123 K1
Canterbury Cres SW9 127 N9
Canterbury PI SE17 127 P3
Canterbury Rd NW6 122 A4
Canterbury Ter NW6 122 A4
Cantium Retail Pk SE1 128 E5
Canton St E14 125 L8
Cantrell Rd E3 125 K6
Canute Gdns SE16 129 H3

Capland St NW8 122 D6
Capper St WC1 123 J6
Capstan Rd SE8 129 K3
Capstan Sq E14 129 N1
Capstan Way SE16 125 J10
Caradoc CI W2 122 A8
Carbis Rd E14 125 K8
Carburton St W1 123 H7
Carden Rd SE15 128 F9
Cardigan Rd E3 125 K4
Cardigan St SE11 127 N4
Cardine Ms SE15 128 F6
Cardinal Bourne St SE1 128 B2
Cardington St NW1 123 J5
Carew St SE5 128 A8
Carey Gdns SW8 127 J7
Carey St WC2 123 M8
Carlile St E3 125 K4
Carlisle La SE1 127 M2
Carlisle Ms NW8 122 D7
Carlisle PI SW1 127 J2
Carlos PI W1 122 G9
Carlton Ct SW9 127 P7
Carlton Gdns SW1 123 K10
Carlton Gro SE15 128 F7
Carlton Hill NW8 122 B4
Carlton Ho Ter SW1 123 K10
Carlton Twr PI SW1 126 F2
Carlton Vale NW6 122 B4
Carlyle Sq SW3 126 D4
Carmelite St EC4 123 N9
Carmen St E14 125 M8
Carnaby St W1 123 J8
Carnegie St N1 123 M3
Carnoustie Dr N1 123 M2
Carnwath Rd SW6 126 A9
Carol St NW1 123 J3
Caroline Gdns SE15 128 F6
Caroline PI SW11 126 G8
Caroline PI W2 122 B9
Caroline St E1 125 H8
Caroline Ter SW1 126 G3
Carpenters PI SW4 127 K10
Carpenters Rd E15 125 M1
Carr St E14 125 J7
Carriage Dr E SW11 126 G6
Carriage Dr N SW11 126 G5
Carriage Dr S SW11 126 F7
Carriage Dr W SW11 126 F6
Carron CI E14 125 M8
Carroun Rd SW8 127 M6
Carter La EC4 123 P8
Carter PI SE17 128 A4
Carter St SE17 128 A5
Carteret St SW1 127 K1
Carteret Way SE8 129 J3
Carting La WC2 123 L9
Cartwright Gdns WC1 123 L5
Cartwright St E1 124 D9
Casella Rd SE14 129 H6
Casey CI NW8 122 E5
Caspian St SE5 128 B6
Cassidy Rd SW6 126 A6
Cassland Rd E9 124 G2
Casson St E1 124 E7
Castellain Rd W9 122 B6
Casterbridge NW6 122 B3
Castle La SW1 127 J2
Castle PI NW1 123 H1
Castle Rd NW1 123 H1
Castlebrook CI SE11 127 P3
Castlehaven Rd NW1 123 H2
Castlemaine Twr SW11 126 F7
Castor La E14 125 M9
Caterham Rd SE13 129 N9
Catesby St SE17 128 B3
Cathay St SE16 128 F1
Cathcart Rd SW10 126 C5
Cathcart St NW5 123 H1
Cathedral St SE1 124 B10
Catherine Gro SE10 129 M7
Catherine PI SW1 127 J2
Catherine St WC2 123 M9
Catlin St SE16 128 E4
Cato Rd SW4 127 K9
Cato St W1 122 E7
Cator St SE15 128 D5
Catton St WC1 123 M7
Caulfield Rd SE15 128 F8
Causeway, The SW18 126 B10
Causton St SW1 127 K3
Cavell St E1 124 F7
Cavendish Av NW8 122 D4
Cavendish CI NW8 122 D5
Cavendish PI W1 123 H8
Cavendish Sq W1 123 H8
Cavendish St N1 124 B4
Caversham Rd NW5 123 J1
Caverswall St SW3 126 F5
Caxton Gro E3 125 L5
Caxton St SW1 127 J2
Cedar CI E3 125 K3
Cedar Way NW1 123 K2
Cedarne Rd SW6 126 B6
Cedars CI SE13 129 P9
Cedars Rd SW4 127 H9
Celandine CI E14 125 L7
Celandine Dr E8 124 D1
Celestial Gdns SE13 129 P10
Celtic St E14 125 M7
Centaur St SE1 127 M2
Central Av SW11 126 F6
Central Mkts EC1 123 P7
Central St EC1 124 A5
Centre St E2 124 F4
Centrepoint WC1 123 K8
Centurion CI N7 123 M2
Cephas Av E1 124 G6
Cephas St E1 124 G6
Cerise Rd SE15 128 E7
Chadbourn St E14 125 M7
Chadwell St EC1 123 N5
Chadwick Rd SE15 128 D8
Chadwick St SW1 127 K2

Chagford St NW1 122 F6
Chalbury Wk N1 123 M4
Chalcot Cres NW1 122 F3
Chalcot Gdns NW3 122 F1
Chalcot Rd NW1 122 G2
Chalcot Sq NW1 122 G2
Chalk Fm Rd NW1 122 G2
Chalsey Rd SE4 129 K10
Chalton St NW1 123 K4
Chamber St E1 124 D9
Chambers St SE16 128 E1
Chambord St E2 124 D5
Champion Gro SE5 128 B9
Champion Hill SE5 128 B9
Champion Hill Est SE5 128 C9
Champion Pk SE5 128 B8
Chance St E1 124 D6
Chance St E2 124 D6
Chancel St SE1 123 P10
Chancery La WC2 123 N7
Chandler Way SE15 128 D6
Chandlers Ms E14 129 L1
Chandos PI WC2 123 L9
Chandos St W1 123 H7
Channelsea Rd E15 125 P3
Chant Sq E15 125 P2
Chant St E15 125 P2
Chantrey Rd SW9 127 M9
Chantry St N1 123 P3
Chapel Ho St E14 129 M4
Chapel Mkt N1 123 N4
Chapel PI W1 123 H8
Chapel Side W2 122 B9
Chapel St NW1 122 E7
Chapel St SW1 126 G2
Chaplin CI SE1 127 N1
Chapman Rd E9 125 K1
Chapman St E1 124 F9
Chapter Rd SE17 128 A4
Chapter St SW1 127 K3
Charing Cross Rd WC2 123 K8
Charlbert St NW8 122 E4
Charles Barry CI SW4 127 J9
Charles Dickens Ho E2 124 F5
Charles II St SW1 123 K10
Charles Sq N1 124 B5
Charles St W1 123 H10
Charleston St SE17 128 A3
Charlotte Despard Av
  SW11 126 G7
Charlotte Rd EC2 124 C6
Charlotte Row SW4 127 J9
Charlotte St W1 123 J7
Charlotte Ter N1 123 M3
Charlton PI N1 123 P4
Charlwood PI SW1 127 J3
Charlwood St SW1 127 J4
Charnwood Gdns E14 129 L3
Charrington St NW1 123 K4
Chart St N1 124 B5
Charterhouse Sq EC1 123 P7
Charterhouse St EC1 123 P7
Chase, The SW4 127 H9
Chaseley St E14 125 J8
Chatfield Rd SW11 126 C9
Chatham PI E9 124 G1
Chatham St SE17 128 B3
Chatsworth Wk E8 124 A3
Chaucer Dr SE1 128 D3
Cheapside EC2 124 A8
Chelsea Br SW1 127 H5
Chelsea Br SW8 127 H5
Chelsea Br Rd SW1 126 G4
Chelsea Embk SW3 126 E5
Chelsea Harbour SW10 126 C7
Chelsea Harbour Dr
  SW10 126 C7
Chelsea Manor Gdns
  SW3 126 E5
Chelsea Manor St SW3 126 E4
Chelsea Pk Gdns SW3 126 D5
Chelsea Sq SW3 126 D4
Chelsea Wf SW10 126 D6
Chelsham Rd SW4 127 K9
Cheltenham Rd SE15 128 G10
Cheltenham Ter SW3 126 F4
Chelwood Wk SE4 129 J10
Chenies PI NW1 123 K4
Chenies St WC1 123 K7
Cheniston Gdns W8 126 B2
Chepstow Cres W11 122 A9
Chepstow PI W2 122 A8
Chepstow Rd W2 122 A8
Chepstow Way SE15 128 D6
Cherbury St N1 124 B4
Cherry Gdn St SE16 128 F1
Cherrywood CI E3 125 J5
Cheryls CI SW6 126 B7
Chesham Ms SW1 126 G2
Chesham PI SW1 126 G2
Chesham St SW1 126 G2
Cheshire CI SE4 129 K8
Cheshire St E2 124 D6
Chesil Ct E2 124 G4
Chesney St SW11 126 G7
Chester CI SW1 126 G1
Chester CI SE5 128 B6
Chester Gate NW1 123 H5
Chester Ms SW1 127 H2
Chester Rd NW1 122 G5
Chester Row SW1 126 G3
Chester Sq SW1 127 H2
Chester St E2 124 E6
Chester St SW1 126 G2
Chester Way SE11 127 N3
Chesterfield Gdns W1 123 H10
Chesterfield Hill W1 123 H9
Chesterfield St W1 123 H10
Chesterfield Wk SE10 129 P7
Chesterfield Way SE15 128 G6
Chestnut CI SE14 129 K7
Cheval PI SW7 126 E2
Cheval St E14 129 L2

Cheyne Gdns SW3 126 E5
Cheyne Ms SW3 126 E5
Cheyne PI SW3 126 F5
Cheyne Row SW3 126 E5
Cheyne Wk SW3 126 E5
Cheyne Wk SW10 126 D6
Chicheley St SE1 127 M1
Chichester Rd NW6 122 A4
Chichester Rd W2 122 B7
Chichester St SW1 127 J4
Chichester Way E14 129 P3
Chicksand St E1 124 D7
Chiddingstone St SW6 126 A8
Childeric Rd SE14 129 J6
Childers St SE8 129 H3
Child's PI SW5 126 A3
Child's St SW5 126 A3
Chiltern Rd E3 125 L6
Chiltern St W1 122 G7
Chilton Gro SE8 129 H3
Chilton St E2 124 D6
Chilworth Ms W2 122 C8
Chilworth St W2 122 C8
Chip St SW4 127 K9
Chipka St E14 129 N1
Chipley St SE14 129 J5
Chippenham Gdns NW6 122 A5
Chippenham Ms W9 122 A6
Chippenham Rd W9 122 A6
Chipstead St SW6 126 A7
Chisenhale Rd E3 125 J4
Chiswell St EC1 124 A7
Chitty St W1 123 J7
Choumert Gro SE15 128 E8
Choumert Ms SE15 128 E8
Choumert Rd SE15 128 D9
Choumert Sq SE15 128 E8
Chrisp St E14 125 M7
Christchurch St SW3 126 F5
Christian Ct SE16 125 K10
Christian St E1 124 E8
Christie Rd E9 125 J1
Christopher CI SE16 129 H1
Christopher St EC2 124 B6
Chryssell Rd SW9 127 N6
Chubworthy St SE14 129 J5
Chudleigh St E1 125 H8
Chumleigh St SE5 128 C5
Church Cres E9 125 H2
Church Gro SE13 129 M10
Church Rd N1 124 A1
Church Rd NW8 122 D7
Church Rd W2 122 D7
Church St Est NW8 122 D6
Church Ter SW8 127 K8
Churchill Gdns SW1 127 J4
Churchill Gdns Rd SW1 127 H4
Churchill PI E14 125 M10
Churchway NW1 123 K5
Churton PI SW1 127 J3
Churton St SW1 127 J3
Cicely Rd SE15 128 E7
Cinnabar Wf E1 124 E10
Cinnamon Row SW11 126 C9
Cinnamon St E1 124 F10
Circus Rd NW8 122 D5
Circus St SE10 129 N6
Cirencester St W2 122 B7
City Gdn Row N1 123 P4
City Mill River Towpath
  E15 125 M2
City Rd EC1 123 P4
Clabon Ms SW1 126 F2
Clack St SE16 128 G1
Claire PI E14 129 L2
Clancarty Rd SW6 126 A8
Clandon St SE8 129 L8
Clanricarde Gdns W2 122 A9
Clapham Common
  N Side SW4 127 H10
Clapham Common
  W Side SW4 126 G10
Clapham Cres SW4 127 K10
Clapham High St SW4 127 K10
Clapham Manor St SW4 127 J9
Clapham Pk Rd SW4 127 K10
Clapham Rd SW9 127 L9
Clapham Rd Est SW4 127 K9
Clare Ho E3 125 K3
Clare La N1 124 A2
Clare Rd SE14 129 K7
Clare St E2 124 F4
Claredale St E2 124 E4
Claremont CI N1 123 N4
Claremont Sq N1 123 N4
Claremont St SE10 129 M5
Clarence Gdns NW1 123 H5
Clarence Ms SE16 125 H10
Clarence Rd SE8 129 M5
Clarence Wk SW4 127 L8
Clarence Way NW1 123 H2
Clarence Way Est NW1 123 H2
Clarendon CI E9 124 G2
Clarendon Gdns W9 122 C6
Clarendon PI W2 122 E9
Clarendon Ri SE13 129 N9
Clarendon St SW1 127 H4
Clareville Gro SW7 126 C3
Clareville St SW7 126 C3
Clarewood Wk SW9 127 N9
Clarges Ms W1 123 H10
Clarges St W1 123 H10
Claribel Rd SW9 127 P8
Clarissa St E8 124 D3
Clark St E1 124 F7
Clarkson Row NW1 123 J4
Claude Rd SE15 128 F8
Claude St E14 129 L3
Clavell St SE10 129 N5
Claverton St SW1 127 J4
Claylands PI SW8 127 N6
Claylands Rd SW8 127 M5
Claypole Rd E15 125 N4

Don Phelan Cl

Clayton Cres **N1** 123 L3
Clayton Ms **SE10** 129 P7
Clayton Rd **SE15** 128 E7
Clayton St **SE11** 127 N5
Clearwell Dr **W9** 122 B6
Cleaver Sq **SE11** 127 N4
Cleaver St **SE11** 127 N4
Clemence St **E14** 125 K7
Clement Av **SW4** 127 K10
Clement's Inn **WC2** 123 M8
Clements La **EC4** 124 B9
Clements Rd **SE16** 128 E2
Clephane Rd **N1** 124 A1
Clerkenwell Cl **EC1** 123 N6
Clerkenwell Grn **EC1** 123 P6
Clerkenwell Rd **EC1** 123 N7
Clermont Rd **E9** 124 G3
Cleve Rd **NW6** 122 A2
Cleveland Gdns **W2** 122 C8
Cleveland Rd **N1** 124 B2
Cleveland Row **SW1** 123 J10
Cleveland Sq **W2** 122 C8
Cleveland St **W1** 123 H6
Cleveland Ter **W2** 122 C8
Cleveland Way **E1** 124 G6
Clichy Est **E1** 124 G7
Cliff Rd **NW1** 123 K1
Cliff Ter **SE8** 129 L8
Cliff Vil **NW1** 123 K1
Clifford Dr **SW9** 127 P10
Clifford St **W1** 123 J9
Cliffview Rd **SE13** 129 L9
Clifton Cres **SE15** 128 F6
Clifton Gdns **W9** 122 C6
Clifton Gro **E8** 124 E1
Clifton Hill **NW8** 122 B4
Clifton Pl **W2** 122 D9
Clifton Ri **SE14** 129 J6
Clifton Rd **N1** 124 A1
Clifton Rd **W9** 122 C6
Clifton St **EC2** 124 C7
Clifton Vil **W9** 122 B7
Clifton Way **SE15** 128 F6
Clink St **SE1** 124 A10
Clinton Rd **E3** 125 J5
Clipper Way **SE13** 129 N10
Clipstone Ms **W1** 123 J6
Clipstone St **W1** 123 J7
Clitheroe Rd **SW9** 127 L8
Cliveden Pl **SW1** 126 G3
Cloak La **EC4** 124 A9
Clock Twr Pl **N7** 123 L1
Cloth Fair **EC1** 123 P7
Cloudesley Pl **N1** 123 N3
Cloudesley Rd **N1** 123 N3
Cloudesley Sq **N1** 123 N3
Cloudesley St **N1** 123 N3
Clove Cres **E14** 125 P9
Clove Hitch Quay **SW11** 126 C9
Cloysters Grn **E1** 124 E10
Club Row **E1** 124 D6
Club Row **E2** 124 D6
Cluny Ms **SW5** 126 A3
Clutton St **E14** 125 M7
Clyde St **SE8** 129 K5
Clyston St **SW8** 127 J8
Coate St **E2** 124 E4
Cobb St **E1** 124 D7
Cobbett St **SW8** 127 M6
Coborn Rd **E3** 125 K5
Coborn St **E3** 125 K5
Cobourg Rd **SE5** 128 D5
Cobourg St **NW1** 123 J5
Cochrane St **NW8** 122 D4
Cock La **EC1** 123 P7
Cockayne Way **SE8** 129 J4
Cockspur St **SW1** 123 K10
Code St **E1** 124 D6
Cody Rd **E16** 125 P6
Cody Rd Business Cen **E16** 125 P6
Coin St **SE1** 123 N10
Coity Rd **NW5** 122 G1
Coke St **E1** 124 E8
Colbeck Ms **SW7** 126 B3
Cold Blow La **SE14** 129 H6
Cold Harbour **E14** 129 N1
Coldbath St **SE13** 129 M7
Coldharbour La **SE5** 127 N10
Coldharbour La **SW9** 127 N10
Cole St **SE1** 128 A1
Colebeck Ms **N1** 123 P1
Colebert Av **E1** 124 G6
Colebrooke Row **N1** 123 P4
Colegrove Rd **SE15** 128 D6
Coleherne Ct **SW5** 126 B4
Coleherne Ms **SW10** 126 B4
Coleherne Rd **SW10** 126 B4
Coleman Flds **N1** 124 A3
Coleman Rd **SE5** 128 C6
Coleman St **EC2** 124 B8
Coleridge Cl **SW8** 127 H8
Coleridge Gdns **SW10** 126 B6
Coleridge Sq **SW10** 126 C6
Colestown St **SW11** 126 E8
Coley St **WC1** 123 M6
College App **SE10** 129 N5
College Cres **NW3** 122 D1
College Cross **N1** 123 N2
College Pk Cl **SE13** 129 P10
College Pl **NW1** 123 J3
College Ter **E3** 125 K5
Collent St **E9** 124 G1
Collett Rd **SE16** 128 E2
Collier St **N1** 123 M4
Collingham Gdns **SW5** 126 B3
Collingham Pl **SW5** 126 B3
Collingham Rd **SW5** 126 B3
Collingwood St **E1** 124 F6
Colls Rd **SE15** 128 G7
Colmore Ms **SE15** 128 F7
Colnbrook St **SE1** 127 P2
Cologne Rd **SW11** 126 D10
Colombo St **SE1** 123 P10
Colonnade **WC1** 123 L6
Colonnade Wk **SW1** 127 H3
Colonnades, The **W2** 122 B8
Columbia Rd **E2** 124 D5
Columbine Way **SE13** 129 N8
Colville Est **N1** 124 C3
Colyer Cl **N1** 123 M4
Comber Gro **SE5** 128 A7
Combermere Rd **SW9** 127 M9
Comerford Rd **SE4** 129 J10
Comet Pl **SE8** 129 L6
Comet St **SE8** 129 L6
Comfort St **SE15** 128 C5
Commercial Rd **E1** 124 E8
Commercial Rd **E14** 124 G8
Commercial St **E1** 124 D6
Commercial Way **SE15** 128 D6
Commodore St **E1** 125 J6
Compayne Gdns **NW6** 122 B2
Compton Av **N1** 123 P1
Compton Cl **E3** 125 L7
Compton Rd **N1** 123 P1
Compton St **EC1** 123 P6
Compton Ter **N1** 123 P1
Comus Pl **SE17** 128 C3
Comyn Rd **SW11** 126 E10
Concanon Rd **SW2** 127 M10
Concert Hall App **SE1** 123 M10
Condell Rd **SW8** 127 J7
Condray Pl **SW11** 126 E6
Conduit Ms **W2** 122 D8
Conduit Pl **W2** 122 D8
Conduit St **W1** 123 H9
Coney Way **SW8** 127 M5
Congreve St **SE17** 128 C3
Coniger Rd **SW6** 126 A8
Conington Rd **SE13** 129 M8
Coniston Ho **SE5** 128 A6
Conistone Way **N7** 123 L2
Connaught Pl **W2** 122 F9
Connaught Sq **W2** 122 F8
Connaught St **W2** 122 E8
Consort Rd **SE15** 128 F7
Constitution Hill **SW1** 127 H1
Content St **SE17** 128 B3
Conway St **W1** 123 J6
Conyer St **E3** 125 J4
Cook's Rd **E15** 125 M4
Cooks Rd **SE17** 127 P5
Coombs St **N1** 123 P4
Coopers Cl **E1** 124 G6
Coopers La **NW1** 123 K4
Coopers Rd **SE1** 128 D4
Cope Pl **W8** 126 A2
Cope St **SE16** 129 H3
Copeland Dr **E14** 129 L3
Copeland Rd **SE15** 128 E8
Copenhagen Pl **E14** 125 K8
Copenhagen St **N1** 123 L3
Copleston Pas **SE15** 128 D9
Copleston Rd **SE15** 128 D9
Copley St **E1** 125 H7
Copper Row **SE1** 124 D10
Copperas St **SE8** 129 M5
Copperfield Rd **E3** 125 J6
Copperfield St **SE1** 127 P1
Coppock Cl **SW11** 126 E8
Copthall Av **EC2** 124 B8
Copthall Ct **EC2** 124 B8
Coptic St **WC1** 123 L7
Coral St **SE1** 127 N1
Coram St **WC1** 123 L6
Corbden Cl **SE15** 128 D7
Corbiere Ho **N1** 124 C3
Corbridge Cres **E2** 124 F4
Cordelia Cl **SE24** 127 P10
Cordelia St **E14** 125 M8
Corfield St **E2** 124 F5
Coriander Av **E14** 125 P8
Cork St **W1** 123 J9
Corlett St **NW1** 122 E7
Cormont Rd **SE5** 127 P7
Cornelia St **N7** 123 M1
Cornhill **EC3** 124 B8
Cornmill La **SE13** 129 M9
Cornwall Av **E2** 124 G5
Cornwall Gdns **SW7** 126 B2
Cornwall Ms S **SW7** 126 C2
Cornwall Rd **SE1** 123 N10
Cornwall Sq **SE11** 127 P4
Cornwood Dr **E1** 124 G8
Coronet St **N1** 124 C5
Corporation Row **EC1** 123 N6
Corrance Rd **SW2** 127 L10
Corry Dr **SW9** 127 P10
Corsham St **N1** 124 B5
Corsica St **N5** 123 P1
Corunna Rd **SW8** 127 J7
Corunna Ter **SW8** 127 J7
Cossall Wk **SE15** 128 F7
Cosser St **SE1** 127 N2
Costa St **SE15** 128 E8
Cosway St **NW1** 122 E7
Cotall St **E14** 125 L8
Cotleigh Rd **NW6** 122 A2
Cottage Grn **SE5** 128 B6
Cottage Gro **SW9** 127 L9
Cottage Pl **SW3** 126 E2
Cottage St **E14** 125 M9
Cottesmore Gdns **W8** 126 B2
Cottingham Rd **SW8** 127 M6
Cotton Row **SW11** 126 C9
Cotton St **E14** 125 N9
Coulgate St **SE4** 129 J9
Coulson St **SW3** 126 F3
Councillor St **SE5** 128 A6
County Gro **SE5** 128 A7
County St **SE1** 128 A2
Courland Gro **SW8** 127 K7
Courland Gro Hall **SW8** 127 K8
Courland St **SW8** 127 K7
Court Gdns **N7** 123 N1
Courtenay St **SE11** 127 N4
Courtfield Gdns **SW5** 126 B3
Courtfield Rd **SW7** 126 B3
Courthill Rd **SE13** 129 N10
Courtnell St **W2** 122 A8
Courtyard, The **N1** 123 M2
Covent Gdn **WC2** 123 L9
Coventry Rd **E1** 124 F6
Coventry Rd **E2** 124 F6
Coventry St **W1** 123 K9
Coverley Cl **E1** 124 E7
Cowcross St **EC1** 123 P7
Cowdenbeath Path **N1** 123 M3
Cowley Rd **SW9** 127 N7
Cowper St **EC2** 124 B6
Cowthorpe Rd **SW8** 127 K7
Crabtree Cl **E2** 124 D4
Crampton St **SE17** 127 P3
Cranbourn St **WC2** 123 K9
Cranbrook Rd **SE8** 129 L7
Cranbury Rd **SW6** 126 B8
Crane Gro **N7** 123 N1
Crane Mead **SE16** 129 H3
Crane St **SE10** 129 P4
Crane St **SE15** 128 D7
Cranfield Rd **SE4** 129 K9
Cranford St **E1** 125 H9
Cranleigh Ms **SW11** 126 E8
Cranleigh St **NW1** 123 J4
Cranley Gdns **SW7** 126 C4
Cranley Ms **SW7** 126 C4
Cranley Pl **SW7** 126 D3
Cranmer Ct **SW4** 127 K9
Cranmer Rd **SW9** 127 N6
Cranston Est **N1** 124 B4
Cranswick Rd **SE16** 128 F4
Cranwell Cl **E3** 125 M6
Cranwood St **EC1** 124 B5
Cranworth Gdns **SW9** 127 N7
Craven Hill **W2** 122 C9
Craven Hill Gdns **W2** 122 C9
Craven Hill Ms **W2** 122 C9
Craven Pas **WC2** 123 L10
Craven Rd **W2** 122 C9
Craven St **WC2** 123 L10
Craven Ter **W2** 122 C9
Crawford Est **SE5** 128 A8
Crawford Pl **W1** 122 E8
Crawford Rd **SE5** 128 A7
Crawford St **W1** 122 F7
Crawthew Gro **SE22** 128 D10
Creasy Est **SE1** 128 C2
Credon Rd **SE16** 128 F4
Creechurch La **EC3** 124 C8
Creek Rd **SE8** 129 L5
Creek Rd **SE10** 129 L5
Creekside **SE8** 129 M6
Cremer St **E2** 124 D4
Cremorne Rd **SW10** 126 C6
Crescent Gro **SW4** 127 J10
Crescent Pl **SW3** 126 E3
Crescent St **N1** 123 M2
Crescent Way **SE4** 129 L9
Cresford Rd **SW6** 126 B7
Cresset Rd **E9** 124 G1
Cresset St **SW4** 127 K9
Cressingham Rd **SE13** 129 N9
Cresswell Gdns **SW5** 126 C4
Cresswell Pl **SW10** 126 C4
Cressy Pl **E1** 124 G7
Crestfield St **WC1** 123 L5
Crewdson Rd **SW9** 127 N6
Crews St **E14** 129 L3
Crewys Rd **SE15** 128 F8
Cricketers Ct **SE11** 127 P3
Crimscott St **SE1** 128 C2
Crimsworth Rd **SW8** 127 K7
Crinan St **N1** 123 L4
Cringle St **SW8** 127 J6
Crispin St **E1** 124 D7
Croft St **SE8** 129 J3
Crofters Way **NW1** 123 K3
Crofton Rd **SE5** 128 C7
Crofts St **E1** 124 E9
Crogsland Rd **NW1** 122 G2
Cromer St **WC1** 123 L5
Crompton St **W2** 122 D6
Cromwell Cres **SW5** 126 A3
Cromwell Gdns **SW7** 126 D2
Cromwell Ms **SW7** 126 D3
Cromwell Pl **SW7** 126 D3
Cromwell Rd **SW5** 126 B3
Cromwell Rd **SW7** 126 B3
Cromwell Rd **SW9** 127 P7
Cromwell Twr **EC2** 124 A7
Crondace Rd **SW6** 126 A7
Crondall St **N1** 124 B4
Cronin St **SE15** 128 D6
Crooke Rd **SE8** 129 J4
Crooms Hill **SE10** 129 P6
Crooms Hill Gro **SE10** 129 N6
Cropley St **N1** 124 B4
Crosby Row **SE1** 128 B1
Cross Av **SE10** 129 P5
Cross Rd **SE5** 128 C8
Cross St **N1** 123 P3
Crossfield Rd **NW3** 122 D2
Crossfield St **SE8** 129 L6
Crossford St **SW9** 127 M8
Crosslet Vale **SE10** 129 M7
Crossley St **N7** 123 N1
Crossmount Ho **SE5** 128 A6
Crossthwaite Av **SE5** 128 B10
Crosswall **EC3** 124 D9
Croston St **E8** 124 E3
Crowder St **E1** 124 F9
Crowhurst Cl **SW9** 127 N8
Crowland Ter **N1** 124 B2
Crown Cl **E3** 125 L3
Crown Cl **NW6** 122 B1
Crown Pas **SW1** 123 J10
Crown Pl **EC2** 124 C7
Crown St **SE5** 128 A6
Crowndale Rd **NW1** 123 J4
Crows Rd **E15** 125 P5
Crucifix La **SE1** 128 C1
Cruden St **N1** 123 P3
Cruikshank St **WC1** 123 N5
Crutched Friars **EC3** 124 C9
Crystal Palace Rd **SE22** 128 E10
Cuba St **E14** 129 L1
Cubitt St **WC1** 123 M5
Cubitt Ter **SW4** 127 J9
Cudworth St **E1** 124 F6
Cuff Pt **E2** 124 D5
Culford Gdns **SW3** 126 F3
Culford Gro **N1** 124 C1
Culford Rd **N1** 124 C2
Culloden Cl **SE16** 128 E4
Culloden St **E14** 125 N8
Culmore Rd **SE15** 128 F6
Culross St **W1** 122 G9
Culvert Pl **SW11** 126 G8
Culvert Rd **SW11** 126 F8
Cumberland Cl **E8** 124 D1
Cumberland Gate **W1** 122 F9
Cumberland Mkt **NW1** 123 H5
Cumberland St **SW1** 127 H4
Cumming St **N1** 123 M4
Cunard Wk **SE16** 129 J3
Cundy St **SW1** 126 G3
Cunningham Pl **NW8** 122 D6
Cupar Rd **SW11** 126 G7
Cureton St **SW1** 127 K3
Curlew St **SE1** 128 D1
Cursitor St **EC4** 123 N8
Curtain Rd **EC2** 124 C6
Curtis St **SE1** 128 D3
Curtis Way **SE1** 128 D3
Curzon Gate **W1** 122 G10
Curzon St **W1** 122 G10
Custom Ho Reach **SE16** 129 K1
Custom Ho Wk **EC3** 124 C9
Cut, The **SE1** 127 N1
Cutcombe Rd **SE5** 128 A8
Cuthbert St **W2** 122 D6
Cuthill Wk **SE5** 128 B7
Cutler St **E1** 124 C8
Cyclops Ms **E14** 129 L3
Cynthia St **N1** 123 M4
Cyntra Pl **E8** 124 F2
Cyprus Pl **E2** 124 G4
Cyprus St **E2** 124 G4
Cyril Mans **SW11** 126 F7
Cyrus St **EC1** 123 P6
Czar St **SE8** 129 L5

D

Dabin Cres **SE10** 129 N7
Dacca St **SE8** 129 K5
Dace Rd **E3** 125 L2
Dacre St **SW1** 127 K2
Dagmar Rd **SE5** 128 C7
Dagmar Ter **N1** 123 P3
Dagnall St **SW11** 126 F8
Dairy Ms **SW9** 127 L9
Daisy La **SW6** 126 A9
Dalberg Rd **SW2** 127 N10
Dalby Rd **SW18** 126 C10
Dalby St **NW5** 123 H1
Dale Rd **SE17** 127 P5
Daleham Ms **NW3** 122 D1
Dalehead **NW1** 123 J4
Daley St **E9** 125 H1
Daley Thompson Way **SW8** 127 H8
Dalgleish St **E14** 125 J8
Daling Way **E3** 125 J3
Dallington St **EC1** 123 P6
Dalrymple Rd **SE4** 129 J10
Dalston La **E8** 124 D1
Dalwood St **SE5** 128 C7
Dalyell Rd **SW9** 127 M9
Dame St **N1** 124 A4
Damien St **E1** 124 F8
Danbury St **N1** 123 P4
Danby St **SE15** 128 D9
Danesdale Rd **E9** 125 J1
Danesfield **SE5** 128 C5
Daneville Rd **SE5** 128 B7
Daniel Gdns **SE15** 128 D6
Daniels Rd **SE15** 128 G9
Dante Rd **SE11** 127 P3
Danvers St **SW3** 126 D5
D'Arblay St **W1** 123 J8
Darien Rd **SW11** 126 D9
Darling Rd **SE4** 129 L9
Darling Row **E1** 124 F6
Darnley Ho **E14** 125 J8
Darnley Rd **E9** 124 F1
Darsley Dr **SW8** 127 L7
Dartford St **SE17** 128 A5
Dartmouth Gro **SE10** 129 N7
Dartmouth Hill **SE10** 129 N7
Dartmouth Row **SE10** 129 N8
Dartmouth St **SW1** 127 K1
Dartmouth Ter **SE10** 129 P7
Darwin St **SE17** 128 B3
Datchelor Pl **SE5** 128 B7
Date St **SE17** 128 A4
Daubeney Twr **SE8** 129 K3
Davenant St **E1** 124 E7
Daventry St **NW1** 122 E7
Davey Cl **N7** 123 M1
Davey Rd **E9** 125 L2
Davey St **SE15** 128 D5
David St **E15** 125 P1
Davidge St **SE1** 127 P1
Davidson Gdns **SW8** 127 L6
Davies St **W1** 123 H9
Dawes St **SE17** 128 B4
Dawson Pl **W2** 122 A9
Dawson St **E2** 124 D4
Dayton Gro **SE15** 128 G7
De Beauvoir Cres **N1** 124 C3
De Beauvoir Est **N1** 124 B3
De Beauvoir Rd **N1** 124 C3
De Beauvoir Sq **N1** 124 C2
De Crespigny Pk **SE5** 128 B8
De Laune St **SE17** 127 P4
De Morgan Rd **SW6** 126 B9
De Vere Gdns **W8** 126 C1
Deacon Ms **N1** 124 B2
Deacon Way **SE17** 128 A3
Deal Porters Way **SE16** 128 G2
Deal St **E1** 124 E7
Dean Bradley St **SW1** 127 L2
Dean Farrar St **SW1** 127 K2
Dean Ryle St **SW1** 127 L3
Dean Stanley St **SW1** 127 L2
Dean St **W1** 123 K8
Dean Trench St **SW1** 127 L2
Deancross St **E1** 124 G8
Deanery St **W1** 122 G10
Deans Bldgs **SE17** 128 B3
Decima St **SE1** 128 C2
Dee St **E14** 125 N8
Deeley Rd **SW8** 127 K7
Deepdene Rd **SE5** 128 B10
Deerdale Rd **SE24** 128 A10
Delaford Rd **SE16** 128 F4
Delamere Ter **W2** 122 B7
Delancey St **NW1** 123 H3
Delaware Rd **W9** 122 B6
Delhi St **N1** 123 L3
Delius Gro **E15** 125 P4
Dell Cl **E15** 125 P3
Dellow St **E1** 124 F9
Deloraine St **SE8** 129 L7
Delverton Rd **SE17** 127 P4
Delvino Rd **SW6** 126 A7
Denbigh Pl **SW1** 127 J4
Denbigh St **SW1** 127 J3
Dene Cl **SE4** 129 J9
Denman Rd **SE15** 128 D7
Denmark Gro **N1** 123 N4
Denmark Hill **SE5** 128 B7
Denmark Hill Est **SE5** 128 B10
Denmark Rd **SE5** 128 A7
Denmark St **WC2** 123 K8
Denne Ter **E8** 124 D3
Dennetts Rd **SE14** 128 G7
Denning Cl **NW8** 122 C5
Dennington Pk Rd **NW6** 122 A1
Dennison Pt **E15** 125 N2
Denny St **SE11** 127 N4
Denyer St **SW3** 126 E3
Deptford Br **SE8** 129 L7
Deptford Bdy **SE8** 129 L7
Deptford Ch St **SE8** 129 L5
Deptford Ferry Rd **E14** 129 L3
Deptford Grn **SE8** 129 L5
Deptford High St **SE8** 129 L5
Deptford Strand **SE8** 129 K3
Deptford Wf **SE8** 129 K3
Derby Rd **E9** 125 H3
Derbyshire St **E2** 124 E5
Dericote St **E8** 124 E3
Dering St **W1** 123 H8
Derry St **W8** 126 B1
Derwent Gro **SE22** 128 D10
Desborough Cl **W2** 122 B7
Desmond St **SE14** 129 J5
Devas St **E3** 125 M6
Deverell St **SE1** 128 B2
Devon St **SE15** 128 F5
Devonia Rd **N1** 123 P4
Devonport St **E1** 124 G8
Devons Est **E3** 125 M5
Devons Rd **E3** 125 L7
Devonshire Cl **W1** 123 H7
Devonshire Dr **SE10** 129 M6
Devonshire Gro **SE15** 128 F5
Devonshire Ms S **W1** 123 H7
Devonshire Ms W **W1** 123 H7
Devonshire Pl **W1** 122 G6
Devonshire St **W1** 123 H7
Devonshire Ter **W2** 122 C8
Dewar St **SE15** 128 E9
Dewberry St **E14** 125 N7
Dewey Rd **N1** 123 N4
D'Eynsford Rd **SE5** 128 B7
Dial Wk, The **W8** 126 B1
Diamond St **SE15** 128 C6
Diamond Ter **SE10** 129 N7
Dibden St **N1** 123 P3
Dickens Est **SE1** 128 D1
Dickens Est **SE16** 128 D1
Dickens Ho **NW6** 122 A5
Dickens Sq **SE1** 128 A2
Dickens St **SW8** 127 H8
Digby Rd **E9** 125 H1
Digby St **E2** 124 G5
Dighton Ct **SE5** 128 A5
Dilke St **SW3** 126 F5
Dimson Cres **E3** 125 L6
Dingle Gdns **E14** 125 L9
Dingley Pl **EC1** 124 A5
Dingley Rd **EC1** 124 A5
Discovery Wk **E1** 124 F10
Diss St **E2** 124 D5
Distaff La **EC4** 124 A9
Distin St **SE11** 127 N3
Ditch All **SE10** 129 M7
Ditchburn St **E14** 125 N9
Dixon Rd **SE14** 129 J7
Dixon's All **SE16** 128 F1
Dobson Cl **NW6** 122 D2
Dock Hill Av **SE16** 129 H1
Dock St **E1** 124 E9
Dockers Tanner Rd **E14** 129 L2
Dockhead **SE1** 128 D1
Dockley Rd **SE16** 128 E2
Docwra's Bldgs **N1** 124 C1
Dod St **E14** 125 K8
Doddington Gro **SE17** 127 P5
Doddington Pl **SE17** 127 P5
Dodson St **SE1** 127 N1
Dog Kennel Hill **SE22** 128 C9
Dog Kennel Hill Est **SE22** 128 C9
Dolben St **SE1** 123 P10
Dolland St **SE11** 127 M4
Dolman St **SW4** 127 M10
Dolphin La **E14** 125 M9
Dolphin Sq **SW1** 127 J4
Dombey St **WC1** 123 M7
Domett Cl **SE5** 128 B10
Don Phelan Cl **SE5** 128 B7

Donegal St

Donegal St **N1** 123 M4
Dongola Rd **E1** 125 J7
Donne Pl **SW3** 126 E3
Dora St **E14** 125 K8
Doran Wk **E15** 125 N2
Doric Way **NW1** 123 K5
Dorking Cl **SE8** 129 K5
Dorman Way **NW8** 122 D3
Dorney **NW3** 122 E2
Dorothy Rd **SW11** 126 F9
Dorrington St **EC1** 123 N7
Dorset Est **E2** 124 D5
Dorset Pl **E15** 125 P1
Dorset Ri **EC4** 123 P8
Dorset Rd **SW8** 127 M6
Dorset Sq **NW1** 122 F6
Dorset St **W1** 122 G7
Doughty Ms **WC1** 123 M6
Doughty St **WC1** 123 M6
Douglas Rd **N1** 124 A2
Douglas St **SW1** 127 K3
Douglas Way **SE8** 129 K6
Douro Pl **W8** 126 B2
Douro St **E3** 125 L4
Dove Ms **SW5** 126 C3
Dove Rd **N1** 124 B1
Dove Row **E2** 124 E3
Dovehouse St **SW3** 126 D4
Dover St **W1** 123 H9
Dovercourt Est **N1** 124 B1
Doves Yd **N1** 123 N3
Dowgate Hill **EC4** 124 B9
Dowlas St **SE5** 128 C6
Down St **W1** 123 H10
Downfield Cl **W9** 122 B6
Downham Rd **N1** 124 B2
Downing St **SW1** 127 L1
Downtown Rd **SE16** 129 J1
Dowson Cl **SE5** 128 B10
D'Oyley St **SW1** 126 G3
Draco St **SE17** 128 A5
Dragon Rd **SE15** 128 C5
Dragoon Rd **SE8** 129 K4
Drake Rd **SE4** 129 L9
Drakefell Rd **SE4** 129 H8
Drakefell Rd **SE14** 129 H8
Drawdock Rd **SE10** 125 P10
Draycott Av **SW3** 126 E3
Draycott Pl **SW3** 126 F3
Draycott Ter **SW3** 126 F3
Drayson Ms **W8** 126 A1
Drayton Gdns **SW10** 126 C4
Dresden Cl **NW6** 122 B1
Driffield Rd **E3** 125 J4
Drovers Pl **SE15** 128 F6
Druid St **SE1** 128 C1
Drummond Cres **NW1** 123 K5
Drummond Gate **SW1** 127 K4
Drummond Rd **SE16** 128 F2
Drummond St **NW1** 123 J6
Drury La **WC2** 123 L8
Dryden Ct **SE11** 127 N3
Drysdale St **N1** 124 C5
Dublin Av **E8** 124 E3
Duchess of Bedford's Wk **W8** 126 A1
Duchess St **W1** 123 H7
Duchy St **SE1** 123 N10
Ducie St **SW4** 127 M10
Duckett St **E1** 125 H6
Dudley St **W2** 122 D7
Duff St **E14** 125 M8
Dufferin St **EC1** 124 A6
Dugard Way **SE11** 127 P3
Duke of Wellington Pl **SW1** 126 G1
Duke of York Sq **SW3** 126 F3
Duke of York St **SW1** 123 J10
Duke St **SW1** 123 J10
Duke St **W1** 122 G8
Dukes La **W8** 126 A1
Dukes Pl **EC3** 124 C8
Duke's Rd **WC1** 123 K5
Dunbridge St **E2** 124 E6
Duncan Rd **E8** 124 F3
Duncan St **N1** 123 P4
Duncan Ter **N1** 123 P4
Duncannon St **WC2** 123 L9
Dundalk Rd **SE4** 129 J9
Dundas Rd **SE15** 128 G8
Dundee St **E1** 124 F10
Dunelm St **E1** 125 H8
Dunloe St **E2** 124 D4
Dunston Rd **E8** 124 D3
Dunston Rd **SW11** 126 G8
Dunston St **E8** 124 D3
Dunton Rd **SE1** 128 D4
Durand Gdns **SW9** 127 M7
Durands Wk **SE16** 129 K1
Durant St **E2** 124 E4
Durham Row **E1** 125 J7
Durham St **SE11** 127 M4
Durham Ter **W2** 122 B8
Durward St **E1** 124 F7
Durweston St **W1** 122 F7
Dutton St **SE10** 129 N7
Dye Ho La **E3** 125 L3
Dylan Rd **SE24** 127 P10
Dylways **SE5** 128 B10
Dymock St **SW6** 126 B9
Dynham Rd **NW6** 122 A2
Dyott St **WC1** 123 K8

E

Eagle Ct **EC1** 123 P7
Eagle St **WC1** 123 M7
Eagle Wf Rd **N1** 124 A4
Eamont St **NW8** 122 E4
Eardley Cres **SW5** 126 A4
Earl St **EC2** 124 B7
Earlham St **WC2** 123 K8
Earls Ct Gdns **SW5** 126 B3
Earls Ct Rd **SW5** 126 A3
Earls Ct Rd **W8** 126 A3
Earls Ct Sq **SW5** 126 B4
Earls Wk **W8** 126 A2
Earlsferry Way **N1** 123 M2
Earlston Gro **E9** 124 F3
Earnshaw St **WC2** 123 K8
East Arbour St **E1** 125 H8
East Cross Cen **E15** 125 L1
East Cross Route **E3** 125 K2
East Cross Route **E9** 125 K2
East Dulwich Rd **SE15** 128 D10
East Dulwich Rd **SE22** 128 D10
East Ferry Rd **E14** 129 M2
East India Dock Rd **E14** 125 L8
East La **SE16** 128 E1
East Mt St **E1** 124 F7
East Rd **N1** 124 B5
East Smithfield **E1** 124 D9
East St **SE17** 128 A4
East Surrey Gro **SE15** 128 D6
East Tenter St **E1** 124 D8
Eastbourne Ms **W2** 122 C8
Eastbourne Ter **W2** 122 C8
Eastbury Ter **E1** 125 H6
Eastcastle St **W1** 123 J8
Eastcheap **EC3** 124 B9
Eastcote St **SW9** 127 M8
Eastdown Pk **SE13** 129 P10
Eastern Rd **SE4** 129 L10
Eastfield St **E14** 125 J7
Eastlake Rd **SE5** 127 P8
Eastney St **SE10** 129 P4
Eastway **E9** 125 K1
Eaton Cl **SW1** 126 G3
Eaton Dr **SW9** 127 P10
Eaton Gate **SW1** 126 G3
Eaton La **SW1** 127 H2
Eaton Ms N **SW1** 126 G2
Eaton Ms S **SW1** 127 H2
Eaton Ms W **SW1** 126 G3
Eaton Pl **SW1** 126 G2
Eaton Row **SW1** 127 H2
Eaton Sq **SW1** 126 G3
Eaton Ter **SW1** 126 G3
Ebbisham Dr **SW8** 127 M5
Ebenezer St **N1** 124 B5
Ebley Cl **SE15** 128 D5
Ebor St **E1** 124 D6
Ebury Br **SW1** 127 H4
Ebury Br Est **SW1** 127 H4
Ebury Br Rd **SW1** 126 G4
Ebury Ms **SW1** 127 H3
Ebury Sq **SW1** 126 G3
Ebury St **SW1** 126 G3
Eccles Rd **SW11** 126 F10
Ecclesbourne Rd **N1** 124 A2
Eccleston Br **SW1** 127 H3
Eccleston Ms **SW1** 126 G2
Eccleston Pl **SW1** 127 H3
Eccleston Sq **SW1** 127 H3
Eccleston Sq Ms **SW1** 127 H3
Eccleston St **SW1** 126 G2
Eckford St **N1** 123 N4
Eckstein Rd **SW11** 126 E10
Edbrooke Rd **W9** 122 A6
Eddystone Twr **SE8** 129 J3
Edenbridge Rd **E9** 125 H2
Edenvale St **SW6** 126 B8
Edgar Kail Way **SE22** 128 C10
Edgar Rd **E3** 125 M5
Edgeley Rd **SW4** 127 K9
Edgware Rd **W2** 122 E8
Edinburgh Gate **SW1** 126 F1
Edinburgh Ho **W9** 122 C5
Edis St **NW1** 122 G3
Edith Gro **SW10** 126 C5
Edith Row **SW6** 126 B7
Edith St **E2** 124 E4
Edith Ter **SW10** 126 C6
Edithna St **SW9** 127 L9
Edmeston Cl **E9** 125 J1
Edmund St **SE5** 128 B6
Edna St **SW11** 126 E7
Edric Rd **SE14** 129 H6
Edrich Ho **SW4** 127 L7
Edward Pl **SE8** 129 K5
Edward St **SE8** 129 K5
Edward St **SE14** 129 J6
Edwardes Sq **W8** 126 A2
Edwards Ms **N1** 123 N2
Edwards Ms **W1** 122 G8
Edwin St **E1** 124 G6
Effie Pl **SW6** 126 A6
Effie Rd **SW6** 126 A6
Effra Rd **SW2** 127 N10
Egbert St **NW1** 122 G3
Egerton Cres **SW3** 126 E3
Egerton Dr **SE10** 129 M7
Egerton Gdns **SW3** 126 E2
Egerton Gdns Ms **SW3** 126 E2
Egerton Pl **SW3** 126 E2
Egerton Ter **SW3** 126 E2
Egmont St **SE14** 129 H6
Elam Cl **SE5** 127 P8
Elam St **SE5** 127 P8
Eland Rd **SW11** 126 F9
Elbe St **SW6** 126 C8
Elcho St **SW11** 126 E6
Elcot Av **SE15** 128 F6
Elder St **E1** 124 D7
Eldon Rd **W8** 126 B2
Eldon St **EC2** 124 B7
Eleanor Cl **SE16** 129 H1
Eleanor Rd **E8** 124 F2
Eleanor St **E3** 125 L5
Electric Av **SW9** 127 N10
Electric La **SW9** 127 N10
Elephant & Castle **SE1** 127 P3
Elephant La **SE16** 128 G1
Elephant Rd **SE17** 128 A3
Elf Row **E1** 124 G9
Elgar St **SE16** 129 J2
Elgin Av **W9** 122 B5
Elia Ms **N1** 123 P4
Elia St **N1** 123 P4
Elias Pl **SW8** 127 N5
Elim Est **SE1** 128 C2
Eliot Hill **SE13** 129 N8
Eliot Ms **NW8** 122 C4
Eliot Pk **SE13** 129 N9
Eliot Vale **SE3** 129 P8
Elizabeth Av **N1** 124 A2
Elizabeth Br **SW1** 127 H3
Elizabeth Est **SE17** 128 B5
Elizabeth Ms **NW3** 122 E1
Elizabeth St **SW1** 126 G3
Elland Rd **SE15** 128 G10
Ellen St **E1** 124 E8
Ellerdale St **SE13** 129 M10
Ellery St **SE15** 128 F8
Ellesmere Rd **E3** 125 J4
Ellesmere St **E14** 125 M8
Ellingfort Rd **E8** 124 F2
Ellington St **N7** 123 N1
Elliott Rd **SW9** 127 P6
Elliott Sq **NW3** 122 E2
Elliotts Row **SE11** 127 P3
Ellis St **SW1** 126 F3
Ellsworth St **E2** 124 F5
Elm Friars Wk **NW1** 123 K2
Elm Gro **SE15** 128 D8
Elm Pk Gdns **SW10** 126 D4
Elm Pk La **SW3** 126 D4
Elm Pk Rd **SW3** 126 D5
Elm Pl **SW7** 126 D4
Elm Quay Ct **SW8** 127 K5
Elm St **WC1** 123 M6
Elm Tree Cl **NW8** 122 D5
Elm Tree Rd **NW8** 122 D5
Elmfield Way **W9** 122 A7
Elmhurst St **SW4** 127 K9
Elmington Est **SE5** 128 B6
Elmington Rd **SE5** 128 B7
Elmira St **SE13** 129 M9
Elmore St **N1** 124 A2
Elms Ms **W2** 122 D9
Elmslie Pt **E3** 125 K7
Elmstone Rd **SW6** 126 A7
Elmwood Ct **SW11** 127 H7
Elrington Rd **E8** 124 E1
Elsa St **E1** 125 J7
Elsdale St **E9** 124 G1
Elsie Rd **SE22** 128 D10
Elsley Rd **SW11** 126 F9
Elspeth Rd **SW11** 126 F10
Elsted St **SE17** 128 B3
Elswick Rd **SE13** 129 M8
Elswick St **SW6** 126 C8
Elsworthy Ri **NW3** 122 E2
Elsworthy Rd **NW3** 122 E3
Elsworthy Ter **NW3** 122 E2
Elthiron Rd **SW6** 126 A7
Elton Ho **E3** 125 K3
Eltringham St **SW18** 126 C10
Elvaston Ms **SW7** 126 C2
Elvaston Pl **SW7** 126 C2
Elverson Ms **SE8** 129 M8
Elverson Rd **SE8** 129 M8
Elverton St **SW1** 127 K3
Elwin St **E2** 124 E5
Elystan Pl **SW3** 126 E4
Elystan St **SW3** 126 E3
Emba St **SE16** 128 E1
Embankment Gdns **SW3** 126 F5
Embankment Pl **WC2** 123 L10
Emberton **SE5** 128 C5
Embleton Rd **SE13** 129 M9
Emden St **SW6** 126 B7
Emerald St **WC1** 123 M7
Emerson St **SE1** 124 A10
Emery Hill St **SW1** 127 J2
Emma St **E2** 124 F4
Emmott Cl **E1** 125 J6
Emperor's Gate **SW7** 126 B2
Empire Wf Rd **E14** 129 P3
Empress Ms **SE5** 128 A8
Empress Pl **SW6** 126 A4
Empress St **SE17** 128 A5
Empson St **E3** 125 M6
Emu Rd **SW8** 127 H8
Endell St **WC2** 123 L8
Endsleigh Gdns **WC1** 123 K6
Endsleigh Pl **WC1** 123 K6
Endsleigh St **WC1** 123 K6
Endwell Rd **SE4** 129 J8
Enfield Rd **N1** 124 C2
Enford St **W1** 122 F7
Engate St **SE13** 129 N10
Englands La **NW3** 122 F1
Englefield Rd **N1** 124 B1
English St **E3** 125 K6
Enid St **SE16** 128 D2
Ennerdale Ho **E3** 125 K6
Ennismore Gdns **SW7** 126 E1
Ennismore Gdns Ms **SW7** 126 E2
Ennismore Ms **SW7** 126 E1
Ennismore St **SW7** 126 E2
Ensign St **E1** 124 E9
Enterprise Way **SW18** 126 A10
Enterprize Way **SE8** 129 K3
Epirus Ms **SW6** 126 A6
Epping Cl **E14** 129 L3
Epworth St **EC2** 124 B6
Erasmus St **SW1** 127 K3
Eresby Pl **NW6** 122 A2
Eric St **E3** 125 K6
Erlanger Rd **SE14** 129 H7
Ermine Rd **SE13** 129 M9
Ernest St **E1** 125 H6
Errol St **EC1** 124 A6
Erskine Rd **NW3** 122 F2
Esmeralda Rd **SE1** 128 E3
Essendine Rd **W9** 122 A6
Essex Rd **N1** 123 P3
Essex Vil **W8** 126 A1
Essian St **E1** 125 J7
Este Rd **SW11** 126 E9
Esterbrooke St **SW1** 127 K3
Ethelburga St **SW11** 126 E7
Ethnard Rd **SE15** 128 F5
Eton Av **NW3** 122 D2
Eton Coll Rd **NW3** 122 F1
Eton Rd **NW3** 122 F2
Eton Vil **NW3** 122 F1
Etta St **SE8** 129 J5
Ettrick St **E14** 125 N8
Eugenia Rd **SE16** 128 G3
Eustace Rd **SW6** 126 A6
Euston Gro **NW1** 123 K5
Euston Rd **N1** 123 K6
Euston Rd **NW1** 123 H6
Euston Sq **NW1** 123 K5
Euston St **NW1** 123 J5
Euston Twr **NW1** 123 J6
Evandale Rd **SW9** 127 N8
Evelina Rd **SE15** 128 G9
Eveline Lowe Est **SE16** 128 E2
Evelyn Gdns **SW7** 126 D4
Evelyn St **SE8** 129 J4
Evelyn Wk **N1** 124 B4
Everest Pl **E14** 125 N7
Evergreen Sq **E8** 124 D2
Everilda St **N1** 123 M3
Eversholt St **NW1** 123 J4
Eversleigh Rd **SW11** 126 F9
Everthorpe Rd **SE15** 128 D9
Evesham Wk **SW9** 127 N8
Evesham Way **SW11** 126 G9
Ewe Cl **N7** 123 L1
Ewer St **SE1** 124 A10
Ewhurst Cl **E1** 124 G7
Excelsior Gdns **SE13** 129 N8
Exchange Sq **EC2** 124 C7
Exeter St **WC2** 123 L9
Exeter Way **SE14** 129 K6
Exhibition Rd **SW7** 126 D2
Exmouth Mkt **EC1** 123 N6
Exmouth Pl **E8** 124 F2
Exon St **SE17** 128 C4
Exton St **SE1** 123 N10
Eythorne Rd **SW9** 127 N7
Ezra St **E2** 124 D5

F

Fairbairn Grn **SW9** 127 N7
Faircharm Trd Est **SE8** 129 M6
Fairclough St **E1** 124 E8
Fairfax Pl **NW6** 122 C2
Fairfax Rd **NW6** 122 C2
Fairfield Rd **E3** 125 L4
Fairfoot Rd **E3** 125 L6
Fairhazel Gdns **NW6** 122 B1
Fakruddin St **E1** 124 E6
Falcon Ct **EC4** 123 N8
Falcon Gro **SW11** 126 E9
Falcon La **SW11** 126 E9
Falcon Rd **SW11** 126 E8
Falcon Ter **SW11** 126 E9
Falcon Way **E14** 129 M3
Falkirk Ho **W9** 122 B5
Falkirk St **N1** 124 C4
Falmouth Rd **SE1** 128 A2
Fann St **EC1** 124 A6
Fann St **EC2** 124 A6
Fanshaw St **N1** 124 C5
Farm La **SW6** 126 A5
Farm St **W1** 123 H9
Farmers Rd **SE5** 127 P6
Farncombe St **SE16** 128 E1
Farnham Royal **SE11** 127 M4
Farrance St **E14** 125 K8
Farrell Ho **E1** 124 G8
Farrier St **NW1** 123 H2
Farrier Wk **SW10** 126 C5
Farringdon La **EC1** 123 N6
Farringdon Rd **EC1** 123 N6
Farringdon St **EC4** 123 P7
Farrins Rents **SE16** 125 J10
Farrow La **SE14** 128 G6
Farthingale Wk **E15** 125 P2
Fashion St **E1** 124 D7
Fassett Rd **E8** 124 E1
Fassett Sq **E8** 124 E1
Faulkner St **SE14** 128 G7
Favart Rd **SW6** 126 A7
Fawcett Cl **SW11** 126 D8
Fawcett St **SW10** 126 C5
Fawe St **E14** 125 M7
Feathers Pl **SE10** 129 P5
Featherstone St **EC1** 124 B6
Featley Rd **SW9** 127 P9
Fellows Ct **E2** 124 D4
Fellows Rd **NW3** 122 D2
Felstead St **E9** 125 K1
Felton St **N1** 124 B3
Fenchurch Av **EC3** 124 C8
Fenchurch St **EC3** 124 C9
Fendall St **SE1** 128 C2
Fenham Rd **SE15** 128 E6
Fentiman Rd **SW8** 127 L5
Fenton Cl **SW9** 127 M8
Fenwick Gro **SE15** 128 E9
Fenwick Pl **SW9** 127 L9
Fenwick Rd **SE15** 128 E9
Ferdinand St **NW1** 122 G1
Ferguson Cl **E14** 129 L3
Fern St **E3** 125 L6
Ferndale Rd **SW4** 127 L10
Ferndale Rd **SW9** 127 M9
Ferndene Rd **SE24** 128 A10
Fernshaw Rd **SW10** 126 C5
Ferrey Ms **SW9** 127 N8
Ferrier St **SW18** 126 B10
Ferris Rd **SE22** 128 E10
Ferry St **E14** 129 N4
Ferryman's Quay **SW6** 126 C8
Fetter La **EC4** 123 N8
Ffinch St **SE8** 129 L6
Field St **WC1** 123 M5
Fieldgate St **E1** 124 E7
Fielding Ho **NW6** 122 A5
Fielding St **SE17** 128 A5
Fields Est **E8** 124 E2
Fife Ter **N1** 123 M4
Finborough Rd **SW10** 126 B4
Finch Ms **SE15** 128 D6
Finchley Pl **NW8** 122 D4
Finchley Rd **NW3** 122 C1
Finchley Rd **NW8** 122 D3
Findhorn St **E14** 125 N8
Finland Rd **SE4** 129 J9
Finland St **SE16** 129 J2
Finnis St **E2** 124 F5
Finsbury Circ **EC2** 124 B7
Finsbury Est **EC1** 123 N5
Finsbury Mkt **EC2** 124 C6
Finsbury Pavement **EC2** 124 B7
Finsbury Sq **EC2** 124 B7
Finsbury St **EC2** 124 B7
Finsen Rd **SE5** 128 A9
Fir Trees Cl **SE16** 125 J10
Firbank Rd **SE15** 128 F8
First St **SW3** 126 E3
Fish St Hill **EC3** 124 B9
Fisher St **WC1** 123 M7
Fishermans Dr **SE16** 129 H1
Fisherman's Wk **E14** 125 L10
Fisherton St **NW8** 122 D6
Fitzalan St **SE11** 127 M3
Fitzgerald Ho **E14** 125 M8
Fitzhardinge St **W1** 122 G8
Fitzmaurice Pl **W1** 123 H9
Fitzroy Rd **NW1** 122 G3
Fitzroy Sq **W1** 123 J6
Fitzroy St **W1** 123 J6
Fitzwilliam Rd **SW4** 127 J9
Fiveways Rd **SW9** 127 N8
Flamborough St **E14** 125 J8
Flanders Way **E9** 125 H1
Flaxman Rd **SE5** 127 P8
Flaxman Ter **WC1** 123 K5
Fleet St **EC4** 123 N8
Fleming Rd **SE17** 127 P5
Fleur de Lis St **E1** 124 C6
Flint St **SE17** 128 B3
Flinton St **SE17** 128 C4
Flodden Rd **SE5** 128 A7
Flood St **SW3** 126 E4
Flood Wk **SW3** 126 E5
Flora Cl **E14** 125 M8
Floral St **WC2** 123 L9
Florence Rd **SE14** 129 K7
Florence St **N1** 123 P2
Florence Ter **SE14** 129 K7
Florida St **E2** 124 E5
Flower Wk, The **SW7** 126 C1
Foley St **W1** 123 J7
Folgate St **E1** 124 C7
Follett St **E14** 125 N8
Folly Wall **E14** 129 N1
Fontarabia Rd **SW11** 126 G10
Ford Rd **E3** 125 J3
Ford Sq **E1** 124 F7
Ford St **E3** 125 J3
Fordham St **E1** 124 E8
Fore St **EC2** 124 A7
Foreign St **SE5** 127 P8
Foreshore **SE8** 129 K3
Forest Gro **E8** 124 D2
Forest Rd **E8** 124 D1
Forester Rd **SE15** 128 F10
Forfar Rd **SW11** 126 G7
Formosa St **W9** 122 B7
Forset St **W1** 122 E8
Forsyth Gdns **SE17** 127 P5
Fort Rd **SE1** 128 D3
Forthbridge Rd **SW11** 126 G10
Fortune St **EC1** 124 A6
Fossil Rd **SE13** 129 L9
Foster La **EC2** 124 A8
Foubert's Pl **W1** 123 J8
Foulis Ter **SW7** 126 D4
Foundry Cl **SE16** 125 J10
Fount St **SW8** 127 K6
Fountain Ms **NW3** 122 F1
Fountain Pl **SW9** 127 N7
Fountain Sq **SW1** 127 H3
Four Seasons Cl **E3** 125 L4
Fournier St **E1** 124 D7
Fowler Cl **SW11** 126 D9
Fownes St **SW11** 126 E9
Fox Cl **E1** 124 G6
Foxberry Rd **SE4** 129 J9
Foxcote **SE5** 128 C4
Foxley Rd **SW9** 127 N6
Foxmore St **SW11** 126 F7
Foxwell St **SE4** 129 J9
Frampton Pk Rd **E9** 124 G1
Frampton St **NW8** 122 D6
Francis Chichester Way **SW11** 126 G7
Francis St **SW1** 127 J3
Frankham St **SE8** 129 L6
Frankland Cl **SE16** 128 F2
Franklin Cl **SE13** 129 M7
Franklin Pl **SE13** 129 M7
Franklin's Row **SW3** 126 F4
Frazier St **SE1** 127 N1
Frean St **SE16** 128 E2
Frederick Cl **W2** 122 E9
Frederick Cres **SW9** 127 P6
Frederick St **WC1** 123 M5
Freedom St **SW11** 126 F8
Freemantle St **SE17** 128 C4
Freke Rd **SW11** 126 G9
Fremont St **E9** 124 G3
Frendsbury Rd **SE4** 129 J10
Frensham St **SE15** 128 E5
Frere St **SW11** 126 E8
Freshfield Av **E8** 124 D2
Friars Mead **E14** 129 N2
Friary Est **SE15** 128 E5
Friary Rd **SE15** 128 E6
Friday St **EC4** 124 A8
Friend St **EC1** 123 P5
Friendly St **SE8** 129 L7
Frimley Way **E1** 125 H6
Friston St **SW6** 126 B8
Frith St **W1** 123 K8

Henry Dent Cl

Frogley Rd SE22 128 D10
Frognal Ct NW3 122 C1
Frome St N1 124 A4
Frostic Wk E1 124 D7
Froude St SW8 127 H8
Fulford St SE16 128 F1
Fulham Bdy SW6 126 A6
Fulham Rd SW3 126 C5
Fulham Rd SW10 126 B6
Fulmead St SW6 126 B7
Fulwood Pl WC1 123 M7
Furley Rd SE15 128 E6
Furlong Rd N7 123 N1
Furness Rd SW6 126 B8
Furnival St EC4 123 N8
Furze St E3 125 L7
Fyfield Rd SW9 127 N9
Fynes St SW1 127 K3

G

Gables Cl SE5 128 C7
Gabrielle Ct NW3 122 D1
Gainsford St SE1 128 D1
Gairloch Rd SE5 128 C8
Gaisford St NW5 123 J1
Gaitskell Ct SW11 126 E8
Galbraith St E14 129 N2
Gale St E3 125 L7
Gales Gdns E2 124 F5
Galleywall Rd SE16 128 F3
Galsworthy Av E14 125 J7
Galway St EC1 124 A5
Gambetta St SW8 127 H8
Garden Rd NW8 122 C5
Garden Row SE1 127 P2
Garden St E1 125 H7
Gardens, The SE22 128 E10
Garfield Rd SW11 126 G9
Garford St E14 125 L9
Garlick Hill EC4 124 A9
Garnet St E1 124 G9
Garnies Cl SE15 128 D6
Garrick Cl SW18 126 C10
Garrick St WC2 123 L9
Garsington Ms SE4 129 K9
Gartons Way SW11 126 C9
Garway Rd W2 122 B8
Gascoigne Pl E2 124 D5
Gascony Av NW6 122 A2
Gascoyne Rd E9 125 H2
Gaselee St E14 125 N9
Gaskell St SW4 127 L8
Gaskin St N1 123 P3
Gataker St SE16 128 F2
Gate Ms SW7 126 E1
Gateforth St NW8 122 E6
Gateley Rd SW9 127 M9
Gateway SE17 128 A5
Gateways, The SW3 126 F3
Gatliff Rd SW1 126 G4
Gatonby St SE15 128 D7
Gauden Cl SW4 127 K9
Gauden Rd SW4 127 K8
Gautrey Rd SE15 128 G8
Gawber St E2 124 G5
Gay Rd E15 125 P4
Gaydon Ho W2 122 B7
Gayfere St SW1 127 L2
Gayhurst Rd E8 124 E2
Gaywood Est SE1 127 P2
Gedling Pl SE1 128 D1
Gee St EC1 124 A6
Geffrye St E2 124 D4
Geldart Rd SE15 128 F6
Gellatly Rd SE14 128 G8
General Wolfe Rd SE10 129 P7
Geneva Dr SW9 127 N10
Geoffrey Cl SE5 128 A8
Geoffrey Rd SE4 129 K9
George Beard Rd SE8 129 K3
George Mathers Rd SE11 127 P3
George Row SE16 128 E1
George St W1 122 G8
George Yd W1 122 G9
Georgiana St NW1 123 J3
Gerald Rd SW1 126 G3
Geraldine St SE11 127 P2
Gerards Cl SE16 128 G4
Gernon Rd E3 125 J4
Gerrard Rd N1 123 P4
Gerrard St W1 123 K9
Gerridge St SE1 127 N2
Gertrude St SW10 126 C5
Gervase St SE15 128 F6
Gibbins Rd E15 125 N2
Gibbon Rd SE15 128 G8
Gibraltar Wk E2 124 D5
Gibson Rd SE11 127 M3
Gibson Sq N1 123 N3
Gideon Rd SW11 126 G9
Giffin St SE8 129 L6
Gifford St N1 123 L2
Gilbert Rd SE11 127 N3
Gilbert St W1 122 G8
Gilbeys Yd NW1 122 G2
Gill St E14 125 K8
Gillender St E3 125 N6
Gillender St E14 125 N6
Gillfoot NW1 123 J4
Gilling Ct NW3 122 E1
Gillingham St SW1 127 H3
Gilmore Rd SE13 129 P10
Gilstead Rd SW6 126 B8
Gilston Rd SW10 126 C4
Giltspur St EC1 123 P8
Giraud St E14 125 M8
Gladstone St SE1 127 P2
Gladys Rd NW6 122 A2
Glaisher St SE8 129 L5
Glamis Pl E1 124 G9
Glamis Rd E1 124 G9
Glasgow Ho W9 122 B4
Glasgow Ter SW1 127 J4
Glasshill St SE1 127 P1
Glasshouse Flds E1 125 H9
Glasshouse St W1 123 J9
Glasshouse Wk SE11 127 L4
Glaucus St E3 125 M7
Glebe Pl SW3 126 E5
Gledhow Gdns SW5 126 C3
Glenaffric Av E14 129 P3
Glendall St SW9 127 M10
Glendower Pl SW7 126 D3
Glenfinlas Way SE5 127 P6
Glengall Causeway E14 129 L2
Glengall Gro E14 129 M2
Glengall Rd SE15 128 D5
Glengall Ter SE15 128 D5
Glengarnock Av E14 129 N3
Glenilla Rd NW3 122 E1
Glenloch Rd NW3 122 E1
Glenmore Rd NW3 122 E1
Glenrosa St SW6 126 C8
Glensdale Rd SE4 129 K9
Glentworth St NW1 122 F6
Glenville Gro SE8 129 K6
Glenworth Av E14 129 P3
Globe Pond Rd SE16 125 J10
Globe Rd E1 124 G5
Globe Rd E2 124 G5
Globe Rope Wk E14 129 N3
Globe St SE1 128 A2
Gloucester Av NW1 122 G2
Gloucester Circ SE10 129 N6
Gloucester Cres NW1 123 H3
Gloucester Gate NW1 123 H4
Gloucester Gro Est SE15 128 C5
Gloucester Ho NW6 122 A4
Gloucester Ms W2 122 C8
Gloucester Pl NW1 122 F6
Gloucester Pl W1 122 F7
Gloucester Rd SW7 126 C2
Gloucester Sq W2 122 D8
Gloucester St SW1 127 J4
Gloucester Ter W2 122 D9
Gloucester Wk W8 126 A1
Gloucester Way EC1 123 N5
Glycena Rd SW11 126 F9
Godalming Rd E14 125 M7
Godfrey St E15 125 N4
Godfrey St SW3 126 E4
Goding St SE11 127 L4
Godliman St EC4 124 A8
Godman Rd SE15 128 F8
Godson St N1 123 N4
Goffers Rd SE3 129 P7
Golden Jubilee Br SE1 123 L10
Golden Jubilee Br WC2 123 L10
Golden La EC1 124 A6
Golden Sq W1 123 J9
Goldhurst Ter NW6 122 B2
Golding St E1 124 E8
Goldington Cres NW1 123 K4
Goldington St NW1 123 K4
Goldman Cl E2 124 E6
Goldney Rd W9 122 A6
Goldsboro Rd SW8 127 K7
Goldsmith Rd SE15 128 E7
Goldsmith's Row E2 124 E4
Goldsmith's Sq E2 124 E4
Goldsworthy Gdns SE16 128 G3
Goldwin Cl SE14 128 G7
Gomm Rd SE16 128 G2
Gonson St SE8 129 M5
Goodge St W1 123 J7
Goodhart Pl E14 125 J9
Goodinge Cl N7 123 L1
Goodman's Stile E1 124 E8
Goodmans Yd E1 124 D9
Goods Way NW1 123 L4
Goodway Gdns E14 125 P8
Goodwin Cl SE16 128 E2
Goodwood Rd SE14 129 J6
Gopsall St N1 124 B3
Gordon Gro SE5 127 P8
Gordon Pl W8 126 A1
Gordon Rd SE15 128 F8
Gordon Sq WC1 123 K6
Gordon St WC1 123 K6
Gore Rd E9 124 G3
Gore St SW7 126 C2
Gorefield Pl NW6 122 A4
Goring St EC3 124 C8
Gorsuch St E2 124 D5
Gosfield St W1 123 J7
Gosling Way SW9 127 N7
Gosset St E2 124 D5
Gosterwood St SE8 129 J5
Goswell Rd EC1 123 P5
Gough Sq EC4 123 N8
Gough St WC1 123 M6
Goulden Ho App SW11 126 E8
Goulston St E1 124 D8
Gower Ms WC1 123 K7
Gower Pl WC1 123 J6
Gower St WC1 123 J6
Gower's Wk E1 124 E8
Gowlett Rd SE15 128 E9
Gowrie Rd SW11 126 G9
Grace St E3 125 M5
Gracechurch St EC3 124 B9
Grace's All E1 124 E9
Graces Ms SE5 128 C8
Graces Rd SE5 128 C8
Grafton Cres NW1 123 H1
Grafton Ho E3 125 L5
Grafton Pl NW1 123 K5
Grafton Sq SW4 127 J9
Grafton St W1 123 H9
Grafton Way W1 123 J6
Grafton Way WC1 123 J6
Graham Rd E8 124 D1
Graham St N1 123 P4
Graham Ter SW1 126 G3
Granary Rd E1 124 F6
Granary St NW1 123 K3
Granby St E2 124 D6
Granby Ter NW1 123 J4
Grand Junct Wf N1 124 A4
Grand Union Cres E8 124 E2
Grand Union Wk NW1 123 H2
Granfield St SW11 126 D7
Grange, The SE1 128 D2
Grange Gro N1 123 P1
Grange Pl NW6 122 A2
Grange Rd SE1 128 C2
Grange St N1 124 B3
Grange Wk SE1 128 C2
Grange Yd SE1 128 D2
Gransden Av E8 124 F2
Grant Rd SW11 126 D10
Grantbridge St N1 123 P4
Grantham Cen, The SW9 127 L8
Grantham Rd SW9 127 L8
Grantley St E1 125 H5
Grantully Rd W9 122 B5
Granville Ct N1 124 B3
Granville Gro SE13 129 N9
Granville Pk SE13 129 N9
Granville Pl W1 122 G8
Granville Rd NW6 122 A4
Granville Sq SE15 128 C6
Granville Sq WC1 123 M5
Grayling Sq E2 124 E5
Gray's Inn WC1 123 N7
Gray's Inn Rd WC1 123 M5
Grayshott Rd SW11 126 G8
Great Castle St W1 123 J8
Great Cen St NW1 122 F7
Great Chapel St W1 123 K8
Great Coll St SW1 127 L2
Great Cumberland Pl W1 122 F8
Great Dover St SE1 128 A1
Great Eastern Rd E15 125 P2
Great Eastern St EC2 124 C5
Great George St SW1 127 K1
Great Guildford St SE1 124 A10
Great James St WC1 123 M7
Great Marlborough St W1 123 J8
Great Maze Pond SE1 128 B1
Great Ormond St WC1 123 L7
Great Percy St WC1 123 M5
Great Peter St SW1 127 K2
Great Portland St W1 123 H6
Great Pulteney St W1 123 J9
Great Queen St WC2 123 L8
Great Russell St WC1 123 L7
Great St. Helens EC3 124 C8
Great Scotland Yd SW1 123 L10
Great Smith St SW1 127 K2
Great Suffolk St SE1 123 P10
Great Sutton St EC1 123 P6
Great Titchfield St W1 123 J8
Great Twr St EC3 124 C9
Great Winchester St EC2 124 B8
Great Windmill St W1 123 K9
Greatfield Cl SE4 129 L10
Greatorex St E1 124 E7
Greek St W1 123 K8
Green Bk E1 124 F10
Green Dale SE5 128 B10
Green Hundred Rd SE15 128 E5
Green St W1 122 G9
Greenberry St NW8 122 E4
Greencoat Pl SW1 127 J3
Greencroft Gdns NW6 122 B2
Greenfield Rd E1 124 E7
Greenham Cl SE1 127 N1
Greenland Quay SE16 129 H3
Greenland Rd NW1 123 J3
Greenman St N1 124 A2
Greenwell St W1 123 H6
Greenwich Ch St SE10 129 N5
Greenwich Foot Tunnel E14 129 N4
Greenwich Foot Tunnel SE10 129 N4
Greenwich High Rd SE10 129 M7
Greenwich Pk St SE10 129 P4
Greenwich Quay SE8 129 M5
Greenwich S St SE10 129 M7
Greenwich Vw Pl E14 129 M2
Greenwood Ct SW1 127 J4
Greenwood Rd E8 124 E1
Greet St SE1 123 N10
Gregory Pl W8 126 B1
Grenade St E14 125 K9
Grendon St NW8 122 E6
Grenville Ms SW7 126 C3
Grenville Pl SW7 126 C2
Grenville St WC1 123 L6
Gresham Rd SW9 127 N9
Gresham St EC2 124 A8
Gresse St W1 123 K7
Greville Hall NW6 122 B4
Greville Pl NW6 122 B4
Greville Rd NW6 122 B3
Greville St EC1 123 N7
Grey Eagle St E1 124 D7
Greycoat Pl SW1 127 K2
Greycoat St SW1 127 K2
Grimwade Cl SE15 128 G9
Grinling Pl SE8 129 L5
Grinstead Rd SE8 129 J4
Grittleton Rd W9 122 A6
Groom Pl SW1 126 G2
Groombridge Rd E9 125 H2
Grosvenor Cres SW1 126 G1
Grosvenor Cres Ms SW1 126 G1
Grosvenor Est SW1 127 K3
Grosvenor Gdns SW1 127 H2
Grosvenor Gate W1 122 F9
Grosvenor Hill W1 123 H9
Grosvenor Pk SE5 128 A5
Grosvenor Pl SW1 126 G1
Grosvenor Rd SW1 127 H5
Grosvenor Sq W1 122 G9
Grosvenor St W1 123 H9
Grosvenor Ter SE5 127 P6
Grosvenor Wf Rd E14 129 P3
Grove Cotts SW3 126 E5
Grove Cres Rd E15 125 P1
Grove End Rd NW8 122 D5
Grove Hill Rd SE5 128 C9
Grove La SE5 128 B7
Grove Pk SE5 128 C8
Grove Pas E2 124 F4
Grove Rd E3 125 H3
Grove St SE8 129 K3
Grove Vale SE22 128 C10
Grove Vil E14 125 M9
Grovelands Cl SE5 128 C8
Groveway SW9 127 M7
Grummant Rd SE15 128 D7
Grundy St E14 125 M8
Guerin Sq E3 125 K5
Guildford Gro SE10 129 M7
Guildford Rd SW8 127 L7
Guildhouse St SW1 127 J3
Guilford Pl WC1 123 M6
Guilford St WC1 123 L6
Guinness Cl E9 125 J2
Guinness Trust Bldgs SE11 127 P4
Guinness Trust Bldgs SW9 127 P10
Gulliver St SE16 129 K2
Gun St E1 124 D7
Gunmakers La E3 125 J3
Gunter Gro SW10 126 C5
Gunthorpe St E1 124 D7
Gunwhale Cl SE16 125 H10
Gurney Rd SW6 126 C9
Gutter La EC2 124 A8
Guy St SE1 128 B1
Gwyn Cl SW6 126 C6
Gwynne Rd SW11 126 D8
Gylcote Cl SE5 128 B10

H

Haberdasher St N1 124 B5
Hackford Rd SW9 127 M7
Hackford Wk SW9 127 M7
Hackney Rd E2 124 D5
Haddo St SE10 129 M5
Haddonfield SE8 129 H3
Hadleigh St E2 124 G6
Hadley St NW1 123 H1
Hadrian Est E2 124 E4
Hafer Rd SW11 126 F10
Haggerston Rd E8 124 D2
Hainford Cl SE4 129 H10
Hainton Cl E1 124 F8
Halcomb St N1 124 C3
Hale St E14 125 M9
Halesworth Rd SE13 129 M9
Half Moon Cres N1 123 M4
Half Moon St W1 123 H10
Halford Rd SW6 126 A5
Halkin Arc SW1 126 F2
Halkin Pl SW1 126 G2
Halkin St SW1 126 G1
Hall Pl W2 122 D6
Hall Rd NW8 122 C5
Hall St EC1 123 P5
Hall Twr W2 122 D7
Hallam St W1 123 H7
Halley Gdns SE13 129 P10
Halley St E14 125 J7
Hallfield Est W2 122 C8
Halliford St N1 124 A2
Halsey St SW3 126 F3
Halsmere Rd SE5 127 P7
Halton Cross St N1 123 P3
Halton Rd N1 123 P2
Hamble St SW6 126 B9
Hamilton Cl NW8 122 D5
Hamilton Gdns NW8 122 C5
Hamilton Pl W1 122 G10
Hamilton Ter NW8 122 B4
Hamlet, The SE5 128 B9
Hamlets Way E3 125 K6
Hammond St NW5 123 J1
Hampson Way SW8 127 M7
Hampstead Rd NW1 123 J4
Hampton Cl NW6 122 A5
Hampton St SE1 127 P3
Hampton St SE17 127 P3
Hanbury St E1 124 D7
Hancock Rd E3 125 N5
Hand Ct WC1 123 M7
Handel St WC1 123 L6
Handforth Rd SW9 127 N6
Handley Rd E9 124 G2
Hankey Pl SE1 128 B1
Hannibal Rd E1 124 G7
Hannington Rd SW4 127 H9
Hanover Gdns SE11 127 N5
Hanover Gate NW1 122 E5
Hanover Pk SE15 128 E7
Hanover Sq W1 123 H8
Hanover St W1 123 H8
Hanover Ter NW1 122 E5
Hans Cres SW1 126 F2
Hans Pl SW1 126 F2
Hans Rd SW3 126 F2
Hanson St W1 123 J7
Hanway St W1 123 K8
Harben Rd NW6 122 C2
Harbet Rd W2 122 D7
Harbinger Rd E14 129 M3
Harbledown Rd SW6 126 A7
Harbour Av SW10 126 C7
Harbour Ex Sq E14 129 M1
Harbour Rd SE5 128 A9
Harbut Rd SW11 126 D10
Harcourt Rd SE4 129 J10
Harcourt St W1 122 E7
Harcourt Ter SW10 126 B4
Harders Rd SE15 128 F8
Hardinge St E1 124 G8
Hardwick St EC1 123 N5
Hare & Billet Rd SE3 129 P7
Hare Row E2 124 F4
Hare Wk N1 124 C4
Harecourt Rd N1 124 A1
Haredale Rd SE24 128 A10
Harefield Ms SE4 129 K9
Harefield Rd SE4 129 K9
Harewood Av NW1 122 E6
Harfield Gdns SE5 128 C9
Harford St E1 125 J6
Hargwyne St SW9 127 M9
Harlescott Rd SE15 129 H10
Harley Gdns SW10 126 C4
Harley Gro E3 125 K5
Harley Pl W1 123 H7
Harley Rd NW3 122 D2
Harley St W1 123 H6
Harleyford Rd SE11 127 M5
Harleyford St SE11 127 N5
Harmood St NW1 123 H2
Harmsworth St SE17 127 P4
Harold Est SE1 128 C2
Harold Pl SE11 127 N4
Harper Rd SE1 128 A2
Harpley Sq E1 124 G5
Harpsden St SW11 126 G7
Harpur St WC1 123 M7
Harrap St E14 125 N9
Harriet Cl E8 124 E3
Harriet Wk SW1 126 F1
Harrington Gdns SW7 126 B3
Harrington Rd SW7 126 D3
Harrington Sq NW1 123 J4
Harrington St NW1 123 J5
Harris St SE5 128 B6
Harrison St WC1 123 L5
Harrow La E14 125 N9
Harrow Pl E1 124 C8
Harroway Rd SW11 126 D8
Harrowby St W1 122 E8
Harrowgate Rd E9 125 J1
Hartfield Ter E3 125 L4
Hartington Rd SW8 127 L7
Hartlake Rd E9 125 H1
Hartland Rd NW1 123 H2
Hartley St E2 124 G5
Harton St SE8 129 L7
Harts La SE14 129 J6
Harvey Rd SE5 128 B7
Harvey St N1 124 B3
Harwood Rd SW6 126 A6
Harwood Ter SW6 126 B7
Haselrigge Rd SW4 127 K10
Hasker St SW3 126 E3
Haslam Cl N1 123 N2
Haslam St SE15 128 D6
Hassett Rd E9 125 H1
Hastings Cl SE15 128 E6
Hastings St WC1 123 L5
Hatcham Pk Rd SE14 129 H7
Hatcham Rd SE15 128 G5
Hatfields SE1 123 P10
Hatherley Gro W2 122 B8
Hathorne Cl SE15 128 F8
Hatton Gdn EC1 123 N7
Hatton Pl EC1 123 N6
Hatton Wall EC1 123 N7
Haul Rd NW1 123 L4
Havannah St E14 129 L1
Havelock St N1 123 L3
Havelock Ter SW8 127 H6
Haverfield Rd E3 125 J5
Haverstock St N1 123 P4
Havil St SE5 128 C6
Hawes St N1 123 P2
Hawgood St E3 125 L7
Hawkstone Rd SE16 128 G3
Hawley Cres NW1 123 H2
Hawley Rd NW1 123 H2
Hawley St NW1 123 H2
Hawthorn Av E3 125 K3
Hawthorne Cl N1 124 C1
Hawtrey Rd NW3 122 E2
Hay Currie St E14 125 M8
Hay Hill W1 123 H9
Hay St E2 124 E3
Haydon Way SW11 126 D10
Hayes Gro SE15 128 D10
Hayles St SE11 127 P3
Haymarket SW1 123 K9
Haymerle Rd SE15 128 E5
Hay's Galleria SE1 124 C10
Hay's Ms W1 123 H9
Hazel Cl SE15 128 E8
Hazelmere Rd NW6 122 A3
Hazlebury Rd SW6 126 B8
Head St E1 125 H8
Headfort Pl SW1 126 G1
Headlam St E1 124 F6
Heald St SE14 129 K7
Healey St NW1 123 H1
Hearn St EC2 124 C6
Heath La SE3 129 P8
Heath Rd SW8 127 H8
Heathcote St WC1 123 M6
Heather Cl SW8 127 H9
Heathwall St SW11 126 F9
Heaton Rd SE15 128 E9
Heddon St W1 123 J9
Hedgers Gro E9 125 J1
Heiron St SE17 127 P5
Helmet Row EC1 124 A6
Helmsley Pl E8 124 F2
Helsinki Sq SE16 129 J2
Hemans St SW8 127 K6
Hemberton Rd SW9 127 L9
Hemingford Rd N1 123 M3
Hemming St E1 124 E6
Hemp Wk SE17 128 B3
Hemstal Rd NW6 122 A2
Hemsworth St N1 124 C4
Heneage St E1 124 D7
Henley Dr SE1 128 D3
Henley St SW11 126 G8
Henning St SW11 126 E7
Henrietta Cl SE8 129 L5
Henrietta Pl W1 123 H8
Henrietta St WC2 123 L9
Henriques St E1 124 E8
Henry Dent Cl SE5 128 B9

Henshall St

Henshall St **N1** 124 B1
Henshaw St **SE17** 128 B3
Henstridge Pl **NW8** 122 E4
Henty Cl **SW11** 126 E6
Hepscott Rd **E9** 125 L2
Herbal Hill **EC1** 123 N6
Herbert St **NW5** 122 G1
Herbrand St **WC1** 123 L6
Hercules Rd **SE1** 127 M2
Hereford Ho **NW6** 122 A4
Hereford Rd **W2** 122 A8
Hereford Sq **SW7** 126 C3
Hereford St **E2** 124 E6
Heritage Cl **SW9** 127 P9
Hermit St **EC1** 123 P5
Hermitage St **W2** 122 D7
Hermitage Wall **E1** 124 E10
Herne Hill Rd **SE24** 128 A9
Heron Pl **SE16** 125 J10
Heron Quay **E14** 125 L10
Heron Rd **SE24** 128 A10
Herrick St **SW1** 127 K3
Hertford Rd **N1** 124 C3
Hertford St **W1** 123 H10
Hertsmere Rd **E14** 125 L9
Hesper Ms **SW5** 126 B4
Hesperus Cres **E14** 129 M3
Hessel St **E1** 124 F8
Hester Rd **SW11** 126 E6
Heston St **SE14** 129 K7
Hetherington Rd **SW4** 127 L10
Hewison St **E3** 125 K4
Hewlett Rd **E3** 125 J4
Heyford Av **SW8** 127 L6
Heygate St **SE17** 128 A3
Hibbert St **SW11** 126 C9
Hickmore Wk **SW4** 127 J9
Hicks Cl **SW11** 126 E9
Hicks St **SE8** 129 J4
Hide Pl **SW1** 127 K3
Hide Twr **SW1** 127 K3
High Br **SE10** 129 P4
High Br Wf **SE10** 129 P4
High Holborn **WC1** 123 L8
High St **E15** 125 N4
High Timber St **EC4** 124 A9
Highbury Cor **N5** 123 N1
Highbury Gro **N5** 123 P1
Highbury Pl **N5** 123 P1
Highbury Sta Rd **N1** 123 N1
Highshore Rd **SE15** 128 D8
Highway, The **E1** 124 F9
Highway, The **E14** 124 F9
Hilary Cl **SW6** 126 B6
Hilda Ter **SW9** 127 N8
Hildyard Rd **SW6** 126 A5
Hilgrove Rd **NW6** 122 C2
Hill Rd **NW8** 122 C4
Hill St **W1** 123 H10
Hillbeck Cl **SE15** 128 G6
Hillgate Pl **W8** 122 A10
Hillgate St **W8** 122 A10
Hillingdon St **SE5** 127 P6
Hillingdon St **SE17** 127 P6
Hillman St **E8** 124 F1
Hillmead Dr **SW9** 127 P10
Hillside Cl **NW8** 122 B4
Hilltop Rd **NW6** 122 A2
Hilly Flds Cres **SE4** 129 L9
Hillyard St **SW9** 127 N7
Hinckley Rd **SE15** 128 E10
Hind Gro **E14** 125 L8
Hinde St **W1** 122 G8
Hinton Rd **SE24** 127 P9
Hitchin Sq **E3** 125 J4
Hobart Pl **SW1** 127 H2
Hobday St **E14** 125 M7
Hobury St **SW10** 126 C5
Hodnet Gro **SE16** 129 H3
Hogarth Rd **SW5** 126 B3
Holbeck Row **SE15** 128 E6
Holbein Ms **SW1** 126 G4
Holbein Pl **SW1** 126 G3
Holborn **EC1** 123 N7
Holborn Viaduct **EC1** 123 N7
Holcroft Rd **E9** 124 G2
Holden St **SW11** 126 G8
Holford St **WC1** 123 N5
Holgate Av **SW11** 126 D9
Holland Gro **SW9** 127 N6
Holland St **SE1** 123 P10
Holland St **W8** 126 A1
Hollen St **W1** 123 J8
Holles St **W1** 123 H8
Holly Gro **SE15** 128 D8
Holly St **E8** 124 D1
Hollybush Gdns **E2** 124 F5
Hollydale Rd **SE15** 128 G7
Hollydene **SE15** 128 F7
Hollymount Cl **SE10** 129 N7
Hollywood Rd **SW10** 126 C5
Holman Rd **SW11** 126 D8
Holmead Rd **SW6** 126 B6
Holmefield Ct **NW3** 122 E1
Holmes Ter **SE1** 127 N1
Holms St **E2** 124 E4
Holton St **E1** 125 H6
Holwood Pl **SW4** 127 K10
Holyhead Cl **E3** 125 L5
Holywell La **EC2** 124 C6
Holywell Row **EC2** 124 C6
Home Rd **SW11** 126 E8
Homefield St **N1** 124 C4
Homer Dr **E14** 129 L3
Homer Rd **E9** 125 J1
Homer Row **W1** 122 E7
Homer St **W1** 122 E7
Hooper St **E1** 124 E8
Hope St **SW11** 126 D9
Hopewell St **SE5** 128 B6
Hopton Gdns **SE1** 123 P10
Hopton St **SE1** 123 P10
Hopwood Rd **SE17** 128 B5
Horatio St **E2** 124 D4
Horbury Cres **W11** 122 A9
Horle Wk **SE5** 127 P8
Hornby Cl **NW3** 122 D2
Hornshay St **SE15** 128 G5
Hornton Pl **W8** 126 A1
Hornton St **W8** 122 A10
Horse Guards Av **SW1** 123 L10
Horse Guards Rd **SW1** 123 K10
Horse Ride **SW1** 123 J10
Horseferry Pl **SE10** 129 N5
Horseferry Rd **E14** 125 J9
Horseferry Rd **SW1** 127 K3
Horselydown La **SE1** 128 D1
Horseshoe Cl **E14** 129 N4
Horsley St **SE17** 128 B5
Hortensia Rd **SW10** 126 C6
Horton Rd **E8** 124 F1
Horton St **SE13** 129 M9
Hosier La **EC1** 123 P7
Hoskins St **SE10** 129 P4
Hotspur St **SE11** 127 N4
Houndsditch **EC3** 124 C8
Howbury Rd **SE15** 128 G9
Howden St **SE15** 128 E9
Howick Pl **SW1** 127 J2
Howie St **SW11** 126 E6
Howitt Rd **NW3** 122 E1
Howland Est **SE16** 128 G2
Howland St **W1** 123 J7
Howland Way **SE16** 129 J1
Howley Pl **W2** 122 C7
Hows St **E2** 124 D4
Howson Rd **SE4** 129 J10
Hoxton Sq **N1** 124 C5
Hoxton St **N1** 124 C3
Hubert Gro **SW9** 127 L9
Huddart St **E3** 125 K7
Huddleston Cl **E2** 124 G4
Hugh St **SW1** 127 H3
Hugon Rd **SW6** 126 B9
Huguenot Pl **E1** 124 D7
Hull Cl **SE16** 129 H1
Humphrey St **SE1** 128 D4
Hungerford Br **SE1** 123 L10
Hungerford Br **WC2** 123 L10
Hunsdon Rd **SE14** 129 H5
Hunter St **WC1** 123 L6
Huntingdon St **N1** 123 M2
Huntley St **WC1** 123 J6
Hunton St **E1** 124 E6
Hunts La **E15** 125 N4
Huntsman St **SE17** 128 B3
Hurlingham Business Pk **SW6** 126 A9
Hurlingham Sq **SW6** 126 B9
Huson Cl **NW3** 122 E2
Hutchings St **E14** 129 L1
Hyde Pk **SW7** 122 E10
Hyde Pk **W1** 122 E10
Hyde Pk **W2** 122 E10
Hyde Pk Cor **W1** 126 G1
Hyde Pk Cres **W2** 122 E8
Hyde Pk Gdns **W2** 122 D9
Hyde Pk Gate **SW7** 126 C1
Hyde Pk Pl **W2** 122 E9
Hyde Pk Sq **W2** 122 E8
Hyde Pk St **W2** 122 E8
Hyde Rd **N1** 124 B3
Hyde Vale **SE10** 129 N6
Hyndman St **SE15** 128 F5

I

Iceland Rd **E3** 125 L3
Ida St **E14** 125 N8
Idonia St **SE8** 129 K6
Ifield Rd **SW10** 126 B5
Ilchester Gdns **W2** 122 B9
Ilderton Rd **SE15** 128 G6
Ilderton Rd **SE16** 128 F4
Iliffe St **SE17** 127 P4
Ilminster Gdns **SW11** 126 E10
Imber St **N1** 124 B3
Imperial Coll Rd **SW7** 126 D2
Imperial Rd **SW6** 126 B7
Imperial Sq **SW6** 126 B7
Imperial St **E3** 125 N5
Imperial Wf **SW6** 126 C8
Indescon Ct **E14** 129 M1
Ingate Pl **SW8** 127 H7
Ingelow Rd **SW8** 127 H8
Ingleborough St **SW9** 127 N8
Inglesham Wk **E9** 125 K1
Ingleton St **SW9** 127 N8
Inglewood Cl **E14** 129 L3
Inglis St **SE5** 127 P7
Ingrave St **SW11** 126 D9
Inkerman Rd **NW5** 123 H1
Inner Circle **NW1** 122 G5
Inverness Pl **W2** 122 B9
Inverness St **NW1** 123 H3
Inverness Ter **W2** 122 B9
Inverton Rd **SE15** 129 H10
Inville Rd **SE17** 128 B4
Inwen Ct **SE8** 129 J4
Inworth St **SW11** 126 E8
Ireland Yd **EC4** 123 P8
Irene Rd **SW6** 126 A7
Ironmonger Row **EC1** 124 A5
Irving Gro **SW9** 127 M8
Irving St **WC2** 123 K9
Isabel St **SW9** 127 M7
Isabella St **SE1** 123 P10
Isambard Ms **E14** 129 N2
Island Row **E14** 125 K8
Islington Grn **N1** 123 P3
Islington High St **N1** 123 P4
Islington Pk St **N1** 123 N2
Ivanhoe Rd **SE5** 128 D9
Iveagh Cl **E9** 125 H3
Iveley Rd **SW4** 127 J8
Iverna Ct **W8** 126 A2
Iverna Gdns **W8** 126 A2
Ives St **SW3** 126 E3
Ivimey St **E2** 124 E5
Ivor Pl **NW1** 122 F6
Ivor St **NW1** 123 J2
Ivy Rd **SE4** 129 K10
Ivy St **N1** 124 C4
Ivydale Rd **SE15** 129 H9
Ixworth Pl **SW3** 126 E4

J

Jacaranda Gro **E8** 124 D2
Jackman St **E8** 124 F3
Jackson Cl **E9** 124 G2
Jacob St **SE1** 128 D1
Jago Wk **SE5** 128 B6
Jamaica Rd **SE1** 128 D1
Jamaica Rd **SE16** 128 D1
Jamaica St **E1** 124 G8
James St **W1** 122 G8
Jameson Ct **E2** 124 G4
Jameson St **W8** 122 A10
Jamestown Rd **NW1** 123 H3
Jamestown Way **E14** 125 P9
Jamuna Cl **E14** 125 J7
Janet St **E14** 129 L2
Janeway St **SE16** 128 E1
Jardine Rd **E1** 125 H9
Jarrow Rd **SE16** 128 G3
Jay Ms **SW7** 126 C1
Jebb St **E3** 125 L4
Jedburgh St **SW11** 126 G10
Jeffreys Rd **SW4** 127 L8
Jeffreys St **NW1** 123 H2
Jeffreys Wk **SW4** 127 L8
Jeger Av **E2** 124 D3
Jerdan Pl **SW6** 126 A6
Jeremiah St **E14** 125 M8
Jermyn St **SW1** 123 K9
Jerningham Rd **SE14** 129 J8
Jerome Cres **NW8** 122 E6
Jerrard St **SE13** 129 M9
Jewry St **EC3** 124 D8
Jew's Row **SW18** 126 B10
Joan St **SE1** 123 P10
Jocelyn St **SE15** 128 E7
Jockey's Flds **WC1** 123 M7
Jodane St **SE8** 129 K3
Jodrell Rd **E3** 125 K3
John Adam St **WC2** 123 L9
John Aird Ct **W2** 122 C7
John Carpenter St **EC4** 123 P9
John Felton Rd **SE16** 128 E1
John Fisher St **E1** 124 E9
John Islip St **SW1** 127 L3
John Maurice Cl **SE17** 128 B3
John Penn St **SE13** 129 M7
John Princes St **W1** 123 H8
John Roll Way **SE16** 128 E2
John Ruskin St **SE5** 127 P6
John Silkin La **SE8** 129 H4
John Spencer Sq **N1** 123 P1
John St **WC1** 123 M6
John Williams Cl **SE14** 129 H5
John's Ms **WC1** 123 M6
Johnson Cl **E8** 124 E3
Johnson's Pl **SW1** 127 J4
Jonathan St **SE11** 127 M4
Joseph Hardcastle Cl **SE14** 129 H6
Joseph St **E3** 125 K6
Joubert St **SW11** 126 F8
Jowett St **SE15** 128 D6
Jubilee Cres **E14** 129 N2
Jubilee Pl **SW3** 126 E4
Jubilee St **E1** 124 G8
Judd St **WC1** 123 L5
Juer St **SW11** 126 E6
Julian Pl **E14** 129 M4
Junction App **SE13** 129 N9
Junction App **SW11** 126 E9
Juniper Cres **NW1** 122 G2
Juniper St **E1** 124 G9
Juno Way **SE14** 129 H5
Jupiter Way **N7** 123 M1
Jupp Rd **E15** 125 P2
Jupp Rd W **E15** 125 N3
Juxon St **SE11** 127 M3

K

Kambala Rd **SW11** 126 D8
Kassala Rd **SW11** 126 F7
Kathleen Rd **SW11** 126 F9
Kay Rd **SW9** 127 L8
Kay St **E2** 124 E4
Kean St **WC2** 123 M8
Keel Cl **SE16** 125 H10
Keeley St **WC2** 123 M8
Keetons Rd **SE16** 128 F2
Keildon Rd **SW11** 126 F10
Kellett Rd **SW2** 127 N10
Kelly Av **SE15** 128 D6
Kelly St **NW1** 123 H1
Kelman Cl **SW4** 127 K8
Kelmore Gro **SE22** 128 E10
Kelsey St **E2** 124 F6
Kelso Pl **W8** 126 B2
Kelson Ho **E14** 129 N2
Kelvedon Ho **SW8** 127 L7
Kemble St **WC2** 123 M8
Kemerton Rd **SE5** 128 A9
Kempsford Gdns **SW5** 126 A4
Kempsford Rd **SE11** 127 N3
Kempson Rd **SW6** 126 A7
Kempthorne Rd **SE8** 129 J3
Kenbury St **SE5** 128 A8
Kenchester Cl **SW8** 127 L6
Kendal Cl **SW9** 127 P6
Kendal St **W2** 122 E8
Kender St **SE14** 128 G6
Kendoa Rd **SW4** 127 K10
Kendrick Pl **SW7** 126 D3
Kenilworth Rd **E3** 125 J4
Kennard Rd **E15** 125 P2
Kennard St **SW11** 126 G8
Kennet St **E1** 124 E10
Kenning Ter **N1** 124 C3
Kennings Way **SE11** 127 N4
Kennington La **SE11** 127 M4
Kennington Oval **SE11** 127 M5
Kennington Pk **SW9** 127 N6
Kennington Pk Gdns **SE11** 127 P5
Kennington Pk Pl **SE11** 127 N5
Kennington Pk Rd **SE11** 127 N5
Kennington Rd **SE1** 127 N2
Kennington Rd **SE11** 127 N3
Kensington Ch Ct **W8** 126 B1
Kensington Ch St **W8** 122 A10
Kensington Ch Wk **W8** 126 B1
Kensington Ct **W8** 126 B1
Kensington Ct Pl **W8** 126 B2
Kensington Gdns **W2** 122 C10
Kensington Gdns Sq **W2** 122 B8
Kensington Gate **W8** 126 C2
Kensington Gore **SW7** 126 D1
Kensington High St **W8** 126 A2
Kensington Mall **W8** 122 A10
Kensington Palace Gdns **W8** 122 B10
Kensington Pl **W8** 122 A10
Kensington Rd **SW7** 126 D1
Kensington Rd **W8** 126 B1
Kensington Sq **W8** 126 B1
Kent Pas **NW1** 122 F5
Kent St **E2** 124 D4
Kent Ter **NW1** 122 E5
Kentish Town Rd **NW1** 123 H2
Kentish Town Rd **NW5** 123 H2
Kenton Rd **E9** 125 H1
Kenton St **WC1** 123 L6
Kentwell Cl **SE4** 129 J10
Kenway Rd **SW5** 126 B3
Kenwyn Rd **SW4** 127 K10
Kepler Rd **SW4** 127 L10
Keppel St **WC1** 123 K7
Kerbey St **E14** 125 M8
Kerfield Cres **SE5** 128 B7
Kerfield Pl **SE5** 128 B7
Kerridge Ct **N1** 124 C1
Kerrison Rd **E15** 125 P3
Kerrison Rd **SW11** 126 E9
Kerry Path **SE14** 129 K5
Kerry Rd **SE14** 129 K5
Kersley Ms **SW11** 126 F8
Kersley St **SW11** 126 F8
Keston Rd **SE15** 128 E9
Kestrel Ho **EC1** 123 P5
Kevan Ho **SE5** 128 A6
Key Cl **E1** 124 F6
Keybridge Ho **SW8** 127 L5
Keyworth St **SE1** 127 P2
Khyber Rd **SW11** 126 E8
Kibworth St **SW8** 127 M6
Kilburn Pk Rd **NW6** 122 A5
Kilburn Pl **NW6** 122 A3
Kilburn Priory **NW6** 122 B3
Kilburn Sq **NW6** 122 A3
Kildare Gdns **W2** 122 A8
Kildare Ter **W2** 122 A8
Kilkie St **SW6** 126 C8
Killick St **N1** 123 M4
Killowen Rd **E9** 125 H1
Killyon Rd **SW8** 127 J8
Killyon Ter **SW8** 127 J8
Kilner St **E14** 125 L7
Kimberley Av **SE15** 128 F8
Kimberley Rd **SW9** 127 L8
Kimpton Rd **SE5** 128 B7
Kinburn St **SE16** 129 H1
Kincaid Rd **SE15** 128 F6
King & Queen St **SE17** 128 A4
King Arthur Cl **SE15** 128 G6
King Charles St **SW1** 127 K1
King David La **E1** 124 G9
King Edward St **EC1** 124 A8
King Edward Wk **SE1** 127 N2
King Edwards Rd **E9** 124 F3
King Frederik IX Twr **SE16** 129 K2
King George St **SE10** 129 N6
King Henry's Rd **NW3** 122 E2
King Henry's Wk **N1** 124 C1
King James St **SE1** 127 P1
King John St **E1** 125 H7
King St **EC2** 124 A8
King St **SW1** 123 J10
King St **WC2** 123 L9
King William St **EC4** 124 B9
King William Wk **SE10** 129 N5
Kingdon Rd **NW6** 122 A1
Kingfield St **E14** 129 N3
Kingfisher Ms **SE13** 129 M10
Kingfisher Sq **SE8** 129 K5
Kinglake St **SE17** 128 C4
Kingly St **W1** 123 J8
Kings Coll Rd **NW3** 122 E2
King's Cross Rd **WC1** 123 M5
Kings Gro **SE15** 128 F6
King's Ms **WC1** 123 M7
King's Reach Twr **SE1** 123 N10
King's Rd **SW1** 126 F4
King's Rd **SW3** 126 F4
King's Rd **SW6** 126 B7
King's Rd **SW10** 126 B7
Kingsbury Rd **N1** 124 C1
Kingsbury Ter **N1** 124 C1
Kingsgate Pl **NW6** 122 A2
Kingsgate Rd **NW6** 122 A2
Kingshold Rd **E9** 124 G2
Kingsland Grn **E8** 124 C1
Kingsland Rd **E2** 124 C4
Kingsland Rd **E8** 124 C4
Kingsland Shop Cen **E8** 124 D1
Kingsley St **SW11** 126 F9
Kingsmill Ter **NW8** 122 D4
Kingstown St **NW1** 122 G3
Kingsway **WC2** 123 M8
Kingswood Cl **SW8** 127 L6
Kinnerton St **SW1** 126 G1
Kinsale Rd **SE15** 128 E9
Kipling Est **SE1** 128 B1
Kipling St **SE1** 128 B1
Kirby Est **SE16** 128 F2
Kirby Gro **SE1** 128 C1
Kirkland Wk **E8** 124 D1
Kirkwall Pl **E2** 124 G5
Kirkwood Rd **SE15** 128 F8
Kirtling St **SW8** 127 J6
Kirwyn Way **SE5** 127 P6
Kitcat Ter **E3** 125 L5
Kitson Rd **SE5** 128 B6
Kitto Rd **SE14** 129 H8
Knapp Rd **E3** 125 L6
Knaresborough Pl **SW5** 126 B3
Knatchbull Rd **SE5** 128 A7
Kneller Rd **SE4** 129 J10
Knighten St **E1** 124 E10
Knighthead Pt **E14** 129 L2
Knightsbridge **SW1** 126 F1
Knightsbridge **SW7** 126 E1
Knivet Rd **SW6** 126 A5
Knobs Hill Rd **E15** 125 M3
Knottisford St **E2** 124 G5
Knowle Cl **SW9** 127 N9
Knowles Wk **SW4** 127 J9
Knowsley Rd **SW11** 126 F8
Knox St **W1** 122 F7
Knoyle St **SE14** 129 J5
Kylemore Rd **NW6** 122 A2
Kynance Ms **SW7** 126 B2
Kynance Pl **SW7** 126 C2

L

Laburnum St **E2** 124 D3
Lacey Wk **E3** 125 L4
Lackington St **EC2** 124 B7
Lacon Rd **SE22** 128 E10
Ladycroft Rd **SE13** 129 M9
Lafone St **SE1** 128 D1
Lagado Ms **SE16** 125 H10
Laird Ho **SE5** 128 A6
Lamb La **E8** 124 F2
Lamb St **E1** 124 D7
Lambert St **N1** 123 N2
Lambeth Br **SE1** 127 L3
Lambeth Br **SW1** 127 L3
Lambeth High St **SE1** 127 M3
Lambeth Hill **EC4** 124 A9
Lambeth Palace Rd **SE1** 127 M2
Lambeth Rd **SE1** 127 M3
Lambeth Rd **SE11** 127 M3
Lambeth Wk **SE11** 127 M3
Lambolle Pl **NW3** 122 E1
Lambolle Rd **NW3** 122 E1
Lambourn Rd **SW4** 127 H9
Lamb's Conduit St **WC1** 123 M6
Lamb's Pas **EC1** 124 B7
Lamerton St **SE8** 129 L5
Lammas Rd **E9** 125 H2
Lamont Rd **SW10** 126 C5
Lanark Pl **W9** 122 C6
Lanark Rd **W9** 122 B4
Lanark Sq **E14** 129 M2
Lanbury Rd **SE15** 129 H10
Lancaster Dr **NW3** 122 E1
Lancaster Gate **W2** 122 C9
Lancaster Gro **NW3** 122 D1
Lancaster Ms **W2** 122 C9
Lancaster Pl **WC2** 123 M9
Lancaster St **SE1** 127 P1
Lancaster Ter **W2** 122 D9
Lancaster Wk **W2** 122 C10
Lancelot Pl **SW7** 126 F1
Lanchester Way **SE14** 128 G7
Lancresse Ct **N1** 124 C3
Landmann Way **SE14** 129 H5
Landon Pl **SW1** 126 F2
Landons Cl **E14** 125 N10
Landor Rd **SW9** 127 L9
Lanfranc Rd **E3** 125 J4
Lang St **E1** 124 G6
Langbourne Pl **E14** 129 M4
Langdale Cl **SE17** 128 A5
Langdale Rd **SE10** 129 N6
Langford Ct **NW8** 122 C4
Langford Grn **SE5** 128 C9
Langford Pl **NW8** 122 C4
Langford Rd **SW6** 126 B8
Langham Pl **W1** 123 H7
Langham St **W1** 123 H7
Langley La **SW8** 127 M5
Langley St **WC2** 123 L8
Langton Rd **SW9** 127 P6
Langton St **SW10** 126 C5
Langtry Rd **NW8** 122 B3
Lanhill Rd **W9** 122 A6
Lanrick Rd **E14** 125 P8
Lansbury Est **E14** 125 M8
Lansbury Gdns **E14** 125 P8
Lanscombe Wk **SW8** 127 L7
Lansdowne Dr **E8** 124 E1
Lansdowne Gdns **SW8** 127 L7
Lansdowne Ter **WC1** 123 L6
Lansdowne Way **SW8** 127 K7
Lant St **SE1** 128 A1
Lanterns Ct **E14** 129 L1
Lanvanor Rd **SE15** 128 G8
Larcom St **SE17** 128 A3
Lark Row **E2** 124 G3
Larkhall La **SW4** 127 K8
Larkhall Ri **SW4** 127 J9
Lassell St **SE10** 129 P4
Latchmere Rd **SW11** 126 F8
Latchmere St **SW11** 126 F8
Latham Ho **E1** 125 H8
Latona Rd **SE15** 128 E5
Lauderdale Rd **W9** 122 B5
Lauderdale Twr **EC2** 124 A7
Launceston Pl **W8** 126 C2
Launch St **E14** 129 N2
Laurel St **E8** 124 D1
Laurie Gro **SE14** 129 J7
Lauriston Rd **E9** 125 H3
Lausanne Rd **SE15** 128 G7
Lavender Gdns **SW11** 126 F10

Name	Page	Grid
Lavender Gro E8	124	D2
Lavender Hill SW11	126	E10
Lavender Rd SE16	125	J10
Lavender Rd SW11	126	D9
Lavender Sweep SW11	126	F10
Lavender Wk SW11	126	F10
Laverton Pl SW5	126	B3
Lavington St SE1	123	P10
Law St SE1	128	B2
Lawford Rd N1	124	C2
Lawford Rd NW5	123	N1
Lawless St E14	125	M9
Lawn Ho Cl E14	129	N1
Lawn La SW8	127	L5
Lawrence Cl E3	125	L4
Lawrence St SW3	126	E5
Lawson Est SE1	128	B2
Lawton Rd E3	125	J5
Laxley Cl SE5	127	P6
Layard Rd SE16	128	F3
Layard Sq SE16	128	F3
Laycock St N1	123	N1
Laystall St EC1	123	N6
Lea Valley Wk E3	125	N6
Lea Valley Wk E14	125	M7
Lea Valley Wk E15	125	N5
Leabank Sq E9	125	L1
Leadenhall St EC3	124	C8
Leake St SE1	127	M1
Leamouth Rd E14	125	P8
Leander Ct SE8	129	L7
Leather La EC1	123	N7
Leathermarket Ct SE1	128	C1
Leathermarket St SE1	128	C1
Leathwaite Rd SW11	126	F10
Leathwell Rd SE8	129	M8
Lecky St SW7	126	D4
Ledbury St SE15	128	F6
Ledbury St SE15	128	E6
Lee Br SE13	129	N9
Lee High Rd SE12	129	P9
Lee High Rd SE13	129	P9
Lee St E8	124	D3
Leeke St WC1	123	M5
Leerdam Dr E14	129	N2
Lees Pl W1	122	G9
Leeson Rd SE24	127	N10
Leeway SE8	129	K4
Lefevre Wk E3	125	K3
Leggatt Rd E15	125	N4
Legion Cl N1	123	N1
Leicester Sq WC2	123	K9
Leigh St WC1	123	L6
Leinster Gdns W2	122	C8
Leinster Ms W2	122	C9
Leinster Pl W2	122	C8
Leinster Sq W2	122	A8
Leinster Ter W2	122	C9
Leman St E1	124	D8
Lendal Ter SW4	127	K9
Lennox Gdns SW1	126	F2
Lennox Gdns Ms SW1	126	F2
Lenthall Rd E8	124	E2
Leo St SE15	128	F6
Leonard St EC2	124	B6
Leontine Cl SE15	128	E6
Leopold St E3	125	K7
Leroy St SE1	128	C3
Lethbridge Cl SE13	129	N7
Lett Rd E15	125	P2
Lettsom St SE5	128	C8
Levehurst Way SW4	127	L8
Leven Rd E14	125	N7
Lever St EC1	123	P5
Lewey Ho E3	125	K6
Lewis Gro SE13	129	N9
Lewis St NW1	123	H1
Lewisham Cen SE13	129	N9
Lewisham High St SE13	129	N9
Lewisham Hill SE13	129	N8
Lewisham Rd SE13	129	M7
Lewisham Way SE4	129	K7
Lewisham Way SE14	129	K7
Lexham Gdns W8	126	B2
Lexham Gdns Ms W8	126	B2
Lexham Ms W8	126	A3
Lexington St W1	123	J8
Leybourne Rd NW1	123	H2
Leylang Rd SE14	129	H6
Liardet St SE14	129	J5
Liberia Rd N5	123	P1
Liberty St SW9	127	M7
Libra Rd E3	125	K3
Library St SE1	127	P1
Lichfield Rd E3	125	J5
Lidcote Gdns SW9	127	N8
Liddell Rd NW6	122	A1
Lidlington Pl NW1	123	J4
Lighter Cl SE16	129	J3
Lighterman Ms E1	125	H8
Lightermans Rd E14	129	L1
Lilac Pl SE11	127	M3
Lilestone St NW8	122	E6
Lilford Rd SE5	127	P8
Lillie Yd SW6	126	A5
Lillieshall Rd SW4	127	H9
Lily Pl EC1	123	N7
Limburg Rd SW11	126	F10
Lime Cl E1	124	E10
Lime St EC3	124	C9
Limeburner La EC4	123	P8
Limehouse Causeway E14	125	K9
Limehouse Flds Est E14	125	J7
Limehouse Link E14	125	J9
Limerston St SW10	126	C5
Limes Gro SE13	129	N10
Limes Wk SE15	128	F10
Limesford Rd SE15	129	H10
Linacre Ct SE15	128	F9
Linberry Wk SE8	129	K3
Lincoln St SW3	126	F3
Lincoln's Inn WC2	123	N8
Lincoln's Inn Flds WC2	123	M8
Lind St SE8	129	M8
Linden Gdns W2	122	A9
Linden Gro SE15	128	F9
Lindfield St E14	125	L8
Lindley St E1	124	G7
Lindore Rd SW11	126	F10
Lindrop St SW6	126	C8
Lindsay Sq SW1	127	K4
Lindsell St SE10	129	N7
Lindsey Ms N1	124	A2
Lindsey St EC1	123	P7
Linford St SW8	127	J7
Lingards Rd SE13	129	N10
Lingham St SW9	127	L8
Linhope St NW1	122	F6
Link St E9	124	G1
Linnell Rd SE5	128	C8
Linom Rd SW4	127	L10
Linsey St SE16	128	E3
Linstead St NW6	122	A2
Linton St N1	124	A3
Linver Rd SW6	126	A8
Linwood Cl SE5	128	D8
Lisford St SE15	128	D7
Lisle St WC2	123	K9
Lisson Grn Est NW8	122	E6
Lisson Gro NW1	122	E6
Lisson Gro NW8	122	D5
Lisson St NW1	122	E7
Liston Rd SW4	127	J9
Litchfield St WC2	123	K9
Lithos Rd NW3	122	B1
Little Boltons, The SW5	126	B4
Little Boltons, The SW10	126	B4
Little Britain EC1	123	P7
Little Chester St SW1	127	H2
Little Dorrit Ct SE1	128	A1
Little Newport St WC2	123	K9
Little Portland St W1	123	H8
Little Russell St WC1	123	L7
Little St. James's St SW1	123	J10
Littlebury Rd SW4	127	K9
Livermere Rd E8	124	D3
Liverpool Gro SE17	128	B4
Liverpool Rd N1	123	N4
Liverpool St EC2	124	C7
Livingstone Rd E15	125	N3
Livingstone Wk SW11	126	D9
Lizard St EC1	124	A5
Lloyd Baker St WC1	123	M5
Lloyd Sq WC1	123	N5
Lloyd St WC1	123	N5
Lloyd's Av EC3	124	C8
Loampit Hill SE13	129	L8
Loampit Vale SE13	129	M9
Lochnagar St E14	125	N7
Lockart Cl N7	123	M1
Lockhart St E3	125	K6
Lockington Rd SW8	127	H7
Lockmead Rd SE13	129	N9
Locksley Est E14	125	K8
Locksley St E14	125	K7
Lockwood Sq SE16	128	F2
Loddiges Rd E9	124	G2
Loder St SE15	128	G7
Lodge Rd NW8	122	D5
Lodore St E14	125	N8
Loftie St SE16	128	E1
Lofting Rd N1	123	M2
Logan Ms W8	126	A3
Logan Pl W8	126	A3
Lollard St SE11	127	M3
Loman St SE1	127	P1
Lomas Dr E8	124	D2
Lomas St E1	124	E7
Lombard Rd SW11	126	D8
Lombard St EC3	124	B8
Lomond Gro SE5	128	B6
Loncroft Rd SE5	128	C5
London Br EC4	124	B10
London Br SE1	124	B10
London Br Wk SE1	124	B10
London Flds E Side E8	124	F2
London Flds W Side E8	124	E2
London La E8	124	F2
London Rd SE1	127	P2
London Silver Vaults WC2	123	N7
London St W2	122	D8
London Wall EC2	124	A7
Long Acre WC2	123	L9
Long La EC1	123	P7
Long La SE1	128	B1
Long Rd SW4	127	H10
Long St E2	124	D5
Long Yd WC1	123	M6
Longbeach Rd SW11	126	F9
Longfield Est SE1	128	D3
Longford St NW1	123	H6
Longhedge St SW11	126	G8
Longhope Cl SE15	128	C5
Longley St SE1	128	E3
Longmoore St SW1	127	J3
Longnor Rd E1	125	H5
Long's Ct WC2	123	K9
Longshore SE8	129	K3
Lonsdale Sq N1	123	N2
Lord Amory Way E14	129	N1
Lord Hills Rd W2	122	B7
Lord N St SW1	127	L2
Lorden Wk E2	124	E5
Lorenzo St WC1	123	M5
Lorn Rd SW9	127	N8
Lorrimore Rd SE17	127	P5
Lorrimore Sq SE17	127	P5
Lothbury EC2	124	B8
Lothian Rd SW9	127	P7
Lots Rd SW10	126	C6
Loudoun Rd NW8	122	C3
Lough Rd N7	123	M1
Loughborough Pk SW9	127	P10
Loughborough Rd SW9	127	N8
Loughborough St SE11	127	M4
Louisa St E1	125	H6
Louvaine Rd SW11	126	D10
Love La EC2	124	A8
Love Wk SE5	128	B8
Lovegrove St SE1	128	E4
Lovegrove Wk E14	125	N10
Lovelinch Cl SE15	128	G5
Lovell Ho E8	124	E2
Lover's Wk W1	122	G10
Lowden Rd SE24	127	P10
Lowell St E14	125	J8
Lower Belgrave St SW1	127	H2
Lower Grosvenor Pl SW1	127	H2
Lower Marsh SE1	127	N1
Lower Merton Ri NW3	122	E2
Lower Rd SE8	128	G2
Lower Rd SE16	128	G2
Lower Sloane St SW1	126	G3
Lower Thames St EC3	124	B9
Lowfield Rd NW6	122	A2
Lowndes Cl SW1	126	G2
Lowndes Pl SW1	126	G2
Lowndes Sq SW1	126	F1
Lowndes St SW1	126	G2
Lowth Rd SE5	128	A8
Lowther Gdns SW7	126	D1
Lubbock St SE14	128	G6
Lucan Pl SW3	126	E3
Lucas St SE8	129	L7
Lucey Rd SE16	128	E2
Lucey Way SE16	128	E2
Ludgate Hill EC4	123	P8
Ludgate Sq EC4	123	P8
Ludwick Ms SE14	129	J6
Lugard Rd SE15	128	F8
Luke Ho E1	124	F8
Luke St EC2	124	C6
Lukin St E1	124	G8
Lulworth Rd SE15	128	F8
Lupus St SW1	127	H5
Lurline Gdns SW11	126	G7
Luscombe Way SW8	127	L6
Luton Pl SE10	129	N6
Luton St NW8	122	D6
Luxborough St W1	122	G6
Luxford St SE16	129	H3
Luxmore St SE4	129	K7
Luxor St SE5	128	A9
Lyal Rd E3	125	J4
Lyall Ms SW1	126	G2
Lyall St SW1	126	G2
Lydney Cl SE15	128	C6
Lydon Rd SW4	127	J9
Lyme St NW1	123	J2
Lymington Rd NW6	122	B1
Lympstone Gdns SE15	128	E6
Lyncott Cres SW4	127	H10
Lyndhurst Gro SE15	128	C8
Lyndhurst Sq SE15	128	D7
Lyndhurst Way SE15	128	D7
Lynton Rd SE1	128	D3
Lyons Pl NW8	122	D6
Lytham St SE17	128	B4
Lyttelton Cl NW3	122	E2

M

Name	Page	Grid
Mabledon Pl WC1	123	K5
Mabley St E9	125	J1
Macaulay Ct SW4	127	H9
Macaulay Rd SW4	127	H9
Macaulay Sq SW4	127	H10
Macauley Ms SE13	129	N8
Macclesfield Br NW1	122	E4
Macclesfield Rd EC1	124	A5
Macclesfield St W1	123	K9
Macduff Rd SW11	126	G7
Mace St E2	125	H4
Machell Rd SE15	128	G9
Mackay Rd SW4	127	H9
Mackennal St NW8	122	E4
Mackenzie Rd N7	123	M1
Mackenzie Wk E14	125	L10
Macklin St WC2	123	L8
Macks Rd SE16	128	E3
Mackworth St NW1	123	J5
Macleod St SE17	128	A4
Maconochies Rd E14	129	M4
Macquarie Way E14	129	M3
Maddams St E3	125	M6
Maddock Way SE17	127	P5
Maddox St W1	123	H9
Madinah Rd E8	124	E1
Madras Pl N7	123	N1
Madrigal La SE5	127	P6
Madron St SE17	128	C4
Magdalen St SE1	124	C10
Magee St SE11	127	N5
Maguire St SE1	128	D1
Mahogany Cl SE16	125	J10
Maida Av W2	122	C7
Maida Vale W9	122	B4
Maiden La NW1	123	K2
Maiden La WC2	123	L9
Maidenstone Hill SE10	129	N7
Maitland Pk Est NW3	122	F1
Maitland Pk Rd NW3	122	F1
Maitland Pk Vil NW3	122	F1
Makins St SW3	126	E3
Malabar St E14	129	L1
Malcolm Pl E2	124	G6
Malcolm Rd E1	124	G6
Malden Cres NW1	122	G1
Malet Pl WC1	123	K6
Malet St WC1	123	K6
Malfort Rd SE5	128	C9
Mall, The E15	125	P2
Mall, The SW1	127	J1
Mallard Cl NW6	122	A4
Mallord St SW3	126	D5
Mallory Cl SE4	129	J10
Mallory St NW8	122	E6
Malmesbury Rd E3	125	K5
Malpas Rd E8	124	F1
Malpas Rd SE4	129	K8
Malt St SE1	128	E5
Malting Ho E14	125	K9
Maltings Pl SW6	126	B7
Malvern Rd E8	124	E2
Malvern Rd NW6	122	A5
Malvern Ter N1	123	N3
Manaton Cl SE15	128	F9
Manchester Gro E14	129	N4
Manchester Rd E14	129	N4
Manchester Sq W1	122	G8
Manchester St W1	122	G7
Manciple St SE1	128	B2
Mandela St NW1	123	J3
Mandela St SW9	127	N6
Mandela Way SE1	128	C3
Mandeville Pl W1	122	G8
Manette St W1	123	K8
Manger Rd N7	123	L1
Manilla St E14	129	L1
Manley St NW1	122	G3
Manor Av SE4	129	K8
Manor Est SE16	128	F3
Manor Gro SE15	128	G5
Manor Ms SE4	129	K8
Manor Pk SE13	129	P10
Manor Pl SE17	127	P4
Manresa Rd SW3	126	E4
Mansell St E1	124	D8
Mansfield St W1	123	H7
Mansford St E2	124	E4
Mansion Ho EC4	124	B8
Manson Ms SW7	126	C3
Manson Pl SW7	126	D3
Mantle Rd SE4	129	J9
Mantua St SW11	126	D9
Mantus Rd E1	124	G6
Maple St W1	123	J7
Mapledene Rd E8	124	D2
Maplin St E3	125	K5
Marble Arch W1	122	F9
Marble Quay E1	124	E10
Marcella Rd SW9	127	N8
Marchant St SE14	129	J5
Marchmont St WC1	123	L6
Marchwood Cl SE5	128	C6
Marcia Rd SE1	128	C3
Marcon Pl E8	124	F1
Marcus Garvey Way SE24	127	N10
Marden Sq SE16	128	F2
Mare St E8	124	F3
Margaret St W1	123	H8
Margaretta Ter SW3	126	E5
Margery St WC1	123	N5
Maria Ter E1	125	H7
Marian Pl E2	124	F4
Marigold St SE16	128	F1
Marinefield Rd SW6	126	B8
Mariners Ms E14	129	P3
Marischal Rd SE13	129	P9
Maritime Quay E14	129	L4
Maritime St E3	125	K6
Marjorie Gro SW11	126	F10
Mark La EC3	124	C9
Market Est N7	123	L1
Market Ms W1	123	H10
Market Pl W1	123	J8
Market Rd N7	123	L1
Markham Sq SW3	126	F4
Markham St SW3	126	E4
Marl Rd SW18	126	B10
Marlborough Av E8	124	E3
Marlborough Ct W8	126	A3
Marlborough Gro SE1	128	E4
Marlborough Hill NW8	122	C3
Marlborough Pl NW8	122	C4
Marlborough Rd SW1	123	J10
Marlborough St SW3	126	E3
Marloes Rd W8	126	B2
Marlow Way SE16	129	H1
Marlowes, The NW8	122	D3
Marmion Rd SW11	126	G10
Marmont Rd SE15	128	E7
Marney Rd SW11	126	G10
Maroon St E14	125	J7
Marquess Rd N1	124	B1
Marquis Rd NW1	123	K1
Marsala Rd SE13	129	M10
Marsden Rd SE15	128	D9
Marsden St NW5	122	G1
Marsh Wall E14	125	L10
Marshall St W1	123	J8
Marshalsea Rd SE1	128	A1
Marsham St SW1	127	K2
Marshfield St E14	129	N2
Marshgate La E15	125	M3
Marshgate Sidings E15	125	M3
Marsland Cl SE17	127	P4
Marston Cl NW6	122	C2
Martello St E8	124	F2
Martello Ter E8	124	F2
Martha St E2	125	H4
Martha St E1	124	G8
Martineau St E1	124	G9
Mary Ann Gdns SE8	129	L5
Mary Datchelor Cl SE5	128	B7
Mary Grn NW8	122	B3
Mary St N1	124	A3
Mary Ter NW1	123	H3
Marylands Rd W9	122	A6
Marylebone High St W1	122	G7
Marylebone La W1	122	G8
Marylebone Ms W1	123	H7
Marylebone Rd NW1	122	E7
Marylebone St W1	122	G7
Marylee Way SE11	127	M3
Maskelyne Cl SW11	126	E7
Mason St SE17	128	B3
Mason's Pl EC1	123	P5
Massingham St E1	125	H6
Mast Leisure Pk SE16	129	H2
Masterman Ho SE5	128	B6
Masters Dr SE16	128	F4
Masters St E1	125	H7
Masthouse Ter E14	129	L3
Mastmaker Rd E14	129	L1
Matham Gro SE22	128	D10
Matilda St N1	123	M3
Matlock Cl SE24	128	A10
Matlock St E14	125	J8
Matrimony Pl SW8	127	J8
Matthew Parker St SW1	127	K1
Matthews St SW11	126	F8
Maude Rd SE5	128	C7
Maunsel St SW1	127	K3
Maverton Rd E3	125	L3
Mawbey Est SE1	128	E4
Mawbey Pl SE1	128	D4
Mawbey St SW8	127	L6
Maxted Rd SE15	128	D9
Maxwell Rd SW6	126	B6
Maya Cl SE15	128	F8
Mayfair Pl W1	123	H10
Mayfield Rd E8	124	D2
Mayflower Rd SW9	127	L9
Mayflower St SE16	128	G1
Maygood St N1	123	M4
Maysoule Rd SW11	126	D10
Mazenod Av NW6	122	A2
McAuley Cl SE1	127	N2
McCullum Rd E3	125	K3
McDermott Cl SW11	126	E9
McDermott Rd SE15	128	E9
McDowall Rd SE5	128	A7
McEwen Way E15	125	P3
McKerrell Rd SE15	128	E7
McMillan St SE8	129	L5
McNeil Rd SE5	128	C8
Mead Pl E9	124	G1
Meadcroft Rd SE11	127	P5
Meadow Ms SW8	127	M5
Meadow Pl SW8	127	L6
Meadow Rd SW8	127	M5
Meadow Row SE1	128	A2
Meadowbank NW3	122	F2
Meakin Est SE1	128	C2
Meard St W1	123	K8
Meath St SW11	127	H7
Mecklenburgh Pl WC1	123	M6
Mecklenburgh Sq WC1	123	M6
Medburn St NW1	123	K4
Medlar St SE5	128	A7
Medley Rd NW6	122	A1
Medway Rd E3	125	J4
Medway St SW1	127	K2
Medwin St SW4	127	M10
Meeting Ho La SE15	128	F7
Mehetabel Rd E9	124	G1
Melba Way SE13	129	M7
Melbourne Gro SE22	128	C10
Melbourne Ms SW9	127	N7
Melbourne Pl WC2	123	M9
Melcombe Pl NW1	122	F7
Melcombe St NW1	122	F6
Melina Pl NW8	122	D5
Melior Pl SE1	128	B1
Melior St SE1	128	B1
Mellish St E14	129	L2
Melon Rd SE15	128	E7
Melton Ct SW7	126	D3
Melton St NW1	123	K5
Mendip Rd SW11	126	C9
Mentmore Ter E8	124	F2
Mepham St SE1	123	M10
Mercator Rd SE13	129	P10
Mercer St WC2	123	L8
Merceron St E1	124	F6
Merchant St E3	125	K5
Mercia Gro SE13	129	N10
Mercury Way SE14	129	H5
Mercy Ter SE13	129	M10
Meredith Ms SE4	129	K10
Meretone Cl SE4	129	J10
Meridian Gate E14	129	N1
Meridian Pl E14	129	M1
Meridian Sq E15	125	P2
Mermaid Ct SE1	128	B1
Mermaid Ct SE16	125	K10
Merriam Av E9	125	K1
Merrick Sq SE1	128	A2
Merrington Rd SW6	126	A5
Merrow St SE17	128	A5
Merton Ri NW3	122	E2
Mervan Rd SW2	127	N10
Messina Av NW6	122	A2
Meteor St SW11	126	G10
Methley St SE11	127	N4
Mews Deck E1	124	F9
Mews St E1	124	E10
Meymott St SE1	123	P10
Meynell Cres E9	125	H2
Meynell Gdns E9	125	H2
Meynell Rd E9	125	H2
Meyrick Rd SW11	126	D9
Micawber St N1	124	A5
Michael Rd SW6	126	B7
Micklethwaite Rd SW6	126	A5
Middle Fld NW8	122	D3
Middle Temple La EC4	123	N8
Middlesex St E1	124	C7
Middleton Dr SE16	129	H1
Middleton Rd E8	124	D2
Middleton St E2	124	F5
Midland Rd NW1	123	K4
Midship Pt E14	129	L1
Milborne Gro SW10	126	C4
Milborne St E9	124	G1
Milcote St SE1	127	P1
Mildmay Av N1	124	B1
Mildmay Pk N1	124	B1
Mile End Pl E1	125	H6
Mile End Rd E1	124	G7
Mile End Rd E3	124	G7

Name	Page	Grid
Miles St SW8	127	L5
Milford La WC2	123	M9
Milk Yd E1	124	C9
Milkwell Yd SE5	128	A7
Mill Row N1	124	C3
Mill St SE1	128	D1
Mill St W1	123	J9
Millbank SW1	127	L2
Millbank Twr SW1	127	L3
Millbrook Rd SW9	127	P9
Millender Wk SE16	128	G3
Millennium Br EC4	124	A9
Millennium Br SE1	124	A9
Millennium Dr E14	129	P3
Millennium Harbour E14	129	K1
Millennium Pl E2	124	F4
Miller St NW1	123	J4
Miller Wk SE1	123	N10
Millgrove St SW11	126	G8
Millharbour E14	129	M2
Milligan St E14	125	K9
Millman Ms WC1	123	M6
Millman St WC1	123	M6
Millmark Gro SE14	129	J8
Millstream Rd SE1	128	D1
Millwall Dock Rd E14	129	L2
Milman's St SW10	126	D5
Milner Pl N1	123	N3
Milner Sq N1	123	P2
Milner St SW3	126	F3
Milton Cl SE1	128	D3
Milton Ct Rd SE14	129	J5
Milton St EC2	124	B7
Milverton St SE11	127	N4
Mina Rd SE17	128	C4
Mincing La EC3	124	C9
Minera Ms SW1	126	G3
Minerva Cl SW9	127	N6
Minerva St E2	124	F4
Minet Rd SW9	127	P8
Ming St E14	125	L9
Minories EC3	124	D8
Minson Rd E9	125	H3
Mintern St N1	124	B4
Mission Pl SE15	128	E7
Mitchell St EC1	124	A6
Mitchison Rd N1	124	B1
Mitre Rd SE1	127	N1
Mitre St EC3	124	C8
Moat Pl SW9	127	M9
Modling Ho E2	125	H4
Molesford Rd SW6	126	A7
Molesworth St SE13	129	N9
Molyneux St W1	122	E7
Mona Rd SE15	128	G8
Monck St SW1	127	K2
Monclar Rd SE5	128	B10
Moncrieff St SE15	128	E8
Monier Rd E3	125	L2
Monkton St SE11	127	N3
Monmouth Rd W2	122	B9
Monmouth St WC2	123	L8
Monnow Rd SE1	128	E3
Monson Rd SE14	129	H6
Montagu Ms N W1	122	F7
Montagu Pl W1	122	F7
Montagu Sq W1	122	F7
Montagu St W1	122	F8
Montague Av SE4	129	K10
Montague Cl SE1	124	B10
Montague Pl WC1	123	K7
Montague St EC1	124	A8
Montague St WC1	123	L7
Monteagle Way SE15	128	F9
Montefiore St SW8	127	H8
Montford Pl SE11	127	N4
Montgomery St E14	125	M10
Montpelier Pl E1	124	G8
Montpelier Pl SW7	126	E2
Montpelier Rd SE15	128	F7
Montpelier Sq SW7	126	E1
Montpelier St SW7	126	E1
Montpelier Wk SW7	126	E2
Montrose Ct SW7	126	D1
Montrose Pl SW1	126	G1
Monument St EC3	124	B9
Monza St E1	125	H9
Moodkee St SE16	128	G2
Moody Rd SE15	128	E8
Moody St E1	125	H5
Moon St N1	123	P3
Moor La EC2	124	B7
Moore Pk Rd SW6	126	B6
Moore St SW3	126	F3
Moorfields EC2	124	B7
Moorgate EC2	124	B8
Moorhouse Rd W2	122	A8
Moorland Rd SW9	127	P10
Moorlands Est SW9	127	N10
Mora St EC1	124	A5
Morant St E14	125	L9
Morat St SW9	127	M7
Moravian St E2	125	G5
Mordaunt St SW9	127	M9
Morden Hill SE13	129	N8
Morden La SE13	129	N7
Morden St SE13	129	M7
Morecambe Cl E1	125	H7
Morecambe St SE17	128	A3
Moreland St EC1	123	P5
Moresby Wk SW8	127	H8
Moreton Pl SW1	127	J4
Moreton St SW1	127	K4
Moreton Ter SW1	127	J4
Morgan Rd E3	125	J4
Morgans La SE1	124	C10
Morley St SE13	129	N10
Morley St SE1	127	N1
Morna Rd SE5	128	B10
Morning La E9	124	G1
Mornington Cres NW1	123	J4
Mornington Gro E3	125	L5
Mornington Ms SE5	128	A7
Mornington Rd SE8	129	K6
Mornington St NW1	123	H4
Mornington Ter NW1	123	H3
Morocco St SE1	128	C1
Morpeth Gro E9	125	H3
Morpeth Rd E9	124	G3
Morpeth St E2	125	H5
Morpeth Ter SW1	127	J2
Morris Rd E14	125	M7
Morris St E1	124	F8
Morrison St SW11	126	G9
Morshead Rd W9	122	A5
Mortham St E15	125	P3
Mortimer Cres NW6	122	B3
Mortimer Est NW6	122	B3
Mortimer Pl NW6	122	B3
Mortimer Rd N1	124	C2
Mortimer St W1	123	H8
Morton Rd N1	124	A2
Morville St E3	125	L4
Moscow Rd W2	122	A9
Mossbury Rd SW11	126	E9
Mossford St E3	125	K6
Mossop St SW3	126	E3
Mostyn Gro E3	125	K4
Mostyn Rd SW9	127	N7
Motcomb St SW1	126	G2
Moulins Rd E9	124	G3
Mount Pleasant WC1	123	N6
Mount Row W1	123	H9
Mount St W1	122	G9
Mountague Pl E14	125	N9
Mounts Pond Rd SE3	129	P8
Mowlem St E2	124	F4
Mowll St SW9	127	N6
Moxon St W1	122	G7
Mozart Ter SW1	126	G3
Mulberry Rd E8	124	D2
Mulberry Wk SW3	126	D5
Mulvaney Way SE1	128	B1
Mundy St N1	124	C5
Munro Ter SW10	126	D6
Munster Sq NW1	123	H5
Munton Rd SE17	128	A3
Murdock St SE15	128	F5
Muriel St N1	123	M4
Murillo Rd SE13	129	P10
Murphy St SE1	127	N1
Murray Gro N1	124	A4
Murray Ms NW1	123	K2
Murray St NW1	123	K2
Mursell Est SW8	127	M7
Musbury St E1	124	G8
Muschamp Rd SE15	128	D9
Museum St WC1	123	L8
Musgrave Cres SW6	126	A7
Musgrove Rd SE14	129	H7
Myatt Rd SW9	127	P7
Myddelton Sq EC1	123	N5
Myddelton St EC1	123	N5
Myers La SE14	129	H5
Mylne St EC1	123	N5
Myrdle St E1	124	E7
Myron Pl SE13	129	N9
Myrtle Wk N1	124	C4
Mysore Rd SW11	126	F9
N		
N1 Shop Cen N1	123	N4
Nairn St E14	125	N7
Nankin St E14	125	L8
Nansen Rd SW11	126	G10
Nantes Cl SW18	126	C10
Napier Av E14	129	L4
Napier Gro N1	124	A4
Narborough St SW6	126	B8
Narrow St E14	125	J9
Naseby Cl NW6	122	C2
Nash Rd SE4	129	H10
Nassau St W1	123	J7
Naval Row E14	125	N9
Navarino Gro E8	124	E1
Navarino Rd E8	124	E1
Navarre St E2	124	D6
Navy St SW4	127	K9
Naylor Rd SE15	128	F6
Nazareth Gdns SE15	128	F8
Nazrul St E2	124	D5
Neal St WC2	123	L8
Nealden St SW9	127	M9
Neate St SE5	128	D5
Nebraska St SE1	128	B1
Neckinger SE16	128	D2
Neckinger Est SE16	128	D2
Neckinger St SE1	128	D1
Nectarine Way SE13	129	M8
Needleman St SE16	129	H1
Nelldale Rd SE16	128	G3
Nelson Cl NW6	122	A4
Nelson Gdns E2	124	E5
Nelson Pl N1	123	P4
Nelson Rd SE10	129	N5
Nelson Sq SE1	127	P1
Nelson St E1	124	F8
Nelson Ter N1	123	P4
Nelson's Row SW4	127	K10
Nepaul Rd SW11	126	E8
Neptune St SE16	128	G2
Netherford Rd SW4	127	J8
Netherhall Gdns NW3	122	C1
Netherton Gro SW10	126	C5
Nettleton Rd SE14	129	H7
Nevada St SE10	129	N5
Nevern Pl SW5	126	A3
Nevern Rd SW5	126	A3
Nevern Sq SW5	126	A3
Neville Cl SE15	128	E6
Neville St SW7	126	D4
Neville Ter SW7	126	D4
New Bond St W1	123	H9
New Br St EC4	123	P8
New Broad St EC2	124	C7
New Burlington St W1	123	J9
New Butt La SE8	129	L6
New Caledonian Wf SE16	129	K2
New Cavendish St W1	122	G7
New Change EC4	122	A8
New Ch Rd SE5	128	A6
New Compton St WC2	123	K8
New Covent Gdn Mkt SW8	127	K6
New Cross Rd SE14	128	G6
New Fetter La EC4	123	N8
New Globe Wk SE1	124	A10
New Inn Yd EC2	124	C6
New Kent Rd SE1	128	A2
New King St SE8	129	L5
New Mt St E15	125	P2
New N Rd N1	124	B4
New N St WC1	123	M7
New Oxford St WC1	123	K8
New Pl Sq SE16	128	F2
New Quebec St W1	122	F8
New Ride SW7	126	E1
New River Wk N1	124	A1
New Rd E1	124	F7
New Row WC2	123	L9
New Sq WC2	123	M8
New St EC2	124	C7
New Union Cl E14	129	N2
New Union St EC2	124	B7
New Wf Rd N1	123	L4
Newark St E1	124	F7
Newburgh St W1	123	J8
Newburn St SE11	127	M4
Newby Pl E14	125	N9
Newby St SW8	127	H9
Newcastle Pl W2	122	D7
Newcomen Rd SW11	126	D9
Newcomen St SE1	128	B1
Newcourt St NW8	122	E4
Newell St E14	125	K8
Newent Cl SE15	128	C6
Newgate St EC1	123	P8
Newington Butts SE1	127	P3
Newington Butts SE11	127	P3
Newington Causeway SE1	127	P2
Newington Grn Rd N1	124	B1
Newlands Quay E1	124	G9
Newman St W1	123	J7
Newport Av E14	125	P9
Newport Ct WC2	123	K9
Newport St SE11	127	M3
Newton Pl E14	125	L3
Newton Rd W2	122	A8
Newton St WC2	123	L8
Nicholas Rd E1	124	G6
Nicholl St E2	124	E3
Nicholson St SE1	123	P10
Nigel Rd SE15	128	E9
Nightingale Rd N1	124	A1
Nile St N1	124	B5
Nile Ter SE15	128	D4
Nine Elms La SW8	127	J6
Noble St EC2	124	A8
Noel Rd N1	123	P4
Noel St W1	123	J8
Norbiton Rd E14	125	K8
Norfolk Cres W2	122	E8
Norfolk Pl W2	122	D8
Norfolk Rd NW8	122	D3
Norfolk Sq W2	122	D8
Norman Gro E3	125	J4
Norman Rd SE10	129	M6
Normandy Rd SW9	127	N7
North Audley St W1	122	G8
North Bk NW8	122	E5
North Carriage Dr W2	122	E9
North Colonnade E14	125	L10
North Cres E16	125	P6
North Cres WC1	123	K7
North Gower St NW1	123	J5
North Ms WC1	123	M6
North Pas SW18	126	A10
North Peckham Est SE15	128	D6
North Ride W2	122	E9
North Row W1	122	F9
North St SW4	127	J9
North Tenter St E1	124	D8
North Ter SW3	126	E2
North Vil NW1	123	K1
North Wf Rd W2	122	D7
Northampton Pk N1	124	A1
Northampton Rd EC1	123	N6
Northampton Sq EC1	123	P5
Northampton St N1	124	A2
Northbourne Rd SW4	127	K10
Northburgh St EC1	123	P6
Northchurch Rd N1	124	B2
Northchurch Ter N1	124	C2
Northcote Rd SW11	126	E10
Northdown St N1	123	M4
Northey St E14	125	J9
Northfields SW18	126	A10
Northiam St E9	124	F3
Northington St WC1	123	M6
Northlands St SE5	128	A8
Northport St N1	124	B3
Northumberland All EC3	124	C8
Northumberland Av WC2	123	L10
Northumberland Pl W2	122	A8
Northumberland St WC2	123	L10
Northumbria St E14	125	L8
Northway Rd SE5	128	A10
Northwick Ter NW8	122	D6
Norton Folgate E1	124	C7
Norway Gate SE16	129	J2
Norway St SE10	129	M5
Norwich St EC4	123	N8
Notley St SE5	128	B6
Notre Dame Est SW4	127	J10
Notting Hill Gate W11	122	A10
Nottingham Pl W1	122	G6
Nottingham St W1	122	G7
Novello St SW6	126	A7
Nuding Cl SE13	129	L9
Nugent Ter NW8	122	C4
Nunhead Cres SE15	128	F9
Nunhead Est SE15	128	F10
Nunhead Grn SE15	128	F9
Nunhead Gro SE15	128	F9
Nunhead La SE15	128	F9
Nursery Cl SE4	129	K8
Nursery La E2	124	D3
Nursery Rd SW9	127	M10
Nutbrook St SE15	128	E9
Nutcroft Rd SE15	128	F6
Nutford Pl W1	122	F8
Nutley Ter NW3	122	C1
Nutmeg La E14	125	P8
Nutt St SE15	128	D6
Nuttall St N1	124	C4
Nynehead St SE14	129	J6
O		
Oak La E14	125	K9
Oak Tree Rd NW8	122	E5
Oakbank Gro SE24	128	A10
Oakbury Rd SW6	126	B8
Oakcroft Rd SE13	129	P8
Oakdale Rd SE15	128	G9
Oakden St SE11	127	N3
Oakey La SE1	127	N2
Oakfield St SW10	126	C5
Oakhill Gro SE22	128	E10
Oakhurst Gro SE22	128	E10
Oakington Rd W9	122	A6
Oakley Gdns SW3	126	E5
Oakley Pl SE1	128	D4
Oakley Rd N1	124	B2
Oakley Sq NW1	123	J4
Oakley St SW3	126	E5
Oat La EC2	124	A8
Oban St E14	125	P8
Oberstein Rd SW11	126	D10
Observatory Gdns W8	126	A1
Occupation Rd SE17	128	A4
Ocean Est E1	125	H6
Ocean St E1	125	H7
Ocean Wf E14	129	L1
Ockendon Rd N1	124	B1
Octavia St SW11	126	E7
Octavius St SE8	129	L6
Odessa St SE16	129	K1
Odger St SW11	126	F8
Offenbach Ho E2	125	H4
Offerton Rd SW4	127	J9
Offley Rd SW9	127	N6
Offord Rd N1	123	M2
Offord St N1	123	M2
Oglander Rd SE15	128	D10
Ogle St W1	123	J7
Old Bailey EC4	123	P8
Old Bellgate Pl E14	129	L2
Old Bethnal Grn Rd E2	124	E5
Old Bond St W1	123	J9
Old Broad St EC2	124	B8
Old Brompton Rd SW5	126	A4
Old Brompton Rd SW7	126	A4
Old Burlington St W1	123	J9
Old Castle St E1	124	D7
Old Cavendish St W1	123	H8
Old Ch Rd E1	125	H8
Old Ch St SW3	126	D4
Old Compton St W1	123	K9
Old Ct Pl W8	126	B1
Old Ford Rd E2	124	G4
Old Ford Rd E3	125	J4
Old Gloucester St WC1	123	L7
Old Jamaica Rd SE16	128	E2
Old James St SE15	128	F9
Old Jewry EC2	124	B8
Old Kent Rd SE1	128	C3
Old Kent Rd SE15	128	C3
Old Marylebone Rd NW1	122	E7
Old Montague St E1	124	D6
Old Nichol St E2	124	D6
Old Palace Yd SW1	127	L2
Old Paradise St SE11	127	M3
Old Pk La W1	122	G10
Old Pye St SW1	127	K2
Old Quebec St W1	122	F8
Old Queen St SW1	127	K1
Old Royal Free Sq N1	123	N3
Old S Lambeth Rd SW8	127	L6
Old Spitalfields Mkt E1	124	D7
Old St WC2	123	N8
Old St EC1	124	A6
Old Town SW4	127	J9
Old Woolwich Rd SE10	129	P5
Oldbury Pl W1	122	G6
Oldfield Gro SE16	129	H3
O'Leary Sq E1	124	G7
Olga St E3	125	J4
Oliver Ms SE15	128	E8
Oliver-Goldsmith Est SE15	128	E7
Ollerton Grn E3	125	K3
Olliffe St E14	129	N2
Olmar St SE1	128	D5
Olney Rd SE17	127	P5
O'Meara St SE1	124	A10
Omega St SE14	129	L7
Ommaney Rd SE14	129	H7
Ondine Rd SE15	128	D10
Onega Gate SE16	129	J2
Ongar Rd SW6	126	A5
Onslow Gdns SW7	126	D4
Onslow Sq SW7	126	D3
Ontario St SE1	127	P2
Ontario Way E14	125	L9
Opal St SE11	127	P3
Ophir Ter SE15	128	E7
Oppenheim Rd SE13	129	N8
Oppidans Rd NW3	122	F2
Orange St WC2	123	K9
Oransay Rd N1	124	A1
Orb St SE17	128	B3
Orbel St SW11	126	E7
Orchard, The SE3	129	P8
Orchard St W1	122	G8
Orchardson St NW8	122	D6
Orde Hall St WC1	123	M6
Ordell Rd E3	125	K4
Ordnance Cres SE10	129	P1
Ordnance Hill NW8	122	D3
Oregano Dr E14	125	P8
Oriel Rd E9	125	H1
Orkney St SW11	126	G8
Orlando Rd SW4	127	J9
Orleston Ms N7	123	N1
Orleston Rd N7	123	N1
Orme Ct W2	122	B9
Orme La W2	122	B9
Ormonde Gate SW3	126	F4
Ormonde Ter NW8	122	F3
Ormsby St E2	124	D4
Ormside St SE15	128	G5
Orpheus St SE5	128	B7
Orsett St SE11	127	M4
Orsett Ter W2	122	C8
Orsman Rd N1	124	C3
Orville Rd SW11	126	D8
Osborn Cl E8	124	E3
Osborn St E1	124	D7
Osborne Rd E9	125	K1
Oscar St SE8	129	L7
Oseney Cres NW5	123	J1
Osier St E1	124	G6
Osiers Rd SW18	126	A10
Oslo Sq SE16	129	J2
Osnaburgh St NW1	123	H6
Osnaburgh St (north section) NW1	123	H5
Osric Path N1	124	C4
Ossington St W2	122	A9
Ossory Rd SE1	128	E4
Ossulston St NW1	123	K5
Oswell Ho E1	124	F10
Oswin St SE11	127	P3
Oswyth Rd SE5	128	C8
Otis St E3	125	N5
Otter Cl E15	125	N3
Otterburn Ho SE5	128	A6
Otto St SE17	127	P5
Outer Circle NW1	123	H4
Outram Pl N1	123	L3
Oval, The E2	124	F4
Oval Pl SW8	127	M6
Oval Rd NW1	123	H3
Oval Way SE11	127	M4
Overcliff Rd SE13	129	L9
Oversley Ho W2	122	A7
Overton Rd SW9	127	N8
Ovex Cl E14	129	N1
Ovington Gdns SW3	126	E2
Ovington Ms SW3	126	E2
Ovington Sq SW3	126	E2
Ovington St SW3	126	E2
Oxenden St SW1	123	K9
Oxenford St SE15	128	D9
Oxenholme E2	123	J4
Oxestalls Rd SE8	129	J4
Oxford Rd E15	125	P1
Oxford Rd NW6	122	A4
Oxford Sq W2	122	E8
Oxford St W1	123	H8
Oxley Cl SE1	128	D4
Oxo Twr Wf SE1	123	N9
Oxonian St SE22	128	D10
P		
Packington Sq N1	124	A3
Packington St N1	123	P3
Padbury SE17	128	C4
Padbury Ct E2	124	D5
Paddington Grn W2	122	D7
Paddington St W1	122	G7
Padfield Rd SE5	128	A9
Pagden St SW8	127	H7
Page St SW1	127	K3
Pages Wk SE1	128	C3
Pagnell St SE14	129	K6
Pagoda Gdns SE3	129	P8
Pakenham St WC1	123	M5
Palace Av W8	122	B10
Palace Ct W2	122	B9
Palace Gdns Ms W8	122	A10
Palace Gdns Ter W8	122	A10
Palace Gate W8	126	C1
Palace Grn W8	126	B1
Palace St SW1	127	J2
Palfrey Pl SW8	127	M6
Palgrave Gdns NW1	122	E6
Pall Mall SW1	123	J10
Pall Mall E SW1	123	K10
Palmer St SW1	127	K2
Palmers Rd E2	125	H4
Palmerston Rd NW6	122	A2
Pancras Rd NW1	123	K4
Pandora Rd NW6	122	A1
Paradise, The SW11	126	F6
Paradise Rd SW4	127	J8
Paradise St SE16	128	F1
Paradise Wk SW3	126	F5
Pardon St EC1	123	P6
Pardoner St SE1	128	B2
Parfett St E1	124	E7
Paris Gdn SE1	123	P10
Park Cl E9	124	G3
Park Cl W14	126	F1
Park Cres W1	123	H6
Park La W1	122	G10
Park Pl E14	125	L10
Park Pl SW1	123	J10
Park Pl Vil W2	122	C7
Park Rd NW1	122	E5
Park Rd NW8	122	E5

Rockingham St

Park Row **SE10** 129 P5
Park Sq E **NW1** 123 H6
Park Sq Ms **NW1** 123 H6
Park Sq W **NW1** 123 H6
Park St **SE1** 124 A10
Park St **W1** 122 G9
Park Vw Est **E2** 125 H4
Park Vw Ms **SW9** 127 M8
Park Village E **NW1** 123 H4
Park Village W **NW1** 123 H4
Park Vista **SE10** 129 P5
Park Wk **SW10** 126 C5
Parker St **WC2** 123 L8
Parkfield Rd **SE14** 129 K7
Parkgate Rd **SW11** 126 E6
Parkham St **SW11** 126 E7
Parkholme Rd **E8** 124 D1
Parkhouse St **SE5** 128 B6
Parkside Rd **SW11** 126 G7
Parkway **NW1** 123 H3
Parliament Sq **SW1** 127 L1
Parliament St **SW1** 127 L1
Parliament Vw Apartments **SE1** 127 M3
Parma Cres **SW11** 126 F10
Parmiter St **E2** 124 F4
Parnell Rd **E3** 125 K3
Parr St **N1** 124 B4
Parry St **SW8** 127 L5
Parsonage St **E14** 129 N3
Parsons Grn **SW6** 126 A7
Parsons Grn La **SW6** 126 A7
Parson's Ho **W2** 122 D6
Parthenia Rd **SW6** 126 A7
Parvin St **SW8** 127 K7
Pascal St **SW8** 127 K6
Passmore St **SW1** 126 G3
Pastor St **SE11** 127 P3
Patcham Ter **SW8** 127 H7
Pater St **W8** 126 A2
Patience Rd **SW11** 126 E8
Patmore Est **SW8** 127 J7
Patmore St **SW8** 127 J7
Patmos Rd **SW9** 127 P6
Paton Cl **E3** 125 L5
Patriot Sq **E2** 124 F4
Patshull Rd **NW5** 123 J1
Patterdale Rd **SE15** 128 G6
Pattina Wk **SE16** 125 K10
Paul Julius Cl **E14** 125 P9
Paul St **E15** 125 P3
Paul St **EC2** 124 B6
Paulet Rd **SE5** 127 P8
Paul's Wk **EC4** 124 A9
Paultons Sq **SW3** 126 D5
Paultons St **SW3** 126 D5
Paveley Dr **SW11** 126 E6
Paveley St **NW8** 122 E6
Pavement, The **SW4** 127 J10
Pavilion Rd **SW1** 126 F1
Paxton Ter **SW1** 127 H5
Payne Rd **E3** 125 M4
Payne St **SE8** 129 K5
Peabody Sq **SE1** 127 P1
Peabody Trust **SE1** 124 A10
Pear Tree Cl **E2** 124 D3
Pear Tree Ct **EC1** 123 N6
Pear Tree St **EC1** 123 P6
Peardon St **SW8** 127 H8
Pearman St **SE1** 127 N1
Pearscroft Ct **SW6** 126 B7
Pearscroft Rd **SW6** 126 B7
Pearson St **E2** 124 C4
Peckford Pl **SW9** 127 N8
Peckham Gro **SE15** 128 C6
Peckham High St **SE15** 128 E7
Peckham Hill St **SE15** 128 E6
Peckham Pk Rd **SE15** 128 E6
Peckham Rd **SE5** 128 C7
Peckham Rd **SE15** 128 C7
Peckham Rye **SE15** 128 E9
Peckham Rye **SE22** 128 E10
Pedlars Wk **N7** 123 L1
Pedley St **E1** 124 D6
Peel Gro **E2** 124 G4
Peel Prec **NW6** 122 A4
Peel St **W8** 122 A10
Peerless St **EC1** 124 B5
Pekin St **E14** 125 L8
Pelham Cl **SE5** 128 C8
Pelham Cres **SW7** 126 E3
Pelham Pl **SW7** 126 E3
Pelham St **SW7** 126 E3
Pelican Est **SE15** 128 D7
Pelling St **E14** 125 L8
Pelter St **E2** 124 D5
Pembridge Cres **W11** 122 A9
Pembridge Gdns **W2** 122 A9
Pembridge Ms **W11** 122 A9
Pembridge Pl **W2** 122 A9
Pembridge Rd **W11** 122 A9
Pembridge Sq **W2** 122 A9
Pembridge Vil **W2** 122 A9
Pembridge Vil **W11** 122 A9
Pembroke Av **N1** 123 L3
Pembroke Cl **SW1** 126 G1
Pembroke Gdns Cl **W8** 126 A2
Pembroke Pl **W8** 126 A2
Pembroke Rd **W8** 126 A3
Pembroke Sq **W8** 126 A2
Pembroke St **N1** 123 L2
Pembroke Vil **W8** 126 A3
Pembroke Wk **W8** 126 A3
Pembry Cl **SW9** 127 N7
Penang St **E1** 124 F10
Penarth St **SE15** 128 G5
Pencraig Way **SE15** 128 F5
Pendrell Rd **SE4** 129 J8
Penfold Pl **NW1** 122 E7
Penfold St **NW1** 122 D6
Penfold St **NW8** 122 D6
Penford St **SE5** 127 P8
Penn St **N1** 124 B3
Pennack Rd **SE15** 128 D5
Pennant Ms **W8** 126 B3
Pennethorne Rd **SE15** 128 F6
Pennington St **E1** 124 E9
Pennyfields **E14** 125 L9
Penpoll Rd **E8** 124 F1
Penrose Gro **SE17** 128 A4
Penrose Ho **SE17** 128 A4
Penrose St **SE17** 128 A4
Penryn St **NW1** 123 K4
Pensbury Pl **SW8** 127 J8
Pensbury St **SW8** 127 J8
Penshurst Rd **E9** 125 H2
Penton Pl **SE17** 127 P4
Penton Ri **WC1** 123 M5
Penton St **N1** 123 N4
Pentonville Rd **N1** 123 M4
Pentridge St **SE15** 128 D6
Penywern Rd **SW5** 126 A4
Pepper St **E14** 129 M2
Pepys Rd **SE14** 129 H7
Pepys St **EC3** 124 C9
Percival St **EC1** 123 P6
Percy Circ **WC1** 123 M5
Percy St **W1** 123 K7
Peregrine Ho **EC1** 123 P5
Perkin's Rents **SW1** 127 K2
Perrymead St **SW6** 126 A7
Perseverance Pl **SW9** 127 N6
Peter St **W1** 123 K9
Peterborough Ms **SW6** 126 A8
Peterborough Rd **SW6** 126 A8
Peterborough Vil **SW6** 126 B7
Petergate **SW11** 126 C10
Petersham La **SW7** 126 C2
Petersham Ms **SW7** 126 C2
Petersham Pl **SW7** 126 C2
Peto Pl **NW1** 123 H6
Petticoat La **E1** 124 C7
Petticoat Sq **E1** 124 D8
Petty France **SW1** 127 J2
Petworth St **SW11** 126 E7
Petyward **SW3** 126 E3
Peyton Pl **SE10** 129 N6
Phelp St **SE17** 128 B5
Phene St **SW3** 126 E5
Philbeach Gdns **SW5** 126 A4
Philip Wk **SE15** 128 E9
Phillimore Gdns **W8** 126 A1
Phillimore Pl **W8** 126 A1
Phillimore Wk **W8** 126 A2
Phillipp St **N1** 124 C3
Philpot St **E1** 124 F8
Phipp St **EC2** 124 C6
Phoenix Pl **WC1** 123 M6
Phoenix Rd **NW1** 123 K5
Piccadilly **W1** 123 H10
Piccadilly Circ **W1** 123 K9
Pickfords Wf **N1** 124 A4
Picton St **SE5** 128 B6
Pier St **E14** 129 N3
Pigott St **E14** 125 L8
Pilgrimage St **SE1** 128 B1
Pilkington Rd **SE15** 128 F8
Pilot Cl **SE8** 129 K5
Pilton Pl **SE17** 128 A4
Pimlico Rd **SW1** 126 G4
Pinchin St **E1** 124 E9
Pincott Pl **SE4** 129 H10
Pindar St **EC2** 124 C7
Pine St **EC1** 123 N6
Pinefield Cl **E14** 125 L9
Pioneer St **SE15** 128 E7
Piper Cl **N7** 123 M1
Pitchford St **E15** 125 P2
Pitfield Est **N1** 124 B5
Pitfield St **N1** 124 C5
Pitman St **SE5** 128 A6
Pitsea St **E1** 125 H8
Pitt St **W8** 126 A1
Pitt's Head Ms **W1** 122 G10
Pixley St **E14** 125 K8
Plantation Wf **SW11** 126 C9
Plato Rd **SW2** 127 L10
Platt St **NW1** 123 K4
Plaza Shop Cen, The **W1** 123 J8
Pleasant Pl **N1** 123 P2
Pleasant Row **NW1** 123 H3
Plender St **NW1** 123 J3
Plevna St **E14** 129 N2
Plough Rd **SW11** 126 D9
Plough Ter **SW11** 126 D10
Plough Way **SE16** 129 H3
Plough Yd **EC2** 124 C6
Plover Way **SE16** 129 J2
Plumbers Row **E1** 124 E7
Plymouth Wf **E14** 129 P3
Plympton St **NW8** 122 E6
Pocock St **SE1** 127 P1
Podmore Rd **SW18** 126 C10
Point Hill **SE10** 129 N6
Point Pleasant **SW18** 126 A10
Pointers Cl **E14** 129 M4
Poland Ho **E15** 125 P3
Poland St **W1** 123 J8
Polesworth Ho **W2** 122 A7
Pollard Row **E2** 124 E5
Pollard St **E2** 124 E5
Polygon Rd **NW1** 123 K4
Pomeroy St **SE14** 128 G7
Pond Pl **SW3** 126 E3
Ponler St **E1** 124 F8
Ponsford St **E9** 124 G1
Ponsonby Pl **SW1** 127 K4
Ponsonby Ter **SW1** 127 K4
Pont St **SW1** 126 F2
Pont St Ms **SW1** 126 F2
Ponton Rd **SW8** 127 K5
Poole Rd **E9** 125 H1
Poole St **N1** 124 B3
Poolmans St **SE16** 129 H1
Pope St **SE1** 128 C1
Popes Rd **SW9** 127 N9
Popham Rd **N1** 124 A3
Popham St **N1** 123 P3
Poplar Business Pk **E14** 125 N9
Poplar High St **E14** 125 L9
Poplar Pl **W2** 122 B9
Poplar Rd **SE24** 128 A10
Poplar Wk **SE24** 128 A10
Porchester Cl **SE5** 128 A10
Porchester Gdns **W2** 122 B9
Porchester Ms **W2** 122 B8
Porchester Pl **W2** 122 E8
Porchester Rd **W2** 122 B7
Porchester Sq **W2** 122 B8
Porchester Ter **W2** 122 C9
Porchester Ter N **W2** 122 B8
Porden Rd **SW2** 127 M10
Porlock St **SE1** 128 B1
Portelet Rd **E1** 125 H5
Porteus Rd **W2** 122 C7
Portia Way **E3** 125 K6
Portland Gro **SW8** 127 M7
Portland Pl **W1** 123 H7
Portland St **SE17** 128 B4
Portman Cl **W1** 122 F8
Portman Ms S **W1** 122 G8
Portman Pl **E2** 124 G5
Portman Sq **W1** 122 F8
Portman St **W1** 122 G8
Portpool La **EC1** 123 N7
Portree St **E14** 125 P8
Portslade Rd **SW8** 127 J8
Portsoken St **E1** 124 D9
Portugal St **WC2** 123 M8
Post Office Way **SW8** 127 K6
Potier St **SE1** 128 B2
Pott St **E2** 124 F5
Potters Rd **SW6** 126 C8
Pottery St **SE16** 128 F1
Poultry **EC2** 124 B8
Pountney Rd **SW11** 126 G9
Powis Pl **WC1** 123 L6
Powis Rd **E3** 125 M5
Pownall Rd **E8** 124 D3
Poyntz Rd **SW11** 126 F8
Poyser St **E2** 124 F4
Praed St **W2** 122 D8
Prairie St **SW8** 126 G8
Pratt St **NW1** 123 J3
Pratt Wk **SE11** 127 M3
Prebend St **N1** 124 A3
Prescot St **E1** 124 D9
Prescott Pl **SW4** 127 K9
Prestage Way **E14** 125 N9
Prestons Rd **E14** 129 N1
Price's Ct **SW11** 126 D9
Price's St **SE1** 123 P10
Price's Yd **N1** 123 M3
Prideaux Pl **WC1** 123 M5
Prideaux Rd **SW9** 127 L9
Prima Rd **SW9** 127 N6
Primrose Gdns **NW3** 122 E1
Primrose Hill Ct **NW3** 122 F2
Primrose Hill Rd **NW3** 122 E2
Primrose Sq **E9** 124 G2
Primrose St **EC2** 124 C7
Prince Albert Rd **NW1** 122 E4
Prince Albert Rd **NW8** 122 E4
Prince Consort Rd **SW7** 126 C2
Prince Edwards Rd **E9** 125 K1
Prince of Wales Dr **SW8** 127 H6
Prince of Wales Dr **SW11** 126 F7
Prince of Wales Gate **SW7** 126 E1
Prince of Wales Rd **NW5** 122 G1
Prince St **SE8** 129 K5
Princelet St **E1** 124 D7
Princes Ct **E1** 124 F9
Princes Ct **SE16** 129 K2
Princes Gdns **SW7** 126 D2
Princes Gate **SW7** 126 E1
Princes Gate Ms **SW7** 126 D2
Princes Ri **SE13** 129 N8
Princes Riverside Rd **SE16** 125 H10
Princes Sq **W2** 122 B9
Princes St **EC2** 124 B8
Princes St **W1** 123 H8
Princess Rd **NW1** 122 G3
Princess Rd **NW6** 122 A4
Princess St **SE1** 127 P2
Princethorpe Ho **W2** 122 B7
Princeton St **WC1** 123 M7
Printers Ms **E3** 125 J3
Prior Bolton St **N1** 123 P1
Prior St **SE10** 129 N6
Prioress St **SE1** 128 B2
Priory Ct **SW8** 127 K7
Priory Grn Est **N1** 123 M4
Priory Gro **SW8** 127 L7
Priory Ms **SW8** 127 K7
Priory Rd **NW6** 122 B3
Priory Ter **NW6** 122 B3
Priory Wk **SW10** 126 C4
Pritchard's Rd **E2** 124 E3
Priter Rd **SE16** 128 E2
Procter St **WC1** 123 M7
Prospect Pl **E1** 124 G10
Prospect Quay **SW18** 126 A10
Providence Ct **W1** 122 G9
Provost Est **N1** 124 B4
Provost Rd **NW3** 122 F2
Provost St **N1** 124 B5
Prusom St **E1** 124 F10
Pudding La **EC3** 124 B9
Pudding Mill La **E15** 125 M3
Pulross Rd **SW9** 127 M9
Pulteney Cl **E3** 125 K3
Pulteney Ter **N1** 123 M3
Pulton Pl **SW6** 126 A6
Pump La **SE14** 128 G6
Pundersons Gdns **E2** 124 F5
Purbrook St **SE1** 128 C2
Purcell St **N1** 124 C4
Purchese St **NW1** 123 K4
Purdy St **E3** 125 M6
Purelake Ms **SE13** 129 P9
Puteaux Ho **E2** 125 H4
Pytchley Rd **SE22** 128 C9

Q

Quaker St **E1** 124 D6
Quality Ct **WC2** 123 N8
Quarrendon St **SW6** 126 A8
Quarterdeck, The **E14** 129 L1
Quebec Way **SE16** 129 H1
Queen Anne Rd **E9** 125 H1
Queen Anne St **W1** 123 H8
Queen Anne's Gate **SW1** 127 K1
Queen Elizabeth St **SE1** 128 D1
Queen of Denmark Ct **SE16** 129 K2
Queen Sq **WC1** 123 L6
Queen St **EC4** 124 A9
Queen St **W1** 123 H10
Queen Victoria St **EC4** 123 P9
Queenhithe **EC4** 124 A9
Queen's Cres **NW5** 122 G1
Queens Gdns **W2** 122 C9
Queen's Gate **SW7** 126 D3
Queen's Gate Gdns **SW7** 126 C2
Queen's Gate Ms **SW7** 126 C1
Queen's Gate Pl **SW7** 126 C2
Queen's Gate Pl Ms **SW7** 126 C2
Queen's Gate Ter **SW7** 126 C2
Queen's Gro **NW8** 122 D3
Queen's Gro Ms **NW8** 122 D3
Queen's Head St **N1** 123 P3
Queens Ms **W2** 122 B9
Queens Rd **SE14** 128 F7
Queens Rd **SE15** 128 F7
Queen's Row **SE17** 128 B5
Queen's Ter **NW8** 122 D4
Queen's Wk **SE1** 124 C10
Queen's Wk **SW1** 123 J10
Queensberry Pl **SW7** 126 D3
Queensborough Ter **W2** 122 B9
Queensbridge Rd **E2** 124 D3
Queensbridge Rd **E8** 124 D2
Queensbury St **N1** 124 A2
Queensgate Pl **NW6** 122 A2
Queensmead **NW8** 122 D3
Queenstown Rd **SW8** 127 H5
Queensway **W2** 122 B8
Querrin St **SW6** 126 C8
Quex Rd **NW6** 122 A3
Quick St **N1** 123 P4
Quilter St **E2** 124 E5
Quince Rd **SE13** 129 M8
Quixley St **E14** 125 P9
Quorn Rd **SE22** 128 C10

R

Racton Rd **SW6** 126 A5
Radcot St **SE11** 127 N4
Radlett Pl **NW8** 122 E3
Radley Ms **W8** 126 A2
Radnor Pl **W2** 122 E8
Radnor Rd **SE15** 128 E6
Radnor St **EC1** 124 A5
Radnor Wk **SW3** 126 E4
Radstock St **SW11** 126 E6
Raeburn St **SW2** 127 L10
Raglan St **NW5** 123 H1
Railton Rd **SE24** 127 N10
Railway App **SE1** 124 B10
Railway Av **SE16** 128 G1
Railway St **N1** 123 L4
Rainbow Av **E14** 129 M4
Rainbow Quay **SE16** 129 J2
Rainbow St **SE5** 128 C6
Raine St **E1** 124 F10
Rainhill Way **E3** 125 L5
Rainsborough Av **SE8** 129 J3
Raleana Rd **E14** 125 N10
Raleigh St **N1** 123 P3
Ramillies Pl **W1** 123 J8
Rampayne St **SW1** 127 K4
Ramsey St **E2** 124 E6
Ramsey Wk **N1** 124 B1
Randall Cl **SW11** 126 E7
Randall Pl **SE10** 129 N6
Randall Rd **SE11** 127 M3
Randell's Rd **N1** 123 L3
Randolph Av **W9** 122 C6
Randolph Cres **W9** 122 C6
Randolph Gdns **NW6** 122 B4
Randolph Ms **W9** 122 C6
Randolph Rd **W9** 122 C6
Randolph St **NW1** 123 J2
Ranelagh Gro **SW1** 126 G4
Rangers Sq **SE10** 129 P7
Ranwell St **E3** 125 K3
Raphael St **SW7** 126 F1
Ratcliffe Cross St **E1** 125 H8
Ratcliffe La **E14** 125 J8
Ratcliffe Orchard **E1** 125 H9
Rathbone Pl **W1** 123 K8
Rathbone St **W1** 123 J7
Rattray Rd **SW2** 127 N10
Raul Rd **SE15** 128 E7
Raven Row **E1** 124 F7
Ravensbourne Pl **SE13** 129 M8
Ravenscroft St **E2** 124 D4
Ravensdon St **SE11** 127 N4
Ravenstone **SE17** 128 C4
Rawlings St **SW3** 126 F3
Rawstorne St **EC1** 123 P5
Ray St **EC1** 123 N6
Raymouth Rd **SE16** 128 F3
Reading La **E8** 124 F1
Reardon Path **E1** 124 F10
Reardon St **E1** 124 F10
Reaston St **SE14** 128 G6
Record St **SE15** 128 G5
Rector St **N1** 124 A3
Rectory Gro **SW4** 127 J9
Rectory Sq **E1** 125 H7
Reculver Rd **SE16** 129 H4
Red Lion Row **SE17** 128 A5
Red Lion Sq **WC1** 123 M7
Red Lion St **WC1** 123 M7
Red Path **E9** 125 K1
Red Post Hill **SE24** 128 B10
Redan Pl **W2** 122 B8
Redbridge Gdns **SE5** 128 C6
Redburn St **SW3** 126 F5
Redcar St **SE5** 128 A6
Redcastle Cl **E1** 124 G9
Redchurch St **E2** 124 D6
Redcliffe Gdns **SW5** 126 B4
Redcliffe Gdns **SW10** 126 B4
Redcliffe Ms **SW10** 126 B4
Redcliffe Pl **SW10** 126 C5
Redcliffe Rd **SW10** 126 C4
Redcliffe Sq **SW10** 126 B4
Redcliffe St **SW10** 126 B5
Redcross Way **SE1** 128 A1
Reddins Rd **SE15** 128 E5
Redesdale St **SW3** 126 F5
Redfield La **SW5** 126 A3
Redhill St **NW1** 123 H4
Redman's Rd **E1** 124 G7
Redriff Est **SE16** 129 K2
Redriff Rd **SE16** 129 H3
Redruth Rd **E9** 125 H3
Redwood Cl **E3** 125 L4
Redwood Cl **SE16** 125 J10
Reece Ms **SW7** 126 D3
Reedham St **SE15** 128 E8
Reedworth St **SE11** 127 N3
Rees St **N1** 124 A3
Reeves Ms **W1** 122 G9
Reeves Rd **E3** 125 M6
Reform St **SW11** 126 F8
Regan Way **N1** 124 C4
Regency St **SW1** 127 K3
Regent Sq **E3** 125 M5
Regent Sq **WC1** 123 L5
Regent St **SW1** 123 K9
Regent St **W1** 123 H8
Regents Br Gdns **SW8** 127 L6
Regent's Pk **NW1** 122 G4
Regents Pk Rd **NW1** 122 F3
Regents Row **E8** 124 E3
Reginald Rd **SE8** 129 L6
Reginald Sq **SE8** 129 L6
Regis Pl **SW2** 127 M10
Relf Rd **SE15** 128 E9
Rembrandt Cl **E14** 129 P2
Remington St **N1** 123 P4
Renforth St **SE16** 128 G1
Renfrew Rd **SE11** 127 P3
Rennell St **SE13** 129 N9
Rennie Est **SE16** 128 F3
Rennie St **SE1** 123 P10
Repton St **E14** 125 J8
Reservoir Rd **SE4** 129 J8
Retreat Pl **E9** 124 G1
Revelon Rd **SE4** 129 J10
Reverdy Rd **SE1** 128 E3
Rewell St **SW6** 126 C6
Rheidol Ter **N1** 123 P4
Rhodesia Rd **SW9** 127 L8
Rhodeswell Rd **E14** 125 J7
Rhondda Gro **E3** 125 J5
Rhyl St **NW5** 122 G1
Ricardo St **E14** 125 M8
Rich St **E14** 125 K9
Richborne Ter **SW8** 127 M6
Richmond Av **N1** 123 M3
Richmond Cres **N1** 123 M3
Richmond Gro **N1** 123 P2
Richmond Rd **E8** 124 D2
Richmond Ter **SW1** 127 L1
Rick Roberts Way **E15** 125 N3
Rickett St **SW6** 126 A5
Ridgdale St **E3** 125 M4
Ridgeway Rd **SW9** 127 P9
Riding Ho St **W1** 123 H7
Rifle Pl **SE11** 127 N5
Rifle St **E14** 125 M7
Rigden St **E14** 125 M8
Rigge Pl **SW4** 127 K10
Riley Rd **SE1** 128 D2
Riley St **SW10** 126 D5
Ring, The **W2** 122 D9
Ripplevale Gro **N1** 123 M2
Risdon St **SE16** 128 G1
Risinghill St **N1** 123 M4
Rita Rd **SW8** 127 M6
Ritchie St **N1** 123 N4
Ritson Rd **E8** 124 E1
Rivaz Pl **E9** 124 G1
River Pl **N1** 124 A2
River St **EC1** 123 N5
Riverside Ct **SW8** 127 K5
Riverside Rd **E15** 125 N4
Riverside Twr **SW6** 126 C8
Rivington St **EC2** 124 C5
Roach Rd **E3** 125 L2
Roan St **SE10** 129 N5
Robert Adam St **W1** 122 G8
Robert Dashwood Way **SE17** 128 A3
Robert Lowe Cl **SE14** 129 H6
Robert St **NW1** 123 H5
Roberta St **E2** 124 E5
Roberts Cl **SE16** 129 H1
Robertson Rd **E15** 125 N3
Robertson St **SW8** 127 H9
Robin Ct **SE16** 128 E3
Robin Hood La **E14** 125 N9
Robinson Rd **E2** 124 G4
Robsart St **SW9** 127 M8
Rochelle Cl **SW11** 126 D10
Rochester Ms **NW1** 123 J2
Rochester Pl **NW1** 123 J1
Rochester Rd **NW1** 123 J1
Rochester Row **SW1** 127 J3
Rochester Sq **NW1** 123 J2
Rochester St **SW1** 127 K2
Rochester Ter **NW1** 123 J1
Rockingham Est **SE1** 128 A2
Rockingham St **SE1** 128 A2

Rodmarton St

Rodmarton St W1 122 F7
Rodney Pl SE17 128 A3
Rodney Rd SE17 128 A3
Rodney St N1 123 M4
Roffey St E14 129 N1
Roger Dowley Ct E2 124 G4
Roger St WC1 123 M6
Rokeby Rd SE4 129 K8
Roland Gdns SW7 126 C4
Roland Way SE17 128 B4
Rollins St SE15 128 G5
Rolls Rd SE1 128 D4
Rolt St SE8 129 J5
Roman Rd E2 124 G5
Roman Rd E3 125 J4
Roman Way N7 123 M1
Romford St E1 124 E7
Romilly St W1 123 K9
Romney Rd SE10 129 N5
Romney St SW1 127 K2
Rood La EC3 124 C9
Rookery Rd SW4 127 J10
Rope St SE16 129 J3
Ropemaker Rd SE16 129 J2
Ropemaker St EC2 124 B7
Ropery St E3 125 K6
Ropley St E2 124 E4
Rosary Gdns SW7 126 C3
Rose All SE1 124 A10
Rose Sq SW3 126 D4
Rosebank Gdns E3 125 K4
Roseberry Pl E8 124 D1
Roseberry St SE16 128 F3
Rosebery Av EC1 123 N6
Rosebury Rd SW6 126 B8
Rosefield Gdns E14 125 L9
Rosemary Dr E14 125 P8
Rosemary Rd SE15 128 D6
Rosemont Rd NW3 122 C1
Rosemoor St SW3 126 F3
Rosenau Cres SW11 126 E7
Rosenau Rd SW11 126 E7
Roserton St E14 129 N1
Rosetta Cl SW8 127 L6
Rosher Cl E15 125 P2
Rosoman St EC1 123 N5
Rossendale Way NW1 123 J2
Rossetti Rd SE16 128 F4
Rossmore Rd NW1 122 E6
Rothbury Rd E9 125 K2
Rotherfield St N1 124 A2
Rotherhithe New Rd SE16 128 E4
Rotherhithe Old Rd SE16 129 H3
Rotherhithe St SE16 128 G1
Rotherhithe Tunnel E1 124 G10
Rotherhithe Tunnel App E14 125 J9
Rotherhithe Tunnel App SE16 128 G1
Rothery Ter SW9 127 P6
Rothsay St SE1 128 C2
Rothwell St NW1 122 F3
Rotten Row SW1 126 F1
Rotten Row SW7 126 E1
Rotterdam Dr E14 129 N2
Rouel Rd SE16 128 E2
Rounton Rd E3 125 L6
Roupell St SE1 123 N10
Rousden St NW1 123 J2
Rowcross St SE1 128 D4
Rowditch La SW11 126 G8
Rowena Cres SW11 126 E8
Rowington Cl W2 122 B7
Rowley Way NW8 122 B3
Rowse Cl E15 125 N2
Roxby Pl SW6 126 A5
Royal Av SW3 126 F4
Royal Cl SE8 129 K5
Royal Coll St NW1 123 J2
Royal Ct SE16 129 K2
Royal Ex EC3 124 B8
Royal Hill SE10 129 N6
Royal Hosp Rd SW3 126 F5
Royal Ms, The SW1 127 H2
Royal Mint Ct EC3 124 D9
Royal Mint St E1 124 D9
Royal Naval Pl SE14 129 K6
Royal Oak Rd E8 124 F1
Royal Opera Arc SW1 123 K10
Royal Pl SE10 129 N6
Royal Rd SE17 127 P5
Royal St SE1 127 M2
Royal Victor Pl E3 125 H4
Royston St E2 124 G4
Rozel Ct N1 124 C3
Rozel Rd SW4 127 J8
Ruby St SE15 128 F5
Rudolph Rd NW6 122 A4
Rufford St N1 123 L3
Rugby St WC1 123 M6
Rugg St E14 125 L9
Rum Cl E1 124 G9
Rumbold Rd SW6 126 B6
Rumsey Rd SW9 127 M9
Rupert Gdns SW9 127 P8
Rupert St W1 123 K9
Rush Hill Rd SW11 126 G9
Rushcroft Rd SW2 127 N10
Rushton St N1 124 B4
Rushworth St SE1 127 P1
Ruskin Pk Ho SE5 128 B9
Russell Gro SW9 127 N6
Russell Sq WC1 123 L7
Russell St WC2 123 M8
Russett Way SE13 129 M8
Russia Dock Rd SE16 125 J10
Russia La E2 124 G4
Russia Wk SE16 129 J1
Rust Sq SE5 128 B6
Ruston St E3 125 K3
Rutherford St SW1 127 K3
Rutland Gdns SW7 126 E1
Rutland Gate SW7 126 E1
Rutland Rd E9 124 G3
Rutland St SW7 126 E2
Rutts Ter SE14 129 H7
Ryder Dr SE16 128 F4
Ryder St SW1 123 J10
Rye Hill Pk SE15 128 G10
Rye La SE15 128 E7
Rye Pas SE15 128 E9
Rye Rd SE15 129 H10
Ryecroft St SW6 126 B7
Ryland Rd NW5 123 H1
Rysbrack St SW3 126 F2

S

Sabella Ct E3 125 K4
Sabine Rd SW11 126 F9
Sable St N1 123 P2
Sackville St W1 123 J9
Saffron Av E14 125 P9
Saffron Hill EC1 123 N6
Sail St SE11 127 M3
St. Agnes Pl SE11 127 N5
St. Albans Gro W8 126 B2
St. Alban's Pl N1 123 P3
St. Alfege Pas SE10 129 N5
St. Alphonsus Rd SW4 127 J10
St. Andrew St EC4 123 N7
St. Andrew's Hill EC4 123 P9
St. Andrews Pl NW1 123 H6
St. Andrews Way E3 125 M6
St. Ann's St SW1 127 K2
St. Ann's Ter NW8 122 D4
St. Anthonys Cl E1 124 E10
St. Asaph Rd SE4 129 H9
St. Augustines Rd NW1 123 K2
St. Austell Rd SE13 129 N8
St. Barnabas St SW1 126 G4
St. Barnabas Vil SW8 127 L7
St. Botolph St EC3 124 D8
St. Bride St EC4 123 P8
St. Chad's Pl WC1 123 L5
St. Chad's St WC1 123 L5
St. Clements St N7 123 N1
St. Cross St EC1 123 N7
St. Davids Sq E14 129 M4
St. Donatts Rd SE14 129 K7
St. Dunstan's Hill EC3 124 C9
St. Edmunds Ter NW8 122 E3
St. Elmos Rd SE16 129 H1
St. Francis Rd SE22 128 C10
St. George St W1 123 H8
St. George Wf SW8 127 L4
St. Georges Circ SE1 127 P2
St. George's Dr SW1 127 H3
St. Georges Flds W2 122 E8
St. Georges Rd SE1 127 N2
St. Georges Sq SE8 129 K3
St. George's Sq SW1 127 K4
St. George's Sq Ms SW1 127 K4
St. Georges Way SE15 128 C5
St. Giles High St WC2 123 K8
St. Giles Rd SE5 128 C6
St. Gilles Ho E2 125 H4
St. Helena Rd SE16 129 H3
St. James Ms E14 129 N2
St. James's SE14 129 J7
St. James's Av E2 124 G4
St. James's Ct SW1 127 J2
St. James's Cres SW9 127 N9
St. James's Palace SW1 123 J10
St. James's Pk SW1 127 K1
St. James's Pl SW1 123 J10
St. James's Rd SE1 128 E4
St. James's Rd SE16 128 E2
St. James's Sq SW1 123 J10
St. James's St SW1 123 J10
St. James's Ter Ms NW8 122 F3
St. James's Wk EC1 123 P6
St. John St EC1 123 P6
St. John's Cres SW9 127 N9
St. John's Est N1 124 B4
St. John's Hill SW11 126 D10
St. John's Hill Gro SW11 126 D10
St. John's La EC1 123 P6
St. John's Rd SW11 126 E10
St. Johns Vale SE8 129 L8
St. John's Wd High St NW8 122 D4
St. John's Wd Pk NW8 122 D3
St. John's Wd Rd NW8 122 D6
St. John's Wd Ter NW8 122 D4
St. Joseph's Vale SE3 129 P8
St. Jude's Rd E2 124 F4
St. Katharine's Way E1 124 D10
St. Lawrence St E14 125 N10
St. Lawrence Way SW9 127 N7
St. Leonards Ct N1 124 B5
St. Leonards Rd E14 125 M7
St. Leonards Sq NW5 122 G1
St. Leonards St E3 125 M5
St. Leonard's Ter SW3 126 F4
St. Loo Av SW3 126 E5
St. Luke's Av SW4 127 K10
St. Luke's Cl EC1 124 A6
St. Luke's Est EC1 124 B5
St. Luke's St SW3 126 E4
St. Margarets La W8 126 B2
St. Margarets Rd SE4 129 K10
St. Margaret's St SW1 127 L1
St. Mark St E1 124 D8
St. Marks Cres NW1 122 G3
St. Mark's Gro SW10 126 B5
St. Marks Sq NW1 122 G3
St. Martins Cl NW1 123 J3
St. Martin's La WC2 123 L9
St. Martin's Pl WC2 123 L9
St. Martin's Rd SW9 127 M8
St. Martin's-le-Grand EC1 124 A8
St. Mary at Hill EC3 124 C9
St. Mary Axe EC3 124 C8
St. Marychurch St SE16 128 G1
St. Mary's Gdns SE11 127 N3
St. Mary's Gate W8 126 B2
St. Mary's Gro N1 123 P1
St. Marys Mans W2 122 C7
St. Marys Path N1 123 P3
St. Mary's Pl W8 126 B2
St. Mary's Rd SE15 128 G7
St. Marys Sq W2 122 D7
St. Marys Ter W2 122 D7
St. Mary's Wk SE11 127 N3
St. Matthew's Rd SW2 127 M10
St. Matthew's Row E2 124 E5
St. Michael's Rd SW9 127 M8
St. Michaels St W2 122 D8
St. Norbert Grn SE4 129 J10
St. Norbert Rd SE4 129 J10
St. Olav's Sq SE16 128 G2
St. Oswald's Pl SE11 127 M4
St. Pancras Way NW1 123 J2
St. Paul St N1 124 A3
St. Paul's Av SE16 125 H10
St. Paul's Chyd EC4 123 P8
St. Paul's Cres NW1 123 K2
St. Paul's Pl N1 124 B1
St. Paul's Rd N1 123 P1
St. Paul's Shrubbery N1 124 B1
St. Pauls Way E3 125 K7
St. Pauls Way E14 125 K7
St. Peter's Cl E2 124 E4
St. Peters St N1 123 P3
St. Peter's Way N1 124 C2
St. Petersburgh Ms W2 122 B9
St. Petersburgh Pl W2 122 B9
St. Philip Sq SW8 127 H8
St. Philip St SW8 127 H8
St. Philip's Rd E8 124 E1
St. Rule St SW8 127 J8
St. Saviour's Est SE1 128 D2
St. Silas Pl NW5 122 G1
St. Silas St Est NW5 122 G1
St. Stephens Cres W2 122 A8
St. Stephens Gdns W2 122 A8
St. Stephens Gro SE13 129 N9
St. Stephen's Rd E3 125 K4
St. Stephens Ter SW8 127 M6
St. Stephen's Wk SW7 126 C3
St. Swithin's La EC4 124 B9
St. Thomas St SE1 124 B10
St. Thomas's Pl E9 124 G2
St. Thomas's Sq E9 124 F2
Salamanca St SE1 127 L3
Sale Pl W2 122 E7
Salem Rd W2 122 B9
Salisbury Ct EC4 123 P8
Salisbury Pl SW9 127 P6
Salisbury Pl W1 122 F7
Salisbury St NW8 122 E6
Salisbury Ter SE15 128 G9
Salmon La E14 125 J8
Salter Rd SE16 125 H10
Salter St E14 125 L9
Saltoun Rd SW2 127 N10
Saltwell St E14 125 L9
Samford St NW8 122 E6
Sampson St E1 124 E10
Samuel Cl SE14 129 H5
Samuel Lewis Trust Dws SW6 126 A6
Samuel St SE15 128 D6
Sancroft St SE11 127 M4
Sandall Rd NW5 123 J1
Sandbourne Rd SE4 129 J8
Sandgate St SE15 128 F5
Sandilands Rd SW6 126 B7
Sandison St SE15 128 D9
Sandland St WC1 123 M7
Sandmere Rd SW4 127 L10
Sandpiper Cl SE16 129 K1
Sandrock Rd SE13 129 L9
Sand's End La SW6 126 B7
Sandwell Cres NW6 122 A1
Sandwich St WC1 123 L5
Sandy's Row E1 124 C7
Sanford St SE14 129 J5
Sangora Rd SW11 126 D10
Sans Wk EC1 123 N6
Sansom St SE5 128 B6
Santley St SW4 127 M10
Saperton Wk SE11 127 M3
Sapphire Rd SE8 129 J3
Saracen St E14 125 L8
Sartor Rd SE15 129 H10
Satchwell Rd E2 124 E5
Saunders Ness Rd E14 129 N4
Saunders St SE11 127 N3
Savile Row W1 123 J9
Savona Est SW8 127 J6
Savona St SW8 127 J6
Savoy Pl WC2 123 L9
Savoy St WC2 123 M9
Sawmill Yd E3 125 J3
Sawyer St SE1 128 A1
Saxon Rd E3 125 K4
Saxton Cl SE13 129 P9
Sayes Ct St SE8 129 K5
Scala St W1 123 J7
Scandrett St E1 124 F10
Scarsdale Vil W8 126 A2
Scawen Rd SE8 129 J4
Scawfell St E2 124 D4
Sceaux Est SE5 128 C7
Sceptre Rd E2 124 G5
Schoolhouse La E1 125 H9
Schooner Cl E14 129 P2
Sclater St E1 124 D6
Scoresby St SE1 123 P10
Scott Ellis Gdns NW8 122 D5
Scott Lidgett Cres SE16 128 E1
Scott St E1 124 F6
Scriven St E8 124 D3
Scrutton St EC2 124 C6
Scylla Rd SE15 128 F9
Seaford St WC1 123 M5
Seagrave Rd SW6 126 A5
Searles Cl SW11 126 E6
Searles Rd SE1 128 B3
Sears St SE5 128 B6
Sebastian St EC1 123 P5
Sebbon St N1 123 P2
Sedding St SW1 126 G3
Sedgmoor Pl SE5 128 C6
Seething La EC3 124 C9
Sekforde St EC1 123 P6
Selby St E1 124 E6
Selden Rd SE15 128 G8
Selsdon Way E14 129 M2
Selsey St E14 125 L7
Selwood Pl SW7 126 D4
Selworthy Ho SW11 126 D7
Selwyn Rd E3 125 K4
Semley Pl SW1 126 G3
Senate St SE15 128 G8
Sendall Ct SW11 126 D9
Senior St W2 122 B7
Senrab St E1 125 H8
Serenaders Rd SW9 127 N8
Serle St WC2 123 M8
Serpentine Rd W2 122 F10
Settles St E1 124 E7
Settrington Rd SW6 126 B8
Severnake Cl E14 129 L3
Severus Rd SW11 126 E10
Seville Ms N1 124 C2
Seville St SW1 126 F1
Sevington St W9 122 B6
Seward St EC1 124 A5
Sewardstone Rd E2 124 G4
Sextant Av E14 129 P3
Seymour Gdns SE4 129 J9
Seymour Ms W1 122 G8
Seymour Pl W1 122 E7
Seymour St W1 122 F8
Seymour St W2 122 F8
Seymour Wk SW10 126 C5
Seyssel St E14 129 N3
Shacklewell St E2 124 D6
Shad Thames SE1 124 D10
Shaftesbury Av W1 123 K9
Shaftesbury Av WC2 123 K9
Shaftesbury St N1 124 A4
Shafton Rd E9 125 H3
Shalbourne Sq E9 125 K1
Shalcomb St SW10 126 C5
Shamrock St SW4 127 K9
Shand St SE1 128 C1
Shandy St E1 125 H7
Shannon Gro SW9 127 M10
Shardeloes Rd SE4 129 K9
Shardeloes Rd SE14 129 K9
Sharon Gdns E9 124 G3
Sharpleshall St NW1 122 F2
Sharratt St SE15 128 G5
Sharsted St SE17 127 P4
Shaw Ct SW11 126 D9
Shaw Rd SE22 128 C10
Shawfield St SW3 126 E4
Shearling Way N7 123 L1
Sheep La E8 124 F3
Sheepcote La SW11 126 F8
Sheffield Ter W8 122 A10
Sheldon Sq W2 122 C7
Shell Rd SE13 129 M9
Shelley Cl SE15 128 F8
Shellwood Rd SW11 126 F8
Shelmerdine Cl E3 125 L7
Shelton St WC2 123 L8
Shenfield St N1 124 C4
Shenley Rd SE5 128 C7
Shepherdess Wk N1 124 A4
Sheppard Dr SE16 128 F4
Shepperton Rd N1 124 A3
Sherborne St N1 124 B3
Sheringham Rd N7 123 M1
Sherriff Rd NW6 122 A1
Sherwin Rd SE14 129 H7
Sherwood Gdns E14 129 L3
Sherwood Gdns SE16 128 E4
Shetland Rd E3 125 K4
Ship St SE8 129 L7
Shipton St E2 124 D5
Shipwright Rd SE16 129 J1
Shirbutt St E14 125 M9
Shirland Rd W9 122 A5
Shirley Gro SW11 126 G9
Shoe La EC4 123 N8
Shooter's Hill Rd SE10 129 P7
Shore Pl E9 124 G2
Shore Rd E9 124 G2
Shoreditch High St E1 124 C6
Shorncliffe Rd SE1 128 D4
Short Rd E15 125 P3
Short Wall E15 125 N5
Shorter St E1 124 D9
Shorts Gdns WC2 123 L8
Shottendane Rd SW6 126 A7
Shouldham St W1 122 E7
Shrewsbury Rd W2 122 A8
Shroton St NW1 122 E7
Shrubland Rd E8 124 E3
Shuttleworth Rd SW11 126 E8
Sibella Rd SW4 127 K8
Sidmouth St WC1 123 L5
Sidney Rd SW9 127 M8
Sidney Sq E1 124 G8
Sidney St E1 124 F7
Sidworth St E8 124 F2
Silex St SE1 127 P1
Silk Mills Sq E9 125 K1
Silk St EC2 124 A7
Silver Rd SE13 129 M9
Silver Wk SE16 125 K10
Silverthorne Rd SW8 127 H8
Silvocea Way E14 125 P8
Silwood Est SE16 128 G3
Silwood St SE16 128 G3
Simms Rd SE1 128 E3
Simpson St SW11 126 E8
Simpsons Rd E14 125 M9
Sirinham Pt SW8 127 M5
Sisters Av SW11 126 F10
Sisulu Pl SW9 127 N9
Sivill Ho E2 124 D5
Six Bridges Trd Est SE1 128 E4
Sketchley Gdns SE16 129 H4
Skinner St EC1 123 N5
Skipworth Rd E9 124 G3
Skylines Village E14 129 N1
Slaidburn St SW10 126 C5
Slaithwaite Rd SE13 129 N10
Sleaford St SW8 127 J6
Slippers Pl SE16 128 F2
Sloane Av SW3 126 E3
Sloane Ct W SW3 126 G4
Sloane Gdns SW1 126 G3
Sloane Sq SW1 126 F3
Sloane St SW1 126 F1
Sloane Ter SW1 126 F3
Smart St E2 125 H5
Smeaton St E1 124 F10
Smedley St SW4 127 K8
Smedley St SW8 127 K8
Smeed Rd E3 125 L2
Smiles Pl SE13 129 N8
Smith Cl SE16 125 H10
Smith Sq SW1 127 L2
Smith St SW3 126 F4
Smith Ter SW3 126 F4
Smithy St E1 124 G7
Smokehouse Yd EC1 123 P7
Smugglers Way SW18 126 B10
Smyrks Rd SE17 128 C4
Smyrna Rd NW6 122 A2
Smythe St E14 125 M9
Snow Hill EC1 123 P7
Snowbury Rd SW6 126 B8
Snowden St EC2 124 C6
Snowman Ho NW6 122 B3
Snowsfields SE1 128 B1
Soames St SE15 128 D9
Soho Sq W1 123 K8
Solebay St E1 125 J6
Solomon's Pas SE15 128 F10
Solon New Rd SW4 127 L10
Solon Rd SW2 127 L10
Solway Rd SE22 128 E10
Somerford St E1 124 F6
Somerford Way SE16 129 J1
Somerleyton Pas SW9 127 P10
Somerleyton Rd SW9 127 N10
Somers Cres W2 122 E8
Somerset Est SW11 126 D7
Somerset Gdns SE13 129 M8
Somerton Rd SE15 128 F10
Sondes St SE17 128 B5
Sopwith Way SW8 127 H6
Sorrel La E14 125 P8
Sotheran Cl E8 124 E3
Sotheron Rd SW6 126 B6
Soudan Rd SW11 126 F7
South Audley St W1 122 G9
South Bolton Gdns SW5 126 B4
South Carriage Dr SW1 126 E1
South Carriage Dr SW7 126 E1
South Colonnade E14 125 L10
South Cres E16 125 P6
South Cres WC1 123 K7
South Eaton Pl SW1 126 G3
South End Row W8 126 B2
South Island Pl SW9 127 M6
South Lambeth Pl SW8 127 L5
South Lambeth Rd SW8 127 L5
South Molton La W1 123 H8
South Molton St W1 123 H8
South Par SW3 126 D4
South Pk SW6 126 A8
South Pk Ms SW6 126 B9
South Pl EC2 124 B7
South Sea St SE16 129 K2
South St W1 122 G10
South Tenter St E1 124 D9
South Ter SW7 126 E3
South Vil NW1 123 K1
South Wf Rd W2 122 D8
Southall Pl SE1 128 B1
Southampton Pl WC1 123 L7
Southampton Row WC1 123 L7
Southampton St WC2 123 L9
Southampton Way SE5 128 B6
Southbank Business Cen SW8 127 K5
Southborough Rd E9 124 G3
Southern Gro E3 125 K5
Southern St N1 123 M4
Southerngate Way SE14 129 J6
Southey Rd SW9 127 N7
Southgate Gro N1 124 B2
Southgate Rd N1 124 B3
Southmoor Way E9 125 K1
Southolm St SW11 127 H7
Southville SW8 127 K7
Southwark Br EC4 124 A10
Southwark Br SE1 124 A10
Southwark Br Rd SE1 127 P2
Southwark Pk Est SE16 128 F3
Southwark Pk Rd SE16 128 D3
Southwark St SE1 123 P10
Southwater Cl E14 125 K8
Southwell Gdns SW7 126 C3
Southwell Rd SE5 128 A9
Southwick Pl W2 122 E8
Southwick St W2 122 E8
Sovereign Cl E1 124 F9
Spa Grn Est EC1 123 N5
Spa Rd SE16 128 D2
Spanby Rd E3 125 L6
Spanish Pl W1 122 G8
Sparkford Ho SW11 126 D7
Sparta St SE10 129 M7
Spear Ms SW5 126 A3
Speke Ho SE5 128 A6
Speldhurst Rd E9 125 H2
Spelman St E1 124 E7
Spencer Rd SW18 126 D10
Spencer St EC1 123 P5
Spenser St SW1 127 J2
Spert St E14 125 J9
Spey St E14 125 N7
Spicer Cl SW9 127 P8
Spindrift Av E14 129 M3

Name	Page	Grid
Spital Sq E1	124	C7
Spital St E1	124	E6
Sporle Ct SW11	126	D9
Sprimont Pl SW3	126	F4
Spring St W2	122	D8
Springall St SE15	128	F6
Springfield La NW6	122	B3
Springfield Rd NW8	122	C3
Springfield Wk NW6	122	B3
Springhill Cl SE5	128	B9
Sprules Rd SE4	129	J8
Spur Rd SE1	127	N1
Spur Rd SW1	127	J1
Spurgeon St SE1	128	B2
Spurling Rd SE22	128	D10
Squirries St E2	124	E5
Stable Yd Rd SW1	123	J10
Stables Way SE11	127	N4
Stacey St WC2	123	K8
Stadium St SW10	126	C6
Stafford Cl NW6	122	A5
Stafford Ct W8	126	A2
Stafford Pl SW1	127	J2
Stafford Rd E3	125	K4
Stafford Rd NW6	122	A5
Stafford St W1	123	J10
Stafford Ter W8	126	A2
Staffordshire St SE15	128	E7
Stag Pl SW1	127	J2
Stainer St SE1	124	B10
Staining La EC2	124	A8
Stainsby Rd E14	125	L8
Stalham St SE16	128	F2
Stamford Rd N1	124	C2
Stamford St SE1	123	N10
Stamp Pl E2	124	D5
Stanbury Rd SE15	128	F7
Stanfield Rd E3	125	J4
Stanford Rd W8	126	B2
Stanhope Gdns SW7	126	C3
Stanhope Gate W1	122	G10
Stanhope Ms E SW7	126	C3
Stanhope Ms S SW7	126	C3
Stanhope Ms W SW7	126	C3
Stanhope Pl W2	122	F8
Stanhope St NW1	123	J5
Stanhope Ter W2	122	D9
Stanley Cl SW8	127	M5
Stanley Gro SW8	126	G8
Stanley Rd E15	125	P3
Stanley St SE8	129	K6
Stanmer St SW11	126	E7
Stannard Ms E8	124	E1
Stannard Rd E8	124	E1
Stannary Pl SE11	127	N4
Stannary St SE11	127	N5
Stansfield Rd SW9	127	M9
Stanswood Gdns SE5	128	C6
Stanway St N1	124	C4
Stanworth St SE1	128	D1
Staple Inn Bldgs WC1	123	N7
Staple St SE1	128	B1
Staples Cl SE16	125	J10
Star St W2	122	E7
Starboard Way E14	129	L2
Starcross St NW1	123	J5
Station App SE1	127	N1
Station Pas SE15	128	G7
Station Rd SE13	129	N9
Station St E15	125	P2
Station Ter SE5	128	A7
Staunton St SE8	129	K5
Stave Yd Rd SE16	125	J10
Stayner's Rd E1	125	H6
Stead St SE17	128	B3
Stean St E8	124	D3
Stebondale St E14	129	N4
Steeles Rd NW3	122	F1
Steers Way SE16	129	J1
Stephan Cl E8	124	E3
Stephen St W1	123	K7
Stephendale Rd SW6	126	B8
Stephenson Way NW1	123	J6
Stepney Causeway E1	125	H8
Stepney Grn E1	124	G7
Stepney High St E1	125	H7
Stepney Way E1	124	F7
Sterling Gdns SE14	129	J5
Sternhall La SE15	128	E9
Sterry St SE1	128	B1
Stevens Av E9	124	G1
Stevenson Cres SE16	128	E4
Steward St E1	124	C7
Stewart St E14	129	N1
Stewart's Gro SW3	126	D3
Stewart's Rd SW8	127	J6
Stillington St SW1	127	J3
Stirling Rd SW9	127	L8
Stockholm Ho E1	124	E9
Stockholm Rd SE16	128	G4
Stockholm Way E1	124	E10
Stockwell Av SW9	127	M9
Stockwell Gdns SW9	127	M8
Stockwell Gdns Est SW9	127	L8
Stockwell Grn SW9	127	M8
Stockwell La SW9	127	M8
Stockwell Pk Cres SW9	127	M8
Stockwell Pk Est SW9	127	M8
Stockwell Pk Rd SW9	127	M7
Stockwell Pk Wk SW9	127	M9
Stockwell Rd SW9	127	M8
Stockwell St SE10	129	N5
Stockwell Ter SW9	127	M7
Stokenchurch St SW6	126	B7
Stone Bldgs WC2	123	M7
Stonecutter St EC4	123	P8
Stonefield St N1	123	N3
Stones End St SE1	128	A1
Stoney La E1	124	B10
Stonhouse St SW4	127	K9
Stopes St SE15	128	D6
Stopford Rd SE17	127	P4
Store St WC1	123	K7
Storers Quay E14	129	P3
Storey's Gate SW1	127	K1
Stories Ms SE5	128	C8
Stories Rd SE5	128	C9
Storks Rd SE16	128	E2
Stormont Rd SW11	126	G9
Stour Rd E3	125	L2
Stourcliffe St W1	122	F8
Stowage SE8	129	L5
Strafford St E14	129	L1
Strahan Rd E3	125	J5
Straightsmouth SE10	129	N6
Straker's Rd SE22	128	F10
Strand WC2	123	L9
Stranraer Way N1	123	L2
Strasburg Rd SW11	127	H7
Stratford Cen, The E15	125	P2
Stratford Pl W1	123	H8
Stratford Rd W8	126	A2
Stratford Vil NW1	123	J2
Strath Ter SW11	126	E10
Strathblaine Rd SW11	126	D10
Stratheam Pl W2	122	E9
Strathnairn St SE1	128	E3
Strathray Gdns NW3	122	E1
Stratton St W1	123	H10
Strattondale St E14	129	N2
Streimer Rd E15	125	N4
Strickland St SE8	129	L8
Stroudley Wk E3	125	M5
Strutton Grd SW1	127	K2
Stuart Rd NW6	122	A5
Stuart Rd SE15	128	G10
Stuart Twr W9	122	C5
Stubbs Dr SE16	128	F4
Studd St N1	123	P3
Studdridge St SW6	126	A8
Studholme St SE15	128	F6
Studley Est SW4	127	L7
Studley Rd SW4	127	L7
Stukeley St WC2	123	L8
Sturdy Rd SE15	128	F8
Sturgeon Rd SE17	128	A4
Sturry St E14	125	M8
Sturt St N1	124	A4
Stutfield St E1	124	E8
Styles Gdns SW9	127	P9
Sudeley St N1	123	P4
Sudlow Rd SW18	126	A10
Sugar Ho La E15	125	N4
Sugar Quay Wk EC3	124	C9
Sugden Rd SW11	126	G9
Sulivan Ct SW6	126	A9
Sulivan Rd SW6	126	A9
Sullivan Cl SW11	126	E9
Sullivan Rd SE11	127	N3
Sultan St SE5	128	A6
Summercourt Rd E1	124	G8
Sumner Est SE15	128	D6
Sumner Pl SW7	126	D3
Sumner Rd SE15	128	D6
Sumner St SE1	124	A10
Sumpter Cl NW3	122	C1
Sun St EC2	124	B7
Sunbury La SW11	126	D7
Sunderland Ter W2	122	B8
Sunlight Sq E2	124	F5
Sunninghill Rd SE13	129	M8
Sunray Av SE24	128	B10
Sunset Rd SE5	128	A10
Surma Cl E1	124	F6
Surrendale Pl W9	122	A6
Surrey Canal Rd SE14	128	G5
Surrey Canal Rd SE15	128	G5
Surrey La SW11	126	E7
Surrey La Est SW11	126	E7
Surrey Quays Retail Cen SE16	129	H2
Surrey Quays Rd SE16	128	G2
Surrey Row SE1	127	P1
Surrey Sq SE17	128	C4
Surrey St WC2	123	M9
Surrey Ter SE17	128	C4
Surrey Water Rd SE16	125	H10
Susannah St E14	125	M8
Sussex Gdns W2	122	D8
Sussex Ms NW1	122	F5
Sussex Pl W2	122	D8
Sussex Sq W2	122	D9
Sussex St SW1	127	H4
Sutherland Av W9	122	C5
Sutherland Pl W2	122	A8
Sutherland Row SW1	127	H4
Sutherland Sq SE17	128	A4
Sutherland St SW1	127	H4
Sutherland Wk SE17	128	A4
Sutterton St N7	123	M1
Sutton Est SW3	126	E4
Sutton Est, The N1	123	P2
Sutton Row W1	123	K8
Sutton St E1	124	G8
Swain St NW8	122	E6
Swallow Cl SE14	128	G7
Swan Mead SE1	128	C2
Swan Rd SE16	128	G1
Swan St SE1	128	A2
Swan Wk SW3	126	F5
Swandon Way SW18	126	B10
Swanfield St E2	124	D5
Swaton Rd E3	125	L6
Sweden Gate SE16	129	J2
Swedenborg Gdns E1	124	E9
Sweeney Cres SE1	128	D1
Swinford Gdns SW9	127	P9
Swinton Pl WC1	123	M5
Swinton St WC1	123	M5
Swiss Ter NW6	122	D2
Sybil Phoenix Cl SE8	129	H1
Sycamore Av E3	125	K3
Sycamore Ms SW4	127	J9
Sydney Cl SW3	126	D3
Sydney Ms SW3	126	D3
Sydney Pl SW7	126	D3
Sydney St SW3	126	E3
Sylvan Gro SE15	128	F6
Sylvester Rd E8	124	F1
Symons St SW3	126	F3

T

Name	Page	Grid
Tabard Gdn Est SE1	128	B1
Tabard St SE1	128	B1
Tabernacle St EC2	124	B6
Tachbrook Est SW1	127	K4
Tachbrook St SW1	127	J3
Tack Ms SE4	129	L9
Tadema Rd SW10	126	C6
Taeping St E14	129	M3
Talacre Rd NW5	122	G1
Talbot Rd SE22	128	C10
Talbot Sq W2	122	D8
Talfourd Pl SE15	128	D7
Talfourd Rd SE15	128	D7
Tallis St EC4	123	N9
Talma Rd SW2	127	N10
Talwin St E3	125	M5
Tamworth St SW6	126	A6
Tanner St SE1	128	C1
Tanners Hill SE8	129	K7
Taplow NW3	122	D2
Taplow St N1	124	A4
Tapp St E1	124	F6
Tappesfield Rd SE15	128	G9
Tariff Cres SE8	129	K3
Tarling St E1	124	F8
Tarling St Est E1	124	G8
Tarragon Cl SE14	129	J6
Tarrant Pl W1	122	F7
Tarver Rd SE17	127	P4
Tarves Way SE10	129	M6
Tasman Rd SW9	127	L9
Tatum St SE17	128	B3
Taunton Pl NW1	122	F6
Tavern La SW9	127	N8
Tavistock Pl WC1	123	L6
Tavistock Sq WC1	123	K6
Tavistock St WC2	123	L9
Taviton St WC1	123	K6
Tavy Cl SE11	127	N4
Tawny Way SE16	129	H3
Taybridge Rd SW11	126	G9
Tayburn Cl E14	125	N8
Taylor Cl SE8	129	K5
Tayport Cl N1	123	L2
Teak Cl SE16	125	J10
Teale St E2	124	E4
Tedworth Sq SW3	126	F4
Teesdale Cl E2	124	F4
Teesdale St E2	124	F4
Teignmouth Cl SW4	127	K10
Telegraph Pl E14	129	M3
Telford Ter SW1	127	J5
Tell Gro SE22	128	D8
Templar St SE5	127	P8
Temple EC4	123	N9
Temple Av EC4	123	N9
Temple Pl WC2	123	M9
Temple St E2	124	F4
Temple W Ms SE11	127	P2
Templecombe Rd E9	124	G3
Templeton Pl SW5	126	A3
Tench St E1	124	F10
Tenison Way SE1	123	M10
Tennis St SE1	128	B1
Tennyson St SW8	127	H8
Tent St E1	124	F6
Tenterden St W1	123	H8
Teredo St SE16	129	H2
Terminus Pl SW1	127	H2
Terrace, The NW6	122	A3
Terrace Rd E9	124	G2
Tessa Sanderson Pl SW8	127	H9
Tetcott Rd SW10	126	C6
Teversham La SW8	127	L7
Teviot St E14	125	N7
Thackeray Rd SW8	126	H8
Thackeray St W8	126	B1
Thalia Cl SE10	129	N5
Thame Rd SE16	129	H1
Thames Av SW10	126	C7
Thames St SE10	129	M5
Thanet St WC1	123	L5
Thayer St W1	122	G7
Theatre St SW11	126	F9
Theberton St N1	123	N3
Theed St SE1	123	N10
Theobald's Rd WC1	123	M7
Thermopylae Gate E14	129	M3
Thessaly Rd SW8	127	J6
Thirleby Rd SW1	127	J2
Thirsk Rd SW11	126	G9
Thistle Gro SW10	126	C4
Thomas Baines Rd SW11	126	D9
Thomas Doyle St SE1	127	P2
Thomas More St E1	124	E9
Thomas Rd E14	125	K8
Thompson's Av SE5	128	A6
Thorburn Sq SE1	128	E3
Thoresby St N1	124	A5
Thorncroft St SW8	127	L6
Thorndike Cl SW10	126	C6
Thorndike Rd N1	124	A1
Thorndike St SW1	127	J3
Thorne Rd SW8	127	L6
Thorney Cres SW11	126	D6
Thorney St SW1	127	L3
Thorngate Rd W9	122	A6
Thornham St SE10	129	M5
Thornhaugh St WC1	123	K6
Thornhill Cres N1	123	M2
Thornhill Rd N1	123	N2
Thornhill Sq N1	123	M2
Thornton Pl W1	122	F7
Thornton St SW9	127	N8
Thornville St SE8	129	L7
Thorparch Rd SW8	127	K7
Thoydon Rd E3	125	J4
Thrale St SE1	124	A10
Thrawl St E1	124	D7
Threadneedle St EC2	124	B8
Three Colt St E14	125	K9
Three Colts La E2	124	F6
Three Kings Yd W1	123	H9
Three Mill La E3	125	N5
Three Quays Wk EC3	124	C9
Throgmorton Av EC2	124	B8
Throgmorton St EC2	124	B8
Thurland Rd SE16	128	E2
Thurloe Cl SW7	126	E2
Thurloe Pl SW7	126	D3
Thurloe Sq SW7	126	E3
Thurloe St SW7	126	D3
Thurlow St SE17	128	B4
Thurston Rd SE13	129	M8
Thurtle Rd E2	124	D3
Tibbatts Rd E3	125	M6
Tideway Ind Est SW8	127	J5
Tidworth Rd E3	125	L6
Tileyard Rd N7	123	L2
Tiller Rd E14	129	L2
Tilney Gdns N1	124	B1
Tilney St W1	122	G10
Timber Mill Way SW4	127	K9
Timber Pond Rd SE16	129	H1
Timberland Rd E1	124	F8
Timothy Rd E3	125	K7
Tindal St SW9	127	P7
Tinsley Rd E1	124	G7
Tintagel Cres SE22	128	D10
Tintern St SW4	127	L10
Tinworth St SE11	127	M4
Tipthorpe Rd SW11	126	G9
Tisdall Pl SE17	128	B3
Titchfield Rd NW8	122	F3
Tite St SW3	126	F4
Tiverton St SE1	128	A2
Tivoli Ct SE16	129	K1
Tobacco Dock E1	124	F9
Tobin Cl NW3	122	E2
Toby La E1	125	J6
Tollet St E1	125	H6
Tollgate Gdns NW6	122	B4
Tolpuddle St N1	123	N4
Tomlins Gro E3	125	L5
Tomlinson Cl E2	124	D5
Tonbridge St WC1	123	L5
Tooley St SE1	124	B10
Topmast Pt E14	129	L1
Tor Gdns W8	126	A1
Torrens St EC1	123	N4
Torridge Gdns SE15	128	G10
Torrington Pl E1	124	E10
Torrington Pl WC1	123	K7
Torrington Sq WC1	123	K6
Tottan Ter E1	125	H8
Tottenham Ct Rd W1	123	J6
Tottenham Rd N1	124	C1
Tottenham St W1	123	J7
Totteridge Ho SW11	126	D8
Toulmin St SE1	128	A1
Toulon St SE5	128	A6
Tours Pas SW11	126	D10
Towcester Rd E3	125	M6
Tower 42 EC2	124	C8
Tower Br E1	124	D10
Tower Br SE1	124	D10
Tower Br App E1	124	D10
Tower Br Rd SE1	128	C2
Tower Br Wf E1	124	E10
Tower Hill EC3	124	C9
Tower Millennium Pier EC3	124	D10
Tower St WC2	123	K8
Town Hall Rd SW11	126	F9
Townmead Rd SW6	126	C8
Townsend St SE17	128	B3
Townshend Est NW8	122	E4
Townshend Rd NW8	122	E3
Toynbee St E1	124	D7
Tradescant Rd SW8	127	L6
Trafalgar Av SE15	128	D4
Trafalgar Gdns E1	125	H7
Trafalgar Gro SE10	129	P5
Trafalgar Ms E9	125	K1
Trafalgar Rd SE10	129	P5
Trafalgar Sq WC2	123	K10
Trafalgar St SE17	128	B4
Trafalgar Way E14	125	N10
Transept St NW1	122	E7
Transom Sq E14	129	M3
Tranton Rd SE16	128	E2
Treadway St E2	124	F4
Treaty St N1	123	M3
Trebovir Rd SW5	126	A4
Treby St E3	125	K6
Tredegar Rd E3	125	K4
Tredegar Sq E3	125	K5
Tredegar Ter E3	125	K5
Trederwen Rd E8	124	E3
Tregarvon Rd SW11	126	G10
Trego Rd E9	125	L2
Tregothnan Rd SW9	127	L9
Tregunter Rd SW10	126	C5
Trelawney Est E9	124	G1
Tremadoc Rd SW4	127	K10
Tremaine Cl SE4	129	L9
Trenchard St SE10	129	P4
Trenchold St SW8	127	L5
Tresco Rd SE15	128	F10
Tresham Cres NW8	122	E6
Tressillian Cres SE4	129	L9
Tressillian Rd SE4	129	K10
Trevithick St SE8	129	L4
Trevor Pl SW7	126	E1
Trevor Sq SW7	126	F1
Trevor St SW7	126	E1
Triangle Pl SW4	127	K10
Triangle Rd E8	124	F3
Trigon Rd SW8	127	M6
Trim St SE14	129	K5
Trinidad St E14	125	L9
Trinity Ch Sq SE1	128	A2
Trinity Cl E8	124	D1
Trinity Gdns SW9	127	M10
Trinity Gro SE10	129	N7
Trinity Sq EC3	124	C9
Trinity St SE1	128	A1
Trinity Wk NW3	122	C1
Triton Sq NW1	123	J6
Trocadero Shop Cen W1	123	K9
Trott St SW11	126	E7
Troutbeck Rd SE14	129	J7
Trowbridge Rd E9	125	K1
Troy Town SE15	128	E9
Trundleys Rd SE8	129	H4
Trundleys Ter SE8	129	H3
Truro St NW5	122	G1
Tryon Cres E9	124	G3
Tryon St SW3	126	F4
Tudor Gro E9	124	G2
Tudor Rd E9	124	G3
Tudor St EC4	123	N9
Tufton St SW1	127	K2
Tuilerie St E2	124	E4
Tunnel Av SE10	129	P1
Tunstall Rd SW9	127	M10
Turenne Cl SW18	126	C10
Turin St E2	124	E5
Turks Row SW3	126	F4
Turner Cl SW9	127	P7
Turner St E1	124	F7
Turners Rd E3	125	K7
Turnmill St EC1	123	N6
Turpin La SE10	129	N5
Turret Gro SW4	127	J9
Tustin Est SE15	128	G5
Twelvetrees Cres E3	125	N6
Twine Ct E1	124	G9
Twyford St N1	123	M3
Tyburn Way W1	122	F9
Tyers Est SE1	128	C1
Tyers St SE11	127	M4
Tyers Ter SE11	127	M4
Tyler Cl E2	124	D4
Tyndale Ct E14	129	M4
Tyneham Rd SW11	126	G8
Tynemouth St SW6	126	C8
Type St E2	125	H4
Tyrawley Rd SW6	126	B7
Tyrrell Rd SE22	128	E10
Tyrwhitt Rd SE4	129	L9
Tyssen Pas E8	124	D1
Tyssen St E8	124	D1

U

Name	Page	Grid
Uamvar St E14	125	M7
Ufford St SE1	127	N1
Ufton Gro N1	124	B2
Ufton Rd N1	124	B2
Undercliff Rd SE13	129	L9
Undershaft EC3	124	C8
Underwood Rd E1	124	E6
Underwood Row N1	124	A5
Underwood St N1	124	A5
Undine Rd E14	129	M3
Union Gro SW8	127	K8
Union Rd SW4	127	K8
Union Rd SW8	127	K8
Union Sq N1	124	A3
Union St E15	125	N3
Union St SE1	123	P10
University St WC1	123	J6
Unwin Cl SE15	128	E5
Upcerne Rd SW10	126	C6
Upper Bk St E14	125	M10
Upper Belgrave St SW1	126	G2
Upper Berkeley St W1	122	F8
Upper Brockley Rd SE4	129	K8
Upper Brook St W1	122	G9
Upper Cheyne Row SW3	126	E5
Upper Grosvenor St W1	122	G9
Upper Grd SE1	123	N10
Upper Marsh SE1	127	M2
Upper Montagu St W1	122	F7
Upper St E14	125	L7
Upper Phillimore Gdns W8	126	A1
Upper St N1	123	N4
Upper Tachbrook St SW1	127	J3
Upper Thames St EC4	124	A9
Upper Wimpole St W1	122	G7
Upper Woburn Pl WC1	123	K5
Upstall St SE5	127	P7
Urlwin St SE5	128	A5
Urlwin Wk SW9	127	N8
Ursula St SW11	126	E7
Usborne Ms SW8	127	M6
Usher Rd E3	125	K4
Usk Rd SW11	126	C10
Usk St E2	125	H5
Uverdale Rd SW10	126	C6
Uxbridge St W8	122	A10

V

Name	Page	Grid
Vale, The SW3	126	D5
Vale Royal N7	123	L2
Valentine Pl SE1	127	P1
Valentine Rd E9	125	H1
Valentine Row SE1	127	P1
Valette St E9	124	F1
Vallance Rd E1	124	E5
Vallance Rd E2	124	E5
Valmar Rd SE5	128	A7
Vandon St SW1	127	J2
Vanguard St SE8	129	L7
Vansittart St SE14	129	J6
Vanston Pl SW6	126	A6
Varcoe Rd SE16	128	F4
Varden St E1	124	F8
Vardens Rd SW11	126	D10
Varndell St NW1	123	J5
Vassall Rd SW9	127	N6
Vauban Est SE16	128	E2

Name	Page	Grid
Vauban St SE16	128	D2
Vaughan Rd SE5	128	A9
Vaughan Rd SE16	129	K1
Vaughan Way E1	124	E9
Vauxhall Br SE1	127	L4
Vauxhall Br SW1	127	L4
Vauxhall Br Rd SW1	127	J3
Vauxhall Gdns Est SE11	127	M4
Vauxhall Gro SW8	127	L5
Vauxhall St SE11	127	M4
Vauxhall Wk SE11	127	M4
Vawdrey Cl E1	124	G6
Veda Rd SE13	129	L10
Velletri Ho E2	125	H4
Venables St NW8	122	D6
Venetian Rd SE5	128	A8
Venn St SW4	127	J10
Ventnor Rd SE14	129	H6
Venue St E14	125	N7
Vere St W1	123	H8
Verney Rd SE16	128	E5
Verney Way SE16	128	F4
Vernon Pl WC1	123	L7
Vernon Ri WC1	123	M5
Vernon Rd E3	125	K4
Vesta Rd SE4	129	J8
Vestry Ms SE5	128	C7
Vestry Rd SE5	128	C7
Vestry St N1	124	B5
Viaduct St E2	124	F5
Vian St SE13	129	M9
Vicarage Cres SW11	126	D7
Vicarage Gdns W8	122	A10
Vicarage Gate W8	126	B1
Vicarage Gro SE5	128	B7
Vicars Hill SE13	129	M10
Viceroy Rd SW8	127	L7
Victoria Embk EC4	123	M9
Victoria Embk SW1	127	L1
Victoria Embk WC2	127	L1
Victoria Gdns W8	122	A10
Victoria Gro W8	126	C2
Victoria Ms NW6	122	A3
Victoria Pk E9	125	J2
Victoria Pk Rd E9	124	G3
Victoria Pk Sq E2	124	G5
Victoria Pl SW1	127	H3
Victoria Ri SW4	127	H9
Victoria Rd W8	126	C2
Victoria Sta SW1	127	H3
Victoria St SW1	127	J2
Victoria Wf E14	125	J9
Victory Pl SE17	128	A3
Victory Way SE16	129	J1
Vigo St W1	123	J9
Viking Ct SW6	126	A5
Villa Rd SW9	127	N9
Villa St SE17	128	B4
Villiers St WC2	123	L9
Vince St EC1	124	B5
Vincent Cl SE16	129	J1
Vincent Ms E3	125	L4
Vincent Sq SW1	127	J3
Vincent St SW1	127	K3
Vincent Ter N1	123	P4
Vine Br EC1	123	N6
Viney Rd SE13	129	M9
Vineyard Wk EC1	123	N6
Vining St SW9	127	N10
Violet Hill NW8	122	C4
Violet Rd E3	125	M6
Virgil St SE1	127	M2
Virginia Rd E2	124	D5
Virginia St E1	124	E9
Vivian Rd E3	125	J4
Voltaire Rd SW4	127	K9
Voss St E2	124	E5
Vulcan Rd SE4	129	K8
Vulcan Ter SE4	129	K8
Vulcan Way N7	123	M1
Vyner St E2	124	F3

W

Name	Page	Grid
Wadding St SE17	128	B3
Waddington St E15	125	P1
Wades Pl E14	125	M9
Wadeson St E2	124	F4
Wadham Gdns NW3	122	E3
Wadhurst Rd SW8	127	J7
Wager St E3	125	K6
Waghorn St SE15	128	E8
Wagner St SE15	128	G6
Waite St SE15	128	D5
Wakefield St WC1	123	L5
Wakeham St N1	124	B1
Wakeling St E14	125	J8
Wakley St EC1	123	P5
Walberswick St SW8	127	L6
Walbrook EC4	124	B9
Walcot Sq SE11	127	N3
Walden St E1	124	F8
Walerand Rd SE13	129	N8
Wales Cl SE15	128	F6
Waley St E1	125	H7
Walham Gro SW6	126	A6
Wall St N1	124	B1
Wallace Rd N1	124	A1
Wallbutton Rd SE4	129	J8
Waller Rd SE14	129	H7
Wallgrave Rd SW5	126	B3
Wallis Cl SW11	126	D9
Wallis Rd E9	125	K1
Wallwood St E14	125	K7
Walnut Tree Wk SE11	127	N3
Walpole St SW3	126	F4
Walsham Rd SE14	129	H8
Walter St E2	125	H5
Walter Ter E1	125	H8
Walton Cl SW8	127	L6
Walton Pl SW3	126	F2
Walton St SW3	126	E3
Walworth Pl SE17	128	A4
Walworth Rd SE1	128	A3
Walworth Rd SE17	128	A3
Wandon Rd SW6	126	B6
Wandsworth Br SW6	126	B9
Wandsworth Br SW18	126	B9
Wandsworth Br Rd SW6	126	B7
Wandsworth Rd SW8	127	K6
Wanless Rd SE24	128	A9
Wanley Rd SE5	128	B10
Wansbeck Rd E3	125	K2
Wansbeck Rd E9	125	K2
Wansey St SE17	128	A3
Wapping High St E1	124	E10
Wapping La E1	124	F9
Wapping Wall E1	124	G10
Ward Rd E15	125	P3
Wardalls Gro SE14	128	G6
Warden Rd NW5	122	G1
Wardour St W1	123	K9
Warham St SE5	127	P6
Warley St E2	125	H5
Warlock Rd W9	122	A6
Warndon St SE16	129	H3
Warneford St E9	124	F3
Warner Pl E2	124	E4
Warner Rd SE5	128	A7
Warner St EC1	123	N6
Warner St N1	123	J6
Warren St W1	123	J6
Warriner Gdns SW11	126	F7
Warrington Cres W9	122	C6
Warton Rd E15	125	N2
Warwick Av W2	122	C6
Warwick Av W9	122	C6
Warwick Ct SE15	128	E8
Warwick Cres W2	122	C7
Warwick Est W2	122	B7
Warwick Ho St SW1	123	K10
Warwick La EC4	123	P8
Warwick Pl W9	122	C7
Warwick Pl N SW1	127	J3
Warwick Row SW1	127	H2
Warwick Sq SW1	127	J4
Warwick Sq Ms SW1	127	J3
Warwick St W1	123	J9
Warwick Way SW1	127	J3
Warwickshire Path SE8	129	K6
Wat Tyler Rd SE3	129	N8
Wat Tyler Rd SE10	129	N8
Water Gdns, The W2	122	E8
Water La SE14	128	G6
Water Ms SE15	128	G10
Waterford Rd SW6	126	B7
Watergate St SE8	129	L5
Waterloo Br SE1	123	M9
Waterloo Br WC2	123	M9
Waterloo Est E2	124	G4
Waterloo Gdns E2	124	G4
Waterloo Pl SW1	123	K10
Waterloo Rd SE1	127	N1
Waterloo Ter N1	123	P2
Waterman Way E1	124	F10
Watermans Wk SE16	129	J2
Watermeadow La SW6	126	C8
Waterside Cl E3	125	K3
Waterside Pt SW11	126	E6
Waterside Twr SW6	126	C7
Waterson St E2	124	C5
Waterview Ho E14	125	J7
Watkinson Rd N7	123	M1
Watling St EC4	124	A8
Watney St E1	124	F8
Watson's St SE8	129	L6
Watts Gro E3	125	M7
Watts St E1	124	F10
Watts St SE15	128	D7
Waveney Av SE15	128	F10
Waverley Pl NW8	122	D4
Waverley Wk W2	122	A4
Waverton Ho E3	125	K3
Wayford St SW11	126	E8
Wayman Ct E8	124	F1
Wear Pl E2	124	F5
Weardale Rd SE13	129	P10
Wearside Rd SE13	129	M10
Weatherley Cl E3	125	K7
Weaver St E1	124	E6
Weavers Ter SW6	126	A5
Weavers Way NW1	123	K3
Webb St SE1	128	C2
Webber Row SE1	127	N1
Webber St SE1	127	N1
Webster Rd SE16	128	E2
Weighhouse St W1	122	G8
Weir's Pas NW1	123	K5
Welbeck St W1	122	G7
Welbeck Way W1	123	H8
Welby St SE5	127	P7
Welland St SE10	129	N5
Wellclose Sq E1	124	E9
Wellesley St E1	125	H7
Wellesley Ter N1	124	A5
Wellington Pl NW8	122	E4
Wellington Rd NW8	122	D4
Wellington Row E2	124	D5
Wellington Sq SW3	126	F4
Wellington St WC2	123	L9
Wellington Ter E1	124	F10
Wellington Way E3	125	L5
Wells Ri NW8	122	F3
Wells St W1	123	J8
Wells Way SE5	128	B5
Welsford St SE1	128	D2
Wendle Ct SW8	127	L5
Wendon St E3	125	K3
Wendover SE17	128	C4
Wenlock Rd N1	124	A4
Wenlock St N1	124	A4
Wennington Rd E3	125	H4
Wentworth Cres SE15	128	E6
Wentworth St E1	124	D8
Werrington St NW1	123	J4
Wesley Cl SE17	127	P3
Wessex St E2	124	G5
West Arbour St E1	125	H8
West Carriage Dr W2	122	D9
West Eaton Pl SW1	126	G3
West End La NW6	122	A2
West Gdns E1	124	F9
West Gro SE10	129	N7
West Halkin St SW1	126	G2
West Hampstead Ms NW6	122	B1
West India Av E14	125	L10
West India Dock Rd E14	125	K8
West La SE16	128	F1
West One Shop Cen W1	123	H8
West Rd SW3	126	F5
West Smithfield EC1	123	P7
West Sq SE11	127	P2
West St E2	124	F4
West Tenter St E1	124	D8
Westbourne Br W2	122	C7
Westbourne Cres W2	122	D9
Westbourne Gdns W2	122	B8
Westbourne Gro W2	122	A8
Westbourne Gro Ter W2	122	B8
Westbourne Pk Rd W2	122	A7
Westbourne Pk Vil W2	122	A7
Westbourne Rd N7	123	N1
Westbourne St W2	122	D9
Westbourne Ter W2	122	D8
Westbourne Ter Ms W2	122	C8
Westbourne Ter Rd W2	122	C7
Westbridge Rd SW11	126	D7
Westbury St SW8	127	J8
Westcott Rd SE17	127	P5
Western Rd SW9	127	N9
Westferry Circ E14	125	K10
Westferry Rd E14	125	L10
Westfield Cl SW10	126	C6
Westfield Way E1	125	J5
Westgate St E8	124	F3
Westgate Ter SW10	126	B4
Westgrove La SE10	129	N7
Westminster Br SE1	127	L1
Westminster Br SW1	127	L1
Westminster Br Rd SE1	127	N2
Westminster Gdns SW1	127	K3
Westmoreland Pl SW1	127	H4
Westmoreland Rd SE17	128	A5
Westmoreland St W1	122	G7
Westmoreland Ter SW1	127	H4
Westmoreland Wk SE17	128	B5
Weston Ri WC1	123	M4
Weston St SE1	128	B2
Westport St E1	125	H8
Westway W2	122	A7
Westway W9	122	A7
Wetherby Gdns SW5	126	C3
Wetherby Pl SW7	126	C3
Wetherell Rd E9	125	H3
Weybridge Pt SW11	126	G8
Weymouth Ms W1	123	H7
Weymouth St W1	123	H7
Weymouth Ter E2	124	D4
Wharf Pl E2	124	E3
Wharf Rd E15	125	P3
Wharf Rd N1	124	A4
Wharfdale Rd N1	123	L4
Wharfedale St SW10	126	B4
Wharton St WC1	123	M5
Wheat Sheaf Cl E14	129	M3
Wheatsheaf La SW8	127	L6
Wheelwright St N7	123	M2
Wheler St E1	124	D6
Whidborne St WC1	123	L5
Whiskin St EC1	123	P5
Whistlers Av SW11	126	D6
Whiston Rd E2	124	D4
Whitbread Rd SE4	129	J10
Whitburn Rd SE13	129	M10
Whitcher Cl SE14	129	J5
Whitcomb St WC2	123	K9
White Ch La E1	124	E8
White Hart St SE11	127	N4
White Horse La E1	125	H6
White Horse Rd E1	125	J8
White Horse St W1	123	H10
White Lion Hill EC4	123	P9
White Lion St N1	123	N4
White Post La E9	125	K2
White Post La SE13	129	L9
White Post St SE15	128	G6
Whiteadder Way E14	129	M3
Whitear Wk E15	125	P1
Whitechapel High St E1	124	D8
Whitechapel Rd E1	124	E8
Whitecross St EC1	124	A6
Whitefriars St EC4	123	N8
Whitehall SW1	123	L10
Whitehall Ct SW1	123	L10
Whitehall Pl SW1	123	L10
Whitehead's Gro SW3	126	E4
Whiteleys Shop Cen W2	122	B8
Whites Grds SE1	128	C1
White's Row E1	124	D7
Whitethorn St E3	125	L6
Whitfield Rd SE3	129	P7
Whitfield St W1	123	K7
Whitgift St SE11	127	M3
Whitmore Est N1	124	C3
Whitmore Rd N1	124	C3
Whittaker St SW1	126	G3
Whittington Rd SE15	128	F9
Whitworth St SE10	129	P5
Whorlton Rd SE15	128	F9
Wick La E3	125	L4
Wick Rd E9	125	H1
Wickersley Rd SW11	126	G8
Wickford St E1	124	G6
Wickham Gdns SE4	129	K9
Wickham Ms SE4	129	K8
Wickham Rd SE4	129	K10
Wickham St SE11	127	M4
Wicklow St WC1	123	M5
Wickwood St SE5	127	P8
Widdin St E15	125	P2
Widley Rd W9	122	A5
Wigmore Pl W1	123	H8
Wigmore St W1	122	G8
Wilbraham Pl SW1	126	F3
Wilcox Cl SW8	127	L6
Wilcox Rd SW8	127	L6
Wild Ct WC2	123	M8
Wild Goose Dr SE14	128	G7
Wild St WC2	123	L8
Wilde Cl E8	124	F2
Wild's Rents SE1	128	C2
Wilfred St SW1	127	J2
Wilkes St E1	124	D7
Wilkin St NW5	123	H1
Wilkinson St SW8	127	M6
Willard St SW8	127	H9
Willes Rd NW5	123	H1
William Bonney Est SW4	127	K10
William Cl SE13	129	N8
William IV St WC2	123	L9
William Morris Way SW6	126	C9
William Rd NW1	123	H5
William St SW1	126	F1
Williams Bldgs E2	124	G6
Willington Rd SW9	127	L9
Willis St E14	125	M8
Willoughby Pas E14	125	L10
Willow Br Rd N1	124	A1
Willow Pl SW1	127	J3
Willow St EC2	124	C6
Willow Wk SE1	128	C3
Willowbrook Rd SE15	128	D5
Wilman Gro E8	124	F2
Wilmcote Ho W2	122	B7
Wilmer Gdns N1	124	C3
Wilmer Lea Cl E15	125	N2
Wilmington Sq WC1	123	N5
Wilmington St WC1	123	N5
Wilmot Cl SE15	128	E6
Wilmot Pl NW1	123	J2
Wilmot St E2	124	F6
Wilshaw St SE14	129	L7
Wilson Gro SE16	128	F1
Wilson Rd SE5	128	C7
Wilson St EC2	124	B7
Wilton Cres SW1	126	G1
Wilton Ms SW1	126	G2
Wilton Pl SW1	126	G1
Wilton Rd SW1	127	H2
Wilton Row SW1	126	G1
Wilton Sq N1	124	B3
Wilton St SW1	127	H2
Wilton Ter SW1	126	G2
Wilton Vil N1	124	B3
Wilton Way E8	124	F2
Wiltshire Rd SW9	127	N9
Wiltshire Row N1	124	B3
Wimbolt St E2	124	E5
Wimbourne St N1	124	B4
Wimpole Ms W1	123	H7
Wimpole St W1	123	H8
Winans Wk SW9	127	N8
Winchester Cl SE17	127	P3
Winchester Rd NW3	122	D2
Winchester Sq SE1	124	B10
Winchester St SW1	127	H4
Winchester Wk SE1	124	B10
Wincott St SE11	127	N3
Winders St SW11	126	E8
Windlass Pl SE8	129	J3
Windmill Cl SE13	129	N8
Windmill La E15	125	P1
Windmill Row SE11	127	N4
Windmill St W1	123	K7
Windmill Wk SE1	123	N10
Windrose Cl SE16	129	H1
Windsock Cl SE16	129	K3
Windsor Gdns W9	122	A7
Windsor St N1	123	P3
Windsor Ter N1	124	A5
Windsor Wk SE5	128	B8
Wine Cl E1	124	G9
Winford Ho E3	125	K2
Winforton St SE10	129	N7
Wingfield St SE15	128	E9
Wingmore Rd SE24	128	A9
Winifred Gro SW11	126	F10
Winkley St E2	124	F4
Winsland St W2	122	D8
Winsley St W1	123	J8
Winslow SE17	128	C4
Winstanley Est SW11	126	D9
Winstanley Rd SW11	126	D9
Winterton Ho E1	124	F8
Winthrop St E1	124	F7
Wise Rd E15	125	P3
Wisteria Rd SE13	129	P10
Witan St E2	124	F5
Wivenhoe Cl SE15	128	F9
Wixs La SW4	127	H10
Woburn Pl WC1	123	K6
Woburn Sq WC1	123	K6
Woburn Wk WC1	123	K5
Wodehouse Av SE5	128	D7
Wolfe Cres SE16	129	H1
Wolftencroft Cl SW11	126	D9
Wolseley St SE1	128	D1
Wolsey Ms NW5	123	J1
Wood Cl E2	124	E6
Wood St EC2	124	A8
Wood Wf SE10	129	M5
Woodbridge St EC1	123	P6
Woodchester Sq W2	122	B7
Woodchurch Rd NW6	122	A2
Woodfall St SW3	126	F4
Woodfarrs SE5	128	B10
Woodland Cres SE16	129	H1
Woodpecker Rd SE14	129	J5
Woods Ms W1	122	F9
Woods Rd SE15	128	F7
Woodseer St E1	124	D7
Woodstock Ter E14	125	M9
Wooler St SE17	128	B4
Woolmore St E14	125	N9
Woolneigh St SW6	126	B9
Woolstaplers Way SE16	128	E3
Wooster Gdns E14	125	P8
Wootton St SE1	123	N10
Worfield St SW11	126	E6
Worgan St SE11	127	M4
World's End Est SW10	126	D6
Worlingham Rd SE22	128	D10
Wormwood St EC2	124	C8
Woronzow Rd NW8	122	D3
Worship St EC2	124	B7
Wotton Rd SE8	129	K5
Wren Rd SE5	128	B7
Wren St WC1	123	M6
Wrexham Rd E3	125	L4
Wrigglesworth St SE14	129	H6
Wrights La W8	126	B1
Wrights Rd E3	125	K4
Wroxton St SE15	128	F8
Wyatt Cl SE16	129	K1
Wycliffe Rd SW11	126	G8
Wye St SW11	126	D8
Wyke Rd E3	125	L2
Wyllen Cl E1	124	G6
Wymering Rd W9	122	A5
Wynan Rd E14	129	M4
Wyndham Est SE5	128	A6
Wyndham Pl W1	122	F7
Wyndham Rd SE5	127	P6
Wyndham St W1	122	F7
Wynford Rd N1	123	M4
Wynne Rd SW9	127	N8
Wynnstay Gdns W8	126	A2
Wynter St SW11	126	C10
Wynyard Ter SE11	127	M4
Wyvil Rd SW8	127	L5
Wyvis St E14	125	M7

Y

Name	Page	Grid
Yabsley St E14	125	N10
Yalding Rd SE16	128	E2
Yardley St WC1	123	N5
Yeate St N1	124	B2
Yelverton Rd SW11	126	D8
Yeo St E3	125	M7
Yeoman St SE8	129	J3
Yeoman's Row SW3	126	E2
York Br NW1	122	G6
York Gate NW1	122	G6
York Ho Pl W8	126	B1
York Pl SW11	126	D9
York Rd SE1	127	M1
York Rd SW11	126	C10
York Rd SW18	126	C10
York Sq E14	125	J8
York St W1	122	G7
York Ter E NW1	122	G6
York Ter W NW1	122	G6
York Way N1	123	L3
York Way N7	123	K1
York Way Ct N1	123	L3
Yorkshire Rd E14	125	J8
Yorkton St E2	124	E4
Young St W8	126	B1

Z

Name	Page	Grid
Zampa Rd SE16	128	G4
Zealand Rd E3	125	J4
Zenoria St SE22	128	D10
Zetland St E14	125	M7

INDEX TO GREAT BRITAIN

Administrative area abbreviations

Aber. Aberdeenshire	*Dur.* Durham	*Inclyde* Inverclyde	*P. & K.* Perth & Kinross	*Surr.* Surrey
Arg. & B. Argyll & Bute	*E.Ayr.* East Ayrshire	*Lancs.* Lancashire	*Pembs.* Pembrokeshire	*Swan.* Swansea
B'burn. Blackburn with Darwen	*E.Dun.* East Dunbartonshire	*Leic.* Leicester	*Peter.* Peterborough	*Swin.* Swindon
B'pool Blackpool	*E.Loth.* East Lothian	*Leics.* Leicestershire	*Plym.* Plymouth	*T. & W.* Tyne & Wear
B. & H. Brighton & Hove	*E.Renf.* East Renfrewshire	*Lincs.* Lincolnshire	*Ports.* Portsmouth	*Tel. & W.* Telford & Wrekin
B. & N.E.Som. Bath & North East Somerset	*E.Riding* East Riding of Yorkshire	*M.K.* Milton Keynes	*R. & C.* Redcar & Cleveland	*Thur.* Thurrock
B.Gwent Blaenau Gwent	*E.Suss.* East Sussex	*M.Tyd.* Merthyr Tydfil	*R.C.T.* Rhondda Cynon Taff	*V. of Glam.* Vale of Glamorgan
Beds. Bedfordshire	*Edin.* Edinburgh	*Med.* Medway	*Read.* Reading	*W'ham* Wokingham
Bourne. Bournemouth	*Falk.* Falkirk	*Mersey.* Merseyside	*Renf.* Renfrewshire	*W. & M.* Windsor & Maidenhead
Brack.F. Bracknell Forest	*Flints.* Flintshire	*Middbro.* Middlesbrough	*Rut.* Rutland	*W.Berks.* West Berkshire
Bucks. Buckinghamshire	*Glas.* Glasgow	*Midloth.* Midlothian	*S'end* Southend	*W.Dun.* West Dunbartonshire
Caerp. Caerphilly	*Glos.* Gloucestershire	*Mon.* Monmouthshire	*S'ham.* Southampton	*W.Isles* Western Isles (Na h-Eileanan an Iar)
Cambs. Cambridgeshire	*Gt.Lon.* Greater London	*N.Ayr.* North Ayrshire	*S.Ayr.* South Ayrshire	*W.Loth.* West Lothian
Carmar. Carmarthenshire	*Gt.Man.* Greater Manchester	*N.E.Lincs.* North East Lincolnshire	*S.Glos.* South Gloucestershire	*W.Mid.* West Midlands
Cere. Ceredigion	*Gwyn.* Gwynedd	*N.Lan.* North Lanarkshire	*S.Lan.* South Lanarkshire	*W.Suss.* West Sussex
Chan.I. Channel Islands	*Hants.* Hampshire	*N.Lincs.* North Lincolnshire	*S.Yorks.* South Yorkshire	*W.Yorks.* West Yorkshire
Ches. Cheshire	*Hart.* Hartlepool	*N.P.T.* Neath Port Talbot	*Sc.Bord.* Scottish Borders	*Warks.* Warwickshire
Cornw. Cornwall	*Here.* Herefordshire	*N.Som.* North Somerset	*Shet.* Shetland	*Warr.* Warrington
Cumb. Cumbria	*Herts.* Hertfordshire	*N.Yorks.* North Yorkshire	*Shrop.* Shropshire	*Wilts.* Wiltshire
D. & G. Dumfries & Galloway	*High.* Highland	*Norf.* Norfolk	*Slo.* Slough	*Worcs.* Worcestershire
Darl. Darlington	*Hull* Kingston upon Hull	*Northants.* Northamptonshire	*Som.* Somerset	*Wrex.* Wrexham
Denb. Denbighshire	*I.o.A.* Isle of Anglesey	*Northumb.* Northumberland	*Staffs.* Staffordshire	
Derbys. Derbyshire	*I.o.M.* Isle of Man	*Nott.* Nottingham	*Stir.* Stirling	
	I.o.S. Isles of Scilly	*Notts.* Nottinghamshire	*Stock.* Stockton-on-Tees	
	I.o.W. Isle of Wight	*Ork.* Orkney	*Stoke* Stoke-on-Trent	
		Oxon. Oxfordshire	*Suff.* Suffolk	

Notes

This index reads in the sequence: Place Name / Postal District / Map Page Number / Grid Reference.

Example: Cheltenham **GL52** 29 J6

Where there is more than one place with the same name, the index reads in the sequence:
Place Name / Administrative Area / Postal District / Map Page Number / Grid Reference.

Example: Prestbury, *Ches.* **SK10** 49 H5
Prestbury, *Glos.* **GL52** 29 J6

Entries in the index shown in **BOLD CAPITALS** indicate the principal post town within a postcode area.

Example: **GLOUCESTER GL** 29 H7

A

Ab Kettleby **LE14** 42 A3
Ab Lench **WR10** 30 B3
Abbas Combe **BA8** 9 G2
Abberley **WR6** 29 G2
Abberley Common **WR6** 29 G2
Abberton, *Essex* **CO5** 34 E7
Abberton, *Worcs.* **WR10** 29 J3
Abberwick **NE66** 71 G2
Abbess Roding **CM5** 33 J7
Abbey Dore **HR2** 28 C5
Abbey Hulton **ST2** 40 B1
Abbey St. Bathans **TD11** 77 F4
Abbey Town **CA7** 60 C1
Abbey Village **PR6** 56 B7
Abbey Wood **SE2** 23 H4
Abbeycwmhir **LD1** 27 K1
Abbeydale **S7** 51 F4
Abbeystead **LA2** 55 J4
Abbotrule **TD9** 70 B2
Abbots Bickington **EX22** 6 B4
Abbots Bromley **WS15** 40 C3
Abbots Langley **WD5** 22 D1
Abbots Leigh **BS8** 19 J4
Abbots Morton **WR7** 30 B3
Abbots Ripton **PE28** 33 F1
Abbot's Salford **WR11** 30 B3
Abbots Worthy **SO21** 11 F1
Abbotsbury **DT3** 8 E6
Abbotsfield Farm **WA9** 48 E3
Abbotsham **EX39** 6 C3
Abbotskerswell **TQ12** 5 J4
Abbotsley **PE19** 33 F3
Abbotstone **SO24** 11 G1
Abbott's Barton **SO23** 11 F1
Abbottswood **SO51** 10 E2
Abdon **SY7** 38 E7
Abdy **S62** 51 G3
Abenhall **GL17** 29 F7
Aber **SA40** 26 D4
Aber Village **LD3** 28 A6
Aberaeron **SA46** 26 D2
Aberaman **CF44** 18 D1
Aberangell **SY20** 37 H5
Aber-Arad **SA38** 26 C4
Aberarder **PH20** 88 B6
Aberarder House **IV2** 88 D2
Aberargie **PH2** 82 C6
Aberarth **SA46** 26 D2
Aberavon **SA12** 18 A3
Aber-banc **SA44** 26 C4
Aberbargoed **CF81** 18 E1
Aberbeeg **NP13** 19 F1
Aberbowlan **SA19** 17 K1
Aberbran **LD3** 27 J6
Abercanaid **CF48** 18 D1
Abercarn **NP11** 19 F2
Abercastle **SA62** 16 B1
Abercegir **SY20** 37 H5
Aberchalder **PH35** 87 K4
Aberchirder **AB54** 98 E5
Abercorn **EH30** 75 J3
Abercraf **SA9** 27 H7
Abercregan **SA13** 18 B2
Abercrombie **KY10** 83 G7
Abercrychan **SA20** 27 G5
Abercwmboi **CF44** 18 D1

Abercych **SA37** 26 B4
Abercynafon **LD3** 27 K7
Abercynon **CF45** 18 D2
Abercywarch **SY20** 37 H4
Aberdalgie **PH2** 82 B5
Aberdare **CF44** 18 C1
Aberdaron **LL53** 36 A3
Aberdaugleddau (Milford Haven) **SA73** 16 B4
ABERDEEN AB 91 H4
Aberdeen Airport **AB21** 91 G3
Aberdesach **LL54** 46 C7
Aberdour **KY3** 75 K2
Aberdovey (Aberdyfi) **LL35** 37 F6
Aberduhonw **LD2** 27 K3
Aberdulais **SA10** 18 A2
Aberdyfi (Aberdovey) **LL35** 37 F6
Aberedw **LD2** 27 K4
Abereiddy **SA62** 16 A1
Abererch **LL53** 36 C2
Aberfan **CF48** 18 D1
Aberfeldy **PH15** 81 K3
Aberffraw **LL63** 46 B6
Aberffrwd **SY23** 27 F1
Aberford **LS25** 57 K6
Aberfoyle **FK8** 81 G7
Abergavenny (Y Fenni) **NP7** 28 B7
Abergele **LL22** 47 H5
Aber-Giâr **SA40** 26 E4
Abergorlech **SA32** 17 J1
Abergwesyn **LD5** 27 H3
Abergwili **SA31** 17 H2
Abergwydol **SY20** 37 G5
Abergwynant **LL40** 37 F4
Abergwynfi **SA13** 18 B2
Abergwyngregyn **LL33** 46 E5
Abergwynolwyn **LL36** 37 F5
Aberhafesp **SY16** 37 K6
Aberhonddu (Brecon) **LD3** 27 K6
Aberhosan **SY20** 37 H6
Aberkenfig **CF32** 18 B3
Aberlady **EH32** 76 C2
Aberlemno **DD8** 83 G2
Aberllefenni **SY20** 37 G5
Aber-llia **CF44** 27 J7
Aberllynfi (Three Cocks) **LD3** 28 A5
Aberlour (Charlestown of Aberlour) **AB38** 97 K7
Abermad **SY23** 26 E1
Abermaw (Barmouth) **LL42** 37 F4
Abermeurig **SA48** 26 E3
Abermule **SY15** 38 A6
Abernaint **SY22** 38 A3
Abernant, *Carmar.* **SA33** 17 G2
Aber-nant, *R.C.T.* **CF44** 18 D1
Abernethy **PH2** 82 C6
Abernyte **PH14** 82 D4
Aberpennar (Mountain Ash) **CF45** 18 D2
Aberporth **SA43** 26 B3
Aberriw (Berriew) **SY21** 38 A5

Aberscross **KW10** 96 E2
Abersky **IV2** 88 C2
Abersoch **LL53** 36 C3
Abersychan **NP4** 19 F1
ABERTAWE (SWANSEA) SA 17 K5
Aberteifi (Cardigan) **SA43** 26 A4
Aberthin **CF71** 18 D4
Abertillery **NP13** 19 F1
Abertridwr, *Caerp.* **CF83** 18 E3
Abertridwr, *Powys* **SY10** 37 K4
Abertysswg **NP22** 18 E1
Aberuthven **PH3** 82 A6
Aberyscir **LD3** 27 J6
Aberystwyth **SY23** 36 E7
Abhainnsuidhe **HS3** 100 C7
Abingdon **OX14** 21 H2
Abinger Common **RH5** 22 E7
Abinger Hammer **RH5** 22 D7
Abington **ML12** 68 E1
Abington Pigotts **SG8** 33 G4
Abingworth **RH20** 12 E5
Ablington, *Glos.* **GL7** 20 E1
Ablington, *Wilts.* **SP4** 20 E7
Abney **S32** 50 D5
Above Church **ST10** 50 C7
Aboyne **AB34** 90 D5
Abram **WN2** 49 F2
Abriachan **IV3** 88 C1
Abridge **RM4** 23 H2
Abronhill **G67** 75 F3
Abson **BS30** 20 A4
Abthorpe **NN12** 31 H4
Abune-the-Hill **KW17** 106 B5
Aby **LN13** 53 H5
Acaster Malbis **YO23** 58 B5
Acaster Selby **YO23** 58 B5
Accrington **BB5** 56 C7
Accurrach **PA33** 80 C5
Acha **PA78** 78 C2
Achacha **PA37** 80 A3
Achadacaie **PA29** 73 G4
Achadh Mòr **HS2** 101 F5
Achadh-chaorrunn **PA29** 73 F5
Achadunan **PA26** 80 D6
Achagavel **PH33** 79 J2
Achaglass **PA29** 73 F6
Achahoish **PA31** 73 F3
Achalader **PH10** 82 C3
Achallader **PA36** 80 E3
Achamore **PA60** 72 D3
Achandunie **IV17** 96 D4
Achany **IV27** 96 C1
Achaphubuil **PH33** 87 G7
Acharacle **PH36** 79 H1
Achargary **KW11** 104 C3
Acharn, *Arg. & B.* **PA35** 80 C4
Acharn, *P. & K.* **PH15** 81 J3
Acharonich **PA73** 79 F4
Acharosson **PA21** 73 H3
Achateny **PH36** 86 B7
Achath **AB32** 91 F3
Achavanich **KW5** 105 G4
Achddu **SA16** 17 H4
Achduart **IV26** 95 G1
Achentoul **KW11** 104 D5
Achfary **IV27** 102 E5
Achgarve **IV22** 94 E2
Achiemore, *High.* **IV27** 103 F2

Achiemore, *High.* **KW13** 104 D3
Achies **KW12** 105 G3
A'Chill **PH44** 85 H4
Achiltibuie **IV26** 95 G1
Achina **KW14** 104 C2
Achindown **IV12** 97 F7
Achinduich **IV27** 96 C2
Achingills **KW12** 105 G2
Achintee **IV54** 95 F7
Achintee House **PH33** 87 H7
Achintraid **IV54** 86 E1
Achlean **PH21** 89 F5
Achleanna **PA34** 79 G2
Achleek **PH33** 79 J2
Achlian **PA33** 80 C5
Achlyness **IV27** 102 E3
Achmelvich **IV27** 102 C6
Achmony **IV63** 88 C1
Achmore, *High.* **IV53** 86 E1
Achmore, *High.* **IV23** 95 G2
Achmore, *Stir.* **FK21** 81 G4
Achnaba **PA31** 73 H2
Achnabat **IV2** 88 C1
Achnabourin **KW14** 104 C3
Achnacarnin **IV27** 102 C5
Achnacarry **PH34** 87 H6
Achnaclerach **IV23** 96 B5
Achnacloich, *Arg. & B.* **PA37** 80 A4
Achnacloich, *High.* **IV46** 86 B4
Achnacraig **PA73** 79 F3
Achnacroish **PA34** 79 K3
Achnadrish **PA75** 79 F2
Achnafalnich **PA33** 80 D5
Achnafauld **PH8** 81 K4
Achnagairn **IV5** 96 C7
Achnagarron **IV18** 96 D4
Achnaha, *High.* **PA34** 79 H3
Achnaha, *High.* **PH36** 79 F1
Achnahanat **IV24** 96 C2
Achnahannet **PH26** 89 G2
Achnairn **IV27** 103 H7
Achnalea **PH33** 79 K1
Achnamara **PA31** 73 F2
Achnanellan **PH37** 79 J1
Achnasaul **PH34** 87 H6
Achnasheen **IV22** 95 H6
Achnashelloch **PA31** 73 G1
Achnastank **AB55** 89 K1
Achorn **KW6** 105 G5
Achosnich, *High.* **IV25** 96 E2
Achosnich, *High.* **PH36** 79 F1
Achreamie **KW14** 105 F2
Achriabhach **PH33** 80 C1
Achriesgill **IV27** 102 E3
Achtoty **KW14** 103 J2
Achurch **PE8** 42 D7
Achuvoldrach **IV27** 103 H3
Achvaich **IV25** 96 E2
Achvarasdal **KW14** 104 E2
Achvlair **PA38** 80 A2
Achvraie **IV26** 95 G1
Ackenthwaite **LA7** 55 J1
Ackergill **KW1** 105 J3
Acklam, *Middbro.* **TS5** 63 F5
Acklam, *N.Yorks.* **YO17** 58 D3
Ackleton **WV6** 39 G6

Acklington **NE65** 71 H3
Ackton **WF7** 57 K7
Ackworth Moor Top **WF7** 51 G1
Acle **NR13** 45 J4
Acock's Green **B27** 40 D7
Acol **CT7** 25 K5
Acomb, *Northumb.* **NE46** 70 E7
Acomb, *York* **YO24** 58 B4
Aconbury **HR2** 28 E5
Acre **BB5** 56 C7
Acrefair **LL14** 38 B1
Acrise Place **CT18** 15 G3
Acton, *Ches.* **CW5** 49 F7
Acton, *Dorset* **BH19** 9 J7
Acton, *Gt.Lon.* **W3** 22 E3
Acton, *Shrop.* **SY9** 38 C7
Acton, *Staffs.* **ST5** 40 A1
Acton, *Suff.* **CO10** 34 C4
Acton, *Worcs.* **DY13** 29 H2
Acton, *Wrex.* **LL12** 48 C7
Acton Beauchamp **WR6** 29 F3
Acton Bridge **CW8** 48 E5
Acton Burnell **SY5** 38 E5
Acton Green **WR6** 29 F3
Acton Pigott **SY5** 38 E5
Acton Round **SY6** 39 F6
Acton Scott **SY6** 38 D7
Acton Trussell **ST17** 40 B4
Acton Turville **GL9** 20 B3
Adamhill **KA1** 74 C7
Adbaston **ST20** 39 G3
Adber **DT9** 8 E2
Adderbury **OX17** 31 F5
Adderley **TF9** 39 F2
Adderstone **NE70** 77 K7
Addiewell **EH55** 75 H4
Addingham **LS29** 57 F5
Addington, *Bucks.* **MK18** 31 J6
Addington, *Gt.Lon.* **CR0** 23 G5
Addington, *Kent* **ME19** 23 K6
Addiscombe **CR0** 23 G5
Addlestone **KT15** 22 D5
Addlethorpe **PE24** 53 J6
Adel **LS16** 57 H6
Adeney **TF10** 39 G4
Adeyfield **HP2** 22 D1
Adfa **SY16** 37 K5
Adforton **SY7** 28 D1
Adisham **CT3** 15 H2
Adlestrop **GL56** 30 D6
Adlingfleet **DN14** 58 E7
Adlington, *Ches.* **SK10** 49 J4
Adlington, *Lancs.* **PR7** 48 E1
Admaston, *Staffs.* **WS15** 40 C3
Admaston, *Tel. & W.* **TF5** 39 F4
Admington **CV36** 30 D4
Adsborough **TA2** 8 B2
Adscombe **TA5** 7 K2
Adstock **MK18** 31 J5
Adstone **NN12** 31 G3
Adversane **RH14** 12 D4
Advie **PH26** 89 J1
Adwalton **BD11** 57 H7
Adwell **OX9** 21 K2
Adwick le Street **DN6** 51 H2
Adwick upon Dearne **S64** 51 G2
Adziel **AB43** 99 H5
Ae Village **DG1** 68 E5
Affetside **BL8** 49 G1

Affleck

Affleck **AB21** 91 G2
Affpuddle **DT2** 9 H5
Afon Wen **LL53** 36 D2
Afon-wen **CH7** 47 K5
Afton **PO40** 10 E6
Afton Bridgend **KA18** 68 B2
Agglethorpe **DL8** 57 F1
Aigburth **L17** 48 C4
Aiginis **HS2** 101 G4
Aike **YO25** 59 G5
Aikerness **KW17** 106 D2
Aikers **KW17** 107 D8
Aiketgate **CA4** 61 F2
Aikshaw **CA7** 60 C2
Aikton **CA7** 60 D1
Aikwood Tower **TD7** 69 K1
Ailby **LN13** 53 H5
Ailey **HR3** 28 C4
Ailsworth **PE5** 42 E6
Aimes Green **EN9** 23 H1
Aimster **KW14** 105 G2
Ainderby Quernhow **YO7** 57 J1
Ainderby Steeple **DL7** 62 E7
Aingers Green **CO7** 35 F6
Ainsdale **PR8** 48 C1
Ainsdale-on-Sea **PR8** 48 C1
Ainstable **CA4** 61 G2
Ainsworth **BL2** 49 G1
Ainthorpe **YO21** 63 J6
Aintree **L10** 48 C3
Aird, *W.Isles* **HS7** 92 C6
Aird, *W.Isles* **HS2** 101 H4
Aird a' Mhachair **HS8** 92 C7
Aird a' Mhulaidh **HS3** 100 D6
Aird Asaig **HS3** 100 D7
Aird Dhail **HS2** 101 G1
Aird Leimhe **HS3** 93 G3
Aird Mhige **HS3** 93 G2
Aird Mhighe **HS3** 93 F3
Aird of Sleat **IV45** 86 B4
Aird Thunga **HS2** 101 G4
Aird Uig **HS2** 100 C4
Airdrie, *Fife* **KY10** 83 G7
Airdrie, *N.Lan.* **ML6** 75 F4
Aire View **BD20** 56 E5
Airidh a' Bhruaich **HS2** 100 E6
Airieland **DG7** 65 H5
Airies **DG9** 66 D7
Airigh-drishaig **IV54** 86 D1
Airmyn **DN14** 58 D7
Airntully **PH1** 82 B4
Airor **PH41** 86 D4
Airth **FK2** 75 G2
Airton **BD23** 56 E4
Airyhassen **DG8** 64 D6
Aisby, *Lincs.* **DN21** 52 B3
Aisby, *Lincs.* **NG32** 42 D2
Aisgernis (Askernish) **HS8** 84 C2
Aisgill **CA17** 61 J7
Aish, *Devon* **TQ10** 5 G4
Aish, *Devon* **TQ9** 5 J5
Aisholt **TA5** 7 K2
Aiskew **DL8** 57 H1
Aislaby, *N.Yorks.* **YO21** 63 K6
Aislaby, *N.Yorks.* **YO18** 58 D1
Aislaby, *Stock.* **TS16** 63 F5
Aisthorpe **LN1** 52 C4
Aith, *Ork.* **KW16** 107 B6
Aith, *Ork.* **KW17** 106 F5
Aith, *Shet.* **ZE2** 109 C7
Aith, *Shet.* **ZE2** 108 F3
Aithsetter **ZE2** 109 D9
Aitnoch **PH26** 89 G1
Akeld **NE71** 70 E1
Akeley **MK18** 31 J5
Akenham **IP1** 35 F4
Albaston **PL18** 4 E3
Albecq **GY5** 3 H5
Alberbury **SY5** 38 C4
Albert Town **SA61** 16 C3
Albourne **BN6** 13 F5
Albourne Green **BN6** 13 F5
Albrighton, *Shrop.* **WV7** 40 A5
Albrighton, *Shrop.* **SY4** 38 D4
Alburgh **IP20** 45 G7
Albury, *Herts.* **SG11** 33 H6
Albury, *Oxon.* **OX9** 21 K1
Albury, *Surr.* **GU5** 22 D7
Albury End **SG11** 33 H6
Albury Heath **GU5** 22 D7
Albyfield **CA8** 61 G1
Alcaig **IV7** 96 C6
Alcaston **SY6** 38 D7
Alcester **B49** 30 B3
Alciston **BN26** 13 J6
Alcombe **TA24** 7 H1
Alconbury **PE28** 32 E1
Alconbury Hill **PE28** 32 E1
Alconbury Weston **PE28** 32 E1
Aldborough, *N.Yorks.* **YO51** 57 K3
Aldborough, *Norf.* **NR11** 45 F2
Aldbourne **SN8** 21 F4
Aldbrough **HU11** 59 J6
Aldbrough St. John **DL11** 62 D5
Aldbury **HP23** 32 C7
Aldclune **PH16** 82 A1
Aldeburgh **IP15** 35 J3
Aldeby **NR34** 45 J6
Aldenham **WD25** 22 E2
Alderbury **SP5** 10 C2
Alderford **NR9** 45 F4
Alderholt **SP6** 10 C3
Alderley **GL12** 20 A2
Alderley Edge **SK9** 49 H5
Aldermaston **RG7** 21 J5
Aldermaston Wharf **RG7** 21 K5
Alderminster **CV37** 30 D4
Alderney **GY9** 3 K4
Alderney Airport **GY9** 3 J4
Alder's End **HR1** 29 F5
Aldersey Green **CH3** 48 D7
Aldershot **GU11** 22 B6
Alderton, *Glos.* **GL20** 29 J5
Alderton, *Northants.* **NN12** 31 J4
Alderton, *Suff.* **IP12** 35 H4
Alderton, *Wilts.* **SN14** 20 B3
Alderwasley **DE56** 51 F7
Aldfield **HG4** 57 H3
Aldford **CH3** 48 D7
Aldham, *Essex* **CO6** 34 D6
Aldham, *Suff.* **IP7** 34 E4
Aldie, *Aber.* **AB42** 99 J6
Aldie, *High.* **IV19** 96 E3
Aldingbourne **PO20** 12 C6
Aldingham **LA12** 55 F2
Aldington, *Kent* **TN25** 15 F4
Aldington, *Worcs.* **WR11** 30 B4
Aldivalloch **AB54** 90 B2
Aldochlay **G83** 74 B1
Aldons **KA26** 67 F5
Aldous's Corner **IP19** 45 H7
Aldreth **CB6** 33 H1
Aldridge **WS9** 40 C5
Aldringham **IP16** 35 J2
Aldsworth, *Glos.* **GL54** 20 E1
Aldsworth, *W.Suss.* **PO10** 11 J4
Aldunie **AB54** 90 B2
Aldville **PH8** 82 A4
Aldwark, *Derbys.* **DE4** 50 E7
Aldwark, *N.Yorks.* **YO61** 57 K3
Aldwick **PO21** 12 C7
Aldwincle **NN14** 42 D7
Aldworth **RG8** 21 J4
Alexandria **G83** 74 B3
Aley **TA5** 7 K2
Aley Green **LU1** 32 D7
Alfardisworthy **EX22** 6 A4
Alfington **EX11** 7 K6
Alfold **GU6** 12 D3
Alfold Crossways **GU6** 12 D3
Alford, *Aber.* **AB33** 90 D3
Alford, *Lincs.* **LN13** 53 H5
Alford, *Som.* **BA7** 9 F1
Alfreton **DE55** 51 G7
Alfrick **WR6** 29 G3
Alfrick Pound **WR6** 29 G3
Alfriston **BN26** 13 J6
Algarkirk **PE20** 43 F2
Alhampton **BA4** 9 F1
Alkborough **DN15** 58 E7
Alkerton **OX15** 30 E4
Alkham **CT15** 15 H3
Alkington **SY13** 38 E2
Alkmonton **DE6** 40 D2
All Cannings **SN10** 20 D5
All Saints South Elmham **IP19** 45 H7
All Stretton **SY6** 38 D6
Allaleigh **TQ9** 5 J5
Allanaquoich **AB35** 89 J5
Allancreich **AB34** 90 D5
Allanfearn **IV2** 96 E7
Allangillfoot **DG13** 69 H4
Allanton, *D. & G.* **DG2** 68 E5
Allanton, *E.Ayr.* **KA17** 74 E7
Allanton, *N.Lan.* **ML7** 75 G5
Allanton, *S.Lan.* **ML3** 75 F5
Allanton, *Sc.Bord.* **TD11** 77 G5
Allardice **DD10** 91 G7
Allathasdal **HS9** 84 B4
Allbrook **SO50** 11 F2
Allendale Town **NE47** 61 K1
Allenheads **NE47** 61 K2
Allen's Green **CM21** 33 H7
Allensford **DH8** 62 B1
Allensmore **HR2** 28 D5
Allenton **DE24** 41 F2
Aller **TA10** 8 D2
Allerby **CA7** 60 B3
Allercombe **EX5** 7 J6
Allerford, *Devon* **EX20** 6 C7
Allerford, *Som.* **TA24** 7 H1
Allerston **YO18** 58 E1
Allerthorpe **YO42** 58 D5
Allerton, *Mersey.* **L18** 48 D4
Allerton, *W.Yorks.* **BD15** 57 G6
Allerton Bywater **WF10** 57 K7
Allerton Mauleverer **HG5** 57 K4
Allesley **CV5** 40 E7
Allestree **DE22** 41 F2
Allet Common **TR4** 2 E4
Allexton **LE15** 42 B5
Allgreave **SK11** 49 J6
Allhallows **ME3** 24 E4
Allhallows-on-Sea **ME3** 24 E4
Alligin Shuas **IV22** 94 E6
Allimore Green **ST18** 40 A4
Allington, *Dorset* **DT6** 8 D5
Allington, *Lincs.* **NG32** 42 B1
Allington, *Wilts.* **SP4** 10 D1
Allington, *Wilts.* **SN10** 20 D5
Allington, *Wilts.* **SN14** 20 B4
Allithwaite **LA11** 55 G2
Allnabad **IV27** 103 G4
Alloa **FK10** 75 G1
Allonby **CA15** 60 B2
Allostock **WA16** 49 G5
Alloway **KA7** 67 H2
Allowenshay **TA17** 8 C3
Allscot **WV15** 39 G6
Allscott **TF6** 39 F4
Allt na h-Airbhe **IV26** 95 H2
Alltachonaich **PA34** 79 J2
Alltbeithe **IV4** 87 G2
Alltforgan **SY10** 37 J3
Alltmawr **LD2** 27 K4
Alltnacaillich **IV27** 103 G4
Allt-na-subh **IV40** 87 F1
Alltsigh **IV63** 88 B3
Alltwalis **SA32** 17 H1
Alltwen **SA8** 18 A1
Alltyblaca **SA40** 26 E4
Allwood Green **IP22** 34 E1
Almeley **HR3** 28 C3
Almeley Wootton **HR3** 28 C3
Almer **DT11** 9 J5
Almington **TF9** 39 G2
Almiston Cross **EX39** 6 B3
Almondbank **PH1** 82 B5
Almondbury **HD4** 50 D1
Almondsbury **BS32** 19 K3
Alne **YO61** 57 K3
Alness **IV17** 96 D5
Alnham **NE66** 70 E2
Alnmouth **NE66** 71 H2
Alnwick **NE66** 71 G2
Alperton **HA0** 22 E3
Alphamstone **CO8** 34 C5
Alpheton **CO10** 34 C3
Alphington **EX2** 7 H6
Alport **DE45** 50 E6
Alpraham **CW6** 48 E7
Alresford **CO7** 34 E6
Alrewas **DE13** 40 D4
Alrick **PH11** 82 C1
Alsager **ST7** 49 G7
Alsagers Bank **ST7** 40 A1
Alsop en le Dale **DE6** 50 D7
Alston, *Cumb.* **CA9** 61 J2
Alston, *Devon* **EX13** 8 C4
Alston Sutton **BS26** 19 H6
Alstone, *Glos.* **GL20** 29 J5
Alstone, *Som.* **TA9** 19 G7
Alstone, *Staffs.* **ST18** 40 A4
Alstonefield **DE6** 50 D7
Alswear **EX36** 7 F3
Alt **OL8** 49 J2
Altandhu **IV26** 102 B7
Altanduin **KW11** 104 D6
Altarnun **PL15** 4 C2
Altass **IV27** 96 C1
Altens **AB12** 91 H4
Alterwall **KW1** 105 H2
Altham **BB5** 56 C6
Althorne **CM3** 25 F2
Althorpe **DN17** 52 B2
Alticry **DG8** 64 C5
Altnafeadh **PH49** 80 D2
Altnaharra **IV27** 103 H5
Altofts **WF6** 57 J7
Alton, *Derbys.* **S42** 51 F6
Alton, *Hants.* **GU34** 11 J1
Alton, *Staffs.* **ST10** 40 C1
Alton Barnes **SN8** 20 E5
Alton Pancras **DT2** 9 G4
Alton Priors **SN8** 20 E5
Altonside **IV30** 97 K6
Altrincham **WA14** 49 G4
Altura **PH34** 87 J5
Alva **FK12** 75 G1
Alvanley **WA6** 48 D5
Alvaston **DE24** 41 F2
Alvechurch **B48** 30 B1
Alvecote **B79** 40 E5
Alvediston **SP5** 9 J2
Alveley **WV15** 39 G7
Alverdiscott **EX31** 6 D3
Alverstoke **PO12** 11 H5
Alverstone **PO36** 11 G6
Alverthorpe **WF2** 57 J7
Alverton **NG13** 42 A1
Alves **IV30** 97 J5
Alvescot **OX18** 21 F1
Alveston, *S.Glos.* **BS35** 19 K3
Alveston, *Warks.* **CV37** 30 D3
Alvie **PH21** 89 F4
Alvingham **LN11** 53 G3
Alvington **GL15** 19 K1
Alwalton **PE2** 42 E6
Alweston **DT9** 9 F3
Alwington **EX39** 6 C3
Alwinton **NE65** 70 E3
Alwoodley **LS17** 57 J5
Alwoodley Gates **LS17** 57 J5
Alyth **PH11** 82 D3
Amalebra **TR20** 2 B5
Ambaston **DE72** 41 G2
Amber Hill **PE20** 43 F1
Ambergate **DE56** 51 F7
Amberley, *Glos.* **GL5** 20 B1
Amberley, *W.Suss.* **BN18** 12 D5
Amble **NE65** 71 H3
Amblecote **DY8** 40 A7
Ambleside **LA22** 60 E6
Ambleston **SA62** 16 D2
Ambrismore **PA20** 73 J5
Ambrosden **OX25** 31 H7
Amcotts **DN17** 52 B1
Amersham **HP6** 22 C2
Amerton **ST18** 40 B3
Amesbury **SP4** 20 E7
Ameysford **BH22** 10 B4
Amington **B77** 40 E5
Amisfield Town **DG1** 69 F5
Amlwch **LL68** 46 C3
Amlwch Port **LL68** 46 C3
Ammanford (Rhydaman) **SA18** 17 K3
Amotherby **YO17** 58 D2
Ampfield **SO51** 10 E2
Ampleforth **YO62** 58 B2
Ampleforth College **YO62** 58 B2
Ampney Crucis **GL7** 20 D1
Ampney St. Mary **GL7** 20 D1
Ampney St. Peter **GL7** 20 D1
Amport **SP11** 21 G7
Ampthill **MK45** 32 D5
Ampton **IP31** 34 C1
Amroth **SA67** 16 E4
Amulree **PH8** 81 K4
An Tairbeart (Tarbert) **HS3** 100 D7
An T-òb (Leverburgh) **HS5** 93 F3
Anaboard **PH26** 89 H1
Anaheilt **PH36** 79 K1
Ancaster **NG32** 42 C1
Anchor **SY7** 38 A7
Anchor Corner **NR17** 44 E6
Ancroft **TD15** 77 H6
Ancrum **TD8** 70 B1
Ancton **PO22** 12 C6
Anderby **PE24** 53 J5
Anderby Creek **PE24** 53 J5
Andersea **TA7** 8 C1
Andersfield **TA5** 8 B1
Anderson **DT11** 9 H5
Anderton **CW9** 49 F5
Andover **SP10** 21 G7
Andover Down **SP11** 21 G7
Andoversford **GL54** 30 B7
Andreas **IM7** 54 D4
Anelog **LL53** 36 A3
Anfield **L4** 48 C3
Angarrack **TR27** 2 C5
Angarrick **TR3** 2 E5
Angelbank **SY8** 28 E1
Angerton **CA7** 60 D1
Angle **SA71** 16 B4
Angler's Retreat **SY20** 37 G6
Anglesey (Ynys Môn) **LL** 46 B4
Angmering **BN16** 12 D6
Angmering-on-Sea **BN16** 12 D6
Angram, *N.Yorks.* **YO23** 58 B5
Angram, *N.Yorks.* **DL11** 61 K7
Anick **NE46** 70 E7
Anie **FK17** 81 G6
Ankerville **IV19** 97 F4
Anlaby **HU10** 59 G7
Anmer **PE31** 44 B3
Anmore **PO7** 11 H3
Anna Valley **SP11** 21 G7
Annan **DG12** 69 G7
Annaside **LA19** 54 D1
Annat, *Arg. & B.* **PA35** 80 B5
Annat, *High.* **IV22** 94 E6
Annbank **KA6** 67 J1
Annesley **NG15** 51 H7
Annesley Woodhouse **NG17** 51 G7
Annfield Plain **DH9** 62 C1
Anniesland **G13** 74 D4
Annscroft **SY5** 38 D5
Ansdell **FY8** 55 G7
Ansford **BA7** 9 F1
Ansley **CV10** 40 E6
Anslow **DE13** 40 E3
Anslow Gate **DE13** 40 D3
Ansteadbrook **GU27** 12 C3
Anstey, *Herts.* **SG9** 33 H5
Anstey, *Leics.* **LE7** 41 H5
Anstruther **KY10** 83 G7
Ansty, *W.Suss.* **RH17** 13 F4
Ansty, *Warks.* **CV7** 41 F7
Ansty, *Wilts.* **SP3** 9 J2
Ansty Coombe **SP3** 9 J2
Ansty Cross **DT2** 9 G4
Anthill Common **PO7** 11 H3
Anthorn **CA7** 60 C1
Antingham **NR28** 45 G2
Anton's Gowt **PE22** 43 F1
Antony **PL11** 4 D5
Antrobus **CW9** 49 F5
Anvil Corner **EX22** 6 B5
Anvil Green **CT4** 15 G3
Anwick **NG34** 52 E7
Anwoth **DG7** 65 F5
Aoradh **PA44** 72 A4
Apethorpe **PE8** 42 D6
Apeton **ST20** 40 A4
Apley **LN8** 52 E5
Apperknowle **S18** 51 F5
Apperley **GL19** 29 H6
Apperley Bridge **BD10** 57 G6
Appersett **DL8** 61 K7
Appin **PA38** 80 A3
Appin House **PA38** 80 A3
Appleby **DN15** 52 C1
Appleby Magna **DE12** 41 F4
Appleby Parva **DE12** 41 F5
Appleby-in-Westmorland **CA16** 61 H4
Applecross **IV54** 94 D7
Appledore, *Devon* **EX39** 6 C2
Appledore, *Devon* **EX16** 7 J4
Appledore, *Kent* **TN26** 14 E5
Appledore Heath **TN26** 14 E4
Appleford **OX14** 21 J2
Appleshaw **SP11** 21 G7
Applethwaite **CA12** 60 D4
Appleton, *Halton* **WA8** 48 E4
Appleton, *Oxon.* **OX13** 21 H1
Appleton Roebuck **YO23** 58 B5
Appleton Thorn **WA4** 49 F4
Appleton Wiske **DL6** 62 E6
Appleton-le-Moors **YO62** 58 D1
Appleton-le-Street **YO17** 58 D2
Appletreehall **TD9** 70 A2
Appletreewick **BD23** 57 F3
Appley **TA21** 7 J3
Appley Bridge **WN6** 48 E2
Apse Heath **PO36** 11 G6
Apsey Green **IP13** 35 G2
Apsley **HP3** 22 D1
Apsley End **SG5** 32 E5
Apuldram **PO20** 12 B6
Arberth (Narberth) **SA67** 16 E3
Arbirlot **DD11** 83 G3
Arborfield **RG2** 22 A5
Arborfield Cross **RG2** 22 A5
Arborfield Garrison **RG2** 22 A5
Arbourthorne **S2** 51 F4
Arbroath **DD11** 83 H3
Arbuthnott **AB30** 91 F7
Archdeacon Newton **DL2** 62 D5
Archiestown **AB38** 97 K7
Arclid **CW11** 49 G6
Ard a' Chapuill **PA22** 73 J2
Ardachearanbeg **PA22** 73 J2
Ardacheranmor **PA22** 73 J2
Ardachoil **PA65** 79 J4
Ardachu **IV28** 96 D1
Ardailly **PA41** 72 E5
Ardalanish **PA67** 78 E6
Ardallie **AB42** 91 J1
Ardanaiseig **PA35** 80 B5
Ardaneaskan **IV54** 86 E1
Ardanstur **PA34** 79 K6
Ardantiobairt **PA34** 79 H2
Ardantrive **PA34** 79 K5
Ardarroch **IV54** 94 E7
Ardbeg, *Arg. & B.* **PA20** 73 J4
Ardbeg, *Arg. & B.* **PA42** 72 C6
Ardbeg, *Arg. & B.* **PA23** 73 K2
Ardblair **IV4** 88 C1
Ardbrecknish **PA33** 80 B5
Ardcharnich **IV23** 95 H3
Ardchiavaig **PA67** 78 E6
Ardchonnel **PA37** 80 A4
Ardchonnell **PA33** 80 A6
Ardchrishnish **PA70** 79 F5
Ardchronie **IV24** 96 D3
Ardchuilk **IV4** 87 J1
Ardchullarie More **FK18** 81 G6
Ardchyle **FK21** 81 G5
Arddlin **SY22** 38 B4
Ardechvie **PH34** 87 H5
Ardeley **SG2** 33 G6
Ardelve **IV40** 86 E2
Arden **G83** 74 B2
Ardencaple House **PA34** 79 J6
Ardens Grafton **B49** 30 C3
Ardentallan **PA34** 79 K5
Ardentinny **PA23** 73 K2
Ardeonaig **FK21** 81 H4
Ardersier **IV2** 96 E6
Ardery **PH36** 79 J1
Ardessie **IV23** 95 G3
Ardfad **PA34** 79 J6
Ardfern **PA31** 79 K7
Ardfin **PA60** 72 C4
Ardgartan **G83** 80 D7
Ardgay **IV24** 96 D2
Ardgenavan **PA26** 80 C6
Ardgowan **PA16** 74 A3
Ardgowse **AB33** 90 E3
Ardgye **IV30** 97 J5
Ardhallow **PA23** 73 K3
Ardheslaig **IV54** 94 D6
Ardiecow **AB45** 98 D4
Ardinamar **PA34** 79 J6
Ardindrean **IV23** 95 H3
Ardingly **RH17** 13 G4
Ardington **OX12** 21 H3
Ardington Wick **OX12** 21 H3
Ardintoul **IV40** 86 E2
Ardkinglas House **PA26** 80 C6
Ardlair **AB52** 90 D2
Ardlamont **PA21** 73 H4
Ardleigh **CO7** 34 E6
Ardleigh Green **RM2** 23 J3
Ardleigh Heath **CO7** 34 E5
Ardleish **G83** 80 E6
Ardler **PH12** 82 D3
Ardley **OX27** 31 G6
Ardley End **CM22** 33 J7
Ardlui **G83** 80 E6
Ardlussa **PA60** 72 E2
Ardmaddy **PA35** 80 B4
Ardmair **IV26** 95 H2
Ardmaleish **PA20** 73 J4
Ardmay **G83** 80 D7
Ardmenish **PA60** 72 D3
Ardmhór **HS9** 84 C4
Ardminish **PA41** 72 E6
Ardmolich **PH36** 86 D7
Ardmore, *Arg. & B.* **PA42** 72 C5
Ardmore, *Arg. & B.* **PA34** 79 J5
Ardmore, *Arg. & B.* **G82** 74 B3
Ardmore, *High.* **IV19** 96 E3
Ardnackaig **PA31** 73 F1
Ardnacross **PA72** 79 G3
Ardnadam **PA23** 73 K2
Ardnadrochit **PA64** 79 J4
Ardnagoine **IV26** 95 F1
Ardnagowan **PA25** 80 C7
Ardnahein **PA24** 73 K1
Ardnahoe **PA46** 72 C3
Ardnarff **IV54** 86 E1
Ardnastang **PH36** 79 K1
Ardnave **PA44** 72 A3
Ardno **PA26** 80 C7
Ardo **AB41** 91 G1
Ardoch, *D. & G.* **DG3** 68 D3
Ardoch, *Moray* **IV36** 97 J6
Ardoch, *P. & K.* **PH1** 82 B4
Ardochrig **G75** 74 E6
Ardoyne **AB52** 90 E2
Ardpatrick **PA29** 73 F4
Ardpeaton **G84** 74 A2
Ardradnaig **PH15** 81 J3
Ardrishaig **PA30** 73 G2
Ardroe **IV27** 102 C6
Ardross **IV17** 96 D4
Ardrossan **KA22** 74 A6
Ardscalpsie **PA20** 73 J5
Ardshave **IV25** 96 E2
Ardshealach **PH36** 79 H1
Ardshellach **PA34** 79 J6
Ardsley **S71** 51 F2
Ardslignish **PH36** 79 G1
Ardtalla **PA42** 72 C5
Ardtalnaig **PH15** 81 J4
Ardtaraig **PA23** 73 J2

Ardteatle **PA33**	80	C5
Ardtoe **PH36**	86	C7
Ardtornish **PA34**	79	J3
Ardtrostan **PH6**	81	H5
Ardtur **PA38**	80	A3
Arduaine **PA34**	79	K6
Ardura **PA65**	79	H4
Ardvar **IV27**	102	D5
Ardvasar **IV45**	86	C4
Ardveenish **HS9**	84	C4
Ardveich **FK19**	81	H5
Ardverikie **PH20**	88	C6
Ardvorlich, *Arg. & B.* **G83**	80	E6
Ardvorlich, *P. & K.* **FK19**	81	H5
Ardwall **DG7**	65	F5
Ardwell, *D. & G.* **DG9**	64	B6
Ardwell, *Moray* **AB54**	90	B1
Ardwell, *S.Ayr.* **KA26**	67	F4
Ardwick **M12**	49	H3
Areley Kings **DY13**	29	H1
Arford **GU35**	12	B3
Argaty **FK16**	81	J7
Argoed **NP12**	18	E2
Argoed Mill **LD1**	27	J2
Argos Hill **TN20**	13	J4
Argrennan House **DG7**	65	H5
Arichamish **PA31**	80	A7
Arichastlich **PA33**	80	D4
Arichonan **PA31**	73	F1
Aridhglas **PA66**	78	E5
Arienskill **PH38**	86	D6
Arileod **PA78**	78	C2
Arinacrinachd **IV54**	94	D6
Arinafad Beg **PA31**	73	F2
Arinagour **PA78**	78	D2
Arinambane **HS8**	84	C2
Arisaig **PH39**	86	C6
Arivegaig **PH36**	79	H1
Arkendale **HG5**	57	J3
Arkesden **CB11**	33	H5
Arkholme **LA6**	55	J2
Arkle Town **DL11**	62	B6
Arkleby **CA7**	60	C3
Arkleside **DL8**	57	F1
Arkleton **DG13**	69	J4
Arkley **EN5**	23	F2
Arksey **DN5**	51	H2
Arkwright Town **S44**	51	G5
Arlary **KY13**	82	C7
Arle **GL51**	29	J6
Arlecdon **CA26**	60	B5
Arlesey **SG15**	32	E5
Arleston **TF1**	39	F4
Arley **CW9**	49	F4
Arlingham **GL2**	29	G7
Arlington, *Devon* **EX31**	6	E1
Arlington, *E.Suss.* **BN26**	13	J6
Arlington, *Glos.* **GL7**	20	E1
Arlington Beccott **EX31**	6	E1
Armadale, *High.* **KW14**	104	C2
Armadale, *High.* **IV45**	86	C4
Armadale, *W.Loth.* **EH48**	75	H4
Armathwaite **CA4**	61	G2
Arminghall **NR14**	45	G5
Armitage **WS15**	40	C4
Armitage Bridge **HD4**	50	D1
Armley **LS12**	57	H6
Armscote **CV37**	30	D4
Armshead **ST9**	40	B1
Armston **PE8**	42	D7
Armthorpe **DN3**	51	J2
Arnabost **PA78**	78	D1
Arnaby **LA18**	54	E1
Arncliffe **BD23**	56	E2
Arncliffe Cote **BD23**	56	E2
Arncroach **KY10**	83	G7
Arne **BH20**	9	J6
Arnesby **LE8**	41	J6
Arngask **PH2**	82	C6
Arngibbon **FK8**	74	E1
Arngomery **FK8**	74	E1
Arnhall **DD9**	83	H1
Arnicle **PA29**	73	F7
Arnipol **PH38**	86	D6
Arnisdale **IV40**	86	E3
Arnish **IV40**	94	B7
Arniston Engine **EH23**	76	B4
Arnol **HS2**	101	F3
Arnold, *E.Riding* **HU11**	59	H5
Arnold, *Notts.* **NG5**	41	H1
Arnprior **FK8**	74	E1
Arnside **LA5**	55	H2
Arowry **SY13**	38	D2
Arrad Foot **LA12**	55	G1
Arradoul **AB56**	98	C4
Arram **HU17**	59	G5
Arran **KA27**	73	H7
Arras **YO43**	59	F5
Arrat **DD9**	83	H2
Arrathorne **DL8**	62	D7
Arreton **PO30**	11	G6
Arrington **SG8**	33	G3
Arrington **PA33**	80	D4
Arrochar **G83**	80	E7
Arrow **B49**	30	B3
Arscaig **IV27**	103	H7
Arscott **SY5**	38	D5
Arthington **LS21**	57	H5
Arthingworth **LE16**	42	A7
Arthog **LL39**	37	F4
Arthrath **AB41**	91	H1
Arthurstone **PH13**	82	D3
Artrochie **AB41**	91	J1
Aruadh **PA49**	72	A4
Arundel **BN18**	12	D6
Aryhoulan **PH33**	80	B1
Asby **CA14**	60	B4
Ascog **PA20**	73	K4
Ascot **SL5**	22	C5
Ascott **CV36**	30	E5

Ascott d'Oyley **OX7**	30	E7
Ascott Earl **OX7**	30	D7
Ascott-under-Wychwood **OX7**	30	E7
Ascreavie **DD8**	82	E2
Asenby **YO7**	57	K2
Asfordby **LE14**	42	A4
Asfordby Hill **LE14**	42	A4
Asgarby, *Lincs.* **PE23**	53	G6
Asgarby, *Lincs.* **NG34**	42	E1
Ash, *Dorset* **DT11**	9	H3
Ash, *Kent* **CT3**	15	H2
Ash, *Kent* **TN15**	24	C5
Ash, *Som.* **TA12**	8	D2
Ash, *Surr.* **GU12**	22	B6
Ash Barton **EX20**	6	D5
Ash Bullayne **EX17**	7	F5
Ash Green, *Surr.* **GU12**	22	C7
Ash Green, *Warks.* **CV7**	41	F7
Ash Magna **SY13**	38	E2
Ash Mill **EX36**	7	F3
Ash Parva **SY13**	38	E2
Ash Priors **TA4**	7	K3
Ash Street **IP7**	34	E4
Ash Thomas **EX16**	7	J4
Ash Vale **GU12**	22	B6
Ashampstead **RG8**	21	J4
Ashbocking **IP6**	35	F3
Ashbourne **DE6**	40	D1
Ashbrittle **TA21**	7	J3
Ashburnham Place **TN33**	13	K5
Ashburton **TQ13**	5	H4
Ashbury, *Devon* **EX20**	6	D6
Ashbury, *Oxon.* **SN6**	21	F3
Ashby **DN16**	52	B2
Ashby by Partney **PE23**	53	H6
Ashby cum Fenby **DN37**	53	F2
Ashby de la Launde **LN4**	52	D7
Ashby de la Zouch **LE65**	41	F4
Ashby Dell **NR32**	45	J6
Ashby Folville **LE14**	42	A4
Ashby Hill **DN37**	53	F2
Ashby Magna **LE17**	41	H6
Ashby Parva **LE17**	41	H7
Ashby Puerorum **LN13**	53	G5
Ashby St. Ledgers **CV23**	31	G2
Ashby St. Mary **NR14**	45	H5
Ashchurch **GL20**	29	J5
Ashcombe, *Devon* **EX7**	5	K3
Ashcombe, *N.Som.* **BS22**	19	G5
Ashcott **TA7**	8	D1
Ashdon **CB10**	33	J4
Ashe **RG25**	21	J7
Asheldham **CM0**	25	F1
Ashen **CO10**	34	B4
Ashenden **TN30**	14	D4
Ashendon **HP18**	31	J7
Ashens **PA29**	73	G3
Ashfield, *Arg. & B.* **PA31**	73	F2
Ashfield, *Here.* **HR9**	28	E6
Ashfield, *Stir.* **FK15**	81	J7
Ashfield, *Suff.* **IP14**	35	G1
Ashfield Green, *Suff.* **IP21**	35	G1
Ashfield Green, *Suff.* **CB8**	34	B3
Ashfold Crossways **RH13**	13	F4
Ashford, *Devon* **TQ7**	5	G6
Ashford, *Devon* **EX31**	6	D2
Ashford, *Hants.* **SP6**	10	C3
Ashford, *Kent* **TN23**	15	F3
Ashford, *Surr.* **TW15**	22	D4
Ashford Bowdler **SY8**	28	E1
Ashford Carbonel **SY8**	28	E1
Ashford Hill **RG19**	21	J5
Ashford in the Water **DE45**	50	D5
Ashgill **ML9**	75	F5
Ashiestiel **TD1**	76	C7
Ashill, *Devon* **EX15**	7	J4
Ashill, *Norf.* **IP25**	44	C5
Ashill, *Som.* **TA19**	8	C3
Ashingdon **SS4**	24	E2
Ashington, *Northumb.* **NE63**	71	H5
Ashington, *Som.* **BA22**	8	E2
Ashington, *W.Suss.* **RH20**	12	E5
Ashkirk **TD7**	69	K1
Ashlett **SO45**	11	F4
Ashleworth **GL19**	29	H6
Ashleworth Quay **GL19**	29	H6
Ashley, *Cambs.* **CB8**	33	K2
Ashley, *Ches.* **WA15**	49	G4
Ashley, *Devon* **EX18**	6	E4
Ashley, *Glos.* **GL8**	20	C2
Ashley, *Hants.* **SO20**	10	E1
Ashley, *Hants.* **BH25**	10	D5
Ashley, *Kent* **CT15**	15	J3
Ashley, *Northants.* **LE16**	42	A6
Ashley, *Staffs.* **TF9**	39	G2
Ashley, *Wilts.* **SN13**	20	B5
Ashley Down **BS7**	19	J4
Ashley Green **HP5**	22	C1
Ashley Heath, *Dorset* **BH24**	10	C4
Ashley Heath, *Staffs.* **TF9**	39	G2
Ashmanhaugh **NR12**	45	H3
Ashmansworth **RG20**	21	H6
Ashmansworthy **EX39**	6	B4
Ashmore, *Dorset* **SP5**	9	J3
Ashmore, *P. & K.* **PH10**	82	C2
Ashmore Green **RG18**	21	J5
Ashorne **CV35**	30	E3
Ashover **S45**	51	F6
Ashover Hay **S45**	51	F6
Ashow **CV8**	30	E1
Ashperton **HR8**	29	F4
Ashprington **TQ9**	5	J5
Ashreigney **EX18**	6	E4
Ashtead **KT21**	22	E6
Ashton, *Ches.* **CH3**	48	E6
Ashton, *Cornw.* **TR13**	2	D6
Ashton, *Cornw.* **PL17**	4	D4

Ashton, *Hants.* **SO32**	11	G3
Ashton, *Here.* **HR6**	28	E2
Ashton, *Inclyde* **PA19**	74	A3
Ashton, *Northants.* **PE8**	42	D7
Ashton, *Northants.* **NN7**	31	J4
Ashton, *Peter.* **PE9**	42	E5
Ashton Common **BA14**	20	B6
Ashton Keynes **SN6**	20	D2
Ashton under Hill **WR11**	29	J5
Ashton upon Mersey **M33**	49	G3
Ashton-in-Makerfield **WN4**	48	E3
Ashton-under-Lyne **OL7**	49	J3
Ashurst, *Hants.* **SO40**	10	E3
Ashurst, *Kent* **TN3**	13	J3
Ashurst, *W.Suss.* **BN44**	12	E5
Ashurst Bridge **SO40**	10	E3
Ashurstwood **RH18**	13	H3
Ashwater **EX21**	6	B6
Ashwell, *Herts.* **SG7**	33	F5
Ashwell, *Rut.* **LE15**	42	B4
Ashwell End **SG7**	33	F4
Ashwellthorpe **NR16**	45	F6
Ashwick **BA3**	19	K7
Ashwicken **PE32**	44	B4
Ashybank **TD9**	70	A2
Askam in Furness **LA16**	55	F2
Askern **DN6**	51	H1
Askernish (Aisgernis) **HS8**	84	C2
Askerswell **DT2**	8	E5
Askett **HP27**	22	B1
Askham, *Cumb.* **CA10**	61	G4
Askham, *Notts.* **NG22**	51	K5
Askham Bryan **YO23**	58	B5
Askham Richard **YO23**	58	B5
Asknish **PA31**	73	H1
Askrigg **DL8**	62	A7
Askwith **LS21**	57	G5
Aslackby **NG34**	42	D2
Aslacton **NR15**	45	F6
Aslockton **NG13**	42	A1
Asloun **AB33**	90	D3
Aspall **IP14**	35	F2
Aspatria **CA7**	60	C2
Aspenden **SG9**	33	G6
Asperton **PE20**	43	F2
Aspley Guise **MK17**	32	C5
Aspley Heath **MK17**	32	C5
Aspull **WN2**	49	F2
Asselby **DN14**	58	D7
Asserby **LN13**	53	H5
Assington **CO10**	34	D5
Assington Green **CO10**	34	B3
Astbury **CW12**	49	H6
Astcote **NN12**	31	H3
Asterby **LN11**	53	F5
Asterley **SY5**	38	C5
Asterton **SY7**	38	D6
Asthall **OX18**	30	D7
Asthall Leigh **OX29**	30	E7
Astle **SK10**	49	H5
Astley, *Gt.Man.* **M29**	49	G2
Astley, *Shrop.* **SY4**	38	E4
Astley, *Warks.* **CV10**	41	F7
Astley, *Worcs.* **DY13**	29	G2
Astley Abbotts **WV16**	39	G6
Astley Bridge **BL1**	49	G1
Astley Cross **DY13**	29	H2
Astley Green **M29**	49	G3
Astley Lodge **SY4**	38	E4
Aston, *Ches.* **CW5**	39	F1
Aston, *Ches.* **WA7**	48	E5
Aston, *Derbys.* **S33**	50	D4
Aston, *Derbys.* **DE6**	40	D2
Aston, *Flints.* **CH5**	48	C6
Aston, *Here.* **SY8**	28	D1
Aston, *Here.* **HR6**	28	D2
Aston, *Herts.* **SG2**	33	F6
Aston, *Oxon.* **OX18**	21	G1
Aston, *S.Yorks.* **S26**	51	G4
Aston, *Shrop.* **SY4**	38	E3
Aston, *Shrop.* **WV5**	40	A6
Aston, *Staffs.* **TF9**	39	G1
Aston, *Tel. & W.* **TF6**	39	F5
Aston, *W'ham* **RG9**	22	A3
Aston, *W.Mid.* **B6**	40	C7
Aston Abbotts **HP22**	32	B6
Aston Botterell **WV16**	39	F7
Aston Cantlow **B95**	30	C3
Aston Clinton **HP22**	32	B7
Aston Crews **HR9**	29	F6
Aston Cross **GL20**	29	J5
Aston End **SG2**	33	F6
Aston Eyre **WV16**	39	F6
Aston Fields **B60**	29	J2
Aston Flamville **LE10**	41	G6
Aston Heath **WA7**	48	E5
Aston Ingham **HR9**	29	F6
Aston juxta Mondrum **CW5**	49	F7
Aston le Walls **NN11**	31	F3
Aston Magna **GL56**	30	C5
Aston Munslow **SY7**	38	E7
Aston on Carrant **GL20**	29	J5
Aston on Clun **SY7**	38	C7
Aston Pigott **SY5**	38	C5
Aston Rogers **SY5**	38	C5
Aston Rowant **OX49**	22	A2
Aston Sandford **HP17**	22	A1
Aston Somerville **WR12**	30	B5
Aston Subedge **GL55**	30	C4
Aston Tirrold **OX11**	21	J3
Aston Upthorpe **OX11**	21	J3
Aston-by-Stone **ST15**	40	B2
Aston-on-Trent **DE72**	41	G3
Astwick **SG5**	33	F5
Astwood **MK16**	32	C4
Astwood Bank **B96**	30	B2
Aswarby **NG34**	42	D1
Aswardby **PE23**	53	G5
Aswick Grange **PE12**	43	G4

Atch Lench **WR11**	30	B3
Atcham **SY5**	38	E5
Ath Linne **HS2**	100	D6
Athelhampton **DT2**	9	G5
Athelington **IP21**	35	G1
Athelney **TA7**	8	C2
Athelstaneford **EH39**	76	D3
Atherington, *Devon* **EX37**	6	D3
Atherington, *W.Suss.* **BN17**	12	D6
Athersley North **S71**	51	F2
Atherstone **CV9**	41	F6
Atherstone on Stour **CV37**	30	D3
Atherton **M46**	49	F2
Atlow **DE6**	40	E1
Attadale **IV54**	87	F1
Attenborough **NG9**	41	H2
Atterby **LN8**	52	C3
Attercliffe **S9**	51	F4
Atterley **TF13**	39	F6
Atterton **CV13**	41	F6
Attleborough, *Norf.* **NR17**	44	E6
Attleborough, *Warks.* **CV11**	41	F6
Attlebridge **NR9**	45	F4
Attleton Green **CB8**	34	B3
Atwick **YO25**	59	H4
Atworth **SN12**	20	B5
Auberrow **HR4**	28	D4
Aubourn **LN5**	52	C6
Auch **PA36**	80	E4
Auchairne **KA26**	67	F5
Auchallater **AB35**	89	J6
Auchameanach **PA29**	73	G5
Auchamore **KA27**	73	G6
Aucharnie **AB54**	98	E6
Aucharrigill **IV27**	96	B1
Auchattie **AB31**	90	E5
Auchavan **PH11**	82	C1
Auchbraad **PA30**	73	G2
Auchbreck **AB37**	89	K2
Auchenback **G78**	74	D5
Auchenblae **AB30**	91	F7
Auchenbothie **PA13**	74	B3
Auchenbrack **DG3**	68	C4
Auchenbreck **PA22**	73	J2
Auchencairn **DG7**	65	H5
Auchencrow **TD14**	77	G4
Auchendinny **EH26**	76	A4
Auchendolly **DG7**	65	H4
Auchenfoyle **PA13**	74	B3
Auchengillan **G63**	74	D2
Auchengray **ML11**	75	H5
Auchenhalrig **IV32**	98	B4
Auchenheath **ML11**	75	G6
Auchenhessnane **DG3**	68	D4
Auchenlochan **PA21**	73	H3
Auchenmalg **DG8**	64	C5
Auchenrivock **DG14**	69	J5
Auchentiber **KA13**	74	B6
Auchenvennel **G84**	74	A2
Auchessan **FK20**	81	F5
Auchgourish **PH24**	89	G3
Auchinafaud **PA29**	73	F5
Auchincruive **KA6**	67	H1
Auchindarrach **PA31**	73	G2
Auchindarroch **PA38**	80	B2
Auchindrain **PA32**	80	B7
Auchininna **AB53**	98	E6
Auchinleck **KA18**	67	K1
Auchinloch **G66**	74	E3
Auchinner **PH6**	81	H6
Auchinroath **AB38**	97	K6
Auchintoul, *Aber.* **AB33**	90	D3
Auchintoul, *Aber.* **AB54**	98	E5
Auchintoul, *High.* **IV27**	96	C2
Auchiries **AB42**	91	J1
Auchleven **AB52**	90	E2
Auchlochan **ML11**	75	G7
Auchlunachan **IV23**	95	H3
Auchlunies **AB12**	91	G5
Auchlunkart **AB55**	98	B6
Auchlyne **FK21**	81	G5
Auchmacoy **AB41**	91	H1
Auchmair **AB54**	90	B2
Auchmantle **DG8**	64	B4
Auchmithie **DD11**	83	H3
Auchmuirbridge **KY6**	82	D7
Auchmull **DD9**	90	D7
Auchnabony **DG6**	65	H6
Auchnabreac **PA32**	80	B7
Auchnacloich **PH8**	81	K4
Auchnacraig **DD8**	79	J4
Auchnacree **DD8**	83	F1
Auchnafree **PH8**	81	K4
Auchnagallin **PH26**	89	H1
Auchnagatt **AB41**	99	H6
Auchnaha **PA21**	73	H2
Auchnangoul **PA32**	80	B7
Aucholzie **AB35**	90	B5
Auchorrie **AB51**	90	E4
Auchrannie **PH11**	82	D2
Auchraw **FK19**	81	G5
Auchreoch **FK20**	80	E5
Auchronie **DD9**	90	C6
Auchterarder **PH3**	82	A6
Auchtercairn **IV21**	94	E4
Auchterderran **KY5**	76	A1
Auchterhouse **DD3**	82	E4
Auchtermuchty **KY14**	82	D6
Auchterneed **IV14**	96	B6
Auchtertool **KY2**	76	A1
Auchtertyre, *Angus* **PH12**	82	D3
Auchtertyre, *High.* **IV40**	86	E2
Auchtertyre, *Moray* **IV30**	97	J6
Auchtertyre, *Stir.* **FK20**	80	E5
Auchtubh **FK19**	81	G5
Auckengill **KW1**	105	J2
Auckley **DN9**	51	J2
Audenshaw **M34**	49	J3
Audlem **CW3**	39	F1

Audley **ST7**	49	G7
Audley End, *Essex* **CB11**	33	J5
Audley End, *Essex* **CO9**	34	C5
Audley End, *Suff.* **IP29**	34	C3
Audmore **ST20**	40	A3
Auds **AB45**	98	E4
Aughton, *E.Riding* **YO42**	58	D6
Aughton, *Lancs.* **L39**	48	C2
Aughton, *Lancs.* **LA2**	55	J3
Aughton, *S.Yorks.* **S26**	51	G4
Aughton, *Wilts.* **SN8**	21	F6
Aughton Park **L39**	48	D2
Auldearn **IV12**	97	G3
Aulden **HR6**	28	D3
Auldgirth **DG2**	68	E5
Auldhame **EH39**	76	D2
Auldhouse **G75**	74	E5
Aulich **PH16**	81	H2
Ault a' chruinn **IV40**	87	F2
Ault Hucknall **S44**	51	G6
Aultanrynie **IV27**	103	F5
Aultbea **IV22**	94	E3
Aultgrishan **IV21**	94	D3
Aultguish Inn **IV23**	95	K4
Aultibea **KW7**	105	F6
Aultiphurst **KW14**	104	D2
Aultmore **AB55**	98	C5
Ault-na-goire **IV2**	88	C2
Aultnamain Inn **IV19**	96	D3
Aultnapaddock **AB55**	98	B6
Aulton **AB52**	90	E2
Aultvaich **IV4**	96	C7
Aultvoulin **PH41**	86	D4
Aunby **PE9**	42	D4
Aundorach **PH25**	89	G3
Aunk **EX15**	7	J5
Aunsby **NG34**	42	D2
Auquhorthies **AB51**	91	G2
Aust **BS35**	19	J3
Austerfield **DN10**	51	J3
Austrey **CV9**	40	E5
Austwick **LA2**	56	C3
Authorpe **LN11**	53	H4
Authorpe Row **PE24**	53	J5
Avebury **SN8**	20	E4
Avebury Trusloe **SN8**	20	D5
Aveley **RM15**	23	J3
Avening **GL8**	20	B2
Averham **NG23**	51	K7
Avery Hill **SE9**	23	H4
Aveton Gifford **TQ7**	5	G6
Avielochan **PH22**	89	G3
Aviemore **PH22**	89	F3
Avington, *Hants.* **SO21**	11	G1
Avington, *W.Berks.* **RG17**	21	G5
Avoch **IV9**	96	D6
Avon **BH23**	10	C5
Avon Dassett **CV47**	31	F3
Avonbridge **FK1**	75	H3
Avoncliff **BA15**	20	B6
Avonmouth **BS11**	19	J4
Avonwick **TQ10**	5	H5
Awbridge **SO51**	10	E2
Awhirk **DG9**	64	A5
Awkley **BS35**	19	J3
Awliscombe **EX14**	7	K5
Awre **GL14**	20	A1
Awsworth **NG16**	41	G1
Axbridge **BS26**	19	H6
Axford, *Hants.* **RG25**	21	K7
Axford, *Wilts.* **SN8**	21	F4
Axminster **EX13**	8	B5
Axmouth **EX12**	8	B5
Axton **CH8**	47	K4
Axtown **PL20**	5	F4
Aycliffe **DL5**	62	D4
Aydon **NE45**	71	F7
Aylburton **GL15**	19	K1
Ayle **CA9**	61	J2
Aylesbeare **EX5**	7	J6
Aylesbury **HP20**	32	B7
Aylesby **DN37**	53	F2
Aylesford **ME20**	14	C2
Aylesham **CT3**	15	H2
Aylestone **LE2**	41	H5
Aylmerton **NR11**	45	F2
Aylsham **NR11**	45	F3
Aylton **HR8**	29	F5
Aymestrey **HR6**	28	D2
Aynho **OX17**	31	G5
Ayot Green **AL6**	33	F7
Ayot St. Lawrence **AL6**	32	E7
Ayot St. Peter **AL6**	33	F7
Ayr **KA7**	67	H1
Aysgarth **DL8**	57	F1
Ayshford **EX16**	7	J4
Ayside **LA11**	55	G1
Ayston **LE15**	42	B5
Aythorpe Roding **CM6**	33	J7
Ayton, *P. & K.* **PH2**	82	C6
Ayton, *Sc.Bord.* **TD14**	77	H4
Aywick **ZE2**	108	E4
Azerley **HG4**	57	H2

B			
Babbacombe **TQ1**	5	K4
Babbinswood **SY11**	38	C2
Babb's Green **SG12**	33	G7
Babcary **TA11**	8	E2
Babel **SA20**	27	H5
Babell **CH8**	47	K5
Babeny **TQ13**	5	G3
Bablock Hythe **OX29**	21	H1
Babraham **CB2**	33	J3
Babworth **DN22**	51	J4
Baby's Hill **AB37**	89	K1
Bac **HS2**	101	G3
Bachau **LL71**	46	C4
Back of Keppoch **PH39**	86	C6
Back Street **CB8**	34	B3

Place	Postcode	Page	Grid
Backaland	KW17	106	E4
Backaskaill	KW17	106	D2
Backbarrow	LA12	55	G1
Backburn	AB54	90	D1
Backe	SA33	17	F3
Backfolds	AB42	99	J5
Backford	CH2	48	D5
Backhill	AB53	91	F1
Backhill of Clackriach	AB42	99	H6
Backhill of Trustach	AB31	90	E5
Backies, *High.*	KW10	97	F1
Backies, *Moray*	AB56	98	D5
Backlass	KW1	105	H3
Backside	AB54	90	C1
Backwell	BS48	19	H5
Backworth	NE23	71	H6
Bacon End	CM6	33	J7
Baconend Green	CM6	33	J7
Baconsthorpe	NR25	45	F2
Bacton, *Here.*	HR2	28	C5
Bacton, *Norf.*	NR12	45	H2
Bacton, *Suff.*	IP14	34	E2
Bacton Green	IP14	34	E2
Bacup	OL13	56	D7
Badachro	IV21	94	D4
Badanloch Lodge	KW11	104	C5
Badavanich	IV22	95	H6
Badbea	KW7	105	F7
Badbury	SN4	20	E3
Badbury Wick	SN4	20	E3
Badby	NN11	31	G3
Badcall, *High.*	IV27	102	D4
Badcall, *High.*	IV27	102	E3
Badcaul	IV23	95	G2
Badden	PA31	73	G2
Baddeley Green	ST2	49	J7
Baddesley Clinton	B93	30	C1
Baddesley Ensor	CV9	40	E6
Baddidarach	IV27	102	C6
Badenscoth	AB51	91	F1
Badenyon	AB36	90	B3
Badgall	PL15	4	C2
Badger	WV6	39	G6
Badgerbank	SK11	49	H5
Badgers Mount	TN14	23	H5
Badgeworth	GL51	29	J7
Badgworth	BS26	19	G6
Badicaul	IV40	86	D2
Badingham	IP13	35	H2
Badintagairt	IV27	103	G7
Badlesmere	ME13	15	F2
Badley	IP6	34	E3
Badlipster	KW1	105	H4
Badluarach	IV23	95	F2
Badminton	GL9	20	B3
Badnaban	IV27	102	C6
Badnabay	IV27	102	E4
Badnafrave	AB37	89	K3
Badnagie	KW6	105	G5
Badnambiast	PH18	88	E7
Badninish	IV25	96	E2
Badrallach	IV23	95	G2
Badsey	WR11	30	B4
Badshot Lea	GU9	22	B7
Badsworth	WF9	51	G1
Badwell Ash	IP31	34	D2
Badworthy	TQ10	5	G4
Badyo	PH16	82	A1
Bae Cinmel (Kinmel Bay)	LL18	47	H4
Bae Colwyn (Colwyn Bay)	LL29	47	G5
Bae Penrhyn (Penrhyn Bay)	LL30	47	G4
Bag Enderby	PE23	53	G5
Bagber	DT10	9	G3
Bagby	YO7	57	K1
Bagendon	GL7	20	D1
Bagginswood	DY14	39	F7
Baggrave Hall	LE7	41	J5
Baggrow	CA7	60	C2
Bàgh a' Chaisteil (Castlebay)	HS9	84	B5
Bàgh Mòr	HS6	92	D6
Baghasdal	HS8	84	C3
Bagillt	CH6	48	B5
Baginton	CV8	30	E1
Baglan	SA12	18	A2
Bagley, *Shrop.*	SY12	38	D3
Bagley, *Som.*	BS28	19	H7
Bagmore	RG25	21	K7
Bagnall	ST9	49	J7
Bagnor	RG20	21	H5
Bagpath	GL8	20	B2
Bagshot, *Surr.*	GU19	22	C5
Bagshot, *Wilts.*	RG17	21	G5
Bagstone	BS37	19	K3
Bagthorpe, *Norf.*	PE31	44	B2
Bagthorpe, *Notts.*	NG16	51	G7
Baguley	M23	49	H4
Bagworth	LE67	41	G5
Bagwyllydiart	HR2	28	D6
Baildon	BD17	57	G6
Baile a' Mhanaich (Balivanich)	HS7	92	C6
Baile Ailein (Balallan)	HS2	100	E5
Baile Boidheach	PA31	73	F3
Baile Gharbhaidh	HS8	92	C7
Baile Glas	HS6	92	D6
Baile Mhartainn	HS6	92	C4
Baile Mhic Phail	HS6	92	D4
Baile Mòr, *Arg. & B.*	PA76	78	D5
Baile Mòr (Balemore), *W.Isles*	HS6	92	C5
Baile nan Cailleach	HS7	92	C6
Baile Raghaill	HS6	92	C5
Bailebeag	IV2	88	C3
Baileguish	PH21	89	F5
Baile-na-Cille	HS6	92	D3
Bailetonach	PH36	86	C7
Bailiesward	AB54	90	C1
Bailiff Bridge	HD6	57	G7
Baillieston	G69	74	E4
Bainsford	FK2	75	G2
Bainshole	AB54	90	E1
Bainton, *E.Riding*	YO25	59	F4
Bainton, *Oxon.*	OX27	31	G6
Bainton, *Peter.*	PE9	42	D5
Bairnkine	TD8	70	B2
Bakebare	AB55	90	B1
Baker Street	RM16	24	C3
Baker's End	SG12	33	G7
Bakewell	DE45	50	E6
Bala	LL23	37	J2
Balachuirn	IV40	94	B7
Balado	KY13	82	B7
Balafark	G63	74	E1
Balaldie	IV20	97	F4
Balallan (Baile Ailein)	HS2	100	E5
Balavil	PH21	88	E4
Balbeg, *High.*	IV63	88	B1
Balbeg, *High.*	IV63	88	B2
Balbeggie	PH2	82	C5
Balbirnie	KY7	82	D7
Balbithan	AB51	91	F3
Balblair, *High.*	IV7	96	E5
Balblair, *High.*	IV24	96	C2
Balblair, *High.*	IV19	96	E3
Balby	DN4	51	H2
Balcharn	IV27	96	C1
Balchers	AB45	99	F5
Balchladich	IV27	102	C5
Balchraggan, *High.*	IV5	96	C7
Balchraggan, *High.*	IV3	88	C1
Balchrick	IV27	102	D3
Balcombe	RH17	13	G3
Balcurvie	KY8	82	E7
Baldernock	G62	74	D3
Baldersby	YO7	57	J2
Baldersby St. James	YO7	57	J2
Balderstone, *Gt.Man.*	OL16	49	J1
Balderstone, *Lancs.*	BB2	56	B6
Balderton, *Ches.*	CH4	48	C6
Balderton, *Notts.*	NG24	52	B7
Baldhu	TR3	2	E4
Baldinnie	KY15	83	F6
Baldock	SG7	33	F5
Baldon Row	OX44	21	J1
Baldovan	DD3	82	E4
Baldovie, *Angus*	DD8	82	E2
Baldovie, *Dundee*	DD5	83	F4
Baldrine	IM4	54	D5
Baldslow	TN37	14	C6
Baldwin	IM4	54	C5
Baldwinholme	CA5	60	E1
Baldwin's Gate	ST5	39	G1
Baldwins Hill	RH19	13	G3
Bale	NR21	44	E2
Balelone	HS6	92	C4
Balemartine	PA77	78	A3
Balemore (Baile Mòr)	HS6	92	C5
Balendoch	PH12	82	D3
Balephuil	PA77	78	A3
Balerno	EH14	75	K4
Balernock	G84	74	A2
Baleromindubh	PA61	72	B1
Balerominmore	PA61	72	B1
Baleshare (Bhaleshear)	HS6	92	C5
Balevulin	PA69	79	F5
Balfield	DD9	83	G1
Balfour, *Aber.*	AB34	90	D5
Balfour, *Ork.*	KW17	107	D6
Balfron	G63	74	D2
Balfron Station	G63	74	D2
Balgonar	KY12	75	J1
Balgove	AB51	91	G1
Balgowan, *D. & G.*	DG9	64	B6
Balgowan, *High.*	PH20	88	D5
Balgown	IV51	93	J5
Balgreen	AB45	99	F5
Balgreggan	DG9	64	A5
Balgy	IV54	94	E6
Balhaldie	FK15	81	K7
Balhalgardy	AB51	91	F2
Balham	SW12	23	F4
Balhary	PH11	82	D3
Balhelvie	KY14	82	E5
Balhousie	KY8	83	F7
Baliasta	ZE2	108	F2
Baligill	KW14	104	D2
Baligrundle	PA34	79	K3
Balindore	PA35	80	A4
Balintore, *Angus*	DD8	82	D2
Balintore, *High.*	IV20	97	F4
Balintraid	IV18	96	E4
Balintyre	PH15	81	H3
Balivanich (Baile a' Mhanaich)	HS7	92	C6
Balkeerie	DD8	82	E3
Balkholme	DN14	58	D7
Balkissock	KA26	67	F5
Ball	SY10	38	C3
Ball Haye Green	ST13	49	J7
Ball Hill	RG20	21	H5
Balla	HS8	84	C3
Ballabeg	IM9	54	B6
Ballacannell	IM4	54	D5
Ballacarnane Beg	IM6	54	B5
Ballachulish	PH49	80	B2
Balladoole	IM9	54	B7
Ballafesson	IM9	54	B6
Ballagyr	IM5	54	B5
Ballajora	IM7	54	D4
Ballakilpheric	IM9	54	B6
Ballamodha	IM9	54	B6
Ballantrae	KA26	66	E5
Ballards Gore	SS4	25	F2
Ballasalla, *I.o.M.*	IM9	54	B6
Ballasalla, *I.o.M.*	IM7	54	C4
Ballater	AB35	90	B5
Ballaterach	AB34	90	C5
Ballaugh	IM7	54	C4
Ballaveare	IM4	54	C6
Ballchraggan	IV18	96	E4
Ballechin	PH9	82	A2
Balleich	FK19	81	G6
Ballencrieff	EH32	76	C3
Ballidon	DE6	50	E7
Balliekine	KA27	73	G6
Balliemeanoch	PA27	80	C7
Balliemore, *Arg. & B.*	PA27	73	K1
Balliemore, *Arg. & B.*	PA34	79	K5
Ballig	IM4	54	B5
Ballimeanoch	PA33	80	B6
Ballimore, *Arg. & B.*	PA21	73	H2
Ballimore, *Stir.*	FK19	81	G6
Ballinaby	PA44	72	A4
Ballindean	PH14	82	D5
Ballingdon	CO10	34	C4
Ballinger Common	HP16	22	C1
Ballingham	HR2	28	E5
Ballingry	KY5	75	K1
Ballinlick	PH8	82	A3
Ballinluig, *P. & K.*	PH9	82	A2
Ballinluig, *P. & K.*	PH10	82	B2
Ballintuim	PH10	82	C2
Balloch, *Angus*	DD8	82	E2
Balloch, *High.*	IV2	96	E7
Balloch, *N.Lan.*	G68	75	F3
Balloch, *W.Dun.*	G83	74	B2
Ballochan	AB31	90	D5
Ballochandrain	PA22	73	H2
Ballochford	AB54	90	B1
Ballochgair	PA28	66	B1
Ballochmartin	KA28	73	K5
Ballochmorrie	KA26	67	G5
Ballochmyle	KA5	67	K1
Ballochroy	PA29	73	F5
Ballogie	AB34	90	D5
Balls Cross	GU28	12	C4
Balls Green, *Essex*	CO7	34	E6
Ball's Green, *Glos.*	GL6	20	B2
Balls Hill	B71	40	B6
Ballyarnan	PA31	73	F3
Ballygown	PA73	79	F3
Ballygrant	PA45	72	B4
Ballyhaugh	PA78	78	C2
Ballymeanoch	PA31	73	G1
Ballymichael	KA27	73	H7
Balmacara	IV40	86	E2
Balmaclellan	DG7	65	G3
Balmacneil	PH9	82	A2
Balmadies	DD8	83	G3
Balmae	DG6	65	G6
Balmaha	DG8	74	C1
Balmalcolm	KY15	82	E7
Balmaqueen	IV51	93	K4
Balmeanach, *Arg. & B.*	PA65	79	H3
Balmeanach, *Arg. & B.*	PA68	79	F4
Balmedie	AB23	91	H3
Balmer Heath	SY12	38	D2
Balmerino	DD6	82	E5
Balmerlawn	SO42	10	E4
Balminnoch	DG8	64	C4
Balmore, *E.Dun.*	G64	74	E3
Balmore, *High.*	IV12	97	F7
Balmore, *High.*	IV4	87	K1
Balmore, *High.*	IV55	93	H7
Balmore, *P. & K.*	PH16	81	J2
Balmullo	KY16	83	F5
Balmungie	IV10	96	E6
Balmyle	PH10	82	B2
Balnaboth	DD8	82	E1
Balnabruaich	IV19	96	E4
Balnacra	IV54	95	F7
Balnafoich	IV2	88	D1
Balnagall	IV20	97	F3
Balnagown Castle	IV18	96	E4
Balnaguard	PH9	82	A2
Balnaguisich	IV18	96	D4
Balnahard, *Arg. & B.*	PA61	72	C1
Balnahard, *Arg. & B.*	PA68	79	F4
Balnain	IV63	88	B1
Balnakeil	IV27	103	F2
Balnaknock	IV51	93	K5
Balnamoon	DD9	83	G1
Balnapaling	IV19	96	E5
Balnespick	PH21	89	F4
Balquhidder	FK19	81	G5
Balsall	CV7	30	D1
Balsall Common	CV7	30	D1
Balsall Heath	B12	40	C7
Balscote	OX15	31	F4
Balsham	CB1	33	J3
Baltasound	ZE2	108	F2
Balterley	CW2	49	G7
Balterley Heath	CW2	49	G7
Baltersan	DG8	64	E4
Balthangie	AB53	99	G5
Balthayock	PH2	82	C5
Baltonsborough	BA6	8	E1
Baluachraig	PA31	73	G1
Balulive	PA31	72	C4
Balure, *Arg. & B.*	PA35	80	B4
Balure, *Arg. & B.*	PA37	79	K4
Balvaird	IV6	96	C6
Balvarran	PH10	82	B1
Balvicar	PA34	79	J6
Balvraid, *High.*	IV40	86	E3
Balvraid, *High.*	IV13	89	F1
Bamber Bridge	PR5	55	J7
Bamber's Green	CM22	33	J6
Bamburgh	NE69	77	K7
Bamff	PH11	82	D2
Bamford, *Derbys.*	S33	50	E4
Bamford, *Gt.Man.*	OL11	49	H1
Bampton, *Cumb.*	CA10	61	G5
Bampton, *Devon*	EX16	7	H3
Bampton, *Oxon.*	OX18	21	G1
Bampton Grange	CA10	61	G5
Banavie	PH33	87	H7
Banbury	OX16	31	F4
Bancffosfelen	SA15	17	H3
Banchor	IV12	97	G2
Banchory	AB31	91	F5
Banchory-Devenick	AB12	91	H4
Bancycapel	SA32	17	H3
Bancyfelin	SA33	17	G3
Bancyffordd	SA44	17	H1
Bandon	KY7	82	D7
Bandrake Head	LA12	55	G1
Banff	AB45	98	E4
Bangor	LL57	46	D5
Bangor-is-y-coed	LL13	38	C1
Bangor's Green	L39	48	C2
Banham	NR16	44	E7
Bank	SO43	10	D4
Bank End	LA20	54	E1
Bank Newton	BD23	56	E4
Bank Street	WR15	29	F2
Bank Top, *Lancs.*	WN8	48	E2
Bank Top, *W.Yorks.*	HX3	57	G7
Bankend	DG1	69	F7
Bankfoot	PH1	82	B4
Bankglen	KA18	67	K2
Bankhead, *Aber.*	AB33	90	E3
Bankhead, *Aber.*	AB51	90	E4
Bankhead, *Aberdeen*	AB21	91	G3
Bankhead, *D. & G.*	DG6	65	H6
Bankland	TA7	8	C2
Banknock	FK4	75	F3
Banks, *Cumb.*	CA8	70	A7
Banks, *Lancs.*	PR9	55	G7
Bankshill	DG11	69	G5
Banningham	NR11	45	G3
Bannister Green	CM6	33	K6
Bannockburn	FK7	75	G1
Banstead	SM7	23	F6
Bantam Grove	LS27	57	H7
Bantham	TQ7	5	G6
Banton	G65	75	F3
Banwell	BS29	19	G6
Banwen Pyrddin	SA10	18	B1
Banyard's Green	IP13	35	H1
Bapchild	ME9	25	F5
Baptiston	G63	74	D2
Bapton	BA12	9	J1
Bar End	SO23	11	F2
Bar Hill	CB3	33	G2
Barabhas (Barvas)	HS2	101	F3
Barachander	PA35	80	B5
Barassie	KA10	74	B7
Baravaville	IV18	96	E4
Barber Booth	S33	50	D4
Barber Green	LA11	55	G1
Barber's Moor	PR26	48	D1
Barbon	LA6	56	B1
Barbridge	CW5	49	F7
Barbrook	EX35	7	F1
Barby	CV23	31	G1
Barcaldine	PA37	80	A3
Barcaple	DG7	65	G5
Barchester	CV36	30	D5
Barclose	CA6	69	K7
Barcombe	BN8	13	H5
Barcombe Cross	BN8	13	H5
Barden	DL8	62	C7
Barden Park	TN9	23	J7
Bardennoch	DG7	67	K4
Bardfield End Green	CM6	33	K5
Bardfield Saling	CM7	33	K6
Bardister	ZE2	108	C5
Bardney	LN3	52	E6
Bardon, *Leics.*	LE67	41	G4
Bardon, *Moray*	IV30	97	K6
Bardon Mill	NE47	70	C7
Bardowie	G62	74	D3
Bardsea	LA12	55	F2
Bardsey	LS17	57	J5
Bardsey Island (Ynys Enlli)	LL53	36	A3
Bardwell	IP31	34	D1
Bare	LA4	55	H3
Barewood	HR6	28	C3
Barfad	PA29	73	G4
Barford, *Norf.*	NR9	45	F5
Barford, *Warks.*	CV35	30	D2
Barford St. John	OX15	31	F5
Barford St. Martin	SP3	10	B1
Barford St. Michael	OX15	31	F5
Barfrestone	CT15	15	H2
Bargaly	DG8	64	E4
Bargany Mains	KA26	67	G3
Bargoed	CF81	18	E2
Bargrennan	DG8	64	D3
Barham, *Cambs.*	PE28	32	E1
Barham, *Kent*	CT4	15	H2
Barham, *Suff.*	IP6	35	F3
Barharrow	DG7	65	G5
Barholm	PE9	42	D4
Barholm Mains	DG8	64	E5
Barkby	LE7	41	J5
Barkby Thorpe	LE7	41	J5
Barkers Green	SY4	38	E3
Barkestone-le-Vale	NG13	42	A2
Barkham	RG41	22	A5
Barking, *Gt.Lon.*	IG11	23	H3
Barking, *Suff.*	IP6	34	E3
Barking Tye	IP6	34	E3
Barkisland	HX4	57	F7
Barkston	NG32	42	C1
Barkston Ash	LS24	57	K6
Barkway	SG8	33	G5
Barlae	DG8	64	C4
Barland	LD8	28	B2
Barlaston	ST12	40	A2
Barlavington	GU28	12	C5
Barlborough	S43	51	G5
Barlby	YO8	58	C6
Barlestone	CV13	41	G5
Barley, *Herts.*	SG8	33	G5
Barley, *Lancs.*	BB12	56	D5
Barley Green	IP21	35	G1
Barleycroft End	SG9	33	H6
Barleyhill	NE44	62	B5
Barleythorpe	LE15	42	B5
Barling	SS3	25	F3
Barlings	LN3	52	D5
Barlow, *Derbys.*	S18	51	F5
Barlow, *N.Yorks.*	YO8	58	C7
Barlow, *T. & W.*	NE21	71	G7
Barmby Moor	YO42	58	D5
Barmby on the Marsh	DN14	58	C7
Barmer	PE31	44	C2
Barmolloch	PA31	73	G1
Barmoor Lane End	TD15	77	J7
Barmouth (Abermaw)	LL42	37	F4
Barmpton	DL1	62	E5
Barmston	YO25	59	H4
Barnaby Green	NR34	35	J1
Barnacabber	PA23	73	K2
Barnacarry	PA27	73	H1
Barnack	PE9	42	D5
Barnacle	CV7	41	F7
Barnamuc	PA38	80	B3
Barnard Castle	DL12	62	B5
Barnard Gate	OX29	31	F7
Barnardiston	CB9	34	B4
Barnbarroch, *D. & G.*	DG8	64	D5
Barnbarroch, *D. & G.*	DG5	65	J5
Barnburgh	DN5	51	G2
Barnby	NR34	45	J7
Barnby Dun	DN3	51	J2
Barnby in the Willows	NG24	52	B7
Barnby Moor	DN22	51	J4
Barndennoch	DG3	68	D5
Barne Barton	PL5	4	E5
Barnehurst	DA7	23	J4
Barnes	SW13	23	F4
Barnes Street	TN11	23	K7
Barnet	EN5	23	F2
Barnet Gate	EN5	23	F2
Barnetby le Wold	DN38	52	D2
Barney	NR21	44	D2
Barnham, *Suff.*	IP24	34	C1
Barnham, *W.Suss.*	PO22	12	C6
Barnham Broom	NR9	44	E5
Barnhead	DD10	83	H2
Barnhill, *Ches.*	CH3	48	D7
Barnhill, *Dundee*	DD5	83	F4
Barnhill, *Moray*	IV30	97	J6
Barnhills	DG9	66	D6
Barningham, *Dur.*	DL11	62	B5
Barningham, *Suff.*	IP31	34	D1
Barningham Green	NR11	45	F2
Barnoldby le Beck	DN37	53	F2
Barnoldswick	BB18	56	D5
Barns Green	RH13	12	E4
Barnsdale Bar	WF8	51	H1
Barnsley, *Glos.*	GL7	20	D1
Barnsley, *S.Yorks.*	S70	51	F2
Barnsole	CT3	15	H2
Barnstaple	EX31	6	D2
Barnston, *Essex*	CM6	33	K7
Barnston, *Mersey.*	CH61	48	B4
Barnstone	NG13	42	A2
Barnt Green	B45	30	B1
Barnton, *Ches.*	CW8	49	F5
Barnton, *Edin.*	EH4	75	K3
Barnwell All Saints	PE8	42	D7
Barnwell St. Andrew	PE8	42	D7
Barnwood	GL4	29	H7
Barons' Cross	HR6	28	D3
Barr, *Arg. & B.*	PA44	72	B4
Barr, *High.*	PA34	79	H2
Barr, *S.Ayr.*	KA26	67	G4
Barr, *Som.*	TA4	7	K3
Barr Hall	CO9	34	B5
Barra (Barraigh)	HS9	84	B4
Barra (Tràigh Mhòr) Airport	HS9	84	B4
Barrachan	DG8	64	D6
Barrackan	PA31	79	J7
Barraer	DG8	64	D4
Barraglom	HS2	100	D4
Barrahormid	PA31	73	F2
Barraigh (Barra)	HS9	84	B4
Barran	PA33	80	C5
Barrapoll	PA77	78	A3
Barrasford	NE48	70	E6
Barravullin	PA31	79	K7
Barregarrow	IM6	54	C5
Barrets Green	CW6	48	E7
Barrhead	G78	74	C5
Barrhill	KA26	67	G5
Barrington, *Cambs.*	CB2	33	G4
Barrington, *Som.*	TA19	8	C3
Barripper	TR14	2	D5
Barrisdale	PH35	86	E4
Barrmill	KA15	74	B5

Beverstone

Barrnacarry **PA34** 79 K5
Barrock **KW14** 105 H1
Barrow, *Glos.* **GL51** 29 H6
Barrow, *Lancs.* **BB7** 56 C6
Barrow, *Rut.* **LE15** 42 B4
Barrow, *Shrop.* **TF12** 39 F5
Barrow, *Som.* **BA9** 9 G1
Barrow, *Som.* **BA4** 19 J7
Barrow, *Suff.* **IP29** 34 B2
Barrow Gurney **BS48** 19 J5
Barrow Hann **DN19** 59 G7
Barrow Haven **DN19** 59 G7
Barrow Hill **S43** 51 G5
Barrow Nook **L39** 48 D2
Barrow Street **BA12** 9 H1
Barrow upon Humber **DN19** 59 G7
Barrow upon Soar **LE12** 41 H4
Barrow upon Trent **DE73** 41 F3
Barroway Drove **PE38** 43 J5
Barrowby **NG32** 42 B2
Barrowcliff **YO12** 59 G1
Barrowden **LE15** 42 C5
Barrowford **BB9** 56 D6
Barrow-in-Furness **LA14** 55 F3
Barrows Green **LA8** 55 J1
Barry, *Angus* **DD7** 83 G4
Barry, *V. of Glam.* **CF62** 18 E5
Barsby **LE7** 41 J4
Barsham **NR34** 45 H7
Barskimming **KA5** 67 J1
Barsloisnoch **PA31** 73 G1
Barston **B92** 30 D1
Bartestree **HR1** 28 E4
Barthol Chapel **AB51** 91 G1
Bartholomew Green **CM77** 34 B6
Barthomley **CW2** 49 G7
Bartley **SO40** 10 E3
Bartley Green **B32** 40 C7
Bartlow **CB1** 33 J4
Barton, *Cambs.* **CB3** 33 H3
Barton, *Ches.* **SY14** 48 D7
Barton, *Cumb.* **CA10** 61 F4
Barton, *Glos.* **GL54** 30 B6
Barton, *Lancs.* **PR3** 55 J6
Barton, *Lancs.* **L39** 48 C2
Barton, *N.Yorks.* **DL10** 62 D6
Barton, *Oxon.* **OX3** 21 J1
Barton, *Torbay* **TQ2** 5 K4
Barton, *Warks.* **B50** 30 C3
Barton Bendish **PE33** 44 B5
Barton End **GL6** 20 B2
Barton Green **DE13** 40 D4
Barton Hartshorn **MK18** 31 H5
Barton Hill **YO60** 58 D3
Barton in Fabis **NG11** 41 H2
Barton in the Beans **CV13** 41 F5
Barton Mills **IP28** 34 B1
Barton on Sea **BH25** 10 D5
Barton St. David **TA11** 8 E1
Barton Seagrave **NN15** 32 B1
Barton Stacey **SO21** 21 H7
Barton Town **EX31** 6 E1
Barton Turf **NR12** 45 H3
Bartongate **OX7** 31 F6
Barton-le-Clay **MK45** 32 D5
Barton-le-Street **YO17** 58 D2
Barton-le-Willows **YO60** 58 D3
Barton-on-the-Heath **GL56** 30 D5
Barton-under-Needwood **DE13** 40 D4
Barton-upon-Humber **DN18** 59 G7
Barvas (Barabhas) **HS2** 101 F3
Barway **CB7** 33 J1
Barwell **LE9** 41 G6
Barwhinnock **DG6** 65 G5
Barwick, *Herts.* **SG11** 33 G7
Barwick, *Som.* **BA22** 8 E3
Barwick in Elmet **LS15** 57 J6
Barwinnock **DG8** 64 D6
Baschurch **SY4** 38 D3
Bascote **CV47** 31 F2
Base Green **IP14** 34 E2
Basford Green **ST13** 49 J7
Bashall Eaves **BB7** 56 B5
Bashall Town **BB7** 56 C5
Bashley **BH25** 10 D5
Basildon, *Essex* **SS14** 24 D3
Basildon, *W.Berks.* **RG8** 21 K4
Basingstoke **RG21** 21 K6
Baslow **DE45** 50 E5
Bason Bridge **TA9** 19 G7
Bassaleg **NP10** 19 F3
Bassenthwaite **CA12** 60 D3
Basset's Cross **EX20** 6 D5
Bassett **SO16** 11 F3
Bassingbourn **SG8** 33 G4
Bassingfield **NG12** 41 J2
Bassingham **LN5** 52 C7
Bassingthorpe **NG33** 42 C3
Basta **ZE2** 108 E3
Baston **PE6** 42 E4
Bastonford **WR2** 29 H3
Bastwick **NR29** 45 J4
Batavaime **FK21** 81 F4
Batch **BS24** 19 G6
Batchley **B97** 30 B2
Batchworth **WD3** 22 D2
Batchworth Heath **WD3** 22 D2
Batcombe, *Dorset* **DT2** 9 F4
Batcombe, *Som.* **BA4** 9 F1
Bate Heath **CW9** 49 F5
BATH BA 20 A5
Bathampton **BA2** 20 A5
Bathealton **TA4** 7 J3
Batheaston **BA1** 20 A5
Bathford **BA1** 20 A5
Bathgate **EH48** 75 H4
Bathley **NG23** 51 K7
Bathpool, *Cornw.* **PL15** 4 C3
Bathpool, *Som.* **TA2** 8 B2
Bathway **BA3** 19 J6
Batley **WF17** 57 H7
Batsford **GL56** 30 C5
Batson **TQ8** 5 H7
Battersby **TS9** 63 G6
Battersea **SW11** 23 F4
Battisborough Cross **PL8** 5 G6
Battisford **IP14** 34 E3
Battisford Tye **IP14** 34 E3
Battle, *E.Suss.* **TN33** 14 C6
Battle, *Powys* **LD3** 27 K5
Battledown **GL52** 29 J6
Battlefield **SY1** 38 E4
Battlesbridge **SS11** 24 D2
Battlesden **MK17** 32 C6
Battlesea Green **IP21** 35 G1
Battleton **TA22** 7 H3
Battlies Green **IP30** 34 D2
Battramsley **SO41** 10 E5
Batt's Corner **GU10** 22 B7
Bauds of Cullen **AB56** 98 C4
Baugh **PA77** 78 B3
Baughton **WR8** 29 H4
Baughurst **RG26** 21 J5
Baulds **AB31** 90 E5
Baulking **SN7** 21 G2
Baumber **LN9** 53 F5
Baunton **GL7** 20 D1
Baveney Wood **DY14** 29 F1
Baverstock **SP3** 10 B1
Bawburgh **NR9** 45 F5
Bawdeswell **NR20** 44 E3
Bawdrip **TA7** 8 C1
Bawdsey **IP12** 35 H4
Bawdsey Manor **IP12** 35 H5
Bawsey **PE32** 44 A4
Bawtry **DN10** 51 J3
Baxenden **BB5** 56 C7
Baxterley **CV9** 40 E6
Baxter's Green **CB8** 34 B3
Bay **SP8** 9 H2
Baybridge **DH8** 62 A2
Baycliff **LA12** 55 F2
Baydon **SN8** 21 F4
Bayford, *Herts.* **SG13** 23 G1
Bayford, *Som.* **BA9** 9 G2
Bayfordbury **SG13** 33 G7
Bayham Abbey **TN3** 13 K3
Bayles **CA9** 61 J2
Baylham **IP6** 35 F3
Baynards Green **OX27** 31 G6
Baysham **HR9** 28 E6
Bayston Hill **SY3** 38 D5
Bayswater **W2** 23 F3
Baythorn End **CO9** 34 B4
Bayton **DY14** 29 F1
Bayworth **OX13** 21 J1
Beach, *High.* **PA34** 79 J2
Beach, *S.Glos.* **BS30** 20 A4
Beachampton **MK19** 31 J5
Beachamwell **PE37** 44 B5
Beacharr **PA29** 72 E6
Beachley **NP16** 19 J2
Beacon, *Devon* **EX14** 7 K5
Beacon, *Devon* **EX14** 8 B4
Beacon Hill, *Dorset* **BH16** 9 J5
Beacon Hill, *Essex* **CM8** 34 C7
Beacon Hill, *Surr.* **GU26** 12 B3
Beacon's Bottom **HP14** 22 A2
Beaconsfield **HP9** 22 C2
Beacravik **HS3** 93 G2
Beadlam **YO62** 58 C1
Beadlow **SG17** 32 E5
Beadnell **NE67** 71 H1
Beaford **EX19** 6 D4
Beal, *N.Yorks.* **DN14** 58 B7
Beal, *Northumb.* **TD15** 77 J6
Bealach **PA38** 80 A2
Bealsmill **PL17** 4 D3
Beambridge **CW5** 49 F7
Beamhurst **ST14** 40 C2
Beaminster **DT8** 8 D4
Beamish **DH9** 62 D1
Beamsley **BD23** 57 F4
Bean **DA2** 23 J4
Beanacre **SN12** 20 C5
Beanley **NE66** 71 F2
Beaquoy **KW17** 106 C5
Beardon **EX20** 6 D7
Beardwood **BB2** 56 B7
Beare **EX5** 7 H5
Beare Green **RH5** 22 E7
Bearley **CV37** 30 C2
Bearnie **AB41** 91 H1
Bearnock **IV63** 88 B1
Bearnus **PA73** 78 E3
Bearpark **DH7** 62 D2
Bearsbridge **NE47** 61 J1
Bearsden **G61** 74 D3
Bearsted **ME14** 14 C2
Bearstone **TF9** 39 G2
Bearwood, *Poole* **BH11** 10 B5
Bearwood, *W.Mid.* **B66** 40 C7
Beattock **DG10** 69 F3
Beauchamp Roding **CM5** 33 J7
Beauchief **S8** 51 F4
Beaudesert **B95** 30 C2
Beaufort **NP23** 28 A7
Beaulieu **SO42** 10 E4
Beauly **IV4** 96 C7
Beaumaris (Biwmaris) **LL58** 46 E5
Beaumont, *Chan.I.* **JE3** 3 J7
Beaumont, *Cumb.* **CA5** 60 E1
Beaumont, *Essex* **CO16** 35 F6
Beaumont Hill **DL1** 62 D5
Beausale **CV35** 30 D1
Beauvale **NG16** 41 G1
Beauworth **SO24** 11 G2
Beaver Green **TN23** 14 E3
Beaworthy **EX21** 6 C6
Beazley End **CM7** 34 B6
Bebington **CH63** 48 C4
Bebside **NE24** 71 H5
Beccles **NR34** 45 J6
Becconsall **PR4** 55 H7
Beck Foot **LA8** 61 H7
Beck Hole **YO22** 63 K6
Beck Row **IP28** 33 K1
Beck Side, *Cumb.* **LA17** 55 F1
Beck Side, *Cumb.* **LA11** 55 G1
Beckbury **TF11** 39 G5
Beckenham **BR3** 23 G5
Beckering **LN8** 52 E4
Beckermet **CA21** 60 B6
Beckermonds **BD23** 56 D1
Beckett End **IP26** 44 B6
Beckfoot, *Cumb.* **CA19** 60 C6
Beckfoot, *Cumb.* **CA7** 60 B2
Beckford **GL20** 29 J5
Beckhampton **SN8** 20 D5
Beckingham, *Lincs.* **LN5** 52 B7
Beckingham, *Notts.* **DN10** 51 K4
Beckington **BA11** 20 B6
Beckley, *E.Suss.* **TN31** 14 D5
Beckley, *Oxon.* **OX3** 31 G7
Beck's Green **NR34** 45 H7
Beckside **LA6** 56 B1
Beckton **E6** 23 H3
Beckwithshaw **HG3** 57 H4
Becontree **RM8** 23 H3
Bedale **DL8** 57 H1
Bedburn **DL13** 62 B3
Bedchester **SP7** 9 H3
Beddau **CF38** 18 D3
Beddgelert **LL55** 36 E1
Beddingham **BN8** 13 H6
Beddington **SM6** 23 F5
Beddington Corner **CR4** 23 F5
Bedfield **IP13** 35 G2
Bedfield Little Green **IP13** 35 G2
Bedford **MK40** 32 D4
Bedgebury Cross **TN17** 14 C4
Bedgrove **HP21** 32 B7
Bedham **RH20** 12 D4
Bedhampton **PO9** 11 J4
Bedingfield **IP23** 35 F2
Bedingfield Green **IP23** 35 F2
Bedingfield Street **IP23** 35 F2
Bedingham Green **NR35** 45 G6
Bedlam, *Lancs.* **BB5** 56 C7
Bedlam, *N.Yorks.* **HG3** 57 H3
Bedlar's Green **CM22** 33 J6
Bedlington **NE22** 71 H5
Bedlinog **CF46** 18 D1
Bedminster **BS3** 19 J4
Bedmond **WD5** 22 D1
Bednall **ST17** 40 B4
Bedol **CH6** 48 B5
Bedrule **TD9** 70 B2
Bedstone **SY7** 28 C1
Bedwas **CF83** 18 E3
Bedwell **SG1** 33 F6
Bedwellty **NP12** 18 E1
Bedworth **CV12** 41 F7
Bedworth Woodlands **CV12** 41 F7
Beeby **LE7** 41 J5
Beech, *Hants.* **GU34** 11 H1
Beech, *Staffs.* **ST4** 40 A2
Beech Hill **RG7** 21 K5
Beechingstoke **SN9** 20 D6
Beechwood **WA7** 48 E4
Beedon **RG20** 21 H4
Beeford **YO25** 59 H4
Beeley **DE4** 50 E6
Beelsby **DN37** 53 F2
Beenham **RG7** 21 J5
Beeny **PL35** 4 B1
Beer **EX12** 8 B6
Beer Hackett **DT9** 9 F3
Beercrocombe **TA3** 8 C2
Beesands **TQ7** 5 J6
Beesby, *Lincs.* **LN13** 53 H4
Beesby, *N.E.Lincs.* **DN36** 53 F3
Beeson **TQ7** 5 J6
Beeston, *Beds.* **SG19** 32 E4
Beeston, *Ches.* **CW6** 48 E7
Beeston, *Norf.* **PE32** 44 D4
Beeston, *Notts.* **NG9** 41 H2
Beeston, *W.Yorks.* **LS11** 57 H6
Beeston Regis **NR26** 45 F1
Beeston St. Lawrence **NR12** 45 H3
Beeswing **DG2** 65 J4
Beetham, *Cumb.* **LA7** 55 H2
Beetham, *Som.* **TA20** 8 B3
Beetley **NR20** 44 D4
Beffcote **ST20** 40 A4
Began **CF3** 19 F3
Begbroke **OX5** 31 F7
Begdale **PE14** 43 H5
Begelly **SA68** 16 E4
Beggar's Bush **LD8** 28 B2
Beggearn Huish **TA23** 7 J2
Beggshill **AB54** 90 D1
Beguildy (Bugeildy) **LD7** 28 A1
Beighton, *Norf.* **NR13** 45 H5
Beighton, *S.Yorks.* **S20** 51 G4
Beili-glas **NP7** 19 G1
Beinn na Faoghla (Benbecula) **HS7** 92 D6
Beith **KA15** 74 B5
Bekesbourne **CT4** 15 G2
Belaugh **NR12** 45 G4
Belbroughton **DY9** 29 J1
Belchalwell **DT11** 9 G4
Belchalwell Street **DT11** 9 G4
Belchamp Otten **CO10** 34 C4
Belchamp St. Paul **CO10** 34 B4
Belchamp Walter **CO10** 34 C4
Belchford **LN9** 53 F5
Belfield **OL16** 49 J1
Belford **NE70** 77 K7
Belgrave **LE4** 41 H5
Belhaven **EH42** 76 E3
Belhelvie **AB23** 91 H3
Belhinnie **AB54** 90 C2
Bell Bar **AL9** 23 F1
Bell Busk **BD23** 56 E4
Bell End **DY9** 29 J1
Bell Heath **DY9** 29 J1
Bell Hill **GU32** 11 J2
Bell o' th' Hill **SY13** 38 E1
Bellabeg **AB36** 90 B3
Belladrum **IV4** 96 C7
Bellanoch **PA31** 73 G1
Bellaty **PH11** 82 D2
Belle Isle **LS10** 57 J7
Belle Vue **CA2** 60 E1
Belleau **LN13** 53 H5
Belleheiglash **AB37** 89 J1
Bellerby **DL8** 62 C7
Bellever **PL20** 5 G3
Bellfields **GU1** 22 C6
Belliehill **DD9** 83 G1
Bellingdon **HP5** 22 C1
Bellingham, *Gt.Lon.* **SE6** 23 G4
Bellingham, *Northumb.* **NE48** 70 D5
Belloch **PA29** 72 E7
Bellochantuy **PA28** 72 E7
Bell's Cross **IP6** 35 F3
Bells Yew Green **TN3** 13 K3
Bellshill, *N.Lan.* **ML4** 75 F4
Bellshill, *Northumb.* **NE70** 77 K7
Bellside **ML1** 75 G5
Bellsquarry **EH54** 75 J4
Belluton **BS39** 19 K5
Belmaduthy **IV8** 96 D6
Belmesthorpe **PE9** 42 D4
Belmont, *B'burn.* **BL7** 49 F1
Belmont, *Gt.Lon.* **SM2** 23 F5
Belmont, *Gt.Lon.* **HA7** 22 E2
Belmont, *Shet.* **ZE2** 108 E2
Belnie **PE11** 43 F2
Belowda **PL26** 3 G2
Belper **DE56** 41 F1
Belper Lane End **DE56** 41 F1
Belsay **NE20** 71 G6
Belsford **TQ9** 5 H5
Belsize **WD3** 22 D1
Belstead **IP8** 35 F4
Belston **KA6** 67 H1
Belstone **EX20** 6 E6
Belstone Corner **EX20** 6 E6
Belsyde **EH49** 75 H3
Belthorn **BB1** 56 C7
Beltinge **CT6** 25 H5
Beltingham **NE47** 70 C7
Beltoft **DN9** 52 B2
Belton, *Leics.* **LE12** 41 G3
Belton, *Lincs.* **NG32** 42 C2
Belton, *N.Lincs.* **DN9** 51 K2
Belton, *Norf.* **NR31** 45 J5
Belton, *Rut.* **LE15** 42 B5
Beltring **TN12** 23 K7
Belvedere **DA17** 23 H4
Belvoir **NG32** 42 B2
Bembridge **PO35** 11 H6
Bemersyde **TD6** 76 D7
Bemerton **SP2** 10 C1
Bempton **YO15** 59 H2
Ben Alder Cottage **PH17** 81 F1
Ben Alder Lodge **PH19** 88 C7
Ben Rhydding **LS29** 57 G5
Benacre **NR34** 45 K7
Benbecula (Beinn na Faoghla) **HS7** 92 D6
Benbecula (Balivanich) Airport **HS7** 92 C6
Benbuie **DG3** 68 C4
Benderloch **PA37** 80 A4
Bendish **SG4** 32 E6
Benenden **TN17** 14 D4
Benfield **DG8** 64 D4
Benfieldside **DH8** 62 B1
Bengate **NR28** 45 H3
Bengeo **SG14** 33 G7
Bengeworth **WR11** 30 B4
Benhall **GL51** 29 J6
Benhall Green **IP17** 35 H2
Benhall Street **IP17** 35 H2
Benholm **DD10** 83 K1
Beningbrough **YO30** 58 B4
Benington, *Herts.* **SG2** 33 F6
Benington, *Lincs.* **PE22** 43 G1
Benington Sea End **PE22** 43 H1
Benllech **LL74** 46 D4
Benmore, *Arg. & B.* **PA23** 73 K2
Benmore, *Stir.* **FK20** 81 F5
Bennacott **PL15** 4 C1
Bennan Cottage **DG7** 65 G3
Bennett End **HP14** 22 A2
Bennetts End **HP3** 22 D1
Benniworth **LN8** 53 F4
Benover **ME18** 14 C3
Benson **OX10** 21 K2
Benston **ZE2** 109 D7
Benthall, *Northumb.* **NE67** 71 H1
Benthall, *Shrop.* **TF12** 39 F5
Bentham **GL51** 29 J7
Benthoul **AB14** 91 G4
Bentlawnt **SY5** 38 C5
Bentley, *E.Riding* **HU17** 59 G6
Bentley, *Essex* **CM15** 23 J2
Bentley, *Hants.* **GU10** 22 A7
Bentley, *S.Yorks.* **DN5** 51 H2
Bentley, *Suff.* **IP9** 35 F5
Bentley, *W.Mid.* **WS2** 40 B6
Bentley, *W.Yorks.* **LS6** 57 H6
Bentley, *Warks.* **CV9** 40 E6
Bentley Heath, *Herts.* **EN5** 23 F2
Bentley Heath, *W.Mid.* **B93** 30 C1
Bentley Rise **DN5** 51 H2
Benton **EX32** 6 E2
Benton Square **NE12** 71 H6
Bentpath **DG13** 69 J4
Bentworth **GU34** 21 K7
Benvie **DD2** 82 E4
Benville Lane **DT2** 8 E4
Benwell **NE15** 71 H7
Benwick **PE15** 43 G6
Beoley **B98** 30 B2
Beoraidbeg **PH40** 86 C5
Bepton **GU29** 12 B5
Berden **CM23** 33 H6
Bere Alston **PL20** 4 E4
Bere Ferrers **PL20** 4 E4
Bere Regis **BH20** 9 H5
Berea **SA62** 16 A1
Berepper **TR12** 2 D6
Bergh Apton **NR15** 45 H5
Berinsfield **OX10** 21 J2
Berkeley **GL13** 19 K2
Berkhamsted **HP4** 22 C1
Berkley **BA11** 20 B7
Berkswell **CV7** 30 D1
Bermondsey **SE16** 23 G4
Bernera **IV40** 86 E2
Berneray (Eilean Bhearnaraigh) **HS6** 92 E3
Berners Roding **CM5** 24 C1
Bernice **PA23** 73 K1
Bernisdale **IV51** 93 K6
Berrick Prior **OX10** 21 K2
Berrick Salome **OX10** 21 K2
Berriedale **KW7** 105 G6
Berriew (Aberriw) **SY21** 38 A5
Berrington, *Northumb.* **TD15** 77 J6
Berrington, *Shrop.* **SY5** 38 E5
Berrington, *Worcs.* **WR15** 28 E2
Berrington Green **WR15** 28 E2
Berriowbridge **PL15** 4 C3
Berrow, *Som.* **TA8** 19 F6
Berrow, *Worcs.* **WR13** 29 G5
Berrow Green **WR6** 29 G3
Berry Cross **EX38** 6 C4
Berry Down Cross **EX34** 6 D1
Berry Hill, *Glos.* **GL16** 28 E7
Berry Hill, *Pembs.* **SA42** 16 D1
Berry Pomeroy **TQ9** 5 J4
Berryhillock **AB56** 98 D4
Berrynarbor **EX34** 6 D1
Berry's Green **TN16** 23 H6
Bersham **LL14** 38 C1
Berstane **KW15** 107 D6
Berthlŵyd **SA4** 17 J5
Berwick **BN26** 13 J6
Berwick Bassett **SN4** 20 E4
Berwick Hill **NE20** 71 G6
Berwick St. James **SP3** 10 B1
Berwick St. John **SP7** 9 J2
Berwick St. Leonard **SP3** 9 J1
Berwick-upon-Tweed **TD15** 77 H5
Bescar **L40** 48 C1
Bescot **WS2** 40 C6
Besford, *Shrop.* **SY4** 38 E3
Besford, *Worcs.* **WR8** 29 J4
Bessacarr **DN4** 51 J2
Bessels Leigh **OX13** 21 H1
Besses o' th' Barn **M45** 49 H2
Bessingby **YO16** 59 H3
Bessingham **NR11** 45 F2
Best Beech Hill **TN5** 13 K3
Besthorpe, *Norf.* **NR17** 44 E6
Besthorpe, *Notts.* **NG23** 52 B6
Bestwood Village **NG5** 41 H1
Beswick, *E.Riding* **YO25** 59 G5
Beswick, *Gt.Man.* **M11** 49 H3
Betchworth **RH3** 23 F6
Bethania, *Cere.* **SY23** 26 E2
Bethania, *Gwyn.* **LL41** 37 G1
Bethel, *Gwyn.* **LL55** 46 D6
Bethel, *Gwyn.* **LL23** 37 J2
Bethel, *I.o.A.* **LL62** 46 B5
Bethersden **TN26** 14 E4
Bethesda, *Gwyn.* **LL57** 46 E6
Bethesda, *Pembs.* **SA67** 16 D3
Bethlehem **SA19** 17 K2
Bethnal Green **E2** 23 G3
Betley **CW3** 39 G1
Betley Common **CW3** 39 G1
Betsham **DA13** 24 C4
Betteshanger **CT14** 15 J2
Bettiscombe **DT6** 8 C5
Bettisfield **SY13** 38 D2
Betton, *Shrop.* **SY5** 38 C5
Betton, *Shrop.* **TF9** 39 F2
Betton Strange **SY5** 38 E5
Bettws **NP20** 19 F2
Bettws Bledrws **SA48** 26 E3
Bettws Cedewain **SY16** 38 A6
Bettws Gwerfil Goch **LL21** 37 K1
Bettws Newydd **NP15** 19 G1
Bettws-y-crwyn **SY7** 38 B7
Bettyhill **KW14** 104 C2
Betws, *Bridgend* **CF32** 18 C3
Betws, *Carmar.* **SA18** 17 K4
Betws Disserth **LD1** 28 A3
Betws Garmon **LL54** 46 D7
Betws Ifan **SA38** 26 C4
Betws-y-coed **LL24** 47 F7
Betws-yn-Rhos **LL22** 47 H5
Beulah, *Cere.* **SA38** 26 B4
Beulah, *Powys* **LD5** 27 J3
Bevendean **BN2** 13 G6
Bevercotes **NG22** 51 J5
Beverley **HU17** 59 G6
Beverstone **GL8** 20 B2

Bevington

Bevington GL13 19 K2
Bewaldeth CA13 60 D3
Bewcastle CA6 70 A6
Bewdley DY12 29 G1
Bewerley HG3 57 G3
Bewholme YO25 59 H4
Bewley Common SN15 20 C5
Bexhill TN40 14 C7
Bexley DA5 23 H4
Bexleyheath DA6 23 H4
Bexwell PE38 44 A5
Beyton IP30 34 D2
Beyton Green IP30 34 D2
Bhalamus HS2 100 E7
Bhaleshear (Baleshare) HS6 92 C5
Bhaltos HS2 100 C4
Bhatarsaigh (Vatersay) HS9 84 B5
Biallaid PH20 88 E5
Bibury GL7 20 E1
Bicester OX26 31 G6
Bickenhall TA3 8 B3
Bickenhill B92 40 D7
Bicker PE20 43 F2
Bickershaw, *Gt.Man.* WN2 49 F2
Bickershaw, *Gt.Man.* WN2 49 F2
Bickerstaffe L39 48 D2
Bickerton, *Ches.* SY14 48 E7
Bickerton, *Devon* TQ7 5 J7
Bickerton, *N.Yorks.* LS22 57 K4
Bickerton, *Northumb.* NE65 70 E3
Bickford ST19 40 A4
Bickham TA24 7 H1
Bickham Bridge TQ9 5 H5
Bickham House EX6 7 H7
Bickington, *Devon* EX31 6 D2
Bickington, *Devon* TQ12 5 H3
Bickleigh, *Devon* PL6 5 F4
Bickleigh, *Devon* EX16 7 H5
Bickleton EX31 6 D2
Bickley BR1 23 H5
Bickley Moss SY13 38 E1
Bickley Town SY14 38 E1
Bicknacre CM3 24 D1
Bicknoller TA4 7 K2
Bicknor ME9 14 D2
Bickton SP6 10 C3
Bicton, *Here.* HR6 28 D2
Bicton, *Shrop.* SY3 38 D4
Bicton, *Shrop.* SY7 38 B7
Bicton Heath SY3 38 D4
Bidborough TN4 23 J7
Biddenden TN27 14 D4
Biddenden Green TN27 14 D3
Biddenham MK40 32 D4
Biddestone SN14 20 B4
Biddick NE38 62 E1
Biddisham BS26 19 G6
Biddlesden NN13 31 H4
Biddlestone NE65 70 E3
Biddulph ST8 49 H7
Biddulph Moor ST8 49 J7
Bideford EX39 6 C3
Bidford-on-Avon B50 30 C3
Bidlake EX20 6 C7
Bidston CH43 48 B3
Bidwell LU5 32 D6
Bielby YO42 58 D5
Bieldside AB15 91 G4
Bierley, *I.o.W.* PO38 11 G7
Bierley, *W.Yorks.* BD4 57 G6
Bierton HP22 32 B7
Big Sand IV21 94 D4
Bigbury TQ7 5 G6
Bigbury-on-Sea TQ7 5 G6
Bigby DN38 52 D2
Bigert Mire LA20 60 C7
Biggar, *Cumb.* LA14 54 E3
Biggar, *S.Lan.* ML12 75 J7
Biggin, *Derbys.* DE6 40 E1
Biggin, *Derbys.* SK17 50 D7
Biggin, *N.Yorks.* LS25 58 B6
Biggin Hill TN16 23 H6
Biggings ZE2 109 A6
Biggleswade SG18 32 E4
Bigholms DG13 69 J5
Bighouse KW14 104 D2
Bighton SO24 11 H1
Biglands CA7 60 D1
Bignor RH20 12 C5
Bigrigg CA24 60 B5
Bigton ZE2 109 C10
Bilberry PL26 4 A5
Bilborough NG8 41 H1
Bilbrook, *Som.* TA24 7 J1
Bilbrook, *Staffs.* WV8 40 A5
Bilbrough YO23 58 B5
Bilbster KW1 105 H3
Bilby DN22 51 J4
Bildershaw DL14 62 C4
Bildeston IP7 34 D4
Billericay CM12 24 C2
Billesdon LE7 42 A5
Billesley B49 30 C3
Billholm DG13 69 H4
Billingborough NG34 42 E2
Billinge WN5 48 E3
Billingford, *Norf.* IP21 35 F1
Billingford, *Norf.* NR20 44 E3
Billingham TS23 63 F4
Billinghay LN4 52 E7
Billingley S72 51 G2
Billingshurst RH14 12 D4
Billingsley WV16 39 G7
Billington, *Beds.* LU7 32 C6
Billington, *Lancs.* BB7 56 C6
Billington, *Staffs.* ST18 40 A3
Billister ZE2 109 D6
Billockby NR29 45 J4
Billy Row DL15 62 C3
Bilsborrow PR3 55 J6
Bilsby LN13 53 H5
Bilsby Field LN13 53 H5
Bilsdean TD13 77 F3
Bilsham BN18 12 C6
Bilsington TN25 15 F4
Bilson Green GL14 29 F7
Bilsthorpe NG22 51 J6
Bilsthorpe Moor NG22 51 J7
Bilston, *Midloth.* EH25 76 A4
Bilston, *W.Mid.* WV14 40 B6
Bilstone CV13 41 F5
Bilting TN25 15 F3
Bilton, *E.Riding* HU11 59 H6
Bilton, *N.Yorks.* HG1 57 J4
Bilton, *Northumb.* NE66 71 H2
Bilton, *Warks.* CV22 31 F1
Bilton-in-Ainsty YO26 57 K5
Bimbister KW17 107 C6
Binbrook LN8 53 F3
Bincombe DT3 9 F6
Bindal IV20 97 G3
Bindon TA21 7 K3
Binegar BA3 19 K7
Bines Green RH13 12 E5
Binfield RG42 22 B4
Binfield Heath RG9 22 A4
Bingfield NE19 70 E6
Bingham NG13 42 A2
Bingham's Melcombe DT2 9 G4
Bingley BD16 57 G6
Bings Heath SY4 38 E4
Binham NR21 44 D2
Binley, *Hants.* SP11 21 H6
Binley, *W.Mid.* CV3 30 E1
Binniehill FK1 75 G3
Binsoe HG4 57 H2
Binstead PO33 11 G5
Binsted, *Hants.* GU34 22 A7
Binsted, *W.Suss.* BN18 12 C6
Binton CV37 30 C3
Bintree NR20 44 E3
Binweston SY5 38 C5
Birch, *Essex* CO2 34 D6
Birch, *Gt.Man.* M24 49 H2
Birch Cross ST14 40 D2
Birch Green, *Essex* CO2 34 D7
Birch Green, *Herts.* SG14 33 F7
Birch Grove RH17 13 H4
Birch Heath CW6 48 E6
Birch Vale SK22 50 C4
Birch Wood TA20 8 B3
Bircham Newton PE31 44 B2
Bircham Tofts PE31 44 B2
Birchanger CM23 33 J6
Bircher HR6 28 D2
Bircher Common HR6 28 D2
Birchfield IV24 96 B2
Birchgrove, *Cardiff* CF14 18 E3
Birchgrove, *Swan.* SA7 18 A2
Birchington CT7 25 K5
Birchmoor B78 40 E5
Birchover DE4 50 E6
Birchwood, *Lincs.* LN6 52 C6
Birchwood, *Warr.* WA3 49 F3
Bircotes DN11 51 J3
Bird Street IP7 34 E3
Birdbrook CO9 34 B4
Birdbush SP7 9 J2
Birdfield PA32 73 H1
Birdforth YO7 57 K2
Birdham PO20 12 B6
Birdingbury CV23 31 F2
Birdlip GL4 29 J7
Birdoswald CA8 70 B7
Birds Green CM5 23 J1
Birdsall YO17 58 E3
Birdsgreen WV15 39 G7
Birdsmoor Gate DT6 8 C4
Birdston G66 74 E3
Birdwell S70 51 F2
Birdwood GL19 29 G7
Birgham TD12 77 F7
Birichen IV25 96 E2
Birkby, *Cumb.* CA15 60 B3
Birkby, *N.Yorks.* DL7 62 E6
Birkdale, *Mersey.* PR8 48 C1
Birkdale, *N.Yorks.* DL11 61 K6
Birkenhead CH41 48 C4
Birkenhills AB53 99 F6
Birkenshaw BD11 57 H7
Birkhall AB35 90 B5
Birkhill, *Angus* DD2 82 E4
Birkhill, *Sc.Bord.* TD4 76 D6
Birkhill, *Sc.Bord.* TD7 69 H2
Birkholme NG33 42 C3
Birkin WF11 58 B7
Birks LS27 57 H7
Birkwood ML11 75 G7
Birley HR4 28 D3
Birley Carr S6 51 F3
Birling, *Kent* ME19 24 C5
Birling, *Northumb.* NE65 71 H3
Birling Gap BN20 13 J7
Birlingham WR10 29 J4
BIRMINGHAM B 40 C7
Birmingham International Airport B26 40 D7
Birnam PH8 82 B3
Birsay KW17 106 B5
Birse AB34 90 D5
Birsemore AB34 90 D5
Birstall LE4 41 H5
Birstall Smithies WF17 57 H7
Birstwith HG3 57 H4
Birthorpe NG34 42 E2
Birtle OL11 49 H1
Birtley, *Here.* SY7 28 C2
Birtley, *Northumb.* NE48 70 D6
Birtley, *T.& W.* DH3 62 D1
Birts Street WR13 29 G5
Birtsmorton WR13 29 H5
Bisbrooke LE15 42 B6
Biscathorpe LN11 53 F4
Bish Mill EX36 7 F3
Bisham SL7 22 B3
Bishampton WR10 29 J3
Bishop Auckland DL14 62 D4
Bishop Burton HU17 59 F5
Bishop Middleham DL17 62 E3
Bishop Monkton HG3 57 J3
Bishop Norton LN8 52 C3
Bishop Sutton BS39 19 J6
Bishop Thornton HG3 57 H3
Bishop Wilton YO42 58 D4
Bishopbridge LN8 52 D3
Bishopbriggs G64 74 E3
Bishopmill IV30 97 K5
Bishops Cannings SN10 20 D5
Bishop's Castle SY9 38 C7
Bishop's Caundle DT9 9 F3
Bishop's Cleeve GL52 29 J6
Bishop's Frome WR6 29 F4
Bishops Gate TW20 22 C4
Bishop's Green, *Essex* CM6 33 K7
Bishop's Green, *Hants.* RG19 21 J5
Bishop's Hull TA1 8 B2
Bishop's Itchington CV47 30 E3
Bishop's Lydeard TA4 7 K3
Bishop's Norton GL2 29 H6
Bishops Nympton EX36 7 F3
Bishop's Offley ST21 39 G3
Bishop's Stortford CM23 33 H6
Bishop's Sutton SO24 11 H1
Bishop's Tachbrook CV33 30 E2
Bishop's Tawton EX32 6 D2
Bishop's Waltham SO32 11 G3
Bishop's Wood ST19 40 A5
Bishopsbourne CT4 15 G2
Bishopsteignton TQ14 5 K3
Bishopstoke SO50 11 F3
Bishopston, *Bristol* BS6 19 J4
Bishopston, *Swan.* SA3 17 J6
Bishopstone, *Bucks.* HP17 32 B7
Bishopstone, *E.Suss.* BN25 13 H6
Bishopstone, *Here.* HR4 28 D4
Bishopstone, *Swin.* SN6 21 F3
Bishopstone, *Wilts.* SP5 10 B2
Bishopstrow BA12 20 B7
Bishopswood TA20 8 B3
Bishopsworth BS13 19 J5
Bishopthorpe YO23 58 B5
Bishopton, *Darl.* TS21 62 E4
Bishopton, *N.Yorks.* HG4 57 H2
Bishopton, *Renf.* PA7 74 C3
Bishopton, *Warks.* CV37 30 C3
Bishton NP18 19 G3
Bisley, *Glos.* GL6 20 C1
Bisley, *Surr.* GU24 22 C6
Bispham FY2 55 G6
Bispham Green L40 48 D1
Bissoe TR4 2 E4
Bisterne BH24 10 C4
Bisterne Close BH24 10 D4
Bitchet Green TN15 23 J6
Bitchfield NG33 42 C3
Bittadon EX31 6 D1
Bittaford PL21 5 G5
Bittering NR19 44 D4
Bitterley SY8 28 E1
Bitterne SO18 11 F3
Bitteswell LE17 41 H7
Bitton BS30 19 K5
Biwmaris (Beaumaris) LL58 46 E5
Bix RG9 22 A3
Bixter ZE2 109 C7
Blaby LE8 41 H6
Black Bourton OX18 21 F1
Black Bridge SA73 16 C4
Black Callerton NE5 71 G7
Black Carr NR17 44 E6
Black Clauchrie KA26 67 G5
Black Corries Lodge PH49 80 D2
Black Crofts PA37 80 A4
Black Cross TR8 3 G2
Black Dog EX17 7 G5
Black Heddon NE20 71 F6
Black Hill CV37 30 D3
Black Marsh SY5 38 C6
Black Moor LS17 57 H5
Black Mount PA36 80 D3
Black Notley CM77 34 B6
Black Pill SA3 17 K5
Black Street NR33 45 K7
Black Torrington EX21 6 C5
Blackaburn NE48 70 C6
Blackacre DG11 69 F4
Blackadder TD11 77 G5
Blackawton TQ9 5 J5
Blackborough, *Devon* EX15 7 J5
Blackborough, *Norf.* PE32 44 A4
Blackborough End PE32 44 A4
Blackboys TN22 13 J4
Blackbraes, *Aber.* AB21 91 G3
Blackbraes, *Falk.* FK1 75 H3
Blackbrook, *Derbys.* DE56 41 F1
Blackbrook, *Leics.* LE12 41 G4
Blackbrook, *Mersey.* WA11 48 E3
Blackbrook, *Staffs.* ST5 39 G2
Blackburn, *Aber.* AB21 91 G3
BLACKBURN, *B'burn.* BB 56 B7
Blackburn, *W.Loth.* EH47 75 H4
Blackbushe GU17 22 A6
Blackcastle IV2 97 F6
Blackchambers AB32 91 F3
Blackcraig, *D.& G.* DG8 64 E4
Blackcraig, *D.& G.* DG7 68 C5
Blackden Heath CW4 49 G5
Blackdog AB23 91 H3
Blackdown, *Devon* PL19 5 F3
Blackdown, *Dorset* DT8 8 C4
Blackdown, *Warks.* CV32 30 E2
Blacker Hill S74 51 F2
Blackfen DA15 23 H4
Blackfield SO45 11 F4
Blackford, *Aber.* AB51 91 F1
Blackford, *Cumb.* CA6 69 J7
Blackford, *P.& K.* PH4 81 K7
Blackford, *Som.* BA22 9 F2
Blackford, *Som.* BS28 19 H7
Blackford Bridge BL9 49 H2
Blackfordby DE11 41 F4
Blackgang PO38 11 F7
Blackhall, *Edin.* EH4 76 A3
Blackhall, *Renf.* PA1 74 C4
Blackhall Colliery TS27 63 F3
Blackhall Mill NE17 62 C1
Blackhall Rocks TS27 63 F3
Blackham TN3 13 J3
Blackhaugh TD1 76 C7
Blackheath, *Essex* CO2 34 E6
Blackheath, *Gt.Lon.* SE3 23 G4
Blackheath, *Suff.* IP19 35 J1
Blackheath, *Surr.* GU4 22 D7
Blackheath, *W.Mid.* B65 40 B7
Blackhill, *Aber.* AB42 99 J5
Blackhill, *Aber.* AB42 99 J6
Blackhillock AB55 98 C6
Blackhills IV30 97 K6
Blackland SN11 20 D5
Blacklands TA24 7 G2
Blackleach PR4 55 H6
Blackley M9 49 H2
Blacklunans PH10 82 C1
Blackmill CF35 18 C3
Blackmoor, *Hants.* GU33 11 J1
Blackmoor, *Som.* TA21 7 K4
Blackmoor Gate EX31 6 E1
Blackmoorfoot HD7 50 C1
Blackmore CM4 24 C1
Blackmore End, *Essex* CM7 34 B5
Blackmore End, *Herts.* AL4 32 E7
Blackness, *Aber.* AB31 90 E5
Blackness, *Falk.* EH49 75 J3
Blackness, *High.* KW3 105 H5
Blacknest GU34 22 A7
Blackney DT6 8 D5
Blacko BB9 56 D5
Blackpole WR3 29 H3
BLACKPOOL, *B'pool* FY 55 G6
Blackpool, *Devon* TQ6 5 J6
Blackpool Airport FY4 55 G6
Blackpool Bridge SA67 16 D3
Blackpool Gate CA6 70 A6
Blackridge EH48 75 G4
Blackrock, *Arg.& B.* PA44 72 B4
Blackrock, *Mon.* NP7 28 B7
Blackrod BL6 49 F1
Blackshaw DG1 69 F7
Blackshaw Head HX7 56 E7
Blacksmith's Green IP14 35 F2
Blacksnape BB3 56 C7
Blackstone BN5 13 F5
Blackthorn OX25 31 H7
Blackthorpe IP30 34 D2
Blacktoft DN14 58 E7
Blacktop AB15 91 G4
Blacktown CF3 19 F3
Blackwater, *Cornw.* TR4 2 E4
Blackwater, *Hants.* GU17 22 B6
Blackwater, *I.o.W.* PO30 11 G6
Blackwater, *Norf.* NR9 44 E3
Blackwater, *Som.* TA20 8 B3
Blackwaterfoot KA27 66 D1
Blackwell, *Darl.* DL3 62 D5
Blackwell, *Derbys.* SK17 50 D5
Blackwell, *Derbys.* DE55 51 G7
Blackwell, *W.Suss.* RH19 13 G3
Blackwell, *Warks.* CV36 30 D4
Blackwell, *Worcs.* B60 29 J1
Blackwells End GL19 29 G6
Blackwood (Coed-duon), *Caerp.* NP12 18 E2
Blackwood, *D.& G.* DG2 68 E5
Blackwood, *S.Lan.* ML11 75 F6
Blackwood Hill ST9 49 J7
Blacon CH1 48 C6
Bladbean CT4 15 G3
Bladnoch DG8 64 E5
Bladon OX20 31 F7
Blaen Clydach CF40 18 C2
Blaenannerch SA43 26 B4
Blaenau Dolwyddelan LL25 46 E7
Blaenau Ffestiniog LL41 37 F1
Blaenavon NP4 19 F1
Blaenawey NP7 28 B7
Blaencelyn SA44 26 C3
Blaencwm CF42 18 C1
Blaendyryn LD3 27 J5
Blaenffos SA37 16 E1
Blaengarw CF32 18 C2
Blaengeuffordd SY23 37 F7
Blaengweche SA18 17 K3
Blaengwrach SA11 18 B1
Blaengwynfi SA13 18 B2
Blaenllechau CF43 18 D2
Blaenos SA20 27 G5
Blaenpennal SY23 27 F2
Blaenplwyf SY23 26 E1
Blaenporth SA43 26 B4
Blaenrhondda CF42 18 C1
Blaenwaun SA34 17 F2
Blaen-y-coed SA33 17 G2
Blagdon, *N.Som.* BS40 19 H6
Blagdon, *Torbay* TQ3 5 J4
Blagdon Hill TA3 8 B3
Blaguegate WN8 48 D2
Blaich PH33 87 G7
Blaina NP13 18 E1
Blair KA24 74 B6
Blair Atholl PH18 81 K1
Blair Drummond FK9 75 F1
Blairannaich G83 80 E7
Blairbuie PA23 73 K3
Blairgowrie PH10 82 C3
Blairhall KY12 75 J2
Blairhoyle FK8 81 H7
Blairhullichan FK8 81 F7
Blairingone FK14 75 H1
Blairkip KA5 74 D7
Blairlogie FK9 75 G1
Blairmore, *Arg.& B.* PA23 73 K2
Blairmore, *High.* IV28 96 E1
Blairmore, *High.* IV27 102 D3
Blairnairn G84 74 A2
Blairnamarrow AB37 89 K3
Blairpark KA24 74 A5
Blairquhan KA19 67 H3
Blairquhosh G63 74 D2
Blair's Ferry PA21 73 H4
Blairshinnoch AB45 98 E4
Blairuskinmore FK8 81 F7
Blairvadach G84 74 A2
Blairydryne AB31 91 F5
Blairythan Cottage AB41 91 H2
Blaisdon GL17 29 G7
Blake End CM77 34 B6
Blakebrook DY11 29 H1
Blakedown DY10 29 H1
Blakelaw, *Sc.Bord.* TD5 77 F7
Blakelaw, *T.& W.* NE5 71 H7
Blakeley WV5 40 A6
Blakelow CW5 49 F7
Blakemere HR2 28 C4
Blakeney, *Glos.* GL15 19 K1
Blakeney, *Norf.* NR25 44 E1
Blakenhall, *Ches.* CW5 39 G1
Blakenhall, *W.Mid.* WV2 40 B6
Blakeshall DY11 40 A7
Blakesley NN12 31 H3
Blanchland DH8 62 A1
Bland Hill HG3 57 H4
Blandford Camp DT11 9 J4
Blandford Forum DT11 9 H4
Blandford St. Mary DT11 9 H4
Blanefield G63 74 D3
Blanerne TD11 77 G5
Blankney LN4 52 D6
Blantyre G72 74 E5
Blar a' Chaorainn PH33 80 C1
Blargie PH20 88 D5
Blarglas G83 74 B2
Blarmachfoldach PH33 80 B1
Blarnalearoch IV23 95 H2
Blashford BH24 10 C4
Blaston LE16 42 B6
Blathaisbhal HS6 92 D4
Blatherwycke PE8 42 C6
Blawith LA12 55 F1
Blaxhall IP12 35 H3
Blaxton DN9 51 J2
Blaydon NE21 71 G7
Bleadney BA5 19 H7
Bleadon BS24 19 G6
Bleak Hey Nook OL3 50 C2
Blean CT2 25 H5
Bleasby, *Lincs.* LN8 52 E4
Bleasby, *Notts.* NG14 42 A1
Bleasby Moor LN8 52 E4
Bleatarn CA16 61 J5
Bleathwood Common SY8 28 E2
Blebocraigs KY15 83 F6
Bleddfa LD7 28 B2
Bledington OX7 30 D6
Bledlow HP27 22 A1
Bledlow Ridge HP14 22 A2
Blencarn CA10 61 H3
Blencogo CA7 60 C2
Blencow CA11 61 F3
Blendworth PO8 11 J3
Blennerhasset CA7 60 C2
Blervie Castle IV36 97 H6
Bletchingdon OX5 31 G7
Bletchingley RH1 23 G6
Bletchley, *M.K.* MK3 32 B5
Bletchley, *Shrop.* TF9 39 F2
Bletherston SA63 16 D2
Bletsoe MK44 32 D3
Blewbury OX11 21 J3
Blickling NR11 45 F3
Blidworth NG21 51 H7
Blidworth Bottoms NG21 51 H7
Blindburn, *Aber.* AB41 91 H1
Blindburn, *Northumb.* NE65 70 D2
Blindcrake CA13 60 C3
Blindley Heath RH7 23 G7
Blisland PL30 4 A3
Bliss Gate DY14 29 G1
Blissford SP6 10 C3
Blisworth NN7 31 J3
Blithbury WS15 40 C3
Blitterlees CA7 60 C1
Blo' Norton IP22 34 E1
Blockley GL56 30 C5

Blofield NR13	45 H5	Boldon NE36	71 J7
Blofield Heath NR13	45 H4	Boldon Colliery NE35	71 J7
Blore DE6	40 D1	Boldre SO41	10 E5
Blossomfield B90	30 C1	Boldron DL12	62 B5
Blowick PR9	48 C1	Bole DN22	51 K4
Bloxham OX15	31 F5	Bolehill DE4	50 E7
Bloxholm LN4	52 D7	Boleigh TR19	2 B6
Bloxwich WS3	40 B5	Bolenowe TR14	2 D5
Bloxworth BH20	9 H5	Boleside TD1	76 C7
Blubberhouses LS21	57 G4	Bolgoed SA4	17 K4
Blue Anchor, Cornw. TR9	3 G3	Bolham, Devon EX16	7 H4
Blue Anchor, Som. TA24	7 J1	Bolham, Notts. DN22	51 K4
Blue Bell Hill ME5	24 D5	Bolham Water EX15	7 K4
Bluewater DA9	23 J4	Bolingey TR6	2 E3
Blundellsands L23	48 C3	Bollington SK10	49 J5
Blundeston NR32	45 K6	Bolney RH17	13 F4
Blunham MK44	32 E3	Bolnhurst MK44	32 D3
Blunsdon St. Andrew SN26	20 E3	Bolshan DD11	83 H2
Bluntington DY10	29 H1	Bolsover S44	51 G5
Bluntisham PE28	33 G1	Bolsterstone S36	50 E3
Blunts PL12	4 D4	Bolstone HR2	28 E5
Blurton ST3	40 A1	Boltby YO7	57 K1
Blyborough DN21	52 C3	Bolter End HP14	22 A2
Blyford IP19	35 J1	Bolton, Cumb. CA16	61 H4
Blymhill TF11	40 A4	Bolton, E.Loth. EH41	76 D3
Blymhill Common TF11	39 G4	Bolton, E.Riding YO42	58 D4
Blymhill Lawn TF11	40 A4	BOLTON, Gt.Man. BL	49 G2
Blyth, Northumb. NE24	71 J5	Bolton, Northumb. NE66	71 G2
Blyth, Notts. S81	51 J4	Bolton Abbey BD23	57 F4
Blyth Bridge EH46	75 K6	Bolton Bridge BD23	57 F4
Blyth End B46	40 E6	Bolton by Bowland BB7	56 C5
Blythburgh IP19	35 J1	Bolton Houses PR4	55 H6
Blythe Bridge ST11	40 B1	Bolton Low Houses CA7	60 D2
Blythe Marsh ST11	40 B1	Bolton Percy YO23	58 B5
Blyton DN21	52 B3	Bolton upon Dearne S63	51 G2
Boarhills KY16	83 G6	Bolton Wood Lane CA7	60 D2
Boarhunt PO17	11 H4	Boltonfellend CA6	69 K7
Boars Hill OX1	21 H1	Boltongate CA7	60 D2
Boarsgreave BB4	56 D7	Bolton-le-Sands LA5	55 H3
Boarshead TN6	13 J3	Bolton-on-Swale DL10	62 D7
Boarstall HP18	31 H7	Bolventor PL15	4 B3
Boarzell TN19	14 C5	Bombie DG6	65 H6
Boasley Cross EX20	6 D6	Bomere Heath SY4	38 D4
Boat o' Brig IV32	98 B5	Bonar Bridge IV24	96 D2
Boat of Garten PH24	89 G3	Bonawe PA37	80 B4
Boath IV17	96 C4	Bonby DN20	52 D1
Bobbing ME9	24 E5	Boncath SA37	17 F1
Bobbington DY7	40 A6	Bonchester Bridge TD9	70 A2
Bobbingworth CM5	23 J1	Bonchurch PO38	11 G7
Bocaddon PL13	4 B5	Bondleigh EX20	6 E5
Bochastle FK17	81 H7	Bonds PR3	55 H5
Bockhampton RG17	21 G4	Bo'ness EH51	75 H2
Bocking CM7	34 B6	Bonhill G83	74 B3
Bocking Churchstreet CM7	34 B6	Boningale WV7	40 A5
Bockleton WR15	28 E2	Bonjedward TD8	70 B1
Boconnoc PL22	4 B4	Bonkle ML2	75 G5
Boddam, Aber. AB42	99 K6	Bonning Gate LA8	61 F7
Boddam, Shet. ZE2	109 F9	Bonnington, Edin. EH27	75 K4
Bodden BA4	19 K7	Bonnington, Kent TN25	15 F4
Boddington GL51	29 H6	Bonnybank KY8	82 E7
Bodedern LL65	46 B4	Bonnybridge FK4	75 G2
Bodelwyddan LL18	47 J5	Bonnykelly AB53	99 G5
Bodenham, Here. HR1	28 E3	Bonnyrigg EH19	76 B4
Bodenham, Wilts. SP5	10 C2	Bonnyton, Aber. AB52	90 E1
Bodenham Moor HR1	28 E3	Bonnyton, Angus DD10	83 G4
Bodesbeck DG10	69 G3	Bonnyton, Angus DD10	83 H2
Bodewryd LL66	46 B3	Bonnyton, Angus DD3	82 E4
Bodfari LL16	47 J5	Bonsall DE4	50 E7
Bodffordd LL77	46 C5	Bont NP7	28 C7
Bodfuan LL53	36 C2	Bont Dolgadfan SY19	37 H5
Bodham NR25	45 F1	Bont Newydd LL40	37 G3
Bodiam TN32	14 C5	Bontddu LL40	37 F4
Bodicote OX15	31 F5	Bont-goch (Elerch) SY24	37 F7
Bodieve PL27	3 G1	Bonthorpe LN13	53 H5
Bodinnick PL23	4 B5	Bont-newydd, Conwy LL17	47 J5
Bodmin PL31	4 A4	Bontnewydd, Gwyn. LL55	46 C6
Bodney IP26	44 C6	Bontuchel LL15	47 J7
Bodorgan LL62	46 B6	Bonvilston CF5	18 D4
Bodrane PL14	4 C4	Bon-y-maen SA1	17 K5
Bodsham Green TN25	15 G3	Boode EX33	6 D2
Bodwen PL26	4 A4	Boohay TQ6	5 K5
Bodymoor Heath B76	40 D6	Booker HP12	22 B2
Bogallan IV1	96 D6	Booleybank SY4	38 E3
Bogbain IV2	96 E7	Boor IV22	94 E3
Bogbrae AB42	91 J1	Boosbeck TS12	63 H5
Bogbuie IV7	96 C6	Boose's Green CO6	34 C5
Bogend KA1	74 B7	Boot CA19	60 C6
Bogfern AB33	90 D4	Boot Street IP6	35 G4
Bogfields AB33	90 D4	Booth HX2	57 F7
Bogfold AB43	99 G5	Booth Bank HD7	50 C1
Boghead, Aber. AB45	98 E5	Booth Green SK10	49 J4
Boghead, E.Ayr. KA18	68 B1	Booth Wood HX6	50 C1
Boghead, S.Lan. ML11	75 F6	Boothby Graffoe LN5	52 C7
Boghole Farm IV12	97 G6	Boothby Pagnell NG33	42 C2
Bogmoor IV32	98 B4	Boothstown M28	49 G2
Bogniebrae AB54	98 D6	Boothville NN3	31 J2
Bognor Regis PO21	12 C7	Bootle, Cumb. LA19	54 E1
Bograxie AB51	91 F3	Bootle, Mersey. L20	48 C3
Bogroy PH23	89 G2	Booton NR10	45 F3
Bogside FK10	75 H1	Boots Green WA16	49 G5
Bogston AB36	90 B4	Booze DL11	62 B6
Bogton AB53	98 E5	Boquhan G63	74 D2
Bogue DG7	68 B5	Boraston WR15	29 F1
Bohemia SP5	10 D3	Bordeaux GY3	3 J5
Bohenie PH31	87 J6	Borden, Kent ME9	24 E5
Bohetherick PL12	4 E4	Borden, W.Suss. GU30	12 B4
Bohortha TR2	3 F5	Bordley BD23	56 E3
Bohuntine PH31	87 J6	Bordon GU35	11 J1
Boirseam HS3	93 F3	Boreham, Essex CM3	24 D1
Bojewyan TR19	2 A5	Boreham, Wilts. BA12	20 B7
Bokiddick PL30	4 A4	Boreham Street BN27	13 K5
Bolam, Dur. DL2	62 C4	Borehamwood WD6	22 E2
Bolam, Northumb. NE61	71 F5	Boreland, D. & G. DG3	68 E4
Bolberry TQ7	5 G7	Boreland, D. & G. DG8	64 D4
Bold Heath WA8	48 E4	Boreland, Stir. FK21	81 G4
Bolderwood SO43	10 D4	Boreley WR9	29 H2
		Boreraig IV55	93 G6
		Borgh, W.Isles HS6	92 E3

Borgh, W.Isles HS9	84 B4	Bourton, Wilts. SN10	20 D5
Borgh (Borve), W.Isles HS2	101 G2	Bourton on Dunsmore CV23	31 F1
Borghastan HS2	100 D3	Bourton-on-the-Hill GL56	30 C5
Borgie KW14	103 J3	Bourton-on-the-Water GL54	30 C6
Borgue, D. & G. DG6	65 G6	Bousd PA78	78 D1
Borgue, High. KW7	105 G6	Boustead Hill CA5	60 D1
Borley CO10	34 C4	Bouth LA12	55 G1
Borley Green, Essex CO10	34 C4	Bouthwaite HG3	57 G2
Borley Green, Suff. IP30	34 D2	Bovain FK21	81 G4
Bornais HS8	84 C2	Boveney SL4	22 C4
Borness DG6	65 G6	Boveridge BH21	10 B3
Bornisketaig IV51	93 J4	Boverton CF61	18 C5
Borough Green TN15	23 K6	Bovey Tracey TQ13	5 J3
Boroughbridge YO51	57 J3	Bovingdon HP3	22 D1
Borras Head LL13	48 C7	Bovinger CM5	23 J1
Borrowash DE72	41 G2	Bovington Camp BH20	9 H6
Borrowby, N.Yorks. TS13	63 J5	Bow, Cumb. CA5	60 E1
Borrowby, N.Yorks. YO7	57 K1	Bow, Devon EX17	7 F5
Borrowdale CA12	60 D5	Bow, Devon TQ9	5 J5
Borrowfield AB39	91 G5	Bow, Ork. KW16	107 C8
Borstal ME1	24 D5	Bow Brickhill MK17	32 C5
Borth SY24	37 F7	Bow of Fife KY15	82 E6
Borthwick EH23	76 B5	Bow Street, Cere. SY24	37 F7
Borthwickbrae TD9	69 K2	Bow Street, Norf. NR17	44 E6
Borthwickshiels TD9	69 K2	Bowbank DL12	62 A4
Borth-y-Gest LL49	36 E2	Bowburn DH6	62 E3
Borve, High. IV51	93 K7	Bowcombe PO30	11 F6
Borve (Borgh), W.Isles HS2	101 G2	Bowd EX10	7 K6
Borwick LA6	55 J2	Bowden, Devon TQ6	5 J6
Borwick Rails LA18	54 E2	Bowden, Sc.Bord. TD6	76 D7
Bosavern TR19	2 A5	Bowden Hill SN15	20 C5
Bosbury HR8	29 F4	Bowdon WA14	49 G4
Boscarne PL30	4 A4	Bower NE48	70 C5
Boscastle PL35	4 A1	Bower Hinton TA12	8 D3
Boscombe, Bourne. BH5	10 C5	Bower House Tye CO6	34 D4
Boscombe, Wilts. SP4	10 D1	Bowerchalke SP5	10 B2
Bosham PO18	12 B6	Bowerhill SN12	20 C5
Bosham Hoe PO18	12 B6	Bowermadden KW1	105 H2
Bosherston SA71	16 C5	Bowers ST21	40 A2
Bosley SK11	49 J6	Bowers Gifford SS13	24 D3
Bossall YO60	58 D3	Bowershall KY12	75 J1
Bossiney PL34	4 A2	Bowertower KW1	105 H2
Bossingham CT4	15 G3	Bowes DL12	62 A5
Bossington, Hants. SO20	10 E1	Bowgreave PR3	55 H5
Bossington, Som. TA24	7 G1	Bowhousebog ML7	75 G5
Bostadh HS2	100 D4	Bowithick PL15	4 B2
Bostock Green CW10	49 F6	Bowker's Green L39	48 D2
Boston PE21	43 G1	Bowland Bridge LA11	55 H1
Boston Spa LS23	57 K5	Bowley HR1	28 E3
Boswarthan TR20	2 B5	Bowley Town HR1	28 E3
Boswinger PL26	3 G4	Bowlhead Green GU8	12 C3
Botallack TR19	2 A5	Bowling, W.Dun. G60	74 C3
Botany Bay EN2	23 G2	Bowling, W.Yorks. BD4	57 G6
Botcheston LE9	41 G5	Bowling Bank LL13	38 C1
Botesdale IP22	34 E1	Bowlish BA4	19 K7
Bothal NE61	71 H5	Bowmanstead LA21	60 E7
Bothamsall DN22	51 J5	Bowmore PA43	72 B4
Bothel CA7	60 C3	Bowness-on-Solway CA7	69 H7
Bothenhampton DT6	8 D5	Bowness-on-Windermere LA23	60 F7
Bothwell G71	75 F5	Bowscale CA11	60 E3
Botley, Bucks. HP5	22 C1	Bowsden TD15	77 H6
Botley, Hants. SO30	11 G3	Bowside Lodge KW14	104 D2
Botley, Oxon. OX2	21 H1	Bowston LA8	61 F7
Botloe's Green GL18	29 G6	Bowthorpe NR5	45 F5
Botolph Claydon MK18	31 J6	Bowtrees FK2	75 H2
Botolphs BN44	12 E6	Box, Glos. GL6	20 B1
Botolph's Bridge CT21	15 G4	Box, Wilts. SN13	20 B5
Bottacks IV14	96 B5	Box End MK43	32 D4
Bottesford, Leics. NG13	42 B2	Boxbush, Glos. GL14	29 G7
Bottesford, N.Lincs. DN16	52 B2	Boxbush, Glos. GL17	29 F6
Bottisham CB5	33 J2	Boxford, Suff. CO10	34 D4
Bottlesford SN9	20 E6	Boxford, W.Berks. RG20	21 H4
Bottom Boat WF3	57 J7	Boxgrove PO18	12 C6
Bottom of Hutton PR4	55 H7	Boxley ME14	14 C2
Bottom o'th'Moor BL6	49 F1	Boxmoor HP1	22 D1
Bottomcraig DD6	82 E5	Box's Shop EX23	6 A5
Bottoms OL14	56 E7	Boxted, Essex CO4	34 D5
Botton Head LA2	56 B3	Boxted, Suff. IP29	34 C3
Botusfleming PL12	4 E4	Boxted Cross CO4	34 D5
Botwnnog LL53	36 B2	Boxwell GL8	20 B2
Bough Beech TN8	23 H7	Boxworth CB3	33 G2
Boughrood LD3	28 A5	Boxworth End CB4	33 G2
Boughspring NP16	19 J2	Boyden Gate CT3	25 J5
Boughton, Norf. PE33	44 B5	Boydston KA1	74 C7
Boughton, Northants. NN2	31 J2	Boylestone DE6	40 D2
Boughton, Notts. NG22	51 J6	Boyndie AB45	98 E4
Boughton Aluph TN25	15 F3	Boynton YO16	59 H3
Boughton Green ME17	14 C2	Boys Hill DT9	9 F4
Boughton Lees TN25	15 F3	Boysack DD11	83 H3
Boughton Malherbe ME17	14 D3	Boyton, Cornw. PL15	6 B6
Boughton Street ME13	15 F2	Boyton, Suff. IP12	35 H4
Boulby TS13	63 J5	Boyton, Wilts. BA12	9 J1
Bouldnor PO41	10 E6	Boyton Cross CM1	24 C1
Bouldon SY7	38 E7	Boyton End CO10	34 B4
Boulge IP13	35 G3	Bozeat NN29	32 C3
Boulmer NE66	71 H2	Braaid IM4	54 C6
Boulston SA62	16 C3	Braal Castle KW12	105 G2
Boultenstone Hotel AB36	90 C3	Brabling Green IP13	35 G2
Boultham LN6	52 C6	Brabourne TN25	15 F3
Boundary, Derbys. DE11	41 F4	Brabourne Lees TN25	15 F3
Boundary, Staffs. ST10	40 B1	Brabster KW1	105 J2
Bourn CB3	33 G3	Bracadale IV56	85 J1
Bourne PE10	42 D3	Braceborough PE9	42 D4
Bourne End, Beds. MK43	32 C4	Bracebridge Heath LN4	52 C6
Bourne End, Bucks. SL8	22 B3	Braceby NG34	42 D2
Bourne End, Herts. HP1	22 D1	Bracewell BD23	56 D5
Bournebridge RM4	23 J2	Brachla IV3	88 C1
BOURNEMOUTH BH	10 B5	Bracken Hill WF14	57 G7
Bournemouth Airport BH23	10 C5	Brackenber CA16	61 J5
Bournheath B61	29 J1	Brackenbottom BD24	56 D2
Bournmoor DH4	62 E1	Brackenfield DE55	51 F7
Bournville B30	40 C7	Brackens AB53	99 F5
Bourton, Bucks. MK18	31 J5	Bracklach AB54	90 B2
Bourton, Dorset SP8	9 G1	Bracklamore AB43	99 G5
Bourton, N.Som. BS22	19 G5	Bracklesham PO20	12 B7
Bourton, Oxon. SN6	21 F3	Brackletter PH34	87 H6
Bourton, Shrop. TF13	38 E6	Brackley, Arg. & B. PA31	73 G2
		Brackley, High. IV2	97 F6

Brackley, Northants. NN13	31 G5
Brackley Gate DE7	41 F1
Brackley Hatch NN13	31 H4
Bracknell RG12	22 B5
Braco PH5	81 K7
Bracobrae AB55	98 D5
Bracon Ash NR14	45 F6
Bracora PH40	86 D5
Bracorina PH40	86 D5
Bradbourne DE6	50 E7
Bradbury TS21	62 E4
Bradda IM9	54 A6
Bradden NN12	31 H4
Braddock PL22	4 B4
Braden Heath SY13	38 D2
Bradenham, Bucks. HP14	22 B2
Bradenham, Norf. IP25	44 D5
Bradenstoke SN15	20 D4
Bradfield, Devon EX15	7 J5
Bradfield, Essex CO11	35 F5
Bradfield, Norf. NR28	45 G2
Bradfield, W.Berks. RG7	21 K4
Bradfield Combust IP30	34 C3
Bradfield Green CW1	49 F7
Bradfield Heath CO11	35 F5
Bradfield St. Clare IP30	34 D3
Bradfield St. George IP30	34 D2
Bradford, Cornw. PL30	4 B3
Bradford, Derbys. DE45	50 E6
Bradford, Devon EX22	6 C5
Bradford, Northumb. NE70	77 K7
Bradford, Northumb. NE20	71 F6
BRADFORD, W.Yorks. BD	57 G6
Bradford Abbas DT9	8 E3
Bradford Leigh BA15	20 B5
Bradford Peverell DT2	9 F5
Bradford-on-Avon BA15	20 B5
Bradford-on-Tone TA4	7 K3
Bradiford EX31	6 D2
Brading PO36	11 H6
Bradley, Ches. WA6	48 E5
Bradley, Derbys. DE6	40 E1
Bradley, Hants. SO24	21 K7
Bradley, N.E.Lincs. DN37	53 F2
Bradley (Low Bradley), N.Yorks. BD20	57 F5
Bradley, Staffs. ST18	40 A4
Bradley, W.Mid. WV14	40 B6
Bradley Fold BL2	49 G2
Bradley Green, Warks. CV9	40 E5
Bradley Green, Worcs. B96	29 J2
Bradley in the Moors ST10	40 C1
Bradley Mills HD5	50 D1
Bradley Stoke BS32	19 K3
Bradmore, Notts. NG11	41 H2
Bradmore, W.Mid. WV3	40 A6
Bradney TA7	8 C1
Bradninch EX5	7 J5
Bradnop ST13	50 C7
Bradnor Green HR5	28 B3
Bradpole DT6	8 D5
Bradshaw, Gt.Man. BL2	49 G1
Bradshaw, W.Yorks. HX2	57 F6
Bradstone PL19	6 B7
Bradwall Green CW11	49 G6
Bradwell, Derbys. S33	50 D4
Bradwell, Devon EX34	6 C1
Bradwell, Essex CM77	34 C6
Bradwell, M.K. MK13	32 B5
Bradwell, Norf. NR31	45 K5
Bradwell Grove OX18	21 F1
Bradwell Waterside CM0	25 F1
Bradwell-on-Sea CM0	25 G1
Bradworthy EX22	6 B4
Brae, D. & G. DG2	65 J3
Brae, High. IV24	96 B1
Brae, Shet. ZE2	109 C6
Brae of Achnahaird IV26	102 C7
Braeantra IV17	96 C4
Braedownie DD8	89 K7
Braefoot AB53	99 F6
Braegrum PH1	82 B5
Braehead, D. & G. DG8	64 E5
Braehead, Glas. G51	74 D4
Braehead, Moray AB55	98 B6
Braehead, Ork. KW17	107 E7
Braehead, Ork. KW17	106 D3
Braehead, S.Lan. ML11	75 G7
Braehead, S.Lan. ML11	75 H5
Braehead of Lunan DD10	83 H2
Braehoulland ZE2	108 B5
Braeleny FK17	81 H6
Braemar AB35	89 J5
Braemore, High. IV27	96 C1
Braemore, High. KW6	105 F5
Braemore, High. IV23	95 H4
Braenaloin AB35	89 K5
Braes of Enzie AB56	98 B5
Braes of Ullapool IV26	95 H2
Braeswick KW17	106 F4
Braeval FK8	81 G7
Braewick ZE2	109 C8
Brafferton, Darl. DL1	62 D4
Brafferton, N.Yorks. YO61	57 K2
Brafield-on-the-Green NN7	32 B3
Bragar HS2	100 E3
Bragbury End SG2	33 F6
Bragenham LU7	32 C6
Bragleenbeg PA34	80 A5
Braichmelyn LL57	46 E6
Braides LA2	55 H4
Braidley DL8	57 F1
Braidwood ML8	75 G6
Braigo PA44	72 A4

173

Brailsford

Brailsford DE6 40 E1
Brain's Green GL15 19 K1
Braintree CM7 34 B6
Braiseworth IP23 35 F1
Braishfield SO51 10 E2
Braithwaite, Cumb. CA12 60 D4
Braithwaite, S.Yorks. DN7 51 J1
Braithwaite, W.Yorks. BD22 57 F5
Braithwell S66 51 H3
Bramber BN44 12 E5
Brambletye RH18 13 H3
Brambridge SO50 11 F2
Bramcote, Notts. NG9 41 H2
Bramcote, Warks. CV11 41 G7
Bramdean SO24 11 H2
Bramerton NR14 45 G5
Bramfield, Herts. SG14 33 F7
Bramfield, Suff. IP19 35 H1
Bramford IP8 35 F4
Bramhall SK7 49 H4
Bramham LS23 57 K5
Bramhope LS16 57 H5
Bramley, Hants. RG26 21 K6
Bramley, S.Yorks. S66 51 G3
Bramley, Surr. GU5 22 D7
Bramley Corner RG26 21 K6
Bramley Head HG3 57 G4
Bramley Vale S44 51 G6
Bramling CT3 15 H2
Brampford Speke EX5 7 H6
Brampton, Cambs. PE28 33 F1
Brampton, Cumb. CA8 70 A7
Brampton, Cumb. CA16 61 H4
Brampton, Derbys. S40 51 F5
Brampton, Lincs. LN1 52 B5
Brampton, Norf. NR10 45 G3
Brampton, S.Yorks. S73 51 G2
Brampton, Suff. NR34 45 J7
Brampton Abbotts HR9 29 F6
Brampton Ash LE16 42 A7
Brampton Bryan SY7 28 C1
Brampton en le Morthen S66 51 G4
Brampton Street NR34 45 J7
Bramshall ST14 40 C2
Bramshaw SO43 10 D3
Bramshill RG27 22 A5
Bramshott GU30 12 B3
Bramwell TA10 8 D2
Bran End CM6 33 K6
Branault PH36 79 G1
Brancaster PE31 44 B1
Brancaster Staithe PE31 44 B1
Brancepeth DH7 62 D3
Branchill IV36 97 H6
Brand Green GL19 29 G6
Brandelhow CA12 60 D4
Branderburgh IV31 97 K4
Brandesburton YO25 59 H5
Brandeston IP13 35 G2
Brandis Corner EX22 6 C5
Brandiston NR10 45 F3
Brandon, Dur. DH7 62 D3
Brandon, Lincs. NG32 42 C1
Brandon, Northumb. NE66 71 F2
Brandon, Suff. IP27 44 B7
Brandon, Warks. CV8 31 F1
Brandon Bank PE38 44 A7
Brandon Creek PE38 44 A6
Brandon Parva NR9 44 E5
Brandsby YO61 58 B2
Brandy Wharf DN21 52 D3
Brane TR20 2 B6
Branksome BH12 10 B5
Branksome Park BH13 10 B5
Bransbury SO21 21 H7
Bransby LN1 52 B5
Branscombe EX12 7 K7
Bransford WR6 29 G3
Bransford Bridge WR6 29 H3
Bransgore BH23 10 C5
Bransholme HU7 59 H6
Branson's Cross B98 30 B1
Branston, Leics. NG32 42 B3
Branston, Lincs. LN4 52 D6
Branston, Staffs. DE14 40 E3
Branston Booths LN4 52 D6
Brant Broughton LN5 52 C7
Brantham CO11 35 F5
Branthwaite, Cumb. CA7 60 D3
Branthwaite, Cumb. CA14 60 B4
Brantingham HU15 59 F7
Branton, Northumb. NE66 71 F2
Branton, S.Yorks. DN3 51 J2
Brantwood LA21 60 E7
Branxholm Bridgend TD9 69 K2
Branxholme TD9 69 K2
Branxton TD12 77 G7
Brassey Green CW6 48 E6
Brassington DE4 50 E7
Brasted TN16 23 H6
Brasted Chart TN16 23 H6
Brathens AB31 90 E5
Bratoft PE24 53 H6
Brattleby LN1 52 C4
Bratton, Som. TA24 7 H1
Bratton, Tel. & W. TF5 39 F4
Bratton, Wilts. BA13 20 C6
Bratton Clovelly EX20 6 C6
Bratton Fleming EX31 6 E2
Bratton Seymour BA9 9 F2
Braughing SG11 33 G6
Brauncewell NG34 52 D7
Braunston, Northants. NN11 31 G2
Braunston, Rut. LE15 42 B5
Braunstone LE3 41 H5
Braunton EX33 6 C2
Brawby YO17 58 D2
Brawdy SA62 16 B2
Brawith TS9 63 G6
Brawl KW14 104 D2
Brawlbin KW12 105 F3
Bray SL6 22 C4
Bray Shop PL17 4 D3
Bray Wick SL6 22 B4
Braybrooke LE16 42 A7
Braydon Side SN15 20 D3
Brayford EX32 6 E2
Brayshaw BD23 56 C4
Braythorn LS21 57 H5
Brayton YO8 58 C6
Braywoodside SL6 22 B4
Brazacott PL15 4 C1
Brea TR15 2 D4
Breach, Kent CT4 15 G3
Breach, Kent ME9 24 E5
Breachwood Green SG4 32 E6
Breacleit HS2 100 D4
Breadsall DE21 41 F2
Breadstone GL13 20 A1
Breage TR13 2 D6
Breakon ZE2 108 E2
Bream GL15 19 K1
Breamore SP6 10 C3
Brean TA8 19 F6
Breanais HS2 100 B5
Brearton HG3 57 J3
Breascleit HS2 100 E4
Breaston DE72 41 G2
Brechfa SA32 17 J1
Brechin DD9 83 H1
Brecklate PA28 66 A2
Breckles NR17 44 D6
Brecon (Aberhonddu) LD3 27 K6
Breconside DG3 68 D3
Bredbury SK6 49 J3
Brede TN31 14 D6
Bredenbury HR7 29 F3
Bredfield IP13 35 G3
Bredgar ME9 24 E5
Bredhurst ME7 24 D5
Bredon GL20 29 J5
Bredon's Hardwick GL20 29 J5
Bredon's Norton GL20 29 J5
Bredwardine HR3 28 C4
Breedon on the Hill DE73 41 G3
Breibhig HS2 101 G4
Breich EH55 75 H4
Breightmet BL2 49 G2
Breighton YO8 58 D6
Breinton HR4 28 D5
Breinton Common HR4 28 D5
Bremhill SN11 20 C4
Bremhill Wick SN11 20 C4
Brenachoille PA32 80 B7
Brenchley TN12 23 K7
Brendon, Devon EX35 7 F1
Brendon, Devon EX22 6 B4
Brendon, Devon EX22 6 B5
Brenkley NE13 71 H6
Brent Eleigh CO10 34 D4
Brent Knoll TA9 19 G6
Brent Pelham SG9 33 H5
Brentford TW8 22 E4
Brentingby LE14 42 A4
Brentwood CM14 23 J2
Brenzett TN29 15 F5
Brenzett Green TN29 15 F5
Breoch DG7 65 H5
Brereton WS15 40 C4
Brereton Green CW11 49 G6
Brereton Heath CW12 49 H6
Breretonhill WS15 40 C4
Bressay ZE2 109 E8
Bressingham IP22 44 E7
Bressingham Common IP22 44 E7
Bretby DE15 40 E3
Bretford CV23 31 F1
Bretforton WR11 30 B4
Bretherdale Head CA10 61 G6
Bretherton PR26 55 H7
Brettabister ZE2 109 D7
Brettenham, Norf. IP24 44 D7
Brettenham, Suff. IP7 34 D3
Bretton, Derbys. S32 50 D5
Bretton, Flints. CH4 48 C6
Brevig HS9 84 B5
Brewood ST19 40 A5
Briach IV36 97 H6
Briantspuddle DT2 9 H5
Brick End CM6 33 J6
Bricket Wood AL2 22 E1
Brickkiln Green CM7 34 B5
Bricklehampton WR10 29 J4
Bride IM7 54 D3
Bridekirk CA13 60 C3
Bridell SA43 26 A4
Bridestones CW12 49 J6
Bridestowe EX20 6 D7
Brideswell AB54 90 D1
Bridford EX6 7 G7
Bridge, Cornw. TR16 2 D4
Bridge, Kent CT4 15 G2
Bridge End, Cumb. LA20 55 F1
Bridge End, Devon TQ7 5 G6
Bridge End, Essex CM7 33 K5
Bridge End, Lincs. NG34 42 E2
Bridge End, Shet. ZE2 109 C9
Bridge Hewick HG4 57 J2
Bridge o' Ess AB34 90 D5
Bridge of Alford AB33 90 D3
Bridge of Allan FK9 75 F1
Bridge of Avon AB37 89 J1
Bridge of Balgie PH15 81 G3
Bridge of Bogendreip AB31 90 E5
Bridge of Brewlands PH11 82 C1
Bridge of Brown AB37 89 J2
Bridge of Cally PH10 82 C2
Bridge of Canny AB31 90 E5
Bridge of Craigisla PH11 82 D2
Bridge of Dee, Aber. AB35 89 J5
Bridge of Dee, Aber. AB31 90 E5
Bridge of Dee, D. & G. DG7 65 H4
Bridge of Don AB23 91 H4
Bridge of Dun DD10 83 H2
Bridge of Dye AB31 90 E6
Bridge of Earn PH2 82 C6
Bridge of Ericht PH17 81 G2
Bridge of Feugh AB31 90 E5
Bridge of Forss KW14 105 F2
Bridge of Gairn AB35 90 B5
Bridge of Gaur PH17 81 G2
Bridge of Muchalls AB39 91 G5
Bridge of Muick AB35 90 B5
Bridge of Orchy PA36 80 D4
Bridge of Tynet AB56 98 B4
Bridge of Walls ZE2 109 B7
Bridge of Weir PA11 74 B4
Bridge Reeve EX18 6 E4
Bridge Sollers HR4 28 D4
Bridge Street CO10 34 C4
Bridge Trafford CH2 48 D5
Bridgefoot, Angus DD3 82 E4
Bridgefoot, Cambs. SG8 33 H4
Bridgefoot, Cumb. CA14 60 B4
Bridgehampton BA22 8 E2
Bridgehaugh AB55 90 B1
Bridgehill DH8 62 B1
Bridgemary PO13 11 G4
Bridgemere CW5 39 G1
Bridgend, Aber. AB54 90 D1
Bridgend, Aber. AB53 99 F6
Bridgend, Angus DD9 83 G1
Bridgend, Arg. & B. PA43 72 B4
Bridgend, Arg. & B. PA31 73 G1
Bridgend (Pen-y-bont ar Ogwr), Bridgend CF31 18 C4
Bridgend, Cornw. PL22 4 B5
Bridgend, Cumb. CA11 60 F5
Bridgend, Fife KY15 82 E6
Bridgend, Moray AB54 90 B1
Bridgend, P. & K. PH2 82 C5
Bridgend, W.Loth. EH49 75 J3
Bridgend of Lintrathen DD8 82 D2
Bridgerule EX22 6 A5
Bridges SY5 38 C6
Bridgeton, Aber. AB33 90 D3
Bridgeton, Glas. G40 74 E4
Bridgetown, Cornw. PL15 6 B7
Bridgetown, Som. TA22 7 H2
Bridgeyate BS30 19 K4
Bridgham NR16 44 D7
Bridgnorth WV16 39 G6
Bridgtown WS11 40 B5
Bridgwater TA6 8 B1
Bridlington YO16 59 H3
Bridport DT6 8 D5
Bridstow HR9 28 E6
Brierfield BB9 56 D6
Brierley, Glos. GL17 29 F7
Brierley, Here. HR6 28 D3
Brierley, S.Yorks. S72 51 G1
Brierley Hill DY5 40 B7
Brierton TS22 63 F4
Briestfield WF12 50 E1
Brig o'Turk FK17 81 G7
Brigg DN20 52 D2
Briggate NR28 45 H3
Briggswath YO21 63 K6
Brigham, Cumb. CA13 60 B3
Brigham, E.Riding YO25 59 G4
Brighouse HD6 57 G7
Brighstone PO30 11 F6
Brightgate DE4 50 E7
Brighthampton OX29 21 G1
Brightholmlee S35 50 E3
Brightling TN32 13 K4
Brightlingsea CO7 34 E7
BRIGHTON, B. & H. BN 13 G6
Brighton, Cornw. TR2 3 G3
Brightons FK2 75 H3
Brightwalton RG20 21 H4
Brightwalton Green RG20 21 H4
Brightwell IP10 35 G4
Brightwell Baldwin OX49 21 K2
Brightwell Upperton OX49 21 K2
Brightwell-cum-Sotwell OX10 21 J2
Brignall DL12 62 B5
Brigsley DN37 53 F2
Brigsteer LA8 55 H1
Brigstock NN14 42 C7
Brill, Bucks. HP18 31 H7
Brill, Cornw. TR11 2 E6
Brilley HR3 28 B4
Brilley Mountain HR3 28 B3
Brimaston SA62 16 C2
Brimfield SY8 28 E2
Brimington S43 51 G5
Brimington Common S43 51 G5
Brimley TQ13 5 J3
Brimpsfield GL4 29 J7
Brimpton RG7 21 J5
Brims KW16 107 B9
Brimscombe GL5 20 B1
Brimstage CH63 48 C4
Brinacory PH41 86 D5
Brindham BA6 19 J7
Brindister, Shet. ZE2 109 D9
Brindister, Shet. ZE2 109 B7
Brindle PR6 55 J7
Brindley Ford ST8 49 H7
Brineton TF11 40 A4
Bringhurst LE16 42 B6
Brington PE28 32 D1
Brinian KW17 106 D5
Briningham NR24 44 E2
Brinkhill LN11 53 G5
Brinkley, Cambs. CB8 33 K3
Brinkley, Notts. NG25 51 K7
Brinklow CV23 31 F1
Brinkworth SN15 20 D3
Brinmore IV2 88 D2
Brinscall PR6 56 B7
Brinsea BS49 19 H5
Brinsley NG16 41 G1
Brinsop HR4 28 D4
Brinsworth S60 51 G3
Brinton NR24 44 E2
Brisco CA4 60 F1
Brisley NR20 44 D3
Brislington BS4 19 K4
Brissenden Green TN26 14 E4
BRISTOL BS 19 J4
Bristol International Airport BS48 19 J5
Briston NR24 44 E2
Britannia OL13 56 D7
Britford SP5 10 C2
Brithdir, Caerp. NP24 18 E1
Brithdir, Gwyn. LL40 37 G4
Brithem Bottom EX15 7 J4
Briton Ferry (Llansawel) SA11 18 A2
Britwell SL2 22 C3
Britwell Salome OX49 21 K2
Brixham TQ5 5 K5
Brixton, Devon PL8 5 F5
Brixton, Gt.Lon. SW2 23 G4
Brixton Deverill BA12 9 H1
Brixworth NN6 31 J1
Brize Norton OX18 21 F1
Broad Alley WR9 29 H2
Broad Blunsdon SN26 20 E2
Broad Campden GL55 30 C5
Broad Carr HX4 50 C1
Broad Chalke SP5 10 B2
Broad Ford TN12 14 C4
Broad Green, Beds. MK43 32 C4
Broad Green, Cambs. CB8 33 K3
Broad Green, Essex CO6 34 C6
Broad Green, Essex SG8 33 H5
Broad Green, Mersey. L14 48 D3
Broad Green, Suff. IP6 34 E3
Broad Green, Worcs. WR6 29 G3
Broad Haven SA62 16 B3
Broad Hill CB7 33 J1
Broad Hinton SN4 20 E4
Broad Laying RG20 21 H5
Broad Marston CV37 30 C4
Broad Oak, Carmar. SA32 17 J2
Broad Oak, Cumb. CA18 60 C7
Broad Oak, E.Suss. TN31 14 D6
Broad Oak, E.Suss. TN21 13 K4
Broad Oak, Here. HR2 28 D6
Broad Road IP21 35 G1
Broad Street, E.Suss. TN36 14 D6
Broad Street, Kent ME17 14 D2
Broad Street, Kent TN25 15 G4
Broad Street, Wilts. SN9 20 E6
Broad Street Green CM9 24 E1
Broad Town SN4 20 D4
Broadbottom SK14 49 J3
Broadbridge PO18 12 B6
Broadbridge Heath RH12 12 E3
Broadclyst EX5 7 H6
Broadfield, Lancs. BB5 56 C7
Broadfield, Lancs. PR25 55 J7
Broadford IV49 86 C2
Broadford Bridge RH14 12 D4
Broadgate LA18 54 E1
Broadhaugh TD9 69 K3
Broadhaven KW1 105 J3
Broadheath, Gt.Man. WA14 49 G4
Broadheath, Worcs. WR15 29 F2
Broadhembury EX14 7 K5
Broadhempston TQ9 5 J4
Broadholme LN1 52 B5
Broadland Row TN31 14 D6
Broadlay SA17 17 G4
Broadley, Lancs. OL12 49 H1
Broadley, Moray AB56 98 B4
Broadley Common EN9 23 H1
Broadmayne DT2 9 G6
Broadmeadows TD7 76 C7
Broadmere RG25 21 K7
Broadmoor SA68 16 D4
Broadnymett EX17 7 F5
Broadoak, Dorset DT6 8 D5
Broadoak, Glos. GL14 29 F7
Broadoak, Kent CT2 25 H5
Broadoak End SG14 33 G7
Broadrashes AB55 98 C5
Broad's Green CM3 33 K7
Broadsea AB43 99 H4
Broadstairs CT10 25 K5
Broadstone, Poole BH18 10 B5
Broadstone, Shrop. SY7 38 E7
Broadstreet Common NP18 19 G3
Broadwas WR6 29 G3
Broadwater, Herts. SG2 33 F6
Broadwater, W.Suss. BN14 12 E6
Broadwater Down TN2 13 J3
Broadwaters DY10 29 H1
Broadway, Carmar. SA17 17 G4
Broadway, Carmar. SA33 17 F3
Broadway, Pembs. SA62 16 B3
Broadway, Som. TA19 8 C3
Broadway, Suff. IP19 35 H1
Broadway, Worcs. WR12 30 C5
Broadwell, Glos. GL56 30 D6
Broadwell, Oxon. GL7 21 F1
Broadwell, Warks. CV23 31 F2
Broadwell House NE47 62 A1
Broadwey DT3 9 F6
Broadwindsor DT8 8 D4
Broadwood Kelly EX19 6 E5
Broadwoodwidger PL16 6 C7
Brobury HR3 28 C4
Brocastle CF35 18 C4
Brochel IV40 94 B7
Brochloch DG7 67 K4
Brock PA77 78 B3
Brockamin WR6 29 G3
Brockbridge SO32 11 H3
Brockdish IP21 35 G1
Brockenhurst SO42 10 D4
Brockford Green IP14 35 F2
Brockford Street IP14 35 F2
Brockhall NN7 31 H2
Brockham RH3 22 E7
Brockhampton, Glos. GL54 30 B6
Brockhampton, Glos. GL51 29 J6
Brockhampton, Here. HR1 28 E5
Brockhampton, Here. WR6 29 F3
Brockhampton Green DT2 9 G4
Brockholes HD9 50 D1
Brockhurst, Hants. PO12 11 G4
Brockhurst, W.Suss. RH19 13 H3
Brocklebank CA7 60 E2
Brocklesby DN41 52 E1
Brockley, N.Som. BS48 19 H5
Brockley, Suff. IP29 34 C3
Brockley Green CO10 34 B4
Brock's Green RG20 21 H5
Brockton, Shrop. TF13 38 E6
Brockton, Shrop. TF11 39 G5
Brockton, Shrop. SY5 38 C5
Brockton, Shrop. SY7 38 C7
Brockton, Tel. & W. TF10 39 G4
Brockweir NP16 19 J1
Brockwood Park SO24 11 H2
Brockworth GL3 29 H7
Brocton ST17 40 B4
Brodick KA27 73 J7
Brodsworth DN5 51 H2
Brogborough MK43 32 C5
Brogden BB18 56 D5
Brogyntyn SY10 38 B2
Broken Cross, Ches. SK11 49 H5
Broken Cross, Ches. CW9 49 F5
Brokenborough SN16 20 C3
Brokes DL11 62 C7
Bromborough CH62 48 C4
Brome IP23 35 F1
Brome Street IP23 35 F1
Bromeswell IP12 35 H3
Bromfield, Cumb. CA7 60 C2
Bromfield, Shrop. SY8 28 D1
Bromham, Beds. MK43 32 D3
Bromham, Wilts. SN15 20 C5
Bromley, Gt.Lon. BR1 23 H5
Bromley, S.Yorks. S35 51 F3
Bromley Cross BL7 49 G1
Bromley Green TN26 14 E4
Brompton, Med. ME7 24 D5
Brompton, N.Yorks. DL6 62 E7
Brompton, N.Yorks. YO13 59 F1
Brompton, Shrop. SY5 38 E5
Brompton on Swale DL10 62 D7
Brompton Ralph TA4 7 J2
Brompton Regis TA22 7 H2
Bromsash HR9 29 F6
Bromsberrow HR8 29 G5
Bromsberrow Heath HR8 29 G5
Bromsgrove B61 29 J1
Bromstead Heath TF10 40 A4
Bromyard HR7 29 F3
Bromyard Downs HR7 29 F3
Bronaber LL41 37 G2
Brondesbury NW6 23 F3
Brongest SA38 26 C4
Bronington SY13 38 D2
Bronllys LD3 28 A5
Bronnant SY23 27 F2
Bronwydd Arms SA33 17 H2
Bronydd HR3 28 B4
Bron-y-gaer SA33 17 G3
Bronygarth SY10 38 B2
Brook, Carmar. SA33 17 F4
Brook, Hants. SO43 10 D3
Brook, Hants. SO20 10 E2
Brook, I.o.W. PO30 10 E6
Brook, Kent TN25 15 F3
Brook, Surr. GU8 12 C3
Brook, Surr. GU5 22 D7
Brook Bottom OL5 49 J2
Brook End, Beds. MK44 32 D2
Brook End, Herts. SG9 33 G6
Brook End, M.K. MK16 32 C4
Brook End, Worcs. WR5 29 H4

Brook Hill SO43 10 D3
Brook Street, Essex CM14 23 J2
Brook Street, Kent TN26 14 E4
Brook Street, Suff. CO10 34 C4
Brook Street, W.Suss. RH17 13 G4
Brooke, Norf. NR15 45 G6
Brooke, Rut. LE15 42 B5
Brookend, Glos. GL15 19 J2
Brookend, Glos. GL13 19 K1
Brookfield SK14 50 C3
Brookhampton OX44 21 K2
Brookhouse, Ches. SK10 49 J5
Brookhouse, Denb. LL16 47 J6
Brookhouse, Lancs. LA2 55 J3
Brookhouse, S.Yorks. S25 51 H4
Brookhouse Green CW11 49 H6
Brookhouses ST10 40 B1
Brookland TN29 14 E5
Brooklands, D. & G. DG2 65 J3
Brooklands, Shrop. SY13 38 E1
Brookmans Park AL9 23 F1
Brooks SY21 38 A6
Brooks Green RH13 12 E4
Brooksby LE14 41 J4
Brookthorpe GL4 29 H7
Brookwood GU24 22 C6
Broom, Beds. SG18 32 E4
Broom, Fife KY8 82 E7
Broom, Warks. B50 30 B3
Broom Green NR20 44 D3
Broom Hill, Dorset BH21 10 B4
Broom Hill, Worcs. DY9 29 J1
Broom of Dalreach PH3 82 B6
Broomcroft SY5 38 E5
Broome, Norf. NR35 45 H6
Broome, Shrop. SY7 38 D7
Broome, Worcs. DY9 29 J1
Broome Wood NE66 71 G2
Broomedge WA13 49 G4
Broomer's Corner RH13 12 E4
Broomfield, Aber. AB41 91 H1
Broomfield, Essex CM1 34 B7
Broomfield, Kent CT5 25 H5
Broomfield, Kent ME17 14 D2
Broomfield, Som. TA5 8 B1
Broomfleet HU15 58 E7
Broomhall Green CW5 39 F1
Broomhaugh NE44 71 F7
Broomhead AB43 99 H4
Broomhill, Bristol BS16 19 K4
Broomhill, Northumb. NE65 71 H3
Broomielaw DL12 62 B5
Broomley NE43 71 F7
Broompark DH7 62 D2
Brora KW9 97 G1
Broseley TF12 39 F5
Brotherlee DL13 62 A3
Brothertoft PE20 43 F1
Brotherton WF11 57 K7
Brotton TS12 63 H5
Broubster KW14 105 F2
Brough, Cumb. CA17 61 J5
Brough, Derbys. S33 50 D4
Brough, E.Riding YO15 59 F7
Brough, High. KW14 105 H1
Brough, Notts. NG23 52 B7
Brough, Ork. KW17 107 C6
Brough, Shet. ZE2 109 E8
Brough, Shet. ZE2 108 D5
Brough, Shet. ZE2 109 E6
Brough, Shet. ZE2 108 E5
Brough Lodge ZE2 108 E3
Brough Sowerby CA17 61 J5
Broughall SY13 38 E1
Brougham CA10 61 G4
Broughton, Bucks. HP20 32 B7
Broughton, Cambs. PE28 33 F1
Broughton, Flints. CH4 48 C6
Broughton, Hants. SO20 10 E1
Broughton, Lancs. PR3 55 J6
Broughton, M.K. MK16 32 B4
Broughton, N.Lincs. DN20 52 C2
Broughton, N.Yorks. YO17 58 D2
Broughton, N.Yorks. BD23 56 E4
Broughton, Northants. NN14 32 B1
Broughton, Ork. KW17 106 D3
Broughton, Oxon. OX15 31 F5
Broughton, Sc.Bord. ML12 75 K7
Broughton, V. of Glam. CF71 18 C4
Broughton Astley LE9 41 H6
Broughton Beck LA12 55 F1
Broughton Gifford SN12 20 B5
Broughton Green WR9 29 J2
Broughton Hackett WR7 29 J3
Broughton in Furness LA20 55 F1
Broughton Mills LA20 60 D7
Broughton Moor CA15 60 B3
Broughton Poggs GL7 21 F1
Broughtown KW17 106 F3
Broughty Ferry DD5 83 F4
Browland ZE2 109 B7
Brown Candover SO24 11 G1
Brown Edge, Lancs. PR8 48 C1
Brown Edge, Staffs. ST6 49 J7
Brown Heath CH3 48 D6
Brown Lees ST7 49 H7
Brown Street IP14 34 E2
Brownber CA17 61 J6
Browndown PO13 11 G5

Brownheath SY12 38 D3
Brownhill AB41 99 G6
Brownhills, Fife KY16 83 G6
Brownhills, W.Mid. WS8 40 C5
Brownieside NE67 71 G1
Brownlow CW12 49 H6
Brownlow Heath CW12 49 H6
Brownsea Island BH15 10 B6
Brownshill GL6 20 B1
Brownshill Green CV5 41 F7
Brownsover CV21 31 G1
Brownston PL21 5 G5
Browston Green NR31 45 J5
Broxa YO13 63 J3
Broxbourne EN10 23 G1
Broxburn, E.Loth. EH42 76 E3
Broxburn, W.Loth. EH52 75 J3
Broxholme LN1 52 C5
Broxted CM6 33 J6
Broxton CH3 48 D7
Broxwood HR6 28 C3
Broyle Side BN8 13 H5
Bru (Brue) HS2 101 F3
Bruachmary IV12 97 F7
Bruan KW2 105 J5
Brue (Bru) HS2 101 F3
Bruera CH3 48 D6
Bruern OX7 30 D6
Bruernish HS9 84 C4
Bruichladdich PA49 72 A4
Bruisyard IP17 35 H2
Bruisyard Street IP17 35 H2
Brumby DN16 52 C1
Brund SK17 50 D6
Brundall NR13 45 H5
Brundish, Norf. NR14 45 H6
Brundish, Suff. IP13 35 G2
Brundish Street IP13 35 G1
Brunstock CA6 60 F1
Brunswick Village NE13 71 H6
Bruntingthorpe LE17 41 J6
Bruntland AB54 90 C2
Brunton, Fife KY15 82 E5
Brunton, Northumb. NE66 71 H1
Brushfield SK17 50 D5
Brushford, Devon EX18 6 E5
Brushford, Som. TA22 7 H3
Bruton BA10 9 F1
Bryanston DT11 9 H4
Bryant's Bottom HP16 22 B2
Brydekirk DG12 69 G6
Brymbo LL11 48 B7
Brympton BA22 8 E3
Bryn, Caerp. NP12 18 E2
Bryn, Carmar. SA14 17 J4
Bryn, Ches. CW8 49 F5
Bryn, Gt.Man. WN4 48 E2
Bryn, N.P.T. SA13 18 B2
Bryn, Shrop. SY9 38 B7
Bryn Bwbach LL47 37 F2
Bryn Gates WN2 48 E2
Bryn Pen-y-lan LL13 38 C1
Brynamman SA18 27 G7
Brynberian SA41 16 E1
Bryncae CF72 18 C3
Bryncethin CF32 18 C3
Bryncir LL51 36 D1
Bryncôch, N.P.T. SA10 18 A2
Bryncroes LL53 36 B2
Bryncrug LL36 37 F5
Bryneglwys LL21 38 A1
Bryngwran LL65 46 B5
Bryngwyn, Mon. NP15 19 G1
Bryngwyn, Powys HR5 28 A4
Bryn-henllan SA42 16 D1
Brynhoffnant SA44 26 C3
Bryning PR4 55 H6
Brynithel NP13 19 F1
Brynmawr, B.Gwent NP23 28 A7
Bryn-mawr, Gwyn. LL53 36 B2
Brynmelyn LD1 28 A1
Brynmenyn CF32 18 C3
Brynna CF72 18 C3
Brynna Gwynion CF72 18 C3
Brynog SA48 26 E3
Bryn-penarth SY21 38 A5
Brynrefail, Gwyn. LL55 46 D6
Brynrefail, I.o.A. LL70 46 C4
Brynsadler CF72 18 D3
Brynsaithmarchog LL21 47 J7
Brynsiencyn LL61 46 C6
Bryn-teg, I.o.A. LL78 46 C4
Brynteg, Wrex. LL11 48 C7
Bryn-y-cochin SY12 38 C2
Bryn-y-maen LL28 47 G5
Bryn-y-maen NP7 28 C7
Buaile nam Bodach HS9 84 C4
Bualadubh HS8 92 C7
Bualintur IV47 85 K2
Bualnaluib IV22 94 E2
Bubbenhall CV8 30 E1
Bubnell DE45 50 E5
Bubwith YO8 58 D6
Buccleuch TD9 69 J2
Buchan IV63 65 H4
Buchanan Castle G63 74 C2
Buchanhaven AB42 99 K6
Buchanty PH1 82 A5
Buchlyvie FK8 74 D1
Buckabank CA5 60 E2
Buckby Wharf NN11 31 H2
Buckden, Cambs. PE19 32 E2
Buckden, N.Yorks. BD23 56 E2
Buckenham NR13 45 H5
Buckerell EX14 7 K5

Buckfast TQ11 5 H4
Buckfastleigh TQ11 5 H4
Buckhaven KY8 76 B1
Buckholm TD1 76 C7
Buckholt NP25 28 E7
Buckhorn Weston SP8 9 G2
Buckhurst Hill IG9 23 H2
Buckie AB56 98 C4
Buckies KW14 105 G2
Buckingham MK18 31 H5
Buckland, Bucks. HP22 32 B7
Buckland, Devon TQ7 5 G6
Buckland, Glos. WR12 30 B5
Buckland, Hants. SO41 10 E5
Buckland, Here. HR6 28 E3
Buckland, Herts. SG9 33 G5
Buckland, Kent CT16 15 J3
Buckland, Oxon. SN7 21 G2
Buckland, Surr. RH3 23 F6
Buckland Brewer EX39 6 C3
Buckland Common HP23 22 C1
Buckland Dinham BA11 20 A6
Buckland Filleigh EX21 6 C5
Buckland in the Moor TQ13 5 H3
Buckland Monachorum PL20 4 E4
Buckland Newton DT2 9 F4
Buckland Ripers DT3 9 F6
Buckland St. Mary TA20 8 B3
Buckland-tout-Saints TQ7 5 H6
Bucklebury RG7 21 J4
Bucklerheads DD5 83 F4
Bucklers Hard SO42 11 F5
Bucklesham IP10 35 G4
Buckley (Bwcle) CH7 48 B6
Buckley Green B95 30 C2
Bucklow Hill WA16 49 G4
Buckman Corner RH14 12 E4
Buckminster NG33 42 B3
Bucknall, Lincs. LN10 52 E6
Bucknall, Stoke ST2 40 B1
Bucknell, Oxon. OX27 31 G6
Bucknell, Shrop. SY7 28 C1
Buckridge DY14 29 G1
Buck's Cross EX39 6 B3
Bucks Green RH12 12 D3
Bucks Hill WD4 22 D1
Bucks Horn Oak GU10 22 B7
Buck's Mills EX39 6 B3
Buckton, E.Riding YO15 59 H2
Buckton, Here. SY7 28 C1
Buckton, Northumb. NE70 77 J7
Buckworth PE28 32 E1
Budbrooke CV35 30 D2
Budby NG22 51 J5
Buddon DD7 83 G4
Bude EX23 6 A5
Budge's Shop PL12 4 D5
Budlake EX5 7 H5
Budle NE69 77 K7
Budleigh Salterton EX9 7 J7
Budock Water TR11 2 E5
Budworth Heath CW9 49 F5
Buerton CW3 39 F1
Bugbrooke NN7 31 H3
Bugeildy (Beguildy) LD7 28 A1
Buglawton CW12 49 H6
Bugle PL26 4 A5
Bugthorpe YO41 58 D4
Building End SG8 33 H5
Buildwas TF8 39 F5
Builth Road LD2 27 K3
Builth Wells LD2 27 K3
Bulby PE10 42 D3
Bulcote NG14 41 J1
Buldoo KW14 104 E2
Bulford SP4 20 E7
Bulford Camp SP4 20 E7
Bulkeley SY14 48 E7
Bulkington, Warks. CV12 41 F7
Bulkington, Wilts. SN10 20 C6
Bulkworthy EX22 6 B4
Bull Bay LL68 46 C3
Bull Green TN26 14 E4
Bullbridge DE56 51 F7
Bullbrook RG12 22 B5
Bullen's Green AL4 23 F1
Bulley GL2 29 G7
Bullington LN3 52 D5
Bullpot Farm LA6 56 B1
Bulls Cross EN2 23 G2
Bull's Green, Herts. SG3 33 F7
Bull's Green, Norf. NR34 45 J6
Bullwood PA23 73 K3
Bulmer, Essex CO10 34 C4
Bulmer, N.Yorks. YO60 58 C3
Bulmer Tye CO10 34 C5
Bulphan RM14 24 C3
Bulstone EX12 7 K7
Bulverhythe TN38 14 C7
Bulwark AB42 99 H6
Bulwell NG6 41 H1
Bulwick NN17 42 C6
Bumble's Green EN9 23 H1
Bun Abhainn Eadarra HS3 100 D7
Bun Loyne IV63 87 H4
Bunarkaig PH34 87 H6
Bunbury CW6 48 E7
Bunbury Heath CW6 48 E7
Bunchrew IV3 96 D7
Bundalloch IV40 86 E2
Buness ZE2 108 F2
Bunessan PA67 78 E5
Bungay NR35 45 H7
Bunker's Hill LN4 53 F7
Bunlarie PA28 73 F7

Bunloit IV63 88 C2
Bunmhullin HS8 84 C3
Bunnahabhain PA46 72 C3
Bunny NG11 41 H3
Buntait IV63 87 K1
Buntingford SG9 33 G6
Bunwell NR16 45 F6
Bunwell Street NR16 45 F6
Burbage, Derbys. SK17 50 C5
Burbage, Leics. LE10 41 G6
Burbage, Wilts. SN8 21 F5
Burchett's Green SL6 22 B3
Burcombe SP2 10 B1
Burcot, Oxon. OX14 21 J2
Burcot, Worcs. B60 29 J1
Burcott LU7 32 B6
Burdale YO17 58 E3
Burdocks RH14 12 D4
Burdon SR3 62 E1
Burdrop OX15 30 E5
Bures CO8 34 D5
Bures Green CO8 34 D5
Burfa LD8 28 B2
Burford, Oxon. OX18 30 D7
Burford, Shrop. WR15 28 E2
Burg PA74 78 E3
Burgate IP22 34 E1
Burgates GU33 11 J2
Burge End SG5 32 E5
Burgess Hill RH15 13 G5
Burgh IP13 35 G3
Burgh by Sands CA5 60 E1
Burgh Castle NR31 45 J5
Burgh Heath KT20 23 F6
Burgh le Marsh PE24 53 H6
Burgh next Aylsham NR11 45 G3
Burgh on Bain LN8 53 F4
Burgh St. Margaret (Fleggburgh) NR29 45 J4
Burgh St. Peter NR34 45 J6
Burghclere RG20 21 H5
Burghead IV30 97 J5
Burghfield RG30 21 K5
Burghfield Common RG7 21 K5
Burghfield Hill RG7 21 K5
Burghill HR4 28 D4
Burghwallis DN6 51 H1
Burham ME1 24 D5
Buriton GU31 11 J2
Burland CW5 49 F7
Burlawn PL27 3 G2
Burleigh SL5 22 C5
Burlescombe EX16 7 J4
Burleston DT2 9 G5
Burley, Hants. BH24 10 D4
Burley, Rut. LE15 42 B4
Burley, W.Yorks. LS6 57 H6
Burley Gate HR1 28 E4
Burley in Wharfedale LS29 57 G5
Burley Street BH24 10 D4
Burley Woodhead LS29 57 G5
Burleydam SY13 39 F1
Burlingjobb LD8 28 B3
Burlow TN21 13 J5
Burlton SY4 38 D3
Burmarsh TN29 15 G4
Burmington CV36 30 D5
Burn YO8 58 B7
Burn Farm DD9 90 E7
Burn Naze FY5 55 G5
Burn of Cambus FK16 81 J7
Burnage M19 49 H3
Burnaston DE65 40 E2
Burnby YO42 58 E5
Burncross S35 51 F3
Burndell BN18 12 C6
Burnden BL3 49 G2
Burnedge OL2 49 J1
Burnend AB41 99 G6
Burneside LA9 61 G7
Burness KW17 106 F3
Burneston DL8 57 J1
Burnett BS31 19 K5
Burnfoot, High. KW11 104 D6
Burnfoot, P. & K. FK14 82 A7
Burnfoot, Sc.Bord. TD9 70 A2
Burnfoot, Sc.Bord. TD9 69 K2
Burnham, Bucks. SL1 22 C3
Burnham, N.Lincs. DN18 52 D1
Burnham Deepdale PE31 44 C1
Burnham Green AL6 33 F7
Burnham Market PE31 44 C1
Burnham Norton PE31 44 C1
Burnham Overy Staithe PE31 44 C1
Burnham Overy Town PE31 44 C1
Burnham Thorpe PE31 44 C1
Burnham-on-Crouch CM0 25 F2
Burnham-on-Sea TA8 19 G7
Burnhaven AB42 99 K6
Burnhead, D. & G. DG7 67 K5
Burnhead, D. & G. DG3 68 D4
Burnhervie AB51 91 F3
Burnhill Green WV6 39 G5
Burnhope DH7 62 C2
Burnhouse KA15 74 B5
Burniston YO13 63 K3
Burnley BB11 56 D6
Burnmouth TD14 77 H4
Burnopfield NE16 62 C1
Burn's Green SG2 33 G6
Burnsall BD23 57 F3
Burnside, Aber. AB32 91 F3
Burnside, Angus DD8 83 G2
Burnside, E.Ayr. KA18 67 K2
Burnside, Fife KY13 82 C7
Burnside, Shet. ZE2 108 B5
Burnside, W.Loth. EH52 75 J3

Burnside of Duntrune DD4 83 F4
Burnstones CA8 61 H1
Burnswark DG11 69 G6
Burnt Hill RG18 21 J4
Burnt Houses DL13 62 C4
Burnt Oak HA8 23 F2
Burnt Yates HG3 57 H3
Burntcliff Top SK11 49 J6
Burntisland KY3 76 A2
Burnton, E.Ayr. KA18 67 J2
Burnton, E.Ayr. KA6 67 J2
Burntwood WS7 40 C5
Burntwood Green WS7 40 C5
Burnworthy TA3 7 K4
Burpham, Surr. GU1 22 D6
Burpham, W.Suss. BN18 12 D6
Burra ZE2 109 C9
Burradon, Northumb. NE65 70 E3
Burradon, T. & W. NE23 71 H6
Burrafirth ZE2 108 F1
Burraland ZE2 108 C5
Burras TR13 2 D5
Burraton, Cornw. PL12 4 E4
Burraton, Cornw. PL12 4 E4
Burravoe, Shet. ZE2 108 E5
Burravoe, Shet. ZE2 109 C6
Burray KW17 107 D8
Burrells CA16 61 H5
Burrelton PH13 82 D4
Burridge, Devon EX13 8 C4
Burridge, Hants. SO31 11 G3
Burrill DL8 57 H1
Burringham DN17 52 B2
Burrington, Devon EX37 6 E4
Burrington, Here. SY8 28 D1
Burrington, N.Som. BS40 19 H6
Burrough Green CB8 33 K3
Burrough on the Hill LE14 42 A4
Burrow, Som. TA24 7 H1
Burrow, Som. TA12 8 D3
Burrow Bridge TA7 8 C1
Burrowhill GU24 22 C5
Burrows Cross GU5 22 D7
Burry SA3 17 H5
Burry Green SA3 17 H5
Burry Port SA16 17 H4
Burscough L40 48 D1
Burscough Bridge L40 48 D1
Bursea YO43 58 E6
Burshill YO25 59 G5
Bursledon SO31 11 F4
Burslem ST6 40 A1
Burstall IP8 35 F4
Burstock DT8 8 D4
Burston, Norf. IP22 45 F7
Burston, Staffs. ST18 40 B2
Burstow RH6 23 G7
Burstwick HU12 59 J7
Burtersett DL8 56 D1
Burthorpe IP29 34 B2
Burthwaite CA4 60 F2
Burtle TA7 19 H7
Burtle Hill TA7 19 G7
Burton, Ches. CH64 48 C5
Burton, Ches. CH6 48 E6
Burton, Dorset BH23 10 C5
Burton, Lincs. LN1 52 C5
Burton, Northumb. NE69 77 K7
Burton, Pembs. SA73 16 C4
Burton, Som. TA5 7 K1
Burton, Wilts. SN14 20 B4
Burton, Wilts. BA12 9 H1
Burton Agnes YO25 59 H3
Burton Bradstock DT6 8 D6
Burton Coggles NG33 42 C3
Burton End CM24 33 J6
Burton Ferry SA73 16 C4
Burton Fleming YO25 59 G2
Burton Green, Warks. CV8 30 D1
Burton Green, Wrex. LL12 48 C7
Burton Hastings CV11 41 G7
Burton in Lonsdale LA6 56 B2
Burton Joyce NG14 41 J1
Burton Latimer NN15 32 C1
Burton Lazars LE14 42 A4
Burton Leonard HG3 57 J3
Burton on the Wolds LE12 41 H3
Burton Overy LE8 41 J6
Burton Pedwardine NG34 42 E1
Burton Pidsea HU12 59 J6
Burton Salmon LS25 57 K7
Burton Stather DN15 52 B1
Burton upon Stather DN15 52 B1
Burton upon Trent DE14 40 E3
Burton-in-Kendal LA6 55 J2
Burton's Green CM77 34 C6
Burtonwood WA5 48 E3
Burwardsley CH3 48 E7
Burwarton WV16 39 F7
Burwash TN19 13 K4
Burwash Common TN19 13 K4
Burwash Weald TN19 13 K4
Burwell, Cambs. CB5 33 J2
Burwell, Lincs. LN11 53 G5
Burwen LL68 46 C3
Burwick, Ork. KW17 107 D9
Burwick, Shet. ZE1 109 C8
Bury, Cambs. PE26 43 F7
Bury, Gt.Man. BL9 49 H1
Bury, Som. TA22 7 H3
Bury, W.Suss. RH20 12 D5
Bury End WR12 30 B5
Bury Green SG11 33 H6
Bury St. Edmunds IP33 34 C2
Buryas Bridge TR20 2 B6
Burythorpe YO17 58 D3

Busbridge

Busbridge GU7 22 C7
Busby, E.Renf. G76 74 D5
Busby, P. & K. PH1 82 B5
Buscot SN7 21 F2
Bush EX23 6 A5
Bush Bank HR4 28 E3
Bush Crathie AB35 89 K5
Bush Green IP21 45 G7
Bushbury WV10 40 B5
Bushby LE7 41 J5
Bushey WD23 22 E2
Bushey Heath WD23 22 E2
Bushley GL20 29 H5
Bushley Green GL20 29 H5
Bushton SN4 20 D4
Bushy Common NR19 44 D4
Busk CA10 61 H2
Buslingthorpe LN8 52 D4
Bussage GL6 20 B1
Busta ZE2 109 C6
Butcher's Common NR12 45 H3
Butcher's Cross TN20 13 J4
Butcher's Pasture CM6 33 K6
Butcombe BS40 19 J5
Bute PA20 73 J4
Bute Town NP22 18 E1
Buthill IV30 97 J5
Butleigh BA6 8 E1
Butleigh Wootton BA6 8 E1
Butler's Cross HP17 22 B1
Butler's Hill NG15 41 H1
Butlers Marston CV35 30 E4
Butlersbank SY4 38 E3
Butley IP12 35 H3
Butley Abbey IP12 35 H4
Butley Low Corner IP12 35 H4
Butley Mills IP12 35 H3
Butley Town SK10 49 J5
Butt Green CW5 49 F7
Butt Lane ST7 49 H7
Butterburn CA8 70 B6
Buttercrambe YO41 58 D4
Butterknowle DL13 62 C4
Butterleigh EX15 7 H5
Butterley DE5 51 G7
Buttermere, Cumb. CA13 60 C5
Buttermere, Wilts. SN8 21 G5
Butters Green ST7 49 H7
Buttershaw BD6 57 G6
Butterstone PH8 82 B3
Butterton, Staffs. ST13 50 C7
Butterton, Staffs. ST5 40 A1
Butterwick, Dur. TS21 62 E4
Butterwick, Lincs. PE22 43 G1
Butterwick, N.Yorks. YO17 59 F2
Butterwick, N.Yorks. YO17 58 D2
Buttington SY21 38 B5
Buttonbridge DY12 29 G1
Buttonoak DY12 29 G1
Buttons' Green IP30 34 D3
Butts EX6 7 G7
Butt's Green, Essex CM2 24 D1
Butt's Green, Hants. SO51 10 D2
Buttsash SO45 11 F4
Buxhall IP14 34 E3
Buxted TN22 13 H4
Buxton, Derbys. SK17 50 C5
Buxton, Norf. NR10 45 G3
Buxton Heath NR10 45 F3
Buxworth SK23 50 C4
Bwcle (Buckley) CH7 48 B6
Bwlch LD3 28 A6
Bwlch-clawdd SA44 17 G1
Bwlch-derwin LL51 36 D1
Bwlchgwyn LL11 48 B7
Bwlch-llan SA48 26 E3
Bwlchnewydd SA33 17 G2
Bwlchtocyn LL53 36 C3
Bwlch-y-cibau SY22 38 A4
Bwlch-y-ddar SY10 38 A3
Bwlchyfadfa SA44 26 D4
Bwlch-y-ffridd SY16 37 K6
Bwlch-y-groes SA35 17 F1
Bwlchyllyn LL54 46 D7
Bwlchymynydd SA4 17 J5
Bwlch-y-sarnau LD6 27 K1
Byers Green DL16 62 D3
Byfield NN11 31 G3
Byfleet KT14 22 D5
Byford HR4 28 C4
Bygrave SG7 33 F5
Byker NE6 71 H7
Byland Abbey YO61 58 B2
Bylane End PL14 4 C5
Bylchau LL16 47 H6
Byley CW10 49 G6
Bynea SA14 17 J5
Byrness NE19 70 C3
Bystock EX8 7 J7
Bythorn PE28 32 D1
Byton LD8 28 C2
Bywell NE43 71 F7
Byworth GU28 12 C4

C

Cabharstadh HS2 101 F5
Cabourne LN7 52 E2
Cabourne Parva LN7 52 E2
Cabrach, Arg. & B. PA60 72 C4
Cabrach, Moray AB54 90 B2
Cabus PR3 55 H5
Cackle Street, E.Suss. TN31 14 D6
Cackle Street, E.Suss. TN22 13 H4
Cacrabank TD7 69 J2
Cadboll IV20 97 F4
Cadbury EX5 7 H5
Cadbury Barton EX18 6 E4

Cadbury Heath BS30 19 K4
Cadder G64 74 E3
Cadderlie PA35 80 B4
Caddington LU1 32 D7
Caddleton PA34 79 J6
Cade Street TN21 13 K4
Cadeby, Leics. CV13 41 G5
Cadeby, S.Yorks. DN5 51 H2
Cadeleigh EX16 7 H5
Cader LL16 47 J6
Cadgwith TR12 2 E7
Cadham KY7 82 D7
Cadishead M44 49 G3
Cadle SA5 17 K5
Cadley, Lancs. PR2 55 J6
Cadley, Wilts. SN8 21 F5
Cadmore End HP14 22 A2
Cadnam SO40 10 D3
Cadney DN20 52 D2
Cadole CH7 48 B6
Cadover Bridge PL7 5 F4
Cadoxton CF63 18 E5
Cadoxton-Juxta-Neath SA10 18 A2
Cadwell SG5 32 E5
Cadwst LL21 37 K2
Cadzow ML3 75 F5
Cae Ddafydd LL48 37 F1
Caeathro LL55 46 D6
Caehopkin SA9 27 H7
Caen KW8 105 F7
Caenby LN8 52 D4
Caenby Corner LN8 52 C4
Caer Llan NP25 19 H1
Caerau, Bridgend CF34 18 B2
Caerau, Cardiff CF5 18 E4
Caerdeon LL42 37 F4
CAERDYDD (CARDIFF) CF 18 E4
Caerfarchell SA62 16 A2
Caerfyrddin (Carmarthen) SA31 17 H2
Caergeiliog LL65 46 B5
Caergwrle LL12 48 C7
Caergybi (Holyhead) LL65 46 A4
Caerhun LL32 47 F5
Caer-Lan SA9 27 H7
Caerleon NP18 19 G2
Caernarfon LL55 46 C6
Caerphilly CF83 18 E3
Caersws SY17 37 K6
Caerwedros SA44 26 C3
Caerwent NP26 19 H2
Caerwys CH7 47 K5
Caethle Farm LL36 37 F6
Caggan PH22 89 F3
Caggle Street NP7 28 C7
Caim, High. PH36 79 G1
Caim, I.o.A. LL58 46 E4
Caio SA19 17 K1
Cairinis (Carinish) HS6 92 D5
Cairisiadar HS2 100 C4
Cairminis HS5 93 F3
Cairnargat AB54 90 C1
Cairnbaan PA31 73 G1
Cairnbeathie AB31 90 D4
Cairnbrogie AB51 91 G2
Cairnbulg AB43 99 J4
Cairncross, Angus DD9 90 D7
Cairncross, Sc.Bord. TD14 77 G4
Cairncurran PA13 74 B4
Cairndoon DG8 64 D7
Cairndow PA26 80 C6
Cairness AB43 99 J4
Cairney Lodge KY15 82 E6
Cairnhill, Aber. AB41 91 H2
Cairnhill, Aber. AB52 90 E1
Cairnie, Aber. AB32 91 G4
Cairnie, Aber. AB54 98 C6
Cairnorrie AB41 99 G6
Cairnryan DG9 64 A4
Cairnsmore DG8 64 E4
Caister-on-Sea NR30 45 K4
Caistor LN7 52 E2
Caistor St. Edmund NR14 45 G5
Caistron NE65 70 E3
Cake Street NR17 44 E6
Cakebole DY10 29 H1
Calanais (Callanish) HS2 100 E4
Calbost HS2 101 G6
Calbourne PO30 11 F6
Calceby LN13 53 G5
Calcoed CH8 47 K5
Calcot RG31 21 K4
Calcott, Kent CT3 25 H5
Calcott, Shrop. SY3 38 D4
Calcotts Green GL2 29 G7
Calcutt SN6 20 E2
Caldarvan G83 74 C2
Caldback ZE2 108 F2
Caldbeck CA7 60 E3
Caldbergh DL8 57 F1
Caldecote, Cambs. CB3 33 G3
Caldecote, Cambs. PE7 42 E7
Caldecote, Herts. SG7 33 F5
Caldecote, Northants. NN12 31 H3
Caldecote, Warks. CV10 41 F6
Caldecott, Northants. NN9 32 C2
Caldecott, Oxon. OX14 21 H2
Caldecott, Rut. LE16 42 B6
Calder Bridge CA20 60 B6
Calder Grove WF4 51 F1
Calder Mains KW12 105 F3
Calder Vale PR3 55 J5
Calderbank ML6 75 F4

Calderbrook OL15 49 J1
Caldercruix ML6 75 G4
Calderglen G72 74 E5
Caldermill ML10 74 E6
Caldey Island SA70 16 E5
Caldhame DD8 83 F3
Caldicot NP26 19 H3
Caldwell, Derbys. DE12 40 E4
Caldwell, E.Renf. G78 74 C5
Caldwell, N.Yorks. DL11 62 C5
Caldy CH48 48 B4
Calebreck CA7 60 E3
Caledrhydiau SA48 26 D3
Calford Green CB9 33 K4
Calfsound KW17 106 E4
Calgary PA75 78 E2
Califer IV36 97 H6
California, Falk. FK1 75 H3
California, Norf. NR29 45 K4
California, Suff. IP4 35 G4
Calke DE73 41 F3
Callakille IV54 94 C6
Callaly NE66 71 F3
Callander FK17 81 H7
Callanish (Calanais) HS2 100 E4
Callaughton TF13 39 F6
Callerton Lane End NE5 71 G7
Calligarry IV45 86 C4
Callington PA28 66 B1
Callingwood DE13 40 D3
Callistermach DG11 69 H5
Callow HR2 28 D5
Callow End WR2 29 H4
Callow Hill, Wilts. SN15 20 D3
Callow Hill, Worcs. DY14 29 G1
Callow Hill, Worcs. B97 30 B2
Callows Grave WR15 28 E2
Calmore SO40 10 E3
Calmsden GL7 20 D1
Calne SN11 20 C4
Calow S44 51 G5
Calrossie IV19 96 E4
Calshot SO45 11 F4
Calstock PL18 4 E4
Calstone Wellington SN11 20 D5
Calthorpe NR11 45 F2
Calthwaite CA11 61 F2
Calton, N.Yorks. BD23 56 E4
Calton, Staffs. ST10 50 D7
Calveley CW6 48 E7
Calver S32 50 E5
Calver Hill HR4 28 C4
Calverhall SY13 39 F2
Calverleigh EX16 7 H4
Calverley LS28 57 H6
Calvert MK18 31 H6
Calverton, M.K. MK19 31 J5
Calverton, Notts. NG14 41 J1
Calvine PH18 81 J1
Calvo CA7 60 C1
Cam GL11 20 A2
Camasnacroise PH33 79 K2
Camastianavaig IV51 86 B1
Camasunary IV49 86 B3
Camault Muir IV4 96 C7
Camb ZE2 108 E3
Camber TN31 14 E6
Camberley GU15 22 B5
Camberwell SE15 23 G4
Camblesforth YO8 58 C7
Cambo NE61 71 F5
Cambois NE24 71 J5
Camborne TR14 2 D5
CAMBRIDGE, Cambs. CB 33 H3
Cambridge, Glos. GL2 20 A1
Cambridge Airport CB5 33 H3
Cambus FK10 75 G1
Cambus o'May AB34 90 C5
Cambusbarron FK7 75 F1
Cambuskenneth FK9 75 G1
Cambuslang G72 74 E4
Cambusnethan ML2 75 G5
Camden Town NW1 23 F3
Camel Hill BA22 8 E2
Cameley BS39 19 K6
Camelford PL32 4 B2
Camelon FK1 75 G2
Camelsdale GU27 12 B3
Camer DA13 24 C5
Cameron House G83 74 B2
Camerory PH26 89 H1
Camer's Green WR13 29 G5
Camerton, B. & N.E.Som. BA2 19 K6
Camerton, Cumb. CA14 60 B3
Camerton, E.Riding HU12 59 J7
Camghouran PH17 81 G2
Camis Eskan G84 74 B2
Cammachmore AB39 91 H5
Cammeringham LN1 52 C4
Camore IV25 96 E2
Camp Hill, Pembs. SA67 16 E3
Camp Hill, Warks. CV10 41 F6
Campbeltown PA28 66 B1
Campbeltown (Machrihanish) Airport PA28 66 A1
Camperdown NE12 71 H6
Campmuir PH13 82 D4
Camps EH27 75 K4
Camps End CB1 33 K4
Camps Heath NR32 45 K6
Campsall DN6 51 H1
Campsea Ashe IP13 35 H3
Campton SG17 32 E5
Camptown TD8 70 B2
Camquhart PA22 73 H2
Camrose SA62 16 C2
Camserney PH15 81 K3

Camstraddan House G83 74 B1
Camus Croise IV43 86 C3
Camus-luinie IV40 87 F2
Camusnagaul, High. PH33 87 G7
Camusnagaul, High. IV23 95 G3
Camusrory PH41 86 E5
Camusteel IV54 94 D7
Camusterrach IV54 94 D7
Camusurich FK21 81 H4
Camusvrachan PH15 81 H3
Canada SO51 10 D3
Canaston Bridge SA67 16 D3
Candacraig AB35 90 B5
Candlesby PE23 53 H6
Candy Mill ML12 75 J6
Cane End RG4 21 K4
Canewdon SS4 24 E2
Canfield End CM6 33 J6
Canford Bottom BH21 10 B4
Canford Cliffs BH13 10 B6
Canford Magna BH21 10 B5
Canham's Green IP14 34 E2
Canisbay KW1 105 J1
Canley CV4 30 E1
Cann SP7 9 H2
Cann Common SP7 9 H2
Canna PH44 85 H4
Cannard's Grave BA4 19 K7
Cannich IV4 87 K1
Canning Town E16 23 H3
Cannington TA5 8 B1
Cannock WS11 40 B5
Cannock Wood WS15 40 C4
Cannop GL16 29 F7
Canon Bridge HR2 28 D4
Canon Frome HR8 29 F4
Canon Pyon HR4 28 D4
Canonbie DG14 69 J6
Canons Ashby NN11 31 G3
Canon's Town TR27 2 C5
Canterbury, Aber. AB45 98 D5
CANTERBURY, Kent CT 15 G2
Cantley, Norf. NR13 45 H5
Cantley, S.Yorks. DN3 51 J2
Cantlop SY5 38 E5
Canton CF11 18 E4
Cantray IV2 96 E7
Cantraydoune IV12 96 E7
Cantraywood IV2 96 E7
Cantsfield LA6 56 B2
Canvey Island SS8 24 D3
Canwell Hall B75 40 D5
Canwick LN4 52 C6
Canworthy Water PL15 4 C1
Caol PH33 87 H7
Caolas, Arg. & B. PA77 78 B3
Caolas, W.Isles HS9 84 B5
Caolas Scalpaigh (Kyles Scalpay) HS3 93 H2
Caolasnacon PH50 80 C1
Capel, Kent TN12 23 K7
Capel, Surr. RH5 22 E7
Capel Bangor SY23 37 F7
Capel Betws Lleucu SY25 27 F3
Capel Carmel LL53 36 A3
Capel Celyn LL23 37 H1
Capel Coch LL77 46 C4
Capel Curig LL24 47 F7
Capel Cynon SA44 26 C4
Capel Dewi, Carmar. SA32 17 H2
Capel Dewi, Cere. SY23 37 F7
Capel Dewi, Cere. SY23 26 D4
Capel Garmon LL26 47 G7
Capel Gwyn, Carmar. SA32 17 H2
Capel Gwyn, I.o.A. LL65 46 B5
Capel Gwynfe SA19 27 G6
Capel Hendre SA18 17 J3
Capel Isaac SA19 17 J2
Capel Iwan SA38 17 F1
Capel le Ferne CT18 15 H4
Capel Llanilltern CF5 18 D3
Capel Mawr LL62 46 C5
Capel Parc LL71 46 C4
Capel St. Andrew IP12 35 H4
Capel St. Mary IP9 34 E5
Capel St. Silin SA48 26 E3
Capel Seion SY23 27 F1
Capel Tygwydd SA38 26 B4
Capeluchaf LL54 36 D1
Capelulo LL34 47 F5
Capel-y-ffin NP7 28 B5
Capel-y-graig LL57 46 D6
Capenhurst CH1 48 C5
Capernwray LA6 55 J2
Capheaton NE19 71 F5
Caplaw G78 74 C5
Capon's Green IP13 35 G2
Cappercleuch TD7 69 H1
Capplegill DG10 69 G3
Capstone ME7 24 D5
Capton, Devon TQ6 5 J5
Capton, Som. TA4 7 J2
Caputh PH1 82 B3
Car Colston NG13 42 A1
Caradon Town PL14 4 C3
Carbellow KA18 68 B1
Carberth G63 74 D3
Carbis Bay TR26 2 C5
Carbost, High. IV51 93 K7
Carbost, High. IV47 85 J1
Carbrain FK4 75 F3
Carbrooke IP25 44 D5
Carburton S80 51 J5
Carcary DD9 83 H2
Carco DG4 68 C2
Carcroft DN6 51 H1
Cardenden KY5 76 A1
Cardeston SY5 38 C4

Cardew CA5 60 E2
CARDIFF (CAERDYDD) CF 18 E4
Cardiff International Airport CF62 18 D5
Cardigan (Aberteifi) SA43 26 A4
Cardinal's Green CB1 33 K4
Cardington, Beds. MK44 32 D4
Cardington, Shrop. SY6 38 E6
Cardinham PL30 4 B4
Cardno AB43 99 H4
Cardonald G52 74 D4
Cardoness EH45 65 F5
Cardow AB38 97 J7
Cardrona EH45 76 A7
Cardross G82 74 B3
Cardurnock CA7 60 C1
Careby PE9 42 D4
Careston DD9 83 G2
Carew SA70 16 D4
Carew Cheriton SA70 16 D4
Carew Newton SA68 16 D4
Carey HR2 28 E5
Carfin ML1 75 F5
Carfrae EH41 76 D4
Carfraemill TD2 76 D5
Cargate Green NR13 45 H4
Cargen DG2 65 K3
Cargenbridge DG2 65 K3
Cargill PH2 82 C4
Cargo CA6 60 E1
Cargreen PL12 4 E4
Carham TD12 77 F7
Carhampton TA24 7 J1
Carharrack TR16 2 E4
Carie, Arg. & B. PH7 81 H2
Carie, P. & K. PH15 81 H4
Carines TR8 2 E3
Carinish (Cairinis) HS6 92 D5
Carisbrooke PO30 11 F6
Cark LA11 55 G2
Carkeel PL12 4 E4
Carlabhagh (Carloway) HS2 100 E3
Carland Cross TR8 3 F3
Carlatton CA8 61 G1
Carlby PE9 42 D4
Carlecotes S36 50 D2
Carleen TR13 2 D6
Carlenrig TR8 69 K2
Carleton, Cumb. CA1 60 F1
Carleton, Cumb. CA11 61 G4
Carleton, Lancs. FY6 55 G5
Carleton, N.Yorks. BD23 56 E5
Carleton, W.Yorks. WF8 57 K7
Carleton Fishery KA26 67 F5
Carleton Forehoe NR9 44 E5
Carleton Rode NR16 45 F6
Carleton St. Peter NR14 45 H5
Carlin How TS13 63 J5
CARLISLE CA 60 F1
Carloggas TR8 3 F2
Carlops EH26 75 K5
Carloway (Carlabhagh) HS2 100 E3
Carlton, Beds. MK43 32 C3
Carlton, Cambs. CB8 33 K3
Carlton, Leics. CV13 41 F5
Carlton, N.Yorks. DN14 58 C7
Carlton, N.Yorks. DL8 57 F1
Carlton, N.Yorks. YO62 58 C1
Carlton, Notts. NG4 41 J1
Carlton, S.Yorks. S71 51 F1
Carlton, Stock. TS21 62 E4
Carlton, Suff. IP17 35 H2
Carlton, W.Yorks. WF3 57 J7
Carlton Colville NR33 45 K6
Carlton Curlieu LE8 41 J6
Carlton Green CB8 33 K3
Carlton Husthwaite YO7 57 K2
Carlton in Lindrick S81 51 H4
Carlton Miniott YO7 57 J1
Carlton Scroop NG32 42 C1
Carlton-in-Cleveland TS9 63 G6
Carlton-le-Moorland LN5 52 C7
Carlton-on-Trent NG23 52 B6
Carluke ML8 75 G5
Carlyon Bay PL25 4 A5
Carmacoup ML11 68 C1
Carmarthen (Caerfyrddin) SA31 17 H2
Carmel, Carmar. SA14 17 J3
Carmel, Flints. CH8 47 K5
Carmel, Gwyn. LL54 46 C7
Carmel, I.o.A. LL71 46 B4
Carmichael ML12 75 H7
Carmont AB39 91 G6
Carmunnock G76 74 E5
Carmyle G32 74 E4
Carmyllie DD11 83 G3
Carn PA48 72 A5
Carn Brea Village TR15 2 D4
Carn Dearg IV21 94 D4
Carnaby YO16 59 H3
Carnach, High. IV40 87 G2
Carnach, High. IV23 95 G2
Carnach, W.Isles HS6 92 D5
Carnan HS8 92 D7
Carnassarie PA31 79 K7
Carnbee KY10 83 G7
Carnbo KY13 82 B7
Carndu IV40 86 E2
Carnduncan PA44 72 A4
Carnforth LA5 55 H2
Carnhedryn SA62 16 B2
Carnhell Green TR14 2 D5
Carnichal AB43 99 H5
Carnkie, Cornw. TR16 2 D5
Carnkie, Cornw. TR13 2 D5
Carnmore PA42 72 B6
Carno SY17 37 J6
Carnoch, High. IV4 87 K1
Carnoch, High. IV6 95 J6

176

Chelwood Common

Carnoch, *High.* **IV12** 97 F7
Carnock **KY12** 75 J2
Carnon Downs **TR3** 3 F4
Carnousie **AB53** 98 E5
Carnoustie **DD7** 83 G4
Carntyne **G32** 74 E4
Carnwath **ML11** 75 H6
Carnyorth **TR19** 2 A5
Carol Green **CV7** 30 D1
Carperby **DL8** 57 F1
Carr **S66** 51 H3
Carr Hill **DN10** 51 J3
Carr Houses **L38** 48 C2
Carr Shield **NE47** 61 K2
Carr Vale **S44** 51 G5
Carradale **PA28** 73 F7
Carradale East **PA28** 73 G7
Carragrich **HS3** 93 G2
Carrbridge **PH23** 89 G2
Carrefour Selous **JE3** 3 J7
Carreg-lefn **LL68** 46 B4
Carreg-wen **SA37** 26 B4
Carrhouse **DN9** 51 K2
Carrick **PA31** 73 H2
Carrick Castle **PA24** 73 K1
Carriden **EH51** 75 J2
Carrine **PA28** 66 A3
Carrington, *Gt.Man.* **M31** 49 G3
Carrington, *Lincs.* **PE22** 53 G7
Carrington, *Midloth.* **EH23** 76 B4
Carroch **DG7** 68 B4
Carrog, *Conwy* **LL24** 37 G1
Carrog, *Denb.* **LL21** 38 A1
Carroglen **PH6** 81 J5
Carrol **KW9** 97 F1
Carron, *Arg. & B.* **PA31** 73 H1
Carron, *Falk.* **FK2** 75 G2
Carron, *Moray* **AB38** 97 K7
Carron Bridge **FK6** 75 F2
Carronbridge **DG3** 68 D4
Carronshore **FK2** 75 G2
Carrot **DD8** 83 F3
Carrow Hill **NP26** 19 H2
Carrutherstown **DG1** 69 G6
Carruthmuir **PA10** 74 B4
Carrville **DH1** 62 E2
Carry **PA21** 73 H4
Carsaig **PA70** 79 G5
Carscreugh **DG8** 64 C4
Carse **PA29** 73 F4
Carse of Ardersier **IV2** 97 F6
Carsegowan **DG8** 64 E5
Carseriggan **DG8** 64 D4
Carsethorn **DG2** 65 K5
Carsgoe **KW12** 105 G2
Carshalton **SM5** 23 F5
Carshalton Beeches **SM5** 23 F5
Carsington **DE4** 50 E7
Carsluith **DG8** 64 E5
Carsphairn **DG7** 67 K4
Carstairs **ML11** 75 H6
Carstairs Junction **ML11** 75 H6
Carswell Marsh **SN7** 21 G2
Carter's Clay **SO51** 10 E2
Carterton **OX18** 21 F1
Carterway Heads **DH8** 62 B1
Carthew **PL26** 4 A5
Carthorpe **DL8** 57 J1
Cartington **NE65** 71 F3
Cartland **ML11** 75 G6
Cartmel **LA11** 55 G2
Cartmel Fell **LA11** 55 H1
Cartworth **HD9** 50 D2
Carway **SA17** 17 H4
Cascob **LD8** 28 B2
Cas-gwent (Chepstow) **NP16** 19 J2
Cashel Farm **G63** 74 C1
Cashes Green **GL5** 20 B1
Cashlie **PH15** 81 F3
Cashmoor **DT11** 9 J3
Caskieberran **KY6** 82 D7
CASNEWYDD (NEWPORT) NP 19 G3
Cassencarie **DG8** 64 E5
Cassington **OX29** 31 F7
Cassop **DH6** 62 E3
Castell **LL32** 47 F6
Castell Gorfod **SA33** 17 F2
Castell Howell **SA44** 26 D4
Castell Newydd Emlyn (Newcastle Emlyn) **SA38** 26 C4
Castellau **CF38** 18 D3
Castell-Nedd (Neath) **SA11** 18 A2
Castell-y-bwch **NP44** 19 F2
Casterton **LA6** 56 B2
Castle Acre **PE32** 44 C4
Castle Ashby **NN7** 32 B3
Castle Bolton **DL8** 62 B7
Castle Bromwich **B36** 40 D7
Castle Bytham **NG33** 42 C4
Castle Caereinion **SY21** 38 A5
Castle Camps **CB1** 33 K4
Castle Carrock **CA8** 61 G1
Castle Cary **BA7** 9 F1
Castle Combe **SN14** 20 B4
Castle Donington **DE74** 41 G3
Castle Douglas **DG7** 65 H4
Castle Eaton **SN6** 20 E2
Castle Eden **TS27** 63 F3
Castle End **CV8** 30 D1
Castle Frome **HR8** 29 F4
Castle Gate **TR20** 2 B5
Castle Goring **BN13** 12 E6
Castle Green **GU24** 22 C5
Castle Gresley **DE11** 40 E4
Castle Heaton **TD12** 77 H6
Castle Hedingham **CO9** 34 B5
Castle Hill, *Kent* **TN12** 23 K7
Castle Hill, *Suff.* **IP1** 35 F4
Castle Kennedy **DG9** 64 B5
Castle Leod **IV14** 96 B6
Castle Levan **PA19** 74 A3
Castle Madoc **LD3** 27 K5
Castle Morris **SA62** 16 C1
Castle O'er **DG13** 69 H4
Castle Rising **PE31** 44 A3
Castle Stuart **IV2** 96 E7
Castlebay (Bàgh a' Chaisteil) **HS9** 84 B5
Castlebythe **SA62** 16 D2
Castlecary **G68** 75 F3
Castlecraig, *High.* **IV19** 97 F5
Castlecraig, *Sc.Bord.* **EH46** 75 K6
Castlefairn **DG3** 68 C5
Castleford **WF10** 57 K7
Castlemartin **SA71** 16 C5
Castlemilk, *D. & G.* **DG11** 69 G6
Castlemilk, *Glas.* **G45** 74 E5
Castlemorton **WR13** 29 G5
Castlerigg **CA12** 60 D4
Castleside **DH8** 62 B2
Castlesteads **CA8** 70 A7
Castlethorpe **MK19** 32 B4
Castleton, *Aber.* **AB45** 99 F5
Castleton, *Angus* **DD8** 82 E3
Castleton, *Arg. & B.* **PA31** 73 G2
Castleton, *Derbys.* **S33** 50 D4
Castleton, *Gt.Man.* **OL11** 49 H1
Castleton, *N.Yorks.* **YO21** 63 H6
Castleton, *Newport* **CF3** 19 F3
Castleton, *Sc.Bord.* **TD9** 70 A4
Castletown, *Dorset* **DT5** 9 F7
Castletown, *High.* **KW14** 105 G2
Castletown, *High.* **IV2** 96 E7
Castletown, *I.o.M.* **IM9** 54 B7
Castletown, *T. & W.* **SR5** 62 E1
Castleweary **TD9** 69 K3
Castlewigg **DG8** 64 E6
Castley **LS21** 57 H5
Caston **NR17** 44 D6
Castor **PE5** 42 E6
Castramont **DG7** 65 F4
Caswell **SA3** 17 J6
Cat and Fiddle Inn **SK11** 50 C5
Catacol **KA27** 73 H6
Catbrain **BS10** 19 J3
Catbrook **NP16** 19 J1
Catchall **TR19** 2 B6
Catcleugh **NE19** 70 C3
Catcliffe **S60** 51 G4
Catcott **TA7** 8 C1
Caterham **CR3** 23 G6
Catfield **NR29** 45 H3
Catfirth **ZE2** 109 D7
Catford **SE6** 23 G4
Catforth **PR4** 55 H6
Cathays **CF24** 18 E4
Cathcart **G44** 74 D4
Cathedine **LD3** 28 A6
Catherine-de-Barnes **B91** 40 D7
Catherington **PO8** 11 H3
Catherston Leweston **DT6** 8 C5
Catherton **DY14** 29 F1
Cathkin **G73** 74 E5
Catisfield **PO15** 11 G4
Catlodge **PH20** 88 D5
Catlowdy **CA6** 69 K6
Catmere End **CB11** 33 H5
Catmore **RG20** 21 H3
Caton, *Devon* **TQ13** 5 H3
Caton, *Lancs.* **LA2** 55 J3
Caton Green **LA2** 55 J3
Cator Court **TQ13** 5 G3
Catrine **KA5** 67 K1
Catsfield **TN33** 14 C6
Catsfield Stream **TN33** 14 C6
Catshaw **S36** 50 E2
Catshill **B61** 29 J1
Cattadale **PA44** 72 B4
Cattal **YO26** 57 K4
Cattawade **CO11** 34 E5
Catterall **PR3** 55 J5
Catterick **DL10** 62 D7
Catterick Bridge **DL10** 62 D7
Catterick Garrison **DL9** 62 C7
Catterlen **CA11** 61 F3
Catterline **AB39** 91 G7
Catterton **LS24** 58 B5
Catteshall **GU7** 22 C7
Catthorpe **LE17** 31 G1
Cattishall **IP31** 34 C2
Cattistock **DT2** 8 E4
Catton, *N.Yorks.* **YO7** 57 J2
Catton, *Norf.* **NR6** 45 G4
Catton, *Northumb.* **NE47** 61 K1
Catton Hall **DE12** 40 E4
Catwick **HU17** 59 H5
Catworth **PE28** 32 D1
Caudle Green **GL53** 29 J7
Caulcott, *Beds.* **MK43** 32 D4
Caulcott, *Oxon.* **OX25** 31 G6
Cauldcots **DD11** 83 H3
Cauldhame, *Stir.* **FK8** 74 E1
Cauldhame, *Stir.* **FK15** 81 K7
Cauldon **ST10** 40 C1
Caulkerbush **DG2** 65 K5
Caulside **DG14** 69 K5
Caundle Marsh **DT9** 9 F3
Caunsall **DY11** 40 A7
Caunton **NG23** 51 K6
Causeway End, *D. & G.* **DG8** 64 E4
Causeway End, *Essex* **CM6** 33 K7
Causeway End, *Lancs.* **L40** 48 D1
Causewayhead, *Cumb.* **CA7** 60 C1
Causewayhead, *Stir.* **FK9** 75 G1
Causey **DH9** 62 D1
Causey Park **NE61** 71 G4
Causeyend **AB23** 91 H3
Cautley **LA10** 61 H7
Cavendish **CO10** 34 C4
Cavendish Bridge **DE72** 41 G3
Cavenham **IP28** 34 B2
Cavens **DG2** 65 K5
Cavers **TD9** 70 A2
Caversfield **OX27** 31 G6
Caversham **RG4** 22 A4
Caverswall **ST11** 40 B1
Cawdor **IV12** 97 F6
Cawkeld **YO25** 59 F4
Cawkwell **LN11** 53 F4
Cawood **YO8** 58 B6
Cawsand **PL10** 4 E6
Cawston, *Norf.* **NR10** 45 F3
Cawston, *Warks.* **CV22** 31 F1
Cawthorn **YO18** 58 D1
Cawthorne **S75** 50 E2
Cawthorpe **PE10** 42 D3
Cawton **YO62** 58 C2
Caxton **CB3** 33 G3
Caxton Gibbet **CB3** 33 F2
Caynham **SY8** 28 E1
Caythorpe, *Lincs.* **NG32** 42 C1
Caythorpe, *Notts.* **NG14** 41 J1
Cayton **YO11** 59 G1
Ceallan **HS6** 92 D6
Ceann a' Bhàigh, *W.Isles* **HS6** 92 C5
Ceann a' Bhàigh, *W.Isles* **HS3** 93 F3
Ceann Loch Shiphoirt **HS2** 100 E6
Ceann Lochroag (Kinlochroag) **HS2** 100 D5
Ceannaridh **HS6** 92 D6
Cearsiadar **HS2** 101 F6
Ceathramh Meadhanach (Middlequarter) **HS6** 92 D4
Cedig **SY10** 37 J3
Cefn Berain **LL16** 47 H6
Cefn Bycharn (Newbridge) **NP11** 19 F2
Cefn Canol **SY10** 38 B2
Cefn Cantref **LD3** 27 K6
Cefn Coch **LL15** 47 K7
Cefn Cribwr **CF32** 18 B3
Cefn Cross **CF32** 18 B3
Cefn Einion **SY9** 38 B7
Cefn Hengoed **CF82** 18 E2
Cefn Llwyd **SY23** 37 F7
Cefn Rhigos **CF44** 18 C1
Cefn-brith **LL21** 47 H7
Cefn-caer-Ferch **LL53** 36 D1
Cefn-coch **SY10** 38 A3
Cefn-coed-y-cymmer **CF48** 18 D1
Cefn-ddwysarn **LL23** 37 J2
Cefndeuddwr **LL40** 37 G3
Cefneithin **SA14** 17 J3
Cefn-gorwydd **LD4** 27 J4
Cefn-gwyn **SY16** 38 A7
Cefn-mawr **LL14** 38 B1
Cefnpennar **CF45** 18 D1
Cefn-y-bedd **LL12** 48 C7
Cefn-y-pant **SA34** 16 E2
Cegidfa (Guilsfield) **SY21** 38 B4
Ceidio **LL71** 46 C4
Ceidio Fawr **LL53** 36 B2
Ceinewydd (New Quay) **SA45** 26 C2
Ceint **LL77** 46 C5
Cellan **SA48** 27 F4
Cellardyke **KY10** 83 G7
Cellarhead **ST9** 40 B1
Cemaes **LL67** 46 B3
Cemmaes **SY20** 37 H5
Cemmaes Road (Glantwymyn) **SY20** 37 H5
Cenarth **SA38** 26 B4
Cennin **LL51** 36 D1
Ceos (Keose) **HS2** 101 F5
Ceres **KY15** 83 F6
Cerist **SY17** 37 J7
Cerne Abbas **DT2** 9 F4
Cerney Wick **GL7** 20 D2
Cerrigceinwen **LL62** 46 C5
Cerrigydrudion **LL21** 37 J1
Cessford **TD5** 70 C1
Ceunant **LL55** 46 D6
Chaceley **GL19** 29 H5
Chacewater **TR4** 2 E4
Chackmore **MK18** 31 H5
Chacombe **OX17** 31 F4
Chad Valley **B15** 40 C7
Chadderton **OL9** 49 J2
Chadderton Fold **OL9** 49 H2
Chaddesden **DE21** 41 F2
Chaddesley Corbett **DY10** 29 H1
Chaddleworth **RG20** 21 H4
Chadlington **OX7** 30 E6
Chadshunt **CV35** 30 E3
Chadstone **NN7** 32 B3
Chadwell, *Leics.* **LE14** 42 A3
Chadwell, *Shrop.* **TF10** 39 G4
Chadwell St. Mary **RM16** 24 C4
Chadwick End **B93** 30 D1
Chaffcombe **TA20** 8 C3
Chafford Hundred **RM16** 24 C3
Chagford **TQ13** 7 F7
Chailey **BN8** 13 G5
Chainhurst **TN12** 14 C3
Chalbury **BH21** 10 B4
Chalbury Common **BH21** 10 B4
Chaldon **CR3** 23 G6
Chaldon Herring (East Chaldon) **DT2** 9 G6
Chale **PO38** 11 F7
Chale Green **PO38** 11 F6
Chalfont Common **SL9** 22 D2
Chalfont St. Giles **HP8** 22 C2
Chalfont St. Peter **SL9** 22 D2
Chalford, *Glos.* **GL6** 20 B1
Chalford, *Wilts.* **BA13** 20 B7
Chalgrove **OX44** 21 K2
Chalk **DA12** 24 C4
Chalk End **CM1** 33 K7
Challacombe **EX31** 6 E1
Challister **ZE2** 109 E6
Challoch **DG8** 64 D4
Challock **TN25** 15 F2
Chalmington **DT2** 8 E4
Chalton, *Beds.* **LU4** 32 D6
Chalton, *Hants.* **PO8** 11 J3
Chalvey **SL1** 22 C4
Chalvington **BN27** 13 J6
Champany **EH49** 75 J3
Chancery **SY23** 26 E1
Chandler's Cross **WD3** 22 D2
Chandler's Ford **SO53** 11 F2
Channel Islands **GY, JE** 3 G7
Channel's End **MK44** 32 E3
Channerwick **ZE2** 109 D10
Chantry, *Som.* **BA11** 20 A7
Chantry, *Suff.* **IP2** 35 F4
Chapel **KY2** 76 A1
Chapel Allerton, *Som.* **BS26** 19 H6
Chapel Allerton, *W.Yorks.* **LS7** 57 J6
Chapel Amble **PL27** 3 G1
Chapel Brampton **NN6** 31 J2
Chapel Chorlton **ST5** 40 A2
Chapel Cleeve **TA24** 7 J1
Chapel Cross **TN21** 13 K4
Chapel End **MK45** 32 D4
Chapel Green, *Warks.* **CV7** 40 E7
Chapel Green, *Warks.* **CV47** 31 F2
Chapel Haddlesey **YO8** 58 B7
Chapel Hill, *Aber.* **AB42** 91 J1
Chapel Hill, *Lincs.* **LN4** 53 F7
Chapel Hill, *Mon.* **NP16** 19 J1
Chapel Hill, *N.Yorks.* **LS22** 57 J5
Chapel Knapp **SN13** 20 B5
Chapel Lawn **SY7** 28 C1
Chapel Leigh **TA4** 7 K3
Chapel Milton **SK23** 50 C4
Chapel of Garioch **AB51** 91 F2
Chapel Rossan **DG9** 64 B6
Chapel Row, *Essex* **CM3** 24 D1
Chapel Row, *W.Berks.* **RG7** 21 J5
Chapel St. Leonards **PE24** 53 J5
Chapel Stile **LA22** 60 E6
Chapel Town **TR8** 3 F3
Chapelbank **PH3** 82 B6
Chapeldonan **KA26** 67 F3
Chapelend Way **CO9** 34 B5
Chapel-en-le-Frith **SK23** 50 C4
Chapelgate **PE12** 43 H3
Chapelhall **ML6** 75 F4
Chapelhill, *High.* **IV20** 97 F4
Chapelhill, *P. & K.* **PH2** 82 D5
Chapelhill, *P. & K.* **PH1** 82 B4
Chapelknowe **DG14** 69 J6
Chapel-le-Dale **LA6** 56 C2
Chapelthorpe **WF2** 51 F1
Chapelton, *Aber.* **AB39** 91 G6
Chapelton, *Angus* **DD11** 83 H3
Chapelton, *Devon* **EX37** 6 D3
Chapelton, *S.Lan.* **ML10** 74 E6
Chapeltown, *B'burn.* **BL7** 49 G1
Chapeltown, *Cumb.* **CA6** 69 K6
Chapeltown, *Moray* **AB37** 89 K2
Chapeltown, *S.Yorks.* **S35** 51 F3
Chapmans Well **PL15** 6 B6
Chapmanslade **BA13** 20 B7
Chapmore End **SG12** 33 G7
Chappel **CO6** 34 C6
Charaton **PL14** 4 D4
Chard **TA20** 8 C4
Chard Junction **TA20** 8 C4
Chardleigh Green **TA20** 8 C3
Chardstock **EX13** 8 C4
Charfield **GL12** 20 A2
Charing **TN27** 14 E3
Charing Cross **SP6** 10 C3
Charing Heath **TN27** 14 E3
Charingworth **GL55** 30 C5
Charlbury **OX7** 30 E7
Charlcombe **BA1** 20 A5
Charlecote **CV35** 30 D3
Charles **EX32** 6 E2
Charles Tye **IP14** 34 E3
Charlesfield **TD6** 70 A1
Charleshill **GU10** 22 B7
Charleston **DD8** 82 E3
Charlestown, *Aber.* **AB43** 99 J4
Charlestown, *Aberdeen* **AB12** 91 H4
Charlestown, *Cornw.* **PL25** 4 A5
Charlestown, *Derbys.* **SK13** 50 C3
Charlestown, *Dorset* **DT3** 9 F7
Charlestown, *Fife* **KY11** 75 J2
Charlestown, *Gt.Man.* **M7** 49 H2
Charlestown, *High.* **IV21** 94 E4
Charlestown, *High.* **IV1** 96 D7
Charlestown, *W.Yorks.* **BD17** 57 G6
Charlestown, *W.Yorks.* **HX7** 56 E7
Charlestown of Aberlour (Aberlour) **AB38** 97 K7
Charlesworth **SK13** 50 C3
Charleton **KY9** 83 F7
Charlinch **TA5** 8 B1
Charlotteville **GU1** 22 D7
Charlton, *Gt.Lon.* **SE7** 23 H4
Charlton, *Hants.* **SP10** 21 G7
Charlton, *Herts.* **SG5** 32 E6
Charlton, *Northants.* **OX17** 31 G5
Charlton, *Northumb.* **NE48** 70 D5
Charlton, *Oxon.* **OX12** 21 H3
Charlton, *Som.* **BA3** 19 K6
Charlton, *Som.* **BA4** 19 K7
Charlton, *Som.* **TA3** 8 B2
Charlton, *Tel. & W.* **TF6** 38 E4
Charlton, *W.Suss.* **PO18** 12 B5
Charlton, *Wilts.* **SP7** 9 J2
Charlton, *Wilts.* **SN16** 20 C3
Charlton, *Wilts.* **SN9** 20 E6
Charlton, *Worcs.* **WR10** 30 B4
Charlton Abbots **GL54** 30 B6
Charlton Adam **TA11** 8 E2
Charlton Horethorne **DT9** 9 F2
Charlton Kings **GL52** 29 J6
Charlton Mackrell **TA11** 8 E2
Charlton Marshall **DT11** 9 H4
Charlton Musgrove **BA9** 9 G2
Charlton on the Hill **DT11** 9 H4
Charlton-All-Saints **SP5** 10 C2
Charlton-on-Otmoor **OX5** 31 G7
Charltons **TS12** 63 H5
Charlwood **RH6** 23 F7
Charminster **DT2** 9 F5
Charmouth **DT6** 8 C5
Charndon **OX27** 31 H6
Charney Bassett **OX12** 21 G2
Charnock Richard **PR7** 48 E1
Charsfield **IP13** 35 G3
Chart Corner **ME17** 14 C3
Chart Sutton **ME17** 14 D3
Charter Alley **RG26** 21 J6
Charterhouse **BS40** 19 H6
Charterville Allotments **OX29** 21 G1
Chartham **CT4** 15 G2
Chartham Hatch **CT4** 15 G2
Chartridge **HP5** 22 C1
Charvil **RG10** 22 A4
Charwelton **NN11** 31 G3
Chase End Street **HR8** 29 G5
Chase Terrace **WS7** 40 C5
Chasetown **WS7** 40 C5
Chastleton **GL56** 30 D6
Chasty **EX22** 6 B5
Chatburn **BB7** 56 C5
Chatcull **ST21** 39 G2
Chatham **ME4** 24 D5
Chatham Green **CM3** 34 B7
Chathill **NE67** 71 G1
Chattenden **ME3** 24 D4
Chatteris **PE16** 43 G7
Chattisham **IP8** 34 E4
Chatto **TD5** 70 C2
Chatton **NE66** 71 F1
Chaul End **LU1** 32 D6
Chavey Down **SL5** 22 B5
Chawleigh **EX18** 7 F4
Chawley **OX2** 21 H1
Chawston **MK44** 32 E3
Chawton **GU34** 11 J1
Chazey Heath **RG4** 21 K4
Cheadle, *Gt.Man.* **SK8** 49 H4
Cheadle, *Staffs.* **ST10** 40 C1
Cheadle Heath **SK3** 49 H4
Cheadle Hulme **SK8** 49 H4
Cheam **SM3** 23 F5
Cheapside **SL5** 22 C5
Chearsley **HP18** 31 J7
Chebsey **ST21** 40 A3
Checkendon **RG8** 21 K3
Checkley, *Ches.* **CW5** 39 G1
Checkley, *Here.* **HR1** 28 E5
Checkley, *Staffs.* **ST10** 40 C2
Checkley Green **CW5** 39 G1
Chedburgh **IP29** 34 B3
Cheddar **BS27** 19 H6
Cheddington **LU7** 32 C7
Cheddleton **ST13** 49 J7
Cheddon Fitzpaine **TA2** 8 B2
Chedglow **SN16** 20 C2
Chedgrave **NR14** 45 H6
Chedington **DT8** 8 D4
Chediston **IP19** 35 H1
Chediston Green **IP19** 35 H1
Chedworth **GL54** 30 B7
Chedzoy **TA7** 8 C1
Cheeklaw **TD11** 77 F5
Cheesden **OL12** 49 H1
Cheeseman's Green **TN24** 15 F4
Cheetham Hill **M8** 49 H2
Cheglinch **EX34** 6 D1
Cheldon **EX18** 7 F4
Chelford **SK11** 49 H5
Chellaston **DE73** 41 F2
Chells **SG2** 33 F6
Chelmarsh **WV16** 39 G7
Chelmondiston **IP9** 35 G5
Chelmorton **SK17** 50 D6
CHELMSFORD CM 24 D1
Chelmsley Wood **B37** 40 D7
Chelsea **SW3** 23 F4
Chelsfield **BR6** 23 H5
Chelsham **CR6** 23 G6
Chelston Heath **TA21** 7 K3
Chelsworth **IP7** 34 D4
Cheltenham **GL50** 29 J6
Chelveston **NN9** 32 C2
Chelvey **BS48** 19 H5
Chelwood **BS39** 19 K5
Chelwood Common **RH17** 13 H4

Chelwood Gate **RH17**	13	H4
Chelworth **SN16**	20	C2
Cheney Longville **SY7**	38	D7
Chenies **WD3**	22	D2
Chepstow (Cas-gwent) **NP16**	19	J2
Cherhill **SN11**	20	D4
Cherington, *Glos.* **GL8**	20	C2
Cherington, *Warks.* **CV36**	30	D5
Cheriton, *Devon* **EX35**	7	F1
Cheriton, *Hants.* **SO24**	11	G2
Cheriton, *Kent* **CT19**	15	G4
Cheriton, *Pembs.* **SA71**	16	C5
Cheriton, *Swan.* **SA3**	17	H5
Cheriton Bishop **EX6**	7	F6
Cheriton Cross **EX6**	7	F6
Cheriton Fitzpaine **EX17**	7	G5
Cherrington **TF6**	39	F3
Cherry Burton **HU17**	59	F5
Cherry Green **CM6**	33	J6
Cherry Hinton **CB1**	33	H3
Cherry Tree **BB2**	56	B7
Cherry Willingham **LN3**	52	D5
Chertsey **KT16**	22	D5
Cheselbourne **DT2**	9	G5
Chesham **HP5**	22	C1
Chesham Bois **HP6**	22	C1
Cheshunt **EN8**	23	G1
Cheslyn Hay **WS6**	40	B5
Chessington **KT9**	22	E5
Chestall **WS15**	40	C4
CHESTER CH	48	D6
Chester Moor **DH2**	62	D2
Chesterblade **BA4**	19	K7
Chesterfield, *Derbys.* **S40**	51	F5
Chesterfield, *Staffs.* **WS14**	40	D5
Chester-le-Street **DH3**	62	D1
Chesters, *Sc.Bord.* **TD9**	70	B2
Chesters, *Sc.Bord.* **TD8**	70	B1
Chesterton, *Cambs.* **CB4**	33	H2
Chesterton, *Cambs.* **PE7**	42	E6
Chesterton, *Oxon.* **OX26**	31	G6
Chesterton, *Shrop.* **WV15**	39	G6
Chesterton, *Staffs.* **ST5**	40	A1
Chesterton, *Warks.* **CV33**	30	E3
Chesterton Green **CV33**	30	E3
Chestfield **CT5**	25	H5
Cheston **TQ10**	5	G5
Cheswardine **TF9**	39	G3
Cheswick **TD15**	77	J6
Cheswick Buildings **TD15**	77	J6
Cheswick Green **B90**	30	C1
Chetnole **DT9**	9	F4
Chettiscombe **EX16**	7	H4
Chettisham **CB6**	43	J7
Chettle **DT11**	9	J3
Chetton **WV16**	39	F6
Chetwode **MK18**	31	H6
Chetwynd Aston **TF10**	39	G4
Chetwynd Park **TF10**	39	G3
Cheveley **CB8**	33	K2
Chevening **TN14**	23	H6
Cheverell's Green **AL3**	32	D7
Chevington **IP29**	34	B3
Chevington Drift **NE61**	71	H4
Chevithorne **EX16**	7	H4
Chew Magna **BS40**	19	J5
Chew Moor **BL6**	49	F2
Chew Stoke **BS40**	19	J5
Chewton Keynsham **BS31**	19	K5
Chewton Mendip **BA3**	19	J6
Chichacott **EX20**	6	E6
Chicheley **MK16**	32	C4
Chichester **PO19**	12	B6
Chickerell **DT3**	9	F6
Chickering **IP21**	35	G1
Chicklade **SP3**	9	J1
Chickney **CM6**	33	J6
Chicksands **SG17**	32	E5
Chidden **PO7**	11	H3
Chidden Holt **PO7**	11	H3
Chiddingfold **GU8**	12	C3
Chiddingly **BN8**	13	J5
Chiddingstone **TN8**	23	H7
Chiddingstone Causeway **TN11**	23	J7
Chiddingstone Hoath **TN8**	23	H7
Chideock **DT6**	8	D5
Chidham **PO18**	11	J4
Chidswell **WF12**	57	H7
Chieveley **RG20**	21	H4
Chignall St. James **CM1**	24	C1
Chignall Smealy **CM1**	33	K7
Chigwell **IG7**	23	H2
Chigwell Row **IG7**	23	H2
Chilbolton **SO20**	21	G7
Chilcomb **SO21**	11	G2
Chilcombe **DT6**	8	E5
Chilcompton **BA3**	19	K6
Chilcote **DE12**	40	E4
Child Okeford **DT11**	9	H3
Childer Thornton **CH66**	48	C5
Childerditch **CM13**	24	C3
Childrey **OX12**	21	G3
Child's Ercall **TF9**	39	F3
Child's Hill **NW3**	23	F3
Childswickham **WR12**	30	B5
Childwall **L16**	48	D4
Childwick Green **AL3**	32	E7
Chilfrome **DT2**	8	E5
Chilgrove **PO18**	12	B5
Chilham **CT4**	15	F2
Chilhampton **SP2**	10	B1
Chilla **EX21**	6	C5
Chillaton **PL16**	6	C7
Chillenden **CT3**	15	H2
Chillerton **PO30**	11	F6
Chillesford **IP12**	35	H3
Chilley **TQ9**	5	H5
Chillingham **NE66**	71	F1
Chillington, *Devon* **TQ7**	5	H6
Chillington, *Som.* **TA19**	8	C3
Chilmark **SP3**	9	J1
Chilson, *Oxon.* **OX7**	30	E7
Chilson, *Som.* **TA20**	8	C4
Chilsworthy, *Cornw.* **PL18**	4	E3
Chilsworthy, *Devon* **EX22**	6	B5
Chilthorne Domer **BA22**	8	E3
Chilton, *Bucks.* **HP18**	31	H7
Chilton, *Devon* **EX17**	7	G5
Chilton, *Dur.* **DL17**	62	D4
Chilton, *Oxon.* **OX11**	21	H3
Chilton, *Suff.* **CO10**	34	C4
Chilton Candover **SO24**	11	G1
Chilton Cantelo **BA22**	8	E2
Chilton Foliat **RG17**	21	G4
Chilton Polden **TA7**	8	C1
Chilton Street **CO10**	34	B4
Chilton Trinity **TA5**	8	B1
Chilvers Coton **CV10**	41	F6
Chilwell **NG9**	41	H2
Chilworth, *Hants.* **SO16**	11	F3
Chilworth, *Surr.* **GU4**	22	D7
Chimney **OX18**	21	G1
Chimney Street **CO10**	34	B4
Chineham **RG24**	21	K6
Chingford **E4**	23	G2
Chinley **SK23**	50	C4
Chinley Head **SK23**	50	C4
Chinnor **OX39**	22	A1
Chipchase Castle **NE48**	70	D6
Chipley **TA21**	7	K3
Chipnall **TF9**	39	G2
Chippenham, *Cambs.* **CB7**	33	K2
Chippenham, *Wilts.* **SN15**	20	C4
Chipperfield **WD4**	22	D1
Chipping, *Herts.* **SG9**	33	G5
Chipping, *Lancs.* **PR3**	56	B5
Chipping Campden **GL55**	30	C5
Chipping Hill **CM8**	34	C7
Chipping Norton **OX7**	30	E6
Chipping Ongar **CM5**	23	J1
Chipping Sodbury **BS37**	20	A3
Chipping Warden **OX17**	31	F4
Chipstable **TA4**	7	J3
Chipstead, *Kent* **TN13**	23	H6
Chipstead, *Surr.* **CR5**	23	F6
Chirbury **SY15**	38	B6
Chirk (Y Waun) **LL14**	38	B2
Chirk Green **LL14**	38	B2
Chirnside **TD11**	77	G5
Chirnsidebridge **TD11**	77	G5
Chirton, *T. & W.* **NE29**	71	J7
Chirton, *Wilts.* **SN10**	20	D6
Chisbury **SN8**	21	F5
Chiscan **PA28**	66	A2
Chiselborough **TA14**	8	D3
Chiseldon **SN4**	20	E4
Chiserley **HX7**	57	F7
Chislehampton **OX44**	21	J2
Chislehurst **BR7**	23	H4
Chislet **CT3**	25	J5
Chiswell Green **AL2**	22	E1
Chiswick **W4**	23	F4
Chiswick End **SG8**	33	G4
Chisworth **SK13**	49	J3
Chithurst **GU31**	12	B4
Chittering **CB5**	33	H1
Chitterne **BA12**	20	C7
Chittlehamholt **EX37**	6	E3
Chittlehampton **EX37**	6	E3
Chittoe **SN15**	20	C5
Chivelstone **TQ7**	5	H7
Chivenor **EX31**	6	D2
Chobham **GU24**	22	C5
Choicelee **TD11**	77	F5
Cholderton **SP4**	21	F7
Cholesbury **HP23**	22	C1
Chollerford **NE46**	70	E6
Chollerton **NE46**	70	E6
Cholsey **OX10**	21	J3
Cholstrey **HR6**	28	D3
Cholwell, *B. & N.E.Som.* **BS39**	19	K6
Cholwell, *Devon* **PL19**	4	E3
Chop Gate **TS9**	63	G7
Choppington **NE62**	71	H5
Chopwell **NE17**	62	C1
Chorley, *Ches.* **CW5**	48	E7
Chorley, *Lancs.* **PR7**	48	E1
Chorley, *Shrop.* **WV16**	39	F7
Chorley, *Staffs.* **WS13**	40	C4
Chorleywood **WD3**	22	D2
Chorlton **CW2**	49	G7
Chorlton Lane **SY14**	38	D1
Chorlton-cum-Hardy **M21**	49	H3
Chowley **CH3**	48	D7
Chrishall **SG8**	33	H5
Chrishall Grange **SG8**	33	H4
Chrisswell **PA16**	74	A3
Christchurch, *Cambs.* **PE14**	43	H6
Christchurch, *Dorset* **BH23**	10	C5
Christchurch, *Glos.* **GL16**	28	E7
Christchurch, *Newport* **NP18**	19	G3
Christian Malford **SN15**	20	C4
Christleton **CH3**	48	D6
Christmas Common **OX49**	22	A2
Christon **BS26**	19	G6
Christon Bank **NE66**	71	H1
Christow **EX6**	7	G7
Christskirk **AB52**	90	E2
Chryston **G69**	74	E3
Chudleigh **TQ13**	5	J3
Chudleigh Knighton **TQ13**	5	J3
Chulmleigh **EX18**	6	E4
Chunal **SK13**	50	C7
Church **BB5**	56	C7
Church Aston **TF10**	39	G4
Church Brampton **NN6**	31	J2
Church Brough **CA17**	61	J5
Church Broughton **DE65**	40	E2
Church Charwelton **NN11**	31	G3
Church Common **IP17**	35	H3
Church Crookham **GU52**	22	B6
Church Eaton **ST20**	40	A4
Church End, *Beds.* **SG15**	32	E5
Church End, *Beds.* **LU6**	32	C6
Church End, *Beds.* **SG19**	32	E4
Church End, *Beds.* **MK43**	32	C5
Church End, *Beds.* **MK17**	32	C5
Church End, *Cambs.* **PE13**	43	G5
Church End, *Cambs.* **CB4**	33	G1
Church End, *Cambs.* **PE28**	43	F7
Church End, *E.Riding* **YO25**	59	G4
Church End, *Essex* **CB10**	33	J4
Church End, *Essex* **CM7**	34	B6
Church End, *Glos.* **GL20**	29	H5
Church End, *Hants.* **RG27**	21	K6
Church End, *Herts.* **AL3**	32	E7
Church End, *Herts.* **SG11**	33	H6
Church End, *Lincs.* **PE11**	43	F2
Church End, *Lincs.* **LN11**	53	H3
Church End, *Warks.* **CV10**	40	E6
Church End, *Wilts.* **SN15**	20	D4
Church Enstone **OX7**	30	E6
Church Fenton **LS24**	58	B6
Church Green **EX24**	7	K6
Church Gresley **DE11**	40	E4
Church Hanborough **OX29**	31	F7
Church Hill, *Ches.* **CW7**	49	F6
Church Hill, *Derbys.* **S45**	51	G6
Church Houses **YO62**	63	H7
Church Knowle **BH20**	9	J6
Church Laneham **DN22**	52	B5
Church Langley **CM17**	23	H1
Church Langton **LE16**	42	A6
Church Lawford **CV23**	31	F1
Church Lawton **ST7**	49	H7
Church Leigh **ST10**	40	C2
Church Lench **WR11**	30	B3
Church Mayfield **DE6**	40	D1
Church Minshull **CW5**	49	F6
Church Norton **PO20**	12	B7
Church Preen **SY6**	38	E6
Church Pulverbatch **SY5**	38	D5
Church Stoke **SY15**	38	B6
Church Stowe **NN7**	31	H3
Church Street, *Essex* **CO10**	34	B4
Church Street, *Kent* **ME3**	24	D4
Church Stretton **SY6**	38	D6
Church Town, *Leics.* **LE67**	41	F4
Church Town, *Surr.* **RH9**	23	G6
Church Village **CF38**	18	D3
Church Warsop **NG20**	51	H6
Church Westcote **OX7**	30	D6
Church Wilne **DE72**	41	G2
Churcham **GL2**	29	G7
Churchdown **GL3**	29	H7
Churchend, *Essex* **SS3**	25	G2
Churchend, *Essex* **CM6**	33	K6
Churchend, *S.Glos.* **GL12**	20	A2
Churchfield **B71**	40	C6
Churchgate **EN7**	23	G1
Churchgate Street **CM17**	33	H7
Churchill, *Devon* **EX31**	6	D1
Churchill, *Devon* **EX13**	8	B4
Churchill, *N.Som.* **BS25**	19	H6
Churchill, *Oxon.* **OX7**	30	D6
Churchill, *Worcs.* **WR7**	29	J3
Churchill, *Worcs.* **DY10**	29	H1
Churchingford **TA3**	8	B3
Churchover **CV23**	41	H7
Churchstanton **TA3**	7	K4
Churchtown **TQ7**	5	H6
Churchtown, *Devon* **EX31**	6	E1
Churchtown, *I.o.M.* **IM7**	54	D4
Churchtown, *Lancs.* **PR3**	55	H5
Churchtown, *Mersey.* **PR9**	48	C1
Churnsike Lodge **NE48**	70	B6
Churston Ferrers **TQ5**	5	K5
Churt **GU10**	12	B3
Churton **CH3**	48	D7
Churwell **LS27**	57	H7
Chute Cadley **SP11**	21	G6
Chute Standen **SP11**	21	G6
Chwilog **LL53**	36	D2
Chwitffordd (Whitford) **CH8**	47	K5
Chyandour **TR18**	2	B5
Chysauster **TR20**	2	B5
Cilan Uchaf **LL53**	36	B3
Cilcain **CH7**	47	K6
Cilcennin **SA48**	26	E2
Cilcewydd **SY21**	38	B5
Cilfrew **SA11**	18	A1
Cilfynydd **CF37**	18	D2
Cilgerran **SA43**	26	A4
Cilgwyn, *Carmar.* **SA20**	27	G5
Cilgwyn, *Pembs.* **SA42**	16	D1
Ciliau Aeron **SA48**	26	E3
Cille Bhrighde **HS8**	84	C3
Cille Pheadair **HS8**	84	C3
Cilmaengwyn **SA8**	18	A1
Cilmery **LD2**	27	K3
Cilrhedyn **SA35**	17	F1
Cilrhedyn Bridge **SA65**	16	D1
Cilsan **SA19**	17	J2
Ciltalgarth **LL23**	37	H1
Cilwendeg **SA37**	17	F1
Cilybebyll **SA8**	18	A1
Cilycwm **SA20**	27	G4
Cimla **SA11**	18	A2
Cinderford **GL14**	29	F7
Cippenham **SL1**	22	C3
Cippyn **SA43**	26	A4
Cirbhig **HS2**	100	D3
Cirencester **GL7**	20	D1
City, *Gt.Lon.* **EC3M**	23	G3
City, *V. of Glam.* **CF71**	18	C4
City Airport **E16**	23	H3
City Dulas **LL70**	46	C4
Clabhach **PA78**	78	C2
Clachaig **PA23**	73	K2
Clachan, *Arg. & B.* **PA26**	80	C6
Clachan, *Arg. & B.* **PA34**	79	K3
Clachan, *Arg. & B.* **PA29**	73	F5
Clachan, *High.* **IV40**	86	B1
Clachan, *W.Isles* **HS8**	92	C7
Clachan Mòr **PA77**	78	A3
Clachan of Campsie **G66**	74	E3
Clachan of Glendaruel **PA22**	73	H2
Clachan Strachur (Strachur) **PA27**	80	B7
Clachan-a-Luib **HS6**	92	D5
Clachandhu **PA68**	79	F4
Clachaneasy **DG8**	64	D3
Clachanmore **DG9**	64	A6
Clachan-Seil **PA34**	79	J6
Clachanturn **AB35**	89	K5
Clachbreck **PA31**	73	F3
Clachnabrain **DD8**	82	E1
Clachnaharry **IV3**	96	D7
Clachtoll **IV27**	102	C6
Clackmannan **FK10**	75	H1
Clackmarras **IV30**	97	K6
Clacton-on-Sea **CO15**	35	F7
Cladach a Bhale Shear **HS6**	92	D5
Cladach a' Chaolais **HS6**	92	C5
Cladach Chircebost **HS6**	92	C5
Cladach Chnoc a Lin **HS6**	92	C5
Cladich **PA33**	80	B5
Cladswell **B49**	30	B3
Claggan, *High.* **PH33**	87	H7
Claggan, *High.* **PA34**	79	J3
Claigan **IV55**	93	H6
Claines **WR3**	29	H3
Clandown **BA3**	19	K6
Clanfield, *Hants.* **PO8**	11	J3
Clanfield, *Oxon.* **OX18**	21	F1
Clannaborough Barton **EX17**	7	F5
Clanville **SP11**	21	G7
Claonaig **PA29**	73	G5
Claonairigh **PA32**	80	B7
Claonel **IV27**	96	C1
Clapgate **SG11**	33	H6
Clapham, *Beds.* **MK41**	32	D3
Clapham, *Devon* **EX6**	7	G7
Clapham, *Gt.Lon.* **SW4**	23	F4
Clapham, *N.Yorks.* **LA2**	56	C3
Clapham, *W.Suss.* **BN13**	12	D6
Clapham Green **MK41**	32	D3
Clapham Hill **CT5**	25	H5
Clappers **TD15**	77	H5
Clappersgate **LA22**	60	E6
Clapton, *Som.* **TA18**	8	D4
Clapton, *Som.* **BA3**	19	K6
Clapton-in-Gordano **BS20**	19	H4
Clapton-on-the-Hill **GL54**	30	C7
Clapworthy **EX36**	6	E3
Clara Vale **NE40**	71	G7
Clarach **SY23**	37	F7
Clarbeston **SA63**	16	D2
Clarbeston Road **SA63**	16	D2
Clarborough **DN22**	51	K4
Clardon **KW14**	105	G2
Clare **CO10**	34	B4
Clarebrand **DG7**	65	H4
Clarencefield **DG1**	69	F7
Clarilaw **TD9**	70	A2
Clark's Green **RH5**	12	E3
Clarkston **G76**	74	D5
Clashban **IV24**	96	D2
Clashcoig **IV24**	96	D2
Clashdorran **IV4**	96	C7
Clashgour **PA36**	80	D3
Clashindarroch **AB54**	90	C1
Clashmore, *High.* **IV25**	96	E3
Clashmore, *High.* **IV27**	102	C5
Clashnessie **IV27**	102	C5
Clashnoir **AB37**	89	K2
Clatford **SN8**	20	E5
Clathy **PH7**	82	A5
Clatt **AB54**	90	D2
Clatter **SY17**	37	J6
Clattercote **OX17**	31	F4
Clatterford **PO30**	11	F6
Clatterford End **CM5**	23	J1
Clatterin Brig **AB30**	90	E7
Clattershaws **DG7**	65	F3
Clatworthy **TA4**	7	J2
Claughton, *Lancs.* **LA2**	55	J3
Claughton, *Lancs.* **PR3**	55	J5
Clavelshay **TA6**	8	B1
Claverdon **CV35**	30	C2
Claverham **BS49**	19	H5
Clavering **CB11**	33	H5
Claverley **WV5**	39	G6
Claverton **BA2**	20	A5
Claverton Down **BA2**	20	A5
Clawdd-côch **CF71**	18	D4
Clawdd-newydd **LL15**	47	J7
Clawfin **KA6**	67	K3
Clawthorpe **LA6**	55	J2
Clawton **EX22**	6	B6
Claxby **LN8**	52	E3
Claxby Pluckacre **LN9**	53	G6
Claxby St. Andrew **LN13**	53	H5
Claxton, *N.Yorks.* **YO60**	58	C3
Claxton, *Norf.* **NR14**	45	H5
Claxton Grange **TS22**	63	F4
Clay Common **NR34**	45	J7
Clay Coton **NN6**	31	G1
Clay Cross **S45**	51	F6
Clay End **SG2**	33	G6
Clay Hill **BS16**	19	K4
Clay of Allan **IV20**	97	F4
Claybrooke Magna **LE17**	41	G7
Claybrooke Parva **LE17**	41	G7
Claydene **TN8**	23	H7
Claydon, *Oxon.* **OX17**	31	F3
Claydon, *Suff.* **IP6**	35	F4
Claygate, *Kent* **TN12**	14	C3
Claygate, *Surr.* **KT10**	22	E5
Claygate Cross **TN15**	23	K6
Clayhanger, *Devon* **EX16**	7	J3
Clayhanger, *W.Mid.* **WS8**	40	C5
Clayhidon **EX15**	7	K4
Clayhill, *E.Suss.* **TN31**	14	D5
Clayhill, *Hants.* **SO43**	10	E4
Clayhithe **CB5**	33	J2
Clayock **KW12**	105	G3
Claypit Hill **CB3**	33	G3
Claypits **GL2**	20	A1
Claypole **NG23**	42	B1
Claythorpe **LN13**	53	H5
Clayton, *S.Yorks.* **DN5**	51	G2
Clayton, *Staffs.* **ST5**	40	A1
Clayton, *W.Suss.* **BN6**	13	F5
Clayton, *W.Yorks.* **BD14**	57	G6
Clayton Green **PR6**	55	J7
Clayton West **HD8**	50	E1
Clayton-le-Moors **BB5**	56	C6
Clayton-le-Woods **PR25**	55	J7
Clayworth **DN22**	51	K4
Cleadale **PH42**	85	K6
Cleadon **SR6**	71	J7
Clearbrook **PL20**	5	F4
Clearwell **GL16**	19	J1
Cleasby **DL2**	62	D5
Cleat, *Ork.* **KW17**	107	D9
Cleat, *W.Isles* **HS9**	84	B4
Cleatlam **DL2**	62	C4
Cleatop **BD24**	56	D3
Cleator **CA23**	60	B5
Cleator Moor **CA25**	60	B5
Cleckheaton **BD19**	57	G7
Clee St. Margaret **SY7**	38	E7
Cleedownton **SY8**	38	E7
Cleehill **SY8**	28	E1
Cleestanton **SY8**	28	E1
Cleethorpes **DN35**	53	G2
Cleeton St. Mary **DY14**	29	F1
Cleeve, *N.Som.* **BS49**	19	H5
Cleeve, *Oxon.* **RG8**	21	K3
Cleeve Hill **GL52**	29	J6
Cleeve Prior **WR11**	30	B4
Cleghorn **ML11**	75	G6
Clehonger **HR2**	28	D5
Cleigh **PA34**	79	K5
Cleish **KY13**	75	J1
Cleland **ML1**	75	F5
Clement's End **LU6**	32	D7
Clench Common **SN8**	20	E5
Clenchwarton **PE34**	43	J3
Clennell **NE65**	70	E3
Clent **DY9**	29	J1
Cleobury Mortimer **DY14**	29	F1
Cleobury North **WV16**	39	F7
Clephanton **IV2**	97	F6
Clerklands **TD6**	70	A1
Clermiston **EH4**	75	K3
Clestrain **KW17**	107	C7
Cleuch Head **TD9**	70	A2
Cleughbrae **DG1**	69	F6
Clevancy **SN11**	20	D4
Clevedon **BS21**	19	H4
Cleveland Tontine Inn **DL6**	63	F7
Cleveley **OX7**	30	E6
Cleveleys **FY5**	55	G5
Clevelode **WR13**	29	H4
Cleverton **SN15**	20	C3
Clewer **BS28**	19	H6
Clewer Green **SL4**	22	C4
Clewer Village **SL4**	22	C4
Cley next the Sea **NR25**	44	E1
Cliburn **CA10**	61	G4
Cliddesden **RG25**	21	K7
Cliff, *Carmar.* **SA17**	17	G4
Cliff, *High.* **PH36**	79	H1
Cliff End **TN35**	14	D6
Cliff Grange **TF9**	39	F2
Cliffe, *Lancs.* **BB6**	56	C6
Cliffe, *Med.* **ME3**	24	D4
Cliffe, *N.Yorks.* **YO8**	58	C6
Cliffe Woods **ME3**	24	D4
Clifford, *Here.* **HR3**	28	B4
Clifford, *W.Yorks.* **LS23**	57	K5
Clifford Chambers **CV37**	30	C3
Clifford's Mesne **GL18**	29	F6
Cliffs End **CT12**	25	K5
Clifton, *Beds.* **SG17**	32	E5
Clifton, *Bristol* **BS8**	19	J4
Clifton, *Cumb.* **CA10**	61	G4
Clifton, *Derbys.* **DE6**	40	D1
Clifton, *Devon* **EX31**	6	D1
Clifton, *Lancs.* **PR4**	55	H6
Clifton, *N.Yorks.* **LS21**	57	G5

Place	Postcode	Page	Grid
Clifton, *Northumb.*	NE61	71	H5
Clifton, *Nott.*	NG11	41	H2
Clifton, *Oxon.*	OX15	31	F5
Clifton, *S.Yorks.*	S66	51	H3
Clifton, *Stir.*	FK20	80	E4
Clifton, *W.Yorks.*	HD6	57	G7
Clifton, *Worcs.*	WR8	29	H4
Clifton, *York*	YO30	58	B4
Clifton Campville	B79	40	E4
Clifton Hampden	OX14	21	J2
Clifton Maybank	BA22	8	E3
Clifton Reynes	MK46	32	C3
Clifton upon Dunsmore	CV23	31	G1
Clifton upon Teme	WR6	29	G2
Cliftonville	CT9	25	K4
Climping	BN17	12	D6
Climpy	ML11	75	H5
Clink	BA11	20	A7
Clint	HG3	57	H4
Clint Green	NR19	44	E4
Clintmains	TD6	76	E7
Clippesby	NR29	45	J4
Clippings Green	NR20	44	E4
Clipsham	LE15	42	C4
Clipston, *Northants.*	LE16	42	A7
Clipston, *Notts.*	NG12	41	J2
Clipstone	NG21	51	H6
Clitheroe	BB7	56	C5
Clivocast	ZE2	108	F2
Clixby	DN38	52	E2
Clocaenog	LL15	47	J7
Clochan	AB56	98	C4
Clochtow	AB41	91	J1
Clock Face	WA9	48	E3
Clockhill	AB42	99	G6
Cloddach	IV30	97	J6
Cloddiau	SY21	38	A5
Clodock	HR2	28	C6
Cloford	BA11	20	A7
Cloichran	FK21	81	H4
Clola	AB42	99	J6
Clonrae	DG3	68	D4
Clophill	MK45	32	D5
Clopton	NN14	42	D7
Clopton Green, *Suff.*	CB8	34	B3
Clopton Green, *Suff.*	IP13	35	G3
Close Clark	IM9	54	B6
Closeburn	DG3	68	D4
Closworth	BA22	8	E3
Clothall	SG7	33	F5
Clothan	ZE2	108	D4
Clotton	CW6	48	E6
Clough, *Cumb.*	LA10	61	J7
Clough, *Gt.Man.*	OL15	49	J1
Clough, *Gt.Man.*	OL2	49	J2
Clough, *W.Yorks.*	HD7	50	C1
Clough Foot	OL14	56	E7
Clough Head	HX6	57	F7
Cloughfold	BB4	56	D7
Cloughton	YO13	63	K3
Cloughton Newlands	YO13	63	K3
Clounlaid	PA34	79	J2
Clousta	ZE2	109	C7
Clouston	KW16	107	C6
Clova, *Aber.*	AB54	90	C2
Clova, *Angus*	DD8	90	B7
Clove Lodge	DL12	62	A5
Clovelly	EX39	6	B3
Clovelly Cross	EX39	6	B3
Clovenfords	TD1	76	C7
Clovenstone	AB51	91	F3
Cloverhill	AB23	91	H3
Cloves	IV30	97	J5
Clovullin	PH33	80	B1
Clow Bridge	BB11	56	D7
Clowne	S43	51	G5
Clows Top	DY14	29	G1
Cloyntie	KA19	67	H3
Cluanach	PA43	72	B5
Clubworthy	PL15	4	C1
Cluddley	TF6	39	F4
Cluer	HS3	93	G2
Clun	SY7	38	B7
Clunas	IV12	97	F7
Clunbury	SY7	38	C7
Clune, *High.*	IV13	88	E2
Clune, *Moray*	AB56	98	D4
Clunes	PH34	87	J6
Clungunford	SY7	28	C1
Clunie, *Aber.*	AB53	98	E5
Clunie, *P. & K.*	PH10	82	C3
Clunton	SY7	38	C7
Cluny	KY2	76	A1
Clutton, *B. & N.E.Som.*	BS39	19	K6
Clutton, *Ches.*	CH3	48	D7
Clwt-y-bont	LL55	46	D6
Clwydyfagwyr	CF48	18	D1
Clydach, *Mon.*	NP7	28	B7
Clydach, *Swan.*	SA6	17	K4
Clydach Terrace	NP23	28	A7
Clydach Vale	CF40	18	C2
Clydebank	G81	74	C3
Clydey	SA35	17	F1
Clyffe Pypard	SN4	20	D4
Clynder	G84	74	A2
Clynderwen	SA66	16	E3
Clyne	SA11	18	B1
Clynelish	KW9	97	F1
Clynfyw	SA37	17	F1
Clynnog-fawr	LL54	36	D1
Clyro	HR3	28	B4
Clyst Honiton	EX5	7	H6
Clyst Hydon	EX15	7	J5
Clyst St. George	EX3	7	H7
Clyst St. Lawrence	EX15	7	J5
Clyst St. Mary	EX5	7	H6
Clyst William	EX15	7	J5
Cnewr	LD3	27	H6
Cnoc	HS2	101	G4
Cnoc an Torrain (Knockintorran)	HS6	92	C5
Cnwch Coch	SY23	27	F1
Coachford	AB54	98	C6
Coad's Green	PL15	4	C3
Coal Aston	S18	51	F5
Coalbrookdale	TF8	39	F5
Coalbrookvale	NP13	18	E1
Coalburn	ML11	75	G7
Coalburns	NE40	71	G7
Coalcleugh	NE47	61	K2
Coaley	GL11	20	A1
Coalmoor	TF6	39	F5
Coalpit Heath	BS36	19	K3
Coalpit Hill	ST7	49	H7
Coalport	TF8	39	G5
Coalsnaughton	FK13	75	H1
Coaltown of Balgonie	KY7	76	B1
Coaltown of Wemyss	KY1	76	B1
Coalville	LE67	41	G4
Coalway	GL16	28	E7
Coanwood	NE49	61	H1
Coast	IV22	95	F2
Coat	TA12	8	D2
Coatbridge	ML5	75	F4
Coate, *Swin.*	SN3	20	E3
Coate, *Wilts.*	SN10	20	D5
Coates, *Cambs.*	PE7	43	G6
Coates, *Glos.*	GL7	20	C1
Coates, *Lincs.*	LN1	52	C4
Coates, *Notts.*	DN22	52	B4
Coates, *W.Suss.*	RH20	12	C5
Coatham	TS10	63	G4
Coatham Mundeville	DL3	62	D4
Cobairdy	AB54	98	D6
Cobbaton	EX37	6	E3
Cobbler's Plain	NP16	19	H1
Cobby Syke	HG3	57	G4
Cobden	EX5	7	J6
Coberley	GL53	29	J7
Cobhall Common	HR2	28	D5
Cobham, *Kent*	DA12	24	C5
Cobham, *Surr.*	KT11	22	E5
Cobleland	FK8	74	D1
Cobley Hill	B60	30	B1
Cobnash	HR6	28	D2
Coburty	AB43	99	H4
Cochno	G81	74	C3
Cock Alley	S44	51	G6
Cock Bank	LL13	38	C1
Cock Bevington	WR11	30	B3
Cock Bridge	AB36	89	K4
Cock Clarks	CM3	24	E1
Cock Green	CM6	34	B7
Cockayne	YO62	63	H7
Cockayne Hatley	SG19	33	F4
Cockburnspath	TD13	77	F3
Cockenzie and Port Seton	EH32	76	C3
Cocker Bar	PR26	55	J7
Cockerham	LA2	55	H4
Cockermouth	CA13	60	C3
Cockernhoe	LU2	32	E6
Cockerton	DL3	62	D5
Cockett	SA2	17	K5
Cockfield, *Dur.*	DL13	62	C4
Cockfield, *Suff.*	IP30	34	D3
Cockfosters	EN4	23	F2
Cocking	GU29	12	B5
Cockington	TQ2	5	J4
Cocklake	BS28	19	H7
Cocklaw	NE46	70	E6
Cockle Park	NE61	71	H4
Cockleford	GL53	29	J7
Cockley Beck	LA20	60	D6
Cockley Cley	PE37	44	B5
Cockpen	EH19	76	B4
Cockpole Green	RG10	22	A3
Cockshutt	SY12	38	D3
Cockthorpe	NR23	44	D1
Cockwood, *Devon*	EX6	7	H7
Cockwood, *Som.*	TA5	19	F7
Cockyard	SK23	50	C4
Codda	PL15	4	B3
Coddenham	IP6	35	F3
Coddington, *Ches.*	CH3	48	D7
Coddington, *Here.*	HR8	29	G4
Coddington, *Notts.*	NG24	52	B7
Codford St. Mary	BA12	9	J1
Codford St. Peter	BA12	9	J1
Codicote	SG4	33	F7
Codmore Hill	RH20	12	D5
Codnor	DE5	41	G1
Codnor Park	NG16	51	G7
Codrington	BS37	20	A4
Codsall	WV8	40	A5
Codsall Wood	WV8	40	A5
Coed Morgan	NP7	28	C7
Coed Ystumgwern	LL44	36	E3
Coedcae	NP4	19	F1
Coed-duon (Blackwood)	NP12	18	E2
Coedely	CF39	18	D3
Coedkernew	NP10	19	F3
Coedpoeth	LL11	48	B7
Coedway	SY5	38	C4
Coed-y-bryn	SA44	26	C4
Coed-y-caerau	NP18	19	G2
Coed-y-paen	NP4	19	G2
Coed-y-parc	LL57	46	E6
Coed-yr-ynys	NP8	28	A6
Coelbren	SA10	27	H7
Coffinswell	TQ12	5	J4
Cofton	EX6	7	H7
Cofton Hackett	B45	30	B1
Cogan	CF64	18	E4
Cogenhoe	NN7	32	B2
Cogges	OX28	21	G1
Coggeshall	CO6	34	C6
Coggeshall Hamlet	CO6	34	C6
Coggins Mill	TN20	13	J4
Cóig Peighinnean	HS2	101	H1
Coilantogle	FK17	81	G7
Coileitir	PH49	80	C3
Coilessan	G83	80	D7
Coillag	PA35	80	B5
Coille Mhorgil	PH35	87	G4
Coille-righ	IV56	87	F2
Coillore	IV56	85	J1
Coity	CF35	18	C3
Col	HS2	101	G4
Col Uarach	HS2	101	G4
Colaboll	IV27	103	H7
Colan	TR8	3	F2
Colaton Raleigh	EX10	7	J7
Colbost	IV55	93	H7
Colburn	DL9	62	C7
Colbury	SO40	10	E3
Colby, *Cumb.*	CA16	61	H4
Colby, *I.o.M.*	IM9	54	B6
Colby, *Norf.*	NR11	45	G2
COLCHESTER	CO	34	D6
Colchester Green	IP30	34	D3
Colcot	CF62	18	E5
Cold Ash	RG18	21	J5
Cold Ashby	NN6	31	H1
Cold Ashton	SN14	20	A4
Cold Aston	GL54	30	C7
Cold Blow	SA67	16	E3
Cold Brayfield	MK46	32	C3
Cold Chapel	ML12	68	E1
Cold Cotes	LA2	56	C2
Cold Hanworth	LN8	52	D4
Cold Harbour	RG8	21	K3
Cold Hatton	TF6	39	F3
Cold Hatton Heath	TF6	39	F3
Cold Hesledon	SR7	63	F2
Cold Higham	NN12	31	H3
Cold Inn	SA68	16	E4
Cold Kirby	YO7	58	B1
Cold Newton	LE7	42	A5
Cold Northcott	PL15	4	C2
Cold Norton	CM3	24	E1
Cold Overton	LE15	42	B5
Cold Row	FY6	55	G5
Coldbackie	IV27	103	J2
Coldblow	DA5	23	J4
Coldean	BN1	13	G6
Coldeast	TQ12	5	J3
Coldeaton	DE6	50	D7
Colden Common	SO21	11	F2
Coldfair Green	IP16	35	J2
Coldham	PE14	43	H5
Coldharbour, *Glos.*	GL15	19	J1
Coldharbour, *Surr.*	RH5	22	E7
Coldingham	TD14	77	H4
Coldrain	KY13	82	B7
Coldred	CT15	15	H3
Coldrey	GU34	22	A7
Coldridge	EX17	6	E5
Coldrife	NE61	71	F4
Coldstream	TD12	77	G7
Coldvreath	PL26	3	G3
Coldwaltham	RH20	12	D5
Coldwells	AB42	99	K6
Cole	BA10	9	F1
Cole End	B46	40	D7
Cole Green	SG14	33	F7
Cole Henley	RG28	21	H6
Colebatch	SY9	38	C7
Colebrook	EX15	7	J5
Colebrooke	EX17	7	F5
Coleburn	IV30	97	K6
Coleby, *Lincs.*	LN5	52	C6
Coleby, *N.Lincs.*	DN15	52	B4
Coleford, *Devon*	EX17	7	F5
Coleford, *Glos.*	GL16	28	E7
Coleford, *Som.*	BA3	19	K7
Colegate End	IP21	45	F7
Colehill	BH21	10	B4
Coleman Green	AL4	32	E7
Coleman's Hatch	TN7	13	H3
Colemere	SY12	38	D2
Colemore	GU34	11	J1
Colemore Green	WV16	39	G6
Colenden	PH2	82	C5
Coleorton	LE67	41	G4
Colerne	SN14	20	B4
Cole's Common	IP21	45	G7
Cole's Cross	TQ9	5	H6
Cole's Green	IP13	35	G2
Colesbourne	GL53	30	B7
Colesden	MK44	32	E3
Coleshill, *Bucks.*	HP7	22	C2
Coleshill, *Oxon.*	SN6	21	F2
Coleshill, *Warks.*	B46	40	E7
Colestocks	EX14	7	J5
Coley, *B. & N.E.Som.*	BS40	19	J6
Coley, *Staffs.*	ST18	40	C3
Colfin	DG9	64	A5
Colgate	RH12	13	F3
Colgrain	G82	74	B3
Colindale	NW9	23	F3
Colinsburgh	KY9	83	F7
Colinton	EH13	76	A4
Colintraive	PA22	73	J3
Colkirk	NR21	44	D3
Coll	PA78	78	C2
Collace	PH2	82	D4
Collafirth	ZE2	109	D6
Collamoor Head	PL32	4	B1
Collaton St. Mary	TQ3	5	J4
Collessie	KY15	82	D6
Colleton Mills	EX37	6	E4
Collett's Green	WR2	29	H3
Collier Row	RM5	23	J2
Collier Street	TN12	14	C3
Collier's End	SG11	33	G6
Collier's Wood	SW19	23	F4
Colliery Row	DH4	62	E2
Colliston	AB41	91	J2
Collin	DG1	69	F6
Collingbourne Ducis	SN8	21	F6
Collingbourne Kingston	SN8	21	F6
Collingham, *Notts.*	NG23	52	B6
Collingham, *W.Yorks.*	LS22	57	J5
Collington	HR7	29	F2
Collingtree	NN4	31	J3
Collins End	RG8	21	K4
Collins Green, *Warr.*	WA5	48	E3
Collins Green, *Worcs.*	WR6	29	G3
Colliston	DD11	83	H3
Colliton	EX14	7	J5
Collmuir	AB31	90	D4
Collycroft	CV12	41	F7
Collyhurst	M8	49	H2
Collynie	AB41	91	G1
Collyweston	PE9	42	C5
Colmonell	KA26	67	F5
Colmworth	MK44	32	E3
Coln Rogers	GL54	20	D1
Coln St. Aldwyns	GL7	20	E1
Coln St. Dennis	GL54	30	B7
Colnabaichin	AB36	89	K4
Colnbrook	SL3	22	D4
Colne, *Cambs.*	PE28	33	G1
Colne, *Lancs.*	BB8	56	D6
Colne Engaine	CO6	34	C5
Colney	NR4	45	F5
Colney Heath	AL4	23	F1
Colney Street	AL2	22	E1
Colonsay	PA61	72	B1
Colonsay House	PA61	72	B1
Colpy	AB52	90	E1
Colquhar	EH44	76	B6
Colsterdale	HG4	57	G1
Colsterworth	NG33	42	C3
Colston Bassett	NG12	42	A2
Coltfield	IV36	97	J5
Colthouse	LA22	60	E7
Coltishall	NR12	45	G4
Coltness	ML2	75	G5
Colton, *Cumb.*	LA12	55	G1
Colton, *N.Yorks.*	LS24	58	B5
Colton, *Norf.*	NR9	45	F5
Colton, *Staffs.*	WS15	40	C3
Colton, *W.Yorks.*	LS15	57	J6
Colva	HR5	28	B3
Colvend	DG5	65	J5
Colvister	ZE2	108	E3
Colwall	WR13	29	G4
Colwall Green	WR13	29	G4
Colwall Stone	WR13	29	G4
Colwell	NE46	70	E6
Colwich	ST18	40	C3
Colwick	NG4	41	J2
Colwinston	CF71	18	C4
Colworth	PO20	12	C6
Colwyn Bay (Bae Colwyn)	LL29	47	G5
Colyford	EX24	8	B5
Colyton	EX24	8	B5
Combe, *Here.*	LD8	28	C2
Combe, *Oxon.*	OX29	31	F7
Combe, *Som.*	TA10	8	D2
Combe, *W.Berks.*	RG17	21	G5
Combe Common	GU8	12	C3
Combe Cross	TQ13	5	H3
Combe Down	BA2	20	A5
Combe Florey	TA4	7	K2
Combe Hay	BA2	20	A6
Combe Martin	EX34	6	D1
Combe Pafford	TQ1	5	K4
Combe Raleigh	EX14	7	K5
Combe St. Nicholas	TA20	8	C3
Combeinteignhead	TQ12	5	J3
Comberbach	CW9	49	F5
Comberford	B79	40	D5
Comberton, *Cambs.*	CB3	33	G3
Comberton, *Here.*	SY8	28	D2
Combpyne	EX13	8	B5
Combridge	ST14	40	C2
Combrook	CV35	30	E3
Combs, *Derbys.*	SK23	50	C5
Combs, *Suff.*	IP14	34	E3
Combs Ford	IP14	34	E3
Combwich	TA5	19	F7
Comer	FK8	80	E7
Comers	AB51	90	E4
Comhampton	DY13	29	H2
Comins Coch	SY23	37	F7
Commercial End	CB5	33	J2
Commins Coch	SY20	37	H5
Common Edge	FY4	55	G6
Common Moor	PL14	4	C3
Common Platt	SN5	20	E3
Common Side	S18	51	F5
Common Square	LN4	52	D5
Commondale	YO21	63	H5
Commonside	DE6	40	E1
Compstall	SK6	49	J3
Compton, *Devon*	TQ3	5	J4
Compton, *Hants.*	SO21	11	F2
Compton, *Plym.*	PL3	4	E5
Compton, *Staffs.*	DY7	40	A7
Compton, *Surr.*	GU3	22	C7
Compton, *W.Berks.*	RG20	21	J4
Compton, *W.Suss.*	PO18	11	J3
Compton, *W.Yorks.*	LS22	57	K5
Compton, *Wilts.*	SN9	20	E6
Compton Abbas	SP7	9	H3
Compton Abdale	GL54	30	B7
Compton Bassett	SN11	20	D4
Compton Beauchamp	SN6	21	F3
Compton Bishop	BS26	19	G6
Compton Chamberlayne	SP3	10	B2
Compton Dando	BS39	19	K5
Compton Dundon	TA11	8	D1
Compton Martin	BS40	19	J6
Compton Pauncefoot	BA22	9	F2
Compton Valence	DT2	8	E5
Compton Verney	CV35	30	E3
Comra	PH20	88	C5
Comrie, *Fife*	KY12	75	J2
Comrie, *P. & K.*	PH6	81	J5
Conchra, *Arg. & B.*	PA22	73	J2
Conchra, *High.*	IV40	86	E2
Concraigie	PH10	82	C3
Conder Green	LA2	55	H4
Conderton	GL20	29	J5
Condicote	GL54	30	C6
Condorrat	G67	75	F3
Condover	SY5	38	D5
Coney Weston	IP31	34	D1
Coneyhurst	RH14	12	E4
Coneysthorpe	YO60	58	D2
Coneythorpe	HG5	57	J4
Conford	GU30	12	B3
Congash	PH26	89	H2
Congdon's Shop	PL15	4	C3
Congerstone	CV13	41	F5
Congham	PE32	44	B3
Congleton	CW12	49	H6
Congresbury	BS49	19	H5
Congreve	ST19	40	B4
Conicavel	IV36	97	G6
Coningsby	LN4	53	F7
Conington, *Cambs.*	PE7	42	E7
Conington, *Cambs.*	CB3	33	G2
Conisbrough	DN12	51	H3
Conisby	PA49	72	A4
Conisholme	LN11	53	H3
Coniston, *Cumb.*	LA21	60	E7
Coniston, *E.Riding*	HU11	59	H6
Coniston Cold	BD23	56	E4
Conistone	BD23	56	E3
Conland	AB54	98	E6
Connah's Quay	CH5	48	B6
Connel	PA37	80	A4
Connel Park	KA18	68	B2
Connor Downs	TR27	2	C5
Conock	SN10	20	D6
Conon Bridge	IV7	96	C6
Cononish	FK20	80	E5
Cononley	BD20	56	E5
Cononsyth	DD11	83	G3
Consall	ST9	40	B1
Consett	DH8	62	C1
Constable Burton	DL8	62	C7
Constantine	TR11	2	E6
Constantine Bay	PL28	3	F1
Contin	IV14	96	B6
Contlaw	AB13	91	G4
Contullich	IV17	96	D4
Conwy	LL32	47	F5
Conyer	ME9	25	F5
Conyer's Green	IP31	34	C2
Cooden	TN39	14	C7
Coodham	KA1	74	C7
Cooil	IM4	54	C6
Cookbury	EX22	6	C5
Cookbury Wick	EX22	6	B5
Cookham	SL6	22	B3
Cookham Dean	SL6	22	B3
Cookham Rise	SL6	22	B3
Cookhill	B49	30	B3
Cookley, *Suff.*	IP19	35	H1
Cookley, *Worcs.*	DY10	40	A7
Cookley Green, *Oxon.*	RG9	21	K2
Cookley Green, *Suff.*	IP19	35	H1
Cookney	AB39	91	G5
Cook's Green	IP7	34	D3
Cooksbridge	BN7	13	G5
Cooksey Green	B61	29	J2
Cookshill	ST11	40	B1
Cooksmill Green	CM1	24	C1
Cookston	AB41	91	H1
Coolham	RH13	12	E4
Cooling	ME3	24	D4
Cooling Street	ME3	24	D4
Coombe, *Cornw.*	PL26	3	G3
Coombe, *Cornw.*	EX23	6	A4
Coombe, *Cornw.*	TR14	2	D4
Coombe, *Cornw.*	TR4	3	F4
Coombe, *Devon*	TQ9	5	H6
Coombe, *Devon*	EX6	7	G7
Coombe, *Devon*	EX10	7	K6
Coombe, *Som.*	TA2	8	B2
Coombe, *Som.*	TA18	8	D4
Coombe, *Wilts.*	SN9	20	E6
Coombe Bissett	SP5	10	C2
Coombe End	TA4	7	J3
Coombe Hill	GL19	29	H6
Coombe Keynes	BH20	9	H6
Coombes	BN15	12	E6
Coombes Moor	LD8	28	C2
Cooper's Corner, *E.Suss.*	TN19	14	C5
Cooper's Corner, *Kent*	TN14	23	H7
Cooper's Green	AL4	22	E1
Coopersale Common	CM16	23	H1
Coopersale Street	CM16	23	H1
Cootham	RH20	12	D5
Cop Street	CT3	15	H5
Copdock	IP8	35	F4
Copford Green	CO6	34	D6
Copgrove	HG3	57	J3
Copister	ZE2	108	D5

Place	Map	Grid
Cople MK44	32	E4
Copley, Dur. DL13	62	B4
Copley, W.Yorks. HX4	57	F7
Coplow Dale SK17	50	D5
Copmanthorpe YO23	58	B5
Copp PR3	55	H6
Coppathorne EX23	6	A5
Coppenhall ST18	40	B4
Coppenhall Moss CW1	49	G7
Copperhouse TR27	2	C5
Coppicegate DY12	39	G7
Coppleridge SP7	9	H2
Copplestone EX17	7	F5
Coppull PR7	48	E1
Coppull Moor PR7	48	E1
Copsale RH13	12	E4
Copse Hill SW20	23	F5
Copster Green BB1	56	B6
Copston Magna LE10	41	G7
Copt Heath B93	30	C1
Copt Hewick HG4	57	J2
Copt Oak LE67	41	G4
Copthall Green EN9	23	H1
Copthorne RH10	13	G3
Copy Lake EX18	6	E4
Copythorne SO40	10	E3
Coralhill AB43	99	J4
Corbets Tey RM14	23	J3
Corbiegoe KW1	105	J4
Corbridge NE45	70	E7
Corby NN17	42	B7
Corby Glen NG33	42	D3
Cordach AB31	90	E5
Coreley SY8	29	F1
Corfcott Green EX22	6	B6
Corfe TA3	8	B3
Corfe Castle BH20	9	J6
Corfe Mullen BH21	9	J5
Corfton SY7	38	D7
Corgarff AB36	89	K4
Corhampton SO32	11	H2
Corley CV7	40	E7
Corley Ash CV7	40	E7
Corley Moor CV7	40	E7
Cornabus PA42	72	B6
Cornard Tye CO10	34	D4
Corndon TQ13	6	E7
Corney LA19	60	C7
Cornforth DH7	62	E3
Cornhill AB45	98	D5
Cornhill on Tweed TD12	77	G7
Cornholme OL14	56	E7
Cornquoy KW17	107	E7
Cornriggs DL13	61	K2
Cornsay DH7	62	C2
Cornsay Colliery DH7	62	C2
Corntown, High. IV7	96	C6
Corntown, V. of Glam. CF35	18	C4
Cornwell OX7	30	D6
Cornwood PL21	5	G5
Cornworthy TQ9	5	J5
Corpach PH33	87	H7
Corpusty NR11	45	F3
Corrachree AB34	90	C4
Corran, Arg. & B. PA24	74	A1
Corran, High. IV40	86	E4
Corran, High. PH33	80	B1
Corranbuie PA29	73	G4
Corranmore PA31	79	J7
Corrany IM7	54	D5
Corribeg PH33	87	F7
Corrie KA27	73	J6
Corrie Common DG11	69	H5
Corriechrevie PA29	73	F5
Corriecravie KA27	66	D1
Corriedoo DG7	68	B5
Corriekinloch IV27	103	F6
Corrielorne PA34	79	K6
Corrievorrie IV13	88	E2
Corrimony IV63	87	K1
Corringham, Lincs. DN21	52	B3
Corringham, Thur. SS17	24	D3
Corris SY20	37	G5
Corris Uchaf SY20	37	G5
Corrlarach PH33	87	F7
Corrour Shooting Lodge PH30	81	F1
Corrow PA24	80	C7
Corry IV49	86	C2
Corrychurrachan PH33	80	B1
Corrylach PA28	73	F7
Corrymuckloch PH8	81	K4
Corsback KW12	105	H2
Corscombe DT2	8	E4
Corse, Aber. AB54	98	E6
Corse, Glos. GL19	29	G6
Corse Lawn GL19	29	H5
Corse of Kinnoir AB54	98	D6
Corsebank DG4	68	D2
Corsegight AB53	99	G5
Corsehill DG11	69	G5
Corsham SN13	20	B4
Corsindae AB51	90	E4
Corsley, Wilts. BA12	20	B7
Corsley Heath BA12	20	B7
Corsock DG7	65	H3
Corston, B. & N.E.Som. BA2	19	K5
Corston, Wilts. SN16	20	C3
Corstorphine EH12	75	K3
Cortachy DD8	82	E2
Corton, Suff. NR32	45	K6
Corton, Wilts. BA12	20	C7
Corton Denham DT9	9	F2
Corwar House KA26	67	G5
Corwen LL21	37	K1
Coryton, Devon EX20	6	C7
Coryton, Thur. SS17	24	D3
Cosby LE9	41	H6
Coscote OX11	21	J3
Coseley WV14	40	B6
Cosford, Shrop. WV7	39	G5
Cosford, Warks. CV21	31	G1
Cosgrove MK19	31	J4
Cosham PO6	11	H4
Cosheston SA72	16	D4
Coshieville PH15	81	J3
Coskills DN38	52	D2
Cosmeston CF64	18	E5
Cossall NG16	41	G1
Cossington, Leics. LE7	41	J4
Cossington, Som. TA7	19	G7
Costa KW17	106	C5
Costessey NR8	45	F4
Costock LE12	41	H3
Coston, Leics. LE14	42	B3
Coston, Norf. NR8	44	E5
Cote, Oxon. OX18	21	G1
Cote, Som. TA9	19	G7
Cotebrook CW6	48	E6
Cotehill CA4	61	F1
Cotes, Cumb. LA8	55	H1
Cotes, Leics. LE12	41	H3
Cotes, Staffs. ST15	40	A4
Cotesbach LE17	41	H7
Cotgrave NG12	41	J2
Cothall AB21	91	G3
Cotham NG23	42	A1
Cothelstone TA4	7	K2
Cotheridge WR6	29	G3
Cotherstone DL12	62	B5
Cothill OX13	21	H2
Cotleigh EX14	8	B4
Cotmanhay DE7	41	G1
Coton, Cambs. CB3	33	H3
Coton, Northants. NN6	31	H1
Coton, Staffs. ST18	40	B2
Coton, Staffs. B79	40	D5
Coton, Staffs. ST20	40	A3
Coton Clanford ST18	40	A3
Coton Hill ST18	40	B2
Coton in the Clay DE6	40	D3
Coton in the Elms DE12	40	E4
Cotonwood, Shrop. SY13	38	E2
Cotonwood, Staffs. ST20	40	A3
Cott TQ9	5	H4
Cottam, Lancs. PR4	55	H6
Cottam, Notts. DN22	52	B4
Cottartown PH26	89	H1
Cottenham CB4	33	H2
Cotterdale DL8	61	K7
Cottered SG9	33	G6
Cotteridge B30	30	B1
Cotterstock PE8	42	D6
Cottesbrooke NN6	31	J1
Cottesmore LE15	42	C4
Cottingham, E.Riding HU16	59	G6
Cottingham, Northants. LE16	42	B6
Cottingley BD16	57	G6
Cottisford NN13	31	G5
Cotton, Staffs. ST10	40	C1
Cotton End MK45	32	E4
Cotton, Suff. IP14	34	E2
Cottonworth SP11	10	E1
Cottown, Aber. AB54	90	D2
Cottown, Aber. AB53	99	G6
Cottown, Aber. AB51	91	F3
Cotts PL20	4	E4
Cottwood EX18	6	E4
Cotwall TF6	39	F4
Cotwalton ST15	40	B2
Couch's Mill PL22	4	B5
Coughton, Here. HR9	28	E6
Coughton, Warks. B49	30	B2
Cougie IV4	87	J2
Coulaghailtro PA29	73	F4
Coulags IV54	95	F7
Coulby Newham TS8	63	G5
Coulderton CA22	60	A6
Coull AB34	90	D4
Coulport G84	74	A2
Coulsdon CR5	23	F6
Coulston BA13	20	C6
Coulter ML12	75	J7
Coultershaw Bridge GU28	12	C5
Coultings TA5	19	F7
Coulton YO62	58	C2
Coultra KY15	82	E5
Cound SY5	38	E5
Coundlane SY5	38	E5
Coundon, Dur. DL14	62	D4
Coundon, W.Mid. CV6	41	F7
Countersett DL8	56	E1
Countess Wear EX2	7	H6
Countesthorpe LE8	41	H6
Countisbury EX35	7	F1
Coup Green PR5	55	J7
Coupar Angus PH13	82	D3
Coupland, Cumb. CA16	61	J5
Coupland, Northumb. NE71	77	H7
Cour PA28	73	G6
Court Colman CF32	18	B3
Court Henry SA32	17	J2
Court House Green CV6	41	F7
Court-at-Street CT21	15	F4
Courteenhall NN7	31	J3
Courtsend SS3	25	G2
Courtway TA5	8	B1
Cousland EH22	76	B4
Cousley Wood TN5	13	K3
Coustonn PA23	73	J3
Cove, Arg. & B. G84	74	A2
Cove, Devon EX16	7	H4
Cove, Hants. GU14	22	B6
Cove, High. IV22	94	E2
Cove, Sc.Bord. TD13	77	F3
Cove Bay AB12	91	H4
Cove Bottom NR34	45	J7
Covehithe NR34	45	K7
Coven WV9	40	B5
Coveney CB6	43	H7
Covenham St. Bartholomew LN11	53	G3
Covenham St. Mary LN11	53	G3
COVENTRY CV	30	E1
Coverack TR12	2	E7
Coverham DL8	57	G1
Covesea IV30	97	J4
Covington, Cambs. PE28	32	D1
Covington, S.Lan. ML12	75	H7
Cowan Bridge LA6	56	B2
Cowbeech BN27	13	K5
Cowbit PE12	43	F4
Cowbridge, Som. TA24	7	H1
Cowbridge, V. of Glam. CF71	18	C4
Cowden TN8	23	H7
Cowden Pound TN8	23	H7
Cowdenbeath KY4	75	K1
Cowdenburn EH46	76	A5
Cowers Lane DE56	41	F1
Cowes PO31	11	F5
Cowesby YO7	57	K1
Cowesfield Green SP5	10	D2
Cowey Green CO7	34	E6
Cowfold RH13	13	F4
Cowgill LA10	56	C1
Cowie, Aber. AB39	91	G6
Cowie, Stir. FK7	75	G2
Cowlam Manor YO25	59	F3
Cowley, Devon EX4	7	H6
Cowley, Glos. GL53	29	J7
Cowley, Gt.Lon. UB8	22	D3
Cowley, Oxon. OX4	21	J1
Cowling, Lancs. PR7	48	E1
Cowling, N.Yorks. BD22	56	E5
Cowling, N.Yorks. DL8	57	H1
Cowlinge CB8	34	B3
Cowmes HD8	50	D1
Cowpe BB4	56	D7
Cowpen NE24	71	H5
Cowpen Bewley TS23	63	F4
Cowplain PO8	11	H3
Cowsden WR7	29	J3
Cowshill DL13	61	K2
Cowthorpe LS22	57	K4
Cox Common IP19	45	H7
Coxbank CW3	39	F1
Coxbench DE21	41	F1
Coxbridge BA6	8	E1
Coxford PE31	44	C3
Coxheath ME17	14	C2
Coxhoe DH6	62	E3
Coxley BA5	19	J7
Coxley Wick BA5	19	J7
Coxpark PL18	4	E3
Coxtie Green CM14	23	J2
Coxwold YO61	58	B2
Coychurch CF35	18	C4
Coylton KA6	67	J2
Coylumbridge PH22	89	G3
Coynach AB34	90	C4
Coynachie AB54	90	C1
Coytrahen CF32	18	B3
Crabbet Park RH10	13	G3
Crabgate NR11	44	E3
Crabtree, Plym. PL3	5	F5
Crabtree, S.Yorks. S4	51	F4
Crabtree, W.Suss. RH13	13	F4
Crabtree Green LL13	38	C1
Crackaig PA60	72	D4
Crackenthorpe CA16	61	H4
Crackington EX23	4	B1
Crackington Haven EX23	4	B1
Crackley ST5	40	A1
Crackleybank TF11	39	G4
Crackpot DL11	62	A7
Crackthorn Corner IP22	34	E1
Cracoe BD23	56	E3
Craddock EX15	7	J4
Cradhlastadh HS2	100	C4
Cradley, Here. WR13	29	G4
Cradley, W.Mid. B63	40	B7
Cradley Heath DY2	40	B7
Crafthole PL11	4	D5
Crafton LU7	32	B7
Cragg HX7	57	F7
Cragg Hill LS18	57	H6
Craggan, Moray AB37	89	J1
Craggan, P. & K. PH5	81	K6
Cragganruar PH15	81	H3
Craggie, High. IV2	88	E1
Craggie, High. KW8	104	D7
Craghead DH9	62	D1
Craibstone, Aberdeen AB21	91	G3
Craibstone, Moray AB56	98	C5
Craichie DD8	83	G3
Craig, Arg. & B. PA35	80	B4
Craig, Arg. & B. PA70	79	G4
Craig, D. & G. DG7	65	H3
Craig, High. IV22	94	D5
Craig, High. IV54	95	G7
Craig, S.Ayr. KA19	67	H3
Craig Berthlŵyd CF46	18	D2
Craigans PA31	73	G1
Craigbeg PH31	88	B6
Craig-cefn-parc SA6	17	K4
Craigcleuch DG13	69	J5
Craigculter AB43	99	H5
Craigdallie PH14	82	D5
Craigdam AB41	91	G1
Craigdarroch, D. & G. DG3	68	C4
Craigdarroch, E.Ayr. KA18	68	B3
Craigdhu, D. & G. DG8	64	D6
Craigdhu, High. IV4	96	B7
Craigearn AB51	91	F3
Craigellachie AB38	97	K7
Craigellie AB43	99	J4
Craigencallie DG7	65	F3
Craigend, Moray IV36	97	J6
Craigend, P. & K. PH2	82	C5
Craigendive PA23	73	J2
Craigendoran G84	74	B2
Craigengillan KA6	67	J3
Craigenputtock DG2	68	C5
Craigens PA44	72	A4
Craigglas PA31	73	G1
Craighall KY15	83	F6
Craighat G63	74	C2
Craighead, Fife KY10	83	H6
Craighead, High. IV11	96	E5
Craighlaw DG8	64	D4
Craighouse PA60	72	D4
Craigie, Aber. AB23	91	H3
Craigie, Dundee DD4	83	F4
Craigie, P. & K. PH13	82	C3
Craigie, S.Ayr. KA1	74	C7
Craigie Brae AB41	91	G1
Craigieburn DG10	69	G3
Craigieholm PH13	82	C4
Craigielaw EH32	76	C3
Craiglockhart EH14	76	A3
Craiglug AB31	91	G5
Craigmaud AB43	99	G5
Craigmillar EH16	76	A3
Craigmore PA20	73	K4
Craigmyle House AB31	90	E4
Craignafeoch PA21	73	H3
Craignant SY10	38	B2
Craignavie FK21	81	G4
Craigneil KA26	67	F5
Craigneuk ML1	75	F5
Craignure PA65	79	J4
Craigo DD10	83	H1
Craigoch KA19	67	G3
Craigow KY13	82	B7
Craigrothie KY15	82	E6
Craigroy IV36	97	J6
Craigroy Farm AB37	89	J1
Craigsanquhar KY15	82	E6
Craigton, Aberdeen AB14	91	G4
Craigton, Angus DD5	83	G4
Craigton, Angus DD8	82	E2
Craigton, High. IV1	96	D7
Craigton, Stir. G63	74	E2
Craigtown KW13	104	D3
Craig-y-nos SA9	27	H7
Craik, Aber. AB54	90	C2
Craik, Sc.Bord. TD9	69	J3
Crail KY10	83	H7
Crailing TD8	70	B1
Crailinghall TD8	70	B1
Crakehill YO7	57	K2
Crakemarsh ST14	40	C2
Crambe YO60	58	D3
Cramlington NE23	71	H6
Cramond EH4	75	K3
Cranage CW4	49	G6
Cranberry ST21	40	A2
Cranborne BH21	10	B3
Cranbourne SL4	22	C4
Cranbrook, Gt.Lon. IG1	23	H3
Cranbrook, Kent TN17	14	C4
Cranbrook Common TN17	14	C4
Crane Moor S35	51	F2
Cranfield MK43	32	C4
Cranford, Devon EX39	6	B3
Cranford, Gt.Lon. TW5	22	E4
Cranford St. Andrew NN14	32	C1
Cranford St. John NN14	32	C1
Cranham, Glos. GL4	29	H7
Cranham, Gt.Lon. RM14	23	J3
Crank WA11	48	E3
Cranleigh GU6	12	D3
Cranmer Green IP31	34	E1
Cranmore, I.o.W. PO41	10	E6
Cranmore, Som. BA4	19	K7
Cranna AB54	98	E5
Crannoch AB55	98	C5
Cranoe LE16	42	A6
Cransford IP13	35	H2
Cranshaws TD11	76	E4
Cranstal IM7	54	D3
Crantock TR8	2	E2
Cranwell NG34	42	D1
Cranwich IP26	44	B6
Cranworth IP25	44	D5
Craobh Haven PA31	79	J7
Crapstone PL20	5	F4
Crarae PA32	73	H1
Crask Inn IV27	103	H6
Crask of Aigas IV4	96	B7
Craskins AB34	90	D4
Craster NE66	71	H2
Craswall HR2	28	B5
Crateford ST19	40	B5
Cratfield IP19	35	H1
Crathes AB31	91	F5
Crathie, Aber. AB35	89	K5
Crathie, High. PH20	88	C5
Crathorne TS15	63	F6
Craven Arms SY7	38	D7
Craw KA27	73	G6
Crawcrook NE40	71	G7
Crawford, Lancs. WN8	48	D2
Crawford, S.Lan. ML12	68	E1
Crawfordjohn ML12	68	D1
Crawfordton DG3	68	C4
Crawick DG4	68	C2
Crawley, Devon EX14	8	B4
Crawley, Hants. SO21	11	F1
Crawley, Oxon. OX29	30	E7
Crawley, W.Suss. RH11	13	F3
Crawley Down RH10	13	G3
Crawleyside DL13	62	A2
Crawshawbooth BB4	56	D7
Crawton AB39	91	G7
Crawyn IM7	54	C4
Cray, N.Yorks. BD23	56	E2
Cray, P. & K. PH10	82	C1
Cray, Powys LD3	27	H6
Crayford DA1	23	J4
Crayke YO61	58	B2
Crays Hill CM11	24	D2
Cray's Pond RG8	21	K3
Crazies Hill RG10	22	A3
Creacombe EX16	7	G4
Creag Ghoraidh (Creagorry) HS7	92	C7
Creagan PA38	80	A3
Creagbheitheachain PH33	80	A1
Creagorry (Creag Ghoraidh) HS7	92	C7
Creamore Bank SY4	38	E2
Creaton NN6	31	J1
Creca DG12	69	H6
Credenhill HR4	28	D4
Crediton EX17	7	G5
Creebridge DG8	64	E4
Creech Heathfield TA3	8	B2
Creech St. Michael TA3	8	B2
Creed TR2	3	G4
Creedy Park EX17	7	G5
Creekmouth IG11	23	H3
Creeting St. Mary IP6	34	E3
Creeton NG33	42	D3
Creetown DG8	64	E5
Creggans PA27	80	B7
Cregneash IM9	54	A7
Cregrina LD1	28	A3
Creich KY15	82	E5
Creigau NP16	19	H2
Creigiau CF15	18	D3
Crelevan IV4	87	K1
Crelly TR13	2	D5
Cremyll PL10	4	E5
Crendell SP6	10	B3
Cressage SY5	38	E5
Cressbrook SK17	50	D5
Cresselly SA68	16	D4
Cressing CM7	34	B6
Cresswell, Northumb. NE61	71	H4
Cresswell, Staffs. ST11	40	B2
Cresswell Quay SA68	16	D4
Creswell S80	51	H5
Cretingham IP13	35	G3
Cretshengan PA29	73	F4
CREWE, Ches. CW	49	G7
Crewe, Ches. CH3	48	D7
Crewe Green CW1	49	G7
Crewgreen SY5	38	C4
Crewkerne TA18	8	D4
Crew's Hole BS5	19	K4
Crewton DE24	41	F2
Crianlarich FK20	80	E5
Cribbs Causeway BS10	19	J3
Cribyn SA48	26	E3
Criccieth LL52	36	D2
Crich DE4	51	F7
Crich Carr DE4	51	F7
Crich Common DE4	51	F7
Crichie AB42	99	H6
Crichton EH37	76	B4
Crick, Mon. NP26	19	H2
Crick, Northants. NN6	31	G1
Crickadarn LD2	27	K4
Cricket Hill GU46	22	B5
Cricket St. Thomas TA20	8	C4
Crickham BS28	19	H7
Crickheath SY10	38	B3
Crickhowell NP8	28	B7
Cricklade SN6	20	E2
Cricklewood NW2	23	F3
Crick's Green HR7	29	F3
Criddlestyle SP6	10	C3
Cridling Stubbs WF11	58	B7
Crieff PH7	81	K5
Criggan PL26	4	A4
Criggion SY5	38	B4
Crigglestone WF4	51	F1
Crimble OL11	49	H1
Crimchard ST20	8	C4
Crimdon Park TS27	63	F3
Crimond AB43	99	J5
Crimonmogate AB43	99	J5
Crimplesham PE33	44	A5
Crinan PA31	73	F1
Crinan Ferry PA31	73	F1
Cringleford NR4	45	F5
Cringletie EH45	76	A6
Crinow SA67	16	E3
Cripplesyle SP6	10	B3
Cripp's Corner TN32	14	C5
Crix CM3	34	B7
Crizeley HR2	28	D5
Croachy IV2	88	D2
Croalchapel DG3	68	D4
Croasdale CA23	60	B5
Crock Street TA19	8	C3
Crockenhill BR8	23	J5
Crocker End RG9	22	A3
Crockerhill PO17	11	G4
Crockernwell EX6	7	F6
Crockerton BA12	20	B7
Crockerton Green BA12	20	B7
Crocketford (Ninemile Bar) DG2	65	J3

Crockey Hill **YO19** 58 C5
Crockham Hill **TN8** 23 H6
Crockhurst Street **TN11** 23 K7
Crockleford Heath **CO7** 34 E6
Croes Hywel **NP7** 28 C7
Croes y pant **NP4** 19 G1
Croesau Bach **SY10** 38 B3
Croesgoch **SA62** 16 B1
Croes-lan **SA44** 26 C4
Croesor **LL48** 37 F1
Croespenmaen **NP11** 18 E2
Croesyceiliog, Carmar. **SA32** 17 H3
Croesyceiliog, Torfaen **NP44** 19 G2
Croes-y-mwyalch **NP44** 19 G2
Croeswlan **LL55** 46 D7
Croford **TA4** 7 K3
Croft, Here. **HR6** 28 D2
Croft, Leics. **LE9** 41 H6
Croft, Lincs. **PE24** 53 J6
Croft, Warr. **WA3** 49 F3
Croftamie **G63** 74 C2
Crofthead **CA6** 69 J6
Croftmore **PH18** 81 K1
Crofton, W.Yorks. **WF4** 51 F1
Crofton, Wilts. **SN8** 21 F5
Croft-on-Tees **DL2** 62 D6
Crofts **DG7** 65 H3
Crofts of Benachielt **KW5** 105 G5
Crofts of Buinach **IV30** 97 J6
Crofts of Haddo **AB41** 91 G1
Crofty **SA4** 17 J5
Crogen **LL21** 37 K2
Croggan **PA63** 79 J5
Croglin **CA4** 61 G2
Croick, High. **IV24** 96 B2
Croick, High. **KW13** 104 D3
Croig **PA75** 79 F2
Crois Dughaill **HS8** 84 C3
Croit e Caley **IM9** 54 B7
Cromarty **IV11** 96 E5
Crombie **KY12** 75 J2
Crombie Mill **DD7** 83 G4
Cromblet **AB51** 91 F1
Cromdale **PH26** 89 H2
Cromer, Herts. **SG2** 33 F6
Cromer, Norf. **NR27** 45 G1
Cromford **DE4** 50 E7
Cromhall **GL12** 19 K2
Cromhall Common **GL12** 19 K3
Crompton Fold **OL2** 49 J1
Cromwell **NG23** 51 K6
Cronberry **KA18** 68 B1
Crondall **GU10** 22 A7
Cronk-y-Voddy **IM6** 54 C5
Cronton **WA8** 48 D4
Crook, Cumb. **LA8** 61 F7
Crook, Dur. **DL15** 62 C3
Crook of Devon **KY13** 82 B7
Crooked Soley **RG17** 21 G4
Crookedholm **KA3** 74 C7
Crookham, Northumb. **TD12** 77 H7
Crookham, W.Berks. **RG19** 21 J5
Crookham Eastfield **TD12** 77 H7
Crookham Village **GU51** 22 A6
Crooklands **LA7** 55 J1
Cropredy **OX17** 31 F4
Cropston **LE7** 41 H4
Cropthorne **WR10** 29 J4
Cropton **YO18** 58 D1
Cropwell Bishop **NG12** 41 J2
Cropwell Butler **NG12** 41 J2
Cros (Cross) **HS2** 101 H1
Crosbie **KA23** 74 A6
Crosbost **HS2** 101 F5
Crosby, Cumb. **CA15** 60 B3
Crosby, I.o.M. **IM4** 54 C6
Crosby, Mersey. **L23** 48 C3
Crosby, N.Lincs. **DN15** 52 B1
Crosby Court **DL6** 62 E7
Crosby Garrett **CA17** 61 J6
Crosby Ravensworth **CA10** 61 H5
Crosby Villa **CA15** 60 B3
Croscombe **BA5** 19 J7
Crosemere **SY12** 38 D3
Crosland Hill **HD4** 50 D1
Cross, Som. **BS26** 19 H6
Cross (Cros), W.Isles **HS2** 101 H1
Cross Ash **NP7** 28 D7
Cross Bank **DY12** 29 G1
Cross End, Beds. **MK44** 32 D3
Cross End, Essex **CO9** 34 C5
Cross Foxes Inn **LL40** 37 G4
Cross Gates **LS15** 57 J6
Cross Green, Devon **PL15** 6 B7
Cross Green, Staffs. **WV10** 40 B5
Cross Green, Suff. **IP7** 34 D3
Cross Green, Suff. **IP30** 34 C3
Cross Green, Suff. **IP29** 34 C3
Cross Hands, Carmar. **SA14** 17 J3
Cross Hands, Pembs. **SA67** 16 D3
Cross Hill **DE5** 41 G1
Cross Hills **BD20** 57 F5
Cross Houses **SY5** 38 E5
Cross in Hand **TN21** 13 J4
Cross Inn, Cere. **SA44** 26 C3
Cross Inn, Cere. **SY23** 26 E2
Cross Inn, R.C.T. **CF72** 18 D3
Cross Keys **PO30** 11 G6
Cross Lane Head **WV16** 39 G6
Cross Lanes, Cornw. **TR4** 2 E4

Cross Lanes, Cornw. **TR12** 2 D6
Cross Lanes, N.Yorks. **YO61** 58 B3
Cross Lanes, Wrex. **LL13** 38 C1
Cross of Jackston **AB51** 91 F1
Cross o'th'hands **DE56** 40 E1
Cross Street **IP21** 35 F1
Crossaig **PA29** 73 G5
Crossapol **PA78** 78 C2
Crossapoll **PA77** 78 A3
Cross-at-Hand **TN12** 14 C3
Crossbush **BN18** 12 D6
Crosscanonby **CA15** 60 B3
Crossdale Street **NR27** 45 G2
Crossens **PR9** 48 C1
Crossflatts **BD16** 57 G5
Crossford, D. & G. **DG3** 68 D5
Crossford, Fife **KY12** 75 J2
Crossford, S.Lan. **ML8** 75 G6
Crossgate, Lincs. **PE11** 43 F3
Crossgate, Staffs. **ST11** 40 B2
Crossgatehall **EH22** 76 B4
Crossgates, Fife **KY4** 75 K2
Crossgates, N.Yorks. **YO12** 59 G1
Crossgates, P. & K. **PH2** 82 B5
Crossgates, Powys **LD1** 27 K2
Crossgill **LA2** 55 J3
Crosshands **KA5** 74 C7
Crosshill, Fife **KY5** 75 K1
Crosshill, S.Ayr. **KA19** 67 H3
Crosshouse **KA2** 74 B7
Crosskeys **NP11** 19 F2
Crosskirk **KW14** 105 F1
Crosslanes **SY10** 38 C4
Crosslee, Renf. **PA6** 74 C4
Crosslee, Sc.Bord. **TD7** 69 J2
Crosslet **G82** 74 C3
Crossmichael **DG7** 65 H4
Crossmoor **PR4** 55 H6
Crossroads, Aber. **AB31** 91 F5
Crossroads, E.Ayr. **KA1** 74 C7
Crossway, Mon. **NP25** 28 D7
Crossway, Powys **LD1** 27 K3
Crossway Green, Mon. **NP16** 19 J2
Crossway Green, Worcs. **DY13** 29 H2
Crossways, Dorset **DT2** 9 G6
Crossways, Glos. **GL16** 28 E7
Crosswell **SA41** 16 E1
Crosswood **SY23** 27 F1
Crosthwaite **LA8** 60 F7
Croston **PR26** 48 D1
Crostwick **NR12** 45 G4
Crostwight **NR28** 45 H3
Crothair **HS2** 100 D4
Crouch **TN15** 23 K6
Crouch End **N8** 23 F3
Crouch Hill **DT9** 9 G3
Crouchestone **SP5** 10 B2
Croughton **NN13** 31 G5
Crovie **AB45** 99 G4
Crow **BH24** 10 C4
Crow Edge **S36** 50 D2
Crow Green **CM15** 23 J2
Crow Hill **HR9** 29 F6
Crowan **TR14** 2 D5
Crowborough **TN6** 13 J3
Crowborough Warren **TN6** 13 J3
Crowcombe **TA4** 7 K2
Crowdecote **SK17** 50 D6
Crowden **SK13** 50 C3
Crowdhill **SO50** 11 F2
Crowell **OX39** 22 A2
Crowfield, Northants. **NN13** 31 H4
Crowfield, Suff. **IP6** 35 F3
Crowhurst, E.Suss. **TN33** 14 C6
Crowhurst, Surr. **RH7** 23 G7
Crowhurst Lane End **RH7** 23 G7
Crowland, Lincs. **PE6** 43 F4
Crowland, Suff. **IP31** 34 E1
Crowlas **TR20** 2 C5
Crowle, N.Lincs. **DN17** 51 K1
Crowle, Worcs. **WR7** 29 J3
Crowle Green **WR7** 29 J3
Crowmarsh Gifford **OX10** 21 K3
Crown Corner **IP13** 35 G1
Crownhill **PL6** 4 E5
Crownthorpe **NR18** 44 E5
Crowntown **TR13** 2 D5
Crow's Nest **PL14** 4 C4
Crows-an-wra **TR19** 2 A6
Crowsnest **SY5** 38 C5
Crowthorne **RG45** 22 B5
Crowton **CW8** 48 E5
Croxall **WS13** 40 E4
Croxby **LN7** 52 E3
Croxdale **DH6** 62 D3
Croxden **ST14** 40 C2
Croxley Green **WD3** 22 D2
Croxton, Cambs. **PE19** 33 F3
Croxton, N.Lincs. **DN39** 52 D1
Croxton, Norf. **IP24** 44 C7
Croxton, Staffs. **ST21** 39 G2
Croxton Green **SY14** 38 E7
Croxton Kerrial **NG32** 42 B3
Croxtonbank **ST21** 39 G2
Croy, High. **IV2** 96 E7
Croy, N.Lan. **G65** 75 F3
Croyde **EX33** 6 C2
Croyde Bay **EX33** 6 C2
Croydon, Cambs. **SG8** 33 G4
Croydon, Gt.Lon. **CR0** 23 G5
Cruach **PA43** 72 B5
Cruchie **AB54** 98 D6
Cruckmeole **SY5** 38 D5
Cruckton **SY5** 38 D4

Cruden Bay **AB42** 91 J1
Crudgington **TF6** 39 F4
Crudwell **SN16** 20 C2
Crug **LD1** 28 A1
Crugmeer **PL28** 3 G1
Crugybar **SA19** 17 K1
Crùlabhig **HS2** 100 D4
Crumlin **NP11** 19 F2
Crumpsall **M8** 49 H2
Crumpsbrook **DY14** 29 F1
Crundale, Kent **CT4** 15 F3
Crundale, Pembs. **SA62** 16 C3
Crunwere Farm **SA67** 16 E3
Crutherland Farm **G75** 74 E5
Cruwys Morchard **EX16** 7 G4
Crux Easton **RG20** 21 H6
Crwbin **SA17** 17 H3
Cryers Hill **HP15** 22 B2
Crymlyn **LL33** 46 E5
Crymych **SA41** 16 E1
Crynant **SA10** 18 A1
Crystal Palace **SE26** 23 G4
Cuaig **IV54** 94 D6
Cubbington **CV32** 30 E2
Cubert **TR8** 2 E3
Cubley **S36** 50 E2
Cublington, Bucks. **LU7** 32 B6
Cublington, Here. **HR2** 28 D5
Cuckfield **RH17** 13 G4
Cucklington **BA9** 9 G2
Cuckney **NG20** 51 H5
Cuckold's Green **NR34** 45 J7
Cuckoo Bridge **PE11** 43 F3
Cuckoo's Corner **GU34** 22 A7
Cuckoo's Nest **CH4** 48 C6
Cuddesdon **OX44** 21 J1
Cuddington, Bucks. **HP18** 31 J7
Cuddington, Ches. **CW8** 48 E5
Cuddington Heath **SY14** 38 D1
Cuddy Hill **PR4** 55 H6
Cudham **TN14** 23 H6
Cudliptown **PL19** 5 F3
Cudworth, S.Yorks. **S72** 51 F2
Cudworth, Som. **TA19** 8 C3
Cuerdley Cross **WA5** 48 E4
Cuffley **EN6** 23 G1
Cuidhaseadair **HS2** 101 H1
Cuidhir **HS9** 84 B4
Cuidhtinis (Quidinish) **HS3** 93 F3
Cuidrach **IV51** 93 J6
Cuilmuich **PA24** 73 K1
Cuil-uaine **PA37** 80 A4
Culag **G83** 74 B1
Culbo **IV7** 96 D5
Culbokie **IV7** 96 D6
Culbone **TA24** 7 G1
Culburnie **IV4** 96 B7
Culcabock **IV2** 96 D7
Culcharan **PA37** 80 A4
Culcharry **IV12** 97 F6
Culcheth **WA3** 49 F3
Culdrain **AB54** 90 D1
Culduie **IV54** 94 D7
Culford **IP28** 34 C2
Culfordheath **IP31** 34 C1
Culgaith **CA10** 61 H4
Culgower **KW8** 104 E7
Culham **OX14** 21 J2
Culindrach **PA29** 73 H5
Culkein **IV27** 102 C5
Culkerton **GL8** 20 C2
Cullachie **PH24** 89 G2
Cullen **AB56** 98 D4
Cullercoats **NE30** 71 J6
Cullicudden **IV7** 96 D5
Culligran **IV4** 95 K7
Cullingworth **BD13** 57 F6
Cullipool **PA34** 79 J6
Cullivoe **ZE2** 108 E2
Culloch **PH6** 81 J6
Culloden **IV2** 96 E7
Cullompton **EX15** 7 J5
Culmaily **KW10** 97 F2
Culmalzie **DG8** 64 D5
Culmington **SY8** 38 D7
Culmstock **EX15** 7 K4
Culnacraig **IV26** 95 G1
Culnadalloch **PA37** 80 A4
Culnaknock **IV51** 94 B5
Culnamean **IV47** 85 K2
Culpho **IP6** 35 G4
Culquhirk **DG8** 64 E5
Culrain **IV24** 96 C2
Culross **KY12** 75 H2
Culroy **KA19** 67 H2
Culsh **AB35** 90 B5
Culshabbin **DG8** 64 D5
Culswick **ZE2** 109 B8
Culter Allers Farm **ML12** 75 J7
Cultercullen **AB41** 91 H2
Cults, Aber. **AB54** 90 D1
Cults, Aberdeen **AB15** 91 G4
Cults, D. & G. **DG8** 64 E6
Cultybraggan Camp **PH6** 81 J6
Culverhouse Cross **CF5** 18 E4
Culverstone Green **TN15** 24 C5
Culverthorpe **NG32** 42 D1
Culvie **AB54** 98 D5
Culworth **OX17** 31 G4
Cumberhead **ML11** 75 F7
Cumberlow Green **SG9** 33 G5
Cumbernauld **G67** 75 F3
Cumberworth **LN13** 53 J5
Cuminestown **AB53** 99 G6
Cumloden **DG8** 64 E4
Cummersdale **CA2** 60 E1
Cummertrees **DG12** 69 G7
Cummingston **IV30** 97 J5
Cumnock **KA18** 67 K1
Cumnor **OX2** 21 H1

Cumrew **CA8** 61 G1
Cumrue **DG11** 69 F5
Cumstoun **DG6** 65 G5
Cumwhinton **CA4** 61 F1
Cumwhitton **CA8** 61 G1
Cundall **YO61** 57 K2
Cunninghamhead **KA3** 74 B6
Cunningsburgh **ZE2** 109 D10
Cunnister **ZE2** 108 E3
Cunnoquhie **KY15** 82 E6
Cupar **KY15** 82 E6
Cupar Muir **KY15** 82 E6
Curbar **S32** 50 E5
Curbridge, Hants. **SO30** 11 G3
Curbridge, Oxon. **OX29** 21 G1
Curdridge **SO32** 11 G3
Curdworth **B76** 40 D6
Curland **TA3** 8 B3
Curlew Green **IP17** 35 H2
Curling Tye Green **CM9** 24 E1
Curload **TA3** 8 C2
Curridge **RG18** 21 H4
Currie **EH14** 75 K4
Curry Mallet **TA3** 8 C2
Curry Rivel **TA10** 8 C2
Curteis' Corner **TN27** 14 D4
Curtisden Green **TN17** 14 C3
Curtisknowle **TQ9** 5 H5
Cury **TR12** 2 D6
Cusgarne **TR4** 2 E4
Cushnie **AB45** 99 F4
Cushuish **TA2** 7 K2
Cusop **HR3** 28 B4
Cusworth **DN5** 51 H2
Cutcloy **DG8** 64 E7
Cutcombe **TA24** 7 H2
Cutgate **OL11** 49 H1
Cuthill **IV25** 96 E3
Cutiau **LL42** 37 F4
Cutlers Green **CM6** 33 J5
Cutnall Green **WR9** 29 H2
Cutsdean **GL54** 30 B5
Cutsyke **WF10** 57 K7
Cutthorpe **S42** 51 F5
Cutts **ZE1** 109 D9
Cuttyhill **AB42** 99 J5
Cuxham **OX49** 21 K2
Cuxton **ME2** 24 D5
Cuxwold **LN7** 52 E2
Cwm, B.Gwent **NP23** 18 E1
Cwm, Denb. **LL18** 47 J5
Cwm Ffrwd-oer **NP4** 19 F1
Cwm Gwaun **SA65** 16 D1
Cwm Head **SY6** 38 D7
Cwm Irfon **LD5** 27 H4
Cwm Penmachno **LL24** 37 G1
Cwm Plysgog **SA43** 26 A4
Cwmafan **SA12** 18 A2
Cwmaman **CF44** 18 D2
Cwmann **SA48** 26 E4
Cwmbach, Carmar. **SA34** 17 F2
Cwmbach, Carmar. **SA15** 17 H4
Cwmbach, Powys **HR3** 28 A5
Cwmbach, Powys **LD2** 27 K3
Cwmbach, R.C.T. **CF44** 18 D1
Cwmbelan **SY18** 37 J7
Cwmbrân **NP44** 19 F2
Cwmbrwyno **SY23** 37 G7
Cwmcarn **NP11** 19 F2
Cwmcarvan **NP25** 19 H1
Cwm-Cewydd **SY20** 37 H4
Cwm-cou **SA38** 26 B4
Cwmcrawnon **LD3** 28 A7
Cwmdare **CF44** 18 C1
Cwmdu, Carmar. **SA19** 17 K1
Cwmdu, Powys **NP8** 28 A6
Cwmduad **SA33** 17 G1
Cwmerfyn **SY23** 37 G7
Cwmfelin **CF46** 18 D1
Cwmfelin Boeth **SA34** 16 E3
Cwmfelin Mynach **SA34** 17 F2
Cwmfelinfach **NP11** 18 E2
Cwmffrwd **SA31** 17 H3
Cwmgiedd **SA9** 27 G7
Cwmgors **SA18** 27 G7
Cwmgwili **SA14** 17 J3
Cwmgwrach **SA11** 18 B1
Cwmgwyn **SA2** 17 K5
Cwmhiraeth **SA44** 17 G1
Cwmifor **SA19** 17 K2
Cwmisfael **SA32** 17 H3
Cwm-Llinau **SY20** 37 H5
Cwmllyfri **SA33** 17 G3
Cwmllynfell **SA9** 27 G7
Cwm-mawr **SA14** 17 J3
Cwm-miles **SA34** 16 E2
Cwm-Morgan **SA38** 17 F1
Cwm-parc **CF42** 18 C2
Cwmpengraig **SA44** 17 G1
Cwmpennar **CF45** 18 D1
Cwmsychbant **SA40** 26 D4
Cwmsymlog **SY23** 37 F7
Cwmtillery **NP13** 19 F1
Cwm-twrch Isaf **SA9** 27 G7
Cwm-twrch Uchaf **SA9** 27 G7
Cwm-y-glo **LL55** 46 D6
Cwmyoy **NP7** 28 C6
Cwm-yr-Eglwys **SA42** 16 D1
Cwmyrhaiadr **SY20** 37 G6
Cwmystwyth **SY23** 27 G1
Cwrt **SY20** 37 F5
Cwrt-newydd **SA40** 26 D4
Cwrt-y-cadno **SA19** 17 K1
Cwrt-y-gollen **NP8** 28 B7
Cydweli (Kidwelly) **SA17** 17 H4
Cyffylliog **LL15** 47 J7
Cyfronydd **SY21** 38 A5
Cymau **LL11** 48 B7
Cymmer, N.P.T. **SA13** 18 B2
Cymmer, R.C.T. **CF39** 18 D2

Cyncoed **CF23** 18 E3
Cynghordy **SA20** 27 H5
Cynheidre **SA15** 17 H4
Cynwyd **LL21** 37 K1
Cynwyl Elfed **SA33** 17 G2

D

Dabton **DG3** 68 D4
Daccombe **TQ12** 5 K4
Dacre, Cumb. **CA11** 61 F4
Dacre, N.Yorks. **HG3** 57 G3
Dacre Banks **HG3** 57 G3
Daddry Shield **DL13** 61 K3
Dadford **MK18** 31 H5
Dadlington **CV13** 41 G6
Dafen **SA14** 17 J4
Daffy Green **IP25** 44 D5
Dagdale **ST14** 40 C2
Dagenham **RM10** 23 H3
Daggons **SP6** 10 C3
Daglingworth **GL7** 20 C1
Dagnall **HP4** 32 C7
Dail **PA35** 80 B4
Dail Beag **HS2** 100 E3
Dail Bho Dheas (South Dell) **HS2** 101 G1
Dail Bho Thuath (North Dell) **HS2** 101 G1
Dail Mòr **HS2** 100 E3
Dailly **KA26** 67 G3
Dailnamac **PA35** 80 A4
Dainton **TQ12** 5 J4
Dairsie (Osnaburgh) **KY15** 83 F6
Dairy House **HU12** 59 J7
Daisy Bank **WS5** 40 C6
Daisy Green **IP31** 34 E2
Dalabrog **HS8** 84 C2
Dalavich **PA35** 80 A6
Dalballoch **PH20** 88 D5
Dalbeattie **DG5** 65 J4
Dalblair **KA18** 68 B2
Dalbog **DD9** 90 D7
Dalbreck **IV28** 104 C7
Dalbury **DE7** 40 E2
Dalby, I.o.M. **IM5** 54 B6
Dalby, Lincs. **PE23** 53 H6
Dalby, N.Yorks. **YO60** 58 C2
Dalcairnie **KA6** 67 J3
Dalchalloch **PH18** 81 J1
Dalchalm **KW9** 97 G1
Dalchenna **PA32** 80 B7
Dalchirach **AB37** 89 J1
Dalchork **IV27** 103 H7
Dalchreichart **IV63** 87 J3
Dalchruin **PH6** 81 J6
Dalcross **IV2** 96 E7
Dalderby **LN9** 53 F6
Dalditch **EX9** 7 J7
Daldownie **AB35** 89 K4
Dale, Cumb. **CA4** 61 G2
Dale, I.o.Man. **OL3** 49 J2
Dale, Pembs. **SA62** 16 B4
Dale Abbey **DE7** 41 G2
Dale End, Derbys. **DE45** 50 E6
Dale End, N.Yorks. **BD20** 56 E5
Dale Head **CA10** 60 F5
Dale of Walls **ZE2** 109 A7
Dale Park **BN18** 12 C5
Dalehouse **TS13** 63 J5
Dalelia **PH36** 79 J1
Daless **IV12** 89 F1
Dalestie **AB37** 89 J3
Dalfad **AB35** 90 B4
Dalganachan **KW12** 105 F4
Dalgarven **KA13** 74 A6
Dalgety Bay **KY11** 75 K2
Dalgig **KA18** 67 K2
Dalginross **PH6** 81 J5
Dalgonar **DG3** 68 C3
Dalguise **PH8** 82 A3
Dalhalvaig **KW13** 104 D3
Dalham **CB8** 34 B2
Daligan **G84** 74 B2
Dalinlongart **PA23** 73 K2
Dalivaddy **PA28** 66 A1
Daljarrock **KA26** 67 F5
Dalkeith **EH22** 76 B4
Dallachulish **PA37** 80 A3
Dallas **IV36** 97 J6
Dallaschyle **IV12** 97 F7
Dallash **DG8** 64 E4
Dalleagles **KA18** 67 K2
Dallinghoo **IP13** 35 G3
Dallington, E.Suss. **TN21** 13 K5
Dallington, Northants. **NN5** 31 J2
Dallow **HG4** 57 G2
Dalmadilly **AB51** 91 F3
Dalmally **PA33** 80 C5
Dalmarnock **PH8** 82 B3
Dalmary **FK8** 74 D1
Dalmellington **KA6** 67 J3
Dalmeny **EH30** 75 K3
Dalmichy **IV27** 103 H7
Dalmigavie **IV13** 88 E3
Dalmore **IV17** 96 D5
Dalmuir **G81** 74 C3
Dalmunzie House Hotel **PH10** 89 H7
Dalnabreck **PH36** 79 J1
Dalnacarn **PH10** 82 B1
Dalnaglar Castle **PH10** 82 C1
Dalnaha **PA35** 79 H5
Dalnahaitnach **PH23** 89 F3
Dalnamain **IV25** 96 E2
Dalnatrat **PA38** 80 A2
Dalnavie **IV17** 96 D4
Dalness **PH49** 80 C2
Dalnessie **IV27** 103 J7

Dalnigap DG8	64 B3
Dalqueich KY13	82 B7
Dalreoch KA26	67 F5
Dalriech PH8	81 J4
Dalroy IV2	96 E7
Dalrulzian PH10	82 C2
Dalry KA24	74 A6
Dalrymple KA6	67 H2
Dalscote NN12	31 H3
Dalserf ML9	75 F5
Dalsetter ZE2	108 E3
Dalshangan DG7	67 K5
Dalskairth DG2	65 K3
Dalston CA5	60 E1
Dalswinton DG2	68 E5
Daltomach IV13	88 E2
Dalton, Cumb. LA6	55 J2
Dalton, D. & G. DG11	69 G6
Dalton, Lancs. WN8	48 D2
Dalton, N.Yorks. YO7	57 K2
Dalton, N.Yorks. DL11	62 C6
Dalton, Northumb. NE18	71 G6
Dalton, Northumb. NE46	62 A1
Dalton, S.Yorks. S65	51 G3
Dalton Magna S65	51 G3
Dalton Piercy TS27	63 F3
Dalton-in-Furness LA15	55 F2
Dalton-le-Dale SR7	63 F2
Dalton-on-Tees DL2	62 D6
Daltote PA31	73 F2
Daltra IV12	97 G7
Dalveich FK19	81 H5
Dalvennan KA19	67 H2
Dalvourn IV2	88 D1
Dalwhinnie PH19	88 D6
Dalwood EX13	8 B4
Dam Green NR16	44 E7
Damask Green SG4	33 F6
Damerham SP6	10 C3
Damgate NR13	45 J5
Damnaglaur DG9	64 B7
Damside PH3	82 A6
Danaway ME9	24 E5
Danbury CM3	24 D1
Danby YO21	63 J6
Danby Wiske DL7	62 E7
Dancers Hill EN5	23 F2
Dandaleith AB38	97 K7
Danderhall EH22	76 B4
Dane Bank M34	49 J3
Dane End SG12	33 G6
Dane Hills LE3	41 H5
Danebridge SK11	49 J6
Danehill RH17	13 H4
Danesmoor S45	51 G6
Danestone AB22	91 H3
Daniel's Water TN26	14 E3
Danskine EH41	76 D4
Danthorpe HU12	59 J6
Danzey Green B94	30 C2
Darby End B64	40 B7
Darby Green GU46	22 B5
Darenth DA2	23 J4
Daresbury WA4	48 E4
Darfield S73	51 G2
Dargate ME13	25 G5
Dargues NE19	70 D4
Darite PL14	4 C4
Darland ME7	24 D5
Darlaston WS10	40 B6
Darley HG3	57 H4
Darley Bridge DE4	50 E6
Darley Dale DE4	50 E6
Darley Head HG3	57 G4
Darley Hillside DE4	50 E6
Darlingscott CV36	30 D4
DARLINGTON DL	62 D5
Darliston SY13	38 E2
Darlton NG22	51 K5
Darnabo AB53	99 F6
Darnall S9	51 F4
Darnconner KA18	67 K1
Darnford AB31	91 F5
Darngarroch DG7	65 G4
Darnick TD6	76 D7
Darowen SY20	37 H5
Darra AB53	99 F6
Darracott EX39	6 A4
Darras Hall NE20	71 G6
Darrington WF8	51 G1
Darrow Green IP20	45 G7
Darsham IP17	35 J2
Dartfield AB43	99 J5
DARTFORD DA	23 J4
Dartington TQ9	5 H4
Dartmeet TQ13	5 G3
Dartmouth TQ6	5 J5
Darton S75	51 F1
Darvel KA17	74 D7
Darwell TN32	14 C5
Darwell Hole TN33	13 K5
Darwen BB3	56 B7
Datchet SL3	22 C4
Datchworth SG3	33 F7
Datchworth Green SG3	33 F7
Daubhill BL3	49 F2
Daugh of Kinermony AB38	97 K7
Dauntsey SN15	20 C3
Dauntsey Green SN15	20 C3
Dauntsey Lock SN15	20 C3
Dava PH26	89 H1
Davaar PA28	66 B2
Davan AB34	90 C4
Davenham CW9	49 F5
Davenport Green WA15	49 H4
Daventry NN11	31 G2
Davidstow PL32	4 B2
Davington DG13	69 H3

Daviot, Aber. AB51	91 F2
Daviot, High. IV2	88 E1
Davoch of Grange AB55	98 C5
Davyhulme M41	49 G3
Dawley TF4	39 F5
Dawlish EX7	5 K3
Dawn LL22	47 G5
Daws Heath SS7	24 E3
Daw's House PL15	6 B7
Dawsmere PE12	43 H2
Day Green CW11	49 G7
Dayhills ST15	40 B2
Dayhouse Bank B62	29 J1
Daylesford GL56	30 D6
Ddôl CH7	47 K5
Deadman's Cross MK45	32 E4
Deadwaters ML11	75 F6
Deal CT14	15 J2
Deal Hall CM0	25 G2
Dean, Cumb. CA14	60 B4
Dean, Devon TQ11	5 H4
Dean, Dorset SP5	9 J3
Dean, Hants. SO32	11 G3
Dean, Oxon. OX7	30 E6
Dean, Som. BA4	19 K7
Dean Bank DL17	62 D3
Dean Cross EX34	6 D1
Dean Head S35	50 E2
Dean Prior TQ11	5 H4
Dean Row SK9	49 H4
Dean Street ME15	14 C2
Deanburnhaugh TD9	69 J2
Deane, Gt.Man. BL3	49 F2
Deane, Hants. RG25	21 J6
Deanland SP5	9 J3
Deanlane End PO9	11 J3
Deans Bottom ME9	24 E5
Deanscales CA13	60 B4
Deansgreen WA13	49 F4
Deanshanger MK19	31 J5
Deanston FK16	81 J7
Dearham CA15	60 B3
Debach IP13	35 G3
Debate DG11	69 H5
Debden CB11	33 J5
Debden Cross CB11	33 J5
Debden Green, Essex CB11	33 J5
Debden Green, Essex IG10	23 H2
Debenham IP14	35 F2
Deblin's Green WR2	29 H4
Dechmont EH52	75 J3
Decker Hill TF11	39 G4
Deddington OX15	31 F5
Dedham CO7	34 E5
Dedham Heath CO7	34 E5
Dedworth SL4	22 C4
Deecastle AB34	90 C5
Deene NN17	42 C6
Deenethorpe NN17	42 C6
Deepcar S36	50 E3
Deepcut GU16	22 C6
Deepdale, Cumb. LA10	56 C1
Deepdale, N.Yorks. BD23	56 D2
Deeping Gate PE6	42 E5
Deeping St. James PE6	42 E5
Deeping St. Nicholas PE11	43 F4
Deepweir NP26	19 H3
Deerhill AB55	98 C5
Deerhurst GL19	29 H6
Deerhurst Walton GL19	29 H6
Deerton Street ME9	25 F5
Defford WR8	29 J4
Defynnog LD3	27 J6
Deganwy LL31	47 F5
Degnish PA34	79 J6
Deighton, N.Yorks. DL6	62 E6
Deighton, W.Yorks. HD2	50 D1
Deighton, York YO19	58 C5
Deiniolen LL55	46 D6
Delabole PL33	4 A2
Delamere CW8	48 E6
Delavorar AB37	89 J1
Delfrigs AB41	91 H2
Dell Lodge PH25	89 H3
Dell Quay PO20	12 B6
Delliefure PH26	89 H1
Delly End OX29	30 E7
Delnabo AB37	89 J3
Delny IV18	96 E4
Delph OL3	49 J2
Delphorrie AB33	90 C3
Delves DH8	62 C2
Delvine PH1	82 C3
Dembleby NG34	42 D2
Denaby DN12	51 G3
Denaby Main DN12	51 G3
Denbigh (Dinbych) LL16	47 J6
Denbury TQ12	5 J4
Denby DE5	41 F1
Denby Dale HD8	50 E2
Denchworth OX12	21 G2
Dendron LA13	55 F2
Denend AB54	90 E1
Denford NN14	32 C1
Dengie CM0	25 F1
Denham, Bucks. UB9	22 D3
Denham, Suff. IP21	35 F1
Denham, Suff. IP29	34 B2
Denham Green UB9	22 D3
Denham Street IP23	35 F1
Denhead, Aber. AB51	91 F3
Denhead, Aber. AB42	99 J5
Denhead, Fife KY16	83 F6
Denhead of Arbirlot DD11	83 G3
Denhead of Gray DD2	82 E4
Denholm TD9	70 A2
Denholme BD13	57 F6
Denholme Clough BD13	57 F6

Denio LL53	36 C2
Denmead PO7	11 H3
Denmill AB51	91 G3
Denmoss AB54	98 E6
Dennington IP13	35 G2
Denny FK6	75 G2
Dennyloanhead FK4	75 G2
Denshaw OL3	49 J1
Denside AB31	91 G5
Densole CT18	15 H3
Denston CB8	34 B3
Denstone ST14	40 C1
Dent LA10	56 C1
Denton, Cambs. PE7	42 E7
Denton, Darl. DL2	62 D5
Denton, E.Suss. BN9	13 H6
Denton, Gt.Man. M34	49 J3
Denton, Kent CT4	15 H3
Denton, Kent DA12	24 C4
Denton, Lincs. NG32	42 B2
Denton, N.Yorks. LS29	57 G5
Denton, Norf. IP20	45 G7
Denton, Northants. NN7	32 B3
Denton, Oxon. OX44	21 J1
Denton's Green WA10	48 D3
Denver PE38	44 A5
Denvilles PO9	11 J4
Denwick NE66	71 H2
Deopham NR18	44 E5
Deopham Green NR18	44 E6
Depden IP29	34 B3
Depden Green IP29	34 B3
Deptford, Gt.Lon. SE8	23 G4
Deptford, Wilts. BA12	10 B1
DERBY DE	41 F2
Derbyhaven IM9	54 B7
Dereham (East Dereham) NR19	44 D4
Dererach PA70	79 G5
Deri CF81	18 E1
Derril EX22	6 B5
Derringstone CT4	15 H3
Derrington ST18	40 A3
Derriton EX22	6 B5
Derry FK19	81 H5
Derry Hill SN11	20 C4
Derrythorpe DN17	52 B2
Dersingham PE31	44 A2
Dervaig PA75	79 F2
Derwen LL21	47 J7
Derwenlas SY20	37 G6
Derwydd SA18	17 K3
Derybruich PA21	73 H3
Desborough NN14	42 B7
Desford LE9	41 G5
Detchant NE70	77 J7
Dethick DE4	51 F7
Detling ME14	14 C2
Deuddwr SY22	38 B4
Deunant LL16	47 H6
Deuxhill WV16	39 F7
Devauden NP16	19 H2
Devil's Bridge (Pontarfynach) SY23	27 G1
Devitts Green CV7	40 E6
Devizes SN10	20 D5
Devonport PL1	4 E5
Devonside FK13	75 H1
Devoran TR3	2 E5
Dewar EH38	76 B6
Dewlish DT2	9 G5
Dewsall Court HR2	28 D5
Dewsbury WF12	57 H7
Dewsbury Moor WF15	57 H7
Dhiseig PA68	79 F4
Dhoon IM7	54 D5
Dhoor IM7	54 D4
Dhowin IM7	54 D3
Dhuhallow IV2	88 C2
Dial Green GU28	12 C4
Dial Post RH13	12 E5
Dibden SO45	11 F4
Dibden Hill HP8	22 C2
Dibden Purlieu SO45	11 F4
Dickleburgh IP21	45 F7
Dickleburgh Moor IP21	45 F7
Didbrook GL54	30 B5
Didcot OX11	21 J2
Diddington PE19	32 E2
Diddlebury SY7	38 E7
Didley HR2	28 D5
Didling GU29	12 B5
Didmarton GL9	20 B3
Didsbury M20	49 H3
Didworthy TQ10	5 G4
Digby LN4	52 D7
Digg IV51	93 K5
Diggle OL3	50 C2
Digmoor WN8	48 D2
Digswell AL6	33 F7
Dihewyd SA48	26 D3
Dildawn DG7	65 H5
Dilham NR28	45 H3
Dilhorne ST10	40 B1
Dillington PE19	32 E2
Dilston NE45	70 E7
Dilton Marsh BA13	20 B7
Dilwyn HR4	28 D3
Dilwyn Common HR4	28 D3
Dimple BL7	49 G1
Dinas, Carmar. SA33	17 F1
Dinas, Gwyn. LL54	46 C7
Dinas, Gwyn. LL53	36 B2
Dinas Cross SA42	16 D1
Dinas Dinlle LL54	46 C7
Dinas Powys CF64	18 E4
Dinas-Mawddwy SY20	37 H4
Dinbych (Denbigh) LL16	47 J6
Dinbych-y-Pysgod (Tenby) SA70	16 E4
Dinckley BB6	56 B6

Dinder BA5	19 J7
Dinedor HR2	28 E5
Dingestow NP25	28 D7
Dingley LE16	42 A7
Dingwall IV15	96 C6
Dinlabyre TD9	70 A4
Dinnet AB34	90 C5
Dinnington, S.Yorks. S25	51 H4
Dinnington, Som. TA17	8 D3
Dinnington, T. & W. NE13	71 H6
Dinorwig LL55	46 D6
Dinton, Bucks. HP17	31 J7
Dinton, Wilts. SP3	10 B1
Dinvin DG9	64 A5
Dinwoodie Mains DG11	69 G4
Dinworthy EX22	6 B4
Dipford TA3	8 B2
Dippen, Arg. & B. PA28	73 F7
Dippen, N.Ayr. KA27	66 E1
Dippenhall GU10	22 B7
Dipple, Moray IV32	98 B5
Dipple, S.Ayr. KA26	67 G3
Diptford TQ9	5 H5
Dipton DH9	62 C1
Dirdhu PH26	89 H2
Dirleton EH39	76 D2
Discoed LD8	28 B2
Diseworth DE74	41 G3
Dishes KW17	106 F5
Dishforth YO7	57 J2
Dishley LE11	41 H3
Disley SK12	49 J4
Diss IP22	45 F7
Disserth LD1	27 K3
Distington CA14	60 B4
Ditcheat BA4	9 F1
Ditchingham NR35	45 H6
Ditchley OX29	30 E6
Ditchling BN6	13 G5
Ditteridge SN13	20 B5
Dittisham TQ6	5 J5
Ditton, Halton WA8	48 D4
Ditton, Kent ME20	14 C2
Ditton Green CB8	33 K3
Ditton Priors WV16	39 F7
Dixton, Glos. GL20	29 J5
Dixton, Mon. NP25	28 E7
Dobcross OL3	49 J2
Dobwalls PL14	4 C4
Doc Penfro (Pembroke Dock) SA72	16 C4
Doccombe TQ13	7 F7
Dochgarroch IV3	88 D1
Dockenfield GU10	22 B7
Docker, Cumb. LA8	61 G7
Docker, Lancs. LA6	55 J2
Docking PE31	44 B2
Docklow HR6	28 E3
Dockray, Cumb. CA11	60 E4
Dockray, Cumb. CA7	60 D1
Dodbrooke TQ7	5 H6
Doddenham WR6	29 G3
Doddinghurst CM15	23 J2
Doddington, Cambs. PE15	43 H6
Doddington, Kent ME9	14 E2
Doddington, Lincs. LN6	52 C5
Doddington, Northumb. NE71	77 H7
Doddington, Shrop. DY14	29 F1
Doddiscombsleigh EX6	7 G7
Doddycross PL14	4 D4
Dodford, Northants. NN7	31 H2
Dodford, Worcs. B61	29 J1
Dodington, S.Glos. BS37	20 A3
Dodington, Som. TA5	7 K1
Dodington Ash BS37	20 A4
Dodleston CH4	48 C6
Dods Leigh ST10	40 C2
Dodscott EX38	6 D4
Dodworth S75	51 F2
Doehole DE55	51 F7
Doffcocker BL1	49 F1
Dog Village EX5	7 H6
Dogdyke LN4	53 F7
Dogmersfield RG27	22 A6
Dogsthorpe PE1	43 F5
Dol Fawr SY19	37 H5
Dolanog SY21	37 K4
Dolau, Powys LD1	28 A2
Dolau, R.C.T. CF72	18 D3
Dolbenmaen LL51	36 E1
Doley ST20	39 G3
Dolfach SY18	27 J1
Dolfor SY18	38 A7
Dolgarreg SA20	27 G5
Dolgarrog LL32	47 F6
Dolgellau LL40	37 G4
Dolgoch SY18	37 F5
Dolgran SA39	17 H1
Doll KW9	97 F1
Dollar FK14	75 H1
Dollarbeg FK14	75 H1
Dolphin CH8	47 K5
Dolphinholme LA2	55 J4
Dolphinton EH46	75 K6
Dolton EX19	6 D4
Dolwen, Conwy LL22	47 G5
Dolwen, Powys SY21	37 J5
Dolwyddelan LL25	47 F7
Dôl-y-bont SY23	37 F7
Dol-y-cannau HR5	28 A4
Dolyhir LD8	28 B3
Dolywern LL20	38 B2
Domgay SY22	38 B4
DONCASTER DN	51 H2
Donhead St. Andrew SP7	9 J2
Donhead St. Mary SP7	9 J2
Donibristle KY4	75 K2
Doniford TA23	7 J1

Donington, Lincs. PE11	43 F2
Donington, Shrop. WV7	40 A5
Donington le Heath LE67	41 G4
Donington on Bain LN11	53 F4
Donisthorpe DE12	41 F4
Donna Nook LN11	53 H3
Donnington, Glos. GL56	30 C6
Donnington, Here. HR8	29 G5
Donnington, Shrop. SY5	38 E5
Donnington, Tel. & W. TF2	39 G4
Donnington, W.Berks. RG14	21 H5
Donnington, W.Suss. PO20	12 B6
Donyatt TA19	8 C3
DORCHESTER, Dorset DT	9 F5
Dorchester, Oxon. OX10	21 J2
Dordon B78	40 E5
Dore S17	51 F4
Dores IV2	88 C1
Dorket Head NG5	41 H1
Dorking RH4	22 E7
Dorley's Corner IP17	35 H2
Dormans Park RH19	23 G7
Dormansland RH7	23 H7
Dormanstown TS10	63 G4
Dormer's Wells UB1	22 E3
Dormington HR1	28 E4
Dormston WR7	29 J3
Dorn GL56	30 D5
Dorney SL4	22 C4
Dorney Reach SL6	22 C4
Dornie IV40	86 E2
Dornoch IV25	96 E3
Dornock DG12	69 H7
Dorrery KW12	105 F3
Dorridge B93	30 C1
Dorrington, Lincs. LN4	52 D7
Dorrington, Shrop. SY5	38 D5
Dorsell AB33	90 D3
Dorsington CV37	30 C4
Dorstone HR3	28 C4
Dorton HP18	31 H7
Dorusduain IV40	87 F2
Dosthill B77	40 E6
Dotland NE46	62 A1
Dottery DT6	8 D5
Doublebois PL14	4 B4
Dougalston G62	74 D3
Dougarie KA27	73 G7
Doughton GL8	20 B2
Douglas, I.o.M. IM1	54 C6
Douglas, S.Lan. ML11	75 G7
Douglas and Angus DD5	83 F4
Douglas Water ML11	75 G7
Douglastown DD8	83 F3
Doulting BA4	19 K7
Dounby KW17	106 B5
Doune, Arg. & B. G83	74 B1
Doune, Arg. & B. FK17	80 E6
Doune, High. PH22	89 F3
Doune, High. IV24	96 B1
Doune, Stir. FK16	81 J7
Dounepark AB45	99 F4
Douneside AB34	90 C4
Dounie, High. IV19	96 D3
Dounie, High. IV24	96 C2
Dounreay KW14	104 E2
Dousland PL20	5 F4
Dovaston SY10	38 C3
Dove Holes SK17	50 C5
Dovenby CA13	60 B3
Dovendale LN11	53 G4
Dover CT16	15 J3
Dovercourt CO12	35 G5
Doverdale WR9	29 H2
Doveridge DE6	40 D2
Doversgreen RH2	23 F7
Dowally PH9	82 B3
Dowdeswell GL54	30 B6
Dowhill KA26	67 G3
Dowlais CF48	18 D1
Dowland EX19	6 D4
Dowlands DT7	8 B5
Dowlish Ford TA19	8 C3
Dowlish Wake TA19	8 C3
Down Ampney GL7	20 E2
Down End TA6	19 G7
Down Hatherley GL2	29 H6
Down St. Mary EX17	7 F5
Down Thomas PL9	5 F6
Downderry PL11	4 D5
Downe BR6	23 H5
Downend, I.o.W. PO30	11 G6
Downend, S.Glos. BS16	19 K4
Downend, W.Berks. RG20	21 H4
Downfield DD3	82 E4
Downfields CB7	33 K1
Downgate PL17	4 D3
Downham, Essex CM11	24 D2
Downham, Lancs. BB7	56 C5
Downham, Northumb. TD12	77 G7
Downham Market PE38	44 A5
Downhead, Cornw. PL15	4 A5
Downhead, Som. BA4	19 K7
Downhead, Som. BA22	8 E2
Downholland Cross L39	48 C2
Downholme DL11	62 C7
Downies AB12	91 H5
Downley HP13	22 B2
Downs CF5	18 E4
Downside, N.Som. BS48	19 H5
Downside, Som. BA4	19 K7
Downside, Som. BA3	19 K6
Downside, Surr. KT11	22 E6
Downton, Devon EX20	6 D7
Downton, Devon TQ6	5 J5
Downton, Hants. SO41	10 D5
Downton, Wilts. SP5	10 C2

Place	Code	Pg	Grid
Downton on the Rock SY8		28	D1
Dowsby PE10		42	E3
Dowthwaitehead CA11		60	E4
Doxey ST16		40	B3
Doynton BS30		20	A4
Drabblegate NR11		45	G3
Draethen NP10		19	F3
Draffan ML11		75	F6
Dragley Beck LA12		55	F2
Drakeland Corner PL7		5	F5
Drakelow DY11		40	A7
Drakemyre KA24		74	A5
Drakes Broughton WR10		29	J4
Drakes Cross B47		30	B1
Draughton, N.Yorks. BD23		57	F4
Draughton, Northants. NN6		31	J1
Drax YO8		58	C7
Draycot Foliat SN4		20	E4
Draycote CV23		31	F2
Draycott, Derbys. DE72		41	G2
Draycott, Glos. GL56		30	C5
Draycott, Shrop. WV5		40	A6
Draycott, Som. BS27		19	H6
Draycott, Worcs. WR9		29	H4
Draycott in the Clay DE6		40	D3
Draycott in the Moors ST10		40	B2
Drayford EX17		7	F4
Draynes PL14		4	C4
Drayton, Leics. LE16		42	B6
Drayton, Lincs. PE20		43	F2
Drayton, Norf. NR8		45	F4
Drayton, Oxon. OX15		31	F4
Drayton, Oxon. OX14		21	H2
Drayton, Ports. PO6		11	H4
Drayton, Som. TA10		8	D2
Drayton, Warks. CV37		30	C3
Drayton, Worcs. DY9		29	J1
Drayton Bassett B78		40	D5
Drayton Beauchamp HP22		32	C7
Drayton Parslow MK17		32	B6
Drayton St. Leonard OX10		21	J2
Drebley BD23		57	F4
Dreemskerry IM7		54	D4
Dreenhill SA62		16	C3
Drefach, Carmar. SA44		17	G1
Drefach, Carmar. SA14		17	J3
Dre-fach, Cere. SA40		26	E4
Drefelin SA44		17	G1
Dreghorn KA11		74	B7
Drem EH39		76	D3
Dreumasdal (Drimsdale) HS8		84	C1
Drewsteignton EX6		7	F6
Driby LN13		53	G5
Driffield, E.Riding YO25		59	G4
Driffield, Glos. GL7		20	D2
Drigg CA19		60	B7
Drighlington BD11		57	H7
Drimfern PA32		80	B6
Drimlee PA32		80	C6
Drimnin PA34		79	G2
Drimore HS8		92	C7
Drimpton DT8		8	D4
Drimsdale (Dreumasdal) HS8		84	C1
Drimsynie PA24		80	C7
Drimvore PA31		73	G1
Drinan IV49		86	B3
Dringhouses YO24		58	B4
Drinisiader HS3		93	G2
Drinkstone IP30		34	D2
Drinkstone Green IP30		34	D2
Drishaig PA32		80	C6
Drissaig PA35		80	A6
Drointon ST18		40	C3
Droitwich Spa WR9		29	H2
Dron PH2		82	C6
Dronfield S18		51	F5
Dronfield Woodhouse S18		51	F5
Drongan KA6		67	J2
Dronley DD3		82	E4
Droop DT10		9	G4
Dropmore SL1		22	C3
Droxford SO32		11	H3
Droylsden M43		49	J3
Druid LL21		37	K1
Druidston SA62		16	B3
Druimarbin PH33		87	G7
Druimavuic PA38		80	B3
Druimdrishaig PA31		73	F3
Druimindarroch PH39		86	C6
Druimkinnerras IV4		88	B1
Drum, Arg. & B. PA21		73	H3
Drum, P. & K. KY13		82	B7
Drumachloy PA20		73	J4
Drumbeg IV27		102	D5
Drumblade AB54		98	D6
Drumblair AB54		98	E6
Drumbuie, D. & G. DG4		68	C2
Drumbuie, High. IV40		86	D1
Drumburgh CA7		60	D1
Drumchapel G15		74	D3
Drumchardine IV5		96	C7
Drumchork IV22		94	E3
Drumclog ML10		74	E7
Drumdelgie AB54		98	C6
Drumderfit IV1		96	D6
Drumeldrie KY8		83	F7
Drumelzier ML12		75	K7
Drumfearn IV43		86	C3
Drumfern PH33		87	F7
Drumgarve PA28		66	B1
Drumgley DD8		83	F2
Drumguish PH21		88	E5
Drumhead AB31		90	E5
Drumin AB37		89	J1
Drumine IV2		96	E6
Drumjohn DG7		67	K4
Drumlamford House KA26		64	C3
Drumlasie AB31		90	E4
Drumlemble PA28		66	A2
Drumlithie AB39		91	F6
Drummond, High. IV16		96	D5
Drummond, Stir. FK17		81	H7
Drummore DG9		64	B7
Drummuir AB55		98	B6
Drummuir Castle AB55		98	B6
Drumnadrochit IV63		88	C2
Drumnagorrach AB54		98	D5
Drumnatorran PH36		79	K1
Drumoak AB31		91	F5
Drumore PA28		66	B1
Drumour PH8		82	A4
Drumrash DG7		65	G3
Drumrunie IV26		95	H1
Drums AB41		91	H2
Drumsturdy DD5		83	F4
Drumuie IV51		93	K7
Drumuillie PH24		89	G2
Drumvaich FK17		81	H7
Drumwhindle AB41		91	H1
Drumwhirn DG7		68	C5
Drunkendub DD11		83	H3
Druridge NE61		71	H4
Drury CH7		48	B6
Drws-y-nant LL40		37	H3
Dry Doddington NG23		42	B1
Dry Drayton CB3		33	G2
Dry Harbour IV40		94	C6
Dry Sandford OX13		21	H1
Dry Street SS16		24	C3
Drybeck CA16		61	H5
Drybridge, Moray AB56		98	C4
Drybridge, N.Ayr. KA11		74	B7
Drybrook GL17		29	F7
Dryburgh TD6		76	D7
Drygrange TD6		76	D7
Dryhope TD7		69	H1
Drymen G63		74	C2
Drymuir AB42		99	H6
Drynoch IV47		85	K1
Dryslwyn SA32		17	J2
Dryton SY5		38	E5
Duachy PA34		79	K5
Dubford AB45		99	F4
Dubhchladach PA29		73	G4
Dubheads PH7		82	A5
Dublin IP23		35	F2
Dubton DD8		83	G2
Duchal PA13		74	B4
Duchally IV27		103	F7
Duchray FK8		81	F7
Duck Bay G83		74	B2
Duck End, Beds. MK45		32	D4
Duck End, Cambs. PE19		33	F2
Duck End, Essex CM6		33	K6
Duck Street HG3		57	G3
Duckington SY14		48	D7
Ducklington OX29		21	G1
Duckmanton S44		51	G5
Duck's Cross MK44		32	E3
Ducks Island EN5		23	F2
Duddenhoe End CB11		33	H5
Duddingston EH15		76	A3
Duddington PE9		42	C5
Duddlestone TA3		8	B2
Duddleswell TN22		13	H4
Duddo TD15		77	H6
Duddon CW6		48	E6
Duddon Bridge LA18		54	E1
Dudleston SY12		38	C2
Dudleston Heath SY12		38	C2
DUDLEY, W.Mid. DY		40	B6
Dudley, T. & W. NE23		71	H6
Dudley Port DY4		40	B6
Dudlow's Green WA4		49	F4
Dudsbury BH22		10	B5
Duffield DE56		41	F1
Duffryn SA13		18	B2
Dufftown AB55		90	B1
Duffus IV30		97	J5
Dufton CA16		61	H4
Duggleby YO17		58	E3
Duiar PH26		89	J1
Duible KW8		104	E6
Duiletter PA33		80	C5
Duinish PH18		81	H1
Duirinish IV40		86	D1
Duisdealmor IV43		86	D3
Duisky PH33		87	G7
Duke End B46		40	E7
Dukestown NP22		28	A7
Dukinfield SK16		49	J3
Dulas LL70		46	C4
Dulax AB36		90	B3
Dulcote BA5		19	J7
Dulford EX15		7	J5
Dull PH15		81	K3
Dullatur G68		75	F3
Dullingham CB8		33	K3
Dullingham Ley CB8		33	K3
Dulnain Bridge PH26		89	G2
Duloe, Beds. PE19		32	E2
Duloe, Cornw. PL14		4	C5
Dulsie IV12		97	G7
Dulverton TA22		7	H3
Dulwich SE21		23	G4
Dumbarton G82		74	B3
Dumbleton WR11		30	B5
Dumcrieff DG10		69	G3
Dumeath AB54		90	C1
Dumfin G84		74	B2
DUMFRIES DG		65	K3
Dumgoyne G63		74	D2
Dummer RG25		21	J7
Dun DD10		83	H2
Dunach PA34		79	K5
Dunalastair PH16		81	J2
Dunan, Arg. & B. PA23		73	K3
Dunan, High. IV49		86	B2
Dunans PA22		73	J1
Dunball TA6		19	G7
Dunbar EH42		76	E3
Dunbeath KW6		105	G5
Dunbeg PA37		79	K4
Dunblane FK15		81	J7
Dunbog KY14		82	D6
Dunbridge SO51		10	E2
Duncanston, Aber. AB52		90	D2
Duncanston, High. IV7		96	C6
Dunchideock EX2		7	G7
Dunchurch CV22		31	F1
Duncote NN12		31	H3
Duncow DG1		68	E5
Duncraggan FK17		81	G7
Duncrievie PH2		82	C7
Duncroist FK21		81	G4
Duncrub PH2		82	B6
Duncryne G83		74	C2
Duncton GU28		12	C5
DUNDEE DD		83	F4
Dundee Airport DD2		82	E5
Dundon TA11		8	D1
Dundon Hayes TA11		8	D1
Dundonald KA2		74	B7
Dundonnell IV23		95	G3
Dundraw CA7		60	D2
Dundreggan IV63		87	K3
Dundrennan DG6		65	H6
Dundridge SO32		11	G3
Dundry BS41		19	J5
Dunearn KY3		76	A2
Dunecht AB32		91	F4
Dunfermline KY12		75	J2
Dunfield GL7		20	E2
Dunford Bridge S36		50	D2
Dungate ME9		14	E2
Dungavel ML10		74	E7
Dungworth S6		50	E3
Dunham NG22		52	B5
Dunham Town WA14		49	G4
Dunham Woodhouses WA14		49	G4
Dunham-on-the-Hill WA6		48	D5
Dunhampton DY13		29	H2
Dunholme LN2		52	D5
Dunino KY16		83	G6
Dunipace FK6		75	G2
Dunira PH6		81	J5
Dunkeld PH8		82	B3
Dunkerton BA2		20	A6
Dunkeswell EX14		7	K5
Dunkeswick LS17		57	J5
Dunkirk, Ches. CH1		48	C5
Dunkirk, Kent ME13		15	F2
Dunk's Green TN11		23	K6
Dunlappie DD9		83	G1
Dunley, Hants. RG28		21	H6
Dunley, Worcs. DY13		29	G2
Dunlop KA3		74	C6
Dunloskin PA23		73	K3
Dunmere PL31		4	A4
Dunmore, Arg. & B. PA29		73	F4
Dunmore, Falk. FK2		75	G2
Dunn KW1		105	G3
Dunn Street ME7		24	D5
Dunnabie DG11		69	H5
Dunnet KW14		105	H1
Dunnichen DD8		83	G3
Dunning PH2		82	B6
Dunnington, E.Riding YO25		59	H4
Dunnington, Warks. B49		30	B3
Dunnington, York YO19		58	C4
Dunnockshaw BB11		56	D7
Dunoon PA23		73	K3
Dunragit DG9		64	B5
Dunrostan PA31		73	F2
Duns TD11		77	F5
Duns Tew OX25		31	F6
Dunsa DE45		50	E5
Dunsby PE10		42	E3
Dunscore DG2		68	D5
Dunscroft DN7		51	J2
Dunsdale TS14		63	H5
Dunsden Green RG4		22	A4
Dunsfold GU8		12	D3
Dunsford EX6		7	G7
Dunshalt KY14		82	D6
Dunshill GL19		29	H5
Dunsinnan PH2		82	C4
Dunsland Cross EX22		6	C5
Dunsley, N.Yorks. YO21		63	K5
Dunsley, Staffs. DY7		40	A7
Dunsmore HP22		22	B1
Dunsop Bridge BB7		56	B4
Dunstable LU6		32	D6
Dunstall DE13		40	D3
Dunstall Green CB8		34	B2
Dunstan NE66		71	H2
Dunstan Steads NE66		71	H1
Dunster TA24		7	H1
Dunston, Lincs. LN4		52	D6
Dunston, Norf. NR14		45	G5
Dunston, Staffs. ST18		40	B4
Dunston Heath ST18		40	B4
Dunston Hill NE11		71	H7
Dunstone, Devon TQ13		5	H3
Dunstone, Devon PL8		5	F5
Dunsville DN7		51	J2
Dunswell HU6		59	G6
Dunsyre ML11		75	J6
Dunterton PL19		4	D3
Duntisbourne Abbots GL7		20	C1
Duntisbourne Leer GL7		20	C1
Duntisbourne Rouse GL7		20	C1
Duntish DT2		9	F4
Duntocher G81		74	C3
Dunton, Beds. SG18		33	F4
Dunton, Bucks. MK18		32	B6
Dunton, Norf. NR21		44	C2
Dunton Bassett LE17		41	H6
Dunton Green TN13		23	J6
Dunton Wayletts CM13		24	C2
Duntulm IV51		93	K4
Dunure KA7		67	G2
Dunure Mains KA7		67	G2
Dunvant SA2		17	J5
Dunvegan IV55		93	H7
Dunwich IP17		35	J1
Dura KY15		83	F6
Durdar CA2		60	F1
Durgan TR11		2	E6
Durgates TN5		13	K3
DURHAM DH		62	D2
Durinemast PA34		79	H2
Durisdeer DG3		68	D3
Durleigh TA5		8	B1
Durley, Hants. SO32		11	G3
Durley, Wilts. SN8		21	F5
Durley Street SO32		11	G3
Durlow Common HR8		29	F5
Durnamuck IV23		95	G2
Durness IV27		103	G2
Durno AB51		91	F2
Duror PA38		80	A2
Durran, Arg. & B. PA33		80	A7
Durran, High. KW14		105	G2
Durrants PO9		11	J4
Durrington, W.Suss. BN13		12	E6
Durrington, Wilts. SP4		20	E7
Dursley GL11		20	A2
Dursley Cross GL17		29	F7
Durston TA3		8	B2
Durweston DT11		9	H4
Dury ZE2		109	D6
Duston NN5		31	J2
Duthil PH23		89	G2
Dutlas LD7		28	B1
Duton Hill CM6		33	K6
Dutson PL15		6	B7
Dutton WA4		48	E5
Duxford CB2		33	H4
Dwygyfylchi LL34		47	F5
Dwyran LL61		46	C6
Dyce AB21		91	G3
Dyfatty SA16		17	H4
Dyffryn, Bridgend CF34		18	B2
Dyffryn (Valley), I.o.A. LL65		46	A5
Dyffryn, Pemb. SA64		16	C1
Dyffryn, V. of Glam. CF5		18	D4
Dyffryn Ardudwy LL44		36	E3
Dyffryn Castell SY23		37	G7
Dyffryn Ceidrych SA19		27	G6
Dyffryn Cellwen SA10		27	H7
Dyke, Devon EX39		6	B3
Dyke, Lincs. PE10		42	E3
Dyke, Moray IV36		97	G6
Dykehead, Angus DD8		82	E1
Dykehead, N.Lan. ML7		75	G5
Dykehead, Stir. FK8		74	D1
Dykelands AB30		83	J1
Dykends PH11		82	D2
Dykeside AB53		99	F6
Dylife SY19		37	H6
Dymchurch TN29		15	G5
Dymock GL18		29	G5
Dyrham SN14		20	A4
Dysart KY1		76	B1
Dyserth LL18		47	J5

E

Place	Code	Pg	Grid
Eabost IV56		85	J1
Eachwick NE18		71	G6
Eadar dha Fhadhail HS2		100	C4
Eagland Hill PR3		55	H5
Eagle LN6		52	B6
Eagle Barnsdale LN6		52	B6
Eagle Moor LN6		52	B6
Eaglescliffe TS16		63	F5
Eaglesfield, Cumb. CA13		60	B4
Eaglesfield, D. & G. DG11		69	H6
Eaglesham G76		74	D5
Eaglethorpe PE8		42	D6
Eagley BL1		49	G1
Eairy IM4		54	B6
Eakley MK16		32	B3
Eakring NG22		51	J6
Ealand DN17		52	B1
Ealing W5		22	E3
Eamont Bridge CA10		61	G4
Earby BB18		56	E5
Earcroft BB3		56	B7
Eardington WV16		39	G6
Eardisland HR6		28	D3
Eardisley HR3		28	C4
Eardiston, Shrop. SY11		38	C3
Eardiston, Worcs. WR15		29	F2
Earith PE28		33	G1
Earl Shilton LE9		41	G6
Earl Soham IP13		35	G2
Earl Sterndale SK17		50	C6
Earl Stonham IP14		35	F3
Earle NE71		70	E1
Earlestown WA12		48	E3
Earley RG6		22	A4
Earlham NR4		45	F5
Earlish IV51		93	J5
Earls Barton NN6		32	B2
Earls Colne CO6		34	C6
Earl's Common WR9		29	J3
Earl's Court SW5		23	F4
Earl's Croome WR8		29	H4
Earl's Green IP14		34	E2
Earlsdon CV5		30	E1
Earlsferry KY9		83	F7
Earlsford AB51		91	G1
Earlsheaton WF12		57	H7
Earlston TD4		76	D7
Earlswood, Mon. NP16		19	H2
Earlswood, Surr. RH1		23	F7
Earlswood, Warks. B94		30	C1
Earnley PO20		12	B7
Earnshaw Bridge PR26		55	J7
Earsairidh HS9		84	C5
Earsdon NE25		71	J6
Earsdon Moor NE61		71	G4
Earsham NR35		45	H7
Earsham Street IP21		35	G1
Earswick YO32		58	C4
Eartham PO18		12	C6
Earthcott Green BS35		19	K3
Easby TS9		63	G6
Easdale, Arg. & B. PA34		79	J6
Easdale, Arg. & B. PA34		79	J6
Easebourne GU29		12	B4
Easenhall CV23		31	F1
Eashing GU7		22	C7
Easington, Bucks. HP18		31	H7
Easington, Dur. SR8		62	E2
Easington, E.Riding HU12		53	G1
Easington, Northumb. NE70		77	K7
Easington, Oxon. OX49		21	K2
Easington, R. & C. TS13		63	J5
Easington Colliery SR8		63	F2
Easington Lane DH5		62	E2
Easingwold YO61		58	B3
Easole Street CT15		15	H2
Eassie DD8		82	E3
East Aberthaw CF62		18	D5
East Acton W3		23	F3
East Allington TQ9		5	H6
East Anstey EX16		7	G3
East Anton SP11		21	G7
East Appleton DL10		62	D7
East Ardsley WF3		57	J7
East Ashey PO33		11	G6
East Ashling PO18		12	B6
East Auchronie AB32		91	G4
East Ayton YO12		59	F1
East Barkwith LN8		52	E4
East Barming ME16		14	C2
East Barnby YO21		63	K5
East Barnet EN4		23	F2
East Barsham NR22		44	D2
East Beckham NR11		45	F2
East Bedfont TW14		22	D4
East Bergholt CO7		34	E5
East Bierley BD4		57	G7
East Bilney NR20		44	D4
East Blatchington BN25		13	H7
East Boldon NE36		71	J7
East Boldre SO42		10	E4
East Bolton NE66		71	G2
East Bower TA6		8	C1
East Brent TA9		19	G6
East Bridge IP16		35	J2
East Bridgford NG13		41	J1
East Brora KW9		97	G1
East Buckland EX32		6	E2
East Budleigh EX9		7	J7
East Burnham SL2		22	C3
East Burra ZE2		109	C9
East Burrafirth ZE2		109	C7
East Burton BH20		9	H6
East Butsfield DL13		62	C2
East Butterleigh EX15		7	H5
East Butterwick DN17		52	B2
East Cairnbeg AB30		91	F7
East Calder EH53		75	J4
East Carleton NR14		45	F5
East Carlton, Northants. LE16		42	B7
East Carlton, W.Yorks. LS19		57	H5
East Chaldon (Chaldon Herring) DT2		9	G6
East Challow OX12		21	G3
East Charleton TQ7		5	H6
East Chelborough DT2		8	E4
East Chiltington BN7		13	G5
East Chinnock BA22		8	D3
East Chisenbury SN9		20	E6
East Clandon GU4		22	D6
East Claydon MK18		31	J6
East Clyne KW9		97	G1
East Clyth KW3		105	H5
East Coker BA22		8	E3
East Compton, Dorset SP7		9	H3
East Compton, Som. BA4		19	K7
East Coombe EX17		7	G5
East Cornworthy TQ9		5	J5
East Cottingwith YO42		58	D5
East Cowes PO32		11	G5
East Cowick DN14		58	C7
East Cowton DL7		62	E6
East Cramlington NE23		71	H6
East Cranmore BA4		19	K7
East Creech BH20		9	J6
East Croachy IV2		88	D2
East Darlochan PA28		66	A1
East Davoch AB34		90	C4
East Dean, E.Suss. BN20		13	J7
East Dean, Hants. SP5		10	D2
East Dean, W.Suss. PO18		12	C5
East Dereham (Dereham) NR19		44	D4
East Down EX31		6	D1
East Drayton DN22		51	K5
East Dundry BS41		19	J5
East Ella HU5		59	G7

East End

East End, *E.Riding* **HU12** 59 H6
East End, *E.Riding* **HU12** 59 J7
East End, *Essex* **CM0** 25 G1
East End, *Hants.* **RG20** 21 H5
East End, *Hants.* **SO41** 10 E5
East End, *Herts.* **SG9** 33 H6
East End, *Kent* **TN17** 14 D4
East End, *Kent* **ME12** 25 F4
East End, *M.K.* **MK16** 32 C4
East End, *N.Som.* **BS48** 19 H4
East End, *Oxon.* **OX29** 30 E7
East End, *Poole* **BH21** 9 J5
East End, *Som.* **BA3** 19 J6
East End, *Suff.* **CO7** 35 F5
East End, *Suff.* **IP14** 35 F3
East Farleigh **ME15** 14 C2
East Farndon **LE16** 42 A7
East Ferry **DN21** 52 B3
East Firsby **LN8** 52 D4
East Fleetham **NE68** 71 H1
East Fortune **EH39** 76 D3
East Garston **RG17** 21 G4
East Ginge **OX12** 21 H3
East Goscote **LE7** 41 J4
East Grafton **SN8** 21 F5
East Green, *Suff.* **IP17** 35 J2
East Green, *Suff.* **CB8** 33 K3
East Grimstead **SP5** 10 D2
East Grinstead **RH19** 13 G3
East Guldeford **TN31** 14 E5
East Haddon **NN6** 31 H2
East Hagbourne **OX11** 21 J3
East Halton **DN40** 52 E1
East Ham **E6** 23 H3
East Hanney **OX12** 21 H2
East Hanningfield **CM3** 24 D1
East Hardwick **WF8** 51 G1
East Harling **NR16** 44 D7
East Harlsey **DL6** 63 F7
East Harnham **SP2** 10 C2
East Harptree **BS40** 19 J6
East Hartford **NE23** 71 H6
East Harting **GU31** 11 J3
East Hatch **SP3** 9 J2
East Hatley **SG19** 33 F3
East Hauxwell **DL8** 62 C7
East Haven **DD7** 83 G4
East Heckington **PE20** 42 E1
East Hedleyhope **DL13** 62 C2
East Helmsdale **KW8** 105 F7
East Hendred **OX12** 21 H3
East Herrington **SR3** 62 E1
East Heslerton **YO17** 59 F2
East Hewish **BS24** 19 H5
East Hoathly **BN8** 13 J5
East Holme **BH20** 9 H6
East Horndon **CM13** 24 C3
East Horrington **BA5** 19 J7
East Horsley **KT24** 22 D6
East Horton **NE71** 77 J7
East Howe **BH10** 10 B5
East Huntspill **TA9** 19 G7
East Hyde **LU2** 32 E7
East Ilsley **RG20** 21 H3
East Keal **PE23** 53 G6
East Kennett **SN8** 20 E5
East Keswick **LS17** 57 J5
East Kilbride **G74** 74 E5
East Kimber **EX20** 6 C6
East Kirkby **PE23** 53 G6
East Knapton **YO17** 58 E2
East Knighton **DT2** 9 H6
East Knowstone **EX36** 7 G3
East Knoyle **SP3** 9 H1
East Kyloe **NE70** 77 J7
East Lambrook **TA13** 8 D3
East Langdon **CT15** 15 J3
East Langton **LE16** 42 A6
East Langwell **IV28** 96 E1
East Lavant **PO18** 12 B6
East Lavington **GU28** 12 C5
East Layton **DL11** 62 C5
East Leake **LE12** 41 H3
East Learmouth **TD12** 77 G7
East Learney **AB31** 90 E4
East Leigh, *Devon* **EX17** 7 F5
East Leigh, *Devon* **EX18** 7 F4
East Leigh, *Devon* **TQ9** 5 H5
East Leigh, *Devon* **PL21** 5 G5
East Lexham **PE32** 44 C4
East Lilburn **NE66** 71 F1
East Linton **EH40** 76 D3
East Liss **GU33** 11 J2
East Lockinge **OX12** 21 H3
East Looe **PL13** 4 C5
East Lound **DN9** 51 K2
East Lulworth **BH20** 9 H6
East Lutton **YO17** 59 F3
East Lydford **TA11** 8 E1
East Lyn **EX35** 7 F1
East Lyng **TA3** 8 C2
East Mains **AB31** 90 E5
East Malling **ME19** 14 C2
East Malling Heath **ME19** 23 K6
East March **DD4** 83 F4
East Marden **PO18** 12 B5
East Markham **NG22** 51 K5
East Martin **SP6** 10 B3
East Marton **BD23** 56 E4
East Meon **GU32** 11 H2
East Mere **EX16** 7 H4
East Mersea **CO5** 34 E7
East Mey **KW14** 105 J1
East Molesey **KT8** 22 E5
East Moor **WF1** 57 J7
East Morden **BH20** 9 J5
East Morriston **TD4** 76 E6
East Morton **BD20** 57 G5
East Ness **YO62** 58 C2
East Newton **HU11** 59 J6
East Norton **LE7** 42 A5
East Oakley **RG23** 21 J6
East Ogwell **TQ12** 5 J3
East Orchard **SP7** 9 H3
East Ord **TD15** 77 H5
East Panson **PL15** 6 B6
East Parley **BH23** 10 C5
East Peckham **TN12** 23 K7
East Pennard **BA4** 8 E1
East Portlemouth **TQ8** 5 H7
East Prawle **TQ7** 5 H7
East Preston **BN16** 12 D6
East Pulham **DT2** 9 G4
East Putford **EX22** 6 B4
East Quantoxhead **TA5** 7 K1
East Rainton **DH5** 62 E2
East Ravendale **DN37** 53 F3
East Raynham **NR21** 44 C3
East Rigton **LS17** 57 J5
East Rolstone **BS24** 19 G5
East Rounton **DL6** 63 F6
East Row **YO21** 63 K5
East Rudham **PE31** 44 C3
East Runton **NR27** 45 G1
East Ruston **NR12** 45 H3
East Saltoun **EH34** 76 C4
East Shefford **RG17** 21 G4
East Sleekburn **NE22** 71 H5
East Somerton **NR29** 45 J4
East Stockwith **DN21** 51 K3
East Stoke, *Dorset* **BH20** 9 H6
East Stoke, *Notts.* **NG23** 42 A1
East Stour **SP8** 9 H2
East Stourmouth **CT3** 25 J5
East Stratton **SO21** 21 J7
East Street **BA6** 8 E1
East Studdal **CT15** 15 J3
East Suisnish **IV40** 86 B1
East Taphouse **PL14** 4 B4
East Thirston **NE65** 71 G4
East Tilbury **RM18** 24 C4
East Tisted **GU34** 11 J1
East Torrington **LN8** 52 E4
East Town **BA4** 19 K7
East Tuddenham **NR20** 44 E4
East Tytherley **SP5** 10 D2
East Tytherton **SN15** 20 C4
East Village **EX17** 7 G5
East Wall **TF13** 38 E6
East Walton **PE32** 44 B4
East Wellow **SO51** 10 E2
East Wemyss **KY1** 76 B1
East Whitburn **EH47** 75 H4
East Wickham **DA16** 23 H4
East Williamston **SA70** 16 D4
East Winch **PE32** 44 A4
East Winterslow **SP5** 10 D1
East Wittering **PO20** 11 J5
East Witton **DL8** 57 G1
East Woodburn **NE48** 70 E5
East Woodhay **RG20** 21 H5
East Woodlands **BA11** 20 A7
East Worldham **GU34** 11 J1
East Worlington **EX17** 7 F4
East Youlstone **EX23** 6 A4
Eastacott **EX37** 6 E3
Eastbourne **BN21** 13 K7
Eastbrook **CF64** 18 E4
Eastburn, *E.Riding* **YO25** 59 F4
Eastburn, *W.Yorks.* **BD20** 57 F5
Eastbury, *Herts.* **HA6** 22 E2
Eastbury, *W.Berks.* **RG17** 21 G4
Eastby **BD23** 57 F4
Eastchurch **ME12** 25 F4
Eastcombe, *Glos.* **GL6** 20 B1
Eastcombe, *Som.* **TA4** 7 K2
Eastcote, *Gt.Lon.* **HA5** 22 E3
Eastcote, *Northants.* **NN12** 31 H3
Eastcote, *W.Mid.* **B92** 30 C1
Eastcott, *Cornw.* **EX23** 6 A4
Eastcott, *Wilts.* **SN10** 20 D6
Eastcourt **SN16** 20 C2
Eastdown **TQ6** 5 J6
Eastend **OX7** 30 E6
Easter Ardross **IV17** 96 D4
Easter Balgedie **KY13** 82 C7
Easter Balmoral **AB35** 89 K5
Easter Boleskine **IV2** 88 C2
Easter Borland **FK8** 81 H7
Easter Brae **IV7** 96 D5
Easter Buckieburn **FK6** 75 F2
Easter Compton **BS35** 19 J3
Easter Drummond **IV2** 88 B3
Easter Dullater **FK17** 81 G7
Easter Ellister **PA48** 72 A5
Easter Fearn **IV24** 96 D3
Easter Galcantray **IV12** 97 F7
Easter Howlaws **TD10** 77 F6
Easter Kinkell **IV7** 96 C6
Easter Knox **DD11** 83 G3
Easter Lednathie **DD8** 82 E1
Easter Moniack **IV5** 96 C7
Easter Ord **AB32** 91 G4
Easter Poldar **FK8** 74 E1
Easter Skeld (Skeld) **ZE2** 109 C8
Easter Suddie **IV8** 96 D6
Easter Tulloch **AB30** 91 F7
Easter Whyntie **AB45** 98 E4
Eastergate **PO20** 12 C6
Easterhouse **G34** 74 E4
Easterton **SN10** 20 D6
Easterton Sands **SN10** 20 D6
Eastertown **BS24** 19 G6
Eastfield, *Bristol* **BS9** 19 J4
Eastfield, *N.Lan.* **ML7** 75 G4
Eastfield, *N.Yorks.* **YO11** 59 G1
Eastfield Hall **NE65** 71 H3
Eastgate, *Dur.* **DL13** 62 A3
Eastgate, *Lincs.* **PE10** 42 E4
Eastgate, *Norf.* **NR10** 45 F3
Easthall **SG4** 33 F6
Eastham, *Mersey.* **CH62** 48 C4
Eastham, *Worcs.* **WR15** 29 F2
Easthampstead **RG12** 22 B5
Easthampton **HR6** 28 D2
Easthaugh **NR9** 44 E4
Eastheath **RG41** 22 B5
Easthope **TF13** 38 E6
Easthorpe, *Essex* **CO6** 34 D6
Easthorpe, *Leics.* **NG13** 42 B2
Easthorpe, *Notts.* **NG25** 51 K7
Easthouses **EH22** 76 B4
Eastington, *Devon* **EX17** 7 F5
Eastington, *Glos.* **GL54** 30 C7
Eastington, *Glos.* **GL10** 20 A1
Eastleach Martin **GL7** 21 F1
Eastleach Turville **GL7** 21 F1
Eastleigh, *Devon* **EX39** 6 C3
Eastleigh, *Hants.* **SO50** 11 F3
Eastling **ME13** 14 E2
Eastmoor, *Derbys.* **S42** 51 F5
Eastmoor, *Norf.* **PE33** 44 B5
Eastnor **HR8** 29 G5
Eastoft **DN17** 52 B1
Eastoke **PO11** 11 J5
Easton, *Cambs.* **PE28** 32 E1
Easton, *Cumb.* **CA6** 69 K6
Easton, *Cumb.* **CA7** 60 D1
Easton, *Devon* **TQ13** 7 F7
Easton, *Dorset* **DT5** 9 F7
Easton, *Hants.* **SO21** 11 G1
Easton, *I.o.W.* **PO40** 10 E6
Easton, *Lincs.* **NG33** 42 C3
Easton, *Norf.* **NR9** 45 F4
Easton, *Som.* **BA5** 19 J7
Easton, *Suff.* **IP13** 35 G3
Easton, *Wilts.* **SN13** 20 B4
Easton Grey **SN16** 20 B3
Easton Maudit **NN29** 32 B3
Easton on the Hill **PE9** 42 D5
Easton Royal **SN9** 21 F5
Easton-in-Gordano **BS20** 19 J4
Eastrea **PE7** 43 F6
Eastriggs **DG12** 69 H7
Eastrington **DN14** 58 D6
Eastry **CT13** 15 J2
Eastside **KW17** 107 D8
East-the-Water **EX39** 6 C3
Eastville **BS16** 19 K4
Eastwell **LE14** 42 A3
Eastwick **CM20** 33 H7
Eastwood, *Notts.* **NG16** 41 G1
Eastwood, *S'end* **SS9** 24 E3
Eastwood, *S.Yorks.* **S65** 51 G3
Eastwood, *W.Yorks.* **OL14** 56 E7
Eastwood End **PE15** 43 H6
Eathorpe **CV33** 30 E2
Eaton, *Ches.* **CW12** 49 H6
Eaton, *Ches.* **CW6** 48 E6
Eaton, *Leics.* **NG32** 42 A3
Eaton, *Norf.* **NR2** 45 G5
Eaton, *Norf.* **PE36** 44 A2
Eaton, *Notts.* **DN22** 51 K5
Eaton, *Oxon.* **OX13** 21 H1
Eaton, *Shrop.* **SY6** 38 E6
Eaton, *Shrop.* **SY9** 38 C7
Eaton Bishop **HR2** 28 D5
Eaton Bray **LU6** 32 C6
Eaton Constantine **SY5** 39 F5
Eaton Ford **PE19** 32 E3
Eaton Hall **CH4** 48 D6
Eaton Hastings **SN7** 21 F2
Eaton Socon **PE19** 32 E3
Eaton upon Tern **TF9** 39 F3
Eaves Green **CV7** 40 E7
Eavestone **HG4** 57 H3
Ebberston **YO13** 58 E1
Ebbesborne Wake **SP5** 9 J2
Ebbw Vale **NP23** 18 E1
Ebchester **DH8** 62 C1
Ebdon **BS22** 19 G5
Ebford **EX3** 7 H7
Ebley **GL5** 20 B1
Ebnal **SY14** 38 D1
Ebrington **GL55** 30 C4
Ebsworthy Town **EX20** 6 D6
Ecchinswell **RG20** 21 H6
Ecclaw **TD13** 77 F4
Ecclefechan **DG11** 69 G6
Eccles, *Gt.Man.* **M30** 49 G3
Eccles, *Kent* **ME20** 24 D5
Eccles, *Sc.Bord.* **TD5** 77 F6
Eccles Green **HR4** 28 C4
Eccles Road **NR16** 44 E6
Ecclesfield **S35** 51 F3
Ecclesgreig **DD10** 83 J1
Eccleshall **ST21** 40 A3
Eccleshill **BD10** 57 G6
Ecclesmachan **EH52** 75 J3
Eccles-on-Sea **NR12** 45 J3
Eccleston, *Ches.* **CH4** 48 D6
Eccleston, *Lancs.* **PR7** 48 E1
Eccleston, *Mersey.* **WA10** 48 D3
Eccup **LS16** 57 H5
Echt **AB32** 91 F4
Eckford **TD5** 70 C1
Eckington, *Derbys.* **S21** 51 G5
Eckington, *Worcs.* **WR10** 29 J4
Ecton, *Northants.* **NN6** 32 B2
Ecton, *Staffs.* **SK17** 50 C7
Edale **S33** 50 D4
Eday **KW17** 106 E4
Edburton **BN5** 13 F5
Edderside **CA15** 60 C2
Edderton **IV19** 96 E3
Eddington **RG17** 21 G5
Eddleston **EH45** 76 A6
Eden Park **BR3** 23 G5
Eden Vale **TS27** 63 F3
Edenbridge **TN8** 23 H7
Edendonich **PA33** 80 C5
Edenfield **BL0** 49 G1
Edenhall **CA11** 61 G3
Edenham **PE10** 42 D3
Edensor **DE45** 50 E5
Edentaggart **G83** 74 B1
Edenthorpe **DN3** 51 J2
Edern **LL53** 36 B2
Edgarley **BA6** 8 E1
Edgbaston **B15** 40 C7
Edgcote **OX17** 31 G4
Edgcott, *Bucks.* **HP18** 31 H6
Edgcott, *Som.* **TA24** 7 G2
Edgcumbe **TR10** 2 E5
Edge, *Glos.* **GL6** 20 B1
Edge, *Shrop.* **SY5** 38 C5
Edge End **GL16** 28 E7
Edge Green, *Ches.* **SY14** 48 D7
Edge Green, *Gt.Man.* **WA3** 48 E3
Edge Green, *Norf.* **NR16** 44 E7
Edgebolton **SY4** 38 E3
Edgefield **NR24** 44 E2
Edgehead **EH37** 76 B4
Edgeley **SY13** 38 E1
Edgerley **SY10** 38 C4
Edgerton **HD2** 50 D1
Edgeworth **GL6** 20 C1
Edginswell **TQ2** 5 J4
Edgmond **TF10** 39 G4
Edgmond Marsh **TF10** 39 G3
Edgton **SY7** 38 C7
Edgware **HA8** 23 F2
Edgworth **BL7** 49 G1
Edinample **FK19** 81 H5
Edinbanchory **AB33** 90 C3
Edinbane **IV51** 93 J6
Edinbarnet **G81** 74 D3
EDINBURGH EH 76 A3
Edinburgh Airport **EH12** 75 K3
Edinchip **FK19** 81 G5
Edingale **B79** 40 E4
Edingley **NG22** 51 J7
Edingthorpe **NR28** 45 H2
Edingthorpe Green **NR28** 45 H2
Edington, *Som.* **TA7** 8 C1
Edington, *Wilts.* **BA13** 20 C6
Edintore **AB55** 98 C6
Edinvale **IV36** 97 J6
Edistone **EX39** 6 A3
Edith Weston **LE15** 42 C5
Edithmead **TA9** 19 G7
Edlaston **DE6** 40 D1
Edlesborough **LU6** 32 C7
Edlingham **NE66** 71 G3
Edlington **LN9** 53 F5
Edmondsham **BH21** 10 B3
Edmondsley **DH7** 62 D2
Edmondstown **CF40** 18 D2
Edmondthorpe **LE14** 42 B4
Edmonstone **KW17** 106 E5
Edmonton, *Cornw.* **PL27** 3 G1
Edmonton, *Gt.Lon.* **N18** 23 G2
Edmundbyers **DH8** 62 B1
Ednam **TD5** 77 F7
Ednaston **DE6** 40 E1
Edney Common **CM1** 24 C1
Edra **FK17** 81 F6
Edradynate **PH15** 81 K2
Edrom **TD11** 77 G5
Edstaston **SY4** 38 E2
Edstone **B95** 30 C2
Edvin Loach **HR7** 29 F3
Edwalton **NG12** 41 H2
Edwardstone **CO10** 34 D4
Edwardsville **CF46** 18 D2
Edwinsford **SA19** 17 K1
Edwinstowe **NG21** 51 J6
Edworth **SG18** 33 F4
Edwyn Ralph **HR7** 29 F3
Edzell **DD9** 83 H1
Efail Isaf **CF38** 18 D3
Efail-fâch **SA12** 18 A2
Efailnewydd **LL53** 36 C2
Efailwen **SA66** 16 E2
Efenechtyd **LL15** 47 K7
Effingham **KT24** 22 E6
Effirth **ZE2** 109 C7
Efflinch **DE13** 40 D4
Efford **EX17** 7 G5
Egbury **SP11** 21 H6
Egdean **RH20** 12 C4
Egdon **WR7** 29 J3
Egerton, *Gt.Man.* **BL7** 49 G1
Egerton, *Kent* **TN27** 14 E3
Egerton Forstal **TN27** 14 D3
Egerton Green **SY14** 48 E7
Egg Buckland **PL6** 4 E5
Eggborough **DN14** 58 B7
Eggerness **DG8** 64 E6
Eggesford Barton **EX18** 6 E4
Eggington **LU7** 32 C6
Egginton **DE65** 40 E3
Egglescliffe **TS16** 63 F5
Eggleston **DL12** 62 A4
Egham **TW20** 22 D4
Egham Wick **TW20** 22 C4
Egilsay **KW17** 106 D5
Egleton **LE15** 42 B5
Eglingham **NE66** 71 G2
Eglinton **KA12** 74 B6
Egloshayle **PL27** 4 A3
Egloskerry **PL15** 4 C2
Eglwys Cross **SY13** 38 D1
Eglwys Fach **SY20** 37 F6
Eglwys Nunydd **SA13** 18 A3
Eglwysbach **LL28** 47 G5
Eglwys-Brewis **CF62** 18 D5
Eglwyswrw **SA41** 16 E1
Egmanton **NG22** 51 K6
Egmere **NR22** 44 D2
Egremont **CA22** 60 B5
Egton **YO21** 63 K6
Egton Bridge **YO21** 63 K6
Egypt **SO21** 21 H7
Eigg **PH42** 85 K6
Eight Ash Green **CO6** 34 D6
Eignaig **PA34** 79 J3
Eil **PH22** 89 F3
Eilanreach **IV40** 86 E3
Eildon **TD6** 76 D7
Eilean Bhearnaraigh (Berneray) **HS6** 92 E3
Eilean Darach **IV23** 95 H3
Eilean Iarmain (Isleornsay) **IV43** 86 C3
Eilean Leodhais (Isle of Lewis) **HS** 101 F3
Eilean Scalpaigh (Scalpay) **HS4** 93 H2
Eilean Shona **PH36** 86 C7
Einacleit **HS2** 100 D5
Eiriosgaigh (Eriskay) **HS8** 84 C3
Eisgean **HS2** 101 F6
Eisingrug **LL47** 37 F2
Eisteddfa Gurig **SY23** 37 G7
Elan Village **LD6** 27 J2
Elberton **BS35** 19 K3
Elburton **PL9** 5 F5
Elcho **PH2** 82 C5
Elcombe **SN4** 20 E3
Elder Street **CB10** 33 J5
Eldernell **PE7** 43 G6
Eldersfield **GL19** 29 G5
Elderslie **PA5** 74 C4
Eldon **DL14** 62 D4
Eldrick **KA26** 67 G5
Eldroth **LA2** 56 C3
Eldwick **BD16** 57 G5
Elemore Vale **DH5** 62 E2
Elerch (Bont-goch) **SY24** 37 F7
Elford, *Northumb.* **NE68** 77 K7
Elford, *Staffs.* **B79** 40 D4
Elford Closes **CB6** 33 J1
Elgin **IV30** 97 K5
Elgol **IV49** 86 B3
Elham **CT4** 15 G3
Elie **KY9** 83 F7
Elilaw **NE65** 70 E3
Elim **LL65** 46 B4
Eling, *Hants.* **SO40** 10 E3
Eling, *W.Berks.* **RG18** 21 J4
Eliock **DG4** 68 D3
Elishader **IV51** 93 K5
Elishaw **NE19** 70 D4
Elkesley **DN22** 51 J5
Elkington **NN6** 31 H1
Elkstone **GL53** 29 J7
Elland **HX5** 57 G7
Elland Upper Edge **HX5** 57 G7
Ellary **PA31** 73 F3
Ellastone **DE6** 40 D1
Ellbridge **PL12** 4 E4
Ellel **LA2** 55 H4
Ellemford **TD11** 77 F4
Ellenborough **CA15** 60 B3
Ellenhall **ST21** 40 A3
Ellen's Green **RH12** 12 D3
Ellerbeck **DL6** 63 F7
Ellerby **TS13** 63 J5
Ellerdine **TF6** 39 F3
Ellerdine Heath **TF6** 39 F3
Ellergreen **LA8** 61 F7
Elleric **PA38** 80 B3
Ellerker **HU15** 59 F7
Ellerton, *E.Riding* **YO42** 58 D5
Ellerton, *N.Yorks.* **DL10** 62 D7
Ellerton, *Shrop.* **TF9** 39 G3
Ellerton Abbey **DL11** 62 B7
Ellesborough **HP17** 22 B1
Ellesmere **SY12** 38 C2
Ellesmere Park **M30** 49 G3
Ellesmere Port **CH65** 48 D5
Ellingham, *Hants.* **BH24** 10 C4
Ellingham, *Norf.* **NR35** 45 H6
Ellingham, *Northumb.* **NE67** 71 G1
Ellingstring **HG4** 57 G1
Ellington, *Cambs.* **PE28** 32 E1
Ellington, *Northumb.* **NE61** 71 H4
Ellington Thorpe **PE28** 32 E1
Elliot's Green **BA11** 20 A7
Ellisfield **RG25** 21 K7
Ellistown **LE67** 41 G4
Ellon **AB41** 91 H1
Ellonby **CA11** 60 F3
Ellough **NR34** 45 J7
Ellough Moor **NR34** 45 J7
Elloughton **HU15** 59 F7
Ellwood **GL16** 19 J1
Elm **PE14** 43 H5
Elm Park **RM12** 23 J3
Elmbridge **WR9** 29 J2
Elmdon, *Essex* **CB11** 33 H5
Elmdon, *W.Mid.* **B26** 40 D7
Elmdon Heath **B92** 40 D7
Elmers End **BR3** 23 G5
Elmer's Green **WN8** 48 D2
Elmesthorpe **LE9** 41 G6
Elmhurst **WS13** 40 D4
Elmley Castle **WR10** 29 J4
Elmley Lovett **WR9** 29 H2
Elmore **GL2** 29 G7
Elmore Back **GL2** 29 G7
Elmscott **EX39** 6 A3
Elmsett **IP7** 34 E4
Elmstead, *Essex* **CO7** 34 E6
Elmstead, *Gt.Lon.* **BR7** 23 H4
Elmstead Market **CO7** 34 E6
Elmstone **CT3** 25 J5
Elmstone Hardwicke **GL51** 29 J6

Elmswell, *E.Riding* YO25	59 F4	Epworth DN9	51 K2
Elmswell, *Suff.* IP30	34 D2	Epworth Turbary DN9	51 K2
Elmton S80	51 H5	Erbistock LL13	38 C1
Elphin IV27	102 E7	Erbusaig IV40	86 D2
Elphinstone EH33	76 B3	Erchless Castle IV4	96 B7
Elrick, *Aber.* AB32	91 G4	Erdington B24	40 D6
Elrick, *Moray* AB54	90 C2	Eredine PA33	80 A7
Elrig DG8	64 D6	Eriboll IV27	103 H3
Elrigbeag PA32	80 C6	Ericstane DG10	69 F2
Elsdon NE19	70 E4	Eridge Green TN3	13 J3
Elsecar S74	51 F2	Eriff DG7	67 K3
Elsenham CM22	33 J6	Erines PA29	73 G3
Elsfield OX3	31 G7	Erisey Barton TR12	2 E7
Elsham DN20	52 D1	Eriskay (Eiriosgaigh) HS8	84 C3
Elsing NR20	44 E4	Eriswell IP28	34 B1
Elslack BD23	56 E5	Erith DA8	23 J4
Elson, *Hants.* PO12	11 H4	Erlestoke SN10	20 C6
Elson, *Shrop.* SY12	38 C2	Ermington PL21	5 G5
Elsrickle ML12	75 J6	Ernesettle PL5	4 E4
Elstead GU8	22 C7	Erpingham NR11	45 F2
Elsted GU29	12 B5	Erringden Grange HX7	56 E7
Elsthorpe PE10	42 D3	Errogie IV2	88 C2
Elstob TS21	62 E4	Errol PH2	82 D5
Elston, *Lancs.* PR2	55 J6	Errollston AB42	91 J1
Elston, *Notts.* NG23	42 A1	Erskine PA8	74 C3
Elstone EX18	6 E4	Ervie DG9	66 D7
Elstow MK42	32 D4	Erwarton IP9	35 G5
Elstree WD6	22 E2	Erwood LD2	27 K4
Elstronwick HU12	59 J6	Eryholme DL2	62 E6
Elswick PR4	55 H6	Eryrys CH7	48 B7
Elsworth CB3	33 G2	Escart PA29	73 G4
Elterwater LA22	60 E6	Escart Farm PA29	73 G5
Eltham SE9	23 H4	Escomb DL14	62 C4
Eltisley PE19	33 F3	Escrick YO19	58 C5
Elton, *Cambs.* PE8	42 D6	Esgair SA33	17 G2
Elton, *Ches.* CH2	48 D5	Esgairgeiliog SY20	37 G5
Elton, *Derbys.* DE4	50 E6	Esgyryn LL31	47 G5
Elton, *Glos.* GL14	29 G7	Esh DH7	62 C2
Elton, *Gt.Man.* BL8	49 G1	Esh Winning DH7	62 C2
Elton, *Here.* SY8	28 D1	Esher KT10	22 E5
Elton, *Notts.* NG13	42 A2	Eshott NE61	71 H4
Elton, *Stock.* TS21	62 F5	Eshton BD23	56 E4
Elton Green CH2	48 D5	Eskadale IV4	88 B1
Elvanfoot ML12	68 E2	Eskbank EH22	76 B4
Elvaston DE72	41 G2	Eskdale Green CA19	60 C6
Elveden IP24	34 C1	Eskdalemuir DG13	69 H4
Elvingston EH33	76 C3	Eskham DN36	53 G3
Elvington, *Kent* CT15	15 H2	Esknish PA44	72 B4
Elvington, *York* YO41	58 D5	Esperley Lane Ends DL13	62 C4
Elwick, *Hart.* TS27	63 F3	Espley Hall NE61	71 G4
Elwick, *Northumb.* NE70	77 K7	Esprick PR4	55 H6
Elworth CW11	49 G6	Essendine PE9	42 D4
Elworthy TA4	7 J2	Essendon AL9	23 F1
Ely, *Cambs.* CB7	33 J1	Essich IV2	88 D1
Ely, *Cardiff* CF5	18 E4	Essington WV11	40 B5
Emberton MK46	32 B4	Esslemont AB41	91 H2
Embleton, *Cumb.* CA13	60 C3	Eston TS6	63 G5
Embleton, *Hart.* TS22	63 F4	Etal TD12	77 H7
Embleton, *Northumb.* NE66	71 H1	Etchilhampton SN10	20 D5
Embo IV25	97 F2	Etchingham TN19	14 C5
Embo Street IV25	97 F2	Etchinghill, *Kent* CT18	15 G4
Emborough BA3	19 K6	Etchinghill, *Staffs.* WS15	40 C4
Embsay BD23	57 F4	Etherdwick Grange HU11	59 J6
Emerson Park RM11	23 J3	Etherley Dene DL14	62 C4
Emery Down SO43	10 D4	Ethie Mains DD11	83 H3
Emley HD8	50 E1	Eton SL4	22 C4
Emmington OX39	22 A1	Eton Wick SL4	22 C4
Emneth PE14	43 H5	Etteridge PH20	88 D5
Emneth Hungate PE14	43 J5	Ettiley Heath CW11	49 G6
Empingham LE15	42 C5	Ettington CV37	30 D4
Empshott GU33	11 J1	Etton, *E.Riding* HU17	59 F5
Empshott Green GU33	11 J1	Etton, *Peter.* PE6	42 E5
Emsworth PO10	11 J4	Ettrick TD7	69 H2
Enborne RG20	21 H5	Ettrickbridge TD7	69 J1
Enborne Row RG20	21 H5	Ettrickhill TD7	69 H2
Enchmarsh SY6	38 E6	Etwall DE65	40 E2
Enderby LE19	41 H6	Eudon George WV16	39 F7
Endmoor LA8	55 J1	Eurach PA31	79 K7
Endon ST9	49 J7	Euston IP24	34 C1
Endon Bank ST9	49 J7	Euxton PR7	48 E1
Enfield EN1	23 G2	Evanstown CF39	18 C3
Enfield Wash EN3	23 G2	Evanton IV16	96 D5
Enford SN9	20 E6	Evedon NG34	42 D1
Engine Common BS37	19 K3	Evelix IV25	96 E2
Englefield RG7	21 K4	Evenjobb LD8	28 B2
Englefield Green TW20	22 C4	Evenley NN13	31 G5
Englesea-brook CW2	49 G7	Evenlode GL56	30 D6
English Bicknor GL16	28 E7	Evenwood DL14	62 C4
English Frankton SY12	38 D3	Evenwood Gate DL14	62 C4
Englishcombe BA2	20 A5	Everbay KW17	106 F5
Enham Alamein SP11	21 G7	Evercreech BA4	9 F1
Enmore TA5	8 B1	Everdon NN11	31 G3
Ennerdale Bridge CA23	60 B5	Everingham YO42	58 E5
Enniscaven PL26	3 G3	Everleigh SN8	21 F6
Ennochdhu PH10	82 B1	Everley, *High.* KW1	105 J2
Ensay PA75	78 E3	Everley, *N.Yorks.* YO13	59 F1
Ensdon SY4	38 D4	Eversholt MK17	32 C5
Ensis EX31	6 D3	Evershot DT2	8 E4
Enson ST18	40 B3	Eversley RG27	22 A5
Enstone OX7	30 E6	Eversley Cross RG27	22 A5
Enterkinfoot DG3	68 D3	Everthorpe HU15	59 F6
Enterpen TS15	63 F6	Everton, *Beds.* SG19	33 F3
Enton Green GU8	22 C7	Everton, *Hants.* SO41	10 D5
Enville DY7	40 A7	Everton, *Mersey.* L5	48 C3
Eolaigearraidh HS9	84 C4	Everton, *Notts.* DN10	51 J3
Eorabus PA67	78 E5	Evertown DG14	69 J6
Eorodal HS2	101 H1	Eves Corner CM0	25 F2
Eoropaidh HS2	101 H1	Evesbatch WR6	29 F4
Epney GL2	29 G7	Evesham WR11	30 B4
Epperstone NG14	41 J1	Evie KW17	106 C5
Epping CM16	23 H1	Evington LE5	41 J5
Epping Green, *Essex* CM16	23 H1	Ewart Newtown NE71	77 H7
Epping Green, *Herts.* SG13	23 G1	Ewden Village S36	50 E3
Epping Upland CM16	23 H1	Ewell KT17	23 F5
Eppleby DL11	62 C5	Ewell Minnis CT15	15 H3
Eppleworth HU16	59 G6	Ewelme OX10	21 K2
Epsom KT17	23 F5	Ewen GL7	20 D2
Epwell OX15	30 E4	Ewenny CF35	18 C4
		Ewerby NG34	42 E1
		Ewerby Thorpe NG34	42 E1

Ewhurst, *E.Suss.* TN32	14 C5	Fanagmore IV27	102 D4
Ewhurst, *Surr.* GU6	22 D7	Fanans PA35	80 B5
Ewhurst Green GU6	12 D3	Fancott LU5	32 D6
Ewloe CH5	48 C6	Fangdale Beck TS9	63 G7
Ewloe Green CH5	48 B6	Fangfoss YO41	58 D4
Ewood BB2	56 B7	Fankerton FK6	75 F2
Ewood Bridge BB4	56 C7	Fanmore PA73	79 F3
Eworthy EX21	6 C6	Fanner's Green CM3	33 K7
Exbourne EX20	6 E5	Fans TD4	76 E6
Exbury SO45	11 F4	Far Cotton NN4	31 J3
Exceat BN25	13 J7	Far Forest DY14	29 G1
Exebridge TA22	7 H3	Far Green GL11	20 A1
Exelby DL8	57 H1	Far Moor WN5	48 E2
EXETER EX	7 H6	Far Oakridge GL6	20 C1
Exeter Airport EX5	7 H6	Far Royds LS12	57 H6
Exford TA24	7 G2	Far Sawrey LA22	60 E7
Exfords Green SY5	38 D5	Farcet PE7	43 F6
Exhall, *Warks.* B49	30 C3	Farden SY8	28 E1
Exhall, *Warks.* CV7	41 F7	Fareham PO16	11 G4
Exlade Street RG8	21 K3	Farewell WS13	40 C4
Exminster EX6	7 H7	Farforth LN11	53 G5
Exmouth EX8	7 J7	Faringdon SN7	21 F2
Exnaboe ZE3	109 F9	Farington PR25	55 J7
Exning CB8	33 K2	Farlam CA8	61 G1
Exton, *Devon* EX3	7 H7	Farlary IV28	96 E1
Exton, *Hants.* SO32	11 H2	Farleigh, *N.Som.* BS48	19 J5
Exton, *Rut.* LE15	42 C4	Farleigh, *Surr.* CR6	23 G5
Exton, *Som.* TA22	7 H2	Farleigh Hungerford BA2	20 B6
Exwick EX4	7 H6	Farleigh Wallop RG25	21 K7
Eyam S32	50 E5	Farlesthorpe LN13	53 H5
Eydon NN11	31 G4	Farleton, *Cumb.* LA6	55 J1
Eye, *Here.* HR6	28 D2	Farleton, *Lancs.* LA2	55 J3
Eye, *Peter.* PE6	43 F5	Farley, *Derbys.* DE4	50 E6
Eye, *Suff.* IP23	35 F1	Farley, *Shrop.* SY5	38 C5
Eye Green PE6	43 F5	Farley, *Staffs.* ST10	40 C1
Eyemouth TD14	77 H4	Farley, *Wilts.* SP5	10 D2
Eyeworth SG19	33 F4	Farley Green, *Suff.* CB8	34 B3
Eyhorne Street ME17	14 D2	Farley Green, *Surr.* GU5	22 D7
Eyke IP12	35 H3	Farley Hill RG7	22 A5
Eynesbury PE19	32 E3	Farleys End GL2	29 G7
Eynort IV47	85 J2	Farlington YO61	58 C3
Eynsford DA4	23 J5	Farlow DY14	39 F7
Eynsham OX29	21 H1	Farm Town LE67	41 F4
Eype DT6	8 D5	Farmborough BA2	19 K5
Eyre IV51	93 K6	Farmcote GL54	30 B6
Eythorne CT15	15 H3	Farmington GL54	30 C7
Eyton, *Here.* HR6	28 D2	Farmoor OX2	21 H1
Eyton, *Shrop.* SY7	38 C7	Farmtown AB55	98 D5
Eyton on Severn SY5	38 E5	Farnborough, *Gt.Lon.* BR6	23 H5
Eyton upon the Weald Moors TF6	39 F4	Farnborough, *Hants.* GU14	22 B6
Eywood HR5	28 C3	Farnborough, *W.Berks.* OX12	21 H3
		Farnborough, *Warks.* OX17	31 F4
F		Farnborough Street GU14	22 B6
Faccombe SP11	21 G6	Farncombe GU7	22 C7
Faceby TS9	63 F6	Farndish NN29	32 C2
Fachwen LL55	46 D6	Farndon, *Ches.* CH3	48 D7
Facit OL12	49 H1	Farndon, *Notts.* NG24	51 K7
Faddiley CW5	48 E7	Farnell DD9	83 H2
Fadmoor YO62	58 C1	Farnham, *Dorset* DT11	9 J3
Faebait IV6	96 B6	Farnham, *Essex* CM23	33 H6
Faifley G81	74 D3	Farnham, *N.Yorks.* HG5	57 J3
Fail KA5	67 J1	Farnham, *Suff.* IP17	35 H2
Failand BS8	19 J4	Farnham, *Surr.* GU9	22 B7
Failford KA5	67 J1	Farnham Common SL2	22 C3
Failsworth M35	49 H2	Farnham Green CM23	33 H6
Fain IV23	95 H4	Farnham Royal SL2	22 C3
Fair Isle ZE2	108 A1	Farningham DA4	23 J5
Fair Oak, *Devon* EX16	7 J4	Farnley, *Leeds* LS21	57 H5
Fair Oak, *Hants.* SO50	11 F3	Farnley, *W.Yorks.* LS12	57 H6
Fair Oak, *Hants.* RG21	21 J5	Farnley Tyas HD4	50 D1
Fair Oak Green RG7	21 K5	Farnsfield NG22	51 J7
Fairbourne LL38	37 F4	Farnworth, *Gt.Man.* BL4	49 G2
Fairburn WF11	57 K7	Farnworth, *Halton* WA8	48 E4
Fairfield, *Derbys.* SK17	50 C5	Farr, *High.* KW14	104 C2
Fairfield, *Gt.Man.* M43	49 J3	Farr, *High.* IV2	88 D1
Fairfield, *Kent* TN29	14 E5	Farr, *High.* PH21	89 F4
Fairfield, *Mersey.* CH63	48 B4	Farr House IV2	88 D1
Fairfield, *Stock.* TS19	63 F5	Farraline IV2	88 C2
Fairfield, *Worcs.* B61	29 J1	Farringdon EX5	7 J6
Fairford GL7	20 E1	Farrington Gurney BS39	19 K6
Fairgirth DG5	65 J5	Farsley LS28	57 H6
Fairhaven FY8	55 G7	Farthing Corner ME8	24 E5
Fairhill ML3	75 F5	Farthing Green TN12	14 D3
Fairholm ML9	75 F5	Farthinghoe NN13	31 G5
Fairley AB15	91 G4	Farthingstone NN12	31 H3
Fairlie KA29	74 A5	Farthorpe LN9	53 F5
Fairlight TN35	14 D6	Fartown HD2	50 D1
Fairlight Cove TN35	14 D6	Farway EX24	7 K6
Fairmile, *Devon* EX11	7 J6	Fasag IV22	94 E6
Fairmile, *Surr.* KT11	22 E5	Fasagrianach IV23	95 H3
Fairmilehead EH10	76 A4	Fascadale PH36	86 B7
Fairnington TD5	70 B1	Faslane G84	74 A2
Fairoak ST21	39 G2	Fasnacloich PA38	80 B3
Fairseat TN15	24 C5	Fasnakyle IV4	87 K2
Fairstead CM3	34 B7	Fassfern PH33	87 G7
Fairwarp TN22	13 H4	Fatfield NE38	62 E1
Fairwater CF5	18 E4	Fattahead AB45	98 E5
Fairy Cross EX39	6 C3	Faugh CA8	61 G1
Fairyhill SA3	17 H5	Fauldhouse EH47	75 H4
Fakenham NR21	44 D3	Faulkbourne CM8	34 B7
Fala EH37	76 C4	Faulkland BA3	20 A6
Fala Dam EH37	76 C4	Fauls SY13	38 E2
Falahill EH37	76 B5	Faulston SP5	10 B2
Faldingworth LN8	52 D4	Faversham ME13	25 G5
Falfield, *Fife* KY15	83 F7	Favillar AB55	89 K1
Falfield, *S.Glos.* GL12	19 K2	Fawdington YO61	57 K2
Falin-Wnda SA44	26 C4	Fawdon NE3	71 H7
Falkenham IP11	35 G5	Fawfieldhead SK17	50 C6
FALKIRK FK	75 G3	Fawkham Green DA3	23 J5
Falkland KY15	82 D7	Fawler OX7	30 E7
Falla TD8	70 C2	Fawley, *Bucks.* RG9	22 A3
Fallgate S45	51 F6	Fawley, *Hants.* SO45	11 F4
Fallin FK7	75 G1	Fawley, *W.Berks.* OX12	21 G3
Falmer BN1	13 G6	Fawley Chapel HR1	28 E6
Falmouth TR11	3 F5	Fawsyde DD10	91 G7
Falsgrave YO12	59 G1		
Falstone NE48	70 C5		

Faxfleet DN14	58 E7
Faxton NN6	31 J1
Faygate RH12	13 F3
Fazakerley L9	48 C3
Fazeley B78	40 E5
Fearby HG4	57 G1
Fearn IV20	97 F4
Fearnan PH15	81 J3
Fearnbeg IV54	94 D6
Fearnhead WA2	49 F3
Fearnmore IV54	94 D5
Fearnoch, *Arg. & B.* PA22	73 H2
Fearnoch, *Arg. & B.* PA21	73 H2
Featherstone, *Staffs.* WV10	40 B5
Featherstone, *W.Yorks.* WF7	57 K7
Featherstone Castle NE49	70 B7
Feckenham B96	30 B2
Feering CO5	34 C6
Feetham DL11	62 A7
Feith-hill AB53	98 E6
Feizor LA2	56 C3
Felbridge RH19	13 G3
Felbrigg NR11	45 G2
Felcourt RH19	23 G7
Felden HP3	22 D1
Felhampton SY6	38 D7
Felindre, *Carmar.* SA19	27 G6
Felindre, *Carmar.* SA32	17 J2
Felindre, *Carmar.* SA44	17 G1
Felindre, *Carmar.* SA19	17 K1
Felindre, *Cere.* SA48	26 E3
Felindre, *Powys.* LD7	38 A7
Felindre, *Powys.* NP8	28 A6
Felindre, *Swan.* SA5	17 K4
Felinfach, *Cere.* SA48	26 E3
Felinfach, *Powys* LD3	27 K5
Felinfoel SA14	17 J4
Felingwmisaf SA32	17 J2
Felingwmuchaf SA32	17 J2
Felixkirk YO7	57 K1
Felixstowe IP11	35 H5
Felixstowe Ferry IP11	35 H5
Felkington TD15	77 H6
Felldownhead PL19	6 B7
Felling NE10	71 H7
Fellonmore PA65	79 H5
Felmersham MK43	32 C3
Felmingham NR28	45 G3
Felpham PO22	12 C7
Felsham IP30	34 D3
Felsted CM6	33 K6
Feltham TW13	22 E4
Felthamhill TW16	22 E4
Felthorpe NR10	45 F4
Felton, *Here.* HR1	28 E4
Felton, *N.Som.* BS40	19 J5
Felton, *Northumb.* NE65	71 G3
Felton Butler SY4	38 C4
Feltwell IP26	44 B6
Fen Ditton CB5	33 H2
Fen Drayton CB4	33 G2
Fen End CV8	30 D1
Fen Street, *Norf.* NR17	44 D6
Fen Street, *Norf.* IP22	34 E1
Fen Street, *Suff.* IP17	35 H2
Fen Street, *Suff.* IP14	35 F2
Fenay Bridge HD8	50 D1
Fence BB12	56 D6
Fence Houses DH4	62 E1
Fencott OX5	31 G7
Fendike Corner PE24	53 H6
Fenham NE15	77 J6
Fenhouses PE20	43 F1
Feniscowles BB2	56 B7
Feniton EX14	7 K6
Fenn Street ME3	24 D4
Fenni-fach LD3	27 K6
Fenny Bentley DE6	50 D7
Fenny Bridges EX14	7 K6
Fenny Compton CV47	31 F3
Fenny Drayton CV13	41 F6
Fenny Stratford MK2	32 B5
Fenrother NE61	71 G4
Fenstanton PE28	33 G2
Fenton, *Cambs.* PE28	33 G1
Fenton, *Lincs.* LN1	52 B5
Fenton, *Lincs.* NG23	52 B7
Fenton, *Northumb.* NE71	77 H7
Fenton, *Notts.* DN22	51 K4
Fenton, *Stoke* ST4	40 A1
Fenton Barns EH39	76 D2
Fenwick, *E.Ayr.* KA3	74 C6
Fenwick, *Northumb.* NE18	71 F6
Fenwick, *Northumb.* TD15	77 J6
Fenwick, *S.Yorks.* DN6	51 H1
Feochaig PA28	66 B2
Feock TR3	3 F5
Feolin PA60	72 D4
Feolin Ferry PA60	72 C4
Feorlan PA28	66 A3
Feorlin PA32	73 H1
Ferguslie Park PA3	74 C4
Feriniquarrie IV55	93 G6
Fern DD8	83 F1
Ferndale CF43	18 C2
Ferndown BH22	10 B4
Ferness IV12	97 G2
Fernham SN7	21 F2
Fernhill Heath WR3	29 H3
Fernhurst GU27	12 B4
Fernie KY15	82 E6
Fernilea IV47	85 J1
Fernilee SK23	50 C5
Fernybank DD9	90 D7
Ferrensby HG5	57 J3
Ferrindonald IV44	86 C4
Ferring BN12	12 D6
Ferry Hill PE16	43 G7

Place	Postcode	Page	Grid
Ferrybridge	WF11	57	K7
Ferryden	DD10	83	J2
Ferryhill	DL17	62	D3
Ferryside (Glanyferi)	SA17	17	G3
Fersfield	IP22	44	E7
Fersit	PH31	87	K7
Ferwig	SA43	26	A4
Feshiebridge	PH21	89	F4
Fetcham	KT22	22	E6
Fetterangus	AB42	99	H5
Fettercairn	AB30	90	E7
Fetternear House	AB51	91	F3
Feus of Caldhame	AB30	83	H1
Fewcott	OX27	31	G6
Fewston	HG3	57	G4
Ffairfach	SA19	17	K2
Ffair-Rhos	SY25	27	G2
Ffaldybrenin	SA19	27	F4
Ffarmers	SA19	27	F4
Ffawyddog	NP8	28	B7
Ffestiniog (Llan Ffestiniog)	LL41	37	G1
Fforddlas, *Denb.*	LL16	47	K6
Ffordd-las, *Powys*	HR3	28	B5
Fforest	SA4	17	J4
Fforest-fach	SA5	17	K5
Ffostrasol	SA44	26	C4
Ffos-y-ffin	SA46	26	D2
Ffridd Uchaf	LL54	46	D7
Ffrith, *Denb.*	LL19	47	J4
Ffrith, *Flints.*	LL11	48	B7
Ffrwdgrech	LD3	27	K6
Ffynnon	SA33	17	G3
Ffynnon Taf (Taff's Well)	CF15	18	E3
Ffynnongroyw	CH8	47	K4
Fibhig	HS2	100	E3
Fichlie	AB33	90	C3
Fidden	PA66	78	E5
Fiddington, *Glos.*	GL20	29	J5
Fiddington, *Som.*	TA5	19	F7
Fiddleford	DT10	9	H3
Fiddler's Green, *Glos.*	GL51	29	J6
Fiddler's Green, *Here.*	HR1	28	E5
Fiddler's Green, *Norf.*	PE32	44	C4
Fiddler's Green, *Norf.*	NR17	44	E6
Fiddlers Hamlet	CM16	23	H1
Field	ST14	40	C2
Field Broughton	LA11	55	G1
Field Dalling	NR25	44	E2
Field Head	LE67	41	G5
Fife Keith	AB55	98	C5
Fifehead Magdalen	SP8	9	G2
Fifehead Neville	DT10	9	G3
Fifehead St. Quintin	DT10	9	G3
Fifield, *Oxon.*	OX7	30	D7
Fifield, *W. & M.*	SL6	22	C4
Fifield Bavant	SP5	10	B2
Figheldean	SP4	20	E7
Filby	NR29	45	J4
Filey	YO14	59	H1
Filgrave	MK16	32	B4
Filham	PL21	5	G5
Filkins	GL7	21	F1
Filleigh, *Devon*	EX32	6	E3
Filleigh, *Devon*	EX17	7	F4
Fillingham	DN21	52	C4
Fillongley	CV7	40	E7
Filmore Hill	GU34	11	H2
Filton	BS34	19	K4
Fimber	YO25	58	E3
Finavon	DD8	83	F2
Fincham	PE33	44	A5
Finchampstead	RG40	22	A5
Finchdean	PO8	11	J3
Finchingfield	CM7	33	K5
Finchley	N3	23	F2
Findern	DE65	41	F2
Findhorn	IV36	97	H5
Findhorn Bridge	IV13	89	F2
Findhuglen	PH6	81	J6
Findo Gask	PH1	82	B5
Findochty	AB56	98	C4
Findon, *Aber.*	AB12	91	H5
Findon, *W.Suss.*	BN14	12	E6
Findon Mains	IV7	96	D5
Findon Valley	BN14	12	E6
Findrassie	IV30	97	J5
Findron	AB37	89	J3
Finedon	NN9	32	C1
Fingal Street	IP13	35	G1
Fingask	AB51	91	F2
Fingerpost	DY14	29	G1
Fingest	RG9	22	A2
Finghall	DL8	57	G1
Fingland, *Cumb.*	CA7	60	D1
Fingland, *D. & G.*	DG13	69	H3
Fingland, *D. & G.*	DG4	68	C3
Finglesham	CT14	15	J2
Fingringhoe	CO5	34	E6
Finkle Street	S35	51	F3
Finlarig	FK21	81	G4
Finmere	MK18	31	H5
Finnart, *Arg. & B.*	G84	74	A1
Finnart, *P. & K.*	PH17	81	G2
Finney Hill	LE12	41	G4
Finningham	IP14	34	E2
Finningley	DN9	51	J3
Finnygaud	AB54	98	E5
Finsbay (Fionnsbhagh)	HS3	93	F3
Finsbury	EC1R	23	G3
Finstall	B60	29	J1
Finsthwaite	LA12	55	G1
Finstock	OX7	30	E7
Finstown	KW17	107	C6
Fintry, *Aber.*	AB53	99	F5
Fintry, *Stir.*	G63	74	E2
Finwood	CV35	30	C2
Finzean	AB31	90	D5
Fionnphort	PA66	78	D5
Fionnsbhagh (Finsbay)	HS3	93	F3
Fir Tree	DL15	62	C3
Firbank	LA10	61	H7
Firbeck	S81	51	H4
Firby, *N.Yorks.*	DL8	57	H1
Firby, *N.Yorks.*	YO60	58	D3
Firgrove	OL16	49	J1
Firs Lane	WN7	49	F2
Firsby	PE23	53	H6
Firsdown	SP5	10	D1
Firth	ZE2	108	D5
Fishbourne, *I.o.W.*	PO33	11	G5
Fishbourne, *W.Suss.*	PO18	12	B6
Fishburn	TS21	62	E3
Fishcross	FK10	75	H1
Fisherford	AB51	90	E1
Fisher's Pond	SO50	11	F2
Fisher's Row	PR3	55	H5
Fishersgate	BN41	13	F6
Fisherstreet	GU8	12	C3
Fisherton, *High.*	IV2	96	E6
Fisherton, *S.Ayr.*	KA7	67	G2
Fisherton de la Mere	BA12	9	J1
Fishguard (Abergwaun)	SA65	16	C1
Fishlake	DN7	51	J1
Fishleigh Barton	EX37	6	D3
Fishley	NR13	45	J4
Fishnish	PA65	79	H3
Fishpond Bottom	DT6	8	C5
Fishponds	BS16	19	K4
Fishpool	BL9	49	H2
Fishtoft	PE21	43	G1
Fishtoft Drove	PE22	43	G1
Fishtown of Usan	DD10	83	J2
Fishwick, *Lancs.*	PR1	55	J6
Fishwick, *Sc.Bord.*	TD15	77	H5
Fiskerton, *Lincs.*	LN3	52	D5
Fiskerton, *Notts.*	NG25	51	K7
Fitling	HU11	59	J6
Fittleton	SP4	20	E7
Fittleworth	RH20	12	D5
Fitton End	PE13	43	H4
Fitz	SY4	38	D4
Fitzhead	TA4	7	K3
Fitzroy	TA2	7	K3
Fitzwilliam	WF9	51	G1
Fiunary	PA34	79	H3
Five Acres	GL16	28	E7
Five Ash Down	TN22	13	H4
Five Ashes	TN20	13	J4
Five Bridges	WR6	29	F4
Five Houses	PO30	11	F6
Five Lanes	NP26	19	H2
Five Oak Green	TN12	23	K7
Five Oaks, *Chan.I.*	JE2	3	K7
Five Oaks, *W.Suss.*	RH14	12	D4
Five Roads	SA15	17	H4
Five Turnings	LD7	28	B1
Five Wents	ME17	14	D2
Fivehead	TA3	8	C2
Fivelanes	PL15	4	C2
Flack's Green	CM3	34	B7
Flackwell Heath	HP10	22	B3
Fladbury	WR10	29	J4
Fladdabister	ZE2	109	D9
Flagg	SK17	50	D6
Flamborough	YO15	59	J2
Flamstead	AL3	32	D7
Flamstead End	EN7	23	G1
Flansham	PO22	12	C6
Flanshaw	WF2	57	J7
Flasby	BD23	56	E4
Flash	SK17	50	C6
Flashader	IV51	93	J6
Flask Inn	YO22	63	J2
Flaunden	HP3	22	D1
Flawborough	NG13	42	A1
Flawith	YO61	57	K3
Flax Bourton	BS48	19	J5
Flax Moss	BB4	56	C7
Flaxby	HG5	57	J4
Flaxholme	DE56	41	F1
Flaxlands	NR16	45	F6
Flaxley	GL14	29	F7
Flaxpool	TA4	7	K2
Flaxton	YO60	58	C3
Fleckney	LE8	41	J6
Flecknoe	CV23	31	G2
Fledborough	NG22	52	B5
Fleet, *Hants.*	GU51	22	B6
Fleet, *Hants.*	PO11	11	J4
Fleet, *Lincs.*	PE12	43	G3
Fleet Hargate	PE12	43	G3
Fleetville	AL1	22	E1
Fleetwood	FY7	55	G5
Fleggburgh (Burgh St. Margaret)	NR29	45	J4
Flemingston	CF62	18	D4
Flemington	G72	74	E5
Flempton	IP28	34	C2
Fleoideabhagh	HS3	93	F3
Flesherin	HS2	101	H4
Fletchersbridge	PL30	4	B4
Fletchertown	CA7	60	D2
Fletching	TN22	13	H4
Flete	PL21	5	G5
Fleuchats	AB36	90	B4
Fleur-de-lis	NP12	18	E2
Flexbury	EX23	6	A5
Flexford	GU3	22	C6
Flimby	CA15	60	B3
Flimwell	TN5	14	C4
Flint (Y Fflint)	CH6	48	B5
Flint Cross	SG8	33	H4
Flint Mountain	CH6	48	B5
Flintham	NG23	42	A1
Flinton	HU11	59	J6
Flint's Green	CV7	30	D1
Flishinghurst	TN17	14	C4
Flitcham	PE31	44	B3
Flitholme	CA16	61	J5
Flitton	MK45	32	D5
Flitwick	MK45	32	D5
Flixborough	DN15	52	B1
Flixton, *Gt.Man.*	M41	49	G3
Flixton, *N.Yorks.*	YO11	59	G2
Flixton, *Suff.*	NR35	45	H7
Flockton	WF4	50	E1
Flockton Green	WF4	50	E1
Flodden	NE71	77	H7
Flodigarry	IV51	93	K4
Flood's Ferry	PE15	43	G6
Flookburgh	LA11	55	G2
Floors	AB55	98	C5
Flordon	NR15	45	F6
Flore	NN7	31	H2
Flotta	KW16	107	C8
Flotterton	NE65	71	F3
Flowton	IP8	34	E4
Flushdyke	WF5	57	H7
Flushing, *Aber.*	AB42	99	J6
Flushing, *Cornw.*	TR5	3	F5
Flushing, *Cornw.*	TR12	2	E6
Fluxton	EX11	7	J6
Flyford Flavell	WR7	29	J3
Foals Green	IP21	35	G1
Fobbing	SS17	24	D3
Fochabers	IV32	98	B5
Fochriw	CF81	18	E1
Fockerby	DN17	52	B1
Fodderletter	AB37	89	J2
Fodderty	IV15	96	C6
Foddington	TA11	8	E2
Foel	SY21	37	J4
Foelgastell	SA14	17	J3
Foggathorpe	YO8	58	D6
Fogo	TD11	77	F6
Fogorig	TD11	77	F6
Fogwatt	IV30	97	K6
Foindle	IV27	102	D4
Folda	PH11	82	C1
Fole	ST14	40	C2
Foleshill	CV6	41	F7
Folke	DT9	9	F3
Folkestone	CT20	15	H4
Folkingham	NG34	42	D2
Folkington	BN26	13	J6
Folksworth	PE7	42	E7
Folkton	YO11	59	G2
Folla Rule	AB51	91	F1
Follifoot	HG3	57	J4
Folly, *Dorset*	DT2	9	G4
Folly, *Pembs.*	SA62	16	C2
Folly Gate	EX20	6	D6
Fonmon	CF62	18	D5
Fonthill Bishop	SP3	9	J1
Fonthill Gifford	SP3	9	J1
Fontmell Magna	SP7	9	H3
Fontmell Parva	DT11	9	H3
Fontwell	BN18	12	C6
Font-y-gary	CF62	18	D5
Foolow	S32	50	D5
Footherley	WS14	40	D5
Foots Cray	DA14	23	H4
Forbestown	AB36	90	B3
Force Forge	LA12	60	E7
Force Green	TN16	23	H6
Forcett	DL11	62	C5
Forches Cross	EX17	7	F5
Ford, *Arg. & B.*	PA31	79	K7
Ford, *Bucks.*	HP17	22	A1
Ford, *Devon*	PL8	5	G5
Ford, *Devon*	EX39	6	C3
Ford, *Devon*	TQ7	5	H6
Ford, *Glos.*	GL54	30	B6
Ford, *Mersey.*	L30	48	C3
Ford, *Midloth.*	EH37	76	B4
Ford, *Northumb.*	TD15	77	H7
Ford, *Pembs.*	SA62	16	C2
Ford, *Plym.*	PL2	4	E5
Ford, *Shrop.*	SY5	38	D4
Ford, *Som.*	TA4	7	J3
Ford, *Staffs.*	ST13	50	C7
Ford, *W.Suss.*	BN18	12	C6
Ford, *Wilts.*	SN14	20	B4
Ford End	CM3	33	K7
Ford Green	PR3	55	H5
Ford Heath	SY5	38	D4
Ford Street	TA21	7	K4
Forda	EX20	6	D6
Fordbridge	B37	40	D7
Fordcombe	TN3	23	J7
Fordell	KY4	75	K2
Forden	SY21	38	B5
Forder Green	TQ13	5	H4
Fordgate	TA7	8	C1
Fordham, *Cambs.*	CB7	33	K1
Fordham, *Essex*	CO6	34	D6
Fordham, *Norf.*	PE38	44	A6
Fordham Abbey	CB7	33	K2
Fordham Heath	CO3	34	D6
Fordhouses	WV10	40	B5
Fordingbridge	SP6	10	C3
Fordon	YO25	59	G2
Fordoun	AB30	91	F7
Ford's Green	IP14	34	E2
Fordstreet	CO6	34	D6
Fordwells	OX29	30	E7
Fordwich	CT2	15	G2
Fordyce	AB45	98	D4
Forebrae	PH1	82	A5
Forebridge	ST17	40	B3
Foredale	BD24	56	D3
Foreland	PA49	72	A4
Foremark	DE65	41	F3
Forest	DL10	62	D6
Forest Coal Pit	NP7	28	B6
Forest Gate	E7	23	H3
Forest Green	RH5	22	E7
Forest Hall, *Cumb.*	LA8	61	G6
Forest Hall, *T. & W.*	NE12	71	H7
Forest Head	CA8	61	G1
Forest Hill, *Gt.Lon.*	SE23	23	G4
Forest Hill, *Oxon.*	OX33	21	J1
Forest Lane Head	HG2	57	J4
Forest Lodge, *Arg. & B.*	PA36	80	D3
Forest Lodge, *P. & K.*	PH18	89	G7
Forest Mill	FK10	75	H1
Forest Row	RH18	13	H3
Forest Side	PO30	11	F6
Forest Town	NG19	51	H6
Forestburn Gate	NE61	71	F4
Forest-in-Teesdale	DL12	61	K4
Forestside	PO9	11	J3
Forfar	DD8	83	F2
Forgandenny	PH2	82	B6
Forge	SY20	37	G6
Forgie	AB55	98	B5
Forhill	B38	30	B1
Formby	L37	48	B2
Forncett End	NR16	45	F6
Forncett St. Mary	NR16	45	F6
Forncett St. Peter	NR16	45	F6
Forneth	PH10	82	B3
Fornham All Saints	IP28	34	C2
Fornham St. Martin	IP31	34	C2
Fornighty	IV12	97	G6
Forres	IV36	97	H6
Forrest	ML6	75	G4
Forrest Lodge	DG7	67	K5
Forsbrook	ST11	40	B1
Forse	KW5	105	H5
Forsie	KW14	105	F2
Forsinain	KW13	104	E4
Forsinard	KW13	104	D4
Forston	DT2	9	F5
Fort Augustus	PH32	87	K4
Fort George	IV2	96	E6
Fort William	PH33	87	H7
Forter	PH11	82	C1
Forteviot	PH2	82	B6
Forth	ML11	75	H5
Forthampton	GL19	29	H5
Fortingall	PH15	81	J3
Fortis Green	N2	23	F3
Forton, *Hants.*	SP11	21	H7
Forton, *Lancs.*	PR3	55	H4
Forton, *Shrop.*	SY4	38	D4
Forton, *Som.*	TA20	8	C4
Forton, *Staffs.*	TF10	39	G3
Fortrie	AB53	98	E6
Fortrose	IV10	96	E6
Fortuneswell	DT5	9	F7
Forty Green	HP9	22	C2
Forty Hill	EN2	23	G2
Forward Green	IP14	34	E3
Fosbury	SN8	21	G6
Foscot	OX7	30	D6
Fosdyke	PE20	43	G2
Foss	PH16	81	J2
Foss Cross	GL54	20	D1
Fossdale	DL8	61	K7
Fossebridge	GL54	30	B7
Foster Street	CM17	23	H1
Fosterhouses	DN14	51	J1
Foster's Booth	NN12	31	H3
Foston, *Derbys.*	DE65	40	D2
Foston, *Leics.*	LE8	41	J6
Foston, *Lincs.*	NG32	42	B1
Foston, *N.Yorks.*	YO60	58	C3
Foston on the Wolds	YO25	59	H4
Fotherby	LN11	53	G3
Fotheringhay	PE8	42	D6
Foubister	KW17	107	E7
Foul Mile	BN27	13	K5
Foula	ZE2	108	B1
Foulbog	DG13	69	H3
Foulden, *Norf.*	IP26	44	B6
Foulden, *Sc.Bord.*	TD15	77	H5
Foulness Island	SS3	25	G2
Foulridge	BB8	56	D5
Foulsham	NR20	44	E3
Foulstone	LA8	55	J1
Foulzie	AB45	99	F4
Fountainhall	TD1	76	C6
Four Ashes, *Staffs.*	WV10	40	B5
Four Ashes, *Staffs.*	DY7	40	A7
Four Ashes, *Suff.*	IP31	34	D1
Four Crosses, *Denb.*	LL21	37	K1
Four Crosses, *Powys*	SY22	38	B4
Four Crosses, *Powys*	SY21	37	K5
Four Crosses, *Staffs.*	WS11	40	B5
Four Elms	TN8	23	H7
Four Forks	TA5	8	B1
Four Gotes	PE13	43	H4
Four Lane Ends, *B'burn.*	BB1	56	B7
Four Lane Ends, *Ches.*	CW6	48	E6
Four Lane Ends, *York*	YO19	58	C4
Four Lanes	TR16	2	D5
Four Marks	GU34	11	H1
Four Mile Bridge	LL65	46	A5
Four Oaks, *E.Suss.*	TN31	14	D5
Four Oaks, *Glos.*	GL18	29	F6
Four Oaks, *W.Mid.*	CV7	40	E7
Four Oaks, *W.Mid.*	B74	40	D6
Four Oaks Park	B74	40	D6
Four Roads	SA17	17	H4
Four Throws	TN18	14	C5
Fourlane Ends	DE55	51	F7
Fourlanes End	CW11	49	H5
Fourpenny	IV25	97	F2
Fourstones	NE47	70	D7
Fovant	SP3	10	B2
Foveran House	AB41	91	H2
Fowey	PL23	4	B5
Fowlis	DD2	82	E4
Fowlis Wester	PH7	82	A5
Fowlmere	SG8	33	H4
Fownhope	HR1	28	E5
Fox Hatch	CM15	23	J2
Fox Lane	GU14	22	B6
Fox Street	CO7	34	E6
Foxbar	PA2	74	C4
Foxcombe Hill	OX1	21	H1
Foxcote, *Glos.*	GL54	30	B7
Foxcote, *Som.*	BA3	20	A6
Foxdale	IM4	54	B6
Foxearth	CO10	34	C4
Foxfield	LA20	55	F1
Foxham	SN15	20	C4
Foxhole, *Cornw.*	PL26	3	G3
Foxhole, *High.*	IV4	88	C1
Foxholes	YO25	59	G2
Foxhunt Green	TN21	13	J5
Foxley, *Here.*	HR4	28	D4
Foxley, *Norf.*	NR20	44	E3
Foxley, *Northants.*	NN12	31	H3
Foxley, *Wilts.*	SN16	20	B3
Foxt	ST10	40	C1
Foxton, *Cambs.*	CB2	33	H4
Foxton, *Dur.*	TS21	62	E4
Foxton, *Leics.*	LE16	41	J6
Foxup	BD23	56	D2
Foxwist Green	CW8	49	F6
Foy	HR9	28	E6
Foyers	IV2	88	B2
Frachadil	PA75	78	E2
Fraddam	TR27	2	C5
Fraddon	TR9	3	G3
Fradley	WS13	40	D4
Fradswell	ST18	40	B2
Fraisthorpe	YO15	59	H3
Framfield	TN22	13	H4
Framingham Earl	NR14	45	G5
Framingham Pigot	NR14	45	G5
Framlingham	IP13	35	G2
Frampton, *Dorset*	DT2	9	F5
Frampton, *Lincs.*	PE20	43	G2
Frampton Cotterell	BS36	19	K3
Frampton Mansell	GL6	20	C1
Frampton on Severn	GL2	20	A1
Frampton West End	PE20	43	F1
Framsden	IP14	35	G3
Framwellgate Moor	DH1	62	D2
France Lynch	GL6	20	C1
Frances Green	PR3	56	B6
Franche	DY11	29	H1
Frandley	CW9	49	F5
Frankby	CH48	48	B4
Frankfort	NR12	45	H3
Frankley	B32	40	C7
Franksbridge	LD1	28	A3
Frankton	CV23	31	F1
Frant	TN3	13	J3
Fraserburgh	AB43	99	H4
Frating	CO7	34	E6
Fratton	PO1	11	H4
Freasley	B78	40	E6
Freathy	PL10	4	D5
Freckenham	IP28	33	K1
Freckleton	PR4	55	H7
Freeby	LE14	42	B3
Freefolk	RG28	21	H7
Freehay	ST10	40	C1
Freeland	OX29	31	F7
Freester	ZE2	109	D7
Freethorpe	NR13	45	J5
Freethorpe Common	NR13	45	J5
Freiston	PE22	43	G1
Freiston Shore	PE22	43	G1
Fremington, *Devon*	EX31	6	D2
Fremington, *N.Yorks.*	DL11	62	B7
Frenchay	BS16	19	K4
Frenchbeer	TQ13	6	E7
Frendraught	AB54	98	E6
French	FK8	81	F7
Frensham	GU10	22	B7
Fresgoe	KW14	104	E2
Freshbrook	SN5	20	E3
Freshfield	L37	48	B2
Freshford	BA2	20	A6
Freshwater	PO40	10	E6
Freshwater Bay	PO40	10	E6
Freshwater East	SA71	16	D5
Fressingfield	IP21	35	G1
Freston	IP9	35	F5
Freswick	KW1	105	J2
Fretherne	GL2	20	A1
Frettenham	NR12	45	G4
Freuchie	KY15	82	D7
Freystrop Cross	SA62	16	C3
Friars Carse	DG2	68	E5
Friar's Gate	TN6	13	H3
Friarton	PH2	82	C5
Friday Bridge	PE14	43	H5
Friday Street, *E.Suss.*	BN23	13	K6
Friday Street, *Suff.*	IP13	35	G3
Friday Street, *Suff.*	IP12	35	H3
Friday Street, *Surr.*	RH5	22	E7
Fridaythorpe	YO25	58	E4

Glasslie

Friern Barnet **N11** 23 F2
Friesthorpe **LN3** 52 D4
Frieston **NG32** 42 C1
Frieth **RG9** 22 A2
Frilford **OX13** 21 H2
Frilsham **RG18** 21 J4
Frimley **GU16** 22 B6
Frimley Green **GU16** 22 B6
Frindsbury **ME2** 24 D5
Fring **PE31** 44 B2
Fringford **OX27** 31 H6
Friningham **ME14** 14 D2
Frinsted **ME9** 14 D2
Frinton-on-Sea **CO13** 35 G7
Friockheim **DD11** 83 G2
Friog **LL38** 37 F4
Frisby on the Wreake **LE14** 41 J4
Friskney **PE22** 53 H7
Friskney Eaudyke **PE22** 53 H7
Friston, *E.Suss.* **BN20** 13 J7
Friston, *Suff.* **IP17** 35 J2
Fritchley **DE56** 51 F7
Frith **ME13** 14 E2
Frith Bank **PE22** 43 G1
Frith Common **WR15** 29 F2
Fritham **SO43** 10 D3
Frithelstock **EX38** 6 C4
Frithelstock Stone **EX38** 6 C4
Frithville **PE22** 53 G7
Frittenden **TN17** 14 D3
Frittiscombe **TQ7** 5 J6
Fritton, *Norf.* **NR15** 45 G6
Fritton, *Norf.* **NR31** 45 J5
Fritwell **OX27** 31 G6
Frizinghall **BD9** 57 G6
Frizington **CA26** 60 B5
Frocester **GL10** 20 A1
Frochas **SY21** 38 B5
Frodesley **SY5** 38 E5
Frodesley Lane **SY5** 38 E5
Frodingham **DN15** 52 B1
Frodsham **WA6** 48 E5
Frog End **CB3** 33 H3
Frog Pool **WR6** 29 G2
Frogden **TD5** 70 C1
Froggatt **S32** 50 E5
Froghall **ST10** 40 C1
Frogham **SP6** 10 C3
Frogland Cross **BS32** 19 K3
Frogmore, *Devon* **TQ7** 5 H6
Frogmore, *Hants.* **GU17** 22 B6
Frogmore, *Herts.* **AL2** 22 E1
Frogwell **PL17** 4 D4
Frolesworth **LE17** 41 H6
Frome **BA11** 20 A7
Frome Market **BA11** 20 B6
Frome St. Quintin **DT2** 8 E4
Frome Whitfield **DT2** 9 F5
Fromes Hill **HR8** 29 F4
Fron, *Gwyn.* **LL53** 36 C2
Fron, *Powys* **SY21** 38 B5
Fron, *Powys* **LD1** 27 K2
Fron, *Powys* **SY15** 38 A6
Fron Isaf **LL14** 38 B2
Froncysyllte **LL20** 38 B1
Fron-goch **LL23** 37 J2
Frostenden **NR34** 45 J7
Frosterley **DL13** 62 B3
Froxfield **SN8** 21 G5
Froxfield Green **GU32** 11 J2
Fryerning **CM4** 24 C1
Fugglestone St. Peter **SP2** 10 C1
Fulbeck **NG32** 52 C7
Fulbourn **CB1** 33 J3
Fulbrook **OX18** 30 D7
Fulflood **SO22** 11 F2
Fulford, *Som.* **TA2** 8 B2
Fulford, *Staffs.* **ST11** 40 B2
Fulford, *York* **YO10** 58 C5
Fulham **SW6** 23 F4
Fulking **BN5** 13 F5
Full Sutton **YO41** 58 D4
Fullaford **EX31** 6 E2
Fuller Street **CM3** 34 B7
Fuller's Moor **CH3** 48 D7
Fullerton **SP11** 10 E1
Fulletby **LN9** 53 F5
Fullwood **KA3** 74 C5
Fulmer **SL3** 22 D3
Fulmodeston **NR21** 44 D2
Fulnetby **LN8** 52 E5
Fulready **CV37** 30 D4
Fulstone **HD9** 50 D2
Fulstow **LN11** 53 G3
Fulwell, *Oxon.* **OX7** 30 E6
Fulwell, *T. & W.* **SR5** 62 E1
Fulwood, *Lancs.* **PR2** 55 J6
Fulwood, *S.Yorks.* **S10** 51 F4
Fundenhall **NR16** 45 F6
Fundenhall Street **NR16** 45 F6
Funtington **PO18** 12 B6
Funtley **PO16** 11 G4
Funzie **ZE2** 108 F3
Furley **EX13** 8 B4
Furnace, *Arg. & B.* **PA32** 80 B7
Furnace, *Carmar.* **SA15** 17 J4
Furnace, *Cere.* **SY20** 37 F6
Furnace, *High.* **IV22** 95 F4
Furnace End **B46** 40 E6
Furner's Green **TN22** 13 H4
Furness Vale **SK23** 50 C4
Furneux Pelham **SG9** 33 H6
Furnham **TA20** 8 C4
Further Quarter **TN26** 14 D4
Furtho **MK19** 31 J4
Furze Green **IP21** 45 G7
Furze Platt **SL6** 22 B3
Furzehill, *Devon* **EX35** 7 F1
Furzehill, *Dorset* **BH21** 10 B4
Furzeley Corner **PO7** 11 H3
Furzey Lodge **SO42** 10 E4
Furzley **SO43** 10 D3
Fyfett **TA20** 8 B3
Fyfield, *Essex* **CM5** 23 J1
Fyfield, *Glos.* **GL7** 21 F1
Fyfield, *Hants.* **SP11** 21 F7
Fyfield, *Oxon.* **OX13** 21 H2
Fyfield, *Wilts.* **SN8** 20 E5
Fyfield, *Wilts.* **SN9** 20 E5
Fylingthorpe **YO22** 63 J2
Fyning **GU31** 12 B4
Fyvie **AB53** 91 F1

G

Gabalfa **CF14** 18 E4
Gabhsunn Bho Dheas **HS2** 101 G2
Gabhsunn Bho Thuath **HS2** 101 G2
Gablon **IV25** 96 E2
Gabroc Hill **KA3** 74 C5
Gaddesby **LE7** 41 J4
Gaddesden Row **HP2** 32 D7
Gadebridge **HP1** 22 D1
Gadshill **ME3** 24 D4
Gaer, *Newport* **NP20** 19 F3
Gaer, *Powys* **NP8** 28 A6
Gaer-fawr **NP15** 19 H2
Gaerllwyd **NP16** 19 H2
Gaerwen **LL60** 46 C5
Gagingwell **OX7** 31 F6
Gaich, *High.* **PH26** 89 H2
Gaich, *High.* **IV2** 88 D1
Gaick Lodge **PH21** 88 E6
Gailes **KA11** 74 B7
Gailey **ST19** 40 B4
Gainford **DL2** 62 C5
Gainsborough **DN21** 52 B3
Gainsford End **CO9** 34 B5
Gairloch **IV21** 94 D4
Gairlochy **PH34** 87 H6
Gairney Bank **KY13** 75 K1
Gairnshiel Lodge **AB35** 89 K4
Gaitsgill **CA5** 60 E2
Galabank **TD1** 76 C6
GALASHIELS TD 76 **C7**
Galdenoch **DG8** 64 B4
Gale **OL15** 49 J1
Galgate **LA2** 55 H4
Galhampton **BA22** 9 F2
Gallanach **PA34** 79 K5
Gallantry Bank **SY14** 48 E7
Gallatown **KY1** 76 A1
Gallchoille **PA31** 73 F1
Gallery **AB30** 83 H1
Galley Common **CV10** 41 F6
Galleyend **CM2** 24 D1
Galleywood **CM2** 24 D1
Gallowfauld **DD8** 83 F3
Gallowhill **PA3** 74 C4
Gallows Green **ST10** 40 C1
Gallowstree Common **RG4** 21 K3
Gallowstree Elm **DY7** 40 A7
Gallt Melyd (Meliden) **LL19** 47 J4
Galltair **IV40** 86 E2
Gallt-y-foel **LL55** 46 D6
Gallypot Street **TN7** 13 H3
Galmington **TA1** 8 B2
Galmisdale **PH42** 85 K6
Galmpton, *Devon* **TQ7** 5 G6
Galmpton, *Torbay* **TQ5** 5 J5
Galmpton Warborough **TQ4** 5 J5
Galphay **HG4** 57 H2
Galston **KA4** 74 C7
Galtrigill **IV55** 93 G6
Gamble's Green **CM3** 34 B7
Gamblesby **CA10** 61 H3
Gamelsby **CA7** 60 D1
Gamesley **SK13** 50 C3
Gamlingay **SG19** 33 F3
Gamlingay Cinques **SG19** 33 F3
Gamlingay Great Heath **SG19** 33 F3
Gammaton **EX39** 6 C3
Gammaton Moor **EX39** 6 C3
Gammersgill **DL8** 57 F1
Gamrie **AB45** 99 F4
Gamston, *Notts.* **DN22** 51 K5
Gamston, *Notts.* **NG2** 41 J2
Ganarew **NP25** 28 E7
Gang **PL14** 4 D4
Ganllwyd **LL40** 37 G3
Gannochy **DD9** 90 E7
Ganstead **HU11** 59 H6
Ganthorpe **YO60** 58 C2
Ganton **YO12** 59 F2
Ganwick Corner **EN5** 23 F2
Gaodhail **PA72** 79 H4
Gappah **TQ13** 5 J3
Gara Bridge **TQ9** 5 H5
Garabal **G83** 80 E6
Garadheancal **IV26** 95 F1
Garbat **IV23** 96 B5
Garbhallt **PA27** 73 J1
Garboldisham **IP22** 44 E7
Garden **FK8** 74 D1
Garden City **CH5** 48 C6
Garden Village **S36** 50 E3
Gardeners Green **RG40** 22 B5
Gardenstown **AB45** 99 F4
Garderhouse **ZE2** 109 C8
Gardham **HU17** 59 F5
Gare Hill **BA11** 20 A7
Garelochhead **G84** 74 A1
Garford **OX13** 21 H2
Garforth **LS25** 57 K6
Gargrave **BD23** 56 E4
Gargunnock **FK8** 75 F1
Gariob **PA31** 73 F2
Garlic Street **IP20** 45 G7
Garlies Castle **DG8** 64 E4
Garlieston **DG8** 64 E6
Garlinge Green **CT4** 15 G2
Garlogie **AB32** 91 F4
Garmelow **ST21** 40 A3
Garmond **AB53** 99 G5
Garmony **PA65** 79 H3
Garmouth **IV32** 98 B4
Garmston **SY5** 39 F5
Garnant **SA18** 17 K3
Garndolbenmaen **LL51** 36 D1
Garneddwen **SY20** 37 G5
Garnett Bridge **LA8** 61 G7
Garnfadryn **LL53** 36 B2
Garnswllt **SA18** 17 K4
Garrabost **HS2** 101 H4
Garrachra **PA23** 73 J2
Garralburn **AB55** 98 C5
Garras **TR12** 2 E6
Garreg **LL48** 37 F1
Garreg Bank **SY21** 38 B4
Garrett's Green **B33** 40 D7
Garrick **FK15** 81 K6
Garrigill **CA9** 61 J2
Garriston **DL8** 62 C7
Garroch **DG7** 67 K5
Garrochty **PA20** 73 J5
Garros **IV51** 93 K5
Garrow **PH8** 81 K4
Garryhorn **DG7** 67 K4
Garrynahine (Gearraidh na h-Aibhne) **HS2** 100 E4
Garsdale **LA10** 56 C1
Garsdale Head **LA10** 61 J7
Garsdon **SN16** 20 C3
Garshall Green **ST18** 40 B2
Garsington **OX44** 21 J1
Garstang **PR3** 55 H5
Garston **L19** 48 D4
Garswood **WN4** 48 E3
Gartachoil **G63** 74 D1
Gartally **IV63** 88 B1
Gartavaich **PA29** 73 G5
Gartbreck **PA43** 72 A5
Gartcosh **G69** 74 E4
Garth, *Bridgend* **CF34** 18 B2
Garth, *Cere.* **SY23** 37 F7
Garth, *Gwyn.* **LL57** 46 D5
Garth, *I.o.M.* **IM4** 54 C6
Garth, *Powys* **LD4** 27 J4
Garth, *Shet.* **ZE2** 109 B7
Garth, *Wrex.* **LL20** 38 B1
Garth Row **LA8** 61 G7
Garthbrengy **LD3** 27 K5
Garthdee **AB15** 91 H4
Gartheli **SA48** 26 E3
Garthmyl **SY21** 38 A6
Garthorpe, *Leics.* **LE14** 42 B3
Garthorpe, *N.Lincs.* **DN17** 52 B1
Garths **LA8** 61 G7
Garthynty **SA20** 27 G4
Gartincaber **FK16** 81 H7
Gartly **AB54** 90 D1
Gartmore **FK8** 74 D1
Gartnagrenach **PA29** 73 F5
Gartnatra **PA43** 72 B4
Gartness **G63** 74 D2
Gartocharn **G83** 74 C2
Garton **HU11** 59 J6
Garton-on-the-Wolds **YO25** 59 F3
Gartymore **KW8** 105 F7
Garvald **EH41** 76 D3
Garvamore **PH20** 88 C5
Garvan **PH33** 87 F7
Garvard **PA61** 72 B1
Garve **IV23** 95 K5
Garveld **PA28** 66 A3
Garvestone **NR9** 44 E5
Garvie **PA22** 73 J2
Garvock, *Aber.* **AB30** 91 F7
Garvock, *Inclyde* **PA16** 74 A3
Garvock, *P. & K.* **PH2** 82 B6
Garwald **DG13** 69 H3
Garwaldwaterfoot **DG13** 69 H3
Garway **HR2** 28 D6
Garway Hill **HR2** 28 D6
Gask, *Aber.* **AB42** 99 J6
Gask, *Aber.* **AB53** 99 F6
Gask, *P. & K.* **PH3** 82 A6
Gaskan **PH37** 86 E7
Gass **KA19** 67 J3
Gastard **SN13** 20 B5
Gasthorpe **IP22** 44 D7
Gaston Green **CM22** 33 J7
Gatcombe **PO30** 11 F6
Gate Burton **DN21** 52 B4
Gate Helmsley **YO41** 58 C4
Gate House **PA60** 72 D3
Gateacre **L25** 48 D4
Gateford **S81** 51 H4
Gateforth **YO8** 58 B7
Gatehead **KA2** 74 B7
Gatehouse **PH15** 81 K3
Gatehouse of Fleet **DG7** 65 G5
Gatelawbridge **DG3** 68 E4
Gateley **NR20** 44 D3
Gatenby **DL7** 57 J1
Gatesgarth **CA13** 60 C5
Gateshaw **TD5** 70 C1
Gateshead **NE8** 71 H7
Gatesheath **CH3** 48 D6
Gateside, *Aber.* **AB33** 90 E3
Gateside, *Angus* **DD8** 83 F3
Gateside, *Fife* **KY14** 82 C7
Gateside, *N.Ayr.* **KA15** 74 B5
Gateslack **DG3** 68 D3
Gathurst **WN5** 48 E2
Gatley **SK8** 49 H4
Gattonside **TD6** 76 D7
Gatwick Airport (London Gatwick Airport) **RH6** 23 F7
Gaufron **LD6** 27 J2
Gaulby **LE7** 41 J5
Gauldry **DD6** 82 E5
Gauntons Bank **SY13** 38 E1
Gaunt's Common **BH21** 10 B4
Gaunt's Earthcott **BS32** 19 K3
Gautby **LN8** 52 E5
Gavinton **TD11** 77 F5
Gawber **S75** 51 F2
Gawcott **MK18** 31 H5
Gawsworth **SK11** 49 H5
Gawthrop **LA10** 56 B1
Gawthwaite **LA12** 55 F1
Gay Bowers **CM3** 24 D1
Gay Street **RH20** 12 D4
Gaydon **CV35** 30 E3
Gayhurst **MK16** 32 B4
Gayle **DL8** 56 D1
Gayles **DL11** 62 C6
Gayton, *Mersey.* **CH60** 48 B4
Gayton, *Norf.* **PE32** 44 B4
Gayton, *Northants.* **NN7** 31 J3
Gayton, *Staffs.* **ST18** 40 B3
Gayton le Marsh **LN13** 53 H4
Gayton le Wold **LN11** 53 F4
Gayton Thorpe **PE32** 44 B4
Gaywood **PE30** 44 A3
Gazeley **CB8** 34 B2
Geanies House **IV20** 97 F4
Gearach **PA48** 72 A5
Gearnsary **KW11** 104 C5
Gearradh **PH33** 80 A1
Gearraidh Bhailteas **HS8** 84 C2
Gearraidh Bhaird **HS2** 101 F5
Gearraidh na h-Aibhne (Garrynahine) **HS2** 100 E4
Gearraidh na Monadh **HS8** 84 C3
Gearrannan **HS2** 100 D3
Geary **IV55** 93 H5
Gedding **IP30** 34 D3
Geddington **NN14** 42 B7
Gedgrave Hall **IP12** 35 J4
Gedintailor **IV51** 86 B1
Gedling **NG4** 41 J1
Gedney **PE12** 43 H3
Gedney Broadgate **PE12** 43 H3
Gedney Drove End **PE12** 43 H3
Gedney Dyke **PE12** 43 H3
Gedney Hill **PE12** 43 G4
Gee Cross **SK14** 49 J3
Geilston **G82** 74 B3
Geirinis **HS8** 92 C7
Geisiadar **HS2** 100 D4
Geldeston **NR34** 45 H6
Gell, *Conwy* **LL22** 47 G6
Gell, *Gwyn.* **LL52** 36 D2
Gelli **CF41** 18 C2
Gelli Gynan **CH7** 47 K7
Gellideg **CF48** 18 D1
Gellifor **LL15** 47 K6
Gelligaer **CF82** 18 E2
Gellilydan **LL41** 37 F2
Gellioedd **LL21** 37 J1
Gelly **SA66** 16 D3
Gellyburn **PH1** 82 B4
Gellywen **SA33** 17 F2
Gelston, *D. & G.* **DG7** 65 H5
Gelston, *Lincs.* **NG32** 42 C1
Gembling **YO25** 59 H4
Gemmil **PA31** 79 J7
Genoch **DG9** 64 B5
Genoch Square **DG9** 64 B5
Gentleshaw **WS15** 40 C4
Geocrab **HS3** 93 G2
George Green **SL3** 22 D3
George Nympton **EX36** 7 F3
Georgeham **EX33** 6 C2
Georgetown **PA6** 74 C4
Gerlan **LL57** 46 E6
Germansweek **EX21** 6 C6
Germoe **TR20** 2 C6
Gerrans **TR2** 3 F5
Gerrards Cross **SL9** 22 D3
Gerston **KW12** 105 G3
Gestingthorpe **CO9** 34 C5
Geuffordd **SY22** 38 B4
Geufron **SY18** 37 H7
Gibbet Hill **BA11** 20 A7
Gibbshill **DG7** 65 H3
Gibraltar, *Lincs.* **PE24** 53 J7
Gibraltar, *Suff.* **IP6** 35 F3
Giddeahall **SN14** 20 B4
Giddy Green **BH20** 9 H6
Gidea Park **RM2** 23 J3
Gidleigh **TQ13** 6 E7
Giffnock **G46** 74 D5
Gifford **EH41** 76 D4
Giffordland **KA24** 74 A6
Giffordtown **KY15** 82 D6
Giggleswick **BD24** 56 D3
Gigha **PA41** 72 E6
Gilberdyke **HU15** 58 E7
Gilbert's End **WR8** 29 H4
Gilchriston **EH36** 76 C4
Gilcrux **CA7** 60 C3
Gildersome **LS27** 57 H7
Gildingwells **S81** 51 H4
Gilesgate Moor **DH1** 62 D2
Gileston **CF62** 18 D5
Gilfach **CF81** 18 E2
Gilfach Goch **CF39** 18 C3
Gilfachrheda **SA45** 26 D3
Gilgarran **CA14** 60 B4
Gill **CA11** 60 F4
Gillamoor **YO62** 58 C1
Gillen **IV55** 93 H5
Gillenbie **DG11** 69 G5
Gillfoot **DG2** 65 K3
Gilling East **YO62** 58 C2
Gilling West **DL10** 62 C6
Gillingham, *Dorset* **SP8** 9 H2
Gillingham, *Med.* **ME7** 24 D5
Gillingham, *Norf.* **NR34** 45 J6
Gillivoan **KW5** 105 G5
Gillock **KW1** 105 H3
Gillow Heath **ST8** 49 H7
Gills **KW1** 105 J1
Gill's Green **TN18** 14 C4
Gilmanscleuch **TD7** 69 J1
Gilmerton, *Edin.* **EH17** 76 A4
Gilmerton, *P. & K.* **PH7** 81 K5
Gilmilnscroft **KA5** 67 K1
Gilmonby **DL12** 62 A5
Gilmorton **LE17** 41 H7
Gilsland **CA8** 70 B7
Gilsland Spa **CA8** 70 B7
Gilson **B46** 40 D7
Gilstead **BD16** 57 G6
Gilston **EH38** 76 C5
Gilston Park **CM20** 33 H7
Giltbrook **NG16** 41 G1
Gilwern **NP7** 28 B7
Gimingham **NR11** 45 G2
Gin Pit **M29** 49 F2
Ginclough **SK10** 49 J5
Ginger's Green **BN27** 13 K5
Giosla **HS2** 100 D5
Gipping **IP14** 34 E2
Gipsey Bridge **PE22** 43 F1
Girlsta **ZE2** 109 D7
Girsby **DL2** 62 E6
Girtford **SG19** 32 E4
Girthon **DG7** 65 G5
Girton, *Cambs.* **CB3** 33 H2
Girton, *Notts.* **NG23** 52 B6
Girvan **KA26** 67 F4
Gisburn **BB7** 56 D5
Gisburn Cotes **BB7** 56 D5
Gisleham **NR33** 45 K7
Gislingham **IP23** 34 E1
Gissing **IP22** 45 F7
Gittisham **EX14** 7 K6
Givons Grove **KT22** 22 E6
Glackour **IV23** 95 H3
Gladestry **HR5** 28 B3
Gladsmuir **EH33** 76 C3
Glaic **PA22** 73 J3
Glais **SA7** 18 A1
Glaisdale **YO21** 63 J6
Glaister **KA27** 73 H7
Glame **IV40** 94 B7
Glamis **DD8** 82 E3
Glan Conwy **LL24** 47 G7
Glanaber Terrace **LL24** 37 G1
Glanaman **SA18** 17 K3
Glanbran **SA20** 27 H5
Glan-Denys **SA48** 26 E3
Glanderston **AB52** 90 D2
Glandford **NR25** 44 E1
Glan-Duar **SA40** 26 E4
Glandwr **SA34** 16 E2
Glan-Dwyfach **LL51** 36 D1
Glangrwyney **NP8** 28 B7
Glanllynfi **CF34** 18 B2
Glanmule **SY16** 38 A6
Glan-rhyd, *N.P.T.* **SA9** 18 A1
Glanrhyd, *Pembs.* **SA43** 26 A4
Glanton **NE66** 71 F2
Glanton Pyke **NE66** 71 F2
Glantwymyn (Cemmaes Road) **SY20** 37 H5
Glanvilles Wootton **DT9** 9 F4
Glanwern **SY24** 37 F7
Glanwydden **LL31** 47 G4
Glan-y-don **CH8** 47 K5
Glanyferi (Ferryside) **SA17** 17 G3
Glan-y-llyn **CF15** 18 E3
Glan-y-nant **SY18** 37 J7
Glan-yr-afon, *Gwyn.* **LL23** 37 J1
Glan-yr-afon, *Gwyn.* **LL21** 37 K1
Glan-yr-afon, *I.o.A.* **LL58** 46 E4
Glan-y-Wern **LL47** 37 F2
Glapthorn **PE8** 42 D6
Glapwell **S44** 51 G6
Glasahoile **FK8** 81 F7
Glasbury **HR3** 28 A5
Glaschoil **PH26** 89 H1
Glascoed, *Mon.* **NP4** 19 G1
Glascoed, *Wrex.* **LL11** 48 B7
Glascorrie **AB35** 90 C5
Glascote **B77** 40 E5
Glascwm **LD1** 28 A3
Glasdrum **PA38** 80 B3
Glasfryn **LL21** 47 H7
GLASGOW G 74 **D4**
Glasgow Airport **PA3** 74 C4
Glasgow Prestwick International Airport (Prestwick International Airport) **KA9** 67 H1
Glashmore **AB31** 91 F4
Glasinfryn **LL57** 46 D6
Glasnacardoch **PH41** 86 C5
Glasnakille **IV49** 86 B3
Glaspant **SA38** 17 F1
Glaspwll **SY20** 37 G6
Glassburn **IV4** 87 K1
Glassel **AB31** 90 E5
Glassenbury **TN17** 14 C4
Glasserton **DG8** 64 E7
Glassford **ML10** 75 F6
Glasshouse **GL17** 29 G6
Glasshouse Hill **GL17** 29 G6
Glasshouses **HG3** 57 G3
Glassingall **FK15** 81 J7
Glasslie **KY6** 82 D7

Glasson

Glasson, *Cumb.* **CA7** 69 H7
Glasson, *Lancs.* **LA2** 55 H4
Glassonby **CA10** 61 G3
Glasterlaw **DD11** 83 G2
Glaston **LE15** 42 B5
Glastonbury **BA6** 8 D1
Glatton **PE28** 42 E7
Glazebrook **WA3** 49 F3
Glazebury **WA3** 49 F3
Glazeley **WV16** 39 G7
Gleadless **S12** 51 F4
Gleadsmoss **SK11** 49 H6
Gleann Ghrabhair **HS2** 101 G5
Gleann Tholastaidh **HS2** 101 H3
Gleaston **LA12** 55 F2
Glecknabae **PA20** 73 J4
Gledhow **LS8** 57 J6
Gledrid **LL14** 38 B2
Glemsford **CO10** 34 C4
Glen, *D. & G.* **DG2** 65 J3
Glen, *D. & G.* **DG7** 65 F5
Glen Auldyn **IM7** 54 D4
Glen Mona **IM7** 54 D5
Glen Parva **LE2** 41 H6
Glen Trool Lodge **DG8** 67 J5
Glen Village **FK1** 75 G3
Glen Vine **IM4** 54 C6
Glenae **DG1** 68 E5
Glenaladale **PH37** 86 E7
Glenald **G84** 74 A1
Glenamachrie **PA34** 80 A5
Glenapp Castle **KA26** 66 E5
Glenarm **DD8** 82 E1
Glenbarr **PA29** 72 E7
Glenbatrick **PA60** 72 D3
Glenbeg, *High.* **IV23** 95 K3
Glenbeg, *High.* **PH26** 89 H2
Glenbeg, *High.* **PH36** 79 G1
Glenbeich **FK19** 81 H5
Glenbervie, *Aber.* **AB39** 91 F6
Glenbervie, *Falk.* **FK5** 75 G2
Glenboig **ML5** 75 F4
Glenborrodale **PH36** 79 H1
Glenbranter **PA27** 73 K1
Glenbreck **ML12** 69 F1
Glenbrittle **IV47** 85 K2
Glenbuck **KA18** 68 C1
Glenburn **PA2** 74 C4
Glenbyre **PA62** 79 G5
Glencaple **DG1** 65 K4
Glencarse **PH2** 82 C5
Glencat **AB34** 90 D5
Glenceitlein **PH49** 80 C3
Glencloy **KA27** 73 J7
Glencoe **PH49** 80 C2
Glenconglass **AB37** 89 J2
Glencraig **KY5** 75 K1
Glencripesdale **PH36** 79 H2
Glencrosh **DG3** 68 C5
Glencruittein **PA34** 79 K5
Glencuie **AB33** 90 C3
Glendearg, *D. & G.* **DG13** 69 H3
Glendearg, *Sc.Bord.* **TD1** 76 D7
Glendessary **PH34** 87 F5
Glendevon **FK14** 82 A7
Glendoebeg **PH32** 88 B4
Glendoick **PH2** 82 D5
Glendoll Lodge **DD8** 89 K7
Glendoune **KA26** 67 F4
Glendrissaig **KA26** 67 F4
Glenduckie **KY14** 82 D6
Glenduisk **KA26** 67 G5
Glendye Lodge **AB31** 90 E6
Gleneagles Hotel **PH3** 82 A6
Gleneagles House **PH3** 82 A7
Glenearn **PH2** 82 C6
Glenegedale **PA42** 72 B5
Glenelg **IV40** 86 E3
Glenfarg **PH2** 82 C6
Glenfeochan **PA34** 79 K5
Glenfield **LE3** 41 H5
Glenfinnan **PH37** 87 F6
Glenfoot **PH2** 82 C6
Glengalmadale **PH33** 79 K2
Glengap **DG6** 65 G5
Glengarnock **KA14** 74 B5
Glengarrisdale **PA60** 72 E1
Glengennet **KA26** 67 G4
Glengolly **KW14** 105 G2
Glengrasco **IV51** 93 K7
Glengyle **FK17** 80 E6
Glenhead **DG2** 68 D5
Glenhead Farm **PH11** 82 D1
Glenhurich **PH37** 79 K1
Glenkerry **TD7** 69 H2
Glenkiln **KA27** 73 J7
Glenkin **PA23** 73 K2
Glenkindie **AB33** 90 C3
Glenlair **DG7** 65 H3
Glenlatterach **IV30** 97 K6
Glenlean **PA23** 73 J2
Glenlee, *Angus* **DD9** 90 C7
Glenlee, *D. & G.* **DG7** 68 B5
Glenlichorn **FK15** 81 J6
Glenlivet **AB37** 89 J2
Glenlochar **DG7** 65 H4
Glenluce **DG8** 64 B5
Glenmallan **G84** 74 A1
Glenmanna **DG3** 68 C3
Glenmavis **ML6** 75 F4
Glenmaye **IM5** 54 B6
Glenmeanie **IV6** 95 J6
Glenmore, *Arg. & B.* **PA20** 73 J4
Glenmore, *High.* **IV51** 93 K7
Glenmore Lodge **PH22** 89 G4
Glenmoy **DD8** 83 F1
Glenmuick **IV27** 103 F7
Glennoe **PA35** 80 B4
Glenochar **ML12** 68 E2
Glenogil **DD8** 83 F1
Glenprosen Village **DD8** 82 E1
Glenquiech **DD8** 83 F1
Glenramskill **PA28** 66 B2
Glenrazie **DG8** 64 D4
Glenridding **CA11** 60 E5
Glenrisdell **PA29** 73 G5
Glenrossal **IV27** 96 B1
Glenrothes **KY7** 82 D7
Glensanda **PA34** 79 K3
Glensaugh **AB30** 90 E7
Glensgaich **IV14** 96 B5
Glenshalg **AB31** 90 D4
Glenshellish **PA27** 73 K1
Glensluain **PA27** 73 J1
Glentaggart **ML11** 68 D1
Glentham **LN8** 52 D3
Glenton **AB51** 90 E2
Glentress **EH45** 76 A7
Glentrool **DG8** 64 D3
Glentruan **IM7** 54 D3
Glentworth **DN21** 52 C4
Glenuachdarach **IV51** 93 K6
Glenuig **PH38** 86 C7
Glenure **PA38** 80 B3
Glenurquhart **IV11** 96 E5
Glenwhilly **DG8** 64 B3
Glespin **ML11** 68 D1
Gletness **ZE2** 109 D7
Glewstone **HR9** 28 E6
Glinton **PE6** 42 E5
Glooston **LE16** 42 A6
Glororum **NE69** 77 K7
Glossop **SK13** 50 C3
Gloster Hill **NE65** 71 H3
GLOUCESTER GL 29 H7
Gloup **ZE2** 108 E2
Gloweth **TR1** 2 E4
Glusburn **BD20** 57 F5
Gluss **ZE2** 108 C5
Glympton **OX20** 31 F6
Glyn **LL24** 47 F7
Glyn Ceiriog **LL20** 38 B2
Glynarthen **SA44** 26 C4
Glyncoch **CF37** 18 D2
Glyncorrwg **SA13** 18 B2
Glyn-Cywarch **LL47** 37 F2
Glynde **BN8** 13 H6
Glyndebourne **BN8** 13 H5
Glyndyfrdwy **LL21** 38 A1
Glynneath **SA11** 18 B1
Glynogwr **CF35** 18 C3
Glyntaff **CF37** 18 D3
Gnosall **ST20** 40 A3
Gnosall Heath **ST20** 40 A3
Goadby **LE7** 42 A6
Goadby Marwood **LE14** 42 A3
Goatacre **SN11** 20 D4
Goatfield **PA32** 80 B7
Goathill **DT9** 9 F3
Goathland **YO22** 63 K6
Goathurst **TA5** 8 B1
Gobernuisgeach **KW12** 104 E5
Gobhaig **HS3** 100 C7
Gobowen **SY11** 38 C2
Godalming **GU7** 22 C7
Goddard's Corner **IP13** 35 G2
Goddards Green **BN6** 13 F4
Godden Green **TN15** 23 J6
Goddington **BR6** 23 H5
Godford Cross **EX14** 7 K5
Godington **OX27** 31 H6
Godleybrook **ST10** 40 B1
Godmanchester **PE29** 33 F1
Godmanstone **DT2** 9 F5
Godmersham **CT4** 15 F2
Godney **BA5** 19 H7
Godolphin Cross **TR13** 2 D5
Godor **SY22** 38 B4
Godre'r-graig **SA9** 18 A1
Godshill, *Hants.* **SP6** 10 C3
Godshill, *I.o.W.* **PO38** 11 G6
Godstone **RH9** 23 G6
Godwick **PE32** 44 D3
Goetre **NP4** 19 G1
Goff's Oak **EN7** 23 G1
Gogar **EH12** 75 K3
Gogarth **LL30** 47 F4
Goginan **SY23** 37 F7
Goirtean a' Chladaich **PH33** 87 G7
Goirtein **PA27** 73 H2
Golan **LL51** 36 E1
Golant **PL23** 4 B5
Golberdon **PL17** 4 D3
Golborne **WA3** 49 F3
Golcar **HD7** 50 D1
Gold Hill, *Cambs.* **PE14** 43 J6
Gold Hill, *Dorset* **DT11** 9 H3
Goldcliff **NP18** 19 G3
Golden Cross **BN27** 13 J5
Golden Green **TN11** 23 K7
Golden Grove **SA32** 17 J3
Golden Pot **GU34** 22 A7
Golden Valley, *Derbys.* **DE55** 51 G7
Golden Valley, *Glos.* **GL51** 29 J6
Goldenhill **ST6** 49 H7
Golders Green **NW11** 23 F3
Goldhanger **CM9** 25 F1
Goldielea **DG2** 65 K3
Golding **SY5** 38 E5
Goldington **MK41** 32 D3
Goldsborough, *N.Yorks.* **YO21** 63 K5
Goldsborough, *N.Yorks.* **HG5** 57 J4
Goldsithney **TR20** 2 C5
Goldstone **TF9** 39 G3
Goldthorn Park **WV2** 40 B6
Goldthorpe **S63** 51 G2
Goldworthy **EX39** 6 B3
Golford **TN17** 14 C4
Gollanfield **IV2** 97 F6
Gollinglith Foot **HG4** 57 G1
Golspie **KW10** 97 F2
Golval **KW13** 104 D2
Gomeldon **SP4** 10 C1
Gomersal **BD19** 57 H7
Gometra **PA73** 78 E3
Gometra House **PA73** 78 E3
Gomshall **GU5** 22 D7
Gonachan Cottage **G63** 74 E2
Gonalston **NG14** 41 J1
Gonerby Hill Foot **NG31** 42 C2
Gonfirth **ZE2** 109 C6
Good Easter **CM1** 33 K7
Gooderstone **PE33** 44 B5
Goodleigh **EX32** 6 E2
Goodmanham **YO43** 58 E5
Goodmayes **IG3** 23 H3
Goodnestone, *Kent* **CT3** 15 H2
Goodnestone, *Kent* **ME13** 25 G5
Goodrich **HR9** 28 E7
Goodrington **TQ4** 5 J5
Goodshaw **BB4** 56 D7
Goodshaw Fold **BB4** 56 D7
Goodwick (Wdig) **SA64** 16 C1
Goodworth Clatford **SP11** 21 G7
Goodyers End **CV12** 41 F7
Goole **DN14** 58 D7
Goom's Hill **WR7** 30 B3
Goonbell **TR5** 2 E4
Goonhavern **TR4** 2 E3
Goonvrea **TR5** 2 E4
Goose Green, *Essex* **CO11** 35 F6
Goose Green, *Essex* **CO16** 35 F6
Goose Green, *Gt.Man.* **WN3** 48 E2
Goose Green, *Kent* **TN11** 23 K6
Goose Green, *S.Glos.* **BS30** 19 K4
Goose Pool **HR2** 28 D5
Gooseham **EX23** 6 A4
Goosehill Green **WR9** 29 J2
Goosewell **PL9** 5 F5
Goosey **SN7** 21 G2
Goosnargh **PR3** 55 J6
Goostrey **CW4** 49 G5
Gorcott Hill **B98** 30 B2
Gorddinog **LL33** 46 E5
Gordon **TD3** 76 E6
Gordonbush **KW9** 97 F1
Gordonstoun **IV30** 97 J5
Gordonstown, *Aber.* **AB45** 98 D5
Gordonstown, *Aber.* **AB51** 91 F1
Gore Cross **SN10** 20 D6
Gore End **RG20** 21 H5
Gore Pit **CO5** 34 C7
Gore Street **CT12** 25 J5
Gorebridge **EH23** 76 B4
Gorefield **PE13** 43 H4
Gorey **JE3** 3 K7
Gorgie **EH11** 76 A3
Goring **RG8** 21 K3
Goring Heath **RG8** 21 K4
Goring-by-Sea **BN12** 12 E6
Gorleston-on-Sea **NR31** 45 K5
Gorllwyn **SA33** 17 G1
Gornalwood **DY3** 40 B6
Gorrachie **AB45** 99 F5
Gorran Churchtown **PL26** 3 G4
Gorran Haven **PL26** 4 A6
Gors **SY23** 27 F1
Gorsedd **CH8** 47 K5
Gorseinon **SA4** 17 J5
Gorseness **KW17** 107 D6
Gorseybank **DE4** 50 E7
Gorsgoch **SA40** 26 D3
Gorslas **SA14** 17 J3
Gorsley **HR9** 29 F6
Gorsley Common **HR9** 29 F6
Gorstage **CW8** 49 F5
Gorstan **IV23** 95 K5
Gorstanvorran **PH37** 86 E7
Gorsty Hill **ST14** 40 D3
Gorten **PA64** 79 J4
Gortenbuie **PA70** 79 G4
Gorteneorn **PH36** 79 H1
Gorton, *Arg. & B.* **PA78** 78 C2
Gorton, *Gt.Man.* **M18** 49 H3
Gosbeck **IP6** 35 F3
Gosberton **PE11** 43 F2
Gosberton Clough **PE11** 42 E3
Goseley Dale **DE11** 41 F3
Gosfield **CO9** 34 B6
Gosford, *Here.* **SY8** 28 E2
Gosford, *Oxon.* **OX5** 31 G7
Gosforth, *Cumb.* **CA20** 60 B6
Gosforth, *T. & W.* **NE3** 71 H7
Gosland Green **CW6** 48 E7
Gosmore **SG4** 32 E6
Gospel End **DY3** 40 B6
Gosport **PO12** 11 H5
Gossabrough **ZE2** 108 E4
Gossington **GL2** 20 A1
Gossops Green **RH11** 13 F3
Goswick **TD15** 77 J6
Gotham **NG11** 41 H2
Gotherington **GL52** 29 J6
Gothers **PL26** 3 G3
Gott **ZE2** 109 D8
Gotton **TA2** 8 B2
Goudhurst **TN17** 14 C4
Goulceby **LN11** 53 F5
Gourdas **AB53** 99 F6
Gourdon **DD10** 91 G7
Gourock **PA19** 74 A3
Govan **G51** 74 D4
Goverton **NG14** 51 K7
Goveton **TQ7** 5 H6
Govilon **NP7** 28 B7
Gowanhill **AB43** 99 J4
Gowdall **DN14** 58 C7
Gowerton **SA4** 17 J5
Gowkhall **KY12** 75 J2
Gowthorpe **YO41** 58 D4
Goxhill, *E.Riding* **HU11** 59 H5
Goxhill, *N.Lincs.* **DN19** 59 H7
Goytre **SA13** 18 A3
Gozzard's Ford **OX13** 21 H2
Grabhair **HS2** 101 F6
Graby **NG34** 42 D3
Gradbach **SK17** 49 J6
Grade **TR12** 2 E7
Gradeley Green **CW5** 48 E7
Graffham **GU28** 12 C5
Grafham, *Cambs.* **PE28** 32 E2
Grafham, *Surr.* **GU5** 22 D7
Grafton, *Here.* **HR2** 28 D5
Grafton, *N.Yorks.* **YO51** 57 K3
Grafton, *Oxon.* **OX18** 21 F1
Grafton, *Shrop.* **SY4** 38 D4
Grafton, *Worcs.* **HR6** 28 E2
Grafton, *Worcs.* **GL20** 29 J5
Grafton Flyford **WR7** 29 J3
Grafton Regis **NN12** 31 J4
Grafton Underwood **NN14** 42 C7
Grafty Green **ME17** 14 D3
Graianrhyd **CH7** 48 B7
Graig, *Carmar.* **SA16** 17 H4
Graig, *Conwy* **LL28** 47 G5
Graig, *Denb.* **LL17** 47 J5
Graig-fechan **LL15** 47 K7
Grain **ME3** 24 E4
Grainel **PA44** 72 A4
Grainhow **AB53** 99 G6
Grains Bar **OL4** 49 J2
Grainsby **DN36** 53 F3
Grainthorpe **LN11** 53 G3
Graiselound **DN9** 51 K3
Gramisdale (Gramsdal) **HS7** 92 D6
Grampound **TR2** 3 G4
Grampound Road **TR2** 3 G3
Gramsdal (Gramisdale) **HS7** 92 D6
Granborough **MK18** 31 J6
Granby **NG13** 42 A2
Grandborough **CV23** 31 F2
Grandes Rocques **GY5** 3 J5
Grandtully **PH9** 82 A2
Grange, *Cumb.* **CA12** 60 D5
Grange, *E.Ayr.* **KA1** 74 C7
Grange, *High.* **IV63** 87 K1
Grange, *Med.* **ME7** 24 D5
Grange, *Mersey.* **CH48** 48 B4
Grange, *P. & K.* **PH2** 82 D5
Grange Crossroads **AB55** 98 C5
Grange de Lings **LN2** 52 C5
Grange Hall **IV36** 97 H5
Grange Hill **IG7** 23 H2
Grange Moor **WF4** 50 E1
Grange of Lindores **KY14** 82 D6
Grange Villa **DH2** 62 D1
Grangemill **DE4** 50 E7
Grangemouth **FK3** 75 H2
Grangemuir **KY10** 83 G7
Grange-over-Sands **LA11** 55 H2
Grangeston **KA26** 67 G4
Grangetown, *Cardiff* **CF11** 18 E4
Grangetown, *R. & C.* **TS6** 63 G4
Granish **PH22** 89 G3
Gransmoor **YO25** 59 H4
Granston **SA62** 16 B1
Grantchester **CB3** 33 H3
Grantham **NG31** 42 C2
Grantley **HG4** 57 H2
Grantlodge **AB51** 91 F3
Granton **EH5** 76 A3
Granton House **DG10** 69 F3
Grantown-on-Spey **PH26** 89 H2
Grantsfield **HR6** 28 E2
Grantshouse **TD11** 77 G4
Grappenhall **WA4** 49 F4
Grasby **DN38** 52 D2
Grasmere **LA22** 60 E6
Grass Green **CO9** 34 B5
Grasscroft **OL4** 49 J2
Grassendale **L19** 48 C4
Grassgarth **LA8** 60 F7
Grassholme **DL12** 62 A4
Grassington **BD23** 57 F3
Grassmoor **S42** 51 G6
Grassthorpe **NG23** 51 K6
Grateley **SP11** 21 F7
Gratwich **ST14** 40 C2
Gravel Hill **SL9** 22 D2
Graveley, *Cambs.* **PE19** 33 F2
Graveley, *Herts.* **SG4** 33 F6
Gravelly Hill **B23** 40 D6
Gravels **SY5** 38 C5
Graven **ZE2** 108 D5
Graveney **ME13** 25 G5
Gravesend **DA11** 24 C4
Grayingham **DN21** 52 C3
Grayrigg **LA8** 61 G7
Grays **RM17** 24 C4
Grayshott **GU26** 12 B3
Grayswood **GU27** 12 C3
Grazeley **RG7** 21 K5
Greasbrough **S61** 51 G3
Greasby **CH49** 48 B4
Great Abington **CB1** 33 J4
Great Addington **NN14** 32 C1
Great Alne **B49** 30 C3
Great Altcar **L37** 48 C2
Great Amwell **SG12** 33 G7
Great Asby **CA16** 61 H5
Great Ashfield **IP31** 34 D2
Great Ayton **TS9** 63 G5
Great Baddow **CM2** 24 D1
Great Bardfield **CM7** 33 K5
Great Barford **MK44** 32 E3
Great Barr **B43** 40 C6
Great Barrington **OX18** 30 D7
Great Barrow **CH3** 48 D6
Great Barton **IP31** 34 C2
Great Barugh **YO17** 58 D2
Great Bavington **NE19** 70 E5
Great Bealings **IP13** 35 G4
Great Bedwyn **SN8** 21 F5
Great Bentley **CO7** 35 F6
Great Bernera **HS2** 100 D4
Great Billing **NN3** 32 B2
Great Bircham **PE31** 44 B2
Great Blakenham **IP6** 35 F3
Great Bolas **TF6** 39 F3
Great Bookham **KT23** 22 E6
Great Bourton **OX17** 31 F4
Great Bowden **LE16** 42 A7
Great Bradley **CB8** 33 K3
Great Braxted **CM8** 34 C7
Great Bricett **IP7** 34 E3
Great Brickhill **MK17** 32 C5
Great Bridgeford **ST18** 40 A3
Great Brington **NN7** 31 H2
Great Bromley **CO7** 34 E6
Great Broughton, *Cumb.* **CA13** 60 B3
Great Broughton, *N.Yorks.* **TS9** 63 G6
Great Buckland **DA13** 24 C5
Great Budworth **CW9** 49 F5
Great Burdon **DL1** 62 E5
Great Burstead **CM12** 24 C2
Great Busby **TS9** 63 G6
Great Cambourne **CB3** 33 G3
Great Canfield **CM6** 33 J7
Great Canney **CM3** 24 E1
Great Carlton **LN11** 53 H4
Great Casterton **PE9** 42 D5
Great Chalfield **SN12** 20 B5
Great Chart **TN23** 14 E3
Great Chatwell **TF10** 39 G4
Great Chell **ST6** 49 H7
Great Chesterford **CB10** 33 J4
Great Cheverell **SN10** 20 C6
Great Chishill **SG8** 33 H5
Great Clacton **CO15** 35 F7
Great Clifton **CA14** 60 B4
Great Coates **DN37** 53 F2
Great Comberton **WR10** 29 J4
Great Corby **CA4** 61 F1
Great Cornard **CO10** 34 C4
Great Cowden **HU11** 59 J5
Great Coxwell **SN7** 21 F2
Great Crakehall **DL8** 57 H1
Great Cransley **NN14** 32 B1
Great Cressingham **IP25** 44 C5
Great Crosby **L23** 48 C2
Great Crosthwaite **CA12** 60 D4
Great Cubley **DE6** 40 D2
Great Cumbrae **KA28** 73 K5
Great Dalby **LE14** 42 A4
Great Doddington **NN29** 32 B2
Great Doward **HR9** 28 E7
Great Dunham **PE32** 44 C4
Great Dunmow **CM6** 33 K6
Great Durnford **SP4** 10 C1
Great Easton, *Essex* **CM6** 33 K6
Great Easton, *Leics.* **LE16** 42 B6
Great Eccleston **PR3** 55 H5
Great Edstone **YO62** 58 D1
Great Ellingham **NR17** 44 E6
Great Elm **BA11** 20 A7
Great Eversden **CB3** 33 G3
Great Fencote **DL7** 62 D7
Great Finborough **IP14** 34 E3
Great Fransham **NR19** 44 C4
Great Gaddesden **HP1** 32 D7
Great Gidding **PE28** 42 E7
Great Givendale **YO42** 58 E4
Great Glemham **IP17** 35 H2
Great Glen **LE8** 41 J6
Great Gonerby **NG31** 42 B2
Great Gransden **SG19** 33 F3
Great Green, *Cambs.* **SG8** 33 F4
Great Green, *Norf.* **IP20** 45 G7
Great Green, *Suff.* **IP30** 34 D3
Great Green, *Suff.* **IP21** 35 F1
Great Green, *Suff.* **IP22** 34 E1
Great Habton **YO17** 58 D2
Great Hale **NG34** 42 E1
Great Hallingbury **CM22** 33 J7
Great Hampden **HP16** 22 B1
Great Harrowden **NN9** 32 B1
Great Harwood **BB6** 56 C6
Great Haseley **OX44** 21 K1
Great Hatfield **HU11** 59 H5
Great Haywood **ST18** 40 C3
Great Heath **CV6** 41 F7
Great Heck **DN14** 58 B7
Great Henny **CO10** 34 C5
Great Hinton **BA14** 20 C6
Great Hockham **IP24** 44 D6
Great Holland **CO13** 35 G7
Great Horkesley **CO6** 34 D5
Great Hormead **SG9** 33 H5
Great Horton **BD7** 57 G6
Great Horwood **MK17** 31 J5
Great Houghton, *Northants.* **NN4** 31 J3
Great Houghton, *S.Yorks.* **S72** 51 G2
Great Hucklow **SK17** 50 D5
Great Kelk **YO25** 59 H4
Great Kimble **HP17** 22 B1

Great Kingshill HP15	22	B2
Great Langton DL7	62	D7
Great Leighs CM3	34	B7
Great Limber DN37	52	E2
Great Linford MK14	32	B4
Great Livermere IP31	34	C1
Great Longstone DE45	50	E5
Great Lumley DH3	62	D2
Great Lyth SY3	38	D5
Great Malvern WR14	29	G4
Great Maplestead CO9	34	C5
Great Marton FY4	55	G6
Great Massingham PE32	44	B3
Great Melton NR9	45	F5
Great Milton OX44	21	K1
Great Missenden HP16	22	B1
Great Mitton BB7	56	C6
Great Mongeham CT14	15	J2
Great Moulton NR15	45	F6
Great Munden SG11	33	G6
Great Musgrave CA17	61	J5
Great Ness SY4	38	D4
Great Notley CM77	34	B6
Great Nurcot TA24	7	H2
Great Oak NP15	19	G1
Great Oakley, Essex CO12	35	F6
Great Oakley, Northants. NN18	42	B7
Great Offley SG5	32	E6
Great Ormside CA16	61	J5
Great Orton CA5	60	E1
Great Ouseburn YO26	57	K3
Great Oxendon LE16	42	A7
Great Oxney Green CM1	24	C1
Great Palgrave PE32	44	C4
Great Parndon CM19	23	H1
Great Paxton PE19	33	F2
Great Plumpton PR4	55	G6
Great Plumstead NR13	45	H5
Great Ponton NG33	42	C2
Great Potheridge EX20	6	D4
Great Preston LS26	57	J7
Great Purston NN13	31	G5
Great Raveley PE26	43	F7
Great Rissington GL54	30	C7
Great Rollright OX7	30	E5
Great Ryburgh NR21	44	D3
Great Ryle NE66	71	F2
Great Ryton SY5	38	D5
Great Saling CM7	34	B6
Great Salkeld CA11	61	G3
Great Sampford CB10	33	K5
Great Sankey WA5	48	E4
Great Saredon WV10	40	B5
Great Saxham IP29	34	B2
Great Shefford RG17	21	G4
Great Shelford CB2	33	H3
Great Smeaton DL6	62	E6
Great Snoring NR21	44	D2
Great Somerford SN15	20	C3
Great Stainton TS21	62	E4
Great Stambridge SS4	25	F2
Great Staughton PE19	32	E2
Great Steeping PE23	53	H6
Great Stonar CT13	15	J2
Great Strickland CA10	61	G4
Great Stukeley PE28	33	F1
Great Sturton LN9	53	F5
Great Sutton, Ches. CH66	48	C5
Great Sutton, Shrop. SY8	38	E7
Great Swinburne NE48	70	E6
Great Tew OX7	30	E6
Great Tey CO6	34	C6
Great Thorness PO31	11	F5
Great Thurlow CB9	33	K4
Great Torr TQ7	5	G6
Great Torrington EX38	6	C4
Great Tosson NE65	71	F3
Great Totham, Essex CM9	34	C7
Great Totham, Essex CM9	34	C7
Great Tows LN8	53	F3
Great Urswick LA12	55	F2
Great Wakering SS3	25	F3
Great Waldingfield CO10	34	D4
Great Walsingham NR22	44	D2
Great Waltham CM3	33	K7
Great Warley CM14	23	J2
Great Washbourne GL20	29	J5
Great Weeke TQ13	7	F7
Great Welnetham IP30	34	C3
Great Wenham CO7	34	E5
Great Whittington NE19	71	F6
Great Wigborough CO5	34	D7
Great Wigsell TN32	14	C5
Great Wilbraham CB1	33	J3
Great Wilne DE72	41	G2
Great Wishford SP2	10	B1
Great Witcombe GL3	29	J7
Great Witley WR6	29	G2
Great Wolford CV36	30	D5
Great Wratting CB9	33	K4
Great Wymondley SG4	33	F6
Great Wyrley WS6	40	B5
Great Wytheford SY4	38	E4
Great Yarmouth NR30	45	K5
Great Yeldham CO9	34	B5
Greatford PE9	42	D4
Greatgate ST10	40	C1
Greatham, Hants. GU33	11	J1
Greatham, Hart. TS25	63	F4
Greatham, W.Suss. RH20	12	D5
Greatness TN14	23	J6
Greatstone-on-Sea TN28	15	F5
Greatworth OX17	31	G4
Green LL16	47	J6
Green Cross GU10	12	B3
Green End, Beds. MK44	32	E3
Green End, Bucks. MK17	32	C5
Green End, Cambs. PE29	33	F1
Green End, Cambs. PE27	33	G1

Green End, Herts. SG12	33	G6
Green End, Herts. SG9	33	G5
Green End, Warks. CV7	40	E7
Green Hammerton YO26	57	K4
Green Hill SN4	20	D3
Green Lane B80	30	B2
Green Moor S35	50	E3
Green Ore BA5	19	J6
Green Quarter LA8	61	F6
Green Street, E.Suss. TN38	14	C6
Green Street, Herts. WD6	22	E2
Green Street, Herts. SG11	33	H6
Green Street, W.Suss. RH13	12	E4
Green Street, Worcs. WR5	29	H4
Green Street Green, Gt.Lon. BR6	23	H5
Green Street Green, Kent DA2	23	J4
Green Tye SG10	33	H7
Greenburn DD5	83	F3
Greencroft DH7	62	C2
Greendams AB31	90	E6
Greendykes NE66	71	F1
Greenend OX7	30	E6
Greenfaulds G67	75	F3
Greenfield, Beds. MK45	32	D5
Greenfield, (Maes-Glas), Flints. CH8	47	K5
Greenfield, Gt.Man. OL3	50	C2
Greenfield, High. PH35	87	J4
Greenfield, Lincs. LN13	53	H5
Greenfield, Oxon. OX49	22	A2
Greenford UB6	22	E3
Greengairs ML6	75	F3
Greengates BD10	57	G6
Greengill CA7	60	C3
Greenhalgh PR4	55	H6
Greenhall AB52	90	E2
Greenham RG14	21	H5
Greenhaugh NE48	70	C5
Greenhead CA8	70	B7
Greenheads AB42	91	J1
Greenheys BL5	49	G2
Greenhill, Gt.Lon. HA1	22	E3
Greenhill, High. KW9	97	G1
Greenhill, S.Yorks. S8	51	F4
Greenholm KA16	74	D7
Greenholme CA10	61	G6
Greenhow Hill HG3	57	G3
Greenigo KW15	107	D7
Greenland KW14	105	H2
Greenlands RG9	22	A3
Greenlaw, Aber. AB45	98	E5
Greenlaw, Sc.Bord. TD10	77	F6
Greenloaning FK15	81	K7
Greenmeadow NP44	19	F2
Greenmoor Hill RG8	21	K3
Greenmount BL8	49	G1
Greenmyre AB53	91	G1
Greenock PA16	74	A3
Greenodd LA12	55	G1
Greens Norton NN12	31	H4
Greenscares FK15	81	J6
Greenside, T. & W. NE40	71	G7
Greenside, W.Yorks. HD5	50	D1
Greenstead CO4	34	E6
Greenstead Green CO9	34	C6
Greensted CM5	23	J1
Greensted Green CM5	23	J1
Greenway, Pembs. SA66	16	D1
Greenway, Som. TA3	8	C2
Greenwell CA8	61	G1
Greenwich SE10	23	G4
Greet GL54	30	B5
Greete SY8	28	E1
Greetham, Lincs. LN9	53	G5
Greetham, Rut. LE15	42	C4
Greetland HX4	57	F7
Gregson Lane PR5	55	J7
Greinetobht (Grenitote) HS6	92	D4
Greinton TA7	8	D1
Grenaby IM9	54	B6
Grendon, Northants. NN7	32	B2
Grendon, Warks. CV9	40	E6
Grendon Common CV9	40	E6
Grendon Green HR6	28	E3
Grendon Underwood HP18	31	H6
Grenitote (Greinetobht) HS6	92	D4
Grenofen PL19	4	E3
Grenoside S35	51	F3
Greosabhagh HS3	93	G2
Gresford LL12	48	C7
Gresham NR11	45	F2
Greshornish IV51	93	J6
Gress (Griais) HS2	101	G3
Gressenhall NR20	44	D4
Gressingham LA2	55	J3
Greta Bridge DL12	62	B5
Gretna DG16	69	J7
Gretna Green DG16	69	J7
Gretton, Glos. GL54	30	B5
Gretton, Northants. NN17	42	C6
Gretton, Shrop. SY6	38	E6
Grewelthorpe HG4	57	H2
Greygarth HG4	57	G2
Greylake TA7	8	C1
Greys Green RG9	22	A3
Greysouthen CA13	60	B4
Greystead NE48	70	C5
Greystoke CA11	60	F3
Greystone, Aber. AB35	89	K5
Greystone, Angus DD11	83	G3
Greystones S11	51	F4

Greywell RG29	22	A6
Griais (Gress) HS2	101	G3
Gribthorpe DN14	58	D6
Gribton DG2	68	E5
Griff CV10	41	F7
Griffithstown NP4	19	F2
Grigadale PH36	79	F1
Grigghall LA8	61	F7
Grimeford Village PR6	49	F1
Grimesthorpe S4	51	F3
Grimethorpe S72	51	G2
Griminis (Griminish) HS7	92	C6
Griminish (Griminis) HS7	92	C6
Grimister ZE2	108	D3
Grimley WR2	29	H2
Grimmet KA19	67	H2
Grimness KW17	107	D8
Grimoldby LN11	53	G4
Grimpo SY11	38	C3
Grimsargh PR2	55	J6
Grimsay (Griomsaigh) HS6	92	D6
Grimsbury OX16	31	F4
Grimsby DN32	53	F2
Grimscote NN12	31	H3
Grimscott EX23	6	A5
Grimshader (Griomsiadar) HS2	101	G5
Grimsthorpe PE10	42	D3
Grimston, E.Riding HU11	59	J6
Grimston, Leics. LE14	41	J3
Grimston, Norf. PE32	44	B3
Grimstone DT2	9	F5
Grimstone End IP31	34	D2
Grindale YO16	59	H2
Grindiscol ZE2	109	D9
Grindle TF11	39	G5
Grindleford S32	50	E5
Grindleton BB7	56	C5
Grindley ST18	40	C3
Grindley Brook SY13	38	E1
Grindlow SK17	50	D5
Grindon, Northum. TD15	77	H6
Grindon, Staffs. ST13	50	C7
Grindon, Stock. TS21	62	E4
Grindon, T. & W. SR4	62	E1
Gringley on the Hill DN10	51	K3
Grinsdale CA5	60	E1
Grinshill SY4	38	E3
Grinton DL11	62	B7
Griomarstaidh HS2	100	E4
Griomsaigh (Grimsay) HS6	92	D6
Griomsiadar (Grimshader) HS2	101	G5
Grisdale CA17	61	J7
Grishipoll PA78	78	C2
Gristhorpe YO14	59	G1
Griston IP25	44	D6
Gritley KW17	107	E7
Grittenham SN15	20	D3
Grittleton SN14	20	B4
Grizebeck LA17	55	F1
Grizedale LA22	60	E7
Grobister KW17	106	F5
Groby LE6	41	H5
Groes LL16	47	J6
Groes-faen CF72	18	D3
Groesffordd LL53	36	B2
Groesffordd Marli LL22	47	J5
Groeslon, Gwyn. LL54	46	C7
Groeslon, Gwyn. LL55	46	D6
Groes-lwyd SY21	38	B4
Groes-wen CF15	18	E3
Grogport PA28	73	G6
Groigearraidh HS8	84	C1
Gromford IP17	35	H3
Gronant LL19	47	J4
Groombridge TN3	13	J3
Grosmont, Mon. NP7	28	D6
Grosmont, N.Yorks. YO22	63	K6
Grotaig IV63	88	B2
Groton CO10	34	D4
Groundistone Heights TD9	69	K2
Grouville JE3	3	K7
Grove, Bucks. LU7	32	C6
Grove, Dorset DT5	9	F7
Grove, Kent CT3	25	J5
Grove, Notts. DN22	51	K5
Grove, Oxon. OX12	21	H2
Grove End ME9	24	E5
Grove Green ME14	14	C2
Grove Park SE12	23	H4
Grove Town WF8	57	K7
Grovehill HP2	22	D1
Grovesend, S.Glos. BS35	19	K3
Grovesend, Swan. SA4	17	J4
Gruids IV27	96	C1
Grula IV47	85	J2
Grumbla TR20	2	B6
Grundcruie PH1	82	B5
Grundisburgh IP13	35	G3
Gruting ZE2	109	B8
Grutness ZE3	109	F10
Gualachulain PH49	80	C3
Guardbridge KY16	83	F6
Guarlford WR13	29	H4
Guay PH9	82	B3
Gubbergill CA19	60	B7
Gubblecote HP23	32	C7
GUERNSEY GY	3	J5
Guernsey Airport GY8	3	H5
Guestling Green TN35	14	D6
Guestling Thorn TN35	14	D6
Guestwick NR20	44	E3
Guestwick Green NR20	44	E3
Guide BB1	56	C7

Guide Post NE62	71	H5
Guilden Down SY7	38	C7
Guilden Morden SG8	33	F4
Guilden Sutton CH3	48	D6
GUILDFORD GU	22	C7
Guildtown PH2	82	C4
Guilsborough NN6	31	H1
Guilsfield (Cegidfa) SY21	38	B4
Guilthwaite S60	51	G4
Guisborough TS14	63	H5
Guiseley LS20	57	G5
Guist NR20	44	E3
Guith KW17	106	E4
Guiting Power GL54	30	B6
Gulberwick ZE2	109	D9
Gullane EH31	76	C2
Gulval TR18	2	B5
Gulworthy PL19	4	E3
Gumfreston SA70	16	E4
Gumley LE16	41	J6
Gunby, Lincs. NG33	42	C3
Gunby, Lincs. PE23	53	H6
Gundleton SO24	11	H1
Gunn EX32	6	E2
Gunnersbury W4	22	E4
Gunnerside DL11	62	A7
Gunnerton NE48	70	E6
Gunness DN15	52	B1
Gunnislake PL18	4	E3
Gunnista ZE2	109	E8
Gunnister ZE2	108	C5
Gunstone WV8	40	A5
Gunter's Bridge GU28	12	C4
Gunthorpe, Norf. NR24	44	E2
Gunthorpe, Notts. NG14	41	J1
Gunthorpe, Rut. LE15	42	B5
Gunville PO30	11	F6
Gunwalloe TR12	2	D6
Gupworthy TA24	7	H2
Gurnard PO31	11	F5
Gurnett SK11	49	J5
Gurney Slade BA3	19	K7
Gurnos, M.Tyd. CF47	18	D1
Gurnos, Powys SA9	18	A1
Gushmere ME13	15	F2
Gussage All Saints BH21	10	B3
Gussage St. Andrew DT11	9	J3
Gussage St. Michael BH21	9	J3
Guston CT15	15	J3
Gutcher ZE2	108	E3
Guthram Gowt PE11	42	E3
Guthrie DD8	83	G2
Guyhirn PE13	43	G5
Guynd DD11	83	G3
Guy's Head PE12	43	H3
Guy's Marsh SP7	9	H2
Guyzance NE65	71	H3
Gwaelod-y-garth CF15	18	E3
Gwaenysgor LL18	47	J4
Gwaithla HR5	28	B3
Gwalchmai LL65	46	B5
Gwastad SA63	16	D2
Gwastadnant LL55	46	E7
Gwaun-Cae-Gurwen SA18	27	G7
Gwaynynog LL16	47	J6
Gwbert SA43	26	A4
Gweek TR12	2	E6
Gwehelog NP15	19	G1
Gwenddwr LD2	27	K4
Gwennap TR16	2	E4
Gwenter TR12	2	E7
Gwernaffield CH7	48	B6
Gwernesney NP15	19	H1
Gwernogle SA32	17	J1
Gwernymynydd CH7	48	B6
Gwern-y-Steeple CF5	18	D4
Gwersyllt LL11	48	C7
Gwespyr CH8	47	K4
Gwinear TR27	2	C5
Gwithian TR27	2	C5
Gwredog LL71	46	C4
Gwrhay NP12	18	E2
Gwyddelwern LL21	37	K1
Gwyddgrug SA39	17	H1
Gwynfryn LL11	48	B7
Gwystre LD1	27	K2
Gwytherin LL22	47	G6
Gyfelia LL13	38	C1
Gyre KW17	107	C7
Gyrn Goch LL54	36	C1

H

Habberley SY5	38	C5
Habin GU31	12	B4
Habrough DN40	52	E1
Haccombe TQ12	5	J3
Hacconby PE10	42	E3
Haceby NG34	42	D2
Hacheston IP13	35	H3
Hackbridge SM6	23	F5
Hackford NR18	44	E5
Hackforth DL8	62	D7
Hackland KW17	106	C5
Hacklet (Haclait) HS7	92	D7
Hacklete (Taclait) HS2	100	D4
Hackleton NN7	32	B3
Hacklinge CT14	15	J2
Hackness, N.Yorks. YO13	63	J3
Hackness, Ork. KW16	107	C8
Hackney E9	23	G3
Hackthorn LN2	52	C4
Hackthorpe CA10	61	G4
Haclait (Hacklet) HS7	92	D7
Hacton RM14	23	J3
Hadden TD5	77	F7
Haddenham, Bucks. HP17	22	A1
Haddenham, Cambs. CB6	33	H1

Haddington, E.Loth. EH41	76	D3
Haddington, Lincs. LN5	52	C6
Haddiscoe NR14	45	J6
Haddon PE7	42	E6
Hade Edge HD9	50	D2
Hademore WS14	40	D5
Hadfield SK13	50	C3
Hadham Cross SG10	33	H7
Hadham Ford SG11	33	H6
Hadleigh, Essex SS7	24	E3
Hadleigh, Suff. IP7	34	E4
Hadleigh Heath IP7	34	D4
Hadley, Tel. & W. TF1	39	F4
Hadley, Worcs. WR9	29	H2
Hadley End DE13	40	D3
Hadley Wood EN4	23	F2
Hadlow TN11	23	K7
Hadlow Down TN22	13	J4
Hadnall SY4	38	E3
Hadspen BA7	9	F1
Hadstock CB1	33	J4
Hadzor WR9	29	J3
Haffenden Quarter TN27	14	D3
Hafod Bridge SA19	17	K1
Hafod-Dinbych LL24	47	G7
Hafodunos LL22	47	G6
Hafodyrynys NP11	19	F2
Haggate BB10	56	D6
Haggbeck CA6	69	K6
Haggerston ZE2	109	C8
Haggerston, Gt.Lon. E2	23	G3
Haggerston, Northumb. TD15	77	J6
Haggrister ZE2	108	C5
Haggs FK4	75	F3
Hagley, Here. HR1	28	E4
Hagley, Worcs. DY9	40	B7
Hagnaby, Lincs. PE23	53	G6
Hagnaby, Lincs. LN13	53	H5
Hague Bar SK22	49	J4
Hagworthingham PE23	53	G6
Haigh WN2	49	F2
Haighton Green PR2	55	J6
Hail Weston PE19	32	E2
Haile CA22	60	B6
Hailes GL54	30	B5
Hailey, Herts. SG13	33	G7
Hailey, Oxon. OX10	21	K3
Hailey, Oxon. OX29	30	E7
Hailsham BN27	13	J6
Haimer KW14	105	G2
Hainault IG6	23	H2
Haine CT12	25	K5
Hainford NR10	45	G4
Hainton LN8	52	E4
Haisthorpe YO25	59	H3
Hakin SA73	16	B4
Halam NG22	51	J7
Halbeath KY11	75	K2
Halberton EX16	7	J4
Halcro KW1	105	H2
Hale, Cumb. LA7	55	J2
Hale, Gt.Man. WA15	49	G4
Hale, Halton L24	48	D4
Hale, Hants. SP6	10	C3
Hale, Surr. GU9	22	B7
Hale Bank WA8	48	D4
Hale Barns WA15	49	G4
Hale Nook PR3	55	G5
Hale Street TN12	23	K7
Hales, Norf. NR14	45	H6
Hales, Staffs. TF9	39	G2
Hales Green DE6	40	D1
Hales Place CT2	15	G2
Halesgate PE12	43	G3
Halesowen B63	40	B7
Halesworth IP19	35	H1
Halewood L26	48	D4
Half Way Inn EX5	7	J7
Halford, Devon TQ12	5	J3
Halford, Shrop. SY7	38	D7
Halford, Warks. CV36	30	D4
Halfpenny LA8	55	J1
Halfpenny Green DY7	40	A6
Halfway, Carmar. SA19	17	K1
Halfway, Carmar. SA15	17	J4
Halfway, Powys SA20	27	H5
Halfway, S.Yorks. S20	51	G4
Halfway, W.Berks. RG20	21	H5
Halfway Bridge GU28	12	C4
Halfway House SY5	38	C4
Halfway Houses, Kent ME12	25	F4
Halfway Houses, Lincs. LN6	52	B6
Halghton Mill LL13	38	D1
HALIFAX HX	57	F7
Halistra IV55	93	H6
Halket KA3	74	C5
Halkirk KW12	105	G3
Halkyn CH8	48	B5
Hall G78	74	C5
Hall Cross PR4	55	H7
Hall Dunnerdale LA20	60	D7
Hall Green, Ches. SY7	49	H7
Hall Green, Lancs. PR4	55	H7
Hall Green, W.Mid. B28	40	D7
Hall Grove AL7	33	F7
Hall of the Forest SY7	38	B7
Halland BN8	13	J5
Hallaton LE16	42	A6
Hallatrow BS39	19	K6
Hallbankgate CA8	61	G1
Hallen BS10	19	J3
Hallfield Gate DE55	51	F7
Hallin IV55	93	H6
Halling ME2	24	D5
Hallington, Lincs. LN11	53	G4
Hallington, Northumb. NE19	70	E6
Halliwell BL1	49	F1

Halloughton NG25 51 J7
Hallow WR2 29 H3
Hallow Heath WR2 29 H3
Hallrule TD9 70 A2
Halls EH42 76 E3
Halls Green, Essex CM19 23 H1
Hall's Green, Herts. SG4 33 F6
Hallsands TQ7 5 J7
Hallthwaites LA18 54 E1
Hallwood Green GL18 29 F5
Hallworthy PL32 4 B2
Hallyne EH45 75 K6
Halmer End ST7 39 G1
Halmond's Frome WR6 29 F4
Halmore GL13 19 K1
Halmyre Mains EH46 75 K6
Halnaker PO18 12 C6
Halsall L39 48 C1
Halse, Northants. NN13 31 G4
Halse, Som. TA4 7 K3
Halsetown TR26 2 C5
Halsham HU12 59 J7
Halsinger EX33 6 D2
Halstead, Essex CO9 34 C5
Halstead, Kent TN14 23 H5
Halstead, Leics. LE7 42 A5
Halstock BA22 8 E4
Halsway TA4 7 K2
Haltemprice Farm HU10 59 G6
Haltham LN9 53 F6
Haltoft End PE22 43 G1
Halton, Bucks. HP22 32 B7
Halton, Halton WA7 48 E4
Halton, Lancs. LA2 55 J3
Halton, Northumb. NE45 70 E7
Halton, Wrex. LL14 38 C2
Halton East BD23 57 F4
Halton Gill BD23 56 D2
Halton Green LA2 55 J3
Halton Holegate PE23 53 H6
Halton Lea Gate CA8 61 H1
Halton Park LA2 55 J3
Halton West BD23 56 D4
Haltwhistle NE49 70 C7
Halvergate NR13 45 J5
Halwell TQ9 5 H5
Halwill EX21 6 C6
Halwill Junction EX21 6 C6
Ham, Devon EX13 8 B4
Ham, Glos. GL13 19 K2
Ham, Glos. GL52 29 J6
Ham, Gt.Lon. TW10 22 E4
Ham, High. KW14 105 H1
Ham, Kent CT14 15 J2
Ham, Plym. PL2 4 E5
Ham, Shet. ZE2 108 B1
Ham, Som. TA3 8 C2
Ham, Som. TA20 8 B3
Ham, Wilts. SN8 21 G5
Ham Common SP8 9 H2
Ham Green, Here. WR13 29 G4
Ham Green, Kent ME9 24 E5
Ham Green, Kent TN30 14 D5
Ham Green, N.Som. BS20 19 J4
Ham Green, Worcs. B97 30 B2
Ham Hill ME6 24 C5
Ham Street BA6 8 E1
Hamble-le-Rice SO31 11 F4
Hambleden RG9 22 A3
Hambledon, Hants. PO7 11 H3
Hambledon, Surr. GU8 12 C3
Hambleton, Lancs. FY6 55 G5
Hambleton, N.Yorks. YO8 58 B6
Hambridge TA10 8 C2
Hambrook, S.Glos. BS16 19 K4
Hambrook, W.Suss. PO18 11 J4
Hameringham LN9 53 G6
Hamerton PE28 32 E1
Hamilton ML3 75 F5
Hamlet, Devon EX14 7 K6
Hamlet, Dorset DT9 8 E4
Hammer GU27 12 B3
Hammerpot BN16 12 D6
Hammersmith W6 23 F4
Hammerwich WS7 40 C5
Hammerwood RH19 13 H3
Hammond Street EN7 23 G1
Hammoon DT10 9 H3
Hamnavoe, Shet. ZE2 109 C9
Hamnavoe, Shet. ZE2 108 D4
Hamnavoe, Shet. ZE2 108 B4
Hamnavoe, Shet. ZE2 108 D5
Hamnish Clifford HR6 28 E3
Hamp TA6 8 B1
Hampden Park BN22 13 K6
Hamperden End CB11 33 J5
Hampnett GL54 30 C7
Hampole DN6 51 H2
Hampreston BH21 10 B5
Hampstead NW3 23 F3
Hampstead Norreys RG18 21 J4
Hampsthwaite HG3 57 H4
Hampton, Devon EX13 8 B5
Hampton, Gt.Lon. TW12 22 E5
Hampton, Kent CT6 25 H5
Hampton, Peter. PE7 42 E6
Hampton, Shrop. WV16 39 G7
Hampton, Swin. SN6 20 E2
Hampton, Worcs. WV11 30 B4
Hampton Bishop HR1 28 E5
Hampton Fields GL6 20 B2
Hampton Heath SY14 38 D1
Hampton in Arden B92 40 E7
Hampton Loade WV15 39 G7
Hampton Lovett WR9 29 H2
Hampton Lucy CV35 30 D3
Hampton on the Hill CV35 30 D2

Hampton Poyle OX5 31 G7
Hampton Wick KT1 22 E5
Hamptworth SP5 10 D3
Hamsey BN8 13 H5
Hamstall Ridware WS15 40 D4
Hamsterley PO41 10 E5
Hamstead Marshall RG20 21 H5
Hamsteels DH7 62 C2
Hamsterley, Dur. DL13 62 C3
Hamsterley, Dur. NE17 62 C1
Hamstreet TN26 15 F4
Hamworthy BH15 9 J5
Hanbury, Staffs. DE13 40 D3
Hanbury, Worcs. B60 29 J2
Hanbury Woodend DE13 40 D3
Hanby NG33 42 D2
Hanchurch ST4 40 A1
Handa Island IV27 102 D4
Handbridge CH4 48 D6
Handcross RH17 13 F3
Handforth SK9 49 H4
Handley, Ches. CH3 48 D7
Handley, Derbys. DE55 51 F6
Handley Green CM4 24 C1
Handsacre WS15 40 C4
Handside AL8 33 F7
Handsworth, S.Yorks. S13 51 G4
Handsworth, W.Mid. B21 40 C6
Handwoodbank SY5 38 D4
Handy Cross SL7 22 B2
Hanford, Dorset DT11 9 H3
Hanford, Stoke ST4 40 A1
Hanging Bridge DE6 40 D1
Hanging Houghton NN6 31 J1
Hanging Langford SP3 10 B1
Hangingshaw DG11 69 G5
Hanham BS15 19 K4
Hankelow CW3 39 F1
Hankerton SN16 20 C2
Hankham BN24 13 K6
Hanley ST1 40 A1
Hanley Castle WR8 29 H4
Hanley Child WR15 29 F2
Hanley Swan WR8 29 H4
Hanley William WR15 29 F2
Hanlith BD23 56 E3
Hanmer SY13 38 D2
Hannah LN13 53 H5
Hannington, Hants. RG26 21 J6
Hannington, Northants. NN6 31 J1
Hannington, Swin. SN6 20 E2
Hannington Wick SN6 20 E2
Hanslope MK19 32 B4
Hanthorpe PE10 42 D3
Hanwell, Gt.Lon. W7 22 E3
Hanwell, Oxon. OX17 31 F4
Hanwood SY5 38 D5
Hanworth, Gt.Lon. TW13 22 E4
Hanworth, Norf. NR11 45 F2
Happisburgh NR12 45 H2
Happisburgh Common NR12 45 H3
Hapsford WA6 48 D5
Hapton, Lancs. BB11 56 C6
Hapton, Norf. NR15 45 F6
Harberton TQ9 5 H5
Harbertonford TQ9 5 H5
Harbledown CT2 15 G2
Harborne B17 40 C7
Harborough Magna CV23 31 F1
Harbost (Tarbost) HS2 101 H1
Harbottle NE65 70 E3
Harbourneford TQ10 5 H4
Harbridge BH24 10 C3
Harbridge Green BH24 10 C3
Harburn EH55 75 J4
Harbury CV33 30 E3
Harby, Leics. LE14 42 A2
Harby, Notts. NG23 52 B5
Harcombe EX10 7 K6
Harcombe Bottom DT6 8 C5
Harden, W.Mid. WS3 40 C5
Harden, W.Yorks. BD16 57 F6
Hardendale CA10 61 G5
Hardenhuish SN14 20 C4
Hardgate, Aber. AB32 91 F4
Hardgate, N.Yorks. HG3 57 H3
Hardham RH20 12 D5
Hardhorn FY3 55 G6
Hardingham NR9 44 E5
Hardingstone NN4 31 J3
Hardington BA11 20 A6
Hardington Mandeville BA22 8 E3
Hardington Marsh BA22 8 E4
Hardington Moor BA22 8 E3
Hardley SO45 11 F4
Hardley Street NR14 45 H5
Hardmead MK16 32 C4
Hardraw DL8 61 K7
Hardstoft S45 51 G6
Hardway, Hants. PO12 11 H4
Hardway, Som. BA10 9 G1
Hardwick, Bucks. HP22 32 B7
Hardwick, Cambs. CB3 33 G3
Hardwick, Lincs. LN1 52 B5
Hardwick, Norf. NR15 45 G6
Hardwick, Northants. NN9 32 B2
Hardwick, Oxon. OX29 31 G1
Hardwick, Oxon. OX27 31 G6
Hardwick, S.Yorks. S26 51 G4
Hardwick, W.Mid. B74 40 C6
Hardwick Village S80 51 J5
Hardwicke, Glos. GL51 29 J6
Hardwicke, Glos. GL2 29 G7

Hardwicke, Here. HR3 28 B4
Hardy's Green CO2 34 D6
Hare Green CO7 34 E6
Hare Hatch RG10 22 B4
Hare Street, Herts. SG2 33 G6
Hare Street, Herts. SG9 33 G6
Hareby PE23 53 G6
Harecroft BD15 57 F6
Hareden BB7 56 B4
Harefield UB9 22 D2
Harehill DE6 40 D2
Harehills LS9 57 J6
Harehope NE66 71 F1
Harelaw ML11 75 H6
Hareplain TN27 14 D4
Haresceugh CA10 61 H2
Harescombe GL4 29 H7
Haresfield GL10 29 H7
Hareshaw, N.Lan. ML1 75 G4
Hareshaw, S.Lan. ML10 74 E6
Harestock SO22 11 F1
Harewood LS17 57 J5
Harewood End HR2 28 E6
Harford, Devon PL21 5 G5
Harford, Devon EX6 7 G6
Hargate NR16 45 F6
Hargatewall SK17 50 D5
Hargrave, Ches. CH3 48 D6
Hargrave, Northants. NN9 32 D1
Hargrave, Suff. IP29 34 B3
Hargrave Green IP29 34 B3
Harker CA6 69 J7
Harkstead IP9 35 F5
Harlaston B79 40 E4
Harlaxton NG32 42 B2
Harle Syke BB10 56 D6
Harlech LL46 36 E2
Harlequin NG12 41 J2
Harlescott SY4 38 E4
Harlesden NW10 23 F3
Harleston, Devon TQ7 5 H6
Harleston, Norf. IP20 45 G7
Harleston, Suff. IP14 34 E2
Harlestone NN7 31 J2
Harley, S.Yorks. S62 51 F3
Harley, Shrop. SY5 38 E5
Harleyholm ML12 75 H7
Harlington, Beds. LU5 32 D5
Harlington, Gt.Lon. UB3 22 D4
Harlosh IV55 93 H7
Harlow CM17 33 H7
Harlow Hill NE15 71 F7
Harlthorpe YO8 58 D6
Harlton CB3 33 G3
Harlyn PL28 3 F1
Harman's Cross BH19 9 J6
Harmby DL8 57 G1
Harmer Green AL6 33 F7
Harmer Hill SY4 38 D3
Harmondsworth UB7 22 D4
Harmston LN5 52 C6
Harnage SY5 38 E5
Harnham SP2 10 C2
Harnhill GL7 20 D1
Harold Hill RM3 23 J2
Harold Park RM3 23 J2
Harold Wood RM3 23 J2
Haroldston West SA62 16 B3
Haroldswick ZE2 108 F1
Harome YO62 58 C1
Harpenden AL5 32 E7
Harpford EX10 7 J6
Harpham YO25 59 G3
Harpley, Norf. PE31 44 B3
Harpley, Worcs. WR6 29 F2
Harpole NN7 31 H2
Harprigg LA6 56 B1
Harpsdale KW12 105 G3
Harpsden RG9 22 A3
Harpswell DN21 52 C4
Harpur Hill SK17 50 C5
Harpurhey M9 49 H2
Harracott EX31 6 D3
Harrapool IV49 86 C2
Harrietfield PH1 82 A4
Harrietsham ME17 14 D2
Harringay N8 23 G3
Harrington, Cumb. CA14 60 A4
Harrington, Lincs. PE23 53 G5
Harrington, Northants. NN6 31 J1
Harringworth NN17 42 C6
Harris PH43 85 J5
Harris Green NR15 45 G6
Harriseahead ST7 49 H7
Harriston CA7 60 C2
Harrogate HG 57 J4
Harrold MK43 32 C3
Harrop Fold BB7 56 C5
Harrow, Gt.Lon. HA1 22 E3
Harrow, High. KW14 105 H1
Harrow Green IP29 34 C3
Harrow on the Hill HA1 22 E3
Harrow Weald HA3 22 E2
Harrowbarrow PL17 4 E3
Harrowden MK42 32 D4
Harrowgate Hill DL3 62 D5
Harry Stoke BS34 19 K4
Harston, Cambs. CB3 33 H3
Harston, Leics. NG32 42 B2
Harswell YO42 58 E5
Hart TS27 63 F3
Hartburn NE61 71 F5
Hartest IP29 34 C3
Hartfield, E.Suss. TN7 13 H3
Hartfield, High. IV54 94 D7
Hartford, Cambs. PE29 33 F1
Hartford, Ches. CW8 49 F5
Hartford, Som. TA4 7 H3
Hartford End CM3 33 K7

Hartfordbridge RG27 22 A6
Hartforth DL10 62 C6
Hartgrove SP7 9 H3
Harthill, Ches. CH3 48 E7
Harthill, N.Lan. ML7 75 H4
Harthill, S.Yorks. S26 51 G4
Hartington SK17 50 D6
Hartington Hall NE61 71 F5
Hartland EX39 6 A3
Hartland Quay EX39 6 A3
Hartlebury DY11 29 H1
Hartlepool TS24 63 G3
Hartley, Cumb. CA17 61 J6
Hartley, Kent DA3 24 C5
Hartley, Kent TN17 14 C4
Hartley, Northumb. NE26 71 J6
Hartley Green ST18 40 B3
Hartley Mauditt GU34 11 J1
Hartley Wespall RG27 21 K6
Hartley Wintney RG27 22 A6
Hartlington BD23 57 F3
Hartlip ME9 24 E5
Hartoft End YO18 63 J7
Harton, N.Yorks. YO60 58 D3
Harton, Shrop. SY6 38 D7
Harton, T.& W. NE34 71 J7
Hartpury GL19 29 H6
Hartridge TD8 70 B1
Hartshead WF15 57 G7
Hartshill CV10 41 F6
Hartshorne DE11 41 F3
Hartsop CA10 60 F5
Hartwell, Bucks. HP17 31 J7
Hartwell, N.Suss. TN7 13 H3
Hartwell, Northants. NN7 31 J3
Hartwith HG3 57 H3
Hartwood ML7 75 G5
Harvel DA13 24 C5
Harvington, Worcs. WR11 30 B4
Harvington, Worcs. DY10 29 H1
Harwell, Notts. DN10 51 J3
Harwell, Oxon. OX11 21 H3
Harwich CO12 35 G5
Harwood, Dur. DL12 61 K3
Harwood, Gt.Man. BL2 49 G1
Harwood, Northumb. NE61 71 F4
Harwood Dale YO13 63 J3
Harwood on Teviot TD9 69 K3
Harworth DN11 51 J3
Hasbury B63 40 B7
Hascombe GU8 22 D7
Haselbech NN6 31 J1
Haselbury Plucknett TA18 8 D3
Haseley CV35 30 D2
Haseley Knob CV35 30 D1
Haselor B49 30 C3
Hasfield GL19 29 H6
Hasguard SA62 16 B4
Haskayne L39 48 C2
Hasketon IP13 35 G3
Hasland S41 51 F6
Hasland Green S41 51 F6
Haslemere GU27 12 C3
Haslingden BB4 56 C7
Haslingden Grane BB4 56 C7
Haslingfield CB3 33 H3
Haslington CW1 49 G7
Hassall CW11 49 G7
Hassall Green CW11 49 G7
Hassall Street TN25 15 F3
Hassendean TD9 70 A1
Hassingham NR13 45 H5
Hassocks BN6 13 G5
Hassop DE45 50 E5
Haster KW1 105 J3
Hasthorpe LN13 53 H6
Hastigrow KW1 105 H2
Hastingleigh TN25 15 F3
Hastings, E.Suss. TN34 14 D7
Hastings, Som. TA19 8 C3
Hastingwood CM17 23 H1
Hastoe HP23 22 C1
Haswell DH6 62 E2
Haswell Plough DH6 62 E2
Hatch, Beds. SG19 32 E4
Hatch End HA5 22 E2
Hatch Beauchamp TA3 8 C2
Hatch End HA5 22 E2
Hatch Green TA3 8 C3
Hatching Green AL5 32 E7
Hatchmere WA6 48 E5
Hatcliffe DN37 53 F2
Hatfield, Here. HR6 28 E3
Hatfield, Herts. AL10 23 F1
Hatfield, S.Yorks. DN7 51 J2
Hatfield Broad Oak CM22 33 J7
Hatfield Heath CM22 33 J7
Hatfield Peverel CM3 34 B7
Hatfield Woodhouse DN7 51 J2
Hatford SN7 21 G2
Hatherden SP11 21 G6
Hatherleigh EX20 6 D5
Hathern LE12 41 G3
Hatherop GL7 20 E1
Hathersage S32 50 E4
Hathershaw OL8 49 J2
Hatherton, Ches. CW5 39 F1
Hatherton, Staffs. WS11 40 B4
Hatley St.George SG19 33 F3
Hatt PL12 4 D4
Hattingley GU34 11 H1
Hatton, Aber. AB42 91 J1
Hatton, Derbys. DE65 40 E3
Hatton, Gt.Lon. TW14 22 E4
Hatton, Lincs. LN8 52 E5
Hatton, Shrop. SY6 38 D6
Hatton, Warks. CV35 30 D2
Hatton, Warr. WA4 48 E4
Hatton Castle AB53 99 F6

Hatton Heath CH3 48 D6
Hatton of Fintray AB21 91 G3
Hattoncrook AB21 91 G2
Haugh LN13 53 H5
Haugh Head NE71 71 F1
Haugh of Glass AB54 90 C1
Haugh of Urr DG7 65 J4
Haugham LN11 53 G4
Haughhead G66 74 E3
Haughley IP14 34 E2
Haughley Green IP14 34 E2
Haughley New Street IP14 34 E2
Haughs AB54 98 D6
Haughton, Ches. CW6 48 E7
Haughton, Notts. DN22 51 J5
Haughton, Powys SY22 38 C4
Haughton, Shrop. WV16 39 F6
Haughton, Shrop. SY4 38 E4
Haughton, Shrop. SY11 38 C3
Haughton, Staffs. ST18 40 A3
Haughton Green M34 49 J3
Haughton Le Skerne DL1 62 E5
Haultwick SG11 33 G6
Haunn HS8 84 C3
Haunton B79 40 E4
Hauxton CB2 33 H3
Havannah CW12 49 H6
Havant PO9 11 J4
Haven HR4 28 D3
Havenstreet PO33 11 G5
Havercroft WF4 51 F1
Haverfordwest (Hwllffordd) SA61 16 C3
Haverhill CB9 33 K4
Haverigg LA18 54 E2
Havering Park RM5 23 H2
Havering-atte-Bower RM4 23 J2
Haversham MK19 32 B4
Haverthwaite LA12 55 G1
Haviker Street TN12 14 C3
Havyat BA6 8 E1
Hawarden CH5 48 C6
Hawbridge WR8 29 J4
Hawbush Green CM77 34 B6
Hawcoat LA14 55 F2
Hawes DL8 56 D1
Hawe's Green NR15 45 G6
Hawick TD9 70 A2
Hawkchurch EX13 8 C4
Hawkedon IP29 34 B3
Hawkenbury, Kent TN2 13 J3
Hawkenbury, Kent TN12 14 D3
Hawkeridge BA13 20 B6
Hawkerland EX10 7 J7
Hawkes End CV5 40 E7
Hawkesbury GL9 20 A3
Hawkesbury Upton GL9 20 A3
Hawkhill NE66 71 H2
Hawkhurst TN18 14 C4
Hawkinge CT18 15 H3
Hawkley GU33 11 J2
Hawkridge TA22 7 G2
Hawksheads LA5 55 H3
Hawkshead LA22 60 E7
Hawkshead Hill LA22 60 E7
Hawksland ML11 75 G6
Hawkswick BD23 56 E2
Hawksworth, Notts. NG13 42 A1
Hawksworth, W.Yorks. LS20 57 G5
Hawksworth, W.Yorks. LS18 57 H6
Hawkwell, Essex SS5 24 E2
Hawkwell, Northumb. NE18 71 F6
Hawley, Hants. GU17 22 B6
Hawley, Kent DA2 23 J4
Hawley's Corner TN16 23 H6
Hawling GL54 30 B6
Hawnby YO62 58 B1
Haworth BD22 57 F6
Hawstead IP29 34 C3
Hawstead Green IP29 34 C3
Hawthorn, Dur. SR7 63 F2
Hawthorn, Hants. GU34 11 H1
Hawthorn, R.C.T. CF37 18 D3
Hawthorn, Wilts. SN13 20 B5
Hawthorn Hill, Brack.F. RG42 22 B4
Hawthorn Hill, Lincs. LN4 53 F7
Hawthorpe PE10 42 D3
Hawton NG24 51 K7
Haxby YO32 58 C4
Haxey DN9 51 K2
Haxted TN8 23 H7
Haxton SP4 20 E7
Hay Green PE34 43 J4
Hay Mills B25 40 D7
Hay Street SG11 33 G6
Haydock WA11 48 E3
Haydon, Dorset DT9 9 F3
Haydon, Swin. SN25 20 E3
Haydon Bridge NE47 70 D7
Haydon Wick SN25 20 E3
Hayes, Gt.Lon. UB3 22 D3
Hayes, Gt.Lon. BR2 23 H5
Hayes End UB4 22 D3
Hayfield, Arg.& B. PA35 80 B5
Hayfield, Derbys. SK22 50 C4
Hayfield, Fife KY2 76 A1
Hayfield, High. KW14 105 G2
Haygrove TA6 8 B1
Hayhillock DD11 83 G3
Hayle TR27 2 C5
Hayling Island PO11 11 J4
Haymoor Green CW5 49 F7
Hayne EX16 7 G4
Haynes MK45 32 E4

Highstreet Green

Haynes Church End MK45 32 D4
Haynes West End MK45 32 D4
Hay-on-Wye HR3 28 B4
Hayscastle SA62 16 B2
Hayscastle Cross SA62 16 C2
Hayton, *Cumb.* CA8 61 G1
Hayton, *Cumb.* CA7 60 C2
Hayton, *E.Riding* YO42 58 E5
Hayton, *Notts.* DN22 51 K4
Hayton's Bent SY8 38 E7
Haytor Vale TQ13 5 H3
Haytown EX22 6 B4
Haywards Heath RH16 13 G4
Haywood Oaks NG21 51 J7
Hazel End CM23 33 H6
Hazel Grove SK7 49 J4
Hazel Street TN12 13 K3
Hazelbank, *Arg. & B.* PA25 80 B7
Hazelbank, *S.Lan.* ML11 75 G6
Hazelbury Bryan DT10 9 G4
Hazeleigh CM3 24 E1
Hazeley RG27 22 A6
Hazelhurst BL8 49 G1
Hazelside ML11 68 D1
Hazelslack LA7 55 H2
Hazelslade WS12 40 C4
Hazelton Walls KY15 82 E5
Hazelwood, *Derbys.* DE56 41 F1
Hazelwood, *Gt.Lon.* TN14 23 H5
Hazlefield DG7 65 H6
Hazlehead, *Aberdeen* AB15 91 G4
Hazlehead, *S.Yorks.* S36 50 D2
Hazlemere HP15 22 B2
Hazlerigg NE13 71 H6
Hazleton GL54 30 B7
Hazon NE65 71 G3
Heacham PE31 44 A2
Head Bridge EX37 6 E4
Headbourne Worthy SO23 11 F1
Headcorn TN27 14 D3
Headingley LS6 57 H6
Headington OX3 21 J1
Headlam DL2 62 C5
Headless Cross B97 30 B2
Headley, *Hants.* GU35 12 B3
Headley, *Hants.* RG19 21 J5
Headley, *Surr.* KT18 23 F6
Headley Down GU35 12 B3
Headley Heath B38 30 B1
Headon DN22 51 K5
Heads Nook CA8 61 F1
Heady Hill OL10 49 H1
Heage DE56 51 F7
Healaugh, *N.Yorks.* DL11 62 B7
Healaugh, *N.Yorks.* LS24 58 B5
Heald Green SK8 49 H4
Heale, *Devon* EX31 6 E1
Heale, *Som.* TA10 8 C2
Healey, *Lancs.* OL12 49 H1
Healey, *N.Yorks.* HG4 57 G1
Healey, *Northumb.* NE44 62 B1
Healey, *W.Yorks.* WF17 57 H7
Healeyfield DH8 62 B2
Healing DN41 53 F1
Heamoor TR18 2 B5
Heaning LA23 60 F7
Heanish PA77 78 B3
Heanor DE75 41 G1
Heanton Punchardon EX31 6 D2
Heanton Satchville EX20 6 D4
Heap Bridge BL9 49 H1
Heapey PR6 56 B7
Heapham DN21 52 B4
Hearn GU35 12 B3
Hearthstane ML12 69 G1
Heasley Mill EX36 7 F2
Heast IV49 86 C3
Heath, *Cardiff* CF14 18 E3
Heath, *Derbys.* S44 51 G6
Heath, *W.Yorks.* WF1 51 F1
Heath and Reach LU7 32 C6
Heath End, *Derbys.* LE65 41 F3
Heath End, *Hants.* RG26 21 J5
Heath End, *Hants.* RG20 21 H5
Heath End, *Surr.* GU9 22 B7
Heath Hayes WS12 40 C4
Heath Hill TF11 39 G4
Heath House BS28 19 H7
Heath Town WV10 40 B6
Heathbrook TF9 39 F3
Heathcot AB12 91 G4
Heathcote, *Derbys.* SK17 50 D6
Heathcote, *Shrop.* TF9 39 F3
Heathencote NN12 31 J4
Heather LE67 41 F4
Heathfield, *Devon* TQ12 5 J3
Heathfield, *E.Suss.* TN21 13 J4
Heathfield, *N.Yorks.* HG3 57 G3
Heathfield, *Som.* TA4 7 K3
Heathrow Airport TW6 22 D4
Heathton WV5 40 A6
Heatley WA13 49 G4
Heaton, *Lancs.* LA3 55 H3
Heaton, *Staffs.* SK11 49 J6
Heaton, *T. & W.* NE6 71 H7
Heaton, *W.Yorks.* BD9 57 G6
Heaton Moor SK4 49 H3
Heaton's Bridge L40 48 D1
Heaverham TN15 23 J6
Heaviley SK2 49 J4
Heavitree EX1 7 H6
Hebburn NE31 71 J7
Hebden BD23 57 F3
Hebden Bridge HX7 56 E7
Hebden Green CW7 49 F6
Hebing End SG2 33 G6
Hebron, *Carmar.* SA34 16 E2
Hebron, *Northumb.* NE61 71 G5
Heck DG11 69 F5
Heckfield RG27 22 A5
Heckfield Green IP21 35 F1
Heckfordbridge CO3 34 D6
Heckingham NR14 45 H6
Heckington NG34 42 E1
Heckmondwike WF16 57 H7
Heddington SN11 20 C5
Heddle KW17 107 C6
Heddon-on-the-Wall NE15 71 G7
Hedenham NR35 45 H6
Hedge End SO30 11 F3
Hedgerley SL2 22 C3
Hedging TA7 8 C2
Hedley on the Hill NE43 62 B1
Hednesford WS12 40 C4
Hedon HU12 59 H7
Hedsor HP10 22 C3
Heeley S8 51 F4
Heglibister ZE2 109 C7
Heighington, *Darl.* DL5 62 D4
Heighington, *Lincs.* LN4 52 D6
Heightington DY12 29 G1
Heights of Brae IV14 96 C5
Heilam IV27 103 G3
Heisker Islands (Monach Islands) HS6 92 B5
Heithat DG11 69 G5
Heiton TD5 77 F7
Hele, *Devon* EX34 6 D1
Hele, *Devon* EX5 7 H5
Hele, *Devon* PL15 6 B6
Hele, *Devon* TQ13 5 H3
Hele, *Som.* TA4 7 K3
Hele, *Torbay* TQ1 5 K4
Hele Bridge EX20 6 D5
Hele Lane EX17 7 F4
Helebridge EX23 6 A5
Helensburgh G84 74 A2
Helford TR12 2 E6
Helhoughton NR21 44 C3
Helions Bumpstead CB9 33 K4
Hell Corner RG17 21 G5
Hellaby S66 51 H3
Helland, *Cornw.* PL30 4 A3
Helland, *Som.* TA3 8 C2
Hellandbridge PL30 4 A3
Hellesdon NR6 45 G4
Hellidon NN11 31 G3
Hellifield BD23 56 D4
Hellingly BN27 13 J5
Hellington NR14 45 H5
Hellister ZE2 109 C8
Helmdon NN13 31 G4
Helmingham IP14 35 F3
Helmington Row DL15 62 C3
Helmsdale KW8 105 F7
Helmshore BB4 56 C7
Helmsley YO62 58 C1
Helperby YO61 57 K3
Helperthorpe YO17 59 F2
Helpringham NG34 42 E1
Helpston PE6 42 E5
Helsby WA6 48 D5
Helsey PE24 53 J5
Helston TR13 2 D6
Helstone PL32 4 A2
Helton CA10 61 G4
Helwith DL11 62 B6
Helwith Bridge BD24 56 D3
Hem SY21 38 B5
Hemborough Post TQ9 5 J5
HEMEL HEMPSTEAD HP 22 D1
Hemerdon PL7 5 F5
Hemingbrough YO8 58 C6
Hemingby LN9 53 F5
Hemingfield S73 51 F2
Hemingford Abbots PE28 33 F1
Hemingford Grey PE28 33 F1
Hemingstone IP6 35 F3
Hemington, *Leics.* DE74 41 G3
Hemington, *Northants.* PE8 42 D7
Hemington, *Som.* BA3 20 A6
Hemley IP12 35 G4
Hemlington TS8 63 F5
Hemp Green IP17 35 H2
Hempholme YO25 59 G4
Hempnall NR15 45 G6
Hempnall Green NR15 45 G6
Hempriggs IV36 97 J5
Hempriggs House KW1 105 J4
Hempstead, *Essex* CB10 33 K5
Hempstead, *Med.* ME7 24 D5
Hempstead, *Norf.* NR12 45 J3
Hempstead, *Norf.* NR25 45 F2
Hempsted GL2 29 H7
Hempton, *Norf.* NR21 44 D3
Hempton, *Oxon.* OX15 31 F5
Hemsby NR29 45 J4
Hemswell DN21 52 C3
Hemswell Cliff DN21 52 C4
Hemsworth WF9 51 G1
Hemyock EX15 7 K4
Henbury, *Bristol* BS10 19 J4
Henbury, *Ches.* SK10 49 H5
Henderland DG2 65 J3
Hendersyde Park TD5 77 F7
Hendham TQ7 5 H5
Hendon, *Gt.Lon.* NW4 23 F3
Hendon, *T. & W.* SR2 62 E1
Hendraburnick PL32 4 B2
Hendre, *Bridgend* CF35 18 C3
Hendre, *Gwyn.* LL53 36 C2
Hendreforgan CF39 18 C3
Hendy SA4 17 J4
Heneglwys LL77 46 C5
Henfield, *S.Glos.* BS36 19 K4
Henfield, *W.Suss.* BN5 13 F5
Henford EX21 6 B6
Henghurst TN26 14 E4
Hengoed, *Caerp.* CF82 18 E2
Hengoed, *Powys* HR5 28 B3
Hengoed, *Shrop.* SY10 38 B2
Hengrave IP28 34 C2
Henham CM22 33 J6
Heniarth SY21 38 A5
Henlade TA3 8 B2
Henley, *Dorset* DT2 9 F4
Henley, *Shrop.* SY8 28 E1
Henley, *Som.* TA10 8 D1
Henley, *Som.* TA18 8 D4
Henley, *Suff.* IP6 35 F3
Henley, *W.Suss.* GU27 12 B4
Henley Corner TA10 8 D1
Henley Park GU3 22 C6
Henley-in-Arden B95 30 C2
Henley-on-Thames RG9 22 A3
Henley's Down TN33 14 C6
Henllan, *Carmar.* SA44 26 C4
Henllan, *Denb.* LL16 47 J6
Henllan Amgoed SA34 16 E2
Henllys NP44 19 F2
Henlow SG16 32 E5
Hennock TQ13 7 G7
Henny Street CO10 34 C5
Henryd LL32 47 F5
Henry's Moat SA63 16 D2
Hensall DN14 58 B7
Henshaw NE47 70 C7
Hensingham CA28 60 A5
Henstead NR34 45 J7
Hensting SO21 11 F2
Henstridge BA8 9 G3
Henstridge Ash BA8 9 G3
Henstridge Bowden BA8 9 F2
Henstridge Marsh BA8 9 G2
Henton, *Oxon.* OX39 22 A1
Henton, *Som.* BA5 19 H7
Henwood PL14 4 C3
Heogan ZE2 109 D8
Heol Senni LD3 27 J6
Heolgerrig CF48 18 D1
Heol-y-Cyw CF35 18 C3
Hepburn NE66 71 F1
Hepburn Bell NE66 71 F1
Hepple NE65 70 E3
Hepscott NE61 71 H5
Hepthorne Lane S42 51 G6
Heptonstall HX7 56 E7
Hepworth, *Suff.* IP22 34 D1
Hepworth, *W.Yorks.* HD9 50 D2
Hepworth South Common IP22 34 D1
Herbrandston SA73 16 B4
HEREFORD HR 28 E4
Heriot EH38 76 B5
Herm GY1 3 J5
Hermiston EH14 75 K3
Hermitage, *D. & G.* DG7 65 H4
Hermitage, *Dorset* DT2 9 F4
Hermitage, *Sc.Bord.* TD9 70 A4
Hermitage, *W.Berks.* RG18 21 J4
Hermitage, *W.Suss.* PO10 11 J4
Hermitage Green WA2 49 F3
Hermon, *Carmar.* SA33 17 G1
Hermon, *I.o.A.* LL62 46 B6
Hermon, *Pembs.* SA36 17 F1
Herne CT6 25 H5
Herne Bay CT6 25 H5
Herne Common CT6 25 H5
Herne Pound ME18 23 K6
Herner EX32 6 D3
Hernhill ME13 25 G5
Herodsfoot PL14 4 C4
Herongate CM13 24 C2
Heron's Ghyll TN22 13 H4
Heronsgate WD3 22 D2
Herriard RG25 21 K7
Herringfleet NR32 45 J6
Herring's Green MK45 32 D4
Herringswell IP28 34 B2
Herringthorpe S65 51 G3
Hersden CT3 25 H5
Hersham, *Cornw.* EX23 6 A5
Hersham, *Surr.* KT12 22 E5
Herstmonceux BN27 13 K5
Herston KW17 107 D8
Hertford SG14 33 G7
Hertford Heath SG13 33 G7
Hertingfordbury SG14 33 G7
Hesket Newmarket CA7 60 E3
Hesketh Bank PR4 55 H7
Hesketh Lane PR3 56 B5
Heskin Green PR7 48 E1
Hesleden TS27 63 F3
Hesleyside NE48 70 D5
Heslington YO10 58 C4
Hessay YO26 58 B4
Hessenford PL11 4 D5
Hessett IP30 34 D2
Hessle HU13 59 G7
Hest Bank LA2 55 H3
Hester's Way GL51 29 J6
Hestley Green IP23 35 F2
Heston TW5 22 E4
Heswall CH60 48 B4
Hethe OX27 31 G6
Hethelpit Cross GL19 29 G6
Hetherington NE48 70 D6
Hethersett NR9 45 F5
Hethersgill CA6 69 K7
Hethpool NE71 70 D1
Hett DH6 62 D3
Hetton BD23 56 E4
Hetton-le-Hole DH5 62 E2
Heugh NE18 71 F6
Heugh-head, *Aber.* AB36 90 B3
Heugh-head, *Aber.* AB34 90 D5
Heveningham IP19 35 H1
Hever TN8 23 H7
Heversham LA7 55 H1
Hevingham NR10 45 F3
Hewas Water PL26 3 G4
Hewell Grange B97 30 B2
Hewell Lane B60 30 B2
Hewelsfield GL15 19 J1
Hewelsfield Common GL15 19 J1
Hewish, *N.Som.* BS24 19 H5
Hewish, *Som.* TA18 8 D4
Hewood TA20 8 C4
Heworth YO31 58 C4
Hewton EX20 6 D6
Hexham NE46 70 E7
Hextable BR8 23 J4
Hexthorpe DN4 51 H2
Hexton SG5 32 E5
Hexworthy PL20 5 G3
Hey BB8 56 D5
Hey Houses FY8 55 G7
Heybridge, *Essex* CM4 24 C2
Heybridge, *Essex* CM9 24 E1
Heybridge Basin CM9 24 E1
Heybrook Bay PL9 4 E6
Heydon, *Cambs.* SG8 33 H4
Heydon, *Norf.* NR11 45 F3
Heydour NG32 42 D2
Heylipoll PA77 78 A3
Heylor ZE2 108 B4
Heyop LD7 28 B1
Heysham LA3 55 H3
Heyshaw HG3 57 G3
Heyshott GU29 12 B5
Heyside OL2 49 J2
Heytesbury BA12 20 C7
Heythrop OX7 30 E6
Heywood, *Gt.Man.* OL10 49 H1
Heywood, *Wilts.* BA13 20 B6
Hibaldstow DN20 52 C2
Hibb's Green IP29 34 C3
Hickleton DN5 51 G2
Hickling, *Norf.* NR12 45 J3
Hickling, *Notts.* LE14 41 J3
Hickling Green NR12 45 J3
Hickling Heath NR12 45 J3
Hickstead RH17 13 F4
Hidcote Bartrim GL55 30 C4
Hidcote Boyce GL55 30 C4
High Ackworth WF7 51 G1
High Angerton NE61 71 F5
High Balantyre PA32 80 B6
High Bankhill CA10 61 G2
High Beach IG10 23 H2
High Bentham LA2 56 B3
High Bickington EX37 6 D3
High Birkwith BD24 56 C2
High Blantyre G72 74 E5
High Bonnybridge FK4 75 G3
High Borgue DG6 65 G5
High Borve HS2 101 G2
High Bradfield S6 50 E3
High Bradley BD20 57 F5
High Bransholme HU7 59 H6
High Bray EX32 6 E2
High Bridge CA5 60 E2
High Brooms TN4 23 J7
High Bullen EX38 6 D3
High Burton HG4 57 H1
High Buston NE66 71 H3
High Callerton NE20 71 G6
High Casterton LA6 56 B2
High Catton YO41 58 D4
High Close DL11 62 C5
High Cogges OX29 21 G1
High Common IP21 45 F7
High Coniscliffe DL2 62 D5
High Crompton OL2 49 J2
High Cross, *Hants.* GU32 11 J2
High Cross, *Herts.* SG11 33 G7
High Cross, *W.Suss.* BN6 13 F5
High Easter CM1 33 K7
High Ellington HG4 57 G1
High Entercommon DL6 62 E6
High Ercall TF6 38 E4
High Etherley DL14 62 C4
High Ferry PE22 43 G1
High Flatts HD8 50 E2
High Garrett CM7 34 B6
High Gate HX7 56 E7
High Grange DL15 62 C3
High Green, *Norf.* NR9 45 F5
High Green, *Norf.* NR19 44 D4
High Green, *Norf.* IP25 44 D5
High Green, *S.Yorks.* S35 51 F3
High Green, *Suff.* IP29 34 C2
High Green, *Worcs.* WR8 29 H4
High Halden TN26 14 D4
High Halstow ME3 24 D4
High Ham TA10 8 D1
High Harrington CA14 60 B4
High Harrogate HG2 57 J4
High Hatton SY4 39 F3
High Hauxley NE65 71 H3
High Hawsker YO22 63 J2
High Heath, *Shrop.* TF9 39 F3
High Heath, *W.Mid.* WS4 40 C5
High Hesket CA4 61 F2
High Hesleden TS27 63 F3
High Hoyland S75 50 E1
High Hunsley YO43 59 F6
High Hurstwood TN22 13 H4
High Hutton YO60 58 D3
High Ireby CA7 60 D3
High Kelling NR25 44 E2
High Kilburn YO61 58 B2
High Kingthorpe YO18 58 E1
High Knipe CA10 61 G5
High Lane, *Derbys.* DE7 41 G1
High Lane, *Gt.Man.* SK6 49 J4
High Lane, *Worcs.* WR6 29 F2
High Laver CM5 23 J1
High Legh WA16 49 G4
High Leven TS17 63 F5
High Littleton BS39 19 K6
High Lorton CA13 60 C4
High Marishes YO17 58 E2
High Marnham NG23 52 B5
High Melton DN5 51 H2
High Moor S21 51 G4
High Newton LA11 55 H1
High Newton-by-the-Sea NE66 71 H1
High Nibthwaite LA12 60 D7
High Offley ST20 39 G3
High Ongar CM5 23 J1
High Onn ST20 40 A4
High Park Corner CO5 34 E6
High Roding CM6 33 K7
High Shaw DL8 61 K7
High Spen NE39 71 G7
High Stoop DL13 62 C2
High Street, *Cornw.* PL26 3 G3
High Street, *Kent* TN18 14 C4
High Street, *Suff.* IP12 35 J3
High Street, *Suff.* NR35 45 H7
High Street, *Suff.* IP17 35 J1
High Street, *Suff.* CO10 34 C4
High Street Green IP14 34 E3
High Throston TS26 63 F3
High Town WS11 40 B4
High Toynton LN9 53 F6
High Trewhitt NE65 71 F3
High Wham DL13 62 C4
High Wigsell TN32 14 C5
High Woolaston GL15 19 J2
High Worsall TS15 62 E6
High Wray LA22 60 E7
High Wych CM21 33 H7
High Wycombe HP13 22 B2
Higham, *Derbys.* DE55 51 F7
Higham, *Kent* ME3 24 D4
Higham, *Lancs.* BB12 56 D6
Higham, *S.Yorks.* S75 51 F2
Higham, *Suff.* IP28 34 B2
Higham, *Suff.* CO7 34 E5
Higham Dykes NE20 71 G6
Higham Ferrers NN10 32 C2
Higham Gobion SG5 32 E5
Higham on the Hill CV13 41 F6
Higham Wood TN10 23 K7
Highampton EX21 6 C5
Highams Park E4 23 G2
Highbridge, *Hants.* SO50 11 F2
Highbridge, *Som.* TA9 19 G7
Highbrook RH17 13 G3
Highburton HD8 50 D1
Highbury BA3 19 K7
Highclere RG20 21 H5
Highcliffe BH23 10 D5
Higher Alham BA4 19 K7
Higher Ansty DT2 9 G4
Higher Ashton EX6 7 G7
Higher Ballam FY8 55 G6
Higher Blackley M9 49 H2
Higher Brixham TQ5 5 K5
Higher Cheriton EX14 7 K5
Higher Combe TA22 7 H2
Higher Gabwell TQ1 5 K4
Higher Green M29 49 G3
Higher Halstock Leigh BA22 8 E4
Higher Kingcombe DT2 8 E5
Higher Kinnerton CH4 48 C6
Higher Muddiford EX31 6 D2
Higher Nyland SP8 9 G2
Higher Prestacott EX21 6 B6
Higher Standen BB7 56 C5
Higher Tale EX14 7 J5
Higher Thrushgill LA2 56 B3
Higher Town, *Cornw.* PL26 4 A4
Higher Town, *I.o.S.* TR25 2 C1
Higher Walreddon PL19 4 E3
Higher Walton, *Lancs.* PR5 55 J7
Higher Walton, *Warr.* WA4 48 E4
Higher Wambrook TA20 8 B4
Higher Whatcombe DT11 9 H4
Higher Wheelton PR6 56 B7
Higher Whiteleigh EX22 4 C1
Higher Whitley WA4 49 F4
Higher Woodhill BL8 49 G1
Higher Woodsford DT2 9 G6
Higher Wraxall DT2 8 E4
Higher Wych SY14 38 D1
Highfield, *E.Riding* YO8 58 D6
Highfield, *N.Ayr.* KA24 74 B5
Highfield, *Oxon.* OX26 31 G6
Highfield, *S.Yorks.* S2 51 F4
Highfield, *T. & W.* NE39 62 C1
Highfields, *Cambs.* CB3 33 G3
Highfields, *Northumb.* TD15 77 H5
Highgate, *E.Suss.* RH18 13 H3
Highgate, *Gt.Lon.* N6 23 F3
Highgreen Manor NE48 70 D4
Highlane, *Ches.* SK11 49 H6
Highlane, *Derbys.* S12 51 G4
Highlaws CA7 60 C2
Highleadon GL18 29 G6
Highleigh, *Devon* TA22 7 H3
Highleigh, *W.Suss.* PO20 12 B7
Highley WV16 39 G7
Highmead SA40 26 E4
Highmoor Cross RG9 21 K3
Highmoor Hill NP26 19 H3
Highnam GL2 29 G7
Highstead CT3 25 J5
Highsted ME9 25 F5
Highstreet ME13 25 G5
Highstreet Green, *Essex* CO9 34 B5

Highstreet Green

Highstreet Green, Surr. GU8	12	C3
Hightae DG11	69	F6
Highter's Heath B14	30	B1
Hightown, Hants. SO20	10	C4
Hightown, Mersey. L38	48	B2
Hightown Green IP30	34	D3
Highway SN11	20	D4
Highweek TQ12	5	J3
Highwood WR15	29	F2
Highwood Hill NW7	23	F2
Highworth SN6	21	F2
Hilborough IP26	44	C5
Hilcote DE55	51	G7
Hilcott SN9	20	E6
Hilden Park TN11	23	J7
Hildenborough TN11	23	J7
Hildenley YO17	58	D2
Hildersham CB1	33	J4
Hilderstone ST15	40	B2
Hilderthorpe YO15	59	H3
Hilfield DT2	9	F4
Hilgay PE38	44	A6
Hill, S.Glos. GL13	19	K2
Hill, Warks. CV23	31	F2
Hill, Worcs. WR10	29	J4
Hill Brow GU33	11	J2
Hill Chorlton ST5	39	G2
Hill Common NR12	45	J3
Hill Cottages YO18	63	J7
Hill Croome WR8	29	H4
Hill Deverill BA12	20	B7
Hill Dyke PE22	43	G1
Hill End, Dur. DL13	62	B3
Hill End, Fife KY12	75	J1
Hill End, Glos. GL20	29	H5
Hill End, Gt.Lon. UB9	22	D2
Hill End, N.Yorks. BD23	57	F4
Hill Green CB11	33	H5
Hill Head PO14	11	G4
Hill Houses DY14	29	F1
Hill Mountain SA62	16	C4
Hill of Beath KY4	75	K2
Hill of Fearn IV20	97	F4
Hill Ridware WS15	40	C4
Hill Row CB6	33	H1
Hill Side HD5	50	D1
Hill Street SO40	10	E3
Hill Top, Hants. SO42	11	F4
Hill Top, S.Yorks. DN12	51	G3
Hill Top, S.Yorks. S6	50	E4
Hill View BH21	9	J5
Hill Wootton CV35	30	E2
Hillam LS25	58	B7
Hillbeck CA17	61	J5
Hillberry IM4	54	C6
Hillborough CT6	25	J5
Hillbrae, Aber. AB54	98	E6
Hillbrae, Aber. AB51	91	F2
Hillbrae, Aber. AB51	91	G1
Hillbutts BH21	9	J4
Hillclifflane DE56	40	E1
Hillend, Aber. AB55	98	C6
Hillend, Fife KY11	75	K2
Hillend, Midloth. EH10	76	A4
Hillend, N.Lan. ML6	75	G4
Hillend, Swan. SA3	17	H5
Hillend Green GL18	29	G6
Hillersland GL16	28	E7
Hillesden MK18	31	H6
Hillesley GL12	20	A3
Hillfarrance TA4	7	K3
Hillfoot End SG5	32	E5
Hillhead, Devon TQ5	5	K5
Hillhead, S.Ayr. KA6	67	J1
Hillhead of Auchentumb AB43	99	H5
Hillhead of Cocklaw AB42	99	J6
Hilliard's Cross WS13	40	D4
Hilliclay KW14	105	G2
Hillingdon UB10	22	D3
Hillington, Glas. G52	74	D4
Hillington, Norf. PE31	44	B3
Hillmorton CV21	31	G1
Hillockhead, Aber. AB36	90	B4
Hillockhead, Aber. AB33	90	C3
Hillowton DG7	65	H4
Hillpound SO32	11	G3
Hill's End MK17	32	C5
Hills Town SA44	51	G6
Hillsborough S6	51	F3
Hillsford Bridge EX35	7	F1
Hillside, Aber. AB12	91	H5
Hillside, Angus DD10	83	J1
Hillside, Moray IV30	97	J5
Hillside, Worcs. WR6	29	G2
Hillswick ZE2	108	B5
Hillway PO35	11	H6
Hillwell ZE2	109	F9
Hillyfields SO16	10	E3
Hilmarton SN11	20	D4
Hilperton BA14	20	B6
Hilsea PO3	11	H4
Hilston HU11	59	J6
Hilton, Cambs. PE28	33	F2
Hilton, Cumb. CA16	61	J4
Hilton, Derbys. DE65	40	E2
Hilton, Dorset DT11	9	G4
Hilton, Dur. DL2	62	C4
Hilton, High. IV20	97	G3
Hilton, Shrop. WV15	39	G6
Hilton, Staffs. WS14	40	C5
Hilton, Stock. TS15	63	F5
Hilton Croft AB41	91	H1
Hilton of Cadboll IV20	97	G3
Hilton of Delnies IV12	97	F6
Himbleton WR9	29	J3
Himley DY3	40	A6
Hincaster LA7	55	J1

Hinchley Wood KT10	22	E5
Hinckley LE10	41	G6
Hinderclay IP22	34	E1
Hinderton CH64	48	C5
Hinderwell TS13	63	J5
Hindford SY11	38	C2
Hindhead GU26	12	B3
Hindley, Gt.Man. WN2	49	F2
Hindley, Northumb. NE43	62	B1
Hindley Green WN2	49	F2
Hindlip WR3	29	H3
Hindolveston NR20	44	E3
Hindon, Som. TA24	7	H1
Hindon, Wilts. SP3	9	J1
Hindringham NR21	44	D2
Hingham NR9	44	E5
Hinstock TF9	39	F3
Hintlesham IP8	34	E4
Hinton, Glos. GL13	19	K1
Hinton, Hants. BH23	10	D5
Hinton, Here. HR2	28	C5
Hinton, Northants. NN11	31	G3
Hinton, S.Glos. SN14	20	A4
Hinton, Shrop. SY5	38	D5
Hinton Admiral BH23	10	D5
Hinton Ampner SO24	11	G2
Hinton Blewett BS39	19	J6
Hinton Charterhouse BA2	20	A6
Hinton Martell BH21	10	B4
Hinton on the Green WR11	30	B4
Hinton Parva, Dorset BH21	9	J4
Hinton Parva, Swin. SN4	21	F3
Hinton St. George TA17	8	D3
Hinton St. Mary DT10	9	G3
Hinton Waldrist SN7	21	G2
Hinton-in-the-Hedges NN13	31	G5
Hints, Shrop. SY8	29	F1
Hints, Staffs. B78	40	D5
Hinwick NN29	32	C2
Hinxhill TN25	15	F3
Hinxton CB10	33	H4
Hinxworth SG7	33	F4
Hipperholme HX3	57	G7
Hipsburn NE66	71	H2
Hipswell DL9	62	C7
Hirn AB31	91	F4
Hirnant SY10	37	K3
Hirst NE63	71	H5
Hirst Courtney YO8	58	C7
Hirwaen LL15	47	K6
Hirwaun CF44	18	C1
Hiscott EX31	6	D3
Histon CB4	33	H2
Hitcham, Bucks. SL1	22	C3
Hitcham, Suff. IP7	34	D3
Hitchin SG5	32	E6
Hither Green SE13	23	G4
Hittisleigh EX6	7	F6
Hittisleigh Barton EX6	7	F6
Hive HU15	58	E6
Hixon ST18	40	C3
Hoaden CT3	15	H2
Hoaldalbert NP7	28	C6
Hoar Cross DE13	40	D3
Hoarwithy HR2	28	E6
Hoath CT3	25	J5
Hobarris SY7	28	C1
Hobbister KW17	107	C7
Hobbles Green CB8	34	B3
Hobbs Cross CM16	23	H2
Hobbs Lots Bridge PE15	43	G5
Hobkirk TD9	70	A2
Hobland Hall NR31	45	K5
Hobson NE16	62	C1
Hoby LE14	41	J4
Hockerill CM23	33	H6
Hockering NR20	44	E4
Hockerton NG25	51	K7
Hockley SS5	24	E2
Hockley Heath B94	30	C1
Hockliffe LU7	32	C6
Hockwold cum Wilton IP26	44	B7
Hockworthy TA21	7	J4
Hoddesdon EN11	23	G1
Hoddlesden BB3	56	C7
Hodgehill SK11	49	H6
Hodgeston SA71	16	D5
Hodnet TF9	39	F3
Hodnetheath TF9	39	F3
Hodsoll Street TN15	24	C5
Hodson SN4	20	E3
Hodthorpe S80	51	H5
Hoe NR20	44	D4
Hoe Gate PO7	11	H3
Hoff CA16	61	H5
Hoffleet Stow PE20	43	F2
Hoggard's Green IP29	34	C3
Hoggeston MK18	32	B6
Hoggie AB56	98	D5
Hoggrill's End B46	40	E6
Hogha Gearraidh HS6	92	C4
Hoghton PR5	56	B7
Hognaston DE6	50	E7
Hogsthorpe PE24	53	J5
Holbeach PE12	43	G3
Holbeach Bank PE12	43	G3
Holbeach Clough PE12	43	G3
Holbeach Drove PE12	43	G4
Holbeach Hurn PE12	43	G3
Holbeach St. Johns PE12	43	G4
Holbeach St. Marks PE12	43	G2
Holbeach St. Matthew PE12	43	H2
Holbeck S80	51	H5
Holbeck Woodhouse S80	51	H5

Holberrow Green B96	30	B3
Holbeton PL8	5	G5
Holborough ME2	24	D5
Holbrook, Derbys. DE56	41	F1
Holbrook, Suff. IP9	35	F5
Holbrooks CV6	41	F7
Holburn TD15	77	J7
Holbury SO45	11	F4
Holcombe, Devon EX7	5	K3
Holcombe, Gt.Man. BL8	49	G1
Holcombe, Som. BA3	19	K7
Holcombe Burnell Barton EX6	7	G6
Holcombe Rogus TA21	7	J4
Holcot NN6	31	J2
Holden BB7	56	C5
Holden Gate OL14	56	D7
Holdenby NN6	31	H2
Holdenhurst BH8	10	C5
Holder's Green CM6	33	K6
Holders Hill NW4	23	F3
Holdgate TF13	38	E7
Holdingham NG34	42	D1
Holditch TA20	8	C4
Hole EX15	7	K4
Hole Park TN17	14	D4
Hole Street BN44	12	E5
Holehouse SK13	50	C3
Hole-in-the-Wall HR9	29	F6
Holford TA5	7	K1
Holgate YO26	58	B4
Holker LA11	55	G2
Holkham NR23	44	C1
Hollacombe, Devon EX22	6	B5
Hollacombe, Devon EX17	7	G5
Hollacombe Town EX18	6	E4
Holland, Ork. KW17	106	D2
Holland, Ork. KW17	106	F5
Holland, Surr. RH8	23	H6
Holland Fen LN4	43	F1
Holland-on-Sea CO15	35	F7
Hollandstoun KW17	106	G2
Hollee DG11	69	H7
Hollesley IP12	35	H4
Hollicombe TQ2	5	K4
Hollingbourne ME17	14	D2
Hollingbury BN1	13	G6
Hollingrove TN32	13	K4
Hollington, Derbys. DE6	40	E2
Hollington, E.Suss. TN38	14	C6
Hollington, Staffs. ST10	40	C2
Hollingworth SK14	50	C3
Hollins S42	51	F5
Hollins Green WA3	49	F3
Hollins Lane PR3	55	H4
Hollinsclough SK17	50	C6
Hollinwood, Gt.Man. OL9	49	J2
Hollinwood, Shrop. SY13	38	E2
Hollocombe EX18	6	E4
Hollow Meadows S6	50	E4
Holloway B4	51	F7
Hollowell NN6	31	H1
Holly Bush LL13	38	D1
Holly End PE14	43	H5
Holly Green HP27	22	A1
Hollybush, Caerp. NP12	18	E1
Hollybush, E.Ayr. KA6	67	H2
Hollybush, Worcs. HR8	29	G5
Hollyhurst SY13	38	E1
Hollym HU19	59	K7
Hollywater GU35	12	B3
Hollywood B47	30	B1
Holm, D. & G. DG13	69	H4
Holm (Tolm), W.Isles HS2	101	G4
Holm of Drumlanrig DG3	68	D4
Holmbridge HD9	50	D2
Holmbury St. Mary RH5	22	E7
Holmbush RH12	13	F3
Holme, Cambs. PE7	42	E7
Holme, Cumb. LA6	55	J2
Holme, N.Lincs. DN16	52	C2
Holme, N.Yorks. YO7	57	J1
Holme, Notts. NG23	52	B7
Holme, W.Yorks. HD9	50	D2
Holme Chapel BB10	56	D7
Holme Hale IP25	44	C5
Holme Lacy HR2	28	E5
Holme Marsh HR5	28	C3
Holme next the Sea PE36	44	B1
Holme on the Wolds HU17	59	F5
Holme Pierrepont NG12	41	J2
Holme St. Cuthbert CA15	60	C2
Holme-on-Spalding-Moor YO43	58	E6
Holmer HR1	28	E4
Holmer Green HP15	22	C2
Holmes PR4	48	D1
Holmes Chapel CW4	49	G6
Holme's Hill BN8	13	J5
Holmesfield S18	51	F5
Holmeswood L40	48	D1
Holmewood S42	51	G6
Holmfield HX2	57	F7
Holmfirth HD9	50	D2
Holmhead, D. & G. DG7	68	C5
Holmhead, E.Ayr. KA18	67	K1
Holmpton HU19	59	K7
Holmrook CA19	60	B6
Holmsgarth ZE1	109	D8
Holmside DH7	62	D2
Holmsleigh Green EX14	8	B4
Holmston KA7	67	H1
Holmwrangle CA4	61	G2
Holne TQ13	5	H4
Holnest DT9	9	F4
Holnicote TA24	7	H1
Holsworthy EX22	6	B5
Holsworthy Beacon EX22	6	B5
Holt, Dorset BH21	10	B4
Holt, Norf. NR25	44	E2

Holt, Wilts. BA14	20	B5
Holt, Worcs. WR6	29	H2
Holt, Wrex. LL13	48	D7
Holt End, Hants. GU34	11	H1
Holt End, Worcs. B98	30	B2
Holt Fleet WR6	29	H2
Holt Heath, Dorset BH21	10	B4
Holt Heath, Worcs. WR6	29	H2
Holt Wood BH21	10	B4
Holtby YO19	58	C4
Holton, Oxon. OX33	21	K1
Holton, Som. BA9	9	F2
Holton, Suff. IP19	35	J1
Holton cum Beckering LN8	52	E4
Holton Heath BH16	9	J5
Holton le Clay DN36	53	F2
Holton le Moor LN7	52	D3
Holton St. Mary CO7	34	E5
Holtspur HP9	22	C3
Holtye TN8	13	H3
Holtye Common TN8	13	H3
Holway TA1	8	B2
Holwell, Dorset DT9	9	F3
Holwell, Herts. SG5	32	E5
Holwell, Leics. LE14	42	A3
Holwell, Oxon. OX18	21	F1
Holwell, Som. BA11	20	A7
Holwick DL12	62	A4
Holworth DT2	9	G6
Holy Cross DY9	29	J1
Holy Island, I.o.A. LL65	46	A5
Holy Island, Northumb. TD15	77	K6
Holybourne GU34	22	A7
Holyfield EN9	23	G1
Holyhead (Caergybi) LL65	46	A4
Holymoorside S42	51	F6
Holyport SL6	22	B4
Holystone NE65	70	E3
Holytown ML1	75	F4
Holywell, Cambs. PE27	33	G1
Holywell, Cornw. TR8	2	E3
Holywell, Dorset DT2	8	E4
Holywell, E.Suss. BN20	13	K7
Holywell (Treffynnon), Flints. CH8	47	K5
Holywell, Northumb. NE25	71	J6
Holywell Green HX4	50	C1
Holywell Lake TA21	7	K3
Holywell Row IP28	34	B1
Holywood DG2	68	E5
Hom Green HR9	28	E6
Homer TF13	39	F5
Homersfield IP20	45	G7
Homington SP5	10	C2
Homore (Tobha Mòr) HS8	84	C1
Honey Hill CT2	25	H5
Honey Street SN9	20	E5
Honey Tye CO6	34	D5
Honeyborough SA73	16	C4
Honeybourne WR11	30	C4
Honeychurch EX20	6	E5
Honicknowle PL5	4	E5
Honiley CV35	30	D1
Honing NR28	45	H3
Honingham NR9	45	F4
Honington, Lincs. NG32	42	C1
Honington, Suff. IP31	34	D1
Honington, Warks. CV36	30	D4
Honiton EX14	7	K5
Honkley LL12	48	C7
Honley HD9	50	D1
Hoo, Med. ME3	24	D4
Hoo, Suff. IP13	35	G3
Hoo Green WA16	49	G4
Hoo Meavy PL20	5	F4
Hood Green S75	51	F2
Hood Hill S35	51	F3
Hooe, E.Suss. TN33	13	K6
Hooe, Plym. PL9	5	F5
Hooe Common TN33	13	K5
Hook, Cambs. PE15	43	H6
Hook, E.Riding DN14	58	D7
Hook, Gt.Lon. KT9	22	E5
Hook, Hants. RG27	22	A6
Hook, Hants. SO31	11	G4
Hook, Pembs. SA62	16	C3
Hook, Wilts. SN4	20	D3
Hook Green, Kent TN3	13	K3
Hook Green, Kent DA13	24	C5
Hook Green, Kent DA13	24	C4
Hook Green, Kent DA2	23	J4
Hook Norton OX15	30	E5
Hook-a-Gate SY5	38	D5
Hooke DT8	8	E4
Hookgate TF9	39	G2
Hookway EX17	7	G6
Hookwood RH6	23	F7
Hoole CH3	48	D6
Hooley CR5	23	F6
Hoop NP25	19	J1
Hooton CH66	48	C5
Hooton Levitt S66	51	H3
Hooton Pagnell DN5	51	G2
Hooton Roberts S65	51	G3
Hop Pole PE11	42	E4
Hopcrofts Holt OX25	31	F6
Hope, Derbys. S33	50	D4
Hope, Devon TQ7	5	G7
Hope, Flints. LL12	48	C7
Hope, Powys SY21	38	B5
Hope, Shrop. SY5	38	C5
Hope, Staffs. DE6	50	D7
Hope Bagot SY8	28	E1
Hope Bowdler SY6	38	D6
Hope End Green CM22	33	J6
Hope Mansell HR9	29	F7
Hope under Dinmore HR6	28	E3

Hopehouse TD7	69	H2
Hopeman IV30	97	J5
Hope's Green SS7	24	D3
Hopesay SY7	38	C7
Hopkinstown CF37	18	D2
Hopley's Green HR3	28	C3
Hopperton HG5	57	K4
Hopsford CV7	41	G7
Hopstone WV5	39	G6
Hopton, Derbys. DE4	50	E7
Hopton, Norf. NR31	45	K6
Hopton, Shrop. TF9	38	E3
Hopton, Shrop. SY4	38	C3
Hopton, Staffs. ST18	40	B3
Hopton, Suff. IP22	34	D1
Hopton Cangeford SY8	38	E7
Hopton Castle SY7	28	C1
Hopton Wafers DY14	29	F1
Hoptonheath SY7	28	C1
Hopwas B78	40	D5
Hopwood B48	30	B1
Horam TN21	13	J5
Horbling NG34	42	E2
Horbury WF4	50	E1
Horden SR8	63	F2
Horderley SY7	38	D7
Hordle SO41	10	D5
Hordley SY12	38	C2
Horeb, Carmar. SA15	17	H4
Horeb, Cere. SA44	26	C4
Horfield BS7	19	J4
Horham IP21	35	G1
Horkesley Heath CO6	34	D6
Horkstow DN18	52	C1
Horley, Oxon. OX15	31	F4
Horley, Surr. RH6	23	F7
Horn Hill SL9	22	D2
Hornblotton BA4	8	E1
Hornblotton Green BA4	8	E1
Hornby, Lancs. LA2	55	J3
Hornby, N.Yorks. DL8	62	D7
Hornby, N.Yorks. DL6	62	E6
Horncastle LN9	53	F6
Hornchurch RM11	23	J3
Horncliffe TD15	77	H6
Horndean, Hants. PO8	11	J3
Horndean, Sc.Bord. TD15	77	H6
Horndon PL19	6	D7
Horndon on the Hill SS17	24	C3
Horne RH6	23	G7
Horne Row CM3	24	D1
Horner TA24	7	G1
Horniehaugh DD8	83	F1
Horning NR12	45	H4
Horninghold LE16	42	B6
Horninglow DE13	40	E3
Horningsea CB5	33	H2
Horningsham BA12	20	B7
Horningtoft NR20	44	D3
Horningtops PL14	4	C4
Horns Cross, Devon EX39	6	B3
Horns Cross, E.Suss. TN31	14	D5
Hornsbury TA20	8	C3
Hornsby CA8	61	G2
Hornsby Gate CA8	61	G1
Hornsea HU18	59	J5
Hornsey N8	23	G3
Hornton OX15	30	E4
Horrabridge PL20	5	F4
Horridge TQ13	5	H3
Horringer IP29	34	C2
Horrocks Fold BL1	49	G1
Horse Bridge ST9	49	J7
Horsebridge, Devon PL19	4	E3
Horsebridge, Hants. SO20	10	E1
Horsebrook ST19	40	A4
Horsecastle BS49	19	H5
Horsehay TF4	39	F5
Horseheath CB1	33	K4
Horsehouse DL8	57	F1
Horsell GU21	22	C6
Horseman's Green SY13	38	D1
Horsenden HP27	22	A1
Horseshoe Green TN8	23	H7
Horseway PE16	43	H7
Horsey NR29	45	J3
Horsey Corner NR29	45	J3
Horsford NR10	45	F4
Horsforth LS18	57	H6
Horsham, W.Suss. RH12	12	E3
Horsham, Worcs. WR6	29	G3
Horsham St. Faith NR10	45	G4
Horsington, Lincs. LN10	52	E6
Horsington, Som. BA8	9	G2
Horsington Marsh BA8	9	G2
Horsley, Derbys. DE21	41	F1
Horsley, Glos. GL6	20	B2
Horsley, Northumb. NE15	71	F7
Horsley, Northumb. NE19	70	D4
Horsley Cross CO11	35	F6
Horsley Woodhouse DE7	41	F1
Horsleycross Street CO11	35	F6
Horsleygate S18	51	F5
Horsleyhill TD9	70	A2
Horsmonden TN12	23	K7
Horspath OX33	21	J1
Horstead NR12	45	G4
Horsted Keynes RH17	13	G4
Horton, Bucks. LU7	32	C7
Horton, Dorset BH21	10	B4
Horton, Lancs. BD23	56	D4
Horton, Northants. NN7	32	B3
Horton, S.Glos. BS37	20	A3
Horton, Shrop. SY4	38	D3
Horton, Som. TA19	8	C3
Horton, Staffs. ST13	49	J7
Horton, Swan. SA3	17	H6

Place	Page	Grid
Horton, *Tel. & W.* TF6	39	F4
Horton, *W. & M.* SL3	22	D4
Horton, *Wilts.* SN10	20	D5
Horton Cross TA19	8	C3
Horton Grange NE13	71	H6
Horton Green SY14	38	D1
Horton Heath SO50	11	F3
Horton in Ribblesdale BD24	56	D2
Horton Inn BH21	10	B4
Horton Kirby DA4	23	J5
Horton-cum-Studley OX33	31	H7
Horwich BL6	49	F1
Horwich End SK23	50	C4
Horwood EX39	6	D3
Hoscar L40	48	D1
Hose LE14	42	A3
Hoses LA20	60	D7
Hosh PH7	81	K5
Hosta HS6	92	C4
Hoswick ZE2	109	D10
Hotham YO43	58	E6
Hothfield TN26	14	E3
Hoton LE12	41	H3
Houbie ZE2	108	F3
Houdston KA26	67	F4
Hough CW2	49	G7
Hough Green WA8	48	D4
Hougham NG32	42	B1
Hough-on-the-Hill NG32	42	C1
Houghton, *Cambs.* PE28	33	F1
Houghton, *Cumb.* CA3	60	F1
Houghton, *Devon* TQ7	5	G6
Houghton, *Hants.* SO20	10	E1
Houghton, *Pembs.* SA73	16	C4
Houghton, *W.Suss.* BN18	12	D5
Houghton Bank DL2	62	D4
Houghton Conquest MK45	32	D4
Houghton le Spring DH4	62	E2
Houghton on the Hill LE7	41	J5
Houghton Regis LU5	32	D6
Houghton St. Giles NR22	44	D2
Houghton-le-Side DL2	62	D4
Houlsyke YO21	63	J6
Hound SO31	11	F4
Hound Green RG27	22	A6
Houndslow TD3	76	E6
Houndsmoor TA4	7	K3
Houndwood TD14	77	G4
Hounsdown SO40	10	E3
Hounslow TW3	22	E4
Housabie KW17	106	F5
Househill IV12	97	F6
Houses Hill HD5	50	D1
Housetter ZE2	108	C4
Housham Tye CM17	33	J7
Houss ZE2	109	C9
Houston PA6	74	C4
Houstry KW6	105	G5
Houstry of Dunn KW1	105	H3
Houton KW17	107	C7
Hove BN3	13	F6
Hove Edge HD6	57	G7
Hoveringham NG14	41	J1
Hoveton NR12	45	H4
Hovingham YO62	58	C2
How CA8	61	G1
How Caple HR1	29	F5
How End MK45	32	D4
How Green TN8	23	H7
How Man CA22	60	A5
Howbrook S35	51	F3
Howden DN14	58	D7
Howden Clough WF17	57	H7
Howden-le-Wear DL15	62	C3
Howe, *Cumb.* LA8	55	H1
Howe, *High.* KW1	105	J2
Howe, *N.Yorks.* YO7	57	J1
Howe, *Norf.* NR15	45	G6
Howe Green CM2	24	D1
Howe of Teuchar AB53	99	F6
Howe Street, *Essex* CM3	33	K7
Howe Street, *Essex* CM7	33	K5
Howegreen CM3	24	E1
Howell NG34	42	E1
Howey LD1	27	K3
Howgate, *Cumb.* CA28	60	A4
Howgate, *Midloth.* EH26	76	A5
Howgill, *Lancs.* BB7	56	D5
Howgill, *N.Yorks.* BD23	57	F4
Howick NE66	71	H2
Howle TF10	39	F3
Howle Hill HR9	29	F6
Howlett End CB10	33	J5
Howley TA20	8	B4
Hownam TD5	70	C2
Hownam Mains TD5	70	C1
Howpasley TD9	69	J3
Howsham, *N.Lincs.* LN7	52	D2
Howsham, *N.Yorks.* YO60	58	D3
Howt Green ME9	24	E5
Howtel TD12	77	G7
Howton HR2	28	D6
Howwood PA9	74	C4
Hoxa KW17	107	D8
Hoxne IP21	35	F1
Hoy, *High.* KW14	105	H2
Hoy, *High.* KW16	107	B8
Hoylake CH47	48	B4
Hoyland S74	51	F2
Hoylandswaine S36	50	E2
Hoyle GU29	12	C5
Hubberholme BD23	56	E2
Hubberston SA73	16	B4
Hubbert's Bridge PE20	43	F1
Huby, *N.Yorks.* YO61	58	B3
Huby, *N.Yorks.* LS17	57	H5
Hucclecote GL3	29	H7
Hucking ME17	14	D2

Place	Page	Grid
Hucknall NG15	41	H1
HUDDERSFIELD HD	50	D1
Huddington WR9	29	J3
Huddlesford WS13	40	D5
Hudnall HP4	32	D7
Hudscott EX37	6	E3
Hudswell DL11	62	C7
Huggate YO42	58	E4
Hugglescote LE67	41	G4
Hugh Town TR21	2	C1
Hughenden Valley HP14	22	B2
Hughley SY5	38	E6
Hugmore LL13	48	C7
Hugus TR3	2	E4
Huish, *Devon* EX20	6	D4
Huish, *Wilts.* SN8	20	E5
Huish Champflower TA4	7	J3
Huish Episcopi TA10	8	D2
Huisinis HS3	100	B6
Hulcote MK17	32	C5
Hulcott HP22	32	B7
HULL HU	59	H7
Hulland DE6	40	E1
Hulland Ward DE6	40	E1
Hullavington SN14	20	B3
Hullbridge SS5	24	E2
Hulme ST3	40	B1
Hulme End SK17	50	D7
Hulme Walfield CW12	49	H6
Hulver Street NR34	45	J7
Hulverstone PO30	10	E6
Humber, *Devon* EX20	5	J3
Humber, *Here.* HR6	28	E3
Humberside International Airport DN39	52	D1
Humberston DN36	53	G2
Humberstone LE5	41	J5
Humberton YO61	57	K3
Humbie EH36	76	C4
Humbleton, *Dur.* DL2	62	B5
Humbleton, *E.Riding* HU11	59	J6
Humbleton, *Northumb.* NE71	70	E1
Humby NG33	42	D2
Hume TD5	77	F6
Humehall TD5	77	F6
Hummer DT9	8	E3
Humshaugh NE46	70	E6
Huna KW1	105	J1
Huncoat BB5	56	C6
Huncote LE9	41	H6
Hundalee TD8	70	B2
Hundall S18	51	F5
Hunderthwaite DL12	62	A4
Hundleby PE23	53	G6
Hundleton SA71	16	C4
Hundon CO10	34	B4
Hundred Acres PO17	11	G3
Hundred End PR9	55	H7
Hundred House LD1	28	A3
Hungarton LE7	41	J5
Hungate End MK19	31	J4
Hungerford, *Hants.* SP6	10	C3
Hungerford, *Shrop.* SY7	38	E7
Hungerford, *W.Berks.* RG17	21	G5
Hungerford Newtown RG17	21	G4
Hungerton NG32	42	B3
Hunglader IV51	93	J4
Hunmanby YO14	59	G2
Hunningham CV33	30	E2
Hunningham Hill CV33	30	E2
Hunny Hill PO30	11	F6
Hunsdon SG12	33	H7
Hunsingore LS22	57	K4
Hunslet LS10	57	J6
Hunsonby CA10	61	G3
Hunspow KW14	105	H1
Hunstanton PE36	44	A1
Hunstanworth DH8	62	A2
Hunston, *Suff.* IP31	34	D2
Hunston, *W.Suss.* PO20	12	B6
Hunsworth BD19	57	G7
Hunt End B97	30	B2
Hunt House YO22	63	K7
Huntercombe End RG9	21	K3
Hunters Forstal CT6	25	H5
Hunter's Inn EX31	6	E1
Hunter's Quay PA23	73	K3
Hunterston KA23	73	K5
Huntford TD8	70	B3
Huntham TA3	8	C2
Huntingdon PE29	33	F1
Huntingfield IP19	35	H1
Huntingford SP8	9	H1
Huntington, *Here.* HR5	28	B3
Huntington, *Here.* HR4	28	D4
Huntington, *Staffs.* WS12	40	B4
Huntington, *Tel. & W.* TF6	39	F5
Huntington, *York* YO32	58	C4
Huntingtower PH1	82	B5
Huntley GL19	29	G7
Huntly AB54	90	D1
Huntlywood TD4	76	E6
Hunton, *Hants.* SO21	21	H7
Hunton, *Kent* ME15	14	C3
Hunton, *N.Yorks.* DL8	62	C7
Hunton Bridge WD4	22	D1
Hunt's Cross L25	48	D4
Huntscott EX16	7	H1
Huntshaw EX38	6	D3
Huntshaw Cross EX31	6	D3
Huntshaw Water EX38	6	D3
Huntspill TA9	19	G7
Huntworth TA7	8	C1
Hunwick DL15	62	C3
Hunworth NR24	44	E2
Hurcott, *Som.* TA11	8	E2

Place	Page	Grid
Hurcott, *Som.* TA19	8	C3
Hurdley SY15	38	B6
Hurdsfield SK10	49	J5
Hurley, *W. & M.* SL6	22	B3
Hurley, *Warks.* CV9	40	E6
Hurley Bottom SL6	22	B3
Hurlford KA1	74	C7
Hurliness KW16	107	B9
Hurlston Green L40	48	C1
Hurn BH23	10	C5
Hursley SO21	11	F2
Hurst, *N.Yorks.* DL11	62	B6
Hurst, *W'ham* RG10	22	A4
Hurst Green, *E.Suss.* TN19	14	C5
Hurst Green, *Essex* CO7	34	E7
Hurst Green, *Lancs.* BB7	56	B6
Hurst Green, *Surr.* RH8	23	G6
Hurst Wickham BN6	13	F5
Hurstbourne Priors RG28	21	H7
Hurstbourne Tarrant SP11	21	G6
Hurstpierpoint BN6	13	F5
Hurstwood BB10	56	D6
Hurtmore GU7	22	C7
Hurworth-on-Tees DL2	62	E5
Hury DL12	62	A4
Husabost IV55	93	G6
Husbands Bosworth LE17	41	J7
Husborne Crawley MK43	32	C5
Husthwaite YO61	58	B2
Hutcherleigh TQ9	5	H5
Huthwaite NG17	51	G7
Huttoft LN13	53	J5
Hutton, *Cumb.* CA11	60	F4
Hutton, *Essex* CM13	24	C2
Hutton, *Lancs.* PR4	55	H7
Hutton, *N.Som.* BS24	19	G6
Hutton, *Sc.Bord.* TD15	77	H5
Hutton Bonville DL7	62	E6
Hutton Buscel YO13	59	F1
Hutton Conyers HG4	57	J2
Hutton Cranswick YO25	59	G4
Hutton End CA11	60	F3
Hutton Hang DL8	57	G1
Hutton Henry TS27	63	F3
Hutton Magna DL11	62	C5
Hutton Mount CM13	24	C2
Hutton Mulgrave YO21	63	K6
Hutton Roof, *Cumb.* LA6	55	J2
Hutton Roof, *Cumb.* CA11	60	E3
Hutton Rudby TS15	63	F6
Hutton Sessay YO7	57	K2
Hutton Wandesley YO26	58	B4
Hutton-le-Hole YO62	63	J7
Huxham EX5	7	H6
Huxham Green BA4	8	E1
Huxley CH3	48	E6
Huxter, *Shet.* ZE2	109	C7
Huxter, *Shet.* ZE2	109	E6
Huyton L36	48	D3
Hwlffordd (Haverfordwest) SA61	16	C3
Hycemoor LA19	54	D1
Hyde, *Glos.* GL6	20	B1
Hyde, *Gt.Man.* SK14	49	J3
Hyde End, *W'ham* RG7	22	A5
Hyde End, *W.Berks.* RG7	21	J5
Hyde Heath HP6	22	C1
Hyde Lea ST18	40	B4
Hydestile GU8	22	C7
Hyndford Bridge ML11	75	H6
Hyndlee TD9	70	A3
Hynish PA77	78	A4
Hyssington SY15	38	C6
Hythe, *Hants.* SO45	11	F4
Hythe, *Kent* CT21	15	G4
Hythe End TW19	22	D4
Hythie AB42	99	J5
Hyton LA19	54	D1

I

Place	Page	Grid
Ianstown AB56	98	C4
Iarsiadar HS2	100	D4
Ibberton DT11	9	G4
Ible DE4	50	E7
Ibsley BH24	10	C4
Ibstock LE67	41	G4
Ibstone HP14	22	A2
Ibthorpe SP11	21	G6
Ibworth RG26	21	J6
Icelton BS22	19	G5
Ickburgh IP26	44	C6
Ickenham UB10	22	D3
Ickford HP18	21	K1
Ickham CT3	15	H2
Ickleford SG5	32	E5
Icklesham TN36	14	D6
Ickleton CB10	33	H4
Icklingham IP28	34	B1
Ickwell Green SG18	32	E4
Icomb GL54	30	D6
Idbury OX7	30	D6
Iddesleigh EX19	6	D5
Ide EX2	7	H6
Ide Hill TN14	23	H6
Ideford TQ13	5	J3
Iden TN31	14	E5
Iden Green, *Kent* TN17	14	C4
Iden Green, *Kent* TN17	14	D4
Idle BD10	57	G6
Idless TR4	3	F4
Idlicote CV36	30	D4
Idmiston SP4	10	C1
Idridgehay DE56	40	E1
Idridgehay Green DE56	40	E1
Idrigil IV51	93	J5
Idstone SN6	21	F3
Idvies DD8	83	G3
Iffley OX4	21	J1

Place	Page	Grid
Ifield (Singlewell), *Kent* DA12	24	C4
Ifield, *W.Suss.* RH11	13	F3
Ifieldwood RH11	13	F3
Ifold RH14	12	D3
Iford, *Bourne.* BH7	10	C5
Iford, *E.Suss.* BN7	13	H6
Ifton NP26	19	H3
Ifton Heath SY11	38	C2
Ightfield SY13	38	E2
Ightham TN15	23	J6
Iken IP12	35	J3
Ilam DE6	50	D7
Ilchester BA22	8	E2
Ilderton NE66	71	F1
ILFORD IG	23	H3
Ilfracombe EX34	6	D1
Ilkeston DE7	41	G1
Ilketshall St. Andrew NR34	45	H7
Ilketshall St. Lawrence NR34	45	H7
Ilketshall St. Margaret NR35	45	H7
Ilkley LS29	57	G5
Illey B62	40	B7
Illidge Green CW11	49	G6
Illington IP24	44	D7
Illingworth HX2	57	F7
Illogan TR16	2	D4
Illston on the Hill LE7	42	A6
Ilmer HP27	22	A1
Ilmington CV36	30	D4
Ilminster TA19	8	C3
Ilsington, *Devon* TQ13	5	H3
Ilsington, *Dorset* DT2	9	G5
Ilston SA2	17	J5
Ilton, *N.Yorks.* HG4	57	G2
Ilton, *Som.* TA19	8	C3
Imachar KA27	73	G6
Imber BA12	20	C7
Immeroin FK19	81	G6
Immingham DN40	52	E1
Immingham Dock DN40	53	F1
Impington CB4	33	H2
Ince CH2	48	D5
Ince Blundell L38	48	C2
Ince-in-Makerfield WN3	48	E2
Inch Kenneth PA68	79	F4
Inch of Arnhall DD9	90	E7
Inchbae Lodge IV23	96	B5
Inchbare DD9	83	H1
Inchberry IV32	98	B5
Inchbraoch DD10	83	J2
Inchgrundle DD9	90	C7
Inchindown IV18	96	E4
Inchinnan PA4	74	C4
Inchkinloch IV27	103	J4
Inchlaggan PH35	87	H4
Inchlumpie IV17	96	C4
Inchmarlo AB31	90	E5
Inchmarnock PA20	73	J5
Inchnabobart AB35	90	B6
Inchnacardoch Hotel PH32	87	K3
Inchnadamph IV27	102	E6
Inchock DD11	83	H3
Inchrory AB37	89	J4
Inchture PH14	82	D5
Inchvuilt IV4	87	J1
Inchyra PH2	82	C5
Indian Queens TR9	3	G3
Inerval PA42	72	B6
Ingatestone CM4	24	C2
Ingbirchworth S36	50	E2
Ingerthorpe HG3	57	H3
Ingestre ST18	40	B3
Ingham, *Lincs.* LN1	52	C4
Ingham, *Norf.* NR12	45	H3
Ingham, *Suff.* IP31	34	C1
Ingham Corner NR12	45	H3
Ingleborough PE14	43	H4
Ingleby, *Derbys.* DE73	41	F3
Ingleby, *Lincs.* LN1	52	B5
Ingleby Arncliffe DL6	63	F6
Ingleby Barwick TS17	63	F5
Ingleby Cross DL6	63	F6
Ingleby Greenhow TS9	63	G6
Ingleigh Green EX19	6	E5
Inglesbatch BA2	20	A5
Inglesham SN6	21	F2
Ingleton, *Dur.* DL2	62	C4
Ingleton, *N.Yorks.* LA6	56	B2
Inglewhite PR3	55	J6
Ingliston EH28	75	K3
Ingmire Hall LA10	61	H7
Ingoe NE20	71	F6
Ingoldisthorpe PE31	44	A2
Ingoldmells PE25	53	J6
Ingoldsby NG33	42	D2
Ingon CV37	30	D3
Ingram NE66	71	F2
Ingrave CM13	24	C2
Ingrow BD21	57	F6
Ings LA8	60	F7
Ingst BS35	19	J3
Ingworth NR11	45	F3
Inistrynich PA33	80	C5
Injebreck IM4	54	C5
Inkberrow WR7	30	B3
Inkersall S43	51	G5
Inkersall Green S43	51	G5
Inkhorn AB41	91	H1
Inkpen RG17	21	G5
Inkstack KW14	105	H1
Inmarsh SN12	20	C5
Innellan PA23	73	K4
Innergellie KY10	83	G7
Innerleithen EH44	76	B7
Innerleven KY8	82	E7

Place	Page	Grid
Innermessan DG9	64	A4
Innerwick, *E.Loth.* EH42	77	F3
Innerwick, *P. & K.* PH15	81	G3
Inninbeg PA34	79	H3
Innsworth GL3	29	H6
Insch AB52	90	E2
Insh PH21	89	F4
Inshore IV27	103	F2
Inskip PR4	55	H6
Instow EX39	6	C2
Intake DN2	51	H6
Intwood NR4	45	F5
Inver, *Aber.* AB35	89	K5
Inver, *Arg. & B.* PA38	80	A3
Inver, *High.* IV20	97	F3
Inver, *High.* KW6	105	G5
Inver, *P. & K.* PH8	82	B3
Inver Mallie PH34	87	H6
Inverailort PH38	86	D6
Inveralligin IV22	94	E6
Inverallochy AB43	99	J4
Inveran IV27	96	C2
Inveraray PA32	80	B7
Inverardoch Mains FK15	81	J7
Inverardran FK20	80	E5
Inverarish IV40	86	B1
Inverarity DD8	83	F3
Inverarnan G83	80	E6
Inverasdale IV22	94	E3
Inverbain IV54	94	D6
Inverbeg G83	74	B1
Inverbervie DD10	91	G7
Inverbroom IV23	95	H3
Inverbrough IV13	89	F2
Invercassley IV27	96	B1
Inverchaolain PA23	73	J3
Invercharnan PH49	80	C3
Inverchorachan PA26	80	D6
Inverchoran IV6	95	J6
Invercreran PA38	80	B3
Inverdruie PH22	89	G3
Inverebrie AB41	91	H1
Invereen IV13	88	E1
Inverernie IV36	97	H5
Inveresk EH21	76	B3
Inverey AB35	89	H6
Inverfarigaig IV2	88	C2
Invergarry PH35	87	K4
Invergelder AB35	89	K5
Invergeldie PH6	81	J5
Invergloy PH34	87	J6
Invergordon IV18	96	E5
Invergowrie DD2	82	E4
Inverguseran PH41	86	D4
Inverhadden PH16	81	H2
Inverharroch Farm AB54	90	B1
Inverherive FK20	80	E5
Inverhope IV27	103	G2
Inverie PH41	86	D4
Inverinan PA35	80	A6
Inverinate IV40	87	F2
Inverkeilor DD11	83	H3
Inverkeithing KY11	75	K2
Inverkeithny AB54	98	E6
Inverkip PA16	74	A3
Inverkirkaig IV27	102	C7
Inverlael IV23	95	H3
Inverlauren G84	74	B2
Inverliever PA31	79	K7
Inverliver PA35	80	B4
Inverlochlarig FK19	81	F6
Inverlochy PA33	80	C5
Inverlussa PA60	72	E2
Invermay PA2	82	B6
Invermoriston IV63	88	B3
Invernaver KW14	104	C2
INVERNESS IV	96	D7
Inverness Airport IV2	96	E6
Invernettie AB42	99	K6
Invernoaden PA27	73	K1
Inveroran Hotel PA36	80	D3
Inverquharity DD8	83	F2
Inverquhomery AB42	99	J6
Inverroy PH31	87	J6
Inversanda PH33	80	A2
Invershiel IV40	87	F3
Invershore KW3	105	H5
Inversnaid Hotel FK8	80	E7
Invertrossachs FK17	81	G7
Inverugie AB42	99	K6
Inveruglas G83	80	E7
Inveruglass PH21	89	F4
Inverurie AB51	91	F2
Invervar PH15	81	H3
Invervegain PA23	73	J3
Invery House AB31	90	E5
Inverythan AB53	99	F6
Inwardleigh EX20	6	D6
Inworth CO5	34	C7
Iochdar HS8	92	C7
Iona PA76	78	D5
Iping GU29	12	B4
Ipplepen TQ12	5	J4
Ipsden OX10	21	K3
Ipstones ST10	40	C1
IPSWICH IP	35	F4
Irby CH61	48	B4
Irby Hill CH61	48	B4
Irby in the Marsh PE24	53	H6
Irby upon Humber DN37	52	E2
Irchester NN29	32	C2
Ireby, *Cumb.* CA7	60	D3
Ireby, *Lancs.* LA6	56	B2
Ireland, *Ork.* KW16	107	C7
Ireland, *Shet.* ZE2	109	C10
Ireland's Cross CW3	39	G1
Ireleth LA16	55	F2
Ireshopeburn DL13	61	K3
Irlam M44	49	G3
Irnham NG33	42	D3

Iron Acton

Iron Acton **BS37** 19 K3
Iron Cross **WR11** 30 B3
Ironbridge **TF8** 39 F5
Irons Bottom **RH2** 23 F7
Ironside **AB53** 99 G5
Ironville **NG16** 51 G7
Irstead **NR12** 45 H3
Irthington **CA6** 69 K7
Irthlingborough **NN9** 32 C1
Irton **YO12** 59 G1
Irvine **KA12** 74 B7
Isauld **KW14** 104 E2
Isbister, *Ork.* **KW17** 107 C6
Isbister, *Ork.* **KW17** 106 B5
Isbister, *Shet.* **ZE2** 109 E6
Isbister, *Shet.* **ZE2** 108 C3
Isfield **TN22** 13 H5
Isham **NN14** 32 B1
Ishriff **PA65** 79 H4
Isington **GU34** 22 A7
Island of Stroma **KW1** 105 J1
Islay **PA** 72 A4
Islay Airport **PA42** 72 B5
Islay House **PA44** 72 B4
Isle Abbotts **TA3** 8 C2
Isle Brewers **TA3** 8 C2
Isle of Lewis (Eilean Leodhais) **HS** 101 F3
ISLE OF MAN IM 54 **C5**
Isle of Man Airport **IM9** 54 B7
Isle of May **KY10** 76 E1
Isle of Noss **ZE2** 109 E8
Isle of Sheppey **ME12** 25 F4
Isle of Walney **LA14** 54 E3
Isle of Whithorn **DG8** 64 E7
Isle of Wight **PO** 11 F6
Isleham **CB7** 33 K1
Isleornsay (Eilean Iarmain) **IV43** 86 C3
Isles of Scilly (Scilly Isles) **TR** 2 C1
Islesburgh **ZE2** 109 C6
Isleworth **TW7** 22 E4
Isley Walton **DE74** 41 G3
Islibhig **HS2** 100 B5
Islip, *Northants.* **NN14** 32 C1
Islip, *Oxon.* **OX5** 31 G7
Isombridge **TF6** 39 F4
Istead Rise **DA13** 24 C5
Itchen **SO19** 11 F3
Itchen Abbas **SO21** 11 G1
Itchen Stoke **SO24** 11 G1
Itchingfield **RH13** 12 E4
Itchington **BS35** 19 K3
Itteringham **NR11** 45 F2
Itton, *Devon* **EX20** 6 E6
Itton, *Mon.* **NP16** 19 H2
Itton Common **NP16** 19 H2
Ivegill **CA4** 60 F2
Ivelet **DL11** 62 A7
Iver **SL0** 22 D3
Iver Heath **SL0** 22 D3
Iveston **DH8** 62 C1
Ivetsey Bank **ST19** 40 A4
Ivinghoe **LU7** 32 C7
Ivinghoe Aston **LU7** 32 C7
Ivington **HR6** 28 D3
Ivington Green **HR6** 28 D3
Ivy Hatch **TN15** 23 J6
Ivy Todd **PE37** 44 C5
Ivybridge **PL21** 5 G5
Ivychurch **TN29** 15 F5
Iwade **ME9** 25 F5
Iwerne Courtney (Shroton) **DT11** 9 H3
Iwerne Minster **DT11** 9 H3
Ixworth **IP31** 34 D1
Ixworth Thorpe **IP31** 34 D1

J

Jack Hill **LS21** 57 G4
Jackfield **TF8** 39 F5
Jacksdale **NG16** 51 G7
Jackstown **AB51** 91 F1
Jackton **G75** 74 D5
Jacobstow **EX23** 4 B1
Jacobstowe **EX20** 6 D5
Jacobswell **GU4** 22 C6
Jameston **SA70** 16 D5
Jamestown, *D. & G.* **DG13** 69 J4
Jamestown, *High.* **IV14** 96 B6
Jamestown, *W.Dun.* **G83** 74 B2
Janefield **IV10** 96 E6
Janetstown, *High.* **KW14** 105 F2
Janetstown, *High.* **KW1** 105 J3
Jarrow **NE32** 71 J7
Jarvis Brook **TN6** 13 J3
Jasper's Green **CM7** 34 B6
Jawcraig **FK1** 75 G3
Jayes Park **RH5** 22 E7
Jaywick **CO15** 35 F7
Jealott's Hill **RG42** 22 B4
Jeater Houses **DL6** 63 F7
Jedburgh **TD8** 70 B1
Jeffreyston **SA68** 16 D4
Jemimaville **IV7** 96 E5
Jericho **BL9** 49 H1
Jersay **ML7** 75 G4
JERSEY JE 3 **J7**
Jersey Airport **JE3** 3 J7
Jersey Marine **SA1** 18 A2
Jerviswood **ML11** 75 G6
Jesmond **NE2** 71 H7
Jevington **BN26** 13 J6
Jockey End **HP2** 32 D7
Jodrell Bank **SK11** 49 G5
John o' Groats **KW1** 105 J1
Johnby **CA11** 60 F3
John's Cross **TN32** 14 C5
Johnshaven **DD10** 83 J1
Johnson Street **NR29** 45 H4
Johnston **SA62** 16 C3
Johnston Mains **AB30** 91 F7
Johnstone **PA5** 74 C4
Johnstone Castle **PA5** 74 C4
Johnstonebridge **DG11** 69 F4
Johnstown, *Carmar.* **SA31** 17 G3
Johnstown, *Wrex.* **LL14** 38 C1
Joppa **KA6** 67 J2
Jordans **HP9** 22 C2
Jordanston **SA62** 16 C1
Jordanstone **PH11** 82 D3
Joy's Green **GL17** 29 F7
Jumpers Common **BH23** 10 C5
Juniper Hill **NN13** 31 G5
Jura **PA60** 72 D2
Jura House **PA60** 72 C4
Jurby East **IM7** 54 C4
Jurby West **IM7** 54 C4

K

Kaber **CA17** 61 J5
Kaimes **EH17** 76 A4
Kames, *Arg. & B.* **PA21** 73 H3
Kames, *Arg. & B.* **PA34** 79 K6
Kames, *E.Ayr.* **KA18** 68 B1
Kea **TR3** 3 F4
Keadby **DN17** 52 B1
Keal Cotes **PE23** 53 G6
Kearsley **BL4** 49 G2
Kearstwick **LA6** 56 B2
Kearton **DL11** 62 B7
Kearvaig **IV27** 102 E1
Keasden **LA2** 56 C3
Kebholes **AB45** 98 E5
Keckwick **WA4** 48 E4
Keddington **LN11** 53 G4
Keddington Corner **LN11** 53 G4
Kedington **CB9** 34 B4
Kedleston **DE22** 40 E1
Keelby **DN41** 52 E1
Keele **ST5** 40 A1
Keeley Green **MK43** 32 D4
Keelham **BD13** 57 F6
Keeres Green **CM6** 33 J7
Keeston **SA62** 16 B3
Keevil **BA14** 20 C6
Kegworth **DE74** 41 G3
Kehelland **TR14** 2 D4
Keig **AB33** 90 E3
Keighley **BD21** 57 F5
Keil, *Arg. & B.* **PA28** 66 A3
Keil, *High.* **PA38** 80 A2
Keilhill **AB45** 99 F5
Keillmore **PA31** 72 E2
Keillor **PH13** 82 D3
Keillour **PH1** 82 A5
Keills **PA46** 72 C4
Keils **PA60** 72 D4
Keinton Mandeville **TA11** 8 E1
Keir House **FK15** 75 F1
Keir Mill **DG3** 68 D4
Keisby **PE10** 42 D3
Keisley **CA16** 61 J4
Keiss **KW1** 105 J2
Keith **AB55** 98 C5
Keithick **PH13** 82 D4
Keithmore **AB55** 90 B1
Keithock **DD9** 83 H1
Kelbrook **BB18** 56 E5
Kelby **NG32** 42 D1
Keld, *Cumb.* **CA10** 61 G5
Keld, *N.Yorks.* **DL11** 61 K6
Keldholme **YO62** 58 D1
Keldy Castle **YO18** 63 J7
Kelfield, *N.Lincs.* **DN9** 52 B2
Kelfield, *N.Yorks.* **YO19** 58 B6
Kelham **NG23** 51 K7
Kella **IM7** 54 C4
Kellacott **PL15** 6 C7
Kellan **PA72** 79 G3
Kellas, *Angus* **DD5** 83 F4
Kellas, *Moray* **IV30** 97 J6
Kellaton **TQ7** 5 H7
Kellaways **SN15** 20 C4
Kelleth **CA10** 61 H6
Kelleythorpe **YO25** 59 G4
Kelling **NR25** 44 E1
Kellington **DN14** 58 B7
Kelloe **DH6** 62 E3
Kelloholm **DG4** 68 C2
Kelly, *Cornw.* **PL27** 4 A3
Kelly, *Devon* **PL16** 6 B7
Kelly Bray **PL17** 4 D3
Kelmarsh **NN6** 31 J1
Kelmscott **GL7** 21 F2
Kelsale **IP17** 35 H2
Kelsall **CW6** 48 E6
Kelsay **PA47** 72 A5
Kelshall **SG8** 33 G5
Kelsick **CA7** 60 D1
Kelso **TD5** 77 F7
Kelstedge **S45** 51 F6
Kelstern **LN11** 53 F3
Kelston **BA1** 20 A5
Keltneyburn **PH15** 81 J3
Kelton **DG1** 65 K3
Kelton Hill (Rhonehouse) **DG7** 65 H5
Kelty **KY4** 75 K1
Kelvedon **CO5** 34 C7
Kelvedon Hatch **CM15** 23 J2
Kelvinside **G12** 74 D4
Kelynack **TR19** 2 A6
Kemacott **EX31** 6 E1
Kemback **KY15** 83 F6
Kemberton **TF11** 39 G5
Kemble **GL7** 20 C2
Kemerton **GL20** 29 J5
Kemeys Commander **NP15** 19 G1
Kemeys Inferior **NP18** 19 G2
Kemnay **AB51** 91 F3
Kemp Town **BN2** 13 G6
Kempe's Corner **TN25** 15 F3
Kempley **GL18** 29 F6
Kempley Green **GL18** 29 F6
Kemps Green **B94** 30 C1
Kempsey **WR5** 29 H4
Kempsford **GL7** 20 E2
Kempshott **RG22** 21 J7
Kempston **MK42** 32 D4
Kempston Hardwick **MK45** 32 D4
Kempston West End **MK43** 32 C4
Kempton **SY7** 38 C7
Kemsing **TN15** 23 J6
Kemsley **ME10** 25 F5
Kenardington **TN26** 14 E4
Kenchester **HR4** 28 D4
Kencott **GL7** 21 F1
Kendal **LA9** 61 G7
Kenderchurch **HR2** 28 D6
Kendleshire **BS36** 19 K4
Kenfig **CF33** 18 A3
Kenfig Hill **CF33** 18 B3
Kenidjack **TR19** 2 A5
Kenilworth **CV8** 30 D1
Kenknock, *P. & K.* **PH15** 81 G3
Kenknock, *Stir.* **FK21** 81 F4
Kenley, *Gt.Lon.* **CR8** 23 G5
Kenley, *Shrop.* **SY5** 38 E5
Kenmore, *Arg. & B.* **PA32** 80 B7
Kenmore, *High.* **IV54** 94 D6
Kenmore, *P. & K.* **PH15** 81 J3
Kenmore, *W.Isles* **HS2** 100 E7
Kenn, *Devon* **EX6** 7 H7
Kenn, *N.Som.* **BS21** 19 H5
Kennacley **HS3** 93 G2
Kennacraig **PA29** 73 G4
Kennards House **PL15** 4 C2
Kennavay **HS4** 93 H2
Kenneggy Downs **TR20** 2 C6
Kennerleigh **EX17** 7 G5
Kennerty **AB31** 90 E5
Kennet **FK10** 75 H1
Kennethmont **AB54** 90 D2
Kennett **CB8** 33 K2
Kennford **EX6** 7 H7
Kenninghall **NR16** 44 E7
Kennington, *Kent* **TN24** 15 F3
Kennington, *Oxon.* **OX1** 21 J1
Kennoway **KY8** 82 E7
Kenny **TA19** 8 C3
Kennyhill **IP28** 33 K1
Kennythorpe **YO17** 58 D3
Kenovay **PA77** 78 A3
Kensaleyre **IV51** 93 K6
Kensington **W8** 23 F3
Kenstone **TF9** 38 E3
Kensworth **LU6** 32 D7
Kent Street, *E.Suss.* **TN33** 14 C6
Kent Street, *Kent* **ME18** 23 K6
Kentallen **PA38** 80 B2
Kentchurch **HR2** 28 D6
Kentford **CB8** 34 B2
Kentisbeare **EX15** 7 J5
Kentisbury **EX31** 6 E1
Kentisbury Ford **EX31** 6 E1
Kentish Town **NW5** 23 F3
Kentmere **LA8** 61 F6
Kenton, *Devon* **EX6** 7 H7
Kenton, *Suff.* **IP14** 35 F2
Kenton, *T. & W.* **NE3** 71 H7
Kenton Corner **IP14** 35 G2
Kentra **PH36** 79 H1
Kents Bank **LA11** 55 G2
Kent's Green **GL18** 29 G6
Kent's Oak **SO51** 10 E2
Kenwick **SY12** 38 D2
Kenwyn **TR1** 3 F4
Kenyon **WA3** 49 F3
Keoldale **IV27** 103 F2
Keose (Ceos) **HS2** 101 F5
Keppanach **PH33** 80 B1
Keppoch, *Arg. & B.* **G82** 74 B3
Keppoch, *High.* **IV40** 86 E2
Keprigan **PA28** 66 A2
Kepwick **YO7** 63 F7
Keresley **CV6** 41 F7
Kernborough **TQ7** 5 H6
Kerrera **PA34** 79 K5
Kerridge **SK10** 49 J5
Kerris **TR19** 2 B6
Kerry **SY16** 38 A6
Kerrycroy **PA20** 73 K4
Kerry's Gate **HR2** 28 C5
Kerrysdale **IV21** 94 E4
Kersall **NG22** 51 K6
Kersey **IP7** 34 E4
Kersey Vale **IP7** 34 E4
Kershopefoot **CA6** 69 K5
Kerswell **EX15** 7 J5
Kerswell Green **WR5** 29 H4
Kerthen Wood **TR27** 2 C5
Kesgrave **IP5** 35 G4
Kessingland **NR33** 45 K7
Kessingland Beach **NR33** 45 K7
Kestle **PL26** 3 G4
Kestle Mill **TR8** 3 F3
Keston **BR2** 23 H5
Keswick, *Cumb.* **CA12** 60 D4
Keswick, *Norf.* **NR4** 45 G5
Keswick, *Norf.* **NR12** 45 H2
Ketley Bank **TF2** 39 F4
Ketsby **LN11** 53 G5
Kettering **NN16** 32 B1
Ketteringham **NR18** 45 F5
Kettins **PH13** 82 D4
Kettle Corner **ME15** 14 C2
Kettlebaston **IP7** 34 D3
Kettlebridge **KY15** 82 E7
Kettlebrook **B77** 40 E5
Kettleburgh **IP13** 35 G2
Kettlehill **KY15** 82 E7
Kettleholm **DG11** 69 G6
Kettleness **YO21** 63 K5
Kettleshulme **SK23** 49 J5
Kettlesing **HG3** 57 H4
Kettlesing Bottom **HG3** 57 H4
Kettlesing Head **HG3** 57 H4
Kettlestone **NR21** 44 D2
Kettlethorpe **LN1** 52 B5
Kettletoft **KW17** 106 F4
Kettlewell **BD23** 56 E2
Ketton **PE9** 42 C5
Kevingtown **BR5** 23 H5
Kew **TW9** 22 E4
Kewstoke **BS22** 19 G5
Kexbrough **S75** 51 F2
Kexby, *Lincs.* **DN21** 52 B4
Kexby, *York* **YO41** 58 D4
Key Green **CW12** 49 H6
Keyham **LE7** 41 J5
Keyhaven **SO41** 10 E5
Keyingham **HU12** 59 J7
Keymer **BN6** 13 G5
Keynsham **BS31** 19 K5
Key's Toft **PE24** 53 H7
Keysoe **MK44** 32 D2
Keysoe Row **MK44** 32 D2
Keyston **PE28** 32 D1
Keyworth **NG12** 41 J2
Kibblesworth **NE11** 62 D1
Kibworth Beauchamp **LE8** 41 J6
Kibworth Harcourt **LE8** 41 J6
Kidbrooke **SE3** 23 H4
Kiddemore Green **ST19** 40 A5
Kidderminster **DY10** 29 H1
Kiddington **OX20** 31 F6
Kidlington **OX5** 31 F7
Kidmore End **RG4** 21 K4
Kidnal **SY14** 38 D1
Kidsdale **DG8** 64 E7
Kidsgrove **ST7** 49 H7
Kidstones **DL8** 56 E1
Kidwelly (Cydweli) **SA17** 17 H4
Kiel Crofts **PA37** 79 K4
Kielder **NE48** 70 B4
Kilbarchan **PA10** 74 C4
Kilbeg **IV44** 86 C4
Kilberry **PA29** 73 F4
Kilbirnie **KA25** 74 B5
Kilblaan **PA32** 80 C6
Kilbraur **KW9** 104 D7
Kilbrennan **PA73** 79 F3
Kilbride, *Arg. & B.* **PA34** 79 K5
Kilbride, *Arg. & B.* **PA20** 73 J4
Kilbride, *High.* **IV49** 86 B2
Kilbride Farm **PA21** 73 H4
Kilbridemore **PA22** 73 J1
Kilburn, *Derbys.* **DE56** 41 F1
Kilburn, *Gt.Lon.* **NW6** 23 F3
Kilburn, *N.Yorks.* **YO61** 58 B2
Kilby **LE18** 41 J6
Kilchattan Bay **PA20** 73 K5
Kilchenzie **PA28** 66 A1
Kilcheran **PA34** 79 K4
Kilchiaran **PA48** 72 A4
Kilchoan, *Arg. & B.* **PA34** 79 J6
Kilchoan, *High.* **PH36** 79 F1
Kilchoman **PA49** 72 A4
Kilchrenan **PA35** 80 B5
Kilchrist **PA28** 66 A2
Kilconquhar **KY9** 83 F7
Kilcot **GL18** 29 F6
Kilcoy **IV6** 96 C6
Kilcreggan **G84** 74 A2
Kildale **YO21** 63 H6
Kildary **IV18** 96 E4
Kildavie **PA28** 66 B2
Kildermorie Lodge **IV17** 96 C4
Kildonan, *N.Ayr.* **KA27** 66 E1
Kildonan (Cilldonnain), *W.Isles* **HS8** 84 C2
Kildonan Lodge **KW8** 104 E6
Kildonnan **PH42** 85 K6
Kildrochet House **DG9** 64 A5
Kildrummy **AB33** 90 C3
Kildwick **BD20** 57 F5
Kilfinan **PA21** 73 H3
Kilfinnan **PH34** 87 J5
Kilgetty **SA68** 16 E4
Kilgwrrwg Common **NP16** 19 H2
Kilham, *E.Riding* **YO25** 59 G3
Kilham, *Northumb.* **TD12** 77 G7
Kilkenneth **PA77** 78 A3
Kilkenny **GL54** 30 B7
Kilkerran, *Arg. & B.* **PA28** 66 B2
Kilkerran, *S.Ayr.* **KA19** 67 H3
Kilkhampton **EX23** 6 A4
Killamarsh **S21** 51 G4
Killay **SA2** 17 K5
Killbeg **PA72** 79 H3
Killean, *Arg. & B.* **PA29** 72 E6
Killean, *Arg. & B.* **PA32** 80 B7
Killearn **G63** 74 D2
Killellan **PA28** 66 A2
Killen **IV9** 96 D6
Killerby **DL2** 62 C4
Killerton **EX5** 7 H5
Killichonan **PH17** 81 G2
Killiechonate **PH34** 87 J6
Killiechronan **PA72** 79 G3
Killiecrankie **PH16** 82 A1
Killiehuntly **PH21** 88 E5
Killiemor **PA72** 79 F4
Killilan **IV40** 87 F1
Killimster **KW1** 105 J3
Killin, *High.* **KW9** 97 F1
Killin, *Stir.* **FK21** 81 G4
Killinallan **PA44** 72 B3
Killinghall **HG3** 57 H4
Killington, *Cumb.* **LA6** 56 B1
Killington, *Devon* **EX31** 6 E1
Killingworth **NE12** 71 H6
Killochyett **TD1** 76 C6
Killocraw **PA28** 72 E7
Killunaig **PA70** 79 F5
Killundine **PA34** 79 G3
Kilmacolm **PA13** 74 B4
Kilmaha **PA35** 80 A7
Kilmahog **FK17** 81 H7
Kilmalieu **PH33** 79 K2
Kilmaluag **IV51** 93 K4
Kilmany **KY15** 82 E5
Kilmarie **IV49** 86 B3
KILMARNOCK KA 74 **C7**
Kilmartin **PA31** 73 G1
Kilmaurs **KA3** 74 C6
Kilmelford **PA34** 79 K6
Kilmeny **PA45** 72 B4
Kilmersdon **BA3** 19 K6
Kilmeston **SO24** 11 G2
Kilmichael **PA28** 66 A1
Kilmichael Glassary **PA31** 73 G1
Kilmichael of Inverlussa **PA31** 73 F2
Kilmington, *Devon* **EX13** 8 B5
Kilmington, *Wilts.* **BA12** 9 G1
Kilmington Common **BA12** 9 G1
Kilmorack **IV4** 96 B7
Kilmore, *Arg. & B.* **PA34** 79 K5
Kilmore, *High.* **IV44** 86 C4
Kilmory, *Arg. & B.* **PA31** 73 F2
Kilmory, *Arg. & B.* **PA31** 73 F3
Kilmory, *High.* **PH43** 85 J4
Kilmory, *High.* **PH36** 86 B7
Kilmory, *N.Ayr.* **KA27** 66 D1
Kilmote **KW8** 104 E7
Kilmuir, *High.* **IV55** 93 H7
Kilmuir, *High.* **IV1** 96 D7
Kilmuir, *High.* **IV18** 96 E4
Kilmuir, *High.* **IV51** 93 J4
Kilmun **PA23** 73 K2
Kilmux **KY8** 82 E7
Kiln Green, *Here.* **HR9** 29 F7
Kiln Green, *W'ham* **RG10** 22 B4
Kiln Pit Hill **DH8** 62 B1
Kilnave **PA44** 72 A3
Kilncadzow **ML8** 75 G6
Kilndown **TN17** 14 C4
Kilnhurst **S64** 51 G3
Kilninian **PA74** 79 F3
Kilninver **PA34** 79 K5
Kilnsea **HU12** 53 H1
Kilnsey **BD23** 56 E3
Kilnwick **YO25** 59 F5
Kilnwick Percy **YO42** 58 E4
Kiloran **PA61** 72 B1
Kilpatrick **KA27** 66 D1
Kilpeck **HR2** 28 D5
Kilphedir **KW8** 104 E7
Kilpin **DN14** 58 D7
Kilpin Pike **DN14** 58 D7
Kilrenny **KY10** 83 G7
Kilsby **CV23** 31 G1
Kilspindie **PH2** 82 D5
Kilstay **DG9** 64 B7
Kilsyth **G65** 75 F3
Kiltarlity **IV4** 96 C7
Kilton, *Notts.* **S81** 51 H5
Kilton, *R. & C.* **TS13** 63 H5
Kilton, *Som.* **TA5** 7 K1
Kilton Thorpe **TS12** 63 H5
Kiltyrie **FK21** 81 H4
Kilvaxter **IV51** 93 J5
Kilve **TA5** 7 K1
Kilverstone **IP24** 44 C7
Kilvington **NG13** 42 B1
Kilwinning **KA13** 74 B6
Kimberley, *Norf.* **NR18** 44 E5
Kimberley, *Notts.* **NG16** 41 H1
Kimberworth **S61** 51 G3
Kimble Wick **HP17** 22 B1
Kimblesworth **DH2** 62 D2
Kimbolton, *Cambs.* **PE28** 32 D2
Kimbolton, *Here.* **HR6** 28 E2
Kimbridge **SO51** 10 E2
Kimcote **LE17** 41 H7
Kimmeridge **BH20** 9 J7
Kimmerston **NE71** 77 H7
Kimpton, *Hants.* **SP11** 21 F7
Kimpton, *Herts.* **SG4** 32 E7
Kinaldy **KY16** 83 G6
Kinblethmont **DD11** 83 H3
Kinbrace **KW11** 104 D5
Kinbreack **PH34** 87 G5
Kinbuck **FK15** 81 J7
Kincaldrum **DD8** 83 F3
Kincaple **KY16** 83 F6
Kincardine, *Fife* **FK10** 75 H2
Kincardine, *High.* **IV24** 96 D3
Kincardine O'Neil **AB34** 90 D5
Kinclaven **PH1** 82 C4
Kincorth **AB12** 91 H4
Kincraig, *Aber.* **AB41** 91 H2
Kincraig, *High.* **PH21** 89 F4
Kincraigie **PH8** 82 A3
Kindallachan **PH9** 82 A2
Kindrogan Field Centre **PH10** 82 B1
Kinellar **AB21** 91 G3
Kineton, *Glos.* **GL54** 30 B6
Kineton, *Warks.* **CV35** 30 E3
Kineton Green **B92** 40 D7

Name	Code		
Kinfauns **PH2**	82	C5
King Sterndale **SK17**	50	C5
Kingarth **PA20**	73	J5
Kingcoed **NP15**	19	H1
Kingerby **LN8**	52	D3
Kingham **OX7**	30	D6
Kingholm Quay **DG1**	65	K3
Kinghorn **KY3**	76	A2
Kinglassie **KY5**	76	A1
Kingoodie **DD2**	82	E5
King's Acre **HR4**	28	D4
King's Bank **TN31**	14	D5
King's Bromley **DE13**	40	D4
Kings Caple **HR1**	28	E6
King's Cliffe **PE8**	42	D6
King's Coughton **B49**	30	B3
King's Green **WR13**	29	G5
King's Heath **B14**	40	C7
Kings Hill, *Kent* **ME19**	23	K6
King's Hill, *W.Mid.* **WS10**	40	B6
King's Hill, *Warks.* **CV3**	30	E1
Kings Langley **WD4**	22	D1
King's Lynn **PE30**	44	A3
King's Meaburn **CA10**	61	H4
Kings Mills **GY5**	3	H5
King's Moss **WA11**	48	E2
Kings Muir **EH45**	76	A7
King's Newnham **CV23**	31	F1
King's Newton **DE73**	41	F3
Kings Norton, *Leics.* **LE7**	41	J5
King's Norton, *W.Mid.* **B30**	30	B1
Kings Nympton **EX37**	6	E4
King's Pyon **HR4**	28	D3
Kings Ripton **PE28**	33	F1
King's Somborne **SO20**	10	E1
King's Stag **DT10**	9	G3
King's Stanley **GL10**	20	B1
King's Sutton **OX17**	31	F5
King'sTamerton **PL5**	4	E5
King's Walden **SG4**	32	E6
Kings Worthy **SO23**	11	F1
Kingsand **PL10**	4	E5
Kingsbarns **KY16**	83	G6
Kingsbridge, *Devon* **TQ7**	5	H6
Kingsbridge, *Som.* **TA23**	7	H2
Kingsburgh **IV51**	93	J6
Kingsbury, *Gt.Lon.* **HA3**	22	E3
Kingsbury, *Warks.* **B78**	40	E6
Kingsbury Episcopi **TA12**	8	D2
Kingscavil **EH49**	75	J3
Kingsclere **RG20**	21	J6
Kingscote **GL8**	20	B2
Kingscott **EX38**	6	D4
Kingscross **KA27**	66	E1
Kingsdale **KY8**	82	E7
Kingsdon **TA11**	8	E2
Kingsdown, *Kent* **CT14**	15	J3
Kingsdown, *Swin.* **SN2**	20	E3
Kingsdown, *Wilts.* **SN13**	20	B5
Kingseat **FK19**	75	K1
Kingsey **HP17**	22	A1
Kingsfold, *Pembs.* **SA71**	16	C5
Kingsfold, *W.Suss.* **RH12**	12	E4
Kingsford, *Aber.* **AB53**	99	F6
Kingsford, *Aber.* **AB33**	90	D3
Kingsford, *Aberdeen* **AB15**	91	G4
Kingsford, *E.Ayr.* **KA3**	74	C6
Kingsford, *Worcs.* **DY11**	40	A7
Kingsgate **CT10**	25	K4
Kingshall Street **IP30**	34	D2
Kingsheanton **EX31**	6	D2
Kingshouse **FK19**	81	G5
Kingshouse Hotel **PH49**	80	D2
Kingshurst **B37**	40	D7
Kingskerswell **TQ12**	5	J4
Kingskettle **KY15**	82	E7
Kingsland, *Here.* **HR6**	28	D2
Kingsland, *I.o.A.* **LL65**	46	A4
Kingsley, *Ches.* **WA6**	48	E5
Kingsley, *Hants.* **GU35**	11	J1
Kingsley, *Staffs.* **ST10**	40	C1
Kingsley Green **GU27**	12	B3
Kingsley Holt **ST10**	40	C1
Kingslow **SY8**	39	G6
Kingsmoor **CM19**	23	H1
Kingsmuir, *Angus* **DD8**	83	F3
Kingsmuir, *Fife* **KY16**	83	G7
Kingsnorth **TN23**	15	F4
Kingsnorth Power Station **ME3**	24	E4
Kingstanding **B44**	40	C6
Kingsteignton **TQ12**	5	J3
Kingsteps **IV12**	97	G6
Kingsthorne **HR2**	28	D5
Kingsthorpe **NN2**	31	J2
Kingston, *Cambs.* **CB3**	33	G3
Kingston, *Cornw.* **PL17**	4	D3
Kingston, *Devon* **TQ7**	5	G6
Kingston, *Devon* **EX10**	7	J7
Kingston, *Dorset* **DT10**	9	G4
Kingston, *Dorset* **BH20**	9	J7
Kingston, *E.Loth.* **EH39**	76	D2
Kingston, *Gt.Man.* **SK14**	49	J3
Kingston, *Hants.* **BH24**	10	C4
Kingston, *I.o.W.* **PO38**	11	F6
Kingston, *Kent* **CT4**	15	G2
Kingston, *Moray* **IV32**	98	B4
Kingston, *W.Suss.* **BN16**	12	D6
Kingston Bagpuize **OX13**	21	G2
Kingston Blount **OX39**	22	A2
Kingston by Sea **BN43**	13	F6
Kingston Deverill **BA12**	9	H1
Kingston Gorse **BN16**	12	D6
Kingston Lisle **OX12**	21	G3
Kingston Maurward **DT2**	9	G5
Kingston near Lewes **BN7**	13	G6
Kingston on Soar **NG11**	41	H3
Kingston Russell **DT2**	8	E5
Kingston St. Mary **TA2**	8	B2
Kingston Seymour **BS21**	19	H5
Kingston Stert **OX39**	22	A1
KINGSTON UPON HULL HU	59	H7
Kingston upon Thames **KT1**	22	E5
Kingston Warren **OX12**	21	G3
Kingstone, *Here.* **HR2**	28	D5
Kingstone, *Here.* **HR9**	29	F6
Kingstone, *Som.* **TA19**	8	C3
Kingstone, *Staffs.* **ST14**	40	C3
Kingstone Winslow **SN6**	21	F3
Kingstown **CA3**	60	E1
Kingswear **TQ6**	5	J5
Kingswell **KA3**	74	D6
Kingswells **AB15**	91	G4
Kingswinford **DY6**	40	A7
Kingswood, *Bucks.* **HP18**	31	H7
Kingswood, *Glos.* **GL12**	20	A2
Kingswood, *Here.* **HR5**	28	B3
Kingswood, *Kent* **ME17**	14	D2
Kingswood, *Powys* **SY21**	38	B5
Kingswood, *S.Glos.* **BS15**	19	K4
Kingswood, *Som.* **TA4**	7	K2
Kingswood, *Surr.* **KT20**	23	F6
Kingswood, *Warks.* **B94**	30	C1
Kingthorpe **LN8**	52	E5
Kington, *Here.* **HR5**	28	B3
Kington, *Worcs.* **WR7**	29	J3
Kington Langley **SN15**	20	C4
Kington Magna **SP8**	9	G2
Kington St. Michael **SN14**	20	C4
Kingussie **PH21**	88	E4
Kingweston **TA11**	8	E1
Kinharrachie **AB41**	91	H1
Kinharvie **DG2**	65	K4
Kinkell **G66**	74	E3
Kinkell Bridge **PH3**	82	A6
Kinknockie **AB42**	99	J6
Kinlet **DY12**	39	G7
Kinloch, *Fife* **KY15**	82	D6
Kinloch, *High.* **IV27**	103	F5
Kinloch, *High.* **PA34**	79	H2
Kinloch, *High.* **PH43**	85	K5
Kinloch, *High.* **IV16**	96	C4
Kinloch, *P.& K.* **PH12**	82	D3
Kinloch, *P.& K.* **PH10**	82	C3
Kinloch Hourn **PH35**	87	F4
Kinloch Laggan **PH20**	88	C6
Kinloch Rannoch **PH16**	81	H2
Kinlochan **PH37**	79	K1
Kinlochard **FK8**	81	F7
Kinlocharkaig **PH34**	87	F5
Kinlochbeoraid **PH38**	86	E6
Kinlochbervie **IV27**	102	E3
Kinlocheil **PH33**	87	F7
Kinlochetive **PH49**	80	C3
Kinlochewe **IV22**	95	G5
Kinlochlaich **PA38**	80	A3
Kinlochleven **PH50**	80	C1
Kinlochmoidart **PH36**	86	D7
Kinlochmorar **PH41**	86	E5
Kinlochmore **PH50**	80	C1
Kinlochroag (Ceann Lochroag) **HS2**	100	D5
Kinlochspelve **PA63**	79	H5
Kinloss **IV36**	97	H5
Kinmel Bay (Bae Cinmel) **LL18**	47	H4
Kinmuck **AB51**	91	G3
Kinnaber **DD10**	83	J1
Kinnadie **AB41**	99	H6
Kinnaird **PH2**	82	D5
Kinneff **DD10**	91	G7
Kinnelhead **DG10**	69	F3
Kinnell, *Angus* **DD11**	83	H2
Kinnell, *Stir.* **FK21**	81	G4
Kinnerley **SY10**	38	C3
Kinnersley, *Here.* **HR3**	28	C4
Kinnersley, *Worcs.* **WR8**	29	H4
Kinnerton **LD8**	28	B2
Kinnerton Green **CH4**	48	C6
Kinnesswood **KY13**	82	C7
Kinnettles **DD8**	83	F3
Kinninvie **DL12**	62	B4
Kinnordy **DD8**	82	E2
Kinoulton **NG12**	41	J2
Kinrara **PH22**	89	F4
Kinross **KY13**	82	C7
Kinrossie **PH2**	82	C4
Kinsbourne Green **AL5**	32	E7
Kinsham, *Here.* **LD8**	28	C2
Kinsham, *Worcs.* **GL20**	29	J5
Kinsley **WF9**	51	G1
Kinson **BH10**	10	B5
Kintarvie **HS2**	100	E6
Kintbury **RG17**	21	G5
Kintessack **IV36**	97	G5
Kintillo **PH2**	82	C6
Kintocher **AB33**	90	D4
Kinton, *Here.* **SY7**	28	D1
Kinton, *Shrop.* **SY4**	38	C4
Kintore **AB51**	91	F3
Kintour **PA42**	72	C5
Kintra, *Arg.& B.* **PA42**	72	B6
Kintra, *Arg.& B.* **PA66**	78	E5
Kintradwell **KW9**	97	G1
Kintraw **PA31**	79	K7
Kinuachdrachd **PA60**	73	F1
Kinveachy **PH24**	89	G3
Kinver **DY7**	40	A7
Kinwarton **B49**	30	C3
Kiplaw Croft **AB42**	91	J1
Kippax **LS25**	57	K6
Kippen, *P.& K.* **PH2**	82	B6
Kippen, *Stir.* **FK8**	74	E1
Kippenross House **FK15**	81	J7
Kippford (Scaur) **DG5**	65	J5
Kipping's Cross **TN12**	23	K7
Kippington **TN13**	23	J6
Kirbister, *Ork.* **KW16**	107	C7
Kirbister, *Ork.* **KW17**	106	F5
Kirbuster **KW17**	106	B5
Kirby Bedon **NR14**	45	G5
Kirby Bellars **LE14**	42	A4
Kirby Cane **NR35**	45	H6
Kirby Corner **CV4**	30	D1
Kirby Cross **CO13**	35	G6
Kirby Fields **LE9**	41	H5
Kirby Green **NR35**	45	H6
Kirby Grindalythe **YO17**	59	F3
Kirby Hill, *N.Yorks.* **DL11**	62	C6
Kirby Hill, *N.Yorks.* **YO51**	57	J3
Kirby Knowle **YO7**	57	K1
Kirby le Soken **CO13**	35	G6
Kirby Misperton **YO17**	58	D2
Kirby Muxloe **LE9**	41	H5
Kirby Row **NR35**	45	H6
Kirby Sigston **DL6**	63	F7
Kirby Underdale **YO41**	58	E4
Kirby Wiske **YO7**	57	J1
Kirdford **RH14**	12	D4
Kirk **KW1**	105	H3
Kirk Bramwith **DN7**	51	J1
Kirk Deighton **LS22**	57	J4
Kirk Ella **HU10**	59	G7
Kirk Hallam **DE7**	41	G1
Kirk Hammerton **YO26**	57	K4
Kirk Ireton **DE6**	50	E7
Kirk Langley **DE6**	40	E2
Kirk Merrington **DL16**	62	D3
Kirk Michael **IM6**	54	C4
Kirk of Shotts **ML7**	75	G4
Kirk Sandall **DN3**	51	J2
Kirk Smeaton **WF8**	51	H1
Kirk Yetholm **TD5**	70	D1
Kirkabister **ZE2**	109	D9
Kirkandrews **DG6**	65	G6
Kirkandrews-upon-Eden **CA5**	60	E1
Kirkbampton **CA5**	60	E1
Kirkbean **DG2**	65	K5
Kirkbride **CA7**	60	D1
Kirkbuddo **DD8**	83	G3
Kirkburn, *E.Riding* **YO25**	59	F4
Kirkburn, *Sc.Bord.* **EH45**	76	A7
Kirkburton **HD8**	50	D1
Kirkby, *Lincs.* **LN8**	52	D3
Kirkby, *Mersey.* **L32**	48	D3
Kirkby, *N.Yorks.* **TS9**	63	G6
Kirkby Fleetham **DL7**	62	D7
Kirkby Green **LN4**	52	D7
Kirkby in Ashfield **NG17**	51	G7
Kirkby la Thorpe **NG34**	42	D1
Kirkby Lonsdale **LA6**	56	B2
Kirkby Malham **BD23**	56	D3
Kirkby Mallory **LE9**	41	G5
Kirkby Malzeard **HG4**	57	H2
Kirkby on Bain **LN10**	53	F6
Kirkby Overblow **HG3**	57	J5
Kirkby Stephen **CA17**	61	J6
Kirkby Thore **CA10**	61	H4
Kirkby Underwood **PE10**	42	D3
Kirkby Wharfe **LS24**	58	B5
Kirkby Woodhouse **NG17**	51	G7
Kirkby-in-Furness **LA17**	55	F1
Kirkbymoorside **YO62**	58	C1
KIRKCALDY KY	76	A1
Kirkcambeck **CA8**	70	A7
Kirkcolm **DG9**	64	A4
Kirkconnel **DG4**	68	C2
Kirkconnell **DG2**	65	K4
Kirkcowan **DG8**	64	D4
Kirkcudbright **DG6**	65	G5
Kirkdale House **DG8**	65	F5
Kirkdean **EH46**	75	K6
Kirkfieldbank **ML11**	75	G6
Kirkgunzeon **DG2**	65	J4
Kirkham, *Lancs.* **PR4**	55	H6
Kirkham, *N.Yorks.* **YO60**	58	D3
Kirkhamgate **WF2**	57	J7
Kirkharle **NE19**	71	F5
Kirkhaugh **CA9**	61	H2
Kirkheaton, *Northumb.* **NE19**	71	F6
Kirkheaton, *W.Yorks.* **HD5**	50	D1
Kirkhill, *Angus* **DD10**	83	H1
Kirkhill, *High.* **IV5**	96	C7
Kirkhill, *Moray* **AB38**	98	B5
Kirkhope **TD7**	69	J1
Kirkibost, *High.* **IV49**	86	B3
Kirkibost, *W.Isles* **HS2**	100	D4
Kirkinch **PH12**	82	E3
Kirkinner **DG8**	64	E5
Kirkintilloch **G66**	74	E3
Kirkland, *Cumb.* **CA10**	61	H3
Kirkland, *Cumb.* **CA26**	60	B5
Kirkland, *D.& G.* **DG3**	68	D4
Kirkland, *D.& G.* **DG4**	68	C2
Kirkland, *D.& G.* **DG11**	69	F5
Kirkland of Longcastle **DG8**	64	D6
Kirkleatham **TS10**	63	G4
Kirklevington **TS15**	63	F5
Kirkley **NR33**	45	K6
Kirklington, *N.Yorks.* **DL8**	57	J1
Kirklington, *Notts.* **NG22**	51	J7
Kirklinton **CA6**	69	K7
Kirkliston **EH29**	75	K3
Kirkmaiden **DG9**	64	B7
Kirkmichael, *P.& K.* **PH10**	82	B1
Kirkmichael, *S.Ayr.* **KA19**	67	H2
Kirkmuirhill **ML11**	75	F6
Kirknewton, *Northumb.* **NE71**	77	H7
Kirknewton, *W.Loth.* **EH27**	75	K4
Kirkney **AB54**	90	D1
Kirkoswald, *Cumb.* **CA10**	61	G2
Kirkoswald, *S.Ayr.* **KA19**	67	G3
Kirkpatrick Durham **DG7**	65	H3
Kirkpatrick-Fleming **DG11**	69	H6
Kirksanton **LA18**	54	E1
Kirkstall **LS5**	57	H6
Kirkstead **LN10**	52	E6
Kirkstile, *Aber.* **AB54**	90	D1
Kirkstile, *D.& G.* **DG13**	69	J4
Kirkstyle **KW1**	105	J1
Kirkthorpe **WF1**	57	J7
Kirkton, *Aber.* **AB52**	90	E2
Kirkton, *Aber.* **AB51**	98	E5
Kirkton, *Aber.* **AB33**	90	E3
Kirkton, *Angus* **DD8**	83	F3
Kirkton, *Arg.& B.* **PA31**	79	J7
Kirkton, *D.& G.* **DG1**	68	E5
Kirkton, *Fife* **DD6**	82	E5
Kirkton, *High.* **IV3**	88	D1
Kirkton, *High.* **KW10**	96	E2
Kirkton, *High.* **IV2**	96	E6
Kirkton, *High.* **IV13**	104	D2
Kirkton, *High.* **IV40**	86	E2
Kirkton, *P.& K.* **PH3**	82	A6
Kirkton, *Sc.Bord.* **TD9**	70	A2
Kirkton Manor **EH45**	76	A7
Kirkton of Airlie **DD8**	82	E2
Kirkton of Auchterhouse **DD3**	82	E4
Kirkton of Barevan **IV12**	97	F7
Kirkton of Bourtie **AB51**	91	G2
Kirkton of Collace **PH2**	82	C4
Kirkton of Craig **DD10**	83	J2
Kirkton of Culsalmond **AB52**	90	E1
Kirkton of Durris **AB31**	91	F5
Kirkton of Glenbuchat **AB36**	90	B3
Kirkton of Glenisla **PH11**	82	D1
Kirkton of Kingoldrum **DD8**	82	E2
Kirkton of Lethendy **PH2**	82	C3
Kirkton of Logie Buchan **AB41**	91	H2
Kirkton of Maryculter **AB12**	91	G5
Kirkton of Menmuir **DD9**	83	G1
Kirkton of Monikie **DD5**	83	G4
Kirkton of Rayne **AB51**	90	E1
Kirkton of Skene **AB32**	91	G4
Kirkton of Tealing **DD4**	83	F4
Kirktonhill, *Aber.* **AB30**	83	H1
Kirktonhill, *W.Dun.* **G82**	74	B3
Kirktown **AB42**	99	J5
Kirktown of Alvah **AB45**	98	E4
Kirktown of Auchterless **AB53**	99	F6
Kirktown of Deskford **AB56**	98	D4
Kirktown of Fetteresso **AB39**	91	G6
Kirktown of Slains **AB41**	91	J2
KIRKWALL KW	107	D6
Kirkwall Airport **KW15**	107	D7
Kirkwhelpington **NE19**	70	E5
Kirmington **DN39**	52	E1
Kirmond le Mire **LN8**	52	E3
Kirn **PA23**	73	K3
Kirriemuir **DD8**	82	E2
Kirstead Green **NR15**	45	G6
Kirtlebridge **DG11**	69	H6
Kirtleton **DG11**	69	H5
Kirtling **CB8**	33	K3
Kirtling Green **CB8**	33	K3
Kirtlington **OX5**	31	G7
Kirtomy **KW14**	104	C2
Kirton, *Lincs.* **PE20**	43	G2
Kirton, *Notts.* **NG22**	51	J6
Kirton, *Suff.* **IP10**	35	G5
Kirton End **PE20**	43	F1
Kirton Holme **PE20**	43	F1
Kirton in Lindsey **DN21**	52	C3
Kiscadale **KA27**	66	E1
Kislingbury **NN7**	31	H3
Kismeldon Bridge **EX22**	6	B4
Kites Hardwick **CV23**	31	F2
Kitley **PL8**	5	F5
Kittisford **TA21**	7	J3
Kittisford Barton **TA21**	7	J3
Kittle **SA3**	17	J6
Kitts End **EN5**	23	F2
Kitt's Green **B33**	40	D7
Kitwood **SO24**	11	H1
Kivernoll **HR2**	28	D5
Kiveton Park **S26**	51	G4
Klibreck **IV27**	103	H5
Knabbygates **AB54**	98	E5
Knaith **DN21**	52	B4
Knaith Park **DN21**	52	B4
Knap Corner **SP8**	9	H2
Knaphill **GU21**	22	C6
Knaplock **TA22**	7	G2
Knapp, *P.& K.* **PH14**	82	D4
Knapp, *Som.* **TA3**	8	C2
Knapthorpe **NG23**	51	K7
Knaptoft **LE17**	41	J7
Knapton, *Norf.* **NR28**	45	H2
Knapton, *York* **YO26**	58	B4
Knapton Green **HR4**	28	D3
Knapwell **CB3**	33	G2
Knaresborough **HG5**	57	J4
Knarsdale **CA8**	61	H1
Knarston **KW17**	106	C5
Knaven **AB42**	99	G6
Knayton **YO7**	57	K1
Knebworth **SG3**	33	F6
Knedlington **DN14**	58	D7
Kneesall **NG22**	51	K6
Kneesworth **SG8**	33	G4
Kneeton **NG13**	42	A1
Knelston **SA3**	17	H6
Knenhall **ST15**	40	B2
Knettishall **IP22**	44	D7
Knightacott **EX31**	6	E2
Knightcote **CV47**	31	F3
Knightley **ST20**	40	A3
Knightley Dale **ST20**	40	A3
Knighton, *Devon* **PL9**	5	F6
Knighton, *Dorset* **DT9**	9	F3
Knighton, *Leic.* **LE2**	41	J5
Knighton, *Poole* **BH21**	10	B5
Knighton (Tref-y-clawdd), *Powys* **LD7**	28	B1
Knighton, *Som.* **TA5**	7	K1
Knighton, *Staffs.* **ST20**	39	G1
Knighton, *Staffs.* **TF9**	39	G1
Knighton, *Wilts.* **SN8**	21	F4
Knighton on Teme **WR15**	29	F1
Knightswood **G15**	74	D4
Knightwick **WR6**	29	G3
Knill **LD8**	28	B2
Knipoch **PA34**	79	K5
Knipton **NG32**	42	B2
Knitsley **DH8**	62	C2
Kniveton **DE6**	50	E7
Knock, *Arg.& B.* **PA71**	79	G4
Knock, *Cumb.* **CA16**	61	H4
Knock, *High.* **IV44**	86	C4
Knock, *Moray* **AB54**	98	D5
Knock of Auchnahannet **PH26**	89	H1
Knockalava **PA31**	73	H1
Knockally **KW6**	105	G6
Knockaloe Moar **IM5**	54	B5
Knockan **IV27**	102	E7
Knockandhu **AB37**	89	K2
Knockando **AB38**	97	J7
Knockarthur **IV28**	96	E1
Knockbain **IV8**	96	D6
Knockban **IV23**	95	J5
Knockbreck **IV19**	96	E3
Knockbrex **DG6**	65	F6
Knockdamph **IV26**	95	J2
Knockdee **KW12**	105	G2
Knockdow **PA23**	73	K3
Knockdown **GL8**	20	B3
Knockenkelly **KA27**	66	E1
Knockentiber **KA2**	74	B7
Knockfin **IV4**	87	K2
Knockgray **DG7**	67	K4
Knockholt **TN14**	23	H6
Knockholt Pound **TN14**	23	H6
Knockin **SY10**	38	C3
Knockinlaw **KA3**	74	C7
Knockintorran (Cnoc an Torrain) **HS6**	92	C5
Knocklearn **DG7**	65	H3
Knockmill **TN15**	23	J5
Knocknaha **PA28**	66	A2
Knocknain **DG9**	66	D7
Knocknalling **DG7**	67	K5
Knockrome **PA60**	72	D3
Knocksharry **IM5**	54	B5
Knockville **DG8**	64	D3
Knockvologan **PA66**	78	E6
Knodishall **IP17**	35	J2
Knodishall Common **IP17**	35	J2
Knodishall Green **IP17**	35	J2
Knole **TA10**	8	D2
Knolls Green **WA16**	49	H5
Knolton **LL13**	38	C2
Knook **BA12**	20	C7
Knossington **LE15**	42	B5
Knott End-on-Sea **FY6**	55	G5
Knotting **MK44**	32	D2
Knotting Green **MK44**	32	D2
Knottingley **WF11**	58	B7
Knotts **BD23**	56	C4
Knotty Green **HP9**	22	C2
Knowbury **SY8**	28	E1
Knowe **DG8**	64	D3
Knowes of Elrick **AB54**	98	E5
Knowesgate **NE19**	70	E5
Knoweside **KA19**	67	G2
Knowetownhead **TD9**	70	A2
Knowhead **AB43**	99	H5
Knowl Green **CO10**	34	B4
Knowl Hill **RG10**	22	B4
Knowl Wall **ST4**	40	A2
Knowle, *Bristol* **BS4**	19	K4
Knowle, *Devon* **EX17**	7	F5
Knowle, *Devon* **EX33**	6	C2
Knowle, *Devon* **EX9**	7	J7
Knowle, *Shrop.* **SY8**	28	E1
Knowle, *Som.* **TA24**	7	H1
Knowle, *W.Mid.* **B93**	30	C1
Knowle Cross **EX5**	7	J6
Knowle Green **PR3**	56	B6
Knowle Hall **TA7**	19	G7
Knowle St. Giles **TA20**	8	C3
Knowlton, *Dorset* **BH21**	10	B3
Knowlton, *Kent* **CT3**	15	H2
Knowsley **L34**	48	D3
Knowstone **EX36**	7	G3
Knox Bridge **TN17**	14	C3
Knucklas **LD7**	28	B1
Knutsford **WA16**	49	G5
Knypersley **ST8**	49	H7
Krumlin **HX4**	50	C1
Kuggar **TR12**	2	E7
Kyle of Lochalsh **IV40**	86	D2
Kyleakin **IV41**	86	D2
Kylerhea **IV40**	86	D2
Kyles Scalpay (Caolas Scalpaigh) **HS3**	93	H2
Kylesbeg **PH36**	86	C7
Kylesknoydart **PH41**	86	E5
Kylesmorar **PH41**	86	E5
Kylestrome **IV27**	102	E3
Kyloag **IV24**	96	D2
Kynaston **SY10**	38	C3
Kynnersley **TF6**	39	F4
Kyre Park **WR15**	29	F2

Labost

L

Labost **HS2** 100 E3
Lacasaigh **HS2** 101 F5
Lacasdal (Laxdale) **HS2** 101 G4
Laceby **DN37** 53 F2
Lacey Green **HP27** 22 B1
Lach Dennis **CW9** 49 G5
Lacharn (Laugharne)
  SA33 17 G3
Lackford **IP28** 34 B1
Lacklee (Leac a' Li) **HS3** 93 G2
Lacock **SN15** 20 C5
Ladbroke **CV47** 31 F3
Laddingford **ME18** 23 K7
Lade Bank **PE22** 53 G7
Ladies Hill **PR3** 55 H5
Ladock **TR2** 3 F3
Lady Hall **LA18** 54 E1
Ladybank **KY15** 82 E6
Ladycross **PL15** 6 B7
Ladyfield **PA32** 80 B6
Ladykirk **TD15** 77 G6
Ladysford **AB43** 99 H4
Ladywood **WR9** 29 H2
Laga **PH36** 79 H1
Lagalochan **PA35** 79 K6
Lagavulin **PA42** 72 C6
Lagg, *Arg. & B.* **PA60** 72 D3
Lagg, *N.Ayr.* **KA27** 66 D1
Lagg, *S.Ayr.* **KA7** 67 G2
Laggan, *Arg. & B.* **PA43** 72 A5
Laggan, *High.* **PH34** 87 J5
Laggan, *High.* **PH20** 88 D5
Laggan, *Moray* **AB55** 90 B1
Laggan, *Stir.* **FK18** 81 G6
Lagganulva **PA73** 79 F3
Lagganvoulin **AB37** 89 J3
Laglingarten **PA25** 80 C7
Lagnalean **IV3** 96 D7
Lagrae **DG4** 68 C2
Laguna **PH1** 82 C4
Laid **IV27** 103 G3
Laide **IV22** 95 F2
Laig **PH42** 85 K6
Laight **KA18** 68 B2
Lainchoil **PH25** 89 H3
Laindon **SS15** 24 C3
Lair **IV27** 82 C1
Lairg **IV27** 96 C1
Lairg Lodge **IV27** 96 C1
Lairigmor **PH33** 80 C1
Laisterdyke **BD4** 57 G6
Laithers **AB53** 98 E6
Laithes **CA11** 61 F3
Lake, *Devon* **EX31** 6 D2
Lake, *Devon* **PL20** 5 F4
Lake, *I.o.W.* **PO36** 11 G6
Lake, *Wilts.* **SP4** 10 C1
Lakenham **NR1** 45 G5
Lakenheath **IP27** 44 B7
Lakesend **PE14** 43 J6
Lakeside, *Cumb.* **LA12** 55 G1
Lakeside, *Thur.* **RM20** 23 J4
Laleham **TW18** 22 D5
Laleston **CF32** 18 B4
Lamancha **EH46** 76 A5
Lamarsh **CO8** 34 C5
Lamas **NR10** 45 G3
Lamb Corner **CO7** 34 E5
Lamb Roe **BB7** 56 C6
Lambden **TD10** 77 F6
Lamberhurst **TN3** 13 K3
Lamberhurst Quarter
  TN3 13 K3
Lamberton **TD15** 77 H5
Lambfell Moar **IM4** 54 B5
Lambley, *Northumb.* **CA8** 61 H1
Lambley, *Notts.* **NG4** 41 J1
Lambourn **RG17** 21 G4
Lambourn Woodlands
  RG17 21 G4
Lambourne End **RM4** 23 H2
Lambs Green **RH12** 13 F3
Lambston **SA62** 16 C3
Lambton **NE38** 62 D1
Lamellion **PL14** 4 C4
Lamerton **PL19** 4 E3
Lamesley **NE11** 62 D1
Lamington, *High.* **IV18** 96 E4
Lamington, *S.Lan.* **ML12** 75 H7
Lamlash **KA27** 73 J7
Lamloch **DG7** 67 K4
Lamonby **CA11** 60 F3
Lamorna **TR19** 2 B6
Lamorran **TR2** 3 F4
Lampert **NE48** 70 B6
Lampeter **SA48** 26 E4
Lampeter Velfrey **SA67** 16 E3
Lamphey **SA71** 16 D4
Lamplugh **CA14** 60 B4
Lamport **NN6** 31 J1
Lamyatt **BA4** 9 F1
Lana, *Devon* **EX22** 6 B6
Lana, *Devon* **EX22** 6 B5
Lanark **ML11** 75 G6
Lanarth **TR12** 2 E6
LANCASTER LA 55 H3
Lanchester **DH7** 62 C2
Lancing **BN15** 12 E6
Landbeach **CB4** 33 H2
Landcross **EX39** 6 C3
Landerberry **AB32** 91 F4
Landewednack **TR12** 2 E7
Landford **SP5** 10 D3
Landhallow **KW5** 105 G5
Landican **CH49** 48 B4
Landkey **SA3** 17 H5
Landkey **DL6** 62 D2
Landmoth **DL6** 63 F7
Landore **SA1** 17 K5
Landrake **PL12** 4 D4

Landscove **TQ13** 5 H4
Landshipping **SA67** 16 D3
Landulph **PL12** 4 E4
Landwade **CB8** 33 K2
Landywood **WS6** 40 B5
Lane Bottom **BB10** 56 D6
Lane End, *Bucks.* **HP14** 22 B2
Lane End, *Cumb.* **LA19** 60 C7
Lane End, *Derbys.* **DE55** 51 G6
Lane End, *Dorset* **BH20** 9 H5
Lane End, *Hants.* **SO21** 11 G2
Lane End, *Here.* **HR9** 29 F7
Lane End, *Kent* **DA2** 23 J4
Lane End, *Wilts.* **BA12** 20 B7
Lane Ends, *Derbys.* **DE6** 40 E2
Lane Ends, *Gt.Man.* **SK6** 49 J3
Lane Ends, *Lancs.* **BB11** 56 C6
Lane Ends, *N.Yorks.*
  BD22 56 E5
Lane Green **WV8** 40 A5
Lane Head, *Dur.* **DL11** 62 C5
Lane Head, *Dur.* **DL13** 62 B4
Lane Head, *Gt.Man.* **WA3** 49 F3
Lane Head, *W.Yorks.* **HD8** 50 D2
Lane Heads **PR3** 55 H6
Lane Side **BB4** 56 C7
Laneast **PL15** 4 C2
Lane-end **PL30** 4 A4
Laneham **DN22** 52 B5
Lanehead, *Dur.* **DL13** 61 K2
Lanehead, *Northumb.*
  NE48 70 C5
Lanesend **SA68** 16 D4
Lanesfield **WV4** 40 B6
Laneshawbridge **BB8** 56 E5
Langais **HS6** 92 D5
Langamull **PA75** 78 E2
Langar **NG13** 42 A2
Langbank **PA14** 74 B3
Langbar **LS29** 57 F4
Langcliffe **BD24** 56 D3
Langdale End **YO13** 63 J3
Langdon, *Cornw.* **EX23** 4 C1
Langdon, *Cornw.* **PL15** 6 B7
Langdon Beck **DL12** 61 K3
Langdon Hills **SS16** 24 C3
Langdon House **EX7** 5 K3
Langdyke **KY8** 82 E7
Langford, *Beds.* **SG18** 32 E4
Langford, *Essex* **CM9** 24 E1
Langford, *Notts.* **NG23** 52 B7
Langford, *Oxon.* **GL7** 21 F1
Langford Budville **TA21** 7 K3
Langham, *Essex* **CO4** 34 E5
Langham, *Norf.* **NR25** 44 E1
Langham, *Rut.* **LE15** 42 B4
Langham, *Suff.* **IP31** 34 D2
Langham Moor **CO4** 34 E5
Langho **BB6** 56 B6
Langholm **DG13** 69 J5
Langland **SA3** 17 K6
Langlands **DG6** 65 G5
Langlee **TD8** 70 B2
Langleeford **NE71** 70 E1
Langley, *Ches.* **SK11** 49 J5
Langley, *Derbys.* **NG16** 41 G1
Langley, *Essex* **CB11** 33 H5
Langley, *Glos.* **GL54** 30 B6
Langley, *Gt.Man.* **M24** 49 H2
Langley, *Hants.* **SO45** 11 F4
Langley, *Herts.* **SG4** 33 F6
Langley, *Kent* **ME17** 14 C2
Langley, *Northumb.*
  NE47 70 D7
Langley, *Oxon.* **OX29** 30 E7
Langley, *Slo.* **SL3** 22 D4
Langley, *Som.* **TA4** 7 J3
Langley, *W.Suss.* **GU33** 12 B4
Langley, *Warks.* **CV37** 30 C2
Langley Burrell **SN15** 20 C4
Langley Corner **SL3** 22 D3
Langley Green, *Derbys.*
  DE6 40 E2
Langley Green, *W.Suss.*
  RH11 13 F3
Langley Green, *Warks.*
  CV35 30 D2
Langley Heath **ME17** 14 C2
Langley Marsh **TA4** 7 J3
Langley Mill **NG16** 41 G1
Langley Moor **DH7** 62 D2
Langley Park **DH7** 62 D2
Langley Street **NR14** 45 H5
Langney **BN23** 13 K6
Langold **S81** 51 H4
Langore **PL15** 4 C2
Langport **TA10** 8 D2
Langrick **PE22** 43 F1
Langrick Bridge **PE22** 43 F1
Langridge, *B. & N.E.Som.*
  BA1 20 A5
Langridge, *Devon* **EX37** 6 D3
Langridgeford **EX37** 6 D3
Langrigg **CA7** 60 C2
Langrish **GU32** 11 J2
Langsett **S36** 50 E2
Langshaw **TD1** 76 D1
Langshawburn **DG13** 69 H3
Langside, *Glas.* **G43** 74 D4
Langside, *P. & K.* **PH6** 81 J6
Langskaill **KW17** 106 D3
Langstone, *Hants.* **PO9** 11 J4
Langstone, *Newport* **NP18** 19 G2
Langthorne **DL8** 62 D7
Langthorpe **YO51** 57 J3
Langthwaite **DL11** 62 B6
Langtoft, *E.Riding* **YO25** 59 G3
Langtoft, *Lincs.* **PE6** 42 E4
Langton, *Dur.* **DL2** 62 C5
Langton, *Lincs.* **PE23** 53 G5

Langton, *Lincs.* **LN9** 53 F6
Langton, *N.Yorks.* **YO17** 58 D3
Langton by Wragby **LN8** 52 E5
Langton Green, *Kent* **TN3** 13 J3
Langton Green, *Suff.*
  IP23 35 F1
Langton Herring **DT3** 9 F6
Langton Long Blandford
  DT11 9 H4
Langton Matravers **BH19** 9 J7
Langtree **EX38** 6 C4
Langtree Week **EX38** 6 C4
Langwathby **CA10** 61 G3
Langwell **IV27** 96 B1
Langwell House **KW7** 105 G6
Langwith **NG20** 51 H5
Langworth **LN3** 52 D5
Lanivet **PL30** 4 A4
Lank **PL30** 4 A3
Lanlivery **PL30** 4 A5
Lanner **TR16** 2 E4
Lanoy **PL15** 4 C3
Lanreath **PL13** 4 B5
Lansallos **PL13** 4 B5
Lansdown **BA1** 20 A5
Lanteglos **PL32** 4 A2
Lanteglos Highway **PL23** 4 B5
Lanton, *Northumb.* **NE71** 77 H7
Lanton, *Sc.Bord.* **TD8** 70 B1
Lanvean **TR8** 3 F2
Lapford **EX17** 7 F5
Laphroaig **PA42** 72 B6
Lapley **ST19** 40 A4
Lapworth **B94** 30 C1
Larach na Gaibhre **PA31** 73 F3
Larachbeg **PA34** 79 H3
Larbert **FK5** 75 G2
Larden Green **CW5** 48 E7
Larg **DG8** 64 D3
Largie **AB52** 90 E1
Largiemore **PA21** 73 H2
Largoward **KY9** 83 F7
Largs **KA30** 74 A5
Largue **AB54** 98 E6
Largybaan **PA28** 66 A2
Largybeg **KA27** 66 E1
Largymore **KA27** 66 E1
Lark Hall **CB1** 33 J3
Larkfield **PA16** 74 A3
Larkhall **ML9** 75 F5
Larkhill **SP4** 20 E7
Larklands **DE7** 41 G1
Larling **NR16** 44 D7
Larriston **TD9** 70 A4
Lartington **DL12** 62 B5
Lary **AB35** 90 B4
Lasborough **GL8** 20 B2
Lasham **GU34** 21 K7
Lashbrook **EX22** 6 C5
Lashenden **TN27** 14 D3
Lassington **GL2** 29 G6
Lassintullich **PH16** 81 J2
Lassodie **KY12** 75 K1
Lasswade **EH18** 76 B4
Lastingham **YO62** 63 J7
Latchford **WA4** 49 F4
Latchingdon **CM3** 24 E1
Latchley **PL18** 4 E3
Lately Common **WN7** 49 F3
Lathallan Mill **KY9** 83 F7
Lathbury **MK16** 32 B4
Latheron **KW5** 105 G5
Latheronwheel **KW5** 105 G5
Lathockar **KY16** 83 F6
Lathones **KY15** 83 F7
Lathrisk **KY15** 82 D7
Latimer **HP5** 22 D2
Latterridge **BS37** 19 K3
Lattiford **BA9** 9 F2
Latton **SN6** 20 D2
Lauchentyre **DG7** 65 F5
Lauchintilly **AB51** 91 F3
Lauder **TD2** 76 D6
Laugharne (Lacharn)
  SA33 17 G3
Laughterton **LN1** 52 B5
Laughton, *E.Suss.* **BN8** 13 J5
Laughton, *Leics.* **LE17** 41 J7
Laughton, *Lincs.* **NG34** 42 D2
Laughton, *Lincs.* **DN21** 52 B3
Laughton en le Morthen
  S25 51 H4
Launcells **EX23** 6 A5
Launcells Cross **EX23** 6 A5
Launceston **PL15** 6 B7
Launde Abbey **LE7** 42 A5
Launton **OX26** 31 H6
Laurencekirk **AB30** 91 F7
Laurieston, *D. & G.* **DG7** 65 G4
Laurieston, *Falk.* **FK2** 75 H3
Lavendon **MK46** 32 C3
Lavenham **CO10** 34 D4
Laverhay **DG10** 69 G4
Lavernock **CF64** 18 E5
Laversdale **CA6** 69 K7
Laverstock **SP1** 10 C1
Laverstoke **RG28** 21 H7
Laverton, *Glos.* **WR12** 30 B5
Laverton, *N.Yorks.* **HG4** 57 H2
Laverton, *Som.* **BA2** 20 A6
Lavister **LL12** 48 C7
Law **ML8** 75 G5
Lawers, *P. & K.* **PH6** 81 J5
Lawers, *P. & K.* **PH15** 81 H4
Lawford, *Essex* **CO11** 34 E5
Lawford, *Som.* **TA4** 7 K2
Lawhitton **PL15** 6 B7
Lawkland **LA2** 56 C3
Lawkland Green **LA2** 56 C3
Lawley **TF4** 39 F5

Lawnhead **ST20** 40 A3
Lawrence Weston **BS11** 19 J4
Lawrenny **SA68** 16 D4
Laws **DD5** 83 F4
Lawshall **IP29** 34 C3
Lawshall Green **IP30** 34 C3
Lawton **HR6** 28 D3
Laxdale (Lacasdal) **HS2** 101 G4
Laxey **IM4** 54 D5
Laxfield **IP13** 35 G1
Laxfirth, *Shet.* **ZE2** 109 D7
Laxfirth, *Shet.* **ZE2** 109 D8
Laxford Bridge **IV27** 102 E4
Laxo **ZE2** 109 D6
Laxton, *E.Riding* **DN14** 58 D7
Laxton, *Northants.* **NN17** 42 C6
Laxton, *Notts.* **NG22** 51 K6
Laycock **BD22** 57 F5
Layer Breton **CO2** 34 D7
Layer de la Haye **CO2** 34 D7
Layer Marney **CO5** 34 D7
Layham **IP7** 34 E4
Laymore **TA20** 8 C4
Layter's Green **SL9** 22 C2
Laytham **YO42** 58 D6
Layton **FY3** 55 G6
Lazenby **TS6** 63 G4
Lazonby **CA10** 61 G3
Lea, *Derbys.* **DE4** 51 F7
Lea, *Here.* **HR9** 29 F6
Lea, *Lincs.* **DN21** 52 B4
Lea, *Shrop.* **SY9** 38 C7
Lea, *Shrop.* **SY5** 38 D5
Lea, *Wilts.* **SN16** 20 C3
Lea Bridge **DE4** 51 F7
Lea Green **WR6** 29 F2
Lea Marston **B76** 40 E6
Lea Town **PR4** 55 H6
Lea Yeat **LA10** 56 C1
Leac a' Li (Lacklee) **HS3** 93 G2
Leachd **PA27** 73 J1
Leachkin **IV3** 96 D7
Leadburn **EH46** 76 A5
Leaden Roding **CM6** 33 J7
Leadenham **LN5** 52 C7
Leaderfoot **TD6** 76 D7
Leadgate, *Cumb.* **CA9** 61 J2
Leadgate, *Dur.* **DH8** 62 C1
Leadgate, *Northumb.*
  NE17 62 C1
Leadhills **ML12** 68 D2
Leadingcross Green **ME17** 14 D2
Leafield **OX29** 30 E7
Leagrave **LU4** 32 D6
Leake Commonside **PE22** 53 G7
Leake Hurn's End **PE22** 43 H1
Lealands **BN27** 13 J5
Lealholm **YO21** 63 J6
Lealt, *Arg. & B.* **PA60** 72 E1
Lealt, *High.* **IV51** 94 B5
Leam **S32** 50 E5
Leamington Hastings
  CV23 31 F2
Leamington Spa **CV32** 30 E2
Leamoor Common **SY7** 38 D7
Leanach, *Arg. & B.* **PA27** 73 J1
Leanach, *High.* **IV2** 96 E7
Leanaig **IV7** 96 C6
Leanoch **IV30** 97 J6
Leargybreck **PA60** 72 D3
Leasgill **LA7** 55 H1
Leasingham **NG34** 42 D1
Leask **AB41** 91 J1
Leason **SA3** 17 H5
Leasowe **CH46** 48 B3
Leat **PL15** 6 B7
Leatherhead **KT22** 22 E6
Leathley **LS21** 57 H5
Leaton, *Shrop.* **SY4** 38 D4
Leaton, *Tel. & W.* **TF6** 39 F4
Leaveland **ME13** 15 F2
Leavenheath **CO6** 34 D5
Leavening **YO17** 58 D3
Leaves Green **BR2** 23 H5
Leavesden Green **WD25** 22 E1
Lebberston **YO11** 59 G1
Lechlade **GL7** 21 F2
Leck **LA6** 56 B2
Leckford **SO20** 10 E1
Leckfurin **KW14** 104 C3
Leckgruinart **PA44** 72 A4
Leckhampstead, *Bucks.*
  MK18 31 J5
Leckhampstead, *W.Berks.*
  RG20 21 H4
Leckhampstead Thicket
  RG20 21 H4
Leckhampton **GL53** 29 J7
Leckie, *High.* **IV22** 95 G5
Leckie, *Stir.* **FK8** 74 E1
Leckmelm **IV23** 95 H3
Leckroy **PH31** 87 K5
Leckuary **PA31** 73 G1
Leckwith **CF11** 18 E4
Leconfield **HU17** 59 G5
Ledaig **PA37** 80 A4
Ledard **FK8** 81 F7
Ledbeg **IV27** 102 E7
Ledburn **LU7** 32 B6
Ledbury **HR8** 29 G5
Ledcharrie **FK20** 81 G5
Ledgemoor **HR4** 28 D3
Ledicot **HR6** 28 D2
Ledmore, *Arg. & B.* **PA72** 79 G3
Ledmore, *High.* **IV27** 102 E7
Lednagullin **KW14** 104 D2
Ledsham, *Ches.* **CH66** 48 C5
Ledsham, *W.Yorks.* **LS25** 57 K7
Ledston **WF10** 57 K7
Ledstone **TQ7** 5 H6
Ledwell **OX7** 31 F6

Lee, *Arg. & B.* **PA67** 79 F5
Lee, *Devon* **EX34** 6 C1
Lee, *Hants.* **SO51** 10 E3
Lee, *Lancs.* **LA2** 55 J4
Lee, *Shrop.* **SY12** 38 D2
Lee Brockhurst **SY4** 38 E3
Lee Chapel **SS15** 24 C3
Lee Clump **HP16** 22 C1
Lee Mill Bridge **PL21** 5 F5
Lee Moor **PL7** 5 F4
Leebotten **ZE2** 109 D10
Leebotwood **SY6** 38 D6
Leece **LA12** 55 F3
Leeds, *Kent* **ME17** 14 D2
LEEDS, *W.Yorks.* LS 57 H6
Leeds Bradford
  International Airport
  LS19 57 H5
Leedstown **TR27** 2 D5
Leegomery **TF1** 39 F4
Leek **ST13** 49 J7
Leek Wootton **CV35** 30 D2
Leekbrook **ST13** 49 J7
Leeming, *N.Yorks.* **DL7** 57 H1
Leeming, *W.Yorks.* **BD22** 57 F6
Leeming Bar **DL7** 57 H1
Lee-on-the-Solent **PO13** 11 G4
Lees, *Derbys.* **DE6** 40 E2
Lees, *Gt.Man.* **OL4** 49 J2
Leeswood **CH7** 48 B7
Leftwich **CW9** 49 F5
Legars **TD5** 77 F6
Legbourne **LN11** 53 G4
Legerwood **TD4** 76 D6
Legsby **LN8** 52 E4
LEICESTER LE 41 H5
Leicester Forest East **LE3** 41 H5
Leideag **HS9** 84 B5
Leigh, *Dorset* **DT9** 9 F3
Leigh, *Dorset* **BH21** 10 B5
Leigh, *Gt.Man.* **WN7** 49 F2
Leigh, *Kent* **TN11** 23 J7
Leigh, *Shrop.* **SY5** 38 C5
Leigh, *Surr.* **RH2** 23 F7
Leigh, *Wilts.* **SN6** 20 D2
Leigh, *Worcs.* **WR6** 29 G3
Leigh Beck **SS8** 24 E3
Leigh Common **BA9** 9 G2
Leigh Delamere **SN14** 20 B4
Leigh Green **TN30** 14 E4
Leigh Park **PO9** 11 J4
Leigh Sinton **WR13** 29 G3
Leigh upon Mendip **BA3** 19 K7
Leigh Woods **BS8** 19 J4
Leigham **PL6** 5 F5
Leighland Chapel **TA23** 7 J2
Leigh-on-Sea **SS9** 24 E3
Leighterton **GL8** 20 B2
Leighton, *N.Yorks.* **HG4** 57 G2
Leighton, *Powys* **SY21** 38 B5
Leighton, *Shrop.* **SY5** 39 F5
Leighton, *Som.* **BA11** 20 A7
Leighton Bromswold
  PE28 32 E1
Leighton Buzzard **LU7** 32 C6
Leinthall Earls **HR6** 28 D2
Leinthall Starkes **SY8** 28 D2
Leintwardine **SY7** 28 D1
Leire **LE17** 41 H7
Leirinmore **IV27** 103 G2
Leiston **IP16** 35 J2
Leitfie **PH11** 82 D3
Leith **EH6** 76 A3
Leitholm **TD12** 77 F6
Lelant **TR26** 2 C5
Lelley **HU12** 59 J6
Lemington **NE15** 71 G7
Lemnas **AB43** 99 G4
Lempitlaw **TD5** 77 F7
Lemsford **AL8** 33 F7
Lenchwick **WR11** 30 B4
Lendalfoot **KA26** 67 F4
Lendrick Lodge **FK17** 81 G7
Lenham **ME17** 14 D2
Lenham Heath **ME17** 14 E3
Lenie **IV63** 88 C2
Lenimore **KA27** 73 G5
Lennel **TD12** 77 G6
Lennox Plunton **DG6** 65 G5
Lennoxtown **G66** 74 E3
Lent Rise **SL6** 22 C3
Lenton, *Lincs.* **NG33** 42 D2
Lenton, *Nott.* **NG7** 41 H2
Lenton Abbey **NG7** 41 H2
Lenwade **NR9** 44 E4
Lenzie **G66** 74 E3
Leoch **DD3** 82 E4
Leochel-Cushnie **AB33** 90 D3
Leominster **HR6** 28 D3
Leonard Stanley **GL10** 20 B1
Leorin **PA42** 72 B6
Lepe **SO45** 11 F5
Lephin **IV55** 93 G7
Lephinchapel **PA27** 73 H1
Lephinmore **PA27** 73 H1
Leppington **YO17** 58 D3
Lepton **HD8** 50 E1
Lerags **PA34** 79 K5
Lerryn **PL22** 4 B5
LERWICK ZE 109 D8
Lesbury **NE66** 71 H2
Leschangie **AB51** 91 F3
Lescrow **PL23** 4 B5
Leslie, *Aber.* **AB52** 90 D2
Leslie, *Fife* **KY6** 82 D7
Lesmahagow **ML11** 75 G7
Lesnewth **PL35** 4 B1
Lessendrum **AB54** 98 D6
Lessingham **NR12** 45 H3
Lessness Heath **DA8** 23 H4
Lessonhall **CA7** 60 D1

Leswalt DG9 64 A4
Letchmore Heath WD25 22 E2
Letchworth Garden City SG6 33 F5
Letcombe Bassett OX12 21 G3
Letcombe Regis OX12 21 G3
Leth Meadhanach HS8 84 C3
Letham, Angus DD8 83 G3
Letham, Falk. FK2 75 G2
Letham, Fife KY15 82 E6
Lethanhill KA6 67 J2
Letheringham IP13 35 G3
Letheringsett NR25 44 E2
Lettaford TQ13 7 F7
Letter Finlay PH34 87 J5
Letterewe IV22 95 F4
Letterfearn IV40 86 E2
Lettermorar PH40 86 D6
Lettermore, Arg. & B. PA72 79 F3
Lettermore, High. IV27 103 J4
Letters IV23 95 H3
Lettershaws ML12 68 D1
Letterston SA62 16 C2
Lettoch, High. PH25 89 H3
Lettoch, High. PH26 89 J1
Letton, Here. SY7 28 C1
Letton, Here. HR3 28 C4
Letty Green SG14 33 F7
Letwell S81 51 H4
Leuchars KY16 83 F5
Leumrabhagh HS2 101 F6
Leurbost (Liurbost) HS2 101 F5
Leusdon TQ13 5 H3
Levedale ST18 40 A4
Level's Green CM23 33 H6
Leven, E.Riding HU17 59 H5
Leven, Fife KY8 82 E7
Levencorroch KA27 66 E1
Levenhall EH21 76 B3
Levens LA8 55 H1
Levens Green SG11 33 G6
Levenshulme M12 49 H3
Levenwick ZE2 109 D10
Leverburgh (An T-òb) HS5 93 F3
Leverington PE13 43 H4
Leverstock Green HP3 22 D1
Leverton PE22 43 G1
Leverton Lucasgate PE22 43 H1
Leverton Outgate PE22 43 H1
Levington IP10 35 G5
Levisham YO18 63 K7
Levishie IV63 88 B3
Lew OX18 21 G1
Lewannick PL15 4 C2
Lewcombe DT2 8 E4
Lewdown EX20 6 C7
Lewes BN7 13 H5
Leweston SA62 16 C2
Lewisham SE13 23 G4
Lewiston IV63 88 C2
Lewistown CF32 18 C3
Lewknor OX49 22 A2
Leworthy EX32 6 E2
Lewson Street ME9 25 F5
Lewth PR4 55 H6
Lewtrenchard EX20 6 C7
Ley, Aber. AB33 90 D3
Ley, Cornw. PL14 4 B4
Ley Green SG4 32 E6
Leybourne ME19 23 K6
Leyburn DL8 62 C7
Leyland PR25 55 J7
Leylodge AB51 91 F3
Leymoor HD3 50 D1
Leys, Aber. AB42 99 J5
Leys, Aber. AB34 90 C4
Leys, P. & K. PH13 82 D4
Leys of Cossans DD8 82 E3
Leysdown-on-Sea ME12 25 G4
Leysmill DD11 83 H3
Leysters HR6 28 E2
Leyton E10 23 G3
Leytonstone E11 23 G3
Lezant PL15 4 D3
Lezerea TR13 2 D5
Lhanbryde IV30 97 K5
Liatrie IV4 87 J1
Libanus LD3 27 J6
Libberton ML11 75 H6
Libbery WR7 29 J3
Liberton EH16 76 A4
Liceasto HS3 93 G2
Lichfield WS13 40 D5
Lickey B60 29 J1
Lickey End B60 29 J1
Lickfold GU28 12 C4
Liddaton Green EX20 6 C7
Liddel KW17 107 D9
Liddesdale PH33 79 J2
Liddington SN4 21 F3
Lidgate, Derbys. S18 51 F5
Lidgate, Suff. CB8 34 B3
Lidget NG21 51 J6
Lidlington MK43 32 C5
Lidsey PO22 12 C6
Lidsing ME7 24 D5
Lidstone OX7 30 E6
Lienassie IV40 87 F2
Lieurary KW14 105 F2
Liff DD2 82 E4
Lifton PL16 6 B7
Liftondown PL15 6 B7
Lightcliffe HX3 57 G7
Lighthorne CV35 30 E3
Lighthorne Heath CV33 30 E3
Lightwater GU18 22 C5
Lightwood ST3 40 B1
Lightwood Green, Ches. CW3 39 F1

Lightwood Green, Wrex. LL13 38 C1
Lilbourne CV23 31 G1
Lilburn Tower NE66 71 F1
Lillesdon TA3 8 C2
Lilleshall TF10 39 G4
Lilley, Herts. LU2 32 E6
Lilley, W.Berks. RG20 21 H4
Lilliesleaf TD6 70 A1
Lilling Green YO32 58 C3
Lillingstone Dayrell MK18 31 J5
Lillingstone Lovell MK18 31 J4
Lillington, Dorset DT9 9 F3
Lillington, Warks. CV32 30 E2
Lilliput BH14 10 B6
Lilstock TA5 7 K1
Lilyhurst TF11 39 G4
Limbury LU3 32 D6
Lime Side OL8 49 J2
Limefield BL9 49 H1
Limehillock AB55 98 D5
Limehurst OL8 49 J2
Limekilnburn ML3 75 F5
Limekilns KY11 75 J2
Limerigg FK1 75 G3
Limerstone PO30 11 F6
Limington BA22 8 E2
Limpenhoe NR13 45 H5
Limpley Stoke BA2 20 A5
Limpsfield RH8 23 H6
Limpsfield Chart TN8 23 H6
Linaclate (Lionacleit) HS7 92 C7
Linbriggs NE65 70 D3
Linby NG15 51 H7
Linchmere GU27 12 B3
Lincluden DG2 65 K3
LINCOLN LN 52 C5
Lincomb DY13 29 H2
Lincombe, Devon TQ9 5 H5
Lincombe, Devon TQ7 5 H6
Lindal in Furness LA12 55 F2
Lindale LA11 55 H1
Lindean TD7 76 C7
Lindertis DD8 82 E2
Lindfield RH16 13 G4
Lindford GU35 12 B3
Lindifferon KY15 82 E6
Lindisfarne (Holy Island) TD15 77 K6
Lindley LS21 57 H5
Lindores KY14 82 D6
Lindow End WA16 49 H5
Lindridge WR15 29 F2
Lindsaig PA21 73 H3
Lindsell CM6 33 K6
Lindsey IP7 34 D4
Lindsey Tye IP7 34 D4
Linfitts OL3 49 J2
Linford, Hants. BH24 10 C4
Linford, Thur. SS17 24 C4
Linford Wood MK13 32 B4
Lingague IM9 54 B6
Lingards Wood HD7 50 C1
Lingdale TS12 63 H5
Lingen SY7 28 C2
Lingfield RH7 23 G7
Lingley Green WA5 48 E4
Lingwood NR13 45 H5
Linhead AB45 98 E5
Linhope TD9 69 K3
Linicro IV51 93 J5
Linkend GL19 29 H5
Linkenholt SP11 21 G6
Linkhill TN18 14 D5
Linkinhorne PL17 4 D3
Linklater KW17 107 D9
Linksness, Ork. KW16 107 B7
Linksness, Ork. KW17 107 E6
Linktown KY1 76 A1
Linley, Shrop. SY9 38 C6
Linley, Shrop. TF12 39 F6
Linley Green WR6 29 F3
Linlithgow EH49 75 J3
Linlithgow Bridge EH49 75 H3
Linn of Muick Cottage AB35 90 B6
Linnels NE46 70 E7
Linney SA71 16 B5
Linshiels NE65 70 D3
Linsiadar HS2 100 E4
Linsidemore IV27 96 C2
Linslade LU7 32 C6
Linstead Parva IP19 35 H1
Linstock CA6 60 F1
Linthwaite HD7 50 D1
Lintlaw TD11 77 G5
Lintmill AB56 98 D4
Linton, Cambs. CB1 33 J4
Linton, Derbys. DE12 40 E4
Linton, Here. HR9 29 F6
Linton, Kent ME17 14 C2
Linton, N.Yorks. BD23 56 E3
Linton, Sc.Bord. TD5 70 C1
Linton, W.Yorks. LS22 57 J5
Linton-on-Ouse YO30 57 K3
Lintzford NE39 62 C1
Linwood, Hants. BH24 10 C4
Linwood, Lincs. LN8 52 E4
Linwood, Renf. PA3 74 C4
Lionacleit (Linaclate) HS7 92 C7
Lional (Lionel) HS2 101 H1
Lionel (Lional) HS2 101 H1
Liphook GU30 12 B3
Lipley TF9 39 G2
Liscard CH45 48 C3
Liscombe TA22 7 G2
Liskeard PL14 4 C4
L'Islet GY2 3 J5
Lismore PA34 79 K4
Liss GU33 11 J2

Liss Forest GU33 11 J2
Lissett YO25 59 H4
Lissington LN3 52 E4
Liston CO10 34 C4
Lisvane CF14 18 E3
Liswerry NP19 19 G3
Litcham PE32 44 C4
Litchborough NN12 31 H3
Litchfield RG28 21 H6
Litherland L21 48 C3
Litlington, Cambs. SG8 33 G4
Litlington, E.Suss. BN26 13 J6
Little Abington CB1 33 J4
Little Addington NN14 32 C1
Little Alne B95 30 C2
Little Altcar L37 48 C2
Little Amwell SG13 33 G7
Little Ann SP11 21 G7
Little Asby CA16 61 H6
Little Assynt IV27 102 D6
Little Aston B74 40 C6
Little Atherfield PO38 11 F7
Little Ayton TS9 63 G5
Little Baddow CM3 24 D1
Little Badminton GL9 20 B3
Little Ballinluig PH15 82 A2
Little Bampton CA7 60 D1
Little Bardfield CM7 33 K5
Little Barford PE19 32 E3
Little Barningham NR11 45 F2
Little Barrington OX18 30 D7
Little Barrow CH3 48 D6
Little Barugh YO17 58 D2
Little Bavington NE19 70 E6
Little Bealings IP13 35 G4
Little Bedwyn SN8 21 F5
Little Beeby LE7 41 J5
Little Bentley CO7 35 F6
Little Berkhamsted SG13 23 F1
Little Billing NN3 32 B2
Little Birch HR2 28 E5
Little Bispham FY5 55 G5
Little Blakenham IP8 35 F4
Little Bloxwich WS3 40 C5
Little Bollington WA14 49 G4
Little Bookham KT23 22 E6
Little Bourton OX17 31 F4
Little Bowden LE16 42 A7
Little Bradley CB9 33 K3
Little Brampton SY7 38 C7
Little Braxted CM8 34 C7
Little Brechin DD9 83 G1
Little Brickhill MK17 32 C5
Little Bridgeford ST18 40 A3
Little Brington NN7 31 H2
Little Bromley CO11 34 E6
Little Broughton CA13 60 B3
Little Budworth CW6 48 E6
Little Burdon DL1 62 E5
Little Burstead CM12 24 C2
Little Burton YO25 59 H5
Little Bytham NG33 42 D4
Little Canford BH21 10 B5
Little Carlton, Lincs. LN11 53 G4
Little Carlton, Notts. NG23 51 K7
Little Casterton PE9 42 D4
Little Catwick HU17 59 H5
Little Catworth PE28 32 D1
Little Cawthorpe LN11 53 G4
Little Chalfield SN12 20 B5
Little Chalfont HP6 22 C2
Little Chart TN27 14 E3
Little Chesterford CB10 33 J4
Little Chesterton OX26 31 G6
Little Cheverell SN10 20 C6
Little Clacton CO16 35 F7
Little Clanfield OX18 21 F1
Little Clifton CA14 60 B4
Little Coates DN34 53 F2
Little Comberton WR10 29 J4
Little Common TN39 14 C7
Little Compton GL56 30 D5
Little Corby CA4 61 F1
Little Cornard CO10 34 C5
Little Cowarne HR7 29 F3
Little Coxwell SN7 21 F2
Little Crakehall DL8 62 D7
Little Cransley NN14 32 B1
Little Crawley MK16 32 C4
Little Creaton NN6 31 J1
Little Creich IV24 96 D3
Little Cressingham IP25 44 C6
Little Crosby L23 48 C2
Little Crosthwaite CA12 60 D4
Little Cubley DE6 40 D2
Little Dalby LE14 42 A4
Little Dens AB42 99 J6
Little Dewchurch HR2 28 E5
Little Ditton CB8 33 K3
Little Doward HR9 28 E7
Little Down SP11 21 G6
Little Downham CB6 43 J7
Little Drayton TF9 39 F2
Little Driffield YO25 59 G4
Little Dunham PE32 44 C4
Little Dunkeld PH8 82 B3
Little Dunmow CM6 33 K6
Little Durnford SP4 10 C1
Little Easton CM6 33 K6
Little Eaton DE21 41 F1
Little Eccleston PR3 55 H6
Little Ellingham NR17 44 E6
Little End CM5 23 J1
Little Everdon NN11 31 G3
Little Eversden CB3 33 G3
Little Fakenham IP24 34 D1
Little Faringdon GL7 21 F1
Little Fencote DL7 62 D7
Little Fenton LS25 58 B6
Little Finborough IP14 34 E3

Little Fransham NR19 44 D4
Little Gaddesden HP4 32 C7
Little Garway HR2 28 D6
Little Gidding PE28 42 E7
Little Glemham IP13 35 H3
Little Gleneshee PH1 82 A4
Little Gorsley HR9 29 F6
Little Gransden SG19 33 F3
Little Green, Cambs. SG8 33 F4
Little Green, Notts. NG13 42 A1
Little Green, Suff. IP23 34 E1
Little Green, Suff. IP22 34 E1
Little Green, Wrex. SY13 38 D1
Little Grimsby LN11 53 G3
Little Gringley DN22 51 K4
Little Gruinard IV22 95 F3
Little Habton YO17 58 D2
Little Hadham SG11 33 H6
Little Hale NG34 42 E1
Little Hallingbury CM22 33 H7
Little Hampden HP16 22 B1
Little Haresfield GL10 20 B1
Little Harrowden NN9 32 B1
Little Haseley OX44 21 K1
Little Hatfield HU11 59 H5
Little Hautbois NR12 45 G3
Little Haven, Pembs. SA62 16 B3
Little Haven, W.Suss. RH12 12 E3
Little Hay WS14 40 D5
Little Hayfield SK22 50 C4
Little Haywood ST18 40 C3
Little Heath CV6 41 F7
Little Hereford SY8 28 E2
Little Hockham IP24 44 D6
Little Horkesley CO6 34 D5
Little Hormead SG9 33 H6
Little Horsted TN22 13 H5
Little Horton SN10 20 D5
Little Horwood MK17 31 J5
Little Houghton NN7 32 B3
Little Hucklow SK17 50 D5
Little Hulton M38 49 G2
Little Hungerford RG18 21 J4
Little Hutton YO7 57 K2
Little Idoch AB53 99 F6
Little Irchester NN8 32 C2
Little Keyford BA11 20 A7
Little Kimble HP17 22 B1
Little Kineton CV35 30 E3
Little Kingshill HP16 22 B2
Little Langdale LA22 60 E6
Little Langford SP3 10 B1
Little Laver CM5 23 J1
Little Lawford CV23 31 F1
Little Leigh CW8 49 F5
Little Leighs CM3 34 B7
Little Lever BL3 49 G2
Little Ley AB51 90 E3
Little Linford MK19 32 B4
Little Linton CB1 33 J4
Little London, Bucks. HP18 31 H7
Little London, E.Suss. TN21 13 J5
Little London, Essex CM23 33 H6
Little London, Hants. SP11 21 G7
Little London, Hants. RG26 21 K6
Little London, I.o.M. IM6 54 C5
Little London, Lincs. PE28 43 H3
Little London, Lincs. PE11 43 F3
Little London, Lincs. LN9 53 G5
Little London, Lincs. LN6 52 E4
Little London, Norf. PE34 43 J3
Little London, Norf. IP26 44 B6
Little London, Oxon. OX14 21 J1
Little London, Powys SY17 37 K7
Little London, Suff. IP14 34 E1
Little London, W.Yorks. LS19 57 H6
Little Longstone DE45 50 D5
Little Lyth SY3 38 D5
Little Malvern WR14 29 G4
Little Maplestead CO9 34 C5
Little Marcle HR8 29 F5
Little Marland EX20 6 D4
Little Marlow SL7 22 B3
Little Marsden BB9 56 D6
Little Massingham PE32 44 B3
Little Melton NR9 45 F5
Little Milford SA62 16 C3
Little Milton OX44 21 K1
Little Missenden HP7 22 C2
Little Musgrave CA17 61 J5
Little Ness SY4 38 D4
Little Neston CH64 48 B5
Little Newcastle SA62 16 C2
Little Newsham DL2 62 C5
Little Oakley, Essex CO12 35 G6
Little Oakley, Northants. NN18 42 B7
Little Odell MK43 32 C3
Little Offley SG5 32 E6
Little Onn ST20 40 A4
Little Orton, Cumb. CA5 60 E1
Little Orton, Leics. CV9 41 F5
Little Ouse CB7 44 A7
Little Ouseburn YO26 57 K3
Little Overton LL13 38 C1
Little Packington CV7 40 E7
Little Parndon CM20 33 H7
Little Paxton PE19 32 E2
Little Petherick PL27 3 G1
Little Plumpton PR4 55 G6
Little Plumstead NR13 45 H4

Little Ponton NG33 42 C2
Little Posbrook PO14 11 G4
Little Potheridge EX20 6 D4
Little Preston NN11 31 G3
Little Raveley PE28 43 F7
Little Ribston LS22 57 J4
Little Rissington GL54 30 C7
Little Rogart IV28 96 E1
Little Rollright OX7 30 D5
Little Ryburgh NR21 44 D3
Little Ryle NE66 71 F2
Little Ryton SY5 38 D5
Little Salkeld CA10 61 G3
Little Sampford CB10 33 K5
Little Saxham IP29 34 C2
Little Scatwell IV14 95 K6
Little Shelford CB2 33 H3
Little Shrawardine SY5 38 C4
Little Silver EX16 7 H5
Little Singleton FY6 55 G6
Little Smeaton, N.Yorks. WF8 51 H1
Little Smeaton, N.Yorks. DL6 62 E6
Little Snoring NR21 44 D2
Little Sodbury BS37 20 A3
Little Sodbury End BS37 20 A3
Little Somborne SO20 10 E1
Little Somerford SN15 20 C3
Little Soudley TF9 39 G3
Little Stainforth BD24 56 D3
Little Stainton TS21 62 E5
Little Stanney CH2 48 D5
Little Staughton MK44 32 E2
Little Steeping PE23 53 H6
Little Stoke ST15 40 B2
Little Stonham IP14 35 F3
Little Street CB6 43 J7
Little Stretton, Leics. LE2 41 J6
Little Stretton, Shrop. SY6 38 D6
Little Strickland CA10 61 G5
Little Stukeley PE28 33 F1
Little Sugnall ST21 40 A2
Little Sutton CH66 48 C5
Little Swinburne NE48 70 E6
Little Tarrington HR1 29 F4
Little Tew OX7 30 E6
Little Tey CO6 34 C6
Little Thetford CB6 33 J1
Little Thornage NR25 44 E2
Little Thornton FY5 55 G5
Little Thorpe SR8 63 F2
Little Thurlow CB9 33 K3
Little Thurlow Green CB9 33 K3
Little Thurrock RM17 24 C4
Little Torboll IV25 96 E2
Little Torrington EX38 6 C4
Little Tosson NE65 71 F3
Little Totham CM9 34 C7
Little Town, Cumb. CA12 60 D5
Little Town, Lancs. PR3 56 B6
Little Town, Warr. WA3 49 F3
Little Twycross CV9 41 F5
Little Urswick LA12 55 F2
Little Wakering SS3 25 F3
Little Walden CB10 33 J4
Little Waldingfield CO10 34 D4
Little Walsingham NR22 44 D2
Little Waltham CM3 34 B7
Little Warley CM13 24 C2
Little Washbourne GL20 29 J5
Little Weighton HU20 59 F6
Little Welland WR13 29 H5
Little Welnetham IP30 34 C2
Little Wenham CO7 34 E5
Little Wenlock TF6 39 F5
Little Whittington NE19 70 E7
Little Wilbraham CB1 33 J3
Little Wishford SP3 10 B1
Little Witcombe GL3 29 J7
Little Witley WR6 29 G2
Little Wittenham OX14 21 J2
Little Wittingham Green IP21 35 G1
Little Wolford CV36 30 D5
Little Woodcote SM5 23 F5
Little Wratting CB9 33 K4
Little Wymington NN10 32 C2
Little Wymondley SG4 33 F6
Little Wyrley WS3 40 C5
Little Wytheford SY4 38 E4
Little Yeldham CO9 34 B5
Littlebeck YO22 63 K6
Littleborough, Devon EX16 7 G4
Littleborough, Gt.Man. OL15 49 J1
Littleborough, Notts. DN22 52 B4
Littlebourne CT3 15 H2
Littlebredy DT2 8 E6
Littlebury CB11 33 J5
Littlebury Green CB11 33 H5
Littledean GL14 29 F7
Littleferry KW10 97 F2
Littleham, Devon EX39 6 C3
Littleham, Devon EX8 7 J7
Littlehampton BN17 12 D6
Littlehempston TQ9 5 J4
Littlehoughton NE66 71 H2
Littlemill, E.Ayr. KA6 67 J2
Littlemill, High. IV12 97 G3
Littlemoor, Derbys. S45 51 F6
Littlemoor, Dorset DT3 9 F6
Littlemore OX4 21 J1
Littlemoss M43 49 J3
Littleover DE23 41 F2
Littleport GU6 22 A4
Littlestead Green RG4 22 A4
Littlestone-on-Sea TN28 15 F5
Littlethorpe HG4 57 J3

Littleton

Littleton, Ches. CH3 48 D6
Littleton, Hants. SO22 11 F1
Littleton, P. & K. PH14 82 D4
Littleton, Som. TA11 8 D1
Littleton, Surr. TW17 22 D5
Littleton Drew SN14 20 B3
Littleton Panell SN10 20 D6
Littleton-on-Severn BS35 19 J2
Littletown, Dur. DH6 62 E2
Littletown, I.o.W. PO33 11 G5
Littlewick Green SL6 22 B4
Littlewindsor DT8 8 D4
Littleworth, Glos. GL55 30 C5
Littleworth, Oxon. SN7 21 G2
Littleworth, S.Yorks. DN11 51 J3
Littleworth, Staffs. WS12 40 C4
Littleworth, Worcs. WR5 29 H4
Littley Green CM3 33 K7
Litton, Derbys. SK17 50 D5
Litton, N.Yorks. BD23 56 E2
Litton, Som. BA3 19 J6
Litton Cheney DT2 8 E5
Liurbost (Leurbost) HS2 101 F5
LIVERPOOL L 48 C3
Liverpool John Lennon Airport L24 48 D4
Liversedge WF15 57 H7
Liverton, Devon TQ12 5 J3
Liverton, R. & C. TS13 63 J5
Liverton Street ME17 14 D3
Livingston EH54 75 J4
Livingston Village EH54 75 J4
Lixwm CH8 47 K5
Lizard TR12 2 E7
Llaingarreglwyd SA47 26 D3
Llaingoch LL65 46 A4
Llaithddu LD1 37 K7
Llampha CF35 18 C4
Llan SY19 37 H5
Llan Ffestiniog (Ffestiniog) LL41 37 G1
Llanaber LL42 37 F4
Llanaelhaearn LL54 36 C1
Llanaeron SA48 26 D2
Llanafan SY23 27 F1
Llanafan-fawr LD2 27 J3
Llanafan-fechan LD4 27 J3
Llanallgo LL72 46 D4
Llanarmon LL53 36 D2
Llanarmon Dyffryn Ceiriog LL20 38 A2
Llanarmon-yn-Ial CH7 47 K7
Llanarth, Cere. SA47 26 D3
Llanarth, Mon. NP15 28 C7
Llanarthney SA32 17 J2
Llanasa CH8 47 K4
Llanbabo LL68 46 B4
Llanbadarn Fawr SY23 36 E7
Llanbadarn Fynydd LD1 27 K1
Llanbadarn-y-garreg LD2 28 A4
Llanbadoc NP15 19 G1
Llanbadrig LL67 46 B3
Llanbeder NP18 19 G2
Llanbedr, Gwyn. LL45 36 E3
Llanbedr, Powys NP8 28 B6
Llanbedr, Powys LD2 28 A4
Llanbedr-Dyffryn-Clwyd LL15 47 K7
Llanbedrgoch LL76 46 D4
Llanbedrog LL53 36 C2
Llanbedr-y-cennin LL32 47 F6
Llanberis LL55 46 D7
Llanbethery CF62 18 D5
Llanbister LD1 28 A1
Llanblethian CF71 18 C4
Llanboidy SA34 17 F2
Llanbradach CF83 18 E2
Llanbryn-mair SY19 37 H5
Llancadle CF62 18 D5
Llancarfan CF62 18 D4
Llancayo NP15 19 G1
Llancynfelyn SY20 37 F6
Llandafal NP13 18 E1
Llandaff CF5 18 E4
Llandaff North CF14 18 E4
Llandanwg LL45 36 E3
Llandawke SA33 17 F3
Llanddaniel Fab LL60 46 C5
Llanddarog SA32 17 H3
Llanddeiniol SY23 26 E1
Llanddeiniolen LL55 46 D6
Llandderfel LL23 37 J2
Llanddeusant, Carmar. SA19 27 G6
Llanddeusant, I.o.A. LL65 46 B4
Llanddew LD3 27 K5
Llanddewi SA3 17 H6
Llanddewi Rhydderch NP7 28 C7
Llanddewi Skirrid NP7 28 C7
Llanddewi Velfrey SA67 16 E3
Llanddewi Ystradenni LD1 28 A2
Llanddewi-Brefi SY25 27 F3
Llanddewi'r Cwm LD2 27 K4
Llanddoged LL26 47 G6
Llanddona LL58 46 D5
Llanddowror SA33 17 F3
Llanddulas LL22 47 H5
Llanddwywe LL44 36 E3
Llanddyfnan LL78 46 D5
Llandefaelog Fach LD3 27 K5
Llandefaelog-tre'r-graig LD3 28 A6
Llandefalle LD3 28 A5
Llandegfan LL59 46 D5
Llandegla LL11 47 K7
Llandegley LD1 28 A2
Llandegveth NP18 19 G2
Llandegwning LL53 36 B2
Llandeilo SA19 17 K2
Llandeilo Abercywyn SA33 17 G3
Llandeilo Graban LD2 27 K4
Llandeilo'r-Fan LD3 27 H5
Llandeloy SA62 16 B2
Llandenny NP15 19 H1
Llandevaud NP18 19 H2
Llandevenny NP26 19 H3
Llandinabo HR2 28 E6
Llandinam SY17 37 K7
Llandissilio SA66 16 E2
Llandogo NP25 19 J1
Llandough, V. of Glam. CF11 18 E4
Llandough, V. of Glam. CF71 18 C4
Llandovery (Llanymddyfri) SA20 27 G5
Llandow CF71 18 C4
Llandre, Carmar. SA19 27 F4
Llandre, Carmar. SA34 16 E2
Llandre, Cere. SY24 37 F7
Llandrillo LL21 37 K2
LLANDRINDOD WELLS LD 27 K2
Llandrinio SY22 38 B4
LLANDUDNO LL 47 F4
Llandudno Junction LL31 47 F5
Llandudoch (St. Dogmaels) SA43 26 A4
Llandwrog LL54 46 C7
Llandybie SA18 17 K3
Llandyfaelog SA17 17 H3
Llandyfan SA18 17 K3
Llandyfriog SA38 26 C4
Llandyfrydog LL71 46 C4
Llandygai LL57 46 D5
Llandygwydd SA43 26 B4
Llandyrnog LL16 47 K6
Llandyry SA17 17 H4
Llandysilio SY22 38 B4
Llandyssil SY15 38 A6
Llandysul SA44 26 D4
Llanedeyrn CF3 19 F3
Llanedy SA4 17 J4
Llaneglwys LD2 27 K5
Llanegryn LL36 37 F5
Llanegwad SA32 17 J2
Llaneilian LL68 46 C3
Llanelian-yn-Rhos LL29 47 G5
Llanelidan LL15 47 K7
Llanelieu LD3 28 A5
Llanellen NP7 28 C7
Llanelli SA15 17 J4
Llanelltyd LL40 37 G4
Llanelly NP7 28 B7
Llanelly Hill NP7 28 B7
Llanelwedd LD2 27 K3
Llanelwy (St. Asaph) LL17 47 J5
Llanenddwyn LL44 36 E3
Llanengan LL53 36 B3
Llanerfyl SY21 37 K5
Llaneuddog LL70 46 C4
Llanfachraeth LL65 46 B4
Llanfachreth LL40 37 G3
Llanfaelog LL63 46 B5
Llanfaelrhys LL53 36 B3
Llanfaenor NP25 28 D7
Llan-faes, I.o.A. LL58 46 E5
Llanfaes, Powys LD3 27 K6
Llanfaethlu LL65 46 B4
Llanfaglan LL54 46 C6
Llanfair LL46 36 E3
Llanfair Caereinion SY21 38 A5
Llanfair Clydogau SA48 27 F3
Llanfair Dyffryn Clwyd LL15 47 K7
Llanfair Talhaiarn LL22 47 H5
Llanfair Waterdine LD7 28 B1
Llanfairfechan LL33 46 E5
Llanfair-Nant-Gwyn SA37 16 E1
Llanfair-Orllwyn SA44 26 C4
Llanfairpwllgwyngyll LL61 46 D5
Llanfairynghornwy LL65 46 B3
Llanfair-yn-neubwll LL65 46 B5
Llanfallteg SA34 16 E3
Llanfaredd LD2 27 K3
Llanfarian SY23 26 E1
Llanfechain SY22 38 A3
Llanfechell LL68 46 B3
Llanfendigaid LL36 36 E5
Llanferres CH7 47 K6
Llanfflewyn LL68 46 B4
Llanfigael LL65 46 B4
Llanfihangel Crucornau (Llanvihangel Crucorney) NP7 28 C6
Llanfihangel Glyn Myfyr LL21 37 J1
Llanfihangel Nant Bran LD3 27 J5
Llanfihangel Rhydithon LD1 28 A2
Llanfihangel Rogiet NP26 19 H3
Llanfihangel Tal-y-llyn LD3 28 A6
Llanfihangel-ar-arth SA39 26 D4
Llanfihangel-nant-Melan LD8 28 A3
Llanfihangel-uwch-Gwili SA32 17 H2
Llanfihangel-y-Creuddyn SY23 27 F1
Llanfihangel-yng-Ngwynfa SY22 37 K4
Llanfihangel-yn-Nhywyn LL65 46 B5
Llanfihangel-y-pennant, Gwyn. LL51 36 E1
Llanfihangel-y-pennant, Gwyn. LL36 37 F5
Llanfilo LD3 28 A5
Llanfoist NP7 28 B7
Llanfor LL23 37 J2
Llanfrechfa NP44 19 G2
Llanfrothen LL48 37 F1
Llanfrynach LD3 27 K6
Llanfwrog, Denb. LL15 47 K7
Llanfwrog, I.o.A. LL65 46 A4
Llanfyllin SY22 38 A4
Llanfynydd, Carmar. SA32 17 J2
Llanfynydd, Flints. LL11 48 B7
Llanfyrnach SA35 17 F1
Llangadfan SY21 37 K4
Llangadog SA19 27 G6
Llangadwaladr, I.o.A. LL62 46 B6
Llangadwaladr, Powys SY10 38 A2
Llangaffo LL60 46 C6
Llangain SA33 17 G3
Llangammarch Wells LD4 27 J4
Llangan CF35 18 C4
Llangarron HR9 28 E6
Llangasty-Talyllyn LD3 28 A6
Llangathen SA32 17 J2
Llangattock NP8 28 B7
Llangattock Lingoed NP7 28 C7
Llangattock-Vibon-Avel NP25 28 D7
Llangedwyn SY10 38 A3
Llangefni LL77 46 C5
Llangeinor CF32 18 C3
Llangeitho SY25 27 F3
Llangeler SA44 17 G1
Llangelynin LL36 36 E5
Llangendeirne SA17 17 H3
Llangennech SA14 17 J4
Llangennith SA3 17 H5
Llangenny NP8 28 B7
Llangernyw LL22 47 G6
Llangian LL53 36 B3
Llangiwg SA8 18 A1
Llangloffan SA62 16 C1
Llanglydwen SA34 16 E2
Llangoed LL58 46 E5
Llangoedmor SA43 26 A4
Llangollen LL20 38 B1
Llangolman SA66 16 E2
Llangorse LD3 28 A6
Llangorwen SY23 37 F7
Llangovan NP25 19 H1
Llangower LL23 37 J2
Llangrannog SA44 26 C3
Llangristiolus LL62 46 C5
Llangrove HR9 28 E7
Llangua NP7 28 C6
Llangunllo LD7 28 B1
Llangunnor SA31 17 H2
Llangurig SY18 27 J1
Llangwm, Conwy LL21 37 J1
Llangwm, Mon. NP15 19 H1
Llangwm, Pembs. SA62 16 C4
Llangwnnadl LL53 36 B2
Llangwyfan LL16 47 K6
Llangwyllog LL77 46 C5
Llangwyryfon SY23 27 F1
Llangybi, Cere. SA48 27 F3
Llangybi, Gwyn. LL53 36 D1
Llangybi, Mon. NP15 19 G2
Llangyfelach SA5 17 K5
Llangynhafal LL16 47 K6
Llangynidr NP8 28 A7
Llangyniew SY21 38 A5
Llangynin SA33 17 F3
Llangynllo SA44 26 C4
Llangynog, Carmar. SA33 17 G3
Llangynog, Powys SY10 37 K3
Llangynwyd CF34 18 B3
Llanhamlach LD3 27 K6
Llanharan CF72 18 D3
Llanharry CF72 18 D3
Llanhennock NP18 19 G2
Llanhilleth NP13 19 F1
Llanidloes SY18 37 J7
Llaniestyn LL53 36 B2
Llanigon HR3 28 B5
Llanilar SY23 27 F1
Llanilid CF35 18 C3
Llanishen, Cardiff CF14 18 E3
Llanishen, Mon. NP16 19 H1
Llanllawddog SA32 17 H2
Llanllechid LL57 46 E6
Llanlleonfel LD4 27 J3
Llanllugan SY21 37 K5
Llanllwch SA31 17 G3
Llanllwchaiarn SY16 38 A6
Llanllwni SA39 26 D4
Llanllyfni LL54 46 C7
Llanllywel NP15 19 G2
Llanmadoc SA3 17 H5
Llanmaes CF61 18 C5
Llanmartin NP18 19 G3
Llanmerewig SY15 38 A6
Llanmihangel CF71 18 C4
Llan-mill SA67 16 E3
Llanmiloe SA33 17 F4
Llanmorlais SA4 17 J5
Llannefydd LL16 47 H5
Llannerch Hall LL17 47 J5
Llannerch-y-medd LL71 46 C4
Llannerch-y-Môr CH8 47 K5
Llannon, Carmar. SA14 17 J4
Llan-non, Cere. SY23 26 E2
Llannor LL53 36 C2
Llanover NP7 19 G1
Llanpumsaint SA33 17 H2
Llanreithan SA62 16 B2
Llanrhaeadr LL16 47 J6
Llanrhaeadr-ym-Mochnant SY10 38 A3
Llanrhian SA62 16 B1
Llanrhidian SA3 17 H5
Llanrhyddlad LL65 46 B4
Llanrhystud SY23 26 E2
Llanrothal NP25 28 D7
Llanrug LL55 46 D6
Llanrumney CF3 19 F3
Llanrwst LL26 47 F6
Llansadurnen SA33 17 F3
Llansadwrn, Carmar. SA19 17 K1
Llansadwrn, I.o.A. LL59 46 D5
Llansaint SA17 17 G4
Llansamlet SA7 17 K5
Llansanffraid SY23 26 E2
Llansanffraid Glan Conwy LL28 47 G5
Llansannan LL16 47 H6
Llansannor CF71 18 C4
Llansantffraed LD3 28 A6
Llansantffraed-Cwmdeuddwr LD6 27 J2
Llansantffraed-in-Elwel LD1 27 K3
Llansantffraid-ym-Mechain SY22 38 B3
Llansawel, Carmar. SA19 17 K1
Llansawel (Briton Ferry), N.P.T. SA11 18 A2
Llansilin SY10 38 B3
Llansoy NP15 19 H1
Llanspyddid LD3 27 K6
Llanstadwell SA73 16 C4
Llansteffan SA33 17 G3
Llanstephan LD3 28 A4
Llantarnam NP44 19 G2
Llanteg SA67 16 E3
Llanthony NP7 28 B6
Llantilio Crossenny NP7 28 C7
Llantilio Pertholey NP7 28 C7
Llantood SA43 26 A4
Llantrisant, I.o.A. LL65 46 B4
Llantrisant, Mon. NP15 19 G2
Llantrisant, R.C.T. CF72 18 D3
Llantrithyd CF71 18 D4
Llantwit Fardre CF38 18 D3
Llantwit Major CF61 18 C5
Llantysilio LL20 38 A1
Llanuwchllyn LL23 37 H3
Llanvaches NP26 19 H2
Llanvair-Discoed NP16 19 H2
Llanvapley NP7 28 C7
Llanvetherine NP7 28 C7
Llanveynoe HR2 28 C5
Llanvihangel Crucorney (Llanfihangel Crucornau) NP7 28 C6
Llanvihangel Gobion NP7 19 G1
Llanvihangel-Ystern-Llewern NP25 28 D7
Llanvithyn CF62 18 D4
Llanwarne HR2 28 E6
Llanwddyn SY10 37 K4
Llanwenog SA40 26 D4
Llanwern NP18 19 G3
Llanwinio SA34 17 F2
Llanwnda, Gwyn. LL54 46 C7
Llanwnda, Pembs. SA64 16 C1
Llanwnen SA48 26 E4
Llanwnog SY17 37 K6
Llanwonno CF37 18 D2
Llanwrda SA19 27 G5
Llanwrin SY20 37 G5
Llanwrthwl LD1 27 J2
Llanwrtyd LD5 27 H4
Llanwrtyd Wells LD5 27 H4
Llanwyddelan SY16 37 K5
Llanyblodwel SY10 38 B3
Llanybri SA33 17 G3
Llanybydder SA40 26 E4
Llanycefn SA66 16 E2
Llanychaer Bridge SA65 16 C1
Llanycil LL23 37 J2
Llanycrwys SA19 27 F4
Llanymawddwy SY20 37 H4
Llanymddyfri (Llandovery) SA20 27 G5
Llanymynech SY22 38 B3
Llanynghenedl LL65 46 B4
Llanynys LL16 47 K6
Llan-y-pwll LL13 48 C7
Llanyre LD1 27 K2
Llanystumdwy LL52 36 D2
Llanywern LD3 28 A6
Llawhaden SA67 16 D3
Llawndy CH8 47 K4
Llawnt SY10 38 B2
Llawr-y-dref LL53 36 B3
Llawryglyn SY17 37 J6
Llay LL12 48 C7
Llechcynfarwy LL71 46 B4
Llecheiddior LL51 36 D1
Llechfaen LD3 27 K6
Llechryd, Caerp. NP22 18 E1
Llechryd, Cere. SA43 26 B4
Llechrydau SY10 38 B2
Lledrod, Cere. SY23 27 F1
Lledrod, Powys SY10 38 B3
Llethrid SA2 17 J5
Llidiad-Nenog SA32 17 J1
Llidiardau LL23 37 H2
Llithfaen LL53 36 C1
Lloc CH8 47 K5
Llong CH7 48 B6
Llowes HR3 28 A4
Lloyney LD7 28 B1
Llundain-fach SA48 26 E3
Llwydcoed CF44 18 C1
Llwydiarth SY21 37 K4
Llwyn, M.Tyd. CF48 27 K7
Llwyn, Shrop. SY7 38 B7
Llwyncelyn SA46 26 D3
Llwyn-croes SA33 17 H2
Llwyndafydd SA44 26 C3
Llwynderw SY21 38 B5
Llwyndyrys LL53 36 C1
Llwyneinion LL14 38 B1
Llwyngwril LL37 36 E5
Llwynhendy SA14 17 J5
Llwyn-Madoc LD5 27 J3
Llwynmawr LL20 38 B2
Llwyn-onn SA45 26 D3
Llwyn-y-brain, Carmar. SA34 16 E3
Llwyn-y-brain, Carmar. SA20 27 G5
Llwyn-y-groes SY25 26 E3
Llwynypia CF40 18 C2
Llynclys SY10 38 B3
Llynfaes LL65 46 C5
Llysfaen LL29 47 G5
Llyswen LD3 28 A5
Llysworney CF71 18 C4
Llys-y-frân SA63 16 D2
Llywel LD3 27 H5
Load Brook S6 50 E4
Loandhu IV20 97 F4
Loanhead, Aber. AB41 91 H1
Loanhead, Midloth. EH20 76 A4
Loans KA10 74 B7
Lobb EX33 6 C2
Lobhillcross EX20 6 C7
Loch a Charnain HS8 92 D7
Loch Baghasdail (Lochboisdale) HS8 84 C3
Loch Choire Lodge KW11 103 J5
Loch Eil Outward Bound PH33 87 G7
Loch Head, D. & G. DG8 64 D6
Loch Head, D. & G. KA6 67 J4
Loch na Madadh (Lochmaddy) HS6 92 E5
Loch Sgioport HS8 84 D1
Lochailort PH38 86 D6
Lochaline PA34 79 H3
Lochans DG9 64 A5
Locharbriggs DG1 68 E5
Lochawe PA33 80 C5
Lochboisdale (Loch Baghasdail) HS8 84 C3
Lochbuie PA62 79 H5
Lochcarron IV54 94 E7
Lochdhu Hotel KW12 105 F4
Lochdon PA64 79 J4
Lochdrum IV23 95 J4
Lochearnhead FK19 81 G5
Lochee DD2 82 E4
Lochend, High. KW14 105 H2
Lochend, High. IV3 88 C1
Locheport (Locheuphort) HS6 92 D5
Locheuphort (Locheport) HS6 92 D5
Lochfoot DG2 65 K3
Lochgair PA31 73 H1
Lochgarthside IV2 88 C3
Lochgelly KY5 75 K1
Lochgilphead PA31 73 G2
Lochgoilhead PA24 80 D7
Lochgoyn KA3 74 D6
Lochhill, E.Ayr. KA18 67 K2
Lochhill, Moray IV30 97 K5
Lochinch Castle DG9 64 B4
Lochinver IV27 102 C6
Lochlair DD8 83 G3
Lochlane PH7 81 K5
Lochlea KA1 74 C7
Lochluichart IV23 95 K5
Lochmaben DG11 69 F5
Lochmaddy (Loch na Madadh) HS6 92 E5
Lochore KY5 75 K1
Lochportain HS6 92 E4
Lochranza KA27 73 H5
Lochside, Aber. DD10 83 J1
Lochside, High. IV27 103 G3
Lochside, High. KW11 104 D5
Lochside, High. KW14 105 H2
Lochslin IV20 97 F3
Lochton KA26 67 G5
Lochty KY10 83 G7
Lochuisge PH33 79 J2
Lochurr DG3 68 C5
Lochussie IV7 96 B6
Lochwinnoch PA12 74 B5
Lockengate PL26 4 A4
Lockerbie DG11 69 G5
Lockeridge SN8 20 E5
Lockerley SO51 10 D2
Lockhills CA4 61 G2
Locking BS24 19 G6
Lockington, E.Riding YO25 59 F5
Lockington, Leics. DE74 41 G3
Lockleywood TF9 39 F3
Locks Heath SO31 11 G4
Lockshottom BR6 23 H5
Locksgreen PO30 11 F5
Lockton YO18 58 E1
Loddington, Leics. LE7 42 A5
Loddington, Northants. NN14 32 B1
Loddiswell TQ7 5 H6
Loddon NR14 45 H6
Lode CB5 33 J2
Loders DT6 8 D5
Lodsworth GU28 12 C4
Lofthouse, N.Yorks. HG3 57 G2

Lofthouse, W.Yorks. WF3 57 J7
Loftus TS13 63 J5
Logan, D. & G. DG9 64 A6
Logan, E.Ayr. KA18 67 K1
Loganlea EH55 75 H4
Loggerheads TF9 39 G2
Loggie IV23 95 H2
Logie, Angus DD10 83 H1
Logie, Angus DD8 82 E2
Logie, Fife KY15 83 F5
Logie, Moray IV36 97 H6
Logie Coldstone AB34 90 C4
Logie Hill IV18 96 E4
Logie Newton AB54 90 E1
Logie Pert DD10 83 H1
Logierait PH9 82 A2
Login SA34 16 E2
Lolworth CB3 33 G2
Lonbain IV54 94 C6
Londesborough YO43 58 E5
LONDON E, EC, N, NW, SE, SW, W, WC 23 G3
London Apprentice PL26 4 A6
London Beach TN30 14 D4
London City Airport E16 23 H3
London Colney AL2 22 E1
London Gatwick Airport (Gatwick Airport) RH6 23 F7
London Heathrow Airport TW6 22 D4
London Luton Airport (Luton Airport) LU2 32 E6
London Minstead SO43 10 D3
London Stansted Airport (Stansted Airport) CM24 33 J6
Londonderry DL7 57 H1
Londonthorpe NG31 42 C2
Londubh IV22 94 E3
Lonemore IV25 96 E3
Long Ashton BS41 19 J4
Long Bank DY12 29 G1
Long Bennington NG23 42 B1
Long Bredy DT2 8 E5
Long Buckby NN6 31 H2
Long Clawson LE14 42 A3
Long Common SO32 11 G3
Long Compton, Staffs. ST18 40 A3
Long Compton, Warks. CV36 30 D5
Long Crendon HP18 21 K1
Long Crichel BH21 9 J3
Long Dean SN14 20 B4
Long Downs TR10 2 E5
Long Drax YO8 58 C7
Long Duckmanton S44 51 G5
Long Eaton NG10 41 G2
Long Gill BD23 56 C4
Long Green, Ches. CH3 48 D5
Long Green, Essex CO6 34 C6
Long Green, Worcs. GL19 29 H5
Long Hanborough OX29 31 F7
Long Itchington CV47 31 F2
Long Lane TF6 39 F4
Long Lawford CV23 31 F1
Long Load TA10 8 D2
Long Marston, Herts. HP23 32 B7
Long Marston, N.Yorks. YO26 58 B4
Long Marston, Warks. CV37 30 C4
Long Marton CA16 61 H4
Long Meadowend SY7 38 D7
Long Melford CO10 34 C4
Long Newton GL8 20 C2
Long Preston BD23 56 D4
Long Riston HU11 59 H5
Long Stratton NR15 45 F6
Long Street MK19 31 J4
Long Sutton, Hants. RG29 22 A7
Long Sutton, Lincs. PE12 43 H3
Long Sutton, Som. TA10 8 D2
Long Thurlow IP31 34 E2
Long Whatton LE12 41 G3
Long Wittenham OX14 21 J2
Longbenton NE7 71 H7
Longborough GL56 30 C6
Longbridge, Plym. PL6 5 F5
Longbridge, W.Mid. B31 30 B1
Longbridge, Warks. CV34 30 D2
Longbridge Deverill BA12 20 B7
Longburgh CA5 60 E1
Longburton DT9 9 F3
Longcliffe DE4 50 E7
Longcombe TQ9 5 J5
Longcot SN7 21 F2
Longcroft FK4 75 F3
Longcross, Devon PL19 4 E3
Longcross, Surr. KT16 22 C5
Longden SY5 38 D5
Longdon, Staffs. WS15 40 C4
Longdon, Worcs. GL20 29 H5
Longdon Green WS15 40 C4
Longdon upon Tern TF6 39 F4
Longdown EX6 7 G6
Longdrum AB23 91 H3
Longfield DA3 24 C5
Longfield Hill DA3 24 C5
Longfleet BH15 10 B5
Longford, Derbys. DE6 40 E2
Longford, Glos. GL2 29 H6
Longford, Gt.Lon. UB7 22 D4
Longford, Shrop. TF9 39 F2
Longford, Tel. & W. TF10 39 G4
Longford, W.Mid. CV6 41 F7
Longforgan DD2 82 E5
Longformacus TD11 76 E5
Longframlington NE65 71 G3
Longham, Dorset BH22 10 B5
Longham, Norf. NR19 44 D4

Longhill AB42 99 H5
Longhirst NE61 71 H5
Longhope, Glos. GL17 29 F7
Longhope, Ork. KW16 107 C8
Longhorsley NE65 71 G4
Longhoughton NE66 71 H2
Longlands, Aber. AB54 90 C2
Longlands, Cumb. CA7 60 D3
Longlane, Derbys. DE6 40 E2
Longlane, W.Berks. RG18 21 H4
Longlevens GL2 29 H7
Longley HD9 50 D2
Longley Green WR6 29 G3
Longmanhill AB45 99 F4
Longmoor Camp GU33 11 J1
Longmorn IV30 97 K6
Longnewton, Sc.Bord. TD6 70 A1
Longnewton, Stock. TS21 62 E5
Longney GL2 29 G7
Longniddry EH32 76 C3
Longnor, Shrop. SY5 38 D5
Longnor, Staffs. SK17 50 C6
Longparish SP11 21 H7
Longridge, Lancs. PR3 56 B6
Longridge, Staffs. ST18 40 B4
Longridge, W.Loth. EH47 75 H4
Longridge End GL19 29 H6
Longridge Towers TD15 77 H5
Longriggend ML6 75 G3
Longrock TR20 2 C5
Longsdon ST9 49 J7
Longshaw WN5 48 E2
Longside AB42 99 J6
Longslow TF9 39 F2
Longsowerby CA2 60 E1
Longstanton CB4 33 H2
Longstock SO20 10 E1
Longstone TR26 2 C5
Longstowe CB3 33 G3
Longstreet SN9 20 E6
Longthorpe PE3 42 E6
Longton, Lancs. PR4 55 H7
Longton, Stoke ST3 40 B1
Longtown, Cumb. CA6 69 J7
Longtown, Here. HR2 28 C6
Longville in the Dale TF13 38 E6
Longwell Green BS30 19 K4
Longwick HP27 22 A1
Longwitton NE61 71 F5
Longworth OX13 21 G2
Longyester EH41 76 D4
Lonmay AB43 99 J5
Lonmore IV55 93 H7
Looe PL13 4 C5
Loose ME15 14 C2
Loosebeare EX17 7 F5
Loosegate PE12 43 G3
Loosley Row HP27 22 B1
Lopcombe Corner SP5 10 D1
Lopen TA13 8 D3
Loppington SY4 38 D3
Lorbottle NE65 71 F3
Lorbottle Hall NE66 71 F3
Lordington PO18 11 J4
Lord's Hill SO16 10 E3
Lorgill IV55 93 G7
Lorn G83 74 B2
Lornty PH10 82 C3
Loscoe DE75 41 G1
Loscombe DT6 8 D5
Losgaintir HS3 93 F2
Lossiemouth IV31 97 K4
Lossit PA47 72 A5
Lostock Gralam CW9 49 F5
Lostock Green CW9 49 F5
Lostock Junction BL6 49 F2
Lostwithiel PL22 4 B5
Loth KW17 106 F4
Lothbeg KW8 104 E7
Lothersdale BD20 56 E5
Lothmore KW8 104 E7
Loudwater HP10 22 C2
Loughborough LE11 41 H4
Loughor SA4 17 J5
Loughton, Essex IG10 23 H2
Loughton, M.K. MK5 32 B5
Loughton, Shrop. WV16 39 F7
Lound, Lincs. PE10 42 D4
Lound, Notts. DN22 51 J4
Lound, Suff. NR32 45 K6
Lount LE65 41 F4
Lour DD8 83 F3
Louth LN11 53 G4
Love Clough BB4 56 D7
Lovedean PO8 11 H3
Lover SP5 10 D3
Loversall DN11 51 H3
Loves Green CM1 24 C1
Lovesome Hill DL6 62 E7
Loveston SA68 16 D4
Lovington BA7 8 E1
Low Ackworth WF7 51 G1
Low Angerton NE61 71 F5
Low Ballevain PA28 66 A1
Low Barlay DG7 65 F5
Low Barlings LN3 52 D5
Low Bentham LA2 56 B3
Low Bolton DL8 62 B7
Low Bradfield S6 50 E3
Low Bradley (Bradley) BD20 57 F5
Low Braithwaite CA4 60 F2
Low Brunton NE46 70 E6
Low Burnham DN9 51 K2
Low Burton HG4 57 H1
Low Buston NE65 71 H3
Low Catton YO41 58 D4
Low Coniscliffe DL2 62 D5

Low Craighead KA26 67 G3
Low Dinsdale DL2 62 E5
Low Ellington HG4 57 H1
Low Entercommon DL6 62 E6
Low Etherley DL14 62 C4
Low Fell NE11 62 D1
Low Gate NE46 70 E7
Low Grantley HG4 57 H1
Low Green IP29 34 C2
Low Habberley DY11 29 H1
Low Ham TA10 8 D2
Low Hawsker YO22 63 J2
Low Haygarth LA10 61 H7
Low Hesket CA4 61 F2
Low Hesleyhurst NE65 71 F4
Low Hutton YO60 58 D3
Low Kingthorpe YO18 58 E1
Low Laithe HG3 57 G3
Low Langton LN8 52 E5
Low Leighton SK22 50 C4
Low Lorton CA13 60 C4
Low Marishes YO17 58 E2
Low Marnham NG23 52 B6
Low Middleton NE70 77 K7
Low Mill YO62 63 H7
Low Moor, Lancs. BB7 56 C5
Low Moor, W.Yorks. BD12 57 G7
Low Moorsley DH5 62 E2
Low Moresby CA28 60 A4
Low Newton-by-the-Sea NE66 71 H1
Low Row, Cumb. CA8 70 A7
Low Row, N.Yorks. DL11 62 A7
Low Stillaig PA21 73 H4
Low Street NR9 44 E5
Low Tharston NR15 45 F6
Low Torry KY12 75 J2
Low Town NE65 71 G3
Low Toynton LN9 53 F5
Low Wood LA12 55 G1
Low Worsall TS15 62 E6
Lowbands GL19 29 G5
Lowdham NG14 41 J1
Lowe SY4 38 E2
Lowe Hill ST13 49 J7
Lower Achachanna PA35 80 B5
Lower Aisholt TA5 8 B1
Lower Apperley GL19 29 H6
Lower Arncott OX25 31 H7
Lower Ashtead KT21 22 E6
Lower Ashton EX6 7 G7
Lower Assendon RG9 22 A3
Lower Auchalick PA21 73 H3
Lower Ballam PR4 55 G6
Lower Barewood HR6 28 C3
Lower Bartle PR4 55 H6
Lower Bayble (Pabail Iarach) HS2 101 H4
Lower Beeding RH13 13 F4
Lower Benefield PE8 42 C7
Lower Bentley B60 29 J2
Lower Berry Hill GL16 28 E7
Lower Birchwood DE55 51 G7
Lower Boddington NN11 31 F3
Lower Boscaswell TR19 2 A5
Lower Bourne GU10 22 B7
Lower Brailes OX15 30 E5
Lower Breakish IV42 86 C2
Lower Bredbury SK6 49 J3
Lower Broadheath WR2 29 H3
Lower Brynamman SA18 27 G7
Lower Bullingham HR2 28 E5
Lower Bullington SO21 21 H7
Lower Burgate SP6 10 C3
Lower Burrow TA12 8 D2
Lower Burton HR6 28 D3
Lower Caldecote SG18 32 E4
Lower Cam GL11 20 A1
Lower Cambourne CB3 33 G3
Lower Camster KW3 105 H4
Lower Canada BS24 19 G6
Lower Chapel LD3 27 K5
Lower Cheriton EX14 7 K5
Lower Chicksgrove SP3 9 J1
Lower Chute SP11 21 G6
Lower Clent DY9 40 B7
Lower Creedy EX17 7 G5
Lower Cumberworth HD8 50 E2
Lower Darwen BB3 56 B7
Lower Dean PE28 32 D2
Lower Diabaig IV22 94 D5
Lower Dicker BN27 13 J5
Lower Dinchope SY7 38 D7
Lower Down SY7 38 C7
Lower Drift TR19 2 B6
Lower Dunsforth YO26 57 K3
Lower Earley RG6 22 A4
Lower Edmonton N9 23 G2
Lower Elkstone SK17 50 C7
Lower End, Bucks. HP18 21 K1
Lower End, M.K. MK17 32 C5
Lower End, Northants. NN7 32 B2
Lower Everleigh SN8 20 E6
Lower Eythorne CT15 15 H3
Lower Failand BS8 19 J4
Lower Farringdon GU34 11 J1
Lower Fittleworth RH20 12 D5
Lower Foxdale IM4 54 B6
Lower Freystrop SA62 16 C3
Lower Froyle GU34 22 A7
Lower Gabwell TQ12 5 K4
Lower Godney BA5 19 H7
Lower Gravenhurst MK45 32 E5
Lower Green, Essex CO6 34 B5
Lower Green, Herts. SG5 32 E5
Lower Green, Kent TN2 23 K7
Lower Green, Norf. NR21 44 D2
Lower Green, Staffs. WV9 40 B5

Lower Green Bank LA2 55 J4
Lower Halstock Leigh BA22 8 E4
Lower Halstow ME9 24 E5
Lower Hardres CT4 15 G2
Lower Harpton LD8 28 B2
Lower Hartshay DE5 51 F7
Lower Hartwell HP17 31 J7
Lower Hawthwaite LA20 55 F1
Lower Hayton SY8 38 E7
Lower Haysden TN11 23 J7
Lower Heath CW12 49 H6
Lower Hergest HR5 28 B3
Lower Heyford OX25 31 F6
Lower Higham ME3 24 D4
Lower Holbrook IP9 35 F5
Lower Hopton WF14 50 D1
Lower Hordley SY12 38 C3
Lower Horncroft RH20 12 D5
Lower Horsebridge BN27 13 J5
Lower Houses HD5 50 D1
Lower Howsell WR14 29 G4
Lower Kersal M25 49 H2
Lower Kilchattan PA61 72 B1
Lower Kilcott GL12 20 A3
Lower Killeyan PA42 72 A6
Lower Kingcombe DT2 8 E5
Lower Kingswood KT20 23 F6
Lower Kinnerton CH4 48 C6
Lower Langford BS40 19 H5
Lower Largo KY8 83 F7
Lower Leigh ST10 40 C2
Lower Lemington GL56 30 D5
Lower Lovacott EX31 6 D3
Lower Loxhore EX31 6 E2
Lower Lydbrook GL17 28 E7
Lower Lye HR6 28 D2
Lower Machen NP10 19 F3
Lower Maes-coed HR2 28 C5
Lower Mannington BH21 10 B4
Lower Middleton Cheney OX17 31 G4
Lower Milton BA5 19 J7
Lower Moor WR10 29 J4
Lower Morton BS35 19 K2
Lower Nash SA72 16 D4
Lower Netchwood WV16 39 F6
Lower Nyland SP8 9 G2
Lower Oddington GL56 30 D6
Lower Ollach IV51 86 B1
Lower Penarth CF64 18 E4
Lower Penn WV4 40 A6
Lower Pennington SO41 10 E5
Lower Peover WA16 49 G5
Lower Pollicott HP18 31 J7
Lower Quinton CV37 30 C4
Lower Race NP4 19 F1
Lower Rainham ME8 24 E5
Lower Roadwater TA23 7 J2
Lower Sapey WR6 29 F2
Lower Seagry SN15 20 C3
Lower Shelton MK43 32 C4
Lower Shiplake RG9 22 A4
Lower Shuckburgh NN11 31 F2
Lower Slaughter GL54 30 C6
Lower Soothill WF17 57 H7
Lower Stanton St. Quintin SN14 20 C3
Lower Stoke ME3 24 E4
Lower Stondon SG16 32 E5
Lower Stone GL13 19 K2
Lower Stonnall WS9 40 C5
Lower Stow Bedon NR17 44 D6
Lower Street, Dorset DT11 9 H5
Lower Street, E.Suss. TN33 14 C6
Lower Street, Norf. NR11 45 G2
Lower Street, Norf. NR12 45 F2
Lower Street, Suff. IP6 35 F3
Lower Stretton WA4 49 F4
Lower Sundon LU3 32 D6
Lower Swanwick SO31 11 F4
Lower Swell GL54 30 C6
Lower Tadmarton OX15 31 F5
Lower Tale EX14 7 J5
Lower Tean ST10 40 C2
Lower Thurlton NR14 45 J6
Lower Thurnham LA2 55 H4
Lower Town, Cornw. TR13 2 D6
Lower Town, Devon TQ13 5 H3
Lower Town, I.o.S. TR25 2 C1
Lower Town, Pembs. SA65 16 C1
Lower Trebullett PL15 4 D3
Lower Tysoe CV35 30 E4
Lower Upcott TQ13 5 H3
Lower Upham SO32 11 G3
Lower Upnor ME2 24 D4
Lower Vexford TA4 7 K2
Lower Wallop SY5 38 C5
Lower Walton WA4 49 F4
Lower Waterhay SN6 20 D2
Lower Weald MK19 31 J5
Lower Wear EX2 7 H7
Lower Weare BS26 19 H6
Lower Welson HR3 28 B3
Lower Whatley BA11 20 A7
Lower Whitley WA4 49 F5
Lower Wick WR2 29 H3
Lower Wield SO24 21 K7
Lower Winchendon (Nether Winchendon) HP18 31 J7
Lower Withington SK11 49 H6
Lower Woodend SL7 22 B3
Lower Woodford SP4 10 C1
Lower Wyche WR14 29 G4
Lowerhouse BB12 56 D6
Lowertown KW17 107 D8
Lowesby LE7 42 A5
Lowestoft NR32 45 K6
Loweswater CA13 60 C4

Lowfield Heath RH11 23 F7
Lowgill, Cumb. LA8 61 H7
Lowgill, Lancs. LA2 56 B3
Lowick, Cumb. LA12 55 F1
Lowick, Northants. NN14 42 C7
Lowick, Northumb. TD15 77 J7
Lowick Bridge LA12 55 F1
Lowick Green LA12 55 F1
Lownie Moor DD8 83 F3
Lowsonford B95 30 C2
Lowther CA10 61 G4
Lowther Castle CA10 61 G4
Lowthorpe YO25 59 G3
Lowton, Devon EX20 6 E5
Lowton, Gt.Man. WA3 49 F3
Lowton, Som. TA3 7 K4
Lowton Common WA3 49 F3
Loxbeare EX16 7 H4
Loxhill GU8 12 D3
Loxhore EX31 6 E2
Loxley CV35 30 D3
Loxley Green ST14 40 C2
Loxton BS26 19 G6
Loxwood RH14 12 D3
Lubachoinnich IV24 96 B2
Lubcroy IV27 95 K1
Lubenham LE16 42 A7
Lubfearn IV23 95 K4
Lubmore IV22 95 G6
Lubreoch PH15 81 F3
Luccombe TA24 7 H1
Luccombe Village PO37 11 G6
Lucker NE70 77 K7
Luckett PL17 4 D3
Luckington SN14 20 B3
Lucklawhill KY16 83 F5
Luckwell Bridge TA24 7 H2
Lucton HR6 28 D2
Lucy Cross DL11 62 D5
Ludag HS8 84 C3
Ludborough DN36 53 F3
Ludbrook PL21 5 G5
Ludchurch SA67 16 E3
Luddenden HX2 57 F7
Luddenden Foot HX2 57 F7
Luddenham Court ME13 25 F5
Luddesdown DA13 24 C5
Luddington, N.Lincs. DN17 52 B1
Luddington, Warks. CV37 30 C3
Luddington in the Brook PE8 42 E7
Ludford, Lincs. LN8 52 E4
Ludford, Shrop. SY8 28 E1
Ludgershall, Bucks. HP18 31 H7
Ludgershall, Wilts. SP11 21 F6
Ludgvan TR20 2 C5
Ludham NR29 45 H4
Ludlow SY8 28 E1
Ludney LN11 53 G3
Ludstock HR8 29 F5
Ludstone WV5 40 A6
Ludwell SP7 9 J2
Ludworth DH6 62 E2
Luffincott EX22 6 B6
Luffness EH32 76 C2
Lufton BA22 8 E3
Lugar KA18 67 K1
Luggate EH41 76 D3
Luggate Burn EH41 76 E3
Luggiebank G67 75 F3
Lugton KA3 74 C5
Lugwardine HR1 28 E4
Luib IV49 86 B2
Luibeilt PH30 80 D1
Luing PA34 79 J6
Lulham HR2 28 D4
Lullington, Derbys. DE12 40 E4
Lullington, Som. BA11 20 A6
Lulsgate Bottom BS40 19 J5
Lulsley WR6 29 G3
Lulworth Camp BH20 9 H6
Lumb, Lancs. BB4 56 D7
Lumb, W.Yorks. HX6 57 F7
Lumbutts OL14 56 E7
Lumby LS25 57 K6
Lumphanan AB31 90 D4
Lumphinnans KY4 75 K1
Lumsdaine TD14 77 G4
Lumsdale DE4 51 F6
Lumsden AB54 90 C2
Lunan DD11 83 H2
Lunanhead DD8 83 F2
Luncarty PH1 82 B5
Lund, E.Riding YO25 59 F5
Lund, N.Yorks. YO8 58 C6
Lund, Shet. ZE2 108 E2
Lundale DE4 50 D4
Lundavra PH33 80 B1
Lunderton AB42 99 K6
Lundie, Angus DD2 82 D4
Lundie, High. IV63 87 H3
Lundin Links KY8 83 F7
Lundwood S71 51 F2
Lundy EX34 6 A1
Lunga PA31 79 K7
Lunna ZE2 109 D6
Lunning ZE2 109 E6
Lunnon SA3 17 J6
Lunsford's Cross TN39 14 C6
Lunt L29 48 C2
Luntley HR6 28 D3
Luppitt EX14 7 K5
Lupset WF2 51 F1
Lupton LA6 55 J1
Lurgashall GU28 12 C4
Lurignich PA38 80 A2
Lusby PE23 53 G6
Luss G83 74 B1
Lussagiven PA60 72 E2
Lusta IV55 93 H6

Lustleigh

Lustleigh **TQ13** 7 F7
Luston **HR6** 28 D2
Luthermuir **AB30** 83 H1
Luthrie **KY15** 82 E6
Luton, Devon **EX14** 7 J5
Luton, Devon **TQ13** 5 J3
LUTON, Luton LU **32 D6**
Luton, Med. **ME5** 24 D5
Luton Airport (London Luton Airport) **LU2** 32 E6
Lutterworth **LE17** 41 H7
Lutton, Devon **PL21** 5 F5
Lutton, Dorset **BH20** 9 J6
Lutton, Lincs. **PE12** 43 H3
Lutton, Northants. **PE8** 42 E7
Luxborough **TA23** 7 H2
Luxulyan **PL30** 4 A5
Lybster, High. **KW14** 105 F2
Lybster, High. **KW3** 105 H5
Lydacott **EX21** 6 C5
Lydbury North **SY7** 38 C7
Lydcott **EX32** 6 E2
Lydd **TN29** 15 F5
Lydd Airport **TN29** 15 F5
Lydden **CT15** 15 H3
Lyddington **LE15** 42 B6
Lydd-on-Sea **TN29** 15 F5
Lyde Green **BS16** 19 K4
Lydeard St. Lawrence **TA4** 7 K2
Lydford **EX20** 6 D7
Lydford-on-Fosse **TA11** 8 E1
Lydgate, Gt.Man. **OL15** 49 J1
Lydgate, Gt.Man. **OL4** 49 J2
Lydgate, W.Yorks. **OL14** 56 E7
Lydham **SY9** 38 C6
Lydiard Millicent **SN5** 20 D3
Lydiard Tregoze **SN5** 20 E3
Lydiate **L31** 48 C2
Lydlinch **DT10** 9 G3
Lydney **GL15** 19 K1
Lydstep **SA70** 16 D5
Lye **DY9** 40 B7
Lye Cross **BS40** 19 H5
Lye Green, Bucks. **HP5** 22 C1
Lye Green, E.Suss. **TN6** 13 J3
Lye Green, Warks. **CV35** 30 C2
Lye's Green **BA12** 20 B7
Lyford **OX12** 21 G2
Lymbridge Green **TN25** 15 G3
Lyme Regis **DT7** 8 C5
Lymekilns **G74** 74 E5
Lyminge **CT18** 15 G3
Lymington **SO41** 10 E5
Lyminster **BN17** 12 D6
Lymm **WA13** 49 F4
Lymore **SO41** 10 D5
Lympne **CT21** 15 G4
Lympsham **BS24** 19 G6
Lympstone **EX8** 7 H7
Lynaberack **PH21** 88 E5
Lynch **TA24** 7 G1
Lynch Green **NR9** 45 F5
Lynchat **PH21** 88 E4
Lyndhurst **SO43** 10 D4
Lyndon **LE15** 42 C5
Lyne, Aber. **AB51** 91 F4
Lyne, Sc.Bord. **EH45** 76 A6
Lyne, Surr. **KT16** 22 D5
Lyne Down **HR8** 29 F5
Lyne of Gorthleck **IV2** 88 C2
Lyne of Skene **AB32** 91 F3
Lyne Station **EH45** 76 A6
Lyneal **SY12** 38 D2
Lynedale House **IV51** 93 J6
Lynegar **KW1** 105 H3
Lyneham, Oxon. **OX7** 30 D6
Lyneham, Wilts. **SN15** 20 D4
Lyneholmeford **CA6** 70 A6
Lynemore, High. **PH26** 89 H2
Lynemore, Moray **AB37** 89 J1
Lynemouth **NE61** 71 H4
Lyness **KW16** 107 C8
Lynford **IP26** 44 C6
Lyng, Norf. **NR9** 44 E4
Lyng, Som. **TA3** 8 C2
Lyngate **NR28** 45 H3
Lynmouth **EX35** 7 F1
Lynn **TF10** 39 G4
Lynsted **ME9** 25 F5
Lynstone **EX23** 6 A5
Lynton **EX35** 7 F1
Lyon's Gate **DT2** 9 F4
Lyonshall **HR5** 28 C3
Lyrabus **PA44** 72 A4
Lytchett Matravers **BH16** 9 J5
Lytchett Minster **BH16** 9 J5
Lyth **KW1** 105 H2
Lytham **FY8** 55 G7
Lytham St. Anne's **FY8** 55 G7
Lythe **YO21** 63 K5
Lythe Hill **GU27** 12 C3
Lythes **KW17** 107 D9
Lythmore **KW14** 105 F2

M

Maaruig (Maraig) **HS3** 100 E7
Mabe Burnthouse **TR10** 2 E5
Mabie **DG2** 65 K3
Mablethorpe **LN12** 53 J4
Macclesfield **SK11** 49 J5
Macclesfield Forest **SK11** 49 J5
Macduff **AB44** 99 F4
Macedonia **KY6** 82 D7
Machan **ML9** 75 F5
Machany **PH3** 81 K6
Macharioch **PA28** 66 B3
Machen **CF83** 19 F3
Machrie, Arg. & B. **PA49** 72 A4
Machrie, Arg. & B. **PA42** 72 B6
Machrie, N.Ayr. **KA27** 73 G7
Machrihanish **PA28** 66 A1
Machrins **PA61** 72 B1
Machynlleth **SY20** 37 G5
McInroy's Point **PA19** 74 A3
Mackerye End **AL4** 32 E7
Mackworth **DE22** 41 F2
Macmerry **EH33** 76 C3
Macterry **AB53** 99 F6
Madderty **PH7** 82 A5
Maddiston **FK2** 75 H3
Madehurst **BN18** 12 C5
Madeley, Staffs. **CW3** 39 G1
Madeley, Tel. & W. **TF7** 39 G5
Madeley Heath **CW3** 39 G1
Maders **PL17** 4 D3
Madford **EX15** 7 K4
Madingley **CB3** 33 G2
Madjeston **SP8** 9 H2
Madley **HR2** 28 D5
Madresfield **WR13** 29 H4
Madron **TR20** 2 B5
Maenaddwyn **LL71** 46 C4
Maenclochog **SA66** 16 D2
Maendy, Cardiff **CF14** 18 E4
Maendy, V. of Glam. **CF71** 18 D4
Maenporth **TR11** 2 E6
Maentwrog **LL41** 37 F1
Maen-y-groes **SA45** 26 C3
Maer, Cornw. **EX23** 6 A5
Maer, Staffs. **ST5** 39 G2
Maerdy, Carmar. **SA19** 17 K2
Maerdy, Carmar. **SA19** 17 K2
Maerdy, Conwy **LL21** 37 K1
Maerdy, R.C.T. **CF43** 18 C2
Maesbrook **SY10** 38 B3
Maesbury Marsh **SY10** 38 C3
Maes-Glas (Greenfield), Flints. **CH8** 47 K5
Maes-glas, Newport **NP20** 19 G3
Maesgwynne **SA34** 17 F2
Maeshafn **CH7** 48 B6
Maesllyn **SA44** 26 C4
Maesmynis **LD2** 27 K4
Maesteg **CF34** 18 B2
Maes-Treylow **LD8** 28 B2
Maesybont **SA14** 17 J3
Maesycrugiau **SA39** 26 D4
Maesycwmmer **CF82** 18 E2
Maesyfed (New Radnor) **LD8** 28 B2
Magdalen Laver **CM5** 23 J1
Maggieknockater **AB38** 98 B6
Maggots End **CM23** 33 H6
Magham Down **BN27** 13 K5
Maghull **L31** 48 C2
Magna Park **LE17** 41 H7
Magor **NP26** 19 H3
Magpie Green **IP22** 34 E1
Maiden Bradley **BA12** 9 G1
Maiden Head **BS41** 19 J5
Maiden Law **DH7** 62 C2
Maiden Newton **DT2** 8 E5
Maiden Wells **SA71** 16 C5
Maidencombe **TQ1** 5 K4
Maidenhayne **EX13** 8 B5
Maidenhead **SL6** 22 B3
Maidens **KA26** 67 G3
Maiden's Green **RG42** 22 B4
Maidensgrove **RG9** 22 A3
Maidenwell, Cornw. **PL30** 4 B3
Maidenwell, Lincs. **LN11** 53 G5
Maidford **NN12** 31 H3
Maids' Moreton **MK18** 31 J5
Maidstone **ME14** 14 C2
Maidwell **NN6** 31 J1
Mail **ZE2** 109 D10
Maindee **NP19** 19 G3
Mainland, Ork. **KW** 107 B6
Mainland, Shet. **ZE** 109 C7
Mains of Ardestie **DD5** 83 G4
Mains of Balgavies **DD8** 83 G2
Mains of Balhall **DD9** 83 G1
Mains of Ballindarg **DD8** 83 F2
Mains of Burgie **IV36** 97 H6
Mains of Culsh **AB53** 99 G6
Mains of Dillavaird **AB30** 91 F6
Mains of Drum **AB31** 91 G4
Mains of Dudwick **AB41** 91 H1
Mains of Faillie **IV2** 88 E1
Mains of Fedderate **AB42** 99 G6
Mains of Glack **AB51** 91 F2
Mains of Glassaugh **AB45** 98 D4
Mains of Glenbuchat **AB36** 90 B3
Mains of Linton **AB51** 91 F3
Mains of Melgund **DD9** 83 G2
Mains of Pitfour **AB42** 99 H6
Mains of Pittrichie **AB21** 91 G2
Mains of Sluie **IV36** 97 H6
Mains of Tannachy **AB56** 98 B4
Mains of Thornton **AB30** 90 E7
Mains of Tig **KA26** 67 F5
Mains of Watten **KW1** 105 H3
Mainsforth **DL17** 62 E3
Mainsriddle **DG2** 65 K5
Mainstone **SY9** 38 B7
Maisemore **GL2** 29 H6
Major's Green **B90** 30 C1
Makendon **NE65** 70 D3
Makeney **DE56** 41 F1
Makerstoun **TD5** 76 E7
Malacleit **HS6** 92 C4
Malborough **TQ7** 5 H7
Malden Rushett **KT9** 22 E5
Maldon **CM9** 24 E1
Malham **BD23** 56 E3
Maligar **IV51** 93 K5
Malinbridge **S6** 51 F4
Mallaig **PH41** 86 C5
Mallaigmore **PH41** 86 C5
Mallaigvaig **PH41** 86 C5
Malleny Mills **EH14** 75 K4
Malletsheugh **G77** 74 D5
Malling **FK8** 81 G7
Mallows Green **CM23** 33 H6
Malltraeth **LL62** 46 C6
Mallwyd **SY20** 37 H4
Malmesbury **SN16** 20 C3
Malmsmead **EX35** 7 F1
Malpas, Ches. **SY14** 38 D1
Malpas, Cornw. **TR1** 3 F4
Malpas, Newport **NP20** 19 G2
Maltby, Lincs. **LN11** 53 G4
Maltby, S.Yorks. **S66** 51 H3
Maltby, Stock. **TS8** 63 F5
Maltby le Marsh **LN13** 53 H4
Malting End **CB8** 34 B3
Malting Green **CO2** 34 D7
Maltman's Hill **TN27** 14 D3
Malton **YO17** 58 D2
Malvern Link **WR14** 29 G4
Malvern Wells **WR14** 29 G4
Mambeg **G84** 74 A2
Mamble **DY14** 29 F1
Mamhead **EX6** 7 H7
Mamhilad **NP4** 19 G1
Manaccan **TR12** 2 E6
Manadon **PL5** 4 E5
Manafon **SY21** 38 A5
Manais (Manish) **HS3** 93 G3
Manaton **TQ13** 7 F7
Manby **LN11** 53 G4
Mancetter **CV9** 41 F6
MANCHESTER M **49 H3**
Manchester Airport **M90** 49 H4
Mancot Royal **CH5** 48 C6
Mandally **PH35** 87 J4
Manea **PE15** 43 H7
Maneight **KA18** 67 K3
Manfield **DL2** 62 D5
Mangaster **ZE2** 108 C5
Mangerton **DT6** 8 D5
Mangotsfield **BS16** 19 K4
Mangrove Green **LU2** 32 E6
Mangurstadh **HS2** 100 C4
Manish (Manais) **HS3** 93 G3
Mankinholes **OL14** 56 E7
Manley **WA6** 48 E5
Manmoel **NP12** 18 E1
Mannal **PA77** 78 A3
Manningford Abbots **SN9** 20 E6
Manningford Bohune **SN9** 20 E6
Manningford Bruce **SN9** 20 E6
Manningham **BD8** 57 G6
Mannings Heath **RH13** 13 F4
Mannington **BH21** 10 B4
Manningtree **CO11** 35 F5
Mannofield **AB15** 91 H4
Manor Park **SL2** 22 C3
Manorbier **SA70** 16 D5
Manorbier Newton **SA70** 16 D4
Manordeifi **SA43** 26 B4
Manordeilo **SA19** 17 K2
Manorowen **SA65** 16 C1
Mansell Gamage **HR4** 28 C4
Mansell Lacy **HR4** 28 D4
Mansergh **LA6** 56 B1
Mansfield **NG18** 51 H6
Mansfield Woodhouse **NG19** 51 H6
Manson Green **NR9** 44 E5
Mansriggs **LA12** 55 F1
Manston, Dorset **DT10** 9 H3
Manston, Kent **CT12** 25 K5
Manston, W.Yorks. **LS15** 57 J6
Manswood **BH21** 9 J4
Manthorpe, Lincs. **PE10** 42 D4
Manthorpe, Lincs. **NG31** 42 C2
Manton, N.Lincs. **DN21** 52 C2
Manton, Notts. **S80** 51 H5
Manton, Rut. **LE15** 42 B5
Manton, Wilts. **SN8** 20 E5
Manuden **CM23** 33 H6
Manwood Green **CM5** 33 J7
Maolachy **PA35** 79 K6
Maperton **BA9** 9 F2
Maple Cross **WD3** 22 D2
Maplebeck **NG22** 51 K6
Mapledurham **RG4** 21 K4
Mapledurwell **RG25** 21 K6
Maplehurst **RH13** 12 E4
Maplescombe **DA4** 23 J5
Mapleton **DE6** 40 D1
Mapperley, Derbys. **DE7** 41 G1
Mapperley, Notts. **NG5** 41 H1
Mapperton, Dorset **DT8** 8 E5
Mapperton, Dorset **DT11** 9 J5
Mappleborough Green **B80** 30 B2
Mappleton **HU18** 59 J5
Mapplewell **S75** 51 F2
Mappowder **DT10** 9 G4
Mar Lodge **AB35** 89 H5
Maraig (Maaruig) **HS3** 100 E7
Marazion **TR17** 2 C5
Marbhig **HS2** 101 G6
Marbury **SY13** 38 E1
March **PE15** 43 H6
Marcham **OX13** 21 H2
Marchamley **SY4** 38 E3
Marchamley Wood **SY4** 38 E2
Marchington **ST14** 40 D2
Marchington Woodlands **ST14** 40 D3
Marchwiel **LL13** 38 C1
Marchwood **SO40** 10 E3
Marcross **CF61** 18 C5
Marcus **DD8** 83 G2
Marden, Here. **HR1** 28 E4
Marden, Kent **TN12** 14 C3
Marden, T. & W. **NE30** 71 J6
Marden, Wilts. **SN10** 20 D6
Marden Ash **CM5** 23 J1
Marden Beech **TN12** 14 C3
Marden Thorn **TN12** 14 C3
Marden's Hill **TN6** 13 H3
Mardon **TD12** 77 H7
Mardy **NP7** 28 C7
Mare Green **TA3** 8 C2
Marefield **LE7** 42 A5
Mareham le Fen **PE22** 53 F6
Mareham on the Hill **LN9** 53 F6
Maresfield **TN22** 13 H4
Marfleet **HU9** 59 H6
Marford **LL12** 48 C7
Margam **SA13** 18 A3
Margaret Marsh **SP7** 9 H3
Margaret Roding **CM6** 33 J7
Margaretting **CM4** 24 C1
Margaretting Tye **CM4** 24 C1
Margate **CT9** 25 K4
Margnaheglish **KA27** 73 J7
Margreig **DG2** 65 J3
Margrove Park **TS12** 63 H5
Marham **PE33** 44 B5
Marhamchurch **EX23** 6 A5
Marholm **PE6** 42 E5
Marian Cwm **LL18** 47 J5
Mariandyrys **LL58** 46 E4
Marian-Glas **LL73** 46 D4
Mariansleigh **EX36** 7 F3
Marine Town **ME12** 25 F4
Marishader **IV51** 93 K5
Maristow House **PL6** 4 E4
Mark **TA9** 19 G7
Mark Causeway **TA9** 19 G7
Mark Cross **TN6** 13 J3
Markbeech **TN8** 23 H7
Markby **LN13** 53 H5
Markdhu **DG8** 64 B3
Markeaton **DE22** 41 F2
Market Bosworth **CV13** 41 G5
Market Deeping **PE6** 42 E4
Market Drayton **TF9** 39 F2
Market Harborough **LE16** 42 A7
Market Lavington **SN10** 20 D6
Market Overton **LE15** 42 B4
Market Rasen **LN8** 52 E4
Market Stainton **LN8** 53 F5
Market Street **NR12** 45 G3
Market Warsop **NG20** 51 H6
Market Weighton **YO43** 58 E5
Market Weston **IP22** 34 D1
Markethill **PH13** 82 D4
Markfield **LE67** 41 G4
Markham **NP12** 18 E1
Markham Moor **DN22** 51 K5
Markinch **KY7** 82 D7
Markington **HG3** 57 H3
Marks Gate **RM6** 23 H2
Marks Tey **CO6** 34 D6
Marksbury **BA2** 19 K5
Markwell **PL12** 4 D5
Markyate **AL3** 32 D7
Marl Bank **WR14** 29 G4
Marland **OL11** 49 H1
Marlborough **SN8** 20 E5
Marlbrook **B60** 29 J1
Marlcliff **B50** 30 B3
Marldon **TQ3** 5 J4
Marle Green **TN21** 13 J5
Marlesford **IP13** 35 H3
Marley Green **SY13** 38 E1
Marley Hill **NE16** 62 D1
Marlingford **NR9** 45 F5
Marloes **SA62** 16 A4
Marlow, Bucks. **SL7** 22 B3
Marlow, Here. **SY7** 28 D1
Marlpit Hill **TN8** 23 H7
Marlpool **DE75** 41 G1
Marnhull **DT10** 9 G3
Marnoch **AB54** 98 D5
Marple **SK6** 49 J4
Marple Bridge **SK6** 49 J4
Marr **DN5** 51 H2
Marrel **KW8** 105 F7
Marrick **DL11** 62 B7
Marrister **ZE2** 109 E6
Marros **SA33** 17 F4
Marsden, T. & W. **NE34** 71 J7
Marsden, W.Yorks. **HD7** 50 C1
Marsett **DL8** 56 E1
Marsh **EX14** 8 B3
Marsh Baldon **OX44** 21 J2
Marsh Benham **RG20** 21 H5
Marsh Gibbon **OX27** 31 H6
Marsh Green, Devon **EX5** 7 J6
Marsh Green, Gt.Man. **WN5** 48 E2
Marsh Green, Kent **TN8** 23 H7
Marsh Green, Tel. & W. **TF6** 39 F4
Marsh Lane **S21** 51 G5
Marsh Street **TA24** 7 H1
Marshall Meadows **TD15** 77 H5
Marshalsea **DT6** 8 C4
Marshalswick **AL1** 22 E1
Marsham **NR10** 45 F3
Marshaw **LA2** 55 J4
Marshborough **CT13** 15 J2
Marshbrook **SY6** 38 D7
Marshchapel **DN36** 53 G3
Marshfield, Newport **CF3** 19 F3
Marshfield, S.Glos. **SN14** 20 A4
Marshgate **PL32** 4 B1
Marshland St. James **PE14** 43 J5
Marshside **PR9** 48 C1
Marshwood **DT6** 8 C5
Marske **DL11** 62 C6
Marske-by-the-Sea **TS11** 63 H4
Marsland Green **M29** 49 F3
Marston, Ches. **CW9** 49 F5
Marston, Here. **HR6** 28 C3
Marston, Lincs. **NG32** 42 B1
Marston, Oxon. **OX3** 21 J1
Marston, Staffs. **ST18** 40 B3
Marston, Staffs. **ST20** 40 A4
Marston, Warks. **B76** 40 E6
Marston, Wilts. **SN10** 20 C6
Marston Doles **CV47** 31 F3
Marston Green **B37** 40 D7
Marston Magna **BA22** 8 E2
Marston Meysey **SN6** 20 E2
Marston Montgomery **DE6** 40 D2
Marston Moretaine **MK43** 32 C4
Marston on Dove **DE65** 40 E3
Marston St. Lawrence **OX17** 31 G4
Marston Stannett **HR6** 28 E3
Marston Trussell **LE16** 41 J7
Marstow **HR9** 28 E7
Marsworth **HP23** 32 C7
Marten **SN8** 21 F5
Marthall **WA16** 49 G5
Martham **NR29** 45 J4
Martin, Hants. **SP6** 10 B3
Martin, Lincs. **LN4** 52 E7
Martin, Lincs. **LN9** 53 F6
Martin Drove End **SP6** 10 B2
Martin Hussingtree **WR3** 29 H2
Martinhoe **EX31** 6 E1
Martinscroft **WA1** 49 F4
Martinstown **DT2** 9 F6
Martlesham **IP12** 35 G4
Martlesham Heath **IP5** 35 G4
Martletwy **SA67** 16 D3
Martley **WR6** 29 G2
Martock **TA12** 8 D3
Marton, Ches. **SK11** 49 H6
Marton, Cumb. **LA12** 55 F2
Marton, E.Riding **HU11** 59 H6
Marton, E.Riding **YO15** 59 J3
Marton, Lincs. **DN21** 52 B4
Marton, Middbro. **TS7** 63 G5
Marton, N.Yorks. **YO51** 57 K3
Marton, N.Yorks. **YO62** 58 D1
Marton, Shrop. **SY21** 38 B5
Marton, Shrop. **SY4** 38 D3
Marton, Warks. **CV23** 31 F2
Marton Abbey **YO61** 58 B3
Marton-in-the-Forest **YO61** 58 B3
Marton-le-Moor **HG4** 57 J2
Martyr Worthy **SO21** 11 G1
Martyr's Green **KT11** 22 D6
Marwick **KW17** 106 B5
Marwood **EX31** 6 D2
Mary Tavy **PL19** 5 F3
Marybank, High. **IV6** 96 B6
Marybank, W.Isles **HS2** 101 G4
Maryburgh **IV7** 96 C6
Maryfield, Cornw. **PL11** 4 E5
Maryfield, Shet. **ZE2** 109 D8
Marygold **TD11** 77 G5
Maryhill, Aber. **AB53** 99 G6
Maryhill, Glas. **G20** 74 D4
Marykirk **AB30** 83 H1
Marylebone, Gt.Lon. **W1G** 23 F3
Marylebone, Gt.Man. **WN1** 48 E2
Marypark **AB37** 89 J1
Maryport, Cumb. **CA15** 60 B3
Maryport, D. & G. **DG9** 64 B7
Marystow **PL16** 6 C7
Maryton **DD10** 83 H2
Marywell, Aber. **AB12** 91 H5
Marywell, Aber. **AB34** 90 D5
Marywell, Angus **DD11** 83 H3
Masham **HG4** 57 H1
Mashbury **CM1** 33 K7
Masongill **LA6** 56 B2
Mastin Moor **S43** 51 G5
Mastrick **AB16** 91 H4
Matchborough **B98** 30 B2
Matching **CM17** 33 J7
Matching Green **CM17** 33 J7
Matching Tye **CM17** 33 J7
Matfen **NE20** 71 F6
Matfield **TN12** 23 K7
Mathern **NP16** 19 J2
Mathon **WR13** 29 G4
Mathry **SA62** 16 B1
Matlaske **NR11** 45 F2
Matlock **DE4** 51 F6
Matlock Bank **DE4** 51 F6
Matlock Bath **DE4** 50 E7
Matson **GL4** 29 H7
Matterdale End **CA11** 60 E4
Mattersey **DN10** 51 J4
Mattersey Thorpe **DN10** 51 J4
Mattingley **RG27** 22 A6
Mattishall **NR20** 44 E4
Mattishall Burgh **NR20** 44 E4
Mauchline **KA5** 67 J1
Maud **AB42** 99 H6
Maufant **JE2** 3 K7
Maugersbury **GL54** 30 C6
Maughold **IM7** 54 D4
Mauld **IV4** 87 K1
Maulden **MK45** 32 D5
Maulds Meaburn **CA10** 61 H5
Maunby **YO7** 57 J1
Maund Bryan **HR1** 28 E3
Maundown **TA4** 7 J3
Mautby **NR29** 45 J4

Milton

Mavesyn Ridware WS15 40 C4
Mavis Enderby PE23 53 G6
Maw Green CW1 49 G7
Mawbray CA15 60 B2
Mawdesley L40 48 D1
Mawdlam CF33 18 B3
Mawgan TR12 2 E6
Mawgan Porth TR8 3 F2
Mawla TR16 2 D4
Mawnan TR11 2 E6
Mawnan Smith TR11 2 E6
Mawsley NN14 32 B1
Mawthorpe LN13 53 H5
Maxey PE6 42 E5
Maxstoke B46 40 E7
Maxted Street CT4 15 G3
Maxton, Kent CT17 15 J3
Maxton, Sc.Bord. TD6 76 E7
Maxwellheugh TD5 77 F7
Maxwelltown DG2 65 K3
Maxworthy PL15 4 C1
Mayals SA3 17 K5
Maybole KA19 67 H3
Maybury GU22 22 D6
Mayen AB54 98 D6
Mayfair W1J 23 F3
Mayfield, E.Suss. TN20 13 J4
Mayfield, Midloth. EH22 76 B4
Mayfield, Staffs. DE6 40 D1
Mayford GU22 22 C6
Mayland CM3 25 F1
Maylandsea CM3 25 F1
Maynard's Green TN21 13 J5
Maypole, I.o.S. TR21 2 C1
Maypole, Kent CT3 25 H5
Maypole, Mon. NP25 28 D7
Maypole Green, Essex CO2 34 D6
Maypole Green, Norf. NR14 45 J6
Maypole Green, Suff. IP13 35 G2
Maypole Green, Suff. IP30 34 D3
May's Green, N.Som. BS24 19 G5
Mays Green, Oxon. RG9 22 A3
Maywick ZE2 109 C10
Mead EX39 6 A4
Mead End SP5 10 B2
Meadgate BA2 19 K6
Meadle HP17 22 B1
Meadow Green WR6 29 G3
Meadowhall S9 51 F3
Meadowmill EH33 76 C3
Meadowtown SY5 38 C5
Meadwell PL16 6 C7
Meaford ST15 40 A2
Meal Bank LA9 61 G7
Mealabost (Melbost Borve) HS2 101 G2
Mealasta HS2 100 B5
Meals LN11 53 H3
Mealsgate CA7 60 D2
Meanley BB7 56 C5
Meanwood LS6 57 H6
Mearbeck BD23 56 D3
Meare BA6 19 H7
Meare Green TA3 8 B2
Mearns G77 74 D5
Mears Ashby NN6 32 B2
Measham DE12 41 F4
Meathop LA11 55 H1
Meavy PL20 5 F4
Medbourne LE16 42 B6
Meddon EX39 6 A4
Meden Vale NG20 51 H6
Medlar PR4 55 H6
Medmenham SL7 22 B3
Medomsley DH8 62 C1
Medstead GU34 11 H1
Meer Common HR3 28 C3
Meer End CV8 30 D1
Meerbrook ST13 49 J6
Meesden SG9 33 H5
Meeson TF6 39 F3
Meeth EX20 6 D5
Meeting House Hill NR28 45 H3
Meggethead TD7 69 G1
Meidrim SA33 17 F2
Meifod, Denb. LL16 47 J7
Meifod, Powys SY22 38 A4
Meigle PH12 82 D3
Meikle Earnock ML3 75 F5
Meikle Grenach PA20 73 J4
Meikle Kilmory PA20 73 J4
Meikle Rahane G84 74 A2
Meikle Strath AB30 90 E7
Meikle Tarty AB41 91 H2
Meikle Wartle AB51 91 F1
Meikleour PH2 82 C4
Meikleyard KA4 74 D7
Meinciau SA17 17 H3
Meir ST3 40 B1
Meirheath ST3 40 B2
Melbost HS2 101 G4
Melbost Borve (Mealabost) HS2 101 G2
Melbourn SG8 33 G4
Melbourne, Derbys. DE73 41 F3
Melbourne, E.Riding YO42 58 D5
Melbury EX39 6 B4
Melbury Abbas SP7 9 H3
Melbury Bubb DT2 8 E4
Melbury Osmond DT2 8 E4
Melbury Sampford DT2 8 E4
Melby ZE2 109 A7
Melchbourne MK44 32 D2
Melcombe Bingham DT2 9 G4
Melcombe Regis DT4 9 F6
Meldon, Devon EX20 6 D6
Meldon, Northumb. NE61 71 G5
Meldreth SG8 33 G4
Meledor PL26 3 G3
Melfort PA34 79 K6
Melgarve PH20 88 B5
Melgum AB34 90 C4
Meliden (Gallt Melyd) LL19 47 J4
Melincourt SA11 18 B1
Melin-y-coed LL26 47 G6
Melin-y-ddol SY21 37 K5
Melin-y-grug SY21 37 K5
Melin-y-Wig LL21 37 K1
Melkinthorpe CA10 61 G4
Melkridge NE49 70 C7
Melksham SN12 20 C5
Melksham Forest SN12 20 C5
Melldalloch PA21 73 H3
Melling, Lancs. LA6 55 J2
Melling, Mersey. L31 48 C2
Melling Mount L31 48 D2
Mellis IP23 34 E1
Mellon Charles IV22 94 E2
Mellon Udrigle IV22 94 E2
Mellor, Gt.Man. SK6 49 J4
Mellor, Lancs. BB2 56 B6
Mellor Brook BB2 56 B6
Mells BA11 20 A7
Melmerby, Cumb. CA10 61 H3
Melmerby, N.Yorks. DL8 57 F1
Melmerby, N.Yorks. HG4 57 J2
Melplash DT6 8 D5
Melrose, Aber. AB45 99 F4
Melrose, Sc.Bord. TD6 76 D7
Melsetter KW16 107 B9
Melsonby DL10 62 C6
Meltham HD9 50 C1
Melton, E.Riding HU15 59 F7
Melton, Suff. IP12 35 G3
Melton Constable NR24 44 E2
Melton Mowbray LE13 42 A4
Melton Ross DN38 52 D1
Meltonby YO42 58 D4
Melvaig IV21 94 D3
Melverley SY10 38 C4
Melverley Green SY10 38 C4
Melvich KW14 104 D2
Membury EX13 8 B4
Memsie AB43 99 H4
Memus DD8 83 F2
Menabilly PL24 4 A5
Menai Bridge (Porthaethwy) LL59 46 D5
Mendham IP20 45 G7
Mendlesham IP14 35 F2
Mendlesham Green IP14 34 E2
Menethorpe YO17 58 D3
Menheniot PL14 4 C4
Menie House AB23 91 H2
Menithwood WR6 29 G2
Mennock DG4 68 D3
Menston LS29 57 G5
Menstrie FK11 75 G1
Mentmore LU7 32 C7
Meoble PH40 86 D6
Meole Brace SY3 38 D4
Meon PO14 11 G4
Meonstoke SO32 11 H3
Meopham DA13 24 C5
Meopham Green DA13 24 C5
Mepal CB6 43 H7
Meppershall SG17 32 E5
Merbach HR3 28 C4
Mercaston DE6 40 E1
Mere, Ches. WA16 49 G4
Mere, Wilts. BA12 9 H1
Mere Brow PR9 48 D1
Mere Green B75 40 D6
Mere Heath CW9 49 F5
Mereclough BB10 56 D6
Mereside FY4 55 G6
Meretown TF10 39 G3
Mereworth ME18 23 K6
Mergie AB39 91 F6
Meriden CV7 40 E7
Merkadale IV47 85 J1
Merkinch IV3 96 D7
Merkland DG7 65 H3
Merley BH21 10 B5
Merlin's Bridge SA61 16 C3
Merridge TA5 8 B1
Merrifield TQ7 5 J6
Merrington SY4 38 D3
Merrion SA71 16 C5
Merriott TA16 8 D3
Merrivale PL19 5 F3
Merrow GU1 22 D6
Merry Hill, Herts. WD23 22 E2
Merry Hill, W.Mid. DY5 40 B7
Merry Hill, W.Mid. WV3 40 A6
Merrymeet PL14 4 C4
Mersea Island CO5 34 E7
Mersham TN25 15 F4
Merstham RH1 23 F6
Merston PO20 12 B6
Merstone PO30 11 G6
Merther TR2 3 F4
Merthyr SA33 17 G2
Merthyr Cynog LD3 27 J5
Merthyr Dyfan CF62 18 E5
Merthyr Mawr CF32 18 B4
Merthyr Tydfil CF47 18 D1
Merthyr Vale CF48 18 D2
Merton, Devon EX20 6 D4
Merton, Norf. IP25 44 D6
Merton, Oxon. OX25 31 G7
Mervinslaw TD8 70 B2
Meshaw EX36 7 F4
Messing CO5 34 D7
Messingham DN17 52 B2
Metcombe EX11 7 J6
Metfield IP20 45 G7
Metheringham LN4 52 D6
Metherwell PL17 4 E4
Methil KY8 76 B1
Methlem LL53 36 A2
Methley LS26 57 J7
Methley Junction LS26 57 J7
Methlick AB41 91 G1
Methven PH1 82 B5
Methwold IP26 44 B6
Methwold Hythe IP26 44 B6
MetroCentre NE11 71 H7
Mettingham NR35 45 H7
Metton NR11 45 F2
Mevagissey PL26 4 A6
Mewith Head LA2 56 C3
Mexborough S64 51 G3
Mey KW14 105 H1
Meysey Hampton GL7 20 E1
Miabhag, W.Isles HS3 93 G2
Miabhag, W.Isles HS3 100 C7
Miabhaig (Miavaig) HS2 100 C4
Mial IV21 94 D4
Miavaig (Miabhaig) HS2 100 C4
Michaelchurch HR2 28 E6
Michaelchurch Escley HR2 28 C5
Michaelchurch-on-Arrow HR5 28 B3
Michaelston-le-Pit CF64 18 E4
Michaelston-super-Ely CF5 18 E4
Michaelston-y-Fedw CF3 19 F3
Michaelstow PL30 4 A3
Michelcombe TQ13 5 G4
Micheldever SO21 11 G1
Michelmersh SO51 10 E2
Mickfield IP14 35 F2
Mickle Trafford CH2 48 D6
Micklebring S66 51 H3
Mickleby TS13 63 K5
Micklefield LS25 57 K6
Micklefield Green WD3 22 D2
Mickleham RH5 22 E6
Micklehurst OL5 49 J2
Mickleover DE3 41 F2
Micklethwaite, Cumb. CA7 60 D1
Micklethwaite, W.Yorks. BD20 57 F5
Mickleton, Dur. DL12 62 A4
Mickleton, Glos. GL55 30 C4
Mickletown LS26 57 J7
Mickley, Derbys. S18 51 F5
Mickley, N.Yorks. HG4 57 H2
Mickley Green IP29 34 C3
Mickley Square NE43 71 F7
Mid Ardlaw AB43 99 H4
Mid Beltie AB31 90 E4
Mid Calder EH53 75 J4
Mid Clyth KW3 105 H5
Mid Lambrook TA13 8 D3
Mid Lavant PO18 12 B6
Mid Letter PA27 80 B7
Mid Lix FK21 81 G4
Mid Mossdale DL8 61 K7
Mid Yell ZE2 108 E3
Midbea KW17 106 D3
Middle Assendon RG9 22 A3
Middle Aston OX25 31 F6
Middle Barton OX7 31 F6
Middle Bickenhill B92 40 E7
Middle Bockhampton BH23 10 C5
Middle Claydon MK18 31 J6
Middle Drift PL14 4 B4
Middle Drums DD9 83 G2
Middle Duntisbourne GL7 20 C1
Middle Handley S21 51 G5
Middle Harling NR16 44 D7
Middle Kames PA31 73 H2
Middle Littleton WR11 30 B4
Middle Maes-coed HR2 28 C5
Middle Marwood EX31 6 D2
Middle Mill SA62 16 B2
Middle Quarter TN26 14 D4
Middle Rasen LN8 52 D4
Middle Rigg PH2 82 B7
Middle Salter LA2 56 B3
Middle Sontley LL13 38 C1
Middle Stoford TA21 7 K3
Middle Taphouse PL14 4 B4
Middle Town TR25 2 C1
Middle Tysoe CV35 30 E4
Middle Wallop SO20 10 D1
Middle Winterslow SP5 10 D1
Middle Woodford SP4 10 C1
Middlebie DG11 69 H6
Middlecliff S72 51 G2
Middlecott EX22 6 C5
Middleham DL8 57 G1
Middlehill, Aber. AB53 99 G6
Middlehill, Cornw. PL14 4 C4
Middlehope SY7 38 E7
Middlemarsh DT9 9 F4
Middlemoor PL19 4 E3
Middlequarter (Ceathramh Meadhanach) HS6 92 D4
Middlesbrough TS1 63 F4
Middlesceugh CA4 60 F2
Middleshaw LA8 55 J1
Middlesmoor HG3 57 F2
Middlestone DL14 62 D3
Middlestone Moor DL16 62 D3
Middlestown WF4 50 E1
Middleton, Aber. AB21 91 G3
Middleton, Angus DD11 83 G3
Middleton, Cumb. LA6 56 B1
Middleton, Derbys. DE4 50 E7
Middleton, Derbys. DE45 50 D6
Middleton, Essex CO10 34 C4
Middleton, Gt.Man. M24 49 H2
Middleton, Hants. SP11 21 H7
Middleton, Here. SY8 28 E2
Middleton, Lancs. LA3 55 H4
Middleton, Midloth. EH23 76 B5
Middleton, N.Yorks. YO18 58 D1
Middleton, Norf. PE32 44 A4
Middleton, Northants. LE16 42 B7
Middleton, Northumb. NE61 71 F5
Middleton, Northumb. NE70 77 J7
Middleton, P. & K. KY13 82 C7
Middleton, P. & K. PH10 82 C3
Middleton, Shrop. SY15 38 B6
Middleton, Shrop. SY8 28 E1
Middleton, Shrop. SY11 38 C3
Middleton, Suff. IP17 35 J2
Middleton, Swan. SA3 17 H6
Middleton, W.Yorks. LS29 57 G5
Middleton, W.Yorks. LS10 57 J7
Middleton, Warks. B78 40 D6
Middleton Baggot WV16 39 F6
Middleton Bank Top NE61 71 F5
Middleton Cheney OX17 31 F4
Middleton Green ST10 40 B2
Middleton Hall NE71 70 E1
Middleton Moor IP17 35 J2
Middleton of Potterton AB23 91 H3
Middleton on the Hill SY8 28 E2
Middleton One Row DL2 62 E5
Middleton Park AB22 91 H3
Middleton Priors WV16 39 F7
Middleton Quernhow HG4 57 J2
Middleton St. George DL2 62 E5
Middleton Scriven WV16 39 F7
Middleton Stoney OX25 31 G6
Middleton Tyas DL10 62 D6
Middleton-in-Teesdale DL12 62 A4
Middleton-on-Leven TS15 63 F5
Middleton-on-Sea PO22 12 C6
Middleton-on-the-Wolds YO25 59 F5
Middletown, Cumb. CA22 60 A6
Middletown, Powys SY21 38 C4
Middlewich CW10 49 G6
Middlewood, Ches. SK12 49 J4
Middlewood, S.Yorks. S6 51 F3
Middlewood Green IP14 34 E2
Middlezoy TA7 8 C1
Middridge DL4 62 D4
Midfield IV27 103 H2
Midford BA2 20 A5
Midge Hall PR26 55 J7
Midgeholme CA8 61 H1
Midgham RG7 21 J5
Midgley, W.Yorks. WF4 50 E1
Midgley, W.Yorks. HX2 57 F7
Midhopestones S36 50 E3
Midhurst GU29 12 B4
Midlem TD7 70 A1
Midloe Grange PE19 32 E2
Midpark PA20 73 J5
Midsomer Norton BA3 19 K6
Midthorpe LN9 53 F5
Midtown, High. IV27 103 H2
Midtown, High. IV22 94 E3
Midtown of Barras AB39 91 G6
Midville PE22 53 G7
Midway DE11 41 F3
Migdale IV24 96 D2
Migvie AB34 90 C4
Milarrochy G63 74 C1
Milber TQ12 5 J3
Milbethill AB54 98 E5
Milborne Port DT9 9 F3
Milborne St. Andrew DT11 9 G5
Milborne Wick DT9 9 F2
Milbourne, Northumb. NE20 71 G6
Milbourne, Wilts. SN16 20 C3
Milburn CA10 61 H4
Milbury Heath GL12 19 K2
Milcombe OX15 31 F5
Milden IP7 34 D4
Mildenhall, Suff. IP28 34 B1
Mildenhall, Wilts. SN8 21 F5
Mile Elm SN11 20 C5
Mile End, Essex CO4 34 D6
Mile End, Glos. GL16 28 E7
Mile Oak TN12 23 K7
Mile Town ME12 25 F4
Milebrook LD7 28 C1
Milebush TN12 14 C3
Mileham PE32 44 D4
Miles Green ST7 40 A1
Miles Hope WR15 28 E2
Milesmark KY12 75 J2
Miles's Green RG7 21 J5
Milfield NE71 77 H7
Milford, Derbys. DE56 41 F1
Milford, Devon EX39 6 A3
Milford, Shrop. SY4 38 D3
Milford, Staffs. ST17 40 B3
Milford, Surr. GU8 22 C7
Milford Haven (Aberdaugleddau) SA73 16 B4
Milford on Sea SO41 10 D5
Milkwall GL16 19 J1
Mill Bank HX6 57 F7
Mill Brow SK6 49 J4
Mill End, Bucks. RG9 22 A3
Mill End, Cambs. CB8 33 K3
Mill End, Herts. SG9 33 G5
Mill End Green CM6 33 K6
Mill Green, Cambs. CB1 33 K4
Mill Green, Essex CM4 24 C1
Mill Green, Herts. AL9 23 F1
Mill Green, Norf. IP22 45 F7
Mill Green, Shrop. TF9 39 F3
Mill Green, Staffs. WS15 40 C3
Mill Green, Suff. IP13 35 H2
Mill Green, Suff. IP14 35 F3
Mill Green, Suff. IP14 34 D3
Mill Green, W.Mid. WS9 40 C5
Mill Hill, B'burn. BB2 56 B7
Mill Hill, Cambs. SG19 33 F3
Mill Hill, Gt.Lon. NW7 23 F2
Mill Houses LA2 56 B3
Mill Lane GU10 22 A6
Mill of Camsail G84 74 A2
Mill of Colp AB53 99 F6
Mill of Elrick AB41 99 H6
Mill of Fortune PH6 81 J5
Mill of Kingoodie AB21 91 G2
Mill of Monquich AB39 91 G5
Mill of Uras AB39 91 G6
Mill Side LA11 55 H1
Mill Street, Kent ME19 23 K6
Mill Street, Norf. NR20 44 E4
Milland GU30 12 B4
Millbank AB42 99 J6
Millbeck CA12 60 D4
Millbounds KW17 106 E4
Millbreck AB42 99 J6
Millbridge GU10 22 B7
Millbrook, Beds. MK45 32 D5
Millbrook, Cornw. PL10 4 E5
Millbrook, Devon EX13 8 C5
Millbrook, S'ham. SO15 10 E3
Millburn, Aber. AB33 90 D2
Millburn, Aber. AB54 90 E1
Millcombe TQ9 5 J6
Millcorner TN31 14 D5
Milldale DE6 50 D7
Millden AB23 91 H3
Milldens DD8 83 G2
Millearne PH7 82 A6
Millend OX7 30 E6
Millenheath SY13 38 E2
Millerhill EH22 76 B4
Miller's Dale SK17 50 D5
Millers Green, Derbys. DE4 50 E7
Miller's Green, Essex CM5 23 J1
Millgate OL12 56 D7
Millhalf HR3 28 B4
Millhayes, Devon EX15 7 K4
Millhayes, Devon EX14 8 B4
Millholme LA8 61 G7
Millhouse, Arg. & B. PA21 73 H3
Millhouse, Cumb. CA7 60 E3
Millhouse Green S36 50 E2
Millhousebridge DG11 69 G5
Millikenpark PA10 74 C4
Millin Cross SA62 16 C3
Millington YO42 58 E4
Millington Green DE6 40 E1
Millmeece ST21 40 A2
Millness IV63 87 K1
Millom LA18 54 E1
Millow SG18 33 F4
Millpool PL30 4 B3
Millport KA28 73 K5
Millthorpe S18 51 F5
Millthrop LA10 61 H7
Milltimber AB13 91 G4
Milltown, Aber. AB36 89 K4
Milltown, Cornw. PL22 4 B5
Milltown, D. & G. DG14 69 J6
Milltown, Devon EX31 6 D2
Milltown, High. IV12 97 G7
Milltown of Aberdalgie PH2 82 B5
Milltown of Auchindoun AB55 90 B1
Milltown of Craigston AB53 99 F5
Milltown of Edinvillie AB38 97 K7
Milltown of Kildrummy AB33 90 C3
Milltown of Rothiemay AB54 98 D6
Milltown of Towie AB33 90 C3
Milnathort KY13 82 C7
Milners Heath CH3 48 D6
Milngavie G62 74 D3
Milnrow OL16 49 J1
Milnsbridge HD3 50 D1
Milnthorpe LA7 55 H1
Milovaig IV55 93 G6
Milrig KA4 74 D7
Milson DY14 29 F1
Milstead ME9 14 E2
Milston SP4 20 E7
Milton, Angus DD8 82 E3
Milton, Cambs. CB4 33 H2
Milton, Cumb. CA8 70 A7
Milton, D. & G. DG2 68 D5
Milton, D. & G. DG2 65 J3
Milton, D. & G. DG8 64 C5
Milton, Derbys. DE65 41 F3
Milton, High. IV6 95 K6
Milton, High. IV18 96 E4
Milton, High. IV12 97 G6
Milton, High. IV54 94 D7
Milton, High. IV6 96 C7
Milton, High. KW1 105 J3
Milton, High. IV63 88 B1
Milton, Moray AB56 98 D4
Milton, N.Som. BS22 19 G5
Milton, Newport NP19 19 G3
Milton, Notts. NG22 51 K5
Milton, Oxon. OX15 31 F5
Milton, Oxon. OX14 21 H2
Milton, P. & K. PH8 82 A4
Milton, Pembs. SA70 16 D4
Milton, Ports. PO4 11 H5

Milton

Place	Page	Ref
Milton, *Som.* TA12	8	D2
Milton, *Stir.* FK8	81	G7
Milton, *Stoke* ST2	49	J7
Milton, *W.Dun.* G82	74	C3
Milton Abbas DT11	9	H4
Milton Abbot PL19	4	E3
Milton Bridge EH26	76	A4
Milton Bryan MK17	32	C5
Milton Clevedon BA4	9	F1
Milton Combe PL20	4	E4
Milton Damerel EX22	6	B4
Milton End GL2	29	G7
Milton Ernest MK44	32	D3
Milton Green CH3	48	D7
Milton Hill OX13	21	H2
MILTON KEYNES MK	32	B5
Milton Keynes Village MK10	32	B5
Milton Lilbourne SN9	20	E5
Milton Malsor NN7	31	J3
Milton Morenish FK21	81	H4
Milton of Auchinhove AB31	90	D4
Milton of Balgonie KY7	82	E7
Milton of Buchanan G63	74	C1
Milton of Cairnborrow AB54	98	C6
Milton of Callander FK17	81	G7
Milton of Campfield AB31	90	E4
Milton of Campsie G66	74	E3
Milton of Coldwells AB41	91	H1
Milton of Cullerlie AB32	91	F4
Milton of Cushnie AB33	90	D3
Milton of Dalcapon PH16	82	A2
Milton of Inveramsay AB51	91	F2
Milton of Noth AB54	90	D2
Milton of Tullich AB35	90	B5
Milton on Stour SP8	9	G2
Milton Regis ME10	24	E5
Milton Street BN26	13	J6
Miltonduff IV30	97	J5
Miltonhill IV36	97	H5
Miltonise DG8	64	B3
Milton-Lockhart ML8	75	G6
Milton-under-Wychwood OX7	30	D7
Milverton, *Som.* TA4	7	K3
Milverton, *Warks.* CV32	30	E2
Milwich ST18	40	B2
Mimbridge GU24	22	C5
Minard PA32	73	H1
Minard Castle PA32	73	H1
Minchington DT11	9	J3
Minchinhampton GL6	20	B1
Mindrum TD12	77	G7
Mindrummill TD12	77	G7
Minehead TA24	7	H1
Minera LL11	48	B7
Minety SN16	20	D2
Minety Lower Moor SN16	20	D2
Minffordd, *Gwyn.* LL40	37	G4
Minffordd, *Gwyn.* LL48	36	E2
Minffordd, *Gwyn.* LL57	46	D5
Miningsby PE22	53	G6
Minions PL14	4	C3
Minishant KA19	67	H2
Minley Manor GU17	22	B6
Minllyn SY20	37	H4
Minnes AB41	91	H2
Minngearraidh HS8	84	C2
Minnigaff DG8	64	E4
Minnonie AB45	99	F4
Minskip YO51	57	J3
Minstead SO43	10	D3
Minsted GU29	12	B4
Minster, *Kent* ME12	25	F4
Minster, *Kent* CT12	25	K5
Minster Lovell OX29	30	E7
Minsteracres NE44	62	B1
Minsterley SY5	38	C5
Minsterworth GL2	29	G7
Minterne Magna DT2	9	F4
Minterne Parva DT2	9	F4
Minting LN9	52	E5
Mintlaw AB42	99	J6
Minto TD9	70	A1
Minton SY6	38	D6
Minwear SA67	16	D3
Minworth B76	40	D6
Miodar PA77	78	B2
Mirbister KW17	107	C6
Mirehouse CA28	60	A5
Mireland KW1	105	J2
Mirfield WF14	57	H7
Miserden GL6	20	C1
Miskin, *R.C.T.* CF72	18	D3
Miskin, *R.C.T.* CF45	18	D2
Misselfore SP5	10	B2
Misson DN10	51	J3
Misterton, *Leics.* LE17	41	H7
Misterton, *Notts.* DN10	51	K3
Misterton, *Som.* TA18	8	D4
Mistley CO11	35	F5
Mitcham CR4	23	F5
Mitchel Troy NP25	28	D7
Mitcheldean GL17	29	F7
Mitchell TR8	3	F3
Mitchelland LA8	60	F7
Mitcheltroy Common NP25	19	H1
Mitford NE61	71	G5
Mithian TR5	2	E3
Mitton ST19	40	A4
Mixbury NN13	31	H5
Mixenden HX2	57	F7
Moar PH15	81	G3
Moat CA6	69	K6
Moats Tye IP14	34	E3
Mobberley, *Ches.* WA16	49	G5
Mobberley, *Staffs.* ST10	40	C1
Moccas HR2	28	C4
Mochdre, *Conwy* LL28	47	G5
Mochdre, *Powys* SY16	37	K7
Mochrum DG8	64	D6
Mockbeggar, *Hants.* BH24	10	C4
Mockbeggar, *Kent* TN12	14	C3
Mockerkin CA13	60	B4
Modbury PL21	5	G5
Moddershall ST15	40	B2
Modsarie KW14	103	J2
Moelfre, *I.o.A.* LL72	46	D4
Moelfre, *Powys* SY10	38	A3
Moffat DG10	69	F3
Mogerhanger MK44	32	E4
Moin'a'choire PA44	72	B4
Moine House IV27	103	H3
Moira DE12	41	F4
Molash CT4	15	F2
Mol-chlach PH41	85	K3
Mold (Yr Wyddgrug) CH7	48	B6
Molehill Green, *Essex* CM6	33	J6
Molehill Green, *Essex* CM6	34	B6
Molescroft HU17	59	G5
Molesden NE61	71	G5
Molesworth PE28	32	D1
Mollance DG7	65	H4
Molland EX36	7	G3
Mollington, *Ches.* CH1	48	C5
Mollington, *Oxon.* OX17	31	F4
Mollinsburn G67	75	F3
Monach Islands (Heisker Islands) HS6	92	B5
Monachty SY23	26	E2
Monachyle FK19	81	F6
Monevechadan PA24	80	C7
Monewden IP13	35	G3
Moneydie PH1	82	B5
Moneyrow Green SL6	22	B4
Moniaive DG3	68	C4
Monifieth DD5	83	G4
Monikie DD5	83	G4
Monimail KY15	82	D6
Monington SA43	26	A4
Monk Bretton S71	51	F2
Monk Fryston LS25	58	B7
Monk Hesleden TS27	63	F3
Monk Sherborne RG26	21	K6
Monk Soham IP13	35	G2
Monk Soham Green IP13	35	G2
Monk Street CM6	33	K6
Monken Hadley EN5	23	F2
Monkerton EX1	7	H6
Monkhide HR8	29	F4
Monkhill CA5	60	E1
Monkhopton WV16	39	F6
Monkland HR6	28	D3
Monkleigh EX39	6	C3
Monknash CF71	18	C4
Monkokehampton EX19	6	D5
Monks Eleigh IP7	34	D4
Monks Eleigh Tye IP7	34	D4
Monk's Gate RH13	13	F4
Monks' Heath SK10	49	H5
Monks Kirby CV23	41	G7
Monks Risborough HP27	22	B1
Monkscross PL17	4	D3
Monkseaton NE25	71	J6
Monkshill AB53	99	F6
Monksilver TA4	7	J2
Monkstadt IV51	93	J5
Monkswood NP15	19	G1
Monkton, *Devon* EX14	7	K5
Monkton, *Kent* CT12	25	J5
Monkton, *Pembs.* SA71	16	C5
Monkton, *S.Ayr.* KA9	67	H1
Monkton, *T. & W.* NE32	71	J7
Monkton, *V. of Glam.* CF71	18	C4
Monkton Combe BA2	20	A5
Monkton Deverill BA12	9	H1
Monkton Farleigh BA15	20	B5
Monkton Heathfield TA2	8	B2
Monkton Up Wimborne BH21	10	B3
Monkton Wyld DT6	8	C5
Monkwearmouth SR6	62	E1
Monkwood SO24	11	H1
Monmouth (Trefynwy) NP25	28	E7
Monnington Court HR2	28	C5
Monnington on Wye HR4	28	C4
Monreith DG8	64	D6
Montacute TA15	8	E3
Monteach AB41	99	G6
Montford SY4	38	D4
Montford Bridge SY4	38	D4
Montgarrie AB33	90	D3
Montgomery (Trefaldwyn) SY15	38	B6
Montgreenan KA13	74	B6
Montrave KY8	82	E7
Montrose DD10	83	J2
Monxton SP11	21	G7
Monyash DE45	50	D6
Monymusk AB51	90	E3
Monzie PH7	81	K5
Moodiesburn G69	74	E3
Moons Moat North B98	30	B2
Moonzie KY15	82	E6
Moor Allerton LS17	57	J6
Moor Cock LA2	56	B3
Moor Crichel BH21	9	J4
Moor End, *Beds.* MK43	32	D3
Moor End, *Beds.* LU6	32	C6
Moor End, *Cumb.* LA5	55	J2
Moor End, *E.Riding* YO43	58	E6
Moor End, *Lancs.* FY6	55	G5
Moor End, *N.Yorks.* YO19	58	B6
Moor End, *W.Yorks.* HX2	57	F7
Moor Green, *W.Mid.* B13	40	C7
Moor Green, *Wilts.* SN13	20	B5
Moor Head BD18	57	G6
Moor Monkton YO26	58	B4
Moor Row CA24	60	B5
Moor Side, *Lancs.* LA16	55	F7
Moor Side, *Lancs.* PR4	55	H6
Moor Side, *Lancs.* PR4	55	H6
Moor Side, *Lincs.* PE22	53	F7
Moor Street ME8	24	E5
Moorby PE22	53	F6
Moorcot HR5	28	C3
Moordown BH9	10	B5
Moore WA4	48	E4
Moorend CA5	60	E1
Moorends DN8	51	J1
Moorfield SK13	50	C3
Moorgreen, *Hants.* SO30	11	F3
Moorgreen, *Notts.* NG16	41	G1
Moorhall S18	51	F5
Moorhampton HR4	28	C4
Moorhouse, *Cumb.* CA5	60	E1
Moorhouse, *Notts.* NG23	51	K6
Moorland (Northmoor Green) TA7	8	C1
Moorlinch TA7	8	C1
Moorsholm TS12	63	H5
Moorside, *Dorset* DT10	9	G3
Moorside, *Gt.Man.* OL1	49	J2
Moorside, *W.Yorks.* LS13	57	H6
Moorthorpe WF9	51	G1
Moortown, *I.o.W.* PO30	11	F6
Moortown, *Lincs.* LN7	52	D3
Moortown, *Tel. & W.* TF6	39	F4
Morangie IV19	96	E3
Morar IV40	86	C5
Morborne PE7	42	E6
Morchard Bishop EX17	7	F5
Morcombelake DT6	8	D5
Morcott LE15	42	C5
Morda SY10	38	B3
Morden, *Dorset* BH20	9	J5
Morden, *Gt.Lon.* SM4	23	F5
Morden Park SM4	23	F5
Mordiford HR1	28	E5
Mordington Holdings TD15	77	H5
Mordon TS21	62	E4
More SY9	38	C6
Morebath EX16	7	H3
Morebattle TD5	70	C1
Morecambe LA4	55	H3
Morefield IV26	95	H2
Moreleigh TQ9	5	H5
Morenish FK21	81	H4
Moresby Parks CA28	60	A5
Morestead SO21	11	G2
Moreton, *Dorset* DT2	9	H6
Moreton, *Essex* CM5	23	J1
Moreton, *Here.* HR6	28	E2
Moreton, *Mersey.* CH46	48	B4
Moreton, *Oxon.* OX9	21	K1
Moreton, *Staffs.* DE6	40	D2
Moreton, *Staffs.* TF10	39	G4
Moreton Corbet SY4	38	E3
Moreton Jeffries HR1	29	F4
Moreton Mill SY4	38	E3
Moreton Morrell CV35	30	E3
Moreton on Lugg HR4	28	E4
Moreton Paddox CV35	30	E3
Moreton Pinkney NN11	31	G4
Moreton Say TF9	39	F2
Moreton Valence GL2	20	A1
Moretonhampstead TQ13	7	F7
Moreton-in-Marsh GL56	30	D5
Morfa, *Carmar.* SA44	17	J3
Morfa, *Cere.* SA44	26	C3
Morfa Bychan LL49	36	E2
Morfa Glas SA11	18	B1
Morfa Nefyn LL53	36	B1
Morgan's Vale SP5	10	C2
Morganstown CF15	18	E3
Mork GL15	19	J1
Morland CA10	61	G4
Morley, *Derbys.* DE7	41	F1
Morley, *Dur.* DL14	62	C4
Morley, *W.Yorks.* LS27	57	H7
Morley Green SK9	49	H4
Morley St. Botolph NR18	44	E6
Mornick PL17	4	D3
Morningside, *Edin.* EH10	76	A3
Morningside, *N.Lan.* ML2	75	G5
Morningthorpe NR15	45	G6
Morpeth NE61	71	H5
Morphie DD10	83	J1
Morrey DE13	40	D4
Morridge Side ST13	50	C7
Morriow Heath ST10	40	B2
Morriston, *S.Ayr.* KA19	67	G3
Morriston, *Swan.* SA6	17	K5
Morristown CF64	18	E4
Morroch PH39	86	C6
Morston NR25	44	E1
Mortehoe EX34	6	C1
Morthen S66	51	G4
Mortimer RG7	21	K5
Mortimer West End RG7	21	K5
Mortimer's Cross HR6	28	D2
Mortlake SW14	23	F4
Morton, *Derbys.* DE55	51	G6
Morton, *Lincs.* PE10	42	D3
Morton, *Lincs.* DN21	52	B3
Morton, *Lincs.* LN6	52	B6
Morton, *Notts.* NG25	51	K7
Morton, *S.Glos.* BS35	19	K2
Morton, *Shrop.* SY10	38	B3
Morton Bagot B80	30	C2
Morton on the Hill NR9	45	F4
Morton Tinmouth DL2	62	C4
Morton-on-Swale DL7	62	E7
Morvah TR20	2	B5
Morval PL13	4	C5
Morvich, *High.* IV40	87	F2
Morvich, *High.* IV28	96	E1
Morvil SA66	16	D1
Morville WV16	39	F6
Morwellham PL19	4	E4
Morwenstow EX23	6	A4
Morwick Hall NE65	71	H3
Mosborough S20	51	G4
Moscow KA4	74	C6
Mosedale CA11	60	E3
Moselden Height HD3	50	C1
Moseley, *W.Mid.* B13	40	C7
Moseley, *W.Mid.* WV10	40	B6
Moseley, *Worcs.* WR2	29	H3
Moses Gate BL3	49	G2
Moss, *Arg. & B.* PA77	78	A3
Moss, *S.Yorks.* DN6	51	H1
Moss, *Wrex.* LL11	48	C7
Moss Bank WA11	48	E3
Moss Houses SK11	49	H5
Moss Nook M22	49	H4
Moss of Barmuckity IV30	97	K5
Moss Side, *Gt.Man.* M14	49	H3
Moss Side, *Lancs.* FY8	55	G6
Moss Side, *Mersey.* L31	48	C2
Mossat AB33	90	C3
Mossbank ZE2	108	D5
Mossblown KA6	67	J1
Mossburnford TD8	70	B2
Mossdale DG7	65	G3
Mossend ML4	75	F4
Mossgiel KA5	67	J1
Mosshead AB54	90	D1
Mosside of Ballinshoe DD8	83	F2
Mossley, *Ches.* CW12	49	H6
Mossley, *Gt.Man.* OL5	49	J2
Mossley Hill L18	48	C4
Mosspaul Hotel DG13	69	J4
Moss-side, *High.* IV12	97	F6
Moss-side, *Moray* AB54	98	D5
Mosstodloch IV32	98	B4
Mosston DD11	83	G3
Mossy Lea WN6	48	E1
Mosterton DT8	8	D4
Moston, *Gt.Man.* M40	49	H2
Moston, *Shrop.* SY4	38	E3
Moston Green CW11	49	G6
Mostyn CH8	47	K4
Motcombe SP7	9	H2
Mothecombe PL8	5	G6
Motherby CA11	60	F4
MOTHERWELL ML	75	F5
Mottingham SE9	23	H4
Mottisfont SO51	10	E2
Mottistone PO30	11	F6
Mottram in Longdendale SK14	49	J3
Mottram St. Andrew SK10	49	H5
Mouldsworth WA6	48	E5
Moulin PH16	82	A2
Moulsecoomb BN2	13	G6
Moulsford OX10	21	J3
Moulsham CM2	24	D1
Moulsoe MK16	32	C4
Moulton, *Ches.* CW9	49	F6
Moulton, *Lincs.* PE12	43	G3
Moulton, *N.Yorks.* DL10	62	D6
Moulton, *Northants.* NN3	31	J2
Moulton, *Suff.* CB8	33	K2
Moulton, *V. of Glam.* CF62	18	D4
Moulton Chapel PE12	43	F4
Moulton St. Mary NR13	45	J5
Moulton Seas End PE12	43	G3
Mounie Castle AB51	91	F2
Mount, *Cornw.* TR8	2	E3
Mount, *Cornw.* PL30	4	B4
Mount, *High.* IV12	97	G2
Mount, *Kent* CT4	15	G3
Mount, *W.Yorks.* HD3	50	D1
Mount Ambrose TR16	2	E4
Mount Bures CO8	34	D5
Mount Charles PL25	4	A5
Mount Hawke TR4	2	E4
Mount Manisty CH65	48	C5
Mount Oliphant KA6	67	H2
Mount Pleasant, *Ches.* ST7	49	H7
Mount Pleasant, *Derbys.* DE56	41	F1
Mount Pleasant, *Derbys.* DE11	40	E4
Mount Pleasant, *E.Suss.* BN8	13	H5
Mount Pleasant, *Flints.* CH6	48	B5
Mount Pleasant, *Gt.Lon.* UB9	22	D2
Mount Pleasant, *Hants.* SO41	10	E5
Mount Pleasant, *Norf.* NR17	44	D6
Mount Pleasant, *Suff.* CO10	34	B4
Mount Sorrel SP5	10	B2
Mount Tabor HX2	57	F6
Mountain HX2	57	F6
Mountain Ash (Aberpennar) CF45	18	D2
Mountain Cross EH46	75	K6
Mountain Water SA62	16	C2
Mountbenger TD7	69	J1
Mountblairy AB53	98	E5
Mountblow G60	74	C3
Mountfield TN32	14	C5
Mountgerald IV15	96	C5
Mountjoy TR8	3	F2
Mountnessing CM15	24	C2
Mounton NP16	19	J2
Mountsorrel LE12	41	H4
Mousa ZE2	109	D10
Mousehole TR19	2	B6
Mouswald DG1	69	F6
Mow Cop ST7	49	H7
Mowden DL3	62	D5
Mowhaugh TD5	70	D1
Mowsley LE17	41	J7
Mowtie AB39	91	G6
Moxley WS10	40	B6
Moy, *High.* PH33	87	H6
Moy, *High.* PH31	88	B6
Moy, *High.* IV13	88	E1
Moy House IV36	97	H6
Moylgrove SA43	26	A4
Muasdale PA29	72	E6
Much Birch HR2	28	E5
Much Cowarne HR7	29	F4
Much Dewchurch HR2	28	D5
Much Hadham SG10	33	H7
Much Hoole PR4	55	H7
Much Hoole Town PR4	55	H7
Much Marcle HR8	29	F5
Much Wenlock TF13	39	F5
Muchalls AB39	91	H5
Muchelney TA10	8	D2
Muchelney Ham TA10	8	D2
Muchlarnick PL13	4	C5
Muchra TD7	69	H2
Muchrachd IV4	87	J1
Muck PH41	85	K7
Mucking SS17	24	C3
Muckle Roe ZE2	109	C6
Muckleford DT2	9	F5
Mucklestone TF9	39	G2
Muckleton TF6	38	E3
Muckletown AB33	90	D2
Muckley WV16	39	F6
Muckley Corner WS14	40	C5
Muckton LN11	53	G4
Muddiford EX31	6	D2
Muddles Green BN8	13	J5
Muddleswood BN6	13	F5
Mudeford BH23	10	C5
Mudford BA21	8	E3
Mudgley BS28	19	H7
Mugdock G62	74	D3
Mugeary IV51	85	K1
Mugginton DE6	40	E1
Muggintonlane End DE6	40	E1
Muggleswick DH8	62	B2
Mugswell KT20	23	F6
Muie IV28	96	D1
Muir IV28	89	H6
Muir of Fowlis AB33	90	D3
Muir of Lochs IV32	98	B4
Muir of Ord IV6	96	C6
Muirden AB53	99	F5
Muirdrum DD7	83	G4
Muiredge KY8	76	B1
Muirhead, *Aber.* AB33	90	D3
Muirhead, *Angus* DD2	82	E4
Muirhead, *Fife* KY15	82	D7
Muirhead, *Moray* IV36	97	H6
Muirhead, *N.Lan.* G69	74	E4
Muirhouses EH51	75	J2
Muirkirk KA18	68	B1
Muirmill FK6	75	F2
Muirtack, *Aber.* AB41	91	H1
Muirtack, *Aber.* AB53	99	G6
Muirton, *High.* IV11	96	E5
Muirton, *P. & K.* PH3	82	A6
Muirton, *P. & K.* PH1	82	C3
Muirton of Ardblair PH10	82	C3
Muirton of Ballochy DD10	83	H1
Muirtown IV6	97	G2
Muiryfold AB53	99	F5
Muker DL11	62	A7
Mulbarton NR14	45	F5
Mulben AB55	98	B5
Mulhagery HS2	101	F7
Mull PA	79	G4
Mullach Charlabhaigh HS2	100	E3
Mullacott Cross EX34	6	D1
Mullion TR12	2	D7
Mumby LN13	53	J5
Munderfield Row HR7	29	F3
Munderfield Stocks HR7	29	F3
Mundesley NR11	45	H2
Mundford IP26	44	C6
Mundham NR14	45	H6
Mundon CM9	24	E1
Mundurno AB23	91	H3
Munerigie PH35	87	J4
Mungasdale IV22	95	F2
Mungoswells EH39	76	C3
Mungrisdale CA11	60	E3
Munlochy IV8	96	D6
Munnoch KA22	74	A6
Munsley HR8	29	F4
Munslow SY7	38	E7
Murchington TQ13	6	E7
Murcott, *Oxon.* OX5	31	G7
Murcott, *Wilts.* SN16	20	C2
Murdostoun ML2	75	G5
Murieston EH54	75	J4
Murkle KW14	105	G2
Murlaganmore FK21	81	G4
Murlaggan, *High.* PH34	87	J3
Murlaggan, *High.* PH31	87	K6
Murra KW16	107	B7
Murrell Green RG27	22	A6
Murroes DD5	83	F4
Murrow PE13	43	G5
Mursley MK17	32	B6

Murston **ME10** 25 F5
Murthill **DD8** 83 F2
Murthly **PH1** 82 B4
Murton, *Cumb.* **CA16** 61 J4
Murton, *Dur.* **SR7** 62 E2
Murton, *Northumb.* **TD15** 77 H6
Murton, *Swan.* **SA3** 17 J6
Murton, *York* **YO19** 58 C4
Musbury **EX13** 8 B5
Muscliff **BH9** 10 B5
Musdale **PA34** 80 A5
Musselburgh **EH21** 76 B3
Mustard Hyrn **NR29** 45 J4
Muston, *Leics.* **NG13** 42 B2
Muston, *N.Yorks.* **YO14** 59 G2
Mustow Green **DY10** 29 H1
Mutford **NR34** 45 J7
Muthill **PH5** 81 K6
Mutterton **EX15** 7 J5
Muxton **TF2** 39 G4
Mybster **KW1** 105 G3
Myddfai **SA20** 27 G5
Myddle **SY4** 38 D3
Myddlewood **SY4** 38 D3
Mydroilyn **SA48** 26 D3
Myerscough College **PR3** 55 H6
Myerscough Smithy **PR5** 56 B6
Mylor **TR11** 3 F5
Mylor Bridge **TR11** 3 F5
Mynachdy **CF14** 18 E4
Mynachlog-ddu **SA66** 16 E1
Myndtown **SY7** 38 C7
Mynydd Fechell **LL68** 46 B3
Mynydd Llandygai **LL57** 46 E6
Mynydd-bach, *Mon.* **NP16** 19 H2
Mynydd-bach, *Swan.* **SA5** 17 K5
Mynyddygarreg **SA17** 17 H4
Mynytho **LL53** 36 C2
Myrebird **AB31** 91 F5
Mytchett **GU16** 22 B6
Mytholm **HX7** 56 E7
Mytholmroyd **HX7** 57 F7
Mythop **FY4** 55 G6
Myton-on-Swale **YO61** 57 K3
Mytton **SY4** 38 D4

N
Naast **IV22** 94 E3
Nab's Head **PR5** 56 B7
Na-Buirgh **HS3** 93 F2
Naburn **YO19** 58 B5
Nackington **CT4** 15 G2
Nacton **IP10** 35 G4
Nadderwater **EX4** 7 G6
Nafferton **YO25** 59 G4
Nailbridge **GL17** 29 F7
Nailsbourne **TA2** 8 B2
Nailsea **BS48** 19 H4
Nailstone **CV13** 41 G5
Nailsworth **GL6** 20 B2
Nairn **IV12** 97 F6
Nancegollan **TR13** 2 D5
Nancekuke **TR16** 2 D4
Nancledra **TR20** 2 B5
Nanhoron **LL53** 36 B2
Nannau **LL40** 37 G3
Nannerch **CH7** 47 K6
Nanpantan **LE11** 41 H4
Nanpean **PL26** 3 G3
Nanstallon **PL30** 4 A4
Nant Peris **LL55** 46 E7
Nant-ddu **CF48** 27 K7
Nanternis **SA45** 26 C3
Nantgaredig **SA32** 17 H2
Nantgarw **CF15** 18 E3
Nant-glas **LD1** 27 J2
Nantglyn **LL16** 47 J6
Nantgwyn **LD6** 27 J1
Nantlle **LL54** 46 D7
Nantmawr **SY10** 38 B3
Nantmel **LD1** 27 K2
Nantmor **LL55** 37 F1
Nantwich **CW5** 49 F7
Nantycaws **SA32** 17 H3
Nant-y-derry **NP7** 19 G1
Nant-y-dugoed **SY21** 37 J4
Nantyffyllon **CF34** 18 B2
Nantyglo **NP23** 28 A7
Nant-y-Gollen **SY10** 38 B3
Nant-y-groes **LD1** 27 K2
Nant-y-moel **CF32** 18 C2
Nant-y-Pandy **LL33** 46 E5
Naphill **HP14** 22 B2
Napley Heath **TF9** 39 G2
Nappa **BD23** 56 D4
Napton on the Hill **CV47** 31 F2
Narberth (Arberth) **SA67** 16 E3
Narborough, *Leics.* **LE19** 41 H6
Narborough, *Norf.* **PE32** 44 B4
Narkurs **PL11** 4 D5
Narrachan **PA35** 80 A6
Nasareth **LL54** 36 D1
Naseby **NN6** 31 H1
Nash, *Bucks.* **MK17** 31 J5
Nash, *Here.* **LD8** 28 C2
Nash, *Newport* **NP18** 19 G3
Nash, *Shrop.* **SY8** 29 F1
Nash, *V. of Glam.* **CF71** 18 C5
Nash Street **DA13** 24 C5
Nassington **PE8** 42 D6
Nasty **SG11** 33 G6
Nateby, *Cumb.* **CA17** 61 J6
Nateby, *Lancs.* **PR3** 55 H5
Nately Scures **RG27** 22 A6
Natland **LA9** 55 J1
Naughton **IP7** 34 E4
Naunton, *Glos.* **GL54** 30 C6
Naunton, *Worcs.* **WR8** 29 H5

Naunton Beauchamp **WR8** 29 J3
Navenby **LN5** 52 C7
Navestock **RM4** 23 J2
Navestock Side **CM14** 23 J2
Navidale **KW8** 105 F7
Navity **IV11** 96 E5
Nawton **YO62** 58 C1
Nayland **CO6** 34 D5
Nazeing **EN9** 23 H1
Neacroft **BH23** 10 C5
Neal's Green **CV7** 41 F7
Neap **ZE2** 109 E4
Neap House **DN15** 52 B1
Near Sawrey **LA22** 60 E7
Nearton End **MK17** 32 B6
Neasden **NW10** 23 F3
Neasham **DL2** 62 E5
Neat Enstone **OX7** 30 E6
Neath (Castell-Nedd) **SA11** 18 A3
Neatham **GU34** 22 A7
Neatishead **NR12** 45 H3
Nebo, *Cere.* **SY23** 26 E2
Nebo, *Conwy* **LL26** 47 G7
Nebo, *Gwyn.* **LL54** 46 C7
Nebo, *I.o.A.* **LL68** 46 C3
Necton **PE37** 44 C5
Nedd **IV27** 102 D5
Nedderton **NE22** 71 H5
Nedging **IP7** 34 D4
Nedging Tye **IP7** 34 E4
Needham **IP20** 45 G7
Needham Market **IP6** 34 E3
Needham Street **CB8** 34 B2
Needingworth **PE27** 33 G1
Needwood **DE13** 40 D3
Neen Savage **DY14** 29 F1
Neen Sollars **DY14** 29 F1
Neenton **WV16** 39 F7
Nefyn **LL53** 36 C1
Neighbourne **BA3** 19 K7
Neilston **G78** 74 C5
Neithrop **OX16** 31 F4
Nelson, *Caerp.* **CF46** 18 E2
Nelson, *Lancs.* **BB9** 56 D6
Nelson Village **NE23** 71 H6
Nemphlar **ML11** 75 G6
Nempnett Thrubwell **BS40** 19 J5
Nenthall **CA9** 61 J2
Nenthead **CA9** 61 J2
Nenthorn **TD5** 76 E7
Neopardy **EX17** 7 F6
Nerabus **PA48** 72 A5
Nercwys **CH7** 48 B6
Neriby **PA43** 72 B4
Nerston **G74** 74 E5
Nesbit **NE71** 77 H7
Nesfield **LS29** 57 F5
Ness **CH64** 48 C5
Ness of Tenston **KW16** 107 B6
Nesscliffe **SY4** 38 C4
Neston, *Ches.* **CH64** 48 B5
Neston, *Wilts.* **SN13** 20 B5
Nether Alderley **SK10** 49 H5
Nether Auchendrane **KA7** 67 H2
Nether Barr **DG8** 64 E4
Nether Blainslie **TD1** 76 D6
Nether Broughton **LE14** 41 J3
Nether Burrow **LA6** 56 B2
Nether Cerne **DT2** 9 F5
Nether Compton **DT9** 8 E3
Nether Crimond **AB51** 91 G2
Nether Dalgliesh **TD7** 69 H3
Nether Dallachy **IV32** 98 B4
Nether Edge **S7** 51 F4
Nether End **DE45** 50 E5
Nether Exe **EX5** 7 H6
Nether Glasslaw **AB43** 99 G5
Nether Handwick **DD8** 82 E3
Nether Haugh **S62** 51 G3
Nether Heage **DE56** 51 F7
Nether Heselden **BD23** 56 D2
Nether Heyford **NN7** 31 H3
Nether Kellet **LA6** 55 J3
Nether Kinmundy **AB42** 99 J6
Nether Langwith **NG20** 51 H5
Nether Lenshie **AB51** 98 E6
Nether Loads **S42** 51 F6
Nether Moor **S42** 51 F6
Nether Padley **S32** 50 E5
Nether Pitforthie **AB30** 91 G7
Nether Poppleton **YO26** 58 B4
Nether Silton **YO7** 63 F7
Nether Skyborry **LD7** 28 B1
Nether Stowey **TA5** 7 K2
Nether Urquhart **KY14** 82 C7
Nether Wallop **SO20** 10 E1
Nether Wasdale **CA20** 60 C6
Nether Wellwood **KA18** 68 B1
Nether Welton **CA5** 60 E2
Nether Westcote **OX7** 30 D6
Nether Whitacre **B46** 40 E6
Nether Winchendon (Lower Winchendon) **HP18** 31 J7
Nether Worton **OX7** 31 F6
Netheravon **SP4** 20 E7
Netherbrae **AB53** 99 F5
Netherbrough **KW17** 107 C6
Netherburn **ML9** 75 G6
Netherbury **DT6** 8 D5
Netherby, *Cumb.* **CA6** 69 J6
Netherby, *N.Yorks.* **HG3** 57 J5
Nethercott **OX5** 31 F6
Netherend **GL15** 19 J1
Netherfield, *E.Suss.* **TN33** 14 C6
Netherfield, *Notts.* **NG4** 41 J1
Netherfield, *S.Lan.* **ML10** 75 F6
Netherhall **KA30** 74 A4
Netherhampton **SP2** 10 C2

Netherhay **DT8** 8 D4
Netherland Green **ST14** 40 D2
Netherley **AB39** 91 G5
Nethermill **DG1** 69 F5
Nethermuir **AB42** 99 H6
Netherseal **DE12** 40 E4
Nethershield **KA5** 67 K1
Netherstreet **SN15** 20 C5
Netherthird, *D. & G.* **DG7** 65 H5
Netherthird, *E.Ayr.* **KA18** 67 K2
Netherthong **HD9** 50 D2
Netherthorpe **S80** 51 H4
Netherton, *Angus* **DD9** 83 G2
Netherton, *Ches.* **WA6** 48 E5
Netherton, *Devon* **TQ12** 5 J3
Netherton, *Hants.* **SP11** 21 G6
Netherton, *Mersey.* **L30** 48 C2
Netherton, *N.Lan.* **ML2** 75 F5
Netherton, *Northumb.* **NE65** 70 E3
Netherton, *Oxon.* **OX13** 21 H1
Netherton, *P. & K.* **PH10** 82 C2
Netherton, *S.Lan.* **ML11** 75 H5
Netherton, *W.Mid.* **DY2** 40 B7
Netherton, *W.Yorks.* **WF4** 50 E1
Netherton, *W.Yorks.* **HD4** 50 D1
Netherton, *Worcs.* **WR10** 29 J4
Netherton Burnfoot **NE65** 70 E3
Netherton Northside **NE65** 70 E3
Nethertown, *Cumb.* **CA22** 60 A6
Nethertown, *Ork.* **KW1** 105 J1
Nethertown, *Staffs.* **WS15** 40 D4
Netherwitton **NE61** 71 G4
Netherwood, *D. & G.* **DG1** 65 K3
Netherwood, *E.Ayr.* **KA18** 68 B1
Nethy Bridge **PH25** 89 H2
Netley Abbey **SO31** 11 F4
Netley Marsh **SO40** 10 E3
Nettlebed **RG9** 21 K3
Nettlebridge **BA3** 19 K7
Nettlecombe, *Dorset* **DT6** 8 E5
Nettlecombe, *I.o.W.* **PO38** 11 G7
Nettlecombe, *Som.* **TA4** 7 J2
Nettleden **HP1** 32 D7
Nettleham **LN2** 52 D5
Nettlestead, *Kent* **ME18** 23 K6
Nettlestead, *Suff.* **IP8** 34 E4
Nettlestead Green **ME18** 23 K6
Nettlestone **PO34** 11 H5
Nettlesworth **DH2** 62 D2
Nettleton, *Lincs.* **LN7** 52 E2
Nettleton, *Wilts.* **SN14** 20 B4
Nettleton Hill **HD7** 50 C1
Netton, *Devon* **PL8** 5 F6
Netton, *Wilts.* **SP4** 10 C1
Neuadd, *Cere.* **SA47** 26 D3
Neuadd, *I.o.A.* **LL67** 46 B3
Neuadd, *Powys* **LD7** 27 J4
Nevendon **SS12** 24 D2
Nevern **SA42** 16 D1
Nevill Holt **LE16** 42 B6
New Abbey **DG2** 65 K4
New Aberdour **AB43** 99 G4
New Addington **CR0** 23 G5
New Alresford **SO24** 11 G1
New Alyth **PH11** 82 D3
New Arley **CV7** 40 E6
New Arram **HU17** 59 G5
New Ash Green **DA3** 24 C5
New Balderton **NG24** 52 B7
New Barn **DA3** 24 C5
New Belses **TD8** 70 A1
New Bewick **NE66** 71 F1
New Bolingbroke **PE22** 53 G7
New Boultham **LN6** 52 C5
New Bradwell **MK13** 32 B4
New Brancepeth **DH7** 62 D2
New Bridge, *D. & G.* **DG2** 65 K3
New Bridge, *Devon* **TQ13** 5 H3
New Brighton, *Flints.* **CH7** 48 B6
New Brighton, *Hants.* **PO10** 11 J4
New Brighton, *Mersey.* **CH45** 48 C3
New Brighton, *W.Yorks.* **LS27** 57 H7
New Brinsley **NG16** 51 G7
New Broughton **LL11** 48 C7
New Buckenham **NR16** 44 E6
New Byth **AB53** 99 G5
New Cheriton **SO24** 11 G2
New Cross, *Cere.* **SY23** 27 F1
New Cross, *Gt.Lon.* **SE14** 23 G4
New Cumnock **KA18** 68 B2
New Deer **AB53** 99 G6
New Duston **NN5** 31 J2
New Earswick **YO31** 58 C4
New Edlington **DN12** 51 H3
New Elgin **IV30** 97 K5
New Ellerby **HU11** 59 H6
New Eltham **SE9** 23 H4
New End **B96** 30 B2
New England **PE1** 42 E5
New Farnley **LS12** 57 H6
New Ferry **CH62** 48 C4
New Galloway **DG7** 65 G3
New Gilston **KY8** 83 F7
New Greens **AL3** 22 E1
New Grimsby **TR24** 2 B1
New Hartley **NE25** 71 J6
New Haw **KT15** 22 D5
New Heaton **TD12** 77 G7
New Hedges **SA70** 16 E4
New Herrington **DH4** 62 E1
New Hinksey **OX1** 21 J1
New Holland **DN19** 59 G7
New Houghton, *Derbys.* **NG19** 51 H6

New Houghton, *Norf.* **PE31** 44 B3
New Houses **BD24** 56 D2
New Hunwick **DL15** 62 C3
New Hutton **LA8** 61 G7
New Hythe **ME20** 14 C2
New Inn, *Carmar.* **SA39** 17 H1
New Inn, *Fife* **KY7** 82 D7
New Inn, *Mon.* **NP16** 19 H1
New Inn, *Torfaen* **NP4** 19 F2
New Invention, *Shrop.* **SY7** 28 B1
New Invention, *W.Mid.* **WV12** 40 B5
New Kelso **IV54** 95 F7
New Lanark **ML11** 75 G6
New Lane **L40** 48 D1
New Lane End **WA3** 49 F3
New Leake **PE22** 53 H7
New Leeds **AB42** 99 H5
New Leslie **AB52** 90 D2
New Lodge **S75** 51 F2
New Longton **PR4** 55 J7
New Luce **DG8** 64 B4
New Mains **ML11** 75 G7
New Mains of Ury **AB39** 91 G6
New Malden **KT3** 23 F5
New Marske **TS11** 63 H4
New Marton **SY11** 38 C2
New Mill, *Cornw.* **TR20** 2 B5
New Mill, *Herts.* **HP23** 32 C7
New Mill, *W.Yorks.* **HD9** 50 D2
New Mill End **LU1** 32 E7
New Mills, *Cornw.* **TR2** 3 F3
New Mills, *Derbys.* **SK22** 50 C4
New Mills, *Glos.* **GL15** 19 K1
New Mills, *Mon.* **NP25** 19 J1
New Mills, *Powys* **SY16** 37 K5
New Milton **BH25** 10 D5
New Mistley **CO11** 35 F5
New Moat **SA63** 16 D2
New Ollerton **NG22** 51 J6
New Orleans **PA28** 66 B2
New Oscott **B44** 40 C6
New Park, *Cornw.* **PL15** 4 B2
New Park, *N.Yorks.* **HG1** 57 H4
New Pitsligo **AB43** 99 G5
New Polzeath **PL27** 3 G1
New Quay (Ceinewydd) **SA45** 26 C2
New Rackheath **NR13** 45 G4
New Radnor (Maesyfed) **LD8** 28 B2
New Rent **CA11** 61 F3
New Ridley **NE43** 71 F7
New Road Side **BD22** 56 E5
New Romney **TN28** 15 F5
New Rossington **DN11** 51 J3
New Row, *Cere.* **SY25** 27 G1
New Row, *Lancs.* **PR3** 56 B6
New Sawley **NG10** 41 G2
New Shoreston **NE69** 77 K7
New Silksworth **SR3** 62 E1
New Swannington **LE67** 41 G4
New Totley **S17** 51 F5
New Town, *Beds.* **SG18** 32 E4
New Town, *Cere.* **SA43** 26 A4
New Town, *Dorset* **SP5** 9 J3
New Town, *Dorset* **BH21** 9 J4
New Town, *E.Loth.* **EH41** 76 C3
New Town, *E.Suss.* **TN22** 13 H4
New Town, *Glos.* **GL54** 30 B5
New Tredegar **NP24** 18 E1
New Tupton **S42** 51 F6
New Ulva **PA31** 73 F2
New Valley **HS2** 101 G4
New Village **DN5** 51 H2
New Walsoken **PE13** 43 H5
New Waltham **DN36** 53 F2
New Winton **EH33** 76 C3
New World **PE15** 43 G6
New Yatt **OX29** 31 F7
New York, *Lincs.* **LN4** 53 F7
New York, *T. & W.* **NE27** 71 J6
Newall **LS21** 57 H5
Newark, *Ork.* **KW17** 106 G3
Newark, *Peter.* **PE1** 43 F5
Newark-on-Trent **NG24** 52 B7
Newarthill **ML1** 75 F5
Newball **LN3** 52 D5
Newbarn **CT18** 15 G4
Newbarns **LA14** 55 F2
Newbattle **EH22** 76 B4
Newbiggin, *Cumb.* **CA11** 61 H4
Newbiggin, *Cumb.* **CA10** 61 H4
Newbiggin, *Cumb.* **CA16** 61 G2
Newbiggin, *Cumb.* **LA12** 55 F3
Newbiggin, *Cumb.* **LA12** 60 B7
Newbiggin, *Dur.* **DL12** 62 A4
Newbiggin, *N.Yorks.* **DL8** 57 F1
Newbiggin, *N.Yorks.* **DL8** 62 A7
Newbiggin, *Northumb.* **NE46** 70 E7
Newbiggin-by-the-Sea **NE64** 71 J5
Newbigging, *Aber.* **AB39** 91 G5
Newbigging, *Aber.* **AB39** 89 J6
Newbigging, *Angus* **DD4** 83 F4
Newbigging, *Angus* **DD5** 83 F4
Newbigging, *Angus* **DD5** 83 G1
Newbigging, *S.Lan.* **ML11** 75 J6
Newbigging-on-Lune **CA17** 61 J6
Newbold, *Derbys.* **S41** 51 F5
Newbold, *Leics.* **LE67** 41 G4
Newbold on Avon **CV21** 31 F1
Newbold on Stour **CV37** 30 D4
Newbold Pacey **CV35** 30 D3
Newbold Verdon **LE9** 41 G5
Newborough, *I.o.A.* **LL61** 46 C6
Newborough, *Peter.* **PE6** 43 F5
Newborough, *Staffs.* **DE13** 40 D3

Newbottle, *Northants.* **OX17** 31 G5
Newbottle, *T. & W.* **DH4** 62 E1
Newbourne **IP12** 35 G4
Newbridge (Cefn Bychan), *Caerp.* **NP11** 19 F2
Newbridge, *Cornw.* **TR20** 2 B5
Newbridge, *Cornw.* **PL17** 4 D3
Newbridge, *E.Suss.* **TN7** 13 H3
Newbridge, *Edin.* **EH28** 75 K3
Newbridge, *Hants.* **SO40** 10 D3
Newbridge, *I.o.W.* **PO41** 11 F6
Newbridge, *N.Yorks.* **YO18** 58 E1
Newbridge, *Oxon.* **OX29** 21 H1
Newbridge, *Pembs.* **SA62** 16 C1
Newbridge, *Wrex.* **LL14** 38 B1
Newbridge Green **WR8** 29 H5
Newbridge on Wye **LD1** 27 K3
Newbridge-on-Usk **NP15** 19 G2
Newbrough **NE47** 70 D7
Newbuildings **EX17** 7 F5
Newburgh, *Aber.* **AB43** 99 H5
Newburgh, *Aber.* **AB41** 91 H2
Newburgh, *Fife* **KY14** 82 D6
Newburgh, *Lancs.* **WN8** 48 D1
Newburgh, *Sc.Bord.* **TD7** 69 J1
Newburn **NE15** 71 G7
Newbury, *Som.* **BA11** 19 K7
Newbury, *W.Berks.* **RG14** 21 H5
Newbury, *Wilts.* **BA12** 20 B7
Newbury Park **IG2** 23 H3
Newby, *Cumb.* **CA10** 61 G4
Newby, *Lancs.* **BB7** 56 D5
Newby, *N.Yorks.* **TS8** 63 G5
Newby, *N.Yorks.* **LA2** 56 C3
Newby, *N.Yorks.* **YO12** 59 G1
Newby Bridge **LA12** 55 G1
Newby Cote **LA2** 56 C2
Newby Cross **CA5** 60 E1
Newby East **CA4** 61 F1
Newby West **CA2** 60 E1
Newby Wiske **DL7** 57 J1
Newcastle, *Bridgend* **CF31** 18 B4
Newcastle, *Mon.* **NP25** 28 D7
Newcastle, *Shrop.* **SY7** 38 B7
Newcastle Emlyn (Castell Newydd Emlyn) **SA38** 26 C4
Newcastle International Airport **NE13** 71 G6
NEWCASTLE UPON TYNE NE 71 H7
Newcastleton **TD9** 69 K5
Newcastle-under-Lyme **ST5** 40 A1
Newchapel, *Pembs.* **SA37** 17 G2
Newchapel, *Stoke* **ST7** 49 H7
Newchapel, *Surr.* **RH7** 23 G7
Newchurch, *Carmar.* **SA33** 17 G2
Newchurch, *I.o.W.* **PO36** 11 G6
Newchurch, *Kent* **TN29** 15 F4
Newchurch, *Lancs.* **BB4** 56 D7
Newchurch, *Lancs.* **BB12** 56 D6
Newchurch, *Mon.* **NP16** 19 H2
Newchurch, *Powys* **HR5** 28 B3
Newchurch, *Staffs.* **DE13** 40 D3
Newcott **EX14** 8 B4
Newcraighall **EH21** 76 B3
Newdigate **RH5** 22 E7
Newell Green **RG42** 22 B4
Newenden **TN18** 14 D5
Newent **GL18** 29 G6
Newerne **GL15** 19 K1
Newfield, *Dur.* **DL14** 62 D3
Newfield, *Dur.* **DH2** 62 D1
Newfield, *High.* **IV19** 96 E4
Newfound **RG23** 21 J6
Newgale **SA62** 16 B2
Newgate **NR25** 44 E1
Newgate Street **SG13** 23 G1
Newgord **ZE2** 108 E2
Newhall, *Ches.* **CW5** 39 F1
Newhall, *Derbys.* **DE11** 40 E3
Newham **NE67** 71 G1
Newham Hall **NE67** 71 G1
Newhaven **BN9** 13 H6
Newhey **OL16** 49 J1
Newholm **YO21** 63 K5
Newhouse **ML1** 75 F4
Newick **BN8** 13 H4
Newingreen **CT21** 15 G4
Newington, *Edin.* **EH9** 76 A3
Newington, *Kent* **CT18** 15 G4
Newington, *Kent* **ME9** 24 E5
Newington, *Notts.* **DN10** 51 J3
Newington, *Oxon.* **OX10** 21 K2
Newington Bagpath **GL8** 20 B2
Newland, *Cumb.* **LA12** 55 G2
Newland, *Glos.* **GL16** 19 J1
Newland, *Hull* **HU6** 59 G6
Newland, *N.Yorks.* **YO8** 58 C7
Newland, *Oxon.* **OX28** 30 E7
Newland, *Worcs.* **WR13** 29 G4
Newlandrig **EH23** 76 B4
Newlands, *Cumb.* **CA5** 60 E3
Newlands, *Essex* **SS8** 24 E3
Newlands, *Northumb.* **DH8** 62 B1
Newlands, *Sc.Bord.* **TD9** 70 A4
Newland's Corner **GU4** 22 D7
Newlands of Geise **KW14** 105 F2
Newlands of Tynet **IV32** 98 B4
Newlyn **TR18** 2 B6
Newlyn East **TR8** 3 F3
Newmachar **AB21** 91 G3
Newmains **ML2** 75 G5
Newman's End **CM22** 33 J7
Newman's Green **CO10** 34 C4
Newmarket, *Suff.* **CB8** 33 K2
Newmarket, *W.Isles* **HS2** 101 G4

Newmill, *Aber.* AB39 91 F6
Newmill, *Aber.* AB41 99 G6
Newmill, *Aber.* AB51 91 G2
Newmill, *Moray* AB55 98 C5
Newmill, *Sc.Bord.* TD9 69 K2
Newmill of Inshewan DD8 83 F1
Newmillerdam WF2 51 F1
Newmills IV7 96 D5
Newmiln, *P. & K.* PH2 82 C4
Newmiln, *P. & K.* PH1 82 B5
Newmilns KA16 74 D7
Newney Green CM1 24 C1
Newnham, *Glos.* GL14 29 F7
Newnham, *Hants.* RG27 22 A6
Newnham, *Herts.* SG7 33 F5
Newnham, *Kent* ME9 14 E2
Newnham, *Northants.* NN11 31 G3
Newnham Bridge WR15 29 F2
Newnham Paddox CV23 41 G7
Newnoth AB54 90 D1
Newport, *Cornw.* PL15 6 B7
Newport, *Devon* EX32 6 D2
Newport, *E.Riding* HU15 58 E6
Newport, *Essex* CB11 33 J5
Newport, *Glos.* GL13 19 K2
Newport, *High.* KW7 105 G6
Newport, *I.o.W.* PO30 11 G6
NEWPORT (CASNEWYDD), *Newport* NP 19 G3
Newport, *Norf.* NR29 45 K4
Newport (Trefdraeth), *Pembs.* SA42 16 D1
Newport, *Som.* TA3 8 C2
Newport, *Tel. & W.* TF10 39 G4
Newport-on-Tay DD6 83 F5
Newpound Common RH14 12 D4
Newquay TR7 3 F2
Newquay Cornwall Airport TR8 3 F2
Newsbank CW12 49 H6
Newseat AB51 91 F1
Newsells SG8 33 G5
Newsham, *Lancs.* PR3 55 J6
Newsham, *N.Yorks.* DL11 62 C6
Newsham, *N.Yorks.* YO7 57 J1
Newsham, *Northumb.* NE24 71 H6
Newsholme, *E.Riding* DN14 58 D7
Newsholme, *Lancs.* BB7 56 D4
Newsome HD4 50 D1
Newstead, *Notts.* NG15 51 H7
Newstead, *Sc.Bord.* TD6 76 D7
Newthorpe, *N.Yorks.* LS25 57 K6
Newthorpe, *Notts.* NG16 41 G1
Newtoft LN8 52 D4
Newton, *Aber.* AB54 98 C6
Newton, *Aber.* AB42 99 J6
Newton, *Arg. & B.* PA27 73 J1
Newton, *Bridgend* CF36 18 B4
Newton, *Cambs.* PE15 43 H4
Newton, *Cambs.* CB2 33 H4
Newton, *Cardiff* CF24 19 F4
Newton, *Ches.* CH3 48 E7
Newton, *Ches.* WA6 48 E5
Newton, *Cumb.* LA13 55 F2
Newton, *D. & G.* DG10 69 G4
Newton, *Derbys.* DE55 51 G7
Newton, *Gt.Man.* SK14 49 J3
Newton, *Here.* SY7 28 C2
Newton, *Here.* HR6 28 D3
Newton, *Here.* HR2 28 C5
Newton, *High.* KW1 105 J3
Newton, *High.* IV2 96 E7
Newton, *High.* IV1 105 H3
Newton, *High.* IV27 102 E5
Newton, *High.* IV6 96 C6
Newton, *High.* IV11 96 E5
Newton, *Lancs.* BB7 56 B4
Newton, *Lancs.* LA6 55 J2
Newton, *Lancs.* FY3 55 G6
Newton, *Lancs.* PR4 55 H6
Newton, *Lincs.* NG34 42 D2
Newton, *Moray* IV30 98 B4
Newton, *N.Ayr.* KA27 73 H5
Newton, *Norf.* PE32 44 C4
Newton, *Northants.* NN14 42 B7
Newton, *Northumb.* NE43 71 F7
Newton, *Northumb.* NE65 70 E3
Newton, *Notts.* NG13 41 J1
Newton, *P. & K.* PH8 81 K4
Newton, *Pembs.* SA62 16 B2
Newton, *Pembs.* SA71 16 C4
Newton, *S.Glos.* BS35 19 K2
Newton, *S.Lan.* ML12 75 H7
Newton, *Sc.Bord.* TD8 70 B1
Newton, *Shrop.* SY12 38 D2
Newton, *Som.* TA4 7 K2
Newton, *Staffs.* WS15 40 C3
Newton, *Suff.* CO10 34 D4
Newton, *Swan.* SA3 17 K6
Newton, *W.Loth.* EH52 75 J3
Newton, *W.Yorks.* WF10 57 K7
Newton, *Warks.* CV23 31 G1
Newton, *Wilts.* SP5 10 D2
Newton Abbot TQ12 5 J3
Newton Arlosh CA7 60 D1
Newton Aycliffe DL5 62 D4
Newton Bewley TS22 63 F4
Newton Blossomville MK43 32 C3

Newton Bromswold MK44 32 C2
Newton Burgoland LE67 41 F5
Newton by Toft LN8 52 D4
Newton Ferrers PL8 5 F6
Newton Flotman NR15 45 G6
Newton Green NP16 19 J2
Newton Harcourt LE8 41 J6
Newton Kyme LS24 57 K5
Newton Longville MK17 32 B5
Newton Mearns G77 74 D5
Newton Morrell, *N.Yorks.* DL10 62 D6
Newton Morrell, *Oxon.* OX27 31 H6
Newton Mountain SA73 16 C4
Newton Mulgrave TS13 63 J5
Newton of Affleck DD5 83 F4
Newton of Ardtoe PH36 86 C7
Newton of Balcanquhal PH2 82 C6
Newton of Dalvey IV36 97 H6
Newton of Falkland KY15 82 D7
Newton of Leys IV2 88 D1
Newton on the Hill SY4 38 D3
Newton on Trent LN1 52 B5
Newton Poppleford EX10 7 J7
Newton Purcell MK18 31 H5
Newton Regis B79 40 E5
Newton Reigny CA11 61 F3
Newton St. Cyres EX5 7 G6
Newton St. Faith NR10 45 G4
Newton St. Loe BA2 20 A5
Newton St. Petrock EX22 6 C4
Newton Solney DE15 40 E3
Newton Stacey SO20 21 H7
Newton Stewart DG8 64 E4
Newton Tony SP4 21 F7
Newton Tracey EX31 6 D3
Newton under Roseberry TS9 63 G5
Newton Underwood NE61 71 G5
Newton upon Derwent YO41 58 D5
Newton Valence GU34 11 J1
Newtonairds DG2 68 D5
Newtongrange EH22 76 B4
Newtonhill AB39 91 H5
Newton-le-Willows, *Mersey.* WA12 48 E3
Newton-le-Willows, *N.Yorks.* DL8 57 H1
Newtonmill DD9 83 H1
Newtonmore PH20 88 E5
Newton-on-Ouse YO30 58 B4
Newton-on-Rawcliffe YO18 63 K7
Newton-on-the-Moor NE65 71 G3
Newtown, *Bucks.* HP5 22 C1
Newtown, *Ches.* CH3 48 E7
Newtown, *Cornw.* PL15 4 C3
Newtown, *Cornw.* TR20 2 C6
Newtown, *Cumb.* CA6 70 A7
Newtown, *Derbys.* SK22 49 J4
Newtown, *Devon* EX36 7 F3
Newtown, *Devon* EX5 7 J6
Newtown, *Dorset* DT8 8 D4
Newtown, *Glos.* GL13 19 K1
Newtown, *Gt.Man.* WN5 48 E2
Newtown, *Gt.Man.* M27 49 G2
Newtown, *Hants.* PO17 11 H3
Newtown, *Hants.* RG20 21 H5
Newtown, *Hants.* SO43 10 D3
Newtown, *Hants.* SO51 10 E2
Newtown, *Hants.* SO32 11 G3
Newtown, *Here.* HR8 29 F4
Newtown, *Here.* HR6 28 D3
Newtown, *High.* PH35 87 K4
Newtown, *I.o.M.* IM4 54 C6
Newtown, *I.o.W.* PO30 11 F5
Newtown, *Northumb.* NE65 71 F3
Newtown, *Northumb.* NE66 71 F1
Newtown, *Oxon.* RG9 22 A3
Newtown (Y Drenewydd), *Powys* SY16 38 A6
Newtown, *R.C.T.* CF45 18 D2
Newtown, *Shrop.* SY4 38 D2
Newtown, *Som.* TA6 8 B1
Newtown, *Som.* TA20 8 B3
Newtown, *Staffs.* ST8 49 J6
Newtown, *Staffs.* SK17 50 C6
Newtown, *Staffs.* WS6 40 B5
Newtown, *Wilts.* SP3 9 J2
Newtown, *Wilts.* SN8 21 G5
Newtown Linford LE6 41 H5
Newtown St. Boswells TD6 76 D7
Newtown Unthank LE9 41 G5
Newtown-in-Saint-Martin TR12 2 E6
Newtyle PH12 82 D3
Newyears Green UB9 22 D3
Neyland SA73 16 C4
Nibley, *Glos.* GL15 19 K1
Nibley, *S.Glos.* BS37 19 K3
Nibley Green GL11 20 A2
Nicholashayne TA21 7 K4
Nicholaston SA3 17 J6
Nidd HG3 57 J3
Nigg, *Aberdeen* AB12 91 H4
Nigg, *High.* IV19 97 F4
Nilig LL15 47 J7
Nilston Rigg NE47 70 D7
Nimlet SN14 20 A4
Nine Ashes CM4 23 J1
Nine Elms SN5 20 E3
Nine Mile Burn EH26 75 K5

Ninebanks NE47 61 J1
Ninemile Bar (Crocketford) DG2 65 J3
Nineveh WR15 29 F2
Ninfield TN33 14 C6
Ningwood PO30 11 F6
Nisbet TD8 70 B1
Niton PO38 11 G7
Nitshill G53 74 D4
No Man's Heath, *Ches.* SY14 38 E1
No Man's Heath, *Warks.* B79 40 E5
No Man's Land PL13 4 C5
Noah's Ark TN15 23 J6
Noak Hill RM4 23 J2
Noblehill DG1 65 K3
Noblethorpe S75 50 E2
Nobottle NN7 31 H2
Nocton LN4 52 D6
Noddsdale KA30 74 A4
Nogdam End NR14 45 H5
Noke OX3 31 G7
Nolton SA62 16 B3
Nolton Haven SA62 16 B3
Nomansland, *Devon* EX16 7 G4
Nomansland, *Wilts.* SP5 10 D3
Noneley SY4 38 D3
Nonington CT15 15 H2
Nook, *Cumb.* CA6 69 K6
Nook, *Cumb.* LA6 55 J1
Noonsbrough ZE2 109 B7
Noranside DD8 83 F1
Norbreck FY5 55 G5
Norbury, *Ches.* SY13 38 E1
Norbury, *Derbys.* DE6 40 D1
Norbury, *Gt.Lon.* SW16 23 G4
Norbury, *Shrop.* SY9 38 C6
Norbury, *Staffs.* ST20 39 G3
Norbury Common SY13 38 E1
Norbury Junction ST20 39 G3
Norchard SA70 16 D5
Norcott Brook WA4 49 F4
Nordelph PE38 43 J5
Norden, *Dorset* BH20 9 J6
Norden, *Gt.Man.* OL11 49 H1
Nordley WV16 39 F6
Norham TD15 77 H6
Norland Town HX6 57 F7
Norley WA6 48 E5
Norleywood SO41 10 E5
Norlington BN8 13 H5
Norman Cross PE7 42 E6
Normanby, *N.Lincs.* DN15 52 B1
Normanby, *N.Yorks.* YO62 58 D1
Normanby, *R. & C.* TS6 63 G5
Normanby by Stow DN21 52 B4
Normanby le Wold LN7 52 E3
Normanby-by-Spital LN8 52 D4
Normandy GU3 22 C6
Norman's Ruh PA74 79 F3
Norman's Bay BN24 13 K6
Norman's Green EX15 7 J5
Normanston NR32 45 K6
Normanton, *Derby* DE23 41 F2
Normanton, *Leics.* NG13 42 B1
Normanton, *Lincs.* NG32 42 C1
Normanton, *Notts.* NG25 51 K7
Normanton, *Rut.* LE15 42 C5
Normanton, *W.Yorks.* WF6 57 J7
Normanton le Heath LE67 41 F4
Normanton on Soar LE12 41 H3
Normanton on Trent NG23 51 K6
Normanton-on-the-Wolds NG12 41 J2
Normoss FY3 55 G6
Norrington Common SN12 20 B5
Norris Green PL17 4 E4
Norris Hill DE12 41 F4
Norristhorpe WF15 57 H7
North Acton W3 23 F3
North Anston S25 51 H4
North Ascot SL5 22 C5
North Aston OX25 31 F6
North Baddesley SO52 10 E3
North Ballachulish PH33 80 B1
North Balloch KA26 67 H4
North Barrow BA22 9 F2
North Barsham NR22 44 D2
North Benfleet SS12 24 D3
North Bersted PO21 12 C6
North Berwick EH39 76 D2
North Boarhunt PO17 11 H3
North Bogbain AB55 98 B5
North Bovey TQ13 7 F7
North Bradley BA14 20 B6
North Brentor PL19 6 C7
North Brewham BA10 9 G1
North Bridge GU8 12 C3
North Buckland EX33 6 C1
North Burlingham NR13 45 H4
North Cadbury BA22 9 F2
North Cairn DG9 66 D6
North Camp GU14 22 B6
North Carlton, *Lincs.* LN1 52 C5
North Carlton, *Notts.* S81 51 H4
North Cave HU15 58 E6
North Cerney GL7 20 D1
North Chailey BN8 13 G4
North Charford SP5 10 C3
North Charlton NE66 71 G1
North Cheriton BA8 9 F2
North Chideock DT6 8 D5
North Cliff YO43 58 E6
North Clifton NG23 52 B5
North Cockerington LN11 53 G3

North Coker BA22 8 E3
North Collafirth ZE2 108 C4
North Common, *S.Glos.* BS30 19 K4
North Common, *Suff.* IP22 34 D1
North Commonty AB53 99 G6
North Connel PA37 80 A4
North Coombe EX17 7 G5
North Cornelly CF33 18 B3
North Corner BS36 19 K3
North Cotes DN36 53 G2
North Cowton DL7 62 D6
North Crawley MK16 32 C4
North Cray DA14 23 H4
North Creake NR21 44 C2
North Curry TA3 8 C2
North Dallens PA38 80 A3
North Dalton YO25 59 F4
North Dawn KW17 107 D7
North Deighton LS22 57 J4
North Dell (Dail Bho Thuath) HS2 101 G1
North Duffield YO8 58 C6
North Elkington LN11 53 F3
North Elmham NR20 44 D3
North Elmsall WF9 51 G1
North End, *Bucks.* LU7 32 B6
North End, *Dorset* SP7 9 H2
North End, *E.Riding* YO25 59 H4
North End, *E.Riding* HU11 59 H5
North End, *E.Riding* HU12 59 J6
North End, *Essex* CM6 33 K7
North End, *Hants.* SO24 11 G2
North End, *Hants.* SP6 10 C3
North End, *Leics.* LE12 41 H4
North End, *N.Som.* BS49 19 H5
North End, *Norf.* NR16 44 E6
North End, *Northumb.* NE65 71 G3
North End, *Ports.* PO2 11 H4
North End, *W.Suss.* BN14 12 E5
North End, *W.Suss.* BN18 12 C6
North Erradale IV21 94 D3
North Essie AB42 99 J5
North Fambridge CM3 24 E2
North Ferriby HU14 59 F7
North Frodingham YO25 59 H4
North Gorley SP6 10 C3
North Green, *Norf.* IP21 45 G7
North Green, *Suff.* IP17 35 H2
North Green, *Suff.* IP17 35 H2
North Grimston YO17 58 E3
North Halling ME2 24 D5
North Harby NG23 52 B5
North Hayling PO11 11 J4
North Hazelrigg NE66 77 J7
North Heasley EX36 7 F2
North Heath, *W.Berks.* RG20 21 H4
North Heath, *W.Suss.* RH20 12 D4
North Hill PL15 4 C3
North Hillingdon UB10 22 D3
North Hinksey OX2 21 H1
North Holmwood RH5 22 E7
North Houghton SO20 10 E1
North Huish TQ10 5 H5
North Hykeham LN6 52 C6
North Johnston SA62 16 C3
North Kelsey LN7 52 D2
North Kessock IV1 96 D7
North Killingholme DN40 52 E1
North Kilvington YO7 57 K1
North Kilworth LE17 41 J7
North Kingston BH24 10 C4
North Kyme LN4 52 E7
North Lancing BN15 12 E6
North Lee HP22 22 B1
North Lees HG4 57 J2
North Leigh OX29 30 E7
North Leverton with Habblesthorpe DN22 51 K4
North Littleton WR11 30 B4
North Lopham IP22 44 E7
North Luffenham LE15 42 C5
North Marden PO18 12 B5
North Marston MK18 31 J6
North Middleton, *Midloth.* EH23 76 B5
North Middleton, *Northumb.* NE71 71 F1
North Millbrex AB53 99 G6
North Molton EX36 7 F3
North Moreton OX11 21 J3
North Mundham PO20 12 B6
North Muskham NG23 51 K7
North Newbald YO43 59 F6
North Newington OX15 31 F4
North Newnton SN9 20 E6
North Nibley GL11 20 A2
North Oakley RG26 21 J6
North Ockendon RM14 23 J3
North Ormesby TS3 63 G5
North Ormsby LN11 53 F3
North Otterington DL7 57 J1
North Owersby LN8 52 D3
North Perrott TA18 8 D4
North Petherton TA6 8 B1
North Petherwin PL15 4 C2
North Pickenham PE37 44 C5
North Piddle WR7 29 J3
North Plain CA7 69 G7
North Pool TQ7 5 H6
North Poorton DT6 8 E5
North Quarme TA24 7 H2
North Queensferry KY11 75 K2
North Radworthy EX36 7 F2

North Rauceby NG34 42 D1
North Reston LN11 53 G4
North Rigton LS17 57 H5
North Rode CW12 49 H6
North Roe ZE2 108 C4
North Ronaldsay KW17 106 G1
North Runcton PE33 44 A4
North Sandwick ZE2 108 E3
North Scale LA14 54 E3
North Scarle LN6 52 B6
North Seaton NE63 71 H5
North Shian PA38 80 A3
North Shields NE30 71 H7
North Shoebury SS3 25 F3
North Side PE6 43 F6
North Skelton TS12 63 H5
North Somercotes LN11 53 H3
North Stainley HG4 57 H2
North Stainmore CA17 61 K5
North Stifford RM16 24 C3
North Stoke, *B. & N.E. Som.* BA1 20 A5
North Stoke, *Oxon.* OX10 21 K3
North Stoke, *W.Suss.* BN18 12 D5
North Stoneham SO50 11 F3
North Street, *Hants.* SO24 11 H1
North Street, *Kent* ME13 15 F2
North Street, *Med.* ME3 24 E4
North Street, *W.Berks.* RG7 21 K4
North Sunderland NE68 77 K7
North Tamerton EX22 6 B6
North Tarbothill AB23 91 H3
North Tawton EX20 6 E5
North Third FK7 75 F2
North Thoresby DN36 53 F3
North Tidworth SP9 21 F7
North Togston NE65 71 H3
North Town, *Devon* EX20 6 D5
North Town, *Hants.* GU12 22 B6
North Town, *W. & M.* SL6 22 B3
North Tuddenham NR20 44 E4
North Uist (Uibhist a Tuath) HS6 92 D4
North Walsham NR28 45 G2
North Waltham RG25 21 J7
North Warnborough RG29 22 A6
North Water Bridge AB30 83 H1
North Watten KW1 105 H3
North Weald Bassett CM16 23 H1
North Wembley HA0 22 E3
North Wheatley DN22 51 K4
North Whilborough TQ12 5 J4
North Wick BS41 19 J5
North Widcombe BS40 19 J6
North Willingham LN8 52 E4
North Wingfield S42 51 G6
North Witham NG33 42 C3
North Wootton, *Dorset* DT9 9 F3
North Wootton, *Norf.* PE30 44 A3
North Wootton, *Som.* BA4 19 J7
North Wraxall SN14 20 B4
North Wroughton SN4 20 E3
North Yardhope NE65 70 E3
Northacre NR17 44 D6
Northall LU6 32 C6
Northall Green NR20 44 D4
Northallerton DL6 62 E7
Northam, *Devon* EX39 6 C3
Northam, *S'ham.* SO14 11 F3
NORTHAMPTON NN 31 J2
Northaw EN6 23 F1
Northay, *Devon* EX13 8 C4
Northay, *Som.* TA20 8 B3
Northbay HS9 84 C4
Northbeck NG34 42 D1
Northborough PE6 42 E5
Northbourne, *Kent* CT14 15 J2
Northbourne, *Oxon.* OX11 21 J3
Northbridge Street TN32 14 C5
Northbrook, *Hants.* SO21 11 G1
Northbrook, *Oxon.* OX5 31 F6
Northburnhill AB53 99 G6
Northchapel GU28 12 C4
Northchurch HP4 22 C1
Northcote Manor EX37 6 E4
Northcott PL15 6 B6
Northcourt OX14 21 J2
Northdyke KW16 106 B5
Northedge S42 51 F6
Northend, *B. & N.E.Som.* BA1 20 A5
Northend, *Bucks.* RG9 22 A2
Northend, *Warks.* CV47 30 E3
Northenden M22 49 H3
Northfield, *Aberdeen* AB16 91 H4
Northfield, *High.* KW1 105 J4
Northfield, *Hull* HU4 59 G7
Northfield, *Sc.Bord.* TD14 77 H4
Northfield, *Som.* TA6 8 B1
Northfield, *W.Mid.* B31 30 B1
Northfields PE9 42 D5
Northfleet DA11 24 C4
Northhouse TD9 69 K3
Northiam TN31 14 D5
Northill SG18 32 E4
Northington, *Glos.* GL14 29 A1
Northington, *Hants.* SO24 11 G1
Northlands PE22 53 G7
Northleach GL54 30 C7
Northleigh, *Devon* EX24 7 K6
Northleigh, *Devon* EX32 6 E2
Northlew EX20 6 D6
Northmoor OX29 21 H1
Northmoor Green (Moorland) TA7 8 C1
Northmuir DD8 82 E2

Over Dinsdale

Northney PO11 11 J4
Northolt UB5 22 E3
Northop CH7 48 B6
Northop Hall CH7 48 B6
Northorpe, Lincs. PE11 43 F2
Northorpe, Lincs. DN21 52 B3
Northorpe, Lincs. PE10 42 D4
Northover, Som. BA22 8 E2
Northover, Som. BA6 8 D1
Northowram HX3 57 G7
Northport BH20 9 J6
Northpunds ZE2 109 D10
Northrepps NR27 45 G2
Northton (Taobh Tuath) HS3 92 E3
Northtown KW17 107 D8
Northway, Glos. GL20 29 J5
Northway, Som. TA4 7 K3
Northwich CW8 49 F5
Northwick, S.Glos. BS35 19 J3
Northwick, Som. TA9 19 G7
Northwick, Worcs. WR3 29 H3
Northwold IP26 44 B6
Northwood, Gt.Lon. HA6 22 D2
Northwood, I.o.W. PO31 11 F5
Northwood, Kent CT12 25 K5
Northwood, Mersey. L33 48 D3
Northwood, Shrop. SY4 38 D2
Northwood Green GL14 29 G7
Northwood Hills HA6 22 E2
Norton, Glos. GL2 29 H6
Norton, Halton WA7 48 E4
Norton, Herts. SG6 33 F5
Norton, I.o.W. PO41 10 E6
Norton, Mon. NP7 28 D6
Norton, N.Som. BS22 19 G5
Norton, N.Yorks. YO17 58 D2
Norton, Northants. NN11 31 H2
Norton, Notts. NG20 51 H5
Norton, Powys LD8 28 C2
Norton, S.Yorks. DN6 51 H1
Norton, S.Yorks. S8 51 F4
Norton, Shrop. SY4 38 E5
Norton, Shrop. TF11 39 G5
Norton, Shrop. SY7 38 D7
Norton, Stock. TS20 63 F4
Norton, Suff. IP31 34 D2
Norton, Swan. SA3 17 K6
Norton, V. of Glam. CF32 18 B4
Norton, W.Mid. DY8 40 A7
Norton, W.Suss. PO20 12 C6
Norton, W.Suss. PO20 12 B7
Norton, Wilts. SN16 20 B3
Norton, Worcs. WR5 29 H3
Norton, Worcs. WR11 30 B4
Norton Bavant BA12 20 C7
Norton Bridge ST15 40 A2
Norton Canes WS11 40 C5
Norton Canon HR4 28 C4
Norton Disney LN6 52 B7
Norton Ferris BA12 9 G1
Norton Fitzwarren TA2 7 K3
Norton Green, Herts. SG1 33 F6
Norton Green, I.o.W. PO40 10 E6
Norton Green, Stoke ST6 49 J7
Norton Hawkfield BS40 19 J5
Norton Heath CM4 24 C1
Norton in Hales TF9 39 G2
Norton in the Moors ST6 49 H7
Norton Lindsey CV35 30 D2
Norton Little Green IP31 34 D2
Norton Malreward BS39 19 K5
Norton Mandeville CM5 23 J1
Norton St. Philip BA2 20 A6
Norton Subcourse NR14 45 J6
Norton Wood HR4 28 C4
Norton Woodseats S8 51 F4
Norton-Juxta-Twycross CV9 41 F5
Norton-le-Clay YO61 57 K2
Norton-sub-Hamdon TA14 8 D3
Norwell NG23 51 K6
Norwell Woodhouse NG23 51 K6
NORWICH NR 45 G5
Norwich Airport NR6 45 G4
Norwick ZE2 108 F1
Norwood End CM5 23 J1
Norwood Green, Gt.Lon. UB2 22 E4
Norwood Green, W.Yorks. HX3 57 G7
Norwood Hill RH6 23 F7
Norwood Park BA6 8 E1
Noseley LE7 42 A6
Noss Mayo PL8 5 F6
Nosterfield DL8 57 H1
Nosterfield End CB1 33 K4
Nostie IV40 86 E2
Notgrove GL54 30 C6
Nottage CF36 18 B4
Notting Hill W11 23 F3
Nottingham, High. KW5 105 H5
NOTTINGHAM, Nott. NG 41 H1
Nottingham East Midlands Airport DE74 41 G3
Nottington DT3 9 F6
Notton, W.Yorks. WF4 51 F1
Notton, Wilts. SN15 20 C5
Nottswood Hill GL17 29 G7
Nounsley CM3 34 B7
Noutard's Green WR6 29 G2
Nowton IP29 34 C2
Nox SY5 38 D4
Noyadd Trefawr SA43 26 B4
Nuffield RG9 21 K3
Nun Monkton YO26 58 B4
Nunburnholme YO42 58 E5
Nuneaton CV11 41 F6
Nuneham Courtenay OX44 21 J2
Nunney BA11 20 A7
Nunnington, Here. HR1 28 E4
Nunnington, N.Yorks. YO62 58 C2
Nunnington Park TA4 7 J3
Nunnykirk NE61 71 F4
Nunsthorpe DN32 53 F2
Nunthorpe, Middbro. TS7 63 G5
Nunthorpe, York YO23 58 B4
Nunton SP5 10 C2
Nunwick, N.Yorks. HG4 57 J2
Nunwick, Northumb. NE48 70 D6
Nup End SG4 33 F7
Nupend GL10 20 A1
Nursling SO16 10 E3
Nursted GU31 11 J2
Nurton WV6 40 A6
Nutbourne, W.Suss. RH20 12 D5
Nutbourne, W.Suss. PO18 11 J4
Nutfield RH1 23 G6
Nuthall NG16 41 H1
Nuthampstead SG8 33 H5
Nuthurst, W.Suss. RH13 12 E4
Nuthurst, Warks. B94 30 C1
Nutley, E.Suss. TN22 13 H4
Nutley, Hants. RG25 21 K7
Nutwell DN3 51 J2
Nyadd FK9 75 F1
Nybster KW1 105 J2
Nyetimber PO21 12 B7
Nyewood GU31 11 J2
Nymet Rowland EX17 7 F5
Nymet Tracey EX17 7 F5
Nympsfield GL10 20 B1
Nynehead TA21 7 K3
Nythe TA7 8 D1
Nyton PO20 12 C6

O

Oad Street ME9 24 E5
Oadby LE2 41 J5
Oak Cross EX20 6 D6
Oak Tree DL2 62 E5
Oakamoor ST10 40 C1
Oakbank, Arg. & B. PA64 79 J4
Oakbank, W.Loth. EH53 75 J4
Oakdale, Caerp. NP12 18 E2
Oakdale, Poole BH15 10 B5
Oake TA4 7 K3
Oaken WV8 40 A5
Oakenclough PR3 55 J5
Oakengates TF2 39 G4
Oakenhead IV31 97 K5
Oakenholt CH6 48 B5
Oakenshaw, Dur. DL15 62 D3
Oakenshaw, W.Yorks. BD12 57 G7
Oakerthorpe DE55 51 F7
Oakes HD3 50 D1
Oakfield, I.o.W. PO33 11 G5
Oakfield, Torfaen NP44 19 F2
Oakford, Cere. SA47 26 D3
Oakford, Devon EX16 7 H3
Oakfordbridge EX16 7 H3
Oakgrove SK11 49 J6
Oakham LE15 42 B5
Oakhanger GU35 11 J1
Oakhill BA3 19 K7
Oakington CB4 33 H2
Oaklands, Conwy LL26 47 G7
Oaklands, Herts. AL6 33 F7
Oakle Street GL2 29 G7
Oakley, Beds. MK43 32 D3
Oakley, Bucks. HP18 31 H7
Oakley, Fife KY12 75 J2
Oakley, Hants. RG23 21 J6
Oakley, Oxon. OX39 22 A1
Oakley, Poole BH21 10 B5
Oakley, Suff. IP21 35 F1
Oakley Green SL4 22 C4
Oakley Park SY17 37 J7
Oakridge Lynch GL6 20 C1
Oaks SY5 38 D5
Oaks Green DE6 40 D2
Oaksey SN16 20 C2
Oakshaw Ford CA6 70 A6
Oakshott GU33 11 J2
Oakthorpe DE12 41 F4
Oaktree Hill DL6 62 E7
Oakwoodhill RH5 12 E3
Oakworth BD22 57 F6
Oare, Kent ME13 25 G5
Oare, Som. EX35 7 G1
Oare, Wilts. SN8 20 E5
Oasby NG32 42 D2
Oatfield PA28 66 A2
Oath TA7 8 C2
Oathlaw DD8 83 F2
Oatlands HG2 57 J4
Oban PA34 79 K5
Obley SY7 28 C1
Oborne DT9 9 F3
Obthorpe PE10 42 D4
Occlestone Green CW10 49 F6
Occold IP23 35 F1
Occumster KW3 105 H5
Ochiltree KA18 67 K1
Ochr-y-foel LL18 47 J5
Ochtermuthill PH5 81 K6
Ochtertyre, P. & K. PH7 81 K5
Ochtertyre, Stir. FK9 75 F1
Ockbrook DE72 41 G2
Ockeridge WR6 29 G2
Ockham GU23 22 D6
Ockle PH36 86 B7
Ockley RH5 12 E3
Ocle Pychard HR1 28 E4
Octon YO25 59 G2
Odcombe BA22 8 E3
Odd Down BA2 20 A5
Oddendale CA10 61 H5
Oddingley WR9 29 J3
Oddington OX5 31 G7
Oddsta ZE2 108 E3
Odell MK43 32 C3
Odham EX21 6 C5
Odie KW17 106 F5
Odiham RG29 22 A6
Odsey SG7 33 F5
Odstock SP5 10 C2
Odstone CV13 41 F5
Offchurch CV33 30 E2
Offenham WR11 30 B4
Offerton SK2 49 J4
Offham, E.Suss. BN8 13 G5
Offham, Kent ME19 23 K6
Offham, W.Suss. BN18 12 D6
Offley Hoo SG5 32 E6
Offleymarsh ST21 39 G3
Offord Cluny PE19 33 F2
Offord D'Arcy PE19 33 F2
Offton IP8 34 E4
Offwell EX14 7 K6
Ogbourne Maizey SN8 20 E4
Ogbourne St. Andrew SN8 20 E4
Ogbourne St. George SN8 20 E4
Ogil DD8 83 F1
Ogle NE20 71 G6
Oglet L24 48 D4
Ogmore CF32 18 B4
Ogmore Vale CF32 18 C2
Ogmore-by-Sea CF32 18 B4
Oil Terminal KW16 107 C8
Okeford Fitzpaine DT11 9 H3
Okehampton EX20 6 D6
Okehampton Camp EX20 6 D6
Okraquoy ZE2 109 D9
Olchard TQ13 5 J3
Olchfa SA2 17 K5
Old NN6 31 J1
Old Aberdeen AB24 91 H4
Old Alresford SO24 11 G1
Old Arley CV7 40 E6
Old Basford NG6 41 H1
Old Basing RG24 21 K6
Old Belses TD6 70 A1
Old Bewick NE66 71 F1
Old Blair PH18 81 K1
Old Bolingbroke PE23 53 G6
Old Bramhope LS16 57 H5
Old Brampton S42 51 F5
Old Bridge of Urr DG7 65 H4
Old Buckenham NR17 44 E6
Old Burdon SR7 62 E1
Old Burghclere RG20 21 H6
Old Byland YO62 58 B1
Old Cassop DH6 62 E3
Old Church Stoke SY15 38 B6
Old Cleeve TA24 7 J1
Old Clipstone NG21 51 J6
Old Colwyn LL29 47 G5
Old Craig AB41 91 H2
Old Craighall EH21 76 B3
Old Crombie AB54 98 D5
Old Dailly KA26 67 G4
Old Dalby LE14 41 J3
Old Dam SK17 50 D5
Old Deer AB42 99 H6
Old Dilton BA13 20 B7
Old Down, S.Glos. BS32 19 K3
Old Down, Som. BA3 19 K6
Old Edlington DN12 51 H3
Old Eldon DL4 62 D4
Old Ellerby HU11 59 H6
Old Felixstowe IP11 35 H5
Old Fletton PE2 42 E6
Old Ford E3 23 G3
Old Glossop SK13 50 C3
Old Goginan SY23 37 F7
Old Goole DN14 58 D7
Old Gore HR9 29 F6
Old Grimsby TR24 2 B1
Old Hall HU12 53 F1
Old Hall Green SG11 33 G6
Old Hall Street NR28 45 H2
Old Harlow CM20 33 H7
Old Heath CO2 34 E6
Old Heathfield TN21 13 J4
Old Hill B64 40 B7
Old Hurst PE28 33 G1
Old Hutton LA8 55 J1
Old Kea TR3 3 F4
Old Kilpatrick G60 74 C3
Old Kinnernie AB32 91 F4
Old Knebworth SG3 33 F6
Old Leake PE22 53 H7
Old Leslie AB52 90 D2
Old Malton YO17 58 E2
Old Milton BH25 10 D5
Old Milverton CV32 30 D2
Old Montsale CM0 25 G2
Old Netley SO31 11 F3
Old Newton IP14 34 E2
Old Philpstoun EH49 75 J3
Old Poltalloch PA31 79 K7
Old Radnor (Pencraig) LD8 28 B3
Old Rattray AB42 99 J5
Old Rayne AB52 90 E2
Old Romney TN29 15 F5
Old Scone PH2 82 C5
Old Shields G67 75 G3
Old Sodbury BS37 20 A3
Old Somerby NG33 42 C2
Old Stratford MK19 31 J4
Old Sunderlandwick YO25 59 G4
Old Swarland NE65 71 G3
Old Swinford DY8 40 B7
Old Thirsk YO7 57 K1
Old Town, Cumb. LA6 55 J1
Old Town, I.o.S. TR21 2 C1
Old Town Farm NE19 70 D4
Old Tupton S42 51 F6
Old Warden SG18 32 E4
Old Weston PE28 32 D1
Old Windsor SL4 22 C4
Old Wives Lees CT4 15 F2
Old Woking GU22 22 D6
Old Woodhall LN9 53 F6
Old Woods SY4 38 D3
Oldberrow B95 30 C2
Oldborough EX17 7 F5
Oldbury, Kent TN15 23 J6
Oldbury, Shrop. WV16 39 G6
Oldbury, W.Mid. B69 40 B7
Oldbury, Warks. CV10 41 F6
Oldbury Naite BS35 19 K2
Oldbury on the Hill GL9 20 B3
Oldbury-on-Severn BS35 19 K2
Oldcastle, Bridgend CF31 18 C4
Oldcastle, Mon. NP7 28 C6
Oldcastle Heath SY14 38 D1
Oldcotes S81 51 H4
Oldcroft GL15 19 K1
Oldeamere PE7 43 G6
Oldfield WR9 29 H2
Oldford BA11 20 A6
Oldhall, Aber. AB34 90 C5
Oldhall, High. KW1 105 H3
OLDHAM OL 49 J2
Oldham Edge OL1 49 J2
Oldhamstocks TD13 77 F3
Oldland BS30 19 K4
Oldmeldrum AB51 91 G2
Oldmill AB31 90 D4
Oldpark TF3 39 F5
Oldridge EX4 7 G6
Oldshore Beg IV27 102 D3
Oldshoremore IV27 102 E3
Oldstead YO61 58 B2
Oldtown IV24 96 C3
Oldtown of Aigas IV4 96 B7
Oldtown of Ord AB45 98 E5
Oldwalls SA3 17 H5
Oldways End EX16 7 G3
Oldwhat AB53 99 G5
Oldwich Lane B93 30 D1
Olgrinmore KW12 105 G3
Oliver ML12 69 G1
Oliver's Battery SO22 11 F2
Ollaberry ZE2 108 C4
Ollerton, Ches. WA16 49 G5
Ollerton, Notts. NG22 51 J6
Ollerton, Shrop. TF9 39 F3
Olmstead Green CB1 33 K4
Olney MK46 32 B3
Olrig House KW14 105 G2
Olton B92 40 D7
Olveston BS35 19 K3
Ombersley WR9 29 H2
Ompton NG22 51 J6
Onchan IM3 54 C6
Onecote ST13 50 C7
Onehouse IP14 34 E3
Ongar Hill PE34 43 J3
Ongar Street HR6 28 C2
Onibury SY7 28 D1
Onich PH33 80 B1
Onllwyn SA10 27 H7
Onneley CW3 39 G1
Onslow Green CM6 33 K7
Onslow Village GU2 22 C7
Opinan, High. IV22 94 E2
Opinan, High. IV21 94 D4
Orange Lane TD12 77 F6
Orasaigh HS2 101 F6
Orbliston IV32 98 B5
Orbost IV55 93 H7
Orby PE24 53 H6
Orcadia PA20 73 K4
Orchard PA23 73 K2
Orchard Portman TA3 8 B2
Orcheston SP3 20 D7
Orcop HR2 28 D6
Orcop Hill HR2 28 D6
Ord IV46 86 C3
Ordhead AB51 90 E3
Ordie AB34 90 C4
Ordiequish IV32 98 B5
Ordsall DN22 51 J5
Ore TN35 14 D6
Oreham Common BN5 13 F5
Oreston PL9 5 F5
Oreton DY14 29 F1
Orford, Suff. IP12 35 J4
Orford, Warr. WA2 49 F3
Organford BH16 9 J5
Orgreave DE13 40 D4
Orlestone TN26 14 E4
Orleton, Here. SY8 28 D2
Orleton, Worcs. WR6 29 F2
Orleton Common SY8 28 D2
Orlingbury NN14 32 B1
Ormacleit HS8 84 C1
Ormesby TS3 63 G5
Ormesby St. Margaret NR29 45 J4
Ormesby St. Michael NR29 45 J4
Ormidale PA22 73 J2
Ormiscaig IV22 94 E2
Ormiston EH35 76 C4
Ormlie KW14 105 G2
Ormsaigmore PH36 79 F1
Ormsary PA31 73 F3
Ormskirk L39 48 D2
Oronsay PA61 72 B2
Orphir KW17 107 C7
Orpington BR6 23 H5
Orrell, Gt.Man. WN5 48 E2
Orrell, Mersey. L20 48 C3
Orrisdale IM6 54 C4
Orrok House AB23 91 H3
Orroland DG6 65 H6
Orsett RM16 24 C3
Orsett Heath RM16 24 C3
Orslow TF10 40 A4
Orston NG13 42 A1
Orton, Cumb. CA10 61 H6
Orton, Northants. NN14 32 B1
Orton Longueville PE2 42 E6
Orton Rigg CA5 60 E1
Orton Waterville PE2 42 E6
Orton-on-the-Hill CV9 41 F5
Orwell SG8 33 G3
Osbaldeston BB2 56 B6
Osbaldwick YO10 58 C4
Osbaston, Leics. CV13 41 G5
Osbaston, Shrop. SY10 38 C3
Osbaston, Tel. & W. TF6 38 E4
Osbaston Hollow CV13 41 G5
Osborne PO32 11 G5
Osbournby NG34 42 D2
Oscroft CH3 48 E6
Ose IV56 93 J7
Osgathorpe LE12 41 G4
Osgodby, Lincs. LN8 52 D3
Osgodby, N.Yorks. YO8 58 C6
Osgodby, N.Yorks. YO11 59 G1
Oskaig IV40 86 B1
Osleston DE6 40 E2
Osmaston, Derby DE24 41 F2
Osmaston, Derbys. DE6 40 D1
Osmington DT3 9 G6
Osmington Mills DT3 9 G6
Osmondthorpe LS9 57 J6
Osmotherley DL6 63 F7
Osnaburgh (Dairsie) KY15 83 F6
Ospringe ME13 25 G5
Ossett WF5 57 H7
Ossett Street Side WF5 57 H7
Ossington NG23 51 K6
Ostend CM0 25 F2
Osterley TW7 22 E4
Oswaldkirk YO62 58 C2
Oswaldtwistle BB5 56 C7
Oswestry SY11 38 B3
Oteley SY12 38 D2
Otford TN14 23 J6
Otham ME15 14 C2
Otherton ST19 40 B4
Othery TA7 8 C1
Otley, Suff. IP6 35 G3
Otley, W.Yorks. LS21 57 H5
Otter PA21 73 H3
Otter Ferry PA21 73 H2
Otterbourne SO21 11 F2
Otterburn, N.Yorks. BD23 56 D4
Otterburn, Northumb. NE19 70 D4
Otterburn Camp NE19 70 D4
Otterden Place ME13 14 E2
Otterham PL32 4 B1
Otterham Quay ME8 24 E5
Otterhampton TA5 19 F7
Otternish HS6 92 E4
Ottershaw KT16 22 D5
Otterswick ZE2 108 E4
Otterton EX9 7 J7
Otterwood SO42 11 F4
Ottery St. Mary EX11 7 J6
Ottinge CT4 15 G3
Ottringham HU12 59 J7
Oughterby CA5 60 D1
Oughtershaw BD23 56 D1
Oughterside CA7 60 C2
Oughtibridge S35 51 F3
Oulston YO61 58 B2
Oulton, Cumb. CA7 60 D1
Oulton, Norf. NR11 45 F3
Oulton, Staffs. ST15 40 B2
Oulton, Staffs. ST20 39 G3
Oulton, Suff. NR32 45 K6
Oulton, W.Yorks. LS26 57 J7
Oulton Broad NR33 45 K6
Oulton Grange ST15 40 B2
Oulton Street NR11 45 F3
Oultoncross ST15 40 B2
Oundle PE8 42 D7
Ousby CA10 61 H3
Ousdale KW7 105 F6
Ousden CB8 34 B3
Ousefleet DN14 58 E7
Ouston, Dur. DH2 62 D1
Ouston, Northumb. NE18 71 F6
Out Newton HU19 59 K7
Out Rawcliffe PR3 55 H5
Outcast LA12 55 G2
Outchester NE70 77 K7
Outertown KW16 107 B6
Outgate LA22 60 E7
Outhgill CA17 61 J6
Outlands ST20 39 G3
Outlane HD3 50 C1
Outwell PE14 43 J5
Outwood, Surr. RH1 23 G7
Outwood, W.Yorks. WF1 57 J7
Outwoods TF10 39 G4
Ouzlewell Green WF3 57 J7
Ovenden HX3 57 F7
Over, Cambs. CB4 33 G1
Over, Ches. CW7 49 F6
Over, Glos. GL2 29 H7
Over, S.Glos. BS32 19 J3
Over Burrows DE6 40 E2
Over Compton DT9 8 E3
Over Dinsdale DL2 62 E5

Over End

Over End **DE45** 50 E5
Over Green **B76** 40 D6
Over Haddon **DE45** 50 E6
Over Hulton **BL5** 49 F2
Over Kellet **LA6** 55 J3
Over Kiddington **OX20** 31 F6
Over Monnow **NP25** 28 D7
Over Norton **OX7** 30 E6
Over Peover **WA16** 49 G5
Over Rankeilour **KY15** 82 E6
Over Silton **YO7** 63 F7
Over Stowey **TA5** 7 K2
Over Stratton **TA13** 8 D3
Over Tabley **WA16** 49 G4
Over Wallop **SO20** 10 D1
Over Whitacre **B46** 40 E6
Over Winchendon (Upper Winchendon) **HP18** 31 J7
Over Worton **OX7** 31 F6
Overbister **KW17** 106 F3
Overbrae **AB53** 99 G5
Overbury **GL20** 29 J5
Overcombe **DT3** 9 F6
Evergreen **S42** 51 F5
Overleigh **BA16** 8 D1
Overpool **CH66** 48 C5
Overscaig Hotel **IV27** 103 G6
Overseal **DE12** 40 E4
Overslade **CV22** 31 F1
Oversland **ME13** 15 F2
Oversley Green **B49** 30 B3
Overstone **NN6** 32 B2
Overstrand **NR27** 45 G1
Overthorpe **OX17** 31 F4
Overton, Aber. **AB51** 91 F3
Overton, Aberdeen **AB21** 91 G3
Overton, Ches. **WA6** 48 E5
Overton, Hants. **RG25** 21 J7
Overton, Lancs. **LA3** 55 H4
Overton, N.Yorks. **YO30** 58 B4
Overton, Shrop. **SY8** 28 E1
Overton, Swan. **SA3** 17 H6
Overton, W.Yorks. **WF4** 50 E1
Overton Bridge **LL13** 38 C1
Overtown, Lancs. **LA6** 56 B2
Overtown, N.Lan. **ML2** 75 G5
Overtown, Swin. **SN4** 20 E4
Overy **OX5** 21 J2
Oving, Bucks. **HP22** 31 J6
Oving, W.Suss. **PO20** 12 C6
Ovingdean **BN2** 13 G6
Ovingham **NE42** 71 F7
Ovington, Dur. **DL11** 62 C5
Ovington, Essex **CO10** 34 B4
Ovington, Hants. **SO24** 11 G1
Ovington, Norf. **IP25** 44 D5
Ovington, Northumb. **NE42** 71 F7
Ower, Hants. **SO51** 10 E3
Ower, Hants. **SO45** 11 F4
Owermoigne **DT2** 9 G6
Owler Bar **S17** 50 E5
Owlpen **GL11** 20 A2
Owl's Green **IP13** 35 G2
Owlswick **HP27** 22 A1
Owmby **DN38** 52 D2
Owmby-by-Spital **LN8** 52 D4
Owslebury **SO21** 11 G2
Owston **LE15** 42 A5
Owston Ferry **DN9** 52 B2
Owstwick **HU12** 59 J6
Owthorpe **NG12** 41 J2
Oxborough **PE33** 44 B5
Oxcliffe Hill **LA3** 55 H3
Oxcombe **LN9** 53 G5
Oxen End **CM7** 33 K6
Oxen Park **LA12** 55 G1
Oxenhall **GL18** 29 G6
Oxenholme **LA9** 61 G7
Oxenhope **BD22** 57 F6
Oxenpill **BA6** 19 H7
Oxenton **GL52** 29 J5
Oxenwood **SN8** 21 G6
OXFORD OX 21 J1
Oxhey **WD17** 22 E2
Oxhill **CV35** 30 E4
Oxley **WV10** 40 B5
Oxley Green **CM9** 34 D7
Oxley's Green **TN32** 13 K4
Oxnam **TD8** 70 C2
Oxnead **NR10** 45 G3
Oxnop Ghyll **DL8** 62 A7
Oxshott **KT22** 22 E5
Oxspring **S36** 50 E2
Oxted **RH8** 23 G6
Oxton, Mersey. **CH43** 48 C4
Oxton, Notts. **NG25** 51 J7
Oxton, Sc.Bord. **TD2** 76 C5
Oxwich **SA3** 17 H6
Oxwich Green **SA3** 17 H6
Oxwick **NR21** 44 D3
Oykel Bridge **IV27** 95 K1
Oyne **AB52** 90 E2
Ozleworth **GL12** 20 A2

P

Pabail Iarach (Lower Bayble) **HS2** 101 H4
Pabail Uarach (Upper Bayble) **HS2** 101 H4
Pabbay **HS6** 92 E3
Packington **LE65** 41 F4
Packwood **B94** 30 C1
Padanaram **DD8** 83 F2
Padbury **MK18** 31 J5
Paddington **W2** 23 F3
Paddlesworth **CT18** 15 G3
Paddock **TN25** 14 E2

Paddock Wood **TN12** 23 K7
Paddockhaugh **IV30** 97 K6
Paddockhole **DG11** 69 H5
Paddolgreen **SY4** 38 E2
Padeswood **CH7** 48 B6
Padfield **SK13** 50 C3
Padiham **BB12** 56 C6
Padside **HG3** 57 G4
Padstow **PL28** 3 G1
Padworth **RG7** 21 K5
Paganhill **GL5** 20 B1
Pagham **PO21** 12 B7
Paglesham Churchend **SS4** 25 F2
Paglesham Eastend **SS4** 25 F2
Paible **HS3** 93 F2
Paignton **TQ3** 5 J4
Pailton **CV23** 41 G7
Paine's Corner **TN21** 13 K4
Painscastle **LD2** 28 A4
Painshawfield **NE43** 71 F7
Painswick **GL6** 20 B1
Pairc **HS2** 100 E3
PAISLEY PA 74 C4
Pakefield **NR33** 45 K6
Pakenham **IP31** 34 D2
Pale **LL23** 37 J2
Palehouse Common **TN22** 13 H5
Palestine **SP11** 21 F7
Paley Street **SL6** 22 B4
Palgowan **DG8** 67 H5
Palgrave **IP22** 35 F1
Pallinsburn House **TD12** 77 G7
Palmarsh **CT21** 15 G4
Palmers Cross **GU5** 22 D7
Palmers Green **N13** 23 G2
Palmerscross **IV30** 97 K5
Palmerstown **CF63** 18 E4
Palnackie **DG7** 65 J5
Palnure **DG8** 64 E4
Palterton **S44** 51 G6
Pamber End **RG26** 21 K6
Pamber Green **RG26** 21 K6
Pamber Heath **RG26** 21 K5
Pamington **GL20** 29 J5
Pamphill **BH21** 9 J5
Pampisford **CB2** 33 H4
Pan **KW16** 107 C8
Panborough **BA5** 19 H7
Panbride **DD7** 83 G4
Pancrasweek **EX22** 6 A5
Pancross **CF62** 18 D5
Pandy, Gwyn. **LL36** 37 F5
Pandy, Mon. **NP7** 28 C6
Pandy, Powys **SY19** 37 J5
Pandy, Wrex. **LL20** 38 A2
Pandy Tudur **LL22** 47 G6
Pandy'r Capel **LL21** 47 J7
Panfield **CM7** 34 B6
Pangbourne **RG8** 21 K4
Pannal **HG3** 57 J4
Pannal Ash **HG3** 57 H4
Panshanger **AL7** 33 F7
Pant **SY10** 38 B3
Pant Glas **LL54** 36 D1
Pant Gwyn **LL40** 37 H3
Pant Mawr **SY18** 37 H7
Pantasaph **CH8** 47 K5
Panteg **NP4** 19 G2
Pantglas **SY20** 37 G6
Pantgwyn, Carmar. **SA19** 17 J2
Pantgwyn, Cere. **SA43** 26 B4
Pant-lasau **SA6** 17 K4
Panton **LN8** 52 E5
Pant-pastynog **LL16** 47 J6
Pantperthog **SY20** 37 G5
Pant-y-dwr **LD6** 27 J1
Pantyffordd **CH7** 48 B7
Pant-y-ffrid **SY21** 38 A5
Pantyffynnon **SA18** 17 K3
Pantygasseg **NP4** 19 F2
Pantygelli **NP7** 28 C7
Panxworth **NR13** 45 H4
Papa Stour **ZE2** 109 A6
Papa Westray **KW17** 106 D2
Papcastle **CA13** 60 C3
Papil **ZE2** 109 C9
Papple **EH41** 76 D3
Papplewick **NG15** 51 H7
Papworth Everard **CB3** 33 F2
Papworth St. Agnes **CB3** 33 F2
Par **PL24** 4 A5
Parbold **WN8** 48 D1
Parbrook, Som. **BA6** 8 E1
Parbrook, W.Suss. **RH14** 12 D4
Parc **LL23** 37 H2
Parcllyn **SA43** 26 B3
Parcrhydderch **SY25** 27 F3
Parc-Seymour **NP26** 19 H2
Parc-y-rhôs **SA48** 26 E4
Pardham **IP13** 35 H2
Pardshaw **CA13** 60 B4
Parham **AB45** 98 D5
Park **LL23** 37 H2
Park Close **BB18** 56 D5
Park Corner, E.Suss. **TN3** 13 J3
Park Corner, Oxon. **RG9** 21 K3
Park End, Northumb. **NE48** 70 D6
Park End, Staffs. **ST7** 49 G2
Park End, Worcs. **DY12** 29 G1
Park Gate, Hants. **SO31** 11 G4
Park Gate, W.Yorks. **LS20** 57 G5
Park Gate, W.Yorks. **HD8** 50 E1
Park Gate, Worcs. **B61** 29 J1
Park Green **IP14** 35 F2
Park Hill **S2** 51 F4
Park Lane **LL13** 38 D2
Park Langley **BR4** 23 G5
Park Street **AL2** 22 E1

Parkend, Cumb. **CA7** 60 E3
Parkend, Glos. **GL15** 19 K1
Parker's Green **TN10** 23 K7
Parkeston **CO12** 35 G5
Parkfield, Cornw. **PL14** 4 D4
Parkfield, S.Glos. **BS16** 19 K4
Parkfield, W.Mid. **WV4** 40 B6
Parkford **DD8** 83 F2
Parkgate, Ches. **CH64** 48 B5
Parkgate, D. & G. **DG1** 69 F5
Parkgate, Kent **TN30** 14 D4
Parkgate, Surr. **RH5** 23 F7
Parkgate, S.Yorks. **S62** 51 G3
Parkham **EX39** 6 B3
Parkham Ash **EX39** 6 B3
Parkhead **G31** 74 E4
Parkhill, Angus **DD11** 83 H3
Parkhill, P. & K. **PH10** 82 C3
Parkhouse **NP25** 19 H1
Parkhurst **PO30** 11 F5
Parkmill **SA3** 17 J6
Parkmore **AB55** 98 B6
Parkneuk **AB30** 91 F7
Parkside **LL12** 48 C7
Parkstone **BH14** 10 B5
Parkway **BA22** 8 E2
Parley Cross **BH22** 10 B5
Parley Green **BH23** 10 C5
Parlington **LS25** 57 K6
Parracombe **EX31** 6 E1
Parrog **SA42** 16 D1
Parson Cross **S5** 51 F3
Parson Drove **PE13** 43 G5
Parsonage Green **CM1** 33 K7
Parsonby **CA7** 60 C3
Partick **G11** 74 D4
Partington **M31** 49 G3
Partney **PE23** 53 H6
Parton, Cumb. **CA28** 60 A4
Parton, D. & G. **DG7** 65 G3
Partridge Green **RH13** 12 E5
Parwich **DE6** 50 D7
Passenham **MK19** 31 J5
Passfield **GU30** 12 B3
Passingford Bridge **RM4** 23 J2
Paston **NR28** 45 H2
Paston Street **NR28** 45 H2
Pasturefields **ST18** 40 B3
Patchacott **EX21** 6 C6
Patcham **BN1** 13 G6
Patchetts Green **WD25** 22 E2
Patching **BN13** 12 D6
Patchole **EX31** 6 E1
Patchway **BS34** 19 K3
Pateley Bridge **HG3** 57 G3
Path of Condie **PH2** 82 B6
Pathe **TA7** 8 C1
Pathfinder Village **EX6** 7 G6
Pathhead, Aber. **DD10** 83 J1
Pathhead, E.Ayr. **KA18** 68 B2
Pathhead, Fife **KY1** 76 A1
Pathhead, Midloth. **EH37** 76 B4
Pathlow **CV37** 30 C3
Patmore Heath **SG11** 33 H6
Patna **KA6** 67 J2
Patney **SN10** 20 D6
Patrick **IM5** 54 B5
Patrick Brompton **DL8** 62 D7
Patrington **HU12** 59 K7
Patrington Haven **HU12** 59 K7
Patrishow **NP7** 28 B6
Patrixbourne **CT4** 15 G2
Patterdale **CA11** 60 E5
Pattingham **WV6** 40 A6
Pattishall **NN12** 31 H3
Pattiswick **CM77** 34 C6
Paul **TR19** 2 B6
Paulerspury **NN12** 31 J4
Paull **HU12** 59 H7
Paull Holme **HU12** 59 H7
Paul's Green **TR27** 2 D5
Paulton **BS39** 19 K6
Pauperhaugh **NE65** 71 F4
Pave Lane **TF10** 39 G4
Pavenham **MK43** 32 C3
Pawlett **TA6** 19 G7
Pawston **TD12** 77 G7
Paxford **GL55** 30 C5
Paxhill Park **RH16** 13 G4
Paxton **TD15** 77 H5
Payden Street **ME17** 14 E2
Payhembury **EX14** 7 J5
Paythorne **BB7** 56 D4
Peacehaven **BN10** 13 H6
Peacemarsh **SP8** 9 H2
Peachley **WR2** 29 H3
Peak Dale **SK17** 50 C5
Peak Forest **SK17** 50 C5
Peakirk **PE6** 42 E5
Pean Hill **CT5** 25 H5
Pear Tree **EX23** 6 B5
Pearsie **DD8** 82 E2
Pearson's Green **TN12** 23 K7
Peartree **AL7** 33 F7
Peartree Green, Essex **CM15** 23 J2
Peartree Green, Here. **HR1** 29 F5
Pease Pottage **RH11** 13 F3
Peasedown St. John **BA2** 20 A6
Peasehill **DE5** 41 G1
Peaseland Green **NR20** 44 E4
Peasemore **RG20** 21 H4
Peasenhall **IP17** 35 H2
Peaslake **GU5** 22 D7
Peasley Cross **WA9** 48 E3
Peasmarsh, E.Suss. **TN31** 14 D5
Peasmarsh, Surr. **GU3** 22 C7
Peaston **EH35** 76 C4

Peastonbank **EH34** 76 C4
Peat Inn **KY15** 83 F7
Peathill **AB43** 99 H4
Peathrow **DL13** 62 C4
Peatling Magna **LE8** 41 H6
Peatling Parva **LE17** 41 H7
Peaton **SY7** 38 E7
Pebble Coombe **KT20** 23 F6
Pebmarsh **CO9** 34 C5
Pebworth **CV37** 30 C4
Pecket Well **HX7** 56 E7
Peckforton **CW6** 48 E7
Peckham **SE15** 23 G4
Peckleton **LE9** 41 G5
Pedham **NR13** 45 H4
Pedmore **DY9** 40 B7
Pedwell **TA7** 8 D1
Peebles **EH45** 76 A6
Peel, I.o.M. **IM5** 54 B5
Peel, Lancs. **FY4** 55 G6
Peening Quarter **TN30** 14 D5
Peggs Green **LE67** 41 G4
Pegsdon **SG5** 32 E5
Pegswood **NE61** 71 H5
Pegwell **CT11** 25 K5
Peighinn nan Aoireann **HS8** 84 C1
Peinchorran **IV51** 86 B1
Peinlich **IV51** 93 K6
Pelaw **NE10** 71 H7
Pelcomb **SA62** 16 C3
Pelcomb Bridge **SA62** 16 C3
Pelcomb Cross **SA62** 16 C3
Peldon **CO5** 34 D7
Pellon **HX2** 57 F7
Pelsall **WS3** 40 C5
Pelton **DH2** 62 D1
Pelutho **CA7** 60 C2
Pelynt **PL13** 4 C5
Pemberton **WN5** 48 E2
Pembrey (Pen-bre) **SA16** 17 H4
Pembridge **HR6** 28 C3
Pembroke (Penfro) **SA71** 16 C4
Pembroke Dock (Doc Penfro) **SA72** 16 C4
Pembury **TN2** 23 K7
Pen-allt **NP25** 28 E7
Penally **SA70** 16 E5
Penalt **HR1** 28 E6
Penare **PL26** 3 G4
Penarran **SY16** 38 A7
Penarth **CF64** 18 E4
Pen-bont Rhydybeddau **SY23** 37 F7
Penboyr **SA44** 17 G1
Pen-bre (Pembrey) **SA16** 17 H4
Penbryn **SA44** 26 B3
Pencader **SA39** 17 H1
Pen-cae **SA47** 26 D3
Pen-cae-cwm **LL16** 47 H6
Pencaenewydd **LL53** 36 D1
Pencaitland **EH34** 76 C4
Pencarnisiog **LL63** 46 B5
Pencarreg **SA40** 26 E4
Pencarrow **PL32** 4 B2
Pencelli **LD3** 27 K6
Pen-clawdd **SA4** 17 J5
Pencoed **CF35** 18 C3
Pencombe **HR7** 28 E3
Pencoyd **HR2** 28 E6
Pencraig, Here. **HR9** 28 E6
Pencraig, Powys **SY10** 37 K3
Pencraig (Old Radnor), Powys **LD8** 28 B3
Pendeen **TR19** 2 A5
Penderyn **CF44** 18 C1
Pendine (Pentywyn) **SA33** 17 F4
Pendlebury **M27** 49 G2
Pendleton **BB7** 56 C6
Pendock **GL19** 29 G5
Pendoggett **PL29** 4 A3
Pendomer **BA22** 8 E3
Pendoylan **CF71** 18 D4
Penegoes **SY20** 37 G5
Penelewey **TR3** 3 F4
Pen-ffordd **SA66** 16 D2
Pen-ffordd-las (Staylittle) **SY19** 37 H6
Penfro (Pembroke) **SA71** 16 C4
Pengam **NP12** 18 E2
Penge **SE20** 23 G4
Pengenffordd **LD3** 28 A6
Pengorffwysfa **LL68** 46 C3
Pengover Green **PL14** 4 C4
Pen-groes-oped **NP7** 19 G1
Pengwern **LL18** 47 J5
Penhale **TR12** 2 D7
Penhallow **TR4** 2 E3
Penhalvean **TR16** 2 E5
Penhelig **LL35** 37 F6
Penhill **SN2** 20 E3
Penhow **NP26** 19 H2
Penhurst **TN33** 13 K5
Peniarth **LL36** 37 F5
Penicuik **EH26** 76 A4
Peniel **SA32** 17 H2
Penifiler **IV51** 93 K7
Peninver **PA28** 66 B1
Penisa'r Waun **LL55** 46 D6
Penisarcwn **SY10** 37 K4
Penishawain **LD3** 27 K5
Penistone **S36** 50 E2
Penjerrick **TR11** 2 E5
Penkill **KA26** 67 G4
Penkridge **ST19** 40 B4
Penlean **EX23** 4 C1
Penley **LL13** 38 D2
Penllech **LL53** 36 B2
Penllergaer **SA4** 17 K5
Pen-llyn, I.o.A. **LL65** 46 B4

Penllyn, V. of Glam. **CF71** 18 C4
Pen-lôn **LL61** 46 C6
Penmachno **LL24** 47 F7
Penmaen **SA3** 17 J6
Penmaenan **LL34** 47 F5
Penmaenmawr **LL34** 47 F5
Penmaenpool **LL40** 37 F4
Penmaen-Rhôs **LL29** 47 G5
Penmark **CF62** 18 D5
Penmon **LL58** 46 E4
Penmorfa **LL49** 36 E1
Penmynydd **LL61** 46 D5
Penn, Bucks. **HP10** 22 C2
Penn, W.Mid. **WV4** 40 A6
Penn Street **HP7** 22 C2
Pennal **SY20** 37 F5
Pennal-isaf **SY20** 37 G5
Pennan **AB43** 99 G4
Pennance **TR16** 2 E4
Pennant, Cere. **SY23** 26 E2
Pennant, Powys **SY19** 37 H6
Pennant Melangell **SY10** 37 K3
Pennar **SA72** 16 C4
Pennard **SA3** 17 J6
Pennerley **SY5** 38 C6
Penninghame **DG8** 64 D4
Pennington, Cumb. **LA12** 55 F2
Pennington, Hants. **SO41** 10 E5
Pennington Green **WN2** 49 F2
Pennorth **LD3** 28 A6
Pennsylvania **SN14** 20 A4
Penny Bridge **LA12** 55 G1
Pennycross **PL5** 4 E5
Pennyfuir **PA34** 79 K4
Pennygate **NR12** 45 H3
Pennyghael **PA70** 79 G5
Pennyglen **KA19** 67 G2
Pennygown **PA72** 79 H3
Pennymoor **EX16** 7 G4
Penny's Green **NR16** 45 F6
Pennyvenie **KA6** 67 J3
Penparc, Cere. **SA43** 26 B4
Penparc, Pembs. **SA62** 16 B1
Penparcau **SY23** 36 E7
Penpedairheol **NP15** 19 G1
Penpethy **PL34** 4 A2
Penpillick **PL24** 4 A5
Penpol **TR3** 3 F5
Penpoll **PL22** 4 B5
Penponds **TR14** 2 D5
Penpont, D. & G. **DG3** 68 D4
Penpont, Powys **LD3** 27 J6
Penprysg **CF35** 18 C3
Penquit **PL21** 5 G5
Penrherber **SA38** 17 F1
Penrhiw **SA37** 26 B4
Penrhiwceiber **CF45** 18 D2
Penrhiwgoch **SA32** 17 J3
Penrhiw-llan **SA44** 26 C4
Penrhiw-pâl **SA44** 26 C4
Penrhiwtyn **SA11** 18 A2
Penrhos, Gwyn. **LL53** 36 C2
Penrhos, I.o.A. **LL65** 46 A4
Penrhos, Mon. **NP15** 28 D7
Penrhos, Powys **SA9** 27 H7
Penrhos-garnedd **LL57** 46 D5
Penrhyn Bay (Bae Penrhyn) **LL30** 47 G4
Penrhyn-coch **SY23** 37 F7
Penrhyndeudraeth **LL48** 37 F2
Penrhyn-side **LL30** 47 G4
Penrhys **CF43** 18 D2
Penrice **SA3** 17 H6
Penrith **CA11** 61 G4
Penrose, Cornw. **PL27** 3 F1
Penrose, Cornw. **PL15** 4 C2
Penruddock **CA11** 60 F4
Penryn **TR10** 2 E5
Pensarn, Carmar. **SA31** 17 H3
Pensarn, Conwy **LL22** 47 H5
Pen-sarn, Gwyn. **LL45** 36 E3
Pen-sarn, Gwyn. **LL54** 36 D1
Pensax **WR6** 29 G2
Pensby **CH61** 48 B4
Penselwood **BA9** 9 G1
Pensford **BS39** 19 K5
Pensham **WR10** 29 J4
Penshaw **DH4** 62 D1
Penshurst **TN11** 23 J7
Pensilva **PL14** 4 C4
Pensnett **DY5** 40 B7
Penston **EH33** 76 C3
Pentewan **PL26** 4 A6
Pentir **LL57** 46 D6
Pentire **TR7** 2 E2
Pentireglaze **PL27** 3 G1
Pentlepoir **SA69** 16 E4
Pentlow **CO10** 34 C4
Pentlow Street **CO10** 34 C4
Pentney **PE32** 44 B4
Penton Mewsey **SP11** 21 G7
Pentonville **N1** 23 G3
Pentraeth **LL75** 46 D5
Pentre, Powys **SY10** 37 K3
Pentre, Powys **SY16** 37 K7
Pentre, Powys **LD8** 28 B2
Pentre, Powys **SY15** 38 B6
Pentre, Powys **SY16** 38 A7
Pentre, R.C.T. **CF41** 18 C2
Pentre, Shrop. **SY4** 38 C1
Pentre, Shrop. **SY7** 28 C1
Pentre, Wrex. **LL14** 38 B1
Pentre, Wrex. **LL14** 38 C1
Pentre Berw **LL60** 46 C5
Pentre Ffwrndan **CH6** 48 B5
Pentre Galar **SA41** 16 E3
Pentre Gwenlais **SA18** 17 K3
Pentre Gwynfryn **LL45** 36 E3
Pentre Halkyn **CH8** 48 B5
Pentre Isaf **LL22** 47 G6
Pentre Llanrhaeadr **LL16** 47 J6

Port Isaac

Pentre Maelor **LL13** 38 C1
Pentre Meyrick **CF71** 18 C4
Pentre Poeth **SA6** 17 K5
Pentre Saron **LL16** 47 J6
Pentre-bach, *Cere.* **SA48** 26 E4
Pentrebach, *M.Tyd.* **CF48** 18 D1
Pentre-bach, *Powys* **LD3** 27 J5
Pentrebach, *R.C.T.* **CF37** 18 D3
Pentrebach, *Swan.* **SA4** 17 J4
Pentre-bont **LL25** 47 F7
Pentre-bwlch **LL11** 38 A1
Pentrecagal **SA38** 26 C4
Pentre-celyn, *Denb.* **LL15** 47 K7
Pentre-celyn, *Powys* **SY19** 37 H5
Pentre-chwyth **SA1** 17 K5
Pentreclwydau **SA11** 18 B1
Pentre-cwrt **SA44** 17 G1
Pentre-Dolau-Honddu **LD3** 27 J4
Pentredwr, *Denb.* **LL20** 38 A1
Pentre-dwr, *Swan.* **SA7** 17 K5
Pentrefelin, *Carmar.* **SA19** 17 K2
Pentrefelin, *Cere.* **SA48** 27 F4
Pentrefelin, *Conwy* **LL28** 47 G5
Pentrefelin, *Gwyn.* **LL52** 36 E2
Pentrefelin, *Powys* **SY10** 38 A3
Pentrefoelas **LL24** 47 G7
Pentregat **SA44** 26 C3
Pentreheyling **SY15** 38 B6
Pentre-llwyn-llŵyd **LD2** 27 J3
Pentre-llyn **SY23** 27 F1
Pentre-llyn-cymmer **LL21** 47 H7
Pentre-piod **LL23** 37 H2
Pentre-poeth **NP10** 19 F3
Pentre'r beirdd **SY21** 38 A4
Pentre'r Felin **LL28** 47 G6
Pentre'r-felin **LD3** 27 J5
Pentre-tafarn-y-fedw **LL26** 47 G6
Pentre-ty-gwyn **SA20** 27 H5
Pentrich **DE5** 51 F7
Pentridge **SP5** 10 B3
Pentwyn, *Caerp.* **CF81** 18 E1
Pen-twyn, *Caerp.* **NP13** 19 F1
Pentwyn, *Cardiff* **CF23** 19 F3
Pen-twyn, *Mon.* **NP25** 19 J1
Pentwyn-mawr **NP11** 18 E2
Pentyrch **CF15** 18 E3
Pentywyn (Pendine) **SA33** 17 F4
Penuwch **SY25** 26 E2
Penwithick **PL26** 4 A5
Penwood **RG20** 21 H5
Penwortham **PR1** 55 J7
Penwortham Lane **PR1** 55 J7
Penwyllt **SA9** 27 H7
Pen-y-banc **SA19** 17 K2
Pen-y-bont, *Carmar.* **SA20** 27 G5
Pen-y-bont, *Carmar.* **SA33** 17 G2
Pen-y-bont, *Powys* **SY21** 37 K4
Pen-y-bont, *Powys* **SY10** 38 B3
Penybont, *Powys* **LD1** 28 A2
Pen-y-bont ar Ogwr (Bridgend) **CF31** 18 C4
Penybontfawr **SY10** 37 K3
Penybryn, *Caerp.* **CF82** 18 E2
Pen-y-bryn, *Gwyn.* **LL40** 37 F4
Pen-y-bryn, *Pembs.* **SA43** 26 A4
Pen-y-bryn, *Wrex.* **LL14** 38 B1
Pen-y-cae, *Powys* **SA9** 27 H7
Penycae, *Wrex.* **LL14** 38 B1
Pen-y-cae-mawr **NP15** 19 H2
Pen-y-cefn **CH7** 47 K5
Pen-y-clawdd **NP25** 19 H1
Pen-y-coedcae **CF37** 18 D3
Penycwm **SA62** 16 B2
Pen-y-Darren **CF47** 18 D1
Pen-y-fai **CF31** 18 B3
Penyffordd, *Flints.* **CH4** 48 C6
Pen-y-ffordd, *Flints.* **CH8** 47 K4
Penyffridd **LL54** 46 D7
Pen-y-gaer **NP8** 28 A6
Pen-y-garn, *Carmar.* **SA32** 17 J1
Pen-y-garn, *Cere.* **SY24** 37 F7
Penygarn, *Torfaen* **NP4** 19 F1
Penygarnedd **SY10** 38 A3
Pen-y-garreg **LD2** 27 K4
Pen-y-Graig, *Gwyn.* **LL53** 36 B2
Penygraig, *R.C.T.* **CF40** 18 D2
Penygroes, *Carmar.* **SA14** 17 J3
Penygroes, *Gwyn.* **LL54** 46 C7
Pen-y-Gwryd Hotel **LL55** 46 E7
Pen-y-lan **CF23** 18 E4
Penymynydd **CH4** 48 C6
Pen-y-parc **CH7** 48 B6
Pen-y-Park **HR3** 28 B4
Pen-yr-englyn **CF42** 18 C2
Pen-yr-heol, *Mon.* **NP25** 28 D7
Penyrheol, *Swan.* **SA4** 17 J5
Pen-y-sarn **LL69** 46 C3
Pen-y-stryt **LL11** 47 K7
Penywaun **CF44** 18 C1
Penzance **TR18** 2 B5
Penzance Heliport **TR18** 2 B5
Peopleton **WR10** 29 J3
Peover Heath **WA16** 49 G5
Peper Harow **GU8** 22 C7
Peplow **TF9** 39 F3
Pepper Arden **DL7** 62 D6
Pepper's Green **CM1** 33 K7
Perceton **KA11** 74 B6
Percie **AB31** 90 D5
Percyhorner **AB43** 99 H4
Perham Down **SP11** 21 F7
Periton **TA24** 7 H1
Perivale **UB6** 22 E3
Perkhill **AB31** 90 D4
Perkins Beach **SY5** 38 C5
Perkin's Village **EX5** 7 J6
Perlethorpe **NG22** 51 J5
Perran Downs **TR20** 2 C5
Perranarworthal **TR3** 2 E5
Perranporth **TR6** 2 E3
Perranuthnoe **TR20** 2 C6
Perranzabuloe **TR4** 2 E3
Perrott's Brook **GL7** 20 D1
Perry Barr **B42** 40 C6
Perry Crofts **B79** 40 E5
Perry Green, *Essex* **CM77** 34 C6
Perry Green, *Herts.* **SG10** 33 H7
Perry Green, *Wilts.* **SN16** 20 C3
Perry Street **DA11** 24 C4
Perrymead **BA2** 20 A5
Pershall **ST21** 40 A3
Pershore **WR10** 29 J4
Persie House **PH10** 82 C2
Pert **AB30** 83 H1
Pertenhall **MK44** 32 D2
PERTH PH **82 C5**
Perthcelyn **CF45** 18 D2
Perthy **SY12** 38 C2
Perton **WV6** 40 A6
Pestalozzi Children's Village **TN33** 14 C6
Peter Tavy **PL19** 5 F3
PETERBOROUGH PE **42 E6**
Peterburn **IV21** 94 D3
Peterchurch **HR2** 28 C5
Peterculter **AB14** 91 G4
Peterhead **AB42** 99 K6
Peterlee **SR8** 63 F2
Peter's Green **LU2** 32 E7
Peters Marland **EX38** 6 C4
Peters Port (Port Pheadair) **HS7** 92 D7
Petersfield **GU32** 11 J2
Petersfinger **SP5** 10 C2
Peterstone Wentlooge **CF3** 19 F3
Peterston-super-Ely **CF5** 18 D4
Peterstow **HR9** 28 E6
Petham **CT4** 15 G2
Petrockstowe **EX20** 6 D5
Pett **TN35** 14 D6
Pettaugh **IP14** 35 F3
Petteril Green **CA11** 61 F2
Pettinain **ML11** 75 H6
Pettistree **IP13** 35 G3
Petton, *Devon* **EX16** 7 J3
Petton, *Shrop.* **SY4** 38 D3
Petts Wood **BR5** 23 H5
Petty **AB53** 91 F1
Pettycur **KY3** 76 A2
Pettymuick **AB41** 91 H2
Petworth **GU28** 12 C4
Pevensey **BN24** 13 K6
Pevensey Bay **BN24** 13 K6
Peverell **PL2** 4 E5
Pewsey **SN9** 20 E5
Pheasant's Hill **RG9** 22 A3
Phesdo **AB30** 90 E7
Philham **EX39** 6 A3
Philiphaugh **TD7** 69 K1
Phillack **TR27** 2 C5
Philleigh **TR2** 3 F5
Philpstoun **EH49** 75 J3
Phocle Green **HR9** 29 F6
Phoenix Green **RG27** 22 A6
Phones **PH20** 88 E5
Phorp **IV36** 97 H6
Pibsbury **TA10** 8 D2
Pica **CA14** 60 B4
Piccadilly Corner **IP20** 45 G7
Pickerells **CM5** 23 J1
Pickering **YO18** 58 D1
Pickering Nook **NE16** 62 C1
Picket Piece **SP11** 21 G7
Picket Post **BH24** 10 C4
Pickford Green **CV5** 40 E7
Pickhill **YO7** 57 J1
Picklescott **SY6** 38 D6
Pickletillem **KY16** 83 F5
Pickmere **WA16** 49 F5
Pickney **TA2** 7 K3
Pickstock **TF10** 39 G3
Pickston **PH1** 82 A5
Pickup Bank **BB3** 56 C7
Pickwell, *Devon* **EX33** 6 C1
Pickwell, *Leics.* **LE14** 42 A4
Pickworth, *Lincs.* **NG34** 42 D2
Pickworth, *Rut.* **PE9** 42 C4
Picton, *Ches.* **CH2** 48 D5
Picton, *N.Yorks.* **TS15** 63 F6
Piddinghoe **BN9** 13 H6
Piddington, *Bucks.* **HP14** 22 B2
Piddington, *Northants.* **NN7** 32 B3
Piddington, *Oxon.* **OX25** 31 H7
Piddlehinton **DT2** 9 G5
Piddletrenthide **DT2** 9 G5
Pidley **PE28** 33 G1
Piercebridge **DL2** 62 D5
Pierowall **KW17** 106 D3
Pigdon **NE61** 71 G5
Pike Hill **BB10** 56 D6
Pikehall **DE4** 50 D7
Pikeshill **SO43** 10 D4
Pilgrims Hatch **CM15** 23 J2
Pilham **DN21** 52 B3
Pill **BS20** 19 J4
Pillaton, *Cornw.* **PL12** 4 D4
Pillaton, *Staffs.* **ST19** 40 B4
Pillerton Hersey **CV35** 30 D4
Pillerton Priors **CV35** 30 D4
Pilleth **LD7** 28 B2
Pilley, *Hants.* **SO41** 10 E5
Pilley, *S.Yorks.* **S75** 51 F2
Pilling **PR3** 55 H5
Pilling Lane **FY6** 55 G5
Pillowell **GL15** 19 K1
Pilning **BS35** 19 J3
Pilsbury **SK17** 50 D6
Pilsdon **DT6** 8 D5
Pilsgate **PE9** 42 D5
Pilsley, *Derbys.* **S45** 51 G6
Pilsley, *Derbys.* **DE45** 50 E5
Pilson Green **NR13** 45 H4
Piltdown **TN22** 13 H4
Pilton, *Devon* **EX31** 6 D2
Pilton, *Northants.* **PE8** 42 D7
Pilton, *Rut.* **LE15** 42 C5
Pilton, *Som.* **BA4** 19 J7
Pilton, *Swan.* **SA3** 17 H6
Pilton Green **SA3** 17 H6
Pimhole **BL9** 49 H1
Pimlico **HP3** 22 D1
Pimperne **DT11** 9 J4
Pin Mill **IP9** 35 G5
Pinchbeck **PE11** 43 F3
Pinchbeck Bars **PE11** 43 F3
Pinchbeck West **PE11** 43 F3
Pincheon Green **DN14** 51 J1
Pinchinthorpe **TS14** 63 G5
Pindon End **MK19** 31 J4
Pinehurst **SN25** 20 E3
Pinfold **L40** 48 C1
Pinged **SA16** 17 H4
Pinhay **DT7** 8 C5
Pinhoe **EX1** 7 H6
Pinkneys Green **SL6** 22 B3
Pinley Green **CV35** 30 D2
Pinminnoch **KA26** 67 F4
Pinmore **KA26** 67 G4
Pinn **EX10** 7 K7
Pinner **HA5** 22 E3
Pinner Green **HA5** 22 E2
Pinvin **WR10** 29 J4
Pinwherry **KA26** 67 F5
Pinxton **NG16** 51 G7
Pipe and Lyde **HR1** 28 E4
Pipe Gate **TF9** 39 G1
Pipe Ridware **WS15** 40 C4
Pipehill **WS13** 40 C5
Piperhall **PA20** 73 J5
Piperhill **IV12** 97 F6
Pipers Pool **PL15** 4 C2
Pipewell **NN14** 42 B7
Pippacott **EX31** 6 D2
Pipton **LD3** 28 A5
Pirbright **GU24** 22 C6
Pirnmill **KA27** 73 G6
Pirton, *Herts.* **SG5** 32 E5
Pirton, *Worcs.* **WR8** 29 H4
Pisgah **FK15** 81 J7
Pishill **RG9** 22 A3
Pistyll **LL53** 36 C1
Pitagowan **PH18** 81 K1
Pitblae **AB43** 99 H4
Pitcairngreen **PH1** 82 B5
Pitcairns **PH2** 82 B6
Pitcaple **AB51** 91 F2
Pitch Green **HP27** 22 A1
Pitch Place, *Surr.* **GU3** 22 C6
Pitch Place, *Surr.* **GU8** 12 B3
Pitchcombe **GL6** 20 B1
Pitchcott **HP22** 31 J6
Pitchford **SY5** 38 E5
Pitcombe **BA10** 9 F1
Pitcot **CF32** 18 B4
Pitcox **EH42** 76 E3
Pitcur **PH13** 82 D4
Pitfichie **AB51** 90 E3
Pitgrudy **IV25** 96 E2
Pitinnan **AB51** 91 F1
Pitkennedy **DD8** 83 G2
Pitkevy **KY6** 82 D7
Pitlessie **KY15** 82 E7
Pitlochry **PH16** 82 A2
Pitman's Corner **IP14** 35 F2
Pitmedden **AB41** 91 G2
Pitminster **TA3** 8 B3
Pitmuies **DD8** 83 G3
Pitmunie **AB51** 90 E3
Pitnacree **PH9** 82 A2
Pitney **TA10** 8 D2
Pitroddie **PH2** 82 D5
Pitscottie **KY15** 83 F6
Pitsea **SS13** 24 D3
Pitsford **NN6** 31 J2
Pitsford Hill **TA4** 7 J2
Pitstone **LU7** 32 C7
Pitstone Green **LU7** 32 C7
Pitt, *Devon* **EX16** 7 J4
Pitt, *Hants.* **SO22** 11 F2
Pittendreich **IV30** 97 J5
Pittentrail **IV28** 96 E1
Pittenweem **KY10** 83 G7
Pitteuchar **KY7** 76 A1
Pittington **DH6** 62 E2
Pittodrie House **AB51** 90 E2
Pitton, *Swan.* **SA3** 17 H6
Pitton, *Wilts.* **SP5** 10 D1
Pittulie **AB43** 99 H4
Pittville **GL52** 29 J6
Pity Me **DH1** 62 D2
Pityme **PL27** 3 G1
Pixey Green **IP21** 35 G1
Pixley **HR8** 29 F5
Place Newton **YO17** 58 E2
Plaidy **AB53** 99 F5
Plain Dealings **SA67** 16 D3
Plainfield **NE65** 70 E3
Plains **ML6** 75 F4
Plainsfield **TA5** 7 K2
Plaish **SY6** 38 E6
Plaistow, *Gt.Lon.* **E13** 23 G3
Plaistow, *W.Suss.* **RH14** 12 D3
Plaitford **SO51** 10 D3
Plaitford Green **SO51** 10 D2
Plas **SA32** 17 H2
Plas Gwynant **LL55** 46 E7
Plas Isaf **LL21** 37 K1
Plas Llwyd **LL18** 47 H5
Plas Llwyngwern **SY20** 37 G5
Plas Llysyn **SY17** 37 J6
Plas Nantyr **LL20** 38 A2
Plashett **SA33** 17 F4
Plasisaf **LL16** 47 H6
Plas-rhiw-Saeson **SY19** 37 J5
Plastow Green **RG19** 21 J5
Plas-yn-Cefn **LL17** 47 J5
Platt **TN15** 23 K6
Platt Bridge **WN2** 49 F2
Platt Lane **SY13** 38 E2
Platt's Heath **ME17** 14 D2
Plawsworth **DH2** 62 D2
Plaxtol **TN15** 23 K6
Play Hatch **RG4** 22 A4
Playden **TN31** 14 E5
Playford **IP6** 35 G4
Playing Place **TR3** 3 F4
Playley Green **GL19** 29 G5
Plealey **SY5** 38 D5
Plean **FK7** 75 G2
Pleasance **KY14** 82 D6
Pleasant Valley **CB11** 33 J5
Pleasington **BB2** 56 B7
Pleasley **NG19** 51 H6
Pleasleyhill **NG19** 51 H6
Pleck, *Dorset* **DT10** 9 G3
Pleck, *W.Mid.* **WS2** 40 B6
Pledgdon Green **CM22** 33 J6
Pledwick **WF2** 51 F1
Plemstall **CH2** 48 D5
Plenmeller **NE49** 70 C7
Pleshey **CM3** 33 K7
Plockton **IV52** 86 E1
Plocropol **HS3** 93 G2
Plomer's Hill **HP13** 22 B2
Plot Gate **TA11** 8 E1
Plough Hill **CV10** 41 F6
Plowden **SY7** 38 C7
Ploxgreen **SY5** 38 C5
Pluckley **TN27** 14 E3
Pluckley Thorne **TN27** 14 E3
Plucks Gutter **CT3** 25 J5
Plumbland **CA7** 60 C3
Plumbley **S20** 51 G4
Plumley **WA16** 49 G5
Plumpton, *Cumb.* **CA11** 61 F3
Plumpton, *E.Suss.* **BN7** 13 G5
Plumpton, *Northants.* **NN12** 31 H4
Plumpton Green **BN7** 13 G5
Plumpton Head **CA11** 61 G3
Plumstead, *Gt.Lon.* **SE18** 23 H4
Plumstead, *Norf.* **NR11** 45 F2
Plumtree **NG12** 41 J2
Plungar **NG13** 42 A2
Plush **DT2** 9 G4
Plusha **PL15** 4 C2
Plushabridge **PL14** 4 D3
Plwmp **SA44** 26 C3
Plym Bridge **PL7** 5 F5
PLYMOUTH PL **4 E5**
Plymouth City Airport **PL6** 5 F4
Plympton **PL7** 5 F5
Plymstock **PL9** 5 F5
Plymtree **EX15** 7 J5
Pockley **YO62** 58 C1
Pocklington **YO42** 58 E5
Pockthorpe **NR20** 44 E3
Pocombe Bridge **EX2** 7 G6
Pode Hole **PE11** 43 F3
Podimore **BA22** 8 E2
Podington **NN29** 32 C2
Podmore **ST21** 39 G2
Podsmead **GL2** 29 H7
Poffley End **OX29** 30 E7
Point Clear **CO16** 34 E7
Pointon **NG34** 42 E2
Polanach **PA38** 80 A2
Polapit Tamar **PL15** 6 B7
Polbae **DG8** 64 C3
Polbain **IV26** 102 B7
Polbathic **PL11** 4 D5
Polbeth **EH55** 75 J4
Poldean **DG10** 69 G4
Pole Moor **HD3** 50 C1
Polebrook **PE8** 42 D7
Polegate **BN26** 13 J6
Poles **IV25** 96 E2
Polesworth **B78** 40 E5
Polglass **IV26** 95 G1
Polgooth **PL26** 3 G3
Polgown **DG3** 68 C3
Poling **BN18** 12 D6
Poling Corner **BN18** 12 D6
Polkerris **PL24** 4 A5
Poll a' Charra **HS8** 84 C3
Polla **IV27** 103 F3
Pollardras **TR13** 2 D5
Polldubh **PH33** 80 C1
Pollie **IV28** 104 C7
Pollington **DN14** 51 J1
Polloch **PH37** 79 J1
Pollok **G53** 74 D4
Pollokshaws **G43** 74 D4
Pollokshields **G41** 74 D4
Polmassick **PL26** 3 G4
Polmont **FK2** 75 H3
Polnoon **G76** 74 D5
Polperro **PL13** 4 C5
Polruan **PL23** 4 B5
Polsham **BA5** 19 J7
Polstead **CO6** 34 D5
Polstead Heath **CO6** 34 D4
Poltalloch **PA31** 73 G1
Poltimore **EX4** 7 H6
Polton **EH18** 76 A4
Polwarth **TD10** 77 F5
Polyphant **PL15** 4 C2
Polzeath **PL27** 3 G1
Pomphlett **PL9** 5 F5
Pond Street **CB11** 33 H5
Ponders End **EN3** 23 G2
Pondersbridge **PE26** 43 F6
Ponsanooth **TR3** 2 E5
Ponsonby **CA20** 60 B6
Ponsongath **TR12** 2 E7
Ponsworthy **TQ13** 5 H3
Pont Aber **SA19** 27 G6
Pont Aberglaslyn **LL55** 36 E1
Pont ar Hydfer **LD3** 27 H6
Pont Crugnant **SY19** 37 H6
Pont Cyfyng **LL24** 47 F7
Pont Dolgarrog **LL32** 47 F6
Pont Pen-y-benglog **LL57** 46 E6
Pont Rhyd-sarn **LL23** 37 H3
Pont Rhyd-y-cyff **CF34** 18 B3
Pont Walby **SA11** 18 B1
Pont yr Alwen **LL21** 47 H7
Pontamman **SA18** 17 K3
Pontantwn **SA17** 17 H3
Pontardawe **SA8** 18 A1
Pontarddulais **SA4** 17 J4
Pontarfynach (Devil's Bridge) **SY23** 27 G1
Pontargothi **SA32** 17 J2
Pont-ar-llechau **SA19** 27 G6
Pontarsais **SA32** 17 H2
Pontblyddyn **CH7** 48 B6
Pontbren Llwyd **CF44** 18 C1
Pontefract **WF8** 57 K7
Ponteland **NE20** 71 G6
Ponterwyd **SY23** 37 G7
Pontesbury **SY5** 38 D5
Pontesbury Hill **SY5** 38 C5
Pontesford **SY5** 38 D5
Pontfadog **LL20** 38 B2
Pontfaen, *Pembs.* **SA65** 16 D1
Pont-faen, *Powys* **LD3** 27 J5
Pontgarreg **SA44** 26 C3
Pont-Henri **SA15** 17 H4
Ponthir **NP18** 19 G2
Ponthirwaun **SA43** 26 B4
Pont-iets (Pontyates) **SA15** 17 H4
Pontllanfraith **NP12** 18 E2
Pontlliw **SA4** 17 K4
Pontllyfni **LL54** 46 C7
Pontlottyn **CF81** 18 E1
Pontneddfechan **SA11** 18 C1
Pontrhydfendigaid **SY25** 27 G2
Pontrhydyfen **SA12** 18 A2
Pont-rhyd-y-groes **SY25** 27 G1
Pontrhydyrun **NP44** 19 F2
Pontrilas **HR2** 28 C6
Pontrobert **SY22** 38 A4
Pont-rug **LL55** 46 D6
Ponts Green **TN33** 13 K5
Pontshill **HR9** 29 F6
Pont-siân **SA44** 26 D4
Pontsticill **CF48** 27 K7
Pontwelly **SA44** 17 H1
Pontyates (Pont-iets) **SA15** 17 H4
Pontyberem **SA15** 17 J3
Pont-y-blew **LL14** 38 C2
Pontybodkin **CH7** 48 B7
Pontyclun **CF72** 18 D3
Pontycymer **CF32** 18 C2
Pontygwaith **CF43** 18 D2
Pontymister **NP11** 19 F2
Pontymoel **NP4** 19 F1
Pont-y-pant **LL25** 47 F7
Pontypool **NP4** 19 F1
Pontypridd **CF37** 18 D2
Pont-y-rhyl **CF32** 18 C3
Pontywaun **NP11** 19 F2
Pooksgreen **SO40** 10 E3
Pool, *Cornw.* **TR15** 2 D4
Pool, *W.Yorks.* **LS21** 57 H5
Pool Bank **LA11** 55 H1
Pool Green **WS9** 40 C5
Pool Head **HR1** 28 E3
Pool of Muckhart **FK14** 82 B7
Pool Quay **SY21** 38 B4
Pool Street **CO9** 34 B5
Poole **BH15** 10 B5
Poole Keynes **GL7** 20 C2
Poolend **ST13** 49 J7
Poolewe **IV22** 94 E3
Pooley Bridge **CA10** 61 F4
Pooley Street **IP22** 44 E7
Poolfold **ST8** 49 H7
Poolhill **GL18** 29 G6
Poolsbrook **S43** 51 G5
Poolthorne Farm **DN20** 52 D2
Pope Hill **SA62** 16 C3
Popeswood **RG42** 22 B5
Popham **SO21** 21 J7
Poplar **E14** 23 G3
Porchfield **PO30** 11 F5
Porin **IV6** 95 K6
Poringland **NR14** 45 G5
Porkellis **TR13** 2 D5
Porlock **TA24** 7 G1
Porlock Weir **TA24** 7 G1
Port Allen **PH2** 82 D5
Port Appin **PA38** 80 A3
Port Askaig **PA46** 72 C4
Port Bannatyne **PA20** 73 J4
Port Carlisle **CA7** 69 H7
Port Charlotte **PA48** 72 A5
Port Clarence **TS2** 63 G4
Port Driseach **PA21** 73 H3
Port e Vullen **IM7** 54 D4
Port Ellen **PA42** 72 B6
Port Elphinstone **AB51** 91 F3
Port Erin **IM9** 54 A7
Port Erroll **AB42** 91 J1
Port Eynon **SA3** 17 H6
Port Gaverne **PL29** 4 A2
Port Glasgow **PA14** 74 B3
Port Henderson **IV21** 94 D4
Port Isaac **PL29** 4 A2

Port Logan

Port Logan **DG9** 64 A6
Port Mòr **PH41** 85 K7
Port Mulgrave **TS13** 63 J5
Port na Craig **PH16** 82 A2
Port nan Giùran (Portnaguran) **HS2** 101 H4
Port nan Long **HS6** 92 D4
Port Ness (Port Nis) **HS2** 101 H1
Port Nis (Port Ness) **HS2** 101 H1
Port o' Warren **DG5** 65 J5
Port of Menteith **FK8** 81 G7
Port Penrhyn **LL57** 46 D5
Port Pheadair (Peters Port) **HS7** 92 D7
Port Quin **PL29** 3 G1
Port Ramsay **PA34** 79 K3
Port St. Mary **IM9** 54 B7
Port Solent **PO6** 11 H4
Port Sunlight **CH62** 48 C4
Port Talbot **SA12** 18 A2
Port Tennant **SA1** 17 K5
Port Wemyss **PA47** 72 A5
Port William **DG8** 64 D6
Portachoillan **PA29** 73 F5
Portavadie **PA21** 73 H4
Portbury **BS20** 19 J4
Portchester **PO16** 11 H4
Portencross **KA23** 73 K6
Portesham **DT3** 9 F6
Portessie **AB56** 98 C4
Portfield, *Arg. & B.* **PA63** 79 J5
Portfield, *W.Suss.* **PO19** 12 B6
Portfield Gate **SA62** 16 C3
Portgate **EX20** 6 C7
Portgordon **AB56** 98 B4
Portgower **KW8** 105 F7
Porth, *Cornw.* **TR7** 3 F2
Porth, *R.C.T.* **CF39** 18 D2
Porth Colmon **LL53** 36 A2
Porth Mellin **TR12** 2 D7
Porth Navas **TR11** 2 E6
Porthaethwy (Menai Bridge) **LL59** 46 D5
Porthallow, *Cornw.* **TR12** 2 E6
Porthallow, *Cornw.* **PL13** 4 C5
Porthcawl **CF36** 18 B4
Porthcothan **PL28** 3 F1
Porthcurno **TR19** 2 A6
Porthgain **SA62** 16 B1
Porthill **ST5** 40 A1
Porthkerry **CF62** 18 D5
Porthleven **TR13** 2 D6
Porthmadog **LL49** 36 E2
Porthmeor **TR20** 2 B5
Portholland **PL26** 3 G4
Porthoustock **TR12** 3 F6
Porthpean **PL26** 4 A5
Porthtowan **TR4** 2 D4
Porthyrhyd, *Carmar.* **SA19** 27 G5
Porthyrhyd, *Carmar.* **SA32** 17 J3
Porth-y-waen **SY10** 38 B3
Portincaple **G84** 74 A1
Portington **DN14** 58 D6
Portinnisherrich **PA33** 80 A6
Portinscale **CA12** 60 D4
Portishead **BS20** 19 H4
Portknockie **AB56** 98 C4
Portlethen **AB12** 91 H5
Portlethen Village **AB12** 91 H5
Portloe **TR2** 3 G5
Portlooe **PL13** 4 C5
Portmahomack **IV20** 97 G3
Portmeirion **LL48** 36 E2
Portmellon **PL26** 4 A6
Portmore **SO41** 10 E5
Port-na-Con **IV27** 103 G2
Portnacroish **PA38** 80 A3
Portnaguran (Port nan Giùran) **HS2** 101 H4
Portnahaven **PA47** 72 A5
Portnalong **IV47** 85 J1
Portnaluchaig **PH39** 86 C6
Portobello **EH15** 76 B3
Porton **SP4** 10 C1
Portpatrick **DG9** 64 A5
Portreath **TR16** 2 D4
Portree **IV51** 93 K7
Portscatho **TR2** 3 F5
Portsea **PO1** 11 H4
Portskerra **KW14** 104 D2
Portskewett **NP26** 19 J3
Portslade **BN41** 13 F6
Portslade-by-Sea **BN41** 13 F6
Portslogan **DG9** 64 A5
PORTSMOUTH PO 11 H5
Portsonachan **PA33** 80 B5
Portsoy **AB45** 98 D4
Portuairk **PH36** 79 F1
Portvoller **HS2** 101 H4
Portway, *Here.* **HR4** 28 C4
Portway, *Here.* **HR4** 28 D4
Portway, *Here.* **HR2** 28 D5
Portway, *Worcs.* **B48** 30 B1
Portwrinkle **PL11** 4 D5
Portyerrock **DG8** 64 E7
Posenhall **TF12** 39 F5
Poslingford **CO10** 34 B4
Postbridge **PL20** 5 G3
Postcombe **OX9** 22 A2
Postling **CT21** 15 G4
Post-mawr (Synod Inn) **SA44** 26 D3
Postwick **NR13** 45 G5
Potarch **AB31** 90 E5
Potsgrove **MK17** 32 C6
Pott Row **PE32** 44 B3
Pott Shrigley **SK10** 49 J5
Potten End **HP4** 22 D1
Potter Brompton **YO12** 59 F2
Potter Heigham **NR29** 45 J4
Potter Street **CM17** 23 H1
Pottergate Street **NR16** 45 F6
Potterhanworth **LN4** 52 D6
Potterhanworth Booths **LN4** 52 D6
Potterne **SN10** 20 C6
Potterne Wick **SN10** 20 D6
Potternewton **LS7** 57 J6
Potters Bar **EN6** 23 F1
Potters Crouch **AL2** 22 E1
Potter's Green **CV2** 41 F7
Potters Marston **LE9** 41 G6
Potterspury **NN12** 31 J4
Potterton, *Aber.* **AB23** 91 H3
Potterton, *W.Yorks.* **LS15** 57 K6
Pottle Street **BA12** 20 B7
Potto **DL6** 63 F6
Potton **SG19** 33 F4
Pott's Green **CO6** 34 D6
Poughill, *Cornw.* **EX23** 6 A5
Poughill, *Devon* **EX17** 7 G5
Poulshot **SN10** 20 C6
Poulton **GL7** 20 E1
Poulton-le-Fylde **FY6** 55 G6
Pound Bank **WR14** 29 G4
Pound Green, *E.Suss.* **TN22** 13 J4
Pound Green, *Suff.* **CB8** 34 B3
Pound Green, *Worcs.* **DY12** 29 G1
Pound Hill **RH10** 13 F3
Pound Street **RG20** 21 H5
Poundbury **DT1** 9 F5
Poundffald **SA4** 17 J5
Poundfield **TN6** 13 J3
Poundgate **TN6** 13 H4
Poundland **KA26** 67 F5
Poundon **OX27** 31 H6
Poundsbridge **TN11** 23 J7
Poundsgate **TQ13** 5 H3
Poundstock **EX23** 4 C1
Povey Cross **RH6** 23 F7
Pow Green **HR8** 29 G4
Powburn **NE66** 71 F2
Powderham **EX6** 7 H7
Powerstock **DT6** 8 E5
Powfoot **DG12** 69 G7
Powick **WR2** 29 H3
Powler's Piece **EX22** 6 B4
Powmill **FK14** 75 J1
Poxwell **DT2** 9 G6
Poyle **SL3** 22 D4
Poynings **BN45** 13 F5
Poyntington **DT9** 9 F2
Poynton, *Ches.* **SK12** 49 J4
Poynton, *Tel. & W.* **TF6** 38 E4
Poynton Green **SY4** 38 E4
Poyntzfield **IV7** 96 E5
Poys Street **IP17** 35 H1
Poyston **SA62** 16 C3
Poyston Cross **SA62** 16 C3
Poystreet Green **IP30** 34 D3
Praa Sands **TR13** 2 C6
Pratis **KY8** 82 E7
Pratt's Bottom **BR6** 23 H5
Praze-an-Beeble **TR14** 2 D5
Predannack Wollas **TR12** 2 D7
Prees **SY13** 38 E2
Prees Green **SY13** 38 E2
Prees Heath **SY13** 38 E2
Prees Higher Heath **SY13** 38 E2
Prees Lower Heath **SY13** 38 E2
Preesall **FY6** 55 G5
Preesgweene **SY10** 38 B2
Prenbrigog **CH7** 48 B6
Prendergast **SA61** 16 C3
Prendwick **NE66** 71 F2
Pren-gwyn **SA44** 26 D4
Prenteg **LL49** 36 E1
Prenton **CH42** 48 C4
Prescot **L34** 48 D3
Prescott, *Devon* **EX15** 7 J4
Prescott, *Shrop.* **SY4** 38 D3
Presley **IV36** 97 H6
Pressen **TD12** 77 G7
Prestatyn **LL19** 47 J4
Prestbury, *Ches.* **SK10** 49 J5
Prestbury, *Glos.* **GL52** 29 J6
Presteigne **LD8** 28 C2
Presthope **TF13** 38 E6
Prestleigh **BA4** 19 K7
Prestolee **M26** 49 G2
Preston, *B. & H.* **BN1** 13 G6
Preston, *Devon* **TQ12** 5 J3
Preston, *Dorset* **DT3** 9 G6
Preston, *E.Loth.* **EH40** 76 D3
Preston, *E.Riding* **HU12** 59 H6
Preston, *Glos.* **HR8** 29 F5
Preston, *Glos.* **GL7** 20 D1
Preston, *Herts.* **SG4** 32 E6
Preston, *Kent* **ME13** 25 G5
Preston, *Kent* **CT3** 25 J5
PRESTON, *Lancs.* PR 55 J7
Preston, *Northumb.* **NE67** 71 G1
Preston, *Rut.* **LE15** 42 B5
Preston, *Sc.Bord.* **TD11** 77 F5
Preston, *Shrop.* **SY4** 38 E4
Preston, *Som.* **TA4** 7 J2
Preston, *Suff.* **CO10** 34 D3
Preston, *Torbay* **TQ3** 5 J4
Preston, *Wilts.* **SN15** 20 D4
Preston Bagot **B95** 30 C2
Preston Bissett **MK18** 31 H5
Preston Bowyer **TA4** 7 K3
Preston Brockhurst **SY4** 38 E3
Preston Brook **WA7** 48 E4
Preston Candover **RG25** 21 K7
Preston Capes **NN11** 31 G3
Preston Deanery **NN7** 31 J3
Preston Gubbals **SY4** 38 D4
Preston on Stour **CV37** 30 D4
Preston on the Hill **WA4** 48 E4
Preston on Wye **HR2** 28 C4
Preston Plucknett **BA20** 8 E3
Preston upon the Weald Moors **TF6** 39 F4
Preston Wynne **HR1** 28 E4
Preston-le-Skerne **DL5** 62 E4
Prestonpans **EH32** 76 B3
Preston-under-Scar **DL8** 62 B7
Prestwich **M25** 49 H2
Prestwick, *Northumb.* **NE20** 71 G6
Prestwick, *S.Ayr.* **KA9** 67 H1
Prestwick International Airport (Glasgow Prestwick International Airport) **KA9** 67 H1
Prestwold **LE12** 41 H3
Prestwood, *Bucks.* **HP16** 22 B1
Prestwood, *Staffs.* **ST14** 40 D1
Price Town **CF32** 18 C2
Prickwillow **CB7** 43 J7
Priddy **BA5** 19 J6
Priest Hill **PR3** 56 B6
Priest Hutton **LA6** 55 J2
Priest Weston **SY15** 38 B6
Priestcliffe **SK17** 50 D5
Priestland **KA17** 74 D7
Priestwood **DA13** 24 C5
Primethorpe **LE9** 41 H6
Primrose Green **NR9** 44 E4
Primrose Hill **NW1** 23 F3
Princes End **DY4** 40 B6
Princes Gate **SA67** 16 E3
Princes Risborough **HP27** 22 B1
Princethorpe **CV23** 31 F1
Princetown, *Caerp.* **NP22** 28 A7
Princetown, *Devon* **PL20** 5 F3
Prior Muir **KY16** 83 G6
Prior's Frome **HR1** 28 E5
Priors Halton **SY8** 28 D1
Priors Hardwick **CV47** 31 F3
Priors Marston **CV47** 31 F3
Prior's Norton **GL2** 29 H6
Priors Park **GL20** 29 H5
Priorslee **TF2** 39 G4
Priory Wood **HR3** 28 B4
Priston **BA2** 19 K5
Pristow Green **NR16** 45 F7
Prittlewell **SS0** 24 E3
Privett **GU34** 11 H2
Prixford **EX31** 6 D2
Proaig **PA44** 72 C5
Probus **TR2** 3 F4
Protstonhill **AB45** 99 G4
Prudhoe **NE42** 71 F7
Prussia Cove **TR20** 2 C6
Pubil **PH15** 81 F3
Publow **BS39** 19 K5
Puckeridge **SG11** 33 G6
Puckington **TA19** 8 C3
Pucklechurch **BS16** 19 K4
Pucknall **SO51** 10 E2
Puckrup **GL20** 29 H5
Puddinglake **CW10** 49 G6
Puddington, *Ches.* **CH64** 48 C5
Puddington, *Devon* **EX16** 7 G4
Puddlebrook **GL17** 29 F7
Puddledock **NR17** 44 E6
Puddletown **DT2** 9 G5
Pudleston **HR6** 28 E3
Pudsey **LS28** 57 H6
Pulborough **RH20** 12 D5
Puldagon **KW1** 105 J4
Puleston **TF10** 39 G3
Pulford **CH4** 48 C7
Pulham **DT2** 9 G4
Pulham Market **IP21** 45 F7
Pulham St. Mary **IP21** 45 G7
Pulley **SY3** 38 D5
Pulloxhill **MK45** 32 D5
Pullrossie **IV25** 96 E3
Pulverbatch **SY5** 38 D5
Pumpherston **EH53** 75 J4
Pumsaint **SA19** 27 F4
Puncheston **SA62** 16 D2
Puncknowle **DT6** 8 E6
Punnett's Town **TN21** 13 K4
Purbrook **PO7** 11 H4
Purewell **BH23** 10 C5
Purfleet **RM19** 23 J4
Puriton **TA7** 19 G7
Purleigh **CM3** 24 E1
Purley **CR8** 23 G5
Purley on Thames **RG8** 21 K4
Purlogue **SY7** 28 B1
Purlpit **SN12** 20 B5
Purls Bridge **PE15** 43 H7
Purse Caundle **DT9** 9 F3
Purslow **SY7** 38 C7
Purston Jaglin **WF7** 51 G1
Purtington **TA20** 8 C4
Purton, *Glos.* **GL13** 19 K1
Purton, *Glos.* **GL15** 19 K1
Purton, *Wilts.* **SN5** 20 D3
Purton Stoke **SN5** 20 D2
Purves Hall **TD10** 77 F6
Pury End **NN12** 31 J4
Pusey **SN7** 21 G2
Putley **HR8** 29 F5
Putley Green **HR8** 29 F5
Putney **SW15** 23 F4
Putsborough **EX33** 6 C1
Puttenham, *Herts.* **HP23** 32 B7
Puttenham, *Surr.* **GU3** 22 C7
Puttock End **CO10** 34 C4
Putts Corner **EX10** 7 K6
Puxton **BS24** 19 H5
Pwll **SA15** 17 H4
Pwllcrochan **SA71** 16 C4
Pwlldefaid **LL53** 36 A3
Pwll-glas **LL15** 47 K7
Pwllgloyw **LD3** 27 K5
Pwllheli **LL53** 36 C2
Pwll-Mawr **CF3** 19 F4
Pwllmeyric **NP16** 19 J2
Pwll-trap **SA33** 17 F3
Pwll-y-glaw **SA12** 18 A2
Pye Corner, *Herts.* **CM20** 33 H7
Pye Corner, *Kent* **ME17** 14 D3
Pye Corner, *Newport* **NP18** 19 G3
Pye Green **WS12** 40 B4
Pyecombe **BN45** 13 F5
Pyle, *Bridgend* **CF33** 18 B3
Pyle, *I.o.W.* **PO38** 11 F7
Pyleigh **TA4** 7 K2
Pylle **BA4** 9 F1
Pymore, *Cambs.* **CB6** 43 H7
Pymore, *Dorset* **DT6** 8 D5
Pyrford **GU22** 22 D6
Pyrford Green **GU22** 22 D6
Pyrton **OX49** 21 K2
Pytchley **NN14** 32 B1
Pyworthy **EX22** 6 B5

Q

Quabbs **LD7** 38 B7
Quadring **PE11** 43 F2
Quadring Eaudike **PE11** 43 F2
Quainton **HP22** 31 J6
Quarff **ZE2** 109 D9
Quarley **SP11** 21 F7
Quarndon **DE22** 41 F1
Quarr Hill **PO33** 11 G5
Quarrier's Village **PA11** 74 B4
Quarrington **NG34** 42 D1
Quarrington Hill **DH6** 62 E3
Quarry Bank **DY5** 40 B7
Quarrybank **CW6** 48 E6
Quarrywood **IV30** 97 J5
Quarter **ML3** 75 F5
Quatford **WV15** 39 G6
Quatt **WV15** 39 G7
Quebec **DH7** 62 C2
Quedgeley **GL2** 29 H7
Queen Adelaide **CB7** 43 J7
Queen Camel **BA22** 8 E2
Queen Charlton **BS31** 19 K5
Queen Dart **EX16** 7 G4
Queen Oak **SP8** 9 G1
Queen Street **TN12** 23 K7
Queenborough **ME11** 25 F4
Queen's Bower **PO36** 11 G6
Queen's Head **SY11** 38 C3
Queensbury, *Gt.Lon.* **HA3** 22 E3
Queensbury, *W.Yorks.* **BD13** 57 G6
Queensferry (South Queensferry), *Edin.* **EH30** 75 K3
Queensferry, *Flints.* **CH5** 48 C6
Queenzieburn **G65** 74 E3
Quemerford **SN11** 20 D5
Quendale **ZE2** 109 F9
Quendon **CB11** 33 J5
Queniborough **LE7** 41 J4
Quenington **GL7** 20 E1
Quernmore **LA2** 55 J3
Queslett **B43** 40 C6
Quethiock **PL14** 4 D4
Quholm **KW16** 107 B6
Quick's Green **RG8** 21 J4
Quidenham **NR16** 44 E7
Quidhampton **RG25** 21 J6
Quidinish (Cuidhtinis) **HS3** 93 F3
Quilquox **AB41** 91 H1
Quina Brook **SY4** 38 E2
Quindry **KW17** 107 D8
Quine's Hill **IM4** 54 C6
Quinhill **PA29** 73 F5
Quinton, *Northants.* **NN7** 31 J3
Quinton, *W.Mid.* **B32** 40 B7
Quinton Green **NN7** 31 J3
Quintrell Downs **TR8** 3 F2
Quixhill **ST14** 40 D1
Quoditch **EX21** 6 C6
Quoig **PH7** 81 K5
Quoiggs House **FK15** 81 K7
Quoisley **SY13** 38 E1
Quorn **LE12** 41 H4
Quothquan **ML12** 75 H7
Quoyloo **KW16** 106 B5
Quoys **ZE2** 108 F1
Quoys of Reiss **KW1** 105 J3

R

Raasay **IV40** 94 B7
Raby **CH63** 48 C5
Rachan **ML12** 75 K7
Rachub **LL57** 46 E6
Rackenford **EX16** 7 G4
Rackham **RH20** 12 D5
Rackheath **NR13** 45 G4
Racks **DG1** 69 F6
Rackwick, *Ork.* **KW16** 107 B8
Rackwick, *Ork.* **KW17** 106 D3
Radbourne **DE6** 40 E2
Radcliffe, *Gt.Man.* **M26** 49 G2
Radcliffe, *Northumb.* **NE65** 71 H3
Radcliffe on Trent **NG12** 41 J2
Radclive **MK18** 31 H5
Radcot **OX18** 21 F2
Raddington **TA4** 7 J3
Radernie **KY15** 83 F7
Radford, *B. & N.E.Som.* **BA2** 19 K6
Radford, *Nott.* **NG7** 41 H1
Radford, *Oxon.* **OX7** 31 F6
Radford, *W.Mid.* **CV6** 41 F7
Radford Semele **CV31** 30 E2
Radipole **DT3** 9 F6
Radlett **WD7** 22 E1
Radley **OX14** 21 J2
Radley Green **CM4** 24 C1
Radmore Green **CW6** 48 E7
Radnage **HP14** 22 A2
Radstock **BA3** 19 K6
Radstone **NN13** 31 G4
Radway **CV35** 30 E4
Radway Green **CW1** 49 G7
Radwell, *Beds.* **MK43** 32 D3
Radwell, *Herts.* **SG7** 33 F5
Radwinter **CB10** 33 K5
Radyr **CF15** 18 E3
Raechester **NE19** 70 E5
Raemoir House **AB31** 90 E5
Raffin **IV27** 102 C5
Rafford **IV36** 97 H6
Ragdale **LE14** 41 J3
Ragged Appleshaw **SP11** 21 G7
Raglan **NP15** 19 H1
Ragnall **NG22** 52 B5
Rahoy **PA34** 79 H2
Rain Shore **OL12** 49 H1
Rainford **WA11** 48 D2
Rainham, *Gt.Lon.* **RM13** 23 J3
Rainham, *Med.* **ME8** 24 E5
Rainhill **L35** 48 D3
Rainhill Stoops **L35** 48 E3
Rainow **SK10** 49 J5
Rainsough **M27** 49 G2
Rainton **YO7** 57 J2
Rainworth **NG21** 51 H7
Raisbeck **CA10** 61 H6
Raise **CA9** 61 J2
Rait **PH2** 82 D5
Raithby, *Lincs.* **PE23** 53 G6
Raithby, *Lincs.* **LN11** 53 G4
Rake **GU33** 12 B4
Raleigh's Cross **TA23** 7 J2
Ram **SA48** 26 E4
Ram Alley **SN8** 21 F5
Ram Lane **TN26** 14 E3
Ramasaig **IV55** 93 G7
Rame, *Cornw.* **TR10** 2 E5
Rame, *Cornw.* **PL10** 4 E6
Rampisham **DT2** 8 E4
Rampside **LA13** 55 F3
Rampton, *Cambs.* **CB4** 33 H2
Rampton, *Notts.* **DN22** 52 B5
Ramsbottom **BL0** 49 G1
Ramsbury **SN8** 21 F4
Ramscraigs **KW6** 105 G6
Ramsdean **GU32** 11 J2
Ramsdell **RG26** 21 J6
Ramsden **OX7** 30 E7
Ramsden Bellhouse **CM11** 24 D2
Ramsden Heath **CM11** 24 D2
Ramsey, *Cambs.* **PE26** 43 F7
Ramsey, *Essex* **CO12** 35 G5
Ramsey, *I.o.M.* **IM8** 54 D4
Ramsey Forty Foot **PE26** 43 G7
Ramsey Heights **PE26** 43 F7
Ramsey Island, *Essex* **CM0** 25 F1
Ramsey Island, *Pembs.* **SA62** 16 A2
Ramsey Mereside **PE26** 43 F7
Ramsey St. Mary's **PE26** 43 F7
Ramsgate **CT11** 25 K5
Ramsgate Street **NR24** 44 E2
Ramsgill **HG3** 57 G2
Ramsholt **IP12** 35 H4
Ramshorn **ST10** 40 C1
Ramsnest Common **GU8** 12 C3
Ranachan **PH36** 79 J1
Ranais (Ranish) **HS2** 101 G5
Ranby, *Lincs.* **LN8** 53 F5
Ranby, *Notts.* **DN22** 51 J4
Rand **LN8** 52 E5
Randwick **GL6** 20 B1
Rangemore **DE13** 40 D3
Rangeworthy **BS37** 19 K3
Ranish (Ranais) **HS2** 101 G5
Rankinston **KA6** 67 J2
Rank's Green **CM3** 34 B7
Ranmoor **S10** 51 F4
Rannoch School **PH17** 81 G2
Ranochan **PH38** 86 E6
Ranscombe **TA24** 7 H1
Ranskill **DN22** 51 J4
Ranton **ST18** 40 A3
Ranton Green **ST18** 40 A3
Ranworth **NR13** 45 H4
Rapness **KW17** 106 E3
Rapps **TA19** 8 C3
Rascarrel **DG7** 65 H6
Rash **LA10** 56 B1
Rashwood **WR9** 29 J2
Raskelf **YO61** 57 K2
Rassau **NP23** 28 A7
Rastrick **HD6** 57 G7
Ratagan **IV40** 87 F3
Ratby **LE6** 41 H5
Ratcliffe Culey **CV9** 41 F6
Ratcliffe on Soar **NG11** 41 G3
Ratcliffe on the Wreake **LE7** 41 J4
Ratford Bridge **SA62** 16 B3
Ratfyn **SP4** 20 E7
Rathen **AB43** 99 H4
Rathillet **KY15** 82 E5
Rathliesbeag **PH34** 87 J6
Rathmell **BD24** 56 D3
Ratho **EH28** 75 K3
Ratho Station **EH28** 75 K3
Rathven **AB56** 98 C4

Ratley OX15 30 E4
Ratling CT3 15 H2
Ratlinghope SY5 38 D6
Ratsloe EX4 7 H6
Rattar KW14 105 H1
Ratten Row, Cumb. CA5 60 E2
Ratten Row, Lancs. PR3 55 H5
Rattery TQ10 5 H4
Rattlesden IP30 34 D3
Rattray PH10 82 C3
Raughton Head CA5 60 E2
Raunds NN9 32 C1
Ravenfield S65 51 G3
Raveningham NR14 45 H6
Raven's Green CO7 35 F6
Ravenscar YO13 63 J2
Ravensdale IM7 54 C4
Ravensden MK44 32 D3
Ravenshaw BD23 56 E5
Ravenshayes EX5 7 H5
Ravenshead NG15 51 H7
Ravensmoor CW5 49 F7
Ravensthorpe, Northants. NN6 31 H1
Ravensthorpe, W.Yorks. WF13 57 H7
Ravenstone, Leics. LE67 41 G4
Ravenstone, M.K. MK46 32 B3
Ravenstonedale CA17 61 J6
Ravenstruther ML11 75 H6
Ravensworth DL11 62 C6
Raw YO22 63 J2
Rawcliffe, E.Riding DN14 58 C7
Rawcliffe, York YO30 58 B4
Rawcliffe Bridge DN14 58 C7
Rawdon LS19 57 H6
Rawmarsh S62 51 G3
Rawnsley WS12 40 C4
Rawreth SS11 24 D2
Rawridge EX14 8 B4
Rawson Green DE56 41 F1
Rawtenstall BB4 56 D7
Rawyards ML6 75 F4
Raxton AB41 91 G1
Raydon IP7 34 E5
Raylees NE19 70 E4
Rayleigh SS6 24 E2
Raymond's Hill EX13 8 C5
Rayne CM77 34 B6
Rayners Lane HA5 22 E3
Raynes Park SW20 23 F5
Reach CB5 33 J2
Read BB12 56 C6
READING RG 22 A4
Reading Green IP21 35 F1
Reading Street TN30 14 E4
Reagill CA10 61 H5
Rearquhar IV25 96 E2
Rearsby LE7 41 J4
Rease Heath CW5 49 F7
Reaster KW1 105 H2
Reaveley NE66 71 F2
Reawick ZE2 109 C8
Reay KW14 104 E2
Reculver CT6 25 J5
Red Ball EX16 7 J4
Red Bull ST7 49 H7
Red Dial CA7 60 D2
Red Hill, Hants. PO9 11 J3
Red Hill, Warks. B49 30 C3
Red Lodge IP28 33 K1
Red Lumb OL11 49 H1
Red Oaks Hill CB10 33 J5
Red Point IV21 94 D5
Red Post, Cornw. EX23 6 A5
Red Post, Devon TQ9 5 J4
Red Rail HR9 28 E6
Red Rock WN2 48 E2
Red Roses SA34 17 F3
Red Row NE61 71 H4
Red Street ST5 49 H7
Red Wharf Bay (Traeth Coch) LL75 46 D4
Redberth SA70 16 D4
Redbourn AL3 32 E7
Redbourne DN21 52 C3
Redbrook, Glos. NP25 28 E7
Redbrook, Wrex. SY13 38 E1
Redbrook Street TN26 14 E4
Redburn, High. IV16 96 C5
Redburn, High. IV12 97 G7
Redburn, Northumb. NE47 70 C7
Redcar TS10 63 H4
Redcastle, Angus DD11 83 H2
Redcastle, High. IV6 96 C7
Redcliff Bay BS20 19 H4
Redcloak AB39 91 G6
Reddingmuirhead FK2 75 H3
Reddish SK5 49 H3
Redditch B97 30 B2
Rede IP29 34 C3
Redenhall IP20 45 G7
Redesmouth NE48 70 D5
Redford, Aber. AB30 91 F7
Redford, Angus DD11 83 G3
Redford, Dur. DL13 62 B3
Redford, W.Suss. GU29 12 B4
Redgrave IP22 34 E1
Redheugh DD8 83 F1
Redhill, Aber. AB51 90 E1
Redhill, Aber. AB31 91 F4
Redhill, Moray AB54 98 D6
Redhill, N.Som. BS40 19 H5
Redhill, Notts. NG5 41 H1
REDHILL, Surr. RH1 23 F6
Redhill Aerodrome & Heliport RH1 23 F7
Redhouse, Aber. AB33 90 D2
Redhouse, Arg. & B. PA29 73 G4

Redhouses PA44 72 B4
Redisham NR34 45 J7
Redland, Bristol BS6 19 J4
Redland, Ork. KW17 106 C5
Redlingfield IP23 35 F1
Redlynch, Som. BA10 9 G1
Redlynch, Wilts. SP5 10 D2
Redmarley D'Abitot GL19 29 G5
Redmarshall TS21 62 E4
Redmile NG13 42 A2
Redmire DL8 62 B7
Redmoor PL30 4 A4
Rednal SY11 38 C3
Redpath TD4 76 D7
Redruth TR15 2 D4
Redscarhead EH45 76 A6
Redshaw ML11 68 D1
Redstone Bank SA67 16 E3
Redwick, Newport NP26 19 H3
Redwick, S.Glos. BS35 19 J3
Redworth DL5 62 D4
Reed SG8 33 G5
Reed End SG8 33 G5
Reedham NR13 45 J5
Reedley BB10 56 D6
Reedness DN14 58 D7
Reef (Riof) HS2 100 D4
Reepham, Lincs. LN3 52 D5
Reepham, Norf. NR10 44 E3
Reeth DL11 62 B7
Regaby IM7 54 D4
Regil BS40 19 J5
Regoul IV12 97 F6
Reiff IV26 102 B7
Reigate RH2 23 F6
Reighton YO14 59 H2
Reinigeadal (Rhenigidale) HS3 100 E7
Reisgill KW3 105 H5
Reiss KW1 105 J3
Rejerrah TR8 2 E3
Releath TR13 2 D5
Relubbus TR20 2 C5
Remenham RG9 22 A3
Remenham Hill RG9 22 A3
Remony PH15 81 J3
Rempstone LE12 41 H3
Rendcomb GL7 30 B7
Rendham IP17 35 H2
Rendlesham IP12 35 H3
Renfrew PA4 74 D4
Renhold MK41 32 D3
Renishaw S21 51 G5
Rennington NE66 71 H2
Renton G82 74 B3
Renwick CA10 61 G2
Repps NR29 45 J4
Repton DE65 41 F3
Rescobie DD8 83 G2
Rescorla PL26 4 A5
Resipole PH36 79 J1
Resolfen SA11 18 B1
Resolis IV7 96 D5
Resolven SA11 18 B1
Resourie PH37 86 E7
Respryn PL30 4 B4
Reston TD14 77 G4
Restormel PL22 4 B4
Reswallie DD8 83 G2
Reterth TR9 3 G2
Retew PL26 3 G3
Retford DN22 51 K4
Rettendon CM3 24 D2
Rettendon Place CM3 24 D2
Retyn TR8 3 F3
Revesby PE22 53 F6
Revesby Bridge PE22 53 G6
Rew TQ13 5 H3
Rew Street PO31 11 F5
Rewe, Devon EX5 7 H6
Rewe, Devon EX5 7 G6
Reybridge SN15 20 C5
Reydon IP18 35 J1
Reydon Smear IP18 35 K1
Reymerston NR9 44 E5
Reynalton SA68 16 D4
Reynoldston SA3 17 H6
Rezare PL15 4 D3
Rhadyr NP15 19 G1
Rhandirmwyn SA20 27 G4
Rhaoine IV28 96 D1
Rhayader LD6 27 J2
Rhedyn LL53 36 B2
Rhegreanoch IV27 102 C7
Rheindown IV4 96 C7
Rhelonie IV24 96 C2
Rhemore PA34 79 G2
Rhenigidale (Reinigeadal) HS3 100 E7
Rheola SA11 18 B1
Rhes-y-cae CH8 47 K6
Rhewl, Denb. LL20 38 A1
Rhewl, Denb. LL15 47 K6
Rhewl, Shrop. SY10 38 C2
Rhian IV27 103 H7
Rhicarn IV27 102 C6
Rhiconich IV27 102 E3
Rhicullen IV18 96 D4
Rhidorroch IV26 95 H2
Rhifail KW11 104 C3
Rhigos CF44 18 C1
Rhilochan IV28 96 E1
Rhinduie IV3 96 C7
Rhireavach IV23 95 G2
Rhiroy IV23 95 H3
Rhiston SY15 38 B6
Rhiw LL53 36 B3
Rhiwargor SY10 37 J3
Rhiwbina CF14 18 E3
Rhiwbryfdir LL41 37 F1
Rhiwderin NP10 19 F3

Rhiwinder CF39 18 D3
Rhiwlas, Gwyn. LL57 46 D6
Rhiwlas, Gwyn. LL23 37 J2
Rhiwlas, Powys SY10 38 B2
Rhode TA5 8 B1
Rhodes Minnis CT4 15 G3
Rhodesia S80 51 H5
Rhodiad-y-brenin SA62 16 A2
Rhodmad SY23 26 E1
Rhonadale PA28 73 F7
Rhonehouse (Kelton Hill) DG7 65 H5
Rhoose CF62 18 D5
Rhos, Carmar. SA44 17 G1
Rhos, N.P.T. SA8 18 A1
Rhos Common SY22 38 B4
Rhôs Lligwy LL70 46 C4
Rhosaman SA18 27 G7
Rhoscolyn LL65 46 A5
Rhoscrowther SA71 16 C4
Rhosesmor CH7 48 B6
Rhos-fawr LL53 36 C2
Rhosgadfan LL54 46 D7
Rhosgoch, I.o.A. LL66 46 C4
Rhosgoch, Powys LD2 28 A4
Rhos-hill SA43 16 A2
Rhoshirwaun LL53 36 A3
Rhoslan LL52 36 D1
Rhoslefain LL36 36 E5
Rhosllanerchrugog LL14 38 B1
Rhosmaen SA19 17 K2
Rhosmeirch LL77 46 C5
Rhosneigr LL64 46 B5
Rhosnesni LL13 48 C7
Rhôs-on-Sea LL28 47 G4
Rhossili SA3 17 H6
Rhosson SA62 16 A2
Rhostrehwfa LL77 46 C5
Rhostryfan LL54 46 C7
Rhostyllen LL14 38 C1
Rhos-y-bol LL68 46 C4
Rhos-y-brithdir SY22 38 A3
Rhosycaerau SA64 16 C1
Rhos-y-garth SY23 27 F1
Rhos-y-gwaliau LL23 37 J2
Rhos-y-llan LL53 36 B2
Rhos-y-mawn LL22 47 G6
Rhos-y-Meirch LD7 28 B2
Rhu G84 74 A2
Rhualt LL17 47 J5
Rhubodach PA20 73 J3
Rhuddall Heath CW6 48 E6
Rhuddlan LL18 47 J5
Rhue IV26 95 H2
Rhulen LD2 28 A4
Rhumach PH39 86 C6
Rhuthun (Ruthin) LL15 47 K7
Rhyd, Gwyn. LL48 37 F1
Rhyd, Powys SY17 37 J5
Rhydaman (Ammanford) SA18 17 K3
Rhydargaeau SA32 17 H2
Rhydcymerau SA19 17 J1
Rhyd-Ddu LL54 46 D7
Rhydding SA10 18 A2
Rhydgaled LL16 47 H6
Rhydlanfair LL24 47 G7
Rhydlewis SA44 26 C4
Rhydlios LL53 36 A2
Rhydlydan, Conwy LL24 47 G7
Rhydlydan, Powys SY16 37 K6
Rhydolion LL53 36 B3
Rhydowen SA44 26 D4
Rhyd-Rosser SY23 26 E2
Rhydspence HR3 28 B4
Rhydtalog CH7 48 B7
Rhyd-uchaf LL23 37 H2
Rhyd-wen LL23 37 J3
Rhyd-wyn LL65 46 B4
Rhyd-y-ceirw CH7 48 B7
Rhyd-y-clafdy LL53 36 C2
Rhydycroesau SY10 38 B2
Rhydyfelin, Cere. SY23 26 E1
Rhydyfelin, R.C.T. CF37 18 D3
Rhyd-y-foel LL22 47 H5
Rhyd-y-fro SA8 18 A1
Rhyd-y-groes LL57 46 D6
Rhydymain LL40 37 H3
Rhydymwyn CH7 48 B6
Rhyd-yr-onnen LL36 37 F5
Rhyd-y-sarn LL41 37 F1
Rhydywrach SA34 16 E3
Rhyl LL18 47 J4
Rhymney NP22 18 E1
Rhyn SY11 38 C2
Rhynd PH2 82 C5
Rhynie, Aber. AB54 90 C2
Rhynie, High. IV20 97 F4
Ribbesford DY12 29 G1
Ribchester PR3 56 B6
Ribigill IV27 103 H3
Riby DN37 52 E2
Riccall YO19 58 C6
Riccarton KA1 74 C7
Richards Castle SY8 28 D2
Richings Park SL0 22 D4
Richmond, Gt.Lon. TW9 22 E4
Richmond, N.Yorks. DL10 62 C6
Richmond, S.Yorks. S13 51 G4
Rich's Holford TA4 7 K2
Rickarton AB39 91 G6
Rickerscote ST17 40 B3
Rickford BS40 19 H6
Rickinghall IP22 34 E1
Rickleton NE38 62 D1
Rickling CB11 33 H5
Rickling Green CB11 33 J6
Rickmansworth WD3 22 D2
Riddell TD6 70 A1
Riddings DE55 51 G7

Riddlecombe EX18 6 E4
Riddlesden BD20 57 F5
Ridge, Dorset BH20 9 J6
Ridge, Herts. EN6 23 F1
Ridge, Wilts. SP3 9 J1
Ridge Green RH1 23 G7
Ridge Lane CV10 40 E6
Ridgebourne LD1 27 K2
Ridgeway S12 51 G4
Ridgeway Cross WR13 29 G4
Ridgeway Moor S12 51 G4
Ridgewell CO9 34 B4
Ridgewood TN22 13 H4
Ridgmont MK43 32 C5
Riding Gate BA9 9 G2
Riding Mill NE44 71 F7
Ridley TN15 24 C5
Ridleywood LL13 48 C7
Ridlington, Norf. NR28 45 H2
Ridlington, Rut. LE15 42 B5
Ridsdale NE48 70 E5
Riechip PH8 82 B3
Rievaulx YO62 58 B1
Rift House TS25 63 F3
Rigg, D. & G. DG16 69 H7
Rigg, High. IV51 94 B6
Riggend ML6 75 F4
Rigifa KW1 105 J1
Rigsby LN13 53 H5
Rigside ML11 75 G7
Riley Green PR5 56 B7
Rileyhill WS13 40 D4
Rilla Mill PL17 4 C3
Rillaton PL17 4 C3
Rillington YO17 58 E2
Rimington BB7 56 D5
Rimpton BA22 9 F2
Rimswell HU19 59 K7
Rinaston SA62 16 C2
Ring o' Bells L40 48 D1
Ringford DG7 65 G5
Ringinglow S11 50 E4
Ringland NR8 45 F4
Ringles Cross TN22 13 H4
Ringmer BN8 13 H5
Ringmore, Devon TQ7 5 G6
Ringmore, Devon TQ12 5 K3
Ringorm AB38 97 K7
Ring's End PE13 43 H5
Ringsfield NR34 45 J7
Ringsfield Corner NR34 45 J7
Ringshall, Herts. HP4 32 C7
Ringshall, Suff. IP14 34 E3
Ringshall Stocks IP14 34 E3
Ringstead, Norf. PE36 44 B1
Ringstead, Northants. NN14 32 C1
Ringwood BH24 10 C4
Ringwould CT14 15 J3
Rinloan AB35 89 K4
Rinmore AB33 90 C3
Rinnigill KW16 107 C8
Rinsey TR13 2 C6
Riof (Reef) HS2 100 D4
Ripe BN8 13 J6
Ripley, Derbys. DE5 51 F7
Ripley, Hants. BH23 10 C5
Ripley, N.Yorks. HG3 57 H3
Ripley, Surr. GU23 22 D6
Riplingham HU15 59 F6
Ripon HG4 57 J2
Rippingale PE10 42 E3
Ripple, Kent CT14 15 J3
Ripple, Worcs. GL20 29 H5
Ripponden HX6 50 C1
Risabus PA42 72 B6
Risbury HR6 28 E3
Risby, E.Riding HU17 59 G6
Risby, Suff. IP28 34 B2
Risca NP11 19 F2
Rise HU11 59 H5
Riseden TN17 14 C4
Risegate PE11 43 F3
Riseholme LN2 52 C5
Riseley, Beds. MK44 32 D2
Riseley, W'ham RG7 22 A5
Rishangles IP23 35 F2
Rishton BB1 56 C6
Rishworth HX6 50 C1
Risinghurst OX3 21 J1
Risley, Derbys. DE72 41 G2
Risley, Warr. WA3 49 F3
Risplith HG4 57 H3
Rispond IV27 103 G2
Rivar SN8 21 G5
Rivenhall CM8 34 C7
Rivenhall End CM8 34 C7
River, Kent CT17 15 H3
River, W.Suss. GU28 12 C4
River Bank CB7 33 J2
River Bridge TA7 19 G7
Riverford Bridge TQ9 5 H4
Riverhead TN13 23 J6
Riverside CF11 18 E4
Riverton EX32 6 E2
Riverview Park DA12 24 C4
Rivington BL6 49 F1
Roa Island LA13 55 F3
Roach Bridge PR5 55 J7
Road Green NR15 45 G6
Road Weedon NN7 31 H3
Roade NN7 31 J3
Roadhead CA6 70 A6
Roadside, High. KW12 105 G2
Roadside, Ork. KW17 106 F3
Roadwater TA23 7 J2
Roag IV55 93 H7
Roast Green CB11 33 H5
Roath CF24 18 E4

Roberton, S.Lan. ML12 68 E1
Roberton, Sc.Bord. TD9 69 K2
Robertsbridge TN32 14 C5
Robertstown, Moray AB38 97 K7
Robertstown, R.C.T. CF44 18 D1
Roberttown WF15 57 G7
Robeston Cross SA73 16 B4
Robeston Wathen SA67 16 D3
Robeston West SA73 16 B4
Robin Hood, Derbys. DE45 50 E5
Robin Hood, Lancs. WN6 48 E1
Robin Hood, W.Yorks. LS26 57 J7
Robin Hood's Bay YO22 63 J2
Robinhood End CO9 34 B5
Robins GU29 12 B4
Roborough, Devon EX19 6 D4
Roborough, Plym. PL6 5 F4
Roby L36 48 D3
Roby Mill WN8 48 E2
Rocester ST14 40 D2
Roch SA62 16 B2
Roch Bridge SA62 16 B2
Roch Gate SA62 16 B2
Rochallie PH10 82 C2
Rochdale OL16 49 H1
Roche PL26 3 G2
Rochester, Med. ME1 24 D5
Rochester, Northumb. NE19 70 D4
Rochford, Essex SS4 24 E2
Rochford, Worcs. WR15 29 F2
Rock, Cornw. PL27 3 G1
Rock, Northumb. NE66 71 H2
Rock, Worcs. DY14 29 G1
Rock Ferry CH42 48 C4
Rockbeare EX5 7 J6
Rockbourne SP6 10 C3
Rockcliffe, Cumb. CA6 69 J7
Rockcliffe, D. & G. DG5 65 J5
Rockcliffe Cross CA6 69 J7
Rockfield, Arg. & B. PA29 73 G5
Rockfield, High. IV20 97 G3
Rockfield, Mon. NP25 28 D7
Rockford BH24 10 C4
Rockhampton GL13 19 K2
Rockhead PL33 4 A2
Rockingham LE16 42 B6
Rockland All Saints NR17 44 D6
Rockland St. Mary NR14 45 H5
Rockland St. Peter NR17 44 D6
Rockley SN8 20 E4
Rockside PA49 72 A4
Rockwell End RG9 22 A3
Rockwell Green TA21 7 K4
Rodborough GL5 20 B1
Rodbourne SN6 20 C3
Rodbridge Corner CO10 34 C4
Rodd LD8 28 C2
Roddam NE66 71 F1
Rodden DT3 9 F6
Rode BA11 20 B6
Rode Heath ST7 49 H7
Rodeheath SK11 49 H6
Roden TF6 38 E4
Rodhuish TA24 7 J2
Rodington SY4 38 E4
Rodington Heath SY4 38 E4
Rodley GL14 29 G7
Rodmarton GL7 20 C2
Rodmell BN7 13 H6
Rodmersham ME9 25 F5
Rodmersham Green ME9 25 F5
Rodney Stoke BS27 19 H6
Rodsley DE6 40 E1
Rodway TA5 19 F7
Roe Cross SK14 49 J3
Roe Green SG9 33 G5
Roecliffe YO51 57 J3
Roehampton SW15 23 F4
Roesound ZE2 109 C6
Roffey RH12 12 E3
Rogart IV28 96 E1
Rogate GU31 12 B4
Rogerstone NP10 19 F3
Roghadal (Rodel) HS5 93 F3
Rogiet NP26 19 H3
Rokemarsh OX10 21 K2
Roker SR6 63 F1
Rollesby NR29 45 J4
Rolleston, Leics. LE7 42 A5
Rolleston, Notts. NG23 51 K7
Rolleston, Staffs. DE13 40 E3
Rollestone SP3 20 D7
Rolston HU18 59 J5
Rolstone BS24 19 G5
Rolvenden TN17 14 D4
Rolvenden Layne TN17 14 D4
Romaldkirk DL12 62 A4
Romanby DL7 62 E7
Romannobridge EH46 75 K6
Romansleigh EX36 7 F3
Romesdal IV51 93 K6
Romford, Dorset BH31 10 B4
ROMFORD, Gt.Lon. RM 23 J3
Romiley SK6 49 J3
Romney Street TN15 23 J5
Romsey SO51 10 E2
Romsley, Shrop. WV15 39 G7
Romsley, Worcs. B62 29 J1
Rona IV40 94 C6
Ronachan PA29 73 F5
Ronague IM9 54 B6
Ronnachmore PA43 72 B5
Rood End B67 40 C7
Rookhope DL13 62 A2
Rookley PO38 11 G6
Rookley Green PO38 11 G6

Place	Ref	Pg	Grid
Rooks Bridge	BS26	19	G6
Rook's Nest	TA4	7	J2
Rookwith	HG4	57	H1
Roos	HU12	59	J6
Roose	LA13	55	F3
Roosebeck	LA12	55	F3
Roosecote	LA13	55	F3
Rootham's Green	MK44	32	D3
Rootpark	ML11	75	H5
Ropley	SO24	11	H1
Ropley Dean	SO24	11	H1
Ropley Soke	SO24	11	H1
Ropsley	NG33	42	C2
Rora	AB42	99	J5
Rorandle	AB51	90	E3
Rorrington	SY15	38	C5
Rosarie	AB55	98	B6
Rose	TR4	2	E3
Rose Ash	EX36	7	F3
Rose Green, Essex	CO6	34	D6
Rose Green, W.Suss.	PO21	12	C7
Rose Hill	TN22	13	H5
Roseacre, Kent	ME14	14	C2
Roseacre, Lancs.	PR4	55	H6
Rosebank	ML8	75	G6
Rosebrough	NE67	71	G1
Rosebush	SA66	16	D2
Rosecare	EX23	4	B1
Rosecliston	TR8	3	F3
Rosedale Abbey	YO18	63	J7
Roseden	NE66	71	F1
Rosehall	IV27	96	B1
Rosehearty	AB43	99	H4
Rosehill, Aber.	AB34	90	D5
Rosehill, Shrop.	SY4	38	D5
Roseisle	IV30	97	J5
Roselands	BN22	13	K6
Rosemarket	SA73	16	C4
Rosemarkie	IV10	96	E6
Rosemary Lane	EX15	7	K4
Rosemount, P. & K.	PH10	82	C3
Rosemount, S.Ayr.	KA9	67	H1
Rosenannon	PL30	3	G2
Rosenithon	TR12	3	F6
Rosepool	SA62	16	B3
Rosevean	PL26	4	A5
Roseville	WV14	40	B6
Rosewell	EH24	76	A4
Roseworth	TS19	63	F4
Rosgill	CA10	61	G5
Roshven	PH38	86	D7
Roskhill	IV55	93	H7
Roskorwell	TR12	2	E6
Rosley	CA7	60	E2
Roslin	EH25	76	A4
Rosliston	DE12	40	E4
Rosneath	G84	74	A2
Ross, D. & G.	DG6	65	G6
Ross, Northumb.	NE70	77	K7
Ross, P. & K.	PH6	81	J5
Ross Priory	G83	74	C2
Rossdhu House	G83	74	B2
Rossett	LL12	48	C7
Rossett Green	HG2	57	J4
Rosside	LA12	55	F2
Rossie Farm School	DD10	83	H2
Rossie Ochill	PH2	82	B6
Rossie Priory	PH14	82	D4
Rossington	DN11	51	J3
Rosskeen	IV18	96	D5
Rossmore	BH12	10	B5
Ross-on-Wye	HR9	29	F6
Roster	KW3	105	H5
Rostherne	WA16	49	G4
Rosthwaite, Cumb.	CA12	60	D5
Rosthwaite, Cumb.	LA20	55	F1
Roston	DE6	40	D1
Rosudgeon	TR20	2	C6
Rosyth	KY11	75	K2
Rothbury	NE65	71	F3
Rotherby	LE14	41	J4
Rotherfield	TN6	13	J3
Rotherfield Greys	RG9	22	A3
Rotherfield Peppard	RG9	22	A3
Rotherham	S60	51	G3
Rothersthorpe	NN7	31	J3
Rotherwick	RG27	22	A6
Rothes	AB38	97	K3
Rothesay	PA20	73	J4
Rothiebrisbane	AB53	91	F1
Rothienorman	AB51	91	F1
Rothiesholm	KW17	106	F5
Rothley, Leics.	LE7	41	H4
Rothley, Northumb.	NE61	71	F5
Rothney	LE52	90	E2
Rothwell, Lincs.	LN7	52	E3
Rothwell, Northants.	NN14	42	B7
Rothwell, W.Yorks.	LS26	57	J7
Rotsea	YO25	59	G4
Rottal	DD8	82	E1
Rotten Row, Bucks.	RG9	22	A3
Rotten Row, W.Mid.	B93	30	C1
Rottingdean	BN2	13	G6
Rottington	CA28	60	A5
Roud	PO38	11	G6
Roudham	NR16	44	D7
Rough Close	ST3	40	B2
Rough Common	CT2	15	G2
Rougham, Norf.	PE32	44	C3
Rougham, Suff.	IP30	34	D2
Rougham Green	IP30	34	D2
Roughburn	PH31	87	K6
Roughlee	BB9	56	D5
Roughley	B75	40	D6
Roughton, Lincs.	LN10	53	F6
Roughton, Norf.	NR11	45	G2
Roughton, Shrop.	WV15	39	G6
Round Bush	WD25	22	E2
Roundbush Green	CM6	33	J7
Roundham	TA18	8	D4
Roundhay	LS8	57	J6
Roundstreet Common	RH14	12	D4
Roundway	SN10	20	D5
Rous Lench	WR11	30	B3
Rousay	KW17	106	C4
Rousdon	DT7	8	B5
Rousham	OX25	31	F6
Rousham Gap	OX25	31	F6
Routenburn	KA30	73	K4
Routh	HU17	59	G5
Rout's Green	HP14	22	A2
Row, Cornw.	PL30	4	A3
Row, Cumb.	LA8	55	H1
Row, Cumb.	CA10	61	H3
Row Heath	CO16	35	F7
Row Town	KT15	22	D5
Rowanburn	DG14	69	K6
Rowardennan Lodge	G63	74	B1
Rowarth	SK22	50	C4
Rowbarton	TA2	8	B2
Rowberrow	BS25	19	H6
Rowchoish	G63	80	E7
Rowde	SN10	20	C5
Rowden	EX20	6	E6
Rowen	LL32	47	F5
Rowfields	DE6	40	D1
Rowfoot	NE49	70	B7
Rowhedge	CO5	34	E6
Rowhook	RH12	12	E3
Rowington	CV35	30	D2
Rowland	DE45	50	E5
Rowland's Castle	PO9	11	J3
Rowlands Gill	NE39	62	C1
Rowledge	GU10	22	B7
Rowlestone	HR2	28	C6
Rowley, Devon	EX36	7	F4
Rowley, Dur.	DH8	62	B2
Rowley, Shrop.	SY5	38	C5
Rowley Park	ST17	40	B3
Rowley Regis	B65	40	B7
Rowly	GU5	22	D7
Rowner	PO13	11	G4
Rowney Green	B48	30	B1
Rownhams	SO16	10	E3
Rowrah	CA26	60	B5
Rowsham	HP22	32	B7
Rowsley	DE4	50	E6
Rowstock	OX11	21	H3
Rowston	LN4	52	D7
Rowthorne	S44	51	G6
Rowton, Ches.	CH3	48	D6
Rowton, Shrop.	SY5	38	C4
Rowton, Tel. & W.	TF6	39	F4
Roxburgh	TD5	77	F7
Roxby, N.Lincs.	DN15	52	C1
Roxby, N.Yorks.	TS13	63	J5
Roxton	MK44	32	E3
Roxwell	CM1	24	C1
Royal British Legion Village	ME20	14	C2
Royal Leamington Spa	CV32	30	E2
Royal Oak	L39	48	D2
ROYAL TUNBRIDGE WELLS	TN	13	J3
Roybridge	PH31	87	J6
Roydon, Essex	CM19	33	H7
Roydon, Norf.	IP22	44	E7
Roydon, Norf.	PE32	44	B3
Roydon Hamlet	CM19	23	H1
Royston, Herts.	SG8	33	G4
Royston, S.Yorks.	S71	51	F1
Royton	OL2	49	J2
Rozel	JE3	3	K6
Ruabon	LL14	38	C1
Ruaig	PA77	78	B3
Ruan Lanihorne	TR2	3	F4
Ruan Major	TR12	2	D7
Ruan Minor	TR12	2	E7
Ruanaich	PA76	78	D5
Ruardean	GL17	29	F7
Ruardean Hill	GL17	29	F7
Ruardean Woodside	GL17	29	J1
Rubery	B45	29	J1
Ruckcroft	CA4	61	G2
Ruckinge	TN26	15	F4
Ruckland	LN11	53	G5
Rucklers Lane	HP3	22	D1
Ruckley	SY5	38	E5
Rudbaxton	SA62	16	C2
Rudby	TS15	63	F6
Rudchester	NE15	71	G7
Ruddington	NG11	41	H2
Ruddlemoor	PL26	4	A5
Rudford	GL2	29	G6
Rudge	BA11	20	B6
Rudgeway	BS35	19	K3
Rudgwick	RH12	12	D3
Rudhall	HR9	29	F6
Rudheath	CW9	49	F5
Rudley Green	CM3	24	E1
Rudloe	SN13	20	B5
Rudry	CF83	18	E3
Rudston	YO25	59	G3
Rudyard	ST13	49	J7
Rufford	L40	48	D1
Rufforth	YO23	58	B4
Ruffside	DH8	62	A1
Rugby	CV21	31	G1
Rugeley	WS15	40	C4
Ruilick	IV4	96	C7
Ruishton	TA3	8	B2
Ruisigearraidh	HS6	92	E3
Ruislip	HA4	22	D3
Ruislip Gardens	HA4	22	D3
Ruislip Manor	HA4	22	D3
Rum	PH43	85	J5
Rumbling Bridge	KY13	75	J1
Rumburgh	IP19	45	H7
Rumford	PL27	3	F1
Rumleigh	PL20	4	E4
Rumney	CF3	19	F4
Rumwell	TA4	7	K3
Runacraig	FK18	81	G6
Runcorn	WA7	48	E4
Runcton	PO20	12	B6
Runcton Holme	PE33	44	A5
Rundlestone	PL20	5	F3
Runfold	GU10	22	B7
Runhall	NR9	44	E5
Runham, Norf.	NR29	45	J4
Runham, Norf.	NR30	45	K5
Runnington	TA21	7	K3
Runshaw Moor	PR7	48	E1
Runswick Bay	TS13	63	K5
Runtaleave	DD8	82	D1
Runwell	SS11	24	D2
Ruscombe, Glos.	GL6	20	B1
Ruscombe, W'ham	RG10	22	A4
Rush Green, Gt.Lon.	RM7	23	J3
Rush Green, Herts.	SG4	33	F6
Rushall, Here.	HR8	29	F5
Rushall, Norf.	IP21	45	F7
Rushall, W.Mid.	WS4	40	C5
Rushall, Wilts.	SN9	20	E6
Rushbrooke	IP30	34	C2
Rushbury	SY6	38	E6
Rushden, Herts.	SG9	33	G5
Rushden, Northants.	NN10	32	C2
Rushford, Devon	PL19	4	E3
Rushford, Norf.	IP24	44	D7
Rushgreen	WA13	49	F4
Rushlake Green	TN21	13	K5
Rushmere	NR33	45	J7
Rushmere St. Andrew	IP5	35	G4
Rushmoor	GU10	22	B7
Rushock	WR9	29	H1
Rusholme	M13	49	H3
Rushton, Ches.	CW6	48	E6
Rushton, Northants.	NN14	42	B7
Rushton, Shrop.	TF6	39	F5
Rushton Spencer	SK11	49	J6
Rushwick	WR2	29	H3
Rushy Green	BN8	13	H5
Rushyford	DL17	62	D4
Ruskie	FK8	81	H7
Ruskington	NG34	52	D7
Rusko	DG7	65	F5
Rusland	LA12	55	G1
Rusper	RH12	13	F3
Ruspidge	GL14	29	F7
Russ Hill	RH6	23	F7
Russel	IV54	94	E7
Russell Green	CM3	34	B7
Russell's Green	TN33	14	C6
Russell's Water	RG9	22	A2
Russel's Green	IP21	35	G1
Rusthall	TN4	13	J3
Rustington	BN16	12	D6
Ruston	YO13	59	F1
Ruston Parva	YO25	59	G3
Ruswarp	YO21	63	K6
Rutherend	ML10	74	E5
Rutherford	TD5	76	E7
Rutherglen	G73	74	E4
Ruthernbridge	PL30	4	A4
Ruthers of Howe	KW1	105	J2
Ruthin (Rhuthun), Denb.	LL15	47	K7
Ruthin, V. of Glam.	CF35	18	C4
Ruthrieston	AB10	91	H4
Ruthven, Aber.	AB54	98	D6
Ruthven, Angus	PH12	82	D3
Ruthven, High.	IV13	89	F1
Ruthven, High.	PH21	88	E5
Ruthvoes	TR9	3	G2
Ruthwaite	CA7	60	D3
Ruthwell	DG1	69	F7
Ruyton-XI-Towns	SY4	38	C3
Ryal	NE20	71	F6
Ryal Fold	BB3	56	B7
Ryall, Dorset	DT6	8	D5
Ryall, Worcs.	WR8	29	H4
Ryarsh	ME19	23	K6
Rydal	LA22	60	E6
Ryde	PO33	11	G5
Rydon	EX22	6	B5
Rye	TN31	14	E5
Rye Foreign	TN31	14	D5
Rye Harbour	TN31	14	E6
Rye Park	EN11	23	G1
Rye Street	WR13	29	G5
Ryebank	SY4	38	E2
Ryeford	HR9	29	F6
Ryehill, Aber.	AB52	90	E2
Ryehill, E.Riding	HU12	59	J7
Ryhall	PE9	42	D4
Ryhill	WF4	51	F1
Ryhope	SR2	63	F1
Rylands	NG9	41	H2
Rylstone	BD23	56	E4
Ryme Intrinseca	DT9	8	E3
Ryther	LS24	58	B6
Ryton, Glos.	GL18	29	G5
Ryton, N.Yorks.	YO17	58	D2
Ryton, Shrop.	TF11	39	G5
Ryton, T. & W.	NE40	71	G7
Ryton-on-Dunsmore	CV8	30	E1

S

Place	Ref	Pg	Grid
Saasaig	IV44	86	C4
Sabden	BB7	56	C6
Sabden Fold	BB12	56	D6
Sackers Green	CO10	34	D5
Sacombe	SG12	33	G7
Sacombe Green	SG12	33	G7
Sacriston	DH7	62	D2
Sadberge	DL2	62	E5
Saddell	PA28	73	F7
Saddington	LE8	41	J6
Saddle Bow	PE34	44	A4
Sadgill	LA8	61	F6
Saffron Walden	CB10	33	J5
Sageston	SA70	16	D4
Saham Hills	IP25	44	D5
Saham Toney	IP25	44	C5
Saighdinis	HS6	92	D5
Saighton	CH3	48	D6
St. Abbs	TD14	77	H4
St. Agnes	TR5	2	E3
ST. ALBANS	AL	22	E1
St. Allen	TR4	3	F3
St. Andrews	KY16	83	G6
St. Andrews Major	CF64	18	E4
St. Anne	GY9	3	K4
St. Anne's	FY8	55	G7
St. Ann's	DG11	69	F4
St. Ann's Chapel, Cornw.	PL18	4	E3
St. Ann's Chapel, Devon	TQ7	5	G6
St. Anthony	TR2	3	F5
St. Anthony-in-Meneage	TR12	2	E6
St. Anthony's Hill	BN23	13	K6
St. Arvans	NP16	19	J2
St. Asaph (Llanelwy)	LL17	47	J5
St. Athan	CF62	18	D5
St. Aubin	JE3	3	J7
St. Audries	TA4	7	K1
St. Austell	PL25	4	A5
St. Bees	CA27	60	A5
St. Blazey	PL24	4	A5
St. Blazey Gate	PL24	4	A5
St. Boswells	TD6	76	D7
St. Brelade	JE3	3	J7
St. Breock	PL27	3	G1
St. Breward	PL30	4	A3
St. Briavels	GL15	19	J1
St. Brides	SA62	16	B3
St. Brides Major	CF32	18	B4
St. Bride's Netherwent	NP26	19	H3
St. Brides Wentlooge	NP10	19	F3
St. Bride's-super-Ely	CF5	18	D4
St. Budeaux	PL5	4	E5
St. Buryan	TR19	2	B6
St. Catherine	BA1	20	A5
St. Catherines	PA25	80	C7
St. Clears	SA33	17	F3
St. Cleer	PL14	4	C4
St. Clement, Chan.I.	JE2	3	K7
St. Clement, Cornw.	TR1	3	F4
St. Clether	PL15	4	C2
St. Colmac	PA20	73	J4
St. Columb Major	TR9	3	G2
St. Columb Minor	TR7	3	F2
St. Columb Road	TR9	3	G3
St. Combs	AB43	99	J4
St. Cross South Elmham	IP20	45	G7
St. Cyrus	DD10	83	J1
St. Davids, Fife	KY11	75	K2
St. David's, P & K.	PH7	82	A5
St. David's (Tyddewi), Pembs.	SA62	16	A2
St. Day	TR16	2	E4
St. Decumans	TA23	7	J1
St. Dennis	PL26	3	G3
St. Denys	SO17	11	F3
St. Dogmaels (Llandudoch)	SA43	26	A4
St. Dogwells	SA62	16	C2
St. Dominick	PL12	4	E4
St. Donats	CF61	18	C5
St. Edith's Marsh	SN15	20	C5
St. Endellion	PL29	3	G1
St. Enoder	TR8	3	F3
St. Erme	TR4	3	F4
St. Erney	PL12	4	D5
St. Erth	TR27	2	C5
St. Erth Praze	TR27	2	C5
St. Ervan	PL27	3	F1
St. Eval	PL27	3	F2
St. Ewe	PL26	3	G4
St. Fagans	CF5	18	E4
St. Fergus	AB42	99	J5
St. Fillans	PH6	81	H5
St. Florence	SA70	16	D4
St. Gennys	EX23	4	B1
St. George, Bristol	BS5	19	K4
St. George, Conwy	LL22	47	H5
St. Georges, N.Som.	BS22	19	G5
St. George's, Tel. & W.	TF2	39	G4
St. George's, V. of Glam.	CF5	18	D4
St. Germans	PL12	4	D5
St. Giles in the Wood	EX38	6	D4
St. Giles on the Heath	PL15	6	B6
St. Harmon	LD6	27	J1
St. Helen Auckland	DL14	62	C4
St. Helena	NR10	45	F4
St. Helen's, E.Suss.	TN34	14	D6
St. Helen's, I.o.W.	PO33	11	H6
St. Helens, Mersey.	WA10	48	E3
St. Helier, Chan.I.	JE2	3	K7
St. Helier, Gt.Lon.	SM5	23	F5
St. Hilary, Cornw.	TR20	2	C5
St. Hilary, V. of Glam.	CF71	18	D4
St. Hill	RH19	13	G3
St. Ibbs	SG4	32	E6
St. Illtyd	NP13	19	F1
St. Ippollitts	SG4	32	E6
St. Ishmael	SA17	17	G4
St. Ishmael's	SA62	16	B4
St. Issey	PL27	3	G1
St. Ive	PL14	4	D4
St. Ives, Cambs.	PE27	33	G1
St. Ives, Cornw.	TR26	2	C4
St. Ives, Dorset	BH24	10	C4
St. James South Elmham	IP19	45	H7
St. John, Chan.I.	JE3	3	J6
St. John, Cornw.	PL11	4	E5
St. John's, Gt.Lon.	SE4	23	G4
St. John's, I.o.M.	IM4	54	B5
St. John's, Surr.	GU21	22	C6
St. John's, Worcs.	WR2	29	H3
St. John's Chapel, Devon	EX31	6	D3
St. John's Chapel, Dur.	DL13	61	K3
St. John's Fen End	PE14	43	J4
St. John's Hall	DL13	62	B3
St. John's Highway	PE14	43	J4
St. John's Kirk	ML12	75	H7
St. John's Town of Dalry	DG7	68	B5
St. Judes	IM7	54	C4
St. Just	TR19	2	A5
St. Just in Roseland	TR2	3	F5
St. Katherines	AB51	91	F1
St. Keverne	TR12	2	E6
St. Kew	TR30	4	A3
St. Kew Highway	PL30	4	A3
St. Keyne	PL14	4	C4
St. Lawrence, Cornw.	PL30	4	A4
St. Lawrence, Essex	CM0	25	F1
St. Lawrence, I.o.W.	PO38	11	G7
St. Leonards, Bucks.	HP23	22	C1
St. Leonards, Dorset	BH24	10	C4
St. Leonards, E.Suss.	TN38	14	D7
St. Leonards Grange	SO42	11	F5
St. Leonard's Street	ME19	23	K6
St. Levan	TR19	2	A6
St. Lythans	CF5	18	E4
St. Mabyn	PL30	4	A3
St. Madoes	PH2	82	C5
St. Margaret South Elmham	IP20	45	H7
St. Margarets, Here.	HR2	28	C5
St. Margarets, Herts.	SG12	33	G7
St. Margarets, Wilts.	SN8	21	F5
St. Margaret's at Cliffe	CT15	15	J3
St. Margaret's Hope	KW17	107	D8
St. Mark's	IM9	54	B6
St. Martin, Chan.I.	GY4	3	J5
St. Martin, Chan.I.	JE3	3	K7
St. Martin, Cornw.	PL13	4	C5
St. Martin, Cornw.	TR12	2	E6
St. Martin's, I.o.S.	TR25	2	C1
St. Martins, P & K.	PH2	82	C4
St. Martin's, Shrop.	SY11	38	C2
St. Mary	JE3	3	J6
St. Mary Bourne	SP11	21	H6
St. Mary Church	CF71	18	D4
St. Mary Cray	BR5	23	H5
St. Mary Hill	CF35	18	C4
St. Mary Hoo	ME3	24	D4
St. Mary in the Marsh	TN29	15	F5
St. Marychurch	TQ1	5	K4
St. Mary's, I.o.S.	TR21	2	C1
St. Mary's, Ork.	KW17	107	D7
St. Mary's Airport	TR21	2	C1
St. Mary's Bay	TN29	15	F5
St. Mary's Croft	DG9	64	A4
St. Mary's Grove	BS48	19	H5
St. Maughans Green	NP25	28	D7
St. Mawes	TR2	3	F5
St. Mawgan	TR8	3	F2
St. Mellion	PL12	4	D4
St. Mellons	CF3	19	F3
St. Merryn	PL28	3	F1
St. Mewan	PL26	3	G3
St. Michael Caerhays	PL26	3	G4
St. Michael Church	TA7	8	C1
St. Michael Penkevil	TR2	3	F4
St. Michael South Elmham	NR35	45	H7
St. Michaels, Fife	KY16	83	F5
St. Michaels, Kent	TN30	14	D4
St. Michaels, Worcs.	WR15	28	E2
St. Michael's on Wyre	PR3	55	H5
St. Minver	PL27	3	G1
St. Monans	KY10	83	G7
St. Neot	PL14	4	B4
St. Neots	PE19	32	E2
St. Nicholas, Pembs.	SA64	16	C1
St. Nicholas, V. of Glam.	CF5	18	D4
St. Nicholas at Wade	CT7	25	J5
St. Ninians	FK7	75	F1
St. Osyth	CO16	35	F7
St. Owen's Cross	HR2	28	E6
St. Paul's Cray	BR5	23	H5
St. Paul's Walden	SG4	32	E6
St. Peter	JE3	3	J6
St. Peter Port	GY1	3	J5

Place	Page	Grid
St. Peter's CT10	25	K5
St. Petrox SA71	16	C5
St. Pinnock PL14	4	C4
St. Quivox KA6	67	H1
St. Ruan TR12	2	E7
St. Sampson GY2	3	J5
St. Saviour, Chan.I. GY7	3	H5
St. Saviour, Chan.I. JE2	3	K7
St. Stephen PL26	3	G3
St. Stephens, Cornw. PL12	4	E5
St. Stephens, Cornw. PL15	6	B7
St. Stephens, Herts. AL1	22	E1
St. Teath PL30	4	A2
St. Thomas EX2	7	H6
St. Tudy PL30	4	A3
St. Twynnells SA71	16	C5
St. Veep PL22	4	B5
St. Vigeans DD11	83	H3
St. Wenn PL30	3	G2
St. Weonards HR2	28	D6
St. Winnow PL22	4	B5
St. y Nyll CF5	18	D4
Saintbury WR12	30	C5
Salachail PA38	80	B2
Salcombe TQ8	5	H7
Salcombe Regis EX10	7	K7
Salcott CM9	34	D7
Sale M33	49	G3
Sale Green WR9	29	J3
Saleby LN13	53	H5
Salehurst TN32	14	C5
Salem, Carmar. SA19	17	K2
Salem, Cere. SY23	37	F7
Salem, Gwyn. LL54	46	D7
Salen, Arg. & B. PA72	79	G3
Salen, High. PH36	79	H1
Salendine Nook HD3	50	D1
Salesbury BB1	56	B6
Saleway WR9	29	J3
Salford, Beds. MK17	32	C5
Salford, Gt.Man. M5	49	H3
Salford, Oxon. OX7	30	D6
Salford Priors WR11	30	B3
Salfords RH1	23	F7
Salhouse NR13	45	H4
Saline KY12	75	J1
SALISBURY SP	10	C2
Salkeld Dykes CA11	61	G3
Sallachan PH33	80	A1
Sallachry PA32	80	B6
Sallachy, High. IV27	96	C1
Sallachy, High. IV40	87	F1
Salle NR10	45	F3
Salmonby LN9	53	G5
Salmond's Muir DD11	83	G4
Salperton GL54	30	B6
Salph End MK41	32	D3
Salsburgh ML7	75	G4
Salt ST18	40	B3
Salt Hill SL1	22	C3
Salt Holme TS2	63	F4
Saltaire BD18	57	G6
Saltash PL12	4	E5
Saltburn IV18	96	E4
Saltburn-by-the-Sea TS12	63	H4
Saltby LE14	42	B3
Saltcoats, Cumb. CA19	60	B7
Saltcoats, N.Ayr. KA21	74	A6
Saltcotes FY8	55	G2
Saltdean BN2	13	G6
Salterbeck CA14	60	A4
Salterforth BB18	56	D5
Saltergate YO18	63	K7
Salterhill IV30	97	K5
Salterswall CW7	49	F6
Saltfleet LN11	53	H3
Saltfleetby All Saints LN11	53	H3
Saltfleetby St. Clements LN11	53	H3
Saltfleetby St. Peter LN11	53	H3
Saltford BS31	19	K5
Salthouse NR25	44	E1
Saltley B8	40	C7
Saltmarshe DN14	58	D7
Saltness KW16	107	B8
Saltney CH4	48	C6
Salton YO62	58	D1
Saltrens EX39	6	C3
Saltwick NE20	71	G6
Saltwood CT21	15	G4
Salum PA77	78	B3
Salvington BN13	12	E6
Salwarpe WR9	29	H2
Salwayash DT6	8	D5
Sambourne B96	30	B2
Sambrook TF10	39	G3
Samhla HS6	92	C5
Samlesbury PR5	56	B6
Sampford Arundel TA21	7	K4
Sampford Brett TA4	7	J1
Sampford Courtenay EX20	6	E5
Sampford Moor TA21	7	K4
Sampford Peverell EX16	7	J4
Sampford Spiney PL20	5	F3
Samuelston EH41	76	C3
Sanaigmore PA44	72	A3
Sancreed TR20	2	B6
Sancton YO43	59	F6
Sand, Shet. ZE2	109	C8
Sand, Som. BS28	19	H7
Sand Hutton YO41	58	C4
Sandaig, Arg. & B. PA77	78	A3
Sandaig, High. PH41	86	D4
Sandaig, High. IV40	86	D3
Sandal Magna WF2	51	F1
Sanday KW17	106	G3
Sandbach CW11	49	G6
Sandbank PA23	73	K2
Sandbanks BH13	10	B6
Sandend AB45	98	D4
Sanderstead CR2	23	G5
Sandford, Cumb. CA16	61	J5
Sandford, Devon EX17	7	G5
Sandford, Dorset BH20	9	J6
Sandford, I.o.W. PO38	11	G6
Sandford, N.Som. BS25	19	H6
Sandford, S.Lan. ML10	75	F6
Sandford, Shrop. SY13	38	E2
Sandford, Shrop. SY13	38	C3
Sandford Orcas DT9	9	F2
Sandford St. Martin OX7	31	F6
Sandfordhill AB42	99	K6
Sandford-on-Thames OX4	21	J1
Sandgarth KW17	107	E6
Sandgate CT20	15	H4
Sandgreen DG7	65	F5
Sandhaven AB43	99	H4
Sandhead DG9	64	A5
Sandhills, Dorset DT9	9	F3
Sandhills, Dorset DT2	8	E4
Sandhills, Surr. GU8	12	C3
Sandhills, W.Yorks. LS14	57	J6
Sandhoe NE46	70	E7
Sandholme, E.Riding HU15	58	E6
Sandholme, Lincs. PE20	43	G2
Sandhurst, Brack.F. GU47	22	B5
Sandhurst, Glos. GL2	29	H6
Sandhurst, Kent TN18	14	C5
Sandhurst Cross TN18	14	C5
Sandhutton YO7	57	J1
Sandiacre NG10	41	G2
Sandilands LN12	53	J4
Sandiway CW8	49	F5
Sandleheath SP6	10	C3
Sandleigh OX13	21	H1
Sandling ME14	14	C2
Sandlow Green CW4	49	G6
Sandness ZE2	109	A7
Sandon, Essex CM2	24	D1
Sandon, Herts. SG9	33	G5
Sandon, Staffs. ST18	40	B3
Sandown PO36	11	H6
Sandplace PL13	4	C5
Sandquoy KW17	106	G3
Sandridge, Devon TQ9	5	J5
Sandridge, Herts. AL4	32	E1
Sandridge, Wilts. SN12	20	C5
Sandringham PE35	44	A3
Sandrocks RH16	13	G4
Sandsend YO21	63	K5
Sandside LA7	55	H1
Sandside House KW14	104	E2
Sandsound ZE2	109	C8
Sandtoft DN8	51	K2
Sandway ME17	14	D2
Sandwell B66	40	C7
Sandwich CT13	15	J2
Sandwick, Cumb. CA10	60	F5
Sandwick, Shet. ZE2	109	D10
Sandwick (Sanndabhaig), W.Isles HS1	101	G4
Sandwith CA28	60	A5
Sandy, Beds. SG19	32	E4
Sandy, Carmar. SA15	17	H4
Sandy Bank LN4	53	F7
Sandy Haven SA62	16	B4
Sandy Lane, W.Yorks. BD15	57	G6
Sandy Lane, Wilts. SN15	20	C5
Sandy Lane, Wrex. LL13	38	D1
Sandy Way PO30	11	F6
Sandycroft CH5	48	C6
Sandygate, Devon TQ12	5	J3
Sandygate, I.o.M. IM7	54	C4
Sandyhills DG5	65	J5
Sandylands LA3	55	H3
Sandypark TQ13	7	F7
Sandyway HR2	28	D6
Sangobeg IV27	103	G2
Sanna PH36	79	F1
Sannaig PA60	72	D4
Sanndabhaig (Sandwick) HS1	101	G4
Sannox KA27	73	J6
Sanquhar DG4	68	C3
Santon Bridge CA19	60	C6
Santon Downham IP27	44	C7
Sapcote LE9	41	G6
Sapey Common WR6	29	G2
Sapiston IP31	34	D1
Sapperton, Derbys. DE65	40	E2
Sapperton, Glos. GL7	20	C1
Sapperton, Lincs. NG34	42	D2
Saracen's Head PE12	43	G3
Sarclet KW1	105	J4
Sardis SA73	16	C4
Sarisbury SO31	11	G4
Sark GY9	3	K6
Sarn, Bridgend CF32	18	C3
Sarn, Powys SY16	38	B6
Sarn Bach LL53	36	C3
Sarn Meyllteyrn LL53	36	B2
Sarnau, Carmar. SA33	17	G3
Sarnau, Cere. SA44	26	C3
Sarnau, Gwyn. LL23	37	J2
Sarnau, Powys SY22	38	B4
Sarnau, Powys LD3	27	K5
Sarnesfield HR4	28	C3
Saron, Carmar. SA18	17	K3
Saron, Carmar. SA44	17	G1
Saron, Gwyn. LL55	46	D6
Saron, Gwyn. LL54	46	C7
Sarratt WD3	22	D2
Sarre CT7	25	J5
Sarsden OX7	30	D6
Sarsgrum IV27	103	F2
Sartfield IM7	54	C4
Satley DL13	62	C2
Satron DL11	62	A7
Satterleigh EX37	6	E3
Satterthwaite LA12	60	E7
Sauchen AB51	90	E3
Saucher PH2	82	C4
Sauchie FK10	75	G1
Sauchieburn AB30	83	H1
Sauchrie KA19	67	H2
Saughall CH1	48	C5
Saughall Massie CH46	48	B4
Saughtree TD9	70	A4
Saul GL2	20	A1
Saundby DN22	51	K4
Saundersfoot SA69	16	E4
Saunderton HP27	22	A1
Saunton EX33	6	C2
Sausthorpe PE23	53	G6
Saval IV27	96	C1
Savalbeg IV27	96	C1
Saverley Green ST11	40	B2
Savile Town WF12	57	H7
Sawbridge CV23	31	G2
Sawbridgeworth CM21	33	H7
Sawdon YO13	59	F1
Sawley, Derbys. NG10	41	G2
Sawley, Lancs. BB7	56	C5
Sawley, N.Yorks. HG4	57	H3
Sawston CB2	33	H4
Sawtry PE28	42	E7
Saxby, Leics. LE14	42	B4
Saxby, Lincs. LN8	52	D4
Saxby All Saints DN20	52	C1
Saxelbye LE14	41	J3
Saxham Street IP14	34	E2
Saxilby LN1	52	B5
Saxlingham NR25	44	E2
Saxlingham Green NR15	45	G6
Saxlingham Nethergate NR15	45	G6
Saxlingham Thorpe NR15	45	G6
Saxmundham IP17	35	H2
Saxon Street CB8	33	K3
Saxondale NG13	41	J2
Saxtead IP13	35	G2
Saxtead Green IP13	35	G2
Saxtead Little Green IP13	35	G2
Saxthorpe NR11	45	F2
Saxton LS24	57	K6
Sayers Common BN6	13	F5
Scackleton YO62	58	C2
Scadabhagh HS3	93	G2
Scaftworth DN10	51	J3
Scagglethorpe YO17	58	E2
Scaitcliffe BB5	56	C7
Scalasaig PA61	72	B1
Scalby, E.Riding HU15	58	E7
Scalby, N.Yorks. YO13	63	K3
Scaldwell NN6	31	J1
Scale Houses CA10	61	G2
Scaleby CA6	69	K7
Scalebyhill CA6	69	K7
Scales, Cumb. CA12	60	E4
Scales, Cumb. LA12	55	F2
Scales, Lancs. PR4	55	H6
Scalford LE14	42	A3
Scaling TS13	63	J5
Scallasaig IV40	86	E3
Scallastle PA65	79	J4
Scalloway ZE1	109	C9
Scalpay HS4	93	H2
Scamblesby LN11	53	F5
Scammadale PA34	79	K5
Scamodale PH37	86	E7
Scampston YO17	58	E2
Scampton LN1	52	C5
Scaniport IV2	88	D1
Scapa KW15	107	D7
Scapegoat Hill HD7	50	C1
Scar KW17	106	F3
Scarborough YO11	59	G1
Scarcewater TR2	3	G3
Scarcliffe S44	51	G6
Scarcroft LS14	57	J5
Scardroy IV6	95	J6
Scarff ZE2	108	B4
Scarfskerry KW14	105	H1
Scargill DL12	62	B5
Scarinish PA77	78	B3
Scarisbrick L40	48	C1
Scarning NR19	44	D4
Scarrington NG13	42	A1
Scarrowhill CA8	61	G1
Scarth Hill L39	48	D2
Scarthingwell LS24	57	K6
Scartho DN33	53	F2
Scarwell KW16	106	B5
Scatraig IV2	88	E1
Scaur, D. & G. DG2	65	J3
Scaur (Kippford), D. & G. DG5	65	J5
Scawby DN20	52	C2
Scawby Brook DN20	52	C2
Scawton YO7	58	B1
Scayne's Hill RH17	13	G4
Scealascro HS2	100	D5
Scethrog LD3	28	A6
Schaw KA5	67	J1
Scholar Green ST7	49	H7
Scholes, S.Yorks. S61	51	F3
Scholes, W.Yorks. LS15	57	J6
Scholes, W.Yorks. HD9	50	D2
Scholes, W.Yorks. BD19	57	G7
School Green CW7	49	F6
School House TA20	8	B4
Schoose CA14	60	B4
Sciberscross IV28	96	E1
Scilly Isles (Isles of Scilly) TR	2	C1
Scissett HD8	50	E1
Scleddau SA65	16	C1
Sco Ruston NR12	45	G3
Scofton S81	51	J4
Scole IP21	35	F1
Scolpaig HS6	92	C4
Scone PH2	82	C5
Scones Lethendy PH2	82	C5
Sconser IV48	86	B1
Scoor PA67	79	F6
Scopwick LN4	52	D7
Scoraig IV23	95	G2
Scorborough YO25	59	G5
Scorrier TR16	2	E4
Scorriton TQ11	5	H4
Scorton, Lancs. PR3	55	J5
Scorton, N.Yorks. DL10	62	D6
Scot Hay ST5	40	A1
Scotby CA4	60	F1
Scotch Corner DL10	62	D6
Scotforth LA1	55	H4
Scothern LN2	52	D5
Scotland NG33	42	D2
Scotland End OX15	30	E5
Scotland Street CO6	34	D5
Scotlandwell KY13	82	C7
Scotnish PA31	73	F2
Scots' Gap NE61	71	F5
Scotsburn IV18	96	E4
Scotston, Aber. AB30	91	F7
Scotston, P. & K. PH8	82	A3
Scotstoun G14	74	D4
Scotstown PH36	79	K1
Scott Willoughby NG34	42	D2
Scotter DN21	52	B2
Scotterthorpe DN21	52	B2
Scottlethorpe PE10	42	D3
Scotton, Lincs. DN21	52	B3
Scotton, N.Yorks. DL9	62	C7
Scotton, N.Yorks. HG5	57	J4
Scottow NR10	45	G3
Scoughall EH39	76	E2
Scoulton NR9	44	D5
Scounslow Green ST14	40	C3
Scourie IV27	102	D4
Scourie More IV27	102	D4
Scousburgh ZE2	109	F9
Scrabster KW14	105	G1
Scrafield LN9	53	G6
Scrainwood NE66	70	E3
Scrane End PE22	43	G1
Scraptoft LE7	41	J5
Scratby NR29	45	K4
Scrayingham YO41	58	D4
Scredington NG34	42	D1
Scremby PE23	53	H6
Scremerston TD15	77	J6
Screveton NG13	42	A1
Scriven HG5	57	J4
Scronkey PR3	55	H5
Scrooby DN10	51	J3
Scropton DE65	40	D2
Scrub Hill LN4	53	F7
Scruton DL7	62	D7
Sculcoates HU...		
Sculthorpe NR21	44	C2
Scunthorpe DN15	52	B1
Scurlage SA3	17	H6
Sea TA19	8	C3
Sea Mills BS9	19	J4
Sea Palling NR12	45	J3
Seabank PA37	80	A3
Seaborough DT8	8	D4
Seaburn SR6	71	K7
Seacombe CH41	48	B3
Seacroft, Lincs. PE25	53	J6
Seacroft, W.Yorks. LS14	57	J6
Seadyke PE20	43	G2
Seafield, Arg. & B. PA37	73	F2
Seafield, S.Ayr. KA7	67	H1
Seafield, W.Loth. EH47	75	J4
Seaford BN25	13	H7
Seaforth L21	48	C3
Seagrave LE12	41	J4
Seagry Heath SN15	20	C3
Seaham SR7	63	F2
Seaham Grange SR7	63	F1
Seahouses NE68	77	K7
Sealand CH1	48	C6
Seale GU10	22	B7
Sealyham SA62	16	C2
Seamer, N.Yorks. TS9	63	F5
Seamer, N.Yorks. YO12	59	G1
Seamill KA23	73	K6
Searby DN38	52	D2
Seasalter CT5	25	G5
Seascale CA20	60	B6
Seathorne PE25	53	J6
Seathwaite, Cumb. CA12	60	D5
Seathwaite, Cumb. CA20	60	D7
Seatle LA11	55	G1
Seatoller CA12	60	D5
Seaton, Cornw. PL11	4	D5
Seaton, Cumb. CA14	60	B3
Seaton, Devon EX12	8	B5
Seaton, Dur. SR7	62	D2
Seaton, E.Riding HU11	59	H5
Seaton, Northumb. NE26	71	J6
Seaton, Rut. LE15	42	C6
Seaton Burn NE13	71	H6
Seaton Delaval NE25	71	J6
Seaton Junction EX13	8	B5
Seaton Ross YO42	58	D5
Seaton Sluice NE26	71	J6
Seatown, Aber. AB56	99	J5
Seatown, Dorset DT6	8	D5
Seatown, Moray AB56	98	D4
Seave Green TS9	63	G6
Seaview PO34	11	H5
Seaville CA7	60	C1
Seavington St. Mary TA19	8	D3
Seavington St. Michael TA19	8	D3
Seawick CO16	35	F7
Sebastopol NP4	19	F2
Sebergham CA5	60	E2
Seckington B79	40	E5
Second Coast IV22	95	F2
Sedbergh LA10	61	H7
Sedbury NP16	19	J2
Sedbusk DL8	61	K7
Seddington SG19	32	E4
Sedgeberrow WR11	30	B5
Sedgebrook NG32	42	B2
Sedgefield TS21	62	E4
Sedgeford PE36	44	B2
Sedgehill SP7	9	H2
Sedgemere CV8	30	D1
Sedgley DY3	40	B6
Sedgwick LA8	55	J1
Sedlescombe TN33	14	C6
Sedlescombe Street TN33	14	C6
Seend SN12	20	C5
Seend Cleeve SN12	20	C5
Seer Green HP9	22	C2
Seething NR15	45	H6
Sefton L29	48	C2
Seghill NE23	71	H6
Seifton SY8	38	D7
Seighford ST18	40	A3
Seil PA34	79	J6
Seilebost HS3	93	F2
Seion LL55	46	D6
Seisdon WV5	40	A6
Seisiadar HS2	101	H4
Selattyn SY10	38	B2
Selborne GU34	11	J1
Selby YO8	58	C6
Selham GU28	12	C4
Selhurst SE25	23	G5
Selkirk TD7	69	K1
Sellack HR9	28	E6
Sellafield CA20	60	B6
Sellafirth ZE2	108	E3
Sellindge TN25	15	F4
Selling ME13	15	F2
Sells Green SN12	20	C5
Selly Oak B29	40	C7
Selmeston BN26	13	J6
Selsdon CR2	23	G5
Selsey PO20	12	B7
Selsfield Common RH19	13	G3
Selside, Cumb. LA8	61	G7
Selside, N.Yorks. BD24	56	C2
Selsley GL5	20	B1
Selstead CT15	15	H3
Selston NG16	51	G7
Selworthy TA24	7	H1
Semblister ZE2	109	C7
Semer IP7	34	D4
Semington BA14	20	B5
Semley SP7	9	H2
Send GU23	22	D6
Send Marsh GU23	22	D6
Senghenydd CF83	18	E2
Sennen TR19	2	A6
Sennen Cove TR19	2	A6
Sennybridge LD3	27	J6
Senwick DG6	65	G6
Sequer's Bridge PL21	5	G5
Serlby DN10	51	J4
Serrington SP3	10	B1
Sessay YO7	57	K2
Setchey PE33	44	A4
Setley SO42	10	E4
Setter, Shet. ZE2	109	E8
Setter, Shet. ZE2	109	C7
Settiscarth KW17	107	C6
Settle BD24	56	D3
Settrington YO17	58	E2
Seven Ash TA4	7	K2
Seven Bridges SN6	20	E2
Seven Kings IG3	23	H3
Seven Sisters SA10	18	B1
Seven Springs GL53	29	J7
Sevenhampton, Glos. GL54	30	B6
Sevenhampton, Swin. SN6	21	F2
Sevenoaks TN13	23	J6
Sevenoaks Weald TN14	23	J6
Severn Beach BS35	19	J3
Severn Stoke WR8	29	H4
Sevick End MK44	32	D3
Sevington TN24	15	F3
Sewards End CB10	33	J3
Sewardstone E4	23	G2
Sewerby YO15	59	H3
Seworgan TR11	2	E5
Sewstern NG33	42	B3
Seymour Villas EX34	6	C1
Sezincote GL56	30	C5
Sgarastaigh HS3	93	F2
Sgiogarstaigh HS2	101	H1
Sgodachail IV24	96	B2
Shabbington HP18	21	K1
Shackerley WV7	40	A5
Shackerstone CV13	41	F5
Shackleford GU8	22	C7
Shadfen NE61	71	H5
Shadforth DH6	62	E2
Shadingfield NR34	45	J7
Shadoxhurst TN26	14	E4
Shadsworth BB1	56	C7
Shadwell, Norf. IP24	44	D7
Shadwell, W.Yorks. LS17	57	J5
Shaftenhoe End SG8	33	H5

Shaftesbury SP7	9	H2	
Shafton S72	51	F1	
Shalbourne SN8	21	G5	
Shalcombe PO41	10	E6	
Shalden GU34	21	K7	
Shalden Green GU34	22	A7	
Shaldon TQ14	5	K3	
Shalfleet PO30	11	F6	
Shalford, Essex CM7	34	B6	
Shalford, Surr. GU4	22	D7	
Shalford Green CM7	34	B6	
Shallowford, Devon EX31	7	F1	
Shallowford, Staffs. ST15	40	A3	
Shalmsford Street CT4	15	F2	
Shalmstry KW14	105	G2	
Shalunt PA20	73	J3	
Shambellie DG2	65	K4	
Shamley Green GU5	22	D7	
Shandon G84	74	A2	
Shandwick IV20	97	F4	
Shangton LE8	42	A6	
Shankend TD9	70	A3	
Shankhouse NE23	71	H6	
Shanklin PO37	11	G6	
Shannochie KA27	66	D1	
Shantron G83	74	B2	
Shantullich IV8	96	D6	
Shanzie PH11	82	D2	
Shap CA10	61	G5	
Shapinsay KW17	107	E6	
Shapwick, Dorset DT11	9	J4	
Shapwick, Som. TA7	8	D1	
Sharcott SN9	20	E6	
Shard End B34	40	D7	
Shardlow DE72	41	G2	
Shareshill WV10	40	B5	
Sharlston WF4	51	F1	
Sharlston Common WF4	51	F1	
Sharnal Street ME3	24	D4	
Sharneyford OL13	56	D7	
Sharnford LE10	41	G6	
Sharnhill Green DT2	9	G4	
Sharow HG4	57	J2	
Sharp Street NR29	45	H3	
Sharpenhoe MK45	32	D5	
Sharperton NE65	70	E3	
Sharpham House TQ9	5	J5	
Sharpness GL13	19	K1	
Sharpthorne RH19	13	G3	
Sharrington NR24	44	E2	
Shatterford DY12	39	G7	
Shatterling CT3	15	H2	
Shaugh Prior PL7	5	F4	
Shave Cross DT6	8	D5	
Shavington CW2	49	G1	
Shaw, Gt.Man. OL2	49	J2	
Shaw, Swin. SN5	20	E3	
Shaw, W.Berks. RG14	21	H5	
Shaw, Wilts. SN12	20	C5	
Shaw Green, Herts. SG7	33	F5	
Shaw Green, N.Yorks. HG3	57	H4	
Shaw Mills HG3	57	H3	
Shaw Side OL2	49	J2	
Shawbost (Siabost) HS2	100	E3	
Shawbury SY4	38	E3	
Shawell LE17	41	H7	
Shawfield, Gt.Man. OL12	49	H1	
Shawfield, Staffs. SK17	50	C6	
Shawford SO21	11	F2	
Shawforth OL12	56	D7	
Shawhead DG2	65	J3	
Shawtonhill ML10	74	E6	
Sheanachie PA28	66	B2	
Sheandow AB38	89	K1	
Shearington DG1	69	F7	
Shearsby LE17	41	J6	
Shebbear EX21	6	C5	
Shebdon ST20	39	G3	
Shebster KW14	105	F2	
Shedfield SO32	11	G3	
Sheen SK17	50	D6	
Sheepridge HD2	50	D1	
Sheepscombe GL6	29	H7	
Sheepstor PL20	5	F4	
Sheepwash, Devon EX21	6	C5	
Sheepwash, Northumb. NE62	71	H5	
Sheepway BS20	19	H4	
Sheepy Magna CV9	41	F5	
Sheepy Parva CV9	41	F5	
Sheering CM22	33	J7	
Sheerness ME12	25	F4	
Sheet GU32	11	J2	
SHEFFIELD S	51	F4	
Sheffield Bottom RG7	21	K5	
Sheffield City Airport S9	51	G4	
Sheffield Green TN22	13	H4	
Shefford SG17	32	E5	
Shefford Woodlands RG17	21	G4	
Sheigra IV27	102	D2	
Sheinton SY5	39	F5	
Shelderton SY7	28	D1	
Sheldon, Derbys. DE45	50	D6	
Sheldon, Devon EX14	7	K5	
Sheldon, W.Mid. B26	40	D7	
Sheldwich ME13	15	F2	
Sheldwich Lees ME13	15	F2	
Shelf, Bridgend CF35	18	C3	
Shelf, W.Yorks. HX3	57	G7	
Shelfanger IP22	45	F7	
Shelfield, W.Mid. WS4	40	C5	
Shelfield, Warks. B49	30	C2	
Shelfield Green B49	30	C2	
Shelford NG12	41	J1	
Shellachan, Arg. & B. PA34	79	K5	
Shellachan, Arg. & B. PA35	80	B5	
Shellbrook LE65	41	F4	
Shellbrook Hill SY12	38	C1	
Shelley, Essex CM5	23	J1	
Shelley, Suff. IP7	34	E5	
Shelley, W.Yorks. HD8	50	E1	
Shellingford SN7	21	G2	
Shellow Bowells CM5	24	C1	
Shelsley Beauchamp WR6	29	G2	
Shelsley Walsh WR6	29	G2	
Shelswell MK18	31	H5	
Shelthorpe LE11	41	H4	
Shelton, Beds. PE28	32	D2	
Shelton, Norf. NR15	45	G6	
Shelton, Notts. NG23	42	A1	
Shelton, Shrop. SY3	38	D4	
Shelve SY5	38	C6	
Shelwick HR1	28	E4	
Shelwick Green HR1	28	E4	
Shenfield CM15	24	C2	
Shenington OX15	30	E4	
Shenley WD7	22	E1	
Shenley Brook End MK5	32	B5	
Shenley Church End MK5	32	B5	
Shenleybury WD7	22	E1	
Shenmore HR2	28	C5	
Shennanton DG8	64	D4	
Shenstone, Staffs. WS14	40	D5	
Shenstone, Worcs. DY10	29	H1	
Shenstone Woodend WS14	40	D5	
Shenton CV13	41	F5	
Shenval AB37	89	K2	
Shepeau Stow PE12	43	G4	
Shephall SG2	33	F6	
Shepherd's Bush W12	23	F4	
Shepherd's Green RG9	22	A3	
Shepherd's Patch GL2	20	A1	
Shepherdswell (Sibertswold) CT15	15	H3	
Shepley HD8	50	D2	
Sheppardstown KW3	105	H5	
Shepperdine BS35	19	K2	
Shepperton TW17	22	D5	
Shepreth SG8	33	G4	
Shepshed LE12	41	G4	
Shepton Beauchamp TA19	8	D3	
Shepton Mallet BA4	19	K7	
Shepton Montague BA9	9	F1	
Shepway ME15	14	C2	
Sheraton TS27	63	F3	
Sherborne, Dorset DT9	9	F3	
Sherborne, Glos. GL54	30	C7	
Sherborne St. John RG24	21	K6	
Sherbourne CV35	30	D2	
Sherbourne Street CO10	34	D4	
Sherburn, Dur. DH6	62	E2	
Sherburn, N.Yorks. YO17	59	F2	
Sherburn Hill DH6	62	E2	
Sherburn in Elmet LS25	57	K6	
Shere GU5	22	D7	
Shereford NR21	44	C3	
Sherfield English SO51	10	D2	
Sherfield on Loddon RG27	21	K6	
Sherford, Devon TQ7	5	H6	
Sherford, Som. TA1	8	B2	
Sheriff Hutton YO60	58	C3	
Sheriffhales TF11	39	G4	
Sheringham NR26	45	F1	
Sherington MK16	32	B4	
Shernal Green WR9	29	J2	
Shernborne PE31	44	B2	
Sherramore PH20	88	C5	
Sherrington BA12	9	J1	
Sherston SN16	20	B3	
Sherwood NG5	41	H1	
Sherwood Green EX31	6	D3	
Shettleston G32	74	E4	
Shevington WN6	48	E2	
Shevington Moor WN6	48	E1	
Sheviock PL11	4	D5	
Shide PO30	11	G6	
Shiel Bridge IV40	87	F3	
Shieldaig, High. IV54	94	E4	
Shieldaig, High. IV21	94	E4	
Shieldhill FK1	75	G3	
Shielfoot PH36	86	C7	
Shielhill DD8	83	F2	
Shiels AB51	90	E4	
Shifford OX29	21	G1	
Shifnal TF11	39	G5	
Shilbottle NE66	71	G3	
Shildon DL4	62	D4	
Shillingford, Devon EX16	7	H3	
Shillingford, Oxon. OX10	21	J2	
Shillingford Abbot EX2	7	H7	
Shillingford St. George EX2	7	H7	
Shillingstone DT11	9	H3	
Shillington SG5	32	E5	
Shillmoor NE65	70	D3	
Shilstone EX20	6	D5	
Shilton, Oxon. OX18	21	F1	
Shilton, Warks. CV7	41	G7	
Shimpling, Norf. IP21	45	F7	
Shimpling, Suff. IP29	34	C3	
Shimpling Street IP29	34	C3	
Shincliffe DH1	62	D2	
Shiney Row DH4	62	E1	
Shinfield RG2	22	A5	
Shingay SG8	33	G4	
Shingham PE37	44	B5	
Shingle Street IP12	35	H4	
Shinness Lodge IV27	103	H7	
Shipbourne TN11	23	J6	
Shipbrookhill CW9	49	F5	
Shipdham IP25	44	D5	
Shipham BS25	19	H6	
Shiphay TQ2	5	J4	
Shiplake RG9	22	A4	
Shiplake Row RG9	22	A4	
Shipley, Northumb. NE66	71	G2	
Shipley, Shrop. WV6	40	A6	
Shipley, W.Suss. RH13	12	E4	
Shipley, W.Yorks. BD18	57	G6	
Shipley Bridge, Devon TQ10	5	G4	
Shipley Bridge, Surr. RH6	23	G7	
Shipley Common DE7	41	G1	
Shipmeadow NR34	45	H6	
Shippea Hill CB7	44	A7	
Shippon OX13	21	H2	
Shipston on Stour CV36	30	D4	
Shipton, Glos. GL54	30	B7	
Shipton, N.Yorks. YO30	58	B4	
Shipton, Shrop. TF13	38	E6	
Shipton Bellinger SP9	21	F7	
Shipton Gorge DT6	8	D5	
Shipton Green PO20	12	B6	
Shipton Moyne GL8	20	B3	
Shipton Oliffe GL54	30	B7	
Shipton Solers GL54	30	B7	
Shipton-on-Cherwell OX5	31	F7	
Shiptonthorpe YO43	58	E5	
Shipton-under-Wychwood OX7	30	D7	
Shira PA32	80	C6	
Shirburn OX49	21	K2	
Shirdley Hill L39	48	C1	
Shire Oak WS8	40	C5	
Shirebrook NG20	51	H6	
Shirecliffe S5	51	F3	
Shiregreen S5	51	F3	
Shirehampton BS11	19	J4	
Shiremoor NE27	71	J6	
Shirenewton NP16	19	H2	
Shireoaks S81	51	H4	
Shirl Heath HR6	28	D3	
Shirland DE55	51	F7	
Shirley, Derbys. DE6	40	E1	
Shirley, Gt.Lon. CR0	23	G5	
Shirley, Hants. BH23	10	C5	
Shirley, S'ham. SO15	11	F3	
Shirley, W.Mid. B90	30	C1	
Shirley Heath B90	30	C1	
Shirley Warren SO16	10	E3	
Shirleywich ST18	40	C3	
Shirrell Heath SO32	11	G3	
Shirwell EX31	6	D2	
Shirwell Cross EX31	6	D2	
Shiskine KA27	66	D1	
Shittlehope DL13	62	B3	
Shobdon HR6	28	C2	
Shobley BH24	10	C4	
Shobrooke EX17	7	G5	
Shocklach SY14	38	D1	
Shocklach Green SY14	38	D1	
Shoeburyness SS3	25	F3	
Sholden CT14	15	J2	
Sholing SO19	11	F3	
Shoot Hill SY5	38	D4	
Shooter's Hill DA16	23	H4	
Shop, Cornw. PL28	3	F1	
Shop, Cornw. EX23	6	A4	
Shop Corner IP9	35	G5	
Shopnoller TA4	7	K2	
Shore OL15	49	J1	
Shoreditch N1	23	G3	
Shoreham TN14	23	J5	
Shoreham-by-Sea BN43	13	F6	
Shoremill IV11	96	E5	
Shoresdean TD15	77	H6	
Shoreswood TD15	77	H6	
Shoreton IV7	96	D5	
Shorley SO24	11	G2	
Shorncote GL7	20	D2	
Shorne DA12	24	C4	
Shorne Ridgeway DA12	24	C4	
Short Cross SY21	38	B5	
Short Green IP22	44	E7	
Short Heath, Derbys. DE12	41	F4	
Short Heath, W.Mid. B23	40	C6	
Shortacombe EX20	6	D7	
Shortbridge TN22	13	H4	
Shortfield Common GU10	22	B7	
Shortgate BN8	13	H5	
Shortgrove CB11	33	J5	
Shorthampton OX7	30	E6	
Shortlands BR2	23	G5	
Shortlanesend TR4	3	F4	
Shorton TQ3	5	J4	
Shorwell PO30	11	F6	
Shoscombe BA2	20	A6	
Shotatton SY4	38	C3	
Shotesham NR15	45	G6	
Shotgate SS11	24	D2	
Shotley, Northants. NN17	42	C6	
Shotley, Suff. IP9	35	G5	
Shotley Bridge DH8	62	B1	
Shotley Gate IP9	35	G5	
Shotleyfield DH8	62	B1	
Shottenden CT4	15	F2	
Shottermill GU27	12	B3	
Shottery CV37	30	C3	
Shotteswell OX17	31	F4	
Shottisham IP12	35	H4	
Shottle DE56	41	F1	
Shottlegate DE56	41	F1	
Shotton, Dur. SR8	63	F3	
Shotton, Dur. TS21	62	E4	
Shotton, Flints. CH5	48	C6	
Shotton, Northumb. NE13	71	H6	
Shotton Colliery DH6	62	E2	
Shotts ML7	75	G4	
Shotwick CH1	48	C5	
Shouldham PE33	44	A5	
Shouldham Thorpe PE33	44	A5	
Shoulton WR2	29	H3	
Shover's Green TN5	13	K3	
Shrawardine SY4	38	C4	
Shrawley WR6	29	H2	
Shreding Green SL0	22	D3	
Shrewley CV35	30	D2	
SHREWSBURY SY	38	D4	
Shrewton SP3	20	D7	
Shripney PO22	12	C6	
Shrivenham SN6	21	F3	
Shropham NR17	44	D6	
Shroton (Iwerne Courtney) DT11	9	H3	
Shrub End CO2	34	D6	
Shucknall HR1	28	E4	
Shudy Camps CB1	33	K4	
Shurdington GL51	29	J7	
Shurlock Row RG10	22	B4	
Shurnock B96	30	B2	
Shurrery KW14	105	F3	
Shurrery Lodge KW14	105	F3	
Shurton TA5	19	F7	
Shustoke B46	40	E6	
Shut Heath ST18	40	A3	
Shute, Devon EX13	8	B5	
Shute, Devon EX17	7	G5	
Shutford OX15	30	E4	
Shuthonger GL20	29	H5	
Shutlanger NN12	31	J4	
Shutt Green ST19	40	A5	
Shuttington B79	40	E5	
Shuttlewood S44	51	G5	
Shuttleworth BL0	49	G1	
Siabost (Shawbost) HS2	100	E3	
Siabost Bho Dheas HS2	100	E3	
Siabost Bho Thuath HS2	100	E3	
Siadar Iarach HS2	101	F2	
Siadar Uarach HS2	101	F2	
Sibbaldbie DG11	69	G5	
Sibbertoft LE16	41	J7	
Sibdon Carwood SY7	38	D7	
Sibertswold (Shepherdswell) CT15	15	H3	
Sibford Ferris OX15	30	E5	
Sibford Gower OX15	30	E5	
Sible Hedingham CO9	34	B5	
Sibley's Green CM6	33	K6	
Sibsey PE22	53	G7	
Sibson, Cambs. PE8	42	D6	
Sibson, Leics. CV13	41	F5	
Sibster IV25	105	J3	
Sibthorpe NG23	42	A1	
Sibton IP17	35	H1	
Sibton Green IP17	35	H1	
Sicklesmere IP30	34	C2	
Sicklinghall LS22	57	J5	
Sidbury, Devon EX10	7	K6	
Sidbury, Shrop. WV16	39	F7	
Sidcot BS25	19	H6	
Sidcup DA14	23	H4	
Siddal HX3	57	G7	
Siddington, Ches. SK11	49	H5	
Siddington, Glos. GL7	20	D2	
Sidemoor B61	29	J1	
Sidestrand NR27	45	G2	
Sidford EX10	7	K6	
Sidlesham PO20	12	B7	
Sidley TN39	14	C7	
Sidlow RH2	23	F7	
Sidmouth EX10	7	K7	
Sigford TQ12	5	H3	
Sigglesthorne HU11	59	H5	
Sigingstone CF71	18	C4	
Signet OX18	30	D7	
Silchester RG7	21	K5	
Sildinis HS2	100	E6	
Sileby LE12	41	J4	
Silecroft LA18	54	E1	
Silfield NR18	45	F6	
Silian SA48	26	E3	
Silk Willoughby NG34	42	D1	
Silkstone S75	50	E2	
Silkstone Common S75	50	E2	
Sill Field LA8	55	J1	
Silloth CA7	60	C1	
Sills NE19	70	D3	
Sillyearn AB55	98	D5	
Silpho YO13	63	J3	
Silsden BD20	57	F5	
Silsoe MK45	32	D5	
Silver End, Beds. MK45	32	E4	
Silver End, Essex CM8	34	C6	
Silver Green NR15	45	G6	
Silver Street, Kent ME9	24	E5	
Silver Street, Som. TA11	8	E1	
Silverburn EH26	76	A4	
Silvercraigs PA31	73	G2	
Silverdale, Lancs. LA5	55	H2	
Silverdale, Staffs. ST5	40	A1	
Silvergate NR11	45	F3	
Silverhill TN38	14	C6	
Silverlace Green IP13	35	H3	
Silverley's Green IP19	35	G1	
Silvermoss AB51	91	G1	
Silverstone NN12	31	H4	
Silverton EX5	7	H5	
Silvington DY14	29	F1	
Silwick ZE2	109	B8	
Simister M25	49	H2	
Simmondley SK13	50	C3	
Simonburn NE48	70	D6	
Simonsbath TA24	7	F2	
Simonstone, Bridgend CF35	18	C3	
Simonstone, Lancs. BB12	56	C6	
Simprim TD12	77	G6	
Simpson MK6	32	B5	
Sinclair's Hill TD11	77	G5	
Sinclairston KA18	67	J2	
Sinderby YO7	57	J1	
Sinderhope NE47	61	K1	
Sindlesham RG41	22	A5	
Sinfin DE24	41	F2	
Singdean TD9	70	A3	
Singleton, Lancs. FY6	55	G6	
Singleton, W.Suss. PO18	12	B5	
Singlewell (Ifield) DA12	24	C4	
Singret LL12	48	C7	
Sinkhurst Green TN12	14	D3	
Sinnahard AB33	90	C3	
Sinnington YO62	58	D1	
Sinton Green WR2	29	H2	
Siop y Fron (Upper Llandwrog) LL54	46	D7	
Sipson UB7	22	D4	
Sirhowy NP22	28	A7	
Sisland NR14	45	H6	
Sissinghurst TN17	14	C4	
Siston BS16	19	K4	
Sithney TR13	2	D6	
Sittingbourne ME10	25	F5	
Siulaisiadar HS2	101	H4	
Six Ashes WV15	39	G7	
Six Hills LE14	41	J3	
Six Mile Bottom CB8	33	J3	
Six Roads End DE6	40	D3	
Sixhills LN8	52	E4	
Sixmile CT4	15	G3	
Sixpenny Handley SP5	10	B3	
Sizewell IP16	35	J2	
Skail KW11	104	C4	
Skaill, Ork. KW16	107	B6	
Skaill, Ork. KW17	107	E7	
Skaill, Ork. KW17	106	D4	
Skares, Aber. AB54	90	E1	
Skares, E.Ayr. KA18	67	K2	
Skarpigarth ZE2	109	A7	
Skateraw EH42	77	F3	
Skaw ZE2	109	E6	
Skeabost IV51	93	K7	
Skeabrae KW17	106	B5	
Skeeby DL10	62	D6	
Skeffington LE7	42	A5	
Skeffling HU12	53	G1	
Skegby NG17	51	H6	
Skegness PE25	53	J6	
Skelberry, Shet. ZE2	109	F9	
Skelberry, Shet. ZE2	109	D6	
Skelbo IV25	96	E2	
Skelbo Street IV25	96	E2	
Skelbrooke DN6	51	H1	
Skeld (Easter Skeld) ZE2	109	C8	
Skeldon KA6	67	H2	
Skeldyke PE20	43	G2	
Skellingthorpe LN6	52	C5	
Skellister ZE2	109	D7	
Skellow DN6	51	H1	
Skelmanthorpe HD8	50	E1	
Skelmersdale WN8	48	D2	
Skelmonae AB41	91	G1	
Skelmorlie PA17	73	K4	
Skelmuir AB42	99	H6	
Skelpick KW14	104	C3	
Skelton, Cumb. CA11	60	F3	
Skelton, E.Riding DN14	58	D7	
Skelton, N.Yorks. DL11	62	B6	
Skelton, R. & C. TS12	63	H5	
Skelton, York YO30	58	B4	
Skelton-on-Ure HG4	57	J3	
Skelwick KW17	106	D3	
Skelwith Bridge LA22	60	E6	
Skendleby PE23	53	H5	
Skendleby Psalter LN13	53	H5	
Skenfrith NP7	28	D6	
Skerne YO25	59	G4	
Skeroblingarry PA28	66	B1	
Skerray KW14	103	J2	
Skerton LA1	55	H3	
Sketchley LE10	41	G6	
Sketty SA2	17	K5	
Skewen SA10	18	A2	
Skewsby YO61	58	C2	
Skeyton NR10	45	G3	
Skeyton Corner NR10	45	G3	
Skidbrooke LN11	53	H3	
Skidbrooke North End LN11	53	H3	
Skidby HU16	59	G6	
Skilgate TA4	7	H3	
Skillington NG33	42	B3	
Skinburness CA7	60	C1	
Skinflats FK2	75	H2	
Skinidin IV55	93	H7	
Skinnet KW12	105	G2	
Skinningrove TS13	63	J5	
Skipness PA29	73	G5	
Skippool FY5	55	G5	
Skipsea YO25	59	H4	
Skipsea Brough YO25	59	H4	
Skipton BD23	56	E4	
Skipton-on-Swale YO7	57	J2	
Skipwith YO8	58	C6	
Skirbeck PE21	43	G1	
Skirbeck Quarter PE21	43	G1	
Skirethorns BD23	56	E3	
Skirlaugh HU11	59	H6	
Skirling ML12	75	J7	
Skirmett RG9	22	A3	
Skirpenbeck YO41	58	D4	
Skirwith, Cumb. CA10	61	H3	
Skirwith, N.Yorks. LA6	56	C2	
Skirza KW1	105	J2	
Skittle Green HP27	22	A1	
Skomer Island SA62	16	A4	
Skulamus IV42	86	C2	
Skullomie IV27	103	J2	
Skyborry Green LD7	28	B1	
Skye IV	85	K1	
Skye Green CO5	34	C6	

Skye of Curr PH26 89 G2
Skyreholme BD23 57 F3
Slack, *Aber.* AB52 90 D1
Slack, *Derbys.* S45 51 F6
Slack, *W.Yorks.* HX7 56 E7
Slackhall SK23 50 C4
Slackhead AB56 98 C4
Slad GL6 20 B1
Slade, *Devon* EX34 6 D1
Slade, *Devon* EX14 7 K5
Slade, *Pembs.* SA61 16 C3
Slade, *Swan.* SA3 17 H6
Slade Green DA8 23 J4
Slade Hooton S25 51 H4
Sladesbridge PL27 4 A3
Slaggyford CA8 61 H1
Slaidburn BB7 56 C4
Slains Park DD10 91 G7
Slaithwaite HD7 50 C1
Slaley NE47 62 A1
Slamannan FK1 75 G3
Slapton, *Bucks.* LU7 32 C6
Slapton, *Devon* TQ7 5 J6
Slapton, *Northants.* NN12 31 H4
Slate Haugh AB56 98 C4
Slatepit Dale S42 51 F6
Slattadale IV22 94 E4
Slaugham RH17 13 F4
Slaughden IP15 35 J3
Slaughterford SN14 20 B4
Slawston LE16 42 A6
Sleaford, *Hants.* GU35 12 B3
Sleaford, *Lincs.* NG34 42 D1
Sleagill CA10 61 G3
Sleap SY4 38 D3
Sledge Green WR13 29 H5
Sledmere YO25 59 F3
Sleights YO22 63 K6
Slepe BH16 9 J5
Slerra EX39 6 B3
Slickly KW1 105 H2
Sliddery KA27 66 D1
Sliemore PH25 89 H2
Sligachan IV47 85 K2
Slimbridge GL2 20 A1
Slindon, *Staffs.* ST21 40 A2
Slindon, *W.Suss.* BN18 12 C6
Slinfold RH13 12 E3
Sling GL16 19 J1
Slingsby YO62 58 C2
Slioch AB54 90 D1
Slip End, *Beds.* LU1 32 D7
Slip End, *Herts.* SG7 33 F6
Slipton NN14 32 C1
Slitting Mill WS15 40 C4
Slochd PH23 89 F2
Slockavullin PA31 73 G1
Slogarie DG7 65 G4
Sloley NR12 45 G3
Slongaber DG2 65 J3
Sloothby LN13 53 H5
SLOUGH SL 22 C3
Slough Green, *Som.* TA3 8 B2
Slough Green, *W.Suss.* RH17 13 F4
Sluggan PH23 89 F2
Slyne LA2 55 H3
Smailholm TD5 76 E7
Small Dole BN5 13 F5
Small Hythe TN30 14 D4
Smallbridge OL16 49 J1
Smallbrook EX5 7 G6
Smallburgh NR12 45 H3
Smallburn, *Aber.* AB42 99 J6
Smallburn, *E.Ayr.* KA18 68 B1
Smalldale SK17 50 C5
Smalley DE7 41 G1
Smallfield RH6 23 G7
Smallford AL4 22 E1
Smallridge EX13 8 B4
Smallthorne ST6 49 H7
Smallworth IP22 44 E7
Smannell SP11 21 G7
Smardale CA17 61 J6
Smarden TN27 14 D3
Smaull PA44 72 A4
Smeatharpe EX14 7 K4
Smeeth TN25 15 F4
Smeeton Westerby LE8 41 J6
Smerclet HS8 84 C3
Smerral KW5 105 G5
Smestow DY3 40 A6
Smethwick B66 40 C7
Smethwick Green CW11 49 H6
Smirisary PH38 86 C1
Smisby LE65 41 F4
Smith End Green WR13 29 G3
Smithfield CA6 69 K7
Smithies S71 51 F2
Smithincott EX15 7 J4
Smith's End SG8 33 G5
Smith's Green, *Essex* CM22 33 J6
Smith's Green, *Essex* CB9 33 K4
Smithstown IV21 94 D4
Smithton IV2 96 E7
Smithy Green WA16 49 G5
Smockington LE10 41 G7
Smyrton KA26 67 F5
Smythe's Green CO5 34 D7
Snailbeach SY5 38 C5
Snailwell CB8 33 K2
Snainton YO13 59 F1
Snaith DN14 58 C7
Snape, *N.Yorks.* DL8 57 H1
Snape, *Suff.* IP17 35 H3
Snape Green PR8 48 C1
Snape Watering IP17 35 H3
Snarestone DE12 41 F5
Snarford LN8 52 D4
Snargate TN29 14 E5

Snave TN29 15 F5
Sneachill WR7 29 J3
Snead SY15 38 C6
Snead's Green DY13 29 H2
Sneath Common NR15 45 F7
Sneaton YO22 63 K6
Sneatonthorpe YO22 63 J2
Snelland LN3 52 D4
Snellings CA22 60 A6
Snelston DE6 40 D1
Snetterton NR16 44 D6
Snettisham PE31 44 A2
Snipeshill ME10 25 F5
Snishival HS8 84 C1
Snitter NE65 71 F3
Snitterby DN21 52 C3
Snitterfield CV37 30 D3
Snitterton DE4 50 E6
Snittlegarth CA7 60 D3
Snitton SY8 28 E1
Snodhill HR3 28 C4
Snodland ME6 24 D5
Snow End SG9 33 H5
Snow Street IP22 44 E7
Snowden Hill S35 50 E2
Snowshill WR12 30 B5
Soar, *Cardiff* CF15 18 D3
Soar, *Carmar.* SA19 17 K2
Soar, *Devon* TQ7 5 H7
Soay PH41 85 K3
Soberton SO32 11 H3
Soberton Heath SO32 11 H3
Sockbridge CA10 61 G4
Sockburn DL2 62 E6
Sodom LL16 47 J5
Sodylt Bank SY12 38 C2
Soham CB7 33 J1
Soham Cotes CB7 33 J1
Solas (Sollas) HS6 92 D4
Soldon EX22 6 B4
Soldon Cross EX22 6 B4
Soldridge GU34 11 H1
Sole Street, *Kent* CT4 15 F3
Sole Street, *Kent* DA12 24 C5
Soleburn DG9 64 A4
Solihull B91 30 C1
Solihull Lodge B90 30 B1
Sollas (Solas) HS6 92 D4
Sollers Dilwyn HR4 28 D3
Sollers Hope HR1 29 F5
Sollom PR4 48 D1
Solomon's Tump GL19 29 G7
Solsgirth KY13 75 H1
Solva SA62 16 A2
Solwaybank DG14 69 J6
Somerby, *Leics.* LE14 42 A4
Somerby, *Lincs.* DN38 52 D2
Somercotes DE55 51 G7
Somerford ST19 40 B5
Somerford Keynes GL7 20 D2
Somerley PO20 12 B7
Somerleyton NR32 45 J6
Somersal Herbert DE6 40 D2
Somersby PE23 53 G5
Somersham, *Cambs.* PE28 33 G1
Somersham, *Suff.* IP8 34 E4
Somerton, *Newport* NP19 19 G3
Somerton, *Oxon.* OX25 31 F6
Somerton, *Som.* TA11 8 D2
Somerton, *Suff.* IP29 34 C3
Sompting BN15 12 E6
Sompting Abbotts BN15 12 E6
Sonning RG4 22 A4
Sonning Common RG4 22 A3
Sonning Eye RG4 22 A4
Sontley LL13 38 C1
Sookholme NG19 51 H6
Sopley BH23 10 C5
Sopworth SN14 20 B3
Sorbie DG8 64 E6
Sordale KW12 105 G2
Sorisdale PA78 78 D1
Sorn KA5 67 K1
Sornhill KA4 74 D7
Soroba PA34 79 K5
Sortat KW1 105 H2
Sotby LN8 53 F5
Sots Hole LN4 52 E6
Sotterley NR34 45 J7
Soudley TF9 39 G3
Soughton CH7 48 B6
Soulbury LU7 32 B6
Soulby CA17 61 J5
Souldern OX27 31 G5
Souldrop MK44 32 C2
Sound, *Shet.* CW5 39 F1
Sound, *Shet.* ZE1 109 D8
Sound, *Shet.* ZE2 109 C7
Sourhope TD5 70 D1
Sourin KW17 106 D4
Sourton EX20 6 D6
Soutergate LA17 55 F1
South Acre PE32 44 C4
South Acton W5 22 E4
South Alkham CT15 15 H3
South Allington TQ7 5 H7
South Alloa FK7 75 G1
South Ambersham GU29 12 C4
South Anston S25 51 H4
South Ascot SL5 22 C5
South Baddesley SO41 10 E5
South Ballachulish PH49 80 B2
South Balloch KA26 67 H4
South Bank TS6 63 G4
South Barrow BA22 9 F2
South Bellsdyke FK2 75 H2
South Benfleet SS7 24 D3
South Bersted PO22 12 C6
South Blackbog AB51 91 F1

South Bockhampton BH23 10 C5
South Bowood DT6 8 D5
South Brent TQ10 5 G4
South Brentor PL19 6 C7
South Brewham BA10 9 G1
South Broomhill NE61 71 H4
South Burlingham NR13 45 H5
South Cadbury BA22 9 F2
South Cairn DG9 66 D7
South Carlton LN1 52 C5
South Cave HU15 59 F6
South Cerney GL7 20 D2
South Charlton NE66 71 G1
South Cheriton BA8 9 F2
South Church DL14 62 D4
South Cliffe YO43 58 E6
South Clifton NG23 52 B5
South Cockerington LN11 53 G4
South Collafirth ZE2 108 C4
South Common BN8 13 G5
South Cornelly CF33 18 B3
South Corriegills KA27 73 J7
South Cove NR34 45 J7
South Creagan PA37 80 A3
South Creake NR21 44 C2
South Crosland HD4 50 D1
South Croxton LE7 41 J4
South Dalton HU17 59 F5
South Darenth DA4 23 J4
South Dell (Dail Bho Dheas) HS2 101 G1
South Duffield YO8 58 C6
South Elkington LN11 53 F4
South Elmsall WF9 51 G1
South End, *Bucks.* LU7 32 B6
South End, *Cumb.* LA14 55 F3
South End, *Hants.* SP6 10 C3
South End, *N.Lincs.* DN19 59 H7
South Erradale IV21 94 D4
South Fambridge SS4 24 E2
South Fawley OX12 21 G3
South Ferriby DN18 59 F7
South Field HU13 59 G7
South Flobbets AB51 91 F1
South Garth ZE2 108 E3
South Godstone RH9 23 G7
South Gorley SP6 10 C3
South Green, *Essex* CM11 24 C2
South Green, *Essex* CO5 34 E7
South Green, *Norf.* NR20 44 E4
South Green, *Suff.* IP23 35 F1
South Gyle EH12 75 K3
South Hall PA22 73 J3
South Hanningfield CM3 24 D2
South Harefield UB9 22 D3
South Harting GU31 11 J3
South Hayling PO11 11 J5
South Hazelrigg NE66 77 J7
South Heath HP16 22 C1
South Heighton BN9 13 H6
South Hetton DH6 62 E2
South Hiendley S72 51 F1
South Hill PL17 4 D3
South Hinksey OX1 21 J1
South Hole EX39 6 A4
South Holme YO62 58 C2
South Holmwood RH5 22 E7
South Hornchurch RM13 23 J3
South Hourat KA24 74 A5
South Huish TQ7 5 G6
South Hykeham LN6 52 C6
South Hylton SR4 62 E1
South Kelsey LN7 52 D3
South Kessock IV3 96 D7
South Killingholme DN40 52 E1
South Kilvington YO7 57 K1
South Kilworth LE17 41 J7
South Kirkby WF9 51 G1
South Kirkton AB32 91 F4
South Knighton TQ12 5 J3
South Kyme LN4 42 E1
South Lancing BN15 12 E6
South Ledaig PA37 80 A4
South Leigh OX29 21 G1
South Leverton DN22 51 K4
South Littleton WR11 30 B4
South Lopham IP22 44 E7
South Luffenham LE15 42 C5
South Malling BN7 13 H5
South Marston SN3 20 E3
South Middleton NE71 70 E1
South Milford LS25 57 K6
South Milton TQ7 5 G6
South Mimms EN6 23 F1
South Molton EX36 7 F3
South Moor DH9 62 C1
South Moreton OX11 21 J3
South Mundham PO20 12 B6
South Muskham NG23 51 K7
South Newbald YO43 59 F6
South Newington OX15 31 F5
South Newton SP2 10 B1
South Normanton DE55 51 G7
South Norwood SE25 23 G5
South Nutfield RH1 23 G7
South Ockendon RM15 23 J3
South Ormsby LN11 53 G5
South Ossett WF5 50 E1
South Otterington DL7 57 J1
South Owersby LN8 52 D3
South Oxhey WD19 22 E2
South Park RH2 23 F7
South Parks KY6 82 D7
South Perrott DT8 8 D4
South Petherton TA13 8 D3
South Petherwin PL15 6 B7
South Pickenham PE37 44 C5
South Pool TQ7 5 H6
South Queensferry (Queensferry) EH30 75 K3

South Radworthy EX36 7 F2
South Rauceby NG34 42 D1
South Raynham NR21 44 C3
South Redbriggs AB53 99 F6
South Reston LN11 53 H4
South Ronaldsay KW17 107 D9
South Ruislip HA4 22 E3
South Runcton PE33 44 A5
South Scarle NG23 52 B6
South Shian PA37 80 A3
South Shields NE33 71 J7
South Somercotes LN11 53 H3
South Somercotes Fen Houses LN11 53 H3
South Stainley HG3 57 J3
South Stoke, *Oxon.* RG8 21 K3
South Stoke, *W.Suss.* BN18 12 D6
South Street, *E.Suss.* BN8 13 G5
South Street, *Gt.Lon.* TN16 23 H6
South Street, *Kent* DA13 24 C5
South Street, *Kent* CT5 25 H5
South Street, *Kent* ME9 24 E5
South Tawton EX20 6 E6
South Thoresby LN13 53 H5
South Tidworth SP9 21 F5
South Tottenham N15 23 G3
South Town, *Devon* EX6 7 H7
South Town, *Hants.* GU34 11 H1
South Uist (Uibhist a Deas) HS8 84 C1
South Upper Barrack AB41 99 H6
South View RG21 21 K6
South Walsham NR13 45 H4
South Warnborough RG29 22 A7
South Weald CM14 23 J2
South Weston OX9 22 A2
South Wheatley, *Cornw.* PL15 4 C1
South Wheatley, *Notts.* DN22 51 K4
South Whiteness ZE2 109 C8
South Wigston LE18 41 H6
South Willingham LN8 52 E4
South Wingfield DE55 51 F7
South Witham NG33 42 C4
South Wonston SO21 11 F1
South Wootton PE30 44 A3
South Wraxall BA15 20 B5
South Yardley B26 40 D7
South Zeal EX20 6 E6
SOUTHALL UB 22 E3
Southam, *Glos.* GL52 29 J6
Southam, *Warks.* CV47 31 F2
Southampton Airport SO18 11 F3
Southbar PA4 74 C4
Southborough, *Gt.Lon.* BR2 23 H5
Southborough, *Kent* TN4 23 J7
Southbourne, *Bourne.* BH6 10 C5
Southbourne, *W.Suss.* PO10 11 J4
Southbrook EX5 7 J6
Southburgh IP25 44 E5
Southburn YO25 59 F4
Southchurch SS1 25 F3
Southcott, *Devon* EX20 6 D6
Southcott, *Wilts.* SN9 20 E6
Southcourt HP21 32 B7
Southdean TD9 70 B3
Southdene L32 48 D3
Southease BN7 13 H6
Southend, *Aber.* AB53 99 F6
Southend, *Arg. & B.* PA28 66 A3
Southend, *Bucks.* RG9 22 A3
Southend, *W.Berks.* RG7 21 J4
Southend, *Wilts.* SN8 20 E4
SOUTHEND-ON-SEA SS 24 E3
Southerfield CA7 60 C2
Southerly EX20 6 D7
Southern Green SG9 33 G5
Southerndown CF32 18 B4
Southerness DG2 65 K5
Southery PE38 44 A6
Southfield KY6 76 A1
Southfields SW18 23 F4
Southfleet DA13 24 C4
Southgate, *Cere.* SY23 36 E3
Southgate, *Gt.Lon.* N14 23 G2
Southgate, *Norf.* NR10 45 F3
Southgate, *Norf.* PE31 44 A2
Southgate, *Swan.* SA3 17 J6
Southill SG18 32 E4
Southington RG25 21 J7
Southleigh EX24 8 B5
Southmarsh BA9 9 G1
Southminster CM0 25 F2
Southmuir DD8 82 E2
Southoe PE38 32 E2
Southolt IP23 35 F2
Southorpe PE9 42 D5
Southowram HX3 57 G7
Southport PR8 48 C1
Southrepps NR11 45 G2
Southrey LN3 52 E6
Southrop GL7 20 E1
Southrope RG25 21 K7
Southsea, *Ports.* PO4 11 H5
Southsea, *Wrex.* LL11 48 B7
Southstoke BA2 20 A5
Southtown, *Norf.* NR31 45 K5
Southtown, *Ork.* KW17 107 D8
Southwaite, *Cumb.* CA17 61 J6

Southwaite, *Cumb.* CA4 61 F2
Southwater RH13 12 E4
Southwater Street RH13 12 E4
Southway BA5 19 J7
Southwell, *Dorset* DT5 9 F7
Southwell, *Notts.* NG25 51 J7
Southwick, *D. & G.* DG2 65 K5
Southwick, *Hants.* PO17 11 H4
Southwick, *Northants.* PE8 42 D6
Southwick, *Som.* TA9 19 G7
Southwick, *T. & W.* SR5 62 E1
Southwick, *W.Suss.* BN42 13 F6
Southwick, *Wilts.* BA14 20 B6
Southwold IP18 35 K1
Southwood BA6 8 E1
Sowden EX8 7 H7
Sower Carr FY6 55 G5
Sowerby, *N.Yorks.* YO7 57 K1
Sowerby, *W.Yorks.* HX6 57 F7
Sowerby Bridge HX6 57 F7
Sowerby Row CA4 60 E2
Sowerhill TA22 7 G3
Sowley Green CB9 34 B3
Sowood HX4 50 C1
Sowton EX5 7 H6
Soyal IV24 96 C2
Spa Common NR28 45 G2
Spadeadam CA8 70 A6
Spalding PE11 43 F3
Spaldington DN14 58 D6
Spaldwick PE28 32 E1
Spalefield KY10 83 G7
Spalford NG23 52 B6
Spanby NG34 42 D2
Sparham NR9 44 E4
Spark Bridge LA12 55 G1
Sparkford BA22 9 F2
Sparkhill B11 40 C7
Sparkwell PL7 5 F5
Sparrow Green NR19 44 D4
Sparrowpit SK17 50 C4
Sparrow's Green TN5 13 K3
Sparsholt, *Hants.* SO21 11 F1
Sparsholt, *Oxon.* OX12 21 G3
Spartylea NE47 61 K2
Spath ST14 40 C2
Spaunton YO62 58 D1
Spaxton TA5 8 B1
Spean Bridge PH34 87 J6
Spear Hill RH20 12 E5
Speddoch DG2 68 D5
Speedwell BS16 19 K4
Speen, *Bucks.* HP27 22 B1
Speen, *W.Berks.* RG14 21 H5
Speeton YO14 59 H2
Speke L24 48 D4
Speldhurst TN3 23 J7
Spellbrook CM23 33 H7
Spelsbury OX7 30 E6
Spen Green CW11 49 H6
Spencers Wood RG7 22 A5
Spennithorne DL8 57 G1
Spennymoor DL16 62 D3
Spernall B80 30 B2
Spetchley WR5 29 H3
Spetisbury DT11 9 J4
Spexhall IP19 45 H7
Spey Bay IV32 98 B4
Speybridge PH26 89 H2
Speyview AB38 97 K7
Spilsby PE23 53 G6
Spindlestone NE70 77 K7
Spinkhill S21 51 G5
Spinningdale IV24 96 D3
Spirthill SN11 20 C4
Spital, *High.* KW1 105 G3
Spital, *W. & M.* SL4 22 C4
Spital in the Street LN8 52 C3
Spitalbrook EN11 23 G1
Spithurst BN8 13 H5
Spittal, *D. & G.* DG8 64 E4
Spittal, *D. & G.* DG8 64 D5
Spittal, *E.Loth.* EH32 76 C3
Spittal, *Northumb.* TD15 77 J5
Spittal, *Pembs.* SA62 16 C2
Spittal of Glenmuick AB35 90 B6
Spittal of Glenshee PH10 82 C1
Spittalfield PH1 82 C3
Spixworth NR10 45 G4
Splayne's Green TN22 13 H4
Splott CF24 19 F4
Spofforth HG3 57 J4
Spondon DE21 41 G2
Spooner Row NR18 44 E6
Spooney TF9 39 F2
Sporle PE32 44 C4
Sportsman's Arms LL16 47 H7
Spott EH42 76 E3
Spratton NN6 31 J1
Spreakley GU10 22 B7
Spreyton EX17 6 E6
Spridlington LN8 52 D4
Spring Grove TW7 22 E4
Spring Vale PO34 11 H5
Springburn G21 74 E4
Springfield, *Arg. & B.* PA22 73 J3
Springfield, *D. & G.* DG16 69 J7
Springfield, *Fife* KY15 82 E6
Springfield, *Moray* IV36 97 H6
Springfield, *P. & K.* PH13 82 C4
Springfield, *W.Mid.* B13 40 C7
Springfields Outlet Village PE12 43 F3
Springhill, *Staffs.* WS14 40 C5
Springhill, *Staffs.* WV11 40 B5
Springholm DG7 65 J4
Springkell DG11 69 H6
Springleys AB51 91 F1

Springside

Springside **KA11** 74 B7
Springthorpe **DN21** 52 B4
Springwell **NE9** 62 D1
Sproatley **HU11** 59 H6
Sproston Green **CW4** 49 G6
Sprotbrough **DN5** 51 H2
Sproughton **IP8** 35 F4
Sprouston **TD5** 77 F7
Sprowston **NR7** 45 G4
Sproxton, *Leics.* **LE14** 42 B3
Sproxton, *N.Yorks.* **YO62** 58 C1
Sprytown **PL16** 6 C7
Spurlands End **HP15** 22 B2
Spurstow **CW6** 48 E7
Spyway **DT2** 8 E5
Square Point **DG7** 65 H3
Squires Gate **FY4** 55 G6
Srondoire **PA30** 73 G3
Sronphadruig Lodge
PH18 88 E7
Stableford, *Shrop.* **WV15** 39 G6
Stableford, *Staffs.* **ST5** 40 A2
Stacey Bank **S6** 50 E3
Stackhouse **BD24** 56 D3
Stackpole **SA71** 16 C5
Stacksteads **OL13** 56 D7
Staddiscombe **PL9** 5 F5
Staddlethorpe **HU15** 58 E7
Staden **SK17** 50 C5
Stadhampton **OX44** 21 K2
Stadhlaigearraidh
(Stilligarry) **HS8** 84 C1
Staffield **CA10** 61 G2
Staffin **IV51** 93 K5
Stafford **ST16** 40 B3
Stagden Cross **CM1** 33 K7
Stagsden **MK43** 32 C4
Stagshaw Bank **NE46** 70 E7
Stain **KW1** 105 J2
Stainburn, *Cumb.* **CA14** 60 B4
Stainburn, *N.Yorks.* **LS21** 57 H5
Stainby **NG33** 42 C3
Staincross **S75** 51 F1
Staindrop **DL2** 62 C4
Staines **TW18** 22 D4
Stainfield, *Lincs.* **PE10** 42 D3
Stainfield, *Lincs.* **LN3** 52 E5
Stainforth, *N.Yorks.* **BD24** 56 D3
Stainforth, *S.Yorks.* **DN7** 51 J1
Staining **FY3** 55 G6
Stainland **HX4** 50 C1
Stainsacre **YO22** 63 J2
Stainsby, *Derbys.* **S44** 51 G6
Stainsby, *Lincs.* **LN9** 53 G5
Stainton, *Cumb.* **LA8** 55 J1
Stainton, *Cumb.* **CA11** 61 F4
Stainton, *Dur.* **DL12** 62 B5
Stainton, *Middbro.* **TS8** 63 F5
Stainton, *N.Yorks.* **DL11** 62 C7
Stainton, *S.Yorks.* **S66** 51 H3
Stainton by Langworth
LN3 52 D5
Stainton le Vale **LN8** 52 E3
Stainton with Adgarley
LA13 55 F2
Staintondale **YO13** 63 J3
Stair, *Cumb.* **CA12** 60 D4
Stair, *E.Ayr.* **KA5** 67 J1
Stairfoot **S70** 51 F2
Staithes **TS13** 63 J5
Stake Pool **PR3** 55 H5
Stakeford **NE62** 71 H5
Stakes **PO7** 11 H4
Stalbridge **DT10** 9 G3
Stalbridge Weston **DT10** 9 G3
Stalham **NR12** 45 H3
Stalham Green **NR12** 45 H3
Stalisfield Green **ME13** 14 E2
Stalling Busk **DL8** 56 E1
Stallingborough **DN41** 52 E1
Stallington **ST11** 40 B2
Stalmine **FY6** 55 G5
Stalybridge **SK15** 49 J3
Stambourne **CO9** 34 B5
Stamford, *Lincs.* **PE9** 42 D5
Stamford, *Northumb.*
NE66 71 H2
Stamford Bridge, *Ches.*
CH3 48 D6
Stamford Bridge, *E.Riding*
YO41 58 D4
Stamfordham **NE18** 71 F6
Stanah **FY5** 55 G5
Stanborough **AL8** 33 F7
Stanbridge, *Beds.* **LU7** 32 C6
Stanbridge, *Dorset* **BH21** 10 B4
Stanbridge Earls **SO51** 10 E2
Stanbury **BD22** 57 F6
Stand **ML6** 75 F4
Standburn **FK1** 75 H3
Standeford **WV10** 40 B5
Standen **TN27** 14 D4
Standen Street **TN17** 14 D4
Standerwick **BA11** 20 B6
Standford **GU35** 12 B3
Standford Bridge **TF10** 39 G3
Standish, *Glos.* **GL10** 20 B1
Standish, *Gt.Man.* **WN6** 48 E1
Standlake **OX29** 21 G1
Standon, *Hants.* **SO21** 11 F2
Standon, *Herts.* **SG11** 33 G6
Standon, *Staffs.* **ST21** 40 A2
Standon Green End **SG11** 33 G7
Stane **ML7** 75 G5
Stanecastle **KA11** 74 B7
Stanfield **NR20** 44 D3
Stanford, *Beds.* **SG18** 32 E4
Stanford, *Kent* **TN25** 15 G4
Stanford, *Shrop.* **SY5** 38 C4
Stanford Bishop **WR6** 29 F3
Stanford Bridge **WR6** 29 G2
Stanford Dingley **RG7** 21 J4
Stanford End **RG7** 22 A5
Stanford in the Vale **SN7** 21 G2
Stanford on Avon **NN6** 31 G1
Stanford on Soar **LE12** 41 H3
Stanford on Teme **WR6** 29 G2
Stanford Rivers **CM5** 23 J1
Stanford-le-Hope **SS17** 24 C3
Stanfree **S44** 51 G5
Stanghow **TS12** 63 H5
Stanground **PE2** 43 F6
Stanhoe **PE31** 44 C2
Stanhope, *Dur.* **DL13** 62 A3
Stanhope, *Sc.Bord.* **ML12** 69 G1
Stanion **NN14** 42 C7
Stanklyn **DY10** 29 H1
Stanley, *Derbys.* **DE7** 41 G1
Stanley, *Dur.* **DH9** 62 C1
Stanley, *Notts.* **NG17** 51 G6
Stanley, *P. & K.* **PH1** 82 C4
Stanley, *Staffs.* **ST9** 49 J7
Stanley, *W.Yorks.* **WF3** 57 J7
Stanley, *Wilts.* **SN15** 20 C4
Stanley Common **DE7** 41 G1
Stanley Crook **DL15** 62 C3
Stanley Gate **L39** 48 D2
Stanley Green **BH15** 10 B5
Stanley Hill **HR8** 29 F4
Stanleygreen **SY13** 38 E2
Stanlow, *Ches.* **CH65** 48 D5
Stanlow, *Shrop.* **WV6** 39 G6
Stanmer **BN1** 13 G5
Stanmore, *Gt.Lon.* **HA7** 22 E2
Stanmore, *W.Berks.* **RG20** 21 H4
Stannersburn **NE48** 70 C5
Stanningfield **IP29** 34 C3
Stanningley **LS28** 57 H6
Stannington, *Northumb.*
NE61 71 H6
Stannington, *S.Yorks.* **S6** 51 F4
Stansbatch **HR6** 28 C2
Stansfield **CO10** 34 B3
Stanshope **DE6** 50 D7
Stanstead **CO10** 34 C4
Stanstead Abbotts **SG12** 33 G7
Stansted **TN15** 24 C5
Stansted Airport (London
Stansted Airport) **CM24** 33 J6
Stansted Mountfitchet
CM24 33 J6
Stanton, *Derbys.* **DE15** 40 E4
Stanton, *Glos.* **WR12** 30 B5
Stanton, *Northumb.*
NE65 71 G4
Stanton, *Staffs.* **DE6** 40 D1
Stanton, *Suff.* **IP31** 34 D1
Stanton by Bridge **DE73** 41 F3
Stanton by Dale **DE7** 41 G2
Stanton Drew **BS39** 19 J5
Stanton Fitzwarren **SN6** 20 E2
Stanton Harcourt **OX29** 21 H1
Stanton Hill **NG17** 51 G6
Stanton in Peak **DE4** 50 E6
Stanton Lacy **SY8** 28 D1
Stanton Lees **DE4** 50 E6
Stanton Long **TF13** 38 E6
Stanton Prior **BA2** 19 K5
Stanton St. Bernard **SN8** 20 D5
Stanton St. John **OX33** 21 J1
Stanton St. Quintin **SN14** 20 C4
Stanton Street **IP31** 34 D2
Stanton under Bardon
LE67 41 G4
Stanton upon Hine Heath
SY4 38 E3
Stanton Wick **BS39** 19 K5
Stanton-on-the-Wolds
NG12 41 J2
Stanwardine in the Fields
SY4 38 D3
Stanwardine in the Wood
SY12 38 D3
Stanway, *Essex* **CO3** 34 D6
Stanway, *Glos.* **GL54** 30 B5
Stanway Green, *Essex*
CO3 34 D6
Stanway Green, *Suff.*
IP13 35 G1
Stanwell **TW19** 22 D4
Stanwell Moor **TW19** 22 D4
Stanwick **NN9** 32 C1
Stanwix **CA3** 60 F1
Stanydale **ZE2** 109 B7
Staoinebrig **HS8** 84 C1
Stapeley **CW5** 39 F1
Stapenhill **DE15** 40 E3
Staple, *Kent* **CT3** 15 H2
Staple, *Som.* **TA4** 7 K1
Staple Cross **TA21** 7 J3
Staple Fitzpaine **TA3** 8 B3
Staplecross **TN32** 14 C5
Staplefield **RH17** 13 F4
Stapleford, *Cambs.* **CB2** 33 H3
Stapleford, *Herts.* **SG14** 33 G7
Stapleford, *Leics.* **LE14** 42 B4
Stapleford, *Lincs.* **LN6** 52 B7
Stapleford, *Notts.* **NG9** 41 G2
Stapleford, *Wilts.* **SP3** 10 B1
Stapleford Abbotts **RM4** 23 H2
Stapleford Tawney **RM4** 23 J2
Staplegrove **TA2** 8 B2
Staplehay **TA3** 8 B2
Staplehurst **TN12** 14 C3
Staplers **PO30** 11 G6
Staplestreet **ME13** 25 G5
Stapleton, *Cumb.* **CA6** 70 A6
Stapleton, *Here.* **LD8** 28 C2
Stapleton, *Leics.* **LE9** 41 G6
Stapleton, *N.Yorks.* **DL2** 62 D5
Stapleton, *Shrop.* **SY5** 38 D5
Stapleton, *Som.* **TA12** 8 D2
Stapley **TA3** 7 K4
Staploe **PE19** 32 E2
Staplow **HR8** 29 F4
Star, *Fife* **KY7** 82 E7
Star, *Pembs.* **SA35** 17 F1
Star, *Som.* **BS25** 19 H6
Starbotton **BD23** 56 E2
Starcross **EX6** 7 H7
Stareton **CV8** 30 E1
Starkholmes **DE4** 51 F7
Starling **BL8** 49 G1
Starling's Green **CB11** 33 H5
Starr **KA6** 67 J4
Starston **IP20** 45 G7
Startforth **DL12** 62 B5
Startley **SN15** 20 C3
Statham **WA13** 49 F4
Stathe **TA7** 8 C2
Stathern **LE14** 42 A2
Station Town **TS28** 63 F3
Staughton Green **PE19** 32 E2
Staughton Highway **PE19** 32 E2
Staunton, *Glos.* **GL16** 28 E7
Staunton, *Glos.* **GL19** 29 G6
Staunton Harold Hall
LE65 41 F3
Staunton in the Vale
NG13 42 B1
Staunton on Arrow **HR6** 28 C2
Staunton on Wye **HR4** 28 C4
Staveley, *Cumb.* **LA8** 61 F7
Staveley, *Derbys.* **S43** 51 G5
Staveley, *N.Yorks.* **HG5** 57 J3
Staveley-in-Cartmel **LA12** 55 G1
Staverton, *Devon* **TQ9** 5 H4
Staverton, *Glos.* **GL51** 29 H6
Staverton, *Northants.*
NN11 31 G2
Staverton, *Wilts.* **BA14** 20 B5
Staverton Bridge **GL51** 29 H6
Stawell **TA7** 8 C1
Stawley **TA21** 7 J3
Staxigoe **KW1** 105 J3
Staxton **YO12** 59 G2
Staylittle (Penffordd-las)
SY19 37 H6
Staynall **FY6** 55 G5
Staythorpe **NG23** 51 K7
Stean **HG3** 57 F2
Steane **NN13** 31 G5
Stearsby **YO61** 58 C2
Steart **TA5** 19 F7
Stebbing **CM6** 33 K6
Stebbing Green **CM6** 33 K6
Stechford **B33** 40 D7
Stedham **GU29** 12 B4
Steel Cross **TN6** 13 J3
Steel Green **LA18** 54 E2
Steele Road **TD9** 70 A4
Steen's Bridge **HR6** 28 E3
Steep **GU32** 11 J2
Steep Marsh **GU32** 11 J2
Steeple, *Dorset* **BH20** 9 J6
Steeple, *Essex* **CM0** 25 F1
Steeple Ashton **BA14** 20 C6
Steeple Aston **OX25** 31 F6
Steeple Barton **OX25** 31 F6
Steeple Bumpstead **CB9** 33 K4
Steeple Claydon **MK18** 31 H6
Steeple Gidding **PE28** 42 E7
Steeple Langford **SP3** 10 B1
Steeple Morden **SG8** 33 F4
Steeraway **TF1** 39 F5
Steeton **BD20** 57 F5
Stein **IV55** 93 H6
Steinmanhill **AB53** 99 F6
Stella **NE21** 71 G7
Stelling Minnis **CT4** 15 G3
Stembridge **TA12** 8 D2
Stemster, *High.* **KW12** 105 G2
Stemster, *High.* **KW5** 105 G4
Stemster House **KW12** 105 G2
Stenalees **PL26** 4 A5
Stenhill **EX15** 7 J4
Stenhousemuir **FK5** 75 G2
Stenigot **LN11** 53 F4
Stenis **HS1** 101 G4
Stenness **ZE2** 108 B5
Stenscholl **IV51** 93 K5
Stenson **DE73** 41 F3
Stenton, *E.Loth.* **EH42** 76 E3
Stenton, *P. & K.* **PH8** 82 B3
Steornabhagh
(Stornoway) **HS1** 101 G4
Stepaside, *Pembs.* **SA67** 16 E4
Stepaside, *Powys* **SY16** 37 K7
Stepney **E1** 23 G3
Steppingley **MK45** 32 D5
Stepps **G33** 74 E4
Sternfield **IP17** 35 H2
Sterridge **EX34** 6 D1
Stert **SN10** 20 D6
Stetchworth **CB8** 33 K3
STEVENAGE SG 33 F6
Stevenston **KA20** 74 A6
Steventon, *Hants.* **RG25** 21 J7
Steventon, *Oxon.* **OX13** 21 H2
Steventon End **CB10** 33 K4
Stevington **MK43** 32 C3
Stewartby **MK43** 32 D4
Stewarton, *D. & G.* **DG8** 64 E6
Stewarton, *E.Ayr.* **KA3** 74 C6
Stewkley **LU7** 32 B6
Stewley **TA19** 8 C3
Stewton **LN11** 53 G4
Steyning **BN44** 12 E5
Steynton **SA73** 16 C4
Stibb **EX23** 6 A4
Stibb Cross **EX38** 6 C4
Stibb Green **SN8** 21 F5
Stibbard **NR21** 44 D3
Stibbington **PE8** 42 D6
Stichill **TD5** 77 F7
Sticker **PL26** 3 G3
Stickford **PE22** 53 G6
Sticklepath, *Devon* **EX20** 6 E6
Sticklepath, *Som.* **TA20** 8 C3
Stickling Green **CB11** 33 H5
Stickney **PE22** 53 G7
Stiff Street **ME9** 24 E5
Stiffkey **NR23** 44 D1
Stifford's Bridge **WR13** 29 G4
Stileway **BA6** 19 H7
Stilligarry
(Stadhlaigearraidh)
HS8 84 C1
Stillingfleet **YO19** 58 B5
Stillington, *N.Yorks.*
YO61 58 B3
Stillington, *Stock.* **TS21** 62 E4
Stilton **PE7** 42 E7
Stinchcombe **GL11** 20 A2
Stinsford **DT2** 9 G5
Stirchley, *Tel. & W.* **TF3** 39 G5
Stirchley, *W.Mid.* **B30** 40 C7
Stirkoke House **KW1** 105 J3
Stirling, *Aber.* **AB42** 99 K6
Stirling, *Stir.* **FK8** 75 F1
Stirton **BD23** 56 E4
Stisted **CM77** 34 C6
Stitchcombe **SN8** 21 F4
Stithians **TR3** 2 E5
Stittenham **IV17** 96 D4
Stivichall **CV3** 30 E1
Stix **PH15** 81 J3
Stixwould **LN10** 52 E6
Stoak **CH2** 48 D5
Stobo **EH45** 75 K7
Stoborough **BH20** 9 J6
Stoborough Green **BH20** 9 J6
Stobwood **ML11** 75 H5
Stocinis (Stockinish) **HS3** 93 G2
Stock **CM4** 24 C2
Stock Green **B96** 29 J3
Stock Lane **SN8** 21 F4
Stock Wood **B96** 30 B3
Stockbridge, *Hants.* **SO20** 10 E1
Stockbridge, *Stir.* **FK15** 81 J7
Stockbridge, *W.Suss.*
PO19 12 B6
Stockbury **ME9** 24 E5
Stockcross **RG20** 21 H5
Stockdale **TR11** 2 E5
Stockdalewath **CA5** 60 E2
Stockerston **LE15** 42 B6
Stocking Green, *Essex*
CB10 33 J5
Stocking Green, *M.K.*
MK19 32 B4
Stocking Pelham **SG9** 33 H6
Stockingford **CV10** 41 F6
Stockinish (Stocinis) **HS3** 93 G2
Stockland, *Cardiff* **CF5** 18 E4
Stockland, *Devon* **EX14** 8 B4
Stockland Bristol **TA5** 19 F7
Stockleigh English **EX17** 7 G5
Stockleigh Pomeroy **EX17** 7 G5
Stockley **SN11** 20 D5
Stocklinch **TA19** 8 C3
STOCKPORT SK 49 H3
Stocksbridge **S36** 50 E3
Stocksfield **NE43** 71 F7
Stockton, *Here.* **HR6** 28 E2
Stockton, *Norf.* **NR34** 45 H6
Stockton, *Shrop.* **TF11** 39 G6
Stockton, *Shrop.* **SY21** 38 B5
Stockton, *Tel. & W.* **TF10** 39 G4
Stockton, *Warks.* **CV47** 31 F2
Stockton, *Wilts.* **BA12** 9 J1
Stockton Heath **WA4** 49 F4
Stockton on Teme **WR6** 29 G2
Stockton on the Forest
YO32 58 C4
Stockton-on-Tees **TS19** 63 F5
Stockwell **GL4** 29 J7
Stockwell Heath **WS15** 40 C3
Stockwood, *Bristol* **BS14** 19 K5
Stockwood, *Dorset* **DT2** 8 E4
Stodday **LA2** 55 H4
Stodmarsh **CT3** 25 J5
Stody **NR24** 44 E2
Stoer **IV27** 102 C6
Stoford, *Som.* **BA22** 8 E3
Stoford, *Wilts.* **SP2** 10 B1
Stogumber **TA4** 7 J2
Stogursey **TA5** 19 F7
Stoke, *Devon* **EX39** 6 A3
Stoke, *Hants.* **SP11** 21 H6
Stoke, *Hants.* **PO11** 11 J4
Stoke, *Med.* **ME3** 24 E4
Stoke, *Plym.* **PL3** 4 E5
Stoke, *W.Mid.* **CV2** 30 E1
Stoke Abbott **DT8** 8 D4
Stoke Albany **LE16** 42 B7
Stoke Ash **IP23** 35 F1
Stoke Bardolph **NG14** 41 J1
Stoke Bishop **BS9** 19 J4
Stoke Bliss **WR15** 29 F2
Stoke Bruerne **NN12** 31 J3
Stoke by Clare **CO10** 34 B4
Stoke Canon **EX5** 7 H6
Stoke Charity **SO21** 11 F1
Stoke Climsland **PL17** 4 D3
Stoke D'Abernon **KT11** 22 E6
Stoke Doyle **PE8** 42 D7
Stoke Dry **LE15** 42 B6
Stoke Edith **HR1** 29 F4
Stoke Farthing **SP5** 10 B2
Stoke Ferry **PE33** 44 B6
Stoke Fleming **TQ6** 5 J6
Stoke Gabriel **TQ9** 5 J5
Stoke Gifford **BS34** 19 K4
Stoke Golding **CV13** 41 F6
Stoke Goldington **MK16** 32 B4
Stoke Green **SL2** 22 C3
Stoke Hammond **MK17** 32 B6
Stoke Heath, *Shrop.* **TF9** 39 F3
Stoke Heath, *Worcs.* **B60** 29 J2
Stoke Holy Cross **NR14** 45 G5
Stoke Lacy **HR7** 29 F4
Stoke Lyne **OX27** 31 G6
Stoke Mandeville **HP22** 32 B7
Stoke Newington **N16** 23 G3
Stoke on Tern **TF9** 39 F3
Stoke Orchard **GL52** 29 J6
Stoke Pero **TA24** 7 G1
Stoke Poges **SL2** 22 C3
Stoke Pound **B60** 29 J2
Stoke Prior, *Here.* **HR6** 28 E3
Stoke Prior, *Worcs.* **B60** 29 J2
Stoke Rivers **EX32** 6 E2
Stoke Rochford **NG33** 42 C3
Stoke Row **RG9** 21 K3
Stoke St. Gregory **TA3** 8 C2
Stoke St. Mary **TA3** 8 B2
Stoke St. Michael **BA3** 19 K7
Stoke St. Milborough **SY8** 38 E7
Stoke sub Hamdon **TA14** 8 D3
Stoke Talmage **OX9** 21 K2
Stoke Trister **BA9** 9 G2
Stoke Villice **BS40** 19 J5
Stoke Wake **DT11** 9 G4
Stoke-by-Nayland **CO6** 34 D5
Stokeford **BH20** 9 H6
Stokeham **DN22** 51 K5
Stokeinteignhead **TQ12** 5 K3
Stokenchurch **HP14** 22 A2
Stokenham **TQ7** 5 J6
STOKE-ON-TRENT ST 40 A1
Stokesay **SY7** 38 D7
Stokesby **NR29** 45 J4
Stokesley **TS9** 63 G6
Stolford **TA5** 19 F7
Ston Easton **BA3** 19 K6
Stonar Cut **CT13** 25 K5
Stondon Massey **CM15** 23 J1
Stone, *Bucks.* **HP17** 31 J7
Stone, *Glos.* **GL13** 19 K2
Stone, *Kent* **DA9** 23 J4
Stone, *Kent* **TN30** 14 E5
Stone, *S.Yorks.* **S66** 51 H4
Stone, *Som.* **BA4** 8 E1
Stone, *Staffs.* **ST15** 40 B2
Stone, *Worcs.* **DY10** 29 H1
Stone Allerton **BS26** 19 H6
Stone Cross, *Dur.* **DL12** 62 B5
Stone Cross, *E.Suss.*
BN24 13 K6
Stone Cross, *E.Suss.* **TN6** 13 J4
Stone Cross, *Kent* **TN25** 15 F4
Stone Cross, *Kent* **TN3** 13 J3
Stone House **LA10** 56 C1
Stone Street, *Kent* **TN15** 23 J6
Stone Street, *Suff.* **IP19** 45 H7
Stone Street, *Suff.* **CO10** 34 D5
Stonea **PE15** 43 H6
Stonebridge, *E.Suss.*
TN22 13 J4
Stonebridge, *N.Som.*
BS29 19 G6
Stonebridge, *Warks.* **CV7** 40 E7
Stonebroom **DE55** 51 G7
Stonecross Green **IP29** 34 C3
Stonefield, *Arg. & B.*
PA29 73 G3
Stonefield, *Staffs.* **ST15** 40 B2
Stonegate, *E.Suss.* **TN5** 13 K4
Stonegate, *N.Yorks.* **YO21** 63 J6
Stonegrave **YO62** 58 C2
Stonehaugh **NE48** 70 C6
Stonehaven **AB39** 91 G6
Stonehill **KT16** 22 C5
Stonehouse, *Ches.* **CH3** 48 E5
Stonehouse, *D. & G.* **DG2** 65 J4
Stonehouse, *Glos.* **GL10** 20 B1
Stonehouse, *Northumb.*
NE49 61 H1
Stonehouse, *Plym.* **PL1** 4 E5
Stonehouse, *S.Lan.* **ML9** 75 F6
Stoneleigh, *Surr.* **KT17** 23 F5
Stoneleigh, *Warks.* **CV8** 30 E1
Stoneley Green **CW5** 49 F7
Stonely **PE19** 32 E2
Stoner Hill **GU32** 11 J2
Stones **OL14** 56 E7
Stones Green **CO12** 35 F6
Stonesby **LE14** 42 B3
Stonesfield **OX29** 30 E7
Stonestreet Green **TN25** 15 F4
Stonethwaite **CA12** 60 D5
Stoney Cross **SO43** 10 D3
Stoney Middleton **S32** 50 E5
Stoney Stanton **LE9** 41 G6
Stoney Stoke **BA9** 9 G1
Stoney Stratton **BA4** 9 F1
Stoney Stretton **SY5** 38 C5
Stoneyburn **EH47** 75 H4
Stoneyford **EX10** 7 J7
Stoneygate **LE2** 41 J5
Stoneyhills **CM0** 25 F2
Stoneykirk **DG9** 64 A5
Stoneywood **AB21** 91 G3
Stonganess **ZE2** 108 E2
Stonham Aspal **IP14** 35 F3
Stonnall **WS9** 40 C5
Stonor **RG9** 22 A3
Stonton Wyville **LE16** 42 A6
Stony Houghton **NG19** 51 G6
Stony Stratford **MK11** 31 J4
Stonybreck **ZE2** 108 A1
Stoodleigh, *Devon* **EX16** 7 H4
Stoodleigh, *Devon* **EX32** 6 E2
Stopham **RH20** 12 D5

Tadmarton

Stopsley **LU2** 32 E6
Stoptide **PL27** 3 G1
Storeton **CH63** 48 C4
Stornoway (Steornabhagh) **HS1** 101 G4
Stornoway Airport **HS2** 101 G4
Storridge **WR13** 29 G4
Storrington **RH20** 12 D5
Storrs **S6** 50 E4
Storth **LA7** 55 H1
Storwood **YO42** 58 D5
Stotfield **IV31** 97 K4
Stotfold **SG5** 33 F5
Stottesdon **DY14** 39 F7
Stoughton, *Leics.* **LE2** 41 J5
Stoughton, *Surr.* **GU2** 22 C6
Stoughton, *W.Suss.* **PO18** 11 J3
Stoughton Cross **BS28** 19 H7
Stoul **PH41** 86 D5
Stoulton **WR7** 29 J4
Stour Provost **SP8** 9 G2
Stour Row **SP7** 9 H2
Stourbridge **DY8** 40 A7
Stourpaine **DT11** 9 H4
Stourport-on-Severn **DY13** 29 H1
Stourton, *Staffs.* **DY7** 40 A7
Stourton, *Warks.* **CV36** 30 D5
Stourton, *Wilts.* **BA12** 9 G1
Stourton Caundle **DT10** 9 G3
Stove **KW17** 106 F4
Stoven **NR34** 45 J7
Stow, *Lincs.* **LN1** 52 B4
Stow, *Sc.Bord.* **TD1** 76 C6
Stow Bardolph **PE34** 44 A5
Stow Bedon **NR17** 44 D6
Stow cum Quy **CB5** 33 J2
Stow Longa **PE28** 32 E1
Stow Maries **CM3** 24 E2
Stow Pasture **LN1** 52 B4
Stowbridge **PE34** 43 J5
Stowe, *Glos.* **GL15** 19 J1
Stowe, *Shrop.* **LD7** 28 C1
Stowe, *Staffs.* **WS13** 40 D4
Stowe-by-Chartley **ST18** 40 C3
Stowehill **NN7** 31 H3
Stowell, *Glos.* **GL54** 30 B7
Stowell, *Som.* **DT9** 9 F2
Stowey **BS39** 19 J6
Stowford, *Devon* **EX20** 6 C7
Stowford, *Devon* **EX37** 6 E3
Stowford, *Devon* **EX10** 7 K7
Stowlangtoft **IP31** 34 D2
Stowmarket **IP14** 34 E3
Stow-on-the-Wold **GL54** 30 C6
Stowting **TN25** 15 G3
Stowupland **IP14** 34 E3
Straad **PA20** 73 J4
Stracathro **DD9** 83 H1
Strachan **AB31** 90 E5
Strachur (Clachan Strachur) **PA27** 80 B7
Stradbroke **IP21** 35 G1
Stradishall **CB8** 34 B3
Stradsett **PE33** 44 A5
Stragglethorpe **LN5** 52 C7
Straight Soley **RG17** 21 G4
Straiton, *Edin.* **EH20** 76 A4
Straiton, *S.Ayr.* **KA19** 67 H3
Straloch, *Aber.* **AB21** 91 G2
Straloch, *P. & K.* **PH10** 82 B1
Stramshall **ST14** 40 C2
Strands **LA18** 54 E1
Strang **IM4** 54 C6
Strangford **HR9** 28 E6
Strannda **HS5** 93 F3
Stranraer **DG9** 64 A4
Strata Florida **SY25** 27 G2
Stratfield Mortimer **RG7** 21 K5
Stratfield Saye **RG7** 21 K5
Stratfield Turgis **RG27** 21 K6
Stratford, *Beds.* **SG19** 32 E4
Stratford, *Glos.* **GL20** 29 H5
Stratford, *Gt.Lon.* **E15** 23 G3
Stratford St. Andrew **IP17** 35 H3
Stratford St. Mary **CO7** 34 E5
Stratford sub Castle **SP1** 10 C1
Stratford Tony **SP5** 10 B2
Stratford-upon-Avon **CV37** 30 C3
Strath **KW1** 105 H3
Strathan, *High.* **IV27** 102 C6
Strathan, *High.* **PH34** 87 F5
Strathaven **ML10** 75 F6
Strathblane **G63** 74 D3
Strathcarron **IV54** 95 F7
Strathdon **AB36** 90 B3
Strathgirnock **AB35** 90 B5
Strathkanaird **IV26** 95 H1
Strathkinness **KY16** 83 F6
Strathmiglo **KY14** 82 D6
Strathpeffer **IV14** 96 B6
Strathrannoch **IV23** 95 K4
Strathtay **PH9** 82 A2
Strathwhillan **KA27** 73 J7
Strathy **KW14** 104 D2
Strathyre **FK18** 81 G6
Stratton, *Cornw.* **EX23** 6 A5
Stratton, *Dorset* **DT2** 9 F5
Stratton, *Glos.* **GL7** 20 D1
Stratton Audley **OX27** 31 H6
Stratton Hall **IP10** 35 G5
Stratton St. Margaret **SN3** 20 E3
Stratton St. Michael **NR15** 45 G6
Stratton Strawless **NR10** 45 G3
Stratton-on-the-Fosse **BA3** 19 K6
Stravanan **PA20** 73 J5
Stravithie **KY16** 83 G6
Strawberry Hill **TW2** 22 E4
Stream **TA4** 7 J2
Streat **BN6** 13 G5
Streatham **SW16** 23 F4
Streatham Vale **SW16** 23 F4
Streatley, *Beds.* **LU3** 32 D6
Streatley, *W.Berks.* **RG8** 21 J3
Street, *Devon* **EX12** 7 K7
Street, *Lancs.* **PR3** 55 J4
Street, *N.Yorks.* **YO21** 63 J6
Street, *Som.* **BA16** 8 D1
Street, *Som.* **TA20** 8 C4
Street Ashton **CV23** 41 G7
Street Dinas **SY11** 38 C2
Street End **PO20** 12 B7
Street Gate **NE16** 62 D1
Street Houses **LS24** 58 B5
Street Lane **DE5** 41 F1
Street on the Fosse **BA4** 9 F1
Streethay **WS13** 40 D4
Streethouse **WF7** 57 J7
Streetlam **DL7** 62 E7
Streetly **B74** 40 C6
Streetly End **CB1** 33 K4
Strefford **SY7** 38 D7
Strelley **NG8** 41 H1
Strensall **YO32** 58 C3
Strensham **WR8** 29 J4
Stretcholt **TA6** 19 F7
Strete **TQ6** 5 J6
Stretford, *Gt.Man.* **M32** 49 G3
Stretford, *Here.* **HR6** 28 D3
Stretford, *Here.* **HR6** 28 E3
Strethall **CB11** 33 H5
Stretham **CB6** 33 J1
Strettington **PO18** 12 B6
Stretton, *Ches.* **SY14** 48 D7
Stretton, *Derbys.* **DE55** 51 F6
Stretton, *Rut.* **LE15** 42 C4
Stretton, *Staffs.* **ST19** 40 A4
Stretton, *Staffs.* **DE13** 40 E3
Stretton, *Warr.* **WA4** 49 F4
Stretton en le Field **DE12** 41 F4
Stretton Grandison **HR8** 29 F4
Stretton Heath **SY5** 38 C4
Stretton Sugwas **HR4** 28 D4
Stretton under Fosse **CV23** 41 G7
Stretton Westwood **TF13** 38 E6
Stretton-on-Dunsmore **CV23** 31 F1
Stretton-on-Fosse **GL56** 30 D5
Stribers **LA12** 55 G1
Strichen **AB43** 99 H5
Strines **SK6** 49 J4
Stringston **TA5** 7 K1
Strixton **NN29** 32 C2
Stroat **NP16** 19 J2
Stromeferry **IV53** 86 E1
Stromemore **IV54** 86 E1
Stromness **KW16** 107 B7
Stronaba **PH34** 87 J6
Stronachlachar **FK8** 81 F6
Strone, *Arg. & B.* **PA23** 73 K2
Strone, *High.* **IV63** 88 C2
Strone, *High.* **PH33** 87 H6
Strone, *Stir.* **FK17** 81 F6
Stronechrubie **IV27** 102 E7
Stronlonag **PA23** 73 K2
Stronmilchan **PA33** 80 C5
Stronsay **KW17** 106 F5
Strontian **PH36** 79 K1
Strontoiller **PA37** 80 A5
Stronvar **FK19** 81 G5
Strood **ME2** 24 D5
Strood Green, *Surr.* **RH3** 23 F7
Strood Green, *W.Suss.* **RH14** 12 D4
Strood Green, *W.Suss.* **RH12** 12 E3
Stroquhan **DG2** 68 D5
Stroud, *Glos.* **GL5** 20 B1
Stroud, *Hants.* **GU32** 11 J2
Stroud Common **GU5** 22 D7
Stroud Green, *Essex* **SS4** 24 E2
Stroud Green, *Glos.* **GL10** 20 B1
Stroude **GU25** 22 D5
Stroul **G84** 74 A2
Stroxton **NG33** 42 C2
Struan, *High.* **IV56** 85 J1
Struan, *P. & K.* **PH18** 81 J1
Strubby, *Lincs.* **LN13** 53 H4
Strubby, *Lincs.* **LN8** 52 E5
Strumpshaw **NR13** 45 H5
Struthers **KY15** 82 E7
Struy **IV4** 88 B1
Stryd y Facsen **LL65** 46 B4
Stryt-cae-rhedyn **CH7** 48 B6
Stryt-issa **LL14** 38 B1
Stuartfield **AB42** 99 H6
Stub Place **LA19** 60 B7
Stubber's Green **WS9** 40 C5
Stubbington **PO14** 11 G4
Stubbins **BL0** 49 G1
Stubbs Green **NR14** 45 H6
Stubhampton **DT11** 9 J3
Stubley **S18** 51 F5
Stubshaw Cross **WN4** 48 E2
Stubton **NG23** 42 B1
Stuck, *Arg. & B.* **PA20** 73 J4
Stuck, *Arg. & B.* **PA23** 73 K1
Stuckbeg **PA24** 74 A1
Stuckgowan **G83** 80 E7
Stuckindroin **G83** 80 E6
Stuckreoch **PA27** 73 J1
Stuckton **SP6** 10 C3
Stud Green **SL6** 22 B4
Studdon **NE47** 61 K1
Studfold **BD24** 56 D2
Studham **LU6** 32 D7
Studholme **CA7** 60 D1
Studland **BH19** 10 B6
Studley, *Warks.* **B80** 30 B2
Studley, *Wilts.* **SN11** 20 C4
Studley Common **B80** 30 B2
Studley Green **HP14** 22 A2
Studley Roger **HG4** 57 H2
Stuggadhoo **IM4** 54 C6
Stump Cross, *Essex* **CB10** 33 J4
Stump Cross, *Lancs.* **PR3** 55 J6
Stuntney **CB7** 33 J1
Stunts Green **BN27** 13 K5
Sturbridge **ST21** 40 A2
Sturgate **DN21** 52 B4
Sturmer **CB9** 33 K4
Sturminster Common **DT10** 9 G3
Sturminster Marshall **BH21** 9 J4
Sturminster Newton **DT10** 9 G3
Sturry **CT2** 25 H5
Sturton by Stow **LN1** 52 B4
Sturton le Steeple **DN22** 51 K4
Stuston **IP21** 35 F1
Stutton, *N.Yorks.* **LS24** 57 K5
Stutton, *Suff.* **IP9** 35 F5
Styal **SK9** 49 H4
Styrrup **DN11** 51 J3
Suainebost (Swainbost) **HS2** 101 H1
Suardail **HS2** 101 G4
Succoth, *Aber.* **AB54** 90 C1
Succoth, *Arg. & B.* **G83** 80 D7
Succothmore **PA27** 80 C7
Suckley **WR6** 29 G3
Suckley Green **WR6** 29 G3
Suckley Knowl **WR6** 29 G3
Sudborough **NN14** 42 C7
Sudbourne **IP12** 35 J3
Sudbrook, *Lincs.* **NG32** 42 C1
Sudbrook, *Mon.* **NP26** 19 J3
Sudbrooke **LN2** 52 D5
Sudbury, *Derbys.* **DE6** 40 D2
Sudbury, *Gt.Lon.* **HA0** 22 E3
Sudbury, *Suff.* **CO10** 34 C4
Sudden **OL11** 49 H1
Sudgrove **GL6** 20 C1
Suffield, *N.Yorks.* **YO13** 63 J3
Suffield, *Norf.* **NR11** 45 G2
Sugarloaf **TN26** 14 E4
Sugnall **ST21** 39 G2
Sugwas Pool **HR4** 28 D4
Suie Lodge Hotel **FK20** 81 F5
Suisnish **IV49** 86 B3
Sulby, *I.o.M.* **IM7** 54 C4
Sulby, *I.o.M.* **IM4** 54 C5
Sulgrave **OX17** 31 G4
Sulham **RG8** 21 K4
Sulhamstead **RG7** 21 K5
Sullington **RH20** 12 D5
Sullom **ZE2** 108 C5
Sullom Voe Oil Terminal **ZE2** 108 C5
Sully **CF64** 18 E5
Sumburgh **ZE3** 109 F10
Sumburgh Airport **ZE3** 109 F9
Summer Bridge **HG3** 57 H3
Summer Isles **IV26** 95 F1
Summer Lodge **DL8** 62 A7
Summercourt **TR8** 3 F3
Summerfield, *Norf.* **PE31** 44 B2
Summerfield, *Worcs.* **DY11** 29 H1
Summerhill **LL11** 48 C7
Summerhouse **DL2** 62 D5
Summerlands **LA8** 55 J1
Summerleaze **NP26** 19 H3
Summertown **OX2** 21 J1
Summit **OL15** 49 J1
Sun Green **SK15** 49 J3
Sunadale **PA28** 73 G6
Sunbiggin **CA10** 61 H6
Sunbury **TW16** 22 E5
Sundaywell **DG2** 68 D5
Sunderland, *Cumb.* **CA13** 60 C3
Sunderland, *Lancs.* **LA3** 55 H4
SUNDERLAND, *T. & W.* SR 62 E1
Sunderland Bridge **DH6** 62 D3
Sundhope **TD7** 69 J1
Sundon Park **LU3** 32 D6
Sundridge **TN14** 23 H6
Sundrum Mains **KA6** 67 J1
Sunhill **GL7** 20 E1
Sunipol **PA75** 78 E2
Sunk Island **HU12** 53 F1
Sunningdale **SL5** 22 C5
Sunninghill **SL5** 22 C5
Sunningwell **OX13** 21 H1
Sunniside, *Dur.* **DL13** 62 C3
Sunniside, *T. & W.* **NE16** 62 D1
Sunny Bank **LA21** 60 D7
Sunny Brow **DL15** 62 C3
Sunnylaw **FK9** 75 F1
Sunnyside, *Aber.* **AB12** 91 G5
Sunnyside, *Northumb.* **NE46** 70 E7
Sunnyside, *S.Yorks.* **S65** 51 G3
Sunnyside, *W.Suss.* **RH19** 13 G3
Sunton **SN8** 21 F6
Sunwick **TD15** 77 G5
Surbiton **KT6** 22 E5
Surfleet **PE11** 43 F3
Surfleet Seas End **PE11** 43 F3
Surlingham **NR14** 45 H5
Sustead **NR11** 45 F2
Susworth **DN17** 52 B2
Sutcombe **EX22** 6 B4
Sutcombemill **EX22** 6 B4
Suton **NR18** 44 E6
Sutors of Cromarty **IV11** 97 F5
Sutterby **LN13** 53 G5
Sutterton **PE20** 43 F2
Sutton, *Beds.* **SG19** 33 F4
Sutton, *Cambs.* **CB6** 33 H1
Sutton, *Devon* **EX17** 7 F5
Sutton, *Devon* **TQ7** 5 H6
Sutton, *Gt.Lon.* **SM1** 23 F5
Sutton, *Kent* **CT15** 15 J3
Sutton, *Lincs.* **LN5** 52 B7
Sutton, *Norf.* **NR12** 45 H3
Sutton, *Notts.* **NG13** 42 A2
Sutton, *Notts.* **DN22** 51 J4
Sutton, *Oxon.* **OX29** 21 H1
Sutton, *Pembs.* **SA62** 16 C3
Sutton, *Peter.* **PE5** 42 D6
Sutton, *S.Yorks.* **DN6** 51 H1
Sutton, *Shrop.* **WV16** 39 G7
Sutton, *Shrop.* **TF9** 39 F2
Sutton, *Shrop.* **SY2** 38 E4
Sutton, *Shrop.* **SY11** 38 C3
Sutton, *Staffs.* **TF10** 39 G3
Sutton, *Suff.* **IP12** 35 H4
Sutton, *W.Suss.* **RH20** 12 C5
Sutton Abinger **RH5** 22 E7
Sutton at Hone **DA4** 23 J4
Sutton Bassett **LE16** 42 A7
Sutton Benger **SN15** 20 C4
Sutton Bingham **BA22** 8 E3
Sutton Bonington **LE12** 41 H3
Sutton Bridge **PE12** 43 H3
Sutton Cheney **CV13** 41 G5
Sutton Coldfield **B74** 40 D6
Sutton Courtenay **OX14** 21 J2
Sutton Crosses **PE12** 43 H3
Sutton Grange **HG4** 57 H2
Sutton Green, *Oxon.* **OX29** 21 H1
Sutton Green, *Surr.* **GU4** 22 D6
Sutton Green, *Wrex.* **LL13** 38 D1
Sutton Holms **BH21** 10 B4
Sutton Howgrave **DL8** 57 J2
Sutton in Ashfield **NG17** 51 G7
Sutton in the Elms **LE9** 41 H6
Sutton Ings **HU8** 59 H6
Sutton Lane Ends **SK11** 49 J5
Sutton le Marsh **LN12** 53 J4
Sutton Leach **WA9** 48 E3
Sutton Maddock **TF11** 39 G5
Sutton Mallet **TA7** 8 C1
Sutton Mandeville **SP3** 9 J2
Sutton Montis **BA22** 9 F2
Sutton on Sea **LN12** 53 J4
Sutton on the Hill **DE6** 40 E2
Sutton on Trent **NG23** 51 K6
Sutton Poyntz **DT3** 9 G6
Sutton St. Edmund **PE12** 43 G4
Sutton St. James **PE12** 43 H4
Sutton St. Nicholas **HR1** 28 E4
Sutton Scarsdale **S44** 51 G6
Sutton Scotney **SO21** 11 F1
Sutton upon Derwent **YO41** 58 D5
Sutton Valence **ME17** 14 D3
Sutton Veny **BA12** 20 B7
Sutton Waldron **DT11** 9 H3
Sutton Weaver **WA7** 48 E5
Sutton Wick, *B. & N.E.Som.* **BS40** 19 J6
Sutton Wick, *Oxon.* **OX14** 21 H2
Sutton-in-Craven **BD20** 57 F5
Sutton-on-Hull **HU7** 59 H6
Sutton-on-the-Forest **YO61** 58 B3
Sutton-under-Brailes **CV36** 30 E5
Sutton-under-Whitestonecliffe **YO7** 57 K1
Swaby **LN13** 53 G5
Swadlincote **DE11** 41 F4
Swaffham **PE37** 44 C5
Swaffham Bulbeck **CB5** 33 J2
Swaffham Prior **CB5** 33 J2
Swafield **NR28** 45 G2
Swainbost (Suainebost) **HS2** 101 H1
Swainby **DL6** 63 F6
Swainsthorpe **NR14** 45 G5
Swainswick **BA1** 20 A5
Swalcliffe **OX15** 30 E5
Swalecliffe **CT5** 25 H5
Swallow **LN7** 52 E2
Swallow Beck **LN6** 52 C6
Swallowcliffe **SP3** 9 J2
Swallowfield **RG7** 22 A5
Swallows Cross **CM15** 24 C2
Swampton **SP11** 21 H6
Swan Green, *Ches.* **WA16** 49 G5
Swan Green, *Suff.* **IP19** 35 G1
Swan Street **CO6** 34 C6
Swanage **BH19** 10 B7
Swanbach **CW3** 39 F1
Swanbourne **MK17** 32 B6
Swanbridge **CF64** 18 E5
Swancote **WV15** 39 G6
Swanland **HU14** 59 F7
Swanlaws **TD8** 70 C2
Swanley **BR8** 23 J5
Swanley Village **BR8** 23 J5
Swanmore, *Hants.* **SO32** 11 G3
Swanmore, *I.o.W.* **PO33** 11 G5
Swannington, *Leics.* **LE67** 41 G4
Swannington, *Norf.* **NR9** 45 F4
Swanscombe **DA10** 24 C4
SWANSEA (ABERTAWE) SA 17 K5
Swanston **EH10** 76 A4
Swanton Abbot **NR10** 45 G3
Swanton Morley **NR20** 44 E4
Swanton Novers **NR24** 44 E2
Swanton Street **ME9** 14 D2
Swanwick, *Derbys.* **DE55** 51 G7
Swanwick, *Hants.* **SO31** 11 G4
Swanwick Green **SY13** 38 E1
Swarby **NG34** 42 D1
Swardeston **NR14** 45 G5
Swarkestone **DE73** 41 F3
Swarland **NE65** 71 G3
Swarraton **SO24** 11 G1
Swarthmoor **LA12** 55 F2
Swaton **NG34** 42 E2
Swavesey **CB4** 33 G2
Sway **SO41** 10 D5
Swayfield **NG33** 42 C3
Swaythling **SO18** 11 F3
Swaythorpe **YO25** 59 G3
Sweetham **EX5** 7 G6
Sweethay **TA3** 8 B2
Sweetshouse **PL30** 4 A4
Swefling **IP17** 35 H2
Swell **TA3** 8 C2
Swepstone **LE67** 41 F4
Swerford **OX7** 30 E5
Swettenham **CW12** 49 H6
Swffryd **NP11** 19 F2
Swift's Green **TN27** 14 D3
Swiftsden **TN19** 14 C5
Swilland **IP6** 35 F3
Swillington **LS26** 57 J6
Swimbridge **EX32** 6 E3
Swimbridge Newland **EX32** 6 D2
Swinbrook **OX18** 30 D7
Swincliffe **HG3** 57 H4
Swincombe **EX31** 6 E1
Swinden **BD23** 56 D4
Swinderby **LN6** 52 B6
Swindon, *Staffs.* **DY3** 40 A6
SWINDON, *Swin.* SN 20 E3
Swindon Village **GL51** 29 J6
Swine **HU11** 59 H6
Swinefleet **DN14** 58 D7
Swineford **BS30** 19 K5
Swineshead, *Beds.* **MK44** 32 D2
Swineshead, *Lincs.* **PE20** 43 F1
Swineshead Bridge **PE20** 43 F1
Swineside **DL8** 57 F1
Swiney **KW3** 105 H5
Swinford, *Leics.* **LE17** 31 G1
Swinford, *Oxon.* **OX29** 21 H1
Swingate **NG16** 41 H1
Swingfield Minnis **CT15** 15 H3
Swingleton Green **IP7** 34 D4
Swinhoe **NE67** 71 H1
Swinhope **LN8** 53 F3
Swining **ZE2** 109 D6
Swinithwaite **DL8** 57 F1
Swinscoe **DE6** 40 D1
Swinside Hall **TD8** 70 C2
Swinstead **NG33** 42 D3
Swinton, *Gt.Man.* **M27** 49 G2
Swinton, *N.Yorks.* **YO17** 58 D2
Swinton, *N.Yorks.* **HG4** 57 H2
Swinton, *S.Yorks.* **S64** 51 G3
Swinton, *Sc.Bord.* **TD11** 77 G6
Swinton Quarter **TD11** 77 G6
Swintonmill **TD11** 77 G6
Swithland **LE12** 41 H4
Swordale **IV16** 96 C5
Swordland **PH41** 86 D5
Swordle **PH36** 86 B7
Swordly **KW14** 104 C2
Sworton Heath **WA16** 49 F4
Swyddffynnon **SY25** 27 F2
Swyncombe **RG9** 21 K2
Swynnerton **ST15** 40 A2
Swyre **DT2** 8 E6
Sychnant **LD6** 27 J1
Syde **GL53** 29 J7
Sydenham, *Gt.Lon.* **SE26** 23 G4
Sydenham, *Oxon.* **OX39** 22 A1
Sydenham Damerel **PL19** 4 E3
Syderstone **PE31** 44 C2
Sydling St. Nicholas **DT2** 9 F5
Sydmonton **RG20** 21 H6
Sydney **CW1** 49 G7
Syerston **NG23** 42 A1
Sykehouse **DN14** 51 J1
Sykes **BB7** 56 B4
Sylen **SA15** 17 J4
Symbister **ZE2** 109 E6
Symington, *S.Ayr.* **KA1** 74 B7
Symington, *S.Lan.* **ML12** 75 H7
Symonds Yat **HR9** 28 E7
Symondsbury **DT6** 8 D5
Synod Inn (Post-mawr) **SA44** 26 D3
Syre **KW11** 103 J4
Syreford **GL54** 30 B6
Syresham **NN13** 31 H4
Syston, *Leics.* **LE7** 41 J4
Syston, *Lincs.* **NG32** 42 C1
Sytchampton **DY13** 29 H2
Sywell **NN6** 32 B2

T

Taagan **IV22** 95 G5
Tableyhill **WA16** 49 G5
Tabost, *W.Isles* **HS2** 101 F6
Tabost (Harbost), *W.Isles* **HS2** 101 H1
Tachbrook Mallory **CV33** 30 E2
Tacher **KW5** 105 G4
Tackley **OX5** 31 F6
Tacleit (Hacklete) **HS2** 100 D4
Tacolneston **NR16** 45 F6
Tadcaster **LS24** 57 K5
Tadden **BH21** 9 J4
Taddington, *Derbys.* **SK17** 50 D5
Taddington, *Glos.* **GL54** 30 B5
Taddiport **EX38** 6 C4
Tadley **RG26** 21 K5
Tadlow **SG8** 33 F4
Tadmarton **OX15** 30 E5

Tadpole Bridge

Tadpole Bridge **SN7** 21 G1
Tadworth **KT20** 23 F6
Tafarnaubach **NP22** 28 A7
Tafarn-y-bwlch **SA41** 16 D1
Tafarn-y-Gelyn **CH7** 47 K6
Taff Merthyr Garden Village **CF46** 18 E2
Taff's Well (Ffynnon Taf) **CF15** 18 E3
Tafolwern **SY19** 37 H5
Taibach, *N.P.T.* **SA13** 18 A3
Tai-bach, *Powys* **SY10** 38 A3
Taicynhaeaf **LL40** 37 F4
Tain, *High.* **KW14** 105 H2
Tain, *High.* **IV19** 96 E3
Tai'n Lôn **LL54** 46 C7
Tai'r Bull **LD3** 27 J6
Tairgwaith **SA18** 27 G7
Tai'r-heol **CF46** 18 E2
Tairlaw **KA19** 67 J3
Tai'r-ysgol **SA7** 17 K5
Takeley **CM22** 33 J6
Takeley Street **CM22** 33 J6
Talachddu **LD3** 27 K5
Talacre **CH8** 47 K4
Talardd **LL23** 37 H3
Talaton **EX5** 7 J6
Talbenny **SA62** 16 B3
Talbot Green **CF72** 18 D3
Talbot Village **BH10** 10 B5
Talerddig **SY19** 37 J5
Talgarreg **SA44** 26 D3
Talgarth **LD3** 28 A5
Taliesin **SY20** 37 F6
Talisker **IV47** 85 J1
Talke Pits **ST7** 49 H7
Talkin **CA8** 61 G1
Talla Linnfoots **ML12** 69 G1
Talladale **IV22** 95 F4
Talladh-a-Bheithe **PH17** 81 G2
Talland **PL13** 4 C5
Tallarn Green **SY14** 38 D1
Tallentire **CA13** 60 C3
Talley (Talyllychau) **SA19** 17 K1
Tallington **PE9** 42 D5
Talmine **IV27** 103 H2
Talog **SA33** 17 G2
Tal-sarn **SA48** 26 E3
Talsarnau **LL47** 37 F2
Talskiddy **TR9** 3 G2
Talwrn, *I.o.A.* **LL77** 46 C5
Talwrn, *Wrex.* **LL14** 38 B1
Talwrn, *Wrex.* **LL13** 38 C1
Talybont, *Cere.* **SY24** 37 F7
Tal-y-bont, *Conwy* **LL32** 47 F6
Tal-y-bont, *Gwyn.* **LL43** 36 E3
Tal-y-bont, *Gwyn.* **LL57** 46 E5
Talybont-on-Usk **LD3** 28 A6
Tal-y-Cae **LL57** 46 E6
Tal-y-cafn **LL28** 47 F5
Tal-y-coed **NP7** 28 D7
Talygarn **CF72** 18 D3
Talyllychau (Talley) **SA19** 17 K1
Tal-y-llyn, *Gwyn.* **LL36** 37 G5
Talyllyn, *Powys* **LD3** 28 A6
Talysarn **LL54** 46 C7
Tal-y-wern **SY20** 37 H5
Tamavoid **FK8** 74 D1
Tamerton Foliot **PL5** 4 E4
Tamworth **B79** 40 E5
Tamworth Green **PE22** 43 G1
Tan Office Green **IP29** 34 B3
Tandem **HD5** 50 D1
Tandridge **RH8** 23 G6
Tanerdy **SA31** 17 H2
Tanfield **DH9** 62 C1
Tanfield Lea **DH9** 62 C1
Tang **HG3** 57 H4
Tang Hall **YO10** 58 C4
Tangiers **SA62** 16 C3
Tanglandford **AB41** 91 G1
Tangley **SP11** 21 G6
Tangmere **PO20** 12 C6
Tangwick **ZE2** 108 B5
Tangy **PA28** 66 A1
Tankerness **KW17** 107 E7
Tankersley **S75** 51 F2
Tankerton **CT5** 25 H5
Tan-lan **LL48** 37 F1
Tannach **KW1** 105 J4
Tannachie **AB39** 91 F6
Tannachy **IV28** 96 E1
Tannadice **DD8** 83 F2
Tannington **IP13** 35 G2
Tannochside **G71** 74 E4
Tansley **DE4** 51 F7
Tansley Knoll **DE4** 51 F7
Tansor **PE8** 42 D6
Tantobie **DH9** 62 C1
Tanton **TS9** 63 G5
Tanworth in Arden **B94** 30 C1
Tan-y-fron **LL16** 47 H6
Tan-y-graig **LL53** 36 C2
Tanygrisiau **LL41** 37 F1
Tan-y-groes **SA43** 26 B4
Tan-y-pistyll **SY10** 37 K3
Tan-yr-allt **LL19** 47 J4
Taobh a' Deas Loch Baghasdail **HS8** 84 C3
Taobh Siar **HS3** 100 D7
Taobh Tuath (Northton) **HS3** 92 E3
Tapeley **EX39** 6 C3
Taplow **SL6** 22 C3
Tapton Grove **S43** 51 G5
Taransay (Tarasaigh) **HS3** 100 C7
Taraphocain **PA38** 80 B3
Tarasaigh (Taransay) **HS3** 100 C7
Tarbat House **IV18** 96 E4
Tarbert, *Arg. & B.* **PA29** 73 G4
Tarbert, *Arg. & B.* **PA41** 72 E5
Tarbert, *Arg. & B.* **PA60** 72 E2
Tarbert, *High.* **PH36** 79 H1
Tarbert (An Tairbeart), *W.Isles* **HS3** 100 D7
Tarbet, *Arg. & B.* **G83** 80 E7
Tarbet, *High.* **PH41** 86 D5
Tarbet, *High.* **IV27** 102 D4
Tarbock Green **L35** 48 D4
Tarbolton **KA5** 67 J1
Tarbrax **EH55** 75 J5
Tardebigge **B60** 29 J2
Tardy Gate **PR5** 55 J7
Tarfside **DD9** 90 C7
Tarland **AB34** 90 C4
Tarleton **PR4** 55 H7
Tarlscough **L40** 48 D1
Tarlton **GL7** 20 C2
Tarnbrook **LA2** 55 J4
Tarnock **BS26** 19 G6
Tarporley **CW6** 48 E6
Tarr **TA4** 7 K2
Tarrant Crawford **DT11** 9 J4
Tarrant Gunville **DT11** 9 J3
Tarrant Hinton **DT11** 9 J3
Tarrant Keyneston **DT11** 9 J4
Tarrant Launceston **DT11** 9 J4
Tarrant Monkton **DT11** 9 J4
Tarrant Rawston **DT11** 9 J4
Tarrant Rushton **DT11** 9 J4
Tarrel **IV20** 97 F3
Tarring Neville **BN9** 13 H6
Tarrington **HR1** 29 F4
Tarrnacraig **KA27** 73 H7
Tarsappie **PH2** 82 C5
Tarskavaig **IV46** 86 B4
Tarves **AB41** 91 G1
Tarvie, *High.* **IV14** 96 B6
Tarvie, *P. & K.* **PH10** 82 B1
Tarvin **CH3** 48 D6
Tarvin Sands **CH3** 48 D6
Tasburgh **NR15** 45 G6
Tasley **WV16** 39 F6
Taston **OX7** 30 E6
Tatenhill **DE13** 40 E3
Tathall End **MK19** 32 B4
Tatham **LA2** 56 B3
Tathwell **LN11** 53 G4
Tatsfield **TN16** 23 H6
Tattenhall **CH3** 48 D7
Tattenhoe **MK4** 32 B5
Tatterford **NR21** 44 C3
Tattersett **PE31** 44 C2
Tattershall **LN4** 53 F7
Tattershall Bridge **LN4** 52 E7
Tattershall Thorpe **LN4** 53 F7
Tattingstone **IP9** 35 F5
Tatworth **TA20** 8 C4
Tauchers **AB55** 98 B6
TAUNTON TA 8 B2
Tavelty **AB51** 91 F3
Taverham **NR8** 45 F4
Tavernspite **SA34** 16 E3
Tavistock **PL19** 4 E3
Taw Bridge **EX18** 6 E5
Taw Green **EX20** 6 E6
Tawstock **EX31** 6 D3
Taxal **SK23** 50 C5
Tayburn **KA3** 74 D6
Taychreggan **PA35** 80 B5
Tayinloan **PA29** 72 E6
Taylors Cross **EX23** 6 A4
Taynafead **PA33** 80 B6
Taynish **PA31** 73 F2
Taynton, *Glos.* **GL19** 29 G6
Taynton, *Oxon.* **OX18** 30 D7
Taynuilt **PA35** 80 B4
Tayock **DD10** 83 H2
Tayovullin **PA44** 72 A3
Tayport **DD6** 83 F5
Tayvallich **PA31** 73 F2
Tea Green **LU2** 32 E6
Tealby **LN8** 52 E3
Tealing **DD4** 83 F4
Team Valley **NE11** 71 H7
Teanamachar **HS6** 92 C5
Teangue **IV44** 86 C4
Teasses **KY8** 83 F7
Tebay **CA10** 61 H6
Tebworth **LU7** 32 C6
Tedburn St. Mary **EX6** 7 G6
Teddington, *Glos.* **GL20** 29 J5
Teddington, *Gt.Lon.* **TW11** 22 E4
Tedstone Delamere **HR7** 29 F3
Tedstone Wafre **HR7** 29 F3
Teesside International Airport **DL2** 62 E5
Teeton **NN6** 31 H1
Teffont Evias **SP3** 9 J1
Teffont Magna **SP3** 9 J1
Tegryn **SA35** 17 F1
Teigh **LE15** 42 B4
Teign Village **TQ13** 7 G7
Teigngrace **TQ12** 5 J3
Teignmouth **TQ14** 5 K3
TELFORD TF 39 **F5**
Telham **TN33** 14 C6
Tellisford **BA2** 20 B6
Telscombe **BN7** 13 H6
Telscombe Cliffs **BN10** 13 H6
Tempar **PH16** 81 H2
Templand **DG11** 69 F5
Temple, *Cornw.* **PL30** 4 B3
Temple, *Midloth.* **EH23** 76 B5
Temple Balsall **B93** 30 D1
Temple Bar **SA48** 26 E3
Temple Cloud **BS39** 19 K6
Temple End **CB9** 33 K3
Temple Ewell **CT16** 15 H3
Temple Grafton **B49** 30 C3
Temple Guiting **GL54** 30 B6
Temple Herdewyke **CV47** 30 E3
Temple Hirst **YO8** 58 C7
Temple Normanton **S42** 51 G6
Temple Sowerby **CA10** 61 H4
Templecombe **BA8** 9 G2
Templeton, *Devon* **EX16** 7 G4
Templeton, *Pembs.* **SA67** 16 E3
Templeton Bridge **EX16** 7 G4
Templewood **DD9** 83 H1
Tempsford **SG19** 32 E3
Ten Mile Bank **PE38** 44 A6
Tenbury Wells **WR15** 28 E2
Tenby (Dinbych-y-Pysgod) **SA70** 16 E4
Tendring **CO16** 35 F6
Tendring Green **CO16** 35 F6
Tenga **PA72** 79 G3
Tenterden **TN30** 14 D4
Tepersie Castle **AB33** 90 D2
Terally **DG9** 64 B6
Terling **CM3** 34 B7
Tern **TF6** 39 F4
Ternhill **TF9** 39 F2
Terregles **DG2** 65 K3
Terriers **HP13** 22 B2
Terrington **YO60** 58 C2
Terrington St. Clement **PE34** 43 J3
Terrington St. John **PE14** 43 J4
Terry's Green **B94** 30 C1
Tervieside **AB37** 89 K1
Teston **ME18** 14 C2
Testwood **SO40** 10 E3
Tetbury **GL8** 20 B2
Tetbury Upton **GL8** 20 B2
Tetchill **SY12** 38 C2
Tetcott **EX22** 6 B6
Tetford **LN9** 53 G5
Tetney **DN36** 53 G2
Tetney Lock **DN36** 53 G2
Tetsworth **OX9** 21 K1
Tettenhall **WV6** 40 A5
Tettenhall Wood **WV6** 40 A6
Tetworth **SG19** 33 F3
Teuchan **AB42** 91 J1
Teversal **NG17** 51 G6
Teversham **CB1** 33 H3
Teviothead **TD9** 69 K3
Tewel **AB39** 91 G6
Tewin **AL6** 33 F7
Tewkesbury **GL20** 29 H5
Teynham **ME9** 25 F5
Thackley **BD10** 57 G6
Thainston **AB30** 90 E7
Thainstone **AB51** 91 F3
Thakeham **RH20** 12 E5
Thame **OX9** 22 A1
Thames Ditton **KT7** 22 E5
Thames Haven **SS17** 24 D3
Thamesmead **SE28** 23 H3
Thanington **CT1** 15 G2
Thankerton **ML12** 75 H7
Tharston **NR15** 45 F6
Thatcham **RG18** 21 J5
Thatto Heath **WA9** 48 E3
Thaxted **CM6** 33 K5
The Apes Hall **CB6** 43 J6
The Bage **HR3** 28 B4
The Balloch **PH7** 81 K6
The Banking **AB51** 91 F1
The Bar **RH13** 12 E4
The Birks **AB32** 91 F4
The Bog **SY5** 38 C6
The Bourne **GU9** 22 B7
The Bratch **WV5** 40 A6
The Broad **HR6** 28 D2
The Bryn **NP7** 19 G1
The Burf **DY13** 29 H2
The Burn **DD9** 90 D7
The Butts **BA11** 20 A7
The Camp **GL6** 20 C1
The Chequer **SY13** 38 D1
The City, *Bucks.* **HP14** 22 A2
The City, *Suff.* **NR34** 45 H7
The Common, *Wilts.* **SP5** 10 D1
The Common, *Wilts.* **SN15** 20 D3
The Craigs **IV24** 96 B2
The Cronk **IM7** 54 C4
The Delves **WS5** 40 C6
The Den **KA24** 74 B5
The Dicker **BN27** 13 J6
The Down **WV16** 39 F6
The Drums **DD8** 82 E1
The Eaves **GL15** 19 K1
The Flatt **CA6** 70 A6
The Folly **AL4** 32 E7
The Forge **HR5** 28 C3
The Forstal, *E.Suss.* **TN3** 13 J3
The Forstal, *Kent* **TN25** 15 F4
The Grange, *Lincs.* **LN13** 53 J5
The Grange, *Shrop.* **SY12** 38 C2
The Grange, *Surr.* **RH9** 23 G7
The Green, *Arg. & B.* **PA77** 78 A3
The Green, *Cumb.* **LA18** 54 E1
The Green, *Essex* **CM8** 34 B7
The Green, *Flints.* **CH7** 48 B6
The Green, *Wilts.* **SP3** 9 H1
The Grove **WR8** 29 H4
The Haven **RH14** 12 D3
The Headland **TS24** 63 G3
The Heath **ST14** 40 C2
The Herberts **CF71** 18 C4
The Hermitage **KT20** 23 F6
The Hill **LA18** 54 E1
The Holme **HG3** 57 H4
The Howe **IM9** 54 A7
The Isle **SY4** 38 D4
The Laurels **NR14** 45 H6
The Leacon **TN26** 14 E4
The Lee **HP16** 22 B1
The Leigh **GL19** 29 H6
The Lhen **IM7** 54 C3
The Lodge **PA24** 73 K1
The Marsh **SY5** 38 C6
The Moor, *E.Suss.* **TN35** 14 D6
The Moor, *Kent* **TN18** 14 C5
The Mumbles **SA3** 17 K6
The Murray **G75** 74 E5
The Mythe **GL20** 29 H5
The Narth **NP25** 19 J1
The Neuk **AB31** 91 F5
The Node **SG4** 33 F7
The Oval **BA2** 20 A5
The Polchar **PH22** 89 G4
The Quarter **TN27** 14 D3
The Reddings **GL51** 29 J6
The Rhos **SA62** 16 D3
The Rookery **ST7** 49 H7
The Rowe **ST5** 40 A2
The Sale **DE13** 40 D4
The Sands **GU10** 22 B7
The Shoe **SN14** 20 B4
The Slade **RG7** 21 J4
The Smithies **WV16** 39 F6
The Stocks **TN30** 14 E5
The Swillett **WD3** 22 D2
The Thrift **SG8** 33 G5
The Vauld **HR1** 28 E4
The Wern **LL14** 48 B7
The Wyke **TF11** 39 G5
Theakston **DL8** 57 J1
Thealby **DN15** 52 B1
Theale, *Som.* **BS28** 19 H7
Theale, *W.Berks.* **RG7** 21 K4
Thearne **HU17** 59 G6
Theberton **IP16** 35 J2
Thedden Grange **GU34** 11 H1
Theddingworth **LE17** 41 J7
Theddlethorpe All Saints **LN12** 53 H4
Theddlethorpe St. Helen **LN12** 53 H4
Thelbridge Barton **EX17** 7 F4
Thelbridge Cross **EX17** 7 F4
Thelnetham **IP22** 34 E1
Thelveton **IP21** 45 F7
Thelwall **WA4** 49 F4
Themelthorpe **NR20** 44 E3
Thenford **OX17** 31 G4
Therfield **SG8** 33 G5
Thetford, *Lincs.* **PE6** 42 E4
Thetford, *Norf.* **IP24** 44 C7
Thethwaite **CA5** 60 E2
Theydon Bois **CM16** 23 H2
Theydon Garnon **CM16** 23 H2
Theydon Mount **CM16** 23 H2
Thickwood **SN14** 20 B4
Thimbleby, *Lincs.* **LN9** 53 F6
Thimbleby, *N.Yorks.* **DL6** 63 F7
Thingley **SN13** 20 B5
Thirkleby **YO7** 57 K2
Thirlby **YO7** 57 K1
Thirlestane **TD2** 76 D6
Thirn **HG4** 57 H1
Thirsk **YO7** 57 K1
Thirston New Houses **NE65** 71 G4
Thirtleby **HU11** 59 H6
Thistleton, *Lancs.* **PR4** 55 H6
Thistleton, *Rut.* **LE15** 42 C4
Thistley Green **IP28** 33 K1
Thixendale **YO17** 58 E3
Thockrington **NE48** 70 E6
Tholomas Drove **PE13** 43 G5
Tholthorpe **YO61** 57 K3
Thomas Chapel **SA68** 16 E4
Thomas Close **CA11** 60 F2
Thomastown **AB54** 90 D1
Thompson **IP24** 44 D6
Thomshill **IV30** 97 K6
Thong **DA12** 24 C4
Thongsbridge **HD9** 50 D2
Thoralby **DL8** 57 F1
Thoresby **NG22** 51 J5
Thoresthorpe **LN13** 53 H5
Thoresway **LN8** 52 E3
Thorganby, *Lincs.* **DN37** 53 F3
Thorganby, *N.Yorks.* **YO19** 58 C5
Thorgill **YO18** 63 J7
Thorington **IP19** 35 J1
Thorington Street **CO6** 34 E5
Thorley **CM23** 33 H7
Thorley Houses **CM23** 33 H6
Thorley Street, *Herts.* **CM23** 33 H7
Thorley Street, *I.o.W.* **PO41** 10 E6
Thormanby **YO61** 57 K2
Thornaby-on-Tees **TS17** 63 F5
Thornage **NR25** 44 E2
Thornborough, *Bucks.* **MK18** 31 J5
Thornborough, *N.Yorks.* **DL8** 57 H2
Thornbury, *Devon* **EX22** 6 B5
Thornbury, *Here.* **HR7** 29 F3
Thornbury, *S.Glos.* **BS35** 19 K2
Thornbury, *W.Yorks.* **BD3** 57 G6
Thornby **NN6** 31 H1
Thorncliff **HD8** 50 E1
Thorncliffe **ST13** 50 C7
Thorncombe **TA20** 8 C4
Thorncombe Street **GU5** 22 D7
Thorncote Green **SG19** 32 E4
Thorncross **PO30** 11 F6
Thorndon **IP23** 35 F2
Thorndon Cross **EX20** 6 D6
Thorne **DN8** 51 J1
Thorne St. Margaret **TA21** 7 J3
Thorner **LS14** 57 J6
Thorney, *Bucks.* **SL0** 22 D4
Thorney, *Notts.* **NG23** 52 B5
Thorney, *Peter.* **PE6** 43 F5
Thorney, *Som.* **TA10** 8 D2
Thorney Close **SR4** 62 E1
Thorney Hill **BH23** 10 D5
Thornfalcon **TA3** 8 B2
Thornford **DT9** 9 F3
Thorngrafton **NE47** 70 C7
Thorngrove **TA7** 8 C1
Thorngumbald **HU12** 59 J7
Thornham **PE36** 44 B1
Thornham Magna **IP23** 35 F1
Thornham Parva **IP23** 35 F1
Thornhaugh **PE8** 42 D5
Thornhill, *Cardiff* **CF83** 18 E3
Thornhill, *Cumb.* **CA22** 60 B6
Thornhill, *D. & G.* **DG3** 68 D4
Thornhill, *Derbys.* **S33** 50 D4
Thornhill, *S'ham.* **SO19** 11 F3
Thornhill, *Stir.* **FK8** 81 H7
Thornhill, *W.Yorks.* **WF12** 50 E1
Thornhill Lees **WF12** 50 E1
Thornholme **YO25** 59 H3
Thornicombe **DT11** 9 H4
Thornley, *Dur.* **DH6** 62 E3
Thornley, *Dur.* **DL13** 62 C3
Thornley Gate **NE47** 61 K1
Thornliebank **G46** 74 D5
Thornroan **AB41** 91 G1
Thorns **CB8** 34 B3
Thorns Green **WA15** 49 G4
Thornsett **SK22** 50 C4
Thornthwaite, *Cumb.* **CA12** 60 D4
Thornthwaite, *N.Yorks.* **HG3** 57 G4
Thornton, *Angus* **DD8** 82 E3
Thornton, *Bucks.* **MK17** 31 J5
Thornton, *E.Riding* **YO42** 58 D5
Thornton, *Fife* **KY1** 76 A1
Thornton, *Lancs.* **FY5** 55 G5
Thornton, *Leics.* **LE67** 41 G5
Thornton, *Lincs.* **LN9** 53 F6
Thornton, *Mersey.* **L23** 48 C2
Thornton, *Middbro.* **TS8** 63 F5
Thornton, *Northumb.* **TD15** 77 H6
Thornton, *P. & K.* **PH1** 82 B3
Thornton, *Pembs.* **SA73** 16 C4
Thornton, *W.Yorks.* **BD13** 57 G6
Thornton Bridge **YO61** 57 K2
Thornton Curtis **DN39** 52 D1
Thornton Heath **CR7** 23 G5
Thornton Hough **CH63** 48 C4
Thornton in Lonsdale **LA6** 56 B2
Thornton le Moor **LN7** 52 D3
Thornton Park **TD15** 77 H6
Thornton Rust **DL8** 56 E1
Thornton Steward **HG4** 57 G1
Thornton Watlass **HG4** 57 H1
Thorntonhall **G74** 74 D5
Thornton-in-Craven **BD23** 56 E5
Thornton-le-Beans **DL6** 63 F7
Thornton-le-Clay **YO60** 58 C3
Thornton-le-Dale **YO18** 58 E1
Thornton-le-Moor **DL7** 57 J1
Thornton-le-Moors **CH2** 48 D5
Thornton-le-Street **YO7** 57 K1
Thorntonloch **EH42** 77 F3
Thornwood Common **CM16** 23 H1
Thornyhill **AB30** 90 E7
Thornylee **TD1** 76 C7
Thoroton **NG13** 42 A1
Thorp Arch **LS23** 57 K5
Thorpe, *Derbys.* **DE6** 50 D7
Thorpe, *E.Riding* **YO25** 59 F5
Thorpe, *Lincs.* **LN12** 53 H4
Thorpe, *N.Yorks.* **BD23** 57 F3
Thorpe, *Norf.* **NR14** 45 J6
Thorpe, *Notts.* **NG23** 51 K7
Thorpe, *Surr.* **TW20** 22 D5
Thorpe Abbotts **IP21** 45 F7
Thorpe Acre **LE11** 41 H4
Thorpe Arnold **LE14** 42 A3
Thorpe Audlin **WF8** 51 G1
Thorpe Bassett **YO17** 58 E2
Thorpe Bay **SS1** 25 F3
Thorpe by Water **LE15** 42 B6
Thorpe Constantine **B79** 40 E5
Thorpe Culvert **PE24** 53 H6
Thorpe End **NR13** 45 G4
Thorpe Green, *Essex* **CO16** 35 F6
Thorpe Green, *Lancs.* **PR6** 55 J7
Thorpe Green, *Suff.* **IP30** 34 D3
Thorpe Hall **YO62** 58 B2
Thorpe Hesley **S61** 51 F3
Thorpe in Balne **DN6** 51 H1
Thorpe in the Fallows **LN1** 52 C4
Thorpe Langton **LE16** 42 A6
Thorpe Larches **TS21** 62 E4
Thorpe le Street **YO42** 58 E5
Thorpe Malsor **NN14** 32 B1
Thorpe Mandeville **OX17** 31 G4
Thorpe Market **NR11** 45 G2
Thorpe Morieux **IP30** 34 D3
Thorpe on the Hill, *Lincs.* **LN6** 52 C6
Thorpe on the Hill, *W.Yorks.* **WF3** 57 J7
Thorpe Row **IP25** 44 D5
Thorpe St. Andrew **NR7** 45 G5
Thorpe St. Peter **PE24** 53 H6
Thorpe Salvin **S80** 51 H4
Thorpe Satchville **LE14** 42 A4
Thorpe Street **IP22** 34 E1

Place	Page	Grid
Thorpe Thewles TS21	63	F4
Thorpe Tilney Dales LN4	52	E7
Thorpe Underwood, N.Yorks. YO26	57	K4
Thorpe Underwood, Northants. NN6	42	A7
Thorpe Waterville NN14	42	D7
Thorpe Willoughby YO8	58	B6
Thorpefield YO7	57	K2
Thorpe-le-Soken CO16	35	F6
Thorpeness IP16	35	J2
Thorpland PE33	44	A5
Thorrington CO7	34	E6
Thorverton EX5	7	H5
Thrandeston IP21	35	F1
Thrapston NN14	32	C1
Threapland BD23	56	E3
Threapwood SY14	38	D1
Threapwood Head ST10	40	C1
Three Ashes BA3	19	K7
Three Bridges RH10	13	F3
Three Burrows TR4	2	E4
Three Chimneys TN27	14	D4
Three Cocks (Aberllynfi) LD3	28	A5
Three Crosses SA4	17	J5
Three Cups Corner TN21	13	K4
Three Hammers PL15	4	C2
Three Holes PE14	43	J5
Three Leg Cross TN5	13	K3
Three Legged Cross BH21	10	B4
Three Mile Cross RG7	22	A5
Three Oaks TN35	14	D6
Threehammer Common NR12	45	H4
Threekingham NG34	42	D2
Threemilestone TR3	2	E4
Threlkeld CA12	60	E4
Threshfield BD23	56	E3
Threxton Hill IP25	44	C5
Thriepley DD2	82	K4
Thringarth DL12	62	A4
Thringstone LE67	41	G4
Thrintoft DL7	62	E7
Thriplow SG8	33	H4
Throapham S25	51	H4
Throckenholt PE12	43	G5
Throcking SG9	33	G5
Throckley NE15	71	G7
Throckmorton WR10	29	J4
Throop DT2	9	H5
Throphill NE61	71	F1
Thropton NE65	71	F3
Througham GL6	20	C1
Throwleigh EX20	6	E6
Throwley ME13	14	E2
Throws CM6	33	K6
Thrumpton, Notts. NG11	41	H2
Thrumpton, Notts. DN22	51	K5
Thrumster KW1	105	J4
Thrunton NE66	71	F2
Thrupp, Glos. GL5	20	B1
Thrupp, Oxon. OX5	31	F7
Thrupp, Oxon. SN7	21	F2
Thruscross HG3	57	G4
Thrushelton EX20	6	C7
Thrussington LE7	41	J4
Thruxton, Hants. SP11	21	F7
Thruxton, Here. HR2	28	D5
Thrybergh S65	51	G3
Thulston DE72	41	G2
Thunder Bridge HD8	50	D1
Thundergay KA27	73	G6
Thundersley SS7	24	E3
Thunderton AB42	99	J6
Thundridge SG12	33	G7
Thurcaston LE7	41	H4
Thurcroft S66	51	G4
Thurdistoft KW14	105	H2
Thurdon EX23	6	A4
Thurgarton, Norf. NR11	45	F2
Thurgarton, Notts. NG14	41	J1
Thurgoland S35	50	E2
Thurlaston, Leics. LE9	41	H6
Thurlaston, Warks. CV23	31	F1
Thurlbear TA3	8	B2
Thurlby, Lincs. PE10	42	E4
Thurlby, Lincs. LN5	52	C6
Thurlby, Lincs. LN13	53	H5
Thurleigh MK44	32	D3
Thurlestone TQ7	5	G6
Thurloxton TA2	8	B1
Thurlstone S36	50	E2
Thurlton NR14	45	J6
Thurlwood ST7	49	H7
Thurmaston LE4	41	J5
Thurnby LE7	41	J5
Thurne NR29	45	J4
Thurnham ME14	14	D2
Thurning, Norf. NR20	44	E3
Thurning, Northants. PE8	42	D7
Thurnscoe S63	51	G2
Thursby CA5	60	E1
Thursden BB10	56	E6
Thursford NR21	44	D2
Thursley GU8	12	C3
Thurso KW14	105	G2
Thurstaston CH61	48	B4
Thurston IP31	34	D2
Thurston Clough OL3	49	J2
Thurstonfield CA5	60	E1
Thurstonland HD4	50	D1
Thurton NR14	45	H5
Thurvaston, Derbys. DE6	40	D2
Thurvaston, Derbys. DE6	40	D2
Thuster KW1	105	H3
Thuxton NR9	44	E5
Thwaite, N.Yorks. DL11	61	K7
Thwaite, Suff. IP23	35	F2
Thwaite Head LA12	60	E7
Thwaite St. Mary NR35	45	H6
Thwaites BD21	57	F5
Thwaites Brow BD21	57	F5
Thwing YO25	59	G2
Tibbermore PH1	82	B5
Tibberton, Glos. GL19	29	G6
Tibberton, Tel. & W. TF10	39	F3
Tibberton, Worcs. WR9	29	J3
Tibbie Shiels Inn TD7	69	H1
Tibenham NR16	45	F6
Tibertich PA31	79	K7
Tibshelf DE55	51	G6
Tibthorpe YO25	59	F4
Ticehurst TN5	13	K3
Tichborne SO24	11	G1
Tickencote PE9	42	C5
Tickenham BS21	19	H4
Tickford End MK16	32	B4
Tickhill DN11	51	H3
Ticklerton SY6	38	D6
Ticknall DE73	41	F3
Tickton HU17	59	G5
Tidbury Green B90	30	C1
Tidcombe SN8	21	F6
Tiddington, Oxon. OX9	21	K1
Tiddington, Warks. CV37	30	D3
Tiddleywink SN14	20	B4
Tidebrook TN5	13	K4
Tideford PL12	4	D5
Tideford Cross PL12	4	D4
Tidenham NP16	19	J2
Tidenham Chase NP16	19	J2
Tideswell SK17	50	D5
Tidmarsh RG8	21	K4
Tidmington CV36	30	D5
Tidpit SP6	10	B3
Tidworth SP9	21	F7
Tiers Cross SA62	16	C3
Tiffield NN12	31	H4
Tifty AB53	99	F6
Tigerton DD9	83	G1
Tigh a' Gearraidh HS6	92	C4
Tighachnoic PA34	79	H3
Tighnablair PH6	81	J6
Tighnabruaich PA21	73	H3
Tighnacomaire PH33	80	A1
Tigley TQ9	5	H4
Tilbrook PE28	32	D2
Tilbury RM18	24	C4
Tilbury Green CO9	34	B4
Tile Hill CV4	30	D1
Tilehurst RG31	21	K4
Tilford GU10	22	B7
Tilgate RH10	13	F3
Tilgate Forest Row RH10	13	F3
Tillathrowie AB54	90	C1
Tilley SY4	38	E3
Tillicoultry FK13	75	H1
Tillingham CM0	25	F1
Tillington, Here. HR4	28	D4
Tillington, W.Suss. GU28	12	C4
Tillington Common HR4	28	D4
Tillyarblet DD9	83	G1
Tillybirloch AB51	90	E4
Tillycairn Castle AB51	90	E3
Tillycorthie AB41	91	H2
Tillydrine AB31	90	E5
Tillyfar AB53	99	G6
Tillyfour AB33	90	D3
Tillyfourie AB51	90	E3
Tillygarmond AB31	90	E5
Tillygreig AB41	91	G2
Tillypronie AB34	90	C4
Tilmanstone CT14	15	J2
Tiln DN22	51	K4
Tilney All Saints PE34	43	J4
Tilney Fen End PE14	43	J4
Tilney High End PE34	43	J4
Tilney St. Lawrence PE34	43	J4
Tilshead SP3	20	D7
Tilstock SY13	38	E2
Tilston SY14	48	D7
Tilstone Fearnall CW6	48	E6
Tilsworth LU7	32	C6
Tilton on the Hill LE7	42	A5
Tiltups End GL6	20	B2
Timberland LN4	52	E7
Timberland Dales LN10	52	E6
Timbersbrook CW12	49	H6
Timberscombe TA24	7	H1
Timble LS21	57	G4
Timperley WA15	49	G4
Timsbury, B. & N.E.Som. BA2	19	K6
Timsbury, Hants. SO51	10	E2
Timsgearraidh HS2	100	C4
Timworth IP31	34	C2
Timworth Green IP31	34	C2
Tincleton DT2	9	G5
Tindale CA8	61	H1
Tindon End CB10	33	K5
Tingewick MK18	31	H5
Tingley WF3	57	H7
Tingrith MK17	32	D5
Tingwall KW17	106	D5
Tinhay PL16	6	B7
Tinney EX22	4	C1
Tinshill LS16	57	H6
Tinsley S9	51	G3
Tinsley Green RH6	13	F3
Tintagel PL34	4	A2
Tintern Parva NP16	19	J1
Tintinhull BA22	8	D3
Tintwistle SK13	50	C3
Tinwald DG1	69	F5
Tinwell PE9	42	D5
Tippacott EX35	7	F1
Tipperty, Aber. AB30	83	H1
Tipperty, Aber. AB41	91	H2
Tips End PE14	43	H6
Tiptoe SO41	10	D5
Tipton DY4	40	B6
Tipton St. John EX10	7	J6
Tiptree CO5	34	C7
Tiptree Heath CO5	34	C7
Tirabad LD4	27	H4
Tirindrish PH34	87	J6
Tirley GL19	29	H6
Tirphil NP24	18	E1
Tir-y-dail SA18	17	K3
Tisbury SP3	9	J2
Tisman's Common RH12	12	D3
Tissington DE6	50	D7
Tister KW12	105	G2
Titchberry EX39	6	A3
Titchfield PO14	11	G4
Titchmarsh NN14	32	D1
Titchwell PE31	44	B1
Tithby NG13	41	J2
Titley HR5	28	C2
Titlington NE66	71	G2
Titmore Green SG4	33	F6
Titsey RH8	23	H6
Titson EX23	6	A5
Tittensor ST12	40	A2
Tittleshall PE32	44	C3
Tiverton, Ches. CW6	48	E6
Tiverton, Devon EX16	7	H4
Tivetshall St. Margaret NR15	45	F7
Tivetshall St. Mary NR15	45	F7
Tivington TA24	7	H1
Tixall ST18	40	B3
Tixover PE9	42	C5
Toab, Ork. KW17	107	E7
Toab, Shet. ZE3	109	F9
Tobermory PA75	79	G2
Toberonochy PA34	79	J7
Tobha Mòr (Homore) HS8	84	C1
Tobson HS2	100	D4
Tocher AB51	90	E1
Tockenham SN4	20	D4
Tockenham Wick SN4	20	D3
Tockholes BB3	56	B7
Tockington BS32	19	K3
Tockwith YO26	57	K4
Todber DT10	9	G2
Toddington, Beds. LU5	32	D6
Toddington, Glos. GL54	30	B5
Todenham GL56	30	D5
Todhills, Angus DD4	83	F4
Todhills, Cumb. CA6	69	J7
Todlachie AB51	90	E3
Todmorden OL14	56	E7
Todwick S26	51	G4
Toft, Cambs. CB3	33	G3
Toft, Lincs. PE10	42	D4
Toft, Shet. ZE2	108	D5
Toft Hill DL14	62	C4
Toft Monks NR34	45	J6
Toft next Newton LN8	52	D4
Toftcarl KW1	105	J4
Toftrees NR21	44	C3
Tofts KW1	105	J2
Toftwood NR19	44	D4
Togston NE65	71	H3
Tokavaig IV46	86	C3
Tokers Green RG4	21	K4
Tolastadh HS2	101	H3
Tolastadh a' Chaolais HS2	100	D4
Tolastadh ur HS2	101	H3
Toll Bar DN5	51	H2
Toll of Birness AB41	91	J1
Tolland TA4	7	K2
Tollard Farnham DT11	9	J3
Tollard Royal SP5	9	J3
Tollcross G32	74	E4
Toller Down Gate DT2	8	E4
Toller Fratrum DT2	8	E5
Toller Porcorum DT2	8	E5
Toller Whelme DT8	8	E4
Tollerton, N.Yorks. YO61	58	B3
Tollerton, Notts. NG12	41	J2
Tollesbury CM9	34	D7
Tollesby TS4	63	G5
Tolleshunt D'Arcy CM9	34	D7
Tolleshunt Knights CM9	34	D7
Tolleshunt Major CM9	34	C7
Tolm (Holm) HS2	101	G4
Tolmachan HS3	100	C7
Tolpuddle DT2	9	G5
Tolvah PH21	89	F5
Tolworth KT6	22	E5
Tom an Fhuadain HS2	101	F6
Tomatin IV13	89	F2
Tombreck IV2	88	D1
Tomchrasky IV63	87	J3
Tomdoun PH35	87	H4
Tomdow IV36	97	H1
Tomich, High. IV4	87	K2
Tomich, High. IV18	96	E4
Tomich, High. IV27	96	D1
Tomintoul AB37	89	J3
Tomnacross IV4	96	C7
Tomnamoon IV36	97	H6
Tomnaven AB54	90	B1
Tomnavoulin AB37	89	K2
Tomvaich PH26	89	H1
Ton Pentre CF41	18	C2
Tonbridge TN9	23	J7
Tondu CF32	18	B3
Tonedale TA21	7	K3
Tonfanau LL36	36	E5
Tong, Kent TN27	14	D3
Tong, Shrop. TF11	39	G5
Tong, W.Yorks. BD4	57	H6
Tong Norton TF11	39	G5
Tong Street BD4	57	G6
Tonge DE73	41	G3
Tongham GU10	22	B7
Tongland DG6	65	G5
Tongue IV27	103	H3
Tongue House IV27	103	H3
Tongwynlais CF15	18	E3
Tonmawr SA12	18	B2
Tonna SA11	18	A2
Tonwell SG12	33	G7
Tonypandy CF40	18	C2
Tonyrefail CF39	18	D3
Toot Baldon OX44	21	J1
Toot Hill CM5	23	J1
Toothill, Hants. SO51	10	E3
Toothill, Swin. SN5	20	E3
Tooting Graveney SW17	23	F4
Top End MK44	32	D2
Top of Hebers M24	49	H2
Topcliffe YO7	57	K2
Topcroft NR35	45	G6
Topcroft Street NR35	45	G6
Toppesfield CO9	34	B5
Toppings BL7	49	G1
Toprow NR16	45	F6
Topsham EX3	7	H7
Topsham Bridge TQ7	5	H5
Torastan PA78	78	D1
Torbain AB37	89	J3
Torbeg, Aber. AB35	90	B5
Torbeg, N.Ayr. KA27	66	D1
Torbothie ML7	75	G5
Torbryan TQ12	5	J4
Torcastle PH33	87	H7
Torcross TQ7	5	J6
Tordarroch IV2	88	D1
Tore IV6	96	D6
Toreduff IV36	97	J5
Toremore, High. PH26	89	J1
Toremore, High. KW6	105	G5
Torfrey PL23	4	B5
Torgyle IV63	87	K3
Torlum HS7	92	C6
Torlundy PH33	87	H7
Tormarton GL9	20	A4
Tormisdale PA47	72	A5
Tormore KA27	73	G7
Tormsdale KW12	105	G3
Tornagrain IV2	96	E6
Tornahaish AB36	89	K4
Tornaveen AB31	90	E4
Torness IV2	88	C2
Toronto DL14	62	C3
Torpenhow CA7	60	D3
Torphichen EH48	75	H3
Torphins AB31	90	E4
Torpoint PL11	4	E5
TORQUAY TQ	5	K4
Torquhan TD1	76	C6
Torr PL8	5	F5
Torran, Arg. & B. PA31	79	K7
Torran, High. IV18	96	E4
Torran, High. IV40	94	B7
Torrance G64	74	E3
Torrance House G75	74	E5
Torrancroy AB36	90	B3
Torre, Som. TA23	7	J1
Torre, Torbay TQ1	5	K4
Torrich IV12	97	F6
Torridon IV22	94	E6
Torrin IV49	86	B2
Torrisdale, Arg. & B. PA28	73	F7
Torrisdale, High. KW14	103	J2
Torrish KW8	104	E7
Torrisholme LA4	55	H3
Torroble IV27	96	C1
Torry, Aber. AB54	98	C6
Torry, Aberdeen AB11	91	H4
Torryburn KY12	75	J2
Torsonce TD1	76	C6
Torterston AB42	99	J6
Torthorwald DG1	69	F6
Tortington BN18	12	C6
Torton DY10	29	H1
Tortworth GL12	20	A2
Torvaig IV51	93	K7
Torver LA21	60	D7
Torwood FK5	75	G2
Torworth DN22	51	J4
Tosberry EX39	6	A3
Toscaig IV54	86	D1
Toseland PE19	33	F2
Tosside BD23	56	C4
Tostarie PA74	78	E3
Tostock IP30	34	D2
Totaig IV55	93	G6
Totamore PA78	78	C2
Tote IV51	93	K7
Tote Hill GU29	12	B4
Totford SO24	11	G1
Totham Hill CM9	34	C7
Tothill LN13	53	H4
Totland PO39	10	E6
Totley S17	51	F5
Totnes TQ9	5	J4
Toton NG9	41	H2
Totronald PA78	78	C2
Totscore IV51	93	J5
Tottenham N17	23	G3
Tottenhill PE33	44	A4
Tottenhill Row PE33	44	A4
Totteridge, Bucks. HP13	22	B2
Totteridge, Gt.Lon. N20	23	F2
Totternhoe LU6	32	C6
Tottington, Gt.Man. BL8	49	G1
Tottington, Norf. IP24	44	C6
Totton SO40	10	E3
Toulton TA4	7	K2
Tournaig IV22	94	E3
Toux AB42	99	H5
Tovil ME15	14	C2
Tow Law DL13	62	C3
Towan Cross TR4	2	E4
Toward PA23	73	K4
Towcester NN12	31	H4
Towednack TR26	2	B5
Tower End PE32	44	A4
Towersey OX9	22	A1
Towie, Aber. AB43	99	G4
Towie, Aber. AB54	90	D2
Towie, Aber. AB33	90	C3
Towiemore AB55	98	B6
Town End, Cambs. PE15	43	H6
Town End, Cumb. LA11	55	H1
Town End, Mersey. WA8	48	D4
Town Green, Lancs. L39	48	D2
Town Green, Norf. NR13	45	H4
Town of Lowton WA3	49	F3
Town Row TN6	13	J3
Town Street IP27	44	B7
Town Yetholm TD5	70	D1
Townend G82	74	C3
Townfield DH8	62	A2
Townhead, D. & G. DG6	65	G6
Townhead, S.Yorks. S36	50	D2
Townhead of Greenlaw DG7	65	H4
Townhill, Fife KY12	75	K2
Townhill, Swan. SA1	17	K5
Towns End RG26	21	J6
Towns Green CW6	49	F6
Townshend TR27	2	C5
Towthorpe, E.Riding YO25	59	F3
Towthorpe, York YO32	58	C4
Towton LS24	57	K6
Towyn LL22	47	H5
Toynton All Saints PE23	53	G6
Toynton Fen Side PE23	53	G6
Toynton St. Peter PE23	53	H6
Toy's Hill TN16	23	H6
Trabboch KA5	67	J1
Traboe TR12	2	E6
Tradespark, High. IV12	97	F6
Tradespark, Ork. KW15	107	D7
Traeth Coch (Red Wharf Bay) LL75	46	D4
Trafford Centre M17	49	G3
Trafford Park M17	49	G3
Trallong LD3	27	J6
Trallwn SA7	17	K5
Tranent EH33	76	C3
Tranmere CH42	48	C4
Trantlebeg KW13	104	D3
Trantlemore KW13	104	D3
Tranwell NE61	71	G5
Trap SA19	17	K3
Trap Street SK11	49	H6
Traprain EH41	76	D3
Trap's Green B94	30	C2
Traquair EH44	76	B7
Trawden BB8	56	E6
Trawsfynydd LL41	37	G2
Trealaw CF40	18	D2
Treales PR4	55	H6
Treardduf LL65	46	A5
Treaslane IV51	93	J6
Tre-Aubrey CF71	18	D4
Trebanog CF39	18	D2
Trebanos SA8	18	A1
Trebarrow EX22	4	C1
Trebartha PL15	4	C3
Trebarvah TR11	2	E5
Trebarwith PL33	4	A2
Trebeath PL15	4	C2
Trebetherick PL27	3	G1
Trebister ZE1	109	D9
Tre-boeth SA5	17	K5
Treborough TA23	7	J2
Trebudannon TR8	3	F2
Trebullett PL15	4	D3
Treburley PL15	4	D3
Treburrick PL27	3	F1
Trebyan PL30	4	A4
Trecastle LD3	27	H6
Trecott EX20	6	E5
Trecrogo PL15	6	B7
Trecwn SA62	16	C1
Trecynon CF44	18	C1
Tredaule PL15	4	C2
Tredavoe TR20	2	B6
Treddiog SA62	16	B2
Tredegar NP22	18	E1
Tredington, Glos. GL20	29	J6
Tredington, Warks. CV36	30	D4
Tredinnick, Cornw. PL27	3	G2
Tredinnick, Cornw. PL14	4	C5
Tredogan CF62	18	D5
Tredomen LD3	28	A5
Tredrissi SA42	16	D1
Tredunnock NP15	19	G2
Tredustan LD3	28	A5
Tredworth GL1	29	H7
Treen, Cornw. TR19	2	A6
Treen, Cornw. TR20	2	B5
Treesmill PL24	4	A5
Treeton S60	51	G4
Trefaldwyn (Montgomery) SY15	38	B6
Trefasser SA64	16	B1
Trefdraeth, I.o.A. LL62	46	C5
Trefdraeth (Newport), Pembs. SA42	16	D1
Trefecca LD3	28	A5
Trefechan CF48	18	D1
Trefeglwys SY17	37	J6
Trefenter SY23	27	F2
Treffgarne SA62	16	C2
Treffynnon (Holywell), Flints. CH8	47	K5

Treffynnon

Name	Code	Page	Grid
Treffynnon, Pembs.	SA62	16	B2
Trefgarn Owen	SA62	16	B2
Trefil	NP22	28	A7
Trefilan	SA48	26	E3
Treflach	SY10	38	B3
Trefnanney	SY22	38	B4
Trefnant	LL16	47	J5
Trefonen	SY10	38	B3
Trefor, Gwyn.	LL54	36	C1
Trefor, I.o.A.	LL65	46	B4
Treforest	CF37	18	D3
Treforest Industrial Estate	CF37	18	E3
Trefriw	LL27	47	F6
Tref-y-clawdd (Knighton)	LD7	28	B1
Trefynwy (Monmouth)	NP25	28	E7
Tregadillett	PL15	4	C2
Tregaian	LL77	46	C5
Tregare	NP15	28	D7
Tregarland	PL13	4	C5
Tregarne	TR12	2	E6
Tregaron	SY25	27	F3
Tregarth	LL57	46	E6
Tregaswith	TR8	3	F2
Tregavethan	TR4	2	E4
Tregear	TR2	3	F3
Tregeare	PL15	4	C2
Tregeiriog	LL20	38	A2
Tregele	LL67	46	B3
Tregidden	TR12	2	E6
Tregiskey	PL26	4	A6
Treglemais	SA62	16	B2
Tregolds	PL28	3	F1
Tregole	EX23	4	B1
Tregonetha	TR9	3	G2
Tregony	TR2	3	G4
Tregoodwell	PL32	4	B2
Tregoss	PL26	3	G2
Tregowris	TR12	2	E6
Tregoyd	LD3	28	A5
Tregrehan Mills	PL25	4	A5
Tre-groes	SA44	26	D4
Treguff	CF71	18	D4
Tregullon	PL30	4	A4
Tregunnon	PL15	4	C2
Tregurrian	TR8	3	F2
Tregynon	SY16	37	K6
Trehafod	CF37	18	D2
Trehan	PL12	4	E5
Treharris	CF46	18	D2
Treherbert	CF42	18	C2
Tre-hill	CF5	18	D4
Trekenner	PL15	4	D3
Treknow	PL34	4	A2
Trelan	TR12	2	E7
Trelash	PL15	4	B1
Trelassick	TR2	3	F3
Trelawnyd	LL18	47	J5
Trelech	SA33	17	F1
Treleddyd-fawr	SA62	16	A2
Trelewis	CF46	18	C2
Treligga	PL33	4	A2
Trelights	PL29	3	G1
Trelill	PL30	4	A3
Trelissick	TR3	3	F5
Trelleck	NP25	19	J1
Trelleck Grange	NP16	19	H1
Trelogan	CH8	47	K4
Trelowla	PL13	4	C5
Trelystan	SY21	38	B5
Tremadog	LL49	36	E1
Tremail	PL32	4	B2
Tremain	SA43	26	B4
Tremaine	PL15	4	C2
Tremar	PL14	4	C4
Trematon	PL12	4	D5
Tremeirchion	LL17	47	J5
Tremethick Cross	TR20	2	B5
Tremore	PL30	4	A4
Trenance, Cornw.	TR8	3	F2
Trenance, Cornw.	PL27	3	G1
Trenarren	PL26	4	A6
Trench, Tel. & W.	TF2	39	F4
Trench, Wrex.	LL13	38	C2
Trencreek	TR7	3	F2
Trenear	TR13	2	D5
Treneglos	PL15	4	C2
Trenewan	PL13	4	B5
Trengune	EX23	4	B1
Trent	DT9	8	E3
Trent Port	DN21	52	B4
Trent Vale	ST4	40	A1
Trentham	ST4	40	A1
Trentishoe	EX31	6	E1
Trenwheal	TR27	2	D5
Treoes	CF35	18	C4
Treorchy	CF42	18	C2
Treowen	NP11	19	F2
Trequite	PL30	4	A3
Tre'r-ddol	SY20	37	F6
Trerhyngyll	CF71	18	D4
Tre-Rhys	SA43	26	A4
Trerulefoot	PL12	4	D5
Tresaith	SA43	26	B3
Tresco	TR24	2	B1
Trescott	WV6	40	A6
Trescowe	TR20	2	C5
Tresean	TR8	2	E3
Tresham	GL12	20	A2
Treshnish	PA75	78	E3
Tresillian	TR2	3	F4
Tresinney	PL32	4	B2
Tresinwen	SA64	16	B1
Treslea	PL30	4	B4
Tresmeer	PL15	4	C2
Tresowes Green	TR13	2	D6
Tresparrett	PL32	4	B1
Tresparrett Posts	PL32	4	B1
Tressait	PH16	81	K1
Tresta, Shet.	ZE2	108	F3
Tresta, Shet.	ZE2	109	C7
Treswell	DN22	51	K5
Trethewey	TR19	2	A6
Trethomas	CF83	18	E3
Trethurgy	PL26	4	A5
Tretio	SA62	16	A2
Tretire	HR2	28	E6
Tretower	NP8	28	A6
Treuddyn	CH7	48	B7
Trevadlock	PL15	4	C3
Trevalga	PL35	4	A1
Trevalyn	LL12	48	C7
Trevanson	PL27	3	G1
Trevarnon	TR27	2	C5
Trevarrack	TR18	2	B5
Trevarren	TR9	3	G2
Trevarrian	TR8	3	F2
Trevarrick	PL26	3	G4
Tre-vaughan, Carmar.	SA31	17	G2
Trevaughan, Carmar.	SA34	16	E3
Treveighan	PL30	4	A3
Trevellas	TR5	2	D5
Trevelmond	PL14	4	C4
Trevenen	TR13	2	D6
Treverva	TR10	2	E5
Trevescan	TR19	2	A6
Trevethin	NP4	19	F1
Trevigro	PL17	4	D4
Trevine, Arg. & B.	PA35	80	B5
Trevine, Pembs.	SA62	16	B1
Treviscoe	PL26	3	G3
Trevivian	PL32	4	B2
Trevone	PL28	3	F1
Trevor	LL20	38	B1
Trewalder	PL33	4	A2
Trewarmett	PL34	4	A2
Trewarthenick	TR2	3	G4
Trewassa	PL32	4	B2
Trewellard	TR19	2	A5
Trewen, Cornw.	PL15	4	C2
Trewen, Here.	HR9	28	E7
Trewennack	TR13	2	D6
Trewent	PL15	16	D5
Trewern	SY21	38	B4
Trewethern	PL27	4	A3
Trewidland	PL14	4	C5
Trewilym	SA41	26	A4
Trewint, Cornw.	EX23	4	B1
Trewint, Cornw.	PL15	4	C2
Trewithian	TR2	3	F5
Trewoon	PL25	3	G3
Treworga	TR2	3	F4
Treworlas	TR2	3	F5
Trewornan	PL27	3	G1
Treworthal	TR2	3	F5
Tre-wyn	NP7	28	C6
Treyarnon	PL28	3	F1
Treyford	GU29	12	B5
Trezaise	PL26	3	G3
Triangle	HX6	57	F7
Trickett's Cross	BH22	10	B4
Triermain	CA8	70	A7
Trimdon	TS29	62	E3
Trimdon Colliery	TS29	62	E3
Trimdon Grange	TS29	62	E3
Trimingham	NR11	45	G2
Trimley Lower Street	IP11	35	G5
Trimley St. Martin	IP11	35	G5
Trimley St. Mary	IP11	35	G5
Trimpley	DY12	29	G1
Trimsaran	SA17	17	H4
Trimstone	EX34	6	C1
Trinafour	PH18	81	J1
Trinant	NP11	19	F2
Tring	HP23	32	C7
Trinity, Angus	DD9	83	H1
Trinity, Chan.I.	JE3	3	K6
Trinity, Edin.	EH5	76	A3
Trisant	SY23	27	G1
Triscombe, Som.	TA24	7	H2
Triscombe, Som.	TA4	7	K2
Trislaig	PH33	87	G7
Trispen	TR4	3	F3
Tritlington	NE61	71	H4
Trochry	PH8	82	A4
Troedyraur	SA38	26	C4
Troedyrhiw	CF48	18	D1
Trofarth	LL22	47	G5
Trondavoe	ZE2	108	C5
Troon, Cornw.	TR14	2	D5
Troon, S.Ayr.	KA10	74	B7
Trosairidh	HS8	84	C3
Troston	IP31	34	C1
Troswell	PL15	4	C1
Trottick	DD3	83	H4
Trottiscliffe	ME19	24	C5
Trotton	GU31	12	B4
Trough Gate	OL13	56	D7
Troughend	NE19	70	D4
Troustan	PA22	73	J3
Troutbeck, Cumb.	LA23	60	F6
Troutbeck, Cumb.	CA11	60	E4
Troutbeck Bridge	LA23	60	F6
Trow Green	GL15	19	J1
Troway	S21	51	F5
Trowbridge, Cardiff	CF3	19	F3
Trowbridge, Wilts.	BA14	20	B6
Trowell	NG9	41	G2
Trowle Common	BA14	20	B6
Trowley Bottom	AL3	32	D7
Trows	TD5	76	E7
Trowse Newton	NR14	45	G5
Troy	LS18	57	H6
Trudernish	PA42	72	C6
Trudoxhill	BA11	20	A7
Trull	TA3	8	B2
Trumaisgearraidh	HS6	92	D4
Trumpan	IV55	93	H5
Trumpet	HR8	29	F5
Trumpington	CB2	33	H3
Trumps Green	GU25	22	C5
Trunch	NR28	45	G2
Trunnah	FY5	55	G5
TRURO	TR	3	F4
Truscott	PL15	6	B7
Trusham	TQ13	7	G7
Trusley	DE6	40	E2
Trusthorpe	LN12	53	J4
Truthan	TR4	3	F3
Trysull	WV5	40	A6
Tubney	OX13	21	H2
Tuckenhay	TQ9	5	J5
Tuckhill	WV15	39	G7
Tuckingmill	TR14	2	D4
Tuddenham, Suff.	IP6	35	F4
Tuddenham, Suff.	IP28	34	B1
Tudeley	TN11	23	K7
Tudeley Hale	TN11	23	K7
Tudhoe	DL16	62	D3
Tudweiliog	LL53	36	B2
Tuesley	GU7	22	C7
Tuffley	GL4	29	H7
Tufton, Hants.	RG28	21	H7
Tufton, Pembs.	SA63	16	D2
Tugby	LE7	42	A5
Tugford	SY7	38	E7
Tughall	NE67	71	H1
Tullibody	FK10	75	G1
Tullich, Arg. & B.	PA35	80	B6
Tullich, Arg. & B.	PA34	79	K6
Tullich, High.	IV20	97	F4
Tullich, High.	IV2	88	D2
Tullich, Moray	AB55	98	B6
Tullich, Stir.	FK21	81	G4
Tullich Muir	IV18	96	E4
Tulliemet	PH9	82	B2
Tulloch, Aber.	AB51	91	G1
Tulloch, High.	IV24	96	D2
Tulloch, Moray	IV36	97	H6
Tullochgorm	PA32	73	H1
Tullochgribban High	PH26	89	G2
Tullochvenus	AB31	90	D4
Tulloes	DD8	83	G3
Tullybannocher	PH6	81	J5
Tullybelton	PH1	82	B4
Tullyfergus	PH11	82	D3
Tullymurdoch	PH11	82	C2
Tullynessle	AB33	90	D3
Tulse Hill	SE21	23	G4
Tumble (Y Tymbl)	SA14	17	J3
Tumby	PE22	53	F7
Tumby Woodside	PE22	53	F7
Tummel Bridge	PH16	81	J2
TUNBRIDGE WELLS	TN	13	J3
Tundergarth Mains	DG11	69	G5
Tunga	HS2	101	G4
Tungate	NR28	45	G3
Tunley	BA2	19	K6
Tunstall, E.Riding	HU12	59	K6
Tunstall, Kent	ME10	24	E5
Tunstall, Lancs.	LA6	56	B2
Tunstall, N.Yorks.	DL10	62	D7
Tunstall, Norf.	NR13	45	J5
Tunstall, Stoke	ST6	49	H7
Tunstall, Suff.	IP12	35	H3
Tunstall, T. & W.	SR2	62	E1
Tunstead, Gt.Man.	OL3	50	C2
Tunstead, Norf.	NR12	45	H3
Tunstead Milton	SK23	50	C4
Tunworth	RG25	21	K7
Tupholme	LN3	52	E6
Tupsley	HR1	28	E5
Tupton	S42	51	F6
Tur Langton	LE8	42	A6
Turbiskill	PA31	73	F2
Turclossie	AB43	99	G5
Turgis Green	RG27	21	K6
Turin	DD8	83	G2
Turkdean	GL54	30	C7
Turleigh	BA15	20	B5
Turn	BL0	49	H1
Turnastone	HR2	28	C5
Turnberry	KA26	67	G3
Turnchapel	PL9	4	E5
Turnditch	DE56	40	E1
Turner's Green	CV35	30	C2
Turners Hill	RH10	13	G3
Turners Puddle	DT2	9	H5
Turnford	EN10	23	G1
Turnworth	DT11	9	H4
Turret Bridge	PH31	87	K5
Turriff	AB53	99	F6
Turton Bottoms	BL7	49	G1
Turvey	MK43	32	C3
Turville	RG9	22	A2
Turville Heath	RG9	22	A2
Turweston	NN13	31	H5
Tutbury	DE13	40	E3
Tutnall	B60	29	J1
Tutshill	NP16	19	J2
Tuttington	NR11	45	G3
Tutts Clump	RG7	21	J4
Tutwell	PL17	4	D3
Tuxford	NG22	51	K5
Twatt, Ork.	KW17	106	B5
Twatt, Shet.	ZE2	109	C7
Twechar	G65	75	F3
Tweedmouth	TD15	77	H5
Tweedsmuir	ML12	69	F1
Twelve Oaks	TN32	13	K4
Twelveheads	TR4	2	E4
Twemlow Green	CW4	49	G6
Twenty	PE10	42	E3
TWICKENHAM	TW	22	E4
Twigworth	GL2	29	H6
Twineham	RH17	13	F4
Twineham Green	RH17	13	F4
Twinhoe	BA2	20	A6
Twinstead	CO10	34	C5
Twiss Green	WA3	49	F3
Twiston	BB7	56	D5
Twitchen, Devon	EX36	7	F2
Twitchen, Shrop.	SY7	28	C1
Twitton	TN14	23	J6
Twizell House	NE70	71	G1
Two Bridges, Devon	PL20	5	G3
Two Bridges, Glos.	GL14	19	K1
Two Dales	DE4	50	E6
Two Gates	B77	40	E5
Two Mills	CH1	48	C5
Twycross	CV9	41	F5
Twyford, Bucks.	MK18	31	H6
Twyford, Derbs.	DE73	41	F3
Twyford, Dorset	SP7	9	H3
Twyford, Hants.	SO21	11	F2
Twyford, Leics.	LE14	42	A4
Twyford, Norf.	NR20	44	E3
Twyford, Oxon.	OX17	31	F5
Twyford, W'ham	RG10	22	A4
Twyford Common	HR2	28	E5
Twyn Shôn-Ifan	CF82	18	E2
Twynholm	DG6	65	G5
Twyning	GL20	29	H5
Twynllanan	SA19	27	G6
Twyn-yr-odyn	CF5	18	E4
Twyn-y-Sheriff	NP15	19	H1
Twywell	NN14	32	C1
Tyberton	HR2	28	C5
Tycroes	SA18	17	K3
Tycrwyn	SY22	38	A4
Tydd Gote	PE13	43	H4
Tydd St. Giles	PE13	43	H4
Tydd St. Mary	PE13	43	H4
Tyddewi (St. David's)	SA62	16	A2
Tye Common	CM12	24	C2
Tye Green, Essex	CM77	34	B6
Tye Green, Essex	CM22	33	J6
Tye Green, Essex	CM1	33	K7
Tye Green, Essex	CM18	23	H1
Tyersal	BD4	57	G6
Ty-hen	LL53	36	A2
Tyldesley	M29	49	F2
Tyle-garw	CF72	18	D3
Tyler Hill	CT2	25	H5
Tylers Green, Bucks.	HP10	22	C2
Tyler's Green, Essex	CM16	23	J1
Tylorstown	CF43	18	D2
Tylwch	LD6	27	J1
Ty-Mawr, Conwy	LL21	37	J1
Ty-mawr, Denb.	LL21	38	A1
Ty-nant, Conwy	LL21	37	J1
Ty-nant, Gwyn.	LL23	37	J3
Tyndrum	FK20	80	E4
Tyneham	BH20	9	H6
Tynehead	EH37	76	B5
Tynemouth	NE30	71	J7
Tynewydd	CF42	18	C2
Tyninghame	EH42	76	E3
Tynron	DG3	68	D4
Tyntesfield	BS48	19	J4
Tyn-y-cefn	LL21	37	K1
Tyn-y-cwm	SY18	37	H7
Tyn-y-ffridd	SY10	38	A2
Tyn-y-garn	CF31	18	B3
Tyn-y-Gongl	LL74	46	D4
Tynygraig, Cere.	SY25	27	F2
Tyn-y-graig, Powys	LD2	27	K4
Ty'n-y-groes	LL32	47	F5
Tyrie	AB43	99	H4
Tyringham	MK16	32	B4
Tyseley	B11	40	D7
Tythegston	CF32	18	B4
Tytherington, Ches.	SK10	49	J5
Tytherington, S.Glos.	GL12	19	K3
Tytherington, Som.	BA11	20	A7
Tytherington, Wilts.	BA12	20	C7
Tytherton Lucas	SN15	20	C4
Tyttenhanger	AL4	22	E1
Ty-uchaf	SY10	37	J3
Tywardreath	PL24	4	A5
Tywardreath Highway	PL24	4	A5
Tywyn	LL36	36	E5

U

Name	Code	Page	Grid
Uachdar	HS7	92	D6
Uags	IV54	86	D1
Ubberley	ST2	40	B1
Ubbeston Green	IP19	35	H1
Ubley	BS40	19	J6
Uckerby	DL10	62	D6
Uckfield	TN22	13	H4
Uckinghall	GL20	29	H5
Uckington	GL51	29	J6
Uddingston	G71	74	E4
Uddington	ML11	75	G7
Udimore	TN31	14	D6
Udley	BS40	19	H5
Udny Green	AB41	91	G2
Udny Station	AB41	91	H2
Udston	ML3	75	F5
Udstonhead	ML10	75	F6
Uffcott	SN4	20	E4
Uffculme	EX15	7	J4
Uffington, Lincs.	PE9	42	D5
Uffington, Oxon.	SN7	21	G3
Uffington, Shrop.	SY4	38	E4
Ufford, Peter.	PE9	42	D5
Ufford, Suff.	IP13	35	G3
Ufton	CV33	30	E2
Ufton Green	RG7	21	K5
Ufton Nervet	RG7	21	K5
Ugborough	PL21	5	G5
Ugford	SP2	10	B1
Uggeshall	NR34	45	J7
Ugglebarnby	YO22	63	K6
Ugley	CM22	33	J6
Ugley Green	CM22	33	J6
Ugthorpe	YO21	63	J5
Uibhist a Deas (South Uist)	HS8	84	C1
Uibhist a Tuath (North Uist)	HS6	92	D4
Uidh	HS9	84	B5
Uig, Arg. & B.	PA78	78	C2
Uig, Arg. & B.	PA23	73	K2
Uig, High.	IV51	93	J5
Uig, High.	IV55	93	G6
Uigen	HS2	100	C4
Uiginish	IV55	93	H7
Uigshader	IV51	93	K7
Uisgebhagh (Uiskevagh)	HS7	92	D6
Uisken	PA67	78	E6
Uiskevagh (Uisgebhagh)	HS7	92	D6
Ulbster	KW2	105	J4
Ulcat Row	CA11	60	F4
Ulceby, Lincs.	LN13	53	H5
Ulceby, N.Lincs.	DN39	52	E1
Ulceby Cross	LN13	53	H5
Ulceby Skitter	DN39	52	E1
Ulcombe	ME17	14	D3
Uldale	CA7	60	D3
Uldale House	CA17	61	J7
Uley	GL11	20	A2
Ulgham	NE61	71	H4
Ullapool	IV26	95	H2
Ullenhall	B95	30	C2
Ullenwood	GL53	29	J7
Ulleskelf	LS24	58	B6
Ullesthorpe	LE17	41	H7
Ulley	S26	51	G4
Ullingswick	HR1	28	E4
Ullinish	IV56	85	J1
Ullock	CA14	60	B4
Ulpha, Cumb.	LA20	60	C7
Ulpha, Cumb.	LA11	55	H1
Ulrome	YO25	59	H4
Ulsta	ZE2	108	D4
Ulting	CM9	24	E1
Uluvalt	PA70	79	G4
Ulva	PA73	79	F4
Ulverston	LA12	55	F2
Ulwell	BH19	10	B6
Ulzieside	DG4	68	C3
Umberleigh	EX37	6	E3
Unapool	IV27	102	E5
Underbarrow	LA8	61	F7
Undercliffe	BD2	57	G6
Underhill	EN5	23	F2
Underhoull	ZE2	108	E2
Underling Green	TN12	14	C3
Underriver	TN15	23	J6
Underwood, Newport	NP18	19	G3
Underwood, Notts.	NG16	51	G7
Underwood, Plym.	PL7	5	F5
Undley	IP27	44	A7
Undy	NP26	19	H3
Ungisiadar	HS2	100	D5
Unifirth	ZE2	109	B7
Union Croft	AB39	91	G5
Union Mills	IM4	54	C6
Union Street	TN5	14	C4
Unst	ZE2	108	F1
Unstone	S18	51	F5
Unstone Green	S18	51	F5
Unsworth	BL9	49	H2
Unthank, Cumb.	CA11	61	F3
Unthank, Derbys.	S18	51	F5
Up Cerne	DT2	9	F4
Up Exe	EX5	7	H5
Up Hatherley	GL51	29	J6
Up Holland	WN8	48	E2
Up Marden	PO18	11	J3
Up Mudford	BA21	8	E3
Up Nately	RG27	21	K6
Up Somborne	SO20	10	E1
Up Sydling	DT2	9	F4
Upavon	SN9	20	E6
Upchurch	ME9	24	E5
Upcott, Devon	EX21	6	C6
Upcott, Devon	EX31	6	D2
Upcott, Here.	HR3	28	C3
Upcott, Som.	TA22	7	H3
Upend	CB8	33	K3
Upgate	NR9	45	F4
Upgate Street, Norf.	NR16	44	E6
Upgate Street, Norf.	NR35	45	G6
Uphall, Dorset	DT2	8	E4
Uphall, W.Loth.	EH52	75	J3
Uphall Station	EH54	75	J4
Upham, Devon	EX17	7	G5
Upham, Hants.	SO32	11	G3
Uphampton, Here.	HR6	28	C2
Uphampton, Worcs.	WR9	29	H2
Uphempston	TQ9	5	J4
Uphill	BS23	19	G6
Uplands, Glos.	GL5	20	B1
Uplands, Swan.	SA2	17	K5
Uplawmoor	G78	74	C5
Upleadon	GL18	29	G6
Upleatham	TS11	63	H5
Uplees	ME13	25	G5
Uploders	DT6	8	E5
Uplowman	EX16	7	J4
Uplyme	DT7	8	C5
Upminster	RM14	23	J3
Uppottery	EX14	8	B4

Upper Affcot SY6 38 D7
Upper Ardroscadale PA20 73 J4
Upper Arley DY12 39 G7
Upper Arncott OX25 31 H7
Upper Astley WV5 38 E4
Upper Aston WV5 40 A6
Upper Astrop OX17 31 G5
Upper Barvas HS2 101 F2
Upper Basildon RG8 21 K4
Upper Bayble
 (Pabail Uarach) HS2 101 H4
Upper Beeding BN44 12 E5
Upper Benefield PE8 42 C7
Upper Bentley B97 29 J2
Upper Berwick SY4 38 D4
Upper Bighouse KW13 104 D3
Upper Boat CF37 18 E3
Upper Boddam AB52 90 E1
Upper Boddington NN11 31 F3
Upper Borth SY24 37 F7
Upper Boyndlie AB43 99 H4
Upper Brailes OX15 30 E5
Upper Breakish IV42 86 C2
Upper Breinton SY4 28 D4
Upper Broadheath WR2 29 H3
Upper Broughton LE14 41 J3
Upper Brynamman SA18 27 G7
Upper Bucklebury RG7 21 J5
Upper Burgate SP6 10 C3
Upper Burnhaugh AB39 91 G5
Upper Caldecote SG18 32 E4
Upper Camster KW3 105 H4
Upper Canada BS24 19 G6
Upper Catesby NN11 31 G3
Upper Catshill B61 29 J1
Upper Chapel LD3 27 K4
Upper Cheddon TA2 8 B2
Upper Chicksgrove SP3 9 J1
Upper Chute SP11 21 F6
Upper Clatford SP11 21 G7
Upper Coberley GL53 29 J7
Upper Colwall WR13 29 G4
Upper Cotton ST10 40 C1
Upper Cound SY5 38 E5
Upper Cumberworth HD8 50 E2
Upper Cwmbran NP44 19 F2
Upper Dallachy IV32 98 B4
Upper Dean PE28 32 D2
Upper Denby HD8 50 E2
Upper Denton CA8 70 B7
Upper Derraid PH26 89 H1
Upper Diabaig IV22 94 E5
Upper Dicker BN27 13 J5
Upper Dovercourt CO12 35 G5
Upper Dunsforth YO26 57 K3
Upper Dunsley HP23 32 C7
Upper Eastern Green CV5 40 E7
Upper Eathie IV11 96 E5
Upper Egleton HR8 29 F4
Upper Elkstone SK17 50 C7
Upper End SK17 50 C5
Upper Enham SP11 21 G7
Upper Farringdon GU34 11 J1
Upper Framilode GL2 29 G7
Upper Froyle GU34 22 A7
Upper Gills KW1 105 J1
Upper Glendessarry PH34 87 F5
Upper Godney BA5 19 H7
Upper Gornal DY3 40 B6
Upper Gravenhurst MK45 32 E5
Upper Green, Essex CB11 33 H5
Upper Green, Essex CB10 33 J5
Upper Green, Mon. NP7 28 C7
Upper Green, W.Berks.
 RG17 21 G5
Upper Grove Common
 HR9 28 E6
Upper Gylen PA34 79 K5
Upper Hackney DE4 50 E6
Upper Halliford TW17 22 D5
Upper Halling ME2 24 C5
Upper Hambleton LE15 42 A5
Upper Harbledown CT2 15 G2
Upper Hardres Court CT4 15 G2
Upper Hartfield TN7 13 H3
Upper Hatton ST21 40 A2
Upper Hawkhillock AB42 91 J1
Upper Hayesden TN11 23 J7
Upper Hayton SY8 38 E7
Upper Heath SY7 38 E7
Upper Heaton HD5 50 D1
Upper Hellesdon NR3 45 G4
Upper Helmsley YO41 58 C4
Upper Hengoed SY10 38 B2
Upper Hergest HR5 28 B3
Upper Heyford,
 Northants. NN7 31 H3
Upper Heyford, Oxon.
 OX25 31 F6
Upper Hill, Here. HR6 28 D3
Upper Hill, S.Glos. GL13 19 K2
Upper Horsebridge BN27 13 J5
Upper Howsell WR14 29 G4
Upper Hulme ST13 50 C6
Upper Inglesham SN6 21 F2
Upper Kilchattan PA61 72 B1
Upper Killay SA2 17 J5
Upper Knockando AB38 97 J7
Upper Lambourn RG17 21 G3
Upper Langford BS40 19 H6
Upper Langwith NG20 51 H6
Upper Largo KY8 83 F7
Upper Leigh ST10 40 C2
Upper Ley GL14 29 G7
Upper Llandwrog
 (Siop y Fron) LL54 46 D7
Upper Loads S42 51 F6
Upper Lochton AB31 90 E5
Upper Longdon WS15 40 C4
Upper Longwood SY5 39 F5
Upper Ludstone WV5 40 A6

Upper Lybster KW3 105 H5
Upper Lydbrook GL17 29 F7
Upper Lyde HR4 28 D4
Upper Lye HR6 28 C2
Upper Maes-coed HR2 28 C5
Upper Midhope S36 50 E3
Upper Milovaig IV55 93 G7
Upper Milton OX7 30 D7
Upper Minety SN16 20 D2
Upper Moor WR10 29 J4
Upper Morton BS35 19 K2
Upper Muirskie AB12 91 G5
Upper Nash SA71 16 D4
Upper Newbold S41 51 F5
Upper North Dean HP14 22 B2
Upper Norwood SE19 23 G4
Upper Obney PH1 82 B4
Upper Oddington GL56 30 D6
Upper Ollach IV51 86 B1
Upper Padley S32 50 E5
Upper Pennington SO41 10 D5
Upper Pollicott HP18 31 J7
Upper Poppleton YO26 58 B4
Upper Quinton CV37 30 C4
Upper Ratley SO51 10 E2
Upper Ridinghill AB43 99 J5
Upper Rissington GL54 30 D6
Upper Rochford WR15 29 F2
Upper Sanday KW17 107 E7
Upper Sapey WR6 29 F2
Upper Scolton SA62 16 C2
Upper Seagry SN15 20 C3
Upper Shelton MK43 32 C4
Upper Sheringham NR26 45 F1
Upper Shuckburgh NN11 31 F2
Upper Siddington GL7 20 D2
Upper Skelmorlie PA17 74 A4
Upper Slaughter GL54 30 C6
Upper Sonachan PA33 80 B5
Upper Soudley GL14 29 F7
Upper Staploe PE19 32 E3
Upper Stoke NR14 45 G5
Upper Stondon SG16 32 E5
Upper Stowe NN7 31 H3
Upper Street, Hants. SP6 10 C3
Upper Street, Norf. NR12 45 H4
Upper Street, Norf. IP21 35 F1
Upper Street, Suff. IP9 35 F5
Upper Street, Suff. IP6 35 F3
Upper Strensham WR8 29 J5
Upper Sundon LU5 32 D6
Upper Swanmore SO32 11 G3
Upper Swell GL54 30 C6
Upper Tean ST10 40 C2
Upper Thurnham LA2 55 H4
Upper Tillyrie KY13 82 C7
Upper Tooting SW17 23 F4

BS40

Upper Tysoe CV35 30 E4
Upper Upham SN8 21 F4
Upper Upnor ME2 24 D4
Upper Victoria DD7 83 G4
Upper Vobster BA3 20 A7
Upper Wardington OX17 31 F4
Upper Waterhay SN6 20 D2
Upper Weald MK19 32 B5
Upper Weedon NN7 31 H3
Upper Welson HR3 28 B3
Upper Weston BA1 20 A5
Upper Whiston S60 51 G4
Upper Wick WR2 29 H3
Upper Wield SO24 11 H1
Upper Winchendon (Over
 Winchendon) HP18 31 J7
Upper Witton B23 40 C6
Upper Woodford SP4 10 C1
Upper Woolhampton RG7 21 J5
Upper Wootton RG26 21 J6
Upper Wraxall SN14 20 B4
Upper Wyche WR13 29 G4
Upperby CA2 60 F1
Uppermill OL3 49 J2
Upperthong HD9 50 D2
Upperton GU28 12 C4
Uppertown, Derbys. S45 51 F6
Uppertown, Ork. KW1 105 J1
Uppingham LE15 42 B5
Uppington TF6 38 E5
Upsall YO7 57 K1
Upsettlington TD15 77 G6
Upshire EN9 23 H1
Upstreet CT3 25 J5
Upthorpe IP31 34 D1
Upton, Bucks. HP17 31 J7
Upton, Cambs. PE28 32 E1
Upton, Ches. CH2 48 D6
Upton, Cornw. PL14 4 C3
Upton, Cornw. EX23 6 A5
Upton, Devon EX14 7 J5
Upton, Devon TQ7 5 H6
Upton, Dorset BH16 9 G6
Upton, Dorset DT2 9 G6
Upton, E.Riding YO25 59 H4
Upton, Hants. SP11 21 G6
Upton, Hants. SO16 10 E3
Upton, Leics. CV13 41 F6
Upton, Lincs. DN21 52 B4
Upton, Mersey. CH49 48 B4
Upton, Norf. NR13 45 H4
Upton, Northants. NN5 31 J2
Upton, Notts. DN22 51 K5
Upton, Notts. NG23 51 K7
Upton, Oxon. OX11 21 J3
Upton, Oxon. OX18 30 D7
Upton, Pembs. SA72 16 D4
Upton, Peter. PE5 42 E5

Upton, Slo. SL1 22 C4
Upton, Som. TA4 7 H3
Upton, Som. TA10 8 D2
Upton, W.Yorks. WF9 51 G1
Upton, Wilts. SP3 9 H1
Upton Bishop HR9 29 F6
Upton Cheyney BS30 19 K5
Upton Cressett WV16 39 F6
Upton Crews HR9 29 F6
Upton Cross PL14 4 C3
Upton End SG5 32 E5
Upton Grey RG25 21 K7
Upton Hellions EX17 7 G5
Upton Lovell BA12 20 C7
Upton Magna SY4 38 E4
Upton Noble BA4 9 G1
Upton Park E13 23 H3
Upton Pyne EX5 7 H6
Upton St. Leonards GL4 29 H7
Upton Scudamore BA12 20 B7
Upton Snodsbury WR7 29 J3
Upton upon Severn WR8 29 H4
Upton Warren B61 29 J2
Upwaltham GU28 12 C5
Upware CB7 33 J1
Upwell PE14 43 J5
Upwey DT3 9 F6
Upwick Green SG11 33 H6
Upwood PE26 43 F7
Uradale ZE1 109 D9
Urafirth ZE2 108 C5
Urchany IV12 97 F7
Urchfont SN10 20 D6
Urdimarsh HR1 28 E4
Ure ZE2 108 B5
Urgha HS3 93 G2
Urlay Nook TS16 63 F5
Urmston M41 49 G3
Urpeth DH2 62 D1
Urquhart, High. IV7 96 C6
Urquhart, Moray IV30 97 K5
Urra TS9 63 G6
Urray IV6 96 C6
Ushaw Moor DH7 62 D2
Usk NP15 19 G1
Usselby LN8 52 D3
Usworth NE37 62 E1
Utley BD20 57 F5
Uton EX17 7 G6
Utterby LN11 53 G3
Uttoxeter ST14 40 C2
Uwchmynydd LL53 36 A3
Uxbridge UB8 22 D3
Uyeasound ZE2 108 E2
Uzmaston SA62 16 C3

V

Valley (Dyffryn) LL65 46 A5
Valley Truckle PL32 4 B2
Valleyfield, D. & G. DG6 65 G5
Valleyfield, Fife KY12 75 J2
Valsgarth ZE2 108 F1
Vange SS16 24 D3
Vardre SA6 17 K4
Varteg NP4 19 F1
Vatersay (Bhatarsaigh)
 HS9 84 B5
Vatsetter ZE2 108 E4
Vatten IV55 93 H7
Vaul PA77 78 B3
Vaynor CF48 27 K7
Vaynor Park SY21 38 A5
Veaullt HR5 28 A3
Veensgarth ZE2 109 D8
Velindre, Pembs. SA41 16 D1
Velindre, Powys LD3 28 A5
Yellow TA4 7 J2
Veness KW17 106 E5
Venn TQ7 5 H6
Venn Ottery EX11 7 J6
Venngreen EX22 6 B4
Vennington SY5 38 C5
Venny Tedburn EX17 7 G6
Venterdon PL17 4 D3
Ventnor PO38 11 G7
Venton PL7 5 F5
Vernham Dean SP11 21 G6
Vernham Street SP11 21 G6
Vernolds Common SY7 38 D7
Verwood BH31 10 B4
Veryan TR2 3 G5
Veryan Green TR2 3 G4
Vickerstown LA14 54 E3
Victoria PL26 3 G2
Vidlin ZE2 109 D6
Viewfield KW14 105 F2
Viewpark G71 75 F4
Vigo WS9 40 C5
Vigo Village DA13 24 C5
Villavin EX19 6 D4
Vinehall Street TN32 14 C5
Vine's Cross TN21 13 J5
Viney Hill GL15 19 K1
Virginia Water GU25 22 C5
Virginstow EX21 6 B6
Virley CM9 34 D7
Vobster BA3 20 A7
Voe, Shet. ZE2 109 D6
Voe, Shet. ZE2 108 C3
Vowchurch HR2 28 C5
Voy KW16 107 B6
Vron Gate SY5 38 C5

W

Waberthwaite CA18 60 C7
Wackerfield DL2 62 C4
Wacton NR15 45 F6
Wadbister ZE2 109 D8
Wadborough WR8 29 J4

Waddesdon HP18 31 J7
Waddeton TQ9 5 J5
Waddicar L31 48 C3
Waddingham DN21 52 C3
Waddington, Lancs. BB7 56 C5
Waddington, Lincs. LN5 52 C6
Waddingworth LN10 52 E5
Waddon, Devon TQ13 5 J3
Waddon, Gt.Lon. CR0 23 G5
Wadebridge PL27 3 G1
Wadeford TA20 8 C3
Wadenhoe PE8 42 D7
Wadesmill SG12 33 G7
Wadhurst TN5 13 K3
Wadshelf S42 51 F5
Wadsley Bridge S5 51 F3
Wadworth DN11 51 H3
Wadworth Hill HU12 59 J7
Waen, Denb. LL16 47 K6
Waen, Denb. LL16 47 J6
Waen Aberwheeler LL16 47 J6
Waen-fâch SY22 38 B4
Waen-wen LL57 46 D6
Wag KW7 105 F6
Wainfleet All Saints PE24 53 H7
Wainfleet Bank PE24 53 H7
Wainford NR35 45 H6
Waingroves DE5 41 G1
Wainhouse Corner EX23 4 B1
Wainscott ME2 24 D4
Wainstalls HX2 57 F7
Waitby CA17 61 J6
WAKEFIELD WF 57 J7
Wakerley LE15 42 C6
Wakes Colne CO6 34 C6
Walberswick IP18 35 J1
Walberton BN18 12 C6
Walbottle NE15 71 G7
Walcot, Lincs. NG34 42 D2
Walcot, Lincs. LN4 52 E7
Walcot, N.Lincs. DN15 58 E7
Walcot, Shrop. SY7 38 C7
Walcot, Tel. & W. TF6 38 E4
Walcot Green IP22 45 F7
Walcote, Leics. LE17 41 H7
Walcote, Warks. B49 30 C3
Walcott NR12 45 H2
Walcott Dales LN4 52 E7
Walden DL8 57 F1
Walden Head DL8 56 E1
Walden Stubbs DN6 51 H1
Walderslade ME5 24 D5
Walderton PO18 11 J3
Walditch DT6 8 D5
Waldley DE6 40 D2
Waldridge DH2 62 D2
Waldringfield IP12 35 G4
Waldron TN21 13 J5
Wales S26 51 G4
Walesby, Lincs. LN8 52 E3
Walesby, Notts. NG22 51 J5
Waleswood S26 51 G4
Walford, Here. SY7 28 C1
Walford, Here. HR9 28 E6
Walford, Shrop. SY4 38 D3
Walford, Staffs. ST21 40 A2
Walford Heath SY4 38 D4
Walgherton CW5 39 F1
Walgrave NN6 32 B1
Walhampton SO41 10 E5
Walk Mill BB10 56 D6
Walkden M28 49 G2
Walker NE6 71 H7
Walker Fold BB7 56 B5
Walkerburn EH43 76 B7
Walkeringham DN10 51 K3
Walkerith DN21 51 K3
Walkern SG2 33 F6
Walker's Green HR1 28 E4
Walkford BH23 10 D5
Walkhampton PL20 5 F4
Walkingham Hill HG3 57 J3
Walkington HU17 59 F6
Walkwood B97 30 B2
Wall, Cornw. TR27 2 D5
Wall, Northumb. NE46 70 E7
Wall, Staffs. WS14 40 D5
Wall End LA17 55 F1
Wall Heath DY6 40 A7
Wall Houses NE20 71 F7
Wall under Heywood SY6 38 E6
Wallacehall DG11 69 H6
Wallacetown KA19 67 G3
Wallasey CH45 48 B3
Wallaston Green SA71 16 C4
Wallend ME3 24 E4
Waller's Green HR8 29 F5
Wallingford OX10 21 K3
Wallington, Gt.Lon. SM6 23 F5
Wallington, Hants. PO16 11 G4
Wallington, Herts. SG7 33 F5
Wallington, Wrex. LL13 38 D1
Wallingwells S81 51 H4
Wallis SA62 16 D2
Wallisdown BH11 10 B5
Walliswood RH5 12 E3
Walls ZE2 109 B8
Wallsend NE28 71 H7
Wallyford EH21 76 B3
Walmer CT14 15 J2
Walmer Bridge PR4 55 H7
Walmersley BL9 49 H1
Walmley B76 40 D6
Walmsgate LN11 53 G5
Walpole IP19 35 H1
Walpole Cross Keys PE34 43 J4
Walpole Highway PE14 43 J4
Walpole Marsh PE14 43 H4
Walpole St. Andrew PE14 43 J4
Walpole St. Peter PE14 43 J4
Walrond's Park TA3 8 C2

Walrow TA9 19 G7
WALSALL WS 40 C6
Walsall Wood WS9 40 C5
Walsden OL14 56 E7
Walsgrave on Sowe CV2 41 F7
Walsham le Willows IP31 34 E1
Walshford LS22 57 K4
Walsoken PE13 43 H4
Walston ML11 75 J6
Walsworth SG4 32 E5
Walterston CF62 18 D4
Walterstone HR2 28 C6
Waltham, Kent CT4 15 G3
Waltham, N.E.Lincs. DN37 53 F2
Waltham Abbey EN9 23 G1
Waltham Chase SO32 11 G3
Waltham Cross EN8 23 G1
Waltham on the Wolds
 LE14 42 A3
Waltham St. Lawrence
 RG10 22 B4
Walthamstow E17 23 G3
Walton, Bucks. HP21 32 B7
Walton, Cumb. CA8 70 A7
Walton, Derbys. S42 51 F6
Walton, Leics. LE17 41 H7
Walton, M.K. MK7 32 B5
Walton, Mersey. L9 48 C3
Walton, Peter. PE4 42 E5
Walton, Powys LD8 28 B3
Walton, Shrop. SY7 28 D1
Walton, Som. BA16 8 D1
Walton, Staffs. ST15 40 A2
Walton, Suff. IP11 35 H5
Walton, Tel. & W. TF6 38 E4
Walton, W.Yorks. WF2 51 F1
Walton, W.Yorks. LS23 57 K5
Walton, Warks. CV35 30 D3
Walton Cardiff GL20 29 J5
Walton East SA63 16 D2
Walton Elm DT10 9 G3
Walton Highway PE14 43 H4
Walton Lower Street IP11 35 G5
Walton on the Hill KT20 23 F6
Walton on the Naze CO14 35 G6
Walton on the Wolds LE12 41 H4
Walton Park, D. & G. DG7 65 H3
Walton Park, N.Som.
 BS21 19 H4
Walton West SA62 16 B3
Walton-in-Gordano BS21 19 H4
Walton-le-Dale PR5 55 J7
Walton-on-Thames KT12 22 E5
Walton-on-the-Hill ST17 40 B3
Walton-on-Trent DE12 40 E4
Walwen, Flints. CH8 47 K5
Walwen, Flints. CH6 48 B5
Walwick NE46 70 E6
Walworth DL2 62 D5
Walworth Gate DL2 62 D4
Walwyn's Castle SA62 16 B3
Wambrook TA20 8 B4
Wanborough, Surr. GU3 22 C7
Wanborough, Swin. SN4 21 F3
Wandel ML12 68 E1
Wandon NE66 71 F1
Wandon End LU2 32 E6
Wandsworth SW15 23 F4
Wandylaw NE67 71 G1
Wangford, Suff. NR34 35 J1
Wangford, Suff. IP27 44 B7
Wanlip LE7 41 J4
Wanlockhead ML12 68 D2
Wannock BN26 13 J6
Wansford, E.Riding YO25 59 G4
Wansford, Peter. PE8 42 D6
Wanshurst Green TN12 14 C3
Wanstrow BA4 20 A7
Wanswell GL13 19 K1
Wantage OX12 21 G3
Wapley BS37 20 A4
Wappenbury CV33 30 E2
Wappenham NN12 31 H4
Warbleton TN21 13 K5
Warblington PO9 11 J4
Warborough OX10 21 J2
Warboys PE28 43 G7
Warbreck FY2 55 G6
Warbstow PL15 4 C1
Warburton WA13 49 F4
Warcop CA16 61 J5
Ward End B8 40 D7
Ward Green IP14 34 E2
Warden, Kent ME12 25 G4
Warden, Northumb. NE46 70 E7
Warden Hill GL51 29 J6
Warden Street SG18 32 E4
Wardhouse AB52 90 D1
Wardington OX17 31 F4
Wardle, Ches. CW5 49 F7
Wardle, Gt.Man. OL12 49 J1
Wardley, Gt.Man. M27 49 G2
Wardley, Rut. LE15 42 B5
Wardley, T. & W. NE10 71 J7
Wardlow SK17 50 D5
Wardsend SK10 49 J4
Wardy Hill CB6 33 H7
Ware, Herts. SG12 33 G7
Ware, Kent CT3 25 J5
Wareham BH20 9 J6
Warehorne TN26 14 E4
Waren Mill NE70 77 K7
Warenford NE70 71 G1
Warenton NE70 77 K7
Wareside SG12 33 G7
Waresley, Cambs. SG19 33 F3
Waresley, Worcs. DY11 29 H1
Warfield RG42 22 B4
Wargrave, Mersey. WA12 48 E3
Wargrave, W'ham RG10 22 A4

Warham

Warham, *Here.* HR4   28 D5
Warham, *Norf.* NR23   44 D1
Wark, *Northumb.* NE48   70 D6
Wark, *Northumb.* TD12   77 H7
Warkleigh EX37   6 E3
Warkton NN16   32 B1
Warkworth, *Northants.* OX17   31 F4
Warkworth, *Northumb.* NE65   71 H3
Warland OL14   56 E7
Warleggan PL30   4 B4
Warley, *Essex* CM14   23 J2
Warley, *W.Mid.* B68   40 C7
Warley Town HX2   57 F7
Warlingham CR6   23 G6
Warmfield WF1   57 J7
Warmingham CW11   49 G6
Warminghurst RH20   12 E5
Warmington, *Northants.* PE8   42 D6
Warmington, *Warks.* OX17   31 F4
Warminster BA12   20 B7
Warmlake ME17   14 D3
Warmley BS30   19 K4
Warmley Hill BS15   19 K4
Warmsworth DN4   51 H2
Warmwell DT2   9 G6
Warndon WR4   29 H3
Warners End HP1   22 D1
Warnford SO32   11 H2
Warnham RH12   12 E3
Warningcamp BN18   12 D6
Warninglid RH17   13 F4
Warren, *Ches.* SK11   49 H5
Warren, *Pembs.* SA71   16 C5
Warren House PL20   6 E7
Warren Row RG10   22 B3
Warren Street ME17   14 E2
Warrenby TS10   63 G4
Warren's Green SG4   33 F6
Warrington, *M.K.* MK46   32 B3
WARRINGTON, *Warr.* WA   49 F4
Warroch KY13   82 B7
Warsash SO31   11 F4
Warslow SK17   50 C7
Warsop Vale NG20   51 H6
Warter YO42   58 E4
Warthill YO19   58 C4
Wartle AB31   90 D4
Wartling BN27   13 K6
Wartnaby LE14   42 A3
Warton, *Lancs.* LA5   55 H1
Warton, *Lancs.* PR4   55 H7
Warton, *Northumb.* NE65   71 F3
Warton, *Warks.* B79   40 E5
Warton Bank PR4   55 H7
Warwick CV34   30 D2
Warwick Bridge CA4   61 F1
Warwick Wold RH1   23 G6
Warwick-on-Eden CA4   61 F1
Wasbister KW17   106 C4
Wasdale Head CA20   60 C6
Wash SK23   50 C4
Wash Common RG14   21 H5
Washall Green SG9   33 H5
Washaway PL30   4 A4
Washbourne TQ9   5 H5
Washbrook BS28   19 H7
Washfield EX16   7 H4
Washfold DL11   62 B6
Washford, *Som.* TA23   7 J1
Washford, *Warks.* B98   30 B2
Washford Pyne EX17   7 G4
Washingborough LN4   52 C6
Washington, *T. & W.* NE38   62 E1
Washington, *W.Suss.* RH20   12 E5
Washmere Green CO10   34 D4
Wasing RG7   21 J5
Waskerley DH8   62 B2
Wasperton CV35   30 D3
Wasps Nest LN4   52 D6
Wass YO61   58 B2
Watchet TA23   7 J1
Watchfield, *Oxon.* SN6   21 F2
Watchfield, *Som.* TA9   19 G7
Watchgate LA8   61 G7
Watcombe TQ1   5 K4
Watendlath CA12   60 D5
Water BB4   56 D7
Water Eaton, *M.K.* MK2   32 B5
Water Eaton, *Oxon.* OX2   31 G7
Water End, *Beds.* MK44   32 C3
Water End, *Beds.* MK45   32 D5
Water End, *E.Riding* YO43   58 D6
Water End, *Essex* CB10   33 J4
Water End, *Herts.* AL9   23 F1
Water End, *Herts.* HP1   32 D7
Water Newton PE8   42 E6
Water Orton B46   40 D6
Water Stratford MK18   31 H5
Water Yeat LA12   55 F1
Waterbeach CB5   33 H2
Waterbeck DG11   69 H6
Watercombe DT2   9 G6
Waterend HP14   22 A2
Waterfall ST10   50 C7
Waterfoot, *E.Renf.* G76   74 D5
Waterfoot, *Lancs.* BB4   56 D7
Waterford SG14   33 G7
Watergate PL32   4 B2
Waterhead, *Cumb.* LA22   60 E6
Waterhead, *D. & G.* DG7   68 C5
Waterheath NR34   45 J6
Waterhill of Bruxie AB42   99 H6
Waterhouses, *Dur.* DH7   62 C2
Waterhouses, *Staffs.* ST10   50 C7
Wateringbury ME18   23 K6
Waterlane GL6   20 C1
Waterloo, *Aber.* AB42   91 J1
Waterloo, *Derbys.* S45   51 G6
Waterloo, *Gt.Man.* OL7   49 J2
Waterloo, *High.* IV42   86 C2
Waterloo, *Mersey.* L22   48 C3
Waterloo, *N.Lan.* ML2   75 G5
Waterloo, *Norf.* NR10   45 G4
Waterloo, *P. & K.* PH1   82 B4
Waterloo, *Pembs.* SA72   16 C4
Waterloo, *Poole* BH17   10 B5
Waterloo Cross EX15   7 J4
Waterlooville PO7   11 H3
Watermeetings ML12   68 E2
Watermillock CA11   60 F4
Waterperry OX33   21 K1
Waterrow TA4   7 J3
Waters Upton TF6   39 F4
Watersfield RH20   12 D5
Watersheddings OL4   49 J2
Waterside, *Aber.* AB36   90 B3
Waterside, *Aber.* AB41   91 J2
Waterside, *B'burn.* BB3   56 C7
Waterside, *Bucks.* HP5   22 C1
Waterside, *E.Ayr.* KA6   67 J3
Waterside, *E.Ayr.* KA3   74 C6
Waterside, *E.Dun.* G66   74 E3
Waterstock OX33   21 K1
Waterston SA73   16 C4
Waterthorpe S20   51 G4
WATFORD, *Herts.* WD   22 E2
Watford, *Northants.* NN6   31 H2
Watford Park CF83   18 E3
Wath, *N.Yorks.* HG4   57 J2
Wath, *N.Yorks.* HG3   57 G3
Wath Brow CA25   60 B5
Wath upon Dearne S63   51 G2
Watley's End BS36   19 K3
Watnall NG16   41 H1
Watten KW1   105 H3
Wattisfield IP22   34 E1
Wattisham IP7   34 E3
Watton, *Dorset* DT6   8 D5
Watton, *E.Riding* YO25   59 G5
Watton, *Norf.* IP25   44 D5
Watton at Stone SG14   33 G7
Watton Green IP25   44 D5
Watton's Green CM14   23 J2
Wattston ML6   75 F4
Wattstown CF39   18 D2
Wattsville NP11   19 F2
Waughtonhill AB43   99 H5
Waun Fawr SY23   37 F7
Waun y Clyn SA17   17 H4
Waunarlwydd SA5   17 K5
Waunclunda SA19   17 K1
Waunfawr LL55   46 D7
Waun-Lwyd NP23   18 E1
Wavendon MK17   32 C5
Waverbridge CA7   60 D2
Waverton, *Ches.* CH3   48 D6
Waverton, *Cumb.* CA7   60 D2
Wavertree L15   48 C4
Wawne HU7   59 G6
Waxham NR12   45 J3
Waxholme HU19   59 K7
Way Gill BD23   56 E3
Way Village EX16   7 G4
Way Wick BS24   19 G5
Wayford TA18   8 D4
Waytown DT6   8 D5
Wdig (Goodwick) SA64   16 C1
Weachyburn AB45   98 E5
Weacombe TA4   7 K1
Weald OX18   21 G1
Wealdstone HA3   22 E2
Weardley LS21   57 H5
Weare BS26   19 H6
Weare Giffard EX39   6 C3
Wearhead DL13   61 K3
Wearne TA10   8 D2
Weasenham All Saints PE32   44 C3
Weasenham St. Peter PE32   44 C3
Weathercote LA6   56 C2
Weatheroak Hill B48   30 B1
Weaverham CW8   49 F5
Weaverthorpe YO17   59 F2
Webheath B97   30 B2
Webton HR2   28 D5
Wedderlairs AB41   91 G1
Weddington CV10   41 F6
Wedhampton SN10   20 D6
Wedmore BS28   19 H7
Wednesbury WS10   40 B6
Wednesfield WV11   40 B6
Weedon HP22   32 B7
Weedon Bec NN7   31 H3
Weedon Lois NN12   31 H4
Weeford WS14   40 D5
Week, *Devon* EX18   7 F4
Week, *Devon* TQ9   5 H4
Week, *Som.* TA22   7 H2
Week Orchard EX23   6 A5
Week St. Mary EX22   4 C1
Weeke SO22   11 F1
Weekley NN16   42 B7
Weel HU17   59 G6
Weeley CO16   35 F6
Weeley Heath CO16   35 F6
Weem PH15   81 K2
Weeping Cross ST17   40 B3
Weethley B49   30 B3
Weeting IP27   44 B7
Weeton, *E.Riding* HU12   59 K7
Weeton, *Lancs.* PR4   55 H6
Weeton, *N.Yorks.* LS17   57 H5
Weetwood LS16   57 H6
Weir, *Essex* SS6   24 E3
Weir, *Lancs.* OL13   56 D7
Weir Quay PL20   4 E4
Weirbrook SY11   38 C3
Weisdale ZE2   109 C7
Welbeck Abbey S80   51 H5
Welborne NR20   44 E5
Welbourn LN5   52 C7
Welburn, *N.Yorks.* YO60   58 D3
Welburn, *N.Yorks.* YO62   58 C1
Welbury DL6   62 E6
Welby NG32   42 C2
Welches Dam PE16   43 H7
Welcombe EX39   6 A4
Weldon NN17   42 C7
Welford, *Northants.* NN6   41 J7
Welford, *W.Berks.* RG20   21 H4
Welford-on-Avon CV37   30 C3
Welham, *Leics.* LE16   42 A6
Welham, *Notts.* DN22   51 K4
Welham Green AL9   23 F1
Well, *Hants.* RG29   22 A7
Well, *Lincs.* LN13   53 H5
Well, *N.Yorks.* DL8   57 H1
Well End, *Bucks.* SL8   22 B3
Well End, *Herts.* WD6   23 F2
Well Hill BR6   23 H5
Well Street ME19   23 K6
Well Town EX16   7 H5
Welland WR13   29 G4
Wellbank DD5   83 F4
Wellesbourne CV35   30 D3
Wellhill IV36   97 G5
Wellhouse, *W.Berks.* RG18   21 J4
Wellhouse, *W.Yorks.* HD7   50 C1
Welling DA16   23 H4
Wellingborough NN8   32 B2
Wellingham PE32   44 C3
Wellingore LN5   52 C7
Wellington, *Cumb.* CA20   60 B6
Wellington, *Here.* HR4   28 D4
Wellington, *Som.* TA21   7 K3
Wellington, *Tel. & W.* TF1   39 F4
Wellington Heath HR8   29 G4
Wellington Marsh HR4   28 D4
Wellow, *B. & N.E.Som.* BA2   20 A6
Wellow, *I.o.W.* PO41   10 E6
Wellow, *Notts.* NG22   51 J6
Wells BA5   19 J7
Wells Green B92   40 D7
Wellsborough CV13   41 F5
Wells-next-the-Sea NR23   44 D1
Wellstye Green CM6   33 K7
Wellwood KY12   75 J2
Welney PE14   43 J6
Welsh Bicknor HR9   28 E7
Welsh End SY13   38 E2
Welsh Frankton SY11   38 C2
Welsh Hook SA62   16 C2
Welsh Newton NP25   28 D7
Welsh St. Donats CF71   18 D4
Welshampton SY12   38 D2
Welshpool (Y Trallwng) SY21   38 B5
Welton, *B. & N.E.Som.* BA3   19 K6
Welton, *Cumb.* CA5   60 E2
Welton, *E.Riding* HU15   59 F7
Welton, *Lincs.* LN2   52 D4
Welton, *Northants.* NN11   31 G2
Welton le Marsh PE23   53 H6
Welton le Wold LN11   53 F4
Welwick HU12   59 K7
Welwyn AL6   33 F7
Welwyn Garden City AL8   33 F7
Wem SY4   38 E3
Wembdon TA6   8 B1
Wembley HA0   22 E3
Wembley Park HA9   22 E3
Wembury PL9   5 F6
Wembworthy EX18   6 E4
Wemyss Bay PA18   73 K4
Wenallt, *Cere.* SY23   27 F1
Wenallt, *Gwyn.* LL21   37 J1
Wendens Ambo CB11   33 J5
Wendlebury OX25   31 G7
Wendling NR19   44 D4
Wendover HP22   22 B1
Wendover Dean HP22   22 B1
Wendron TR13   2 D5
Wendy SG8   33 G4
Wenfordbridge PL30   4 A3
Wenhaston IP19   35 J1
Wenlli LL22   47 G6
Wennington, *Cambs.* PE28   33 F1
Wennington, *Gt.Lon.* RM13   23 J3
Wennington, *Lancs.* LA2   56 B2
Wensley, *Derbys.* DE4   50 E6
Wensley, *N.Yorks.* DL8   57 F1
Wentbridge WF8   51 G1
Wentnor SY9   38 C6
Wentworth, *Cambs.* CB6   33 H1
Wentworth, *S.Yorks.* S62   51 F3
Wenvoe CF5   18 E4
Weobley HR4   28 D3
Weobley Marsh HR4   28 D3
Weoley Castle B29   40 C7
Wepham BN18   12 D6
Wepre CH5   48 B6
Wereham PE33   44 A5
Wergs WV6   40 A5
Wern, *Gwyn.* LL49   36 E2
Wern, *Powys* SY21   38 B4
Wern, *Powys* NP8   28 A7
Wern, *Shrop.* SY10   38 B2
Wernffrwd SA4   17 J5
Wern-olau SA4   17 J5
Wernrheolydd NP15   28 C7
Wern-y-cwrt NP15   19 G1
Werrington, *Cornw.* PL15   6 B7
Werrington, *Peter.* PE4   42 E5
Werrington, *Staffs.* ST9   40 B1
Wervil Grange SA44   26 C3
Wervin CH2   48 D5
Wesham PR4   55 H6
Wessington DE55   51 F7
West Aberthaw CF62   18 D5
West Acre PE32   44 B4
West Allerdean TD15   77 H6
West Alvington TQ7   5 H6
West Amesbury SP4   20 E7
West Anstey EX36   7 G3
West Ashby LN9   53 F5
West Ashford EX31   6 D2
West Ashling PO18   12 B6
West Ashton BA14   20 B6
West Auckland DL14   62 C4
West Ayton YO13   59 F1
West Bagborough TA4   7 K2
West Barkwith LN8   52 E4
West Barnby YO21   63 K5
West Barns EH42   76 E3
West Barsham NR21   44 D2
West Bay DT6   8 D5
West Beckham NR25   45 F2
West Benhar ML7   75 G4
West Bergholt CO6   34 D6
West Bexington DT2   8 E6
West Bilney PE32   44 B4
West Blatchington BN3   13 F6
West Boldon NE36   71 J7
West Bourton SP8   9 G2
West Bowling BD5   57 G6
West Brabourne TN25   15 F3
West Bradford BB7   56 C5
West Bradley BA6   8 E1
West Bretton WF4   50 E1
West Bridgford NG2   41 H2
West Bromwich B70   40 C6
West Buckland, *Devon* EX32   6 E2
West Buckland, *Som.* TA21   7 K3
West Burrafirth ZE2   109 B7
West Burton, *N.Yorks.* DL8   57 F1
West Burton, *W.Suss.* RH20   12 C5
West Butsfield DL13   62 B2
West Butterwick DN17   52 B2
West Byfleet KT14   22 D5
West Cairncake AB53   99 G6
West Caister NR30   45 K4
West Calder EH55   75 J4
West Camel BA22   8 E2
West Carbeth G63   74 D2
West Carr Houses DN9   51 K2
West Cauldcoats ML10   74 E6
West Chaldon DT2   9 G6
West Challow OX12   21 G3
West Charleton TQ7   5 H6
West Chevington NE61   71 H4
West Chiltington RH20   12 D5
West Chiltington Common RH20   12 D5
West Chinnock TA18   8 D3
West Chisenbury SN9   20 E6
West Clandon GU4   22 D6
West Cliffe CT15   15 J3
West Clyne KW9   97 F1
West Coker BA22   8 E3
West Compton, *Dorset* DT2   8 E5
West Compton, *Som.* BA4   19 J7
West Cowick DN14   58 C7
West Cross SA3   17 K6
West Crudwell SN16   20 C2
West Curry EX22   4 C1
West Curthwaite CA7   60 E2
West Dean, *W.Suss.* PO18   12 B5
West Dean, *Wilts.* SP5   10 D2
West Deeping PE6   42 E5
West Derby L12   48 C3
West Dereham PE33   44 A5
West Ditchburn NE66   71 G1
West Down EX34   6 D1
West Drayton, *Gt.Lon.* UB7   22 D4
West Drayton, *Notts.* DN22   51 K5
West Dullater FK17   81 G7
West Dunnet KW14   105 H1
West Edington NE61   71 G5
West Ella HU10   59 G7
West End, *Beds.* MK43   32 C3
West End, *Brack.F.* RG42   22 B4
West End, *Cambs.* PE15   43 H6
West End, *E.Riding* YO25   59 G3
West End, *Hants.* SO30   11 F3
West End, *Herts.* EN10   23 G1
West End, *Kent* CT6   25 H5
West End, *Lancs.* LA4   55 H4
West End, *Lincs.* DN36   53 G3
West End, *N.Som.* BS48   19 H5
West End, *N.Yorks.* HG3   57 G4
West End, *Norf.* NR30   45 J4
West End, *Norf.* IP25   44 D5
West End, *Oxon.* OX29   21 H1
West End, *Oxon.* OX10   21 J3
West End, *S.Lan.* ML11   75 H6
West End, *Suff.* NR34   45 J7
West End, *Surr.* KT10   22 E5
West End, *Surr.* GU24   22 C5
West End, *Wilts.* SN15   20 C4
West End, *Wilts.* SP7   9 J2
West End, *Wilts.* SP5   9 J2
West End Green RG7   21 K5
West Farleigh ME15   14 C2
West Farndon NN11   31 G3
West Felton SY11   38 C3
West Firle BN8   13 H6
West Fleetham NE67   71 G1
West Flotmanby YO14   59 G2
West Garforth LS25   57 J6
West Ginge OX12   21 H3
West Glen PA21   73 H3
West Grafton SN8   21 F5
West Green, *Gt.Lon.* N15   23 G3
West Green, *Hants.* RG27   22 A6
West Grimstead SP5   10 D2
West Grinstead RH13   12 E4
West Haddlesey YO8   58 B7
West Haddon NN6   31 H1
West Hagbourne OX11   21 J3
West Hagley DY9   40 B7
West Hall CA8   70 A7
West Hallam DE7   41 G1
West Halton DN15   59 F7
West Ham E15   23 G3
West Handley S21   51 F5
West Hanney OX12   21 H2
West Hanningfield CM2   24 D2
West Hardwick WF4   51 G1
West Harnham SP2   10 C2
West Harptree BS40   19 J6
West Harrow HA1   22 E3
West Harting GU31   11 J2
West Hatch, *Som.* TA3   8 B2
West Hatch, *Wilts.* SP3   9 J2
West Head PE34   43 J5
West Heath, *Ches.* CW12   49 H6
West Heath, *Gt.Lon.* SE2   23 H4
West Heath, *Hants.* GU14   22 B6
West Heath, *Hants.* RG26   21 J6
West Heath, *W.Mid.* B31   30 B1
West Helmsdale KW8   105 F7
West Hendon NW9   23 F3
West Hendred OX12   21 H3
West Heslerton YO17   59 F2
West Hewish BS24   19 G5
West Hill, *Devon* EX11   7 J6
West Hill, *E.Riding* YO16   59 H3
West Hill, *N.Som.* BS20   19 H4
West Hoathly RH19   13 G3
West Holme BH20   9 H6
West Horndon CM13   24 C3
West Horrington BA5   19 J7
West Horsley KT24   22 D6
West Horton NE71   77 J7
West Hougham CT15   15 H3
West Howe BH11   10 B5
West Howetown TA24   7 H2
West Huntspill TA9   19 G7
West Hyde WD3   22 D2
West Hythe CT21   15 G4
West Ilsley RG20   21 H3
West Itchenor PO20   11 J4
West Keal PE23   53 G6
West Kennett SN8   20 E5
West Kilbride KA23   74 A6
West Kingsdown TN15   23 J5
West Kington SN14   20 B4
West Kington Wick SN14   20 B4
West Kirby CH48   48 B4
West Knapton YO17   58 E2
West Knighton DT2   9 G6
West Knoyle BA12   9 H1
West Kyloe TD15   77 J6
West Lambrook TA13   8 D3
West Langdon CT15   15 J3
West Langwell IV28   96 D1
West Lavington, *W.Suss.* GU29   12 B4
West Lavington, *Wilts.* SN10   20 D6
West Layton DL11   62 C6
West Leake LE12   41 H3
West Learmouth TD12   77 H7
West Lees DL6   63 F6
West Leigh, *Devon* EX17   6 E5
West Leigh, *Devon* TQ9   5 H5
West Leigh, *Som.* TA4   7 K2
West Leith HP23   32 C7
West Lexham PE32   44 C4
West Lilling YO60   58 C3
West Lingo KY9   83 F7
West Linton EH46   75 K5
West Liss GU33   11 J2
West Littleton SN14   20 A4
West Lockinge OX12   21 H3
West Looe PL13   4 C5
West Lulworth BH20   9 H6
West Lutton YO17   59 F3
West Lydford TA11   8 E2
West Lyn EX35   7 F1
West Lyng TA3   8 C2
West Lynn PE34   44 A4
West Mains TD15   77 J6
West Malling ME19   23 K6
West Malvern WR14   29 G4
West Marden PO18   11 J3
West Markham NG22   51 K5
West Marsh DN31   53 F2
West Marton BD23   56 D4
West Melbury SP7   9 H2
West Melton S63   51 G2
West Meon GU32   11 H2
West Meon Hut GU32   11 H2
West Mersea CO5   34 E7
West Milton DT6   8 D5
West Minster ME12   25 F4
West Molesey KT8   22 E5
West Monkton TA2   8 B2
West Moors BH22   10 B4
West Morden BH20   9 J5
West Morriston TD4   76 E6

Whitley

West Morton **BD20** 57 F5
West Mostard **LA10** 61 J7
West Mudford **BA22** 8 E2
West Muir **DD9** 83 G1
West Ness **YO62** 58 C2
West Newbiggin **DL2** 62 E5
West Newton, *E.Riding* **HU11** 59 H6
West Newton, *Norf.* **PE31** 44 A3
West Norwood **SE27** 23 G4
West Ogwell **TQ12** 5 J4
West Orchard **SP7** 9 H3
West Overton **SN8** 20 E5
West Panson **PL15** 6 B6
West Park, *Aber.* **AB31** 91 F5
West Park, *Mersey.* **WA10** 48 E3
West Parley **BH22** 10 B5
West Peckham **ME18** 23 K6
West Pelton **DH9** 62 D1
West Pennard **BA6** 8 E1
West Pentire **TR8** 2 E2
West Perry **PE28** 32 E2
West Porlock **TA24** 7 G1
West Prawle **TQ8** 5 H7
West Preston **BN16** 12 D6
West Pulham **DT2** 9 G4
West Putford **EX22** 6 B4
West Quantoxhead **TA4** 7 K1
West Raddon **EX17** 7 G5
West Rainton **DH4** 62 E2
West Rasen **LN8** 52 D4
West Raynham **NR21** 44 C3
West Retford **DN22** 51 J4
West Rounton **DL6** 63 F6
West Row **IP28** 33 K1
West Rudham **PE31** 44 C3
West Runton **NR27** 45 F1
West Saltoun **EH34** 76 C4
West Sandford **EX17** 7 G5
West Sandwick **ZE2** 108 D4
West Scrafton **DL8** 57 F1
West Shepton **BA4** 19 K7
West Shinness Lodge **IV27** 103 H7
West Somerton **NR29** 45 J4
West Stafford **DT2** 9 G6
West Stockwith **DN10** 51 K3
West Stoke **PO18** 12 B6
West Stonesdale **DL11** 61 K6
West Stoughton **BS28** 19 H7
West Stour **SP8** 9 G2
West Stourmouth **CT3** 25 J5
West Stow **IP28** 34 C1
West Stowell **SN8** 20 E5
West Stratton **SO21** 21 J7
West Street, *Kent* **ME17** 14 E2
West Street, *Med.* **ME3** 24 D4
West Street, *Suff.* **IP31** 34 D1
West Tanfield **HG4** 57 H2
West Taphouse **PL22** 4 B4
West Tarbert **PA29** 73 G4
West Tarring **BN13** 12 E6
West Thirston **NE65** 71 G3
West Thorney **PO10** 11 J4
West Thurrock **RM20** 23 J4
West Tilbury **RM18** 24 C4
West Tisted **SO24** 11 H2
West Tofts, *Norf.* **IP26** 44 C6
West Tofts, *P. & K.* **PH1** 82 C4
West Torrington **LN8** 52 E4
West Town, *B. & N.E.Som.* **BS40** 19 J5
West Town, *Hants.* **PO11** 11 J5
West Town, *N.Som.* **BS48** 19 H5
West Town, *Som.* **BA6** 8 E1
West Tytherley **SP5** 10 D2
West Walton **PE14** 43 H4
West Wellow **SO51** 10 D3
West Wembury **PL9** 5 F6
West Wemyss **KY1** 76 B1
West Wick **BS24** 19 G5
West Wickham, *Cambs.* **CB1** 33 K4
West Wickham, *Gt.Lon.* **BR4** 23 G5
West Williamston **SA68** 16 D4
West Winch **PE33** 44 A4
West Winterslow **SP5** 10 D1
West Wittering **PO20** 11 J5
West Witton **DL8** 57 F1
West Woodburn **NE48** 70 D5
West Woodhay **RG20** 21 G5
West Woodlands **BA11** 20 A7
West Worldham **GU34** 11 J1
West Worlington **EX17** 7 F4
West Worthing **BN11** 12 E6
West Wratting **CB1** 33 K3
West Wycombe **HP14** 22 B2
West Yatton **SN14** 20 B4
West Yell **ZE2** 108 D4
West Youlstone **EX23** 6 A4
Westbere **CT2** 25 H5
Westborough **NG23** 42 B1
Westbourne, *Bourne.* **BH4** 10 B5
Westbourne, *W.Suss.* **PO10** 11 J4
Westbourne Green **W2** 23 F3
Westbrook, *Kent* **CT9** 25 K4
Westbrook, *W.Berks.* **RG20** 21 H4
Westbrook, *Wilts.* **SN15** 20 C5
Westbury, *Bucks.* **NN13** 31 H5
Westbury, *Shrop.* **SY5** 38 C5
Westbury, *Wilts.* **BA13** 20 B6
Westbury Leigh **BA13** 20 B6
Westbury on Trym **BS9** 19 J4
Westbury-on-Severn **GL14** 29 G7
Westbury-sub-Mendip **BA5** 19 J7
Westby, *Lancs.* **PR4** 55 G6
Westby, *Lincs.* **NG33** 42 C3
Westcliff-on-Sea **SS0** 24 E3
Westcombe **BA4** 9 F1
Westcot **OX12** 21 G3
Westcott, *Bucks.* **HP18** 31 J7
Westcott, *Devon* **EX15** 7 J5
Westcott, *Surr.* **RH4** 22 E7
Westcott Barton **OX7** 31 F6
Westcourt **SN8** 21 F5
Westdean **BN25** 13 J7
Westdowns **PL33** 4 A2
Westend Town **SN14** 20 A4
Wester Aberchalder **IV2** 88 C2
Wester Badentyre **AB53** 99 F5
Wester Balgedie **KY13** 82 C7
Wester Culbeuchly **AB45** 98 E4
Wester Dechmont **EH52** 75 J3
Wester Fintray **AB51** 91 G3
Wester Foffarty **DD8** 83 F3
Wester Greenskares **AB45** 99 F4
Wester Gruinards **IV24** 96 C2
Wester Hailes **EH14** 76 A4
Wester Lealty **IV17** 96 D4
Wester Lonvine **IV18** 96 E4
Wester Newburn **KY8** 83 F7
Wester Ord **AB32** 91 G4
Wester Quarff **ZE2** 109 D9
Wester Skeld **ZE2** 109 B8
Westerdale, *High.* **KW12** 105 G3
Westerdale, *N.Yorks.* **YO21** 63 H6
Westerfield, *Shet.* **ZE2** 109 C7
Westerfield, *Suff.* **IP6** 35 F4
Westergate **PO20** 12 C6
Westerham **TN16** 23 H6
Westerhope **NE5** 71 G7
Westerleigh **BS37** 19 K4
Westerloch **KW1** 105 J3
Westerton, *Aber.* **AB31** 91 F5
Westerton, *Angus* **DD10** 83 H2
Westerton, *Dur.* **DL14** 62 D3
Westerton, *P. & K.* **PH5** 81 K6
Westerwick **ZE2** 109 B8
Westfield, *Cumb.* **CA14** 60 A4
Westfield, *E.Suss.* **TN35** 14 D6
Westfield, *High.* **KW14** 105 F2
Westfield, *N.Lan.* **G68** 75 F3
Westfield, *Norf.* **NR19** 44 D5
Westfield, *R. & C.* **TS10** 63 G4
Westfield, *W.Loth.* **EH48** 75 H3
Westfield, *W.Yorks.* **WF16** 57 H7
Westfield Sole **ME14** 24 D5
Westgate, *Dur.* **DL13** 62 A3
Westgate, *N.Lincs.* **DN9** 51 K2
Westgate, *Norf.* **NR21** 44 D1
Westgate, *Northumb.* **NE20** 71 G6
Westgate Hill **BD4** 57 H7
Westgate on Sea **CT8** 25 K4
Westhall, *Aber.* **AB52** 90 E2
Westhall, *Suff.* **IP19** 45 J7
Westham, *Dorset* **DT4** 9 F7
Westham, *E.Suss.* **BN24** 13 K6
Westham, *Som.* **TA7** 19 H7
Westhampnett **PO18** 12 B6
Westhay, *Devon* **EX13** 8 C4
Westhay, *Som.* **BA6** 19 H7
Westhead **L40** 48 D2
Westhide **HR1** 28 E4
Westhill, *Aber.* **AB32** 91 G4
Westhill, *High.* **IV2** 96 E7
Westhope, *Here.* **HR4** 28 D3
Westhope, *Shrop.* **SY7** 38 D7
Westhorp **NN11** 31 G3
Westhorpe, *Lincs.* **PE11** 43 F2
Westhorpe, *Notts.* **NG25** 51 J7
Westhorpe, *Suff.* **IP14** 34 E2
Westhoughton **BL5** 49 F2
Westhouse **LA6** 56 B2
Westhouses **DE55** 51 G7
Westhumble **RH5** 22 E6
Westing **ZE2** 108 E2
Westlake **PL21** 5 G5
Westlands **ST5** 40 A1
Westlea **SN5** 20 E3
Westleigh, *Devon* **EX39** 6 C3
Westleigh, *Devon* **EX16** 7 J4
Westleigh, *Gt.Man.* **WN7** 49 F2
Westleton **IP17** 35 J2
Westley, *Shrop.* **SY5** 38 C5
Westley, *Suff.* **IP33** 34 C2
Westley Heights **SS16** 24 C3
Westley Waterless **CB8** 33 K3
Westlington **HP17** 31 J7
Westlinton **CA6** 69 J7
Westloch **EH45** 76 A5
Westmancote **GL20** 29 J5
Westmarsh **CT3** 25 J5
Westmeston **BN6** 13 G5
Westmill **SG9** 33 G6
Westminster **SW1H** 23 F4
Westmuir **DD8** 82 E2
Westness **KW17** 106 C5
Westnewton, *Cumb.* **CA7** 60 C2
Westnewton, *Northumb.* **NE71** 77 H7
Westoe **NE33** 71 J7
Weston, *B. & N.E.Som.* **BA1** 20 A5
Weston, *Ches.* **CW2** 49 G7
Weston, *Devon* **EX12** 7 K7
Weston, *Devon* **EX14** 7 K5
Weston, *Dorset* **DT5** 9 F7
Weston, *Halton* **WA7** 48 E4
Weston, *Hants.* **GU32** 11 J2
Weston, *Here.* **HR5** 28 C3
Weston, *Herts.* **SG4** 33 F5
Weston, *Lincs.* **PE12** 43 F3
Weston, *Moray* **AB56** 98 C4
Weston, *N.Yorks.* **LS21** 57 G5
Weston, *Northants.* **NN12** 31 G4
Weston, *Notts.* **NG23** 51 K6
Weston, *S'ham.* **SO19** 11 F3
Weston, *Shrop.* **SY4** 38 E3
Weston, *Shrop.* **TF13** 38 E6
Weston, *Shrop.* **SY7** 28 C1
Weston, *Staffs.* **ST18** 40 B3
Weston, *W.Berks.* **RG20** 21 H4
Weston Bampfylde **BA22** 9 F2
Weston Beggard **HR1** 28 E4
Weston by Welland **LE16** 42 A6
Weston Colville **CB1** 33 K3
Weston Corbett **RG25** 21 K7
Weston Coyney **ST3** 40 B1
Weston Favell **NN3** 31 J2
Weston Green, *Cambs.* **CB1** 33 K3
Weston Green, *Norf.* **NR9** 45 F4
Weston Heath **TF11** 39 G4
Weston Hills **PE12** 43 F3
Weston in Arden **CV12** 41 F7
Weston Jones **TF10** 39 G3
Weston Longville **NR9** 45 F4
Weston Lullingfields **SY4** 38 D3
Weston Patrick **RG25** 21 K7
Weston Point **WA7** 48 D4
Weston Rhyn **SY10** 38 B2
Weston Subedge **GL55** 30 C4
Weston Town **BA4** 20 A7
Weston Turville **HP22** 32 B7
Weston under Penyard **HR9** 29 F6
Weston under Wetherley **CV33** 30 E2
Weston Underwood, *Derbys.* **DE6** 40 E1
Weston Underwood, *M.K.* **MK46** 32 B3
Westonbirt **GL8** 20 B3
Westoning **MK45** 32 D5
Weston-in-Gordano **BS20** 19 H4
Weston-on-Avon **CV37** 30 C3
Weston-on-the-Green **OX25** 31 G7
Weston-on-Trent **DE72** 41 G3
Weston-super-Mare **BS23** 19 G5
Weston-under-Lizard **TF11** 40 A4
Westonzoyland **TA7** 8 C1
Westow **YO60** 58 D3
Westport, *Arg. & B.* **PA28** 66 A1
Westport, *Som.* **TA10** 8 C2
Westra **CF64** 18 E4
Westray **KW17** 106 D3
Westridge Green **RG8** 21 J4
Westrigg **EH48** 75 H4
Westruther **TD3** 76 E6
Westry **PE15** 43 G6
Westside **AB12** 91 G5
Westvale **L32** 48 D3
Westville **NG15** 41 H1
Westward **CA7** 60 D2
Westward Ho! **EX39** 6 C3
Westwell, *Kent* **TN25** 14 E3
Westwell, *Oxon.* **OX18** 21 F1
Westwell Leacon **TN27** 14 E3
Westwick, *Cambs.* **CB4** 33 H2
Westwick, *Dur.* **DL12** 62 B5
Westwick, *N.Yorks.* **YO51** 57 J3
Westwick, *Norf.* **NR10** 45 G3
Westwood, *Devon* **EX5** 7 J6
Westwood, *Peter.* **PE3** 42 E6
Westwood, *S.Lan.* **G75** 74 E5
Westwood, *Wilts.* **BA15** 20 B6
Westwood Heath **CV4** 30 D1
Westwoodside **DN9** 51 K3
Wetham Green **ME9** 24 E5
Wetheral **CA4** 61 F1
Wetherby **LS22** 57 K5
Wetherden **IP14** 34 E2
Wetherden Upper Town **IP14** 34 E2
Wetheringsett **IP14** 35 F2
Wethersfield **CM7** 34 B5
Wethersta **ZE2** 109 C6
Wetherup Street **IP14** 35 F2
Wetley Abbey **ST9** 40 B1
Wetley Rocks **ST9** 40 B1
Wettenhall **CW7** 49 F6
Wettenhall Green **CW7** 49 F6
Wetton **DE6** 50 D7
Wetwang **YO25** 59 F4
Wetwood **ST21** 39 G2
Wexcombe **SN8** 21 F6
Wexham Street **SL3** 22 C3
Weybourne, *Norf.* **NR25** 45 F1
Weybourne, *Surr.* **GU9** 22 B7
Weybread **IP21** 45 G7
Weybread Street **IP21** 35 G1
Weybridge **KT13** 22 D5
Weycroft **EX13** 8 C4
Weydale **KW14** 105 G2
Weyhill **SP11** 21 G7
Weymouth **DT4** 9 F7
Whaddon, *Bucks.* **MK17** 32 B5
Whaddon, *Cambs.* **SG8** 33 G4
Whaddon, *Glos.* **GL4** 29 H7
Whaddon, *Glos.* **GL52** 29 J6
Whaddon, *Wilts.* **SP5** 10 C2
Whaddon, *Wilts.* **BA14** 20 B5
Whaddon Gap **SG8** 33 G4
Whale **CA10** 61 G4
Whaley **NG20** 51 H5
Whaley Bridge **SK23** 50 C4
Whaley Thorns **NG20** 51 H5
Whaligoe **KW2** 105 J4
Whalley **BB7** 56 C6
Whalsay **ZE2** 109 E6
Whalton **NE61** 71 G5
Wham **BD24** 56 C3
Whaplode **PE12** 43 G3
Whaplode Drove **PE12** 43 G4
Whaplode St. Catherine **PE12** 43 G4
Wharfe **LA2** 56 C3
Wharles **PR4** 55 H6
Wharley End **MK43** 32 C4
Wharncliffe Side **S35** 50 E3
Wharram le Street **YO17** 58 E3
Wharram Percy **YO17** 58 E3
Wharton, *Ches.* **CW7** 49 F6
Wharton, *Here.* **HR6** 28 E3
Whashton **DL11** 62 C6
Whatcote **CV36** 30 E4
Whateley **B78** 40 E6
Whatfield **IP7** 34 E4
Whatley **BA11** 20 A7
Whatlington **TN33** 14 C6
Whatsole Street **TN25** 15 G3
Whatstandwell **DE4** 51 F7
Whatton **NG13** 42 A2
Whauphill **DG8** 64 E6
Whaw **DL11** 62 A6
Wheatacre **NR34** 45 J6
Wheatcroft **DE4** 51 F7
Wheatenhurst **GL2** 20 A1
Wheatfield **OX9** 21 K2
Wheathampstead **AL4** 32 E7
Wheathill, *Shrop.* **WV16** 39 F7
Wheathill, *Som.* **TA11** 8 E1
Wheatley, *Hants.* **GU34** 11 J1
Wheatley, *Oxon.* **OX33** 21 K1
Wheatley, *W.Yorks.* **HX3** 57 F7
Wheatley Hill **DH6** 62 E3
Wheatley Lane **BB12** 56 D6
Wheatley Park **DN2** 51 H2
Wheaton Aston **ST19** 40 A4
Wheddon Cross **TA24** 7 H2
Wheedlemont **AB54** 90 C2
Wheelerstreet **GU8** 22 C7
Wheelock **CW11** 49 G7
Wheelock Heath **CW11** 49 G7
Wheelton **PR6** 56 B7
Wheen **DD8** 90 B7
Wheldale **WF10** 57 K7
Wheldrake **YO19** 58 C5
Whelford **GL7** 20 E2
Whelley **WN1** 48 E2
Whelpley Hill **HP5** 22 C1
Whelpo **CA7** 60 E3
Whelston **CH6** 48 B5
Whenby **YO61** 58 C3
Whepstead **IP29** 34 C3
Wherstead **IP9** 35 F4
Wherwell **SP11** 21 G7
Wheston **SK17** 50 D5
Whetley Cross **DT8** 8 D4
Whetsted **TN12** 23 K7
Whetstone, *Gt.Lon.* **N20** 23 F2
Whetstone, *Leics.* **LE8** 41 H6
Whicham **LA18** 54 E1
Whichford **CV36** 30 E5
Whickham **NE16** 71 H7
Whiddon **EX21** 6 C5
Whiddon Down **EX6** 6 E6
Whifflet **ML5** 75 F4
Whigstreet **DD8** 83 F3
Whilton **NN11** 31 H2
Whim **EH46** 76 A5
Whimble **EX22** 6 B5
Whimple **EX5** 7 J6
Whimpwell Green **NR12** 45 H3
Whin Lane End **PR3** 55 G5
Whinburgh **NR19** 44 E5
Whinny Hill **TS21** 62 E5
Whinnyfold **AB42** 91 J1
Whippingham **PO32** 11 G5
Whipsnade **LU6** 32 D7
Whipton **EX1** 7 H6
Whirlow **S11** 51 F4
Whisby **LN6** 52 C6
Whissendine **LE15** 42 B4
Whissonsett **NR20** 44 D3
Whisterfield **SK11** 49 H5
Whistley Green **RG10** 22 A4
Whiston, *Mersey.* **L35** 48 D3
Whiston, *Northants.* **NN7** 32 B2
Whiston, *S.Yorks.* **S60** 51 G3
Whiston, *Staffs.* **ST10** 40 C1
Whiston, *Staffs.* **ST19** 40 A4
Whiston Cross **WV7** 39 G5
Whiston Eaves **ST10** 40 C1
Whitacre Fields **B46** 40 E6
Whitacre Heath **B46** 40 E6
Whitbeck **LA19** 54 E1
Whitbourne **WR6** 29 G3
Whitburn, *T. & W.* **SR6** 71 K7
Whitburn, *W.Loth.* **EH47** 75 H4
Whitby, *Ches.* **CH65** 48 C5
Whitby, *N.Yorks.* **YO21** 63 K5
Whitbyheath **CH65** 48 C5
Whitchurch, *B. & N.E.Som.* **BS14** 19 K5
Whitchurch, *Bucks.* **HP22** 32 B6
Whitchurch, *Cardiff* **CF14** 18 E3
Whitchurch, *Devon* **PL19** 4 E3
Whitchurch, *Hants.* **RG28** 21 H7
Whitchurch, *Here.* **HR9** 28 E7
Whitchurch, *Pembs.* **SA62** 16 A2
Whitchurch, *Shrop.* **SY13** 38 E1
Whitchurch, *Warks.* **CV37** 30 D4
Whitchurch Canonicorum **DT6** 8 C5
Whitchurch Hill **RG8** 21 K4
Whitchurch-on-Thames **RG8** 21 K4
Whitcombe **DT2** 9 G6
Whitcott Keysett **SY7** 38 B7
White Ball **TA21** 7 J4
White Colne **CO6** 34 C6
White Coppice **PR6** 49 F1
White Cross, *Cornw.* **TR8** 3 F3
White Cross, *Devon* **EX5** 7 J6
White Cross, *Here.* **HR4** 28 D4
White Cross, *Wilts.* **BA12** 9 G1
White End **GL19** 29 H6
White Hill **BA12** 9 H1
White Houses **DN22** 51 K5
White Kirkley **DL13** 62 B3
White Lackington **DT2** 9 G5
White Ladies Aston **WR7** 29 J3
White Lund **LA3** 55 H3
White Mill **SA32** 17 H2
White Moor **DE56** 41 F1
White Notley **CM8** 34 B7
White Ox Mead **BA2** 20 A6
White Pit **LN13** 53 G5
White Rocks **HR2** 28 D6
White Roding **CM6** 33 J7
White Waltham **SL6** 22 B4
Whiteacen **AB38** 97 K7
Whiteash Green **CO9** 34 B5
Whitebirk **BB1** 56 C7
Whitebog **AB43** 99 H5
Whitebridge, *High.* **KW14** 105 H1
Whitebridge, *High.* **IV2** 88 B3
Whitebrook **NP25** 19 J1
Whiteburn **TD2** 76 D6
Whitecairn **DG8** 64 C5
Whitecairns **AB23** 91 H3
Whitecastle **ML12** 75 J6
Whitechapel **PR3** 55 J5
Whitechurch **SA41** 16 E1
Whitecote **LS13** 57 H6
Whitecraig **EH21** 76 B3
Whitecroft **GL15** 19 K1
Whitecrook **DG9** 64 B5
Whitecross, *Cornw.* **TR20** 2 C5
Whitecross, *Cornw.* **PL27** 3 G1
Whitecross, *Dorset* **DT6** 8 D5
Whiteface **IV25** 96 E3
Whitefield, *Aber.* **AB51** 91 F2
Whitefield, *Devon* **EX32** 7 F2
Whitefield, *Dorset* **BH20** 9 J5
Whitefield, *Gt.Man.* **M45** 49 H2
Whitefield, *High.* **IV2** 88 C2
Whitefield, *High.* **KW1** 105 H3
Whitefield, *P. & K.* **PH13** 82 C4
Whiteford **AB51** 91 F2
Whitegate **CW8** 49 F6
Whitehall, *Devon* **EX15** 7 K4
Whitehall, *Hants.* **RG29** 22 A6
Whitehall, *Ork.* **KW17** 106 F5
Whitehall, *W.Suss.* **RH13** 12 E4
Whitehaven **CA28** 60 A5
Whitehill, *Aber.* **AB42** 99 H5
Whitehill, *Hants.* **GU35** 11 J1
Whitehill, *Kent* **ME13** 14 E2
Whitehill, *Midloth.* **EH22** 76 B4
Whitehill, *N.Ayr.* **KA24** 74 A5
Whitehills **AB45** 98 E4
Whitehouse, *Aber.* **AB33** 90 E3
Whitehouse, *Arg. & B.* **PA29** 73 G4
Whitehouse Common **B75** 40 D6
Whitekirk **EH42** 76 D2
Whitelackington **TA19** 8 C3
Whitelaw **TD11** 77 G5
Whiteleen **KW2** 105 J4
Whitelees **KA1** 74 B7
Whiteley **PO15** 11 G4
Whiteley Bank **PO38** 11 G6
Whiteley Green **SK10** 49 J5
Whiteley Village **KT12** 22 D5
Whiteleys **DG9** 64 A5
Whitemans Green **RH17** 13 G4
Whitemire **IV36** 97 G6
Whitemoor **PL26** 3 G3
Whiteness **ZE2** 109 C8
Whiteoak Green **OX29** 30 E7
Whiteparish **SP5** 10 D2
Whiterashes **AB21** 91 G2
Whiterow **KW1** 105 J4
Whiteshill **GL6** 20 B1
Whiteside, *Northumb.* **NE49** 70 C7
Whiteside, *W.Loth.* **EH48** 75 H4
Whitesmith **BN8** 13 J5
Whitestaunton **TA20** 8 B3
Whitestone, *Aber.* **AB31** 90 E5
Whitestone, *Arg. & B.* **PA28** 73 F7
Whitestone, *Devon* **EX4** 7 G6
Whitestreet Green **CO10** 34 D5
Whitestripe **AB43** 99 H5
Whiteway **GL6** 29 J7
Whitewell, *Aber.* **AB43** 99 H4
Whitewell, *Lancs.* **BB7** 56 B5
Whitewell, *Wrex.* **SY13** 38 D1
Whiteworks **PL20** 5 G3
Whitewreath **IV30** 97 K6
Whitfield, *Here.* **HR2** 28 D5
Whitfield, *Kent* **CT16** 15 J3
Whitfield, *Northants.* **NN13** 31 H5
Whitfield, *Northumb.* **NE47** 61 J1
Whitfield, *S.Glos.* **GL12** 19 K2
Whitford, *Devon* **EX13** 8 B5
Whitford (Chwitffordd), *Flints.* **CH8** 47 K5
Whitgift **DN14** 58 E7
Whitgreave **ST18** 40 A3
Whithorn **DG8** 64 E6
Whiting Bay **KA27** 66 E1
Whitkirk **LS15** 57 J6
Whitlam **AB21** 91 G2
Whitland **SA34** 17 F3
Whitland Abbey **SA34** 17 F3
Whitleigh **PL5** 4 E4
Whitletts **KA8** 67 H1
Whitley, *N.Yorks.* **DN14** 58 B7
Whitley, *Read.* **RG2** 22 A5
Whitley, *W.Mid.* **CV3** 30 E1
Whitley, *Wilts.* **SN12** 20 B5

Whitley Bay

Whitley Bay **NE26** 71 J6
Whitley Chapel **NE47** 62 A1
Whitley Heath **ST21** 40 A3
Whitley Lower **WF12** 50 E1
Whitley Row **TN14** 23 H6
Whitlock's End **B90** 30 C1
Whitminster **GL2** 20 A1
Whitmore, *Dorset* **BH21** 10 B4
Whitmore, *Staffs.* **ST5** 40 A1
Whitnage **EX16** 7 J4
Whitnash **CV31** 30 E2
Whitnell **TA5** 19 F7
Whitney-on-Wye **HR3** 28 B4
Whitrigg, *Cumb.* **CA7** 60 D1
Whitrigg, *Cumb.* **CA7** 60 D3
Whitsbury **SP6** 10 C3
Whitsome **TD11** 77 G5
Whitson **NP18** 19 G3
Whitstable **CT5** 25 H5
Whitstone **EX22** 4 C1
Whittingham **NE66** 71 F2
Whittingslow **SY6** 38 D7
Whittington, *Derbys.* **S41** 51 F5
Whittington, *Glos.* **GL54** 30 B6
Whittington, *Lancs.* **LA6** 56 B2
Whittington, *Norf.* **PE33** 44 B6
Whittington, *Shrop.* **SY11** 38 C2
Whittington, *Staffs.* **WS14** 40 D5
Whittington, *Staffs.* **DY7** 40 A7
Whittington, *Worcs.* **WR5** 29 H3
Whittlebury **NN12** 31 H4
Whittle-le-Woods **PR6** 55 J7
Whittlesey **PE7** 43 F6
Whittlesford **CB2** 33 H4
Whittlestone Head **BL7** 49 G1
Whitton, *Gt.Lon.* **TW2** 22 E4
Whitton, *N.Lincs.* **DN15** 59 F7
Whitton, *Northumb.* **NE65** 71 F3
Whitton, *Powys* **LD7** 28 B2
Whitton, *Shrop.* **SY8** 28 E1
Whitton, *Stock.* **TS21** 62 E4
Whitton, *Suff.* **IP1** 35 F4
Whittonditch **SN8** 21 F4
Whittonstall **DH8** 62 B1
Whitway **RG20** 21 H6
Whitwell, *Derbys.* **S80** 51 H5
Whitwell, *Herts.* **SG4** 32 E6
Whitwell, *I.o.W.* **PO38** 11 G7
Whitwell, *N.Yorks.* **DL10** 62 D7
Whitwell, *Rut.* **LE15** 42 C5
Whitwell Street **NR10** 45 F3
Whitwell-on-the-Hill **YO60** 58 D3
Whitwick **LE67** 41 G4
Whitwood **WF10** 57 K7
Whitworth **OL12** 49 H1
Whixall **SY13** 38 E2
Whixley **YO26** 57 K4
Whorlton, *Dur.* **DL12** 62 C5
Whorlton, *N.Yorks.* **DL6** 63 F6
Whygate **NE48** 70 C6
Whyle **HR6** 28 E2
Whyteleafe **CR3** 23 G6
Wibdon **NP16** 19 J2
Wibsey **BD6** 57 G6
Wibtoft **LE17** 41 G7
Wichenford **WR6** 29 G2
Wichling **ME9** 14 E2
Wick, *Bourne.* **BH6** 10 C5
Wick, *Devon* **EX14** 7 K5
Wick, *High.* **KW1** 105 J3
Wick, *S.Glos.* **BS30** 20 A4
Wick, *Som.* **TA5** 19 F7
Wick, *Som.* **BA6** 8 E1
Wick, *V. of Glam.* **CF71** 18 C4
Wick, *W.Suss.* **BN17** 12 D6
Wick, *Wilts.* **SP5** 10 C2
Wick, *Worcs.* **WR10** 29 J4
Wick Airport **KW1** 105 J3
Wick Hill, *Kent* **TN27** 14 D3
Wick Hill, *W'ham* **RG40** 22 A5
Wick St. Lawrence **BS22** 19 G5
Wicken, *Cambs.* **CB7** 33 J1
Wicken, *Northants.* **MK19** 31 J5
Wicken Bonhunt **CB11** 33 H5
Wickenby **LN3** 52 D4
Wicker Street Green **CO10** 34 D4
Wickerslack **CA10** 61 H5
Wickersley **S66** 51 G3
Wicketwood Hill **NG4** 41 J1
Wickford **SS12** 24 D2
Wickham, *Hants.* **PO17** 11 G3
Wickham, *W.Berks.* **RG20** 21 G4
Wickham Bishops **CM8** 34 C7
Wickham Heath **RG20** 21 H5
Wickham Market **IP13** 35 H3
Wickham St. Paul **CO9** 34 C5
Wickham Skeith **IP23** 34 E2
Wickham Street, *Suff.* **CB8** 34 B3
Wickham Street, *Suff.* **IP23** 34 E2
Wickhambreaux **CT3** 15 H2
Wickhambrook **CB8** 34 B3
Wickhamford **WR11** 30 B4
Wickhampton **NR13** 45 J5
Wicklewood **NR18** 44 E5
Wickmere **NR11** 45 F2
Wickstreet **BN26** 13 J6
Wickwar **GL12** 20 A3
Widcombe **BA2** 20 A5
Widdington **CB11** 33 J5
Widdop **HX7** 56 E6
Widdrington **NE61** 71 H4
Widdrington Station **NE61** 71 H4
Wide Open **NE13** 71 H6
Widecombe in the Moor **TQ13** 5 H3
Widegates **PL13** 4 C5
Widemouth Bay **EX23** 6 A5
Widewall **KW17** 107 D8
Widford, *Essex* **CM2** 24 C1
Widford, *Herts.* **SG12** 33 H7
Widford, *Oxon.* **OX18** 30 D7
Widgham Green **CB8** 33 K3
Widmer End **HP15** 22 B2
Widmerpool **NG12** 41 J3
Widnes **WA8** 48 E4
Widworthy **EX14** 8 B5
WIGAN WN 48 E2
Wiganthorpe **YO60** 58 C2
Wigborough **TA13** 8 D3
Wiggaton **EX11** 7 K6
Wiggenhall St. Germans **PE34** 43 J4
Wiggenhall St. Mary Magdalen **PE34** 43 J4
Wiggenhall St. Mary the Virgin **PE34** 43 J4
Wiggenhall St. Peter **PE34** 44 A4
Wiggens Green **CB9** 33 K4
Wigginton, *Herts.* **HP23** 32 C7
Wigginton, *Oxon.* **OX15** 30 E5
Wigginton, *Shrop.* **SY11** 38 C2
Wigginton, *Staffs.* **B79** 40 E5
Wigginton, *York* **YO32** 58 C4
Wigglesworth **BD23** 56 D4
Wiggonby **CA7** 60 E1
Wiggonholt **RH20** 12 D5
Wighill **LS24** 57 K5
Wighton **NR23** 44 D2
Wightwizzle **S36** 50 E3
Wigley **SO51** 10 E3
Wigmore, *Here.* **HR6** 28 D2
Wigmore, *Med.* **ME8** 24 E5
Wigsley **NG23** 52 B5
Wigsthorpe **NN14** 42 D7
Wigston **LE18** 41 J6
Wigston Parva **LE10** 41 G7
Wigthorpe **S81** 51 H4
Wigtoft **PE20** 43 F2
Wigton **CA7** 60 D2
Wigtown **DG8** 64 E5
Wike **LS17** 57 J5
Wilbarston **LE16** 42 B7
Wilberfoss **YO41** 58 D4
Wilburton **CB6** 33 H1
Wilby, *Norf.* **NR16** 44 E6
Wilby, *Northants.* **NN8** 32 B2
Wilby, *Suff.* **IP21** 35 G1
Wilcot **SN9** 20 E5
Wilcott **SY4** 38 C4
Wilcrick **NP26** 19 H3
Wilday Green **S18** 51 F5
Wildboarclough **SK11** 49 J6
Wilde Street **IP28** 34 B1
Wilden, *Beds.* **MK44** 32 D3
Wilden, *Worcs.* **DY13** 29 H1
Wildhern **SP11** 21 G6
Wildhill **AL9** 23 F1
Wildmoor **B61** 29 J1
Wildsworth **DN21** 52 B3
Wilford **NG11** 41 H2
Wilkesley **SY13** 39 F1
Wilkhaven **IV20** 97 G3
Wilkieston **EH27** 75 K4
Wilksby **PE22** 53 F6
Willand, *Devon* **EX15** 7 J4
Willand, *Som.* **TA3** 7 K4
Willaston, *Ches.* **CH64** 48 C5
Willaston, *Ches.* **CW5** 49 F7
Willaston, *Shrop.* **SY13** 38 E2
Willen **MK15** 32 B4
Willenhall, *W.Mid.* **WV13** 40 B6
Willenhall, *W.Mid.* **CV3** 30 E1
Willerby, *E.Riding* **HU10** 59 G6
Willerby, *N.Yorks.* **YO12** 59 G2
Willersey **WR12** 30 C5
Willersley **HR3** 28 C4
Willesborough **TN24** 15 F3
Willesborough Lees **TN24** 15 F3
Willesden **NW10** 23 F3
Willesleigh **EX32** 6 D2
Willesley **GL8** 20 B3
Willett **TA4** 7 K2
Willey, *Shrop.* **TF12** 39 F6
Willey, *Warks.* **CV23** 41 G7
Willey Green **GU3** 22 C6
William's Green **IP7** 34 D4
Williamscot **OX17** 31 F4
Williamthorpe **S42** 51 G6
Willian **SG6** 33 F5
Willimontswick **NE47** 70 C7
Willingale **CM5** 23 J1
Willingdon **BN20** 13 J6
Willingham **CB4** 33 H1
Willingham by Stow **DN21** 52 B4
Willingham Green **CB8** 33 K3
Willington, *Beds.* **MK44** 32 E3
Willington, *Derbys.* **DE65** 40 E3
Willington, *Dur.* **DL15** 62 C3
Willington, *Kent* **ME15** 14 C2
Willington, *T. & W.* **NE28** 71 J7
Willington, *Warks.* **CV36** 30 D5
Willington Corner **CW6** 48 E6
Willisham **IP8** 34 E3
Willitoft **YO8** 58 D6
Williton **TA4** 7 J1
Willoughbridge **TF9** 39 G1
Willoughby, *Lincs.* **LN13** 53 H5
Willoughby, *Warks.* **CV23** 31 G2
Willoughby Waterleys **LE8** 41 H6
Willoughby-on-the-Wolds **LE12** 41 J3
Willoughton **DN21** 52 C3
Willow Green **CW8** 49 F5
Willows Green **CM3** 34 B7
Willsbridge **BS30** 19 K4
Willslock **ST14** 40 C2
Willsworthy **PL19** 6 D7
Willtown **TA10** 8 C2
Wilmcote **CV37** 30 C3
Wilmington, *B. & N.E.Som.* **BA2** 19 K5
Wilmington, *Devon* **EX14** 8 B4
Wilmington, *E.Suss.* **BN26** 13 J6
Wilmington, *Kent* **DA2** 23 J4
Wilmslow **SK9** 49 H4
Wilnecote **B77** 40 E5
Wilney Green **IP22** 44 E7
Wilpshire **BB1** 56 B6
Wilsden **BD15** 57 F6
Wilsford, *Lincs.* **NG32** 42 D1
Wilsford, *Wilts.* **SP4** 10 C1
Wilsford, *Wilts.* **SN9** 20 E6
Wilsham **EX35** 7 F1
Wilshaw **HD9** 50 D2
Wilsill **HG3** 57 G3
Wilsley Green **TN17** 14 C4
Wilsley Pound **TN17** 14 C4
Wilson **DE73** 41 G3
Wilstead **MK45** 32 D4
Wilsthorpe, *E.Riding* **YO15** 59 H3
Wilsthorpe, *Lincs.* **PE9** 42 D4
Wilstone **HP23** 32 C7
Wilton, *Cumb.* **CA22** 60 B5
Wilton, *Here.* **HR9** 28 E6
Wilton, *N.Yorks.* **YO18** 58 E1
Wilton, *R. & C.* **TS10** 63 G4
Wilton, *Sc.Bord.* **TD9** 69 K2
Wilton, *Wilts.* **SN8** 21 F5
Wilton, *Wilts.* **SP2** 10 B1
Wiltown **EX15** 7 K4
Wimbish **CB10** 33 J5
Wimbish Green **CB10** 33 K5
Wimblebury **WS12** 40 C4
Wimbledon **SW19** 23 F4
Wimblington **PE15** 43 H6
Wimborne Minster **BH21** 10 B4
Wimborne St. Giles **BH21** 10 B3
Wimbotsham **PE34** 44 A5
Wimpole **SG8** 33 G3
Wimpole Lodge **SG8** 33 G4
Wimpstone **CV37** 30 D4
Wincanton **BA9** 9 G2
Winceby **LN9** 53 G6
Wincham **CW9** 49 F5
Winchburgh **EH52** 75 J3
Winchcombe **GL54** 30 B6
Winchelsea **TN36** 14 E6
Winchelsea Beach **TN36** 14 E6
Winchester **SO23** 11 F2
Winchet Hill **TN17** 14 C3
Winchfield **RG27** 22 A6
Winchmore Hill, *Bucks.* **HP7** 22 C2
Winchmore Hill, *Gt.Lon.* **N21** 23 G2
Wincle **SK11** 49 J6
Wincobank **S9** 51 F3
Windermere **LA23** 60 F7
Winderton **OX15** 30 E4
Windhill **IV4** 96 C7
Windle Hill **CH64** 48 C5
Windlehurst **SK6** 49 J4
Windlesham **GU20** 22 C5
Windley **DE56** 41 F1
Windmill Hill, *E.Suss.* **BN27** 13 K5
Windmill Hill, *Som.* **TA19** 8 C3
Windmill Hill, *Worcs.* **WR7** 29 J4
Windrush **OX18** 30 C7
Windsor **SL4** 22 C4
Windsor Green **IP30** 34 C3
Windy Nook **NE10** 71 H7
Windygates **KY8** 82 E7
Windy-Yett **KA3** 74 C5
Wineham **BN5** 13 F4
Winestead **HU12** 59 J7
Winewall **BB8** 56 E6
Winfarthing **IP22** 45 F7
Winford, *I.o.W.* **PO36** 11 G6
Winford, *N.Som.* **BS40** 19 J5
Winforton **HR3** 28 B4
Winfrith Newburgh **DT2** 9 H6
Wing, *Bucks.* **LU7** 32 B6
Wing, *Rut.* **LE15** 42 B5
Wingate **TS28** 62 E3
Wingates, *Gt.Man.* **BL5** 49 F2
Wingates, *Northumb.* **NE65** 71 F4
Wingerworth **S42** 51 F6
Wingfield, *Beds.* **LU7** 32 D6
Wingfield, *Suff.* **IP21** 35 G1
Wingfield, *Wilts.* **BA14** 20 B6
Wingfield Green **IP21** 35 G1
Wingham **CT3** 15 H2
Wingham Well **CT3** 15 H2
Wingmore **CT4** 15 G3
Wingrave **HP22** 32 B7
Winkburn **NG22** 51 K7
Winkfield **SL4** 22 C4
Winkfield Row **RG42** 22 B4
Winkhill **ST13** 50 C7
Winkleigh **EX19** 6 E5
Winksley **HG4** 57 H2
Winkton **BH23** 10 C5
Winlaton **NE21** 71 G7
Winlaton Mill **NE21** 71 G7
Winless **KW1** 105 J3
Winmarleigh **PR3** 55 H5
Winnard's Perch **TR9** 3 G2
Winnersh **RG41** 22 A4
Winnington **CW8** 49 F5
Winscombe **BS25** 19 H6
Winsford, *Ches.* **CW7** 49 F6
Winsford, *Som.* **TA24** 7 H2
Winsham, *Devon* **EX33** 6 C2
Winsham, *Som.* **TA20** 8 C4
Winshill **DE15** 40 E3
Winsh-wen **SA7** 17 K5
Winskill **CA10** 61 G3
Winslade **RG25** 21 K7
Winsley **BA15** 20 B5
Winslow **MK18** 31 J6
Winson **GL7** 20 D1
Winsor **SO40** 10 E3
Winster, *Cumb.* **LA23** 60 F7
Winster, *Derbys.* **DE4** 50 E6
Winston, *Dur.* **DL2** 62 C5
Winston, *Suff.* **IP14** 35 F2
Winston Green **IP14** 35 F2
Winstone **GL7** 20 C1
Winswell **EX38** 6 C4
Winterborne Came **DT2** 9 G6
Winterborne Clenston **DT11** 9 H4
Winterborne Herringston **DT2** 9 F6
Winterborne Houghton **DT11** 9 H4
Winterborne Kingston **DT11** 9 H5
Winterborne Monkton **DT2** 9 F6
Winterborne Stickland **DT11** 9 H4
Winterborne Whitechurch **DT11** 9 H4
Winterborne Zelston **DT11** 9 H5
Winterbourne, *S.Glos.* **BS36** 19 K3
Winterbourne, *W.Berks.* **RG20** 21 H4
Winterbourne Abbas **DT2** 9 F5
Winterbourne Bassett **SN4** 20 E4
Winterbourne Dauntsey **SP4** 10 C1
Winterbourne Earls **SP4** 10 C1
Winterbourne Gunner **SP4** 10 C1
Winterbourne Monkton **SN4** 20 E4
Winterbourne Steepleton **DT2** 9 F6
Winterbourne Stoke **SP3** 20 D7
Winterbrook **OX10** 21 K3
Winterburn **BD23** 56 E4
Wintercleugh **ML12** 68 E2
Winteringham **DN15** 59 F7
Winterley **CW11** 49 G7
Wintersett **WF4** 51 F1
Wintershill **SO32** 11 G3
Winterslow **SP5** 10 D1
Winterton **DN15** 52 C1
Winterton-on-Sea **NR29** 45 J4
Winthorpe, *Lincs.* **PE25** 53 J6
Winthorpe, *Notts.* **NG24** 52 B7
Winton, *Bourne.* **BH9** 10 B5
Winton, *Cumb.* **CA17** 61 J5
Wintringham **YO17** 58 E2
Winwick, *Cambs.* **PE28** 42 E7
Winwick, *Northants.* **NN6** 31 H1
Winwick, *Warr.* **WA2** 49 F3
Wirksworth **DE4** 50 E7
Wirksworth Moor **DE4** 51 F7
Wirswall **SY13** 38 E1
Wisbech **PE13** 43 H5
Wisbech St. Mary **PE13** 43 H5
Wisborough Green **RH14** 12 D4
Wiseton **DN10** 51 K4
Wishaw, *N.Lan.* **ML2** 75 F5
Wishaw, *Warks.* **B76** 40 D6
Wisley **GU23** 22 D6
Wispington **LN9** 53 F5
Wissett **IP19** 35 H1
Wissington **CO6** 34 D5
Wistanstow **SY7** 38 D7
Wistanswick **TF9** 39 F3
Wistaston **CW2** 49 F7
Wiston, *Pembs.* **SA62** 16 D3
Wiston, *S.Lan.* **ML12** 75 H7
Wistow, *Cambs.* **PE28** 43 F7
Wistow, *N.Yorks.* **YO8** 58 B6
Wiswell **BB7** 56 C6
Witcham **CB6** 33 H1
Witchampton **BH21** 9 J4
Witchburn **PA28** 66 B1
Witchford **CB6** 33 J1
Witcombe **TA12** 8 D2
Witham **CM8** 34 C7
Witham Friary **BA11** 20 A7
Witham on the Hill **PE10** 42 D4
Withcall **LN11** 53 F4
Withcote **LE15** 42 A5
Withdean **BN1** 13 G6
Witherenden Hill **TN19** 13 K4
Witherhurst **TN19** 13 K4
Witheridge **EX16** 7 G4
Witherley **CV9** 41 F6
Withern **LN13** 53 H4
Withernsea **HU19** 59 K7
Withernwick **HU11** 59 H5
Withersdale Street **IP20** 45 G7
Withersfield **CB9** 33 K4
Witherslack **LA11** 55 H1
Witherslack Hall **LA11** 55 H1
Withiel **PL30** 3 G2
Withiel Florey **TA24** 7 H2
Withielgoose **PL30** 4 A4
Withington, *Glos.* **GL54** 30 B7
Withington, *Gt.Man.* **M20** 49 H3
Withington, *Here.* **HR1** 28 E4
Withington, *Shrop.* **SY4** 38 E4
Withington, *Staffs.* **ST10** 40 C2
Withington Green **SK11** 49 H5
Withington Marsh **HR1** 28 E4
Withleigh **EX16** 7 H4
Withnell **PR6** 56 B7
Withnell Fold **PR6** 56 B7
Withybrook, *Som.* **BA3** 19 K7
Withybrook, *Warks.* **CV7** 41 G7
Withycombe **TA24** 7 J1
Withycombe Raleigh **EX8** 7 J7
Withyham **TN7** 13 H3
Withypool **TA24** 7 G2
Witley **GU8** 12 C3
Witnesham **IP6** 35 F3
Witney **OX28** 21 G1
Wittering **PE8** 42 D5
Wittersham **TN30** 14 D5
Witton, *Angus* **DD9** 90 D7
Witton, *Norf.* **NR13** 45 H5
Witton, *Worcs.* **WR9** 29 H2
Witton Bridge **NR28** 45 H2
Witton Gilbert **DH7** 62 D2
Witton Park **DL14** 62 C3
Witton-le-Wear **DL14** 62 C3
Wiveliscombe **TA4** 7 J3
Wivelsfield **RH17** 13 G4
Wivelsfield Green **RH17** 13 G5
Wivenhoe **CO7** 34 E6
Wiveton **NR25** 44 E1
Wix **CO11** 35 F6
Wixford **B49** 30 B3
Wixhill **SY4** 38 E3
Wixoe **CO10** 34 B4
Woburn **MK17** 32 C5
Woburn Sands **MK17** 32 C5
Wokefield Park **RG7** 21 K5
Woking **GU22** 22 D6
Wokingham **RG40** 22 B5
Wolborough **TQ12** 5 J3
Wold Newton, *E.Riding* **YO25** 59 G2
Wold Newton, *N.E.Lincs.* **LN8** 53 F3
Woldingham **CR3** 23 G6
Wolfelee **TD9** 70 A3
Wolferlow **HR7** 29 F2
Wolferton **PE31** 44 A3
Wolfhampcote **CV23** 31 G2
Wolfhill **PH2** 82 C4
Wolfpits **LD8** 28 B3
Wolf's Castle **SA62** 16 C2
Wolfsdale **SA62** 16 C2
Woll **TD7** 69 K1
Wollaston, *Northants.* **NN29** 32 C2
Wollaston, *Shrop.* **SY5** 38 C4
Wollaston, *W.Mid.* **DY8** 40 A7
Wollaton **NG8** 41 H2
Wollerton **TF9** 39 F3
Wollescote **DY9** 40 B7
Wolsingham **DL13** 62 B3
Wolston **CV8** 31 F1
Wolsty **CA7** 60 C1
Wolvercote **OX2** 21 J1
WOLVERHAMPTON WV 40 B6
Wolverley, *Shrop.* **SY4** 38 D2
Wolverley, *Worcs.* **DY11** 29 H1
Wolverton, *Hants.* **RG26** 21 J6
Wolverton, *M.K.* **MK12** 32 B4
Wolverton, *Warks.* **CV35** 30 D2
Wolverton, *Wilts.* **BA12** 9 G1
Wolverton Common **RG26** 21 J6
Wolvesnewton **NP16** 19 H2
Wolvey **LE10** 41 G7
Wolvey Heath **LE10** 41 G7
Wolviston **TS22** 63 F4
Womaston **LD8** 28 B2
Wombleton **YO62** 58 C1
Wombourne **WV5** 40 A6
Wombwell **S73** 51 F2
Womenswold **CT4** 15 H2
Womersley **DN6** 51 H1
Wonastow **NP25** 28 D7
Wonersh **GU5** 22 D7
Wonford **EX2** 7 H6
Wonson **EX20** 6 E7
Wonston **SO21** 11 F1
Wooburn **HP10** 22 C3
Wooburn Green **HP10** 22 C3
Wood Bevington **B49** 30 B3
Wood Burcote **NN12** 31 H4
Wood Dalling **NR11** 44 E3
Wood Eaton **ST20** 40 A4
Wood End, *Beds.* **MK43** 32 D4
Wood End, *Beds.* **MK44** 32 D2
Wood End, *Bucks.* **MK17** 31 J5
Wood End, *Herts.* **SG2** 33 G6
Wood End, *W.Mid.* **WV11** 40 B5
Wood End, *Warks.* **CV9** 40 E6
Wood End, *Warks.* **B94** 30 C1
Wood End, *Warks.* **CV7** 40 E7
Wood Enderby **PE22** 53 F6
Wood Green, *Essex* **EN9** 23 H1
Wood Green, *Gt.Lon.* **N22** 23 G2
Wood Green, *Norf.* **NR15** 45 G6
Wood Lane **SY12** 38 D2
Wood Norton **NR20** 44 E3
Wood Seats **S35** 51 F3
Wood Stanway **GL54** 30 B5
Wood Street **NR29** 45 H3
Wood Street Village **GU3** 22 C6
Woodacott **EX22** 6 B5
Woodale **DL8** 57 F2
Woodall **S26** 51 G4
Woodbastwick **NR13** 45 H4
Woodbeck **DN22** 51 K5
Woodborough, *Notts.* **NG14** 41 J1
Woodborough, *Wilts.* **SN9** 20 E6
Woodbridge, *Devon* **EX24** 7 K6
Woodbridge, *Dorset* **DT10** 9 G3
Woodbridge, *Suff.* **IP12** 35 G4
Woodbury, *Devon* **EX5** 7 J7
Woodbury, *Som.* **BA5** 19 J7
Woodbury Salterton **EX5** 7 J7

223

Woodchester **GL5** 20 B1
Woodchurch, *Kent* **TN26** 14 E4
Woodchurch, *Mersey.* **CH49** 48 B4
Woodcombe **TA24** 7 H1
Woodcote, *Oxon.* **RG8** 21 K3
Woodcote, *Tel. & W.* **TF10** 39 G4
Woodcote Green **B61** 29 J1
Woodcott **RG28** 21 H6
Woodcroft **NP16** 19 J2
Woodcutts **SP5** 9 J3
Woodditton **CB8** 33 K3
Woodeaton **OX3** 31 G7
Woodend, *Aber.* **AB51** 90 E3
Woodend, *Cumb.* **CA18** 60 C7
Woodend, *High.* **IV13** 88 E2
Woodend, *High.* **PH36** 79 J2
Woodend, *Northants.* **NN12** 31 H4
Woodend, *P. & K.* **PH15** 81 J3
Woodend, *W.Suss.* **PO18** 12 B6
Woodend Green **CM22** 33 J6
Woodfalls **SP5** 10 C2
Woodfield, *Oxon.* **OX26** 31 G6
Woodfield, *S.Ayr.* **KA8** 67 H1
Woodfoot **CA10** 61 H5
Woodford, *Cornw.* **EX23** 6 A4
Woodford, *Devon* **TQ9** 5 H5
Woodford, *Glos.* **GL13** 19 K2
Woodford, *Gt.Lon.* **IG8** 23 H2
Woodford, *Gt.Man.* **SK7** 49 H4
Woodford, *Northants.* **NN14** 32 C1
Woodford, *Som.* **TA4** 7 J2
Woodford Bridge **IG8** 23 H2
Woodford Green **IG8** 23 H2
Woodford Halse **NN11** 31 G3
Woodgate, *Devon* **EX15** 7 K4
Woodgate, *Norf.* **NR20** 44 E4
Woodgate, *W.Mid.* **B32** 40 B7
Woodgate, *W.Suss.* **PO20** 12 C6
Woodgate, *Worcs.* **B60** 29 J2
Woodgreen **SP6** 10 C3
Woodhall, *Inclyde* **PA14** 74 B3
Woodhall, *N.Yorks.* **DL8** 62 A7
Woodhall Hills **LS28** 57 G6
Woodhall Spa **LN10** 52 E6
Woodham, *Bucks.* **HP18** 31 H7
Woodham, *Dur.* **DL17** 62 D4
Woodham, *Surr.* **KT15** 22 D5
Woodham Ferrers **CM3** 24 D2
Woodham Mortimer **CM9** 24 E1
Woodham Walter **CM9** 24 E1
Woodhaven **DD6** 83 F5
Woodhead, *Aber.* **AB53** 91 F1
Woodhead, *Staffs.* **ST10** 40 C1
Woodhey **CH42** 48 C4
Woodhey Green **CW5** 48 E7
Woodhill, *Shrop.* **WV16** 39 G7
Woodhill, *Som.* **TA3** 8 C2
Woodhorn **NE63** 71 H5
Woodhouse, *Cumb.* **LA7** 55 J1
Woodhouse, *Leics.* **LE12** 41 H4
Woodhouse, *S.Yorks.* **S13** 51 G4
Woodhouse, *W.Yorks.* **LS2** 57 H6
Woodhouse, *W.Yorks.* **WF6** 57 J7
Woodhouse, *W.Yorks.* **HD6** 57 G7
Woodhouse Down **BS32** 19 K3
Woodhouse Eaves **LE12** 41 H4
Woodhouse Green **SK11** 49 J6
Woodhouses, *Gt.Man.* **M35** 49 H2
Woodhouses, *Staffs.* **DE13** 40 D4
Woodhouses, *Staffs.* **WS7** 40 C5
Woodhuish **TQ6** 5 K5
Woodhurst **PE28** 33 G1
Woodingdean **BN2** 13 G6
Woodington **SO51** 10 E2
Woodland, *Devon* **TQ13** 5 H4
Woodland, *Dur.* **DL13** 62 B4
Woodland, *Kent* **CT18** 15 G3
Woodland Head **EX17** 7 F6
Woodlands, *Dorset* **BH21** 10 B4
Woodlands, *Hants.* **SO40** 10 E3
Woodlands, *N.Yorks.* **HG2** 57 J4
Woodlands, *Shrop.* **WV16** 39 G7
Woodlands, *Som.* **TA5** 7 K1
Woodlands Park **SL6** 22 B4
Woodlands St. Mary **RG17** 21 G4
Woodlane **DE13** 40 D3
Woodleigh **TQ7** 5 H6
Woodlesford **LS26** 57 J7
Woodley, *Gt.Man.* **SK6** 49 J3
Woodley, *W'ham* **RG5** 22 A4
Woodmancote, *Glos.* **GL7** 20 D1
Woodmancote, *Glos.* **GL52** 29 J6
Woodmancote, *Glos.* **GL11** 20 A2
Woodmancote, *W.Suss.* **BN5** 13 F5
Woodmancote, *W.Suss.* **PO10** 11 J4
Woodmancott **SO21** 21 J7
Woodmansey **HU17** 59 G6
Woodmansterne **SM7** 23 F6
Woodmanton **EX5** 7 J7
Woodmill **DE13** 40 D3
Woodminton **SP5** 10 B2
Woodnesborough **CT13** 15 J2
Woodnewton **PE8** 42 D6
Woodperry **OX33** 31 G7
Woodplumpton **PR4** 55 J6
Woodrising **NR9** 44 D5
Woodrow **DT10** 9 G3
Wood's Corner **TN21** 13 K5
Woods Eaves **HR3** 28 B4
Wood's Green **TN5** 13 K3
Woodseaves, *Shrop.* **TF9** 39 F2
Woodseaves, *Staffs.* **ST20** 39 G3
Woodsend **SN8** 21 F4

Woodsetts **S81** 51 H4
Woodsford **DT2** 9 G5
Woodside, Aberdeen **AB24** 91 H4
Woodside, *Beds.* **LU1** 32 D7
Woodside, *Brack.F.* **SL4** 22 C4
Woodside, *Cumb.* **CA15** 60 B3
Woodside, *D. & G.* **DG1** 69 F6
Woodside, *Fife* **KY8** 83 F7
Woodside, *Fife* **KY7** 82 D7
Woodside, *Gt.Lon.* **SE25** 23 G5
Woodside, *Hants.* **SO41** 10 E5
Woodside, *Herts.* **AL9** 23 F1
Woodside, *N.Ayr.* **KA15** 74 B5
Woodside, *P. & K.* **PH13** 82 C4
Woodside, *Shrop.* **SY7** 38 C7
Woodside, *W.Mid.* **DY5** 40 B7
Woodside Green **ME17** 14 E2
Woodstock, *Oxon.* **OX20** 31 F7
Woodstock, *Pembs.* **SA63** 16 D2
Woodthorpe, *Derbys.* **S43** 51 G5
Woodthorpe, *Leics.* **LE12** 41 H4
Woodthorpe, *Lincs.* **LN13** 53 H4
Woodthorpe, *S.Yorks.* **S2** 51 F4
Woodton **NR35** 45 G6
Woodtown **EX39** 6 C3
Woodvale **PR8** 48 C1
Woodville **DE11** 41 F4
Woodwall Green **ST21** 39 G2
Woodwalton **PE28** 43 F7
Woodwick **KW17** 106 C5
Woodworth Green **CW6** 48 E7
Woodyates **SP5** 10 B3
Woofferton **SY8** 28 E2
Wookey **BA5** 19 J7
Wookey Hole **BA5** 19 J7
Wool **BH20** 9 H6
Woolacombe **EX34** 6 C1
Woolage Green **CT4** 15 H3
Woolage Village **CT4** 15 H2
Woolaston **GL15** 19 J2
Woolaston Slade **GL15** 19 J1
Woolavington **TA7** 19 G7
Woolbeding **GU29** 12 B4
Woolcotts **TA22** 7 H2
Wooldale **HD9** 50 D2
Wooler **NE71** 70 E1
Woolfardisworthy, *Devon* **EX17** 7 G5
Woolfardisworthy, *Devon* **EX39** 6 B3
Woolfold **BL8** 49 G1
Woolfords Cottages **EH55** 75 J5
Woolgarston **BH20** 9 J6
Woolgreaves **WF2** 51 F1
Woolhampton **RG7** 21 J5
Woolhope **HR1** 29 F5
Woolland **DT11** 9 G4
Woollard **BS39** 19 K5
Woollaton **EX38** 6 C4
Woollensbrook **EN11** 23 G1
Woolley, *B. & N.E.Som.* **BA1** 20 A5
Woolley, *Cambs.* **PE28** 32 E1
Woolley, *Cornw.* **EX23** 6 A4
Woolley, *Derbys.* **DE55** 51 F6
Woolley, *W.Yorks.* **WF4** 51 F1
Woolley Green, *W. & M.* **SL6** 22 B4
Woolley Green, *Wilts.* **BA15** 20 B5
Woolmer Green **SG3** 33 F7
Woolmere Green **B60** 29 J2
Woolmersdon **TA5** 8 B1
Woolpit **IP30** 34 D2
Woolpit Green **IP30** 34 D2
Woolscott **CV23** 31 F2
Woolsgrove **EX17** 7 F5
Woolstaston **SY6** 38 D6
Woolsthorpe **NG32** 42 B2
Woolsthorpe by Colsterworth **NG33** 42 C3
Woolston, *Devon* **TQ7** 5 H6
Woolston, *S'ham.* **SO19** 11 F3
Woolston, *Shrop.* **SY10** 38 C3
Woolston, *Shrop.* **SY6** 38 D7
Woolston, *Warr.* **WA1** 49 F4
Woolston Green **TQ13** 5 H4
Woolstone, *Glos.* **GL52** 29 J5
Woolstone, *M.K.* **MK15** 32 B5
Woolstone, *Oxon.* **SN7** 21 F3
Woolton **L25** 48 D4
Woolton Hill **RG20** 21 H5
Woolverstone **IP9** 35 F5
Woolverton **BA2** 20 A6
Woolwich **SE18** 23 H4
Woonton **HR3** 28 C3
Wooperton **NE66** 71 F2
Woore **CW3** 39 G1
Wootten Green **IP21** 35 G1
Wootton, *Beds.* **MK43** 32 D4
Wootton, *Hants.* **BH25** 10 D5
Wootton, *I.o.W.* **PO33** 11 G5
Wootton, *Kent* **CT4** 15 H3
Wootton, *N.Lincs.* **DN39** 52 D1
Wootton, *Northants.* **NN4** 31 J3
Wootton, *Oxon.* **OX20** 31 F7
Wootton, *Oxon.* **OX1** 21 H1
Wootton, *Shrop.* **SY7** 28 D1
Wootton, *Shrop.* **SY3** 38 C3
Wootton, *Staffs.* **ST21** 40 A3
Wootton, *Staffs.* **DE6** 40 D1
Wootton Bassett **SN4** 20 D3
Wootton Bridge **PO33** 11 G5
Wootton Common **PO33** 11 G5
Wootton Courtenay **TA24** 7 H1
Wootton Fitzpaine **DT6** 8 C5
Wootton Green **MK43** 32 D4
Wootton Rivers **SN8** 20 E5
Wootton St. Lawrence **RG23** 21 J6
Wootton Wawen **B95** 30 C2

WORCESTER **WR** 29 H3
Worcester Park **KT4** 23 F5
Wordsley **DY8** 40 A7
Wordwell **IP28** 34 C1
Worfield **WV15** 39 G6
Worgret **BH20** 9 J6
Work **KW15** 107 D6
Workhouse End **MK41** 32 E3
Workington **CA14** 60 B4
Worksop **S80** 51 H5
Worlaby, *Lincs.* **LN11** 53 G5
Worlaby, *N.Lincs.* **DN20** 52 D1
World's End, *Bucks.* **HP22** 22 B1
Worlds End, *Hants.* **PO7** 11 H3
World's End, *W.Berks.* **RG20** 21 H4
Worldham **GU34** 11 J1
Worle **BS22** 19 G5
Worleston **CW5** 49 F7
Worlingham **NR34** 45 J7
Worlington **IP28** 33 K1
Worlingworth **IP13** 35 G2
Wormald Green **HG3** 57 J3
Wormbridge **HR2** 28 D5
Wormegay **PE33** 44 A4
Wormelow Tump **HR2** 28 D5
Wormhill **SK17** 50 D5
Wormiehills **DD11** 83 H4
Wormingford **CO6** 34 D5
Worminghall **HP18** 21 K1
Wormington **WR12** 30 B5
Worminster **BA4** 19 J7
Wormiston **KY10** 83 H7
Wormit **DD6** 82 E5
Wormleighton **CV47** 31 F3
Wormley, *Herts.* **EN10** 23 G1
Wormley, *Surr.* **GU8** 12 C3
Wormley West End **AL9** 23 F1
Wormshill **ME9** 14 D2
Wormsley **HR4** 28 D4
Worplesdon **GU3** 22 C6
Worrall **S35** 51 F3
Worsbrough **S70** 51 F2
Worsley **M28** 49 G2
Worstead **NR28** 45 H3
Worsted Lodge **CB1** 33 J3
Worsthorne **BB10** 56 D6
Worston **BB7** 56 C5
Worswell **PL8** 5 F6
Worth, *Kent* **CT14** 15 J2
Worth, *W.Suss.* **RH10** 13 F3
Worth Matravers **BH19** 9 J7
Wortham **IP22** 34 E1
Worthen **SY5** 38 C5
Worthenbury **LL13** 38 D1
Worthing, *Norf.* **NR20** 44 D4
Worthing, *W.Suss.* **BN11** 12 E6
Worthington **LE65** 41 G3
Worting **RG23** 21 K6
Wortley, *Glos.* **GL12** 20 A2
Wortley, *S.Yorks.* **S35** 51 F3
Wortley, *W.Yorks.* **LS12** 57 H6
Worton, *N.Yorks.* **DL8** 56 E1
Worton, *Wilts.* **SN10** 20 C6
Wortwell **IP20** 45 G7
Wothersome **LS23** 57 K5
Wotherton **SY15** 38 B5
Wotter **PL7** 5 F4
Wotton **RH5** 22 E7
Wotton Underwood **HP18** 31 H7
Wotton-under-Edge **GL12** 20 A2
Woughton on the Green **MK6** 32 B5
Wouldham **ME1** 24 D5
Wrabness **CO11** 35 F5
Wrae **AB53** 99 F5
Wrafton **EX33** 6 C2
Wragby **LN8** 52 E5
Wragholme **LN11** 53 G3
Wramplingham **NR18** 45 F5
Wrangaton **PL21** 5 G5
Wrangham **AB52** 90 E1
Wrangle **PE22** 53 H7
Wrangle Lowgate **PE22** 53 H7
Wrangway **TA21** 7 K4
Wrantage **TA3** 8 C2
Wrawby **DN20** 52 D2
Wraxall, *N.Som.* **BS48** 19 H4
Wraxall, *Som.* **BA4** 9 F1
Wray **LA2** 56 B3
Wray Castle **LA22** 60 E6
Wrays **RH6** 23 F7
Wraysbury **TW19** 22 D4
Wrayton **LA6** 56 B2
Wrea Green **PR4** 55 G6
Wreay, *Cumb.* **CA11** 60 F4
Wreay, *Cumb.* **CA4** 60 F2
Wrecclesham **GU10** 22 B7
Wrecsam (Wrexham) **LL13** 38 C1
Wrekenton **NE9** 62 D1
Wrelton **YO18** 58 D1
Wrenbury **CW5** 38 E1
Wrench Green **YO13** 59 F1
Wreningham **NR16** 45 F6
Wrentham **NR34** 45 J7
Wrenthorpe **WF2** 57 J7
Wrentnall **SY5** 38 D5
Wressle, *E.Riding* **YO8** 58 D6
Wressle, *N.Lincs.* **DN20** 52 C2
Wrestlingworth **SG19** 33 F4
Wretham **IP24** 44 D6
Wretton **PE33** 44 A5
Wrexham (Wrecsam) **LL13** 38 C1
Wrexham Industrial Estate **LL13** 38 C1
Wribbenhall **DY12** 29 G1
Wrightington Bar **WN6** 48 E1
Wrightbenhall **DY12** 29 G1
Wrightpark **FK8** 74 E1
Wright's Green **CM22** 33 J7

Wrinehill **CW3** 39 G1
Wrington **BS40** 19 H5
Writhlington **BA3** 19 K6
Writtle **CM1** 24 C1
Wrockwardine **TF6** 39 F4
Wroot **DN9** 51 K2
Wrose **BD18** 57 G6
Wrotham **TN15** 23 K6
Wrotham Heath **TN15** 23 K6
Wrotham Hill Park **TN15** 24 C5
Wrottesley **WV8** 40 A5
Wroughton **SN4** 20 E3
Wroxall, *I.o.W.* **PO38** 11 G7
Wroxall, *Warks.* **CV35** 30 D1
Wroxeter **SY5** 38 E5
Wroxham **NR12** 45 H4
Wroxton **OX15** 31 F4
Wstrws **SA44** 26 C4
Wyaston **DE6** 40 D1
Wyberton **PE21** 43 G1
Wyboston **MK44** 32 E3
Wybunbury **CW5** 39 F1
Wych Cross **RH18** 13 H3
Wychbold **WR9** 29 J2
Wychnor **DE13** 40 D4
Wychnor Bridges **DE13** 40 D4
Wyck **GU34** 11 J1
Wyck Rissington **GL54** 30 C6
Wycliffe **DL12** 62 C5
Wycoller **BB8** 56 E6
Wycomb **LE14** 42 A3
Wycombe Marsh **HP11** 22 B2
Wyddial **SG9** 33 G5
Wye **TN25** 15 F3
Wyesham **NP25** 28 E7
Wyfordby **LE14** 42 A4
Wyke, *Devon* **EX17** 7 G6
Wyke, *Dorset* **SP8** 9 G2
Wyke, *Shrop.* **TF13** 39 F5
Wyke, *Surr.* **GU3** 22 C6
Wyke, *W.Yorks.* **BD12** 57 G7
Wyke Champflower **BA10** 9 F1
Wyke Regis **DT4** 9 F7
Wykeham, *N.Yorks.* **YO13** 59 F1
Wykeham, *N.Yorks.* **YO17** 58 E2
Wyken, *Shrop.* **WV15** 39 G6
Wyken, *W.Mid.* **CV2** 41 F7
Wykey **SY4** 38 C3
Wylam **NE41** 71 G7
Wylde Green **B72** 40 D6
Wyllie **NP1** 18 E2
Wylye **BA12** 10 B1
Wymering **PO6** 11 H4
Wymeswold **LE12** 41 J3
Wymington **NN10** 32 C2
Wymondham, *Leics.* **LE14** 42 B4
Wymondham, *Norf.* **NR18** 45 F5
Wyndham **CF32** 18 C2
Wynford Eagle **DT2** 8 E5
Wynnstay Park **LL14** 38 C1
Wynyard **TS22** 63 F4
Wyre Piddle **WR10** 29 J4
Wyresdale Tower **LA2** 56 B4
Wysall **NG12** 41 J3
Wyson **SY8** 28 E2
Wythall **B47** 30 B1
Wytham **OX2** 21 H1
Wythburn **CA12** 60 E5
Wythenshawe **M22** 49 H4
Wyton, *Cambs.* **PE28** 33 F1
Wyton, *E.Riding* **HU11** 59 H6
Wyverstone **IP14** 34 E2
Wyverstone Street **IP14** 34 E2
Wyville **NG32** 42 B3
Wyvis Lodge **IV16** 96 B4

Y

Y Bryn **LL23** 37 H3
Y Drenewydd (Newtown) **SY16** 38 A6
Y Fan **SY18** 37 J7
Y Felinheli **LL56** 46 D6
Y Fenni (Abergavenny) **NP7** 28 B7
Y Fflint (Flint) **CH6** 48 B5
Y Ffôr **LL53** 36 C2
Y Trallwng (Welshpool) **SY21** 38 B5
Y Tymbl (Tumble) **SA14** 17 J3
Y Waun (Chirk) **LL14** 38 B2
Yaddlethorpe **DN17** 52 B2
Yafford **PO30** 11 F6
Yafforth **DL7** 62 E7
Yalberton **TQ4** 5 J5
Yalding **ME18** 23 K7
Yanley **BS41** 19 J5
Yanwath **CA10** 61 G4
Yanworth **GL54** 30 B7
Yapham **YO42** 58 D4
Yapton **BN18** 12 C6
Yarburgh **LN11** 53 G3
Yarcombe **EX14** 8 B4
Yardley **B26** 40 D7
Yardley Gobion **NN12** 31 J4
Yardley Hastings **NN7** 32 B3
Yardro **LD8** 28 B3
Yarford **TA2** 8 B2
Yarkhill **HR1** 29 F4
Yarlet **ST18** 40 B3
Yarley **BA5** 19 J7
Yarlington **BA9** 9 F2
Yarm **TS15** 63 F5
Yarmouth **PO41** 10 E6
Yarnacott **EX32** 6 E2
Yarnbrook **BA14** 20 B6
Yarnfield **ST15** 40 A2
Yarnscombe **EX31** 6 D3
Yarnton **OX5** 31 F7
Yarpole **HR6** 28 D2
Yarrow, *Sc.Bord.* **TD7** 69 J1

Yarrow, *Som.* **TA9** 19 G7
Yarrow Feus **TD7** 69 J1
Yarrowford **TD7** 69 K1
Yarsop **HR4** 28 D4
Yarwell **PE8** 42 D6
Yate **BS37** 20 A3
Yatehouse Green **CW10** 49 G6
Yateley **GU46** 22 B5
Yatesbury **SN11** 20 D4
Yattendon **RG18** 21 J4
Yatton, *Here.* **HR6** 28 D2
Yatton, *N.Som.* **BS49** 19 H5
Yatton Keynell **SN14** 20 B4
Yaverland **PO36** 11 H6
Yawl **DT7** 8 C5
Yaxham **NR19** 44 E4
Yaxley, *Cambs.* **PE7** 42 E6
Yaxley, *Suff.* **IP23** 35 F1
Yazor **HR4** 28 D4
Yeabridge **TA13** 8 D3
Yeading **UB4** 22 E3
Yeadon **LS19** 57 H5
Yealand Conyers **LA5** 55 J2
Yealand Redmayne **LA5** 55 J2
Yealand Storrs **LA5** 55 J2
Yealmbridge **PL8** 5 F5
Yealmpton **PL8** 5 F5
Yearby **TS11** 63 H4
Yearsley **YO61** 58 B2
Yeaton **SY4** 38 D4
Yeaveley **DE6** 40 D1
Yeavering **NE71** 77 H7
Yedingham **YO17** 58 E2
Yelford **OX29** 21 G1
Yell **ZE2** 108 D4
Yelland, *Devon* **EX31** 6 C2
Yelland, *Devon* **EX20** 6 D6
Yelling **PE19** 33 F2
Yelvertoft **NN6** 31 G1
Yelverton, *Devon* **PL20** 5 F4
Yelverton, *Norf.* **NR14** 45 G5
Yenston **BA8** 9 G2
Yeo Mill **EX36** 7 G3
Yeo Vale **EX39** 6 C3
Yeoford **EX17** 7 F6
Yeolmbridge **PL15** 6 B7
Yeomadon **EX22** 6 B5
Yeovil **BA20** 8 E3
Yeovil Marsh **BA21** 8 E3
Yeovilton **BA22** 8 E2
Yerbeston **SA68** 16 D4
Yesnaby **KW16** 107 B6
Yetholm Mains **TD5** 70 D1
Yetlington **NE66** 71 F2
Yetminster **DT9** 8 E3
Yettington **EX9** 7 J7
Yetts o'Muckhart **FK14** 82 B7
Yew Green **CV35** 30 D2
Yielden **MK44** 32 D2
Yieldshields **ML8** 75 G5
Ynys **LL47** 36 E2
Ynys Enlli (Bardsey Island) **LL53** 36 A3
Ynys Môn (Anglesey) **LL** 46 B4
Ynys Tachwedd **SY24** 37 F6
Ynysboeth **CF45** 18 D2
Ynysddu **NP11** 18 E2
Ynyshir **CF39** 18 D2
Ynyslas **SY24** 37 F6
Ynysmaerdy **CF72** 18 D3
Ynysmeudwy **SA8** 18 A1
Ynystawe **SA6** 17 K4
Ynyswen **CF42** 18 C2
Ynysybwl **CF37** 18 D2
Yockenthwaite **BD23** 56 E2
Yockleton **SY5** 38 C4
Yokefleet **DN14** 58 E7
Yoker **G14** 74 D4
Yonder Bognie **AB54** 98 E6
YORK YO 58 C4
Yorkletts **CT5** 25 G5
Yorkley **GL15** 19 K1
Yorton **SY4** 38 E3
Yorton Heath **SY4** 38 E3
Youldon **EX22** 6 B5
Youldonmoor Cross **EX22** 6 B5
Youlgreave **DE45** 50 E6
Youlthorpe **YO41** 58 D4
Youlton **YO61** 57 K3
Young's End **CM3** 34 B7
Yoxall **DE13** 40 D4
Yoxford **IP17** 35 H2
Yr Wyddgrug (Mold) **CH7** 48 B6
Ysbyty Cynfyn **SY23** 27 G1
Ysbyty Ifan **LL24** 37 H1
Ysbyty Ystwyth **SY25** 27 G1
Ysceifiog **CH8** 47 K5
Ysgubor-y-coed **SY20** 37 F6
Ystalyfera **SA9** 18 A1
Ystrad **CF41** 18 C2
Ystrad Aeron **SA48** 26 E3
Ystrad Meurig **SY25** 27 G2
Ystrad Mynach **CF82** 18 E2
Ystradfellte **CF44** 27 J7
Ystradffin **SA20** 27 G4
Ystradgynlais **SA9** 27 G7
Ystradowen, *N.P.T.* **SA9** 27 G7
Ystradowen, *V. of Glam.* **CF71** 18 D4
Ystumtuen **SY23** 27 G1
Ythanwells **AB54** 90 E1
Ythsie **AB41** 91 G1

Z

Zeal Monachorum **EX17** 7 F5
Zeals **BA12** 9 G1
Zelah **TR4** 3 F3
Zennor **TR26** 2 B5
Zouch **LE12** 41 H3

INDEX TO NORTHERN IRELAND

Administrative area abbreviations

Banbr.   Banbridge   *London.*   Londonderry
Ferm.   Fermanagh   *N. & M.*   Newry & Mourne

A

Aghagallon **BT67** 111 F4
Aghalee **BT67** 111 F3
Aghanloo **BT49** 110 D1
Agivey **BT51** 111 E1
Ahoghill **BT42** 111 E2
Aldergrove **BT29** 111 F3
Annahilt **BT26** 111 F4
Annalong **BT34** 111 G5
Annsborough **BT31** 111 G4
Antrim **BT41** 111 F3
Ardglass **BT30** 111 G5
Ardkeen **BT22** 111 G4
Ardmore **BT49** 110 D1
Ardstraw **BT78** 110 C3
Armagh **BT60** 111 E4
Armoy **BT53** 111 E1
Articlave **BT51** 110 D1
Artigarvan **BT82** 110 C2
Attical **BT34** 111 F5
Aughamullan **BT71** 111 E3
Augher **BT77** 110 C4
Aughnacloy **BT69** 110 D4

B

Ballinamallard **BT94** 110 B4
Ballintoy **BT54** 111 E1
Ballybogy **BT53** 111 E1
Ballycarry **BT38** 111 G2
Ballycastle **BT54** 111 F1
Ballyclare **BT39** 111 F3
Ballygalley **BT40** 111 G2
Ballygawley **BT70** 110 D4
Ballygowan **BT23** 111 G4
Ballyhalbert **BT22** 111 H4
Ballyhoe Bridge **BT53** 111 E1
Ballyhornan **BT30** 111 G4
Ballykelly **BT49** 110 D1
Ballyleny **BT61** 111 E4
Ballymackilroy **BT70** 110 D4
Ballymagorry **BT82** 110 C2
Ballymartin **BT34** 111 F5
Ballymena **BT43** 111 F2
Ballymoney **BT53** 111 E1
Ballynahinch **BT24** 111 G4
Ballyneaner **BT82** 110 C2
Ballynoe **BT30** 111 G4
Ballynure **BT39** 111 F2
Ballyronan **BT45** 111 E3
Ballyvoy **BT54** 111 F1
Ballywalter **BT22** 111 H3
Ballyward **BT31** 111 F4
Balnamore **BT53** 111 E1
Banbridge **BT32** 111 F4
Bangor **BT20** 111 G3
Barnmeen **BT34** 111 F5
Belcoo **BT93** 110 B4
BELFAST BT 111 F3
Belfast City Airport **BT3** 111 G3
Belfast International Airport **BT29** 111 F3
Bellaghy **BT45** 111 E2
Bellanaleck **BT92** 110 B4
Belleek, *Ferm.* **BT93** 110 A4
Belleek, *N. & M.* **BT35** 111 E5
Benburb **BT71** 111 E4
Beragh **BT79** 110 C3
Bessbrook **BT35** 111 E5
Blacktown **BT81** 110 B3
Blackwatertown **BT71** 111 E4
Blaney **BT93** 110 B4
Bodoney **BT78** 110 C4
Boho **BT74** 110 B4
Bolea **BT49** 110 D1
Boviel **BT47** 110 D2
Brookeborough **BT94** 110 C4
Broughderg **BT79** 110 D3
Broughshane **BT42** 111 F2
Buckna **BT42** 111 F2
Burnfoot **BT47** 110 D2
Burren **BT34** 111 F5
Bushmills **BT57** 111 E1

C

Caddy **BT41** 111 E2
Caledon **BT68** 110 D4
Cappagh **BT70** 110 D3
Carland **BT71** 110 D3
Carnagh **BT60** 111 E5
Carnanreagh **BT47** 110 C2
Carnduff **BT54** 111 F1
Carnlough **BT44** 111 F2
Carnteel **BT69** 110 D4
Carrickfergus **BT38** 111 G3
Carrickmore **BT79** 110 D3
Carrowdore **BT22** 111 G3
Carryduff **BT8** 111 G3
Castlecaulfield **BT70** 110 D4

Castledawson **BT45** 111 E2
Castlederg **BT81** 110 B3
Castlereagh **BT6** 111 G3
Castlerock **BT51** 110 D1
Castleroe **BT51** 111 E1
Castlewellan **BT31** 111 F5
Causeway Head **BT57** 111 E1
Chapeltown **BT42** 111 F2
Charlemont **BT71** 111 E4
Church Ballee **BT30** 111 G4
Churchtown **BT30** 111 G4
City of Derry Airport **BT47** 110 C1
Clady, *London.* **BT44** 111 E2
Clady, *Strabane* **BT82** 110 C2
Clanabogan **BT78** 110 C3
Claudy **BT47** 110 C2
Clogh **BT44** 111 F2
Clogh Mills **BT44** 111 E1
Clogher **BT76** 110 C4
Cloghy **BT22** 111 H4
Clough **BT30** 111 G4
Cloyfin **BT52** 111 E1
Coagh **BT45** 111 E3
Coalisland **BT71** 111 E3
Coleraine **BT52** 111 E1
Comber **BT23** 111 G3
Conlig **BT2** 111 G3
Connor **BT42** 111 F2
Cookstown **BT80** 110 D3
Cooneen **BT75** 110 C4
Corkey **BT44** 111 E1
Craig **BT47** 110 C2
Craigantlet **BT23** 111 G3
Craigavad **BT18** 111 G3
Craigavon **BT65** 111 E4
Craigs **BT42** 111 E2
Cranagh **BT79** 110 D2
Crawfordsburn **BT19** 111 G3
Creagh **BT94** 110 C4
Creggan, *N. & M.* **BT35** 111 E5
Creggan, *Omagh* **BT79** 110 D3
Crilly **BT69** 110 D4
Crossgar **BT30** 111 G4
Crossgare **BT51** 111 E1
Crossmaglen **BT35** 111 E5
Crumlin **BT29** 111 F3
Culkey **BT92** 110 B4
Cullybackey **BT42** 111 E2
Cullyhanna **BT35** 111 E5
Culmore **BT48** 110 C1
Curran **BT45** 111 E2
Cushendall **BT44** 111 F1
Cushendun **BT44** 111 F1

D

Damhead **BT52** 111 E1
Darkley **BT60** 111 E5
Derry (Londonderry) **BT48** 110 C2
Derrygonnelly **BT93** 110 B4
Derrylin **BT92** 110 B5
Derrynawilt **BT92** 110 C5
Derrytrasna **BT66** 111 E4
Dervock **BT53** 111 E1
Desertmartin **BT45** 111 E2
Doagh **BT39** 111 F3
Donagh **BT92** 110 C5
Donaghadee **BT21** 111 G3
Donaghcloney **BT66** 111 F4
Donaghmore **BT70** 110 D3
Donemana **BT82** 110 C2
Dooish **BT78** 110 C3
Douglas Bridge **BT82** 110 C3
Downhill **BT51** 110 D1
Downpatrick **BT30** 111 G4
Draperstown **BT45** 110 D2
Dromara **BT25** 111 F4
Dromore, *Banbr.* **BT25** 111 F4
Dromore, *Omagh* **BT78** 110 C4
Drumahoe **BT47** 110 C2
Drumaness **BT24** 111 G4
Drumcard **BT92** 110 B5
Drumduff **BT94** 110 B4
Drumlegagh **BT78** 110 C3
Drumnakilly **BT79** 110 C3
Drumquin **BT78** 110 C3
Drumskinny **BT93** 110 B3
Drumsurn **BT49** 110 D2
Dundonald **BT16** 111 G3
Dundrod **BT29** 111 F3
Dundrum **BT33** 111 G5
Dungannon **BT71** 110 D4
Dungiven **BT47** 110 D2
Dunloy **BT44** 111 E1
Dunmurry **BT17** 111 F3
Dunnamore **BT80** 110 D3
Dunseverick **BT57** 111 E1
Dyan **BT68** 110 D4

E

Eden **BT38** 111 G3
Ederny **BT93** 110 B3
Eglinton **BT47** 110 C1
Eglish **BT70** 110 D4
Enniskillen **BT74** 110 B4
Ervey Cross Roads **BT47** 110 C2
Eshnadarragh **BT92** 110 C4
Eskragh **BT78** 110 C4

F

Feeny **BT47** 110 D2
Feystown **BT44** 111 F2
Finnis **BT25** 111 F4
Fintona **BT78** 110 C4
Finvoy **BT53** 111 E1
Fivemiletown **BT75** 110 C4
Forkhill **BT35** 111 E5

G

Garrison **BT93** 110 A4
Garvagh **BT51** 111 E2
Garvaghy **BT70** 110 C4
Garvary **BT94** 110 B4
Gilford **BT63** 111 E4
Glarryford **BT44** 111 E2
Glenariff **BT44** 111 F1
Glenarm **BT44** 111 F2
Glenavy **BT29** 111 F3
Glenhead **BT49** 110 D1
Glenhull **BT79** 110 D3
Glenoe **BT40** 111 G2
Glynn **BT40** 111 G2
Gortaclare **BT79** 110 C3
Gortavoy Bridge **BT70** 110 D3
Gortin **BT79** 110 C3
Gortnagallon **BT29** 111 F3
Gracehill **BT42** 111 E2
Gransha **BT25** 111 F4
Greencastle, *N. & M.* **BT34** 111 F5
Greencastle, *Omagh* **BT79** 110 D3
Greenisland **BT38** 111 G3
Greyabbey **BT22** 111 G3
Groomsport **BT19** 111 G3
Gulladuff **BT45** 111 E2

H

Hamilton's Bawn **BT60** 111 E4
Helen's Bay **BT19** 111 G3
Hillsborough **BT26** 111 F4
Hilltown **BT34** 111 F5
Holywell **BT93** 110 B4
Holywood **BT18** 111 G3

I

Irvinestown **BT94** 110 B4

J

Jonesborough **BT35** 111 E5

K

Katesbridge **BT32** 111 F4
Keady **BT60** 111 E5
Kearney **BT22** 111 H4
Kells **BT42** 111 F2
Kesh **BT93** 110 B3
Kildress **BT80** 110 D3
Kilkeel **BT34** 111 F5
Kilkinamurry **BT32** 111 F4
Killadeas **BT94** 110 B4
Killagan Bridge **BT44** 111 E1
Killen **BT81** 110 B3
Killeter **BT81** 110 B3
Killinchy **BT23** 111 G4
Killough **BT30** 111 G5
Killyclogher **BT79** 110 C3
Killylea **BT60** 110 D4
Kilrea **BT51** 111 E2
Kilskeery **BT78** 110 B4
Kilwaughter **BT40** 111 F2
Kircubbin **BT22** 111 G4
Knocknacarry **BT44** 111 F1

L

Lack **BT93** 110 B3
Lagavara **BT54** 111 E1

Larne **BT40** 111 G2
Lawrencetown **BT63** 111 F4
Leggs **BT93** 110 A4
Leitrim **BT31** 111 F4
Letterbreen **BT74** 110 B4
Limavady **BT49** 110 D1
Lisbane **BT23** 111 G3
Lisbellaw **BT94** 110 C4
Lisburn **BT28** 111 F3
Liscolman **BT53** 111 E1
Lislea **BT44** 111 E2
Lisnamuck **BT46** 110 D2
Lisnarrick **BT94** 110 B4
Lisnaskea **BT92** 110 C5
Lisrodden **BT44** 111 E2
Lissan **BT80** 110 D3
Listooder **BT30** 111 G4
Londonderry (Derry) **BT48** 110 C2
Loughbrickland **BT32** 111 F4
Loughgall **BT61** 111 E4
Loughinisland **BT30** 111 G4
Lower Ballinderry **BT28** 111 F3
Lurgan **BT67** 111 E4

M

McGregor's Corner **BT43** 111 F2
Macosquin **BT51** 110 D1
Maghera **BT46** 111 E2
Magherafelt **BT45** 111 E3
Magheralin **BT67** 111 F4
Magheramason **BT47** 110 C2
Maghery **BT71** 111 E4
Magilligan **BT49** 110 D1
Maguiresbridge **BT94** 110 C4
Markethill **BT60** 111 E4
Martinstown **BT43** 111 F2
Mayobridge **BT34** 111 F5
May's Corner **BT32** 111 F4
Meigh **BT35** 111 E5
Middletown **BT60** 110 D4
Milebush **BT38** 111 G3
Millford **BT60** 111 E4
Millisle **BT22** 111 G3
Milltown, *N. & M.* **BT34** 111 F5
Milltown, *Omagh* **BT79** 110 D3
Minerstown **BT30** 111 G4
Moira **BT67** 111 F4
Monea **BT74** 110 B4
Moneydig **BT51** 111 E2
Moneyglass **BT41** 111 E2
Moneymore **BT45** 111 E3
Moneyneany **BT45** 110 D2
Moneyreagh **BT23** 111 G3
Moorfields **BT42** 111 F2
Moortown **BT80** 111 E3
Mossley **BT3** 111 F3
Moss-side **BT53** 111 E1
Mount Hamilton **BT79** 110 D2
Mount Norris **BT60** 111 E5
Mountfield **BT79** 110 C3
Mountjoy, *Dungannon* **BT71** 111 E3
Mountjoy, *Omagh* **BT78** 110 C3
Moy **BT71** 111 E4
Moyarget **BT54** 111 E1
Moygashel **BT71** 110 D4
Moys **BT49** 110 D2
Mullan **BT92** 110 B5
Mullartown **BT34** 111 G5
Murley **BT75** 110 C4

N

New Buildings **BT47** 110 C2
New Ferry **BT41** 111 E2
Newcastle **BT33** 111 G5
Newry **BT34** 111 E5
Newtown Crommelin **BT43** 111 F2
Newtownabbey **BT37** 111 F3
Newtownards **BT2** 111 G3
Newtownbutler **BT92** 110 C5
Newtownhamilton **BT35** 111 E5
Newtownstewart **BT78** 110 C3
Nutt's Corner **BT29** 111 F3

O

Omagh **BT79** 110 C3

P

Park **BT47** 110 D2
Pettigo **BT93** 110 B3

Pharis **BT53** 111 E1
Plumbridge **BT79** 110 C3
Pomeroy **BT70** 110 D3
Portadown **BT62** 111 E4
Portaferry **BT22** 111 G4
Portavogie **BT22** 111 H4
Portballintrae **BT57** 111 E1
Portglenone **BT44** 111 E2
Portmuck **BT40** 111 G2
Portrush **BT56** 111 E1
Portstewart **BT55** 110 D1
Poyntz Pass **BT35** 111 E4

R

Raffrey **BT30** 111 G4
Randalstown **BT41** 111 E3
Rasharkin **BT44** 111 E2
Rathfriland **BT34** 111 F5
Richhill **BT61** 111 E4
Ringsend **BT51** 110 D1
Rosscor **BT93** 110 A4
Rosslea **BT92** 110 C5
Rostrevor **BT34** 111 F5
Rousky **BT79** 110 C3
Rubane **BT22** 111 G4

S

Saintfield **BT24** 111 G4
Saul **BT30** 111 G4
Scarva **BT63** 111 E4
Scotch Town **BT79** 110 C3
Scribbagh **BT93** 110 A4
Seapatrick **BT32** 111 F4
Seskinore **BT78** 110 C4
Shoptown **BT42** 111 F2
Shrigley **BT30** 111 G4
Sion Mills **BT82** 110 C2
Six Road Ends **BT19** 111 G3
Sixmilecross **BT79** 110 D3
Springfield **BT74** 110 B4
Staffordstown **BT41** 111 E3
Stewartstown **BT71** 111 E3
Stonyford **BT28** 111 F3
Strabane **BT82** 110 C2
Strangford **BT30** 111 G4
Stranocum **BT53** 111 E1
Swatragh **BT46** 111 E2

T

Tamlaght O'Crilly **BT46** 111 E2
Tandragee **BT62** 111 E4
Tassagh **BT60** 111 E5
Teemore **BT92** 110 C5
Templepatrick **BT39** 111 F3
Tempo **BT94** 110 C4
The Diamond, *Cookstown* **BT71** 111 E3
The Diamond, *Omagh* **BT78** 110 C3
The Loup **BT45** 111 E3
The Rock **BT70** 110 D3
The Sheddings **BT42** 111 F2
The Six Towns **BT45** 110 D2
The Temple **BT27** 111 F4
Tildarg **BT39** 111 F2
Tobermore **BT45** 111 E2
Toome **BT41** 111 E3
Torr **BT54** 111 F1
Trillick **BT78** 110 C4
Trory **BT94** 110 B4
Tully, *Ferm.* **BT92** 110 C5
Tully, *Ferm.* **BT93** 110 A4
Tullyhogue **BT80** 110 D3
Tynan **BT60** 110 D4
Tyrella **BT30** 111 G5

U

Upper Ballinderry **BT28** 111 F3
Upperlands **BT46** 111 E2

V

Vow **BT53** 111 E2

W

Waringsford **BT25** 111 F4
Waringstown **BT66** 111 F4
Warrenpoint **BT34** 111 F5
Waterside **BT47** 110 C2
Wattlebridge **BT92** 110 C5
Wheathill **BT93** 110 B5
Whitecross **BT60** 111 E5
Whitehead **BT38** 111 G2
Whitehouse **BT36** 111 F3